FEDERAL RULES OF CIVIL PROCEDURE
2018 Edition
Casebook Supplement

Updated through January 1, 2018

Michigan Legal Publishing Ltd.

Grand Rapids, Michigan

Academic and bulk discounts available at
www.michlp.com

WE WELCOME YOUR FEEDBACK: info@michlp.com

ISBN-13: 978-1-64002-020-7
ISBN-10: 1-64002-020-9

Table of Contents

Federal Rules of Civil Procedure With Advisory Committee Notes

TITLE I. SCOPE OF RULES; FORM OF ACTION

Rule 1. Scope and Purpose

These rules govern the procedure in all civil actions and proceedings in the United States district courts, except as stated in Rule 81. They should be construed, administered, and employed by the court and the parties to secure the just, speedy, and inexpensive determination of every action and proceeding.

———

(As amended Dec. 29, 1948, eff. Oct. 20, 1949; Feb. 28, 1966, eff. July 1, 1966; Apr. 22, 1993, eff. Dec. 1, 1993; Apr. 30, 2007, eff. Dec. 1, 2007; Apr. 29, 2015, eff. Dec. 1, 2015.)

Notes of Advisory Committee on Rules—1937

1. Rule 81 states certain limitations in the application of these rules to enumerated special proceedings.

2. The expression "district courts of the United States" appearing in the statute authorizing the Supreme Court of the United States to promulgate rules of civil procedure does not include the district courts held in the Territories and insular possessions. See Mookini et al. v. United States, 303 U.S. 201, 58 S.Ct. 543, 82 L.Ed. 748 (1938).

3. These rules are drawn under the authority of the act of June 19, 1934, U.S.C., Title 28, §723b [see 2072] (Rules in actions at law; Supreme Court authorized to make), and §723c [see 2072] (Union of equity and action at law rules; power of Supreme Court) and also other grants of rule making power to the Court. See Clark and Moore, A New Federal Civil Procedure—I. The Background, 44 Yale L.J. 387, 391 (1935). Under §723b after the rules have taken effect all laws in conflict therewith are of no further force or effect. In accordance with §723c the Court has united the general rules prescribed for cases in equity with those in actions at law so as to secure one form of civil action and procedure for both. See Rule 2 (One Form of Action). For the former practice in equity and at law see U.S.C., Title 28, §§723 and 730 [see 2071 et seq.] (conferring power on the Supreme Court to make rules of practice in equity) and the [former] Equity Rules promulgated thereunder; U.S.C., Title 28, [former] §724 (Conformity act): [former] Equity Rule 22 (Action at Law Erroneously Begun as Suit in Equity—Transfer); [former] Equity Rule 23 (Matters Ordinarily Determinable at Law When Arising in Suit in Equity to be Disposed of Therein); U.S.C., Title 28, [former] §§397 (Amendments to pleadings when case brought to wrong side of court), and 398 (Equitable defenses and equitable relief in actions at law).

4. With the second sentence compare U.S.C., Title 28, [former] §§777 (Defects of form; amendments), 767 (Amendment of process); [former] Equity Rule 19 (Amendments Generally).

Notes of Advisory Committee on Rules—1948 Amendment

The change in nomenclature conforms to the official designation of district courts in Title 28, U.S.C., §132(a).

Notes of Advisory Committee on Rules—1966 Amendment

This is the fundamental change necessary to effect unification of the civil and admiralty procedure. Just as the 1938 rules abolished the distinction between actions at law and suits in equity, this change would abolish the distinction between civil actions and suits in admiralty. See also Rule 81.

Notes of Advisory Committee on Rules—1993 Amendment

The purpose of this revision, adding the words "and administered" to the second sentence, is to recognize the affirmative duty of the court to exercise the authority conferred by these rules to ensure that civil litigation is resolved not only fairly, but also without undue cost or delay. As officers of the court, attorneys share this responsibility with the judge to whom the case is assigned.

Committee Notes on Rules—2007 Amendment

The language of Rule 1 has been amended as part of the general restyling of the Civil Rules to make them more easily understood and to make style and terminology consistent throughout the rules. These changes are intended to be stylistic only.

The merger of law, equity, and admiralty practice is complete. There is no need to carry forward the phrases that initially accomplished the merger.

The former reference to "suits of a civil nature" is changed to the more modern "civil actions and proceedings." This change does not affect such questions as whether the Civil Rules apply to summary proceedings created by statute. See SEC v. McCarthy, 322 F.3d 650 (9th Cir. 2003); see also New Hampshire Fire Ins. Co. v Scanlon, 362 U.S. 404 (1960).

The Style Project

The Civil Rules are the third set of the rules to be restyled. The restyled Rules of Appellate Procedure took effect in 1998. The restyled Rules of Criminal Procedure took effect in 2002. The restyled Rules of Civil Procedure apply the same general drafting guidelines and principles used in restyling the Appellate and Criminal Rules.

1. General Guidelines. Guidance in drafting, usage, and style was provided by Bryan Garner, Guidelines for Drafting and Editing Court Rules, Administrative Office of the United States Courts (1996) and Bryan Garner, Dictionary of Modern Legal Usage (2d ed. 1995). See also Joseph Kimble, Guiding Principles for Restyling the Civil Rules, in Preliminary Draft of Proposed Style Revision of the Federal Rules of Civil Procedure, at x [sic] (Feb. 2005) (available at http://www.uscourts.gov/rules/Prelim—draft—proposed—ptl.pdf).

2. Formatting Changes. Many of the changes in the restyled Civil Rules result from using format to achieve clearer presentation. The rules are broken down into constituent parts, using progressively indented subparagraphs with headings and substituting vertical for horizontal lists. "Hanging indents" are used throughout. These formatting changes make the structure of the rules graphic and make the restyled rules easier to read and understand even when the words are not changed. Rule 14(a) illustrates the benefits of formatting changes.

3. Changes to Reduce Inconsistent, Ambiguous, Redundant, Repetitive, or Archaic Words. The restyled rules reduce the use of inconsistent terms that say the same thing in different ways. Because different words are presumed to have different meanings, such inconsistencies can result in confusion. The restyled rules reduce inconsistencies by using the same words to express the same meaning. For example, consistent expression is achieved without affecting meaning by the changes from "infant" in many rules to "minor" in all rules; from "upon motion or on its own initiative" in Rule 4(m) and variations in many other rules to "on motion or on its own"; and from "deemed" to "considered" in Rules 5(c), 12(e), and elsewhere. Some variations of expression have been carried forward when the context made that appropriate. As an example, "stipulate," "agree," and "consent"

appear throughout the rules, and "written" qualifies these words in some places but not others. The number of variations has been reduced, but at times the former words were carried forward. None of the changes, when made, alters the rule's meaning.

The restyled rules minimize the use of inherently ambiguous words. For example, the word "shall" can mean "must," "may," or something else, depending on context. The potential for confusion is exacerbated by the fact that "shall" is no longer generally used in spoken or clearly written English. The restyled rules replace "shall" with "must," "may," or "should," depending on which one the context and established interpretation make correct in each rule.

The restyled rules minimize the use of redundant "intensifiers." These are expressions that attempt to add emphasis, but instead state the obvious and create negative implications for other rules. "The court in its discretion may" becomes "the court may"; "unless the order expressly directs otherwise" becomes "unless the court orders otherwise." The absence of intensifiers in the restyled rules does not change their substantive meaning. For example, the absence of the word "reasonable" to describe the written notice of foreign law required in Rule 44.1 does not mean that "unreasonable" notice is permitted.

The restyled rules also remove words and concepts that are outdated or redundant. The reference to "at law or in equity" in Rule 1 has become redundant with the merger of law and equity. Outdated words and concepts include the reference to "demurrers, pleas, and exceptions" in Rule 7(c); the reference to "mesne" process in Rule 77(c); and the reference in Rule 81(f) to a now-abolished official position.

The restyled rules remove a number of redundant cross-references. For example, Rule 8(b) states that a general denial is subject to the obligations of Rule 11, but all pleadings are subject to Rule 11. Removing such cross-references does not defeat application of the formerly cross-referenced rule.

4. Rule Numbers. The restyled rules keep the same rule numbers to minimize the effect on research. Subdivisions have been rearranged within some rules to achieve greater clarity and simplicity. The only change that moves one part of a rule to another is the transfer of former Rule 25(d)(2) to Rule 17(d). The restyled rules include a comparison chart to make it easy to identify transfers of provisions between subdivisions and redesignations of some subdivisions.

5. Other Changes. The style changes to the rules are intended to make no changes in substantive meaning. A very small number of minor technical amendments that arguably do change meaning were approved separately from the restyled rules, but become effective at the same time. An example is adding "e-mail address" to the information that must be included in pleadings[.] These minor changes occur in Rules 4(k), 9(h), 11(a), 14(b), 16(c)(1), 26(g)(1), 30(b), 31, 40, 71.1, and 78.

Changes Made After Publication and Comment.

Style Rules 1–86

Most of the changes in Styles Rule [sic] 1–86 reflect style improvements made in response to public comments and continuing work by consultants, reporters, Subcommittees A and B, the Standing Committee Style Subcommittee, and the Advisory Committee. They are marked above [omitted] as changes made after publication. An explanation of each would be both burdensome and unnecessary. Many are self-explanatory. Some are set out in the introduction to the Style Project materials. Others are explained in the minutes of the May 2006 Civil Rules Committee meeting. A few changes—and decisions against change—deserve individual mention here as well.

Present Rule 1 says that the Rules govern "in all suits of a civil nature." Style Rule 1 as published changed this to "all civil actions and proceedings." Comments suggested that the addition of "proceedings" might inadvertently expand the domain governed by the Civil Rules. The Standing Committee Style Subcommittee was persuaded that "and proceedings" should be removed. Subcommittee A accepted this recommendation. Further consideration, however, persuaded the Advisory Committee that "and proceedings" should be retained. The reasons for concluding that the term "civil actions" does not express all of the events properly governed by the Rules are described in the draft Minutes for the May meeting. As noted in the introduction, the Committee Note to Rule 1 is expanded to include a general description of the Style Project.

Present Rule 25(a)(1) is a classic illustration of the "shall" trap. It says that "the action shall be dismissed as to" a deceased party unless a motion to substitute is made within 90 days after death is suggested on the record. Style Rule 25(a)(1) translated "shall" as "may," providing that the action "may be dismissed." This choice was bolstered by considering the effects of the Rule 6(b) authority to extend the 90-day period even after it expires. To say that the court "must" dismiss might distract attention from the alternative authority to extend the time and grant a motion to substitute. Comments suggested that "may" effects a substantive change. The comments took pains to express no view on the desirability of substantive change. The Committee concluded that it is better to replace "may" with "must," and to delete the Committee Note explanation of the Rule 6(b) reasons for concluding that "may" does not work a substantive change.

A syntactic ambiguity in Rule 65(d) was corrected in response to comments and further research demonstrating that the ambiguity resulted from inadvertent omission of a comma when the Rule was adopted to carry forward former 28 U.S.C. §363. As revised, Rule 65(d) clearly provides that an injunction binds a party only after actual notice. It also clearly provides that after actual notice of an injunction, the injunction binds a person in active concert or participation with a party's officers, agents, servants, employees, and attorneys. The change is explained further in the new paragraph added to the Rule 65 Committee Note.

Finally, the Committee decided not to change the approach taken to identifying shifts of material among subdivisions. The Bankruptcy Rules Committee urged that the Committee Notes should identify decisions to rearrange material among subdivisions of the same rule to improve clarity and simplicity. In Rule 12, for example, subdivision (c) was divided between Style Rule 12(c) and (d), while former subdivision (d) became Style Rule 12(i). The purpose of expanding the Committee Notes would be to alert future researchers—particularly those who rely on tightly focused electronic searches—to define search terms that will reach back before the Style Amendments took effect. The approach taken in the published Style Rules was to identify in Committee Notes only the one instance in which material was shifted between Rules—from Rule 25 to Rule 17. Forty-four shifts among subdivisions of the same rule were charted in Appendix B, "Current and Restyled Rules Comparison Chart" The chart is set out below [omitted]. The Committee decided again that this approach is better than the alternative of adding length to many of the Committee Notes. It can be expected that many rules publications will draw attention to the changes identified in the chart.

Style-Substance Track

Two rules published on the Style-Substance Track were abandoned.

Rule 8 would have been revised to call for "a demand for the relief sought, which may include alternative forms or different types of relief." Comments showed that the old-fashioned "relief in the alternative" better describes circumstances in which the pleader is uncertain as to the available forms of relief, or prefers a form of relief that may not be available.

Rule 36 would have been amended to make clear the rule that an admission adopted at a final pretrial conference can be withdrawn or amended only on satisfying the "manifest injustice" standard of Style Rule 16(e). Revisions of Style Rule 16(e) make this clear, avoiding the need to further amend Rule 36.

"E-Discovery" Style Amendments: Rules 16, 26, 33, 34, 37, and 45

As noted above [omitted], the Style revisions to the "e-discovery" amendments published for comment in 2004, before the Style Project was published for comment in 2005, are all "changes made after publication." All involve pure style. They can be evaluated by reading the overstrike-underline version set out above [omitted].

Committee Notes on Rules—2015 Amendment

Rule 1 is amended to emphasize that just as the court should construe and administer these rules to secure the just, speedy, and inexpensive determination of every action, so the parties share the responsibility to employ the rules in the same way. Most lawyers and parties cooperate to achieve these ends. But discussions of ways to improve the administration of civil justice regularly include pleas to discourage over-use, misuse, and abuse of procedural tools that increase cost and result in delay. Effective advocacy is consistent with—and indeed depends upon—cooperative and proportional use of procedure.

This amendment does not create a new or independent source of sanctions. Neither does it abridge the scope of any other of these rules.

Rule 2. One Form of Action

There is one form of action—the civil action.

———

(As amended Apr. 30, 2007, eff. Dec. 1, 2007.)

Notes of Advisory Committee on Rules—1937

1. This rule modifies U.S.C., Title 28, [former] §384 (Suits in equity, when not sustainable). U.S.C., Title 28, §§723 and 730 [see 2071 et seq.] (conferring power on the Supreme Court to make rules of practice in equity), are unaffected insofar as they relate to the rule making power in admiralty. These sections, together with §723b [see 2072] (Rules in actions at law; Supreme Court authorized to make) are continued insofar as they are not inconsistent with §723c [see 2072] (Union of equity and action at law rules; power of Supreme Court). See Note 3 to Rule 1. U.S.C., Title 28, [former] §§724 (Conformity act), 397 (Amendments to pleadings when case brought to wrong side of court) and 398 (Equitable defenses and equitable relief in actions at law) are superseded.

2. Reference to actions at law or suits in equity in all statutes should now be treated as referring to the civil action prescribed in these rules.

3. This rule follows in substance the usual introductory statements to code practices which provide for a single action and mode of procedure, with abolition of forms of action and procedural distinctions. Representative statutes are N.Y. Code 1848 (Laws 1848, ch. 379) §62; N.Y.C.P.A. (1937) §8; Calif.Code Civ.Proc. (Deering, 1937) §307; 2 Minn.Stat. (Mason, 1927) §9164; 2 Wash.Rev.Stat.Ann. (Remington, 1932) §§153, 255.

Committee Notes on Rules—2007 Amendment

The language of Rule 2 has been amended as part of the general restyling of the Civil Rules to make them more easily understood and to make style and terminology consistent throughout the rules. These changes are intended to be stylistic only.

TITLE II. COMMENCING AN ACTION; SERVICE OF PROCESS, PLEADINGS, MOTIONS, AND ORDERS

Rule 3. Commencing an Action

A civil action is commenced by filing a complaint with the court.

———

(As amended Apr. 30, 2007, eff. Dec. 1, 2007.)

Notes of Advisory Committee on Rules—1937

1. Rule 5(e) defines what constitutes filing with the court.

2. This rule governs the commencement of all actions, including those brought by or against the United States or an officer or agency thereof, regardless of whether service is to be made personally pursuant to Rule 4(d), or otherwise pursuant to Rule 4(e).

3. With this rule compare [former] Equity Rule 12 (Issue of Subpoena—Time for Answer) and the following statutes (and other similar statutes) which provide a similar method for commencing an action:

U.S.C., Title 28:

- §45 [former] (District courts; practice and procedure in certain cases under interstate commerce laws).
- §762 [see 1402] (Petition in suit against United States).
- §766 [see 2409] (Partition suits where United States is tenant in common or joint tenant).

4. This rule provides that the first step in an action is the filing of the complaint. Under Rule 4(a) this is to be followed forthwith by issuance of a summons and its delivery to an officer for service. Other rules providing for dismissal for failure to prosecute suggest a method available to attack unreasonable delay in prosecuting an action after it has been commenced. When a Federal or State statute of limitations is pleaded as a defense, a question may arise under this rule whether the mere filing of the complaint stops the running of the statute, or whether any further step is required, such as, service of the summons and complaint or their delivery to the marshal for service. The answer to this question may depend on whether it is competent for the Supreme Court, exercising the power to make rules of procedure without affecting substantive rights, to vary the operation of statutes of limitations. The requirement of Rule 4(a) that the clerk shall forthwith issue the summons and deliver it to the marshal for service will reduce the chances of such a question arising.

Committee Notes on Rules—2007 Amendment

The caption of Rule 3 has been amended as part of the general restyling of the Civil Rules to make them more easily understood

and to make style and terminology consistent throughout the rules. These changes are intended to be stylistic only.

Rule 4. Summons

(a) Contents; Amendments.

(1) Contents. A summons must:

(A) name the court and the parties;

(B) be directed to the defendant;

(C) state the name and address of the plaintiff's attorney or—if unrepresented—of the plaintiff;

(D) state the time within which the defendant must appear and defend;

(E) notify the defendant that a failure to appear and defend will result in a default judgment against the defendant for the relief demanded in the complaint;

(F) be signed by the clerk; and

(G) bear the court's seal.

(2) Amendments. The court may permit a summons to be amended.

(b) Issuance. On or after filing the complaint, the plaintiff may present a summons to the clerk for signature and seal. If the summons is properly completed, the clerk must sign, seal, and issue it to the plaintiff for service on the defendant. A summons—or a copy of a summons that is addressed to multiple defendants—must be issued for each defendant to be served.

(c) Service.

(1) In General. A summons must be served with a copy of the complaint. The plaintiff is responsible for having the summons and complaint served within the time allowed by Rule 4(m) and must furnish the necessary copies to the person who makes service.

(2) By Whom. Any person who is at least 18 years old and not a party may serve a summons and complaint.

(3) By a Marshal or Someone Specially Appointed. At the plaintiff's request, the court may order that service be made by a United States marshal or deputy marshal or by a person specially appointed by the court. The court must so order if the plaintiff is authorized to proceed in forma pauperis under 28 U.S.C. §1915 or as a seaman under 28 U.S.C. §1916.

(d) Waiving Service.

(1) Requesting a Waiver. An individual, corporation, or association that is subject to service under Rule 4(e), (f), or (h) has a duty to avoid unnecessary expenses of serving the summons. The plaintiff may notify such a defendant that an action has been commenced and request that the defendant waive service of a summons. The notice and request must:

(A) be in writing and be addressed:

(i) to the individual defendant; or

(ii) for a defendant subject to service under Rule 4(h), to an officer, a managing or general agent, or any other agent authorized by appointment or by law to receive service of process;

(B) name the court where the complaint was filed;

(C) be accompanied by a copy of the complaint, 2 copies of the waiver form appended to this Rule 4, and a prepaid means for returning the form;

(D) inform the defendant, using the form appended to this Rule 4, of the consequences of waiving and not waiving service;

(E) state the date when the request is sent;

(F) give the defendant a reasonable time of at least 30 days after the request was sent—or at least 60 days if sent to the defendant outside any judicial district of the United States—to return the waiver; and

(G) be sent by first-class mail or other reliable means.

(2) Failure to Waive. If a defendant located within the United States fails, without good cause, to sign and return a waiver requested by a plaintiff located within the United States, the court must impose on the defendant:

(A) the expenses later incurred in making service; and

(B) the reasonable expenses, including attorney's fees, of any motion required to collect those service expenses.

(3) Time to Answer After a Waiver. A defendant who, before being served with process, timely returns a waiver need not serve an answer to the complaint until 60 days after the request was sent—or until 90 days after it was sent to the defendant outside any judicial district of the United States.

(4) Results of Filing a Waiver. When the plaintiff files a waiver, proof of service is not required and these rules apply as if a summons and complaint had been served at the time of filing the waiver.

(5) Jurisdiction and Venue Not Waived. Waiving service of a summons does not waive any objection to personal jurisdiction or to venue.

(e) Serving an Individual Within a Judicial District of the United States. Unless federal law provides otherwise, an individual—other than a minor, an incompetent person, or a person whose waiver has been filed—may be served in a judicial district of the United States by:

(1) following state law for serving a summons in an action brought in courts of general jurisdiction in the state where the district court is located or where service is made; or

(2) doing any of the following:

(A) delivering a copy of the summons and of the complaint to the individual personally;

(B) leaving a copy of each at the individual's dwelling or usual place of abode with someone of suitable age and discretion who resides there; or

(C) delivering a copy of each to an agent authorized by appointment or by law to receive service of process.

(f) Serving an Individual in a Foreign Country. Unless federal law provides otherwise, an individual—other than a minor, an incompetent person, or a person whose waiver has been filed—may be served at a place not within any judicial district of the United States:

(1) by any internationally agreed means of service that is reasonably calculated to give notice, such as those authorized by the Hague Convention on the Service Abroad of Judicial and Extrajudicial Documents;

(2) if there is no internationally agreed means, or if an international agreement allows but does not specify

other means, by a method that is reasonably calculated to give notice:

(A) as prescribed by the foreign country's law for service in that country in an action in its courts of general jurisdiction;

(B) as the foreign authority directs in response to a letter rogatory or letter of request; or

(C) unless prohibited by the foreign country's law, by:

(i) delivering a copy of the summons and of the complaint to the individual personally; or

(ii) using any form of mail that the clerk addresses and sends to the individual and that requires a signed receipt; or

(3) by other means not prohibited by international agreement, as the court orders.

(g) Serving a Minor or an Incompetent Person. A minor or an incompetent person in a judicial district of the United States must be served by following state law for serving a summons or like process on such a defendant in an action brought in the courts of general jurisdiction of the state where service is made. A minor or an incompetent person who is not within any judicial district of the United States must be served in the manner prescribed by Rule 4(f)(2)(A), (f)(2)(B), or (f)(3).

(h) Serving a Corporation, Partnership, or Association. Unless federal law provides otherwise or the defendant's waiver has been filed, a domestic or foreign corporation, or a partnership or other unincorporated association that is subject to suit under a common name, must be served:

(1) in a judicial district of the United States:

(A) in the manner prescribed by Rule 4(e)(1) for serving an individual; or

(B) by delivering a copy of the summons and of the complaint to an officer, a managing or general agent, or any other agent authorized by appointment or by law to receive service of process and—if the agent is one authorized by statute and the statute so requires—by also mailing a copy of each to the defendant; or

(2) at a place not within any judicial district of the United States, in any manner prescribed by Rule 4(f) for serving an individual, except personal delivery under (f)(2)(C)(i).

(i) Serving the United States and Its Agencies, Corporations, Officers, or Employees.

(1) United States. To serve the United States, a party must:

(A)

(i) deliver a copy of the summons and of the complaint to the United States attorney for the district where the action is brought—or to an assistant United States attorney or clerical employee whom the United States attorney designates in a writing filed with the court clerk—or

(ii) send a copy of each by registered or certified mail to the civil-process clerk at the United States attorney's office;

(B) send a copy of each by registered or certified mail to the Attorney General of the United States at Washington, D.C.; and

(C) if the action challenges an order of a nonparty agency or officer of the United States, send a copy of each by registered or certified mail to the agency or officer.

(2) Agency; Corporation; Officer or Employee Sued in an Official Capacity. To serve a United States agency or corporation, or a United States officer or employee sued only in an official capacity, a party must serve the United States and also send a copy of the summons and of the complaint by registered or certified mail to the agency, corporation, officer, or employee.

(3) Officer or Employee Sued Individually. To serve a United States officer or employee sued in an individual capacity for an act or omission occurring in connection with duties performed on the United States' behalf (whether or not the officer or employee is also sued in an official capacity), a party must serve the United States and also serve the officer or employee under Rule 4(e), (f), or (g).

(4) Extending Time. The court must allow a party a reasonable time to cure its failure to:

(A) serve a person required to be served under Rule 4(i)(2), if the party has served either the United States attorney or the Attorney General of the United States; or

(B) serve the United States under Rule 4(i)(3), if the party has served the United States officer or employee.

(j) Serving a Foreign, State, or Local Government.

(1) Foreign State. A foreign state or its political subdivision, agency, or instrumentality must be served in accordance with 28 U.S.C. §1608.

(2) State or Local Government. A state, a municipal corporation, or any other state-created governmental organization that is subject to suit must be served by:

(A) delivering a copy of the summons and of the complaint to its chief executive officer; or

(B) serving a copy of each in the manner prescribed by that state's law for serving a summons or like process on such a defendant.

(k) Territorial Limits of Effective Service.

(1) In General. Serving a summons or filing a waiver of service establishes personal jurisdiction over a defendant:

(A) who is subject to the jurisdiction of a court of general jurisdiction in the state where the district court is located;

(B) who is a party joined under Rule 14 or 19 and is served within a judicial district of the United States and not more than 100 miles from where the summons was issued; or

(C) when authorized by a federal statute.

(2) Federal Claim Outside State-Court Jurisdiction. For a claim that arises under federal law, serving a summons or filing a waiver of service establishes personal jurisdiction over a defendant if:

(A) the defendant is not subject to jurisdiction in any state's courts of general jurisdiction; and

(B) exercising jurisdiction is consistent with the United States Constitution and laws.

(l) Proving Service.

(1) Affidavit Required. Unless service is waived, proof of service must be made to the court. Except for service by

a United States marshal or deputy marshal, proof must be by the server's affidavit.

(2) Service Outside the United States. Service not within any judicial district of the United States must be proved as follows:

(A) if made under Rule 4(f)(1), as provided in the applicable treaty or convention; or

(B) if made under Rule 4(f)(2) or (f)(3), by a receipt signed by the addressee, or by other evidence satisfying the court that the summons and complaint were delivered to the addressee.

(3) Validity of Service; Amending Proof. Failure to prove service does not affect the validity of service. The court may permit proof of service to be amended.

(m) Time Limit for Service. If a defendant is not served within 90 days after the complaint is filed, the court—on motion or on its own after notice to the plaintiff—must dismiss the action without prejudice against that defendant or order that service be made within a specified time. But if the plaintiff shows good cause for the failure, the court must extend the time for service for an appropriate period. This subdivision (m) does not apply to service in a foreign country under Rule 4(f), 4(h)(2), or 4(j)(1).1, or to service of a notice under Rule 71.1(d)(3)(A).

(n) Asserting Jurisdiction over Property or Assets.

(1) Federal Law. The court may assert jurisdiction over property if authorized by a federal statute. Notice to claimants of the property must be given as provided in the statute or by serving a summons under this rule.

(2) State Law. On a showing that personal jurisdiction over a defendant cannot be obtained in the district where the action is brought by reasonable efforts to serve a summons under this rule, the court may assert jurisdiction over the defendant's assets found in the district. Jurisdiction is acquired by seizing the assets under the circumstances and in the manner provided by state law in that district.

(As amended Jan. 21, 1963, eff. July 1, 1963; Feb. 28, 1966, eff. July 1, 1966; Apr. 29, 1980, eff. Aug. 1, 1980; Pub. L. 97–462, §2, Jan. 12, 1983, 96 Stat. 2527, eff. Feb. 26, 1983; Mar. 2, 1987, eff. Aug. 1, 1987; Apr. 22, 1993, eff. Dec. 1, 1993; Apr. 17, 2000, eff. Dec. 1, 2000; Apr. 30, 2007, eff. Dec. 1, 2007; Apr. 29, 2015, eff. Dec. 1, 2015; Apr. 28, 2016, eff. Dec. 1, 2016; Apr. 27, 2017, eff. Dec. 1, 2017.)

Rule 4 Notice of a Lawsuit and Request to Waive Service of Summons.

(Caption)

To (name the defendant or—if the defendant is a corporation, partnership, or association—name an officer or agent authorized to receive service):

Why are you getting this?

A lawsuit has been filed against you, or the entity you represent, in this court under the number shown above. A copy of the complaint is attached.

This is not a summons, or an official notice from the court. It is a request that, to avoid expenses, you waive formal service of a summons by signing and returning the enclosed waiver. To avoid these expenses, you must return the signed waiver within (give at least 30 days or at least 60 days if the defendant is outside any judicial district of the United States) from the date shown below, which is the date this notice was sent. Two copies of the waiver form are enclosed, along with a stamped, self-addressed envelope or other prepaid means for returning one copy. You may keep the other copy.

What happens next?

If you return the signed waiver, I will file it with the court. The action will then proceed as if you had been served on the date the waiver is filed, but no summons will be served on you and you will have 60 days from the date this notice is sent (see the date below) to answer the complaint (or 90 days if this notice is sent to you outside any judicial district of the United States).

If you do not return the signed waiver within the time indicated, I will arrange to have the summons and complaint served on you. And I will ask the court to require you, or the entity you represent, to pay the expenses of making service.

Please read the enclosed statement about the duty to avoid unnecessary expenses.

I certify that this request is being sent to you on the date below.

Date:______________________

____

(Signature of the attorney

or unrepresented party)

____

(Printed name)

____

(Address)

____

(E-mail address)

____

(Telephone number)

Rule 4 Waiver of the Service of Summons.

(Caption)

To (name the plaintiff's attorney or the unrepresented plaintiff):

I have received your request to waive service of a summons in this action along with a copy of the complaint, two copies of this waiver form, and a prepaid means of returning one signed copy of the form to you.

I, or the entity I represent, agree to save the expense of serving a summons and complaint in this case.

I understand that I, or the entity I represent, will keep all defenses or objections to the lawsuit, the court's jurisdiction, and the venue of the action, but that I waive any objections to the absence of a summons or of service.

I also understand that I, or the entity I represent, must file and serve an answer or a motion under Rule 12 within 60 days from ______________________, the date when this request was sent (or 90 days if it was sent outside the United States). If I fail to do so, a default judgment will be entered against me or the entity I represent.

Date:____________________

____

(Signature of the attorney

or unrepresented party)

____

(Printed name)

____

(Address)

____

(E-mail address)

____

(Telephone number)

(Attach the following)

Duty to Avoid Unnecessary Expenses of Serving a Summons

Rule 4 of the Federal Rules of Civil Procedure requires certain defendants to cooperate in saving unnecessary expenses of serving a summons and complaint. A defendant who is located in the United States and who fails to return a signed waiver of service requested by a plaintiff located in the United States will be required to pay the expenses of service, unless the defendant shows good cause for the failure.

"Good cause" does not include a belief that the lawsuit is groundless, or that it has been brought in an improper venue, or that the court has no jurisdiction over this matter or over the defendant or the defendant's property.

If the waiver is signed and returned, you can still make these and all other defenses and objections, but you cannot object to the absence of a summons or of service.

If you waive service, then you must, within the time specified on the waiver form, serve an answer or a motion under Rule 12 on the plaintiff and file a copy with the court. By signing and returning the waiver form, you are allowed more time to respond than if a summons had been served.

Notes of Advisory Committee on Rules—1937

Note to Subdivision (a). With the provision permitting additional summons upon request of the plaintiff compare [former] Equity Rule 14 (Alias Subpoena) and the last sentence of [former] Equity Rule 12 (Issue of Subpoena—Time for Answer).

Note to Subdivision (b). This rule prescribes a form of summons which follows substantially the requirements stated in [former] Equity Rules 12 (Issue of Subpoena—Time for Answer) and 7 (Process, Mesne and Final).

U.S.C., Title 28, §721 [now 1691] (Sealing and testing of writs) is substantially continued insofar as it applies to a summons, but its requirements as to teste of process are superseded. U.S.C., Title 28, [former] §722 (Teste of process, day of), is superseded.

See Rule 12(a) for a statement of the time within which the defendant is required to appear and defend.

Note to Subdivision (c). This rule does not affect U.S.C., Title 28, §503 [see 566], as amended June 15, 1935 (Marshals; duties) and such statutes as the following insofar as they provide for service of process by a marshal, but modifies them insofar as they may imply service by a marshal only:

U.S.C., Title 15:

- §5 (Bringing in additional parties) (Sherman Act)
- §10 (Bringing in additional parties)
- §25 (Restraining violations; procedure)

U.S.C., Title 28:

- §45 [former] (Practice and procedure in certain cases under the interstate commerce laws)

Compare [former] Equity Rule 15 (Process, by Whom Served).

Note to Subdivision (d). Under this rule the complaint must always be served with the summons.

Paragraph (1). For an example of a statute providing for service upon an agent of an individual see U.S.C., Title 28, §109 [now 1400, 1694] (Patent cases).

Paragraph (3). This enumerates the officers and agents of a corporation or of a partnership or other unincorporated association upon whom service of process may be made, and permits service of process only upon the officers, managing or general agents, or agents authorized by appointment or by law, of the corporation, partnership or unincorporated association against which the action is brought. See Christian v. International Ass'n of Machinists, 7 F.(2d) 481 (D.C.Ky., 1925) and Singleton v. Order of Railway Conductors of America, 9 F.Supp. 417 (D.C.Ill., 1935). Compare Operative Plasterers' and Cement Finishers' International Ass'n of the United States and Canada v. Case, 93 F.(2d) 56 (App.D.C., 1937).

For a statute authorizing service upon a specified agent and requiring mailing to the defendant, see U.S.C., Title 6, §7 [now Title 31, §9306] (Surety companies as sureties; appointment of agents; service of process).

Paragraphs (4) and (5) provide a uniform and comprehensive method of service for all actions against the United States or an officer or agency thereof. For statutes providing for such service see U.S.C., Title 7, §§217 (Proceedings for suspension of orders), 499k (Injunctions; application of injunction laws governing orders of Interstate Commerce Commission), 608c(15)(B) (Court review of ruling of Secretary of Agriculture), and 855 (making §608c(15)(B) applicable to orders of the Secretary of Agriculture as to handlers of anti-hog-cholera serum and hog-cholera virus); U.S.C., Title 26, [former] §1569 (Bill in chancery to clear title to realty on which the United States has a lien for taxes); U.S.C., Title 28, [former] §§45 (District Courts; practice and procedure in certain cases under the interstate commerce laws), [former] 763 (Petition in suit against the United States; service; appearance by district attorney), 766 [now 2409] (Partition suits where United States is tenant in common or joint tenant), 902 [now 2410] (Foreclosure of mortgages or other liens on property in which the United States has an interest). These and similar statutes are modified insofar as they prescribe a different method of service or dispense with the service of a summons.

For the [former] Equity Rule on service, see [former] Equity Rule 13 (Manner of Serving Subpoena).

Note to Subdivision (e). The provisions for the service of a summons or of notice or of an order in lieu of summons contained in U.S.C., Title 8, §405 [see 1451] (Cancellation of certificates of citizenship fraudulently or illegally procured) (service by publication in accordance with State law); U.S.C., Title 28, §118 [now 1655] (Absent defendants in suits to enforce liens); U.S.C., Title 35, §72a [now 146, 291] (Jurisdiction of District Court of United States for the District of Columbia in certain equity suits where adverse parties reside elsewhere) (service by publication against parties residing in foreign countries); U.S.C., Title 38, §445 [now 1984] (Action against the United States on a veteran's contract of insurance) (parties not inhabitants of or not found within the District may be served with an order of the court, personally or by publication) and similar statutes are continued by this rule. Title 24, §378 [now Title 13, §336] of the Code of the District of Columbia (Publication against nonresident; those absent for six months; unknown heirs or devisees; for divorce or in rem; actual service beyond District) is continued by this rule.

Note to Subdivision (f). This rule enlarges to some extent the present rule as to where service may be made. It does not, however, enlarge the jurisdiction of the district courts.

U.S.C., Title 28, §§113 [now 1392] (Suits in States containing more than one district) (where there are two or more defendants residing in different districts), [former] 115 (Suits of a local nature), 116 [now 1392] (Property in different districts in same State), [former] 838 (Executions run in all districts of State); U.S.C., Title 47, §13 (Action for damages against a railroad or telegraph company whose officer or agent in control of a telegraph line refuses or fails to operate such line in a certain manner—"upon any agent of the company found in such state"); U.S.C., Title 49, §321(c) [see 13304(a)] (Requiring designation of a process agent by interstate motor carriers and in case of failure so to do, service may be made upon any agent in the State) and similar statutes, allowing the running of process throughout a State, are substantially continued.

U.S.C., Title 15, §§5 (Bringing in additional parties) (Sherman Act), 25 (Restraining violations; procedure); U.S.C., Title 28, §§44 [now 2321] (Procedure in certain cases under interstate commerce laws; service of processes of court), 117 [now 754, 1692] (Property in different States in same circuit; jurisdiction of receiver), 839 [now 2413] (Executions; run in every State and Territory) and similar statutes, providing for the running of process beyond the territorial limits of a State, are expressly continued.

Note to Subdivision (g). With the second sentence compare [former] Equity Rule 15 (Process, by Whom Served).

Note to Subdivision (h). This rule substantially continues U.S.C., Title 28, [former] §767 (Amendment of process).

Notes of Advisory Committee on Rules—1963 Amendment

Subdivision (b). Under amended subdivision (e) of this rule, an action may be commenced against a nonresident of the State in which the district court is held by complying with State procedures. Frequently the form of the summons or notice required in these cases by State law differs from the Federal form of summons described in present subdivision (b) and exemplified in Form 1. To avoid confusion, the amendment of subdivision (b) states that a form of summons or notice, corresponding "as nearly as may be" to the State form, shall be employed. See also a corresponding amendment of Rule 12(a) with regard to the time to answer.

Subdivision (d)(4). This paragraph, governing service upon the United States, is amended to allow the use of certified mail as an alternative to registered mail for sending copies of the papers to the Attorney General or to a United States officer or agency. Cf. N.J. Rule 4:5–2. See also the amendment of Rule 30(f)(1).

Subdivision (d)(7). Formerly a question was raised whether this paragraph, in the context of the rule as a whole, authorized service in original Federal actions pursuant to State statutes permitting service on a State official as a means of bringing a nonresident motorist defendant into court. It was argued in McCoy v. Siler, 205 F.2d 498, 501–2 (3d Cir.) (concurring opinion), cert. denied, 346 U.S. 872, 74 S.Ct. 120, 98 L.Ed. 380 (1953), that the effective service in those cases occurred not when the State official was served but when notice was given to the defendant outside the State, and that subdivision (f) (Territorial limits of effective service), as then worded, did not authorize out-of-State service. This contention found little support. A considerable number of cases held the service to be good, either by fixing upon the service on the official within the State as the effective service, thus satisfying the wording of subdivision (f) as it then stood, see Holbrook v. Cafiero, 18 F.R.D. 218 (D.Md. 1955); Pasternack v. Dalo, 17 F.R.D. 420; (W.D.Pa. 1955); cf. Super Prods. Corp. v. Parkin, 20 F.R.D. 377 (S.D.N.Y. 1957), or by reading paragraph (7) as not limited by subdivision (f). See Griffin v. Ensign, 234 F.2d 307 (3d Cir. 1956); 2 Moore's Federal Practice, 4.19 (2d ed. 1948); 1 Barron & Holtzoff, Federal Practice & Procedure §182.1 (Wright ed. 1960); Comment, 27 U. of Chi.L.Rev. 751 (1960). See also Olberding v. Illinois Central R.R., 201 F.2d 582 (6th Cir.), rev'd on other grounds, 346 U.S. 338, 74 S.Ct. 83, 98 L.Ed. 39 (1953); Feinsinger v. Bard, 195 F.2d 45 (7th Cir. 1952).

An important and growing class of State statutes base personal jurisdiction over nonresidents on the doing of acts or on other contacts within the State, and permit notice to be given the defendant outside the State without any requirement of service on a local State official. See, e.g., Ill.Ann.Stat. ch. 110, §§16, 17 (Smith-Hurd 1956); Wis.Stat. §262.06 (1959). This service, employed in original Federal actions pursuant to paragraph (7), has also been held proper. See Farr & Co. v. Cia. Intercontinental de Nav. de Cuba, 243 F.2d 342 (2d Cir. 1957); Kappus v. Western Hills Oil, Inc., 24 F.R.D. 123 (E.D.Wis. 1959); Star v. Rogalny, 162 F.Supp. 181 (E.D.Ill. 1957). It has also been held that the clause of paragraph (7) which permits service "in the manner prescribed by the law of the state," etc., is not limited by subdivision (c) requiring that service of all process be made by certain designated persons. See Farr & Co. v. Cia. Intercontinental de Nav. de Cuba, supra. But cf. Sappia v. Lauro Lines, 130 F.Supp. 810 (S.D.N.Y. 1955).

The salutary results of these cases are intended to be preserved. See paragraph (7), with a clarified reference to State law, and amended subdivisions (e) and (f).

Subdivision (e). For the general relation between subdivisions (d) and (e), see 2 Moore, supra, 4.32.

The amendment of the first sentence inserting the word "thereunder" supports the original intention that the "order of court" must be authorized by a specific United States statute. See 1 Barron & Holtzoff, supra, at 731. The clause added at the end of the first sentence expressly adopts the view taken by commentators that, if no manner of service is prescribed in the statute or order, the service may be made in a manner stated in Rule 4. See 2 Moore, supra, 4.32, at 1004; Smit, International Aspects of Federal Civil Procedure, 61 Colum.L.Rev. 1031, 1036–39 (1961). But see Commentary, 5 Fed. Rules Serv. 791 (1942).

Examples of the statutes to which the first sentence relates are 28 U.S.C. §2361 (Interpleader; process and procedure); 28 U.S.C. §1655 (Lien enforcement; absent defendants).

The second sentence, added by amendment, expressly allows resort in original Federal actions to the procedures provided by State law for effecting service on nonresident parties (as well as on domiciliaries not found within the State). See, as illustrative, the discussion under amended subdivision (d)(7) of service pursuant to State nonresident motorist statutes and other comparable State statutes. Of particular interest is the change brought about by the reference in this sentence to State procedures for commencing actions against nonresidents by attachment and the like, accompanied by notice. Although an action commenced in a State court by attachment may be removed to the Federal court if ordinary conditions for removal are satisfied, see 28 U.S.C. §1450; Rorick v. Devon Syndicate, Ltd., 307 U.S. 299, 59 S.Ct. 877, 83 L.Ed. 1303 (1939); Clark v. Wells, 203 U.S. 164, 27 S.Ct. 43, 51 L.Ed. 138 (1906), there has heretofore been no provision recognized by the courts for commencing an original Federal civil action by attachment. See Currie, Attachment and Garnishment in the Federal Courts, 59 Mich.L.Rev. 337 (1961), arguing that this result came about through historical anomaly. Rule 64, which refers to attachment, garnishment, and similar procedures under State law, furnishes only provisional remedies in actions otherwise validly commenced. See Big Vein Coal Co. v. Read, 229 U.S. 31, 33 S.Ct. 694, 57 L.Ed. 1953 (1913); Davis v. Ensign-Bickford Co., 139 F.2d 624 (8th Cir. 1944); 7 Moore's Federal Practice 64.05 (2d ed. 1954); 3 Barron & Holtzoff, Federal Practice & Procedure §1423 (Wright ed. 1958); but cf. Note, 13 So.Calif.L.Rev. 361 (1940). The amendment will now permit the institution of original Federal actions against nonresidents through the use of familiar State procedures by which property of these defendants is brought within the custody of the court and some appropriate service is made up them.

The necessity of satisfying subject-matter jurisdictional requirements and requirements of venue will limit the practical utilization of these methods of effecting service. Within those limits, however, there appears to be no reason for denying plaintiffs means of commencing actions in Federal courts which are generally available in the State courts. See 1 Barron & Holtzoff, supra, at 374–80; Nordbye, Comments on Proposed Amendments to Rules of Civil Procedure for the United States District Courts, 18 F.R.D. 105, 106 (1956); Note, 34 Corn.L.Q. 103 (1948); Note, 13 So.Calif.L.Rev. 361 (1940).

If the circumstances of a particular case satisfy the applicable Federal law (first sentence of Rule 4(e), as amended) and the applicable State law (second sentence), the party seeking to make the service may proceed under the Federal or the State law, at his option.

See also amended Rule 13(a), and the Advisory Committee's Note thereto.

Subdivision (f). The first sentence is amended to assure the effectiveness of service outside the territorial limits of the State in all the cases in which any of the rules authorize service beyond those boundaries. Besides the preceding provisions of Rule 4, see Rule 71A(d)(3). In addition, the new second sentence of the subdivision permits effective service within a limited area outside the State in certain special situations, namely, to bring in additional parties to a counterclaim or cross-claim (Rule 13(h)), impleaded parties (Rule 14), and indispensable or conditionally necessary parties to a pending action (Rule 19); and to secure compliance with an order of commitment for civil contempt. In those situations effective service can be made at points not more than 100 miles distant from the courthouse in which the action is commenced, or to which it is assigned or transferred for trial.

The bringing in of parties under the 100-mile provision in the limited situations enumerated is designed to promote the objective of enabling the court to determine entire controversies. In the light of present-day facilities for communication and travel, the territorial range of the service allowed, analogous to that which applies to the service of a subpoena under Rule 45(e)(1), can hardly work hardship on the parties summoned. The provision will be especially useful in metropolitan areas spanning more than one State. Any requirements of subject-matter jurisdiction and venue will still have to be satisfied as to the parties brought in, although these requirements will be eased in some instances when the parties can be regarded as "ancillary." See Pennsylvania R.R. v. Erie Avenue Warehouse Co., 5 F.R.Serv.2d 14a.62, Case 2 (3d Cir. 1962); Dery v. Wyer, 265 F.2d 804 (2d Cir. 1959); United Artists Corp. v. Masterpiece Productions, Inc., 221 F.2d 213 (2d Cir. 1955); Lesnik v. Public Industrials Corp., 144 F.2d 968 (2d Cir. 1944); Vaughn v. Terminal Transp. Co., 162 F.Supp. 647 (E.D.Tenn. 1957); and compare the fifth paragraph of the Advisory Committee's Note to Rule 4(e), as amended. The amendment is but a moderate extension of the territorial reach of Federal process and has ample practical justification. See 2 Moore, supra. §4.01[13] (Supp. 1960); 1 Barron & Holtzoff, supra, §184; Note, 51 Nw.U.L.Rev. 354 (1956). But cf. Nordbye, Comments on Proposed Amendments to Rules of Civil Procedure for the United States District Courts, 18 F.R.D 105, 106 (1956).

As to the need for enlarging the territorial area in which orders of commitment for civil contempt may be served, see Graber v. Graber, 93 F.Supp. 281 (D.D.C. 1950); Teele Soap Mfg. Co. v. Pine Tree Products Co., Inc., 8 F.Supp. 546 (D.N.H. 1934); Mitchell v. Dexter, 244 Fed. 926 (1st Cir. 1917); in re Graves, 29 Fed. 60 (N.D. Iowa 1886).

As to the Court's power to amend subdivisions (e) and (f) as here set forth, see Mississippi Pub. Corp. v. Murphree, 326 U.S. 438, 66 S.Ct. 242, 90 L.Ed. 185 (1946).

Subdivision (i). The continual increase of civil litigation having international elements makes it advisable to consolidate, amplify, and clarify the provisions governing service upon parties in foreign countries. See generally Jones, International Judicial Assistance: Procedural Chaos and a Program for Reform, 62 Yale L.J. 515 (1953); Longley, Serving Process, Subpoenas and Other Documents in Foreign Territory, Proc. A.B.A., Sec. Int'l & Comp. L. 34 (1959); Smit, International Aspects of Federal Civil Procedure, 61 Colum.L.Rev. 1031 (1961).

As indicated in the opening lines of new subdivision (i), referring to the provisions of subdivision (e), the authority for effecting foreign service must be found in a statute of the United States or a statute or rule of court of the State in which the district court is held providing in terms or upon proper interpretation for service abroad upon persons not inhabitants of or found within the State. See the Advisory Committee's Note to amended Rule 4(d)(7) and Rule 4(e). For examples of Federal and State statutes expressly authorizing such service, see 8 U.S.C. §1451(b); 35 U.S.C. §§146, 293; Me.Rev.Stat., ch. 22, §70 (Supp. 1961); Minn.Stat.Ann. §303.13 (1947); N.Y.Veh. & Tfc.Law §253. Several decisions have construed statutes to permit service in foreign countries, although the matter is not expressly mentioned in the statutes. See, e.g., Chapman v. Superior Court, 162 Cal.App.2d 421, 328 P.2d 23 (Dist.Ct.App. 1958); Sperry v. Fliegers, 194 Misc. 438, 86 N.Y.S.2d 830 (Sup.Ct. 1949); Ewing v. Thompson, 233 N.C. 564, 65 S.E.2d 17 (1951); Rushing v. Bush, 260 S.W.2d 900 (Tex.Ct.Civ.App. 1953). Federal and State statutes authorizing service on nonresidents in such terms as to warrant the interpretation that service abroad is permissible include 15 U.S.C. §§77v(a), 78aa, 79y; 28 U.S.C. §1655; 38 U.S.C. §784(a); Ill.Ann.Stat. ch. 110, §§16, 17 (Smith-Hurd 1956); Wis.Stat. §262.06 (1959).

Under subdivisions (e) and (i), when authority to make foreign service is found in a Federal statute or statute or rule of court of a State, it is always sufficient to carry out the service in the manner indicated therein. Subdivision (i) introduces considerable further flexibility by permitting the foreign service and return thereof to be carried out in any of a number of other alternative ways that are also declared to be sufficient. Other aspects of foreign service continue to be governed by the other provisions of Rule 4. Thus, for example, subdivision (i) effects no change in the form of the summons, or the issuance of separate or additional summons, or the amendment of service.

Service of process beyond the territorial limits of the United States may involve difficulties not encountered in the case of domestic service. Service abroad may be considered by a foreign country to require the performance of judicial, and therefore "sovereign," acts within its territory, which that country may conceive to be offensive to its policy or contrary to its law. See Jones, supra, at 537. For example, a person not qualified to serve process according to the law of the foreign country may find himself subject to sanctions if he attempts service therein. See Inter-American Judicial Committee, Report on Uniformity of Legislation on International Cooperation in Judicial Procedures 20 (1952). The enforcement of a judgment in the foreign country in which the service was made may be embarrassed or prevented if the service did not comport with the law of that country. See ibid.

One of the purposes of subdivision (i) is to allow accommodation to the policies and procedures of the foreign country. It is emphasized, however, that the attitudes of foreign countries vary considerably and that the question of recognition of United States judgments abroad is complex. Accordingly, if enforcement is to be sought in the country of service, the foreign law should be examined before a choice is made among the methods of service allowed by subdivision (i).

Subdivision (i)(1). Subparagraph (a) of paragraph (1), permitting service by the method prescribed by the law of the foreign country for service on a person in that country in a civil action in any of its courts of general jurisdiction, provides an alternative that is likely to create least objection in the place of service and also is likely to enhance the possibilities of securing ultimate enforcement of the judgment abroad. See Report on Uniformity of Legislation on International Cooperation in Judicial Procedures, supra.

In certain foreign countries service in aid of litigation pending in other countries can lawfully be accomplished only upon request to the foreign court, which in turn directs the service to be made. In many countries this has long been a customary way of accomplishing the service. See In re Letters Rogatory out of First Civil Court of City of Mexico, 261 Fed. 652 (S.D.N.Y. 1919); Jones, supra, at 543; Comment, 44 Colum.L.Rev. 72 (1944); Note, 58 Yale L.J. 1193 (1949). Subparagraph (B) of paragraph (1), referring to a letter rogatory, validates this method. A proviso, applicable to this subparagraph and the preceding one, requires, as a safeguard, that the service made shall be reasonably calculated to give actual notice of the proceedings to the party. See Milliken v. Meyer, 311 U.S. 457, 61 S.Ct. 339, 85 L.Ed. 278 (1940).

Subparagraph (C) of paragraph (1), permitting foreign service by personal delivery on individuals and corporations, partnerships, and associations, provides for a manner of service that is not only traditionally preferred, but also is most likely to lead to actual notice. Explicit provision for this manner of service was thought desirable because a number of Federal and State statutes permitting foreign service do not specifically provide for service by personal delivery abroad, see e.g., 35 U.S.C. §§146, 293; 46 [App.] U.S.C. §1292; Calif.Ins.Code §1612; N.Y.Veh. & Tfc.Law §253, and it also may be unavailable under the law of the country in which the service is made.

Subparagraph (D) of paragraph (1), permitting service by certain types of mail, affords a manner of service that is inexpensive and expeditious, and requires a minimum of activity within the foreign country. Several statutes specifically provide for service in a foreign country by mail, e.g., Hawaii Rev.Laws §§230–31, 230–32 (1955); Minn.Stat.Ann. §303.13 (1947); N.Y.Civ.Prac.Act, §229–b; N.Y.Veh. & Tfc.Law §253, and it has been sanctioned by the courts even in the absence of statutory provision specifying that form of service. Zurini v. United States, 189 F.2d 722 (8th Cir. 1951); United States v. Cardillo, 135 F.Supp. 798 (W.D.Pa. 1955); Autogiro Co. v. Kay Gyroplanes, Ltd., 55 F.Supp. 919 (D.D.C. 1944). Since the reliability of postal service may vary from country to country, service by mail is proper only when it is addressed to the party to be served and a form of mail requiring a signed receipt is used. An additional safeguard is provided by the requirement that the mailing be attended to be the clerk of the court. See also the provisions of paragraph (2) of this subdivision (i) regarding proof of service by mail.

Under the applicable law it may be necessary, when the defendant is an infant or incompetent person, to deliver the summons and complaint to a guardian, committee, or similar fiduciary. In such a case it would be advisable to make service under subparagraph (A), (B), or (E).

Subparagraph (E) of paragraph (1) adds flexibility by permitting the court by order to tailor the manner of service to fit the necessities of a particular case or the peculiar requirements of the law of the country in which the service is to be made. A similar provision appears in a number of statutes, e.g., 35 U.S.C. §§146, 293; 38 U.S.C. §784(a); 46 [App.] U.S.C. §1292.

The next-to-last sentence of paragraph (1) permits service under (C) and (E) to be made by any person who is not a party and is not less than 18 years of age or who is designated by court order or by the foreign court. Cf. Rule 45(c); N.Y.Civ.Prac.Act §§233, 235. This alternative increases the possibility that the plaintiff will be able to find a process server who can proceed unimpeded in the foreign country; it also may improve the chances of enforcing the judgment in the country of service. Especially is the alternative valuable when authority for the foreign service is found in a statute or rule of court that limits the group of eligible process servers to designated officials or special appointees who, because directly connected with another "sovereign," may be particularly offensive to the foreign country. See generally Smit, supra, at 1040–41. When recourse is had to subparagraph (A) or (B) the identity of the process server always will be determined by the law of the foreign country in which the service is made.

The last sentence of paragraph (1) sets forth an alternative manner for the issuance and transmission of the summons for service. After obtaining the summons from the clerk, the plaintiff must ascertain the best manner of delivering the summons and complaint to the person, court, or officer who will make the service. Thus the clerk is not burdened with the task of determining who is permitted to serve process under the law of a particular country or the appropriate governmental or nongovernmental channel for forwarding a letter rogatory. Under (D), however, the papers must always be posted by the clerk.

Subdivision (i)(2). When service is made in a foreign country, paragraph (2) permits methods for proof of service in addition to those prescribed by subdivision (g). Proof of service in accordance with the law of the foreign country is permitted because foreign process servers, unaccustomed to the form or the requirement of return of service prevalent in the United States, have on occasion been unwilling to execute the affidavit required by Rule 4(g). See Jones, supra, at 537; Longley, supra, at 35. As a corollary of the alternate manner of service in subdivision (i)(1)(E), proof of service as directed by order of the court is permitted. The special provision for proof of service by mail is intended as an additional safeguard when that method is used. On the type of evidence of delivery that may be satisfactory to a court in lieu of a signed receipt, see Aero Associates, Inc. v. La Metropolitana, 183 F.Supp. 357 (S.D.N.Y. 1960).

Notes of Advisory Committee on Rules—1966 Amendment

The wording of Rule 4(f) is changed to accord with the amendment of Rule 13(h) referring to Rule 19 as amended.

Notes of Advisory Committee on Rules—1980 Amendment

Subdivision (a). This is a technical amendment to conform this subdivision with the amendment of subdivision (c).

Subdivision (c). The purpose of this amendment is to authorize service of process to be made by any person who is authorized to make service in actions in the courts of general jurisdiction of the state in which the district court is held or in which service is made.

There is a troublesome ambiguity in Rule 4. Rule 4(c) directs that all process is to be served by the marshal, by his deputy, or by a person specially appointed by the court. But Rule 4(d)(7) authorizes service in certain cases "in the manner prescribed by the law of the state in which the district court is held. . . ." And Rule 4(e), which authorizes service beyond the state and service in quasi in rem cases when state law permits such service, directs that "service may be made . . . under the circumstances and in the manner prescribed in the [state] statute or rule." State statutes and rules of the kind referred to in Rule 4(d)(7) and Rule 4(e) commonly designate the persons who are to make the service provided for, e.g., a sheriff or a plaintiff. When that is so, may the persons so designated by state law make service, or is service in all cases to be made by a marshal or by one specially appointed under present Rule 4(c)? The commentators have noted the ambiguity and have suggested the desirability of an amendment. See 2 Moore's Federal Practice 4.08 (1974); Wright & Miller, Federal Practice and Procedure: Civil §1092 (1969). And the ambiguity has given rise to unfortunate results. See United States for the use of Tanos v. St. Paul Mercury Ins. Co., 361 F. 2d 838 (5th Cir. 1966); Veeck v. Commodity Enterprises, Inc., 487 F. 2d 423 (9th Cir. 1973).

The ambiguity can be resolved by specific amendments to Rules 4(d)(7) and 4(e), but the Committee is of the view that there is no reason why Rule 4(c) should not generally authorize service of process in all cases by anyone authorized to make service in the courts of general jurisdiction of the state in which the district court is held or in which service is made. The marshal continues to be the obvious, always effective officer for service of process.

Legislative Statement—1983 Amendment

128 Congressional Record H9848, Dec. 15, 1982

Mr. EDWARDS of California. Mr. Speaker, in July Mr. McClory and I brought before the House a bill to delay the effective date of proposed changes in rule 4 of the Federal Rules of Civil Procedure, dealing with service of process. The Congress enacted that legislation and delayed the effective date so that we could cure certain problems in the proposed amendments to rule 4.

Since that time, Mr. McClory and I introduced a bill, H.R. 7154, that cures those problems. It was drafted in consultation with representatives of the Department of Justice, the Judicial Conference of the United States, and others.

The Department of Justice and the Judicial Conference have endorsed the bill and have urged its prompt enactment. Indeed, the Department of Justice has indicated that the changes occasioned by the bill will facilitate its collection of debts owned to the Government.

I have a letter from the Office of Legislative Affairs of the Department of Justice supporting the bill that I will submit for the Record. Also, I am submitting for the Record a section-by-section analysis of the bill.

H.R. 7154 makes much needed changes in rule 4 of the Federal Rules of Civil Procedure and is supported by all interested parties. I urge my colleagues to support it.

U.S. Department of Justice.
Office of Legislative Affairs,
Washington, D.C., December 10, 1982.
Hon. Peter W. Rodino, Jr.,
Chairman, Committee on the Judiciary, House of Representatives,
Washington, D.C.

Dear Mr. Chairman: This is to proffer the views of the Department of Justice on H.R. 7154, the proposed Federal Rules of Civil Procedure Amendments Act of 1982. While the agenda is extremely tight and we appreciate that fact, we do reiterate that this Department strongly endorses the enactment of H.R. 7154. We would greatly appreciate your watching for any possible way to enact this legislation expeditiously.

H.R. 7154 would amend Rule 4 of the Federal Rules of Civil Procedure to relieve effectively the United States Marshals Service of the duty of routinely serving summonses and complaints for private parties in civil actions and would thus achieve a goal this Department has long sought. Experience has shown that the Marshals Service's increasing workload and limited budget require such major relief from the burdens imposed by its role as process-server in all civil actions.

The bill would also amend Rule 4 to permit certain classes of defendants to be served by first class mail with a notice and acknowledgment of receipt form enclosed. We have previously expressed a preference for the service-by-mail provisions of the proposed amendments to Rule 4 which the Supreme Court transmitted to Congress on April 28, 1982.

The amendments proposed by the Supreme Court would permit service by registered or certified mail, return receipt requested. We had regarded the Supreme Court proposal as the more efficient because it would not require and affirmative act of signing and mailing on the part of a defendant. Moreover, the Supreme Court proposal would permit the entry of a default judgment if the record contained a returned receipt showing acceptance by the defendant or a returned envelope showing refusal of the process by the defendant and subsequent service and notice by first class mail. However, critics of that system of mail service have argued that certified mail is not an effective method of providing actual notice to defendants of claims against them because signatures may be illegible or may not match the name of the defendant, or because it may be difficult to determine whether mail has been "unclaimed" or "refused," the latter providing the sole basis for a default judgment.

As you know, in light of these criticisms the Congress enacted Public Law 97–227 (H.R. 6663) postponing the effective date of the proposed amendments to Rule 4 until October 1, 1983, so as to facilitate further review of the problem. This Department opposed the delay in the effective date, primarily because the Supreme Court's proposed amendments also contained urgently needed provisions designed to relieve the United States Marshals of the burden of serving summonses and complaints in private civil actions. In our view, these necessary relief provisions are readily separable from the issues of service by certified mail and the propriety of default judgment after service by certified mail which the Congress felt warranted additional review.

During the floor consideration of H.R. 6663 Congressman Edwards and other proponents of the delayed effective date pledged to expedite the review of the proposed amendments to Rule 4, given the need to provide prompt relief for the Marshals Service in the service of process area. In this spirit Judiciary Committee staff consulted with representatives of this Department, the Judicial Conference, and others who had voiced concern about the proposed amendments.

H.R. 7154 is the product of those consultations and accommodated the concerns of the Department in a very workable and acceptable manner.

Accordingly, we are satisfied that the provisions of H.R. 7154 merit the support of all three branches of the Federal Government and everyone else who has a stake in the fair and efficient service of process in civil actions. We urge prompt consideration of H.R. 7154 by the Committee.1

The Office of Management and Budget has advised that there is no objection to the submission of this report from the standpoint of the Administration's program.

Sincerely,
Robert A. McConnell,
Assistant Attorney General.

1 In addition to amending Rule 4, we have previously recommended: (a) amendments to 28 U.S.C. §569(b) redefining the Marshals traditional role by eliminating the statutory requirement that they serve subpoenas, as well as summonses and complaints, and; (b) amendments to 28 U.S.C. §1921 changing the manner and level in which marshal fees are charged for serving private civil process. These legislative changes are embodied in Section 10 of S. 2567 and the Department's proposed fiscal year 1983 Appropriations Authorization bill. If, in the Committee's judgment, efforts to incorporate these suggested amendments in H.R. 7154 would in any way impede consideration of the bill during the few remaining legislative days in the 97th Congress, we would urge that they be separately considered early in the 98th Congress.

H.R. 7154—Federal Rules of Civil Procedure Amendments Act of 1982

Background

The Federal Rules of Civil Procedure set forth the procedures to be followed in civil actions and proceedings in United States district courts. These rules are usually amended by a process established by 28 U.S.C. 2072, often referred to as the "Rules Enabling Act". The Rules Enabling Act provides that the Supreme Court can propose new rules of "practice and procedure" and amendments to existing rules by transmitting them to Congress after the start of a regular session but not later than May 1. The rules and amendments so proposed take effect 90 days after transmittal unless legislation to the contrary is enacted.1

On April 28, 1982, the Supreme Court transmitted to Congress several proposed amendments to the Federal Rules of Civil Procedure, the Federal Rules of Criminal Procedure (which govern criminal cases and proceedings in Federal courts), and the Rules and Forms Governing Proceedings in the United States District Courts under sections 2254 and 2255 of Title 28, United States Code (which govern habeas corpus proceedings). These amendments were to have taken effect on August 1, 1982.

The amendments to Rule 4 of the Federal Rules of Civil Procedure were intended primarily to relieve United States marshals of the burden of serving summonses and complaints in private civil actions. Appendix II, at 7 (Report of the Committee on Rules of Practice and Procedure), 16 (Advisory Committee Note). The Committee received numerous complaints that the changes not only failed to achieve that goal, but that in the process the changes saddled litigators with flawed mail service, deprived litigants of the use of effective local procedures for service, and created a time limit for service replete with ambiguities that could only be resolved by costly litigation. See House Report No. 97–662, at 2–4 (1982).

In order to consider these criticisms, Congress enacted Public Law 97–227, postponing the effective date of the proposed amendments to Rule 4 until October 1, 1983.2 Accordingly, in order to help shape the policy behind, and the form of, the proposed amendments, Congress must enact legislation before October 1, 1983.3

With that deadline and purpose in mind, consultations were held with representatives of the Judicial Conference, the Department of Justice, and others who had voiced concern about the proposed amendments. H.R. 7154 is the product of those consultations. The bill seeks to effectuate the policy of relieving the Marshals Service of the duty of routinely serving summonses and complaints. It provides a system of service by mail modeled upon a system found to be effective in California, and finally, it makes appropriate stylistic, grammatical, and other changes in Rule 4.

Need for the legislation

1. Current Rule 4

Rule 4 of the Federal Rules of Civil Procedure relates to the issuance and service of process. Subsection (c) authorizes service of process by personnel of the Marshals Service, by a person specially appointed by the Court, or "by a person authorized to serve process in an action brought in the courts of general jurisdiction of the state in which the district court is held or in which service is made." Subsection (d) describes how a summons and complaint must be served and designates those persons who must be served in cases involving specified categories of defendants. Mail service is not directly authorized. Subsection (d)(7), however, authorizes service under the law of the state in which the district court sits upon defendants described in subsections (d)(1) (certain individuals) and (d)(3) (organizations). Thus, if state law authorizes service by mail of a summons and complaint upon an individual or organization described in subsections (d)(1) or (3), then subsection (d)(7) authorizes service by mail for United States district courts in that state.4

2. Reducing the role of marshals

The Supreme Court's proposed modifications of Rule 4 were designed to alleviate the burden on the Marshals Service of serving summonses and complaints in private civil actions. Appendix II, at 7 (Report of the Committee on Rules of Practice and Procedure), 16 (Advisory Committee Note). While the Committee received no complaints about the goal of reducing the role of the Marshals Service, the Court's proposals simply failed to achieve that goal. See House Report No. 97–662, at 2–3 (1982).

The Court's proposed Rule 4(c)(2)(B) required the Marshals Service to serve summonses and complaints "pursuant to any statutory provision expressly providing for service by a United States Marshal or his deputy." 5 One such statutory provision is 28 U.S.C. 569(b), which compels marshals to "execute all lawful writs, process and orders issued under authority of the United States, including those of the courts * * *." (emphasis added). Thus, any party could have invoked 28 U.S.C. 569(b) to utilize a marshal for service of a summons and complaint, thereby thwarting the intent of the new subsection to limit the use of marshals. The Justice Department acknowledges that the proposed subsection did not accomplish its objectives.6

Had 28 U.S.C. 569(b) been inconsistent with proposed Rule 4(c)(2)(B), the latter would have nullified the former under 28 U.S.C. 2072, which provides that "All laws in conflict with such rules shall be of no further force or effect after such rules have taken effect." Since proposed Rule 4(c)(2)(B) specifically referred to statutes such as 28 U.S.C. 569(b), however, the new subsection did not conflict with 28 U.S.C. 569(b) and did not, therefore, supersede it.

H.R. 7154 cures this problem and achieves the desired reduction in the role of the Marshals Service by authorizing marshals to serve summonses and complaints "on behalf of the United States". By so doing, H.R. 7154 eliminates the loophole in the Court's proposed language and still provides for service by marshals on behalf of the Government.7

3. Mail service

The Supreme Court's proposed subsection (d)(7) and (8) authorized, as an alternative to personal service, mail service of summonses and complaints on individuals and organizations described in subsection (d)(1) and (3), but only through registered or certified mail, restricted delivery. Critics of that system of mail service argued that registered and certified mail were not necessarily effective methods of providing actual notice to defendants of claims against them. This was so, they argued, because signatures may be illegible or may not match the name of the defendant, or because it may be difficult to determine whether mail has been "unclaimed" or "refused", the latter apparently providing the sole basis for a default judgment.8

H.R. 7154 provides for a system of service by mail similar to the system now used in California. See Cal. Civ. Pro. §415.30 (West 1973). Service would be by ordinary mail with a notice and acknowledgment of receipt form enclosed. If the defendant returns the acknowledgment form to the sender within 20 days of mailing, the sender files the return and service is complete. If the acknowledgment is not returned within 20 days of mailing, then service must be effected through some other means provided for in the Rules.

This system of mail service avoids the notice problems created by the registered and certified mail procedures proposed by the Supreme Court. If the proper person receives the notice and returns the acknowledgment, service is complete. If the proper person does not receive the mailed form, or if the proper person receives the notice but fails to return the acknowledgment form, another method of service authorized by law is required.9 In either instance, however, the defendant will receive actual notice of the claim. In order to encourage defendants to return the acknowledgment form, the court can order a defendant who does not return it to pay the costs of service unless the defendant can show good cause for the failure to return it.

4. The local option

The Court's proposed amendments to Rule 4 deleted the provision in current subsection (d)(7) that authorizes service of a summons and complaint upon individuals and organizations "in the manner prescribed by the law of the state in which the district court is held for the service of summons or other like process upon any such defendant in an action brought in the courts of general jurisdiction of that state." The Committee received a variety of complaints about the deletion of this provision. Those in favor of preserving the local option saw no reason to forego systems of service that had been successful in achieving effective notice.10

H.R. 7154 carries forward the policy of the current rule and permits a party to serve a summons and complaint upon individuals and organizations described in Rule 4(d)(1) and (3) in accordance with the law of the state in which the district court sits. Thus, the bill authorizes four methods of serving a summons and complaint on such defendants: (1) service by a nonparty adult (Rule 4(c)(2)(A)); (2) service by personnel of the Marshals Service, if the party qualifies, such as because the party is proceeding in forma pauperis (Rule 4(c)(2)(B)); (3) service in any manner authorized by the law of the state in which the district court is held (Rule 4(c)(2)(C)(i)); or (4) service by regular mail with a notice and acknowledgment of receipt form enclosed (Rule 4(c)(2)(C)(ii)).11

5. Time limits

Rule 4 does not currently provide a time limit within which service must be completed. Primarily because United States marshals currently effect service of process, no time restriction has been deemed necessary. Appendix II, at 18 (Advisory Committee Note). Along with the proposed changes to subdivisions (c) and (d) to reduce the role of the Marshals Service, however, came new subdivision (j), requiring that service of a summons and complaint be made within 120 days of the filing of the complaint. If service were not accomplished within that time, proposed subdivision (j) required that the action "be dismissed as to that defendant without prejudice upon motion or upon the court's own initiative". Service by mail was deemed made for purposes of subdivision (j) "as of the date on which the process was accepted, refused, or returned as unclaimed".12

H.R. 7154 adopts a policy of limiting the time to effect service. It provides that if a summons and complaint have not been served within 120 days of the filing of the complaint and the plaintiff fails to show "good cause" for not completing service within that time, then the court must dismiss the action as to the unserved defendant. H.R. 7154 ensures that a plaintiff will be notified of an attempt to dismiss the action. If dismissal for failure to serve is raised by the court upon its own motion, the legislation requires that the court provide notice to the plaintiff. If dismissal is sought by someone else, Rule 5(a) of the Federal Rules of Civil Procedure requires that the motion be served upon the plaintiff.

Like proposed subsection (j), H.R. 7154 provides that a dismissal for failure to serve within 120 days shall be "without prejudice". Proposed subsection (j) was criticized by some for ambiguity because, it was argued, neither the text of subsection (j) nor the Advisory Committee Note indicated whether a dismissal without prejudice would toll a statute of limitation. See House Report 97–662, at 3–4 (1982). The problem would arise when a plaintiff files the complaint within the applicable statute of limitation period but does not effect service within 120 days. If the statute of limitation period expires during that period, and if the plaintiff's action is dismissed "without prejudice", can the plaintiff refile the complaint and maintain the action? The answer depends upon how the statute of limitation is tolled.13

If the law provides that the statute of limitation is tolled by filing and service of the complaint, then a dismissal under H.R. 7154 for failure to serve within the 120 days would, by the terms of the law controlling the tolling, bar the plaintiff from later maintaining the cause of action.14 If the law provides that the statute of limitation is tolled by filing alone, then the status of the plaintiff's cause of action turns upon the plaintiff's diligence. If the plaintiff has not been diligent, the court will dismiss the complaint for failure to serve within 120 days, and the plaintiff will be barred from later maintaining the cause of action because the statute of limitation has run. A dismissal without prejudice does not confer upon the plaintiff any rights that the plaintiff does not otherwise possess and leaves a plaintiff whose action has been dismissed in the same position as if the action had never been filed.15 If, on the other hand, the plaintiff has made reasonable efforts to effect service, then the plaintiff can move under Rule 6(b) to enlarge the time within which to serve or can oppose dismissal for failure to serve. A court would undoubtedly permit such a plaintiff additional time within which to effect service. Thus, a diligent plaintiff can preserve the cause of action. This result is consistent with the policy behind the time limit for service and with statutes of limitation, both of which are designed to encourage prompt movement of civil actions in the federal courts.

6. Conforming and clarifying subsections (d)(4) and (5)

Current subsections (d)(4) and (5) prescribe which persons must be served in cases where an action is brought against the United States or an officer or agency of the United States. Under subsection (d)(4), where the United States is the named defendant, service must be made as follows: (1) personal service upon the United States attorney, an assistant United States attorney, or a designated clerical employee of the United States attorney in the district in which the action is brought; (2) registered or certified mail service to the Attorney General of the United States in Washington, D.C.; and (3) registered or certified mail service to the appropriate officer or agency if the action attacks an order of that officer or agency but does not name the officer or agency as a defendant. Under subsection (d)(5), where an officer or agency of the United States is named as a defendant, service must be made as in subsection (d)(4), except that personal service upon the officer or agency involved is required.16

The time limit for effecting service in H.R. 7154 would present significant difficulty to a plaintiff who has to arrange for personal service upon an officer or agency that may be thousands of miles away. There is little reason to require different types of service when the officer or agency is named as a party, and H.R. 7154 therefore conforms the manner of service under subsection (d)(5) to the manner of service under subsection (d)(4).

Section-by-Section Analysis

Section 1

Section 1 provides that the short title of the bill is the "Federal Rules of Civil Procedure Amendments Act of 1982".

Section 2

Section 2 of the bill consists of 7 numbered paragraphs, each amending a different part of Rule 4 of the Federal Rules of Civil Procedure.

Paragraph (1) deletes the requirement in present Rule 4(a) that a summons be delivered for service to the marshal or other person authorized to serve it. As amended by the legislation, Rule 4(a) provides that the summons be delivered to "the plaintiff or the plaintiff's attorney, who shall be responsible for prompt service of the summons and complaint". This change effectuates the policy proposed by the Supreme Court. See Appendix II, at — (Advisory Committee Note).

Paragraph (2) amends current Rule 4(c), which deals with the service of process. New Rule 4(c)(1) requires that all process, other than a subpoena or a summons and complaint, be served by the Marshals Service or by a person especially appointed for that purpose. Thus, the Marshals Service or persons specially appointed will continue to serve all process other than subpoenas and summonses and complaints, a policy identical to that proposed by the Supreme Court. See Appendix II, at 8 (Report of the Judicial Conference Committee on Rules of Practice and Procedure). The service of subpoenas is governed by Rule 45,17 and the service of summonses and complaints is governed by new Rule 4(c)(2).

New Rule 4(c)(2)(A) sets forth the general rule that summonses and complaints shall be served by someone who is at least 18 years old and not a party to the action or proceeding. This is consistent with the Court's proposal. Appendix II, at 16 (Advisory Committee Note). Subparagraphs (B) and (C) of new Rule 4(c)(2) set forth exceptions to this general rule.

Subparagraph (B) sets forth 3 exceptions to the general rule. First, subparagraph (B)(i) requires the Marshals Service (or someone specially appointed by the court) to serve summonses and complaints on behalf of a party proceeding in forma pauperis or a seaman authorized to proceed under 28 U.S.C. 1916. This is identical to the Supreme Court's proposal. See Appendix II, at 3 (text of proposed rule), 16 (Advisory Committee Note). Second, subparagraph (B)(ii) requires the Marshals Service (or someone specially appointed by the court) to serve a summons and complaint when the court orders the marshals to do so in order properly to effect service in that particular action.18 This, except for nonsubstantive changes in phrasing, is identical to the Supreme Court's proposal. See Appendix II, at 3 (text of proposed rule), 16 (Advisory Committee Note).

Subparagraph (C) of new Rule 4(c)(2) provides 2 exceptions to the general rule of service by a nonparty adult. These exceptions apply only when the summons and complaint is to be served upon persons described in Rule 4(d)(1) (certain individuals) or Rule 4(d)(3) (organizations).19 First, subparagraph (C)(i) permits service of a summons and complaint in a manner authorized by the law of the state in which the court sits. This restates the option to follow local law currently found in Rule 4(d)(7) and would authorize service by mail if the state law so allowed. The method of mail service in that instance would, of course, be the method permitted by state law.

Second, subparagraph (C)(ii) permits service of a summons and complaint by regular mail. The sender must send to the defendant, by first-class mail, postage prepaid, a copy of the summons and complaint, together with 2 copies of a notice and acknowledgment of receipt of summons and complaint form and a postage prepaid return envelope addressed to the sender. If a copy of the notice and acknowledgment form is not received by the sender within 20 days after the date of mailing, then service must be made under Rule 4(c)(2)(A) or (B) (i.e., by a nonparty adult or, if the person qualifies,20 by personnel of the Marshals Service or a person specially appointed by the court) in the manner prescribed by Rule 4(d)(1) or (3) (i.e., personal or substituted service).

New Rule 4(c)(2)(D) permits a court to penalize a person who avoids service by mail. It authorizes the court to order a person who does not return the notice and acknowledgment form within 20 days after mailing to pay the costs of service, unless that person can show good cause for failing to return the form. The purpose of this provision is to encourage the prompt return of the form so that the action can move forward without unnecessary delay. Fairness requires that a person who causes another additional and unnecessary expense in effecting service ought to reimburse the party who was forced to bear the additional expense.

Subparagraph (E) of rule 4(c)(2) requires that the notice and acknowledgment form described in new Rule 4(c)(2)(C)(ii) be executed under oath or affirmation. This provision tracks the language of 28 U.S.C. 1746, which permits the use of unsworn declarations under penalty of perjury whenever an oath or affirmation is required. Statements made under penalty of perjury are subject to 18 U.S,C. 1621(2), which provides felony penalties for someone who "willfully subscribes as true any material matter which he does not believe to be true". The requirement that the form be executed under oath or affirmation is intended to encourage truthful submissions to the court, as the information contained in the form is important to the parties.21

New Rule 4(c)(3) authorizes the court freely to make special appointments to serve summonses and complaints under Rule 4(c)(2)(B) and all other process under Rule 4(c)(1). This carries forward the policy of present Rule 4(c).

Paragraph (3) of section 2 of the bill makes a non-substantive change in the caption of Rule 4(d) in order to reflect more accurately the provisions of Rule 4(d). Paragraph (3) also deletes a provision on service of a summons and complaint pursuant to state law. This provision is redundant in view of new Rule 4(c)(2)(C)(i).

Paragraph (4) of section 2 of the bill conforms Rule 4(d)(5) to present Rule 4(d)(4). Rule 4(d)(5) is amended to provide that service upon a named defendant agency or officer of the United States shall be made by "sending" a copy of the summons and complaint "by registered or certified mail" to the defendant.22 Rule 4(d)(5) currently provides for service by "delivering" the copies to the defendant, but 28 U.S.C. 1391(e) authorizes delivery upon a defendant agency or officer outside of the district in which the action is brought by means of certified mail. Hence, the change is not a marked departure from current practice.

Paragraph (5) of section 2 of the bill amends the caption of Rule 4(e) in order to describe subdivision (e) more accurately.

Paragraph (6) of section 2 of the bill amends Rule 4(g), which deals with return of service. Present rule 4(g) is not changed except to provide that, if service is made pursuant to the new system of mail service (Rule 4(c)(2)(C)(ii)), the plaintiff or the plaintiff's attorney must file with the court the signed acknowledgment form returned by the person served.

Paragraph (7) of section 2 of the bill adds new subsection (j) to provide a time limitation for the service of a summons and complaint. New Rule 4(j) retains the Supreme Court's requirement that a summons and complaint be served within 120 days of the filing of the complaint. See Appendix II, at 18 (Advisory Committee Note).23 The plaintiff must be notified of an effort or intention to dismiss the action. This notification is mandated by subsection (j) if the dismissal is being raised on the court's own initiative and will be provided pursuant to Rule 5 (which requires service of motions upon the adverse party) if the dismissal is sought by someone else.24 The plaintiff may move under Rule 6(b) to enlarge the time period. See Appendix II, at 1d. (Advisory Committee Note). If service is not made within the time period or enlarged time period, however, and if the plaintiff fails to show "good cause" for not completing service, then the court must dismiss the action as to the unserved defendant. The dismissal is "without prejudice". The term "without prejudice" means that the dismissal does not constitute an adjudication of the merits of the complaint. A dismissal "without prejudice" leaves a plaintiff whose action has been dismissed in the position in which that person would have been if the action had never been filed.

Section 3

Section 3 of the bill amends the Appendix of Forms at the end of the Federal Rules of Civil Procedure by adding a new form 18A, "Notice and Acknowledgment for Service by Mail". This new form is required by new Rule 4(c)(2)(C)(ii), which requires that the notice and acknowledgment form used with service by regular mail conform substantially to Form 18A.

Form 18A as set forth in section 3 of the bill is modeled upon a form used in California.25 It contains 2 parts. The first part is a notice to the person being served that tells that person that the enclosed summons and complaint is being served pursuant to Rule 4(c)(2)(C)(ii); advises that person to sign and date the acknowledgment form and indicate the authority to receive service if the person served is not the party to the action (e.g., the person served is an officer of the organization being served); and warns that failure to return the form to the sender within 20 days may result in the court ordering the party being served to pay the expenses involved in effecting service. The notice also warns that if the complaint is not responded to within 20 days, a default judgment can be entered against the party being served. The notice is dated under penalty of perjury by the plaintiff or the plaintiff's attorney.26

The second part of the form contains the acknowledgment of receipt of the summons and complaint. The person served must declare on this part of the form, under penalty of perjury, the date and place of service and the person's authority to receive service.

Section 4

Section 4 of the bill provides that the changes in Rule 4 made by H.R. 7154 will take effect 45 days after enactment, thereby giving the bench and bar, as well as other interested persons and organizations (such as the Marshals Service), an opportunity to prepare to implement the changes made by the legislation. The delayed effective date means that service of process issued before the effective date will be made in accordance with current Rule 4. Accordingly, all process in the hands of the Marshals Service prior to the effective date will be served by the Marshals Service under the present rule.

Section 5

Section 5 of the bill provides that the amendments to Rule 4 proposed by the Supreme Court (whose effective date was postponed by Public Law 97–227) shall not take effect. This is necessary because under Public Law 97–227 the proposed amendments will take effect on October 1, 1983.

---

1 The drafting of the rules and amendments is actually done by a committee of the Judicial Conference of the United States. In the case of the Federal Rules of Civil Procedure, the initial draft is prepared by the Advisory Committee on Civil Rules. The Advisory Committee's draft is then reviewed by the Committee on Rules of Practice and Procedure, which must give its approval to the draft. Any draft approved by that committee is forwarded to the Judicial Conference. If the Judicial Conference approves the draft, it forwards the draft to the Supreme Court. The Judicial Conference's role in the rule-making process is defined by 28 U.S.C. 331.

For background information about how the Judicial Conference committees operate, see Wright, "Procedural Reform: Its

Limitation and Its Future," 1 Ga.L.Rev. 563, 565–66 (1967) (civil rules); statement of United States District Judge Roszel C. Thomsen, Hearings on Proposed Amendments to the Federal Rules of Criminal Procedure Before the Subcommittee on Criminal Justice of the House Committee on the Judiciary, 93d Cong., 2d Sess. at 25 (1974) (criminal rules); statement of United States Circuit Judge J. Edward Lumbard, id. at 203 (criminal rules); J. Weinstein, Reform of Federal Court Rulemaking Procedure (1977); Weinstein, "Reform of Federal Rulemaking Procedures," 76 Colum.L.Rev. 905 (1976).

2 All of the other amendments, including all of the proposed amendments to the Federal Rules of Criminal Procedure and the Rules and Forms Governing Proceedings in the United States District Courts under sections 2254 and 2255 of Title 28, United States Code, took effect on August 1, 1982, as scheduled.

3 The President has urged Congress to act promptly. See President's Statement on Signing H.R. 6663 into Law, 18 Weekly Comp. of Pres. Doc. 982 (August 2, 1982).

4 Where service of a summons is to be made upon a party who is neither an inhabitant of, nor found within, the state where the district court sits, subsection (e) authorizes service under a state statute or rule of court that provides for service upon such a party. This would authorize mail service if the state statute or rule of court provided for service by mail.

5 The Court's proposal authorized service by the Marshals Service in other situations. This authority, however, was not seen as thwarting the underlying policy of limiting the use of marshals. See Appendix II, at 16, 17 (Advisory Committee Note).

6 Appendix I, at 2 (letter of Assistant Attorney General Robert A. McConnell).

7 The provisions of H.R. 7154 conflict with 28 U.S.C. 569(b) because the latter is a broader command to marshals to serve all federal court process. As a later statutory enactment, however, H.R. 7154 supersedes 28 U.S.C. 569(b), thereby achieving the goal of reducing the role of marshals.

8 Proposed Rule 4(d)(8) provided that "Service . . . shall not be the basis for the entry of a default or a judgment by default unless the record contains a return receipt showing acceptance by the defendant or a returned envelope showing refusal of the process by the defendant." This provision reflects a desire to preclude default judgments on unclaimed mail. See Appendix II, at 7 (Report of the Committee on Rules of Practice and Procedure).

The interpretation of Rule 4(d)(8) to require a refusal of delivery in order to have a basis for a default judgment, while undoubtedly the interpretation intended and the interpretation that reaches the fairest result, may not be the only possible interpretation. Since a default judgment can be entered for defendant's failure to respond to the complaint once defendant has been served and the time to answer the complaint has run, it can be argued that a default judgment can be obtained where the mail was unclaimed because proposed subsection (j), which authorized dismissal of a complaint not served within 120 days, provided that mail service would be deemed made "on the date on which the process was accepted, refused, or returned as unclaimed" (emphasis added).

9 See p. 15 infra.

10 Proponents of the California system of mail service, in particular, saw no reason to supplant California's proven method of mail service with a certified mail service that they believed likely to result in default judgments without actual notice to defendants. See House Report No. 97–662, at 3 (1982).

11 The parties may, of course, stipulate to service, as is frequently done now.

12 While return of the letter as unclaimed was deemed service for the purpose of determining whether the plaintiff's action could be dismissed, return of the letter as unclaimed was not service for the purpose of entry of a default judgment against the defendant. See note 8 supra.

13 The law governing the tolling of a statute of limitation depends upon the type of civil action involved. In adversity action, state law governs tolling. Walker v. Armco Steel Corp., 446 U.S. 740 (1980). In Walker, plaintiff had filed his complaint and thereby commenced the action under Rule 3 of the Federal Rules of Civil Procedure within the statutory period. He did not, however, serve the summons and complaint until after the statutory period had run. The Court held that state law (which required both filing and service within the statutory period) governed, barring plaintiff's action.

In the federal question action, the courts of appeals have generally held that Rule 3 governs, so that the filing of the complaint tolls a statute of limitation. United States v. Wahl, 538 F.2d 285 (6th Cir. 1978); Windbrooke Dev. Co. v. Environmental Enterprises Inc. of Fla., 524 F.2d 461 (5th Cir. 1975); Metropolitan Paving Co. v. International Union of Operating Engineers, 439 F.2d 300 (10th Cir. 1971); Moore Co. v. Sid Richardson Carbon & Gasoline Co., 347 F.2d 921 (8th Cir.), cert. denied, 383 U.S. 925, reh. denied, 384 U.S. 914 (1965); Hoffman v. Halden, 268 F.2d 280 (9th Cir. 1959). The continued validity of this line of cases, however, must be questioned in light of the Walker case, even though the Court in that case expressly reserved judgment about federal question actions, see Walker v. Armco Steel Corp., 446 U.S. 741, 751 n.11 (1980).

14 The same result obtains even if service occurs within the 120 day period, if the service occurs after the statute of limitation has run.

15 See p. 19 infra.

16 See p. 17 infra.

17 Rule 45(c) provides that "A subpoena may be served by the marshal, by his deputy, or by any other person who is not a party and is not less than 18 years of age."

18 Some litigators have voiced concern that there may be situations in which personal service by someone other than a member of the Marshals Service may present a risk of injury to the person attempting to make the service. For example, a hostile defendant may have a history of injuring persons attempting to serve process. Federal judges undoubtedly will consider the risk of harm to private persons who would be making personal service when deciding whether to order the Marshals Service to make service under Rule 4(c)(2)(B)(iii).

19 The methods of service authorized by Rule 4(c)(2)(C) may be invoked by any person seeking to effect service. Thus, a nonparty adult who receives the summons and complaint for service under Rule 4(c)(1) may serve them personally or by mail in the manner authorized by Rule 4(c)(2)(C)(ii). Similarly, the Marshals Service may utilize the mail service authorized by Rule 4(c)(2)(C)(ii) when serving a summons and complaint under Rule 4(c)(2)(B)(i)(iii). When serving a summons and complaint under Rule 4(c)(2)(B)(ii), however, the Marshals Service must serve in the manner set forth in the court's order. If no particular manner of service is specified, then the Marshals Service may utilize Rule 4(c)(2)(C)(ii).

It would not seem to be appropriate, however, for the Marshals Service to utilize Rule 4(c)(2)(C)(ii) in a situation where a previous attempt to serve by mail failed. Thus, it would not seem to be appropriate for the Marshals Service to attempt service by regular mail when serving a summons and complaint on behalf of a plaintiff who is proceeding in forma pauperis if that plaintiff previously attempted unsuccessfully to serve the defendant by mail.

20 To obtain service by personnel of the Marshals Service or someone specially appointed by the court, a plaintiff who has unsuccessfully attempted mail service under Rule 4(c)(2)(C)(ii) must meet the conditions of Rule 4(c)(2)(B)—for example, the plaintiff must be proceeding in forma pauperis.

21 For example, the sender must state the date of mailing on the form. If the form is not returned to the sender within 20 days of that date, then the plaintiff must serve the defendant in another manner and the defendant may be liable for the costs of such service. Thus, a defendant would suffer the consequences of a misstatement about the date of mailing.

22 See p. 12 supra.

23 The 120 day period begins to run upon the filing of each complaint. Thus, where a defendant files a cross-claim against the plaintiff, the 120 day period begins to run upon the filing of the cross-complaint, not upon the filing of the plaintiff's complaint initiating the action.

24 The person who may move to dismiss can be the putative defendant (i.e., the person named as defendant in the complaint filed with the court) or, in multi-party actions, another party to the action. (If the putative defendant moves to dismiss and the failure to effect service is due to that person's evasion of service, a court should not dismiss because the plaintiff has "good cause" for not completing service.)

25 See Cal. Civ. Pro. §415.30 (West 1973).

26 See p. 16 supra.

Notes of Advisory Committee on Rules—1987 Amendment

The amendments are technical. No substantive change is intended.

Notes of Advisory Committee on Rules—1993 Amendment

Purposes of Revision. The general purpose of this revision is to facilitate the service of the summons and complaint. The revised rule explicitly authorizes a means for service of the summons and complaint on any defendant. While the methods of service so authorized always provide appropriate notice to persons against whom claims are made, effective service under this rule does not assure that personal jurisdiction has been established over the defendant served.

First, the revised rule authorizes the use of any means of service provided by the law not only of the forum state, but also of the state in which a defendant is served, unless the defendant is a minor or incompetent.

Second, the revised rule clarifies and enhances the cost-saving practice of securing the assent of the defendant to dispense with actual service of the summons and complaint. This practice was introduced to the rule in 1983 by an act of Congress authorizing "service-by-mail," a procedure that effects economic service with cooperation of the defendant. Defendants that magnify costs of service by requiring expensive service not necessary to achieve full notice of an action brought against them are required to bear the wasteful costs. This provision is made available in actions against defendants who cannot be served in the districts in which the actions are brought.

Third, the revision reduces the hazard of commencing an action against the United States or its officers, agencies, and corporations. A party failing to effect service on all the offices of the United States as required by the rule is assured adequate time to cure defects in service.

Fourth, the revision calls attention to the important effect of the Hague Convention and other treaties bearing on service of documents in foreign countries and favors the use of internationally agreed means of service. In some respects, these treaties have facilitated service in foreign countries but are not fully known to the bar.

Finally, the revised rule extends the reach of federal courts to impose jurisdiction over the person of all defendants against whom federal law claims are made and who can be constitutionally subjected to the jurisdiction of the courts of the United States. The present territorial limits on the effectiveness of service to subject a defendant to the jurisdiction of the court over the defendant's person are retained for all actions in which there is a state in which personal jurisdiction can be asserted consistently with state law and the Fourteenth Amendment. A new provision enables district courts to exercise jurisdiction, if permissible under the Constitution and not precluded by statute, when a federal claim is made against a defendant not subject to the jurisdiction of any single state.

The revised rule is reorganized to make its provisions more accessible to those not familiar with all of them. Additional subdivisions in this rule allow for more captions; several overlaps among subdivisions are eliminated; and several disconnected provisions are removed, to be relocated in a new Rule 4.1.

The Caption of the Rule. Prior to this revision, Rule 4 was entitled "Process" and applied to the service of not only the summons but also other process as well, although these are not covered by the revised rule. Service of process in eminent domain proceedings is governed by Rule 71A. Service of a subpoena is governed by Rule 45, and service of papers such as orders, motions, notices, pleadings, and other documents is governed by Rule 5.

The revised rule is entitled "Summons" and applies only to that form of legal process. Unless service of the summons is waived, a summons must be served whenever a person is joined as a party against whom a claim is made. Those few provisions of the former rule which relate specifically to service of process other than a summons are relocated in Rule 4.1 in order to simplify the text of this rule.

Subdivision (a). Revised subdivision (a) contains most of the language of the former subdivision (b). The second sentence of the former subdivision (b) has been stricken, so that the federal court summons will be the same in all cases. Few states now employ distinctive requirements of form for a summons and the applicability of such a requirement in federal court can only serve as a trap for an unwary party or attorney. A sentence is added to this subdivision authorizing an amendment of a summons. This sentence replaces the rarely used former subdivision 4(h). See 4A Wright & Miller, Federal Practice and Procedure §1131 (2d ed. 1987).

Subdivision (b). Revised subdivision (b) replaces the former subdivision (a). The revised text makes clear that the responsibility for filling in the summons falls on the plaintiff, not the clerk of the court. If there are multiple defendants, the plaintiff may secure issuance of a summons for each defendant or may serve copies of a single original bearing the names of multiple defendants if the addressee of the summons is effectively identified.

Subdivision (c). Paragraph (1) of revised subdivision (c) retains language from the former subdivision (d)(1). Paragraph (2) retains language from the former subdivision (a), and adds an appropriate caution regarding the time limit for service set forth in subdivision (m).

The 1983 revision of Rule 4 relieved the marshals' offices of much of the burden of serving the summons. Subdivision (c) eliminates the requirement for service by the marshal's office in actions in which the party seeking service is the United States. The United States, like other civil litigants, is now permitted to designate any person who is 18 years of age and not a party to serve its summons.

The court remains obligated to appoint a marshal, a deputy, or some other person to effect service of a summons in two classes of cases specified by statute: actions brought in forma pauperis or by a seaman. 28 U.S.C. §§1915, 1916. The court also retains discretion to appoint a process server on motion of a party. If a law enforcement presence appears to be necessary or advisable to keep the peace, the court should appoint a marshal or deputy or other official person to make the service. The Department of Justice may also call upon the Marshals Service to perform services in actions brought by the United States. 28 U.S.C. §651.

Subdivision (d). This text is new, but is substantially derived from the former subdivisions (c)(2)(C) and (D), added to the rule by Congress in 1983. The aims of the provision are to eliminate the costs of service of a summons on many parties and to foster cooperation among adversaries and counsel. The rule operates to impose upon the defendant those costs that could have been avoided if the defendant had cooperated reasonably in the manner prescribed. This device is useful in dealing with defendants who are furtive, who reside in places not easily reached by process servers, or who are outside the United States and can be served only at substantial and unnecessary expense. Illustratively, there is no useful purpose achieved by requiring a plaintiff to comply with all the formalities of service in a foreign country, including costs of translation, when suing a defendant manufacturer, fluent in English, whose products are widely distributed in the United States. See Bankston v. Toyota Motor Corp., 889 F.2d 172 (8th Cir. 1989).

The former text described this process as service-by-mail. This language misled some plaintiffs into thinking that service could be effected by mail without the affirmative cooperation of the defendant. E.g., Gulley v. Mayo Foundation, 886 F.2d 161 (8th Cir. 1989). It is more accurate to describe the communication sent to the defendant as a request for a waiver of formal service.

The request for waiver of service may be sent only to defendants subject to service under subdivision (e), (f), or (h). The United States is not expected to waive service for the reason that its mail receiving facilities are inadequate to assure that the notice is actually received by the correct person in the Department of Justice. The same principle is applied to agencies, corporations, and officers of the United States and to other governments and entities subject to service under subdivision (j). Moreover, there are policy reasons why governmental entities should not be confronted with the potential for bearing costs of service in cases in which they ultimately prevail. Infants or incompetent persons likewise are not called upon to waive service because, due to their presumed inability to understand the request and its consequences, they must generally be served through fiduciaries.

It was unclear whether the former rule authorized mailing of a request for "acknowledgement of service" to defendants outside the forum state. See 1 R. Casad, Jurisdiction in Civil Actions (2d Ed.) 5–29, 30 (1991) and cases cited. But, as Professor Casad observed, there was no reason not to employ this device in an effort to obtain service outside the state, and there are many instances in which it was in fact so used, with respect both to defendants within the United States and to defendants in other countries.

The opportunity for waiver has distinct advantages to a foreign defendant. By waiving service, the defendant can reduce the costs that may ultimately be taxed against it if unsuccessful in the lawsuit, including the sometimes substantial expense of translation that may be wholly unnecessary for defendants fluent in English. Moreover, a foreign defendant that waives service is afforded substantially more time to defend against the action than if it had been formally served: under Rule 12, a defendant ordinarily has only 20 days after service in which to file its answer or raise objections by motion, but by signing a waiver it is allowed 90 days after the date the request for waiver was mailed in which to submit its defenses. Because of the additional time needed for mailing and the unreliability of some foreign mail services, a period of 60 days (rather than the 30 days required for domestic transmissions) is provided for a return of a waiver sent to a foreign country.

It is hoped that, since transmission of the notice and waiver forms is a private nonjudicial act, does not purport to effect service, and is not accompanied by any summons or directive from a court, use of the procedure will not offend foreign sovereignties, even those that have withheld their assent to formal service by mail or have objected to the "service-by-mail" provisions of the former rule. Unless the addressee consents, receipt of the request under the revised rule does not give rise to any obligation to answer the lawsuit, does not provide a basis for default judgment, and does not suspend the statute of limitations in those states where the period continues to run until service. Nor are there any adverse consequences to a foreign defendant, since the provisions for shifting the expense of service to a defendant that declines to waive service apply only if the plaintiff and defendant are both located in the United States.

With respect to a defendant located in a foreign country like the United Kingdom, which accepts documents in English, whose Central Authority acts promptly in effecting service, and whose policies discourage its residents from waiving formal service, there will be little reason for a plaintiff to send the notice and request under subdivision (d) rather than use convention methods. On the other hand, the procedure offers significant potential benefits to a plaintiff when suing a defendant that, though fluent in English, is located in a country where, as a condition to formal service under a convention, documents must be translated into another language or where formal service will be otherwise costly or time-consuming.

Paragraph (1) is explicit that a timely waiver of service of a summons does not prejudice the right of a defendant to object by means of a motion authorized by Rule 12(b)(2) to the absence of jurisdiction over the defendant's person, or to assert other defenses that may be available. The only issues eliminated are those involving the sufficiency of the summons or the sufficiency of the method by which it is served.

Paragraph (2) states what the present rule implies: the defendant has a duty to avoid costs associated with the service of a summons not needed to inform the defendant regarding the commencement of an action. The text of the rule also sets forth the requirements for a Notice and Request for Waiver sufficient to put the cost-shifting provision in place. These requirements are illustrated in Forms 1A and 1B, which replace the former Form 18–A.

Paragraph (2)(A) is explicit that a request for waiver of service by a corporate defendant must be addressed to a person qualified to receive service. The general mail rooms of large organizations cannot be required to identify the appropriate individual recipient for an institutional summons.

Paragraph (2)(B) permits the use of alternatives to the United States mails in sending the Notice and Request. While private messenger services or electronic communications may be more expensive than the mail, they may be equally reliable and on occasion more convenient to the parties. Especially with respect to transmissions to foreign countries, alternative means may be desirable, for in some countries facsimile transmission is the most efficient and economical means of communication. If electronic means such as facsimile transmission are employed, the sender should maintain a record of the transmission to assure proof of transmission if receipt is denied, but a party receiving such a transmission has a duty to cooperate and cannot avoid liability for the resulting cost of formal service if the transmission is prevented at the point of receipt.

A defendant failing to comply with a request for waiver shall be given an opportunity to show good cause for the failure, but sufficient cause should be rare. It is not a good cause for failure to waive service that the claim is unjust or that the court lacks jurisdiction. Sufficient cause not to shift the cost of service would exist, however, if the defendant did not receive the request or was insufficiently literate in English to understand it. It should be noted that the provisions for shifting the cost of service apply only if the plaintiff and the defendant are both located in the United States, and accordingly a foreign defendant need not show "good cause" for its failure to waive service.

Paragraph (3) extends the time for answer if, before being served with process, the defendant waives formal service. The extension is intended to serve as an inducement to waive service and to assure that a defendant will not gain any delay by declining to waive service and thereby causing the additional time needed to effect service. By waiving service, a defendant is not called upon to respond to the complaint until 60 days from the date the notice was sent to it—90 days if the notice was sent to a foreign country—rather than within the 20 day period from date of service specified in Rule 12.

Paragraph (4) clarifies the effective date of service when service is waived; the provision is needed to resolve an issue arising when applicable law requires service of process to toll the statute of limitations. E.g., Morse v. Elmira Country Club, 752 F.2d 35 (2d Cir. 1984). Cf. Walker v. Armco Steel Corp., 446 U.S. 740 (1980).

The provisions in former subdivision (c)(2)(C)(ii) of this rule may have been misleading to some parties. Some plaintiffs, not reading the rule carefully, supposed that receipt by the defendant of the mailed complaint had the effect both of establishing the jurisdiction of the court over the defendant's person and of tolling the statute of limitations in actions in which service of the summons is required to toll the limitations period. The revised rule is clear that, if the waiver is not returned and filed, the limitations period under such a law is not tolled and the action will not otherwise proceed until formal service of process is effected.

Some state limitations laws may toll an otherwise applicable statute at the time when the defendant receives notice of the action. Nevertheless, the device of requested waiver of service is not suitable if a limitations period which is about to expire is not tolled by filing the action. Unless there is ample time, the plaintiff should proceed directly to the formal methods for service identified in subdivisions (e), (f), or (h).

The procedure of requesting waiver of service should also not be used if the time for service under subdivision (m) will expire before the date on which the waiver must be returned. While a plaintiff has been allowed additional time for service in that situation, e.g., Prather v. Raymond Constr. Co., 570 F. Supp. 278 (N.D. Ga. 1983), the court could refuse a request for additional time unless the defendant appears to have evaded service pursuant to subdivision (e) or (h). It may be noted that the presumptive time limit for service under subdivision (m) does not apply to service in a foreign country.

Paragraph (5) is a cost-shifting provision retained from the former rule. The costs that may be imposed on the defendant could include, for example, the cost of the time of a process server required to make contact with a defendant residing in a guarded apartment house or residential development. The paragraph is explicit that the costs of enforcing the cost-shifting provision are themselves recoverable from a defendant who fails to return the waiver. In the absence of such a provision, the purpose of the rule would be frustrated by the cost of its enforcement, which is likely to be high in relation to the small benefit secured by the plaintiff.

Some plaintiffs may send a notice and request for waiver and, without waiting for return of the waiver, also proceed with efforts to effect formal service on the defendant. To discourage this practice, the cost-shifting provisions in paragraphs (2) and (5) are limited to costs of effecting service incurred after the time expires for the defendant to return the waiver. Moreover, by returning the waiver within the time allowed and before being served with process, a defendant receives the benefit of the longer period for responding to the complaint afforded for waivers under paragraph (3).

Subdivision (e). This subdivision replaces former subdivisions (c)(2)(C)(i) and (d)(1). It provides a means for service of summons on individuals within a judicial district of the United States. Together with subdivision (f), it provides for service on persons anywhere, subject to constitutional and statutory constraints.

Service of the summons under this subdivision does not conclusively establish the jurisdiction of the court over the person of the defendant. A defendant may assert the territorial limits of the court's reach set forth in subdivision (k), including the constitutional limitations that may be imposed by the Due Process Clause of the Fifth Amendment.

Paragraph (1) authorizes service in any judicial district in conformity with state law. This paragraph sets forth the language of former subdivision (c)(2)(C)(i), which authorized the use of the law of the state in which the district court sits, but adds as an alternative the use of the law of the state in which the service is effected.

Paragraph (2) retains the text of the former subdivision (d)(1) and authorizes the use of the familiar methods of personal or abode service or service on an authorized agent in any judicial district.

To conform to these provisions, the former subdivision (e) bearing on proceedings against parties not found within the state is stricken. Likewise stricken is the first sentence of the former subdivision (f), which had restricted the authority of the federal process server to the state in which the district court sits.

Subdivision (f). This subdivision provides for service on individuals who are in a foreign country, replacing the former subdivision (i) that was added to Rule 4 in 1963. Reflecting the pattern of Rule 4 in incorporating state law limitations on the exercise of jurisdiction over persons, the former subdivision (i) limited service outside the United States to cases in which extraterritorial service was authorized by state or federal law. The new rule eliminates the requirement of explicit authorization. On occasion, service in a foreign country was held to be improper for lack of statutory authority. E.g., Martens v. Winder, 341 F.2d 197 (9th Cir.), cert. denied, 382 U.S. 937 (1965). This authority, however, was found to exist by implication. E.g., SEC v. VTR, Inc., 39 F.R.D. 19 (S.D.N.Y. 1966). Given the substantial increase in the number of international transactions and events that are the subject of litigation in federal courts, it is appropriate to infer a general legislative authority to effect service on defendants in a foreign country.

A secondary effect of this provision for foreign service of a federal summons is to facilitate the use of federal long-arm law in actions brought to enforce the federal law against defendants who cannot be served under any state law but who can be constitutionally subjected to the jurisdiction of the federal court. Such a provision is set forth in paragraph (2) of subdivision (k) of this rule, applicable only to persons not subject to the territorial jurisdiction of any particular state.

Paragraph (1) gives effect to the Hague Convention on the Service Abroad of Judicial and Extrajudicial Documents, which entered into force for the United States on February 10, 1969. See 28 U.S.C.A., Fed.R.Civ.P. 4 (Supp. 1986). This Convention is an important means of dealing with problems of service in a foreign country. See generally 1 B. Ristau, International Judicial Assistance §§4–1–1 to 4–5–2 (1990). Use of the Convention procedures, when available, is mandatory if documents must be transmitted abroad to effect service. See Volkswagenwerk Aktiengesellschaft v. Schlunk, 486 U.S. 694 (1988) (noting that voluntary use of these procedures may be desirable even when service could constitutionally be effected in another manner); J. Weis, The Federal Rules and the Hague Conventions: Concerns of Conformity and Comity, 50 U. Pitt. L. Rev. 903 (1989). Therefore, this paragraph provides that, when service is to be effected outside a judicial district of the United States, the methods of service appropriate under an applicable treaty shall be employed if available and if the treaty so requires.

The Hague Convention furnishes safeguards against the abridgment of rights of parties through inadequate notice. Article 15 provides for verification of actual notice or a demonstration that process was served by a method prescribed by the internal laws of the foreign state before a default judgment may be entered. Article 16 of the Convention also enables the judge to extend the time for appeal after judgment if the defendant shows a lack of adequate notice either to defend or to appeal the judgment, or has disclosed a prima facie case on the merits.

The Hague Convention does not specify a time within which a foreign country's Central Authority must effect service, but Article 15 does provide that alternate methods may be used if a Central Authority does not respond within six months. Generally, a Central Authority can be expected to respond much more quickly than that limit might permit, but there have been occasions when the signatory state was dilatory or refused to cooperate for substantive reasons. In such cases, resort may be had to the provision set forth in subdivision (f)(3).

Two minor changes in the text reflect the Hague Convention. First, the term "letter of request" has been added. Although these words are synonymous with "letter rogatory," "letter of request" is preferred in modern usage. The provision should not be interpreted to authorize use of a letter of request when there is in fact no treaty obligation on the receiving country to honor such a request from this country or when the United States does not extend diplomatic recognition to the foreign nation. Second, the passage formerly found in subdivision (i)(1)(B), "when service in either case is reasonably calculated to give actual notice," has been relocated.

Paragraph (2) provides alternative methods for use when internationally agreed methods are not intended to be exclusive, or where there is no international agreement applicable. It contains most of the language formerly set forth in subdivision (i) of the rule. Service by methods that would violate foreign law is not generally authorized. Subparagraphs (A) and (B) prescribe the more appropriate methods for conforming to local practice or using a local authority. Subparagraph (C) prescribes other methods authorized by the former rule.

Paragraph (3) authorizes the court to approve other methods of service not prohibited by international agreements. The Hague Convention, for example, authorizes special forms of service in cases of urgency if convention methods will not permit service within the time required by the circumstances. Other circumstances that might justify the use of additional methods include the failure of the foreign country's Central Authority to effect service within the six-month period provided by the Convention, or the refusal of the Central Authority to serve a complaint seeking punitive damages or to enforce the antitrust laws of the United States. In such cases, the court may direct a special method of service not explicitly authorized by international agreement if not prohibited by the agreement. Inasmuch as our Constitution requires that reasonable notice be given, an earnest effort should be made to devise a method of communication that is consistent with due process and minimizes offense to foreign law. A court may in some instances specially authorize use of ordinary mail. Cf. Levin v. Ruby Trading Corp., 248 F. Supp. 537 (S.D.N.Y. 1965).

Subdivision (g). This subdivision retains the text of former subdivision (d)(2). Provision is made for service upon an infant or incompetent person in a foreign country.

Subdivision (h). This subdivision retains the text of former subdivision (d)(3), with changes reflecting those made in subdivision (e). It also contains the provisions for service on a corporation or association in a foreign country, as formerly found in subdivision (i).

Frequent use should be made of the Notice and Request procedure set forth in subdivision (d) in actions against corporations. Care must be taken, however, to address the request to an individual officer or authorized agent of the corporation. It is not effective use of the Notice and Request procedure if the mail is sent undirected to the mail room of the organization.

Subdivision (i). This subdivision retains much of the text of former subdivisions (d)(4) and (d)(5). Paragraph (1) provides for service of a summons on the United States; it amends former subdivision (d)(4) to permit the United States attorney to be served by registered or certified mail. The rule does not authorize the use of the Notice and Request procedure of revised subdivision (d) when the United States is the defendant. To assure proper handling of mail in the United States attorney's office, the authorized mail service must be specifically addressed to the civil process clerk of the office of the United States attorney.

Paragraph (2) replaces former subdivision (d)(5). Paragraph (3) saves the plaintiff from the hazard of losing a substantive right because of failure to comply with the complex requirements of multiple service under this subdivision. That risk has proved to be more than nominal. E.g., Whale v. United States, 792 F.2d 951

(9th Cir. 1986). This provision should be read in connection with the provisions of subdivision (c) of Rule 15 to preclude the loss of substantive rights against the United States or its agencies, corporations, or officers resulting from a plaintiff's failure to correctly identify and serve all the persons who should be named or served.

Subdivision (j). This subdivision retains the text of former subdivision (d)(6) without material change. The waiver-of-service provision is also inapplicable to actions against governments subject to service pursuant to this subdivision.

The revision adds a new paragraph (1) referring to the statute governing service of a summons on a foreign state and its political subdivisions, agencies, and instrumentalities, the Foreign Sovereign Immunities Act of 1976, 28 U.S.C. §1608. The caption of the subdivision reflects that change.

Subdivision (k). This subdivision replaces the former subdivision (f), with no change in the title. Paragraph (1) retains the substance of the former rule in explicitly authorizing the exercise of personal jurisdiction over persons who can be reached under state long-arm law, the "100-mile bulge" provision added in 1963, or the federal interpleader act. Paragraph (1)(D) is new, but merely calls attention to federal legislation that may provide for nationwide or even world-wide service of process in cases arising under particular federal laws. Congress has provided for nationwide service of process and full exercise of territorial jurisdiction by all district courts with respect to specified federal actions. See 1 R. Casad, Jurisdiction in Civil Actions (2d Ed.) chap. 5 (1991).

Paragraph (2) is new. It authorizes the exercise of territorial jurisdiction over the person of any defendant against whom is made a claim arising under any federal law if that person is subject to personal jurisdiction in no state. This addition is a companion to the amendments made in revised subdivisions (e) and (f).

This paragraph corrects a gap in the enforcement of federal law. Under the former rule, a problem was presented when the defendant was a non-resident of the United States having contacts with the United States sufficient to justify the application of United States law and to satisfy federal standards of forum selection, but having insufficient contact with any single state to support jurisdiction under state long-arm legislation or meet the requirements of the Fourteenth Amendment limitation on state court territorial jurisdiction. In such cases, the defendant was shielded from the enforcement of federal law by the fortuity of a favorable limitation on the power of state courts, which was incorporated into the federal practice by the former rule. In this respect, the revision responds to the suggestion of the Supreme Court made in Omni Capital Int'l v. Rudolf Wolff & Co., Ltd., 484 U.S. 97, 111 (1987).

There remain constitutional limitations on the exercise of territorial jurisdiction by federal courts over persons outside the United States. These restrictions arise from the Fifth Amendment rather than from the Fourteenth Amendment, which limits state-court reach and which was incorporated into federal practice by the reference to state law in the text of the former subdivision (e) that is deleted by this revision. The Fifth Amendment requires that any defendant have affiliating contacts with the United States sufficient to justify the exercise of personal jurisdiction over that party. Cf. Wells Fargo & Co. v. Wells Fargo Express Co., 556 F.2d 406, 418 (9th Cir. 1977). There also may be a further Fifth Amendment constraint in that a plaintiff's forum selection might be so inconvenient to a defendant that it would be a denial of "fair play and substantial justice" required by the due process clause, even though the defendant had significant affiliating contacts with the United States. See DeJames v. Magnificent Carriers, 654 F.2d 280, 286 n.3 (3rd Cir.), cert. denied, 454 U.S. 1085 (1981). Compare World-Wide Volkswagen Corp. v. Woodson, 444 U.S. 286, 293–294 (1980); Insurance Corp. of Ireland v. Compagnie des Bauxites de Guinee, 456 U.S. 694, 702–03 (1982); Burger King Corp. v. Rudzewicz, 471 U.S. 462, 476–78 (1985); Asahi Metal Indus. v. Superior Court of Cal., Solano County, 480 U.S. 102, 108–13 (1987). See generally R. Lusardi, Nationwide Service of Process: Due Process Limitations on the Power of the Sovereign, 33 Vill. L. Rev. 1 (1988).

This provision does not affect the operation of federal venue legislation. See generally 28 U.S.C. §1391. Nor does it affect the operation of federal law providing for the change of venue. 28 U.S.C. §§1404, 1406. The availability of transfer for fairness and convenience under §1404 should preclude most conflicts between the full exercise of territorial jurisdiction permitted by this rule and the Fifth Amendment requirement of "fair play and substantial justice."

The district court should be especially scrupulous to protect aliens who reside in a foreign country from forum selections so onerous that injustice could result. "[G]reat care and reserve should be exercised when extending our notions of personal jurisdiction into the international field." Asahi Metal Indus. v. Superior Court of Cal., Solano County, 480 U.S. 102, 115 (1987), quoting United States v. First Nat'l City Bank, 379 U.S. 378, 404 (1965) (Harlan, J., dissenting).

This narrow extension of the federal reach applies only if a claim is made against the defendant under federal law. It does not establish personal jurisdiction if the only claims are those arising under state law or the law of another country, even though there might be diversity or alienage subject matter jurisdiction as to such claims. If, however, personal jurisdiction is established under this paragraph with respect to a federal claim, then 28 U.S.C. §1367(a) provides supplemental jurisdiction over related claims against that defendant, subject to the court's discretion to decline exercise of that jurisdiction under 28 U.S.C. §1367(c).

Subdivision (l). This subdivision assembles in one place all the provisions of the present rule bearing on proof of service. No material change in the rule is effected. The provision that proof of service can be amended by leave of court is retained from the former subdivision (h). See generally 4A Wright & Miller, Federal Practice and Procedure §1132 (2d ed. 1987).

Subdivision (m). This subdivision retains much of the language of the present subdivision (j).

The new subdivision explicitly provides that the court shall allow additional time if there is good cause for the plaintiff's failure to effect service in the prescribed 120 days, and authorizes the court to relieve a plaintiff of the consequences of an application of this subdivision even if there is no good cause shown. Such relief formerly was afforded in some cases, partly in reliance on Rule 6(b). Relief may be justified, for example, if the applicable statute of limitations would bar the refiled action, or if the defendant is evading service or conceals a defect in attempted service. E.g., Ditkof v. Owens-Illinois, Inc., 114 F.R.D. 104 (E.D. Mich. 1987). A specific instance of good cause is set forth in paragraph (3) of this rule, which provides for extensions if necessary to correct oversights in compliance with the requirements of multiple service in actions against the United States or its officers, agencies, and corporations. The district court should also take care to protect pro se plaintiffs from consequences of confusion or delay attending the resolution of an in forma pauperis petition. Robinson v. America's Best Contacts & Eyeglasses, 876 F.2d 596 (7th Cir. 1989).

The 1983 revision of this subdivision referred to the "party on whose behalf such service was required," rather than to the "plaintiff," a term used generically elsewhere in this rule to refer to any party initiating a claim against a person who is not a party to the action. To simplify the text, the revision returns to the usual practice in the rule of referring simply to the plaintiff even though its principles apply with equal force to defendants who may assert claims against non-parties under Rules 13(h), 14, 19, 20, or 21.

Subdivision (n). This subdivision provides for in rem and quasi-in-rem jurisdiction. Paragraph (1) incorporates any requirements of 28 U.S.C. §1655 or similar provisions bearing on seizures or liens.

Paragraph (2) provides for other uses of quasi-in-rem jurisdiction but limits its use to exigent circumstances. Provisional remedies may be employed as a means to secure jurisdiction over the property of a defendant whose person is not within reach of the court, but occasions for the use of this provision should be rare, as where the defendant is a fugitive or assets are in imminent danger of disappearing. Until 1963, it was not possible under Rule 4 to assert jurisdiction in a federal court over the property of a defendant not personally served. The 1963 amendment to subdivision (e) authorized the use of state law procedures authorizing seizures of assets as a basis for jurisdiction. Given the liberal availability of long-arm jurisdiction, the exercise of power quasi-in-rem has become almost an anachronism. Circumstances too spare to affiliate the defendant to the forum state sufficiently to support long-arm jurisdiction over the defendant's person are also inadequate to support seizure of the defendant's assets fortuitously found within the state. Shaffer v. Heitner, 433 U.S. 186 (1977).

Committee Notes on Rules—2000 Amendment

Paragraph (2)(B) is added to Rule 4(i) to require service on the United States when a United States officer or employee is sued in an individual capacity for acts or omissions occurring in connection with duties performed on behalf of the United States. Decided cases provide uncertain guidance on the question whether the United States must be served in such actions. See Vaccaro v. Dobre, 81 F.3d 854, 856–857 (9th Cir. 1996); Armstrong v. Sears, 33 F.3d 182, 185–187 (2d Cir. 1994); Ecclesiastical Order of the Ism of Am v. Chasin, 845 F.2d 113, 116 (6th Cir. 1988); Light v. Wolf, 816 F.2d 746 (D.C. Cir. 1987); see also Simpkins v. District of Columbia, 108 F.3d 366, 368–369 (D.C. Cir. 1997). Service on the United States will help to protect the interest of the individual defendant in securing representation by the United States, and will expedite the process of determining whether the United States will provide representation. It has been understood that the individual defendant must be served as an individual defendant, a requirement that is made explicit. Invocation of the individual service provisions of subdivisions (e), (f), and (g) invokes also the waiver-of-service provisions of subdivision (d).

Paragraph 2(B) reaches service when an officer or employee of the United States is sued in an individual capacity "for acts or omissions occurring in connection with the performance of duties on behalf of the United States." This phrase has been chosen as a functional phrase that can be applied without the occasionally distracting associations of such phrases as "scope of employment," "color of office," or "arising out of the employment." Many actions are brought against individual federal officers or employees of the United States for acts or omissions that have no connection whatever to their governmental roles. There is no reason to require service on the United States in these actions. The connection to federal employment that requires service on the United States must be determined as a practical matter, considering whether the individual defendant has reasonable grounds to look to the United States for assistance and whether the United States has reasonable grounds for demanding formal notice of the action.

An action against a former officer or employee of the United States is covered by paragraph (2)(B) in the same way as an action against a present officer or employee. Termination of the relationship between the individual defendant and the United States does not reduce the need to serve the United States.

Paragraph (3) is amended to ensure that failure to serve the United States in an action governed by paragraph 2(B) does not defeat an action. This protection is adopted because there will be cases in which the plaintiff reasonably fails to appreciate the need to serve the United States. There is no requirement, however, that the plaintiff show that the failure to serve the United States was reasonable. A reasonable time to effect service on the United States must be allowed after the failure is pointed out. An additional change ensures that if the United States or United States attorney is served in an action governed by paragraph 2(A), additional time is to be allowed even though no officer, employee, agency, or corporation of the United States was served.

GAP Report. The most important changes were made to ensure that no one would read the seemingly independent provisions of paragraphs 2(A) and 2(B) to mean that service must be made twice both on the United States and on the United States employee when the employee is sued in both official and individual capacities. The word "only" was added in subparagraph (A) and the new phrase "whether or not the officer or employee is sued also in an individual capacity" was inserted in subparagraph (B).

Minor changes were made to include "Employees" in the catchline for subdivision (i), and to add "or employee" in paragraph 2(A). Although it may seem awkward to think of suit against an employee in an official capacity, there is no clear definition that separates "officers" from "employees" for this purpose. The published proposal to amend Rule 12(a)(3) referred to actions against an employee sued in an official capacity, and it seemed better to make the rules parallel by adding "employee" to Rule 4(i)(2)(A) than by deleting it from Rule 12(a)(3)(A).

Committee Notes on Rules—2007 Amendment

The language of Rule 4 has been amended as part of the general restyling of the Civil Rules to make them more easily understood and to make style and terminology consistent throughout the rules. These changes are intended to be stylistic only.

Rule 4(d)(1)(C) corrects an inadvertent error in former Rule 4(d)(2)(G). The defendant needs two copies of the waiver form, not an extra copy of the notice and request.

Rule 4(g) changes "infant" to "minor." "Infant" in the present rule means "minor." Modern word usage suggests that "minor" will better maintain the intended meaning. The same change from "infant" to "minor" is made throughout the rules. In addition, subdivision (f)(3) is added to the description of methods of service that the court may order; the addition ensures the evident intent that the court not order service by means prohibited by international agreement.

Rule 4(i)(4) corrects a misleading reference to "the plaintiff" in former Rule 4(i)(3). A party other than a plaintiff may need a reasonable time to effect service. Rule 4(i)(4) properly covers any party.

Former Rule 4(j)(2) refers to service upon an "other governmental organization subject to suit." This is changed to "any other state-created governmental organization that is subject to suit." The change entrenches the meaning indicated by the caption ("Serving a Foreign, State, or Local Government"), and the invocation of state law. It excludes any risk that this rule might be read to govern service on a federal agency, or other entities not created by state law.

The former provision describing service on interpleader claimants [former subd. (k)(1)(C)] is deleted as redundant in light of the general provision in (k)(1)(C) recognizing personal jurisdiction authorized by a federal statute.

Committee Notes on Rules—2015 Amendment

Subdivision (d). Abrogation of Rule 84 and the other official forms requires that former Forms 5 and 6 be directly incorporated into Rule 4.

Subdivision (m). The presumptive time for serving a defendant is reduced from 120 days to 90 days. This change, together with the shortened times for issuing a scheduling order set by amended Rule 16(b)(2), will reduce delay at the beginning of litigation.

Shortening the presumptive time for service will increase the frequency of occasions to extend the time. More time may be needed, for example, when a request to waive service fails, a defendant is difficult to serve, or a marshal is to make service in an in forma pauperis action.

The final sentence is amended to make it clear that the reference to Rule 4 in Rule 71.1(d)(3)(A) does not include Rule 4(m). Dismissal under Rule 4(m) for failure to make timely service would be inconsistent with the limits on dismissal established by Rule 71.1(i)(1)(C).

Shortening the time to serve under Rule 4(m) means that the time of the notice required by Rule 15(c)(1)(C) for relation back is also shortened.

Committee Notes on Rules—2016 Amendment

Rule 4(m) is amended to correct a possible ambiguity that appears to have generated some confusion in practice. Service in a foreign country often is accomplished by means that require more than the time set by Rule 4(m). This problem is recognized by the two clear exceptions for service on an individual in a foreign country under Rule 4(f) and for service on a foreign state under Rule 4(j)(1). The potential ambiguity arises from the lack of any explicit reference to service on a corporation, partnership, or other unincorporated association. Rule 4(h)(2) provides for service on such defendants at a place outside any judicial district of the United States "in any manner prescribed by Rule 4(f) for serving an individual, except personal delivery under (f)(2)(C)(i)." Invoking service "in the manner prescribed by Rule 4(f)" could easily be read to mean that service under Rule 4(h)(2) is also service "under" Rule 4(f). That interpretation is in keeping with the purpose to recognize the delays that often occur in effecting service in a foreign country. But it also is possible to read the words for what they seem to say—service is under Rule 4(h)(2), albeit in a manner borrowed from almost all, but not quite all, of Rule 4(f).

The amendment resolves this possible ambiguity.

References in Text

Rule 4(m) is set out above as it appears in the Supreme Court order of Apr. 28, 2016. As amended by the Supreme Court order of Apr. 29, 2015, the last sentence of Rule 4(m) reads as follows: "This subdivision (m) does not apply to service in a foreign country under Rule 4(f) or 4(j)(1) or to service of a notice under Rule 71.1(d)(3)(A)." The language added to the last sentence in 2015, "or to service of a notice under Rule 71.1(d)(3)(A)", probably should be part of Rule 4(m), but does not appear in the 2016 amendment.

Committee Notes on Rules—2017 Amendment

This is a technical amendment that integrates the intended effect of the amendments adopted in 2015 and 2016.

Civil Rule 4(m) addresses the time limit for service of a summons and was amended in two consecutive years, 2015 and 2016. In addition to shortening the presumptive time for service from 120 days to 90 days, the 2015 amendment added an exemption from the time limit for Rule 71.1(d)(3)(A) notices of a condemnation action. The 2016 amendment added another exemption for Rule 4(h)(2) service on a corporation, partnership, or association at a place not within any judicial district of the United States.

The sequential amendments resulted in an error. The 2016 amendment exempting Rule 4(h)(2) was prepared in 2014, before the 2015 amendment exempting Rule 71.1(d)(3)(A) was in effect. Once the 2015 amendment became effective, it should have been incorporated into the proposed 2016 amendment then making its way through the Rules Enabling Act process, but such a revision of the 2016 materials was overlooked. As a result, Rule 71.1(d)(3)(A) was not included in the list of exemptions in Rule 4(m) when the 2016 amendment became effective. The Advisory and Standing Committees unanimously recommend restoring Rule 71.1(d)(3)(A) to the list of exemptions in Rule 4(m) without re-publication.

Amendment by Public Law

1983—Subd. (a). Pub. L. 97–462, §2(1), substituted "deliver the summons to the plaintiff or the plaintiff's attorney, who shall be responsible for prompt service of the summons and a copy of the complaint" for "deliver it for service to the marshal or to any other person authorized by Rule 4(c) to serve it".

Subd. (c). Pub. L. 97–462, §2(2), substituted provision with subd heading "Service" for provision with subd. heading "By Whom Served" which read: "Service of process shall be made by a United States marshal, by his deputy, or by some person specially appointed by the court for that purpose, except that a subpoena may be served as provided in Rule 45. Special appointments to serve process shall be made freely. Service of process may also be made by a person authorized to serve process in an action brought in the courts of general jurisdiction of the state in which the district court is held or in which service is made."

Subd. (d). Pub. L. 97–462, §2(3), (4), substituted "Summons and Complaint: Person to be Served" for "Summons: Personal Service" in subd. heading.

Subd. (d)(5). Pub. L. 97–462, §2(4), substituted "sending a copy of the summons and of the complaint by registered or certified mail" for "delivering a copy of the summons and of the complaint".

Subd. (d)(7). Pub. L. 97–462, §2(3)(B), struck out par. (7) which read: "Upon a defendant of any class referred to in paragraph (1) or (3) of this subdivision of this rule, it is also sufficient if the summons and complaint are served in the manner prescribed by any statute of the United States or in the manner prescribed by the law of the state in which the district court is held for the service of summons or other like process upon any such defendant in an action brought in the courts of general jurisdiction of that state.". See subd. (c)(2)(C) of this rule.

Subd. (e). Pub. L. 97–462, §2(5), substituted "Summons" for "Same" as subd. heading.

Subd. (g). Pub. L. 97–462, §2(6), substituted in second sentence "deputy United States marshal" and "such person" for "his deputy" and "he" and inserted third sentence "If service is made under subdivision (c)(2)(C)(ii) of this rule, return shall be made by the sender's filing with the court the acknowledgment received pursuant to such subdivision.".

Subd. (j). Pub. L. 97–462, §2(7), added subd. (j).

Effective Date of 1983 Amendment

Amendment by Pub. L. 97–462 effective 45 days after Jan. 12, 1983, see section 4 of Pub. L. 97–462, set out as a note under section 2071 of this title.

Rule 4.1. Serving Other Process

(a) In General. Process—other than a summons under Rule 4 or a subpoena under Rule 45—must be served by a United States marshal or deputy marshal or by a person specially appointed for that purpose. It may be served anywhere within the territorial limits of the state where the district court is located and, if authorized by a federal statute, beyond those limits. Proof of service must be made under Rule 4(l).

(b) Enforcing Orders: Committing for Civil Contempt. An order committing a person for civil contempt of a decree or injunction issued to enforce federal law may be served and enforced in any district. Any other order in a civil-contempt proceeding may be served only in the state where the issuing court is located or elsewhere in the United States within 100 miles from where the order was issued.

(As added Apr. 22, 1993, eff. Dec. 1, 1993; amended Apr. 30, 2007, eff. Dec. 1, 2007.)

Notes of Advisory Committee on Rules—1993

This is a new rule. Its purpose is to separate those few provisions of the former Rule 4 bearing on matters other than service of a summons to allow greater textual clarity in Rule 4. Subdivision (a) contains no new language.

Subdivision (b) replaces the final clause of the penultimate sentence of the former subdivision 4(f), a clause added to the rule in 1963. The new rule provides for nationwide service of orders of civil commitment enforcing decrees of injunctions issued to compel compliance with federal law. The rule makes no change in the practice with respect to the enforcement of injunctions or decrees not involving the enforcement of federally-created rights.

Service of process is not required to notify a party of a decree or injunction, or of an order that the party show cause why that party should not be held in contempt of such an order. With respect to a party who has once been served with a summons, the service of the decree or injunction itself or of an order to show cause can be made pursuant to Rule 5. Thus, for example, an injunction may be served on a party through that person's attorney. Chagas v. United States, 369 F.2d 643 (5th Cir. 1966). The same is true for service of an order to show cause. Waffenschmidt v. Mackay, 763 F.2d 711 (5th Cir. 1985).

The new rule does not affect the reach of the court to impose criminal contempt sanctions. Nationwide enforcement of federal decrees and injunctions is already available with respect to criminal contempt: a federal court may effect the arrest of a criminal contemnor anywhere in the United States, 28 U.S.C. §3041, and a contemnor when arrested may be subject to removal to the district in which punishment may be imposed. Fed. R. Crim. P. 40. Thus, the present law permits criminal contempt enforcement against a contemnor wherever that person may be found.

The effect of the revision is to provide a choice of civil or criminal contempt sanctions in those situations to which it applies. Contempt proceedings, whether civil or criminal, must be brought in the court that was allegedly defied by a contumacious act. Ex parte Bradley, 74 U.S. 366 (1869). This is so even if the offensive conduct or inaction occurred outside the district of the court in which the enforcement proceeding must be conducted. E.g., McCourtney v. United States, 291 Fed. 497 (8th Cir.), cert. denied, 263 U.S. 714 (1923). For this purpose, the rule as before does not distinguish between parties and other persons subject to contempt sanctions by reason of their relation or connection to parties.

Committee Notes on Rules—2007 Amendment

The language of Rule 4.1 has been amended as part of the general restyling of the Civil Rules to make them more easily understood and to make style and terminology consistent throughout the rules. These changes are intended to be stylistic only.

Rule 5. Serving and Filing Pleadings and Other Papers

(a) Service: When Required.

(1) In General. Unless these rules provide otherwise, each of the following papers must be served on every party:

(A) an order stating that service is required;

(B) a pleading filed after the original complaint, unless the court orders otherwise under Rule 5(c) because there are numerous defendants;

(C) a discovery paper required to be served on a party, unless the court orders otherwise;

(D) a written motion, except one that may be heard ex parte; and

(E) a written notice, appearance, demand, or offer of judgment, or any similar paper.

(2) If a Party Fails to Appear. No service is required on a party who is in default for failing to appear. But a pleading that asserts a new claim for relief against such a party must be served on that party under Rule 4.

(3) Seizing Property. If an action is begun by seizing property and no person is or need be named as a defendant, any service required before the filing of an appearance, answer, or claim must be made on the person who had custody or possession of the property when it was seized.

(b) Service: How Made.

(1) Serving an Attorney. If a party is represented by an attorney, service under this rule must be made on the attorney unless the court orders service on the party.

(2) Service in General. A paper is served under this rule by:

(A) handing it to the person;

(B) leaving it:

(i) at the person's office with a clerk or other person in charge or, if no one is in charge, in a conspicuous place in the office; or

(ii) if the person has no office or the office is closed, at the person's dwelling or usual place of abode with someone of suitable age and discretion who resides there;

(C) mailing it to the person's last known address—in which event service is complete upon mailing;

(D) leaving it with the court clerk if the person has no known address;

(E) sending it by electronic means if the person consented in writing—in which event service is complete upon transmission, but is not effective if the serving party learns that it did not reach the person to be served; or

(F) delivering it by any other means that the person consented to in writing—in which event service is complete when the person making service delivers it to the agency designated to make delivery.

(3) Using Court Facilities. If a local rule so authorizes, a party may use the court's transmission facilities to make service under Rule 5(b)(2)(E).

(c) Serving Numerous Defendants.

(1) In General. If an action involves an unusually large number of defendants, the court may, on motion or on its own, order that:

(A) defendants' pleadings and replies to them need not be served on other defendants;

(B) any crossclaim, counterclaim, avoidance, or affirmative defense in those pleadings and replies to them will be treated as denied or avoided by all other parties; and

(C) filing any such pleading and serving it on the plaintiff constitutes notice of the pleading to all parties.

(2) Notifying Parties. A copy of every such order must be served on the parties as the court directs.

(d) Filing.

(1) Required Filings; Certificate of Service. Any paper after the complaint that is required to be served—together with a certificate of service—must be filed within a reasonable time after service. But disclosures under Rule 26(a)(1) or (2) and the following discovery requests and responses must not be filed until they are used in the proceeding or the court orders filing: depositions, interrogatories, requests for documents or tangible things or to permit entry onto land, and requests for admission.

(2) How Filing Is Made—In General. A paper is filed by delivering it:

(A) to the clerk; or

(B) to a judge who agrees to accept it for filing, and who must then note the filing date on the paper and promptly send it to the clerk.

(3) Electronic Filing, Signing, or Verification. A court may, by local rule, allow papers to be filed, signed, or verified by electronic means that are consistent with any technical standards established by the Judicial Conference of the United States. A local rule may require electronic filing only if reasonable exceptions are allowed. A paper filed electronically in compliance with a local rule is a written paper for purposes of these rules.

(4) Acceptance by the Clerk. The clerk must not refuse to file a paper solely because it is not in the form prescribed by these rules or by a local rule or practice.

(As amended Jan. 21, 1963, eff. July 1, 1963; Mar. 30, 1970, eff. July 1, 1970; Apr. 29, 1980, eff. Aug. 1, 1980; Mar. 2, 1987, eff. Aug. 1, 1987; Apr. 30, 1991, eff. Dec. 1, 1991; Apr. 22, 1993, eff. Dec. 1, 1993; Apr. 23, 1996, eff. Dec. 1, 1996; Apr. 17, 2000, eff. Dec. 1, 2000; Apr. 23, 2001, eff. Dec. 1, 2001; Apr. 12, 2006, eff. Dec. 1, 2006; Apr. 30, 2007, eff. Dec. 1, 2007.)

Notes of Advisory Committee on Rules—1937

Note to Subdivisions (a) and (b). Compare 2 Minn.Stat. (Mason, 1927) §§9240, 9241, 9242; N.Y.C.P.A. (1937) §§163, 164, and N.Y.R.C.P. (1937) Rules 20, 21; 2 Wash.Rev.Stat.Ann. (Remington, 1932) §§244–249.

Note to Subdivision (d). Compare the present practice under [former] Equity Rule 12 (Issue of Subpoena—Time for Answer).

Notes of Advisory Committee on Rules—1963 Amendment

The words "affected thereby," stricken out by the amendment, introduced a problem of interpretation. See 1 Barron & Holtzoff, Federal Practice & Procedure 760–61 (Wright ed. 1960). The amendment eliminates this difficulty and promotes full exchange of information among the parties by requiring service of papers on all the parties to the action, except as otherwise provided in the rules. See also subdivision (c) of Rule 5. So, for example, a third-party defendant is required to serve his answer to the third-party complaint not only upon the defendant but also upon the plaintiff. See amended Form 22–A and the Advisory Committee's Note thereto.

As to the method of serving papers upon a party whose address is unknown, see Rule 5(b).

Notes of Advisory Committee on Rules—1970 Amendment

The amendment makes clear that all papers relating to discovery which are required to be served on any party must be served on all parties, unless the court orders otherwise. The present language expressly includes notices and demands, but it is not explicit as to answers or responses as provided in Rules 33, 34, and 36. Discovery papers may be voluminous or the parties numerous, and the court is empowered to vary the requirement if in a given case it proves needlessly onerous.

In actions begun by seizure of property, service will at times have to be made before the absent owner of the property has filed an appearance. For example, a prompt deposition may be needed in a maritime action in rem. See Rules 30(a) and 30(b)(2) and the related notes. A provision is added authorizing service on the person having custody or possession of the property at the time of its seizure.

Notes of Advisory Committee on Rules—1980 Amendment

Subdivision (d). By the terms of this rule and Rule 30(f)(1) discovery materials must be promptly filed, although it often happens that no use is made of the materials after they are filed. Because the copies required for filing are an added expense and the large volume of discovery filings presents serious problems of storage in some districts, the Committee in 1978 first proposed that discovery materials not be filed unless on order of the court or for use in the proceedings. But such materials are sometimes of interest to those who may have no access to them except by a requirement of filing, such as members of a class, litigants similarly situated, or the public generally. Accordingly, this amendment and a change in Rule 30(f)(1) continue the requirement of filing but make it subject to an order of the court that discovery materials not be filed unless filing is requested by the court or is effected by parties who wish to use the materials in the proceeding.

Notes of Advisory Committee on Rules—1987 Amendment

The amendments are technical. No substantive change is intended.

Notes of Advisory Committee on Rules—1991 Amendment

Subdivision (d). This subdivision is amended to require that the person making service under the rule certify that service has been effected. Such a requirement has generally been imposed by local rule.

Having such information on file may be useful for many purposes, including proof of service if an issue arises concerning the effectiveness of the service. The certificate will generally specify the date as well as the manner of service, but parties employing private delivery services may sometimes be unable to specify the date of delivery. In the latter circumstance, a specification of the date of transmission of the paper to the delivery service may be sufficient for the purposes of this rule.

Subdivision (e). The words "pleading and other" are stricken as unnecessary. Pleadings are papers within the meaning of the rule. The revision also accommodates the development of the use of facsimile transmission for filing.

Several local district rules have directed the office of the clerk to refuse to accept for filing papers not conforming to certain requirements of form imposed by local rules or practice. This is not a suitable role for the office of the clerk, and the practice exposes litigants to the hazards of time bars; for these reasons, such rules are proscribed by this revision. The enforcement of these rules and of the local rules is a role for a judicial officer. A clerk may of course advise a party or counsel that a particular instrument is not in proper form, and may be directed to so inform the court.

Notes of Advisory Committee on Rules—1993 Amendment

This is a technical amendment, using the broader language of Rule 25 of the Federal Rules of Appellate Procedure. The district court—and the bankruptcy court by virtue of a cross-reference in Bankruptcy Rule 7005—can, by local rule, permit filing not only by facsimile transmissions but also by other electronic means, subject to standards approved by the Judicial Conference.

Notes of Advisory Committee on Rules—1996 Amendment

The present Rule 5(e) has authorized filing by facsimile or other electronic means on two conditions. The filing must be authorized by local rule. Use of this means of filing must be authorized by the Judicial Conference of the United States and must be consistent with standards established by the Judicial Conference. Attempts to develop Judicial Conference standards have demonstrated the value of several adjustments in the rule.

The most significant change discards the requirement that the Judicial Conference authorize local electronic filing rules. As before, each district may decide for itself whether it has the equipment and personnel required to establish electronic filing, but a district that wishes to establish electronic filing need no longer await Judicial Conference action.

The role of the Judicial Conference standards is clarified by specifying that the standards are to govern technical matters. Technical standards can provide nationwide uniformity, enabling ready use of electronic filing without pausing to adjust for the otherwise inevitable variations among local rules. Judicial Conference adoption of technical standards should prove superior to specification in these rules. Electronic technology has advanced with great speed. The process of adopting Judicial Conference standards should prove speedier and more flexible in determining the time for the first uniform standards, in adjusting standards at appropriate intervals, and in sparing the Supreme Court and Congress the need to consider technological details. Until Judicial Conference standards are adopted, however, uniformity will occur only to the extent that local rules deliberately seek to copy other local rules.

It is anticipated that Judicial Conference standards will govern such technical specifications as data formatting, speed of transmission, means to transmit copies of supporting documents, and security of communication. Perhaps more important, standards must be established to assure proper maintenance and integrity of the record and to provide appropriate access and retrieval mechanisms. Local rules must address these issues until Judicial Conference standards are adopted.

The amended rule also makes clear the equality of filing by electronic means with written filings. An electronic filing that complies with the local rule satisfies all requirements for filing on paper, signature, or verification. An electronic filing that otherwise satisfies the requirements of 28 U.S.C. §1746 need not be separately made in writing. Public access to electronic filings is governed by the same rules as govern written filings.

The separate reference to filing by facsimile transmission is deleted. Facsimile transmission continues to be included as an electronic means.

Committee Notes on Rules—2000 Amendment

Subdivision (d). Rule 5(d) is amended to provide that disclosures under Rule 26(a)(1) and (2), and discovery requests and responses under Rules 30, 31, 33, 34, and 36 must not be filed until they are used in the action. "Discovery requests" includes deposition notices and "discovery responses" includes objections. The rule supersedes and invalidates local rules that forbid, permit, or require filing of these materials before they are used in the action. The former Rule 26(a)(4) requirement that disclosures under Rule 26(a)(1) and (2) be filed has been removed. Disclosures under Rule 26(a)(3), however, must be promptly filed as provided in Rule 26(a)(3). Filings in connection with Rule 35 examinations, which involve a motion proceeding when the parties do not agree, are unaffected by these amendments.

Recognizing the costs imposed on parties and courts by required filing of discovery materials that are never used in an action, Rule 5(d) was amended in 1980 to authorize court orders that excuse filing. Since then, many districts have adopted local rules that excuse or forbid filing. In 1989 the Judicial Conference Local Rules Project concluded that these local rules were inconsistent with Rule 5(d), but urged the Advisory Committee to consider amending the rule. Local Rules Project at 92 (1989). The Judicial Conference of the Ninth Circuit gave the Committee similar advice in 1997. The reality of nonfiling reflected in these local rules has even been assumed in drafting the national rules. In 1993, Rule 30(f)(1) was amended to direct that the officer presiding at a deposition file it with the court or send it to the attorney who arranged for the transcript or recording. The Committee Note explained that this alternative to filing was designed for "courts which direct that depositions not be automatically filed." Rule 30(f)(1) has been amended to conform to this change in Rule 5(d).

Although this amendment is based on widespread experience with local rules, and confirms the results directed by these local rules, it is designed to supersede and invalidate local rules. There is no apparent reason to have different filing rules in different districts. Even if districts vary in present capacities to store filed materials that are not used in an action, there is little reason to continue expending court resources for this purpose. These costs and burdens would likely change as parties make increased use of audio- and videotaped depositions. Equipment to facilitate review and reproduction of such discovery materials may prove costly to acquire, maintain, and operate.

The amended rule provides that discovery materials and disclosures under Rule 26(a)(1) and (a)(2) must not be filed until they are "used in the proceeding." This phrase is meant to refer to proceedings in court. This filing requirement is not triggered by "use" of discovery materials in other discovery activities, such as depositions. In connection with proceedings in court, however, the rule is to be interpreted broadly; any use of discovery materials in court in connection with a motion, a pretrial conference under Rule 16, or otherwise, should be interpreted as use in the proceeding.

Once discovery or disclosure materials are used in the proceeding, the filing requirements of Rule 5(d) should apply to them. But because the filing requirement applies only with regard to materials that are used, only those parts of voluminous materials that are actually used need be filed. Any party would be free to file other pertinent portions of materials that are so used. See Fed. R. Evid. 106; cf. Rule 32(a)(4). If the parties are unduly sparing in their submissions, the court may order further filings. By local rule, a court could provide appropriate direction regarding the filing of discovery materials, such as depositions, that are used in proceedings.

"Shall" is replaced by "must" under the program to conform amended rules to current style conventions when there is no ambiguity.

GAP Report. The Advisory Committee recommends no changes to either the amendments to Rule 5(d) or the Committee Note as published.

Committee Notes On Rules—2001 Amendment

Rule 5(b) is restyled.

Rule 5(b)(1) makes it clear that the provision for service on a party's attorney applies only to service made under Rules 5(a) and 77(d). Service under Rules 4, 4.1, 45(b), and 71A(d)(3)—as well as rules that invoke those rules—must be made as provided in those rules.

Subparagraphs (A), (B), and (C) of Rule 5(b)(2) carry forward the method-of-service provisions of former Rule 5(b).

Subparagraph (D) of Rule 5(b)(2) is new. It authorizes service by electronic means or any other means, but only if consent is obtained from the person served. The consent must be express, and cannot be implied from conduct. Early experience with electronic filing as authorized by Rule 5(d) is positive, supporting service by electronic means as well. Consent is required, however, because it is not yet possible to assume universal entry into the world of electronic communication. Subparagraph (D) also authorizes service by nonelectronic means. The Rule 5(b)(2)(B) provision making mail service complete on mailing is extended in subparagraph (D) to make service by electronic means complete on transmission; transmission is effected when the sender does the last act that must be performed by the sender. Service by other agencies is complete on delivery to the designated agency.

Finally, subparagraph (D) authorizes adoption of local rules providing for service through the court. Electronic case filing systems will come to include the capacity to make service by using the court's facilities to transmit all documents filed in the case. It may prove most efficient to establish an environment in which a party can file with the court, making use of the court's transmission facilities to serve the filed paper on all other parties. Transmission might be by such means as direct transmission of the paper, or by transmission of a notice of filing that includes an electronic link for direct access to the paper. Because service is under subparagraph (D), consent must be obtained from the persons served.

Consent to service under Rule 5(b)(2)(D) must be in writing, which can be provided by electronic means. Parties are encouraged to specify the scope and duration of the consent. The specification should include at least the persons to whom service should be made, the appropriate address or location for such service—such as the e-mail address or facsimile machine number, and the format to be used for attachments. A district court may establish a registry or other facility that allows advance consent to service by specified means for future actions.

Rule 6(e) is amended to allow additional time to respond when service is made under Rule 5(b)(2)(D). The additional time does not relieve a party who consents to service under Rule 5(b)(2)(D) of the responsibilities to monitor the facility designated for receiving service and to provide prompt notice of any address change.

Paragraph (3) addresses a question that may arise from a literal reading of the provision that service by electronic means is complete on transmission. Electronic communication is rapidly improving, but lawyers report continuing failures of transmission, particularly with respect to attachments. Ordinarily the risk of non-receipt falls on the person being served, who has consented to this form of service. But the risk should not extend to situations in which the person attempting service learns that the attempted service in fact did not reach the person to be served. Given actual knowledge that the attempt failed, service is not effected. The person attempting service must either try again or show circumstances that justify dispensing with service.

Paragraph (3) does not address the similar questions that may arise when a person attempting service learns that service by means other than electronic means in fact did not reach the person to be served. Case law provides few illustrations of circumstances in which a person attempting service actually knows that the attempt failed but seeks to act as if service had been made. This negative history suggests there is no need to address these problems in Rule 5(b)(3). This silence does not imply any view on these issues, nor on the circumstances that justify various forms of judicial action even though service has not been made.

Changes Made After Publication and Comments Rule 5(b)(2)(D) was changed to require that consent be "in writing."

Rule 5(b)(3) is new. The published proposal did not address the question of failed service in the text of the rule. Instead, the Committee Note included this statement: "As with other modes of service, however, actual notice that the transmission was not received defeats the presumption of receipt that arises from the provision that service is complete on transmission. The sender must take additional steps to effect service. Service by other agencies is complete on delivery to the designated agency." The addition of paragraph (3) was prompted by consideration of the draft Appellate Rule 25(c) that was prepared for the meeting of the Appellate Rules Advisory Committee. This draft provided: "Service by electronic means is complete on transmission, unless the party making service is notified that the paper was not received." Although Appellate Rule 25(c) is being prepared for publication and comment, while Civil Rule 5(b) has been published and otherwise is ready to recommend for adoption, it seemed desirable to achieve some parallel between the two rules.

The draft Rule 5(b)(3) submitted for consideration by the Advisory Committee covered all means of service except for leaving a copy with the clerk of the court when the person to be served has no known address. It was not limited to electronic service for fear that a provision limited to electronic service might generate unintended negative implications as to service by other means, particularly mail. This concern was strengthened by a small number of opinions that say that service by mail is effective, because complete on mailing, even when the person making service has prompt actual notice that the mail was not delivered. The Advisory Committee voted to limit Rule 5(b)(3) to service by electronic means because this means of service is relatively new, and seems likely to miscarry more frequently than service by post. It was suggested during the Advisory Committee meeting that the question of negative implication could be addressed in the Committee Note. There was little discussion of this possibility. The Committee Note submitted above includes a "no negative implications" paragraph prepared by the Reporter for consideration by the Standing Committee.

The Advisory Committee did not consider at all a question that was framed during the later meeting of the Appellate Rules Advisory Committee. As approved by the Advisory Committee, Rule 5(b)(3) defeats service by electronic means "if the party making service learns that the attempted service did not reach the person to be served." It says nothing about the time relevant to learning of the failure. The omission may seem glaring. Curing the omission, however, requires selection of a time. As revised, proposed Appellate Rule 25(c) requires that the party making service learn of the failure within three calendar days. The Appellate Rules Advisory Committee will have the luxury of public comment and another year to consider the desirability of this short period. If Civil Rule 5(b) is to be recommended for adoption now, no such luxury is available. This issue deserves careful consideration by the Standing Committee.

Several changes are made in the Committee Note. (1) It requires that consent "be express, and cannot be implied from conduct." This addition reflects a more general concern stimulated by a reported ruling that an e-mail address on a firm's letterhead implied consent to email service. (2) The paragraph discussing service through the court's facilities is expanded by describing alternative methods, including an "electronic link." (3) There is a new paragraph that states that the requirement of written consent can be satisfied by electronic means, and that suggests matters that should be addressed by the consent. (4) A paragraph is added to note the additional response time provided by amended Rule 6(e). (5) The final two paragraphs address newly added Rule 5(b)(3). The first explains the rule that electronic service is not effective if the person making service learns that it did not reach the person to be served. The second paragraph seeks to defeat any negative implications that might arise from limiting Rule 5(b)(3) to electronic service, not mail, not other means consented to such as commercial express service, and not service on another person on behalf of the person to be served.

Rule 6(e)

The Advisory Committee recommended that no change be made in Civil Rule 6(e) to reflect the provisions of Civil Rule 5(b)(2)(D) that, with the consent of the person to be served, would allow service by electronic or other means. Absent change, service by these means would not affect the time for acting in response to the paper served. Comment was requested, however, on the alternative that would allow an additional 3 days to respond. The alternative Rule 6(e) amendments are cast in a form that permits ready incorporation in the Bankruptcy Rules. Several of the comments suggest that the added three days should be provided. Electronic transmission is not always instantaneous, and may fail for any of a number of reasons. It may take three days to arrange for transmission in readable form. Providing added time to respond will not discourage people from asking for consent to electronic transmission, and may encourage people to give consent. The more who consent, the quicker will come the improvements that will make electronic service ever more attractive. Consistency with the Bankruptcy Rules will be a good thing, and the Bankruptcy Rules Advisory Committee believes the additional three days should be allowed.

Committee Notes on Rules—2006 Amendment

Amended Rule 5(e) acknowledges that many courts have required electronic filing by means of a standing order, procedures manual, or local rule. These local practices reflect the advantages that courts and most litigants realize from electronic filing. Courts that mandate electronic filing recognize the need to make exceptions when requiring electronic filing imposes a hardship on a party. Under amended Rule 5(e), a local rule that requires electronic filing must include reasonable exceptions, but Rule 5(e) does not define the scope of those exceptions. Experience with the local rules that have been adopted and that will emerge will aid in drafting new local rules and will facilitate gradual convergence on uniform exceptions, whether in local rules or in an amended Rule 5(e).

Changes Made after Publication and Comment. This recommendation is of a modified version of the proposal as published. The changes from the published version limit local rule authority to implement a caution stated in the published Committee Note. A local rule that requires electronic filing must include reasonable exceptions. This change was accomplished by a separate sentence stating that a "local rule may require filing by electronic means only if reasonable exceptions are allowed." Corresponding changes were made in the Committee Note, in collaboration with the Appellate Rules Committee. The changes from the published proposal are shown below. [Omitted]

Committee Notes on Rules—2007 Amendment

The language of Rule 5 has been amended as part of the general restyling of the Civil Rules to make them more easily understood and to make style and terminology consistent throughout the rules. These changes are intended to be stylistic only.

Rule 5(a)(1)(E) omits the former reference to a designation of record on appeal. Appellate Rule 10 is a self-contained provision for the record on appeal, and provides for service.

Former Rule 5(b)(2)(D) literally provided that a local rule may authorize use of the court's transmission facilities to make service by non-electronic means agreed to by the parties. That was not intended. Rule 5(b)(3) restores the intended meaning—court transmission facilities can be used only for service by electronic means.

Rule 5(d)(2)(B) provides that "a" judge may accept a paper for filing, replacing the reference in former Rule 5(e) to "the" judge. Some courts do not assign a designated judge to each case, and it may be important to have another judge accept a paper for filing even when a case is on the individual docket of a particular judge. The ministerial acts of accepting the paper, noting the time, and transmitting the paper to the court clerk do not interfere with the assigned judge's authority over the action.

Rule 5.1. Constitutional Challenge to a Statute—Notice, Certification, and Intervention

(a) Notice by a Party. A party that files a pleading, written motion, or other paper drawing into question the constitutionality of a federal or state statute must promptly:

(1) file a notice of constitutional question stating the question and identifying the paper that raises it, if:

(A) a federal statute is questioned and the parties do not include the United States, one of its agencies, or one of its officers or employees in an official capacity; or

(B) a state statute is questioned and the parties do not include the state, one of its agencies, or one of its officers or employees in an official capacity; and

(2) serve the notice and paper on the Attorney General of the United States if a federal statute is questioned—or on the state attorney general if a state statute is questioned—either by certified or registered mail or by sending it to an electronic address designated by the attorney general for this purpose.

(b) Certification by the Court. The court must, under 28 U.S.C. §2403, certify to the appropriate attorney general that a statute has been questioned.

(c) Intervention; Final Decision on the Merits. Unless the court sets a later time, the attorney general may intervene within 60 days after the notice is filed or after the court certifies the challenge, whichever is earlier. Before the time to intervene expires, the court may reject the constitutional challenge, but may not enter a final judgment holding the statute unconstitutional.

(d) No Forfeiture. A party's failure to file and serve the notice, or the court's failure to certify, does not forfeit a constitutional claim or defense that is otherwise timely asserted.

(As added Apr. 12, 2006, eff. Dec. 1, 2006; amended Apr. 30, 2007, eff. Dec. 1, 2007.)

Committee Notes on Rules—2006

Rule 5.1 implements 28 U.S.C. §2403, replacing the final three sentences of Rule 24(c). New Rule 5.1 requires a party that files a pleading, written motion, or other paper drawing in question the constitutionality of a federal or state statute to file a notice of constitutional question and serve it on the United States Attorney General or state attorney general. The party must promptly file and serve the notice of constitutional question. This notice requirement supplements the court's duty to certify a constitutional challenge to the United States Attorney General or state attorney general. The notice of constitutional question will ensure that the attorney general is notified of constitutional challenges and has an opportunity to exercise the statutory right to intervene at the earliest possible point in the litigation. The court's certification obligation remains, and is the only notice when the constitutionality of a federal or state statute is drawn in question by means other than a party's pleading, written motion, or other paper.

Moving the notice and certification provisions from Rule 24(c) to a new rule is designed to attract the parties' attention to these provisions by locating them in the vicinity of the rules that require notice by service and pleading.

Rule 5.1 goes beyond the requirements of §2403 and the former Rule 24(c) provisions by requiring notice and certification of a constitutional challenge to any federal or state statute, not only those "affecting the public interest." It is better to assure, through notice, that the attorney general is able to determine whether to seek intervention on the ground that the act or statute affects a public interest. Rule 5.1 refers to a "federal statute," rather than the §2403 reference to an "Act of Congress," to maintain consistency in the Civil Rules vocabulary. In Rule 5.1 "statute" means any congressional enactment that would qualify as an "Act of Congress."

Unless the court sets a later time, the 60-day period for intervention runs from the time a party files a notice of constitutional question or from the time the court certifies a constitutional challenge, whichever is earlier. Rule 5.1(a) directs that a party promptly serve the notice of constitutional question. The court may extend the 60-[day] period on its own or on motion. One occasion for extension may arise if the court certifies a challenge under §2403 after a party files a notice of constitutional question. Pretrial activities may continue without interruption during the intervention period, and the court retains authority to grant interlocutory relief. The court may reject a constitutional challenge to a statute at any time. But the court may not enter a final judgment holding a statute unconstitutional before the attorney general has responded or the intervention period has expired without response. This rule does not displace any of the statutory or rule procedures that permit dismissal of al or part of an action—including a constitutional challenge—at any time, even before service of process.

Changes Made After Publication and Comment. Rule 5.1 as proposed for adoption incorporates several changes from the published draft. The changes were made in response to public comments and Advisory Committee discussion.

The Advisory Committee debated at length the question whether the party who files a notice of constitutional question should be required to serve the notice on the appropriate attorney general. The service requirement was retained, but the time for intervention was set to run from the earlier of the notice filing or the court's certification. The definition of the time to intervene was changed in tandem with this change. The published rule directed the court to set an intervention time not less than 60 days from the court's certification. This was changed to set a 60-day period in the rule "[u]nless the court sets a later time." The Committee Note points out that the court may extend the 60-day period on its own or on motion, and recognizes that an occasion for extension may arise if the 60-day period begins with the filing of the notice of constitutional question.

The method of serving the notice of constitutional question set by the published rule called for serving the United States Attorney General under Civil Rule 4, and for serving a state attorney general by certified or registered mail. This proposal has been changed to provide service in all cases either by certified or registered mail or by sending the Notice to an electronic address designated by the attorney general for this purpose.

The rule proposed for adoption brings into subdivision (c) matters that were stated in the published Committee Note but not in the rule text. The court may reject a constitutional challenge at any time, but may not enter a final judgment holding a statute unconstitutional before the time set to intervene expires.

The published rule would have required notice and certification when an officer of the United States or a state brings suit in an official capacity. There is no need for notice in such circumstances. The words "is sued" were deleted to correct this oversight.

Several style changes were made at the Style Subcommittee's suggestion. One change that straddles the line between substance and style appears in Rule 5.1(d). The published version adopted the language of present Rule 24(c): failure to comply with the Notice or certification requirements does not forfeit a constitutional "right." This expression is changed to "claim or defense" from concern that reference to a "right" may invite confusion of the no-forfeiture provision with the merits of the claim or defense that is not forfeited.

Committee Notes on Rules—2007 Amendment

The language of Rule 5.1 has been amended as part of the general restyling of the Civil Rules to make them more easily understood and to make style and terminology consistent throughout the rules. These changes are intended to be stylistic only.

Rule 5.2. Privacy Protection For Filings Made with the Court

(a) Redacted Filings. Unless the court orders otherwise, in an electronic or paper filing with the court that contains an individual's social-security number, taxpayer-identification number, or birth date, the name of an individual known to be a minor, or a financial-account number, a party or nonparty making the filing may include only:

(1) the last four digits of the social-security number and taxpayer-identification number;
(2) the year of the individual's birth;
(3) the minor's initials; and
(4) the last four digits of the financial-account number.

(b) Exemptions from the Redaction Requirement. The redaction requirement does not apply to the following:

(1) a financial-account number that identifies the property allegedly subject to forfeiture in a forfeiture proceeding;
(2) the record of an administrative or agency proceeding;
(3) the official record of a state-court proceeding;
(4) the record of a court or tribunal, if that record was not subject to the redaction requirement when originally filed;
(5) a filing covered by Rule 5.2(c) or (d); and
(6) a pro se filing in an action brought under 28 U.S.C. §§2241, 2254, or 2255.

(c) Limitations on Remote Access to Electronic Files; Social-Security Appeals and Immigration Cases. Unless the court orders otherwise, in an action for benefits under the Social Security Act, and in an action or proceeding relating to an order of removal, to relief from removal, or to immigration benefits or detention, access to an electronic file is authorized as follows:

(1) the parties and their attorneys may have remote electronic access to any part of the case file, including the administrative record;
(2) any other person may have electronic access to the full record at the courthouse, but may have remote electronic access only to:
 (A) the docket maintained by the court; and
 (B) an opinion, order, judgment, or other disposition of the court, but not any other part of the case file or the administrative record.

(d) Filings Made Under Seal. The court may order that a filing be made under seal without redaction. The court may later unseal the filing or order the person who made the filing to file a redacted version for the public record.

(e) Protective Orders. For good cause, the court may by order in a case:

(1) require redaction of additional information; or
(2) limit or prohibit a nonparty's remote electronic access to a document filed with the court.

(f) Option for Additional Unredacted Filing Under Seal. A person making a redacted filing may also file an unredacted copy under seal. The court must retain the unredacted copy as part of the record.

(g) Option for Filing a Reference List. A filing that contains redacted information may be filed together with a reference list that identifies each item of redacted information and specifies an appropriate identifier that uniquely corresponds to each item listed. The list must be filed under seal and may be amended as of right. Any reference in the case to a listed identifier will be construed to refer to the corresponding item of information.

(h) Waiver of Protection of Identifiers. A person waives the protection of Rule 5.2(a) as to the person's own information by filing it without redaction and not under seal.

(As added Apr. 30, 2007, eff. Dec. 1, 2007.)

Committee Notes on Rules—2007

The rule is adopted in compliance with section 205(c)(3) of the E-Government Act of 2002, Public Law 107–347. Section 205(c)(3) requires the Supreme Court to prescribe rules "to protect privacy and security concerns relating to electronic filing of documents and the public availability . . . of documents filed electronically." The rule goes further than the E-Government Act in regulating paper filings even when they are not converted to electronic form. But the number of filings that remain in paper form is certain to diminish over time. Most districts scan paper filings into the electronic case file, where they become available to the public in the same way as documents initially filed in electronic form. It is electronic availability, not the form of the initial filing, that raises the privacy and security concerns addressed in the E-Government Act.

The rule is derived from and implements the policy adopted by the Judicial Conference in September 2001 to address the privacy concerns resulting from public access to electronic case files. See http://www.privacy.uscourts.gov/Policy.htm. The Judicial Conference policy is that documents in case files generally should be made available electronically to the same extent they are available at the courthouse, provided that certain "personal data identifiers" are not included in the public file.

While providing for the public filing of some information, such as the last four digits of an account number, the rule does not intend to establish a presumption that this information never could or should be protected. For example, it may well be necessary in individual cases to prevent remote access by nonparties to any part of an account number or social security number. It may also be necessary to protect information not covered by the redaction requirement—such as driver's license numbers and alien registration numbers—in a particular case. In such cases, protection may be sought under subdivision (d) or (e). Moreover, the Rule does not affect the protection available under other rules, such as Civil Rules 16 and 26(c), or under other sources of protective authority.

Parties must remember that any personal information not otherwise protected by sealing or redaction will be made available over the internet. Counsel should notify clients of this fact so that an informed decision may be made on what information is to be included in a document filed with the court.

The clerk is not required to review documents filed with the court for compliance with this rule. The responsibility to redact filings rests with counsel and the party or nonparty making the filing.

Subdivision (c) provides for limited public access in Social Security cases and immigration cases. Those actions are entitled to special treatment due to the prevalence of sensitive information and the volume of filings. Remote electronic access by nonparties is limited to the docket and the written dispositions of the court unless the court orders otherwise. The rule contemplates, however, that nonparties can obtain full access to the case file at the courthouse, including access through the court's public computer terminal.

Subdivision (d) reflects the interplay between redaction and filing under seal. It does not limit or expand the judicially developed rules that govern sealing. But it does reflect the possibility that redaction may provide an alternative to sealing.

Subdivision (e) provides that the court can by order in a particular case for good cause require more extensive redaction than otherwise required by the Rule. Nothing in this subdivision is intended to affect the limitations on sealing that are otherwise applicable to the court.

Subdivision (f) allows a person who makes a redacted filing to file an unredacted document under seal. This provision is derived from section 205(c)(3)(iv) of the E-Government Act.

Subdivision (g) allows the option to file a register of redacted information. This provision is derived from section 205(c)(3)(v) of the E-Government Act, as amended in 2004. In accordance with the E-Government Act, subdivision (g) refers to "redacted" information. The term "redacted" is intended to govern a filing that is prepared with abbreviated identifiers in the first instance, as well as a filing in which a personal identifier is edited after its preparation.

Subdivision (h) allows a person to waive the protections of the rule as to that person's own personal information by filing it unsealed and in unredacted form. One may wish to waive the protection if it is determined that the costs of redaction outweigh the benefits to privacy. If a person files an unredacted identifier by mistake, that person may seek relief from the court.

Trial exhibits are subject to the redaction requirements of Rule 5.2 to the extent they are filed with the court. Trial exhibits that are not initially filed with the court must be redacted in accordance with the rule if and when they are filed as part of an appeal or for other reasons.

Changes Made After Publication and Comment. The changes made after publication were made in conjunction with the E-Government Act Subcommittee and the other Advisory Committees.

Subdivision (a) was amended to incorporate a suggestion from the Federal Magistrate Judges Association that the rule text state that the responsibility to redact filings rests on the filer, not the court clerk.

As published, subdivision (b)(6) exempted from redaction all filings in habeas corpus proceedings under 28 U.S.C. §§2241, 2254, or 2255. The exemption is revised to apply only to pro se filings. A petitioner represented by counsel, and respondents represented by counsel, must redact under Rule 5.2(a).

Subdivision (e) was published with a standard for protective orders, referring to a need to protect private or sensitive information not otherwise protected by Rule 5.2(a). This standard has been replaced by a general reference to "good cause."

Rule 6. Computing and Extending Time; Time for Motion Papers

(a) Computing Time. The following rules apply in computing any time period specified in these rules, in any local rule or court order, or in any statute that does not specify a method of computing time.

(1) Period Stated in Days or a Longer Unit. When the period is stated in days or a longer unit of time:

(A) exclude the day of the event that triggers the period;

(B) count every day, including intermediate Saturdays, Sundays, and legal holidays; and

(C) include the last day of the period, but if the last day is a Saturday, Sunday, or legal holiday, the period continues to run until the end of the next day that is not a Saturday, Sunday, or legal holiday.

(2) Period Stated in Hours. When the period is stated in hours:

(A) begin counting immediately on the occurrence of the event that triggers the period;

(B) count every hour, including hours during intermediate Saturdays, Sundays, and legal holidays; and

(C) if the period would end on a Saturday, Sunday, or legal holiday, the period continues to run until the same time on the next day that is not a Saturday, Sunday, or legal holiday.

(3) Inaccessibility of the Clerk's Office. Unless the court orders otherwise, if the clerk's office is inaccessible:

(A) on the last day for filing under Rule 6(a)(1), then the time for filing is extended to the first accessible day that is not a Saturday, Sunday, or legal holiday; or

(B) during the last hour for filing under Rule 6(a)(2), then the time for filing is extended to the same time on the first accessible day that is not a Saturday, Sunday, or legal holiday.

(4) "Last Day" Defined. Unless a different time is set by a statute, local rule, or court order, the last day ends:

(A) for electronic filing, at midnight in the court's time zone; and
(B) for filing by other means, when the clerk's office is scheduled to close.

(5) "Next Day" Defined. The "next day" is determined by continuing to count forward when the period is measured after an event and backward when measured before an event.

(6) "Legal Holiday" Defined. "Legal holiday" means:

(A) the day set aside by statute for observing New Year's Day, Martin Luther King Jr.'s Birthday, Washington's Birthday, Memorial Day, Independence Day, Labor Day, Columbus Day, Veterans' Day, Thanksgiving Day, or Christmas Day;
(B) any day declared a holiday by the President or Congress; and
(C) for periods that are measured after an event, any other day declared a holiday by the state where the district court is located.

(b) Extending Time.

(1) In General. When an act may or must be done within a specified time, the court may, for good cause, extend the time:

(A) with or without motion or notice if the court acts, or if a request is made, before the original time or its extension expires; or
(B) on motion made after the time has expired if the party failed to act because of excusable neglect.

(2) Exceptions. A court must not extend the time to act under Rules 50(b) and (d), 52(b), 59(b), (d), and (e), and 60(b).

(c) Motions, Notices of Hearing, and Affidavits.

(1) In General. A written motion and notice of the hearing must be served at least 14 days before the time specified for the hearing, with the following exceptions:

(A) when the motion may be heard ex parte;
(B) when these rules set a different time; or
(C) when a court order—which a party may, for good cause, apply for ex parte—sets a different time.

(2) Supporting Affidavit. Any affidavit supporting a motion must be served with the motion. Except as Rule 59(c) provides otherwise, any opposing affidavit must be served at least 7 days before the hearing, unless the court permits service at another time.

(d) Additional Time After Certain Kinds of Service. When a party may or must act within a specified time after being served and service is made under Rule 5(b)(2)(C) (mail), (D) (leaving with the clerk), or (F) (other means consented to), 3 days are added after the period would otherwise expire under Rule 6(a).

(As amended Dec. 27, 1946, eff. Mar. 19, 1948; Jan. 21, 1963, eff. July 1, 1963; Feb. 28, 1966, eff. July 1, 1966; Dec. 4, 1967, eff. July 1, 1968; Mar. 1, 1971, eff. July 1, 1971; Apr. 28, 1983, eff. Aug. 1, 1983; Apr. 29, 1985, eff. Aug. 1, 1985; Mar. 2, 1987, eff. Aug. 1, 1987; Apr. 26, 1999, eff. Dec. 1, 1999; Apr. 23, 2001, eff. Dec. 1, 2001; Apr. 25, 2005, eff. Dec. 1, 2005; Apr. 30, 2007, eff. Dec. 1, 2007; Mar. 26, 2009, eff. Dec. 1, 2009; Apr. 28, 2016, eff. Dec. 1, 2016.)

Notes of Advisory Committee on Rules—1937

Note to Subdivisions (a) and (b). These are amplifications along lines common in state practices, of [former] Equity Rule 80 (Computation of Time—Sundays and Holidays) and of the provisions for enlargement of time found in [former] Equity Rules 8 (Enforcement of Final Decrees) and 16 (Defendant to Answer—Default—Decree Pro Confesso). See also Rule XIII, Rules and Forms in Criminal Cases, 292 U.S. 661, 666 (1934). Compare Ala.Code Ann. (Michie, 1928) §13 and former Law Rule 8 of the Rules of the Supreme Court of the District of Columbia (1924), superseded in 1929 by Law Rule 8, Rules of the District Court of the United States for the District of Columbia (1937).

Note to Subdivision (c). This eliminates the difficulties caused by the expiration of terms of court. Such statutes as U.S.C. Title 28, [former] §12 (Trials not discontinued by new term) are not affected. Compare Rules of the United States District Court of Minnesota, Rule 25 (Minn.Stat. (Mason, Supp. 1936), p. 1089).

Note to Subdivision (d). Compare 2 Minn.Stat. (Mason, 1927) §9246; N.Y.R.C.P. (1937) Rules 60 and 64.

Notes of Advisory Committee on Rules—1946 Amendment

Subdivision (b). The purpose of the amendment is to clarify the finality of judgments. Prior to the advent of the Federal Rules of Civil Procedure, the general rule that a court loses jurisdiction to disturb its judgments, upon the expiration of the term at which they were entered, had long been the classic device which (together with the statutory limits on the time for appeal) gave finality to judgments. See Note to Rule 73(a). Rule 6(c) abrogates that limit on judicial power. That limit was open to many objections, one of them being inequality of operation because, under it, the time for vacating a judgment rendered early in a term was much longer than for a judgment rendered near the end of the term.

The question to be met under Rule 6(b) is: how far should the desire to allow correction of judgments be allowed to postpone their finality? The rules contain a number of provisions permitting the vacation or modification of judgments on various grounds. Each of these rules contains express time limits on the motions for granting of relief. Rule 6(b) is a rule of general application giving wide discretion to the court to enlarge these time limits or revive them after they have expired, the only exceptions stated in the original rule being a prohibition against enlarging the time specified in Rule 59(b) and (d) for making motions for or granting new trials, and a prohibition against enlarging the time fixed by law for taking an appeal. It should also be noted that Rule 6(b) itself contains no limitation of time within which the court may exercise its discretion, and since the expiration of the term does not end its power, there is now no time limit on the exercise of its discretion under Rule 6(b).

Decisions of lower federal courts suggest that some of the rules containing time limits which may be set aside under Rule 6(b) are Rules 25, 50(b), 52(b), 60(b), and 73(g).

In a number of cases the effect of Rule 6(b) on the time limitations of these rules has been considered. Certainly the rule is susceptible of the interpretation that the court is given the power in its discretion to relieve a party from failure to act within the times specified in any of these other rules, with only the exceptions stated in Rule 6(b), and in some cases the rule has been so construed.

With regard to Rule 25(a) for substitution, it was held in Anderson v. Brady (E.D.Ky. 1941) 4 Fed.Rules Service 25a.1, Case 1, and in Anderson v. Yungkau (C.C.A. 6th, 1946) 153 F.(2d) 685, cert. granted (1946) 66 S.Ct. 1025, that under Rule 6(b) the court had no authority to allow substitution of parties after the expiration of the limit fixed in Rule 25(a).

As to Rules 50(b) for judgments notwithstanding the verdict and 52(b) for amendment of findings and vacation of judgment, it was recognized in Leishman v. Associated Wholesale Electric Co. (1943) 318 U.S. 203, that Rule 6(b) allowed the district court to enlarge the time to make a motion for amended findings and judgment beyond the limit expressly fixed in Rule 52(b). See Coca-Cola v. Busch (E.D.Pa. 1943) 7 Fed.Rules Service 59b.2, Case 4. Obviously, if the time limit in Rule 52(b) could be set aside under Rule 6(b), the time limit in Rule 50(b) for granting judgment notwithstanding the verdict (and thus vacating the judgment entered "forthwith" on the verdict) likewise could be set aside.

As to Rule 59 on motions for a new trial, it has been settled that the time limits in Rule 59(b) and (d) for making motions for or granting new trial could not be set aside under Rule 6(b), because Rule 6(b) expressly refers to Rule 59, and forbids it. See Safeway Stores, Inc. v. Coe (App.D.C. 1943) 136 F.(2d) 771; Jusino v. Morales & Tio (C.C.A. 1st, 1944) 139 F.(2d) 946; Coca-Cola Co. v. Busch (E.D.Pa. 1943) 7 Fed.Rules Service 59b.2, Case 4; Peterson v. Chicago Great Western Ry. Co. (D.Neb. 1943) 7 Fed.Rules Service 59b.2, Case 1; Leishman v. Associated Wholesale Electric Co. (1943) 318 U.S. 203.

As to Rule 60(b) for relief from a judgment, it was held in Schram v. O'Connor (E.D.Mich. 1941) 5 Fed.Rules Serv. 6b.31, Case 1, 2 F.R.D. 192, s. c. 5 Fed.Rules Serv. 6b.31, Case 2, F.R.D. 192, that the six-months time limit in original Rule 60(b) for making a motion for relief from a judgment for surprise, mistake, or excusable neglect could be set aside under Rule 6(b). The contrary result was reached in Wallace v. United States (C.C.A.2d, 1944) 142 F.(2d) 240, cert. den. (1944) 323 U.S. 712; Reed v. South Atlantic Steamship Co. of Del. (D.Del. 1942) 6 Fed.Rules Serv. 60b.31, Case 1.

As to Rule 73(g), fixing the time for docketing an appeal, it was held in Ainsworth v. Gill Glass & Fixture Co. (C.C.A.3d, 1939) 104 F.(2d) 83, that under Rule 6(b) the district court, upon motion made after the expiration of the forty-day period, stated in Rule 73(g), but before the expiration of the ninety-day period therein specified, could permit the docketing of the appeal on a showing of excusable neglect. The contrary was held in Mutual Benefit Health & Accident Ass'n v. Snyder (C.C.A. 6th, 1940) 109 F.(2d) 469 and in Burke v. Canfield (App.D.C. 1940) 111 F.(2d) 526.

The amendment of Rule 6(b) now proposed is based on the view that there should be a definite point where it can be said a judgment is final; that the right method of dealing with the problem is to list in Rule 6(b) the various other rules whose time limits may not be set aside, and then, if the time limit in any of those other rules is too short, to amend that other rule to give a longer time. The further argument is that Rule 6(c) abolished the long standing device to produce finality in judgments through expiration of the term, and since that limitation on the jurisdiction of courts to set aside their own judgments has been removed by Rule 6(c), some other limitation must be substituted or judgments never can be said to be final.

In this connection reference is made to the established rule that if a motion for new trial is seasonably made, the mere making or pendency of the motion destroys the finality of the judgment, and even though the motion is ultimately denied, the full time for appeal starts anew from the date of denial. Also, a motion to amend the findings under Rule 52(b) has the same effect on the time for appeal. Leishman v. Associated Wholesale Electric Co. (1943) 318 U.S. 203. By the same reasoning a motion for judgment under Rule 50(b), involving as it does the vacation of a judgment entered "forthwith" on the verdict (Rule 58), operates to postpone, until an order is made, the running of the time for appeal. The Committee believes that the abolition by Rule 6(c) of the old rule that a court's power over its judgments ends with the term, requires a substitute limitation, and that unless Rule 6(b) is amended to prevent enlargement of the times specified in Rules 50(b), 52(b) and 60(b), and the limitation as to Rule 59(b) and (c) is retained, no one can say when a judgment is final. This is also true with regard to proposed Rule 59(e), which authorizes a motion to alter or amend a judgment, hence that rule is also included in the enumeration in amended Rule 6(b). In consideration of the amendment, however, it should be noted that Rule 60(b) is also to be amended so as to lengthen the six-months period originally prescribed in that rule to one year.

As to Rule 25 on substitution, while finality is not involved, the limit there fixed should be controlling. That rule, as amended, gives the court power, upon showing of a reasonable excuse, to permit substitution after the expiration of the two-year period.

As to Rule 73(g), it is believed that the conflict in decisions should be resolved and not left to further litigation, and that the rule should be listed as one whose limitation may not be set aside under Rule 6(b).

As to Rule 59(c), fixing the time for serving affidavits on motion for new trial, it is believed that the court should have authority under Rule 6(b) to enlarge the time, because, once the motion for new trial is made, the judgment no longer has finality, and the extension of time for affidavits thus does not of itself disturb finality.

Other changes proposed in Rule 6(b) are merely clarifying and conforming. Thus "request" is substituted for "application" in clause (1) because an application is defined as a motion under Rule 7(b). The phrase "extend the time" is substituted for "enlarge the period" because the former is a more suitable expression and relates more clearly to both clauses (1) and (2). The final phrase in Rule 6(b), "or the period for taking an appeal as provided by law", is deleted and a reference to Rule 73(a) inserted, since it is proposed to state in that rule the time for appeal to a circuit court of appeals, which is the only appeal governed by the Federal Rules, and allows an extension of time See Rule 72.

Subdivision (c). The purpose of this amendment is to prevent reliance upon the continued existence of a term as a source of power to disturb the finality of a judgment upon grounds other than those stated in these rules. See Hill v. Hawes (1944) 320 U.S. 520; Boaz v. Mutual Life Ins. Co. of New York (C.C.A. 8th, 1944) 146 F.(2d) 321; Bucy v. Nevada Construction Co. (C.C.A. 9th, 1942) 125 F.(2d) 213.

Notes of Advisory Committee on Rules—1963 Amendment

Subdivision (a). This amendment is related to the amendment of Rule 77(c) changing the regulation of the days on which the clerk's office shall be open.

The wording of the first sentence of Rule 6(a) is clarified and the subdivision is made expressly applicable to computing periods of time set forth in local rules.

Saturday is to be treated in the same way as Sunday or a "legal holiday" in that it is not to be included when it falls on the last day of a computed period, nor counted as an intermediate day when the period is less than 7 days. "Legal holiday" is defined for purposes of this subdivision and amended Rule 77(c). Compare the definition of "holiday" in 11 U.S.C. §1(18); also 5 U.S.C. §86a; Executive Order No. 10358, "Observance of Holidays," June 9, 1952, 17 Fed.Reg. 5269. In the light of these changes the last sentence of the present subdivision, dealing with half holidays, is eliminated.

With Saturdays and State holidays made "dies non" in certain cases by the amended subdivision, computation of the usual 5–day notice of motion or the 2–day notice to dissolve or modify a temporary restraining order may work out so as to cause embarrassing delay in urgent cases. The delay can be obviated by applying to the court to shorten the time, see Rules 6(d) and 65(b).

Subdivision (b). The prohibition against extending the time for taking action under Rule 25 (Substitution of parties) is eliminated. The only limitation of time provided for in amended Rule 25 is the 90–day period following a suggestion upon the record of the death of a party within which to make a motion to substitute the proper parties for the deceased party. See Rule 25(a)(1), as amended, and the Advisory Committee's Note thereto. It is intended that the court shall have discretion to enlarge that period.

Notes of Advisory Committee on Rules—1968 Amendment

The amendment eliminates the references to Rule 73, which is to be abrogated.

P. L. 88–139, §1, 77 Stat. 248, approved on October 16, 1963, amended 28 U.S.C. §138 to read as follows: "The district court shall not hold formal terms." Thus Rule 6(c) is rendered unnecessary, and it is rescinded.

Notes of Advisory Committee on Rules—1971 Amendment

The amendment adds Columbus Day to the list of legal holidays to conform the subdivision to the Act of June 28, 1968, 82 Stat. 250, which constituted Columbus Day a legal holiday effective after January 1, 1971.

The Act, which amended Title 5, U.S.C., §6103(a), changes the day on which certain holidays are to be observed. Washington's Birthday, Memorial Day and Veterans Day are to be observed on the third Monday in February, the last Monday in May and the fourth Monday in October, respectively, rather than, as heretofore, on February 22, May 30, and November 11, respectively. Columbus Day is to be observed on the second Monday in October. New Year's Day, Independence Day, Thanksgiving Day and Christmas continue to be observed on the traditional days.

Notes of Advisory Committee on Rules—1983 Amendment

Subdivision (b). The amendment confers finality upon the judgments of magistrates by foreclosing enlargement of the time for appeal except as provided in new Rule 74(a) (20 day period for demonstration of excusable neglect).

Notes of Advisory Committee on Rules—1985 Amendment

Rule 6(a) is amended to acknowledge that weather conditions or other events may render the clerk's office inaccessible one or more days. Parties who are obliged to file something with the court during that period should not be penalized if they cannot do so. The amendment conforms to changes made in Federal Rule of Criminal Procedure 45(a), effective August 1, 1982.

The Rule also is amended to extend the exclusion of intermediate Saturdays, Sundays, and legal holidays to the computation of time periods less than 11 days. Under the current version of the Rule, parties bringing motions under rules with 10-day periods could have as few as 5 working days to prepare their motions. This hardship would be especially acute in the case of Rules 50(b) and (c)(2), 52(b), and 59(b), (d), and (e), which may not be enlarged at the discretion of the court. See Rule 6(b). If the exclusion of Saturdays, Sundays, and legal holidays will operate to cause excessive delay in urgent cases, the delay can be obviated by applying to the court to shorten the time, See Rule 6(b).

The Birthday of Martin Luther King, Jr., which becomes a legal holiday effective in 1986, has been added to the list of legal holidays enumerated in the Rule.

Notes of Advisory Committee on Rules—1987 Amendment

The amendments are technical. No substantive change is intended.

Committee Notes on Rules—1999 Amendment

The reference to Rule 74(a) is stricken from the catalogue of time periods that cannot be extended by the district court. The change reflects the 1997 abrogation of Rule 74(a).

Committee Notes on Rules—2001 Amendment

The additional three days provided by Rule 6(e) is extended to the means of service authorized by the new paragraph (D) added to Rule 5(b), including—with the consent of the person served—service by electronic or other means. The three-day addition is provided as well for service on a person with no known address by leaving a copy with the clerk of the court.

Changes Made After Publication and Comments. Proposed Rule 6(e) is the same as the "alternative proposal" that was published in August 1999.

Committee Notes on Rules—2005 Amendment

Rule 6(e) is amended to remove any doubt as to the method for extending the time to respond after service by mail, leaving with the clerk of court, electronic means, or other means consented to by the party served. Three days are added after the prescribed period otherwise expires under Rule 6(a). Intermediate Saturdays, Sundays, and legal holidays are included in counting these added three days. If the third day is a Saturday, Sunday, or legal holiday, the last day to act is the next day that is not a Saturday, Sunday, or legal holiday. The effect of invoking the day when the prescribed period would otherwise expire under Rule 6(a) can be illustrated by assuming that the thirtieth day of a thirty-day period is a Saturday. Under Rule 6(a) the period expires on the next day that is not a Sunday or legal holiday. If the following Monday is a legal holiday, under Rule 6(a) the period expires on Tuesday. Three days are then added—Wednesday, Thursday, and Friday as the third and final day to act. If the period prescribed expires on a Friday, the three added days are Saturday, Sunday, and Monday, which is the third and final day to act unless it is a legal holiday. If Monday is a legal holiday, the next day that is not a legal holiday is the third and final day to act.

Application of Rule 6(e) to a period that is less than eleven days can be illustrated by a paper that is served by mailing on a Friday. If ten days are allowed to respond, intermediate Saturdays, Sundays, and legal holidays are excluded in determining when the period expires under Rule 6(a). If there is no legal holiday, the period expires on the Friday two weeks after the paper was mailed. The three added Rule 6(e) days are Saturday, Sunday, and Monday, which is the third and final day to act unless it is a legal holiday. If Monday is a legal holiday, the next day that is not a legal holiday is the final day to act.

Changes Made After Publication and Comment. Changes were made to clarify further the method of counting the three days added after service under Rule 5(b)(2)(B), (C), or (D).

Committee Notes on Rules—2007 Amendment

The language of Rule 6 has been amended as part of the general restyling of the Civil Rules to make them more easily understood and to make style and terminology consistent throughout the rules. These changes are intended to be stylistic only.

Committee Notes on Rules—2009 Amendment

Subdivision (a). Subdivision (a) has been amended to simplify and clarify the provisions that describe how deadlines are computed. Subdivision (a) governs the computation of any time period found in these rules, in any local rule or court order, or in any statute that does not specify a method of computing time. In accordance with Rule 83(a)(1), a local rule may not direct that a deadline be computed in a manner inconsistent with subdivision (a).

The time-computation provisions of subdivision (a) apply only when a time period must be computed. They do not apply when a fixed time to act is set. The amendments thus carry forward the approach taken in Violette v. P.A. Days, Inc., 427 F.3d 1015, 1016 (6th Cir. 2005) (holding that Civil Rule 6(a) "does not apply to situations where the court has established a specific calendar day as a deadline"), and reject the contrary holding of In re American Healthcare Management, Inc., 900 F.2d 827, 832 (5th Cir. 1990) (holding that Bankruptcy Rule 9006(a) governs treatment of date-certain deadline set by court order). If, for example, the date for filing is "no later than November 1, 2007," subdivision (a) does not govern. But if a filing is required to be made "within 10 days" or "within 72 hours," subdivision (a) describes how that deadline is computed.

Subdivision (a) does not apply when computing a time period set by a statute if the statute specifies a method of computing time. See, e.g., 2 U.S.C. §394 (specifying method for computing time periods prescribed by certain statutory provisions relating to contested elections to the House of Representatives).

Subdivision (a)(1). New subdivision (a)(1) addresses the computation of time periods that are stated in days. It also applies to time periods that are stated in weeks, months, or years. See, e.g., Rule 60(c)(1). Subdivision (a)(1)(B)'s directive to "count every day" is relevant only if the period is stated in days (not weeks, months or years).

Under former Rule 6(a), a period of 11 days or more was computed differently than a period of less than 11 days. Intermediate Saturdays, Sundays, and legal holidays were included in computing the longer periods, but excluded in computing the shorter periods. Former Rule 6(a) thus made computing deadlines unnecessarily complicated and led to counterintuitive results. For example, a 10-day period and a 14-day period that started on the same day usually ended on the same day—and the 10-day period not infrequently ended later than the 14-day period. See Miltimore Sales, Inc. v. Int'l Rectifier, Inc., 412 F.3d 685, 686 (6th Cir. 2005).

Under new subdivision (a)(1), all deadlines stated in days (no matter the length) are computed in the same way. The day of the event that triggers the deadline is not counted. All other days—including intermediate Saturdays, Sundays, and legal holidays—are counted, with only one exception: If the period ends on a Saturday, Sunday, or legal holiday, then the deadline falls on the next day that is not a Saturday, Sunday, or legal holiday. An illustration is provided below in the discussion of subdivision (a)(5). Subdivision (a)(3) addresses filing deadlines that expire on a day when the clerk's office is inaccessible.

Where subdivision (a) formerly referred to the "act, event, or default" that triggers the deadline, new subdivision (a) refers simply to the "event" that triggers the deadline; this change in terminology is adopted for brevity and simplicity, and is not intended to change meaning.

Periods previously expressed as less than 11 days will be shortened as a practical matter by the decision to count intermediate Saturdays, Sundays, and legal holidays in computing all periods. Many of those periods have been lengthened to compensate for the change. See, e.g., Rule 14(a)(1).

Most of the 10-day periods were adjusted to meet the change in computation method by setting 14 days as the new period. A 14-day period corresponds to the most frequent result of a 10-day period under the former computation method—two Saturdays and two Sundays were excluded, giving 14 days in all. A 14-day period has an additional advantage. The final day falls on the same day of the week as the event that triggered the period—the 14th day after a Monday, for example, is a Monday. This advantage of using week-long periods led to adopting 7-day periods to replace some of the periods set at less than 10 days, and 21-day periods to replace 20-day periods. Thirty-day and longer periods, however, were generally retained without change.

Subdivision (a)(2). New subdivision (a)(2) addresses the computation of time periods that are stated in hours. No such deadline currently appears in the Federal Rules of Civil Procedure. But some statutes contain deadlines stated in hours, as do some court orders issued in expedited proceedings.

Under subdivision (a)(2), a deadline stated in hours starts to run immediately on the occurrence of the event that triggers the deadline. The deadline generally ends when the time expires. If, however, the time period expires at a specific time (say, 2:17 p.m.) on a Saturday, Sunday, or legal holiday, then the deadline is extended to the same time (2:17 p.m.) on the next day that is not a Saturday, Sunday, or legal holiday. Periods stated in hours are not to be "rounded up" to the next whole hour. Subdivision (a)(3) addresses situations when the clerk's office is inaccessible during the last hour before a filing deadline expires.

Subdivision (a)(2)(B) directs that every hour be counted. Thus, for example, a 72-hour period that commences at 10:23 a.m. on Friday, November 2, 2007, will run until 9:23 a.m. on Monday, November 5; the discrepancy in start and end times in this example results from the intervening shift from daylight saving time to standard time.

Subdivision (a)(3). When determining the last day of a filing period stated in days or a longer unit of time, a day on which the clerk's office is not accessible because of the weather or another reason is treated like a Saturday, Sunday, or legal holiday. When determining the end of a filing period stated in hours, if the clerk's office is inaccessible during the last hour of the filing period computed under subdivision (a)(2) then the period is extended to the same time on the next day that is not a weekend, holiday, or day when the clerk's office is inaccessible.

Subdivision (a)(3)'s extensions apply "[u]nless the court orders otherwise." In some circumstances, the court might not wish a period of inaccessibility to trigger a full 24-hour extension; in those instances, the court can specify a briefer extension.

The text of the rule no longer refers to "weather or other conditions" as the reason for the inaccessibility of the clerk's office. The reference to "weather" was deleted from the text to underscore that inaccessibility can occur for reasons unrelated to weather, such as an outage of the electronic filing system. Weather can still be a reason for inaccessibility of the clerk's office. The rule does not attempt to define inaccessibility. Rather, the concept will continue to develop through caselaw, see, e.g., William G. Phelps, When Is Office of Clerk of Court Inaccessible Due to Weather or Other Conditions for Purpose of Computing Time Period for Filing Papers under Rule 6(a) of Federal Rules of Civil Procedure, 135 A.L.R. Fed. 259 (1996) (collecting cases). In addition, many local provisions address inaccessibility for purposes of electronic filing, see, e.g., D. Kan. Rule 5.4.11 ("A Filing User whose filing is made untimely as the result of a technical failure may seek appropriate relief from the court.").

Subdivision (a)(4). New subdivision (a)(4) defines the end of the last day of a period for purposes of subdivision (a)(1). Subdivision (a)(4) does not apply in computing periods stated in hours under subdivision (a)(2), and does not apply if a different time is set by a statute, local rule, or order in the case. A local rule may, for example, address the problems that might arise if a single district has clerk's offices in different time zones, or provide that papers filed in a drop box after the normal hours of the clerk's office are filed as of the day that is date-stamped on the papers by a device in the drop box.

28 U.S.C. §452 provides that "[a]ll courts of the United States shall be deemed always open for the purpose of filing proper papers, issuing and returning process, and making motions and orders." A corresponding provision exists in Rule 77(a). Some courts have held that these provisions permit an after-hours filing by handing the papers to an appropriate official. See, e.g., Casalduc v. Diaz, 117 F.2d 915, 917 (1st Cir. 1941). Subdivision (a)(4) does not address the effect of the statute on the question of after-hours filing; instead, the rule is designed to deal with filings in the ordinary course without regard to Section 452.

Subdivision (a)(5). New subdivision (a)(5) defines the "next" day for purposes of subdivisions (a)(1)(C) and (a)(2)(C). The Federal Rules of Civil Procedure contain both forward-looking time periods and backward-looking time periods. A forward-looking time period requires something to be done within a period of time after an event. See, e.g., Rule 59(b) (motion for new trial "must be filed no later than 28 days after entry of the judgment"). A backward-looking time period requires something to be done within a period of time before an event. See, e.g., Rule 26(f) (parties must hold Rule 26(f) conference "as soon as practicable and in any event at least 21 days before a scheduling conference is held or a scheduling order is due under Rule 16(b)"). In determining what is the "next" day for purposes of subdivisions (a)(1)(C) and (a)(2)(C), one should continue counting in the same direction—that is, forward when computing a forward-looking period and backward when computing a backward-looking period. If, for example, a filing is due within 30 days after an event, and the thirtieth day falls on Saturday, September 1, 2007, then the filing is due on Tuesday, September 4, 2007 (Monday, September 3, is Labor Day). But if a filing is due 21 days before an event, and the twenty-first day falls on Saturday, September 1, then the filing is due on Friday, August 31. If the clerk's office is inaccessible on August 31, then subdivision (a)(3) extends the filing deadline forward to the next accessible day that is not a Saturday, Sunday, or legal holiday—no later than Tuesday, September 4.

Subdivision (a)(6). New subdivision (a)(6) defines "legal holiday" for purposes of the Federal Rules of Civil Procedure, including the time-computation provisions of subdivision (a). Subdivision (a)(6) continues to include within the definition of "legal holiday" days that are declared a holiday by the President or Congress.

For forward-counted periods—i.e., periods that are measured after an event—subdivision (a)(6)(C) includes certain state holidays within the definition of legal holidays. However, state legal holidays are not recognized in computing backward-counted periods. For both forward- and backward-counted periods, the rule thus protects those who may be unsure of the effect of state holidays. For forward-counted deadlines, treating state holidays the same as federal holidays extends the deadline. Thus, someone who thought that the federal courts might be closed on a state holiday would be safeguarded against an inadvertent late filing. In contrast, for backward-counted deadlines, not giving state holidays the treatment of federal holidays allows filing on the state holiday itself rather than the day before. Take, for example, Monday, April 21, 2008 (Patriot's Day, a legal holiday in the relevant state). If a filing is due 14 days after an event, and the fourteenth day is April 21, then the filing is due on Tuesday, April 22 because Monday, April 21 counts as a legal holiday. But if a filing is due 14 days before an event, and the fourteenth day is April 21, the filing is due on Monday, April 21; the fact that April 21 is a state holiday does not make April 21 a legal holiday for purposes of computing this backward-counted deadline. But note that if the clerk's office is inaccessible on Monday, April 21, then subdivision (a)(3) extends the April 21 filing deadline forward to the next accessible day that is not a Saturday, Sunday or legal holiday—no earlier than Tuesday, April 22.

Changes Made after Publication and Comment. The Standing Committee changed Rule 6(a)(6) to exclude state holidays from the definition of "legal holiday" for purposes of computing backward-counted periods; conforming changes were made to the Committee Note.

[Subdivisions (b) and (c).] The times set in the former rule at 1 or 5 days have been revised to 7 or 14 days. See the Note to Rule 6 [above].

Committee Notes on Rules—2016 Amendment

Rule 6(d) is amended to remove service by electronic means under Rule 5(b)(2)(E) from the modes of service that allow 3 added days to act after being served.

Rule 5(b)(2) was amended in 2001 to provide for service by electronic means. Although electronic transmission seemed virtually instantaneous even then, electronic service was included in the modes of service that allow 3 added days to act after being served. There were concerns that the transmission might be delayed for some time, and particular concerns that incompatible systems might make it difficult or impossible to open attachments. Those concerns have been substantially alleviated by advances in technology and in widespread skill in using electronic transmission.

A parallel reason for allowing the 3 added days was that electronic service was authorized only with the consent of the person to be served. Concerns about the reliability of electronic transmission might have led to refusals of consent; the 3 added days were calculated to alleviate these concerns.

Diminution of the concerns that prompted the decision to allow the 3 added days for electronic transmission is not the only reason for discarding this indulgence. Many rules have been changed to ease the task of computing time by adopting 7-, 14-, 21-, and 28-day periods that allow "day-of-the-week" counting. Adding 3 days at the end complicated the counting, and increased the occasions for further complication by invoking the provisions that apply when the last day is a Saturday, Sunday, or legal holiday.

Electronic service after business hours, or just before or during a weekend or holiday, may result in a practical reduction in the time available to respond. Extensions of time may be warranted to prevent prejudice.

Eliminating Rule 5(b) subparagraph (2)(E) from the modes of service that allow 3 added days means that the 3 added days cannot be retained by consenting to service by electronic means. Consent to electronic service in registering for electronic case filing, for example, does not count as consent to service "by any other means" of delivery under subparagraph (F).

What is now Rule 6(d) was amended in 2005 "to remove any doubt as to the method for calculating the time to respond after service by mail, leaving with the clerk of court, electronic means, or by other means consented to by the party served." A potential ambiguity was created by substituting "after service" for the earlier references to acting after service "upon the party" if a paper or notice "is served upon the party" by the specified means. "[A]fter service" could be read to refer not only to a party that has been served but also to a party that has made service. That reading would mean that a party who is allowed a specified time to act after making service can extend the time by choosing one of the means of service specified in the rule, something that was never intended by the original rule or the amendment. Rules setting a time to act after making service include Rules 14(a)(1), 15(a)(1)(A), and 38(b)(1). "[A]fter being served" is substituted for "after service" to dispel any possible misreading.

TITLE III. PLEADINGS AND MOTIONS

Rule 7. Pleadings Allowed; Form of Motions and Other Papers

(a) Pleadings. Only these pleadings are allowed:
(1) a complaint;
(2) an answer to a complaint;
(3) an answer to a counterclaim designated as a counterclaim;
(4) an answer to a crossclaim;
(5) a third-party complaint;
(6) an answer to a third-party complaint; and
(7) if the court orders one, a reply to an answer.

(b) Motions and Other Papers.
(1) In General. A request for a court order must be made by motion. The motion must:
(A) be in writing unless made during a hearing or trial;
(B) state with particularity the grounds for seeking the order; and
(C) state the relief sought.
(2) Form. The rules governing captions and other matters of form in pleadings apply to motions and other papers.

(As amended Dec. 27, 1946, eff. Mar. 19, 1948; Jan. 21, 1963, eff. July 1, 1963; Apr. 28, 1983, eff. Aug. 1, 1983; Apr. 30, 2007, eff. Dec. 1, 2007.)

Notes of Advisory Committee on Rules—1937

1. A provision designating pleadings and defining a motion is common in the State practice acts. See Ill.Rev.Stat. (1937), ch. 110, §156 (Designation and order of pleadings); 2 Minn.Stat. (Mason, 1927) §9246 (Definition of motion); and N.Y.C.P.A. (1937) §113 (Definition of motion). Former Equity Rules 18 (Pleadings—Technical Forms Abrogated), 29 (Defenses—How Presented), and 33 (Testing Sufficiency of Defense) abolished technical forms of pleading, demurrers, and pleas, and exceptions for insufficiency of an answer.

2. Note to Subdivision (a). This preserves the substance of [former] Equity Rule 31 (Reply—When Required—When Cause at Issue). Compare the English practice, English Rules Under the Judicature Act (The Annual Practice, 1937) O. 23, r.r. 1, 2 (Reply to counterclaim; amended, 1933, to be subject to the rules applicable to defenses, O. 21). See O. 21, r.r. 1–14; O. 27, r. 13 (When pleadings deemed denied and put in issue). Under the codes the pleadings are generally limited. A reply is sometimes required to an affirmative defense in the answer. 1 Colo.Stat.Ann. (1935) §66; Ore.Code Ann. (1930) §§1–614, 1–616. In other jurisdictions no reply is necessary to an affirmative defense in the answer, but a reply may be ordered by the court. N.C.Code Ann (1935) §525; 1 S.D.Comp.Laws (1929) §2357. A reply to a counterclaim is usually required. Ark.Civ.Code (Crawford, 1934) §§123–125; Wis.Stat. (1935) §§263.20, 263.21. U.S.C., Title 28, [former] §45 (District courts; practice and procedure in certain cases) is modified insofar as it may dispense with a reply to a counterclaim.

For amendment of pleadings, see Rule 15 dealing with amended and supplemental pleadings.

3. All statutes which use the words "petition", "bill of complaint", "plea", "demurrer", and other such terminology are modified in form by this rule.

Notes of Advisory Committee on Rules—1946 Amendment

This amendment [to subdivision (a)] eliminates any question as to whether the compulsory reply, where a counterclaim is pleaded, is a reply only to the counterclaim or is a general reply to the answer containing the counterclaim. See Commentary, Scope of Reply Where Defendant Has Pleaded Counterclaim (1939) 1 Fed.Rules Serv. 672; Fort Chartres and Ivy Landing Drainage and Levee District No. Five v. Thompson (E.D.Ill. 1945) 8 Fed.Rules Serv. 13.32, Case 1.

Notes of Advisory Committee on Rules—1963 Amendment

Certain redundant words are eliminated and the subdivision is modified to reflect the amendment of Rule 14(a) which in certain cases eliminates the requirement of obtaining leave to bring in a third-party defendant.

Notes of Advisory Committee on Rules—1983 Amendment

One of the reasons sanctions against improper motion practice have been employed infrequently is the lack of clarity of Rule 7 That rule has stated only generally that the pleading requirements relating to captions, signing, and other matters of form also apply to motions and other papers. The addition of Rule 7(b)(3) makes explicit the applicability of the signing requirement and the sanctions of Rule 11, which have been amplified.

Committee Notes on Rules—2007 Amendment

The language of Rule 7 has been amended as part of the general restyling of the Civil Rules to make them more easily understood and to make style and terminology consistent throughout the rules. These changes are intended to be stylistic only.

Former Rule 7(a) stated that "there shall be * * * an answer to a cross-claim, if the answer contains a cross-claim * * *." Former Rule 12(a)(2) provided more generally that "[a] party served with a pleading stating a cross-claim against that party shall serve an answer thereto * * *." New Rule 7(a) corrects this inconsistency by providing for an answer to a crossclaim.

For the first time, Rule 7(a)(7) expressly authorizes the court to order a reply to a counterclaim answer. A reply may be as useful in this setting as a reply to an answer, a third-party answer, or a crossclaim answer.

Former Rule 7(b)(1) stated that the writing requirement is fulfilled if the motion is stated in a written notice of hearing. This statement was deleted as redundant because a single written document can satisfy the writing requirements both for a motion and for a Rule 6(c)(1) notice.

The cross-reference to Rule 11 in former Rule 7(b)(3) is deleted as redundant. Rule 11 applies by its own terms. The force and application of Rule 11 are not diminished by the deletion.

Former Rule 7(c) is deleted because it has done its work. If a motion or pleading is described as a demurrer, plea, or exception for insufficiency, the court will treat the paper as if properly captioned.

Rule 7.1. Disclosure Statement

(a) Who Must File; Contents. A nongovernmental corporate party must file 2 copies of a disclosure statement that:

(1) identifies any parent corporation and any publicly held corporation owning 10% or more of its stock; or

(2) states that there is no such corporation.

(b) Time to File; Supplemental Filing. A party must:

(1) file the disclosure statement with its first appearance, pleading, petition, motion, response, or other request addressed to the court; and

(2) promptly file a supplemental statement if any required information changes.

(As added Apr. 29, 2002, eff. Dec. 1, 2002; amended Apr. 30, 2007, eff. Dec. 1, 2007.)

Committee Notes on Rules—2002

Rule 7.1 is drawn from Rule 26.1 of the Federal Rules of Appellate Procedure, with changes to adapt to the circumstances of district courts that dictate different provisions for the time of filing, number of copies, and the like. The information required by Rule 7.1(a) reflects the "financial interest" standard of Canon 3C(1)(c) of the Code of Conduct for United States Judges. This information will support properly informed disqualification decisions in situations that call for automatic disqualification under Canon 3C(1)(c). It does not cover all of the circumstances that may call for disqualification under the financial interest standard, and does not deal at all with other circumstances that may call for disqualification.

Although the disclosures required by Rule 7.1(a) may seem limited, they are calculated to reach a majority of the circumstances that are likely to call for disqualification on the basis of financial information that a judge may not know or recollect. Framing a rule that calls for more detailed disclosure will be difficult. Unnecessary disclosure requirements place a burden on the parties and on courts. Unnecessary disclosure of volumes of information may create a risk that a judge will overlook the one bit of information that might require disqualification, and also may create a risk that unnecessary disqualifications will be made rather than attempt to unravel a potentially difficult question. It has not been feasible to dictate more detailed disclosure requirements in Rule 7.1(a).

Rule 7.1 does not prohibit local rules that require disclosures in addition to those required by Rule 7.1. Developing experience with local disclosure practices and advances in electronic technology may provide a foundation for adopting more detailed disclosure requirements by future amendments of Rule 7.1.

Changes Made After Publication and Comments. The provisions that would require disclosure of additional information that may be required by the Judicial Conference have been deleted.

Committee Notes on Rules—2007 Amendment

The language of Rule 7.1 has been amended as part of the general restyling of the Civil Rules to make them more easily understood and to make style and terminology consistent throughout the rules. These changes are intended to be stylistic only.

Rule 8. General Rules of Pleading

(a) Claim for Relief. A pleading that states a claim for relief must contain:

(1) a short and plain statement of the grounds for the court's jurisdiction, unless the court already has jurisdiction and the claim needs no new jurisdictional support;

(2) a short and plain statement of the claim showing that the pleader is entitled to relief; and

(3) a demand for the relief sought, which may include relief in the alternative or different types of relief.

(b) Defenses; Admissions and Denials.

(1) In General. In responding to a pleading, a party must:

(A) state in short and plain terms its defenses to each claim asserted against it; and

(B) admit or deny the allegations asserted against it by an opposing party.

(2) Denials—Responding to the Substance. A denial must fairly respond to the substance of the allegation.

(3) General and Specific Denials. A party that intends in good faith to deny all the allegations of a pleading—including the jurisdictional grounds—may do so by a general denial. A party that does not intend to deny all the allegations must either specifically deny designated allegations or generally deny all except those specifically admitted.

(4) Denying Part of an Allegation. A party that intends in good faith to deny only part of an allegation must admit the part that is true and deny the rest.

(5) Lacking Knowledge or Information. A party that lacks knowledge or information sufficient to form a belief about the truth of an allegation must so state, and the statement has the effect of a denial.

(6) Effect of Failing to Deny. An allegation—other than one relating to the amount of damages—is admitted if a responsive pleading is required and the allegation is not denied. If a responsive pleading is not required, an allegation is considered denied or avoided.

(c) Affirmative Defenses.

(1) In General. In responding to a pleading, a party must affirmatively state any avoidance or affirmative defense, including:

- accord and satisfaction;
- arbitration and award;
- assumption of risk;

- contributory negligence;
- duress;
- estoppel;
- failure of consideration;
- fraud;
- illegality;
- injury by fellow servant;
- laches;
- license;
- payment;
- release;
- res judicata;
- statute of frauds;
- statute of limitations; and
- waiver.

(2) Mistaken Designation. If a party mistakenly designates a defense as a counterclaim, or a counterclaim as a defense, the court must, if justice requires, treat the pleading as though it were correctly designated, and may impose terms for doing so.

(d) Pleading to Be Concise and Direct; Alternative Statements; Inconsistency.

(1) In General. Each allegation must be simple, concise, and direct. No technical form is required.

(2) Alternative Statements of a Claim or Defense. A party may set out 2 or more statements of a claim or defense alternatively or hypothetically, either in a single count or defense or in separate ones. If a party makes alternative statements, the pleading is sufficient if any one of them is sufficient.

(3) Inconsistent Claims or Defenses. A party may state as many separate claims or defenses as it has, regardless of consistency.

(e) Construing Pleadings. Pleadings must be construed so as to do justice.

(As amended Feb. 28, 1966, eff. July 1, 1966; Mar. 2, 1987, eff. Aug. 1, 1987; Apr. 30, 2007, eff. Dec. 1, 2007; Apr. 28, 2010, eff. Dec. 1, 2010.)

Notes of Advisory Committee on Rules—1937

Note to Subdivision (a). See [former] Equity Rules 25 (Bill of Complaint—Contents), and 30 (Answer—Contents—Counterclaim). Compare 2 Ind.Stat.Ann. (Burns, 1933) §§2–1004, 2–1015; 2 Ohio Gen.Code Ann. (Page, 1926) §§11305, 11314; Utah Rev.Stat.Ann. (1933), §§104–7–2, 104–9–1.

See Rule 19(c) for the requirement of a statement in a claim for relief of the names of persons who ought to be parties and the reason for their omission.

See Rule 23(b) for particular requirements as to the complaint in a secondary action by shareholders.

Note to Subdivision (b). 1. This rule supersedes the methods of pleading prescribed in U.S.C., Title 19, §508 (Persons making seizures pleading general issue and providing special matter); U.S.C., Title 35, [former] §§40d (Providing under general issue, upon notice, that a statement in application for an extended patent is not true), 69 [now 282] (Pleading and proof in actions for infringement) and similar statutes.

2. This rule is, in part, [former] Equity Rule 30 (Answer—Contents—Counterclaim), with the matter on denials largely from the Connecticut practice. See Conn.Practice Book (1934) §§107, 108, and 122; Conn.Gen.Stat. (1930) §§5508–5514. Compare the English practice, English Rules Under the Judicature Act (The Annual Practice, 1937) O. 19, r.r. 17–20.

Note to Subdivision (c). This follows substantially English Rules Under the Judicature Act (The Annual Practice, 1937) O. 19, r. 15 and N.Y.C.P.A. (1937) §242, with "surprise" omitted in this rule.

Note to Subdivision (d). The first sentence is similar to [former] Equity Rule 30 (Answer—Contents—Counterclaim). For the second sentence see [former] Equity Rule 31 (Reply—When Required—When Cause at Issue). This is similar to English Rules Under the Judicature Act (The Annual Practice, 1937) O. 19, r.r. 13, 18; and to the practice in the States.

Note to Subdivision (e). This rule is an elaboration upon [former] Equity Rule 30 (Answer—Contents—Counterclaim), plus a statement of the actual practice under some codes. Compare also [former] Equity Rule 18 (Pleadings—Technical Forms Abrogated). See Clark, Code Pleading (1928), pp. 171–4, 432–5; Hankin, Alternative and Hypothetical Pleading (1924), 33 Yale L.J. 365.

Note to Subdivision (f). A provision of like import is of frequent occurrence in the codes. Ill.Rev.Stat. (1937) ch. 110, §157(3); 2 Minn.Stat. (Mason, 1927) §9266; N.Y.C.P.A. (1937) §275; 2 N.D.Comp.Laws Ann. (1913) §7458.

Notes of Advisory Committee on Rules—1966 Amendment

The change here is consistent with the broad purposes of unification.

Notes of Advisory Committee on Rules—1987 Amendment

The amendments are technical. No substantive change is intended.

Committee Notes on Rules—2007 Amendment

The language of Rule 8 has been amended as part of the general restyling of the Civil Rules to make them more easily understood and to make style and terminology consistent throughout the rules. These changes are intended to be stylistic only.

The former Rule 8(b) and 8(e) cross-references to Rule 11 are deleted as redundant. Rule 11 applies by its own terms. The force and application of Rule 11 are not diminished by the deletion.

Former Rule 8(b) required a pleader denying part of an averment to "specify so much of it as is true and material and * * * deny only the remainder." "[A]nd material" is deleted to avoid the implication that it is proper to deny something that the pleader believes to be true but not material.

Deletion of former Rule 8(e)(2)'s "whether based on legal, equitable, or maritime grounds" reflects the parallel deletions in Rule 1 and elsewhere. Merger is now successfully accomplished.

Changes Made After Publication and Comment. See Note to Rule 1, supra.

Committee Notes on Rules—2010 Amendment

Subdivision (c)(1). "[D]ischarge in bankruptcy" is deleted from the list of affirmative defenses. Under 11 U.S.C. §524(a)(1) and (2) a discharge voids a judgment to the extent that it determines a personal liability of the debtor with respect to a discharged debt. The discharge also operates as an injunction against commencement or continuation of an action to collect, recover, or offset a discharged debt. For these reasons it is confusing to describe discharge as an affirmative defense. But §524(a) applies only to a claim that was actually discharged. Several categories of debt set out in 11 U.S.C. §523(a) are excepted from discharge. The issue whether a claim was excepted from discharge may be determined either in the court that entered the discharge or—in most instances—in another court with jurisdiction over the creditor's claim.

Changes Made After Publication and Comment. No changes were made in the rule text.

The Committee Note was revised to delete statements that were over-simplified. New material was added to provide a reminder of the means to determine whether a debt was in fact discharged.

Rule 9. Pleading Special Matters

(a) Capacity or Authority to Sue; Legal Existence.

(1) In General. Except when required to show that the court has jurisdiction, a pleading need not allege:

(A) a party's capacity to sue or be sued;

(B) a party's authority to sue or be sued in a representative capacity; or

(C) the legal existence of an organized association of persons that is made a party.

(2) Raising Those Issues. To raise any of those issues, a party must do so by a specific denial, which must state any supporting facts that are peculiarly within the party's knowledge.

(b) Fraud or Mistake; Conditions of Mind. In alleging fraud or mistake, a party must state with particularity the circumstances constituting fraud or mistake. Malice, intent, knowledge, and other conditions of a person's mind may be alleged generally.

(c) Conditions Precedent. In pleading conditions precedent, it suffices to allege generally that all conditions precedent have occurred or been performed. But when denying that a condition precedent has occurred or been performed, a party must do so with particularity.

(d) Official Document or Act. In pleading an official document or official act, it suffices to allege that the document was legally issued or the act legally done.

(e) Judgment. In pleading a judgment or decision of a domestic or foreign court, a judicial or quasi-judicial tribunal, or a board or officer, it suffices to plead the judgment or decision without showing jurisdiction to render it.

(f) Time and Place. An allegation of time or place is material when testing the sufficiency of a pleading.

(g) Special Damages. If an item of special damage is claimed, it must be specifically stated.

(h) Admiralty or Maritime Claim.

(1) How Designated. If a claim for relief is within the admiralty or maritime jurisdiction and also within the court's subject-matter jurisdiction on some other ground, the pleading may designate the claim as an admiralty or maritime claim for purposes of Rules 14(c), 38(e), and 82 and the Supplemental Rules for Admiralty or Maritime Claims and Asset Forfeiture Actions. A claim cognizable only in the admiralty or maritime jurisdiction is an admiralty or maritime claim for those purposes, whether or not so designated.

(2) Designation for Appeal. A case that includes an admiralty or maritime claim within this subdivision (h) is an admiralty case within 28 U.S.C. §1292(a)(3).

(As amended Feb. 28, 1966, eff. July 1, 1966; Dec. 4, 1967, eff. July 1, 1968; Mar. 30, 1970, eff. July 1, 1970; Mar. 2, 1987, eff. Aug. 1, 1987; Apr. 11, 1997, eff. Dec. 1, 1997; Apr. 12, 2006, eff. Dec. 1, 2006; Apr. 30, 2007, eff. Dec. 1, 2007.)

Notes of Advisory Committee on Rules—1937

Note to Subdivision (a). Compare [former] Equity Rule 25 (Bill of Complaint—Contents) requiring disability to be stated; Utah Rev.Stat.Ann. (1933) §104–13–15, enumerating a number of situations where a general averment of capacity is sufficient. For provisions governing averment of incorporation, see 2 Minn.Stat. (Mason, 1927) §9271; N.Y.R.C.P. (1937) Rule 93; 2 N.D.Comp.Laws Ann. (1913) §7981 et seq.

Note to Subdivision (b). See English Rules Under the Judicature Act (The Annual Practice, 1937) O. 19, r. 22.

Note to Subdivision (c). The codes generally have this or a similar provision. See English Rules Under the Judicature Act (The Annual Practice, 1937) O. 19, r. 14; 2 Minn.Stat. (Mason, 1927) §9273; N.Y.R.C.P. (1937) Rule 92; 2 N.D.Comp.Laws Ann. (1913) §7461; 2 Wash.Rev.Stat.Ann. (Remington, 1932) §288.

Note to Subdivision (e). The rule expands the usual code provisions on pleading a judgment by including judgments or decisions of administrative tribunals and foreign courts. Compare Ark.Civ.Code (Crawford, 1934) §141; 2 Minn.Stat. (Mason, 1927) §9269; N.Y.R.C.P. (1937) Rule 95; 2 Wash.Rev.Stat.Ann. (Remington, 1932) §287.

Notes of Advisory Committee on Rules—1966 Amendment

Certain distinctive features of the admiralty practice must be preserved for what are now suits in admiralty. This raises the question: After unification, when a single form of action is established, how will the counterpart of the present suit in admiralty be identifiable? In part the question is easily answered. Some claims for relief can only be suits in admiralty, either because the admiralty jurisdiction is exclusive or because no nonmaritime ground of federal jurisdiction exists. Many claims, however, are cognizable by the district courts whether asserted in admiralty or in a civil action, assuming the existence of a nonmaritime ground of jurisdiction. Thus at present the pleader has power to determine procedural consequences by the way in which he exercises the classic privilege given by the saving-to-suitors clause (28 U.S.C. §1333) or by equivalent statutory provisions. For example, a longshoreman's claim for personal injuries suffered by reason of the unseaworthiness of a vessel may be asserted in a suit in admiralty or, if diversity of citizenship exists, in a civil action. One of the important procedural consequences is that in the civil action either party may demand a jury trial, while in the suit in admiralty there is no right to jury trial except as provided by statute.

It is no part of the purpose of unification to inject a right to jury trial into those admiralty cases in which that right is not provided by statute. Similarly as will be more specifically noted below, there is no disposition to change the present law as to interlocutory appeals in admiralty, or as to the venue of suits in admiralty; and, of course, there is no disposition to inject into the civil practice as it now is the distinctively maritime remedies (maritime attachment and garnishment, actions in rem, possessory, petitory and partition actions and limitation of liability). The unified rules must therefore provide some device for preserving the present power of the pleader to determine whether these historically maritime procedures shall be applicable to his claim or not; the pleader must be afforded some means of designating his claim as the counterpart of the present suit in admiralty, where its character as such is not clear.

The problem is different from the similar one concerning the identification of claims that were formerly suits in equity. While that problem is not free from complexities, it is broadly true that the modern counterpart of the suit in equity is distinguishable from the former action at law by the character of the relief sought. This mode of identification is possible in only a limited category of admiralty cases. In large numbers of cases the relief sought in admiralty is simple money damages, indistinguishable from the remedy afforded by the common law. This is true, for example, in the case of the longshoreman's action for personal injuries stated above. After unification has abolished the distinction between civil actions and suits in admiralty, the complaint in such an action would be almost completely ambiguous as to the pleader's intentions regarding the procedure invoked. The allegation of diversity of citizenship might be regarded as a clue indicating an intention to proceed as at present under the saving-to-suitors clause; but this, too, would be ambiguous if there were also reference to the admiralty jurisdiction, and the pleader ought not be required to forego mention of all available jurisdictional grounds.

Other methods of solving the problem were carefully explored, but the Advisory Committee concluded that the preferable solution is to allow the pleader who now has power to determine procedural consequences by filing a suit in admiralty to exercise that power under unification, for the limited instances in which procedural differences will remain, by a simple statement in his pleading to the effect that the claim is an admiralty or maritime claim.

The choice made by the pleader in identifying or in failing to identify his claim as an admiralty or maritime claim is not an irrevocable election. The rule provides that the amendment of a pleading to add or withdraw an identifying statement is subject to the principles of Rule 15.

Notes of Advisory Committee on Rules—1968 Amendment

The amendment eliminates the reference to Rule 73 which is to be abrogated and transfers to Rule 9(h) the substance of Subsection (h) of Rule 73 which preserved the right to an interlocutory appeal in admiralty cases which is provided by 28 U.S.C. §1292(a)(3).

Notes of Advisory Committee on Rules—1970 Amendment

The reference to Rule 26(a) is deleted, in light of the transfer of that subdivision to Rule 30(a) and the elimination of the de bene esse procedure therefrom. See the Advisory Committee's note to Rule 30(a).

Notes of Advisory Committee on Rules—1987 Amendment

The amendment is technical. No substantive change is intended.

Notes of Advisory Committee on Rules—1997 Amendment

Section 1292(a)(3) of the Judicial Code provides for appeal from "[i]nterlocutory decrees of * * * district courts * * * determining the rights and liabilities of the parties to admiralty cases in which appeals from final decrees are allowed."

Rule 9(h) was added in 1966 with the unification of civil and admiralty procedure. Civil Rule 73(h) was amended at the same time to provide that the §1292(a)(3) reference "to admiralty cases shall be construed to mean admiralty and maritime claims within the meaning of Rule 9(h)." This provision was transferred to Rule 9(h) when the Appellate Rules were adopted.

A single case can include both admiralty or maritime claims and nonadmiralty claims or parties. This combination reveals an ambiguity in the statement in present Rule 9(h) that an admiralty "claim" is an admiralty "case." An order "determining the rights and liabilities of the parties" within the meaning of §1292(a)(3) may resolve only a nonadmiralty claim, or may simultaneously resolve interdependent admiralty and nonadmiralty claims. Can appeal be taken as to the nonadmiralty matter, because it is part of a case that includes an admiralty claim, or is appeal limited to the admiralty claim?

The courts of appeals have not achieved full uniformity in applying the §1292(a)(3) requirement that an order "determin[e] the rights and liabilities of the parties." It is common to assert that the statute should be construed narrowly, under the general policy that exceptions to the final judgment rule should be construed narrowly. This policy would suggest that the ambiguity should be resolved by limiting the interlocutory appeal right to orders that determine the rights and liabilities of the parties to an admiralty claim.

A broader view is chosen by this amendment for two reasons. The statute applies to admiralty "cases," and may itself provide for appeal from an order that disposes of a nonadmiralty claim that is joined in a single case with an admiralty claim. Although a rule of court may help to clarify and implement a statutory grant of jurisdiction, the line is not always clear between permissible implementation and impermissible withdrawal of jurisdiction. In addition, so long as an order truly disposes of the rights and liabilities of the parties within the meaning of §1292(a)(3), it may prove important to permit appeal as to the nonadmiralty claim. Disposition of the nonadmiralty claim, for example, may make it unnecessary to consider the admiralty claim and have the same effect on the case and parties as disposition of the admiralty claim. Or the admiralty and nonadmiralty claims may be interdependent. An illustration is provided by Roco Carriers, Ltd. v. M/V Nurnberg Express, 899 F.2d 1292 (2d Cir. 1990). Claims for losses of ocean shipments were made against two defendants, one subject to admiralty jurisdiction and the other not. Summary judgment was granted in favor of the admiralty defendant and against the nonadmiralty defendant. The nonadmiralty defendant's appeal was accepted, with the explanation that the determination of its liability was "integrally linked with the determination of non-liability" of the admiralty defendant, and that "section 1292(a)(3) is not limited to admiralty claims; instead, it refers to admiralty cases." 899 F.2d at 1297. The advantages of permitting appeal by the nonadmiralty defendant would be particularly clear if the plaintiff had appealed the summary judgment in favor of the admiralty defendant.

It must be emphasized that this amendment does not rest on any particular assumptions as to the meaning of the §1292(a)(3) provision that limits interlocutory appeal to orders that determine the rights and liabilities of the parties. It simply reflects the conclusion that so long as the case involves an admiralty claim and an order otherwise meets statutory requirements, the opportunity to appeal should not turn on the circumstance that the order does—or does not—dispose of an admiralty claim. No attempt is made to invoke the authority conferred by 28 U.S.C. §1292(e) to provide by rule for appeal of an interlocutory decision that is not otherwise provided for by other subsections of §1292.

GAP Report on Rule 9(h). No changes have been made in the published proposal.

Committee Notes on Rules—2006 Amendment

Rule 9(h) is amended to conform to the changed title of the Supplemental Rules.

Committee Notes on Rules—2007 Amendment

The language of Rule 9 has been amended as part of the general restyling of the Civil Rules to make them more easily understood and to make style and terminology consistent throughout the rules. These changes are intended to be stylistic only.

Rule 15 governs pleading amendments of its own force. The former redundant statement that Rule 15 governs an amendment that adds or withdraws a Rule 9(h) designation as an admiralty or maritime claim is deleted. The elimination of paragraph (2) means that "(3)" will be redesignated as "(2)" in Style Rule 9(h).

Rule 10. Form of Pleadings

(a) Caption; Names of Parties. Every pleading must have a caption with the court's name, a title, a file number, and a Rule 7(a) designation. The title of the complaint must name all the parties; the title of other pleadings, after naming the first party on each side, may refer generally to other parties.
(b) Paragraphs; Separate Statements. A party must state its claims or defenses in numbered paragraphs, each limited as far as practicable to a single set of circumstances. A later pleading may refer by number to a paragraph in an earlier pleading. If doing so would promote clarity, each claim founded on a separate transaction or occurrence—and each defense other than a denial—must be stated in a separate count or defense.
(c) Adoption by Reference; Exhibits. A statement in a pleading may be adopted by reference elsewhere in the same pleading or in any other pleading or motion. A copy of a written instrument that is an exhibit to a pleading is a part of the pleading for all purposes.

(As amended Apr. 30, 2007, eff. Dec. 1, 2007.)

Notes of Advisory Committee on Rules—1937

The first sentence is derived in part from the opening statement of [former] Equity Rule 25 (Bill of Complaint—Contents). The remainder of the rule is an expansion in conformity with usual state provisions. For numbered paragraphs and separate statements, see Conn.Gen.Stat. (1930) §5513; Ill.Rev.Stat. (1937) ch. 110, §157 (2); N.Y.R.C.P. (1937) Rule 90. For incorporation by reference, see N.Y.R.C.P. (1937) Rule 90. For written instruments as exhibits, see Ill.Rev.Stat. (1937) ch. 110, §160.

Committee Notes on Rules—2007 Amendment

The language of Rule 10 has been amended as part of the general restyling of the Civil Rules to make them more easily understood and to make style and terminology consistent throughout the rules. These changes are intended to be stylistic only.

Rule 11. Signing Pleadings, Motions, and Other Papers; Representations to the Court; Sanctions

(a) Signature. Every pleading, written motion, and other paper must be signed by at least one attorney of record in the attorney's name—or by a party personally if the party is unrepresented. The paper must state the signer's address, e-mail address, and telephone number. Unless a rule or statute specifically states otherwise, a pleading need not be verified or accompanied by an affidavit. The court must strike an unsigned paper unless the omission is promptly corrected after being called to the attorney's or party's attention.
(b) Representations to the Court. By presenting to the court a pleading, written motion, or other paper—whether by signing, filing, submitting, or later advocating it—an attorney or unrepresented party certifies that to the best of the person's knowledge, information, and belief, formed after an inquiry reasonable under the circumstances:

(1) it is not being presented for any improper purpose, such as to harass, cause unnecessary delay, or needlessly increase the cost of litigation;
(2) the claims, defenses, and other legal contentions are warranted by existing law or by a nonfrivolous argument for extending, modifying, or reversing existing law or for establishing new law;
(3) the factual contentions have evidentiary support or, if specifically so identified, will likely have evidentiary support after a reasonable opportunity for further investigation or discovery; and
(4) the denials of factual contentions are warranted on the evidence or, if specifically so identified, are reasonably based on belief or a lack of information.

(c) Sanctions.

(1) In General. If, after notice and a reasonable opportunity to respond, the court determines that Rule 11(b) has been violated, the court may impose an appropriate sanction on any attorney, law firm, or party that violated the rule or is responsible for the violation. Absent exceptional circumstances, a law firm must be held jointly responsible for a violation committed by its partner, associate, or employee.
(2) Motion for Sanctions. A motion for sanctions must be made separately from any other motion and must describe the specific conduct that allegedly violates Rule 11(b). The motion must be served under Rule 5, but it must not be filed or be presented to the court if the challenged paper, claim, defense, contention, or denial is withdrawn or appropriately corrected within 21 days after service or within another time the court sets. If warranted, the court may award to the prevailing party the reasonable expenses, including attorney's fees, incurred for the motion.
(3) On the Court's Initiative. On its own, the court may order an attorney, law firm, or party to show cause why conduct specifically described in the order has not violated Rule 11(b).
(4) Nature of a Sanction. A sanction imposed under this rule must be limited to what suffices to deter repetition of the conduct or comparable conduct by others similarly situated. The sanction may include nonmonetary directives; an order to pay a penalty into court; or, if imposed on motion and warranted for effective deterrence, an order directing payment to the movant of part or all of the reasonable attorney's fees and other expenses directly resulting from the violation.

(5) Limitations on Monetary Sanctions. The court must not impose a monetary sanction:

(A) against a represented party for violating Rule 11(b)(2); or

(B) on its own, unless it issued the show-cause order under Rule 11(c)(3) before voluntary dismissal or settlement of the claims made by or against the party that is, or whose attorneys are, to be sanctioned.

(6) Requirements for an Order. An order imposing a sanction must describe the sanctioned conduct and explain the basis for the sanction.

(d) Inapplicability to Discovery. This rule does not apply to disclosures and discovery requests, responses, objections, and motions under Rules 26 through 37.

———

(As amended Apr. 28, 1983, eff. Aug. 1, 1983; Mar. 2, 1987, eff. Aug. 1, 1987; Apr. 22, 1993, eff. Dec. 1, 1993; Apr. 30, 2007, eff. Dec. 1, 2007.)

Notes of Advisory Committee on Rules—1937

This is substantially the content of [former] Equity Rules 24 (Signature of Counsel) and 21 (Scandal and Impertinence) consolidated and unified. Compare [former] Equity Rule 36 (Officers Before Whom Pleadings Verified). Compare to similar purposes, English Rules Under the Judicature Act (The Annual Practice, 1937) O. 19, r. 4, and Great Australian Gold Mining Co. v. Martin, L. R., 5 Ch.Div. 1, 10 (1877). Subscription of pleadings is required in many codes. 2 Minn.Stat. (Mason, 1927) §9265; N.Y.R.C.P. (1937) Rule 91; 2 N.D.Comp.Laws Ann. (1913) §7455.

This rule expressly continues any statute which requires a pleading to be verified or accompanied by an affidavit, such as:

U.S.C., Title 28:

- §381 [former] (Preliminary injunctions and temporary restraining orders)
- §762 [now 1402] (Suit against the United States).

U.S.C., Title 28, §829 [now 1927] (Costs; attorney liable for, when) is unaffected by this rule.

For complaints which must be verified under these rules, see Rules 23(b) (Secondary Action by Shareholders) and 65 (Injunctions).

For abolition of the rule in equity that the averments of an answer under oath must be overcome by the testimony of two witnesses or of one witness sustained by corroborating circumstances, see Pa.Stat.Ann. (Purdon, 1931) see 12 P.S.Pa., §1222; for the rule in equity itself, see Greenfield v. Blumenthal, 69 F.2d 294 (C.C.A. 3d, 1934).

Notes of Advisory Committee on Rules—1983 Amendment

Since its original promulgation, Rule 11 has provided for the striking of pleadings and the imposition of disciplinary sanctions to check abuses in the signing of pleadings. Its provisions have always applied to motions and other papers by virtue of incorporation by reference in Rule 7(b)(2). The amendment and the addition of Rule 7(b)(3) expressly confirms this applicability.

Experience shows that in practice Rule 11 has not been effective in deterring abuses. See 6 Wright & Miller, Federal Practice and Procedure: Civil §1334 (1971). There has been considerable confusion as to (1) the circumstances that should trigger striking a pleading or motion or taking disciplinary action, (2) the standard of conduct expected of attorneys who sign pleadings and motions, and (3) the range of available and appropriate sanctions. See Rodes, Ripple & Mooney, Sanctions Imposable for Violations of the Federal Rules of Civil Procedure 64–65, Federal Judicial Center (1981). The new language is intended to reduce the reluctance of courts to impose sanctions, see Moore, Federal Practice 7.05, at 1547, by emphasizing the responsibilities of the attorney and reenforcing those obligations by the imposition of sanctions.

The amended rule attempts to deal with the problem by building upon and expanding the equitable doctrine permitting the court to award expenses, including attorney's fees, to a litigant whose opponent acts in bad faith in instituting or conducting litigation. See, e.g., Roadway Express, Inc. v. Piper, 447 U.S. 752, (1980); Hall v. Cole, 412 U.S. 1, 5 (1973). Greater attention by the district courts to pleading and motion abuses and the imposition of sanctions when appropriate, should discourage dilatory or abusive tactics and help to streamline the litigation process by lessening frivolous claims or defenses.

The expanded nature of the lawyer's certification in the fifth sentence of amended Rule 11 recognizes that the litigation process may be abused for purposes other than delay. See, e.g., Browning Debenture Holders' Committee v. DASA Corp., 560 F.2d 1078 (2d Cir. 1977).

The words "good ground to support" the pleading in the original rule were interpreted to have both factual and legal elements. See, e.g., Heart Disease Research Foundation v. General Motors Corp., 15 Fed.R.Serv. 2d 1517, 1519 (S.D.N.Y. 1972). They have been replaced by a standard of conduct that is more focused.

The new language stresses the need for some prefiling inquiry into both the facts and the law to satisfy the affirmative duty imposed by the rule. The standard is one of reasonableness under the circumstances. See Kinee v. Abraham Lincoln Fed. Sav. & Loan Ass'n, 365 F.Supp. 975 (E.D.Pa. 1973). This standard is more stringent than the original good-faith formula and thus it is expected that a greater range of circumstances will trigger its violation. See Nemeroff v. Abelson, 620 F.2d 339 (2d Cir. 1980).

The rule is not intended to chill an attorney's enthusiasm or creativity in pursuing factual or legal theories. The court is expected to avoid using the wisdom of hindsight and should test the signer's conduct by inquiring what was reasonable to believe at the time the pleading, motion, or other paper was submitted. Thus, what constitutes a reasonable inquiry may depend on such factors as how much time for investigation was available to the signer; whether he had to rely on a client for information as to the facts underlying the pleading, motion, or other paper; whether the pleading, motion, or other paper was based on a plausible view of the law; or whether he depended on forwarding counsel or another member of the bar.

The rule does not require a party or an attorney to disclose privileged communications or work product in order to show that the signing of the pleading, motion, or other paper is substantially justified. The provisions of Rule 26(c), including appropriate orders after in camera inspection by the court, remain available to protect a party claiming privilege or work product protection.

Amended Rule 11 continues to apply to anyone who signs a pleading, motion, or other paper. Although the standard is the same for unrepresented parties, who are obliged themselves to sign the pleadings, the court has sufficient discretion to take account of the special circumstances that often arise in pro se situations. See Haines v. Kerner 404 U.S. 519 (1972).

The provision in the original rule for striking pleadings and motions as sham and false has been deleted. The passage has rarely been utilized, and decisions thereunder have tended to confuse the issue of attorney honesty with the merits of the action. See generally Risinger, Honesty in Pleading and its Enforcement: Some "Striking" Problems with Fed. R. Civ. P. 11, 61 Minn.L.Rev. 1 (1976). Motions under this provision generally present issues better dealt with under Rules 8, 12, or 56. See Murchison v. Kirby, 27 F.R.D. 14 (S.D.N.Y. 1961); 5 Wright & Miller, Federal Practice and Procedure: Civil §1334 (1969).

The former reference to the inclusion of scandalous or indecent matter, which is itself strong indication that an improper purpose underlies the pleading, motion, or other paper, also has been deleted as unnecessary. Such matter may be stricken under Rule 12(f) as well as dealt with under the more general language of amended Rule 11.

The text of the amended rule seeks to dispel apprehensions that efforts to obtain enforcement will be fruitless by insuring that the rule will be applied when properly invoked. The word "sanctions" in the caption, for example, stresses a deterrent orientation in dealing with improper pleadings, motions or other papers. This corresponds to the approach in imposing sanctions for discovery abuses. See National Hockey League v. Metropolitan Hockey Club, 427 U.S. 639 (1976) (per curiam). And the words "shall impose" in the last sentence focus the court's attention on the need to impose sanctions for pleading and motion abuses. The court, however, retains the necessary flexibility to deal appropriately with violations of the rule. It has discretion to tailor sanctions to the particular facts of the case, with which it should be well acquainted.

The reference in the former text to wilfullness as a prerequisite to disciplinary action has been deleted. However, in considering the nature and severity of the sanctions to be imposed, the court should take account of the state of the attorney's or party's actual or presumed knowledge when the pleading or other paper was signed. Thus, for example, when a party is not represented by counsel, the absence of legal advice is an appropriate factor to be considered.

Courts currently appear to believe they may impose sanctions on their own motion. See North American Trading Corp. v. Zale Corp., 73 F.R.D. 293 (S.D.N.Y. 1979). Authority to do so has been made explicit in order to overcome the traditional reluctance of courts to intervene unless requested by one of the parties. The detection and punishment of a violation of the signing requirement, encouraged by the amended rule, is part of the court's responsibility for securing the system's effective operation.

If the duty imposed by the rule is violated, the court should have the discretion to impose sanctions on either the attorney, the party the signing attorney represents, or both, or on an unrepresented party who signed the pleading, and the new rule so provides. Although Rule 11 has been silent on the point, courts have claimed the power to impose sanctions on an attorney personally, either by imposing costs or employing the contempt technique. See 5 Wright & Miller, Federal Practice and Procedure: Civil §1334 (1969); 2A Moore, Federal Practice 11.02, at 2104 n.8. This power has been used infrequently. The amended rule should eliminate any doubt as to the propriety of assessing sanctions against the attorney.

Even though it is the attorney whose signature violates the rule, it may be appropriate under the circumstances of the case to impose a sanction on the client. See Browning Debenture Holders' Committee v. DASA Corp., supra. This modification brings Rule 11 in line with practice under Rule 37, which allows sanctions for abuses during discovery to be imposed upon the party, the attorney, or both.

A party seeking sanctions should give notice to the court and the offending party promptly upon discovering a basis for doing so. The time when sanctions are to be imposed rests in the discretion of the trial judge. However, it is anticipated that in the case of pleadings the sanctions issue under Rule 11 normally will be determined at the end of the litigation, and in the case of motions at the time when the motion is decided or shortly thereafter. The procedure obviously must comport with due process requirements. The particular format to be followed should depend on the circumstances of the situation and the severity of the sanction under consideration. In many situations the judge's participation in the proceedings provides him with full knowledge of the relevant facts and little further inquiry will be necessary.

To assure that the efficiencies achieved through more effective operation of the pleading regimen will not be offset by the cost of satellite litigation over the imposition of sanctions, the court must to the extent possible limit the scope of sanction proceedings to the record. Thus, discovery should be conducted only by leave of the court, and then only in extraordinary circumstances.

Although the encompassing reference to "other papers" in new Rule 11 literally includes discovery papers, the certification requirement in that context is governed by proposed new Rule 26(g). Discovery motions, however, fall within the ambit of Rule 11.

Notes of Advisory Committee on Rules—1987 Amendment

The amendments are technical. No substantive change is intended.

Notes of Advisory Committee on Rules—1993 Amendment

Purpose of revision. This revision is intended to remedy problems that have arisen in the interpretation and application of the 1983 revision of the rule. For empirical examination of experience under the 1983 rule, see, e.g., New York State Bar Committee on Federal Courts, Sanctions and Attorneys' Fees (1987); T. Willging, The Rule 11 Sanctioning Process (1989); American Judicature Society, Report of the Third Circuit Task Force on Federal Rule of Civil Procedure 11 (S. Burbank ed., 1989); E. Wiggins, T. Willging, and D. Stienstra, Report on Rule 11 (Federal Judicial Center 1991). For book-length analyses of the case law, see G. Joseph, Sanctions: The Federal Law of Litigation Abuse (1989); J. Solovy, The Federal Law of Sanctions (1991); G. Vairo, Rule 11 Sanctions: Case Law Perspectives and Preventive Measures (1991).

The rule retains the principle that attorneys and pro se litigants have an obligation to the court to refrain from conduct that frustrates the aims of Rule 1. The revision broadens the scope of this obligation, but places greater constraints on the imposition of sanctions and should reduce the number of motions for sanctions presented to the court. New subdivision (d) removes from the ambit of this rule all discovery requests, responses, objections, and motions subject to the provisions of Rule 26 through 37.

Subdivision (a). Retained in this subdivision are the provisions requiring signatures on pleadings, written motions, and other papers. Unsigned papers are to be received by the Clerk, but then are to be stricken if the omission of the signature is not corrected promptly after being called to the attention of the attorney or pro se litigant. Correction can be made by signing the paper on file or by submitting a duplicate that contains the signature. A court may require by local rule that papers contain additional identifying information regarding the parties or attorneys, such as telephone numbers to facilitate facsimile transmissions, though, as for omission of a signature, the paper should not be rejected for failure to provide such information.

The sentence in the former rule relating to the effect of answers under oath is no longer needed and has been eliminated. The provision in the former rule that signing a paper constitutes a certificate that it has been read by the signer also has been eliminated as unnecessary. The obligations imposed under subdivision (b) obviously require that a pleading, written motion, or other paper be read before it is filed or submitted to the court.

Subdivisions (b) and (c). These subdivisions restate the provisions requiring attorneys and pro se litigants to conduct a reasonable inquiry into the law and facts before signing pleadings, written motions, and other documents, and prescribing sanctions for violation of these obligations. The revision in part expands the responsibilities of litigants to the court, while providing greater constraints and flexibility in dealing with infractions of the rule. The rule continues to require litigants to "stop-and-think" before initially making legal or factual contentions. It also, however, emphasizes the duty of candor by subjecting litigants to potential sanctions for insisting upon a position after it is no longer tenable and by generally providing protection against sanctions if they withdraw or correct contentions after a potential violation is called to their attention.

The rule applies only to assertions contained in papers filed with or submitted to the court. It does not cover matters arising for the first time during oral presentations to the court, when counsel may make statements that would not have been made if there had been more time for study and reflection. However, a litigant's obligations with respect to the contents of these papers are not measured solely as of the time they are filed with or submitted to the court, but include reaffirming to the court and advocating positions contained in those pleadings and motions after learning that they cease to have any merit. For example, an attorney who during a pretrial conference insists on a claim or defense should be viewed as "presenting to the court" that contention and would be subject to the obligations of subdivision (b) measured as of that time. Similarly, if after a notice of removal is filed, a party urges in federal court the allegations of a pleading filed in state court (whether as claims, defenses, or in disputes regarding removal or remand), it would be viewed as "presenting"—and hence certifying to the district court under Rule 11—those allegations.

The certification with respect to allegations and other factual contentions is revised in recognition that sometimes a litigant may have good reason to believe that a fact is true or false but may need discovery, formal or informal, from opposing parties or third persons to gather and confirm the evidentiary basis for the allegation. Tolerance of factual contentions in initial pleadings by plaintiffs or defendants when specifically identified as made on information and belief does not relieve litigants from the obligation to conduct an appropriate investigation into the facts that is reasonable under the circumstances; it is not a license to join parties, make claims, or present defenses without any factual basis or justification. Moreover, if evidentiary support is not obtained after a reasonable opportunity for further investigation or discovery, the party has a duty under the rule not to persist with that contention. Subdivision (b) does not require a formal amendment to pleadings for which evidentiary support is not obtained, but rather calls upon a litigant not thereafter to advocate such claims or defenses.

The certification is that there is (or likely will be) "evidentiary support" for the allegation, not that the party will prevail with respect to its contention regarding the fact. That summary judgment is rendered against a party does not necessarily mean, for purposes of this certification, that it had no evidentiary support for its position. On the other hand, if a party has evidence with respect to a contention that would suffice to defeat a motion for summary judgment based thereon, it would have sufficient "evidentiary support" for purposes of Rule 11.

Denials of factual contentions involve somewhat different considerations. Often, of course, a denial is premised upon the existence of evidence contradicting the alleged fact. At other times a denial is permissible because, after an appropriate investigation, a party has no information concerning the matter or, indeed, has a reasonable basis for doubting the credibility of the only evidence relevant to the matter. A party should not deny an allegation it knows to be true; but it is not required, simply because it lacks contradictory evidence, to admit an allegation that it believes is not true.

The changes in subdivisions (b)(3) and (b)(4) will serve to equalize the burden of the rule upon plaintiffs and defendants, who under Rule 8(b) are in effect allowed to deny allegations by stating that from their initial investigation they lack sufficient information to form a belief as to the truth of the allegation. If, after further investigation or discovery, a denial is no longer warranted, the defendant should not continue to insist on that denial. While sometimes helpful, formal amendment of the pleadings to withdraw an allegation or denial is not required by subdivision (b).

Arguments for extensions, modifications, or reversals of existing law or for creation of new law do not violate subdivision (b)(2) provided they are "nonfrivolous." This establishes an objective standard, intended to eliminate any "empty-head pure-heart" justification for patently frivolous arguments. However, the extent to which a litigant has researched the issues and found some support for its theories even in minority opinions, in law review articles, or through consultation with other attorneys should certainly be taken into account in determining whether paragraph (2) has been violated. Although arguments for a change of law are not required to be specifically so identified, a contention that is so identified should be viewed with greater tolerance under the rule.

The court has available a variety of possible sanctions to impose for violations, such as striking the offending paper; issuing an admonition, reprimand, or censure; requiring participation in seminars or other educational programs; ordering a fine payable to the court; referring the matter to disciplinary authorities (or, in the case of government attorneys, to the Attorney General, Inspector General, or agency head), etc. See Manual for Complex Litigation, Second, §42.3. The rule does not attempt to enumerate the factors a court should consider in deciding whether to impose a sanction or what sanctions would be appropriate in the circumstances; but, for emphasis, it does specifically note that a sanction may be nonmonetary as well as monetary. Whether the improper conduct was willful, or negligent; whether it was part of a pattern of activity, or an isolated event; whether it infected the entire pleading, or only one particular count or defense; whether the person has engaged in similar conduct in other litigation; whether it was intended to injure; what effect it had on the litigation process in time or expense; whether the responsible person is trained in the law; what amount, given the financial resources of the responsible person, is needed to deter that person from repetition in the same case; what amount is needed to deter similar activity by other litigants: all of these may in a particular case be proper considerations. The court has significant discretion in determining what sanctions, if any, should be imposed for a violation, subject to the principle that the sanctions should not be more severe than reasonably necessary to deter repetition of the conduct by the offending person or comparable conduct by similarly situated persons.

Since the purpose of Rule 11 sanctions is to deter rather than to compensate, the rule provides that, if a monetary sanction is imposed, it should ordinarily be paid into court as a penalty. However, under unusual circumstances, particularly for [subdivision] (b)(1) violations, deterrence may be ineffective unless the sanction not only requires the person violating the rule to make a monetary payment, but also directs that some or all of this payment be made to those injured by the violation. Accordingly, the rule authorizes the court, if requested in a motion and if so warranted, to award attorney's fees to another party. Any such award to another party, however, should not exceed the expenses and attorneys' fees for the services directly and unavoidably caused by the violation of the certification requirement. If, for example, a wholly unsupportable count were included in a multi-count complaint or counterclaim for the purpose of needlessly increasing the cost of litigation to an impecunious adversary, any award of expenses should be limited to those directly caused by inclusion of the improper count, and not those resulting from the filing of the complaint or answer itself. The award should not provide compensation for services that could have been avoided by an earlier disclosure of evidence or an earlier challenge to the groundless claims or defenses. Moreover, partial reimbursement of fees may constitute a sufficient deterrent with respect to violations by persons having modest financial resources. In cases brought under statutes providing for fees to be awarded to prevailing parties, the court should not employ cost-shifting under this rule in a manner that would be inconsistent with the standards that govern the statutory award of fees, such as stated in Christiansburg Garment Co. v. EEOC, 434 U.S. 412 (1978).

The sanction should be imposed on the persons—whether attorneys, law firms, or parties—who have violated the rule or who may be determined to be responsible for the violation. The person signing, filing, submitting, or advocating a document has a nondelegable responsibility to the court, and in most situations is the person to be sanctioned for a violation. Absent exceptional circumstances, a law firm is to be held also responsible when, as a result of a motion under subdivision (c)(1)(A), one of its partners, associates, or employees is determined to have violated the rule. Since such a motion may be filed only if the offending paper is not withdrawn or corrected within 21 days after service of the motion, it is appropriate that the law firm ordinarily be viewed as jointly responsible under established principles of agency. This provision is designed to remove the restrictions of the former rule. Cf. Pavelic & LeFlore v. Marvel Entertainment Group, 493 U.S. 120 (1989) (1983 version of Rule 11 does not permit sanctions against law firm of attorney signing groundless complaint).

The revision permits the court to consider whether other attorneys in the firm, co-counsel, other law firms, or the party itself should be held accountable for their part in causing a violation. When appropriate, the court can make an additional inquiry in order to determine whether the sanction should be imposed on such persons, firms, or parties either in addition to or, in unusual circumstances, instead of the person actually making the presentation to the court. For example, such an inquiry may be appropriate in cases involving governmental agencies or other institutional parties that frequently impose substantial restrictions on the discretion of individual attorneys employed by it.

Sanctions that involve monetary awards (such as a fine or an award of attorney's fees) may not be imposed on a represented party for causing a violation of subdivision (b)(2), involving frivolous contentions of law. Monetary responsibility for such violations is more properly placed solely on the party's attorneys. With this limitation, the rule should not be subject to attack under the Rules Enabling Act. See Willy v. Coastal Corp., ____ U.S. ____ (1992); Business Guides, Inc. v. Chromatic Communications Enter. Inc., ____ U.S. ____ (1991). This restriction does not limit the court's power to impose sanctions or remedial orders that may have collateral financial consequences upon a party, such as dismissal of a claim, preclusion of a defense, or preparation of amended pleadings.

Explicit provision is made for litigants to be provided notice of the alleged violation and an opportunity to respond before sanctions are imposed. Whether the matter should be decided solely on the basis of written submissions or should be scheduled for oral argument (or, indeed, for evidentiary presentation) will depend on the circumstances. If the court imposes a sanction, it must, unless waived, indicate its reasons in a written order or on the record; the court should not ordinarily have to explain its denial of a motion for sanctions. Whether a violation has occurred and what sanctions, if any, to impose for a violation are matters committed to the discretion of the trial court; accordingly, as under current law, the standard for appellate review of these decisions will be for abuse of discretion. See Cooter & Gell v. Hartmarx Corp., 496 U.S. 384 (1990) (noting, however, that an abuse would be established if the court based its ruling on an erroneous view of the law or on a clearly erroneous assessment of the evidence).

The revision leaves for resolution on a case-by-case basis, considering the particular circumstances involved, the question as to when a motion for violation of Rule 11 should be served and when, if filed, it should be decided. Ordinarily the motion should be served promptly after the inappropriate paper is filed, and, if delayed too long, may be viewed as untimely. In other circumstances, it should not be served until the other party has had a reasonable opportunity for discovery. Given the "safe harbor" provisions discussed below, a party cannot delay serving its Rule 11 motion until conclusion of the case (or judicial rejection of the offending contention).

Rule 11 motions should not be made or threatened for minor, inconsequential violations of the standards prescribed by subdivision (b). They should not be employed as a discovery device or to test the legal sufficiency or efficacy of allegations in the pleadings; other motions are available for those purposes. Nor should Rule 11 motions be prepared to emphasize the merits of a party's position, to exact an unjust settlement, to intimidate an adversary into withdrawing contentions that are fairly debatable, to increase the costs of litigation, to create a conflict of interest between attorney and client, or to seek disclosure of matters otherwise protected by the attorney-client privilege or the work-product doctrine. As under the prior rule, the court may defer its ruling (or its decision as to the identity of the persons to be sanctioned) until final resolution of the case in order to avoid immediate conflicts of interest and to reduce the disruption created if a disclosure of attorney-client communications is needed to determine whether a violation occurred or to identify the person responsible for the violation.

The rule provides that requests for sanctions must be made as a separate motion, i.e., not simply included as an additional prayer for relief contained in another motion. The motion for sanctions is not, however, to be filed until at least 21 days (or such other period as the court may set) after being served. If, during this period, the alleged violation is corrected, as by withdrawing (whether formally or informally) some allegation or contention, the motion should not be filed with the court. These provisions are intended to provide a type of "safe harbor" against motions under Rule 11 in that a party will not be subject to sanctions on the basis of another party's motion unless, after receiving the motion, it refuses to withdraw that position or to acknowledge candidly that it does not currently have evidence to support a specified allegation. Under the former rule, parties were sometimes reluctant to abandon a questionable contention lest that be viewed as evidence of a violation of Rule 11; under the revision, the timely withdrawal of a contention will protect a party against a motion for sanctions.

To stress the seriousness of a motion for sanctions and to define precisely the conduct claimed to violate the rule, the revision provides that the "safe harbor" period begins to run only upon service of the motion. In most cases, however, counsel should be expected to give informal notice to the other party, whether in person or by a telephone call or letter, of a potential violation before proceeding to prepare and serve a Rule 11 motion.

As under former Rule 11, the filing of a motion for sanctions is itself subject to the requirements of the rule and can lead to sanctions. However, service of a cross motion under Rule 11 should rarely be needed since under the revision the court may award to the person who prevails on a motion under Rule 11—whether the movant or the target of the motion—reasonable expenses, including attorney's fees, incurred in presenting or opposing the motion.

The power of the court to act on its own initiative is retained, but with the condition that this be done through a show cause order. This procedure provides the person with notice and an opportunity to respond. The revision provides that a monetary sanction imposed after a court-initiated show cause order be limited to a penalty payable to the court and that it be imposed only if the show cause order is issued before any voluntary dismissal or an agreement of the parties to settle the claims made by or against the litigant. Parties settling a case should not be subsequently faced with an unexpected order from the court leading to monetary sanctions that might have affected their willingness to settle or voluntarily dismiss a case. Since show cause orders will ordinarily be issued only in situations that are akin to a contempt of court, the rule does not provide a "safe harbor" to a litigant for withdrawing a claim, defense, etc., after a show cause order has been issued on the court's own initiative. Such corrective action, however, should be taken into account in deciding what—if any—sanction to impose if, after consideration of the litigant's response, the court concludes that a violation has occurred.

Subdivision (d). Rules 26(g) and 37 establish certification standards and sanctions that apply to discovery disclosures, requests, responses, objections, and motions. It is appropriate that Rules 26 through 37, which are specially designed for the discovery process, govern such documents and conduct rather than the more general provisions of Rule 11. Subdivision (d) has been added to accomplish this result.

Rule 11 is not the exclusive source for control of improper presentations of claims, defenses, or contentions. It does not supplant statutes permitting awards of attorney's fees to prevailing parties or alter the principles governing such awards. It does not inhibit the court in punishing for contempt, in exercising its inherent powers, or in imposing sanctions, awarding expenses, or directing remedial action authorized under other rules or under 28 U.S.C. §1927. See Chambers v. NASCO, ____ U.S. ____ (1991). Chambers cautions, however, against reliance upon inherent powers if appropriate sanctions can be imposed under provisions such as Rule 11, and the procedures specified in Rule 11—notice, opportunity to respond, and findings—should ordinarily be employed when imposing a sanction under the court's inherent powers. Finally, it should be noted that Rule 11 does not preclude a party from initiating an independent action for malicious prosecution or abuse of process.

Committee Notes on Rules—2007 Amendment

The language of Rule 11 has been amended as part of the general restyling of the Civil Rules to make them more easily understood and to make style and terminology consistent throughout the rules. These changes are intended to be stylistic only.

Providing an e-mail address is useful, but does not of itself signify consent to filing or service by e-mail.

Rule 12. Defenses and Objections: When and How Presented; Motion for Judgment on the Pleadings; Consolidating Motions; Waiving Defenses; Pretrial Hearing

(a) Time to Serve a Responsive Pleading.

(1) In General. Unless another time is specified by this rule or a federal statute, the time for serving a responsive pleading is as follows:

(A) A defendant must serve an answer:

(i) within 21 days after being served with the summons and complaint; or

(ii) if it has timely waived service under Rule 4(d), within 60 days after the request for a waiver was sent, or within 90 days after it was sent to the defendant outside any judicial district of the United States.

(B) A party must serve an answer to a counterclaim or crossclaim within 21 days after being served with the pleading that states the counterclaim or crossclaim.

(C) A party must serve a reply to an answer within 21 days after being served with an order to reply, unless the order specifies a different time.

(2) United States and Its Agencies, Officers, or Employees Sued in an Official Capacity. The United States, a United States agency, or a United States officer or employee sued only in an official capacity must serve an answer to a complaint, counterclaim, or crossclaim within 60 days after service on the United States attorney.

(3) United States Officers or Employees Sued in an Individual Capacity. A United States officer or employee sued in an individual capacity for an act or omission occurring in connection with duties performed on the United States' behalf must serve an answer to a complaint, counterclaim, or crossclaim within 60 days after service on the officer or employee or service on the United States attorney, whichever is later.

(4) Effect of a Motion. Unless the court sets a different time, serving a motion under this rule alters these periods as follows:

(A) if the court denies the motion or postpones its disposition until trial, the responsive pleading must be served within 14 days after notice of the court's action; or

(B) if the court grants a motion for a more definite statement, the responsive pleading must be served within 14 days after the more definite statement is served.

(b) How to Present Defenses. Every defense to a claim for relief in any pleading must be asserted in the responsive pleading if one is required. But a party may assert the following defenses by motion:

(1) lack of subject-matter jurisdiction;

(2) lack of personal jurisdiction;

(3) improper venue;

(4) insufficient process;

(5) insufficient service of process;

(6) failure to state a claim upon which relief can be granted; and

(7) failure to join a party under Rule 19.

A motion asserting any of these defenses must be made before pleading if a responsive pleading is allowed. If a pleading sets out a claim for relief that does not require a responsive pleading, an opposing party may assert at trial any defense to that claim. No defense or objection is waived by joining it with one or more other defenses or objections in a responsive pleading or in a motion.

(c) Motion for Judgment on the Pleadings. After the pleadings are closed—but early enough not to delay trial—a party may move for judgment on the pleadings.

(d) Result of Presenting Matters Outside the Pleadings. If, on a motion under Rule 12(b)(6) or 12(c), matters outside the pleadings are presented to and not excluded by the court, the motion must be treated as one for summary judgment under Rule 56. All parties must be given a reasonable opportunity to present all the material that is pertinent to the motion.

(e) Motion for a More Definite Statement. A party may move for a more definite statement of a pleading to which a responsive pleading is allowed but which is so vague or ambiguous that the party cannot reasonably prepare a response. The motion must be made before filing a responsive pleading and must point out the defects complained of and the details desired. If the court orders a more definite statement and the order is not obeyed within 14 days after notice of the order or within the time the court sets, the court may strike the pleading or issue any other appropriate order.

(f) Motion to Strike. The court may strike from a pleading an insufficient defense or any redundant, immaterial, impertinent, or scandalous matter. The court may act:

(1) on its own; or

(2) on motion made by a party either before responding to the pleading or, if a response is not allowed, within 21 days after being served with the pleading.

(g) Joining Motions.

(1) Right to Join. A motion under this rule may be joined with any other motion allowed by this rule.

(2) Limitation on Further Motions. Except as provided in Rule 12(h)(2) or (3), a party that makes a motion under this rule must not make another motion under this rule raising a defense or objection that was available to the party but omitted from its earlier motion.

(h) Waiving and Preserving Certain Defenses.

(1) When Some Are Waived. A party waives any defense listed in Rule 12(b)(2)–(5) by:

(A) omitting it from a motion in the circumstances described in Rule 12(g)(2); or

(B) failing to either:

(i) make it by motion under this rule; or

(ii) include it in a responsive pleading or in an amendment allowed by Rule 15(a)(1) as a matter of course.

(2) When to Raise Others. Failure to state a claim upon which relief can be granted, to join a person required by Rule 19(b), or to state a legal defense to a claim may be raised:

(A) in any pleading allowed or ordered under Rule 7(a);

(B) by a motion under Rule 12(c); or

(C) at trial.

(3) Lack of Subject-Matter Jurisdiction. If the court determines at any time that it lacks subject-matter jurisdiction, the court must dismiss the action.

(i) Hearing Before Trial. If a party so moves, any defense listed in Rule 12(b)(1)–(7)—whether made in a pleading or by motion—and a motion under Rule 12(c) must be heard and decided before trial unless the court orders a deferral until trial.

(As amended Dec. 27, 1946, eff. Mar. 19, 1948; Jan. 21, 1963, eff. July 1, 1963; Feb. 28, 1966, eff. July 1, 1966; Mar. 2, 1987, eff. Aug. 1, 1987; Apr. 22, 1993, eff. Dec. 1, 1993; Apr. 17, 2000, eff. Dec. 1, 2000; Apr. 30, 2007, eff. Dec. 1, 2007; Mar. 26, 2009, eff. Dec. 1, 2009.)

Notes of Advisory Committee on Rules—1937

Note to Subdivision (a). 1. Compare [former] Equity Rules 12 (Issue of Subpoena—Time for Answer) and 31 (Reply—When Required—When Cause at Issue); 4 Mont.Rev.Codes Ann. (1935) §§9107, 9158; N.Y.C.P.A. (1937) §263; N.Y.R.C.P. (1937) Rules 109–111.

2. U.S.C., Title 28, §763 [now 547] (Petition in action against United States; service; appearance by district attorney) provides that the United States as a defendant shall have 60 days within which to answer or otherwise defend. This and other statutes which provide 60 days for the United States or an officer or agency thereof to answer or otherwise defend are continued by this rule. Insofar as any statutes not excepted in Rule 81 provide a different time for a defendant to defend, such statutes are modified. See U.S.C., Title 28, [former] §45 (District courts; practice and procedure in certain cases under the interstate commerce laws) (30 days).

3. Compare the last sentence of [former] Equity Rule 29 (Defenses—How Presented) and N.Y.C.P.A. (1937) §283. See Rule 15(a) for time within which to plead to an amended pleading.

Note to Subdivisions (b) and (d). 1. See generally [former] Equity Rules 29 (Defenses—How Presented), 33 (Testing Sufficiency of

Defense), 43 (Defect of Parties—Resisting Objection), and 44 (Defect of Parties—Tardy Objection); N.Y.C.P.A. (1937) §§277–280; N.Y.R.C.P. (1937) Rules 106–112; English Rules Under the Judicature Act (The Annual Practice, 1937) O. 25, r.r. 1–4; Clark, Code Pleading (1928) pp. 371–381.

2. For provisions authorizing defenses to be made in the answer or reply see English Rules Under the Judicature Act (The Annual Practice, 1937) O. 25, r.r. 1–4; 1 Miss.Code Ann. (1930) §§378, 379. Compare [former] Equity Rule 29 (Defenses—How Presented); U.S.C., Title 28, [former] §45 (District Courts; practice and procedure in certain cases under the interstate commerce laws). U.S.C., Title 28, [former] §45, substantially continued by this rule, provides: "No replication need be filed to the answer, and objections to the sufficiency of the petition or answer as not setting forth a cause of action or defense must be taken at the final hearing or by motion to dismiss the petition based on said grounds, which motion may be made at any time before answer is filed." Compare Calif.Code Civ.Proc. (Deering, 1937) §433; 4 Nev.Comp.Laws (Hillyer, 1929) §8600. For provisions that the defendant may demur and answer at the same time, see Calif.Code Civ.Proc. (Deering, 1937) §431; 4 Nev.Comp.Laws (Hillyer, 1929) §8598.

3. [Former] Equity Rule 29 (Defenses—How Presented) abolished demurrers and provided that defenses in point of law arising on the face of the bill should be made by motion to dismiss or in the answer, with further provision that every such point of law going to the whole or material part of the cause or causes stated might be called up and disposed of before final hearing "at the discretion of the court." Likewise many state practices have abolished the demurrer, or retain it only to attack substantial and not formal defects. See 6 Tenn.Code Ann. (Williams, 1934) §8784; Ala.Code Ann. (Michie, 1928) §9479; 2 Mass.Gen.Laws (Ter.Ed., 1932) ch. 231, §§15–18; Kansas Gen.Stat.Ann. (1935) §§60–705, 60–706.

Note to Subdivision (c). Compare [former] Equity Rule 33 (Testing Sufficiency of Defense); N.Y.R.C.P. (1937) Rules 111 and 112.

Note to Subdivisions (e) and (f). Compare [former] Equity Rules 20 (Further and Particular Statement in Pleading May Be Required) and 21 (Scandal and Impertinence); English Rules Under the Judicature Act (The Annual Practice, 1937) O. 19, r.r. 7, 7a, 7b, 8; 4 Mont.Rev.Codes Ann. (1935) §§9166, 9167; N.Y.C.P.A. (1937) §247; N.Y.R.C.P. (1937) Rules 103, 115, 116, 117; Wyo.Rev.Stat.Ann. (Courtright, 1931) §§89–1033, 89–1034.

Note to Subdivision (g). Compare Rules of the District Court of the United States for the District of Columbia (1937), Equity Rule 11; N.M. Rules of Pleading, Practice and Procedure, 38 N.M.Rep. vii [105–408] (1934); Wash.Gen.Rules of the Superior Courts, 1 Wash.Rev.Stat.Ann. (Remington, 1932) p. 160, Rule VI (e) and (f).

Note to Subdivision (h). Compare Calif.Code Civ.Proc. (Deering, 1937) §434; 2 Minn.Stat. (Mason, 1927) §9252; N.Y.C.P.A. (1937) §§278 and 279; Wash.Gen.Rules of the Superior Courts, 1 Wash.Rev.Stat.Ann. (Remington, 1932) p. 160, Rule VI (e). This rule continues U.S.C., Title 28, §80 [now 1359, 1447, 1919] (Dismissal or remand) (of action over which district court lacks jurisdiction), while U.S.C., Title 28, §399 [now 1653] (Amendments to show diverse citizenship) is continued by Rule 15.

Notes of Advisory Committee on Rules—1946 Amendment

Subdivision (a). Various minor alterations in language have been made to improve the statement of the rule. All references to bills of particulars have been stricken in accordance with changes made in subdivision (e).

Subdivision (b). The addition of defense (7), "failure to join an indispensable party", cures an omission in the rules, which are silent as to the mode of raising such failure. See Commentary, Manner of Raising Objection of Non-Joinder of Indispensable Party (1940) 2 Fed.Rules Serv. 658 and (1942) 5 Fed.Rules Serv. 820. In one case, United States v. Metropolitan Life Ins. Co. (E.D.Pa. 1941) 36 F.Supp. 399, the failure to join an indispensable party was raised under Rule 12(c).

Rule 12(b)(6), permitting a motion to dismiss for failure of the complaint to state a claim on which relief can be granted, is substantially the same as the old demurrer for failure of a pleading to state a cause of action. Some courts have held that as the rule by its terms refers to statements in the complaint, extraneous matter on affidavits, depositions or otherwise, may not be introduced in support of the motion, or to resist it. On the other hand, in many cases the district courts have permitted the introduction of such material. When these cases have reached circuit courts of appeals in situations where the extraneous material so received shows that there is no genuine issue as to any material question of fact and that on the undisputed facts as disclosed by the affidavits or depositions, one party or the other is entitled to judgment as a matter of law, the circuit courts, properly enough, have been reluctant to dispose of the case merely on the face of the pleading, and in the interest of prompt disposition of the action have made a final disposition of it. In dealing with such situations the Second Circuit has made the sound suggestion that whatever its label or original basis, the motion may be treated as a motion for summary judgment and disposed of as such. Samara v. United States (C.C.A.2d, 1942) 129 F.(2d) 594, cert. den. (1942) 317 U.S. 686; Boro Hall Corp. v. General Motors Corp. (C.C.A.2d, 1942) 124 F.(2d) 822, cert. den. (1943) 317 U.S. 695. See also Kithcart v. Metropolitan Life Ins. Co. (C.C.A.8th, 1945) 150 F.(2d) 997, aff'g 62 F.Supp. 93.

It has also been suggested that this practice could be justified on the ground that the federal rules permit "speaking" motions. The Committee entertains the view that on motion under Rule 12(b)(6) to dismiss for failure of the complaint to state a good claim, the trial court should have authority to permit the introduction of extraneous matter, such as may be offered on a motion for summary judgment, and if it does not exclude such matter the motion should then be treated as a motion for summary judgment and disposed of in the manner and on the conditions stated in Rule 56 relating to summary judgments, and, of course, in such a situation, when the case reaches the circuit court of appeals, that court should treat the motion in the same way. The Committee believes that such practice, however, should be tied to the summary judgment rule. The term "speaking motion" is not mentioned in the rules, and if there is such a thing its limitations are undefined. Where extraneous matter is received, by tying further proceedings to the summary judgment rule the courts have a definite basis in the rules for disposing of the motion.

The Committee emphasizes particularly the fact that the summary judgment rule does not permit a case to be disposed of by judgment on the merits on affidavits, which disclose a conflict on a material issue of fact, and unless this practice is tied to the summary judgment rule, the extent to which a court, on the introduction of such extraneous matter, may resolve questions of fact on conflicting proof would be left uncertain.

The decisions dealing with this general situation may be generally grouped as follows: (1) cases dealing with the use of affidavits and other extraneous material on motions; (2) cases reversing judgments to prevent final determination on mere pleading allegations alone.

Under group (1) are: Boro Hall Corp. v. General Motors Corp. (C.C.A.2d, 1942) 124 F.(2d) 822, cert. den. (1943) 317 U.S. 695; Gallup v. Caldwell (C.C.A.3d, 1941) 120 F.(2d) 90; Central Mexico Light & Power Co. v. Munch (C.C.A.2d, 1940) 116 F.(2d) 85; National Labor Relations Board v. Montgomery Ward & Co. (App.D.C. 1944) 144 F.(2d) 528, cert. den. (1944) 65 S.Ct. 134; Urquhart v. American-La France Foamite Corp. (App.D.C. 1944) 144 F.(2d) 542; Samara v. United States (C.C.A.2d, 1942) 129 F.(2d) 594; Cohen v. American Window Glass Co. (C.C.A.2d, 1942) 126 F.(2d) 111; Sperry Products Inc. v. Association of American Railroads (C.C.A.2d, 1942) 132 F.(2d) 408; Joint Council Dining Car Employees Local 370 v. Delaware, Lackawanna and Western R. Co. (C.C.A.2d, 1946) 157 F.(2d) 417; Weeks v. Bareco Oil Co. (C.C.A.7th, 1941) 125 F.(2d) 84; Carroll v. Morrison Hotel Corp. (C.C.A.7th, 1945) 149 F.(2d) 404; Victory v. Manning (C.C.A.3rd, 1942) 128 F.(2d) 415; Locals No. 1470, No. 1469, and 1512 of International Longshoremen's Association v. Southern Pacific Co. (C.C.A.5th, 1942) 131 F.(2d) 605; Lucking v. Delano (C.C.A.6th, 1942) 129 F.(2d) 283; San Francisco Lodge No. 68 of International Association of Machinists v. Forrestal (N.D.Cal. 1944) 58 F.Supp. 466; Benson v. Export Equipment Corp. (N. Mex. 1945) 164 P.2d 380 (construing New Mexico rule identical with Rule 12(b)(6); F. E. Myers & Bros. Co. v. Gould Pumps, Inc. (W.D.N.Y. 1946) 9 Fed.Rules Serv. 12b.33, Case 2, 5 F.R.D. 132. Cf. Kohler v. Jacobs (C.C.A.5th, 1943) 138 F.(2d) 440; Cohen v. United States (C.C.A.8th, 1942) 129 F.(2d) 733.

Under group (2) are: Sparks v. England (C.C.A.8th, 1940) 113 F.(2d) 579; Continental Collieries, Inc. v. Shober (C.C.A.3d, 1942) 130 F.(2d) 631; Downey v. Palmer (C.C.A.2d 1940) 114 F.(2d) 116; DeLoach v. Crowley's Inc. (C.C.A.5th, 1942) 128 F.(2d) 378; Leimer v. State Mutual Life Assurance Co. of Worcester, Mass. (C.C.A.8th, 1940) 108 F.(2d) 302; Rossiter v. Vogel (C.C.A.2d, 1943) 134 F.(2d) 908, compare s. c. (C.C.A.2d, 1945) 148 F.(2d) 292; Karl Kiefer Machine Co. v. United States Bottlers Machinery Co. (C.C.A.7th, 1940) 113 F.(2d) 356; Chicago Metallic Mfg. Co. v. Edward Katzinger Co. (C.C.A.7th, 1941) 123 F.(2d) 518; Louisiana Farmers' Protective Union, Inc. v. Great Atlantic & Pacific Tea Co. of America, Inc. (C.C.A.8th, 1942) 131 F.(2d) 419; Publicity Bldg. Realty Corp. v. Hannegan (C.C.A.8th, 1943) 139 F.(2d) 583; Dioguardi v. Durning (C.C.A.2d, 1944) 139 F.(2d) 774; Package Closure Corp. v. Sealright Co., Inc. (C.C.A.2d, 1944) 141 F.(2d) 972; Tahir Erk v. Glenn L. Martin Co. (C.C.A.4th, 1941) 116 F.(2d) 865; Bell v. Preferred Life Assurance Society of Montgomery, Ala. (1943) 320 U.S. 238.

The addition at the end of subdivision (b) makes it clear that on a motion under Rule 12(b)(6) extraneous material may not be considered if the court excludes it, but that if the court does not exclude such material the motion shall be treated as a motion for summary judgment and disposed of as provided in Rule 56. It will also be observed that if a motion under Rule 12(b)(6) is thus converted into a summary judgment motion, the amendment insures that both parties shall be given a reasonable opportunity to submit affidavits and extraneous proofs to avoid taking a party by surprise through the conversion of the motion into a motion for summary judgment. In this manner and to this extent the amendment regularizes the practice above described. As the courts are already dealing with cases in this way, the effect of this amendment is really only to define the practice carefully and apply the requirements of the summary judgment rule in the disposition of the motion.

Subdivision (c). The sentence appended to subdivision (c) performs the same function and is grounded on the same reasons as the corresponding sentence added in subdivision (b).

Subdivision (d). The change here was made necessary because of the addition of defense (7) in subdivision (b).

Subdivision (e). References in this subdivision to a bill of particulars have been deleted, and the motion provided for is confined to one for a more definite statement, to be obtained only in cases where the movant cannot reasonably be required to frame an answer or other responsive pleading to the pleading in question. With respect to preparations for trial, the party is properly relegated to the various methods of examination and discovery provided in the rules for that purpose. Slusher v. Jones (E.D.Ky. 1943) 7 Fed.Rules Serv. 12e.231, Case 5, 3 F.R.D. 168; Best Foods, Inc. v. General Mills, Inc. (D.Del. 1943) 7 Fed.Rules Serv. 12e.231, Case 7, 3 F.R.D. 275; Braden v. Callaway (E.D.Tenn. 1943) 8 Fed.Rules Serv. 12e.231, Case 1 (". . . most courts . . . conclude that the definiteness required is only such as will be sufficient for the party to prepare responsive pleadings"). Accordingly, the reference to the 20 day time limit has also been eliminated, since the purpose of this present provision is to state a time period where the motion for a bill is made for the purpose of preparing for trial.

Rule 12(e) as originally drawn has been the subject of more judicial rulings than any other part of the rules, and has been much criticized by commentators, judges and members of the bar. See general discussion and cases cited in 1 Moore's Federal Practice (1938), Cum.Supplement §12.07, under "Page 657"; also, Holtzoff, New Federal Procedure and the Courts (1940) 35–41. And compare vote of Second Circuit Conference of Circuit and District Judges (June 1940) recommending the abolition of the bill of particulars; Sun Valley Mfg. Co. v. Mylish (E.D.Pa. 1944) 8 Fed.Rules Serv. 12e.231, Case 6 ("Our experience . . . has demonstrated not only that 'the office of the bill of particulars is fast becoming obsolete' . . . but that in view of the adequate discovery procedure available under the Rules, motions for bills of particulars should be abolished altogether."); Walling v. American Steamship Co. (W.D.N.Y. 1945) 4 F.R.D. 355, 8 Fed.Rules Serv. 12e.244, Case 8 (". . . the adoption of the rule was ill advised. It has led to confusion, duplication and delay.") The tendency of some courts freely to grant extended bills of particulars has served to neutralize any helpful benefits derived from Rule 8, and has overlooked the intended use of the rules on depositions and discovery. The words "or to prepare for trial"—eliminated by the proposed amendment—have sometimes been seized upon as grounds for compulsory statement in the opposing pleading of all the details which the movant would have to meet at the trial. On the other hand, many courts have in effect read these words out of the rule. See Walling v. Alabama Pipe Co. (W.D.Mo. 1942) 6 Fed.Rules Serv. 12e.244, Case 7; Fleming v. Mason & Dixon Lines, Inc. (E.D.Tenn. 1941) 42 F.Supp. 230; Kellogg Co. v. National Biscuit Co. (D.N.J. 1941) 38 F.Supp. 643; Brown v. H. L. Green Co. (S.D.N.Y. 1943) 7 Fed.Rules Serv. 12e.231, Case 6; Pedersen v. Standard Accident Ins. Co. (W.D.Mo. 1945) 8 Fed.Rules Serv. 12e.231, Case 8; Bowles v. Ohse (D.Neb. 1945) 4 F.R.D. 403, 9 Fed.Rules Serv. 12e.231, Case 1; Klages v. Cohen (E.D.N.Y. 1945) 9 Fed.Rules Serv. 8a.25, Case 4; Bowles v. Lawrence (D.Mass. 1945) 8 Fed.Rules Serv. 12e.231, Case 19; McKinney Tool & Mfg. Co. v. Hoyt (N.D.Ohio 1945) 9 Fed.Rules Serv. 12e.235, Case 1; Bowles v. Jack (D.Minn. 1945) 5 F.R.D. 1, 9 Fed.Rules Serv. 12e.244, Case 9. And it has been urged from the bench that the phrase be stricken. Poole v. White (N.D.W.Va. 1941). 5 Fed.Rules Serv. 12e.231, Case 4, 2 F.R.D. 40. See also Bowles v. Gabel (W.D.Mo. 1946) 9 Fed.Rules Serv. 12e.244, Case

10 ("The courts have never favored that portion of the rules which undertook to justify a motion of this kind for the purpose of aiding counsel in preparing his case for trial.").

Subdivision (f). This amendment affords a specific method of raising the insufficiency of a defense, a matter which has troubled some courts, although attack has been permitted in one way or another. See Dysart v. Remington-Rand, Inc. (D.Conn. 1939) 31 F.Supp. 296; Eastman Kodak Co. v. McAuley (S.D.N.Y. 1941) 4 Fed.Rules Serv. 12f.21, Case 8, 2 F.R.D. 21; Schenley Distillers Corp. v. Renken (E.D.S.C. 1940) 34 F.Supp. 678; Yale Transport Corp. v. Yellow Truck & Coach Mfg. Co. (S.D.N.Y. 1944) 3 F.R.D. 440; United States v. Turner Milk Co. (N.D.Ill. 1941) 4 Fed.Rules Serv. 12b.51, Case 3, 1 F.R.D. 643; Teiger v. Stephan Oderwald, Inc. (S.D.N.Y. 1940) 31 F.Supp. 626; Teplitsky v. Pennsylvania R. Co. (N.D.Ill. 1941) 38 F.Supp. 535; Gallagher v. Carroll (E.D.N.Y. 1939) 27 F.Supp. 568; United States v. Palmer (S.D.N.Y. 1939) 28 F.Supp. 936. And see Indemnity Ins. Co. of North America v. Pan American Airways, Inc. (S.D.N.Y. 1944) 58 F.Supp. 338; Commentary, Modes of Attacking Insufficient Defenses in the Answer (1939) 1 Fed.Rules Serv. 669 (1940) 2 Fed.Rules Serv. 640.

Subdivision (g). The change in title conforms with the companion provision in subdivision (h).

The alteration of the "except" clause requires that other than provided in subdivision (h) a party who resorts to a motion to raise defenses specified in the rule, must include in one motion all that are then available to him. Under the original rule defenses which could be raised by motion were divided into two groups which could be the subjects of two successive motions.

Subdivision (h). The addition of the phrase relating to indispensable parties is one of necessity.

Notes of Advisory Committee on Rules—1963 Amendment

This amendment conforms to the amendment of Rule 4(e). See also the Advisory Committee's Note to amended Rule 4(b).

Notes of Advisory Committee on Rules—1966 Amendment

Subdivision (b)(7). The terminology of this subdivision is changed to accord with the amendment of Rule 19. See the Advisory Committee's Note to Rule 19, as amended, especially the third paragraph therein before the caption "Subdivision (c)."

Subdivision (g). Subdivision (g) has forbidden a defendant who makes a preanswer motion under this rule from making a further motion presenting any defense or objection which was available to him at the time he made the first motion and which he could have included, but did not in fact include therein. Thus if the defendant moves before answer to dismiss the complaint for failure to state a claim, he is barred from making a further motion presenting the defense of improper venue, if that defense was available to him when he made his original motion. Amended subdivision (g) is to the same effect. This required consolidation of defenses and objections in a Rule 12 motion is salutary in that it works against piecemeal consideration of a case. For exceptions to the requirement of consolidation, see the last clause of subdivision (g), referring to new subdivision (h)(2).

Subdivision (h). The question has arisen whether an omitted defense which cannot be made the basis of a second motion may nevertheless be pleaded in the answer. Subdivision (h) called for waiver of "* * * defenses and objections which he [defendant] does not present * * * by motion * * * or, if he has made no motion, in his answer * * *." If the clause "if he has made no motion," was read literally, it seemed that the omitted defense was waived and could not be pleaded in the answer. On the other hand, the clause might be read as adding nothing of substance to the preceding words; in that event it appeared that a defense was not waived by reason of being omitted from the motion and might be set up in the answer. The decisions were divided. Favoring waiver, see Keefe v. Derounian, 6 F.R.D. 11 (N.D.Ill. 1946); Elbinger v. Precision Metal Workers Corp., 18 F.R.D. 467 (E.D.Wis. 1956); see also Rensing v. Turner Aviation Corp., 166 F.Supp. 790 (N.D.Ill. 1958); P. Beiersdorf & Co. v. Duke Laboratories, Inc., 10 F.R.D. 282 (S.D.N.Y. 1950); Neset v. Christensen, 92 F.Supp. 78 (E.D.N.Y. 1950). Opposing waiver, see Phillips v. Baker, 121 F.2d 752 (9th Cir. 1941); Crum v. Graham, 32 F.R.D. 173 (D.Mont. 1963) (regretfully following the Phillips case); see also Birnbaum v. Birrell, 9 F.R.D. 72 (S.D.N.Y. 1948); Johnson v. Joseph Schlitz Brewing Co., 33 F.Supp. 176 (E.D.Tenn. 1940); cf. Carter v. American Bus Lines, Inc., 22 F.R.D. 323 (D.Neb. 1958).

Amended subdivision (h)(1)(A) eliminates the ambiguity and states that certain specified defenses which were available to a party when he made a preanswer motion, but which he omitted from the motion, are waived. The specified defenses are lack of jurisdiction over the person, improper venue, insufficiency of process, and insufficiency of service of process (see Rule 12(b)(2)–(5)). A party who by motion invites the court to pass upon a threshold defense should bring forward all the specified defenses he then has and thus allow the court to do a reasonably complete job. The waiver reinforces the policy of subdivision (g) forbidding successive motions.

By amended subdivision (h)(1)(B), the specified defenses, even if not waived by the operation of (A), are waived by the failure to raise them by a motion under Rule 12 or in the responsive pleading or any amendment thereof to which the party is entitled as a matter of course. The specified defenses are of such a character that they should not be delayed and brought up for the first time by means of an application to the court to amend the responsive pleading.

Since the language of the subdivisions is made clear, the party is put on fair notice of the effect of his actions and omissions and can guard himself against unintended waiver. It is to be noted that while the defenses specified in subdivision (h)(1) are subject to waiver as there provided, the more substantial defenses of failure to state a claim upon which relief can be granted, failure to join a party indispensable under Rule 19, and failure to state a legal defense to a claim (see Rule 12(b)(6), (7), (f)), as well as the defense of lack of jurisdiction over the subject matter (see Rule 12(b)(1)), are expressly preserved against waiver by amended subdivision (h)(2) and (3).

Notes of Advisory Committee on Rules—1987 Amendment

The amendments are technical. No substantive change is intended.

Notes of Advisory Committee on Rules—1993 Amendment

Subdivision (a) is divided into paragraphs for greater clarity, and paragraph (1)(B) is added to reflect amendments to Rule 4. Consistent with Rule 4(d)(3), a defendant that timely waives service is allowed 60 days from the date the request was mailed in which to respond to the complaint, with an additional 30 days afforded if the request was sent out of the country. Service is timely waived if the waiver is returned within the time specified in the request (30 days after the request was mailed, or 60 days if mailed out of the country) and before being formally served with process. Sometimes a plaintiff may attempt to serve a defendant with process while also sending the defendant a request for waiver of service; if the defendant executes the waiver of service within the time specified and before being served with process, it should have the longer time to respond afforded by waiving service.

The date of sending the request is to be inserted by the plaintiff on the face of the request for waiver and on the waiver itself. This date is used to measure the return day for the waiver form, so that the plaintiff can know on a day certain whether formal service of process will be necessary; it is also a useful date to measure the time for answer when service is waived. The defendant who returns the waiver is given additional time for answer in order to assure that it loses nothing by waiving service of process.

Committee Notes on Rules—2000 Amendment

Rule 12(a)(3)(B) is added to complement the addition of Rule 4(i)(2)(B). The purposes that underlie the requirement that service be made on the United States in an action that asserts individual liability of a United States officer or employee for acts occurring in connection with the performance of duties on behalf of the United States also require that the time to answer be extended to 60 days. Time is needed for the United States to determine whether to provide representation to the defendant officer or employee. If the United States provides representation, the need for an extended answer period is the same as in actions against the United States, a United States agency, or a United States officer sued in an official capacity.

An action against a former officer or employee of the United States is covered by subparagraph (3)(B) in the same way as an action against a present officer or employee. Termination of the relationship between the individual defendant and the United States does not reduce the need for additional time to answer.

GAP Report. No changes are recommended for Rule 12 as published.

Committee Notes on Rules—2007 Amendment

The language of Rule 12 has been amended as part of the general restyling of the Civil Rules to make them more easily understood and to make style and terminology consistent throughout the rules. These changes are intended to be stylistic only.

Former Rule 12(a)(4)(A) referred to an order that postpones disposition of a motion "until the trial on the merits." Rule 12(a)(4) now refers to postponing disposition "until trial." The new expression avoids the ambiguity that inheres in "trial on the merits," which may become confusing when there is a separate trial of a single issue or another event different from a single all-encompassing trial.

Changes Made After Publication and Comment. See Note to Rule 1, supra.

Committee Notes on Rules—2009 Amendment

The times set in the former rule at 10 or 20 days have been revised to 14 or 21 days. See the Note to Rule 6.

Rule 13. Counterclaim and Crossclaim

(a) Compulsory Counterclaim.

(1) In General. A pleading must state as a counterclaim any claim that—at the time of its service—the pleader has against an opposing party if the claim:

(A) arises out of the transaction or occurrence that is the subject matter of the opposing party's claim; and

(B) does not require adding another party over whom the court cannot acquire jurisdiction.

(2) Exceptions. The pleader need not state the claim if:

(A) when the action was commenced, the claim was the subject of another pending action; or

(B) the opposing party sued on its claim by attachment or other process that did not establish personal jurisdiction over the pleader on that claim, and the pleader does not assert any counterclaim under this rule.

(b) Permissive Counterclaim. A pleading may state as a counterclaim against an opposing party any claim that is not compulsory.

(c) Relief Sought in a Counterclaim. A counterclaim need not diminish or defeat the recovery sought by the opposing party. It may request relief that exceeds in amount or differs in kind from the relief sought by the opposing party.

(d) Counterclaim Against the United States. These rules do not expand the right to assert a counterclaim—or to claim a credit—against the United States or a United States officer or agency.

(e) Counterclaim Maturing or Acquired After Pleading. The court may permit a party to file a supplemental pleading asserting a counterclaim that matured or was acquired by the party after serving an earlier pleading.

(f) [Abrogated.]

(g) Crossclaim Against a Coparty. A pleading may state as a crossclaim any claim by one party against a coparty if the claim arises out of the transaction or occurrence that is the subject matter of the original action or of a counterclaim, or if the claim relates to any property that is the subject matter of the original action. The crossclaim may include a claim that the coparty is or may be liable to the crossclaimant for all or part of a claim asserted in the action against the crossclaimant.

(h) Joining Additional Parties. Rules 19 and 20 govern the addition of a person as a party to a counterclaim or crossclaim.

(i) Separate Trials; Separate Judgments. If the court orders separate trials under Rule 42(b), it may enter judgment on a counterclaim or crossclaim under Rule 54(b) when it has jurisdiction to do so, even if the opposing party's claims have been dismissed or otherwise resolved.

(As amended Dec. 27, 1946, eff. Mar. 19, 1948; Jan. 21, 1963, eff. July 1, 1963; Feb. 28, 1966, eff. July 1, 1966; Mar. 2, 1987, eff. Aug. 1, 1987; Apr. 30, 2007, eff. Dec. 1, 2007; Mar. 26, 2009, eff. Dec. 1, 2009.)

Notes of Advisory Committee on Rules—1937

1. This is substantially [former] Equity Rule 30 (Answer—Contents—Counterclaim), broadened to include legal as well as equitable counterclaims.

2. Compare the English practice, English Rules Under the Judicature Act (The Annual Practice, 1937) O. 19, r.r. 2 and 3, and O. 21, r.r. 10—17; Beddall v. Maitland, L.R. 17 Ch.Div. 174, 181, 182 (1881).

3. Certain States have also adopted almost unrestricted provisions concerning both the subject matter of and the parties to a counterclaim. This seems to be the modern tendency. Ark.Civ.Code (Crawford, 1934) §§117 (as amended) and 118; N.J.Comp.Stat. (2 Cum.Supp. 1911–1924), N.Y.C.P.A. (1937)

§§262, 266, 267 (all as amended, Laws of 1936, ch. 324), 268, 269, and 271; Wis.Stat. (1935) §263.14 (1)(c).

4. Most codes do not expressly provide for a counterclaim in the reply. Clark, Code Pleading (1928), p. 486. Ky.Codes (Carroll, 1932) Civ.Pract. §98 does provide, however, for such counterclaim.

5. The provisions of this rule respecting counterclaims are subject to Rule 82 (Jurisdiction and Venue Unaffected). For a discussion of Federal jurisdiction and venue in regard to counterclaims and cross-claims, see Shulman and Jaegerman, Some Jurisdictional Limitations in Federal Procedure (1936), 45 Yale L.J. 393, 410 et seq.

6. This rule does not affect such statutes of the United States as U.S.C., Title 28, §41(1) [now 1332, 1345, 1359] (United States as plaintiff; civil suits at common law and in equity), relating to assigned claims in actions based on diversity of citizenship.

7. If the action proceeds to judgment without the interposition of a counterclaim as required by subdivision (a) of this rule, the counterclaim is barred. See American Mills Co. v. American Surety Co., 260 U.S. 360 (1922); Marconi Wireless Telegraph Co. v. National Electric Signalling Co., 206 Fed. 295 (E.D.N.Y., 1913); Hopkins, Federal Equity Rules (8th ed., 1933), p. 213; Simkins, Federal Practice (1934), p. 663

8. For allowance of credits against the United States see U.S.C., Title 26, §§1672–1673 [see 7442] (Suits for refunds of internal revenue taxes—limitations); U.S.C., Title 28, §§774 [now 2406] (Suits by United States against individuals; credits), [former] 775 (Suits under postal laws; credits); U.S.C., Title 31, §227 [now 3728] (Offsets against judgments and claims against United States).

Notes of Advisory Committee on Rules—1946 Amendment

Subdivision (a). The use of the word "filing" was inadvertent. The word "serving" conforms with subdivision (e) and with usage generally throughout the rules.

The removal of the phrase "not the subject of a pending action" and the addition of the new clause at the end of the subdivision is designed to eliminate the ambiguity noted in Prudential Insurance Co. of America v. Saxe (App.D.C. 1943) 134 F.(2d) 16, 33–34, cert. den. (1943) 319 U.S. 745. The rewording of the subdivision in this respect insures against an undesirable possibility presented under the original rule whereby a party having a claim which would be the subject of a compulsory counterclaim could avoid stating it as such by bringing an independent action in another court after the commencement of the federal action but before serving his pleading in the federal action.

Subdivision (g). The amendment is to care for a situation such as where a second mortgagee is made defendant in a foreclosure proceeding and wishes to file a cross-complaint against the mortgagor in order to secure a personal judgment for the indebtedness and foreclose his lien. A claim of this sort by the second mortgagee may not necessarily arise out of the transaction or occurrence that is the subject matter of the original action under the terms of Rule 13(g).

Subdivision (h). The change clarifies the interdependence of Rules 13(i) and 54(b).

Notes of Advisory Committee on Rules—1963 Amendment

When a defendant, if he desires to defend his interest in property, is obliged to come in and litigate in a court to whose jurisdiction he could not ordinarily be subjected, fairness suggests that he should not be required to assert counterclaims, but should rather be permitted to do so at his election. If, however, he does elect to assert a counterclaim, it seems fair to require him to assert any other which is compulsory within the meaning of Rule 13(a). Clause (2), added by amendment to Rule 13(a), carries out this idea. It will apply to various cases described in Rule 4(e), as amended, where service is effected through attachment or other process by which the court does not acquire jurisdiction to render a personal judgment against the defendant. Clause (2) will also apply to actions commenced in State courts jurisdictionally grounded on attachment or the like, and removed to the Federal courts.

Notes of Advisory Committee on Rules—1966 Amendment

Rule 13(h), dealing with the joinder of additional parties to a counterclaim or cross-claim, has partaken of some of the textual difficulties of Rule 19 on necessary joinder of parties. See Advisory Committee's Note to Rule 19, as amended; cf. 3 Moore's Federal Practice, Par. 13.39 (2d ed. 1963), and Supp. thereto; 1A Barron & Holtzoff, Federal Practice and Procedure §399 (Wright ed. 1960). Rule 13(h) has also been inadequate in failing to call attention to the fact that a party pleading a counterclaim or cross-claim may join additional persons when the conditions for permissive joinder of parties under Rule 20 are satisfied.

The amendment of Rule 13(h) supplies the latter omission by expressly referring to Rule 20, as amended, and also incorporates by direct reference the revised criteria and procedures of Rule 19, as amended. Hereafter, for the purpose of determining who must or may be joined as additional parties to a counterclaim or cross-claim, the party pleading the claim is to be regarded as a plaintiff and the additional parties as plaintiffs or defendants as the case may be, and amended Rules 19 and 20 are to be applied in the usual fashion. See also Rules 13(a) (compulsory counterclaims) and 22 (interpleader).

The amendment of Rule 13(h), like the amendment of Rule 19, does not attempt to regulate Federal jurisdiction or venue. See Rule 82. It should be noted, however, that in some situations the decisional law has recognized "ancillary" Federal jurisdiction over counterclaims and cross-claims and "ancillary" venue as to parties to these claims.

Notes of Advisory Committee on Rules—1987 Amendment

The amendments are technical. No substantive change is intended.

Committee Notes on Rules—2007 Amendment

The language of Rule 13 has been amended as part of the general restyling of the Civil Rules to make them more easily understood and to make style and terminology consistent throughout the rules. These changes are intended to be stylistic only.

The meaning of former Rule 13(b) is better expressed by deleting "not arising out of the transaction or occurrence that is the subject matter of the opposing party's claim." Both as a matter of intended meaning and current practice, a party may state as a permissive counterclaim a claim that does grow out of the same transaction or occurrence as an opposing party's claim even though one of the exceptions in Rule 13(a) means the claim is not a compulsory counterclaim.

Committee Notes on Rules—2009 Amendment

Rule 13(f) is deleted as largely redundant and potentially misleading. An amendment to add a counterclaim will be governed by Rule 15. Rule 15(a)(1) permits some amendments to be made as a matter of course or with the opposing party's written consent. When the court's leave is required, the reasons described in Rule 13(f) for permitting amendment of a pleading to add an omitted counterclaim sound different from the general amendment standard in Rule 15(a)(2), but seem to be administered—as they should be—according to the same standard directing that leave should be freely given when justice so requires. The independent existence of Rule 13(f) has, however, created some uncertainty as to the availability of relation back of the amendment under Rule 15(c). See 6 C. Wright, A. Miller & M. Kane, Federal Practice & Procedure: Civil 2d, §1430 (1990). Deletion of Rule 13(f) ensures that relation back is governed by the tests that apply to all other pleading amendments.

Rule 14. Third-Party Practice

(a) When a Defending Party May Bring in a Third Party.

(1) Timing of the Summons and Complaint. A defending party may, as third-party plaintiff, serve a summons and complaint on a nonparty who is or may be liable to it for all or part of the claim against it. But the third-party plaintiff must, by motion, obtain the court's leave if it files the third-party complaint more than 14 days after serving its original answer.

(2) Third-Party Defendant's Claims and Defenses. The person served with the summons and third-party complaint—the "third-party defendant":

(A) must assert any defense against the third-party plaintiff's claim under Rule 12;

(B) must assert any counterclaim against the third-party plaintiff under Rule 13(a), and may assert any counterclaim against the third-party plaintiff under Rule 13(b) or any crossclaim against another third-party defendant under Rule 13(g);

(C) may assert against the plaintiff any defense that the third-party plaintiff has to the plaintiff's claim; and

(D) may also assert against the plaintiff any claim arising out of the transaction or occurrence that is the subject matter of the plaintiff's claim against the third-party plaintiff.

(3) Plaintiff's Claims Against a Third-Party Defendant. The plaintiff may assert against the third-party defendant any claim arising out of the transaction or occurrence that is the subject matter of the plaintiff's claim against the third-party plaintiff. The third-party defendant must then assert any defense under Rule 12 and any counterclaim under Rule 13(a), and may assert any counterclaim under Rule 13(b) or any crossclaim under Rule 13(g).

(4) Motion to Strike, Sever, or Try Separately. Any party may move to strike the third-party claim, to sever it, or to try it separately.

(5) Third-Party Defendant's Claim Against a Nonparty. A third-party defendant may proceed under this rule against a nonparty who is or may be liable to the third-party defendant for all or part of any claim against it.

(6) Third-Party Complaint In Rem. If it is within the admiralty or maritime jurisdiction, a third-party complaint may be in rem. In that event, a reference in this rule to the "summons" includes the warrant of arrest, and a reference to the defendant or third-party plaintiff includes, when appropriate, a person who asserts a right under Supplemental Rule C(6)(a)(i) in the property arrested.

(b) When a Plaintiff May Bring in a Third Party. When a claim is asserted against a plaintiff, the plaintiff may bring in a third party if this rule would allow a defendant to do so.

(c) Admiralty or Maritime Claim.

(1) Scope of Impleader. If a plaintiff asserts an admiralty or maritime claim under Rule 9(h), the defendant or a person who asserts a right under Supplemental Rule C(6)(a)(i) may, as a third-party plaintiff, bring in a third-party defendant who may be wholly or partly liable—either to the plaintiff or to the third-party plaintiff— for remedy over, contribution, or otherwise on account of the same transaction, occurrence, or series of transactions or occurrences.

(2) Defending Against a Demand for Judgment for the Plaintiff. The third-party plaintiff may demand judgment in the plaintiff's favor against the third-party defendant. In that event, the third-party defendant must defend under Rule 12 against the plaintiff's claim as well as the third-party plaintiff's claim; and the action proceeds as if the plaintiff had sued both the third-party defendant and the third-party plaintiff.

(As amended Dec. 27, 1946, eff. Mar. 19, 1948; Jan. 21, 1963, eff. July 1, 1963; Feb. 28, 1966, eff. July 1, 1966; Mar. 2, 1987, eff. Aug. 1, 1987; Apr. 17, 2000, eff. Dec. 1, 2000; Apr. 12, 2006, eff. Dec. 1, 2006; Apr. 30, 2007, eff. Dec. 1, 2007; Mar. 26, 2009, eff. Dec. 1, 2009.)

Notes of Advisory Committee on Rules—1937

Third-party impleader is in some aspects a modern innovation in law and equity although well known in admiralty. Because of its many advantages a liberal procedure with respect to it has developed in England, in the Federal admiralty courts, and in some American State jurisdictions. See English Rules Under the Judicature Act (The Annual Practice, 1937) O. 16A, r.r. 1–13; United States Supreme Court Admiralty Rules (1920), Rule 56 (Right to Bring in Party Jointly Liable); Pa.Stat.Ann. (Purdon, 1936) Title 12, §141; Wis.Stat. (1935) §§260.19, 260.20; N.Y.C.P.A. (1937) §§193 (2), 211(a). Compare La.Code Pract. (Dart, 1932) §§378–388. For the practice in Texas as developed by judicial decision, see Lottman v. Cuilla, 288 S.W. 123, 126 (Tex., 1926). For a treatment of this subject see Gregory, Legislative Loss Distribution in Negligence Actions (1936); Shulman and Jaegerman, Some Jurisdictional Limitations on Federal Procedure (1936), 45 Yale L.J. 393, 417, et seq.

Third-party impleader under the conformity act has been applied in actions at law in the Federal courts. Lowry and Co., Inc., v. National City Bank of New York, 28 F.(2d) 895 (S.D.N.Y., 1928); Yellow Cab Co. of Philadelphia v. Rodgers, 61 F.(2d) 729 (C.C.A.3d, 1932).

Notes of Advisory Committee on Rules—1946 Amendment

The provisions in Rule 14(a) which relate to the impleading of a third party who is or may be liable to the plaintiff have been deleted by the proposed amendment. It has been held that under Rule 14(a) the plaintiff need not amend his complaint to state a claim against such third party if he does not wish to do so. Satink v. Holland Township (D.N.J. 1940) 31 F.Supp. 229, noted (1940) 88 U.Pa.L.Rev. 751; Connelly v. Bender (E.D.Mich. 1941) 36

F.Supp. 368; Whitmire v. Partin v. Milton (E.D.Tenn. 1941) 5 Fed.Rules Serv. 14a.513, Case 2; Crim v. Lumbermen's Mutual Casualty Co. (D.D.C. 1939) 26 F.Supp. 715; Carbola Chemical Co., Inc. v. Trundle (S.D.N.Y. 1943) 7 Fed.Rules Serv. 14a.224, Case 1; Roadway Express, Inc. v. Automobile Ins. Co. of Hartford, Conn. v. Providence Washington Ins. Co. (N.D.Ohio 1945) 8 Fed.Rules Serv. 14a.513, Case 3. In Delano v. Ives (E.D.Pa. 1941) 40 F.Supp. 672, the court said: ". . . the weight of authority is to the effect that a defendant cannot compel the plaintiff, who has sued him, to sue also a third party whom he does not wish to sue, by tendering in a third party complaint the third party as an additional defendant directly liable to the plaintiff." Thus impleader here amounts to no more than a mere offer of a party to the plaintiff, and if he rejects it, the attempt is a time-consuming futility. See Satink v. Holland Township, supra; Malkin v. Arundel Corp. (D.Md. 1941) 36 F.Supp. 948; also Koenigsberger, Suggestions for Changes in the Federal Rules of Civil Procedure, (1941) 4 Fed.Rules Serv. 1010. But cf. Atlantic Coast Line R. Co. v. United States Fidelity & Guaranty Co. (M.D.Ga. 1943) 52 F.Supp. 177. Moreover, in any case where the plaintiff could not have joined the third party originally because of jurisdictional limitations such as lack of diversity of citizenship, the majority view is that any attempt by the plaintiff to amend his complaint and assert a claim against the impleaded third party would be unavailing. Hoskie v. Prudential Ins. Co. of America v. Lorrac Real Estate Corp. (E.D.N.Y. 1941) 39 F.Supp. 305; Johnson v. G. J. Sherrard Co. v. New England Telephone & Telegraph Co. (D.Mass. 1941) 5 Fed.Rules Serv. 14a.511, Case 1, 2 F.R.D. 164; Thompson v. Cranston (W.D.N.Y. 1942) 6 Fed.Rules Serv. 14a.511, Case 1, 2 F.R.D. 270, aff'd (C.C.A.2d, 1942) 132 F.(2d) 631, cert. den. (1943) 319 U.S. 741; Friend v. Middle Atlantic Transportation Co. (C.C.A.2d, 1946) 153 F.(2d) 778, cert. den. (1946) 66 S.Ct. 1370; Herrington v. Jones (E.D.La. 1941) 5 Fed.Rules Serv. 14a.511, Case 2, 2 F.R.D. 108; Banks v. Employers' Liability Assurance Corp. v. Central Surety & Ins. Corp. (W.D.Mo. 1943) 7 Fed.Rules Serv. 14a.11, Case 2; Saunders v. Baltimore & Ohio R. Co. (S.D.W.Va. 1945) 9 Fed.Rules Serv. 14a.62, Case 2; Hull v. United States Rubber Co. v. Johnson Larsen & Co. (E.D.Mich. 1945) 9 Fed.Rules Serv. 14a.62, Case 3. See also concurring opinion of Circuit Judge Minton in People of State of Illinois for use of Trust Co. of Chicago v. Maryland Casualty Co. (C.C.A.7th, 1942) 132 F.(2d) 850, 853. Contra: Sklar v. Hayes v. Singer (E.D.Pa. 1941) 4 Fed.Rules Serv. 14a.511, Case 2, 1 F.R.D. 594. Discussion of the problem will be found in Commentary, Amendment of Plaintiff's Pleading to Assert Claim Against Third-Party Defendant (1942) 5 Fed.Rules Serv. 811; Commentary, Federal Jurisdiction in Third-Party Practice (1943) 6 Fed.Rules Serv. 766; Holtzoff, Some Problems Under Federal Third-Party Practice (1941) 3 La.L.Rev. 408, 419–420; 1. Moore's Federal Practice (1938) Cum.Supplement §14.08. For these reasons therefore, the words "or to the plaintiff" in the first sentence of subdivision (a) have been removed by the amendment; and in conformance therewith the words "the plaintiff" in the second sentence of the subdivision, and the words "or to the third-party plaintiff" in the concluding sentence thereof have likewise been eliminated.

The third sentence of Rule 14(a) has been expanded to clarify the right of the third-party defendant to assert any defenses which the third-party plaintiff may have to the plaintiff's claim. This protects the impleaded third-party defendant where the third-party plaintiff fails or neglects to assert a proper defense to the plaintiff's action. A new sentence has also been inserted giving the third-party defendant the right to assert directly against the original plaintiff any claim arising out of the transaction or occurrence that is the subject matter of the plaintiff's claim against the third-party plaintiff. This permits all claims arising out of the same transaction or occurrence to be heard and determined in the same action. See Atlantic Coast Line R. Co. v. United States Fidelity & Guaranty Co. (M.D.Ga. 1943) 52 F.Supp. 177. Accordingly, the next to the last sentence of subdivision (a) has also been revised to make clear that the plaintiff may, if he desires, assert directly against the third-party defendant either by amendment or by a new pleading any claim he may have against him arising out of the transaction or occurrence that is the subject matter of the plaintiff's claim against the third-party plaintiff. In such a case, the third-party defendant then is entitled to assert the defenses, counterclaims and cross-claims provided in Rules 12 and 13.

The sentence reading "The third-party defendant is bound by the adjudication of the third-party plaintiff's liability to the plaintiff, as well as of his own to the plaintiff, or to the third-party plaintiff" has been stricken from Rule 14(a), not to change the law, but because the sentence states a rule of substantive law which is not within the scope of a procedural rule. It is not the purpose of the rules to state the effect of a judgment.

The elimination of the words "the third-party plaintiff, or any other party" from the second sentence of Rule 14(a), together with the insertion of the new phrases therein, are not changes of substance but are merely for the purpose of clarification.

Notes of Advisory Committee on Rules—1963 Amendment

Under the amendment of the initial sentences of the subdivision, a defendant as a third-party plaintiff may freely and without leave of court bring in a third-party defendant if he files the third-party complaint not later than 10 days after he serves his original answer. When the impleader comes so early in the case, there is little value in requiring a preliminary ruling by the court on the propriety of the impleader.

After the third-party defendant is brought in, the court has discretion to strike the third-party claim if it is obviously unmeritorious and can only delay or prejudice the disposition of the plaintiff's claim, or to sever the third-party claim or accord it separate trial if confusion or prejudice would otherwise result. This discretion, applicable not merely to the cases covered by the amendment where the third-party defendant is brought in without leave, but to all impleaders under the rule, is emphasized in the next-to-last sentence of the subdivision, added by amendment.

In dispensing with leave of court for an impleader filed not later than 10 days after serving the answer, but retaining the leave requirement for impleaders sought to be effected thereafter, the amended subdivision takes a moderate position on the lines urged by some commentators, see Note, 43 Minn.L.Rev. 115 (1958); cf. Pa.R.Civ.P. 2252–53 (60 days after service on the defendant); Minn.R.Civ.P. 14.01 (45 days). Other commentators would dispense with the requirement of leave regardless of the time when impleader is effected, and would rely on subsequent action by the court to dismiss the impleader if it would unduly delay or complicate the litigation or would be otherwise objectionable. See 1A Barron & Holtzoff, Federal Practice & Procedure 649–50 (Wright ed. 1960); Comment, 58 Colum.L.Rev. 532, 546 (1958); cf. N.Y.Civ.Prac. Act §193–a; Me.R.Civ.P. 14. The amended subdivision preserves the value of a preliminary screening, through the leave procedure, of impleaders attempted after the 10-day period.

The amendment applies also when an impleader is initiated by a third-party defendant against a person who may be liable to him, as provided in the last sentence of the subdivision.

Notes of Advisory Committee on Rules—1966 Amendment

Rule 14 was modeled on Admiralty Rule 56. An important feature of Admiralty Rule 56 was that it allowed impleader not only of a person who might be liable to the defendant by way of remedy over, but also of any person who might be liable to the plaintiff. The importance of this provision was that the defendant was entitled to insist that the plaintiff proceed to judgment against the third-party defendant. In certain cases this was a valuable implementation of a substantive right. For example, in a case of ship collision where a finding of mutual fault is possible, one shipowner, if sued alone, faces the prospect of an absolute judgment for the full amount of the damage suffered by an innocent third party; but if he can implead the owner of the other vessel, and if mutual fault is found, the judgment against the original defendant will be in the first instance only for a moiety of the damages; liability for the remainder will be conditioned on the plaintiff's inability to collect from the third-party defendant.

This feature was originally incorporated in Rule 14, but was eliminated by the amendment of 1946, so that under the amended rule a third party could not be impleaded on the basis that he might be liable to the plaintiff. One of the reasons for the amendment was that the Civil Rule, unlike the Admiralty Rule, did not require the plaintiff to go to judgment against the third-party defendant. Another reason was that where jurisdiction depended on diversity of citizenship the impleader of an adversary having the same citizenship as the plaintiff was not considered possible.

Retention of the admiralty practice in those cases that will be counterparts of a suit in admiralty is clearly desirable.

Notes of Advisory Committee on Rules—1987 Amendment

The amendments are technical. No substantive change is intended.

Committee Notes on Rules—2000 Amendment

Subdivisions (a) and (c) are amended to reflect revisions in Supplemental Rule C(6).

GAP Report. Rule B(1)(a) was modified by moving "in an in personam action" out of paragraph (a) and into the first line of subdivision (1). This change makes it clear that all paragraphs of subdivision (1) apply when attachment is sought in an in personam action. Rule B(1)(d) was modified by changing the requirement that the clerk deliver the summons and process to the person or organization authorized to serve it. The new form requires only that the summons and process be delivered, not that the clerk effect the delivery. This change conforms to present practice in some districts and will facilitate rapid service. It matches the spirit of Civil Rule 4(b), which directs the clerk to issue the summons "to the plaintiff for service on the defendant." A parallel change is made in Rule C(3)(b).

Committee Notes on Rules—2006 Amendment

Rule 14 is amended to conform to changes in designating the paragraphs of Supplemental Rule C(6).

Committee Notes on Rules—2007 Amendment

The language of Rule 14 has been amended as part of the general restyling of the Civil Rules to make them more easily understood and to make style and terminology consistent throughout the rules. These changes are intended to be stylistic only.

Former Rule 14 twice refers to counterclaims under Rule 13. In each case, the operation of Rule 13(a) depends on the state of the action at the time the pleading is filed. If plaintiff and third-party defendant have become opposing parties because one has made a claim for relief against the other, Rule 13(a) requires assertion of any counterclaim that grows out of the transaction or occurrence that is the subject matter of that claim. Rules 14(a)(2)(B) and (a)(3) reflect the distinction between compulsory and permissive counterclaims.

A plaintiff should be on equal footing with the defendant in making third-party claims, whether the claim against the plaintiff is asserted as a counterclaim or as another form of claim. The limit imposed by the former reference to "counterclaim" is deleted.

Committee Notes on Rules—2009 Amendment

The time set in the former rule at 10 days has been revised to 14 days. See the Note to Rule 6.

Rule 15. Amended and Supplemental Pleadings

(a) Amendments Before Trial.

(1) Amending as a Matter of Course. A party may amend its pleading once as a matter of course within:

(A) 21 days after serving it, or

(B) if the pleading is one to which a responsive pleading is required, 21 days after service of a responsive pleading or 21 days after service of a motion under Rule 12(b), (e), or (f), whichever is earlier.

(2) Other Amendments. In all other cases, a party may amend its pleading only with the opposing party's written consent or the court's leave. The court should freely give leave when justice so requires.

(3) Time to Respond. Unless the court orders otherwise, any required response to an amended pleading must be made within the time remaining to respond to the original pleading or within 14 days after service of the amended pleading, whichever is later.

(b) Amendments During and After Trial.

(1) Based on an Objection at Trial. If, at trial, a party objects that evidence is not within the issues raised in the pleadings, the court may permit the pleadings to be amended. The court should freely permit an amendment when doing so will aid in presenting the merits and the objecting party fails to satisfy the court that the evidence would prejudice that party's action or defense on the merits. The court may grant a continuance to enable the objecting party to meet the evidence.

(2) For Issues Tried by Consent. When an issue not raised by the pleadings is tried by the parties' express or implied consent, it must be treated in all respects as if raised in the pleadings. A party may move—at any time, even after judgment—to amend the pleadings to conform them to the evidence and to raise an unpleaded issue. But failure to amend does not affect the result of the trial of that issue.

(c) Relation Back of Amendments.

(1) When an Amendment Relates Back. An amendment to a pleading relates back to the date of the original pleading when:

(A) the law that provides the applicable statute of limitations allows relation back;

(B) the amendment asserts a claim or defense that arose out of the conduct, transaction, or occurrence set out—or attempted to be set out—in the original pleading; or

(C) the amendment changes the party or the naming of the party against whom a claim is asserted, if Rule 15(c)(1)(B) is satisfied and if, within the period provided by Rule 4(m) for serving the summons and complaint, the party to be brought in by amendment:

(i) received such notice of the action that it will not be prejudiced in defending on the merits; and

(ii) knew or should have known that the action would have been brought against it, but for a mistake concerning the proper party's identity.

(2) Notice to the United States. When the United States or a United States officer or agency is added as a defendant by amendment, the notice requirements of Rule 15(c)(1)(C)(i) and (ii) are satisfied if, during the stated period, process was delivered or mailed to the United States attorney or the United States attorney's designee, to the Attorney General of the United States, or to the officer or agency.

(d) Supplemental Pleadings. On motion and reasonable notice, the court may, on just terms, permit a party to serve a supplemental pleading setting out any transaction, occurrence, or event that happened after the date of the pleading to be supplemented. The court may permit supplementation even though the original pleading is defective in stating a claim or defense. The court may order that the opposing party plead to the supplemental pleading within a specified time.

(As amended Jan. 21, 1963, eff. July 1, 1963; Feb. 28, 1966, eff. July 1, 1966; Mar. 2, 1987, eff. Aug. 1, 1987; Apr. 30, 1991, eff. Dec. 1, 1991; Pub. L. 102–198, §11(a), Dec. 9, 1991, 105 Stat. 1626; Apr. 22, 1993, eff. Dec. 1, 1993; Apr. 30, 2007, eff. Dec. 1, 2007; Mar. 26, 2009, eff. Dec. 1, 2009.)

Notes of Advisory Committee on Rules—1937

See generally for the present federal practice, [former] Equity Rules 19 (Amendments Generally), 28 (Amendment of Bill as of Course), 32 (Answer to Amended Bill), 34 (Supplemental Pleading), and 35 (Bills of Revivor and Supplemental Bills—Form); U.S.C., Title 28, §§399 [now 1653] (Amendments to show diverse citizenship) and [former] 777 (Defects of Form; amendments). See English Rules Under the Judicature Act (The Annual Practice, 1937) O. 28, r.r. 1–13; O. 20, r. 4; O. 24, r.r. 1–3.

Note to Subdivision (a). The right to serve an amended pleading once as of course is common. 4 Mont.Rev.Codes Ann. (1935) §9186; 1 Ore.Code Ann. (1930) §1–904; 1 S.C.Code (Michie, 1932) §493; English Rules Under the Judicature Act (The Annual Practice, 1937) O. 28, r. 2. Provision for amendment of pleading before trial, by leave of court, is in almost every code. If there is no statute the power of the court to grant leave is said to be inherent. Clark, Code Pleading, (1928) pp. 498, 509.

Note to Subdivision (b). Compare [former] Equity Rule 19 (Amendments Generally) and code provisions which allow an amendment "at any time in furtherance of justice," (e. g., Ark.Civ.Code (Crawford, 1934) §155) and which allow an amendment of pleadings to conform to the evidence, where the adverse party has not been misled and prejudiced (e.g., N.M.Stat.Ann. (Courtright, 1929) §§105–601, 105–602).

Note to Subdivision (c). "Relation back" is a well recognized doctrine of recent and now more frequent application. Compare Ala.Code Ann. (Michie, 1928) §9513; Ill.Rev.Stat. (1937) ch. 110, §170(2); 2 Wash.Rev.Stat.Ann. (Remington, 1932) §308–3(4). See U.S.C., Title 28, §399 [now 1653] (Amendments to show diverse citizenship) for a provision for "relation back."

Note to Subdivision (d). This is an adaptation of Equity Rule 34 (Supplemental Pleading).

Notes of Advisory Committee on Rules—1963 Amendment

Rule 15(d) is intended to give the court broad discretion in allowing a supplemental pleading. However, some cases, opposed by other cases and criticized by the commentators, have taken the rigid and formalistic view that where the original complaint fails to state a claim upon which relief can be granted, leave to serve a supplemental complaint must be denied. See Bonner v. Elizabeth Arden, Inc., 177 F.2d 703 (2d Cir. 1949); Bowles v. Senderowitz, 65 F.Supp. 548 (E.D.Pa.), rev'd on other grounds, 158 F.2d 435 (3d Cir. 1946), cert. denied, Senderowitz v. Fleming, 330 U.S. 848, 67 S.Ct. 1091, 91 L.Ed. 1292 (1947); cf. LaSalle Nat. Bank v. 222 East Chestnut St. Corp., 267 F.2d 247 (7th Cir.), cert. denied, 361 U.S. 836, 80 S.Ct. 88, 4 L.Ed.2d 77 (1959). But see Camilla Cotton Oil Co. v. Spencer Kellogg & Sons, 257 F.2d 162 (5th Cir. 1958); Genuth v. National Biscuit Co., 81 F.Supp. 213 (S.D.N.Y. 1948), app. dism., 177 F.2d 962 (2d Cir. 1949); 3 Moore's Federal Practice 15.01 [5] (Supp. 1960); 1A Barron & Holtzoff, Federal Practice & Procedure 820–21 (Wright ed. 1960). Thus plaintiffs have sometimes been needlessly remitted to the difficulties of commencing a new action even though events occurring after the commencement of the original action have made clear the right to relief.

Under the amendment the court has discretion to permit a supplemental pleading despite the fact that the original pleading is defective. As in other situations where a supplemental pleading is offered, the court is to determine in the light of the particular circumstances whether filing should be permitted, and if so, upon what terms. The amendment does not attempt to deal with such questions as the relation of the statute of limitations to supplemental pleadings, the operation of the doctrine of laches, or the availability of other defenses. All these questions are for decision in accordance with the principles applicable to supplemental pleadings generally. Cf. Blau v. Lamb, 191 F.Supp. 906 (S.D.N.Y. 1961); Lendonsol Amusement Corp. v. B. & Q. Assoc., Inc., 23 F.R.Serv. 15d. 3, Case 1 (D.Mass. 1957).

Notes of Advisory Committee on Rules—1966 Amendment

Rule 15(c) is amplified to state more clearly when an amendment of a pleading changing the party against whom a claim is asserted (including an amendment to correct a misnomer or misdescription of a defendant) shall "relate back" to the date of the original pleading.

The problem has arisen most acutely in certain actions by private parties against officers or agencies of the United States. Thus an individual denied social security benefits by the Secretary of Health, Education, and Welfare may secure review of the decision by bringing a civil action against that officer within sixty days. 42 U.S.C. §405(g) (Supp. III, 1962). In several recent cases the claimants instituted timely action but mistakenly named as defendant the United States, the Department of HEW, the "Federal Security Administration" (a nonexistent agency), and a Secretary who had retired from the office nineteen days before. Discovering their mistakes, the claimants moved to amend their complaints to name the proper defendant; by this time the statutory sixty-day period had expired. The motions were denied on the ground that the amendment "would amount to the commencement of a new proceeding and would not relate back in time so as to avoid the statutory provision * * * that suit be brought within sixty days * * *" Cohn v. Federal Security Adm.,

199 F.Supp. 884, 885 (W.D.N.Y. 1961); see also Cunningham v. United States, 199 F.Supp. 541 (W.D.Mo. 1958); Hall v. Department of HEW, 199 F.Supp. 833 (S.D.Tex. 1960); Sandridge v. Folsom, Secretary of HEW, 200 F.Supp. 25 (M.D.Tenn. 1959). [The Secretary of Health, Education, and Welfare has approved certain ameliorative regulations under 42 U.S.C. §405(g). See 29 Fed.Reg. 8209 (June 30, 1964); Jacoby, The Effect of Recent Changes in the Law of "Nonstatutory" Judicial Review, 53 Geo.L.J. 19, 42–43 (1964); see also Simmons v. United States Dept. HEW, 328 F.2d 86 (3d Cir. 1964).]

Analysis in terms of "new proceeding" is traceable to Davis v. L. L. Cohen & Co., 268 U.S. 638 (1925), and Mellon v. Arkansas Land & Lumber Co., 275 U.S. 460 (1928), but those cases antedate the adoption of the Rules which import different criteria for determining when an amendment is to "relate back". As lower courts have continued to rely on the Davis and Mellon cases despite the contrary intent of the Rules, clarification of Rule 15(c) is considered advisable.

Relation back is intimately connected with the policy of the statute of limitations. The policy of the statute limiting the time for suit against the Secretary of HEW would not have been offended by allowing relation back in the situations described above. For the government was put on notice of the claim within the stated period—in the particular instances, by means of the initial delivery of process to a responsible government official (see Rule 4(d)(4) and (5). In these circumstances, characterization of the amendment as a new proceeding is not responsive to the realty, but is merely question-begging; and to deny relation back is to defeat unjustly the claimant's opportunity to prove his case. See the full discussion by Byse, Suing the "Wrong" Defendant in Judicial Review of Federal Administrative Action: Proposals for Reform, 77 Harv.L.Rev. 40 (1963); see also Ill.Civ.P.Act §46(4).

Much the same question arises in other types of actions against the government (see Byse, supra, at 45 n. 15). In actions between private parties, the problem of relation back of amendments changing defendants has generally been better handled by the courts, but incorrect criteria have sometimes been applied, leading sporadically to doubtful results. See 1A Barron & Holtzoff, Federal Practice & Procedure §451 (Wright ed. 1960); 1 id. §186 (1960); 2 id. §543 (1961); 3 Moore's Federal Practice, par. 15.15 (Cum.Supp. 1962); Annot., Change in Party After Statute of Limitations Has Run, 8 A.L.R.2d 6 (1949). Rule 15(c) has been amplified to provide a general solution. An amendment changing the party against whom a claim is asserted relates back if the amendment satisfies the usual condition of Rule 15(c) of "arising out of the conduct * * * set forth * * * in the original pleading," and if, within the applicable limitations period, the party brought in by amendment, first, received such notice of the institution of the action—the notice need not be formal—that he would not be prejudiced in defending the action, and, second, knew or should have known that the action would have been brought against him initially had there not been a mistake concerning the identity of the proper party. Revised Rule 15(c) goes on to provide specifically in the government cases that the first and second requirements are satisfied when the government has been notified in the manner there described (see Rule 4(d)(4) and (5). As applied to the government cases, revised Rule 15(c) further advances the objectives of the 1961 amendment of Rule 25(d) (substitution of public officers).

The relation back of amendments changing plaintiffs is not expressly treated in revised Rule 15(c) since the problem is generally easier. Again the chief consideration of policy is that of the statute of limitations, and the attitude taken in revised Rule 15(c) toward change of defendants extends by analogy to amendments changing plaintiffs. Also relevant is the amendment of Rule 17(a) (real party in interest). To avoid forfeitures of just claims, revised Rule 17(a) would provide that no action shall be dismissed on the ground that it is not prosecuted in the name of the real party in interest until a reasonable time has been allowed for correction of the defect in the manner there stated.

Notes of Advisory Committee on Rules—1987 Amendment

The amendments are technical. No substantive change is intended.

Notes of Advisory Committee on Rules—1991 Amendment

The rule has been revised to prevent parties against whom claims are made from taking unjust advantage of otherwise inconsequential pleading errors to sustain a limitations defense.

Paragraph (c)(1). This provision is new. It is intended to make it clear that the rule does not apply to preclude any relation back that may be permitted under the applicable limitations law. Generally, the applicable limitations law will be state law. If federal jurisdiction is based on the citizenship of the parties, the primary reference is the law of the state in which the district court sits. Walker v. Armco Steel Corp., 446 U.S. 740 (1980). If federal jurisdiction is based on a federal question, the reference may be to the law of the state governing relations between the parties. E.g., Board of Regents v. Tomanio, 446 U.S. 478 (1980). In some circumstances, the controlling limitations law may be federal law. E.g., West v. Conrail, Inc., 107 S.Ct. 1538 (1987). Cf. Burlington Northern R. Co. v. Woods, 480 U.S. 1 (1987); Stewart Organization v. Ricoh, 108 S.Ct. 2239 (1988). Whatever may be the controlling body of limitations law, if that law affords a more forgiving principle of relation back than the one provided in this rule, it should be available to save the claim. Accord, Marshall v. Mulrenin, 508 F.2d 39 (1st cir. 1974). If Schiavone v. Fortune, 106 S.Ct. 2379 (1986) implies the contrary, this paragraph is intended to make a material change in the rule.

Paragraph (c)(3). This paragraph has been revised to change the result in Schiavone v. Fortune, supra, with respect to the problem of a misnamed defendant. An intended defendant who is notified of an action within the period allowed by Rule 4(m) for service of a summons and complaint may not under the revised rule defeat the action on account of a defect in the pleading with respect to the defendant's name, provided that the requirements of clauses (A) and (B) have been met. If the notice requirement is met within the Rule 4(m) period, a complaint may be amended at any time to correct a formal defect such as a misnomer or misidentification. On the basis of the text of the former rule, the Court reached a result in Schiavone v. Fortune that was inconsistent with the liberal pleading practices secured by Rule 8. See Bauer, Schiavone: An Un-Fortune-ate Illustration of the Supreme Court's Role as Interpreter of the Federal Rules of Civil Procedure, 63 NOTRE DAME L. REV. 720 (1988); Brussack, Outrageous Fortune: The Case for Amending Rule 15(c) Again, 61 S. CAL. L. REV. 671 (1988); Lewis, The Excessive History of Federal Rule 15(c) and Its Lessons for Civil Rules Revision, 86 MICH. L. REV. 1507 (1987).

In allowing a name-correcting amendment within the time allowed by Rule 4(m), this rule allows not only the 120 days specified in that rule, but also any additional time resulting from any extension ordered by the court pursuant to that rule, as may be granted, for example, if the defendant is a fugitive from service of the summons.

This revision, together with the revision of Rule 4(i) with respect to the failure of a plaintiff in an action against the United States to effect timely service on all the appropriate officials, is intended to produce results contrary to those reached in Gardner v. Gartman, 880 F.2d 797 (4th cir. 1989), Rys v. U.S. Postal Service, 886 F.2d 443 (1st cir. 1989), Martin's Food & Liquor, Inc. v. U.S. Dept. of Agriculture, 14 F.R.S.3d 86 (N.D. Ill. 1988). But cf. Montgomery v. United States Postal Service, 867 F.2d 900 (5th cir. 1989), Warren v. Department of the Army, 867 F.2d 1156 (8th cir. 1989); Miles v. Department of the Army, 881 F.2d 777 (9th cir. 1989), Barsten v. Department of the Interior, 896 F.2d 422 (9th cir. 1990); Brown v. Georgia Dept. of Revenue, 881 F.2d 1018 (11th cir. 1989).

Congressional Modification of Proposed 1991 Amendment

Section 11(a) of Pub. L. 102–198 [set out as a note under section 2074 of this title] provided that Rule 15(c)(3) of the Federal Rules of Civil Procedure as transmitted to Congress by the Supreme Court to become effective on Dec. 1, 1991, is amended. See 1991 Amendment note below.

Notes of Advisory Committee on Rules—1993 Amendment

The amendment conforms the cross reference to Rule 4 to the revision of that rule.

Committee Notes on Rules—2007 Amendment

The language of Rule 15 has been amended as part of the general restyling of the Civil Rules to make them more easily understood and to make style and terminology consistent throughout the rules. These changes are intended to be stylistic only.

Former Rule 15(c)(3)(A) called for notice of the "institution" of the action. Rule 15(c)(1)(C)(i) omits the reference to "institution" as potentially confusing. What counts is that the party to be brought in have notice of the existence of the action, whether or not the notice includes details as to its "institution."

Committee Notes on Rules—2009 Amendment

Rule 15(a)(1) is amended to make three changes in the time allowed to make one amendment as a matter of course.

Former Rule 15(a) addressed amendment of a pleading to which a responsive pleading is required by distinguishing between the means used to challenge the pleading. Serving a responsive pleading terminated the right to amend. Serving a motion attacking the pleading did not terminate the right to amend, because a motion is not a "pleading" as defined in Rule 7. The right to amend survived beyond decision of the motion unless the decision expressly cut off the right to amend.

The distinction drawn in former Rule 15(a) is changed in two ways. First, the right to amend once as a matter of course terminates 21 days after service of a motion under Rule 12(b), (e), or (f). This provision will force the pleader to consider carefully and promptly the wisdom of amending to meet the arguments in the motion. A responsive amendment may avoid the need to decide the motion or reduce the number of issues to be decided, and will expedite determination of issues that otherwise might be raised seriatim. It also should advance other pretrial proceedings.

Second, the right to amend once as a matter of course is no longer terminated by service of a responsive pleading. The responsive pleading may point out issues that the original pleader had not considered and persuade the pleader that amendment is wise. Just as amendment was permitted by former Rule 15(a) in response to a motion, so the amended rule permits one amendment as a matter of course in response to a responsive pleading. The right is subject to the same 21-day limit as the right to amend in response to a motion.

The 21-day periods to amend once as a matter of course after service of a responsive pleading or after service of a designated motion are not cumulative. If a responsive pleading is served after one of the designated motions is served, for example, there is no new 21-day period.

Finally, amended Rule 15(a)(1) extends from 20 to 21 days the period to amend a pleading to which no responsive pleading is allowed and omits the provision that cuts off the right if the action is on the trial calendar. Rule 40 no longer refers to a trial calendar, and many courts have abandoned formal trial calendars. It is more effective to rely on scheduling orders or other pretrial directions to establish time limits for amendment in the few situations that otherwise might allow one amendment as a matter of course at a time that would disrupt trial preparations. Leave to amend still can be sought under Rule 15(a)(2), or at and after trial under Rule 15(b).

Abrogation of Rule 13(f) establishes Rule 15 as the sole rule governing amendment of a pleading to add a counterclaim.

Amended Rule 15(a)(3) extends from 10 to 14 days the period to respond to an amended pleading.

Amendment by Public Law

1991—Subd. (c)(3). Pub. L. 102–198 substituted "Rule 4(j)" for "Rule 4(m)".

Rule 16. Pretrial Conferences; Scheduling; Management

(a) Purposes of a Pretrial Conference. In any action, the court may order the attorneys and any unrepresented parties to appear for one or more pretrial conferences for such purposes as:

(1) expediting disposition of the action;

(2) establishing early and continuing control so that the case will not be protracted because of lack of management;

(3) discouraging wasteful pretrial activities;

(4) improving the quality of the trial through more thorough preparation; and

(5) facilitating settlement.

(b) Scheduling.

(1) Scheduling Order. Except in categories of actions exempted by local rule, the district judge—or a magistrate judge when authorized by local rule—must issue a scheduling order:

(A) after receiving the parties' report under Rule 26(f); or

(B) after consulting with the parties' attorneys and any unrepresented parties at a scheduling conference.

(2) Time to Issue. The judge must issue the scheduling order as soon as practicable, but unless the judge finds good cause for delay, the judge must issue it within the earlier of 90 days after any defendant has been served with the complaint or 60 days after any defendant has appeared.

(3) Contents of the Order.

(A) Required Contents. The scheduling order must limit the time to join other parties, amend the pleadings, complete discovery, and file motions.

(B) Permitted Contents. The scheduling order may:

(i) modify the timing of disclosures under Rules 26(a) and 26(e)(1);
(ii) modify the extent of discovery;
(iii) provide for disclosure, discovery, or preservation of electronically stored information;
(iv) include any agreements the parties reach for asserting claims of privilege or of protection as trial-preparation material after information is produced, including agreements reached under Federal Rule of Evidence 502;
(v) direct that before moving for an order relating to discovery, the movant must request a conference with the court;
(vi) set dates for pretrial conferences and for trial; and
(vii) include other appropriate matters.

(4) Modifying a Schedule. A schedule may be modified only for good cause and with the judge's consent.

(c) Attendance and Matters for Consideration at a Pretrial Conference.

(1) Attendance. A represented party must authorize at least one of its attorneys to make stipulations and admissions about all matters that can reasonably be anticipated for discussion at a pretrial conference. If appropriate, the court may require that a party or its representative be present or reasonably available by other means to consider possible settlement.

(2) Matters for Consideration. At any pretrial conference, the court may consider and take appropriate action on the following matters:

(A) formulating and simplifying the issues, and eliminating frivolous claims or defenses;
(B) amending the pleadings if necessary or desirable;
(C) obtaining admissions and stipulations about facts and documents to avoid unnecessary proof, and ruling in advance on the admissibility of evidence;
(D) avoiding unnecessary proof and cumulative evidence, and limiting the use of testimony under Federal Rule of Evidence 702;
(E) determining the appropriateness and timing of summary adjudication under Rule 56;
(F) controlling and scheduling discovery, including orders affecting disclosures and discovery under Rule 26 and Rules 29 through 37;
(G) identifying witnesses and documents, scheduling the filing and exchange of any pretrial briefs, and setting dates for further conferences and for trial;
(H) referring matters to a magistrate judge or a master;
(I) settling the case and using special procedures to assist in resolving the dispute when authorized by statute or local rule;
(J) determining the form and content of the pretrial order;
(K) disposing of pending motions;
(L) adopting special procedures for managing potentially difficult or protracted actions that may involve complex issues, multiple parties, difficult legal questions, or unusual proof problems;
(M) ordering a separate trial under Rule 42(b) of a claim, counterclaim, crossclaim, third-party claim, or particular issue;
(N) ordering the presentation of evidence early in the trial on a manageable issue that might, on the evidence, be the basis for a judgment as a matter of law under Rule 50(a) or a judgment on partial findings under Rule 52(c);
(O) establishing a reasonable limit on the time allowed to present evidence; and
(P) facilitating in other ways the just, speedy, and inexpensive disposition of the action.

(d) Pretrial Orders. After any conference under this rule, the court should issue an order reciting the action taken. This order controls the course of the action unless the court modifies it.

(e) Final Pretrial Conference and Orders. The court may hold a final pretrial conference to formulate a trial plan, including a plan to facilitate the admission of evidence. The conference must be held as close to the start of trial as is reasonable, and must be attended by at least one attorney who will conduct the trial for each party and by any unrepresented party. The court may modify the order issued after a final pretrial conference only to prevent manifest injustice.

(f) Sanctions.

(1) In General. On motion or on its own, the court may issue any just orders, including those authorized by Rule 37(b)(2)(A)(ii)–(vii), if a party or its attorney:

(A) fails to appear at a scheduling or other pretrial conference;
(B) is substantially unprepared to participate—or does not participate in good faith—in the conference; or
(C) fails to obey a scheduling or other pretrial order.

(2) Imposing Fees and Costs. Instead of or in addition to any other sanction, the court must order the party, its attorney, or both to pay the reasonable expenses—including attorney's fees—incurred because of any noncompliance with this rule, unless the noncompliance was substantially justified or other circumstances make an award of expenses unjust.

(As amended Apr. 28, 1983, eff. Aug. 1, 1983; Mar. 2, 1987, eff. Aug. 1, 1987; Apr. 22, 1993, eff. Dec. 1, 1993; Apr. 12, 2006, eff. Dec. 1, 2006; Apr. 30, 2007, eff. Dec. 1, 2007; Apr. 29, 2015, eff. Dec. 1, 2015.)

Notes of Advisory Committee on Rules—1937

1. Similar rules of pre-trial procedure are now in force in Boston, Cleveland, Detroit, and Los Angeles, and a rule substantially like this one has been proposed for the urban centers of New York state. For a discussion of the successful operation of pre-trial procedure in relieving the congested condition of trial calendars of the courts in such cities and for the proposed New York plan, see A Proposal for Minimizing Calendar Delay in Jury Cases (Dec. 1936—published by The New York Law Society); Pre-Trial Procedure and Administration, Third Annual Report of the Judicial Council of the State of New York (1937), pp. 207–243; Report of the Commission on the Administration of Justice in New York State (1934), pp. (288)–(290). See also Pre-Trial Procedure in the Wayne Circuit Court, Detroit, Michigan, Sixth Annual Report of

the Judicial Council of Michigan (1936), pp. 63–75; and Sunderland, The Theory and Practice of Pre-Trial Procedure (Dec. 1937) 36 Mich.L.Rev. 215–226, 21 J.Am.Jud.Soc. 125. Compare the English procedure known as the "summons for directions," English Rules Under the Judicature Act (The Annual Practice, 1937) O. 38a; and a similar procedure in New Jersey, N.J.Comp.Stat. (2 Cum.Supp. 1911–1924); N.J. Supreme Court Rules, 2 N.J.Misc.Rep. (1924) 1230, Rules 94, 92, 93, 95 (the last three as amended 1933, 11 N.J.Misc.Rep. (1933) 955).

2. Compare the similar procedure under Rule 56(d) (Summary Judgment—Case Not Fully Adjudicated on Motion). Rule 12(g) (Consolidation of Motions), by requiring to some extent the consolidation of motions dealing with matters preliminary to trial, is a step in the same direction. In connection with clause (5) of this rule, see Rules 53(b) (Masters; Reference) and 53(e)(3) (Master's Report; In Jury Actions).

Notes of Advisory Committee on Rules—1983 Amendment

Introduction

Rule 16 has not been amended since the Federal Rules were promulgated in 1938. In many respects, the rule has been a success. For example, there is evidence that pretrial conferences may improve the quality of justice rendered in the federal courts by sharpening the preparation and presentation of cases, tending to eliminate trial surprise, and improving, as well as facilitating, the settlement process. See 6 Wright & Miller, Federal Practice and Procedure: Civil §1522 (1971). However, in other respects particularly with regard to case management, the rule has not always been as helpful as it might have been. Thus there has been a widespread feeling that amendment is necessary to encourage pretrial management that meets the needs of modern litigation. See Report of the National Commission for the Review of Antitrust Laws and Procedures (1979).

Major criticism of Rule 16 has centered on the fact that its application can result in over-regulation of some cases and under-regulation of others. In simple, run-of-the-mill cases, attorneys have found pretrial requirements burdensome. It is claimed that over-administration leads to a series of mini-trials that result in a waste of an attorney's time and needless expense to a client. Pollack, Pretrial Procedures More Effectively Handled, 65 F.R.D. 475 (1974). This is especially likely to be true when pretrial proceedings occur long before trial. At the other end of the spectrum, the discretionary character of Rule 16 and its orientation toward a single conference late in the pretrial process has led to under-administration of complex or protracted cases. Without judicial guidance beginning shortly after institution, these cases often become mired in discovery.

Four sources of criticism of pretrial have been identified. First, conferences often are seen as a mere exchange of legalistic contentions without any real analysis of the particular case. Second, the result frequently is nothing but a formal agreement on minutiae. Third, the conferences are seen as unnecessary and time-consuming in cases that will be settled before trial. Fourth, the meetings can be ceremonial and ritualistic, having little effect on the trial and being of minimal value, particularly when the attorneys attending the sessions are not the ones who will try the case or lack authority to enter into binding stipulations. See generally McCargo v. Hedrick, 545 F.2d 393 (4th Cir. 1976); Pollack, Pretrial Procedures More Effectively Handled, 65 F.R.D. 475 (1974); Rosenberg, The Pretrial Conference and Effective Justice 45 (1964).

There also have been difficulties with the pretrial orders that issue following Rule 16 conferences. When an order is entered far in advance of trial, some issues may not be properly formulated. Counsel naturally are cautious and often try to preserve as many options as possible. If the judge who tries the case did not conduct the conference, he could find it difficult to determine exactly what was agreed to at the conference. But any insistence on a detailed order may be too burdensome, depending on the nature or posture of the case.

Given the significant changes in federal civil litigation since 1938 that are not reflected in Rule 16, it has been extensively rewritten and expanded to meet the challenges of modern litigation. Empirical studies reveal that when a trial judge intervenes personally at an early stage to assume judicial control over a case and to schedule dates for completion by the parties of the principal pretrial steps, the case is disposed of by settlement or trial more efficiently and with less cost and delay than when the parties are left to their own devices. Flanders, Case Management and Court Management in United States District Courts 17, Federal Judicial Center (1977). Thus, the rule mandates a pretrial scheduling order. However, although scheduling and pretrial conferences are encouraged in appropriate cases, they are not mandated.

Discussion

Subdivision (a); Pretrial Conferences; Objectives. The amended rule makes scheduling and case management an express goal of pretrial procedure. This is done in Rule 16(a) by shifting the emphasis away from a conference focused solely on the trial and toward a process of judicial management that embraces the entire pretrial phase, especially motions and discovery. In addition, the amendment explicitly recognizes some of the objectives of pretrial conferences and the powers that many courts already have assumed. Rule 16 thus will be a more accurate reflection of actual practice.

Subdivision (b); Scheduling and Planning. The most significant change in Rule 16 is the mandatory scheduling order described in Rule 16(b), which is based in part on Wisconsin Civil Procedure Rule 802.10. The idea of scheduling orders is not new. It has been used by many federal courts. See, e.g., Southern District of Indiana, Local Rule 19.

Although a mandatory scheduling order encourages the court to become involved in case management early in the litigation, it represents a degree of judicial involvement that is not warranted in many cases. Thus, subdivision (b) permits each district court to promulgate a local rule under Rule 83 exempting certain categories of cases in which the burdens of scheduling orders exceed the administrative efficiencies that would be gained. See Eastern District of Virginia, Local Rule 12(1). Logical candidates for this treatment include social security disability matters, habeas corpus petitions, forfeitures, and reviews of certain administrative actions.

A scheduling conference may be requested either by the judge, a magistrate when authorized by district court rule, or a party within 120 days after the summons and complaint are filed. If a scheduling conference is not arranged within that time and the case is not exempted by local rule, a scheduling order must be issued under Rule 16(b), after some communication with the parties, which may be by telephone or mail rather than in person. The use of the term "judge" in subdivision (b) reflects the Advisory Committee's judgment that is it preferable that this task should be handled by a district judge rather than a magistrate, except when the magistrate is acting under 28 U.S.C. §636(c). While personal supervision by the trial judge is preferred, the rule, in recognition of the impracticality or difficulty of complying with such a requirement in some districts, authorizes a district by local rule to delegate the duties to a magistrate. In order to formulate a practicable scheduling order, the judge, or a magistrate when authorized by district court rule, and attorneys are required to develop a timetable for the matters listed in Rule 16(b)(1)–(3). As indicated in Rule 16(b)(4)–(5), the order may also deal with a wide range of other matters. The rule is phrased permissively as to clauses (4) and (5), however, because scheduling these items at an early point may not be feasible or appropriate. Even though subdivision (b) relates only to scheduling, there is no reason why some of the procedural matters listed in Rule 16(c) cannot be addressed at the same time, at least when a scheduling conference is held.

Item (1) assures that at some point both the parties and the pleadings will be fixed, by setting a time within which joinder of parties shall be completed and the pleadings amended.

Item (2) requires setting time limits for interposing various motions that otherwise might be used as stalling techniques.

Item (3) deals with the problem of procrastination and delay by attorneys in a context in which scheduling is especially important—discovery. Scheduling the completion of discovery can serve some of the same functions as the conference described in Rule 26(f).

Item (4) refers to setting dates for conferences and for trial. Scheduling multiple pretrial conferences may well be desirable if the case is complex and the court believes that a more elaborate pretrial structure, such as that described in the Manual for Complex Litigation, should be employed. On the other hand, only one pretrial conference may be necessary in an uncomplicated case.

As long as the case is not exempted by local rule, the court must issue a written scheduling order even if no scheduling conference is called. The order, like pretrial orders under the former rule and those under new Rule 16(c), normally will "control the subsequent course of the action." See Rule 16(e). After consultation with the attorneys for the parties and any unrepresented parties—a formal motion is not necessary—the court may modify the schedule on a showing of good cause if it cannot reasonably be met despite the diligence of the party seeking the extension. Since the scheduling order is entered early in the litigation, this standard seems more appropriate than a "manifest injustice" or "substantial hardship" test. Otherwise, a fear that extensions will not be granted may encourage counsel to request the longest possible periods for completing pleading, joinder, and discovery. Moreover, changes in the court's calendar sometimes will oblige the judge or magistrate when authorized by district court rule to modify the scheduling order.

The district courts undoubtedly will develop several prototype scheduling orders for different types of cases. In addition, when no formal conference is held, the court may obtain scheduling information by telephone, mail, or otherwise. In many instances this will result in a scheduling order better suited to the individual case than a standard order, without taking the time that would be required by a formal conference.

Rule 16(b) assures that the judge will take some early control over the litigation, even when its character does not warrant holding a scheduling conference. Despite the fact that the process of preparing a scheduling order does not always bring the attorneys and judge together, the fixing of time limits serves to stimulate litigants to narrow the areas of inquiry and advocacy to those they believe are truly relevant and material. Time limits not only compress the amount of time for litigation, they should also reduce the amount of resources invested in litigation. Litigants are forced to establish discovery priorities and thus to do the most important work first. Report of the National Commission for the Review of Antitrust Laws and Procedures 28 (1979).

Thus, except in exempted cases, the judge or a magistrate when authorized by district court rule will have taken some action in every case within 120 days after the complaint is filed that notifies the attorneys that the case will be moving toward trial. Subdivision (b) is reenforced by subdivision (f), which makes it clear that the sanctions for violating a scheduling order are the same as those for violating a pretrial order.

Subdivision (c); Subjects to be Discussed at Pretrial Conferences. This subdivision expands upon the list of things that may be discussed at a pretrial conference that appeared in original Rule 16. The intention is to encourage better planning and management of litigation. Increased judicial control during the pretrial process accelerates the processing and termination of cases. Flanders, Case Management and Court Management in United States District Courts, Federal Judicial Center (1977). See also Report of the National Commission for the Review of Antitrust Laws and Procedures (1979).

The reference in Rule 16(c)(1) to "formulation" is intended to clarify and confirm the court's power to identify the litigable issues. It has been added in the hope of promoting efficiency and conserving judicial resources by identifying the real issues prior to trial, thereby saving time and expense for everyone. See generally Meadow Gold Prods. Co. v. Wright, 278 F.2d 867 (D.C. Cir. 1960). The notion is emphasized by expressly authorizing the elimination of frivolous claims or defenses at a pretrial conference. There is no reason to require that this await a formal motion for summary judgment. Nor is there any reason for the court to wait for the parties to initiate the process called for in Rule 16(c)(1).

The timing of any attempt at issue formulation is a matter of judicial discretion. In relatively simple cases it may not be necessary or may take the form of a stipulation between counsel or a request by the court that counsel work together to draft a proposed order.

Counsel bear a substantial responsibility for assisting the court in identifying the factual issues worthy of trial. If counsel fail to identify an issue for the court, the right to have the issue tried is waived. Although an order specifying the issues is intended to be binding, it may be amended at trial to avoid manifest injustice. See Rule 16(e). However, the rule's effectiveness depends on the court employing its discretion sparingly.

Clause (6) acknowledges the widespread availability and use of magistrates. The corresponding provision in the original rule referred only to masters and limited the function of the reference to the making of "findings to be used as evidence" in a case to be tried to a jury. The new text is not limited and broadens the potential use of a magistrate to that permitted by the Magistrate's Act.

Clause (7) explicitly recognizes that it has become commonplace to discuss settlement at pretrial conferences. Since it obviously eases crowded court dockets and results in savings to the litigants and the judicial system, settlement should be facilitated at as early a stage of the litigation as possible. Although it is not the purpose of Rule 16(b)(7) to impose settlement negotiations on unwilling litigants, it is believed that providing a neutral forum for discussing the subject might foster it. See Moore's Federal Practice 16.17; 6 Wright & Miller, Federal Practice and Procedure: Civil §1522 (1971). For instance, a judge to whom a case has been assigned may arrange, on his own motion or a at a party's request, to have settlement conferences handled by another member of the court or by a magistrate. The rule does not make settlement conferences mandatory because they would be a waste of time in many cases. See Flanders, Case Management and Court Management in the United States District Courts, 39, Federal Judicial Center (1977). Requests for a conference from a party indicating a willingness to talk settlement normally should be honored, unless thought to be frivolous or dilatory.

A settlement conference is appropriate at any time. It may be held in conjunction with a pretrial or discovery conference, although various objectives of pretrial management, such as moving the case toward trial, may not always be compatible with settlement negotiations, and thus a separate settlement conference may be desirable. See 6 Wright & Miller, Federal Practice and Procedure: Civil §1522, at p. 751 (1971).

In addition to settlement, Rule 16(c)(7) refers to exploring the use of procedures other than litigation to resolve the dispute. This includes urging the litigants to employ adjudicatory techniques outside the courthouse. See, for example, the experiment described in Green, Marks & Olson, Settling Large Case Litigation: An Alternative Approach, 11 Loyola of L.A. L.Rev. 493 (1978).

Rule 16(c)(10) authorizes the use of special pretrial procedures to expedite the adjudication of potentially difficult or protracted cases. Some district courts obviously have done so for many years. See Rubin, The Managed Calendar: Some Pragmatic Suggestions About Achieving the Just, Speedy and Inexpensive Determination of Civil Cases in Federal Courts, 4 Just. Sys. J. 135 (1976). Clause 10 provides an explicit authorization for such procedures and encourages their use. No particular techniques have been described; the Committee felt that flexibility and experience are the keys to efficient management of complex cases. Extensive guidance is offered in such documents as the Manual for Complex Litigation.

The rule simply identifies characteristics that make a case a strong candidate for special treatment. The four mentioned are illustrative, not exhaustive, and overlap to some degree. But experience has shown that one or more of them will be present in every protracted or difficult case and it seems desirable to set them out. See Kendig, Procedures for Management of Non-Routine Cases, 3 Hofstra L.Rev. 701 (1975).

The last sentence of subdivision (c) is new. See Wisconsin Civil Procedure Rule 802.11(2). It has been added to meet one of the criticisms of the present practice described earlier and insure proper preconference preparation so that the meeting is more than a ceremonial or ritualistic event. The reference to "authority" is not intended to insist upon the ability to settle the litigation. Nor should the rule be read to encourage the judge conducting the conference to compel attorneys to enter into stipulations or to make admissions that they consider to be unreasonable, that touch on matters that could not normally have been anticipated to arise at the conference, or on subjects of a dimension that normally require prior consultation with and approval from the client.

Subdivision (d); Final Pretrial Conference. This provision has been added to make it clear that the time between any final pretrial conference (which in a simple case may be the only pretrial conference) and trail should be as short as possible to be certain that the litigants make substantial progress with the case and avoid the inefficiency of having that preparation repeated when there is a delay between the last pretrial conference and trial. An optimum time of 10 days to two weeks has been suggested by one federal judge. Rubin, The Managed Calendar: Some Pragmatic Suggestions About Achieving the Just, Speedy and Inexpensive Determination of Civil Cases in Federal Courts, 4 Just. Sys. J. 135, 141 (1976). The Committee, however, concluded that it would be inappropriate to fix a precise time in the rule, given the numerous variables that could bear on the matter. Thus the timing has been left to the court's discretion.

At least one of the attorneys who will conduct the trial for each party must be present at the final pretrial conference. At this late date there should be no doubt as to which attorney or attorneys this will be. Since the agreements and stipulations made at this final conference will control the trial, the presence of lawyers who will be involved in it is especially useful to assist the judge in structuring the case, and to lead to a more effective trial.

Subdivision (e); Pretrial Orders. Rule 16(e) does not substantially change the portion of the original rule dealing with pretrial orders. The purpose of an order is to guide the course of the litigation and the language of the original rule making that clear has been retained. No compelling reason has been found for major revision, especially since this portion of the rule has been interpreted and clarified by over forty years of judicial decisions with comparatively little difficulty. See 6 Wright & Miller, Federal Practice and Procedure: Civil §§1521–30 (1971). Changes in language therefore have been kept to a minimum to avoid confusion.

Since the amended rule encourages more extensive pretrial management than did the original, two or more conferences may be held in many cases. The language of Rule 16(e) recognizes this possibility and the corresponding need to issue more than one pretrial order in a single case.

Once formulated, pretrial orders should not be changed lightly; but total inflexibility is undesirable. See, e.g., Clark v. Pennsylvania R.R. Co., 328 F.2d 591 (2d Cir. 1964). The exact words used to describe the standard for amending the pretrial order probably are less important than the meaning given them in practice. By not imposing any limitation on the ability to modify a pretrial order, the rule reflects the reality that in any process of continuous management what is done at one conference may have to be altered at the next. In the case of the final pretrial order, however, a more stringent standard is called for and the words "to prevent manifest injustice," which appeared in the original rule, have been retained. They have the virtue of familiarity and adequately describe the restraint the trial judge should exercise.

Many local rules make the plaintiff's attorney responsible for drafting a proposed pretrial order, either before or after the conference. Others allow the court to appoint any of the attorneys to perform the task, and others leave it to the court. See Note, Pretrial Conference: A Critical Examination of Local Rules Adopted by Federal District Courts, 64 Va.L.Rev. 467 (1978). Rule 16 has never addressed this matter. Since there is no consensus about which method of drafting the order works best and there is no reason to believe that nationwide uniformity is needed, the rule has been left silent on the point. See Handbook for Effective Pretrial Procedure, 37 F.R.D. 225 (1964).

Subdivision (f); Sanctions. Original Rule 16 did not mention the sanctions that might be imposed for failing to comply with the rule. However, courts have not hesitated to enforce it by appropriate measures. See, e.g., Link v. Wabash R. Co., 370 U.S. 628 (1962) (district court's dismissal under Rule 41(b) after plaintiff's attorney failed to appear at a pretrial conference upheld); Admiral Theatre Corp. v. Douglas Theatre, 585 F.2d 877 (8th Cir. 1978) (district court has discretion to exclude exhibits or refuse to permit the testimony of a witness not listed prior to trial in contravention of its pretrial order).

To reflect that existing practice, and to obviate dependence upon Rule 41(b) or the court's inherent power to regulate litigation, cf. Societe Internationale Pour Participations Industrielles et Commerciales, S.A. v. Rogers, 357 U.S. 197 (1958), Rule 16(f) expressly provides for imposing sanctions on disobedient or recalcitrant parties, their attorneys, or both in four types of situations. Rodes, Ripple & Mooney, Sanctions Imposable for Violations of the Federal Rules of Civil Procedure 65–67, 80–84, Federal Judicial Center (1981). Furthermore, explicit reference to sanctions reenforces the rule's intention to encourage forceful judicial management.

Rule 16(f) incorporates portions of Rule 37(b)(2), which prescribes sanctions for failing to make discovery. This should facilitate application of Rule 16(f), since courts and lawyers already are familiar with the Rule 37 standards. Among the sanctions authorized by the new subdivision are: preclusion order, striking a pleading, staying the proceeding, default judgment, contempt, and charging a party, his attorney, or both with the expenses, including attorney's fees, caused by noncompliance. The contempt sanction, however, is only available for a violation of a court order. The references in Rule 16(f) are not exhaustive.

As is true under Rule 37(b)(2), the imposition of sanctions may be sought by either the court or a party. In addition, the court has discretion to impose whichever sanction it feels is appropriate under the circumstances. Its action is reviewable under the abuse-of-discretion standard. See National Hockey League v. Metropolitan Hockey Club, Inc., 427 U.S. 639 (1976).

Notes of Advisory Committee on Rules—1987 Amendment

The amendments are technical. No substantive change is intended.

Notes of Advisory Committee on Rules—1993 Amendment

Subdivision (b). One purpose of this amendment is to provide a more appropriate deadline for the initial scheduling order required by the rule. The former rule directed that the order be entered within 120 days from the filing of the complaint. This requirement has created problems because Rule 4(m) allows 120 days for service and ordinarily at least one defendant should be available to participate in the process of formulating the scheduling order. The revision provides that the order is to be entered within 90 days after the date a defendant first appears (whether by answer or by a motion under Rule 12) or, if earlier (as may occur in some actions against the United States or if service is waived under Rule 4), within 120 days after service of the complaint on a defendant. The longer time provided by the revision is not intended to encourage unnecessary delays in entering the scheduling order. Indeed, in most cases the order can and should be entered at a much earlier date. Rather, the additional time is intended to alleviate problems in multi-defendant cases and should ordinarily be adequate to enable participation by all defendants initially named in the action.

In many cases the scheduling order can and should be entered before this deadline. However, when setting a scheduling conference, the court should take into account the effect this setting will have in establishing deadlines for the parties to meet under revised Rule 26(f) and to exchange information under revised Rule 26(a)(1). While the parties are expected to stipulate to additional time for making their disclosures when warranted by the circumstances, a scheduling conference held before defendants have had time to learn much about the case may result in diminishing the value of the Rule 26(f) meeting, the parties' proposed discovery plan, and indeed the conference itself.

New paragraph (4) has been added to highlight that it will frequently be desirable for the scheduling order to include provisions relating to the timing of disclosures under Rule 26(a). While the initial disclosures required by Rule 26(a)(1) will ordinarily have been made before entry of the scheduling order, the timing and sequence for disclosure of expert testimony and of the witnesses and exhibits to be used at trial should be tailored to the circumstances of the case and is a matter that should be considered at the initial scheduling conference. Similarly, the scheduling order might contain provisions modifying the extent of discovery (e.g., number and length of depositions) otherwise permitted under these rules or by a local rule.

The report from the attorneys concerning their meeting and proposed discovery plan, as required by revised Rule 26(f), should be submitted to the court before the scheduling order is entered. Their proposals, particularly regarding matters on which they agree, should be of substantial value to the court in setting the timing and limitations on discovery and should reduce the time of the court needed to conduct a meaningful conference under Rule 16(b). As under the prior rule, while a scheduling order is mandated, a scheduling conference is not. However, in view of the benefits to be derived from the litigants and a judicial officer meeting in person, a Rule 16(b) conference should, to the extent practicable, be held in all cases that will involve discovery.

This subdivision, as well as subdivision (c)(8), also is revised to reflect the new title of United States Magistrate Judges pursuant to the Judicial Improvements Act of 1990.

Subdivision (c). The primary purposes of the changes in subdivision (c) are to call attention to the opportunities for structuring of trial under Rules 42, 50, and 52 and to eliminate questions that have occasionally been raised regarding the authority of the court to make appropriate orders designed either to facilitate settlement or to provide for an efficient and economical trial. The prefatory language of this subdivision is revised to clarify the court's power to enter appropriate orders at a conference notwithstanding the objection of a party. Of course settlement is dependent upon agreement by the parties and, indeed, a conference is most effective and productive when the parties participate in a spirit of cooperation and mindful of their responsibilities under Rule 1.

Paragraph (4) is revised to clarify that in advance of trial the court may address the need for, and possible limitations on, the use of expert testimony under Rule 702 of the Federal Rules of Evidence. Even when proposed expert testimony might be admissible under the standards of Rules 403 and 702 of the evidence rules, the court may preclude or limit such testimony if the cost to the litigants—which may include the cost to adversaries of securing testimony on the same subjects by other experts—would be unduly expensive given the needs of the case and the other evidence available at trial.

Paragraph (5) is added (and the remaining paragraphs renumbered) in recognition that use of Rule 56 to avoid or reduce the scope of trial is a topic that can, and often should, be considered at a pretrial conference. Renumbered paragraph (11) enables the court to rule on pending motions for summary adjudication that are ripe for decision at the time of the conference. Often, however, the potential use of Rule 56 is a matter that arises from discussions during a conference. The court may then call for motions to be filed.

Paragraph (6) is added to emphasize that a major objective of pretrial conferences should be to consider appropriate controls on the extent and timing of discovery. In many cases the court should also specify the times and sequence for disclosure of written reports from experts under revised Rule 26(a)(2)(B) and perhaps direct changes in the types of experts from whom written reports are required. Consideration should also be given to possible changes in the timing or form of the disclosure of trial witnesses and documents under Rule 26(a)(3).

Paragraph (9) is revised to describe more accurately the various procedures that, in addition to traditional settlement conferences, may be helpful in settling litigation. Even if a case cannot immediately be settled, the judge and attorneys can explore possible use of alternative procedures such as mini-trials, summary jury trials, mediation, neutral evaluation, and nonbinding arbitration that can lead to consensual resolution of the dispute without a full trial on the merits. The rule acknowledges the presence of statutes and local rules or plans that may authorize use of some of these procedures even when not agreed to by the parties. See 28 U.S.C. §§473(a)(6), 473(b)(4), 651–58; Section 104(b)(2), Pub. L. 101–650. The rule does not attempt to resolve questions as to the extent a court would be authorized to require such proceedings as an exercise of its inherent powers.

The amendment of paragraph (9) should be read in conjunction with the sentence added to the end of subdivision (c), authorizing the court to direct that, in appropriate cases, a responsible representative of the parties be present or available by telephone during a conference in order to discuss possible settlement of the case. The sentence refers to participation by a party or its representative. Whether this would be the individual party, an officer of a corporate party, a representative from an insurance carrier, or someone else would depend on the circumstances. Particularly in litigation in which governmental agencies or large amounts of money are involved, there may be no one with on-the-spot settlement authority, and the most that should be expected is access to a person who would have a major role in submitting a recommendation to the body or board with ultimate decision-making responsibility. The selection of the appropriate representative should ordinarily be left to the party and its counsel. Finally, it should be noted that the unwillingness of a party to be available, even by telephone, for a settlement conference may be a clear signal that the time and expense involved in pursuing settlement is likely to be unproductive and that personal participation by the parties should not be required.

The explicit authorization in the rule to require personal participation in the manner stated is not intended to limit the reasonable exercise of the court's inherent powers, e.g., G. Heileman Brewing Co. v. Joseph Oat Corp., 871 F.2d 648 (7th Cir. 1989), or its power to require party participation under the Civil Justice Reform Act of 1990. See 28 U.S.C. §473(b)(5) (civil justice expense and delay reduction plans adopted by district courts may include requirement that representatives "with authority to bind [parties] in settlement discussions" be available during settlement conferences).

New paragraphs (13) and (14) are added to call attention to the opportunities for structuring of trial under Rule 42 and under revised Rules 50 and 52.

Paragraph (15) is also new. It supplements the power of the court to limit the extent of evidence under Rules 403 and 611(a) of the Federal Rules of Evidence, which typically would be invoked as a result of developments during trial. Limits on the length of trial established at a conference in advance of trial can provide the parties with a better opportunity to determine priorities and exercise selectivity in presenting evidence than when limits are imposed during trial. Any such limits must be reasonable under the circumstances, and ordinarily the court should impose them only after receiving appropriate submissions from the parties outlining the nature of the testimony expected to be presented through various witnesses, and the expected duration of direct and cross-examination.

Committee Notes on Rules—2006 Amendment

The amendment to Rule 16(b) is designed to alert the court to the possible need to address the handling of discovery of electronically stored information early in the litigation if such discovery is expected to occur. Rule 26(f) is amended to direct the parties to discuss discovery of electronically stored information if such discovery is contemplated in the action. Form 35 is amended to call for a report to the court about the results of this discussion. In many instances, the court's involvement early in the litigation will help avoid difficulties that might otherwise arise.

Rule 16(b) is also amended to include among the topics that may be addressed in the scheduling order any agreements that the parties reach to facilitate discovery by minimizing the risk of waiver of privilege or work-product protection. Rule 26(f) is amended to add to the discovery plan the parties' proposal for the court to enter a case-management or other order adopting such an agreement. The parties may agree to various arrangements. For example, they may agree to initial provision of requested materials without waiver of privilege or protection to enable the party seeking production to designate the materials desired or protection for actual production, with the privilege review of only those materials to follow. Alternatively, they may agree that if privileged or protected information is inadvertently produced, the producing party may by timely notice assert the privilege or protection and obtain return of the materials without waiver. Other arrangements are possible. In most circumstances, a party who receives information under such an arrangement cannot assert that production of the information waived a claim of privilege or of protection as trial-preparation material.

An order that includes the parties' agreement may be helpful in avoiding delay and excessive cost in discovery. See Manual for Complex Litigation (4th) §11.446. Rule 16(b)(6) recognizes the propriety of including such agreements in the court's order. The rule does not provide the court with authority to enter such a case-management or other order without party agreement, or limit the court's authority to act on motion.

Changes Made After Publication and Comment. This recommendation is of a modified version of the proposal as published. Subdivision (b)(6) was modified to eliminate the references to "adopting" agreements for "protection against waiving" privilege. It was feared that these words might seem to promise greater protection than can be assured. In keeping with changes to Rule 26(b)(5)(B), subdivision (b)(6) was expanded to include agreements for asserting claims of protection as trial-preparation materials. The Committee Note was revised to reflect the changes in the rule text.

The proposed changes from the published rule are set out below. [Omitted]

Committee Notes on Rules—2007 Amendment

The language of Rule 16 has been amended as part of the general restyling of the Civil Rules to make them more easily understood and to make style and terminology consistent throughout the rules. These changes are intended to be stylistic only.

When a party or its representative is not present, it is enough to be reasonably available by any suitable means, whether telephone or other communication device.

Changes Made After Publication and Comment. See Note to Rule 1, supra.

Committee Notes on Rules—2015 Amendment

The provision for consulting at a scheduling conference by "telephone, mail, or other means" is deleted. A scheduling conference is more effective if the court and parties engage in direct simultaneous communication. The conference may be held in person, by telephone, or by more sophisticated electronic means.

The time to issue the scheduling order is reduced to the earlier of 90 days (not 120 days) after any defendant has been served, or 60 days (not 90 days) after any defendant has appeared. This change, together with the shortened time for making service under Rule 4(m), will reduce delay at the beginning of litigation. At the same time, a new provision recognizes that the court may find good cause to extend the time to issue the scheduling order. In some cases it may be that the parties cannot prepare adequately for a meaningful Rule 26(f) conference and then a scheduling conference in the time allowed. Litigation involving complex issues, multiple parties, and large organizations, public or private, may be more likely to need extra time to establish meaningful collaboration between counsel and the people who can supply the information needed to participate in a useful way. Because the time for the Rule 26(f) conference is geared to the time for the scheduling conference or order, an order extending the time for the scheduling conference will also extend the time for the Rule 26(f) conference. But in most cases it will be desirable to hold at least a first scheduling conference in the time set by the rule.

Three items are added to the list of permitted contents in Rule 16(b)(3)(B).

The order may provide for preservation of electronically stored information, a topic also added to the provisions of a discovery plan under Rule 26(f)(3)(C). Parallel amendments of Rule 37(e) recognize that a duty to preserve discoverable information may arise before an action is filed.

The order also may include agreements incorporated in a court order under Evidence Rule 502 controlling the effects of disclosure of information covered by attorney-client privilege or work-product protection, a topic also added to the provisions of a discovery plan under Rule 26(f)(3)(D).

Finally, the order may direct that before filing a motion for an order relating to discovery the movant must request a conference with the court. Many judges who hold such conferences find them an efficient way to resolve most discovery disputes without the delay and burdens attending a formal motion, but the decision whether to require such conferences is left to the discretion of the judge in each case.

TITLE IV. PARTIES

Rule 17. Plaintiff and Defendant; Capacity; Public Officers

(a) Real Party in Interest.

(1) Designation in General. An action must be prosecuted in the name of the real party in interest. The following may sue in their own names without joining the person for whose benefit the action is brought:

(A) an executor;
(B) an administrator;
(C) a guardian;
(D) a bailee;
(E) a trustee of an express trust;
(F) a party with whom or in whose name a contract has been made for another's benefit; and
(G) a party authorized by statute.

(2) Action in the Name of the United States for Another's Use or Benefit. When a federal statute so provides, an action for another's use or benefit must be brought in the name of the United States.

(3) Joinder of the Real Party in Interest. The court may not dismiss an action for failure to prosecute in the name of the real party in interest until, after an objection, a reasonable time has been allowed for the real party in interest to ratify, join, or be substituted into the action. After ratification, joinder, or substitution, the action proceeds as if it had been originally commenced by the real party in interest.

(b) Capacity to Sue or Be Sued. Capacity to sue or be sued is determined as follows:

(1) for an individual who is not acting in a representative capacity, by the law of the individual's domicile;
(2) for a corporation, by the law under which it was organized; and
(3) for all other parties, by the law of the state where the court is located, except that:

(A) a partnership or other unincorporated association with no such capacity under that state's law may sue or be sued in its common name to enforce a substantive right existing under the United States Constitution or laws; and
(B) 28 U.S.C. §§754 and 959(a) govern the capacity of a receiver appointed by a United States court to sue or be sued in a United States court.

(c) Minor or Incompetent Person.

(1) With a Representative. The following representatives may sue or defend on behalf of a minor or an incompetent person:

(A) a general guardian;
(B) a committee;
(C) a conservator; or
(D) a like fiduciary.

(2) Without a Representative. A minor or an incompetent person who does not have a duly appointed representative may sue by a next friend or by a guardian ad litem. The court must appoint a guardian ad litem—or issue another appropriate order—to protect a minor or incompetent person who is unrepresented in an action.

(d) Public Officer's Title and Name. A public officer who sues or is sued in an official capacity may be designated by official title rather than by name, but the court may order that the officer's name be added.

(As amended Dec. 27, 1946, eff. Mar. 19, 1948; Dec. 29, 1948, eff. Oct. 20, 1949; Feb. 28, 1966, eff. July 1, 1966; Mar. 2, 1987, eff. Aug. 1, 1987; Apr. 25, 1988, eff. Aug. 1, 1988; Pub. L. 100–690, title VII, §7049, Nov. 18, 1988, 102 Stat. 4401; Apr. 30, 2007, eff. Dec. 1, 2007.)

Notes of Advisory Committee on Rules—1937

Note to Subdivision (a). The real party in interest provision, except for the last clause which is new, is taken verbatim from [former] Equity Rule 37 (Parties Generally—Intervention), except that the word "expressly" has been omitted. For similar provisions see N.Y.C.P.A. (1937) §210; Wyo.Rev.Stat.Ann. (1931) §§89–501, 89–502, 89–503; English Rules Under the Judicature Act (The Annual Practice, 1937) O. 16, r. 8. See also Equity Rule 41 (Suit to Execute Trusts of Will—Heir as Party). For examples of statutes of the United States providing particularly for an action for the use or benefit of another in the name of the United States, see U.S.C., [former] Title 40, §270b (Suit by persons furnishing labor and material for work on public building contracts * * * may sue on a payment bond, "in the name of the United States for the use of the person suing") [now 40 U.S.C. §3133(b), (c)]; and U.S.C., Title 25, §201 (Penalties under laws relating to Indians—how recovered). Compare U.S.C., Title 26, [former] §1645(c) (Suits for penalties, fines, and forfeitures, under this title, where not otherwise provided for, to be in name of United States).

Note to Subdivision (b). For capacity see generally Clark and Moore, A New Federal Civil Procedure—II. Pleadings and Parties, 44 Yale L.J. 1291, 1312–1317 (1935) and specifically Coppedge v. Clinton, 72 F.(2d) 531 (C.C.A.10th, 1934) (natural person); David Lupton's Sons Co. v. Automobile Club of America, 225 U.S. 489 (1912) (corporation); Puerto Rico v. Russell & Co., 288 U.S. 476 (1933) (unincorporated ass'n.); United Mine Workers of America v. Coronado Coal Co., 259 U.S. 344 (1922) (federal substantive right enforced against unincorporated association by suit against the association in its common name without naming all its members as parties). This rule follows the existing law as to such associations, as declared in the case last cited above. Compare Moffat Tunnel League v. United States, 289 U.S. 113 (1933). See note to Rule 23, clause (1).

Note to Subdivision (c). The provision for infants and incompetent persons is substantially [former] Equity Rule 70 (Suits by or Against Incompetents) with slight additions. Compare the more detailed English provisions, English Rules Under the Judicature Act (The Annual Practice, 1937) O. 16, r.r. 16–21.

Notes of Advisory Committee on Rules—1946 Amendment

The new matter [in subdivision (b)] makes clear the controlling character of Rule 66 regarding suits by or against a federal receiver in a federal court.

Notes of Advisory Committee on Rules—1948 Amendment

Since the statute states the capacity of a federal receiver to sue or be sued, a repetitive statement in the rule is confusing and undesirable.

Notes of Advisory Committee on Rules—1966 Amendment

The minor change in the text of the rule is designed to make it clear that the specific instances enumerated are not exceptions to, but illustrations of, the rule. These illustrations, of course, carry no negative implication to the effect that there are not other instances of recognition as the real party in interest of one whose standing as such may be in doubt. The enumeration is simply of cases in which there might be substantial doubt as to the issue but for the specific enumeration. There are other potentially arguable cases that are not excluded by the enumeration. For example, the enumeration states that the promisee in a contract for the benefit of a third party may sue as real party in interest; it does not say, because it is obvious, that the third-party beneficiary may sue (when the applicable law gives him that right.)

The rule adds to the illustrative list of real parties in interest a bailee—meaning, of course, a bailee suing on behalf of the bailor with respect to the property bailed. (When the possessor of property other than the owner sues for an invasion of the possessory interest he is the real party in interest.) The word "bailee" is added primarily to preserve the admiralty practice whereby the owner of a vessel as bailee of the cargo, or the master of the vessel as bailee of both vessel and cargo, sues for damage to either property interest or both. But there is no reason to limit such a provision to maritime situations. The owner of a warehouse in which household furniture is stored is equally entitled to sue on behalf of the numerous owners of the furniture stored. Cf. Gulf Oil Corp. v. Gilbert, 330 U.S. 501 (1947).

The provision that no action shall be dismissed on the ground that it is not prosecuted in the name of the real party in interest until a reasonable time has been allowed, after the objection has been raised, for ratification, substitution, etc., is added simply in the interests of justice. In its origin the rule concerning the real party in interest was permissive in purpose: it was designed to allow an assignee to sue in his own name. That having been accomplished, the modern function of the rule in its negative aspect is simply to protect the defendant against a subsequent action by the party actually entitled to recover, and to insure generally that the judgment will have its proper effect as res judicata.

This provision keeps pace with the law as it is actually developing. Modern decisions are inclined to be lenient when an honest mistake has been made in choosing the party in whose name the action is to be filed—in both maritime and nonmaritime cases. See Levinson v. Deupree, 345 U.S. 648 (1953); Link Aviation, Inc. v. Downs, 325 F.2d 613 (D.C.Cir. 1963). The provision should not be misunderstood or distorted. It is intended to prevent forfeiture when determination of the proper party to sue is difficult or when an understandable mistake has been made. It does not mean, for example, that, following an airplane crash in which all aboard were killed, an action may be filed in the name of John Doe (a fictitious person), as personal representative of Richard Roe (another fictitious person), in the hope that at a later time the attorney filing the action may substitute the real name of the real personal representative of a real victim, and have the benefit of suspension of the limitation period. It does not even mean, when an action is filed by the personal representative of John Smith, of Buffalo, in the good faith belief that he was aboard the flight, that upon discovery that Smith is alive and well, having missed the fatal flight, the representative of James Brown, of San Francisco, an actual victim, can be substituted to take advantage of the suspension of the limitation period. It is, in cases of this sort, intended to insure against forfeiture and injustice—in short, to codify in broad terms the salutary principle of Levinson v. Deupree, 345 U.S. 648 (1953), and Link Aviation, Inc. v. Downs, 325 F.2d 613 (D.C.Cir. 1963).

Notes of Advisory Committee on Rules—1987 Amendment

The amendments are technical. No substantive change is intended.

Notes of Advisory Committee on Rules—1988 Amendment

The amendment is technical. No substantive change is intended.

Committee Notes on Rules—2007 Amendment

The language of Rule 17 has been amended as part of the general restyling of the Civil Rules to make them more easily understood and to make style and terminology consistent throughout the rules. These changes are intended to be stylistic only.

Rule 17(d) incorporates the provisions of former Rule 25(d)(2), which fit better with Rule 17.

Amendment by Public Law

1988—Subd. (a). Pub. L. 100–690, which directed amendment of subd. (a) by striking "with him", could not be executed because of the intervening amendment by the Court by order dated Apr. 25, 1988, eff. Aug. 1, 1988.

Rule 18. Joinder of Claims

(a) In General. A party asserting a claim, counterclaim, crossclaim, or third-party claim may join, as independent or alternative claims, as many claims as it has against an opposing party.

(b) Joinder of Contingent Claims. A party may join two claims even though one of them is contingent on the disposition of the other; but the court may grant relief only in accordance with the parties' relative substantive rights. In particular, a plaintiff may state a claim for money and a claim to set aside a conveyance that is fraudulent as to that plaintiff, without first obtaining a judgment for the money.

(As amended Feb. 28, 1966, eff. July 1, 1966; Mar. 2, 1987, eff. Aug. 1, 1987; Apr. 30, 2007, eff. Dec. 1, 2007.)

Notes of Advisory Committee on Rules—1937

Note to Subdivision (a). 1. Recent development, both in code and common law states, has been toward unlimited joinder of actions. See Ill.Rev.Stat. (1937) ch. 110, §168; N.J.S.A. 2:27–37, as modified by N.J.Sup.Ct.Rules, Rule 21, 2 N.J.Misc. 1208 (1924); N.Y.C.P.A. (1937) §258 as amended by Laws of 1935, ch. 339.

2. This provision for joinder of actions has been patterned upon [former] Equity Rule 26 (Joinder of Causes of Action) and broadened to include multiple parties. Compare the English practice, English Rules Under the Judicature Act (The Annual Practice, 1937) O. 18, r.r. 1–9 (noting rules 1 and 6). The earlier American codes set forth classes of joinder, following the now abandoned New York rule. See N.Y.C.P.A. §258 before amended in 1935; Compare Kan.Gen.Stat.Ann. (1935) §60–601; Wis.Stat. (1935) §263.04 for the more liberal practice.

3. The provisions of this rule for the joinder of claims are subject to Rule 82 (Jurisdiction and Venue Unaffected). For the jurisdictional aspects of joinder of claims, see Shulman and Jaegerman, Some Jurisdictional Limitations on Federal Procedure (1936), 45 Yale L.J. 393, 397–410. For separate trials of joined claims, see Rule 42(b).

Note to Subdivision (b). This rule is inserted to make it clear that in a single action a party should be accorded all the relief to which he is entitled regardless of whether it is legal or equitable or both. This necessarily includes a deficiency judgment in foreclosure actions formerly provided for in [former] Equity Rule 10 (Decree for Deficiency in Foreclosures, Etc.). In respect to fraudulent conveyances the rule changes the former rule requiring a prior judgment against the owner (Braun v. American Laundry Mach. Co., 56 F.(2d) 197 (S.D.N.Y. 1932)) to conform to the provisions of the Uniform Fraudulent Conveyance Act, §§9 and 10. See McLaughlin, Application of the Uniform Fraudulent Conveyance Act, 46 Harv.L.Rev. 404, 444 (1933).

Notes of Advisory Committee on Rules—1966 Amendment

The Rules "proceed upon the theory that no inconvenience can result from the joinder of any two or more matters in the pleadings, but only from trying two or more matters together which have little or nothing in common." Sunderland, The New Federal Rules, 45 W.Va.L.Q. 5, 13 (1938); see Clark, Code Pleading 58 (2d ed. 1947). Accordingly, Rule 18(a) has permitted a party to plead multiple claims of all types against an opposing party, subject to the court's power to direct an appropriate procedure for trying the claims. See Rules 42(b), 20(b), 21.

The liberal policy regarding joinder of claims in the pleadings extends to cases with multiple parties. However, the language used in the second sentence of Rule 18(a)—"if the requirements of Rules 19 [necessary joinder of parties], 20 [permissive joinder of parties], and 22 [interpleader] are satisfied"—has led some courts to infer that the rules regulating joinder of parties are intended to carry back to Rule 18(a) and to impose some special limits on joinder of claims in multiparty cases. In particular, Rule 20(a) has been read as restricting the operation of Rule 18(a) in certain situations in which a number of parties have been permissively joined in an action. In Federal Housing Admr. v. Christianson, 26 F.Supp. 419 (D.Conn. 1939), the indorsee of two notes sued the three comakers of one note, and sought to join in the action a count on a second note which had been made by two of the three defendants. There was no doubt about the propriety of the joinder of the three parties defendant, for a right to relief was being asserted against all three defendants which arose out of a single "transaction" (the first note) and a question of fact or law "common" to all three defendants would arise in the action. See the text of Rule 20(a). The court, however, refused to allow the joinder of the count on the second note, on the ground that this right to relief, assumed to arise from a distinct transaction, did not involve a question common to all the defendants but only two of them. For analysis of the Christianson case and other authorities, see 2 Barron & Holtzoff, Federal Practice & Procedure, §533.1 (Wright ed. 1961); 3 Moore's Federal Practice, par. 18.04[3] (2d ed. 1963).

If the court's view is followed, it becomes necessary to enter at the pleading stage into speculations about the exact relation between the claim sought to be joined against fewer than all the defendants properly joined in the action, and the claims asserted against all the defendants. Cf. Wright, Joinder of Claims and Parties Under Modern Pleading Rules, 36 Minn.L.Rev. 580, 605–06 (1952). Thus if it could be found in the Christianson situation that the claim on the second note arose out of the same transaction as the claim on the first or out of a transaction forming part of a "series," and that any question of fact or law with respect to the second note also arose with regard to the first, it would be held that the claim on the second note could be joined in the complaint. See 2 Barron & Holtzoff, supra, at 199; see also id. at 198 n. 60.4; cf. 3 Moore's Federal Practice, supra, at 1811. Such pleading niceties provide a basis for delaying and wasteful maneuver. It is more compatible with the design of the Rules to allow the claim to be joined in the pleading, leaving the question of possible separate trial of that claim to be later decided. See 2 Barron & Holtzoff, supra, §533.1; Wright, supra, 36 Minn.L.Rev. at 604–11; Developments in the Law—Multiparty Litigation in the Federal Courts, 71 Harv. 874, 970–71 (1958); Commentary, Relation Between Joinder of Parties and Joinder of Claims, 5 F.R.Serv. 822 (1942). It is instructive to note that the court in the Christianson case, while holding that the claim on the second note could not be joined as a matter of pleading, held open the possibility that both claims would later be consolidated for trial under Rule 42(a). See 26 F.Supp. 419.

Rule 18(a) is now amended not only to overcome the Christianson decision and similar authority, but also to state clearly as a comprehensive proposition, that a party asserting a claim (an original claim, counterclaim, cross-claim, or third-party claim) may join as many claims as he has against an opposing party. See Noland Co., Inc. v. Graver Tank & Mfg. Co., 301 F.2d 43, 49–51 (4th Cir. 1962); but cf. C. W. Humphrey Co. v. Security Alum. Co., 31 F.R.D. 41 (E.D.Mich. 1962) This permitted joinder of claims is not affected by the fact that there are multiple parties in the action. The joinder of parties is governed by other rules operating independently.

It is emphasized that amended Rule 18(a) deals only with pleading. As already indicated, a claim properly joined as a matter of pleading need not be proceeded with together with the other claim if fairness or convenience justifies separate treatment.

Amended Rule 18(a), like the rule prior to amendment, does not purport to deal with questions of jurisdiction or venue which may arise with respect to claims properly joined as a matter of pleading. See Rule 82.

See also the amendment of Rule 20(a) and the Advisory Committee's Note thereto.

Free joinder of claims and remedies is one of the basic purposes of unification of the admiralty and civil procedure. The amendment accordingly provides for the inclusion in the rule of maritime claims as well as those which are legal and equitable in character.

Notes of Advisory Committee on Rules—1987 Amendment

The amendments are technical. No substantive change is intended.

Committee Notes on Rules—2007 Amendment

The language of Rule 18 has been amended as part of the general restyling of the Civil Rules to make them more easily understood and to make style and terminology consistent throughout the rules. These changes are intended to be stylistic only.

Modification of the obscure former reference to a claim "heretofore cognizable only after another claim has been prosecuted to a conclusion" avoids any uncertainty whether Rule 18(b)'s meaning is fixed by retrospective inquiry from some particular date.

Rule 19. Required Joinder of Parties

(a) Persons Required to Be Joined if Feasible.

(1) Required Party. A person who is subject to service of process and whose joinder will not deprive the court of subject-matter jurisdiction must be joined as a party if:

(A) in that person's absence, the court cannot accord complete relief among existing parties; or

(B) that person claims an interest relating to the subject of the action and is so situated that disposing of the action in the person's absence may:

(i) as a practical matter impair or impede the person's ability to protect the interest; or

(ii) leave an existing party subject to a substantial risk of incurring double, multiple, or otherwise inconsistent obligations because of the interest.

(2) Joinder by Court Order. If a person has not been joined as required, the court must order that the person be made a party. A person who refuses to join as a plaintiff may be made either a defendant or, in a proper case, an involuntary plaintiff.

(3) Venue. If a joined party objects to venue and the joinder would make venue improper, the court must dismiss that party.

(b) When Joinder Is Not Feasible. If a person who is required to be joined if feasible cannot be joined, the court must determine whether, in equity and good conscience, the action should proceed among the existing parties or should be dismissed. The factors for the court to consider include:

(1) the extent to which a judgment rendered in the person's absence might prejudice that person or the existing parties;

(2) the extent to which any prejudice could be lessened or avoided by:

(A) protective provisions in the judgment;

(B) shaping the relief; or

(C) other measures;

(3) whether a judgment rendered in the person's absence would be adequate; and

(4) whether the plaintiff would have an adequate remedy if the action were dismissed for nonjoinder.

(c) Pleading the Reasons for Nonjoinder. When asserting a claim for relief, a party must state:

(1) the name, if known, of any person who is required to be joined if feasible but is not joined; and

(2) the reasons for not joining that person.

(d) Exception for Class Actions. This rule is subject to Rule 23.

(As amended Feb. 28, 1966, eff. July 1, 1966; Mar. 2, 1987, eff. Aug. 1, 1987; Apr. 30, 2007, eff. Dec. 1, 2007.)

Notes of Advisory Committee on Rules—1937

Note to Subdivision (a). The first sentence with verbal differences (e.g., "united" interest for "joint" interest) is to be found in [former] Equity Rule 37 (Parties Generally—Intervention). Such compulsory joinder provisions are common. Compare Alaska Comp. Laws (1933) §3392 (containing in same sentence a "class suit" provision); Wyo.Rev.Stat.Ann. (Courtright, 1931) §89–515 (immediately followed by "class suit" provisions, §89–516). See also [former] Equity Rule 42 (Joint and Several Demands). For example of a proper case for involuntary plaintiff, see Independent Wireless Telegraph Co. v. Radio Corp. of America, 269 U.S. 459 (1926).

The joinder provisions of this rule are subject to Rule 82 (Jurisdiction and Venue Unaffected).

Note to Subdivision (b). For the substance of this rule see [former] Equity Rule 39 (Absence of Persons Who Would be Proper Parties) and U.S.C., Title 28, §111 [now 1391] (When part of several defendants cannot be served); Camp v. Gress, 250 U.S. 308 (1919). See also the second and third sentences of [former] Equity Rule 37 (Parties Generally—Intervention).

Note to Subdivision (c). For the substance of this rule see the fourth subdivision of [former] Equity Rule 25 (Bill of Complaint—Contents).

Notes of Advisory Committee on Rules—1966 Amendment

General Considerations

Whenever feasible, the persons materially interested in the subject of an action—see the more detailed description of these persons in the discussion of new subdivision (a) below—should be joined as parties so that they may be heard and a complete disposition made. When this comprehensive joinder cannot be accomplished—a situation which may be encountered in Federal courts because of limitations on service of process, subject matter jurisdiction, and venue—the case should be examined pragmatically and a choice made between the alternatives of proceeding with the action in the absence of particular interested persons, and dismissing the action.

Even if the court is mistaken in its decision to proceed in the absence of an interested person, it does not by that token deprive itself of the power to adjudicate as between the parties already before it through proper service of process. But the court can make a legally binding adjudication only between the parties actually joined in the action. It is true that an adjudication between the parties before the court may on occasion adversely affect the absent person as a practical matter, or leave a party exposed to a later inconsistent recovery by the absent person. These are factors which should be considered in deciding whether the action should proceed, or should rather be dismissed; but they do not themselves negate the court's power to adjudicate as between the parties who have been joined.

Defects in the Original Rule

The foregoing propositions were well understood in the older equity practice, see Hazard, Indispensable Party: The Historical Origin of a Procedural Phantom, 61 Colum.L.Rev. 1254 (1961), and Rule 19 could be and often was applied in consonance with them. But experience showed that the rule was defective in its phrasing and did not point clearly to the proper basis of decision.

Textual defects.—(1) The expression "persons * * * who ought to be parties if complete relief is to be accorded between those already parties," appearing in original subdivision (b), was apparently intended as a description of the persons whom it would be desirable to join in the action, all questions of feasibility of joinder being put to one side; but it was not adequately descriptive of those persons.

(2) The word "Indispensable," appearing in original subdivision (b), was apparently intended as an inclusive reference to the interested persons in whose absence it would be advisable, all factors having been considered, to dismiss the action. Yet the sentence implied that there might be interested persons, not "indispensable." in whose absence the action ought also to be dismissed. Further, it seemed at least superficially plausible to equate the word "indispensable" with the expression "having a joint interest," appearing in subdivision (a). See United States v. Washington Inst. of Tech., Inc., 138 F.2d 25, 26 (3d Cir. 1943); cf. Chidester v. City of Newark, 162 F.2d 598 (3d Cir. 1947). But persons holding an interest technically "joint" are not always so related to an action that it would be unwise to proceed without joining all of them, whereas persons holding an interest not technically "joint" may have this relation to an action. See Reed, Compulsory Joinder of Parties in Civil Actions, 55 Mich.L.Rev. 327, 356 ff., 483 (1957).

(3) The use of "indispensable" and "joint interest" in the context of original Rule 19 directed attention to the technical or abstract character of the rights or obligations of the persons whose joinder was in question, and correspondingly distracted attention from the pragmatic considerations which should be controlling.

(4) The original rule, in dealing with the feasibility of joining a person as a party to the action, besides referring to whether the person was "subject to the jurisdiction of the court as to both service of process and venue," spoke of whether the person could be made a party "without depriving the court of jurisdiction of the parties before it." The second quoted expression used "jurisdiction" in the sense of the competence of the court over the subject matter of the action, and in this sense the expression was apt. However, by a familiar confusion, the expression seems to have suggested to some that the absence from the lawsuit of a person who was "indispensable" or "who ought to be [a] part[y]" itself deprived the court of the power to adjudicate as between the parties already joined. See Samuel Goldwyn, Inc. v. United Artists Corp., 113 F.2d 703, 707 (3d Cir. 1940); McArthur v. Rosenbaum Co. of Pittsburgh, 180 F.2d 617, 621 (3d Cir. 1949); cf. Calcote v. Texas Pac. Coal & Oil Co., 157 F.2d 216 (5th Cir. 1946), cert. denied, 329 U.S. 782 (1946), noted in 56 Yale L.J. 1088 (1947); Reed, supra, 55 Mich.L.Rev. at 332–34.

Failure to point to correct basis of decision. The original rule did not state affirmatively what factors were relevant in deciding whether the action should proceed or be dismissed when joinder of interested persons was infeasible. In some instances courts did not undertake the relevant inquiry or were misled by the "jurisdiction" fallacy. In other instances there was undue preoccupation with abstract classifications of rights or obligations, as against consideration of the particular consequences of proceeding with the action and the ways by which these consequences might be ameliorated by the shaping of final relief or other precautions.

Although these difficulties cannot be said to have been general analysis of the cases showed that there was good reason for attempting to strengthen the rule. The literature also indicated how the rule should be reformed. See Reed, supra (discussion of the important case of Shields v. Barrow, 17 How. (58 U.S.) 130 (1854), appears at 55 Mich.L.Rev., p. 340 ff.); Hazard, supra; N.Y. Temporary Comm. on Courts, First Preliminary Report, Legis.Doc. 1957, No. 6(b), pp. 28, 233; N.Y. Judicial Council, Twelfth Ann.Rep., Legis.Doc. 1946, No. 17, p. 163; Joint Comm. on Michigan Procedural Revision, Final Report, Pt. III, p. 69 (1960); Note, Indispensable Parties in the Federal Courts, 65 Harv.L.Rev. 1050 (1952); Developments in the Law—Multiparty Litigation in the Federal Courts, 71 Harv.L.Rev. 874, 879 (1958); Mich.Gen.Court Rules, R. 205 (effective Jan. 1, 1963); N.Y.Civ.Prac.Law & Rules, §1001 (effective Sept. 1, 1963).

The Amended Rule

New subdivision (a) defines the persons whose joinder in the action is desirable. Clause (1) stresses the desirability of joining those persons in whose absence the court would be obliged to grant partial or "hollow" rather than complete relief to the parties before the court. The interests that are being furthered here are not only those of the parties, but also that of the public in avoiding repeated lawsuits on the same essential subject matter. Clause (2)(i) recognizes the importance of protecting the person whose joinder is in question against the practical prejudice to him which may arise through a disposition of the action in his absence. Clause (2)(ii) recognizes the need for considering whether a party may be left, after the adjudication, in a position where a person not joined can subject him to a double or otherwise inconsistent liability. See Reed, supra, 55 Mich.L.Rev. at 330, 338; Note, supra, 65 Harv.L.Rev. at 1052–57; Developments in the Law, supra, 71 Harv.L.Rev. at 881–85.

The subdivision (a) definition of persons to be joined is not couched in terms of the abstract nature of their interests—"joint," "united," "separable," or the like. See N.Y. Temporary Comm. on Courts, First Preliminary Report, supra; Developments in the Law, supra, at 880. It should be noted particularly, however, that the description is not at variance with the settled authorities holding that a tortfeasor with the usual "joint-and-several" liability is merely a permissive party to an action against another with like liability. See 3 Moore's Federal Practice 2153 (2d ed. 1963); 2 Barron & Holtzoff, Federal Practice & Procedure §513.8 (Wright ed. 1961). Joinder of these tortfeasors continues to be regulated by Rule 20; compare Rule 14 on third-party practice.

If a person as described in subdivision (a)(1)(2) is amenable to service of process and his joinder would not deprive the court of jurisdiction in the sense of competence over the action, he should be joined as a party; and if he has not been joined, the court should order him to be brought into the action. If a party joined has a valid objection to the venue and chooses to assert it, he will be dismissed from the action.

Subdivision (b).—When a person as described in subdivision (a)(1)–(2) cannot be made a party, the court is to determine whether in equity and good conscience the action should proceed among the parties already before it, or should be dismissed. That this decision is to be made in the light of pragmatic considerations has often been acknowledged by the courts. See Roos v. Texas Co., 23 F.2d 171 (2d Cir. 1927), cert. denied, 277 U.S. 587 (1928); Niles-Bement-Pond Co. v. Iron Moulders, Union, 254 U.S. 77, 80 (1920). The subdivision sets out four relevant considerations drawn from the experience revealed in the decided cases. The factors are to a certain extent overlapping, and they are not intended to exclude other considerations which may be applicable in particular situations.

The first factor brings in a consideration of what a judgment in the action would mean to the absentee. Would the absentee be adversely affected in a practical sense, and if so, would the prejudice be immediate and serious, or remote and minor? The possible collateral consequences of the judgment upon the parties already joined are also to be appraised. Would any party be exposed to a fresh action by the absentee, and if so, how serious is the threat? See the elaborate discussion in Reed, supra; cf. A. L. Smith Iron Co. v. Dickson, 141 F.2d 3 (2d Cir. 1944); Caldwell Mfg. Co. v. Unique Balance Co., 18 F.R.D. 258 (S.D.N.Y. 1955).

The second factor calls attention to the measures by which prejudice may be averted or lessened. The "shaping of relief" is a familiar expedient to this end. See, e.g., the award of money damages in lieu of specific relief where the latter might affect an absentee adversely. Ward v. Deavers, 203 F.2d 72 (D.C.Cir. 1953); Miller & Lux, Inc. v. Nickel, 141 F.Supp. 41 (N.D.Calif. 1956). On the use of "protective provisions," see Roos v. Texas Co., supra; Atwood v. Rhode Island Hosp. Trust Co., 275 Fed. 513, 519 (1st Cir. 1921), cert. denied, 257 U.S. 661 (1922); cf. Stumpf v. Fidelity Gas Co., 294 F.2d 886 (9th Cir. 1961); and the general statement in National Licorice Co. v. Labor Board, 309 U.S. 350, 363 (1940).

Sometimes the party is himself able to take measures to avoid prejudice. Thus a defendant faced with a prospect of a second suit by an absentee may be in a position to bring the latter into the action by defensive interpleader. See Hudson v. Newell, 172 F.2d 848, 852 mod., 176 F.2d 546 (5th Cir. 1949); Gauss v. Kirk, 198 F.2d 83, 86 (D.C.Cir. 1952); Abel v. Brayton Flying Service, Inc., 248 F.2d 713, 716 (5th Cir. 1957) (suggestion of possibility of counterclaim under Rule 13(h)); cf. Parker Rust-Proof Co. v. Western Union Tel. Co., 105 F.2d 976 (2d Cir. 1939) cert. denied, 308 U.S. 597 (1939). See also the absentee may sometimes be able to avert prejudice to himself by voluntarily appearing in the action or intervening on an ancillary basis. See Developments in the Law, supra, 71 Harv.L.Rev. at 882; Annot., Intervention or Subsequent Joinder of Parties as Affecting Jurisdiction of Federal Court Based on Diversity of Citizenship, 134 A.L.R. 335 (1941); Johnson v. Middleton, 175 F.2d 535 (7th Cir. 1949); Kentucky Nat. Gas Corp. v. Duggins, 165 F.2d 1011 (6th Cir. 1948); McComb v. McCormack, 159 F.2d 219 (5th Cir. 1947). The court should consider whether this, in turn, would impose undue hardship on the absentee. (For the possibility of the court's informing an absentee of the pendency of the action, see comment under subdivision (c) below.)

The third factor—whether an "adequate" judgment can be rendered in the absence of a given person—calls attention to the extent of the relief that can be accorded among the parties joined. It meshes with the other factors, especially the "shaping of relief" mentioned under the second factor. Cf. Kroese v. General Steel Castings Corp., 179 F.2d 760 (3d Cir. 1949), cert. denied, 339 U.S. 983 (1950).

The fourth factor, looking to the practical effects of a dismissal, indicates that the court should consider whether there is any assurance that the plaintiff, if dismissed, could sue effectively in another forum where better joinder would be possible. See Fitzgerald v. Haynes, 241 F.2d 417, 420 (3d Cir. 1957); Fouke v. Schenewerk, 197 F.2d 234, 236 (5th Cir. 1952); cf. Warfield v. Marks, 190 F.2d 178 (5th Cir. 1951).

The subdivision uses the word "indispensable" only in a conclusory sense, that is, a person is "regarded as indispensable" when he cannot be made a party and, upon consideration of the factors above mention, it is determined that in his absence it would be preferable to dismiss the action, rather than to retain it.

A person may be added as a party at any stage of the action on motion or on the court's initiative (see Rule 21); and a motion to dismiss, on the ground that a person has not been joined and justice requires that the action should not proceed in his absence, may be made as late as the trial on the merits (see Rule 12(h)(2), as amended; cf. Rule 12(b)(7), as amended). However, when the moving party is seeking dismissal in order to protect himself against a later suit by the absent person (subdivision (a)(2)(ii)), and is not seeking vicariously to protect the absent person against a prejudicial judgment (subdivision (a)(2)(i)), his undue delay in making the motion can properly be counted against him as a reason for denying the motion. A joinder question should be decided with reasonable promptness, but decision may properly be deferred if adequate information is not available at the time. Thus the relationship of an absent person to the action, and the practical effects of an adjudication upon him and others, may not be sufficiently revealed at the pleading stage; in such a case it would be appropriate to defer decision until the action was further advanced. Cf. Rule 12(d).

The amended rule makes no special provision for the problem arising in suits against subordinate Federal officials where it has often been set up as a defense that some superior officer must be joined. Frequently this defense has been accompanied by or intermingled with defenses of sovereign community or lack of consent of the United States to suit. So far as the issue of joinder can be isolated from the rest, the new subdivision seems better adapted to handle it than the predecessor provision. See the discussion in Johnson v. Kirkland, 290 F.2d 440, 446–47 (5th Cir. 1961) (stressing the practical orientation of the decisions); Shaughnessy v. Pedreiro, 349 U.S. 48, 54 (1955). Recent legislation, P.L. 87–748, 76 Stat. 744, approved October 5, 1962, adding §§1361, 1391(e) to Title 28, U.S.C., vests original jurisdiction in the District Courts over actions in the nature of mandamus to compel officials of the United States to perform their legal duties, and extends the range of service of process and liberalizes venue in these actions. If, then, it is found that a particular official should be joined in the action, the legislation will make it easy to bring him in.

Subdivision (c) parallels the predecessor subdivision (c) of Rule 19. In some situations it may be desirable to advise a person who has not been joined of the fact that the action is pending, and in particular cases the court in its discretion may itself convey this information by directing a letter or other informal notice to the absentee.

Subdivision (d) repeats the exception contained in the first clause of the predecessor subdivision (a).

Notes of Advisory Committee on Rules—1987 Amendment

The amendments are technical. No substantive change is intended.

Committee Notes on Rules—2007 Amendment

The language of Rule 19 has been amended as part of the general restyling of the Civil Rules to make them more easily understood and to make style and terminology consistent throughout the rules. These changes are intended to be stylistic only.

Former Rule 19(b) described the conclusion that an action should be dismissed for inability to join a Rule 19(a) party by carrying forward traditional terminology: "the absent person being thus regarded as indispensable." "Indispensable" was used only to express a conclusion reached by applying the tests of Rule 19(b). It has been discarded as redundant.

Rule 20. Permissive Joinder of Parties

(a) Persons Who May Join or Be Joined.

(1) Plaintiffs. Persons may join in one action as plaintiffs if:

(A) they assert any right to relief jointly, severally, or in the alternative with respect to or arising out of the same transaction, occurrence, or series of transactions or occurrences; and

(B) any question of law or fact common to all plaintiffs will arise in the action.

(2) Defendants. Persons—as well as a vessel, cargo, or other property subject to admiralty process in rem—may be joined in one action as defendants if:

(A) any right to relief is asserted against them jointly, severally, or in the alternative with respect to or arising out of the same transaction, occurrence, or series of transactions or occurrences; and

(B) any question of law or fact common to all defendants will arise in the action.

(3) Extent of Relief. Neither a plaintiff nor a defendant need be interested in obtaining or defending against all the relief demanded. The court may grant judgment to one or more plaintiffs according to their rights, and against one or more defendants according to their liabilities.

(b) Protective Measures. The court may issue orders—including an order for separate trials—to protect a party against embarrassment, delay, expense, or other prejudice that arises from including a person against whom the party asserts no claim and who asserts no claim against the party.

———

(As amended Feb. 28, 1966, eff. July 1, 1966; Mar. 2, 1987, eff. Aug. 1, 1987; Apr. 30, 2007, eff. Dec. 1, 2007.)

Notes of Advisory Committee on Rules—1937

The provisions for joinder here stated are in substance the provisions found in England, California, Illinois, New Jersey, and New York. They represent only a moderate expansion of the present federal equity practice to cover both law and equity actions.

With this rule compare also [former] Equity Rules 26 (Joinder of Causes of Action), 37 (Parties Generally—Intervention), 40 (Nominal Parties), and 42 (Joint and Several Demands).

The provisions of this rule for the joinder of parties are subject to Rule 82 (Jurisdiction and Venue Unaffected).

Note to Subdivision (a). The first sentence is derived from English Rules Under the Judicature Act (The Annual Practice, 1937) O. 16, r. 1. Compare Calif.Code Civ.Proc. (Deering, 1937) §§378, 379a; Ill.Rev.Stat. (1937) ch. 110, §§147–148; N.J.Comp.Stat. (2 Cum.Supp., 1911–1924), N.Y.C.P.A. (1937) §§209, 211. The second sentence is derived from English Rules Under the Judicature Act (he Annual Practice, 1937) O. 16, r. 4. The third sentence is derived from O. 16, r. 5, and the fourth from O. 16, r.r. 1 and 4.

Note to Subdivision (b). This is derived from English Rules Under the Judicature Act (The Annual Practice, 1937) O. 16, r.r. 1 and 5.

Notes of Advisory Committee on Rules—1966 Amendment

See the amendment of Rule 18(a) and the Advisory Committee's Note thereto. It has been thought that a lack of clarity in the antecedent of the word "them," as it appeared in two places in Rule 20(a), contributed to the view, taken by some courts, that this rule limited the joinder of claims in certain situations of permissive party joinder. Although the amendment of Rule 18(a) should make clear that this view is untenable, it has been considered advisable to amend Rule 20(a) to eliminate any ambiguity. See 2 Barron & Holtzoff, Federal Practice & Procedure 202 (Wright Ed. 1961).

A basic purpose of unification of admiralty and civil procedure is to reduce barriers to joinder; hence the reference to "any vessel," etc.

Notes of Advisory Committee on Rules—1987 Amendment

The amendments are technical. No substantive change is intended.

Committee Notes on Rules—2007 Amendment

The language of Rule 20 has been amended as part of the general restyling of the Civil Rules to make them more easily understood and to make style and terminology consistent throughout the rules. These changes are intended to be stylistic only.

Rule 21. Misjoinder and Nonjoinder of Parties

Misjoinder of parties is not a ground for dismissing an action. On motion or on its own, the court may at any time, on just terms, add or drop a party. The court may also sever any claim against a party.

———

(As amended Apr. 30, 2007, eff. Dec. 1, 2007.)

Notes of Advisory Committee on Rules—1937

See English Rules Under the Judicature Act (The Annual Practice, 1937) O. 16, r. 11. See also [former] Equity Rules 43 (Defect of

Parties—Resisting Objection) and 44 (Defect of Parties—Tardy Objection).

For separate trials see Rules 13(i) (Counterclaims and Cross-Claims: Separate Trials; Separate Judgments), 20(b) (Permissive Joinder of Parties: Separate Trials), and 42(b) (Separate Trials, generally) and the note to the latter rule.

Committee Notes on Rules—2007 Amendment

The language of Rule 21 has been amended as part of the general restyling of the Civil Rules to make them more easily understood and to make style and terminology consistent throughout the rules. These changes are intended to be stylistic only.

Rule 22. Interpleader

(a) Grounds.

(1) By a Plaintiff. Persons with claims that may expose a plaintiff to double or multiple liability may be joined as defendants and required to interplead. Joinder for interpleader is proper even though:

(A) the claims of the several claimants, or the titles on which their claims depend, lack a common origin or are adverse and independent rather than identical; or

(B) the plaintiff denies liability in whole or in part to any or all of the claimants.

(2) By a Defendant. A defendant exposed to similar liability may seek interpleader through a crossclaim or counterclaim.

(b) Relation to Other Rules and Statutes. This rule supplements—and does not limit—the joinder of parties allowed by Rule 20. The remedy this rule provides is in addition to—and does not supersede or limit—the remedy provided by 28 U.S.C. §§1335, 1397, and 2361. An action under those statutes must be conducted under these rules.

—

(As amended Dec. 29, 1948, eff. Oct. 20, 1949; Mar. 2, 1987, eff. Aug. 1, 1987; Apr. 30, 2007, eff. Dec. 1, 2007.)

Notes of Advisory Committee on Rules—1937

The first paragraph provides for interpleader relief along the newer and more liberal lines of joinder in the alternative. It avoids the confusion and restrictions that developed around actions of strict interpleader and actions in the nature of interpleader. Compare John Hancock Mutual Life Insurance Co. v. Kegan et al., (D.C.Md., 1938) [22 F.Supp. 326]. It does not change the rules on service of process, jurisdiction, and venue, as established by judicial decision.

The second paragraph allows an action to be brought under the recent interpleader statute when applicable. By this paragraph all remedies under the statute are continued, but the manner of obtaining them is in accordance with these rules. For temporary restraining orders and preliminary injunctions under this statute, see Rule 65(e).

This rule substantially continues such statutory provisions as U.S.C., Title 38, §445 [now 1984] (Actions on claims; jurisdiction; parties; procedure; limitation; witnesses; definitions) (actions upon veterans' contracts of insurance with the United States), providing for interpleader by the United States where it acknowledges indebtedness under a contract of insurance with the United States; U.S.C., Title 49, §97 [now 80110(e)] (Interpleader of conflicting claimants) (by carrier which has issued bill of lading). See Chafee, The Federal Interpleader Act of 1936: I and II (1936), 45 Yale L.J. 963, 1161.

Notes of Advisory Committee on Rules—1948 Amendment

The amendment substitutes the present statutory reference.

Notes of Advisory Committee on Rules—1987 Amendment

The amendment is technical. No substantive change is intended.

Committee Notes on Rules—2007 Amendment

The language of Rule 22 has been amended as part of the general restyling of the Civil Rules to make them more easily understood and to make style and terminology consistent throughout the rules. These changes are intended to be stylistic only.

Rule 23. Class Actions

(a) Prerequisites. One or more members of a class may sue or be sued as representative parties on behalf of all members only if:

(1) the class is so numerous that joinder of all members is impracticable;

(2) there are questions of law or fact common to the class;

(3) the claims or defenses of the representative parties are typical of the claims or defenses of the class; and

(4) the representative parties will fairly and adequately protect the interests of the class.

(b) Types of Class Actions. A class action may be maintained if Rule 23(a) is satisfied and if:

(1) prosecuting separate actions by or against individual class members would create a risk of:

(A) inconsistent or varying adjudications with respect to individual class members that would establish incompatible standards of conduct for the party opposing the class; or

(B) adjudications with respect to individual class members that, as a practical matter, would be dispositive of the interests of the other members not parties to the individual adjudications or would substantially impair or impede their ability to protect their interests;

(2) the party opposing the class has acted or refused to act on grounds that apply generally to the class, so that final injunctive relief or corresponding declaratory relief is appropriate respecting the class as a whole; or

(3) the court finds that the questions of law or fact common to class members predominate over any questions affecting only individual members, and that a class action is superior to other available methods for fairly and efficiently adjudicating the controversy. The matters pertinent to these findings include:

(A) the class members' interests in individually controlling the prosecution or defense of separate actions;

(B) the extent and nature of any litigation concerning the controversy already begun by or against class members;

(C) the desirability or undesirability of concentrating the litigation of the claims in the particular forum; and

(D) the likely difficulties in managing a class action.

(c) Certification Order; Notice to Class Members; Judgment; Issues Classes; Subclasses.

(1) Certification Order.

(A) Time to Issue. At an early practicable time after a person sues or is sued as a class representative, the court must determine by order whether to certify the action as a class action.

(B) Defining the Class; Appointing Class Counsel. An order that certifies a class action must define the class and the class claims, issues, or defenses, and must appoint class counsel under Rule 23(g).

(C) Altering or Amending the Order. An order that grants or denies class certification may be altered or amended before final judgment.

(2) Notice.

(A) For (b)(1) or (b)(2) Classes. For any class certified under Rule 23(b)(1) or (b)(2), the court may direct appropriate notice to the class.

(B) For (b)(3) Classes. For any class certified under Rule 23(b)(3), the court must direct to class members the best notice that is practicable under the circumstances, including individual notice to all members who can be identified through reasonable effort. The notice must clearly and concisely state in plain, easily understood language:

(i) the nature of the action;

(ii) the definition of the class certified;

(iii) the class claims, issues, or defenses;

(iv) that a class member may enter an appearance through an attorney if the member so desires;

(v) that the court will exclude from the class any member who requests exclusion;

(vi) the time and manner for requesting exclusion; and

(vii) the binding effect of a class judgment on members under Rule 23(c)(3).

(3) Judgment. Whether or not favorable to the class, the judgment in a class action must:

(A) for any class certified under Rule 23(b)(1) or (b)(2), include and describe those whom the court finds to be class members; and

(B) for any class certified under Rule 23(b)(3), include and specify or describe those to whom the Rule 23(c)(2) notice was directed, who have not requested exclusion, and whom the court finds to be class members.

(4) Particular Issues. When appropriate, an action may be brought or maintained as a class action with respect to particular issues.

(5) Subclasses. When appropriate, a class may be divided into subclasses that are each treated as a class under this rule.

(d) Conducting the Action.

(1) In General. In conducting an action under this rule, the court may issue orders that:

(A) determine the course of proceedings or prescribe measures to prevent undue repetition or complication in presenting evidence or argument;

(B) require—to protect class members and fairly conduct the action—giving appropriate notice to some or all class members of:

(i) any step in the action;

(ii) the proposed extent of the judgment; or

(iii) the members' opportunity to signify whether they consider the representation fair and adequate, to intervene and present claims or defenses, or to otherwise come into the action;

(C) impose conditions on the representative parties or on intervenors;

(D) require that the pleadings be amended to eliminate allegations about representation of absent persons and that the action proceed accordingly; or

(E) deal with similar procedural matters.

(2) Combining and Amending Orders. An order under Rule 23(d)(1) may be altered or amended from time to time and may be combined with an order under Rule 16.

(e) Settlement, Voluntary Dismissal, or Compromise. The claims, issues, or defenses of a certified class may be settled, voluntarily dismissed, or compromised only with the court's approval. The following procedures apply to a proposed settlement, voluntary dismissal, or compromise:

(1) The court must direct notice in a reasonable manner to all class members who would be bound by the proposal.

(2) If the proposal would bind class members, the court may approve it only after a hearing and on finding that it is fair, reasonable, and adequate.

(3) The parties seeking approval must file a statement identifying any agreement made in connection with the proposal.

(4) If the class action was previously certified under Rule 23(b)(3), the court may refuse to approve a settlement unless it affords a new opportunity to request exclusion to individual class members who had an earlier opportunity to request exclusion but did not do so.

(5) Any class member may object to the proposal if it requires court approval under this subdivision (e); the objection may be withdrawn only with the court's approval.

(f) Appeals. A court of appeals may permit an appeal from an order granting or denying class-action certification under this rule if a petition for permission to appeal is filed with the circuit clerk within 14 days after the order is entered. An appeal does not stay proceedings in the district court unless the district judge or the court of appeals so orders.

(g) Class Counsel.

(1) Appointing Class Counsel. Unless a statute provides otherwise, a court that certifies a class must appoint class counsel. In appointing class counsel, the court:

(A) must consider:

(i) the work counsel has done in identifying or investigating potential claims in the action;

(ii) counsel's experience in handling class actions, other complex litigation, and the types of claims asserted in the action;

(iii) counsel's knowledge of the applicable law; and

(iv) the resources that counsel will commit to representing the class;

(B) may consider any other matter pertinent to counsel's ability to fairly and adequately represent the interests of the class;

(C) may order potential class counsel to provide information on any subject pertinent to the appointment and to propose terms for attorney's fees and nontaxable costs;

(D) may include in the appointing order provisions about the award of attorney's fees or nontaxable costs under Rule 23(h); and

(E) may make further orders in connection with the appointment.

(2) Standard for Appointing Class Counsel. When one applicant seeks appointment as class counsel, the court may appoint that applicant only if the applicant is adequate under Rule 23(g)(1) and (4). If more than one adequate applicant seeks appointment, the court must appoint the applicant best able to represent the interests of the class.

(3) Interim Counsel. The court may designate interim counsel to act on behalf of a putative class before determining whether to certify the action as a class action.

(4) Duty of Class Counsel. Class counsel must fairly and adequately represent the interests of the class.

(h) Attorney's Fees and Nontaxable Costs. In a certified class action, the court may award reasonable attorney's fees and nontaxable costs that are authorized by law or by the parties' agreement. The following procedures apply:

(1) A claim for an award must be made by motion under Rule 54(d)(2), subject to the provisions of this subdivision (h), at a time the court sets. Notice of the motion must be served on all parties and, for motions by class counsel, directed to class members in a reasonable manner.

(2) A class member, or a party from whom payment is sought, may object to the motion.

(3) The court may hold a hearing and must find the facts and state its legal conclusions under Rule 52(a).

(4) The court may refer issues related to the amount of the award to a special master or a magistrate judge, as provided in Rule 54(d)(2)(D).

(As amended Feb. 28, 1966, eff. July 1, 1966; Mar. 2, 1987, eff. Aug. 1, 1987; Apr. 24, 1998, eff. Dec. 1, 1998; Mar. 27, 2003, eff. Dec. 1, 2003; Apr. 30, 2007, eff. Dec. 1, 2007; Mar. 26, 2009, eff. Dec. 1, 2009.)

Notes of Advisory Committee on Rules—1937

Note to Subdivision (a). This is a substantial restatement of [former] Equity Rule 38 (Representatives of Class) as that rule has been construed. It applies to all actions, whether formerly denominated legal or equitable. For a general analysis of class actions, effect of judgment, and requisites of jurisdiction see Moore, Federal Rules of Civil Procedure: Some Problems Raised by the Preliminary Draft, 25 Georgetown L.J. 551, 570 et seq. (1937); Moore and Cohn, Federal Class Actions, 32 Ill.L.Rev. 307 (1937); Moore and Cohn, Federal Class Actions—Jurisdiction and Effect of Judgment, 32 Ill.L.Rev. 555—567 (1938); Lesar, Class Suits and the Federal Rules, 22 Minn.L.Rev. 34 (1937); cf. Arnold and James, Cases on Trials, Judgments and Appeals (1936) 175; and see Blume, Jurisdictional Amount in Representative Suits, 15 Minn.L.Rev. 501 (1931).

The general test of [former] Equity Rule 38 (Representatives of Class) that the question should be "one of common or general interest to many persons constituting a class so numerous as to make it impracticable to bring them all before the court," is a common test. For states which require the two elements of a common or general interest and numerous persons, as provided for in [former] Equity Rule 38, see Del.Ch.Rule 113; Fla.Comp.Gen.Laws Ann. (Supp., 1936) §4918 (7); Georgia Code (1933) §37–1002, and see English Rules Under the Judicature Act (The Annual Practice, 1937) O. 16, r. 9. For statutory provisions providing for class actions when the question is one of common or general interest or when the parties are numerous, see Ala.Code Ann. (Michie, 1928) §5701; 2 Ind.Stat.Ann. (Burns, 1933) §2–220; N.Y.C.P.A. (1937) §195; Wis.Stat. (1935) §260.12. These statutes have, however, been uniformly construed as though phrased in the conjunctive. See Garfein v. Stiglitz, 260 Ky. 430, 86 S.W.(2d) 155 (1935). The rule adopts the test of [former] Equity Rule 38, but defines what constitutes a "common or general interest". Compare with code provisions which make the action dependent upon the propriety of joinder of the parties. See Blume, The "Common Questions" Principle in the Code Provision for Representative Suits, 30 Mich.L.Rev. 878 (1932). For discussion of what constitutes "numerous persons" see Wheaton, Representative Suits Involving Numerous Litigants, 19 Corn.L.Q. 399 (1934); Note, 36 Harv.L.Rev. 89 (1922).

Clause (1), Joint, Common, or Secondary Right. This clause is illustrated in actions brought by or against representatives of an unincorporated association. See Oster v. Brotherhood of Locomotive Firemen and Enginemen, 271 Pa. 419, 114 Atl. 377 (1921); Pickett v. Walsh, 192 Mass. 572, 78 N.E. 753, 6 L.R.A. (N.S.) 1067 (1906); Colt v. Hicks, 97 Ind.App. 177, 179 N.E. 335 (1932). Compare Rule 17(b) as to when an unincorporated association has capacity to sue or be sued in its common name; United Mine Workers of America v. Coronado Coal Co., 259 U.S. 344 (1922) (an unincorporated association was sued as an entity for the purpose of enforcing against it a federal substantive right); Moore, Federal Rules of Civil Procedure: Some Problems Raised by the Preliminary Draft, 25 Georgetown L.J. 551, 566 (for discussion of jurisdictional requisites when an unincorporated association sues or is sued in its common name and jurisdiction is founded upon diversity of citizenship). For an action brought by representatives of one group against representatives of another group for distribution of a fund held by an unincorporated association, see Smith v. Swormstedt, 16 How. 288 (U.S. 1853). Compare Christopher, et al. v. Brusselback, 58 S.Ct. 350 [302 U.S. 500] (1938).

For an action to enforce rights held in common by policyholders against the corporate issuer of the policies, see Supreme Tribe of Ben Hur v. Cauble, 255 U.S. 356 (1921). See also Terry v. Little, 101 U.S. 216 (1880); John A. Roebling's Sons Co. v. Kinnicutt, 248 Fed. 596 (D.C.N.Y., 1917) dealing with the right held in common by creditors to enforce the statutory liability of stockholders.

Typical of a secondary action is a suit by stockholders to enforce a corporate right. For discussion of the general nature of these actions see Ashwander v. Tennessee Valley Authority, 297 U.S. 288 (1936); Glenn, The Stockholder's Suit—Corporate and Individual Grievances, 33 Yale L.J. 580 (1924); McLaughlin, Capacity of Plaintiff-Stockholder to Terminate a Stockholder's Suit, 46 Yale L.J. 421 (1937). See also Subdivision (b) of this rule which deals with Shareholder's Action; Note, 15 Minn.L.Rev. 453 (1931).

Clause (2). A creditor's action for liquidation or reorganization of a corporation is illustrative of this clause. An action by a stockholder against certain named defendants as representatives of numerous claimants presents a situation converse to the creditor's action.

Clause (3). See Everglades Drainage League v. Napoleon Broward Drainage Dist., 253 Fed. 246 (D.C.Fla., 1918); Gramling v. Maxwell, 52 F.(2d) 256 (D.C.N.C., 1931), approved in 30 Mich.L.Rev. 624 (1932); Skinner v. Mitchell, 108 Kan. 861, 197 Pac. 569 (1921); Duke of Bedford v. Ellis (1901) A.C. 1, for class actions when there were numerous persons and there was only a question of law or fact common to them; and see Blume, The "Common Questions" Principle in the Code Provision for Representative Suits, 30 Mich.L.Rev. 878 (1932).

Note to Subdivision (b). This is [former] Equity Rule 27 (Stockholder's Bill) with verbal changes. See also Hawes v. Oakland, 104 U.S. 450, 26 L.Ed. 827 (1882) and former Equity Rule 94, promulgated January 23, 1882, 104 U.S. IX.

Note to Subdivision (c). See McLaughlin, Capacity of Plaintiff-Stockholder to Terminate a Stockholder's Suit, 46 Yale L.J. 421 (1937).

Notes of Advisory Committee on Rules—1946 Amendment

Subdivision (b), relating to secondary actions by shareholders, provides among other things, that in, such an action the complainant "shall aver (1) that the plaintiff was a shareholder at the time of the transaction of which he complains or that his share thereafter devolved on him by operation of law . . ."

As a result of the decision in Erie R. Co. v. Tompkins, 304 U.S. 64 (decided April 25, 1938, after this rule was promulgated by the Supreme Court, though before it took effect) a question has arisen as to whether the provision above quoted deals with a matter of substantive right or is a matter of procedure. If it is a matter of substantive law or right, then under Erie R. Co. v. Tompkins clause (1) may not be validly applied in cases pending in states whose local law permits a shareholder to maintain such actions, although not a shareholder at the time of the transactions complained of. The Advisory Committee, believing the question should be settled in the courts, proposes no change in Rule 23 but thinks rather that the situation should be explained in an appropriate note.

The rule has a long history. In Hawes v. Oakland (1882) 104 U.S. 450, the Court held that a shareholder could not maintain such an action unless he owned shares at the time of the transactions complained of, or unless they devolved on him by operation of law. At that time the decision in Swift v. Tyson (1842) 16 Peters 1, was the law, and the federal courts considered themselves free to establish their own principles of equity jurisprudence, so the Court was not in 1882 and has not been, until Erie R. Co. v. Tompkins in 1938, concerned with the question whether Hawes v. Oakland dealt with substantive right or procedure.

Following the decision in Hawes v. Oakland, and at the same term, the Court, to implement its decision, adopted [former] Equity Rule 94, which contained the same provision above quoted from Rule 23 F.R.C.P. The provision in [former] Equity Rule 94 was later embodied in [former] Equity Rule 27, of which the present Rule 23 is substantially a copy.

In City of Quincy v. Steel (1887) 120 U.S. 241, 245, the Court referring to Hawes v. Oakland said: "In order to give effect to the principles there laid down, this Court at that term adopted Rule 94 of the rules of practice for courts of equity of the United States."

Some other cases dealing with [former] Equity Rules 94 or 27 prior to the decision in Erie R. Co. v. Tompkins are Dimpfel v. Ohio & Miss. R. R. (1884) 110 U.S. 209; Illinois Central R. Co. v. Adams (1901) 180 U.S. 28, 34; Venner v. Great Northern Ry. (1908) 209 U.S. 24, 30; Jacobson v. General Motors Corp. (S.D.N.Y. 1938) 22 F.Supp. 255, 257. These cases generally treat Hawes v. Oakland as establishing a "principle" of equity, or as dealing not with jurisdiction but with the "right" to maintain an action, or have said that the defense under the equity rule is analogous to the defense that the plaintiff has no "title" and results in a dismissal "for want of equity."

Those state decisions which held that a shareholder acquiring stock after the event may maintain a derivative action are founded on the view that it is a right belonging to the shareholder at the time of the transaction and which passes as a right to the subsequent purchaser. See Pollitz v. Gould (1911) 202 N.Y. 11.

The first case arising after the decision in Erie R. Co. v. Tompkins, in which this problem was involved, was Summers v. Hearst (S.D.N.Y. 1938) 23 F.Supp. 986. It concerned [former] Equity Rule 27, as Federal Rule 23 was not then in effect. In a well considered opinion Judge Leibell reviewed the decisions and said: "The federal cases that discuss this section of Rule 27 support the view that it states a principle of substantive law." He quoted Pollitz v. Gould (1911) 202 N.Y. 11, as saying that the United States Supreme Court "seems to have been more concerned with establishing this rule as one of practice than of substantive law" but that "whether it be regarded as establishing a principle of law or a rule of practice, this authority has been subsequently followed in the United States courts."

He then concluded that, although the federal decisions treat the equity rule as "stating a principle of substantive law", if [former] "Equity Rule 27 is to be modified or revoked in view of Erie R. Co. v. Tompkins, it is not the province of this Court to suggest it, much less impliedly to follow that course by disregarding the mandatory provisions of the Rule."

Some other federal decisions since 1938 touch the question.

In Piccard v. Sperry Corporation (S.D.N.Y. 1941) 36 F.Supp. 1006, 1009–10, affirmed without opinion (C.C.A.2d, 1941) 120 F.(2d) 328, a shareholder, not such at the time of the transactions complained of, sought to intervene. The court held an intervenor was as much subject to Rule 23 as an original plaintiff; and that the requirement of Rule 23(b) was "a matter of practice," not substance, and applied in New York where the state law was otherwise, despite Erie R. Co. v. Tompkins. In York v. Guaranty Trust Co. of New York (C.C.A.2d, 1944) 143 F.(2d) 503, rev'd on other grounds (1945) 65 S.Ct. 1464, the court said: "Restrictions on the bringing of stockholders' actions, such as those imposed by F.R.C.P. 23(b) or other state statutes are procedural," citing the Piccard and other cases.

In Gallup v. Caldwell (C.C.A.3d, 1941) 120 F.(2d) 90, 95, arising in New Jersey, the point was raised but not decided, the court saying that it was not satisfied that the then New Jersey rule differed from Rule 23(b), and that "under the circumstances the proper course was to follow Rule 23(b)."

In Mullins v. De Soto Securities Co. (W.D.La. 1942) 45 F.Supp. 871, 878, the point was not decided, because the court found the Louisiana rule to be the same as that stated in Rule 23(b).

In Toebelman v. Missouri-Kansas Pipe Line Co. (D.Del. 1941) 41 F.Supp. 334, 340, the court dealt only with another part of Rule 23(b), relating to prior demands on the stockholders and did not discuss Erie R. Co. v. Tompkins, or its effect on the rule.

In Perrott v. United States Banking Corp. (D.Del. 1944) 53 F.Supp. 953, it appeared that the Delaware law does not require the plaintiff to have owned shares at the time of the transaction complained of. The court sustained Rule 23(b), after discussion of the authorities, saying:

"It seems to me the rule does not go beyond procedure. * * * Simply because a particular plaintiff cannot qualify as a proper party to maintain such an action does not destroy or even whittle at the cause of action. The cause of action exists until a qualified plaintiff can get it started in a federal court."

In Bankers Nat. Corp. v. Barr (S.D.N.Y. 1945) 9 Fed.Rules Serv. 23b.11, Case 1, the court held Rule 23(b) to be one of procedure, but that whether the plaintiff was a stockholder was a substantive question to be settled by state law.

The New York rule, as stated in Pollitz v. Gould, supra, has been altered by an act of the New York Legislature (Chapter 667, Laws of 1944, effective April 9, 1944, General Corporation Law, §61) which provides that "in any action brought by a shareholder in the right of a . . . corporation, it must appear that the plaintiff was a stockholder at the time of the transaction of which he complains, or that his stock thereafter devolved upon him by operation of law." At the same time a further and separate provision was enacted, requiring under certain circumstances the giving of security for reasonable expenses and attorney's fees, to which security the corporation in whose right the action is brought and the defendants therein may have recourse. (Chapter 668, Laws of 1944, effective April 9, 1944, General Corporation Law, §61–b.) These provisions are aimed at so-called "strike" stockholders' suits and their attendant abuses. Shielcrawt v. Moffett (Ct.App. 1945) 294 N.Y. 180, 61 N.E.(2d) 435, rev'g 51 N.Y.S.(2d) 188, aff'g 49 N.Y.S.(2d) 64; Noel Associates, Inc. v. Merrill (Sup.Ct. 1944) 184 Misc. 646, 53 N.Y.S.(2d) 143.

Insofar as §61 is concerned, it has been held that the section is procedural in nature. Klum v. Clinton Trust Co. (Sup.Ct. 1944) 183 Misc. 340, 48 N.Y.S.(2d) 267; Noel Associates, Inc. v. Merrill, supra. In the latter case the court pointed out that "The 1944 amendment to Section 61 rejected the rule laid down in the Pollitz case and substituted, in place thereof, in its precise language, the rule which has long prevailed in the Federal Courts and which is now Rule 23(b) . . ." There is, nevertheless, a difference of opinion regarding the application of the statute to pending actions. See Klum v. Clinton Trust Co., supra (applicable); Noel Associates, Inc. v. Merrill, supra (inapplicable).

With respect to §61–b, which may be regarded as a separate problem (Noel Associates, Inc. v. Merrill, supra), it has been held that even though the statute is procedural in nature—a matter not definitely decided—the Legislature evinced no intent that the provision should apply to actions pending when it became effective. Shielcrawt v. Moffett, supra. As to actions instituted after the effective date of the legislation, the constitutionality of §61–b is in dispute. See Wolf v. Atkinson (Sup.Ct. 1944) 182 Misc. 675, 49 N.Y.S.(2d) 703 (constitutional); Citron v. Mangel Stores Corp. (Sup.Ct. 1944) — Misc. —, 50 N.Y.S.(2d) 416 (unconstitutional); Zlinkoff, The American Investor and the Constitutionality of Section 61–B of the New York General Corporation Law (1945) 54 Yale L.J. 352.

New Jersey also enacted a statute, similar to Chapters 667 and 668 of the New York law. See P.L. 1945, Ch. 131, R.S.Cum.Supp. 14:3–15. The New Jersey provision similar to Chapter 668 (§61–b) differs, however, in that it specifically applies retroactively. It has been held that this provision is procedural and hence will not govern a pending action brought against a New Jersey corporation in the New York courts. Shielcrawt v. Moffett (Sup.Ct.N.Y. 1945) 184 Misc. 1074, 56 N.Y.S.(2d) 134.

See also generally, 2 Moore's Federal Practice (1938) 2250–2253, and Cum.Supplement §23.05.

The decisions here discussed show that the question is a debatable one, and that there is respectable authority for either view, with a recent trend towards the view that Rule 23(b)(1) is procedural. There is reason to say that the question is one which should not be decided by the Supreme Court ex parte, but left to await a judicial decision in a litigated case, and that in the light of the material in this note, the only inference to be drawn from a failure to amend Rule 23(b) would be that the question is postponed to await a litigated case.

The Advisory Committee is unanimously of the opinion that this course should be followed.

If, however, the final conclusion is that the rule deals with a matter of substantive right, then the rule should be amended by adding a provision that Rule 23(b)(1) does not apply in jurisdictions where state law permits a shareholder to maintain a secondary action, although he was not a shareholder at the time of the transactions of which he complains.

Notes of Advisory Committee on Rules—1966 Amendment

Difficulties with the original rule. The categories of class actions in the original rule were defined in terms of the abstract nature of the rights involved: the so-called "true" category was defined as involving "joint, common, or secondary rights"; the "hybrid" category, as involving "several" rights related to "specific property"; the "spurious" category, as involving "several" rights affected by a common question and related to common relief. It was thought that the definitions accurately described the situations amendable to the class-suit device, and also would indicate the proper extent of the judgment in each category, which would in turn help to determine the res judicata effect of the judgment if questioned in a later action. Thus the judgments in "true" and "hybrid" class actions would extend to the class (although in somewhat different ways); the judgment in a "spurious" class action would extend only to the parties including intervenors. See Moore, Federal Rules of Civil Procedure: Some Problems Raised by the Preliminary Draft, 25 Geo.L.J. 551, 570–76 (1937).

In practice, the terms "joint," "common," etc., which were used as the basis of the Rule 23 classification proved obscure and uncertain. See Chaffee, Some Problems of Equity 245–46, 256–57 (1950); Kalven & Rosenfield, The Contemporary Function of the Class Suit, 8 U. of Chi.L.Rev. 684, 707 & n. 73 (1941); Keeffe, Levy & Donovan, Lee Defeats Ben Hur, 33 Corn.L.Q. 327, 329–36 (1948); Developments in the Law: Multiparty Litigation in the Federal Courts, 71 Harv.L.Rev. 874, 931 (1958); Advisory Committee's Note to Rule 19, as amended. The courts had considerable difficulty with these terms. See, e.g., Gullo v. Veterans' Coop. H. Assn., 13 F.R.D. 11 (D.D.C. 1952); Shipley v. Pittsburgh & L. E. R. Co., 70 F.Supp. 870 (W.D.Pa. 1947); Deckert v. Independence Shares Corp., 27 F.Supp. 763 (E.D.Pa. 1939), rev'd, 108 F.2d 51 (3d Cir. 1939), rev'd, 311 U.S. 282 (1940), on remand, 39 F.Supp. 592 (E.D.Pa. 1941), rev'd sub nom. Pennsylvania Co. for Ins. on Lives v. Deckert, 123 F.2d 979 (3d Cir. 1941) (see Chafee, supra, at 264–65).

Nor did the rule provide an adequate guide to the proper extent of the judgments in class actions. First, we find instances of the courts classifying actions as "true" or intimating that the judgments would be decisive for the class where these results seemed appropriate but were reached by dint of depriving the word "several" of coherent meaning. See, e.g., System Federation No. 91 v. Reed, 180 F.2d 991 (6th Cir. 1950); Wilson v. City of Paducah, 100 F.Supp. 116 (W.D.Ky. 1951); Citizens Banking Co. v. Monticello State Bank, 143 F.2d 261 (8th Cir. 1944); Redmond v. Commerce Trust Co., 144 F.2d 140 (8th Cir. 1944), cert. denied, 323 U.S. 776 (1944); United States v. American Optical Co., 97 F.Supp. 66 (N.D.Ill. 1951); National Hairdressers' & C. Assn. v. Philad. Co., 34 F.Supp. 264 (D.Del. 1940); 41 F.Supp. 701 (D.Del. 1940), aff'd mem., 129 F.2d 1020 (3d Cir. 1942). Second, we find cases classified by the courts as "spurious" in which, on a realistic view, it would seem fitting for the judgments to extend to the class. See, e.g., Knapp v. Bankers Sec. Corp., 17 F.R.D. 245 (E.D.Pa. 1954); aff'd 230 F.2d 717 (3d Cir. 1956); Giesecke v. Denver Tramway Corp., 81 F.Supp. 957 (D.Del. 1949); York v. Guaranty Trust Co., 143 F.2d 503 (2d Cir. 1944), rev'd on grounds not here relevant, 326 U.S. 90 (1945) (see Chafee, supra, at 208); cf. Webster Eisenlohr, Inc. v. Kalodner, 145 F.2d 316, 320 (3d Cir. 1944), cert. denied, 325 U.S. 807 (1945). But cf. the early decisions, Duke of Bedford v. Ellis [1901], A.C. 1; Sheffield Waterworks v. Yeomans, L.R. 2 Ch.App. 8 (1866); Brown v. Vermuden, 1 Ch.Cas. 272, 22 Eng.Rep. 796 (1676).

The "spurious" action envisaged by original Rule 23 was in any event an anomaly because, although denominated a "class" action and pleaded as such, it was supposed not to adjudicate the rights or liabilities of any person not a party. It was believed to be an advantage of the "spurious" category that it would invite decisions that a member of the "class" could, like a member of the class in a "true" or "hybrid" action, intervene on an ancillary basis without being required to show an independent basis of Federal jurisdiction, and have the benefit of the date of the commencement of the action for purposes of the statute of limitations. See 3 Moore's Federal Practice, pars. 23.10[1], 23.12 (2d ed. 1963). These results were attained in some instances but not in others. On the statute of limitations, see Union Carbide & Carbon Corp. v. Nisley, 300 F.2d 561 (10th Cir. 1961), pet. cert. dism., 371 U.S. 801 (1963); but cf. P. W. Husserl, Inc. v. Newman, 25 F.R.D. 264 (S.D.N.Y. 1960); Athas v. Day, 161 F.Supp. 916 (D.Colo. 1958). On ancillary intervention, see Amen v. Black, 234 F.2d 12 (10th Cir. 1956), cert. granted, 352 U.S. 888 (1956), dism. on stip., 355 U.S. 600 (1958); but. cf. Wagner v. Kemper, 13 F.R.D. 128 (W.D.Mo. 1952). The results, however, can hardly depend upon the mere appearance of a "spurious" category in the rule; they should turn no more basic considerations. See discussion of subdivision (c)(1) below.

Finally, the original rule did not squarely address itself to the question of the measures that might be taken during the course of the action to assure procedural fairness, particularly giving notice to members of the class, which may in turn be related in some instances to the extension of the judgment to the class. See Chafee, supra, at 230–31; Keeffe, Levy & Donovan, supra; Developments in the Law, supra, 71 Harv.L.Rev. at 937–38; Note, Binding Effect of Class Actions, 67 Harv.L.Rev. 1059, 1062–65 (1954); Note, Federal Class Actions: A Suggested Revision of Rule 23, 46 Colum.L.Rev. 818, 833–36 (1946); Mich.Gen.Court R. 208.4 (effective Jan. 1, 1963); Idaho R.Civ.P. 23(d); Minn.R.Civ.P. 23.04; N.Dak.R.Civ.P. 23(d).

The amended rule describes in more practical terms the occasions for maintaining class actions; provides that all class actions maintained to the end as such will result in judgments including those whom the court finds to be members of the class, whether or not the judgment is favorable to the class; and refers to the measures which can be taken to assure the fair conduct of these actions.

Subdivision (a) states the prerequisites for maintaining any class action in terms of the numerousness of the class making joinder of the members impracticable, the existence of questions common to the class, and the desired qualifications of the representative parties. See Weinstein, Revision of Procedure; Some Problems in Class Actions, 9 Buffalo L.Rev. 433, 458–59 (1960); 2 Barron & Holtzoff, Federal Practice & Procedure §562, at 265, §572, at 351–52 (Wright ed. 1961). These are necessary but not sufficient conditions for a class action. See, e.g., Giordano v. Radio Corp. of Am., 183 F.2d 558, 560 (3d Cir. 1950); Zachman v. Erwin, 186 F.Supp. 681 (S.D.Tex. 1959); Baim & Blank, Inc. v. Warren Connelly Co., Inc., 19 F.R.D. 108 (S.D.N.Y. 1956). Subdivision (b) describes the additional elements which in varying situations justify the use of a class action.

Subdivision (b)(1). The difficulties which would be likely to arise if resort were had to separate actions by or against the individual members of the class here furnish the reasons for, and the principal key to, the propriety and value of utilizing the class-action device. The considerations stated under clauses (A) and (B) are comparable to certain of the elements which define the persons whose joinder in an action is desirable as stated in Rule 19(a), as amended. See amended Rule 19(a)(2)(i) and (ii), and the Advisory Committee's Note thereto; Hazard, Indispensable Party; The Historical Origin of a Procedural Phantom, 61 Colum.L.Rev. 1254, 1259–60 (1961); cf. 3 Moore, supra, par. 23.08, at 3435.

Clause (A): One person may have rights against, or be under duties toward, numerous persons constituting a class, and be so positioned that conflicting or varying adjudications in lawsuits with individual members of the class might establish incompatible standards to govern his conduct. The class action device can be used effectively to obviate the actual or virtual dilemma which would thus confront the party opposing the class. The matter has been stated thus: "The felt necessity for a class action is greatest when the courts are called upon to order or sanction the alteration of the status quo in circumstances such that a large number of persons are in a position to call on a single person to alter the status quo, or to complain if it is altered, and the possibility exists that [the] actor might be called upon to act in inconsistent ways." Louisell & Hazard, Pleading and Procedure; State and Federal 719 (1962); see Supreme Tribe of Ben-Hur v. Cauble, 255 U.S. 356, 366–67 (1921). To illustrate: Separate actions by individuals against a municipality to declare a bond issue invalid or condition or limit it, to prevent or limit the making of a particular appropriation or to compel or invalidate an assessment, might create a risk of inconsistent or varying determinations. In the same way, individual litigations of the rights and duties of riparian owners, or of landowners' rights and duties respecting a claimed nuisance, could create a possibility of incompatible adjudications. Actions by or against a class provide a ready and fair means of achieving unitary adjudication. See Maricopa County Mun. Water Con. Dist. v. Looney, 219 F.2d 529 (9th Cir. 1955); Rank v. Krug, 142 F.Supp. 1, 154–59 (S.D.Calif. 1956), on app., State of California v. Rank, 293 F.2d 340, 348 (9th Cir. 1961); Gart v. Cole, 263 F.2d 244 (2d Cir. 1959), cert. denied 359 U.S. 978 (1959); cf. Martinez v. Maverick Cty. Water Con. & Imp. Dist., 219 F.2d 666 (5th Cir. 1955); 3 Moore, supra, par. 23.11[2], at 3458–59.

Clause (B): This clause takes in situations where the judgment in a nonclass action by or against an individual member of the class, while not technically concluding the other members, might do so as a practical matter. The vice of an individual actions would lie in the fact that the other members of the class, thus practically concluded, would have had no representation in the lawsuit. In an action by policy holders against a fraternal benefit association attacking a financial reorganization of the society, it would hardly have been practical, if indeed it would have been possible, to confine the effects of a validation of the reorganization to the individual plaintiffs. Consequently a class action was called for with adequate representation of all members of the class. See Supreme Tribe of Ben-Hur v. Cauble, 255 U.S. 356 (1921); Waybright v. Columbian Mut. Life Ins. Co., 30 F.Supp. 885 (W.D.Tenn. 1939); cf. Smith v. Swormstedt, 16 How. (57 U.S.) 288 (1853). For much the same reason actions by shareholders to compel the declaration of a dividend the proper recognition and handling of redemption or pre-emption rights, or the like (or actions by the corporation for corresponding declarations of rights), should ordinarily be conducted as class actions, although the matter has been much obscured by the insistence that each shareholder has an individual claim. See Knapp v. Bankers Securities Corp., 17 F.R.D. 245 (E.D.Pa. 1954), aff'd, 230 F.2d 717 (3d Cir. 1956); Giesecke v. Denver Tramway Corp., 81 F.Supp. 957 (D.Del. 1949); Zahn v. Transamerica Corp., 162 F.2d 36 (3d Cir. 1947); Speed v. Transamerica Corp., 100 F.Supp. 461 (D.Del. 1951); Sobel v. Whittier Corp., 95 F.Supp. 643 (E.D.Mich. 1951), app. dism., 195 F.2d 361 (6th Cir. 1952); Goldberg v. Whittier Corp., 111 F.Supp. 382 (E.D.Mich. 1953); Dann v. Studebaker-Packard Corp., 288 F.2d 201 (6th Cir. 1961); Edgerton v. Armour & Co.,94 F.Supp. 549 (S.D.Calif. 1950); Ames v. Mengel Co., 190 F.2d 344 (2d Cir. 1951). (These shareholders' actions are to be distinguished from derivative actions by shareholders dealt with in new Rule 23.1). The same reasoning applies to an action which charges a breach of trust by an indenture trustee or other fiduciary similarly affecting the members of a large class of security holders or other beneficiaries, and which requires an accounting or like measures to restore the subject of the trust. See Bosenberg v. Chicago T. & T. Co., 128 F.2d 245 (7th Cir. 1942); Citizens Banking Co. v. Monticello State Bank, 143 F.2d 261 (8th Cir. 1944); Redmond v. Commerce Trust Co., 144 F.2d 140 (8th Cir. 1944), cert. denied, 323 U.S. 776 (1944); cf. York v. Guaranty Trust Co., 143 F.2d 503 (2d Cir. 1944), rev'd on grounds not here relevant, 326 U.S. 99 (1945).

In various situations an adjudication as to one or more members of the class will necessarily or probably have an adverse practical effect on the interests of other members who should therefore be represented in the lawsuit. This is plainly the case when claims are made by numerous persons against a fund insufficient to satisfy all claims. A class action by or against representative members to settle the validity of the claims as a whole, or in groups, followed by separate proof of the amount of each valid claim and proportionate distribution of the fund, meets the problem. Cf. Dickinson v. Burnham, 197 F.2d 973 (2d Cir. 1952), cert. denied, 344 U.S. 875 (1952); 3 Moore, supra, at par. 23.09. The same reasoning applies to an action by a creditor to set aside a fraudulent conveyance by the debtor and to appropriate the property to his claim, when the debtor's assets are insufficient to pay all creditors' claims. See Hefferman v. Bennett & Armour, 110 Cal.App.2d 564, 243 P.2d 846 (1952); cf. City & County of San Francisco v. Market Street Ry., 95 Cal.App.2d 648, 213 P.2d 780 (1950). Similar problems, however, can arise in the absence of a fund either present or potential. A negative or mandatory injunction secured by one of a numerous class may disable the opposing party from performing claimed duties toward the other members of the class or materially affect his ability to do so. An adjudication as to movie "clearances and runs" nominally affecting only one exhibitor would often have practical effects on all the exhibitors in the same territorial area. Cf. United States v. Paramount Pictures, Inc., 66 F.Supp. 323, 341–46 (S.D.N.Y. 1946); 334 U.S. 131, 144–48 (1948). Assuming a sufficiently numerous class of exhibitors, a class action would be advisable. (Here representation of subclasses of exhibitors could become necessary; see subdivision (c)(3)(B).)

Subdivision (b)(2). This subdivision is intended to reach situations where a party has taken action or refused to take action with respect to a class, and final relief of an injunctive nature or of a corresponding declaratory nature, settling the legality of the behavior with respect to the class as a whole, is appropriate. Declaratory relief "corresponds" to injunctive relief when as a practical matter it affords injunctive relief or serves as a basis for later injunctive relief. The subdivision does not extend to cases in which the appropriate final relief relates exclusively or predominantly to money damages. Action or inaction is directed to a class within the meaning of this subdivision even if it has taken effect or is threatened only as to one or a few members of the class, provided it is based on grounds which have general application to the class.

Illustrative are various actions in the civil-rights field where a party is charged with discriminating unlawfully against a class, usually one whose members are incapable of specific enumeration. See Potts v. Flax, 313 F.2d 284 (5th Cir. 1963); Bailey v. Patterson, 323 F.2d 201 (5th Cir. 1963), cert. denied, 377 U.S. 972 (1964); Brunson v. Board of Trustees of School District No. 1, Clarendon City, S.C., 311 F.2d 107 (4th Cir. 1962), cert. denied, 373 U.S. 933 (1963); Green v. School Bd. of Roanoke, Va., 304 F.2d 118 (4th Cir. 1962); Orleans Parish School Bd. v. Bush, 242 F.2d 156 (5th Cir. 1957), cert. denied, 354 U.S. 921 (1957); Mannings v. Board of Public Inst. of Hillsborough County, Fla., 277 F.2d 370 (5th Cir. 1960); Northcross v. Board of Ed. of City of Memphis, 302 F.2d 818 (6th Cir. 1962), cert. denied 370 U.S. 944 (1962); Frasier v. Board of Trustees of Univ. of N.C., 134 F.Supp. 589 (M.D.N.C. 1955, 3-judge court), aff'd, 350 U.S. 979 (1956). Subdivision (b)(2) is not limited to civil-rights cases. Thus an action looking to specific or declaratory relief could be brought by a numerous class of purchasers, say retailers of a given description, against a seller alleged to have undertaken to sell to that class at prices higher than those set for other purchasers, say retailers of another description, when the applicable law forbids such a pricing differential. So also a patentee of a machine, charged with selling or licensing the machine on condition that purchasers or licensees also purchase or obtain licenses to use an ancillary unpatented machine, could be sued on a class basis by a numerous group of purchasers or licensees, or by a numerous group of competing sellers or licensors of the unpatented machine, to test the legality of the "tying" condition.

Subdivision (b)(3). In the situations to which this subdivision relates, class-action treatment is not as clearly called for as in those described above, but it may nevertheless be convenient and desirable depending upon the particular facts. Subdivision (b)(3) encompasses those cases in which a class action would achieve economies of time, effort, and expense, and promote, uniformity of decision as to persons similarly situated, without sacrificing procedural fairness or bringing about other undesirable results. Cf. Chafee, supra, at 201.

The court is required to find, as a condition of holding that a class action may be maintained under this subdivision, that the questions common to the class predominate over the questions affecting individual members. It is only where this predominance exists that economies can be achieved by means of the class-action device. In this view, a fraud perpetrated on numerous persons by the use of similar misrepresentations may be an appealing situation for a class action, and it may remain so despite the need, if liability is found, for separate determination of the damages suffered by individuals within the class. On the other hand, although having some common core, a fraud case may be unsuited for treatment as a class action if there was material variation in the representation made or in the kinds or degrees of reliance by the persons to whom they were addressed. See Oppenheimer v. F. J. Young & Co., Inc., 144 F.2d 387 (2d Cir. 1944); Miller v. National City Bank of N.Y., 166 F.2d 723 (2d Cir. 1948); and for like problems in other contexts, see Hughes v. Encyclopaedia Brittanica, 199 F.2d 295 (7th Cir. 1952); Sturgeon v. Great Lakes Steel Corp., 143 F.2d 819 (6th Cir. 1944). A "mass accident" resulting in injuries to numerous persons is ordinarily not appropriate for a class action because of the likelihood that significant questions, not only of damages but of liability and defenses of liability, would be present, affecting the individuals in different ways. In these circumstances an action conducted nominally as a class action would degenerate in practice into multiple lawsuits separately tried. See Pennsylvania R.R. v. United States, 111 F.Supp. 80 (D.N.J. 1953); cf. Weinstein, supra, 9 Buffalo L.Rev. at 469. Private damage claims by numerous individuals arising out of concerted antitrust violations may or may not involve predominating common questions. See Union Carbide & Carbon Corp. v. Nisley, 300 F.2d 561 (10th Cir. 1961), pet. cert. dism., 371 U.S. 801 (1963); cf. Weeks v. Bareco Oil Co., 125 F.2d 84 (7th Cir. 1941); Kainz v. Anheuser-Busch, Inc., 194 F.2d 737 (7th Cir. 1952); Hess v. Anderson, Clayton & Co., 20 F.R.D. 466 (S.D.Calif. 1957).

That common questions predominate is not itself sufficient to justify a class action under subdivision (b)(3), for another method of handling the litigious situation may be available which has greater practical advantages. Thus one or more actions agreed to by the parties as test or model actions may be preferable to a class action; or it may prove feasible and preferable to consolidate actions. Cf. Weinstein, supra, 9 Buffalo L.Rev. at 438–54. Even when a number of separate actions are proceeding simultaneously, experience shows that the burdens on the parties and the courts can sometimes be reduced by arrangements for avoiding repetitious discovery or the like. Currently the Coordinating Committee on Multiple Litigation in the United States District Courts (a subcommittee of the Committee on Trial Practice and Technique of the Judicial Conference of the United States) is charged with developing methods for expediting such massive litigation. To reinforce the point that the court with the aid of the parties ought to assess the relative advantages of alternative procedures for handling the total controversy, subdivision (b)(3) requires, as a further condition of maintaining the class action, that the court shall find that that procedure is "superior" to the others in the particular circumstances.

Factors (A)–(D) are listed, non-exhaustively, as pertinent to the findings. The court is to consider the interests of individual members of the class in controlling their own litigations and carrying them on as they see fit. See Weeks v. Bareco Oil Co., 125 F.2d 84, 88–90, 93–94 (7th Cir. 1941) (anti-trust action); see also Pentland v. Dravo Corp., 152 F.2d 851 (3d Cir. 1945), and Chaffee, supra, at 273–75, regarding policy of Fair Labor Standards Act of 1938, §16(b), 29 U.S.C. §216(b), prior to amendment by Portal-to-Portal Act of 1947, §5(a). [The present provisions of 29 U.S.C. §216(b) are not intended to be affected by Rule 23, as amended.]

In this connection the court should inform itself of any litigation actually pending by or against the individuals. The interests of individuals in conducting separate lawsuits may be so strong as to call for denial of a class action. On the other hand, these interests may be theoretic rather than practical; the class may have a high degree of cohesion and prosecution of the action through representatives would be quite unobjectionable, or the amounts at stake for individuals may be so small that separate suits would be impracticable. The burden that separate suits would impose on the party opposing the class, or upon the court calendars, may also fairly be considered. (See the discussion, under subdivision (c)(2) below, of the right of members to be excluded from the class upon their request.)

Also pertinent is the question of the desirability of concentrating the trial of the claims in the particular forum by means of a class action, in contrast to allowing the claims to be litigated separately in forums to which they would ordinarily be brought. Finally, the court should consider the problems of management which are likely to arise in the conduct of a class action.

Subdivision (c)(1). In order to give clear definition to the action, this provision requires the court to determine, as early in the proceedings as may be practicable, whether an action brought as a class action is to be so maintained. The determination depends in each case on satisfaction of the terms of subdivision (a) and the relevant provisions of subdivision (b).

An order embodying a determination can be conditional; the court may rule, for example, that a class action may be maintained only if the representation is improved through intervention of additional parties of a stated type. A determination once made can be altered or amended before the decision on the merits if, upon fuller development of the facts, the original determination appears unsound. A negative determination means that the action should be stripped of its character as a class action. See subdivision (d)(4). Although an action thus becomes a nonclass action, the court may still be receptive to interventions before the decision on the merits so that the litigation may cover as many interests as can be conveniently handled; the questions whether the intervenors in the nonclass action shall be permitted to claim "ancillary" jurisdiction or the benefit of the date of the commencement of the action for purposes of the statute of limitations are to be decided by reference to the laws governing jurisdiction and limitations as they apply in particular contexts.

Whether the court should require notice to be given to members of the class of its intention to make a determination, or of the order embodying it, is left to the court's discretion under subdivision (d)(2).

Subdivision (c)(2) makes special provision for class actions maintained under subdivision (b)(3). As noted in the discussion of the latter subdivision, the interests of the individuals in pursuing their own litigations may be so strong here as to warrant denial of a class action altogether. Even when a class action is maintained under subdivision (b)(3), this individual interest is respected. Thus the court is required to direct notice to the members of the class of the right of each member to be excluded from the class upon his request. A member who does not request exclusion may, if he wishes, enter an appearance in the action through his counsel; whether or not he does so, the judgment in the action will embrace him.

The notice setting forth the alternatives open to the members of the class, is to be the best practicable under the circumstances, and shall include individual notice to the members who can be identified through reasonable effort. (For further discussion of this notice, see the statement under subdivision (d)(2) below.)

Subdivision (c)(3). The judgment in a class action maintained as such to the end will embrace the class, that is, in a class action under subdivision (b)(1) or (b)(2), those found by the court to be class members; in a class action under subdivision (b)(3), those to whom the notice prescribed by subdivision (c)(2) was directed, excepting those who requested exclusion or who are ultimately found by the court not to be members of the class. The judgment has this scope whether it is favorable or unfavorable to the class. In a (b)(1) or (b)(2) action the judgment "describes" the members of the class, but need not specify the individual members; in a (b)(3) action the judgment "specifies" the individual members who have been identified and described the others.

Compare subdivision (c)(4) as to actions conducted as class actions only with respect to particular issues. Where the class-action character of the lawsuit is based solely on the existence of a "limited fund," the judgment, while extending to all claims of class members against the fund, has ordinarily left unaffected the personal claims of nonappearing members against the debtor. See 3 Moore, supra, par. 23.11[4].

Hitherto, in a few actions conducted as "spurious" class actions and thus nominally designed to extend only to parties and others intervening before the determination of liability, courts have held or intimated that class members might be permitted to intervene after a decision on the merits favorable to their interests, in order to secure the benefits of the decision for themselves, although they would presumably be unaffected by an unfavorable decision. See, as to the propriety of this so-called "one-way" intervention in "spurious" actions, the conflicting views expressed in Union Carbide & Carbon Corp. v. Nisley, 300 F.2d 561 (10th Cir. 1961), pet. cert. dism., 371 U.S. 801 (1963); York v. Guaranty Trust Co., 143 F.2d 503, 529 (2d Cir. 1944), rev'd on grounds not here relevant, 326 U.S. 99 (1945); Pentland v. Dravo Corp., 152 F.2d 851, 856 (3d Cir. 1945); Speed v. Transamerica Corp., 100 F.Supp. 461, 463 (D.Del. 1951); State Wholesale Grocers v. Great Atl. & Pac. Tea Co., 24 F.R.D. 510 (N.D.Ill. 1959); Alabama Ind. Serv. Stat. Assn. v. Shell Pet Corp., 28 F.Supp. 386, 390 (N.D.Ala. 1939); Tolliver v. Cudahy Packing Co., 39 F.Supp. 337, 339 (E.D.Tenn. 1941); Kalven & Rosenfield, supra, 8 U. of Chi.L.Rev. 684 (1941); Comment, 53 Nw.U.L.Rev. 627, 632–33 (1958); Developments in the Law, supra, 71 Harv.L.Rev. at 935; 2 Barron & Holtzoff, supra, §568; but cf. Lockwood v. Hercules Powder Co., 7 F.R.D. 24, 28–29 (W.D.Mo. 1947); Abram v. San Joaquin Cotton Oil Co., 46 F.Supp. 969, 976–77 (S.D.Calif. 1942); Chaffee, supra, at 280, 285; 3 Moore, supra, par. 23.12, at 3476. Under proposed subdivision (c)(3), one-way intervention is excluded; the action will have been early determined to be a class or nonclass action, and in the former case the judgment, whether or not favorable, will include the class, as above stated.

Although thus declaring that the judgment in a class action includes the class, as defined, subdivision (c)(3) does not disturb the recognized principle that the court conducting the action cannot predetermine the res judicata effect of the judgment; this can be tested only in a subsequent action. See Restatement, Judgments §86, comment (h), §116 (1942). The court, however, in framing the judgment in any suit brought as a class action, must decide what its extent or coverage shall be, and if the matter is carefully considered, questions of res judicata are less likely to be raised at a later time and if raised will be more satisfactorily answered. See Chafee, supra, at 294; Weinstein, supra, 9 Buffalo L.Rev. at 460.

Subdivision (c)(4). This provision recognizes that an action may be maintained as a class action as to particular issues only. For example, in a fraud or similar case the action may retain its "class" character only through the adjudication of liability to the class; the members of the class may thereafter be required to come in individually and prove the amounts of their respective claims.

Two or more classes may be represented in a single action. Where a class is found to include subclasses divergent in interest, the class may be divided correspondingly, and each subclass treated as a class.

Subdivision (d) is concerned with the fair and efficient conduct of the action and lists some types of orders which may be appropriate.

The court should consider how the proceedings are to be arranged in sequence, and what measures should be taken to simplify the proof and argument. See subdivision (d)(1). The orders resulting from this consideration, like the others referred to in subdivision (d), may be combined with a pretrial order under Rule 16, and are subject to modification as the case proceeds.

Subdivision (d)(2) sets out a non-exhaustive list of possible occasions for orders requiring notice to the class. Such notice is not a novel conception. For example, in "limited fund" cases, members of the class have been notified to present individual claims after the basic class decision. Notice has gone to members of a class so that they might express any opposition to the representation, see United States v. American Optical Co., 97 F.Supp. 66 (N.D.Ill. 1951), and 1950–51 CCH Trade Cases 64573–74 (par. 62869); cf. Weeks v. Bareco Oil Co., 125 F.2d 84, 94 (7th Cir. 1941), and notice may encourage interventions to improve the representation of the class. Cf. Oppenheimer v. F. J. Young & Co., 144 F.2d 387 (2d Cir. 1944). Notice has been used to poll members on a proposed modification of a consent decree. See record in Sam Fox Publishing Co. v. United States, 366 U.S. 683 (1961).

Subdivision (d)(2) does not require notice at any stage, but rather calls attention to its availability and invokes the court's discretion. In the degree that there is cohesiveness or unity in the class and the representation is effective, the need for notice to the class will tend toward a minimum. These indicators suggest that notice under subdivision (d)(2) may be particularly useful and advisable in certain class actions maintained under subdivision (b)(3), for example, to permit members of the class to object to the representation. Indeed, under subdivision (c)(2), notice must be ordered, and is not merely discretionary, to give the members in a subdivision (b)(3) class action an opportunity to secure exclusion from the class. This mandatory notice pursuant to subdivision (c)(2), together with any discretionary notice which the court may find it advisable to give under subdivision (d)(2), is designed to fulfill requirements of due process to which the class action procedure is of course subject. See Hansberry v. Lee, 311 U.S. 32 (1940); Mullane v. Central Hanover Bank & Trust Co., 339 U.S. 306 (1950); cf. Dickinson v. Burnham, 197 F.2d 973, 979 (2d Cir. 1952), and studies cited at 979 n. 4; see also All American Airways, Inc. v. Elderd, 209 F.2d 247, 249 (2d Cir. 1954); Gart v. Cole, 263 F.2d 244, 248–49 (2d Cir. 1959), cert. denied, 359 U.S. 978 (1959).

Notice to members of the class, whenever employed under amended Rule 23, should be accommodated to the particular purpose but need not comply with the formalities for service of process. See Chafee, supra, at 230–31; Brendle v. Smith, 7 F.R.D. 119 (S.D.N.Y. 1946). The fact that notice is given at one stage of the action does not mean that it must be given at subsequent stages. Notice is available fundamentally "for the protection of the members of the class or otherwise for the fair conduct of the action" and should not be used merely as a device for the undesirable solicitation of claims. See the discussion in Cherner v. Transitron Electronic Corp., 201 F.Supp. 934 (D.Mass. 1962); Hormel v. United States, 17 F.R.D. 303 (S.D.N.Y. 1955).

In appropriate cases the court should notify interested government agencies of the pendency of the action or of particular steps therein.

Subdivision (d)(3) reflects the possibility of conditioning the maintenance of a class action, e.g., on the strengthening of the representation, see subdivision (c)(1) above; and recognizes that the imposition of conditions on intervenors may be required for the proper and efficient conduct of the action.

As to orders under subdivision (d)(4), see subdivision (c)(1) above.

Subdivision (e) requires approval of the court, after notice, for the dismissal or compromise of any class action.

Notes of Advisory Committee on Rules—1987 Amendment

The amendments are technical. No substantive change is intended.

Committee Notes on Rules—1998 Amendment

Subdivision (f). This permissive interlocutory appeal provision is adopted under the power conferred by 28 U.S.C. §1292(e). Appeal from an order granting or denying class certification is permitted in the sole discretion of the court of appeals. No other type of Rule 23 order is covered by this provision. The court of appeals is given unfettered discretion whether to permit the appeal, akin to the discretion exercised by the Supreme Court in acting on a petition for certiorari. This discretion suggests an analogy to the provision in 28 U.S.C. §1292(b) for permissive appeal on certification by a district court. Subdivision (f), however, departs from the §1292(b) model in two significant ways. It does not require that the district court certify the certification ruling for appeal, although the district court often can assist the parties and court of appeals by offering advice on the desirability of appeal. And it does not include the potentially limiting requirements of §1292(b) that the district court order "involve[] a controlling question of law as to which there is substantial ground for difference of opinion and that an immediate appeal from the order may materially advance the ultimate termination of the litigation."

The courts of appeals will develop standards for granting review that reflect the changing areas of uncertainty in class litigation. The Federal Judicial Center study supports the view that many suits with class-action allegations present familiar and almost routine issues that are no more worthy of immediate appeal than many other interlocutory rulings. Yet several concerns justify expansion of present opportunities to appeal. An order denying certification may confront the plaintiff with a situation in which the only sure path to appellate review is by proceeding to final judgment on the merits of an individual claim that, standing alone, is far smaller than the costs of litigation. An order granting certification, on the other hand, may force a defendant to settle rather than incur the costs of defending a class action and run the risk of potentially ruinous liability. These concerns can be met at low cost by establishing in the court of appeals a discretionary power to grant interlocutory review in cases that show appeal-worthy certification issues.

Permission to appeal may be granted or denied on the basis of any consideration that the court of appeals finds persuasive. Permission is most likely to be granted when the certification decision turns on a novel or unsettled question of law, or when, as a practical matter, the decision on certification is likely dispositive of the litigation.

The district court, having worked through the certification decision, often will be able to provide cogent advice on the factors that bear on the decision whether to permit appeal. This advice can be particularly valuable if the certification decision is tentative. Even as to a firm certification decision, a statement of reasons bearing on the probable benefits and costs of immediate appeal can help focus the court of appeals decision, and may persuade the disappointed party that an attempt to appeal would be fruitless.

The 10-day period for seeking permission to appeal is designed to reduce the risk that attempted appeals will disrupt continuing proceedings. It is expected that the courts of appeals will act quickly in making the preliminary determination whether to permit appeal. Permission to appeal does not stay trial court proceedings. A stay should be sought first from the trial court. If the trial court refuses a stay, its action and any explanation of its views should weigh heavily with the court of appeals.

Appellate Rule 5 has been modified to establish the procedure for petitioning for leave to appeal under subdivision (f).

Changes Made after Publication (GAP Report). No changes were made in the text of Rule 23(f) as published.

Several changes were made in the published Committee Note. (1) References to 28 U.S.C. §1292(b) interlocutory appeals were revised to dispel any implication that the restrictive elements of §1292(b) should be read in to Rule 23(f). New emphasis was placed on court of appeals discretion by making explicit the analogy to certiorari discretion. (2) Suggestions that the new procedure is a "modest" expansion of appeal opportunities, to be applied with "restraint," and that permission "almost always will be denied when the certification decision turns on case-specific matters of fact and district court discretion," were deleted. It was thought better simply to observe that courts of appeals will develop standards "that reflect the changing areas of uncertainty in class litigation."

Committee Notes on Rules—2003 Amendment

Subdivision (c). Subdivision (c) is amended in several respects. The requirement that the court determine whether to certify a class "as soon as practicable after commencement of an action" is replaced by requiring determination "at an early practicable time." The notice provisions are substantially revised.

Paragraph (1). Subdivision (c)(1)(A) is changed to require that the determination whether to certify a class be made "at an early practicable time." The "as soon as practicable" exaction neither reflects prevailing practice nor captures the many valid reasons that may justify deferring the initial certification decision. See Willging, Hooper & Niemic, Empirical Study of Class Actions in Four Federal District Courts: Final Report to the Advisory Committee on Civil Rules 26–36 (Federal Judicial Center 1996).

Time may be needed to gather information necessary to make the certification decision. Although an evaluation of the probable outcome on the merits is not properly part of the certification decision, discovery in aid of the certification decision often includes information required to identify the nature of the issues that actually will be presented at trial. In this sense it is appropriate to conduct controlled discovery into the "merits," limited to those aspects relevant to making the certification decision on an informed basis. Active judicial supervision may be required to achieve the most effective balance that expedites an informed certification determination without forcing an artificial and ultimately wasteful division between "certification discovery" and "merits discovery." A critical need is to determine how the case will be tried. An increasing number of courts require a party requesting class certification to present a "trial plan" that describes the issues likely to be presented at trial and tests whether they are susceptible of class-wide proof. See Manual For Complex Litigation Third, §21.213, p. 44; §30.11, p. 214; §30.12, p. 215.

Other considerations may affect the timing of the certification decision. The party opposing the class may prefer to win dismissal or summary judgment as to the individual plaintiffs without certification and without binding the class that might have been certified. Time may be needed to explore designation of class counsel under Rule 23(g), recognizing that in many cases the need to progress toward the certification determination may require designation of interim counsel under Rule 23(g)(2)(A).

Although many circumstances may justify deferring the certification decision, active management may be necessary to ensure that the certification decision is not unjustifiably delayed.

Subdivision (c)(1)(C) reflects two amendments. The provision that a class certification "may be conditional" is deleted. A court that is not satisfied that the requirements of Rule 23 have been met should refuse certification until they have been met. The provision that permits alteration or amendment of an order granting or denying class certification is amended to set the cut-off point at final judgment rather than "the decision on the merits." This change avoids the possible ambiguity in referring to "the decision on the merits." Following a determination of liability, for example, proceedings to define the remedy may demonstrate the need to amend the class definition or subdivide the class. In this setting the final judgment concept is pragmatic. It is not the same as the concept used for appeal purposes, but it should be flexible, particularly in protracted litigation.

The authority to amend an order under Rule 23(c)(1) before final judgment does not restore the practice of "one-way intervention" that was rejected by the 1966 revision of Rule 23. A determination of liability after certification, however, may show a need to amend the class definition. Decertification may be warranted after further proceedings.

If the definition of a class certified under Rule 23(b)(3) is altered to include members who have not been afforded notice and an opportunity to request exclusion, notice—including an opportunity to request exclusion—must be directed to the new class members under Rule 23(c)(2)(B).

Paragraph (2). The first change made in Rule 23(c)(2) is to call attention to the court's authority—already established in part by Rule 23(d)(2)—to direct notice of certification to a Rule 23(b)(1) or (b)(2) class. The present rule expressly requires notice only in actions certified under Rule 23(b)(3). Members of classes certified under Rules 23(b)(1) or (b)(2) have interests that may deserve protection by notice.

The authority to direct notice to class members in a (b)(1) or (b)(2) class action should be exercised with care. For several reasons, there may be less need for notice than in a (b)(3) class action. There is no right to request exclusion from a (b)(1) or (b)(2) class. The characteristics of the class may reduce the need for formal notice. The cost of providing notice, moreover, could easily cripple actions that do not seek damages. The court may decide not to direct notice after balancing the risk that notice costs may deter the pursuit of class relief against the benefits of notice.

When the court does direct certification notice in a (b)(1) or (b)(2) class action, the discretion and flexibility established by subdivision (c)(2)(A) extend to the method of giving notice. Notice facilitates the opportunity to participate. Notice calculated to reach a significant number of class members often will protect the interests of all. Informal methods may prove effective. A simple posting in a place visited by many class members, directing attention to a source of more detailed information, may suffice. The court should consider the costs of notice in relation to the probable reach of inexpensive methods.

If a Rule 23(b)(3) class is certified in conjunction with a (b)(2) class, the (c)(2)(B) notice requirements must be satisfied as to the (b)(3) class.

The direction that class-certification notice be couched in plain, easily understood language is a reminder of the need to work unremittingly at the difficult task of communicating with class members. It is difficult to provide information about most class actions that is both accurate and easily understood by class members who are not themselves lawyers. Factual uncertainty, legal complexity, and the complication of class-action procedure raise the barriers high. The Federal Judicial Center has created illustrative clear-notice forms that provide a helpful starting point for actions similar to those described in the forms.

Subdivision (e). Subdivision (e) is amended to strengthen the process of reviewing proposed class-action settlements. Settlement may be a desirable means of resolving a class action. But court review and approval are essential to assure adequate representation of class members who have not participated in shaping the settlement.

Paragraph (1). Subdivision (e)(1)(A) expressly recognizes the power of a class representative to settle class claims, issues, or defenses.

Rule 23(e)(1)(A) resolves the ambiguity in former Rule 23(e)'s reference to dismissal or compromise of "a class action." That language could be—and at times was—read to require court approval of settlements with putative class representatives that resolved only individual claims. See Manual for Complex Litigation Third, §30.41. The new rule requires approval only if the claims, issues, or defenses of a certified class are resolved by a settlement, voluntary dismissal, or compromise.

Subdivision (e)(1)(B) carries forward the notice requirement of present Rule 23(e) when the settlement binds the class through claim or issue preclusion; notice is not required when the settlement binds only the individual class representatives. Notice of a settlement binding on the class is required either when the settlement follows class certification or when the decisions on certification and settlement proceed simultaneously.

Reasonable settlement notice may require individual notice in the manner required by Rule 23(c)(2)(B) for certification notice to a Rule 23(b)(3) class. Individual notice is appropriate, for example, if class members are required to take action—such as filing claims—to participate in the judgment, or if the court orders a settlement opt-out opportunity under Rule 23(e)(3).

Subdivision (e)(1)(C) confirms and mandates the already common practice of holding hearings as part of the process of approving settlement, voluntary dismissal, or compromise that would bind members of a class.

Subdivision (e)(1)(C) states the standard for approving a proposed settlement that would bind class members. The settlement must be fair, reasonable, and adequate. A helpful review of many factors that may deserve consideration is provided by In re: Prudential Ins. Co. America Sales Practice Litigation Agent Actions, 148 F.3d 283, 316–324 (3d Cir. 1998). Further guidance can be found in the Manual for Complex Litigation.

The court must make findings that support the conclusion that the settlement is fair, reasonable, and adequate. The findings must be set out in sufficient detail to explain to class members and the appellate court the factors that bear on applying the standard.

Settlement review also may provide an occasion to review the cogency of the initial class definition. The terms of the settlement themselves, or objections, may reveal divergent interests of class members and demonstrate the need to redefine the class or to designate subclasses. Redefinition of a class certified under Rule 23(b)(3) may require notice to new class members under Rule 23(c)(2)(B). See Rule 23(c)(1)(C).

Paragraph (2). Subdivision (e)(2) requires parties seeking approval of a settlement, voluntary dismissal, or compromise under Rule 23(e)(1) to file a statement identifying any agreement made in connection with the settlement. This provision does not change the basic requirement that the parties disclose all terms of the settlement or compromise that the court must approve under Rule 23(e)(1). It aims instead at related undertakings that, although seemingly separate, may have influenced the terms of the settlement by trading away possible advantages for the class in return for advantages for others. Doubts should be resolved in favor of identification.

Further inquiry into the agreements identified by the parties should not become the occasion for discovery by the parties or objectors. The court may direct the parties to provide to the court or other parties a summary or copy of the full terms of any agreement identified by the parties. The court also may direct the parties to provide a summary or copy of any agreement not identified by the parties that the court considers relevant to its review of a proposed settlement. In exercising discretion under this rule, the court may act in steps, calling first for a summary of any agreement that may have affected the settlement and then for a complete version if the summary does not provide an adequate basis for review. A direction to disclose a summary or copy of an agreement may raise concerns of confidentiality. Some agreements may include information that merits protection against general disclosure. And the court must provide an opportunity to claim work-product or other protections.

Paragraph (3). Subdivision (e)(3) authorizes the court to refuse to approve a settlement unless the settlement affords class members a new opportunity to request exclusion from a class certified under Rule 23(b)(3) after settlement terms are known. An agreement by the parties themselves to permit class members to elect exclusion at this point by the settlement agreement may be one factor supporting approval of the settlement. Often there is an opportunity to opt out at this point because the class is certified and settlement is reached in circumstances that lead to simultaneous notice of certification and notice of settlement. In these cases, the basic opportunity to elect exclusion applies without further complication. In some cases, particularly if settlement appears imminent at the time of certification, it may be possible to achieve equivalent protection by deferring notice and the opportunity to elect exclusion until actual settlement terms are known. This approach avoids the cost and potential confusion of providing two notices and makes the single notice more meaningful. But notice should not be delayed unduly after certification in the hope of settlement.

Rule 23(e)(3) authorizes the court to refuse to approve a settlement unless the settlement affords a new opportunity to elect exclusion in a case that settles after a certification decision if the earlier opportunity to elect exclusion provided with the certification notice has expired by the time of the settlement notice. A decision to remain in the class is likely to be more carefully considered and is better informed when settlement terms are known.

The opportunity to request exclusion from a proposed settlement is limited to members of a (b)(3) class. Exclusion may be requested only by individual class members; no class member may purport to opt out other class members by way of another class action.

The decision whether to approve a settlement that does not allow a new opportunity to elect exclusion is confided to the court's discretion. The court may make this decision before directing notice to the class under Rule 23(e)(1)(B) or after the Rule 23(e)(1)(C) hearing. Many factors may influence the court's decision. Among these are changes in the information available to class members since expiration of the first opportunity to request exclusion, and the nature of the individual class members' claims.

The terms set for permitting a new opportunity to elect exclusion from the proposed settlement of a Rule 23(b)(3) class action may address concerns of potential misuse. The court might direct, for example, that class members who elect exclusion are bound by rulings on the merits made before the settlement was proposed for approval. Still other terms or conditions may be appropriate.

Paragraph (4). Subdivision (e)(4) confirms the right of class members to object to a proposed settlement, voluntary dismissal, or compromise. The right is defined in relation to a disposition that, because it would bind the class, requires court approval under subdivision (e)(1)(C).

Subdivision (e)(4)(B) requires court approval for withdrawal of objections made under subdivision (e)(4)(A). Review follows automatically if the objections are withdrawn on terms that lead to modification of the settlement with the class. Review also is required if the objector formally withdraws the objections. If the objector simply abandons pursuit of the objection, the court may inquire into the circumstances.

Approval under paragraph (4)(B) may be given or denied with little need for further inquiry if the objection and the disposition go only to a protest that the individual treatment afforded the objector under the proposed settlement is unfair because of factors that distinguish the objector from other class members. Different considerations may apply if the objector has protested that the proposed settlement is not fair, reasonable, or adequate on grounds that apply generally to a class or subclass. Such objections, which purport to represent class-wide interests, may augment the opportunity for obstruction or delay. If such objections are surrendered on terms that do not affect the class settlement or the objector's participation in the class settlement, the court often can approve withdrawal of the objections without elaborate inquiry.

Once an objector appeals, control of the proceeding lies in the court of appeals. The court of appeals may undertake review and approval of a settlement with the objector, perhaps as part of appeal settlement procedures, or may remand to the district court to take advantage of the district court's familiarity with the action and settlement.

Subdivision (g). Subdivision (g) is new. It responds to the reality that the selection and activity of class counsel are often critically important to the successful handling of a class action. Until now, courts have scrutinized proposed class counsel as well as the class representative under Rule 23(a)(4). This experience has recognized the importance of judicial evaluation of the proposed lawyer for the class, and this new subdivision builds on that experience rather than introducing an entirely new element into the class certification process. Rule 23(a)(4) will continue to call for scrutiny of the proposed class representative, while this subdivision will guide the court in assessing proposed class counsel as part of the certification decision. This subdivision recognizes the importance of class counsel, states the obligation to represent the interests of the class, and provides a framework for selection of class counsel. The procedure and standards for appointment vary depending on whether there are multiple applicants to be class counsel. The new subdivision also provides a method by which the court may make directions from the outset about the potential fee award to class counsel in the event the action is successful.

Paragraph (1) sets out the basic requirement that class counsel be appointed if a class is certified and articulates the obligation of class counsel to represent the interests of the class, as opposed to the potentially conflicting interests of individual class members. It also sets out the factors the court should consider in assessing proposed class counsel.

Paragraph (1)(A) requires that the court appoint class counsel to represent the class. Class counsel must be appointed for all classes, including each subclass that the court certifies to represent divergent interests.

Paragraph (1)(A) does not apply if "a statute provides otherwise." This recognizes that provisions of the Private Securities Litigation Reform Act of 1995, Pub. L. No. 104–67, 109 Stat. 737 (1995) (codified in various sections of 15 U.S.C.), contain directives that bear on selection of a lead plaintiff and the retention of counsel. This subdivision does not purport to supersede or to affect the interpretation of those provisions, or any similar provisions of other legislation.

Paragraph 1(B) recognizes that the primary responsibility of class counsel, resulting from appointment as class counsel, is to represent the best interests of the class. The rule thus establishes the obligation of class counsel, an obligation that may be different from the customary obligations of counsel to individual clients. Appointment as class counsel means that the primary obligation of counsel is to the class rather than to any individual members of it. The class representatives do not have an unfettered right to "fire" class counsel. In the same vein, the class representatives cannot command class counsel to accept or reject a settlement proposal. To the contrary, class counsel must determine whether seeking the court's approval of a settlement would be in the best interests of the class as a whole.

Paragraph (1)(C) articulates the basic responsibility of the court to appoint class counsel who will provide the adequate representation called for by paragraph (1)(B). It identifies criteria that must be considered and invites the court to consider any other pertinent matters. Although couched in terms of the court's duty, the listing also informs counsel seeking appointment about the topics that should be addressed in an application for appointment or in the motion for class certification.

The court may direct potential class counsel to provide additional information about the topics mentioned in paragraph (1)(C) or about any other relevant topic. For example, the court may direct applicants to inform the court concerning any agreements about a prospective award of attorney fees or nontaxable costs, as such agreements may sometimes be significant in the selection of class counsel. The court might also direct that potential class counsel indicate how parallel litigation might be coordinated or consolidated with the action before the court.

The court may also direct counsel to propose terms for a potential award of attorney fees and nontaxable costs. Attorney fee awards are an important feature of class action practice, and attention to this subject from the outset may often be a productive technique. Paragraph (2)(C) therefore authorizes the court to provide directions about attorney fees and costs when appointing class counsel. Because there will be numerous class actions in which this information is not likely to be useful, the court need not consider it in all class actions.

Some information relevant to class counsel appointment may involve matters that include adversary preparation in a way that should be shielded from disclosure to other parties. An appropriate protective order may be necessary to preserve confidentiality.

In evaluating prospective class counsel, the court should weigh all pertinent factors. No single factor should necessarily be determinative in a given case. For example, the resources counsel will commit to the case must be appropriate to its needs, but the court should be careful not to limit consideration to lawyers with the greatest resources.

If, after review of all applicants, the court concludes that none would be satisfactory class counsel, it may deny class certification, reject all applications, recommend that an application be modified, invite new applications, or make any other appropriate order regarding selection and appointment of class counsel.

Paragraph (2). This paragraph sets out the procedure that should be followed in appointing class counsel. Although it affords substantial flexibility, it provides the framework for appointment of class counsel in all class actions. For counsel who filed the action, the materials submitted in support of the motion for class certification may suffice to justify appointment so long as the information described in paragraph (g)(1)(C) is included. If there are other applicants, they ordinarily would file a formal application detailing their suitability for the position.

In a plaintiff class action the court usually would appoint as class counsel only an attorney or attorneys who have sought appointment. Different considerations may apply in defendant class actions.

The rule states that the court should appoint "class counsel." In many instances, the applicant will be an individual attorney. In other cases, however, an entire firm, or perhaps numerous attorneys who are not otherwise affiliated but are collaborating on the action will apply. No rule of thumb exists to determine when such arrangements are appropriate; the court should be alert to the need for adequate staffing of the case, but also to the risk of overstaffing or an ungainly counsel structure.

Paragraph (2)(A) authorizes the court to designate interim counsel during the pre-certification period if necessary to protect the interests of the putative class. Rule 23(c)(1)(B) directs that the order certifying the class include appointment of class counsel. Before class certification, however, it will usually be important for an attorney to take action to prepare for the certification decision. The amendment to Rule 23(c)(1) recognizes that some discovery is often necessary for that determination. It also may be important to make or respond to motions before certification. Settlement may be discussed before certification. Ordinarily, such work is handled by the lawyer who filed the action. In some cases, however, there may be rivalry or uncertainty that makes formal designation of interim counsel appropriate. Rule 23(g)(2)(A) authorizes the court to designate interim counsel to act on behalf of the putative class before the certification decision is made. Failure to make the formal designation does not prevent the attorney who filed the action from proceeding in it. Whether or not formally designated interim counsel, an attorney who acts on behalf of the class before certification must act in the best interests of the class as a whole. For example, an attorney who negotiates a pre-certification settlement must seek a settlement that is fair, reasonable, and adequate for the class.

Rule 23(c)(1) provides that the court should decide whether to certify the class "at an early practicable time," and directs that class counsel should be appointed in the order certifying the class. In some cases, it may be appropriate for the court to allow a reasonable period after commencement of the action for filing applications to serve as class counsel. The primary ground for deferring appointment would be that there is reason to anticipate competing applications to serve as class counsel. Examples might include instances in which more than one class action has been filed, or in which other attorneys have filed individual actions on behalf of putative class members. The purpose of facilitating competing applications in such a case is to afford the best possible representation for the class. Another possible reason for deferring appointment would be that the initial applicant was found inadequate, but it seems appropriate to permit additional applications rather than deny class certification.

Paragraph (2)(B) states the basic standard the court should use in deciding whether to certify the class and appoint class counsel in the single applicant situation—that the applicant be able to provide the representation called for by paragraph (1)(B) in light of the factors identified in paragraph (1)(C).

If there are multiple adequate applicants, paragraph (2)(B) directs the court to select the class counsel best able to represent the interests of the class. This decision should also be made using the factors outlined in paragraph (1)(C), but in the multiple applicant situation the court is to go beyond scrutinizing the adequacy of counsel and make a comparison of the strengths of the various applicants. As with the decision whether to appoint the sole applicant for the position, no single factor should be dispositive in selecting class counsel in cases in which there are multiple applicants. The fact that a given attorney filed the instant action, for example, might not weigh heavily in the decision if that lawyer had not done significant work identifying or investigating claims. Depending on the nature of the case, one important consideration might be the applicant's existing attorney-client relationship with the proposed class representative.

Paragraph (2)(C) builds on the appointment process by authorizing the court to include provisions regarding attorney fees in the order appointing class counsel. Courts may find it desirable to adopt guidelines for fees or nontaxable costs, or to direct class counsel to report to the court at regular intervals on the efforts undertaken in the action, to facilitate the court's later determination of a reasonable attorney fee.

Subdivision (h). Subdivision (h) is new. Fee awards are a powerful influence on the way attorneys initiate, develop, and conclude class actions. Class action attorney fee awards have heretofore been handled, along with all other attorney fee awards, under Rule 54(d)(2), but that rule is not addressed to the particular concerns of class actions. This subdivision is designed to work in tandem with new subdivision (g) on appointment of class counsel, which may afford an opportunity for the court to provide an early framework for an eventual fee award, or for monitoring the work of class counsel during the pendency of the action.

Subdivision (h) applies to "an action certified as a class action." This includes cases in which there is a simultaneous proposal for class certification and settlement even though technically the class may not be certified unless the court approves the settlement pursuant to review under Rule 23(e). When a settlement is proposed for Rule 23(e) approval, either after certification or with a request for certification, notice to class members about class counsel's fee motion would ordinarily accompany the notice to the class about the settlement proposal itself.

This subdivision does not undertake to create new grounds for an award of attorney fees or nontaxable costs. Instead, it applies when such awards are authorized by law or by agreement of the parties. Against that background, it provides a format for all awards of attorney fees and nontaxable costs in connection with a class action, not only the award to class counsel. In some situations, there may be a basis for making an award to other counsel whose work produced a beneficial result for the class, such as attorneys who acted for the class before certification but were not appointed class counsel, or attorneys who represented objectors to a proposed settlement under Rule 23(e) or to the fee motion of class counsel. Other situations in which fee awards are authorized by law or by agreement of the parties may exist.

This subdivision authorizes an award of "reasonable" attorney fees and nontaxable costs. This is the customary term for measurement of fee awards in cases in which counsel may obtain an award of fees under the "common fund" theory that applies in many class actions, and is used in many fee-shifting statutes. Depending on the circumstances, courts have approached the determination of what is reasonable in different ways. In particular, there is some variation among courts about whether in "common fund" cases the court should use the lodestar or a percentage method of determining what fee is reasonable. The rule does not attempt to resolve the question whether the lodestar or percentage approach should be viewed as preferable.

Active judicial involvement in measuring fee awards is singularly important to the proper operation of the class-action process. Continued reliance on caselaw development of fee-award measures does not diminish the court's responsibility. In a class action, the district court must ensure that the amount and mode of payment of attorney fees are fair and proper whether the fees come from a common fund or are otherwise paid. Even in the absence of objections, the court bears this responsibility.

Courts discharging this responsibility have looked to a variety of factors. One fundamental focus is the result actually achieved for class members, a basic consideration in any case in which fees are sought on the basis of a benefit achieved for class members. The Private Securities Litigation Reform Act of 1995 explicitly makes this factor a cap for a fee award in actions to which it applies. See 15 U.S.C. §§77z–1(a)(6); 78u–4(a)(6) (fee award should not exceed a "reasonable percentage of the amount of any damages and prejudgment interest actually paid to the class"). For a percentage approach to fee measurement, results achieved is the basic starting point.

In many instances, the court may need to proceed with care in assessing the value conferred on class members. Settlement regimes that provide for future payments, for example, may not result in significant actual payments to class members. In this connection, the court may need to scrutinize the manner and operation of any applicable claims procedure. In some cases, it may be appropriate to defer some portion of the fee award until actual payouts to class members are known. Settlements involving nonmonetary provisions for class members also deserve careful scrutiny to ensure that these provisions have actual value to the class. On occasion the court's Rule 23(e) review will provide a solid basis for this sort of evaluation, but in any event it is also important to assessing the fee award for the class.

At the same time, it is important to recognize that in some class actions the monetary relief obtained is not the sole determinant of an appropriate attorney fees award. Cf. Blanchard v. Bergeron, 489 U.S. 87, 95 (1989) (cautioning in an individual case against an "undesirable emphasis" on "the importance of the recovery of damages in civil rights litigation" that might "shortchange efforts to seek effective injunctive or declaratory relief").

Any directions or orders made by the court in connection with appointing class counsel under Rule 23(g) should weigh heavily in making a fee award under this subdivision.

Courts have also given weight to agreements among the parties regarding the fee motion, and to agreements between class counsel and others about the fees claimed by the motion. Rule 54(d)(2)(B) provides: "If directed by the court, the motion shall also disclose the terms of any agreement with respect to fees to be paid for the services for which claim is made." The agreement by a settling party not to oppose a fee application up to a certain amount, for example, is worthy of consideration, but the court remains responsible to determine a reasonable fee. "Side agreements" regarding fees provide at least perspective pertinent to an appropriate fee award.

In addition, courts may take account of the fees charged by class counsel or other attorneys for representing individual claimants or objectors in the case. In determining a fee for class counsel, the court's objective is to ensure an overall fee that is fair for counsel and equitable within the class. In some circumstances individual fee agreements between class counsel and class members might have provisions inconsistent with those goals, and the court might determine that adjustments in the class fee award were necessary as a result.

Finally, it is important to scrutinize separately the application for an award covering nontaxable costs. If costs were addressed in the order appointing class counsel, those directives should be a presumptive starting point in determining what is an appropriate award.

Paragraph (1). Any claim for an award of attorney fees must be sought by motion under Rule 54(d)(2), which invokes the provisions for timing of appeal in Rule 58 and Appellate Rule 4. Owing to the distinctive features of class action fee motions, however, the provisions of this subdivision control disposition of fee motions in class actions, while Rule 54(d)(2) applies to matters not addressed in this subdivision.

The court should direct when the fee motion must be filed. For motions by class counsel in cases subject to court review of a proposed settlement under Rule 23(e), it would be important to require the filing of at least the initial motion in time for inclusion of information about the motion in the notice to the class about the proposed settlement that is required by Rule 23(e). In cases litigated to judgment, the court might also order class counsel's motion to be filed promptly so that notice to the class under this subdivision (h) can be given.

Besides service of the motion on all parties, notice of class counsel's motion for attorney fees must be "directed to the class in a reasonable manner." Because members of the class have an interest in the arrangements for payment of class counsel whether that payment comes from the class fund or is made directly by another party, notice is required in all instances. In cases in which settlement approval is contemplated under Rule 23(e), notice of class counsel's fee motion should be combined with notice of the proposed settlement, and the provision regarding notice to the class is parallel to the requirements for notice under Rule 23(e). In adjudicated class actions, the court may calibrate the notice to avoid undue expense.

Paragraph (2). A class member and any party from whom payment is sought may object to the fee motion. Other parties—for example, nonsettling defendants—may not object because they lack a sufficient interest in the amount the court awards. The rule does not specify a time limit for making an objection. In setting the date objections are due, the court should provide sufficient time after the full fee motion is on file to enable potential objectors to examine the motion.

The court may allow an objector discovery relevant to the objections. In determining whether to allow discovery, the court should weigh the need for the information against the cost and delay that would attend discovery. See Rule 26(b)(2). One factor in determining whether to authorize discovery is the completeness of the material submitted in support of the fee motion, which depends in part on the fee measurement standard applicable to the case. If the motion provides thorough information, the burden should be on the objector to justify discovery to obtain further information.

Paragraph (3). Whether or not there are formal objections, the court must determine whether a fee award is justified and, if so, set a reasonable fee. The rule does not require a formal hearing in all cases. The form and extent of a hearing depend on the circumstances of the case. The rule does require findings and conclusions under Rule 52(a).

Paragraph (4). By incorporating Rule 54(d)(2), this provision gives the court broad authority to obtain assistance in determining the appropriate amount to award. In deciding whether to direct submission of such questions to a special master or magistrate judge, the court should give appropriate consideration to the cost and delay that such a process might entail.

Changes Made After Publication and Comment. Rule 23(c)(1)(B) is changed to incorporate the counsel-appointment provisions of Rule 23(g). The statement of the method and time for requesting exclusion from a (b)(3) class has been moved to the notice of certification provision in Rule 23(c)(2)(B).

Rule 23(c)(1)(C) is changed by deleting all references to "conditional" certification.

Rule 23(c)(2)(A) is changed by deleting the requirement that class members be notified of certification of a (b)(1) or (b)(2) class. The new version provides only that the court may direct appropriate notice to the class.

Rule 23(c)(2)(B) is revised to require that the notice of class certification define the certified class in terms identical to the terms used in (c)(1)(B), and to incorporate the statement transferred from (c)(1)(B) on "when and how members may elect to be excluded."

Rule 23(e)(1) is revised to delete the requirement that the parties must win court approval for a precertification dismissal or settlement.

Rule 23(e)(2) is revised to change the provision that the court may direct the parties to file a copy or summary of any agreement or understanding made in connection with a proposed settlement. The new provision directs the parties to a proposed settlement to identify any agreement made in connection with the settlement.

Rule 23(e)(3) is proposed in a restyled form of the second version proposed for publication.

Rule 23(e)(4)(B) is restyled.

Rule 23(g)(1)(C) is a transposition of criteria for appointing class counsel that was published as Rule 23(g)(2)(B). The criteria are rearranged, and expanded to include consideration of experience in handling claims of the type asserted in the action and of counsel's knowledge of the applicable law.

Rule 23(g)(2)(A) is a new provision for designation of interim counsel to act on behalf of a putative class before a certification determination is made.

Rule 23(g)(2)(B) is revised to point up the differences between appointment of class counsel when there is only one applicant and when there are competing applicants. When there is only one applicant the court must determine that the applicant is able to fairly and adequately represent class interests. When there is more than one applicant the court must appoint the applicant best able to represent class interests.

Rule 23(h) is changed to require that notice of an attorney-fee motion by class counsel be "directed to class members," rather than "given to all class members."

Committee Notes on Rules—2007 Amendment

The language of Rule 23 has been amended as part of the general restyling of the Civil Rules to make them more easily understood and to make style and terminology consistent throughout the rules. These changes are intended to be stylistic only.

Amended Rule 23(d)(2) carries forward the provisions of former Rule 23(d) that recognize two separate propositions. First, a Rule 23(d) order may be combined with a pretrial order under Rule 16. Second, the standard for amending the Rule 23(d) order continues to be the more open-ended standard for amending Rule 23(d) orders, not the more exacting standard for amending Rule 16 orders.

As part of the general restyling, intensifiers that provide emphasis but add no meaning are consistently deleted. Amended Rule 23(f) omits as redundant the explicit reference to court of appeals discretion in deciding whether to permit an interlocutory appeal. The omission does not in any way limit the unfettered discretion established by the original rule.

Committee Notes on Rules—2009 Amendment

The time set in the former rule at 10 days has been revised to 14 days. See the Note to Rule 6.

Rule 23.1. Derivative Actions

(a) Prerequisites. This rule applies when one or more shareholders or members of a corporation or an unincorporated association bring a derivative action to enforce a right that the corporation or association may properly assert but has failed to enforce. The derivative action may not be maintained if it appears that the plaintiff does not fairly and adequately represent the interests of shareholders or members who are similarly situated in enforcing the right of the corporation or association.

(b) Pleading Requirements. The complaint must be verified and must:

(1) allege that the plaintiff was a shareholder or member at the time of the transaction complained of, or that the plaintiff's share or membership later devolved on it by operation of law;

(2) allege that the action is not a collusive one to confer jurisdiction that the court would otherwise lack; and

(3) state with particularity:

(A) any effort by the plaintiff to obtain the desired action from the directors or comparable authority and, if necessary, from the shareholders or members; and

(B) the reasons for not obtaining the action or not making the effort.

(c) Settlement, Dismissal, and Compromise. A derivative action may be settled, voluntarily dismissed, or compromised only with the court's approval. Notice of a proposed settlement, voluntary dismissal, or compromise must be given to shareholders or members in the manner that the court orders.

(As added Feb. 28, 1966, eff. July 1, 1966; amended Mar. 2, 1987, eff. Aug. 1, 1987; Apr. 30, 2007, eff. Dec. 1, 2007.)

Notes of Advisory Committee on Rules—1966

A derivative action by a shareholder of a corporation or by a member of an unincorporated association has distinctive aspects which require the special provisions set forth in the new rule. The next-to-the-last sentence recognizes that the question of adequacy of representation may arise when the plaintiff is one of a group of shareholders or members. Cf. 3 Moore's Federal Practice, par. 23.08 (2d ed. 1963).

The court has inherent power to provide for the conduct of the proceedings in a derivative action, including the power to determine the course of the proceedings and require that any appropriate notice be given to shareholders or members.

Notes of Advisory Committee on Rules—1987 Amendment

The amendments are technical. No substantive change is intended.

Committee Notes on Rules—2007 Amendment

The language of Rule 23.1 has been amended as part of the general restyling of the Civil Rules to make them more easily understood and to make style and terminology consistent throughout the rules. These changes are intended to be stylistic only.

Rule 23.2. Actions Relating to Unincorporated Associations

This rule applies to an action brought by or against the members of an unincorporated association as a class by naming certain members as representative parties. The action may be maintained only if it appears that those parties will fairly and adequately protect the interests of the association and its members. In conducting the action, the court may issue any appropriate orders corresponding with those in Rule 23(d), and the procedure for settlement, voluntary dismissal, or compromise must correspond with the procedure in Rule 23(e).

(As added Feb. 28, 1966, eff. July 1, 1966; amended Apr. 30, 2007, eff. Dec. 1, 2007.)

Notes of Advisory Committee on Rules—1966

Although an action by or against representatives of the membership of an unincorporated association has often been viewed as a class action, the real or main purpose of this characterization has been to give "entity treatment" to the association when for formal reasons it cannot sue or be sued as a jural person under Rule 17(b). See Louisell & Hazard, Pleading and Procedure: State and Federal 718 (1962); 3 Moore's Federal Practice, par. 23.08 (2d ed. 1963); Story, J. in West v. Randall, 29 Fed.Cas. 718, 722–23, No. 17,424 (C.C.D.R.I. 1820); and, for examples, Gibbs v. Buck, 307 U.S. 66 (1939); Tunstall v. Brotherhood of Locomotive F. & E., 148 F.2d 403 (4th Cir. 1945); Oskoian v. Canuel, 269 F.2d 311 (1st Cir. 1959). Rule 23.2 deals separately with these actions, referring where appropriate to Rule 23.

Committee Notes on Rules—2007 Amendment

The language of Rule 23.2 has been amended as part of the general restyling of the Civil Rules to make them more easily understood and to make style and terminology consistent throughout the rules. These changes are intended to be stylistic only.

Rule 24. Intervention

(a) Intervention of Right. On timely motion, the court must permit anyone to intervene who:

(1) is given an unconditional right to intervene by a federal statute; or

(2) claims an interest relating to the property or transaction that is the subject of the action, and is so situated that disposing of the action may as a practical matter impair or impede the movant's ability to protect its interest, unless existing parties adequately represent that interest.

(b) Permissive Intervention.

(1) In General. On timely motion, the court may permit anyone to intervene who:

(A) is given a conditional right to intervene by a federal statute; or

(B) has a claim or defense that shares with the main action a common question of law or fact.

(2) By a Government Officer or Agency. On timely motion, the court may permit a federal or state governmental officer or agency to intervene if a party's claim or defense is based on:

(A) a statute or executive order administered by the officer or agency; or

(B) any regulation, order, requirement, or agreement issued or made under the statute or executive order.

(3) Delay or Prejudice. In exercising its discretion, the court must consider whether the intervention will unduly delay or prejudice the adjudication of the original parties' rights.

(c) Notice and Pleading Required. A motion to intervene must be served on the parties as provided in Rule 5. The motion must state the grounds for intervention and be accompanied by a pleading that sets out the claim or defense for which intervention is sought.

(As amended Dec. 27, 1946, eff. Mar. 19, 1948; Dec. 29, 1948, eff. Oct. 20, 1949; Jan. 21, 1963, eff. July 1, 1963; Feb. 28, 1966, eff. July 1, 1966; Mar. 2, 1987, eff. Aug. 1, 1987; Apr. 30, 1991, eff. Dec. 1, 1991; Apr. 12, 2006, eff. Dec. 1, 2006; Apr. 30, 2007, eff. Dec. 1, 2007.)

Notes of Advisory Committee on Rules—1937

The right to intervene given by the following and similar statutes is preserved, but the procedure for its assertion is governed by this rule:

U.S.C., Title 28:

- §45a [now 2323] (Special attorneys; participation by Interstate Commerce Commission; intervention) (in certain cases under interstate commerce laws)
- §48 [now 2322] (Suits to be against United States; intervention by United States)
- §401 [now 2403] (Intervention by United States; constitutionality of Federal statute)

U.S.C., Title 40:

- §276a–2(b) [now 3144] (Bonds of contractors for public buildings or works; rights of persons furnishing labor and materials).

Compare with the last sentence of [former] Equity Rule 37 (Parties Generally—Intervention). This rule amplifies and restates the present federal practice at law and in equity. For the practice in admiralty see Admiralty Rules 34 (How Third Party May Intervene) and 42 (Claims Against Proceeds in Registry). See generally Moore and Levi, Federal Intervention: I The Right to Intervene and Reorganization (1936), 45 Yale L.J. 565. Under the codes two types of intervention are provided, one for the recovery of specific real or personal property (2 Ohio Gen.Code Ann. (Page, 1926) §11263; Wyo.Rev.Stat.Ann. (Courtright, 1931) §89–522), and the other allowing intervention generally when the applicant has an interest in the matter in litigation (1 Colo.Stat.Ann. (1935) Code Civ.Proc. §22; La.Code Pract. (Dart, 1932) Arts. 389–394; Utah Rev.Stat.Ann. (1933) §104–3–24). The English intervention practice is based upon various rules and decisions and falls into the two categories of absolute right and discretionary right. For the absolute right see English Rules Under the Judicature Act (The Annual Practice, 1937) O. 12, r. 24 (admiralty), r. 25 (land), r. 23 (probate); O. 57, r. 12 (execution); J. A. (1925) §§181, 182, 183(2) (divorce); In re Metropolitan Amalgamated Estates, Ltd., (1912) 2 Ch. 497 (receivership); Wilson v. Church, 9 Ch.D. 552 (1878) (representative action). For the discretionary right see O. 16, r. 11 (nonjoinder) and Re Fowler, 142 L. T. Jo. 94 (Ch. 1916), Vavasseur v. Krupp, 9 Ch.D. 351 (1878) (persons out of the jurisdiction).

Notes of Advisory Committee on Rules—1946 Amendments

Note. Subdivision (a). The addition to subdivision (a)(3) covers the situation where property may be in the actual custody of some other officer or agency—such as the Secretary of the Treasury—but the control and disposition of the property is lodged in the court wherein the action is pending.

Subdivision (b). The addition in subdivision (b) permits the intervention of governmental officers or agencies in proper cases and thus avoids exclusionary constructions of the rule. For an example of the latter, see Matter of Bender Body Co. (Ref.Ohio 1941) 47 F.Supp. 224, aff'd as moot (N.D.Ohio 1942) 47 F.Supp. 224, 234, holding that the Administrator of the Office of Price Administration, then acting under the authority of an Executive Order of the President, could not intervene in a bankruptcy proceeding to protest the sale of assets above ceiling prices. Compare, however, Securities and Exchange Commission v. United States Realty & Improvement Co. (1940) 310 U.S. 434, where permissive intervention of the Commission to protect the public interest in an arrangement proceeding under Chapter XI of the Bankruptcy Act was upheld. See also dissenting opinion in Securities and Exchange Commission v. Long Island Lighting Co. (C.C.A.2d, 1945) 148 F.(2d) 252, judgment vacated as moot and case remanded with direction to dismiss complaint (1945) 325 U.S. 833. For discussion see Commentary, Nature of Permissive Intervention Under Rule 24b (1940) 3 Fed.Rules Serv. 704; Berger, Intervention by Public Agencies in Private Litigation in the Federal Courts (1940) 50 Yale L.J. 65.

Regarding the construction of subdivision (b)(2), see Allen Calculators, Inc. v. National Cash Register Co. (1944) 322 U.S. 137.

Notes of Advisory Committee on Rules—1948 Amendment

The amendment substitutes the present statutory reference.

Notes of Advisory Committee on Rules—1963 Amendment

This amendment conforms to the amendment of Rule 5(a). See the Advisory Committee's Note to that amendment.

Notes of Advisory Committee on Rules—1966 Amendment

In attempting to overcome certain difficulties which have arisen in the application of present Rule 24(a)(2) and (3), this amendment draws upon the revision of the related Rules 19 (joinder of persons needed for just adjudication) and 23 (class actions), and the reasoning underlying that revision.

Rule 24(a)(3) as amended in 1948 provided for intervention of right where the applicant established that he would be adversely affected by the distribution or disposition of property involved in an action to which he had not been made a party. Significantly, some decided cases virtually disregarded the language of this provision. Thus Professor Moore states: "The concept of a fund has been applied so loosely that it is possible for a court to find a fund in almost any in personam action." 4 Moore's Federal Practice, par. 24.09[3], at 55 (2d ed. 1962), and see, e.g., Formulabs, Inc. v. Hartley Pen Co., 275 F.2d 52 (9th Cir. 1960). This development was quite natural, for Rule 24(a)(3) was unduly restricted. If an absentee would be substantially affected in a practical sense by the determination made in an action, he should, as a general rule, be entitled to intervene, and his right to do so should not depend on whether there is a fund to be distributed or otherwise disposed of. Intervention of right is here seen to be a kind of counterpart to Rule 19(a)(2)(i) on joinder of persons needed for a just adjudication: where, upon motion of a party in an action, an absentee should be joined so that he may protect his interest which as a practical matter may be substantially impaired by the disposition of the action, he ought to have a right to intervene in the action on his own motion. See Louisell & Hazard, Pleading and Procedure: State and Federal 749–50 (1962).

The general purpose of original Rule 24(a)(2) was to entitle an absentee, purportedly represented by a party, to intervene in the action if he could establish with fair probability that the representation was inadequate. Thus, where an action is being prosecuted or defended by a trustee, a beneficiary of the trust should have a right to intervene if he can show that the trustee's representation of his interest probably is inadequate; similarly a member of a class should have the right to intervene in a class action if he can show the inadequacy of the representation of his interest by the representative parties before the court.

Original Rule 24(a)(2), however, made it a condition of intervention that "the applicant is or may be bound by a judgment in the action," and this created difficulties with intervention in class actions. If the "bound" language was read literally in the sense of res judicata, it could defeat intervention in some meritorious cases. A member of a class to whom a judgment in a class action extended by its terms (see Rule 23(c)(3), as amended) might be entitled to show in a later action, when the judgment in the class action was claimed to operate as res judicata against him, that the "representative" in the class action had not in fact adequately represented him. If he could make this showing, the class-action judgment might be held not to bind him. See Hansberry v. Lee, 311 U.S. 32 (1940). If a class member sought to intervene in the class action proper, while it was still pending, on grounds of inadequacy of representation, he could be met with the argument: if the representation was in fact inadequate, he would not be "bound" by the judgment when it was subsequently asserted against him as res judicata, hence he was not entitled to intervene; if the representation was in fact adequate, there was no occasion or ground for intervention. See Sam Fox Publishing Co. v. United States, 366 U.S. 683 (1961); cf. Sutphen Estates, Inc. v. United States, 342 U.S. 19 (1951). This reasoning might be linguistically justified by original Rule 24(a)(2); but it could lead to poor results. Compare the discussion in International M. & I. Corp. v. Von Clemm, 301 F.2d 857 (2d Cir. 1962); Atlantic Refining Co. v. Standard Oil Co., 304 F.2d 387 (D.C.Cir. 1962). A class member who claims that his "representative" does not adequately represent him, and is able to establish that proposition with sufficient probability, should not be put to the risk of having a judgment entered in the action which by its terms extends to him, and be obliged to test the validity of the judgment as applied to his interest by a later collateral attack. Rather he should, as a general rule, be entitled to intervene in the action.

The amendment provides that an applicant is entitled to intervene in an action when his position is comparable to that of a person under Rule 19(a)(2)(i), as amended, unless his interest is already adequately represented in the action by existing parties. The Rule 19(a)(2)(i) criterion imports practical considerations, and the deletion of the "bound" language similarly frees the rule from undue preoccupation with strict considerations of res judicata.

The representation whose adequacy comes into question under the amended rule is not confined to formal representation like that provided by a trustee for his beneficiary or a representative party in a class action for a member of the class. A party to an action may provide practical representation to the absentee seeking intervention although no such formal relationship exists between them, and the adequacy of this practical representation will then have to be weighed. See International M. & I. Corp. v. Von Clemm, and Atlantic Refining Co. v. Standard Oil Co., both supra; Wolpe v. Poretsky, 144 F.2d 505 (D.C.Cir. 1944), cert. denied, 323 U.S. 777 (1944); cf. Ford Motor Co. v. Bisanz Bros., 249 F.2d 22 (8th Cir. 1957); and generally, Annot., 84 A.L.R.2d 1412 (1961).

An intervention of right under the amended rule may be subject to appropriate conditions or restrictions responsive among other things to the requirements of efficient conduct of the proceedings.

Notes of Advisory Committee on Rules—1987 Amendment

The amendments are technical. No substantive change is intended.

Notes of Advisory Committee on Rules—1991 Amendment

Language is added to bring Rule 24(c) into conformity with the statute cited, resolving some confusion reflected in district court rules. As the text provides, counsel challenging the constitutionality of legislation in an action in which the appropriate government is not a party should call the attention of the court to its duty to notify the appropriate governmental officers. The statute imposes the burden of notification on the court, not the party making the constitutional challenge, partly in order to protect against any possible waiver of constitutional rights by parties inattentive to the need for notice. For this reason, the failure of a party to call the court's attention to the matter cannot be treated as a waiver.

Committee Notes on Rules—2006 Amendment

New Rule 5.1 replaces the final three sentences of Rule 24(c), implementing the provisions of 28 U.S.C. §2403. Section 2403 requires notification to the Attorney General of the United States when the constitutionality of an Act of Congress is called in question, and to the state attorney general when the constitutionality of a state statute is drawn into question.

Committee Notes on Rules—2007 Amendment

The language of Rule 24 has been amended as part of the general restyling of the Civil Rules to make them more easily understood and to make style and terminology consistent throughout the rules. These changes are intended to be stylistic only.

The former rule stated that the same procedure is followed when a United States statute gives a right to intervene. The statement is deleted because it added nothing.

Rule 25. Substitution of Parties

(a) Death.

(1) Substitution if the Claim Is Not Extinguished. If a party dies and the claim is not extinguished, the court may order substitution of the proper party. A motion for substitution may be made by any party or by the decedent's successor or representative. If the motion is not made within 90 days after service of a statement noting the death, the action by or against the decedent must be dismissed.

(2) Continuation Among the Remaining Parties. After a party's death, if the right sought to be enforced survives only to or against the remaining parties, the action does not abate, but proceeds in favor of or against the remaining parties. The death should be noted on the record.

(3) Service. A motion to substitute, together with a notice of hearing, must be served on the parties as provided in Rule 5 and on nonparties as provided in Rule 4. A statement noting death must be served in the same manner. Service may be made in any judicial district.

(b) Incompetency. If a party becomes incompetent, the court may, on motion, permit the action to be continued by or against the party's representative. The motion must be served as provided in Rule 25(a)(3).

(c) Transfer of Interest. If an interest is transferred, the action may be continued by or against the original party unless the court, on motion, orders the transferee to be substituted in the action or joined with the original party. The motion must be served as provided in Rule 25(a)(3).

(d) Public Officers; Death or Separation from Office. An action does not abate when a public officer who is a party in an official capacity dies, resigns, or otherwise ceases to hold office while the action is pending. The officer's successor is automatically substituted as a party. Later proceedings should be in the substituted party's name, but any misnomer not affecting the parties' substantial rights must be disregarded. The court may order substitution at any time, but the absence of such an order does not affect the substitution.

(As amended Dec. 29, 1948, eff. Oct. 20, 1949; Apr. 17, 1961, eff. July 19, 1961; Jan. 21, 1963, eff. July 1, 1963; Mar. 2, 1987, eff. Aug. 1, 1987; Apr. 30, 2007, eff. Dec. 1, 2007.)

Notes of Advisory Committee on Rules—1937

Note to Subdivision (a). 1. The first paragraph of this rule is based upon [former] Equity Rule 45 (Death of Party—Revivor) and U.S.C., Title 28, [former] §778 (Death of parties; substitution of executor or administrator). The scire facias procedure provided for in the statute cited is superseded and the writ is abolished by Rule 81 (b). Paragraph two states the content of U.S.C., Title 28, [former] §779 (Death of one of several plaintiffs or defendants). With these two paragraphs compare generally English Rules Under the Judicature Act (The Annual Practice, 1937) O. 17, r.r. 1–10.

2. This rule modifies U.S.C., Title 28, [former] §§778 (Death of parties; substitution of executor or administrator), 779 (Death of one of several plaintiffs or defendants), and 780 (Survival of actions, suits, or proceedings, etc.) insofar as they differ from it.

Note to Subdivisions (b) and (c). These are a combination and adaptation of N.Y.C.P.A. (1937) §83 and Calif.Code Civ.Proc. (Deering, 1937) §385; see also 4 Nev.Comp.Laws (Hillyer, 1929) §8561.

Note to Subdivision (d). With the first and last sentences compare U.S.C., Title 28, [former] §780 (Survival of actions, suits, or proceedings, etc.). With the second sentence of this subdivision compare Ex parte La Prade, 289 U.S. 444 (1933).

Notes of Advisory Committee on Rules—1948 Amendment

The Act of February 13, 1925, 43 Stat. 941, U.S.C. Title 28, §780, is repealed and not included in revised Title 28, for the stated reason that it is "Superseded by Rules 25 and 81 of the Federal Rules of Civil Procedure." See Report from the Committee on the Judiciary, House of Representatives, to Accompany H.R. 3214, House Rept. 308 (80th Cong., 1st Sess.), p. A239. Those officers which that Act specified but which were not enumerated in Rule 25(d), namely, officers of "the Canal Zone, or of a Territory or an insular possession of the United States, . . . or other governmental agency of such Territory or insular possession," should now be specifically enumerated in the rule and the amendment so provides.

Notes of Advisory Committee on Rules—1961 Amendment

Subdivision (d)(1). Present Rule 25(d) is generally considered to be unsatisfactory. 4 Moore's Federal Practice 25.01[7] (2d ed. 1950); Wright, Amendments to the Federal Rules: The Function of a Continuing Rules Committee, 7 Vand.L.Rev. 521, 529 (1954); Developments in the Law—Remedies Against the United States and Its Officials, 70 Harv.L.Rev. 827, 931–34 (1957). To require, as a condition of substituting a successor public officer as a party to a pending action, that an application be made with a showing that there is substantial need for continuing the litigation, can rarely serve any useful purpose and fosters a burdensome formality. And to prescribe a short, fixed time period for substitution which cannot be extended even by agreement, see Snyder v. Buck, 340 U.S. 15, 19 (1950), with the penalty of dismissal of the action, "makes a trap for unsuspecting litigants which seems unworthy of a great government." Vibra Brush Corp. v. Schaffer, 256 F.2d 681, 684 (2d Cir. 1958). Although courts have on occasion found means of undercutting the rule, e.g. Acheson v. Furusho, 212 F.2d 284 (9th Cir. 1954) (substitution of defendant officer unnecessary on theory that only a declaration of status was sought), it has operated harshly in many instances, e.g. Snyder v. Buck, supra; Poindexter v. Folsom, 242 F.2d 516 (3d Cir. 1957).

Under the amendment, the successor is automatically substituted as a party without an application or showing of need to continue the action. An order of substitution is not required, but may be entered at any time if a party desires or the court thinks fit.

The general term "public officer" is used in preference to the enumeration which appears in the present rule. It comprises Federal, State, and local officers.

The expression "in his official capacity" is to be interpreted in its context as part of a simple procedural rule for substitution; care should be taken not to distort its meaning by mistaken analogies to the doctrine of sovereign immunity from suit or the Eleventh Amendment. The amended rule will apply to all actions brought by public officers for the government, and to any action brought in form against a named officer, but intrinsically against the government or the office or the incumbent thereof whoever he may be from time to time during the action. Thus the amended rule will apply to actions against officers to compel performance of official duties or to obtain judicial review of their orders. It will also apply to actions to prevent officers from acting in excess of their authority or under authority not validly conferred, cf. Philadelphia Co. v. Stimson, 223 U.S. 605 (1912), or from enforcing unconstitutional enactments, cf. Ex parte Young, 209 U.S. 123 (1908); Ex parte La Prade, 289 U.S. 444 (1933). In general it will apply whenever effective relief would call for corrective behavior by the one then having official status and power, rather than one who has lost that status and power through ceasing to hold office. Cf. Land v. Dollar, 330 U.S. 731 (1947); Larson v. Domestic & Foreign Commerce Corp., 337 U.S. 682 (1949). Excluded from the operation of the amended rule will be the relatively infrequent actions which are directed to securing money judgments against the named officers enforceable against their personal assets; in these cases Rule 25(a)(1), not Rule 25(d), applies to the question of substitution. Examples are actions against officers seeking to make them pay damages out of their own pockets for defamatory utterances or other misconduct in some way related to the office, see Barr v. Matteo, 360 U.S. 564 (1959); Howard v. Lyons, 360 U.S. 593 (1959); Gregoire v. Biddle, 177 F.2d 579 (2d Cir. 1949), cert. denied, 339 U.S. 949 (1950). Another example is the anomalous action for a tax refund against a collector of internal revenue, see Ignelzi v. Granger, 16 F.R.D. 517 (W.D.Pa. 1955), 28 U.S.C. §2006, 4 Moore, supra, 25.05, p. 531; but see 28 U.S.C. §1346(a)(1), authorizing the bringing of such suits against the United States rather than the officer.

Automatic substitution under the amended rule, being merely a procedural device for substituting a successor for a past officeholder as a party, is distinct from and does not affect any substantive issues which may be involved in the action. Thus a defense of immunity from suit will remain in the case despite a substitution.

Where the successor does not intend to pursue the policy of his predecessor which gave rise to the lawsuit, it will be open to him, after substitution, as plaintiff to seek voluntary dismissal of the action, or as defendant to seek to have the action dismissed as moot or to take other appropriate steps to avert a judgment or decree. Contrast Ex parte La Prade, supra; Allen v. Regents of the University System, 304 U.S. 439 (1938); McGrath v. National Assn. of Mfgrs., 344 U.S. 804 (1952); Danenberg v. Cohen, 213 F.2d 944 (7th Cir. 1954).

As the present amendment of Rule 25(d)(1) eliminates a specified time period to secure substitution of public officers, the reference in Rule 6(b) (regarding enlargement of time) to Rule 25 will no longer apply to these public-officer substitutions.

As to substitution on appeal, the rules of the appellate courts should be consulted.

Subdivision (d)(2). This provision, applicable in "official capacity" cases as described above, will encourage the use of the official title without any mention of the officer individually, thereby recognizing the intrinsic character of the action and helping to eliminate concern with the problem of substitution. If for any reason it seems necessary or desirable to add the individual's name, this may be done upon motion or on the court's initiative without dismissal of the action; thereafter the procedure of amended Rule 25(d)(1) will apply if the individual named ceases to hold office.

For examples of naming the office or title rather than the officeholder, see Annot., 102 A.L.R. 943, 948–52; Comment, 50 Mich.L.Rev. 443, 450 (1952); cf. 26 U.S.C. §7484. Where an action is brought by or against a board or agency with continuity of existence, it has been often decided that there is no need to name the individual members and substitution is unnecessary when the personnel changes. 4 Moore, supra, 25.09, p. 536. The practice encouraged by amended Rule 25(d)(2) is similar.

Notes of Advisory Committee on Rules—1963 Amendment

Present Rule 25(a)(1), together with present Rule 6(b), results in an inflexible requirement that an action be dismissed as to a deceased party if substitution is not carried out within a fixed period measured from the time of the death. The hardships and inequities of this unyielding requirement plainly appear from the cases. See e.g., Anderson v. Yungkau, 329 U.S. 482, 67 S.Ct. 428, 91 L.Ed. 436 (1947); Iovino v. Waterson, 274 F.2d 41 (1959), cert. denied, Carlin v. Sovino, 362 U.S. 949, 80 S.Ct. 860, 4 L.Ed.2d 867 (1960); Perry v. Allen, 239 F.2d 107 (5th Cir. 1956); Starnes v. Pennsylvania R.R., 26 F.R.D. 625 (E.D.N.Y.), aff'd per curiam, 295 F.2d 704 (2d Cir. 1961), cert. denied, 369 U.S. 813, 82 S.Ct. 688, 7 L.Ed.2d 612 (1962); Zdanok v. Glidden Co., 28 F.R.D. 346 (S.D.N.Y. 1961). See also 4 Moore's Federal Practice 25.01[9] (Supp. 1960); 2 Barron & Holtzoff, Federal Practice & Procedure §621, at 420–21 (Wright ed. 1961).

The amended rule establishes a time limit for the motion to substitute based not upon the time of the death, but rather upon the time information of the death as provided by the means of a suggestion of death upon the record, i.e., service of a statement of the fact of the death. Cf. Ill.Ann.Stat., ch. 110, §54(2) (Smith-Hurd 1956). The motion may not be made later than 90 days after the service of the statement unless the period is extended pursuant to Rule 6(b), as amended. See the Advisory Committee's Note to amended Rule 6(b). See also the new Official Form 30.

A motion to substitute may be made by any party or by the representative of the deceased party without awaiting the suggestion of death. Indeed, the motion will usually be so made. If a party or the representative of the deceased party desires to limit the time within which another may make the motion, he may do so by suggesting the death upon the record.

A motion to substitute made within the prescribed time will ordinarily be granted, but under the permissive language of the first sentence of the amended rule ("the court may order") it may be denied by the court in the exercise of a sound discretion if made long after the death—as can occur if the suggestion of death is not made or is delayed—and circumstances have arisen rendering it unfair to allow substitution. Cf. Anderson v. Yungkau, supra, 329 U.S. at 485, 486, 67 S.Ct. at 430, 431, 91 L.Ed. 436, where it was noted under the present rule that settlement and distribution of the state of a deceased defendant might be so far advanced as to warrant denial of a motion for substitution even though made within the time limit prescribed by that rule. Accordingly, a party interested in securing substitution under the amended rule should not assume that he can rest indefinitely awaiting the suggestion of death before he makes his motion to substitute.

Notes of Advisory Committee on Rules—1987 Amendment

The amendments are technical. No substantive change is intended.

Committee Notes on Rules—2007 Amendment

The language of Rule 25 has been amended as part of the general restyling of the Civil Rules to make them more easily understood and to make style and terminology consistent throughout the rules. These changes are intended to be stylistic only.

Former Rule 25(d)(2) is transferred to become Rule 17(d) because it deals with designation of a public officer, not substitution.

Changes Made After Publication and Comment. See Note to Rule 1, supra.

TITLE V. DISCLOSURES AND DISCOVERY

Notes of Advisory Committee on Rules—1970 Amendments to Discovery Rules

This statement is intended to serve as a general introduction to the amendments of Rules 26–37, concerning discovery, as well as related amendments of other rules. A separate note of customary scope is appended to amendments proposed for each rule. This statement provides a framework for the consideration of individual rule changes.

Changes in the Discovery Rules

The discovery rules, as adopted in 1938, were a striking and imaginative departure from tradition. It was expected from the outset that they would be important, but experience has shown them to play an even larger role than was initially foreseen. Although the discovery rules have been amended since 1938, the changes were relatively few and narrowly focused, made in order to remedy specific defects. The amendments now proposed reflect the first comprehensive review of the discovery rules undertaken since 1938. These amendments make substantial changes in the discovery rules. Those summarized here are among the more important changes.

Scope of Discovery. New provisions are made and existing provisions changed affecting the scope of discovery: (1) The contents of insurance policies are made discoverable (Rule 26(b)(2)). (2) A showing of good cause is no longer required for discovery of documents and things and entry upon land (Rule 34). However, a showing of need is required for discovery of "trial preparation" materials other than a party's discovery of his own statement and a witness' discovery of his own statement; and protection is afforded against disclosure in such documents of mental impressions, conclusions, opinions, or legal theories concerning the litigation. (Rule 26(b)(3)). (3) Provision is made for discovery with respect to experts retained for trial preparation, and particularly those experts who will be called to testify at trial (Rule 26(b)(4)). (4) It is provided that interrogatories and requests for admission are not objectionable simply because they relate to matters of opinion or contention, subject of course to the supervisory power of the court (Rules 33(b), 36(a)). (5) Medical examination is made available as to certain nonparties. (Rule 35(a)).

Mechanics of Discovery. A variety of changes are made in the mechanics of the discovery process, affecting the sequence and timing of discovery, the respective obligations of the parties with respect to requests, responses, and motions for court orders, and the related powers of the court to enforce discovery requests and to protect against their abusive use. A new provision eliminates the automatic grant of priority in discovery to one side (Rule 26(d)). Another provides that a party is not under a duty to supplement his responses to requests for discovery, except as specified (Rule 26(e)).

Other changes in the mechanics of discovery are designed to encourage extrajudicial discovery with a minimum of court intervention. Among these are the following: (1) The requirement that a plaintiff seek leave of court for early discovery requests is eliminated or reduced, and motions for a court order under Rule 34 are made unnecessary. Motions under Rule 35 are continued. (2) Answers and objections are to be served together and an enlargement of the time for response is provided. (3) The party seeking discovery, rather than the objecting party, is made responsible for invoking judicial determination of discovery disputes not resolved by the parties. (4) Judicial sanctions are tightened with respect to unjustified insistence upon or objection to discovery. These changes bring Rules 33, 34, and 36 substantially into line with the procedure now provided for depositions.

Failure to amend Rule 35 in the same way is based upon two considerations. First, the Columbia Survey (described below) finds that only about 5 percent of medical examinations require court motions, of which about half result in court orders. Second and of greater importance, the interest of the person to be examined in the privacy of his person was recently stressed by the Supreme Court in Schlagenhauf v. Holder, 379 U.S. 104 (1964). The court emphasized the trial judge's responsibility to assure that the medical examination was justified, particularly as to its scope.

Rearrangement of Rules. A limited rearrangement of the discovery rules has been made, whereby certain provisions are transferred from one rule to another. The reasons for this rearrangement are discussed below in a separate section of this statement, and the details are set out in a table at the end of this statement.

Optional Procedures. In two instances, new optional procedures have been made available. A new procedure is provided to a party seeking to take the deposition of a corporation or other organization (Rule 30(b)(6)). A party on whom interrogatories have been served requesting information derivable from his business records may under specified circumstances produce the records rather than give answers (Rule 33(c)).

Other Changes. This summary of changes is by no means exhaustive. Various changes have been made in order to improve, tighten, or clarify particular provisions, to resolve conflicts in the case law, and to improve language. All changes, whether mentioned here or not, are discussed in the appropriate note for each rule.

A Field Survey of Discovery Practice

Despite widespread acceptance of discovery as an essential part of litigation, disputes have inevitably arisen concerning the values claimed for discovery and abuses alleged to exist. Many disputes about discovery relate to particular rule provisions or court decisions and can be studied in traditional fashion with a view to specific amendment. Since discovery is in large measure extra-judicial, however, even these disputes may be enlightened by a study of discovery "in the field." And some of the larger questions concerning discovery can be pursued only by a study of its operation at the law office level and in unreported cases.

The Committee, therefore, invited the Project for Effective Justice of Columbia Law School to conduct a field survey of discovery. Funds were obtained from the Ford Foundation and the Walter E.

Meyer Research Institute of Law, Inc. The survey was carried on under the direction of Prof. Maurice Rosenberg of Columbia Law School. The Project for Effective Justice has submitted a report to the Committee entitled "Field Survey of Federal Pretrial Discovery" (hereafter referred to as the Columbia Survey). The Committee is deeply grateful for the benefit of this extensive undertaking and is most appreciative of the cooperation of the Project and the funding organizations. The Committee is particularly grateful to Professor Rosenberg who not only directed the survey but has given much time in order to assist the Committee in assessing the results.

The Columbia Survey concludes, in general, that there is no empirical evidence to warrant a fundamental change in the philosophy of the discovery rules. No widespread or profound failings are disclosed in the scope or availability of discovery. The costs of discovery do not appear to be oppressive, as a general matter, either in relation to ability to pay or to the stakes of the litigation. Discovery frequently provides evidence that would not otherwise be available to the parties and thereby makes for a fairer trial or settlement. On the other hand, no positive evidence is found that discovery promotes settlement.

More specific findings of the Columbia Survey are described in other Committee notes, in relation to particular rule provisions and amendments. Those interested in more detailed information may obtain it from the Project for Effective Justice.

Rearrangement of the Discovery Rules

The present discovery rules are structured entirely in terms of individual discovery devices, except for Rule 27 which deals with perpetuation of testimony, and Rule 37 which provides sanctions to enforce discovery. Thus, Rules 26 and 28 to 32 are in terms addressed only to the taking of a deposition of a party or third person. Rules 33 to 36 then deal in succession with four additional discovery devices: Written interrogatories to parties, production for inspection of documents and things, physical or mental examination and requests for admission.

Under the rules as promulgated in 1938, therefore, each of the discovery devices was separate and self-contained. A defect of this arrangement is that there is no natural location in the discovery rules for provisions generally applicable to all discovery or to several discovery devices. From 1938 until the present, a few amendments have applied a discovery provision to several rules. For example, in 1948, the scope of deposition discovery in Rule 26(b) and the provision for protective orders in Rule 30(b) were incorporated by reference in Rules 33 and 34. The arrangement was adequate so long as there were few provisions governing discovery generally and these provisions were relatively simple.

As will be seen, however, a series of amendments are now proposed which govern most or all of the discovery devices. Proposals of a similar nature will probably be made in the future. Under these circumstances, it is very desirable, even necessary, that the discovery rules contain one rule addressing itself to discovery generally.

Rule 26 is obviously the most appropriate rule for this purpose. One of its subdivisions, Rule 26(b), in terms governs only scope of deposition discovery, but it has been expressly incorporated by reference in Rules 33 and 34 and is treated by courts as setting a general standard. By means of a transfer to Rule 26 of the provisions for protective orders now contained in Rule 30(b), and a transfer from Rule 26 of provisions addressed exclusively to depositions, Rule 26 is converted into a rule concerned with discovery generally. It becomes a convenient vehicle for the inclusion of new provisions dealing with the scope, timing, and regulation of discovery. Few additional transfers are needed. See table showing rearrangement of rules, set out below.

There are, to be sure, disadvantages in transferring any provision from one rule to another. Familiarity with the present pattern, reinforced by the references made by prior court decisions and the various secondary writings about the rules, is not lightly to be sacrificed. Revision of treatises and other references works is burdensome and costly. Moreover, many States have adopted the existing pattern as a model for their rules.

On the other hand, the amendments now proposed will in any event require revision of texts and reference works as well as reconsideration by States following the Federal model. If these amendments are to be incorporated in an understandable way, a rule with general discovery provisions is needed. As will be seen, the proposed rearrangement produces a more coherent and intelligible pattern for the discovery rules taken as a whole. The difficulties described are those encountered whenever statutes are reexamined and revised. Failure to rearrange the discovery rules now would freeze the present scheme, making future change even more difficult.

Table Showing Rearrangement of Rules

Existing Rule No.	New Rule No.
26(a)	30(a), 31(a)
26(c)	30(c)
26(d)	32(a)
26(e)	32(b)
26(f)	32(c)
30(a)	30(b)
30(b)	26(c)
32	32(d)

Rule 26. Duty to Disclose; General Provisions Governing Discovery

(a) Required Disclosures.

(1) Initial Disclosure.

(A) In General. Except as exempted by Rule 26(a)(1)(B) or as otherwise stipulated or ordered by the court, a party must, without awaiting a discovery request, provide to the other parties:

(i) the name and, if known, the address and telephone number of each individual likely to have discoverable information—along with the subjects of that information—that the disclosing party may use to support its claims or defenses, unless the use would be solely for impeachment;

(ii) a copy—or a description by category and location—of all documents, electronically stored information, and tangible things that the disclosing party has in its possession, custody, or control and may use to support its claims or defenses, unless the use would be solely for impeachment;

(iii) a computation of each category of damages claimed by the disclosing party—who must also make available for inspection and copying as under Rule 34 the documents or other evidentiary material, unless privileged or protected from disclosure, on which each computation is based, including materials bearing on the nature and extent of injuries suffered; and

(iv) for inspection and copying as under Rule 34, any insurance agreement under which an insurance business may be liable to satisfy all or part of a possible judgment in the action or to indemnify or reimburse for payments made to satisfy the judgment.

(B) Proceedings Exempt from Initial Disclosure. The following proceedings are exempt from initial disclosure:

(i) an action for review on an administrative record;
(ii) a forfeiture action in rem arising from a federal statute;
(iii) a petition for habeas corpus or any other proceeding to challenge a criminal conviction or sentence;
(iv) an action brought without an attorney by a person in the custody of the United States, a state, or a state subdivision;
(v) an action to enforce or quash an administrative summons or subpoena;
(vi) an action by the United States to recover benefit payments;
(vii) an action by the United States to collect on a student loan guaranteed by the United States;
(viii) a proceeding ancillary to a proceeding in another court; and
(ix) an action to enforce an arbitration award.

(C) Time for Initial Disclosures—In General. A party must make the initial disclosures at or within 14 days after the parties' Rule 26(f) conference unless a different time is set by stipulation or court order, or unless a party objects during the conference that initial disclosures are not appropriate in this action and states the objection in the proposed discovery plan. In ruling on the objection, the court must determine what disclosures, if any, are to be made and must set the time for disclosure.

(D) Time for Initial Disclosures—For Parties Served or Joined Later. A party that is first served or otherwise joined after the Rule 26(f) conference must make the initial disclosures within 30 days after being served or joined, unless a different time is set by stipulation or court order.

(E) Basis for Initial Disclosure; Unacceptable Excuses. A party must make its initial disclosures based on the information then reasonably available to it. A party is not excused from making its disclosures because it has not fully investigated the case or because it challenges the sufficiency of another party's disclosures or because another party has not made its disclosures.

(2) Disclosure of Expert Testimony.

(A) In General. In addition to the disclosures required by Rule 26(a)(1), a party must disclose to the other parties the identity of any witness it may use at trial to present evidence under Federal Rule of Evidence 702, 703, or 705.

(B) Witnesses Who Must Provide a Written Report. Unless otherwise stipulated or ordered by the court, this disclosure must be accompanied by a written report—prepared and signed by the witness—if the witness is one retained or specially employed to provide expert testimony in the case or one whose duties as the party's employee regularly involve giving expert testimony. The report must contain:

(i) a complete statement of all opinions the witness will express and the basis and reasons for them;
(ii) the facts or data considered by the witness in forming them;
(iii) any exhibits that will be used to summarize or support them;
(iv) the witness's qualifications, including a list of all publications authored in the previous 10 years;
(v) a list of all other cases in which, during the previous 4 years, the witness testified as an expert at trial or by deposition; and
(vi) a statement of the compensation to be paid for the study and testimony in the case.

(C) Witnesses Who Do Not Provide a Written Report. Unless otherwise stipulated or ordered by the court, if the witness is not required to provide a written report, this disclosure must state:

(i) the subject matter on which the witness is expected to present evidence under Federal Rule of Evidence 702, 703, or 705; and
(ii) a summary of the facts and opinions to which the witness is expected to testify.

(D) Time to Disclose Expert Testimony. A party must make these disclosures at the times and in the sequence that the court orders. Absent a stipulation or a court order, the disclosures must be made:

(i) at least 90 days before the date set for trial or for the case to be ready for trial; or
(ii) if the evidence is intended solely to contradict or rebut evidence on the same subject matter identified by another party under Rule 26(a)(2)(B) or (C), within 30 days after the other party's disclosure.

(E) Supplementing the Disclosure. The parties must supplement these disclosures when required under Rule 26(e).

(3) Pretrial Disclosures.

(A) In General. In addition to the disclosures required by Rule 26(a)(1) and (2), a party must provide to the other parties and promptly file the following information about the evidence that it may present at trial other than solely for impeachment:

(i) the name and, if not previously provided, the address and telephone number of each witness—separately identifying those the party expects to present and those it may call if the need arises;
(ii) the designation of those witnesses whose testimony the party expects to present by deposition and, if not taken stenographically, a transcript of the pertinent parts of the deposition; and
(iii) an identification of each document or other exhibit, including summaries of other evidence—separately identifying those items the party expects to offer and those it may offer if the need arises.

(B) Time for Pretrial Disclosures; Objections. Unless the court orders otherwise, these disclosures must be made at least 30 days before trial. Within 14 days after they are made, unless the court sets a different time, a party may serve and promptly file a list of the following objections: any objections to the use under Rule 32(a) of a deposition designated by another party under Rule 26(a)(3)(A)(ii); and any objection, together with the grounds for it, that may be made to the admissibility of materials identified under Rule 26(a)(3)(A)(iii). An objection not so made—except for one under Federal Rule of Evidence 402 or 403—is waived unless excused by the court for good cause.

(4) Form of Disclosures. Unless the court orders otherwise, all disclosures under Rule 26(a) must be in writing, signed, and served.

(b) Discovery Scope and Limits.

(1) Scope in General. Unless otherwise limited by court order, the scope of discovery is as follows: Parties may obtain discovery regarding any nonprivileged matter that is relevant to any party's claim or defense and proportional to the needs of the case, considering the importance of the issues at stake in the action, the amount in controversy, the parties' relative access to relevant information, the parties' resources, the importance of the discovery in resolving the issues, and whether the burden or expense of the proposed discovery outweighs its likely benefit. Information within this scope of discovery need not be admissible in evidence to be discoverable.

(2) Limitations on Frequency and Extent.

(A) When Permitted. By order, the court may alter the limits in these rules on the number of depositions and interrogatories or on the length of depositions under Rule 30. By order or local rule, the court may also limit the number of requests under Rule 36.

(B) Specific Limitations on Electronically Stored Information. A party need not provide discovery of electronically stored information from sources that the party identifies as not reasonably accessible because of undue burden or cost. On motion to compel discovery or for a protective order, the party from whom discovery is sought must show that the information is not reasonably accessible because of undue burden or cost. If that showing is made, the court may nonetheless order discovery from such sources if the requesting party shows good cause, considering the limitations of Rule 26(b)(2)(C). The court may specify conditions for the discovery.

(C) When Required. On motion or on its own, the court must limit the frequency or extent of discovery otherwise allowed by these rules or by local rule if it determines that:

(i) the discovery sought is unreasonably cumulative or duplicative, or can be obtained from some other source that is more convenient, less burdensome, or less expensive;

(ii) the party seeking discovery has had ample opportunity to obtain the information by discovery in the action; or

(iii) the proposed discovery is outside the scope permitted by Rule 26(b)(1).

(3) Trial Preparation: Materials.

(A) Documents and Tangible Things. Ordinarily, a party may not discover documents and tangible things that are prepared in anticipation of litigation or for trial by or for another party or its representative (including the other party's attorney, consultant, surety, indemnitor, insurer, or agent). But, subject to Rule 26(b)(4), those materials may be discovered if:

(i) they are otherwise discoverable under Rule 26(b)(1); and

(ii) the party shows that it has substantial need for the materials to prepare its case and cannot, without undue hardship, obtain their substantial equivalent by other means.

(B) Protection Against Disclosure. If the court orders discovery of those materials, it must protect against disclosure of the mental impressions, conclusions, opinions, or legal theories of a party's attorney or other representative concerning the litigation.

(C) Previous Statement. Any party or other person may, on request and without the required showing, obtain the person's own previous statement about the action or its subject matter. If the request is refused, the person may move for a court order, and Rule 37(a)(5) applies to the award of expenses. A previous statement is either:

(i) a written statement that the person has signed or otherwise adopted or approved; or

(ii) a contemporaneous stenographic, mechanical, electrical, or other recording—or a transcription of it—that recites substantially verbatim the person's oral statement.

(4) Trial Preparation: Experts.

(A) Deposition of an Expert Who May Testify. A party may depose any person who has been identified as an expert whose opinions may be presented at trial. If Rule 26(a)(2)(B) requires a report from the expert, the deposition may be conducted only after the report is provided.

(B) Trial-Preparation Protection for Draft Reports or Disclosures. Rules 26(b)(3)(A) and (B) protect drafts of any report or disclosure required under Rule 26(a)(2), regardless of the form in which the draft is recorded.

(C) Trial-Preparation Protection for Communications Between a Party's Attorney and Expert Witnesses. Rules 26(b)(3)(A) and (B) protect communications between the party's attorney and any witness required to provide a report under Rule 26(a)(2)(B), regardless of the form of the communications, except to the extent that the communications:

(i) relate to compensation for the expert's study or testimony;

(ii) identify facts or data that the party's attorney provided and that the expert considered in forming the opinions to be expressed; or

(iii) identify assumptions that the party's attorney provided and that the expert relied on in forming the opinions to be expressed.

(D) Expert Employed Only for Trial Preparation. Ordinarily, a party may not, by interrogatories or deposition, discover facts known or opinions held by an expert who has been retained or specially employed by another party in anticipation of litigation or to prepare for trial and who is not expected to be called as a witness at trial. But a party may do so only:

(i) as provided in Rule 35(b); or

(ii) on showing exceptional circumstances under which it is impracticable for the party to obtain facts or opinions on the same subject by other means.

(E) Payment. Unless manifest injustice would result, the court must require that the party seeking discovery:

(i) pay the expert a reasonable fee for time spent in responding to discovery under Rule 26(b)(4)(A) or (D); and

(ii) for discovery under (D), also pay the other party a fair portion of the fees and expenses it reasonably incurred in obtaining the expert's facts and opinions.

(5) Claiming Privilege or Protecting Trial-Preparation Materials.

(A) Information Withheld. When a party withholds information otherwise discoverable by claiming that the information is privileged or subject to protection as trial-preparation material, the party must:

(i) expressly make the claim; and

(ii) describe the nature of the documents, communications, or tangible things not produced or disclosed—and do so in a manner that, without revealing information itself privileged or protected, will enable other parties to assess the claim.

(B) Information Produced. If information produced in discovery is subject to a claim of privilege or of protection as trial-preparation material, the party making the claim may notify any party that received the information of the claim and the basis for it. After being notified, a party must promptly return, sequester, or destroy the specified information and any copies it has; must not use or disclose the information until the claim is resolved; must take reasonable steps to retrieve the information if the party disclosed it before being notified; and may promptly present the information to the court under seal for a determination of the claim. The producing party must preserve the information until the claim is resolved.

(c) Protective Orders.

(1) In General. A party or any person from whom discovery is sought may move for a protective order in the court where the action is pending—or as an alternative on matters relating to a deposition, in the court for the district where the deposition will be taken. The motion must include a certification that the movant has in good faith conferred or attempted to confer with other affected parties in an effort to resolve the dispute without court action. The court may, for good cause, issue an order to protect a party or person from annoyance, embarrassment, oppression, or undue burden or expense, including one or more of the following:

(A) forbidding the disclosure or discovery;

(B) specifying terms, including time and place or the allocation of expenses, for the disclosure or discovery;

(C) prescribing a discovery method other than the one selected by the party seeking discovery;

(D) forbidding inquiry into certain matters, or limiting the scope of disclosure or discovery to certain matters;

(E) designating the persons who may be present while the discovery is conducted;

(F) requiring that a deposition be sealed and opened only on court order;

(G) requiring that a trade secret or other confidential research, development, or commercial information not be revealed or be revealed only in a specified way; and

(H) requiring that the parties simultaneously file specified documents or information in sealed envelopes, to be opened as the court directs.

(2) Ordering Discovery. If a motion for a protective order is wholly or partly denied, the court may, on just terms, order that any party or person provide or permit discovery.

(3) Awarding Expenses. Rule 37(a)(5) applies to the award of expenses.

(d) Timing and Sequence of Discovery.

(1) Timing. A party may not seek discovery from any source before the parties have conferred as required by Rule 26(f), except in a proceeding exempted from initial disclosure under Rule 26(a)(1)(B), or when authorized by these rules, by stipulation, or by court order.

(2) Early Rule 34 Requests.

(A) Time to Deliver. More than 21 days after the summons and complaint are served on a party, a request under Rule 34 may be delivered:

(i) to that party by any other party, and

(ii) by that party to any plaintiff or to any other party that has been served.

(B) When Considered Served. The request is considered to have been served at the first Rule 26(f) conference.

(3) Sequence. Unless the parties stipulate or the court orders otherwise for the parties' and witnesses' convenience and in the interests of justice:

(A) methods of discovery may be used in any sequence; and

(B) discovery by one party does not require any other party to delay its discovery.

(e) Supplementing Disclosures and Responses.

(1) In General. A party who has made a disclosure under Rule 26(a)—or who has responded to an interrogatory, request for production, or request for admission—must supplement or correct its disclosure or response:

(A) in a timely manner if the party learns that in some material respect the disclosure or response is incomplete or incorrect, and if the additional or corrective information has not otherwise been made known to the other parties during the discovery process or in writing; or

(B) as ordered by the court.

(2) Expert Witness. For an expert whose report must be disclosed under Rule 26(a)(2)(B), the party's duty to supplement extends both to information included in the report and to information given during the expert's deposition. Any additions or changes to this information must be disclosed by the time the party's pretrial disclosures under Rule 26(a)(3) are due.

(f) Conference of the Parties; Planning for Discovery.

(1) Conference Timing. Except in a proceeding exempted from initial disclosure under Rule 26(a)(1)(B) or when the court orders otherwise, the parties must confer as soon as practicable—and in any event at least 21 days before a scheduling conference is to be held or a scheduling order is due under Rule 16(b).

(2) Conference Content; Parties' Responsibilities. In conferring, the parties must consider the nature and basis of their claims and defenses and the possibilities for promptly settling or resolving the case; make or arrange for the disclosures required by Rule 26(a)(1); discuss any issues about preserving discoverable information; and develop a proposed discovery plan. The attorneys of record and all unrepresented parties that have appeared in the case are jointly responsible for arranging the conference, for attempting in good faith to agree on the proposed discovery plan, and for submitting to the court within 14 days after the conference a written report outlining the plan. The court may order the parties or attorneys to attend the conference in person.

(3) Discovery Plan. A discovery plan must state the parties' views and proposals on:

(A) what changes should be made in the timing, form, or requirement for disclosures under Rule 26(a), including a statement of when initial disclosures were made or will be made;

(B) the subjects on which discovery may be needed, when discovery should be completed, and whether discovery should be conducted in phases or be limited to or focused on particular issues;

(C) any issues about disclosure, discovery, or preservation of electronically stored information, including the form or forms in which it should be produced;

(D) any issues about claims of privilege or of protection as trial-preparation materials, including—if the parties agree on a procedure to assert these claims after production—whether to ask the court to include their agreement in an order under Federal Rule of Evidence 502;

(E) what changes should be made in the limitations on discovery imposed under these rules or by local rule, and what other limitations should be imposed; and

(F) any other orders that the court should issue under Rule 26(c) or under Rule 16(b) and (c).

(4) Expedited Schedule. If necessary to comply with its expedited schedule for Rule 16(b) conferences, a court may by local rule:

(A) require the parties' conference to occur less than 21 days before the scheduling conference is held or a scheduling order is due under Rule 16(b); and

(B) require the written report outlining the discovery plan to be filed less than 14 days after the parties' conference, or excuse the parties from submitting a written report and permit them to report orally on their discovery plan at the Rule 16(b) conference.

(g) Signing Disclosures and Discovery Requests, Responses, and Objections.

(1) Signature Required; Effect of Signature. Every disclosure under Rule 26(a)(1) or (a)(3) and every discovery request, response, or objection must be signed by at least one attorney of record in the attorney's own name—or by the party personally, if unrepresented—and must state the signer's address, e-mail address, and telephone number. By signing, an attorney or party certifies that to the best of the person's knowledge, information, and belief formed after a reasonable inquiry:

(A) with respect to a disclosure, it is complete and correct as of the time it is made; and

(B) with respect to a discovery request, response, or objection, it is:

(i) consistent with these rules and warranted by existing law or by a nonfrivolous argument for extending, modifying, or reversing existing law, or for establishing new law;

(ii) not interposed for any improper purpose, such as to harass, cause unnecessary delay, or needlessly increase the cost of litigation; and

(iii) neither unreasonable nor unduly burdensome or expensive, considering the needs of the case, prior discovery in the case, the amount in controversy, and the importance of the issues at stake in the action.

(2) Failure to Sign. Other parties have no duty to act on an unsigned disclosure, request, response, or objection until it is signed, and the court must strike it unless a signature is promptly supplied after the omission is called to the attorney's or party's attention.

(3) Sanction for Improper Certification. If a certification violates this rule without substantial justification, the court, on motion or on its own, must impose an appropriate sanction on the signer, the party on whose behalf the signer was acting, or both. The sanction may include an order to pay the reasonable expenses, including attorney's fees, caused by the violation.

(As amended Dec. 27, 1946, eff. Mar. 19, 1948; Jan. 21, 1963, eff. July 1, 1963; Feb. 28, 1966, eff. July 1, 1966; Mar. 30, 1970, eff. July 1, 1970; Apr. 29, 1980, eff. Aug. 1, 1980; Apr. 28, 1983, eff. Aug. 1, 1983; Mar. 2, 1987, eff. Aug. 1, 1987; Apr. 22, 1993, eff. Dec. 1, 1993; Apr. 17, 2000, eff. Dec. 1, 2000; Apr. 12, 2006, eff. Dec. 1, 2006; Apr. 30, 2007, eff. Dec. 1, 2007; Apr. 28, 2010, eff. Dec. 1, 2010; Apr. 29, 2015, eff. Dec. 1, 2015.)

Notes of Advisory Committee on Rules—1937

Note to Subdivision (a). This rule freely authorizes the taking of depositions under the same circumstances and by the same methods whether for the purpose of discovery or for the purpose of obtaining evidence. Many states have adopted this practice on account of its simplicity and effectiveness, safeguarding it by imposing such restrictions upon the subsequent use of the deposition at the trial or hearing as are deemed advisable. See Ark.Civ.Code (Crawford, 1934) §§606–607; Calif.Code Civ.Proc. (Deering, 1937) §2021; 1 Colo.Stat.Ann. (1935) Code Civ.Proc. §376; Idaho Code Ann. (1932) §16–906; Ill. Rules of Pract., Rule 19 (Ill.Rev.Stat. (1937) ch. 110, §259.19); Ill.Rev.Stat. (1937) ch. 51, §24; 2 Ind.Stat.Ann. (Burns, 1933) §§2–1501, 2–1506; Ky.Codes (Carroll, 1932) Civ.Pract. §557; 1 Mo.Rev.Stat. (1929) §1753; 4 Mont.Rev.Codes Ann. (1935) §10645; Neb.Comp.Stat. (1929) ch. 20, §§1246–7; 4 Nev.Comp.Laws (Hillyer, 1929) §9001; 2 N.H.Pub.Laws (1926) ch. 337, §1; N.C.Code Ann. (1935) §1809; 2 N.D.Comp.Laws Ann. (1913) §§7889–7897; 2 Ohio Gen.Code Ann. (Page, 1926) §§11525–6; 1 Ore.Code Ann. (1930) Title 9, §1503; 1 S.D.Comp.Laws (1929) §§2713–16; Tex.Stat. (Vernon, 1928) arts. 3738, 3752, 3769; Utah Rev.Stat.Ann. (1933) §104–51–7; Wash. Rules of Practice adopted by the Supreme Ct., Rule 8, 2 Wash.Rev.Stat.Ann. (Remington, 1932) §308–8; W.Va.Code (1931) ch. 57, art. 4, §1. Compare [former] Equity Rules 47 (Depositions—To be Taken in Exceptional Instances); 54 (Depositions Under Revised Statutes, Sections 863, 865, 866, 867—Cross-Examination); 58 (Discovery—Interrogatories—Inspection and Production of Documents—Admission of Execution or Genuineness).

This and subsequent rules incorporate, modify, and broaden the provisions for depositions under U.S.C., Title 28, [former] §§639 (Depositions de bene esse; when and where taken; notice), 640 (Same; mode of taking), 641 (Same; transmission to court), 644 (Depositions under dedimus potestatem and in perpetuam), 646 (Deposition under dedimus potestatem; how taken). These statutes are superseded insofar as they differ from this and subsequent rules. U.S.C., Title 28, [former] §643 (Depositions; taken in mode prescribed by State laws) is superseded by the third sentence of Subdivision (a).

While a number of states permit discovery only from parties or their agents, others either make no distinction between parties or agents of parties and ordinary witnesses, or authorize the taking of ordinary depositions, without restriction, from any persons who have knowledge of relevant facts. See Ark.Civ.Code (Crawford, 1934) §§606–607; 1 Idaho Code Ann. (1932) §16–906; Ill. Rules of Pract., Rule 19 (Ill.Rev.Stat. (1937) ch. 110, §259.19); Ill.Rev.Stat. (1937) ch. 51, §24; 2 Ind.Stat.Ann. (Burns, 1933) §2–1501; Ky.Codes (Carroll, 1932) Civ.Pract. §§554–558; 2 Md.Ann.Code (Bagby, 1924) Art. 35, §21; 2 Minn.Stat. (Mason, 1927) §9820; 1 Mo.Rev.Stat. (1929) §§1753, 1759; Neb.Comp.Stat. (1929) ch. 20, §§1246–7; 2 N.H.Pub.Laws (1926) ch. 337, §1; 2 N.D.Comp.Laws Ann. (1913) §7897; 2 Ohio Gen.Code Ann. (Page, 1926) §§11525–6; 1 S.D.Comp.Laws (1929) §§2713–16; Tex.Stat. (Vernon, 1928) arts. 3738, 3752, 3769; Utah Rev.Stat.Ann. (1933) §104–51–7; Wash. Rules of Practice adopted by Supreme Ct., Rule 8, 2 Wash.Rev.Stat.Ann. (Remington, 1932) §308–8; W.Va.Code (1931) ch. 57, art. 4, §1.

The more common practice in the United States is to take depositions on notice by the party desiring them, without any order from the court, and this has been followed in these rules. See Calif.Code Civ.Proc. (Deering 1937) §2031; 2 Fla.Comp.Gen.Laws Ann. (1927) §§4405–7; 1 Idaho Code Ann. (1932) §16–902; Ill. Rules of Pract., Rule 19 (Ill.Rev.Stat. (1937) ch. 110, §25919); Ill.Rev.Stat. (1937) ch. 51, §24; 2 Ind.Stat.Ann. (Burns, 1933) §2–1502; Kan.Gen.Stat.Ann. (1935) §60–2827; Ky.Codes (Carroll, 1932) Civ.Pract. §565; 2 Minn.Stat. (Mason, 1927) §9820; 1 Mo.Rev.Stat. (1929) §1761; 4 Mont.Rev.Codes Ann. (1935) §10651; Nev.Comp.Laws (Hillyer, 1929) §9002; N.C.Code Ann. (1935) §1809; 2 N.D.Comp.Laws Ann. (1913) §7895; Utah Rev.Stat.Ann. (1933) §104–51–8.

Note to Subdivision (b). While the old chancery practice limited discovery to facts supporting the case of the party seeking it, this limitation has been largely abandoned by modern legislation. See Ala.Code Ann. (Michie, 1928) §§7764–7773; 2 Ind.Stat.Ann. (Burns, 1933) §§2–1028, 2–1506, 2–1728–2–1732; Iowa Code (1935) §11185; Ky.Codes (Carroll, 1932) Civ.Pract. §§557, 606 (8); La.Code Pract. (Dart, 1932) arts. 347–356; 2 Mass.Gen.Laws (Ter.Ed., 1932) ch. 231, §§61–67; 1 Mo.Rev.Stat. (1929) §§1753, 1759; Neb.Comp.Stat. (1929) §§20–1246, 20–1247; 2 N.H.Pub.Laws (1926) ch. 337, §1; 2 Ohio Gen.Code Ann. (Page, 1926) §§11497, 11526; Tex.Stat. (Vernon, 1928) arts. 3738, 3753, 3769; Wis.Stat. (1935) §326.12; Ontario Consol.Rules of Pract. (1928) Rules 237–347; Quebec Code of Civ.Proc. (Curran, 1922) §§286–290.

Note to Subdivisions (d), (e), and (f). The restrictions here placed upon the use of depositions at the trial or hearing are substantially the same as those provided in U.S.C., Title 28, [former] §641, for depositions taken, de bene esse, with the additional provision that any deposition may be used when the court finds the existence of exceptional circumstances. Compare English Rules Under the Judicature Act (The Annual Practice, 1937) O. 37, r. 18 (with additional provision permitting use of deposition by consent of the parties). See also [former] Equity Rule 64 (Former Depositions, Etc., May be Used Before Master); and 2 Minn. Stat. (Mason, 1927) §9835 (Use in a subsequent action of a deposition filed in a previously dismissed action between the same parties and involving the same subject matter).

Notes of Advisory Committee on Rules—1946 Amendment

Subdivision (a). The amendment eliminates the requirement of leave of court for the taking of a deposition except where a plaintiff seeks to take a deposition within 20 days after the commencement of the action. The retention of the requirement where a deposition is sought by a plaintiff within 20 days of the commencement of the action protects a defendant who has not had an opportunity to retain counsel and inform himself as to the nature of the suit; the plaintiff, of course, needs no such protection. The present rule forbids the plaintiff to take a deposition, without leave of court, before the answer is served. Sometimes the defendant delays the serving of an answer for more than 20 days, but as 20 days are sufficient time for him to obtain a lawyer, there is no reason to forbid the plaintiff to take a deposition without leave merely because the answer has not been served. In all cases, Rule 30(a) empowers the court, for cause shown, to alter the time of the taking of a deposition, and Rule 30(b) contains provisions giving ample protection to persons who are unreasonably pressed. The modified practice here adopted is along the line of that followed in various states. See, e.g., 8 Mo.Rev.Stat.Ann. (1939) §1917; 2 Burns' Ind.Stat.Ann. (1933) §2–1506.

Subdivision (b). The amendments to subdivision (b) make clear the broad scope of examination and that it may cover not only evidence for use at the trial but also inquiry into matters in themselves inadmissible as evidence but which will lead to the discovery of such evidence. The purpose of discovery is to allow a broad search for facts, the names of witnesses, or any other matters which may aid a party in the preparation or presentation of his case. Engl v. Aetna Life Ins. Co. (C.C.A.2d, 1943) 139 F.(2d) 469; Mahler v. Pennsylvania R. Co. (E.D.N.Y. 1945) 8 Fed.Rules Serv. 33.351, Case 1. In such a preliminary inquiry admissibility at trial should not be the test as to whether the information sought is within the scope of proper examination. Such a standard unnecessarily curtails the utility of discovery practice. Of course, matters entirely without bearing either as direct evidence or as leads to evidence are not within the scope of inquiry, but to the extent that the examination develops useful information, it functions successfully as an instrument of discovery, even if it produces no testimony directly admissible. Lewis v. United Air Lines Transportation Corp. (D.Conn. 1939) 27 F.Supp. 946; Engl v. Aetna Life Ins. Co., supra; Mahler v. Pennsylvania R. Co., supra; Bloomer v. Sirian Lamp Co. (D.Del. 1944) 8 Fed.Rules Serv. 26b.31, Case 3; Rousseau v. Langley (S.D.N.Y. 1945) 9 Fed.Rules Serv. 34.41, Case 1 (Rule 26 contemplates "examinations not merely for the narrow purpose of adducing testimony which may be offered in evidence but also for the broad discovery of information which may be useful in preparation for trial."); Olson Transportation Co. v. Socony-Vacuum Co. (E.D.Wis. 1944) 8 Fed.Rules Serv. 34.41, Case 2 (". . . the Rules . . . permit 'fishing' for evidence as they should."); Note (1945) 45 Col.L.Rev. 482. Thus hearsay, while inadmissible itself, may suggest testimony which properly may be proved. Under Rule 26 (b) several cases, however, have erroneously limited discovery on the basis of admissibility, holding that the word "relevant" in effect meant "material and competent under the rules of evidence". Poppino v. Jones Store Co. (W.D.Mo. 1940) 3 Fed.Rules Serv. 26b.5, Case 1; Benevento v. A. & P. Food Stores, Inc. (E.D.N.Y. 1939) 26 F.Supp. 424. Thus it has been said that inquiry might not be made into statements or other matters which, when disclosed, amounted only to hearsay. See Maryland for use of Montvila v. Pan-American Bus Lines, Inc. (D.Md. 1940) 3 Fed.Rules Serv. 26b.211, Case 3; Gitto v. "Italia," Societa Anonima Di Navigazione (E.D.N.Y. 1940) 31 F.Supp. 567; Rose Silk Mills, Inc. v. Insurance Co. of North America (S.D.N.Y. 1939) 29 F.Supp. 504; Colpak v. Hetterick (E.D.N.Y. 1941) 40 F.Supp. 350; Matthies v. Peter F. Connolly Co. (E.D.N.Y. 1941) 6 Fed.Rules Serv. 30a.22, Case 1, 2 F.R.D. 277; Matter of Examination of Citizens Casualty Co. of New York (S.D.N.Y. 1942) 7 Fed.Rules Serv. 26b.211, Case 1; United States v. Silliman (D.N.J. 1944) 8 Fed.Rules Serv. 26b.52, Case 1. The contrary and better view, however, has often been stated. See, e.g., Engl v. Aetna Life Ins. Co., supra; Stevenson v. Melady (S.D.N.Y. 1940) 3 Fed.Rules Serv. 26b.31, Case 1, 1 F.R.D. 329; Lewis v. United Air Lines Transport Corp., supra; Application of Zenith Radio Corp. (E.D.Pa. 1941) 4 Fed.Rules Serv. 30b.21, Case 1, 1 F.R.D. 627; Steingut v. Guaranty Trust Co. of New York (S.D.N.Y. 1941) 4 Fed.Rules Serv. 26b.5. Case 2; DeSeversky v. Republic Aviation Corp (E.D.N.Y. 1941) 5 Fed.Rules Serv. 26b.31, Case 5; Moore v. George A. Hormel & Co. (S.D.N.Y. 1942) 6 Fed.Rules Serv. 30b.41, Case 1, 2 F.R.D. 340; Hercules Powder Co. v. Rohm & Haas Co. (D.Del. 1943) 7 Fed.Rules Serv. 45b.311, Case 2, 3 F.R.D. 302; Bloomer v. Sirian Lamp Co., supra; Crosby Steam Gage & Valve Co. v. Manning, Maxwell & Moore, Inc. (D.Mass. 1944) 8 Fed.Rules Serv. 26b.31, Case 1; Patterson Oil Terminals, Inc. v. Charles Kurz & Co., Inc. (E.D.Pa. 1945) 9 Fed.Rules Serv. 33.321, Case 2; Pueblo Trading Co. v. Reclamation Dist. No. 1500 (N.D.Cal. 1945) 9 Fed.Rules Serv. 33.321, Case 4, 4 F.R.D. 471. See also discussion as to the broad scope of discovery in Hoffman v. Palmer (C.C.A.2d, 1942) 129 F.(2d) 976, 995–997, aff'd on other grounds (1942) 318 U.S. 109; Note (1945) 45 Col.L.Rev. 482.

Notes of Advisory Committee on Rules—1963 Amendment

This amendment conforms to the amendment of Rule 28(b). See the next-to-last paragraph of the Advisory Committee's Note to that amendment.

Notes of Advisory Committee on Rules—1966 Amendment

The requirement that the plaintiff obtain leave of court in order to serve notice of taking of a deposition within 20 days after commencement of the action gives rises to difficulties when the prospective deponent is about to become unavailable for examination. The problem is not confined to admiralty, but has been of special concern in that context because of the mobility of vessels and their personnel. When Rule 26 was adopted as Admiralty Rule 30A in 1961, the problem was alleviated by permitting depositions de bene esse, for which leave of court is not required. See Advisory Committee's Note to Admiralty Rule 30A (1961).

A continuing study is being made in the effort to devise a modification of the 20-day rule appropriate to both the civil and admiralty practice to the end that Rule 26(a) shall state a uniform rule applicable alike to what are now civil actions and suits in admiralty. Meanwhile, the exigencies of maritime litigation require preservation, for the time being at least, of the traditional de bene esse procedure for the post-unification counterpart of the present suit in admiralty. Accordingly, the amendment provides for continued availability of that procedure in admiralty and maritime claims within the meaning of Rule 9(h).

Notes of Advisory Committee on Rules—1970 Amendment

A limited rearrangement of the discovery rules is made, whereby certain rule provisions are transferred, as follows: Existing Rule 26(a) is transferred to Rules 30(a) and 31(a). Existing Rule 26(c) is transferred to Rule 30(c). Existing Rules 26(d), (e), and (f) are transferred to Rule 32. Revisions of the transferred provisions, if any, are discussed in the notes appended to Rules 30, 31, and 32. In addition, Rule 30(b) is transferred to Rule 26(c). The purpose of this rearrangement is to establish Rule 26 as a rule governing discovery in general. (The reasons are set out in the Advisory Committee's explanatory statement.)

Subdivision (a)—Discovery Devices. This is a new subdivision listing all of the discovery devices provided in the discovery rules and establishing the relationship between the general provisions of Rule 26 and the specific rules for particular discovery devices. The provision that the frequency of use of these methods is not limited confirms existing law. It incorporates in general form a provision now found in Rule 33.

Subdivision (b)—Scope of Discovery. This subdivision is recast to cover the scope of discovery generally. It regulates the discovery obtainable through any of the discovery devices listed in Rule 26(a).

All provisions as to scope of discovery are subject to the initial qualification that the court may limit discovery in accordance with these rules. Rule 26(c) (transferred from 30(b)) confers broad powers on the courts to regulate or prevent discovery even though the materials sought are within the scope of 26(b), and these powers have always been freely exercised. For example, a party's income tax return is generally held not privileged, 2A Barron & Holtzoff, Federal Practice and Procedure, §65.2 (Wright ed. 1961), and yet courts have recognized that interests in privacy may call for a measure of extra protection. E.g., Wiesenberger v. W. E. Hutton & Co., 35 F.R.D. 556 (S.D.N.Y. 1964). Similarly, the courts have in appropriate circumstances protected materials that are primarily of an impeaching character. These two types of materials merely illustrate the many situations, not capable of governance by precise rule, in which courts must exercise judgment. The new subsections in Rule 26(d) do not change existing law with respect to such situations.

Subdivision (b)(1)—In General. The language is changed to provide for the scope of discovery in general terms. The existing subdivision, although in terms applicable only to depositions, is incorporated by reference in existing Rules 33 and 34. Since decisions as to relevance to the subject matter of the action are made for discovery purposes well in advance of trial, a flexible treatment of relevance is required and the making of discovery, whether voluntary or under court order, is not a concession or determination of relevance for purposes of trial. Cf. 4 Moore's Federal Practice 26–16[1] (2d ed. 1966).

Subdivision (b)(2)—Insurance Policies. Both cases and commentators are sharply in conflict on the question whether defendant's liability insurance coverage is subject to discovery in the usual situation when the insurance coverage is not itself admissible and does not bear on another issue on the case. Examples of Federal cases requiring disclosure and supporting comments: Cook v. Welty, 253 F.Supp. 875 (D.D.C. 1966) (cases cited); Johanek v. Aberle, 27 F.R.D. 272 (D.Mont. 1961); Williams, Discovery of Dollar Limits in Liability Policies in Automobile Tort Cases, 10 Ala.L.Rev. 355 (1958); Thode, Some Reflections on the 1957 Amendments to the Texas Rules, 37 Tex.L.Rev. 33, 40–42 (1958). Examples of Federal cases refusing disclosure and supporting comments: Bisserier v. Manning, 207 F.Supp. 476 (D.N.J. 1962); Cooper v. Stender, 30 F.R.D. 389 (E.D.Tenn. 1962); Frank, Discovery and Insurance Coverage, 1959 Ins.L.J. 281; Fournier, Pre-Trial Discovery of Insurance Coverage and Limits, 28 Ford L.Rev. 215 (1959).

The division in reported cases is close. State decisions based on provisions similar to the federal rules are similarly divided. See cases collected in 2A Barron & Holtzoff, Federal Practice and Procedure §647.1, nn. 45.5, 45.6 (Wright ed. 1961). It appears to be difficult if not impossible to obtain appellate review of the issue. Resolution by rule amendment is indicated. The question is essentially procedural in that it bears upon preparation for trial and settlement before trial, and courts confronting the question, however, they have decided it, have generally treated it as procedural and governed by the rules.

The amendment resolves this issue in favor of disclosure. Most of the decisions denying discovery, some explicitly, reason from the text of Rule 26(b) that it permits discovery only of matters which will be admissible in evidence or appear reasonably calculated to lead to such evidence; they avoid considerations of policy, regarding them as foreclosed. See Bisserier v. Manning, supra. Some note also that facts about a defendant's financial status are not discoverable as such, prior to judgment with execution unsatisfied, and fear that, if courts hold insurance coverage discoverable, they must extend the principle to other aspects of the defendant's financial status. The cases favoring disclosure rely heavily on the practical significance of insurance in the decisions lawyers make about settlement and trial preparation. In Clauss v. Danker, 264 F.Supp. 246 (S.D.N.Y. 1967), the court held that the rules forbid disclosure but called for an amendment to permit it.

Disclosure of insurance coverage will enable counsel for both sides to make the same realistic appraisal of the case, so that settlement and litigation strategy are based on knowledge and not speculation. It will conduce to settlement and avoid protracted litigation in some cases, though in others it may have an opposite effect. The amendment is limited to insurance coverage, which should be distinguished from any other facts concerning defendant's financial status (1) because insurance is an asset created specifically to satisfy the claim; (2) because the insurance company ordinarily controls the litigation; (3) because information about coverage is available only from defendant or his insurer; and (4) because disclosure does not involve a significant invasion of privacy.

Disclosure is required when the insurer "may be liable" on part or all of the judgment. Thus, an insurance company must disclose even when it contests liability under the policy, and such disclosure does not constitute a waiver of its claim. It is immaterial whether the liability is to satisfy the judgment directly or merely to indemnify or reimburse another after he pays the judgment.

The provision applies only to persons "carrying on an insurance business" and thus covers insurance companies and not the ordinary business concern that enters into a contract of indemnification. Cf. N.Y.Ins. Law §41. Thus, the provision makes no change in existing law on discovery of indemnity agreements other than insurance agreements by persons carrying on an insurance business. Similarly, the provision does not cover the business concern that creates a reserve fund for purposes of self-insurance.

For some purposes other than discovery, an application for insurance is treated as a part of the insurance agreement. The provision makes clear that, for discovery purposes, the application is not to be so treated. The insurance application may contain personal and financial information concerning the insured, discovery of which is beyond the purpose of this provision.

In no instance does disclosure make the facts concerning insurance coverage admissible in evidence.

Subdivision (b)(3)—Trial Preparation: Materials. Some of the most controversial and vexing problems to emerge from the discovery rules have arisen out of requests for the production of documents or things prepared in anticipation of litigation or for trial. The existing rules make no explicit provision for such materials. Yet, two verbally distinct doctrines have developed, each conferring a qualified immunity on these materials—the "good cause" requirement in Rule 34 (now generally held applicable to discovery of documents via deposition under Rule 45 and interrogatories under Rule 33) and the work-product doctrine of Hickman v. Taylor, 329 U.S. 495 (1947). Both demand a showing of justification before production can be had, the one of "good cause" and the other variously described in the Hickman case: "necessity or justification," "denial * * * would unduly prejudice the preparation of petitioner's case," or "cause hardship or injustice" 329 U.S. at 509–510.

In deciding the Hickman case, the Supreme Court appears to have expressed a preference in 1947 for an approach to the problem of trial preparation materials by judicial decision rather than by rule. Sufficient experience has accumulated, however, with lower court applications of the Hickman decision to warrant a reappraisal.

The major difficulties visible in the existing case law are (1) confusion and disagreement as to whether "good cause" is made out by a showing of relevance and lack of privilege, or requires an additional showing of necessity, (2) confusion and disagreement as to the scope of the Hickman work-product doctrine, particularly whether it extends beyond work actually performed by lawyers, and (3) the resulting difficulty of relating the "good cause" required by Rule 34 and the "necessity or justification" of the work-product doctrine, so that their respective roles and the distinctions between them are understood.

Basic Standard. Since Rule 34 in terms requires a showing of "good cause" for the production of all documents and things, whether or not trial preparation is involved, courts have felt that a single formula is called for and have differed over whether a showing of relevance and lack of privilege is enough or whether more must be shown. When the facts of the cases are studied, however, a distinction emerges based upon the type of materials. With respect to documents not obtained or prepared with an eye to litigation, the decisions, while not uniform, reflect a strong and increasing tendency to relate "good cause" to a showing that the documents are relevant to the subject matter of the action. E.g.,

Connecticut Mutual Life Ins. Co. v. Shields, 17 F.R.D. 273 (S.D.N.Y. 1959), with cases cited; Houdry Process Corp. v. Commonwealth Oil Refining Co., 24 F.R.D. 58 (S.D.N.Y. 1955); see Bell v. Commercial Ins. Co., 280 F.2d 514, 517 (3d Cir. 1960). When the party whose documents are sought shows that the request for production is unduly burdensome or oppressive, courts have denied discovery for lack of "good cause", although they might just as easily have based their decision on the protective provisions of existing Rule 30(b) (new Rule 26(c)). E.g., Lauer v. Tankrederi, 39 F.R.D. 334 (E.D.Pa. 1966).

As to trial-preparation materials, however, the courts are increasingly interpreting "good cause" as requiring more than relevance. When lawyers have prepared or obtained the materials for trial, all courts require more than relevance; so much is clearly commanded by Hickman. But even as to the preparatory work of nonlawyers, while some courts ignore work-product and equate "good cause" with relevance, e.g., Brown v. New York, N.H. & H. RR., 17 F.R.D. 324 (S.D.N.Y. 1955), the more recent trend is to read "good cause" as requiring inquiry into the importance of and need for the materials as well as into alternative sources for securing the same information. In Guilford Nat'l Bank v. Southern Ry., 297 F.2d 921 (4th Cir. 1962), statements of witnesses obtained by claim agents were held not discoverable because both parties had had equal access to the witnesses at about the same time, shortly after the collision in question. The decision was based solely on Rule 34 and "good cause"; the court declined to rule on whether the statements were work-product. The court's treatment of "good cause" is quoted at length and with approval in Schlagenhauf v. Holder, 379 U.S. 104, 117–118 (1964). See also Mitchell v. Bass, 252 F.2d 513 (8th Cir. 1958); Hauger v. Chicago, R.I. & Pac. RR., 216 F.2d 501 (7th Cir. 1954); Burke v. United States, 32 F.R.D. 213 (E.D.N.Y. 1963). While the opinions dealing with "good cause" do not often draw an explicit distinction between trial preparation materials and other materials, in fact an overwhelming proportion of the cases in which special showing is required are cases involving trial preparation materials.

The rules are amended by eliminating the general requirement of "good cause" from Rule 34 but retaining a requirement of a special showing for trial preparation materials in this subdivision. The required showing is expressed, not in terms of "good cause" whose generality has tended to encourage confusion and controversy, but in terms of the elements of the special showing to be made: substantial need of the materials in the preparation of the case and inability without undue hardship to obtain the substantial equivalent of the materials by other means.

These changes conform to the holdings of the cases, when viewed in light of their facts. Apart from trial preparation, the fact that the materials sought are documentary does not in and of itself require a special showing beyond relevance and absence of privilege. The protective provisions are of course available, and if the party from whom production is sought raises a special issue of privacy (as with respect to income tax returns or grand jury minutes) or points to evidence primarily impeaching, or can show serious burden or expense, the court will exercise its traditional power to decide whether to issue a protective order. On the other hand, the requirement of a special showing for discovery of trial preparation materials reflects the view that each side's informal evaluation of its case should be protected, that each side should be encouraged to prepare independently, and that one side should not automatically have the benefit of the detailed preparatory work of the other side. See Field and McKusick, Maine Civil Practice 264 (1959).

Elimination of a "good cause" requirement from Rule 34 and the establishment of a requirement of a special showing in this subdivision will eliminate the confusion caused by having two verbally distinct requirements of justification that the courts have been unable to distinguish clearly. Moreover, the language of the subdivision suggests the factors which the courts should consider in determining whether the requisite showing has been made. The importance of the materials sought to the party seeking them in preparation of his case and the difficulty he will have obtaining them by other means are factors noted in the Hickman case. The courts should also consider the likelihood that the party, even if he obtains the information by independent means, will not have the substantial equivalent of the documents the production of which he seeks.

Consideration of these factors may well lead the court to distinguish between witness statements taken by an investigator, on the one hand, and other parts of the investigative file, on the other. The court in Southern Ry. v. Lanham, 403 F.2d 119 (5th Cir. 1968), while it naturally addressed itself to the "good cause" requirements of Rule 34, set forth as controlling considerations the factors contained in the language of this subdivision. The analysis of the court suggests circumstances under which witness statements will be discoverable. The witness may have given a fresh and contemporaneous account in a written statement while he is available to the party seeking discovery only a substantial time thereafter. Lanham, supra at 127–128; Guilford, supra at 926. Or he may be reluctant or hostile. Lanham, supra at 128–129; Brookshire v. Pennsylvania RR., 14 F.R.D. 154 (N.D.Ohio 1953); Diamond v. Mohawk Rubber Co., 33 F.R.D. 264 (D.Colo. 1963). Or he may have a lapse of memory. Tannenbaum v. Walker, 16 F.R.D. 570 (E.D.Pa. 1954). Or he may probably be deviating from his prior statement. Cf. Hauger v. Chicago, R.I. & Pac. RR., 216 F.2d 501 (7th Cir. 1954). On the other hand, a much stronger showing is needed to obtain evaluative materials in an investigator's reports. Lanham, supra at 131–133; Pickett v. L. R. Ryan, Inc., 237 F.Supp. 198 (E.D.S.C. 1965).

Materials assembled in the ordinary course of business, or pursuant to public requirements unrelated to litigation, or for other nonlitigation purposes are not under the qualified immunity provided by this subdivision. Gossman v. A. Duie Pyle, Inc., 320 F.2d 45 (4th Cir. 1963); cf. United States v. New York Foreign Trade Zone Operators, Inc., 304 F.2d 792 (2d Cir. 1962). No change is made in the existing doctrine, noted in the Hickman case, that one party may discover relevant facts known or available to the other party, even though such facts are contained in a document which is not itself discoverable.

Treatment of Lawyers; Special Protection of Mental Impressions, Conclusions, Opinions, and Legal Theories Concerning the Litigation.—The courts are divided as to whether the work-product doctrine extends to the preparatory work only of lawyers. The Hickman case left this issue open since the statements in that case were taken by a lawyer. As to courts of appeals, compare Alltmont v. United States, 177 F.2d 971, 976 (3d Cir. 1949), cert. denied, 339 U.S. 967 (1950) (Hickman applied to statements obtained by FBI agents on theory it should apply to "all statements of prospective witnesses which a party has obtained for his trial counsel's use"), with Southern Ry. v. Campbell, 309 F.2d 569 (5th Cir. 1962) (statements taken by claim agents not work-product), and Guilford Nat'l Bank v. Southern Ry., 297 F.2d 921 (4th Cir. 1962) (avoiding issue of work-product as to claim agents, deciding case instead under Rule 34 "good cause"). Similarly, the district courts are divided on statements obtained by claim agents, compare, e.g., Brown v. New York, N.H. & H. RR., 17 F.R.D. 324 (S.D.N.Y. 1955) with Hanke v. Milwaukee Electric Ry. & Transp. Co., 7 F.R.D. 540 (E.D. Wis. 1947);

investigators, compare Burke v. United States, 32 F.R.D. 213 (E.D.N.Y.1963) with Snyder v. United States, 20 F.R.D. 7 (E.D.N.Y.1956); and insurers, compare Gottlieb v. Bresler, 24 F.R.D. 371 (D.D.C.1959) with Burns v. Mulder, 20 F.R.D. 605 (ED.Pa 1957). See 4 Moore's Federal Practice 26.23 [8.1] (2d ed. 1966); 2A Barron & Holtzoff, Federal Practice and Procedure §652.2 (Wright ed. 1961).

A complication is introduced by the use made by courts of the "good cause" requirement of Rule 34, as described above. A court may conclude that trial preparation materials are not work-product because not the result of lawyer's work and yet hold that they are not producible because "good cause" has not been shown. Cf. Guilford Nat'l Bank v. Southern Ry., 297 F.2d 921 (4th Cir. 1962), cited and described above. When the decisions on "good cause" are taken into account, the weight of authority affords protection of the preparatory work of both lawyers and nonlawyers (though not necessarily to the same extent) by requiring more than a showing of relevance to secure production.

Subdivision (b)(3) reflects the trend of the cases by requiring a special showing, not merely as to materials prepared by an attorney, but also as to materials prepared in anticipation of litigation or preparation for trial by or for a party or any representative acting on his behalf. The subdivision then goes on to protect against disclosure the mental impressions, conclusions, opinions, or legal theories concerning the litigation of an attorney or other representative of a party. The Hickman opinion drew special attention to the need for protecting an attorney against discovery of memoranda prepared from recollection of oral interviews. The courts have steadfastly safeguarded against disclosure of lawyers' mental impressions and legal theories, as well as mental impressions and subjective evaluations of investigators and claim-agents. In enforcing this provision of the subdivision, the courts will sometimes find it necessary to order disclosure of a document but with portions deleted.

Rules 33 and 36 have been revised in order to permit discovery calling for opinions, contentions, and admissions relating not only to fact but also to the application of law to fact. Under those rules, a party and his attorney or other representative may be required to disclose, to some extent, mental impressions, opinions, or conclusions. But documents or parts of documents containing these matters are protected against discovery by this subdivision. Even though a party may ultimately have to disclose in response to interrogatories or requests to admit, he is entitled to keep confidential documents containing such matters prepared for internal use.

Party's Right to Own Statement.—An exception to the requirement of this subdivision enables a party to secure production of his own statement without any special showing. The cases are divided. Compare, e.g., Safeway Stores, Inc. v. Reynolds, 176 F.2d 476 (D.C. Cir. 1949); Shupe v. Pennsylvania RR., 19 F.R.D. 144 (W.D.Pa. 1956); with e.g., New York Central RR. v. Carr, 251 F.2d 433 (4th Cir. 1957); Belback v. Wilson Freight Forwarding Co., 40 F.R.D. 16 (W.D.Pa. 1966).

Courts which treat a party's statement as though it were that of any witness overlook the fact that the party's statement is, without more, admissible in evidence. Ordinarily, a party gives a statement without insisting on a copy because he does not yet have a lawyer and does not understand the legal consequences of his actions. Thus, the statement is given at a time when he functions at a disadvantage. Discrepancies between his trial testimony and earlier statement may result from lapse of memory or ordinary inaccuracy; a written statement produced for the first time at trial may give such discrepancies a prominence which they do not deserve. In appropriate cases the court may order a party to be deposed before his statement is produced. E.g., Smith v. Central Linen Service Co., 39 F.R.D. 15 (D.Md. 1966); McCoy v. General Motors Corp., 33 F.R.D. 354 (W.D.Pa. 1963).

Commentators strongly support the view that a party be able to secure his statement without a showing. 4 Moore's Federal Practice 26.23 [8.4] (2d ed. 1966); 2A Barron & Holtzoff, Federal Practice and Procedure §652.3 (Wright ed. 1961); see also Note, Developments in the Law—Discovery, 74 Harv.L.Rev. 940, 1039 (1961). The following states have by statute or rule taken the same position: Statutes: Fla.Stat.Ann. §92.33; Ga.Code Ann. §38–2109(b); La.Stat.Ann.R.S. 13:3732; Mass.Gen.Laws Ann. c. 271, §44; Minn.Stat.Ann. §602.01; N.Y.C.P.L.R. §3101(e). Rules: Mo.R.C.P. 56.01(a); N.Dak.R.C.P. 34(b); Wyo.R.C.P. 34(b); cf. Mich.G.C.R. 306.2.

In order to clarify and tighten the provision on statements by a party, the term "statement" is defined. The definition is adapted from 18 U.S.C. §3500(e) (Jencks Act). The statement of a party may of course be that of plaintiff or defendant, and it may be that of an individual or of a corporation or other organization.

Witness' Right to Own Statement.—A second exception to the requirement of this subdivision permits a nonparty witness to obtain a copy of his own statement without any special showing. Many, though not all, of the considerations supporting a party's right to obtain his statement apply also to the non-party witness. Insurance companies are increasingly recognizing that a witness is entitled to a copy of his statement and are modifying their regular practice accordingly.

Subdivision (b)(4)—Trial Preparation: Experts. This is a new provision dealing with discovery of information (including facts and opinions) obtained by a party from an expert retained by that party in relation to litigation or obtained by the expert and not yet transmitted to the party. The subdivision deals separately with those experts whom the party expects to call as trial witnesses and with those experts who have been retained or specially employed by the party but who are not expected to be witnesses. It should be noted that the subdivision does not address itself to the expert whose information was not acquired in preparation for trial but rather because he was an actor or viewer with respect to transactions or occurrences that are part of the subject matter of the lawsuit. Such an expert should be treated as an ordinary witness.

Subsection (b)(4)(A) deals with discovery of information obtained by or through experts who will be called as witnesses at trial. The provision is responsive to problems suggested by a relatively recent line of authorities. Many of these cases present intricate and difficult issues as to which expert testimony is likely to be determinative. Prominent among them are food and drug, patent, and condemnation cases. See, e.g., United States v. Nysco Laboratories, Inc., 26 F.R.D. 159, 162 (E.D.N.Y. 1960) (food and drug); E. I. du Pont de Nemours & Co. v. Phillips Petroleum Co., 24 F.R.D. 416, 421 (D.Del. 1959) (patent); Cold Metal Process Co. v. Aluminum Co. of America, 7 F.R.D. 425 (N.D.Ohio 1947), aff'd. Sachs v. Aluminum Co. of America, 167 F.2d 570 (6th Cir. 1948) (same); United States v. 50.34 Acres of Land, 13 F.R.D. 19 (E.D.N.Y. 1952) (condemnation).

In cases of this character, a prohibition against discovery of information held by expert witnesses produces in acute form the very evils that discovery has been created to prevent. Effective cross-examination of an expert witness requires advance preparation. The lawyer even with the help of his own experts frequently cannot anticipate the particular approach his adversary's expert will take or the data on which he will base his judgment on the stand. McGlothlin, Some Practical Problems in Proof of Economic, Scientific, and Technical Facts, 23 F.R.D. 467, 478 (1958). A California study of discovery and pretrial in condemnation cases notes that the only substitute for discovery of experts' valuation materials is "lengthy—and often fruitless—cross-examination during trial," and recommends pretrial exchange of such material. Calif.Law Rev.Comm'n, Discovery in Eminent Domain Proceedings 707–710 (Jan.1963). Similarly, effective rebuttal requires advance knowledge of the line of testimony of the other side. If the latter is foreclosed by a rule against discovery, then the narrowing of issues and elimination of surprise which discovery normally produces are frustrated.

These considerations appear to account for the broadening of discovery against experts in the cases cited where expert testimony was central to the case. In some instances, the opinions are explicit in relating expanded discovery to improved cross-examination and rebuttal at trial. Franks v. National Dairy Products Corp., 41 F.R.D. 234 (W.D.Tex. 1966); United States v. 23.76 Acres, 32 F.R.D. 593 (D.Md. 1963); see also an unpublished opinion of Judge Hincks, quoted in United States v. 48 Jars, etc., 23 F.R.D. 192, 198 (D.D.C. 1958). On the other hand, the need for a new provision is shown by the many cases in which discovery of expert trial witnesses is needed for effective cross-examination and rebuttal, and yet courts apply the traditional doctrine and refuse disclosure. E.g., United States v. Certain Parcels of Land, 25 F.R.D. 192 (N.D.Cal. 1959); United States v. Certain Acres, 18 F.R.D. 98 (M.D.Ga. 1955).

Although the trial problems flowing from lack of discovery of expert witnesses are most acute and noteworthy when the case turns largely on experts, the same problems are encountered when a single expert testifies. Thus, subdivision (b)(4)(A) draws no line between complex and simple cases, or between cases with many experts and those with but one. It establishes by rule substantially the procedure adopted by decision of the court in Knighton v. Villian & Fassio, 39 F.R.D. 11 (D.Md. 1965). For a full analysis of the problem and strong recommendations to the same effect, see Friedenthal, Discovery and Use of an Adverse Party's Expert Information, 14 Stan.L.Rev. 455, 485–488 (1962); Long, Discovery and Experts under the Federal Rules of Civil Procedure, 38 F.R.D. 111 (1965).

Past judicial restrictions on discovery of an adversary's expert, particularly as to his opinions, reflect the fear that one side will benefit unduly from the other's better preparation. The procedure established in subsection (b)(4)(A) holds the risk to a minimum. Discovery is limited to trial witnesses, and may be obtained only at a time when the parties know who their expert witnesses will be. A party must as a practical matter prepare his own case in advance of that time, for he can hardly hope to build his case out of his opponent's experts.

Subdivision (b)(4)(A) provides for discovery of an expert who is to testify at the trial. A party can require one who intends to use the expert to state the substance of the testimony that the expert is expected to give. The court may order further discovery, and it has ample power to regulate its timing and scope and to prevent abuse. Ordinarily, the order for further discovery shall compensate the expert for his time, and may compensate the party who intends to use the expert for past expenses reasonably incurred in obtaining facts or opinions from the expert. Those provisions are likely to discourage abusive practices.

Subdivision (b)(4)(B) deals with an expert who has been retained or specially employed by the party in anticipation of litigation or preparation for trial (thus excluding an expert who is simply a general employee of the party not specially employed on the case), but who is not expected to be called as a witness. Under its provisions, a party may discover facts known or opinions held by such an expert only on a showing of exceptional circumstances under which it is impracticable for the party seeking discovery to obtain facts or opinions on the same subject by other means.

Subdivision (b)(4)(B) is concerned only with experts retained or specially consulted in relation to trial preparation. Thus the subdivision precludes discovery against experts who were informally consulted in preparation for trial, but not retained or specially employed. As an ancillary procedure, a party may on a proper showing require the other party to name experts retained or specially employed, but not those informally consulted.

These new provisions of subdivision (b)(4) repudiate the few decisions that have held an expert's information privileged simply because of his status as an expert, e.g., American Oil Co. v. Pennsylvania Petroleum Products Co., 23 F.R.D. 680, 685–686 (D.R.I. 1959). See Louisell, Modern California Discovery 315–316 (1963). They also reject as ill-considered the decisions which have sought to bring expert information within the work-product doctrine. See United States v. McKay, 372 F.2d 174, 176–177 (5th Cir. 1967). The provisions adopt a form of the more recently developed doctrine of "unfairness". See e.g., United States v. 23.76 Acres of Land, 32 F.R.D. 593, 597 (D.Md. 1963); Louisell, supra, at 317–318; 4 Moore's Federal Practice §26.24 (2d ed. 1966).

Under subdivision (b)(4)(C), the court is directed or authorized to issue protective orders, including an order that the expert be paid a reasonable fee for time spent in responding to discovery, and that the party whose expert is made subject to discovery be paid a fair portion of the fees and expenses that the party incurred in obtaining information from the expert. The court may issue the latter order as a condition of discovery, or it may delay the order until after discovery is completed. These provisions for fees and expenses meet the objection that it is unfair to permit one side to obtain without cost the benefit of an expert's work for which the other side has paid, often a substantial sum. E.g., Lewis v. United Air Lines Transp. Corp., 32 F.Supp. 21 (W.D.Pa. 1940); Walsh v. Reynolds Metal Co., 15 F.R.D. 376 (D.N.J. 1954). On the other hand, a party may not obtain discovery simply by offering to pay fees and expenses. Cf. Boynton v. R. J. Reynolds Tobacco Co., 36 F.Supp. 593 (D.Mass. 1941).

In instances of discovery under subdivision (b)(4)(B), the court is directed to award fees and expenses to the other party, since the information is of direct value to the discovering party's preparation of his case. In ordering discovery under (b)(4)(A)(ii), the court has discretion whether to award fees and expenses to the other party; its decision should depend upon whether the discovering party is simply learning about the other party's case or is going beyond this to develop his own case. Even in cases where the court is directed to issue a protective order, it may decline to do so if it finds that manifest injustice would result. Thus, the court can protect, when necessary and appropriate, the interests of an indigent party.

Subdivision (c)—Protective Orders. The provisions of existing Rule 30(b) are transferred to this subdivision (c), as part of the rearrangement of Rule 26. The language has been changed to give it application to discovery generally. The subdivision recognizes the power of the court in the district where a deposition is being taken to make protective orders. Such power is needed when the deposition is being taken far from the court where the action is pending. The court in the district where the deposition is being taken may, and frequently will, remit the deponent or party to the court where the action is pending.

In addition, drafting changes are made to carry out and clarify the sense of the rule. Insertions are made to avoid any possible implication that a protective order does not extend to "time" as well as to "place" or may not safeguard against "undue burden or expense."

The new reference to trade secrets and other confidential commercial information reflects existing law. The courts have not given trade secrets automatic and complete immunity against disclosure, but have in each case weighed their claim to privacy against the need for disclosure. Frequently, they have been afforded a limited protection. See, e.g., Covey Oil Co. v. Continental Oil Co., 340 F.2d 993 (10th Cir. 1965); Julius M. Ames Co. v. Bostitch, Inc., 235 F.Supp. 856 (S.D.N.Y. 1964).

The subdivision contains new matter relating to sanctions. When a motion for a protective order is made and the court is disposed to deny it, the court may go a step further and issue an order to provide or permit discovery. This will bring the sanctions of Rule 37(b) directly into play. Since the court has heard the contentions of all interested persons, an affirmative order is justified. See Rosenberg, Sanctions to Effectuate Pretrial Discovery, 58 Col.L.Rev. 480, 492–493 (1958). In addition, the court may require the payment of expenses incurred in relation to the motion.

Subdivision (d)—Sequence and Priority. This new provision is concerned with the sequence in which parties may proceed with discovery and with related problems of timing. The principal effects of the new provision are first, to eliminate any fixed priority in the sequence of discovery, and second, to make clear and explicit the court's power to establish priority by an order issued in a particular case.

A priority rule developed by some courts, which confers priority on the party who first serves notice of taking a deposition, is unsatisfactory in several important respects:

First, this priority rule permits a party to establish a priority running to all depositions as to which he has given earlier notice. Since he can on a given day serve notice of taking many depositions he is in a position to delay his adversary's taking of depositions for an inordinate time. Some courts have ruled that deposition priority also permits a party to delay his answers to interrogatories and production of documents. E.g., E. I. du Pont de Nemours & Co. v. Phillips Petroleum Co., 23 F.R.D. 237 (D.Del. 1959); but cf. Sturdevant v. Sears, Roebuck & Co., 32 F.R.D. 426 (W.D.Mo. 1963).

Second, since notice is the key to priority, if both parties wish to take depositions first a race results. See Caldwell-Clements, Inc. v. McGraw-Hill Pub. Co., 11 F.R.D. 156 (S.D.N.Y. 1951) (description of tactics used by parties). But the existing rules on notice of deposition create a race with runners starting from different positions. The plaintiff may not give notice without leave of court until 20 days after commencement of the action, whereas the defendant may serve notice at any time after commencement. Thus, a careful and prompt defendant can almost always secure priority. This advantage of defendants is fortuitous, because the purpose of requiring plaintiff to wait 20 days is to afford defendant an opportunity to obtain counsel, not to confer priority.

Third, although courts have ordered a change in the normal sequence of discovery on a number of occasions, e.g., Kaeppler v. James H. Matthews & Co., 200 F.Supp. 229 (E.D.Pa. 1961); Park & Tilford Distillers Corp. v. Distillers Co., 19 F.R.D. 169 (S.D.N.Y. 1956), and have at all times avowed discretion to vary the usual priority, most commentators are agreed that courts in fact grant relief only for "the most obviously compelling reasons." 2A Barron & Holtzoff, Federal Practice and Procedure 447–47 (Wright ed. 1961); see also Younger, Priority of Pretrial Examination in the Federal Courts—A Comment, 34 N.Y.U.L.Rev. 1271 (1959); Freund, The Pleading and Pretrial of an Antitrust Claim, 46 Corn.L.Q. 555, 564, (1964). Discontent with the fairness of actual practice has been evinced by other observers. Comments, 59 Yale L.J. 117, 134–136 (1949); Yudkin, Some Refinements in Federal Discovery Procedure, 11 Fed.B.J. 289, 296–297 (1951); Developments in the Law-Discovery, 74 Harv.L.Rev. 940, 954–958 (1961).

Despite these difficulties, some courts have adhered to the priority rule, presumably because it provides a test which is easily understood and applied by the parties without much court intervention. It thus permits deposition discovery to function extrajudicially, which the rules provide for and the courts desire. For these same reasons, courts are reluctant to make numerous exceptions to the rule.

The Columbia Survey makes clear that the problem of priority does not affect litigants generally. It found that most litigants do not move quickly to obtain discovery. In over half of the cases, both parties waited at least 50 days. During the first 20 days after commencement of the action—the period when defendant might assure his priority by noticing depositions—16 percent of the defendants acted to obtain discovery. A race could not have occurred in more than 16 percent of the cases and it undoubtedly occurred in fewer. On the other hand, five times as many defendants as plaintiffs served notice of deposition during the first 19 days. To the same effect, see Comment, Tactical Use and Abuse of Depositions Under the Federal Rules, 59 Yale L.J. 117, 134 (1949).

These findings do not mean, however, that the priority rule is satisfactory or that a problem of priority does not exist. The court decisions show that parties do bottle on this issue and carry their disputes to court. The statistics show that these court cases are not typical. By the same token, they reveal that more extensive exercise of judicial discretion to vary the priority will not bring a flood of litigation, and that a change in the priority rule will in fact affect only a small fraction of the cases.

It is contended by some that there is no need to alter the existing priority practice. In support, it is urged that there is no evidence that injustices in fact result from present practice and that, in any event, the courts can and do promulgate local rules, as in New York, to deal with local situations and issue orders to avoid possible injustice in particular cases.

Subdivision (d) is based on the contrary view that the rule of priority based on notice is unsatisfactory and unfair in its operation. Subdivision (d) follows an approach adapted from Civil Rule 4 of the District Court for the Southern District of New York. That rule provides that starting 40 days after commencement of the action, unless otherwise ordered by the court, the fact that one part is taking a deposition shall not prevent another party from doing so "concurrently." In practice, the depositions are not usually taken simultaneously; rather, the parties work out arrangements for alternation in the taking of depositions. One party may take a complete deposition and then the other, or, if the depositions are extensive, one party deposes for a set time, and then the other. See Caldwell-Clements, Inc. v. McGraw-Hill Pub. Co., 11 F.R.D. 156 (S.D.N.Y. 1951).

In principle, one party's initiation of discovery should not wait upon the other's completion, unless delay is dictated by special considerations. Clearly the principle is feasible with respect to all methods of discovery other than depositions. And the experience of the Southern District of New York shows that the principle can be applied to depositions as well. The courts have not had an increase in motion business on this matter. Once it is clear to lawyers that they bargain on an equal footing, they are usually able to arrange for an orderly succession of depositions without judicial intervention. Professor Moore has called attention to Civil Rule 4 and suggested that it may usefully be extended to other areas. 4 Moore's Federal Practice 1154 (2d ed. 1966).

The court may upon motion and by order grant priority in a particular case. But a local court rule purporting to confer priority in certain classes of cases would be inconsistent with this subdivision and thus void.

Subdivision (e)—Supplementation of Responses. The rules do not now state whether interrogatories (and questions at deposition as well as requests for inspection and admissions) impose a "continuing burden" on the responding party to supplement his answers if he obtains new information. The issue is acute when new information renders substantially incomplete or inaccurate an answer which was complete and accurate when made. It is essential that the rules provide an answer to this question. The parties can adjust to a rule either way, once they know what it is. See 4 Moore's Federal Practice 33.25[4] (2d ed. 1966).

Arguments can be made both ways. Imposition of a continuing burden reduces the proliferation of additional sets of interrogatories. Some courts have adopted local rules establishing such a burden. E.g., E.D.Pa.R. 20(f), quoted in Taggart v. Vermont Transp. Co., 32 F.R.D. 587 (E.D.Pa. 1963); D.Me.R.15(c). Others have imposed the burden by decision, E.g., Chenault v. Nebraska Farm Products, Inc., 9 F.R.D. 529, 533 (D.Nebr. 1949). On the other hand, there are serious objections to the burden, especially in protracted cases. Although the party signs the answers, it is his lawyer who understands their significance and bears the responsibility to bring answers up to date. In a complex case all sorts of information reaches the party, who little understands its bearing on answers previously given to interrogatories. In practice, therefore, the lawyer under a continuing burden must periodically recheck all interrogatories and canvass all new information. But a full set of new answers may no longer be needed by the interrogating party. Some issues will have been dropped from the case, some questions are now seen as unimportant, and other questions must in any event be reformulated. See Novick v. Pennsylvania RR., 18 F.R.D. 296, 298 (W.D.Pa. 1955).

Subdivision (e) provides that a party is not under a continuing burden except as expressly provided. Cf. Note, 68 Harv.L.Rev. 673, 677 (1955). An exception is made as to the identity of persons having knowledge of discoverable matters, because of the obvious importance to each side of knowing all witnesses and because information about witnesses routinely comes to each lawyer's attention. Many of the decisions on the issue of a continuing burden have in fact concerned the identity of witnesses. An exception is also made as to expert trial witnesses in order to carry out the provisions of Rule 26(b)(4). See Diversified Products Corp. v. Sports Center Co., 42 F.R.D. 3 (D.Md. 1967).

Another exception is made for the situation in which a party, or more frequently his lawyer, obtains actual knowledge that a prior response is incorrect. This exception does not impose a duty to check the accuracy of prior responses, but it prevents knowing concealment by a party or attorney. Finally, a duty to supplement may be imposed by order of the court in a particular case (including an order resulting from a pretrial conference) or by agreement of the parties. A party may of course make a new discovery request which requires supplementation of prior responses.

The duty will normally be enforced, in those limited instances where it is imposed, through sanctions imposed by the trial court, including exclusion of evidence, continuance, or other action, as the court may deem appropriate.

Notes of Advisory Committee on Rules—1980 Amendment

Subdivision (f). This subdivision is new. There has been widespread criticism of abuse of discovery. The Committee has considered a number of proposals to eliminate abuse, including a change in Rule 26(b)(1) with respect to the scope of discovery and a change in Rule 33(a) to limit the number of questions that can be asked by interrogatories to parties.

The Committee believes that abuse of discovery, while very serious in certain cases, is not so general as to require such basic changes in the rules that govern discovery in all cases. A very recent study of discovery in selected metropolitan districts tends to support its belief. P. Connolly, E. Holleman, & M. Kuhlman, Judicial Controls and the Civil Litigative Process: Discovery (Federal Judicial Center, 1978). In the judgment of the Committee abuse can best be prevented by intervention by the court as soon as abuse is threatened.

To this end this subdivision provides that counsel who has attempted without success to effect with opposing counsel a reasonable program or plan for discovery is entitled to the assistance of the court.

It is not contemplated that requests for discovery conferences will be made routinely. A relatively narrow discovery dispute should be resolved by resort to Rules 26(c) or 37(a), and if it appears that a request for a conference is in fact grounded in such a dispute, the court may refer counsel to those rules. If the court is persuaded that a request is frivolous or vexatious, it can strike it. See Rules 11 and 7(b)(2).

A number of courts routinely consider discovery matters in preliminary pretrial conferences held shortly after the pleadings are closed. This subdivision does not interfere with such a practice. It authorizes the court to combine a discovery conference with a pretrial conference under Rule 16 if a pretrial conference is held sufficiently early to prevent or curb abuse.

Notes of Advisory Committee on Rules—1983 Amendment

Excessive discovery and evasion or resistance to reasonable discovery requests pose significant problems. Recent studies have made some attempt to determine the sources and extent of the difficulties. See Brazil, Civil Discovery: Lawyers' Views of its Effectiveness, Principal Problems and Abuses, American Bar Foundation (1980); Connolly, Holleman & Kuhlman, Judicial Controls and the Civil Litigative Process: Discovery, Federal Judicial Center (1978); Ellington, A Study of Sanctions for Discovery Abuse, Department of Justice (1979); Schroeder & Frank, The Proposed Changes in the Discovery Rules, 1978 Ariz.St.L.J. 475.

The purpose of discovery is to provide a mechanism for making relevant information available to the litigants. "Mutual knowledge of all the relevant facts gathered by both parties is essential to proper litigation." Hickman v. Taylor, 329 U.S. 495, 507 (1947). Thus the spirit of the rules is violated when advocates attempt to use discovery tools as tactical weapons rather than to expose the facts and illuminate the issues by overuse of discovery or unnecessary use of defensive weapons or evasive responses. All of this results in excessively costly and time-consuming activities that are disproportionate to the nature of the case, the amount involved, or the issues or values at stake.

Given our adversary tradition and the current discovery rules, it is not surprising that there are many opportunities, if not incentives, for attorneys to engage in discovery that, although authorized by the broad, permissive terms of the rules, nevertheless results in delay. See Brazil, The Adversary Character of Civil Discovery: A Critique and Proposals for Change, 31 Vand.L.Rev. 1259 (1978). As a result, it has been said that the rules have "not infrequently [been] exploited to the disadvantage of justice." Herbert v. Lando, 441 U.S. 153, 179 (1979) (Powell, J., concurring). These practices impose costs on an already overburdened system and impede the fundamental goal of the "just, speedy, and inexpensive determination of every action." Fed.R.Civ.P. 1.

Subdivision (a); Discovery Methods. The deletion of the last sentence of Rule 26(a)(1), which provided that unless the court ordered otherwise under Rule 26(c) "the frequency of use" of the various discovery methods was not to be limited, is an attempt to address the problem of duplicative, redundant, and excessive discovery and to reduce it. The amendment, in conjunction with the changes in Rule 26(b)(1), is designed to encourage district judges to identify instances of needless discovery and to limit the use of the various discovery devices accordingly. The question may be raised by one of the parties, typically on a motion for a protective order, or by the court on its own initiative. It is entirely appropriate to consider a limitation on the frequency of use of discovery at a discovery conference under Rule 26(f) or at any other pretrial conference authorized by these rules. In considering the discovery needs of a particular case, the court should consider the factors described in Rule 26(b)(1).

Subdivision (b); Discovery Scope and Limits. Rule 26(b)(1) has been amended to add a sentence to deal with the problem of over-discovery. The objective is to guard against redundant or disproportionate discovery by giving the court authority to reduce the amount of discovery that may be directed to matters that are otherwise proper subjects of inquiry. The new sentence is intended to encourage judges to be more aggressive in identifying and discouraging discovery overuse. The grounds mentioned in the amended rule for limiting discovery reflect the existing practice of many courts in issuing protective orders under Rule 26(c). See e.g., Carlson Cos. v. Sperry & Hutchinson Co., 374 F.Supp. 1080 (D.Minn. 1974); Dolgow v. Anderson, 53 F.R.D. 661 (E.D.N.Y. 1971); Mitchell v. American Tobacco Co., 33 F.R.D. 262 (M.D.Pa. 1963); Welty v. Clute, 1 F.R.D. 446 (W.D.N.Y. 1941). On the whole, however, district judges have been reluctant to limit the use of the discovery devices. See, e.g., Apco Oil Co. v. Certified Transp., Inc., 46 F.R.D. 428 (W.D.Mo. 1969). See generally 8 Wright & Miller, Federal Practice and Procedure: Civil §§2036, 2037, 2039, 2040 (1970).

The first element of the standard, Rule 26(b)(1)(i), is designed to minimize redundancy in discovery and encourage attorneys to be sensitive to the comparative costs of different methods of securing information. Subdivision (b)(1)(ii) also seeks to reduce repetitiveness and to oblige lawyers to think through their discovery activities in advance so that full utilization is made of each deposition, document request, or set of interrogatories. The elements of Rule 26(b)(1)(iii) address the problem of discovery that is disproportionate to the individual lawsuit as measured by such matters as its nature and complexity, the importance of the issues at stake in a case seeking damages, the limitations on a financially weak litigant to withstand extensive opposition to a discovery program or to respond to discovery requests, and the significance of the substantive issues, as measured in philosophic, social, or institutional terms. Thus the rule recognizes that many cases in public policy spheres, such as employment practices, free speech, and other matters, may have importance far beyond the monetary amount involved. The court must apply the standards in an even-handed manner that will prevent use of discovery to wage a war of attrition or as a device to coerce a party, whether financially weak or affluent.

The rule contemplates greater judicial involvement in the discovery process and thus acknowledges the reality that it cannot always operate on a self-regulating basis. See Connolly, Holleman & Kuhlman, Judicial Controls and the Civil Litigative Process: Discovery 77, Federal Judicial Center (1978). In an appropriate case the court could restrict the number of depositions, interrogatories, or the scope of a production request. But the court must be careful not to deprive a party of discovery that is reasonably necessary to afford a fair opportunity to develop and prepare the case.

The court may act on motion, or its own initiative. It is entirely appropriate to resort to the amended rule in conjunction with a discovery conference under Rule 26(f) or one of the other pretrial conferences authorized by the rules.

Subdivision (g); Signing of Discovery Requests, Responses, and Objections. Rule 26(g) imposes an affirmative duty to engage in pretrial discovery in a responsible manner that is consistent with the spirit and purposes of Rules 26 through 37. In addition, Rule 26(g) is designed to curb discovery abuse by explicitly encouraging the imposition of sanctions. The subdivision provides a deterrent to both excessive discovery and evasion by imposing a certification requirement that obliges each attorney to stop and think about the legitimacy of a discovery request, a response thereto, or an objection. The term "response" includes answers to interrogatories and to requests to admit as well as responses to production requests.

If primary responsibility for conducting discovery is to continue to rest with the litigants, they must be obliged to act responsibly and avoid abuse. With this in mind, Rule 26(g), which parallels the amendments to Rule 11, requires an attorney or unrepresented party to sign each discovery request, response, or objection. Motions relating to discovery are governed by Rule 11. However, since a discovery request, response, or objection usually deals with more specific subject matter than motions or papers, the elements that must be certified in connection with the former are spelled out more completely. The signature is a certification of the elements set forth in Rule 26(g).

Although the certification duty requires the lawyer to pause and consider the reasonableness of his request, response, or objection, it is not meant to discourage or restrict necessary and legitimate discovery. The rule simply requires that the attorney make a reasonable inquiry into the factual basis of his response, request, or objection.

The duty to make a "reasonable inquiry" is satisfied if the investigation undertaken by the attorney and the conclusions drawn therefrom are reasonable under the circumstances. It is an objective standard similar to the one imposed by Rule 11. See the Advisory Committee Note to Rule 11. See also Kinee v. Abraham Lincoln Fed. Sav. & Loan Ass'n, 365 F.Supp. 975 (E.D.Pa. 1973). In making the inquiry, the attorney may rely on assertions by the client and on communications with other counsel in the case as long as that reliance is appropriate under the circumstances. Ultimately, what is reasonable is a matter for the court to decide on the totality of the circumstances.

Rule 26(g) does not require the signing attorney to certify the truthfulness of the client's factual responses to a discovery request. Rather, the signature certifies that the lawyer has made a reasonable effort to assure that the client has provided all the information and documents available to him that are responsive to the discovery demand. Thus, the lawyer's certification under Rule 26(g) should be distinguished from other signature requirements in the rules, such as those in Rules 30(e) and 33.

Nor does the rule require a party or an attorney to disclose privileged communications or work product in order to show that a discovery request, response, or objection is substantially justified. The provisions of Rule 26(c), including appropriate orders after in camera inspection by the court, remain available to protect a party claiming privilege or work product protection.

The signing requirement means that every discovery request, response, or objection should be grounded on a theory that is reasonable under the precedents or a good faith belief as to what should be the law. This standard is heavily dependent on the circumstances of each case. The certification speaks as of the time it is made. The duty to supplement discovery responses continues to be governed by Rule 26(e).

Concern about discovery abuse has led to widespread recognition that there is a need for more aggressive judicial control and supervision. ACF Industries, Inc. v. EEOC, 439 U.S. 1081 (1979) (certiorari denied) (Powell, J., dissenting). Sanctions to deter discovery abuse would be more effective if they were diligently applied "not merely to penalize those whose conduct may be deemed to warrant such a sanction, but to deter those who might be tempted to such conduct in the absence of such a deterrent." National Hockey League v. Metropolitan Hockey Club, 427 U.S. 639, 643 (1976). See also Note, The Emerging Deterrence Orientation in the Imposition of Discovery Sanctions, 91 Harv. L. Rev. 1033 (1978). Thus the premise of Rule 26(g) is that imposing sanctions on attorneys who fail to meet the rule's standards will significantly reduce abuse by imposing disadvantages therefor.

Because of the asserted reluctance to impose sanctions on attorneys who abuse the discovery rules, see Brazil, Civil Discovery: Lawyers' Views of its Effectiveness, Principal Problems and Abuses, American Bar Foundation (1980); Ellington, A Study of Sanctions for Discovery Abuse, Department of Justice (1979), Rule 26(g) makes explicit the authority judges now have to impose appropriate sanctions and requires them to use it. This authority derives from Rule 37, 28 U.S.C. §1927, and the court's inherent power. See Roadway Express, Inc., v. Piper, 447 U.S. 752 (1980); Martin v. Bell Helicopter Co., 85 F.R.D. 654, 661–62 (D.Col. 1980); Note, Sanctions Imposed by Courts on Attorneys Who Abuse the Judicial Process, 44 U.Chi.L.Rev. 619 (1977). The new rule mandates that sanctions be imposed on attorneys who fail to meet the standards established in the first portion of Rule 26(g). The nature of the sanction is a matter of judicial discretion to be exercised in light of the particular circumstances. The court may take into account any failure by the party seeking sanctions to invoke protection under Rule 26(c) at an early stage in the litigation.

The sanctioning process must comport with due process requirements. The kind of notice and hearing required will depend on the facts of the case and the severity of the sanction being considered. To prevent the proliferation of the sanction procedure and to avoid multiple hearings, discovery in any sanction proceeding normally should be permitted only when it is clearly required by the interests of justice. In most cases the court will be aware of the circumstances and only a brief hearing should be necessary.

Notes of Advisory Committee on Rules—1987 Amendment

The amendments are technical. No substantive change is intended.

Notes of Advisory Committee on Rules—1993 Amendment

Subdivision (a). Through the addition of paragraphs (1)–(4), this subdivision imposes on parties a duty to disclose, without awaiting formal discovery requests, certain basic information that is needed in most cases to prepare for trial or make an informed decision about settlement. The rule requires all parties (1) early in the case to exchange information regarding potential witnesses, documentary evidence, damages, and insurance, (2) at an appropriate time during the discovery period to identify expert witnesses and provide a detailed written statement of the testimony that may be offered at trial through specially retained experts, and (3) as the trial date approaches to identify the particular evidence that may be offered at trial. The enumeration in Rule 26(a) of items to be disclosed does not prevent a court from requiring by order or local rule that the parties disclose additional information without a discovery request. Nor are parties precluded from using traditional discovery methods to obtain further information regarding these matters, as for example asking an expert during a deposition about testimony given in other litigation beyond the four-year period specified in Rule 26(a)(2)(B).

A major purpose of the revision is to accelerate the exchange of basic information about the case and to eliminate the paper work involved in requesting such information, and the rule should be applied in a manner to achieve those objectives. The concepts of imposing a duty of disclosure were set forth in Brazil, The Adversary Character of Civil Discovery: A Critique and Proposals for Change, 31 Vand. L. Rev. 1348 (1978), and Schwarzer, The Federal Rules, the Adversary Process, and Discovery Reform, 50 U. Pitt. L. Rev. 703, 721–23 (1989).

The rule is based upon the experience of district courts that have required disclosure of some of this information through local rules, court-approved standard interrogatories, and standing orders. Most have required pretrial disclosure of the kind of information described in Rule 26(a)(3). Many have required written reports from experts containing information like that specified in Rule 26(a)(2)(B). While far more limited, the experience of the few state and federal courts that have required pre-discovery exchange of core information such as is contemplated in Rule 26(a)(1) indicates that savings in time and expense can be achieved, particularly if the litigants meet and discuss the issues in the case as a predicate for this exchange and if a judge supports the process, as by using the results to guide further proceedings in the case. Courts in Canada and the United Kingdom have for many years required disclosure of certain information without awaiting a request from an adversary.

Paragraph (1). As the functional equivalent of court-ordered interrogatories, this paragraph requires early disclosure, without need for any request, of four types of information that have been customarily secured early in litigation through formal discovery. The introductory clause permits the court, by local rule, to exempt all or particular types of cases from these disclosure requirement[s] or to modify the nature of the information to be disclosed. It is expected that courts would, for example, exempt cases like Social Security reviews and government collection cases in which discovery would not be appropriate or would be unlikely. By order the court may eliminate or modify the disclosure requirements in a particular case, and similarly the parties, unless precluded by order or local rule, can stipulate to elimination or modification of the requirements for that case. The disclosure obligations specified in paragraph (1) will not be appropriate for all cases, and it is expected that changes in these obligations will be made by the court or parties when the circumstances warrant.

Authorization of these local variations is, in large measure, included in order to accommodate the Civil Justice Reform Act of 1990, which implicitly directs districts to experiment during the study period with differing procedures to reduce the time and expense of civil litigation. The civil justice delay and expense reduction plans adopted by the courts under the Act differ as to the type, form, and timing of disclosures required. Section 105(c)(1) of the Act calls for a report by the Judicial Conference to Congress by December 31, 1995, comparing experience in twenty of these courts; and section 105(c)(2)(B) contemplates that some changes in the Rules may then be needed. While these studies may indicate the desirability of further changes in Rule 26(a)(1), these changes probably could not become effective before December 1998 at the earliest. In the meantime, the present revision puts in place a series of disclosure obligations that, unless a court acts affirmatively to impose other requirements or indeed to reject all such requirements for the present, are designed to eliminate certain discovery, help focus the discovery that is needed, and facilitate preparation for trial or settlement.

Subparagraph (A) requires identification of all persons who, based on the investigation conducted thus far, are likely to have discoverable information relevant to the factual disputes between the parties. All persons with such information should be disclosed, whether or not their testimony will be supportive of the position of the disclosing party. As officers of the court, counsel are expected to disclose the identity of those persons who may be used by them as witnesses or who, if their potential testimony were known, might reasonably be expected to be deposed or called as a witness by any of the other parties. Indicating briefly the general topics on which such persons have information should not be burdensome, and will assist other parties in deciding which depositions will actually be needed.

Subparagraph (B) is included as a substitute for the inquiries routinely made about the existence and location of documents and other tangible things in the possession, custody, or control of the disclosing party. Although, unlike subdivision (a)(3)(C), an itemized listing of each exhibit is not required, the disclosure should describe and categorize, to the extent identified during the initial investigation, the nature and location of potentially relevant documents and records, including computerized data and other electronically-recorded information, sufficiently to enable opposing parties (1) to make an informed decision concerning which documents might need to be examined, at least initially, and (2) to frame their document requests in a manner likely to avoid squabbles resulting from the wording of the requests. As with potential witnesses, the requirement for disclosure of documents applies to all potentially relevant items then known to the party, whether or not supportive of its contentions in the case.

Unlike subparagraphs (C) and (D), subparagraph (B) does not require production of any documents. Of course, in cases involving few documents a disclosing party may prefer to provide copies of the documents rather than describe them, and the rule is written to afford this option to the disclosing party. If, as will be more typical, only the description is provided, the other parties are expected to obtain the documents desired by proceeding under Rule 34 or through informal requests. The disclosing party does not, by describing documents under subparagraph (B), waive its right to object to production on the basis of privilege or work product protection, or to assert that the documents are not sufficiently relevant to justify the burden or expense of production.

The initial disclosure requirements of subparagraphs (A) and (B) are limited to identification of potential evidence "relevant to disputed facts alleged with particularity in the pleadings." There is no need for a party to identify potential evidence with respect to allegations that are admitted. Broad, vague, and conclusory allegations sometimes tolerated in notice pleading—for example, the assertion that a product with many component parts is defective in some unspecified manner—should not impose upon responding parties the obligation at that point to search for and identify all persons possibly involved in, or all documents affecting, the design, manufacture, and assembly of the product. The greater the specificity and clarity of the allegations in the pleadings, the more complete should be the listing of potential witnesses and types of documentary evidence. Although paragraphs (1)(A) and (1)(B) by their terms refer to the factual disputes defined in the pleadings, the rule contemplates that these issues would be informally refined and clarified during the meeting of the parties under subdivision (f) and that the disclosure obligations would be adjusted in the light of these discussions. The disclosure requirements should, in short, be applied with common sense in light of the principles of Rule 1, keeping in mind the salutary purposes that the rule is intended to accomplish. The litigants should not indulge in gamesmanship with respect to the disclosure obligations.

Subparagraph (C) imposes a burden of disclosure that includes the functional equivalent of a standing Request for Production under Rule 34. A party claiming damages or other monetary relief must, in addition to disclosing the calculation of such damages, make available the supporting documents for inspection and copying as if a request for such materials had been made under Rule 34. This obligation applies only with respect to documents then reasonably available to it and not privileged or protected as work product. Likewise, a party would not be expected to provide a calculation of damages which, as in many patent infringement actions, depends on information in the possession of another party or person.

Subparagraph (D) replaces subdivision (b)(2) of Rule 26, and provides that liability insurance policies be made available for inspection and copying. The last two sentences of that subdivision have been omitted as unnecessary, not to signify any change of law. The disclosure of insurance information does not thereby render such information admissible in evidence. See Rule 411, Federal Rules of Evidence. Nor does subparagraph (D) require disclosure of applications for insurance, though in particular cases such information may be discoverable in accordance with revised subdivision (a)(5).

Unless the court directs a different time, the disclosures required by subdivision (a)(1) are to be made at or within 10 days after the meeting of the parties under subdivision (f). One of the purposes of this meeting is to refine the factual disputes with respect to which disclosures should be made under paragraphs (1)(A) and (1)(B), particularly if an answer has not been filed by a defendant, or, indeed, to afford the parties an opportunity to modify by stipulation the timing or scope of these obligations. The time of this meeting is generally left to the parties provided it is held at least 14 days before a scheduling conference is held or before a scheduling order is due under Rule 16(b). In cases in which no scheduling conference is held, this will mean that the meeting must ordinarily be held within 75 days after a defendant has first appeared in the case and hence that the initial disclosures would be due no later than 85 days after the first appearance of a defendant.

Before making its disclosures, a party has the obligation under subdivision (g)(1) to make a reasonable inquiry into the facts of the case. The rule does not demand an exhaustive investigation at this stage of the case, but one that is reasonable under the circumstances, focusing on the facts that are alleged with particularity in the pleadings. The type of investigation that can be expected at this point will vary based upon such factors as the number and complexity of the issues; the location, nature, number, and availability of potentially relevant witnesses and documents; the extent of past working relationships between the attorney and the client, particularly in handling related or similar litigation; and of course how long the party has to conduct an investigation, either before or after filing of the case. As provided in the last sentence of subdivision (a)(1), a party is not excused from the duty of disclosure merely because its investigation is incomplete. The party should make its initial disclosures based on the pleadings and the information then reasonably available to it. As its investigation continues and as the issues in the pleadings are clarified, it should supplement its disclosures as required by subdivision (e)(1). A party is not relieved from its obligation of disclosure merely because another party has not made its disclosures or has made an inadequate disclosure.

It will often be desirable, particularly if the claims made in the complaint are broadly stated, for the parties to have their Rule 26(f) meeting early in the case, perhaps before a defendant has answered the complaint or had time to conduct other than a cursory investigation. In such circumstances, in order to facilitate more meaningful and useful initial disclosures, they can and should stipulate to a period of more than 10 days after the meeting in which to make these disclosures, at least for defendants who had no advance notice of the potential litigation. A stipulation at an early meeting affording such a defendant at least 60 days after receiving the complaint in which to make its disclosures under subdivision (a)(1)—a period that is two weeks longer than the time formerly specified for responding to interrogatories served with a complaint—should be adequate and appropriate in most cases.

Paragraph (2). This paragraph imposes an additional duty to disclose information regarding expert testimony sufficiently in advance of trial that opposing parties have a reasonable opportunity to prepare for effective cross examination and perhaps arrange for expert testimony from other witnesses. Normally the court should prescribe a time for these disclosures in a scheduling order under Rule 16(b), and in most cases the party with the burden of proof on an issue should disclose its expert testimony on that issue before other parties are required to make their disclosures with respect to that issue. In the absence of such a direction, the disclosures are to be made by all parties at least 90 days before the trial date or the date by which the case is to be ready for trial, except that an additional 30 days is allowed (unless the court specifies another time) for disclosure of expert testimony to be used solely to contradict or rebut the testimony that may be presented by another party's expert. For a discussion of procedures that have been used to enhance the reliability of expert testimony, see M. Graham, Expert Witness Testimony and the Federal Rules of Evidence: Insuring Adequate Assurance of Trustworthiness, 1986 U. Ill. L. Rev. 90.

Paragraph (2)(B) requires that persons retained or specially employed to provide expert testimony, or whose duties as an employee of the party regularly involve the giving of expert testimony, must prepare a detailed and complete written report, stating the testimony the witness is expected to present during direct examination, together with the reasons therefor. The information disclosed under the former rule in answering interrogatories about the "substance" of expert testimony was frequently so sketchy and vague that it rarely dispensed with the need to depose the expert and often was even of little help in preparing for a deposition of the witness. Revised Rule 37(c)(1) provides an incentive for full disclosure; namely, that a party will not ordinarily be permitted to use on direct examination any expert testimony not so disclosed. Rule 26(a)(2)(B) does not preclude counsel from providing assistance to experts in preparing the reports, and indeed, with experts such as automobile mechanics, this assistance may be needed. Nevertheless, the report, which is intended to set forth the substance of the direct examination, should be written in a manner that reflects the testimony to be given by the witness and it must be signed by the witness.

The report is to disclose the data and other information considered by the expert and any exhibits or charts that summarize or support the expert's opinions. Given this obligation of disclosure, litigants should no longer be able to argue that materials furnished to their experts to be used in forming their opinions—whether or not ultimately relied upon by the expert—are privileged or otherwise protected from disclosure when such persons are testifying or being deposed.

Revised subdivision (b)(4)(A) authorizes the deposition of expert witnesses. Since depositions of experts required to prepare a written report may be taken only after the report has been served, the length of the deposition of such experts should be reduced, and in many cases the report may eliminate the need for a deposition. Revised subdivision (e)(1) requires disclosure of any material changes made in the opinions of an expert from whom a report is required, whether the changes are in the written report or in testimony given at a deposition.

For convenience, this rule and revised Rule 30 continue to use the term "expert" to refer to those persons who will testify under Rule 702 of the Federal Rules of Evidence with respect to scientific, technical, and other specialized matters. The requirement of a written report in paragraph (2)(B), however, applies only to those experts who are retained or specially employed to provide such testimony in the case or whose duties as an employee of a party regularly involve the giving of such testimony. A treating physician, for example, can be deposed or called to testify at trial without any requirement for a written report. By local rule, order, or written stipulation, the requirement of a written report may be waived for particular experts or imposed upon additional persons who will provide opinions under Rule 702.

Paragraph (3). This paragraph imposes an additional duty to disclose, without any request, information customarily needed in final preparation for trial. These disclosures are to be made in accordance with schedules adopted by the court under Rule 16(b) or by special order. If no such schedule is directed by the court, the disclosures are to be made at least 30 days before commencement of the trial. By its terms, rule 26(a)(3) does not require disclosure of evidence to be used solely for impeachment purposes; however, disclosure of such evidence—as well as other items relating to conduct of trial—may be required by local rule or a pretrial order.

Subparagraph (A) requires the parties to designate the persons whose testimony they may present as substantive evidence at trial, whether in person or by deposition. Those who will probably be called as witnesses should be listed separately from those who are not likely to be called but who are being listed in order to preserve the right to do so if needed because of developments during trial. Revised Rule 37(c)(1) provides that only persons so listed may be used at trial to present substantive evidence. This restriction does not apply unless the omission was "without substantial justification" and hence would not bar an unlisted witness if the need for such testimony is based upon developments during trial that could not reasonably have been anticipated—e.g., a change of testimony.

Listing a witness does not obligate the party to secure the attendance of the person at trial, but should preclude the party from objecting if the person is called to testify by another party who did not list the person as a witness.

Subparagraph (B) requires the party to indicate which of these potential witnesses will be presented by deposition at trial. A party expecting to use at trial a deposition not recorded by stenographic means is required by revised Rule 32 to provide the court with a transcript of the pertinent portions of such depositions. This rule requires that copies of the transcript of a nonstenographic deposition be provided to other parties in advance of trial for verification, an obvious concern since counsel often utilize their own personnel to prepare transcripts from audio or video tapes. By order or local rule, the court may require that parties designate the particular portions of stenographic depositions to be used at trial.

Subparagraph (C) requires disclosure of exhibits, including summaries (whether to be offered in lieu of other documentary evidence or to be used as an aid in understanding such evidence), that may be offered as substantive evidence. The rule requires a separate listing of each such exhibit, though it should permit voluminous items of a similar or standardized character to be described by meaningful categories. For example, unless the court has otherwise directed, a series of vouchers might be shown collectively as a single exhibit with their starting and ending dates. As with witnesses, the exhibits that will probably be offered are to be listed separately from those which are unlikely to be offered but which are listed in order to preserve the right to do so if needed because of developments during trial. Under revised Rule 37(c)(1) the court can permit use of unlisted documents the need for which could not reasonably have been anticipated in advance of trial.

Upon receipt of these final pretrial disclosures, other parties have 14 days (unless a different time is specified by the court) to disclose any objections they wish to preserve to the usability of the deposition testimony or to the admissibility of the documentary evidence (other than under Rules 402 and 403 of the Federal Rules of Evidence). Similar provisions have become commonplace either in pretrial orders or by local rules, and significantly expedite the presentation of evidence at trial, as well as eliminate the need to have available witnesses to provide "foundation" testimony for most items of documentary evidence. The listing of a potential objection does not constitute the making of that objection or require the court to rule on the objection; rather, it preserves the right of the party to make the objection when and as appropriate during trial. The court may, however, elect to treat the listing as a motion "in limine" and rule upon the objections in advance of trial to the extent appropriate.

The time specified in the rule for the final pretrial disclosures is relatively close to the trial date. The objective is to eliminate the time and expense in making these disclosures of evidence and objections in those cases that settle shortly before trial, while affording a reasonable time for final preparation for trial in those cases that do not settle. In many cases, it will be desirable for the court in a scheduling or pretrial order to set an earlier time for disclosures of evidence and provide more time for disclosing potential objections.

Paragraph (4). This paragraph prescribes the form of disclosures. A signed written statement is required, reminding the parties and counsel of the solemnity of the obligations imposed; and the signature on the initial or pretrial disclosure is a certification under subdivision (g)(1) that it is complete and correct as of the time when made. Consistent with Rule 5(d), these disclosures are to be filed with the court unless otherwise directed. It is anticipated that many courts will direct that expert reports required under paragraph (2)(B) not be filed until needed in connection with a motion or for trial.

Paragraph (5). This paragraph is revised to take note of the availability of revised Rule 45 for inspection from non-parties of documents and premises without the need for a deposition.

Subdivision (b). This subdivision is revised in several respects. First, former paragraph (1) is subdivided into two paragraphs for ease of reference and to avoid renumbering of paragraphs (3) and (4). Textual changes are then made in new paragraph (2) to enable the court to keep tighter rein on the extent of discovery. The information explosion of recent decades has greatly increased both the potential cost of wide-ranging discovery and the potential for discovery to be used as an instrument for delay or oppression. Amendments to Rules 30, 31, and 33 place presumptive limits on the number of depositions and interrogatories, subject to leave of court to pursue additional discovery. The revisions in Rule 26(b)(2) are intended to provide the court with broader discretion to impose additional restrictions on the scope and extent of discovery and to authorize courts that develop case tracking systems based on the complexity of cases to increase or decrease by local rule the presumptive number of depositions and interrogatories allowed in particular types or classifications of cases. The revision also dispels any doubt as to the power of the court to impose limitations on the length of depositions under Rule 30 or on the number of requests for admission under Rule 36.

Second, former paragraph (2), relating to insurance, has been relocated as part of the required initial disclosures under subdivision (a)(1)(D), and revised to provide for disclosure of the policy itself.

Third, paragraph (4)(A) is revised to provide that experts who are expected to be witnesses will be subject to deposition prior to trial, conforming the norm stated in the rule to the actual practice followed in most courts, in which depositions of experts have become standard. Concerns regarding the expense of such depositions should be mitigated by the fact that the expert's fees for the deposition will ordinarily be borne by the party taking the deposition. The requirement under subdivision (a)(2)(B) of a complete and detailed report of the expected testimony of certain forensic experts may, moreover, eliminate the need for some such depositions or at least reduce the length of the depositions. Accordingly, the deposition of an expert required by subdivision (a)(2)(B) to provide a written report may be taken only after the report has been served.

Paragraph (4)(C), bearing on compensation of experts, is revised to take account of the changes in paragraph (4)(A).

Paragraph (5) is a new provision. A party must notify other parties if it is withholding materials otherwise subject to disclosure under the rule or pursuant to a discovery request because it is asserting a claim of privilege or work product protection. To withhold materials without such notice is contrary to the rule, subjects the party to sanctions under Rule 37(b)(2), and may be viewed as a waiver of the privilege or protection.

The party must also provide sufficient information to enable other parties to evaluate the applicability of the claimed privilege or protection. Although the person from whom the discovery is sought decides whether to claim a privilege or protection, the court ultimately decides whether, if this claim is challenged, the privilege or protection applies. Providing information pertinent to the applicability of the privilege or protection should reduce the need for in camera examination of the documents.

The rule does not attempt to define for each case what information must be provided when a party asserts a claim of privilege or work product protection. Details concerning time, persons, general subject matter, etc., may be appropriate if only a few items are withheld, but may be unduly burdensome when voluminous documents are claimed to be privileged or protected, particularly if the items can be described by categories. A party can seek relief through a protective order under subdivision (c) if compliance with the requirement for providing this information would be an unreasonable burden. In rare circumstances some of the pertinent information affecting applicability of the claim, such as the identity of the client, may itself be privileged; the rule provides that such information need not be disclosed.

The obligation to provide pertinent information concerning withheld privileged materials applies only to items "otherwise discoverable." If a broad discovery request is made—for example, for all documents of a particular type during a twenty year period—and the responding party believes in good faith that production of documents for more than the past three years would be unduly burdensome, it should make its objection to the breadth of the request and, with respect to the documents generated in that three year period, produce the unprivileged documents and describe those withheld under the claim of privilege. If the court later rules that documents for a seven year period are properly discoverable, the documents for the additional four years should then be either produced (if not privileged) or described (if claimed to be privileged).

Subdivision (c). The revision requires that before filing a motion for a protective order the movant must confer—either in person or by telephone—with the other affected parties in a good faith effort to resolve the discovery dispute without the need for court intervention. If the movant is unable to get opposing parties even to discuss the matter, the efforts in attempting to arrange such a conference should be indicated in the certificate.

Subdivision (d). This subdivision is revised to provide that formal discovery—as distinguished from interviews of potential witnesses and other informal discovery—not commence until the parties have met and conferred as required by subdivision (f). Discovery can begin earlier if authorized under Rule 30(a)(2)(C) (deposition of person about to leave the country) or by local rule, order, or stipulation. This will be appropriate in some cases, such as those involving requests for a preliminary injunction or motions challenging personal jurisdiction. If a local rule exempts any types of cases in which discovery may be needed from the requirement of a meeting under Rule 26(f), it should specify when discovery may commence in those cases.

The meeting of counsel is to take place as soon as practicable and in any event at least 14 days before the date of the scheduling conference under Rule 16(b) or the date a scheduling order is due under Rule 16(b). The court can assure that discovery is not unduly delayed either by entering a special order or by setting the case for a scheduling conference.

Subdivision (e). This subdivision is revised to provide that the requirement for supplementation applies to all disclosures required by subdivisions (a)(1)–(3). Like the former rule, the duty, while imposed on a "party," applies whether the corrective information is learned by the client or by the attorney. Supplementations need not be made as each new item of information is learned but should be made at appropriate intervals during the discovery period, and with special promptness as the trial date approaches. It may be useful for the scheduling order to specify the time or times when supplementations should be made.

The revision also clarifies that the obligation to supplement responses to formal discovery requests applies to interrogatories, requests for production, and requests for admissions, but not ordinarily to deposition testimony. However, with respect to experts from whom a written report is required under subdivision (a)(2)(B), changes in the opinions expressed by the expert whether in the report or at a subsequent deposition are subject to a duty of supplemental disclosure under subdivision (e)(1).

The obligation to supplement disclosures and discovery responses applies whenever a party learns that its prior disclosures or responses are in some material respect incomplete or incorrect. There is, however, no obligation to provide supplemental or corrective information that has been otherwise made known to the parties in writing or during the discovery process, as when a witness not previously disclosed is identified during the taking of a deposition or when an expert during a deposition corrects information contained in an earlier report.

Subdivision (f). This subdivision was added in 1980 to provide a party threatened with abusive discovery with a special means for obtaining judicial intervention other than through discrete motions under Rules 26(c) and 37(a). The amendment envisioned a two-step process: first, the parties would attempt to frame a mutually agreeable plan; second, the court would hold a "discovery conference" and then enter an order establishing a schedule and limitations for the conduct of discovery. It was contemplated that the procedure, an elective one triggered on request of a party, would be used in special cases rather than as a routine matter. As expected, the device has been used only sparingly in most courts, and judicial controls over the discovery process have ordinarily been imposed through scheduling orders under Rule 16(b) or through rulings on discovery motions.

The provisions relating to a conference with the court are removed from subdivision (f). This change does not signal any lessening of the importance of judicial supervision. Indeed, there is a greater need for early judicial involvement to consider the scope and timing of the disclosure requirements of Rule 26(a) and the presumptive limits on discovery imposed under these rules or by local rules. Rather, the change is made because the provisions addressing the use of conferences with the court to control discovery are more properly included in Rule 16, which is being revised to highlight the court's powers regarding the discovery process.

The desirability of some judicial control of discovery can hardly be doubted. Rule 16, as revised, requires that the court set a time for completion of discovery and authorizes various other orders affecting the scope, timing, and extent of discovery and disclosures. Before entering such orders, the court should consider the views of the parties, preferably by means of a conference, but at the least through written submissions. Moreover, it is desirable that the parties' proposals regarding discovery be developed through a process where they meet in person, informally explore the nature and basis of the issues, and discuss how discovery can be conducted most efficiently and economically.

As noted above, former subdivision (f) envisioned the development of proposed discovery plans as an optional procedure to be used in relatively few cases. The revised rule directs that in all cases not exempted by local rule or special order the litigants must meet in person and plan for discovery. Following this meeting, the parties submit to the court their proposals for a discovery plan and can begin formal discovery. Their report will assist the court in seeing that the timing and scope of disclosures under revised Rule 26(a) and the limitations on the extent of discovery under these rules and local rules are tailored to the circumstances of the particular case.

To assure that the court has the litigants' proposals before deciding on a scheduling order and that the commencement of discovery is not delayed unduly, the rule provides that the meeting of the parties take place as soon as practicable and in any event at least 14 days before a scheduling conference is held or before a scheduling order is due under Rule 16(b). (Rule 16(b) requires that a scheduling order be entered within 90 days after the first appearance of a defendant or, if earlier, within 120 days after the complaint has been served on any defendant.) The obligation to participate in the planning process is imposed on all parties that have appeared in the case, including defendants who, because of a pending Rule 12 motion, may not have yet filed an answer in the case. Each such party should attend the meeting, either through one of its attorneys or in person if unrepresented. If more parties are joined or appear after the initial meeting, an additional meeting may be desirable.

Subdivision (f) describes certain matters that should be accomplished at the meeting and included in the proposed discovery plan. This listing does not exclude consideration of other subjects, such as the time when any dispositive motions should be filed and when the case should be ready for trial.

The parties are directed under subdivision (a)(1) to make the disclosures required by that subdivision at or within 10 days after this meeting. In many cases the parties should use the meeting to exchange, discuss, and clarify their respective disclosures. In other cases, it may be more useful if the disclosures are delayed until after the parties have discussed at the meeting the claims and defenses in order to define the issues with respect to which the initial disclosures should be made. As discussed in the Notes to subdivision (a)(1), the parties may also need to consider whether a stipulation extending this 10-day period would be appropriate, as when a defendant would otherwise have less than 60 days after being served in which to make its initial disclosure. The parties should also discuss at the meeting what additional information, although not subject to the disclosure requirements, can be made available informally without the necessity for formal discovery requests.

The report is to be submitted to the court within 10 days after the meeting and should not be difficult to prepare. In most cases counsel should be able to agree that one of them will be responsible for its preparation and submission to the court. Form 35 has been added in the Appendix to the Rules, both to illustrate the type of report that is contemplated and to serve as a checklist for the meeting.

The litigants are expected to attempt in good faith to agree on the contents of the proposed discovery plan. If they cannot agree on all aspects of the plan, their report to the court should indicate the competing proposals of the parties on those items, as well as the matters on which they agree. Unfortunately, there may be cases in which, because of disagreements about time or place or for other reasons, the meeting is not attended by all parties or, indeed, no meeting takes place. In such situations, the report—or reports—should describe the circumstances and the court may need to consider sanctions under Rule 37(g).

By local rule or special order, the court can exempt particular cases or types of cases from the meet-and-confer requirement of subdivision (f). In general this should include any types of cases which are exempted by local rule from the requirement for a scheduling order under Rule 16(b), such as cases in which there will be no discovery (e.g., bankruptcy appeals and reviews of social security determinations). In addition, the court may want to exempt cases in which discovery is rarely needed (e.g., government collection cases and proceedings to enforce administrative summonses) or in which a meeting of the parties might be impracticable (e.g., actions by unrepresented prisoners). Note that if a court exempts from the requirements for a meeting any types of cases in which discovery may be needed, it should indicate when discovery may commence in those cases.

Subdivision (g). Paragraph (1) is added to require signatures on disclosures, a requirement that parallels the provisions of paragraph (2) with respect to discovery requests, responses, and objections. The provisions of paragraph (3) have been modified to be consistent with Rules 37(a)(4) and 37(c)(1); in combination, these rules establish sanctions for violation of the rules regarding disclosures and discovery matters. Amended Rule 11 no longer applies to such violations.

Committee Notes on Rules—2000 Amendment

Purposes of amendments. The Rule 26(a)(1) initial disclosure provisions are amended to establish a nationally uniform practice. The scope of the disclosure obligation is narrowed to cover only information that the disclosing party may use to support its position. In addition, the rule exempts specified categories of proceedings from initial disclosure, and permits a party who contends that disclosure is not appropriate in the circumstances of the case to present its objections to the court, which must then determine whether disclosure should be made. Related changes are made in Rules 26(d) and (f).

The initial disclosure requirements added by the 1993 amendments permitted local rules directing that disclosure would not be required or altering its operation. The inclusion of the "opt out" provision reflected the strong opposition to initial disclosure felt in some districts, and permitted experimentation with differing disclosure rules in those districts that were favorable to disclosure. The local option also recognized that—partly in response to the first publication in 1991 of a proposed disclosure rule—many districts had adopted a variety of disclosure programs under the aegis of the Civil Justice Reform Act. It was hoped that developing experience under a variety of disclosure systems would support eventual refinement of a uniform national disclosure practice. In addition, there was hope that local experience could identify categories of actions in which disclosure is not useful.

A striking array of local regimes in fact emerged for disclosure and related features introduced in 1993. See D. Stienstra, Implementation of Disclosure in United States District Courts, With Specific Attention to Courts' Responses to Selected Amendments to Federal Rule of Civil Procedure 26 (Federal Judicial Center, March 30, 1998) (describing and categorizing local regimes). In its final report to Congress on the CJRA experience, the Judicial Conference recommended reexamination of the need for national uniformity, particularly in regard to initial disclosure. Judicial Conference, Alternative Proposals for Reduction of Cost and Delay: Assessment of Principles, Guidelines and Techniques, 175 F.R.D. 62, 98 (1997).

At the Committee's request, the Federal Judicial Center undertook a survey in 1997 to develop information on current disclosure and discovery practices. See T. Willging, J. Shapard, D. Stienstra & D. Miletich, Discovery and Disclosure Practice, Problems, and Proposals for Change (Federal Judicial Center, 1997). In addition, the Committee convened two conferences on discovery involving lawyers from around the country and received reports and recommendations on possible discovery amendments from a number of bar groups. Papers and other proceedings from the second conference are published in 39 Boston Col. L. Rev. 517–840 (1998).

The Committee has discerned widespread support for national uniformity. Many lawyers have experienced difficulty in coping with divergent disclosure and other practices as they move from one district to another. Lawyers surveyed by the Federal Judicial Center ranked adoption of a uniform national disclosure rule second among proposed rule changes (behind increased availability of judges to resolve discovery disputes) as a means to reduce litigation expenses without interfering with fair outcomes. Discovery and Disclosure Practice, supra, at 44–45. National uniformity is also a central purpose of the Rules Enabling Act of 1934, as amended, 28 U.S.C. §§2072–2077.

These amendments restore national uniformity to disclosure practice. Uniformity is also restored to other aspects of discovery by deleting most of the provisions authorizing local rules that vary the number of permitted discovery events or the length of depositions. Local rule options are also deleted from Rules 26(d) and (f).

Subdivision (a)(1). The amendments remove the authority to alter or opt out of the national disclosure requirements by local rule, invalidating not only formal local rules but also informal "standing" orders of an individual judge or court that purport to create exemptions from—or limit or expand—the disclosure provided under the national rule. See Rule 83. Case-specific orders remain proper, however, and are expressly required if a party objects that initial disclosure is not appropriate in the circumstances of the action. Specified categories of proceedings are excluded from initial disclosure under subdivision (a)(1)(E). In addition, the parties can stipulate to forgo disclosure, as was true before. But even in a case excluded by subdivision (a)(1)(E) or in which the parties stipulate to bypass disclosure, the court can order exchange of similar information in managing the action under Rule 16.

The initial disclosure obligation of subdivisions (a)(1)(A) and (B) has been narrowed to identification of witnesses and documents that the disclosing party may use to support its claims or defenses. "Use" includes any use at a pretrial conference, to support a motion, or at trial. The disclosure obligation is also triggered by intended use in discovery, apart from use to respond to a discovery request; use of a document to question a witness during a deposition is a common example. The disclosure obligation attaches both to witnesses and documents a party intends to use and also to witnesses and to documents the party intends to use if—in the language of Rule 26(a)(3)—"the need arises."

A party is no longer obligated to disclose witnesses or documents, whether favorable or unfavorable, that it does not intend to use. The obligation to disclose information the party may use connects directly to the exclusion sanction of Rule 37(c)(1). Because the disclosure obligation is limited to material that the party may use, it is no longer tied to particularized allegations in the pleadings. Subdivision (e)(1), which is unchanged, requires supplementation if information later acquired would have been subject to the disclosure requirement. As case preparation continues, a party must supplement its disclosures when it determines that it may use a witness or document that it did not previously intend to use.

The disclosure obligation applies to "claims and defenses," and therefore requires a party to disclose information it may use to support its denial or rebuttal of the allegations, claim, or defense of another party. It thereby bolsters the requirements of Rule 11(b)(4), which authorizes denials "warranted on the evidence," and disclosure should include the identity of any witness or document that the disclosing party may use to support such denials.

Subdivision (a)(3) presently excuses pretrial disclosure of information solely for impeachment. Impeachment information is similarly excluded from the initial disclosure requirement.

Subdivisions (a)(1)(C) and (D) are not changed. Should a case be exempted from initial disclosure by Rule 26(a)(1)(E) or by agreement or order, the insurance information described by subparagraph (D) should be subject to discovery, as it would have been under the principles of former Rule 26(b)(2), which was added in 1970 and deleted in 1993 as redundant in light of the new initial disclosure obligation.

New subdivision (a)(1)(E) excludes eight specified categories of proceedings from initial disclosure. The objective of this listing is to identify cases in which there is likely to be little or no discovery, or in which initial disclosure appears unlikely to contribute to the effective development of the case. The list was developed after a review of the categories excluded by local rules in various districts from the operation of Rule 16(b) and the conference requirements of subdivision (f). Subdivision (a)(1)(E) refers to categories of "proceedings" rather than categories of "actions" because some might not properly be labeled "actions." Case designations made by the parties or the clerk's office at the time of filing do not control application of the exemptions. The descriptions in the rule are generic and are intended to be administered by the parties—and, when needed, the courts—with the flexibility needed to adapt to gradual evolution in the types of proceedings that fall within these general categories. The exclusion of an action for review on an administrative record, for example, is intended to reach a proceeding that is framed as an "appeal" based solely on an administrative record. The exclusion should not apply to a proceeding in a form that commonly permits admission of new evidence to supplement the record. Item (vii), excluding a proceeding ancillary to proceedings in other courts, does not refer to bankruptcy proceedings; application of the Civil Rules to bankruptcy proceedings is determined by the Bankruptcy Rules.

Subdivision (a)(1)(E) is likely to exempt a substantial proportion of the cases in most districts from the initial disclosure requirement. Based on 1996 and 1997 case filing statistics, Federal Judicial Center staff estimate that, nationwide, these categories total approximately one-third of all civil filings.

The categories of proceedings listed in subdivision (a)(1)(E) are also exempted from the subdivision (f) conference requirement and from the subdivision (d) moratorium on discovery. Although there is no restriction on commencement of discovery in these cases, it is not expected that this opportunity will often lead to abuse since there is likely to be little or no discovery in most such cases. Should a defendant need more time to respond to discovery requests filed at the beginning of an exempted action, it can seek relief by motion under Rule 26(c) if the plaintiff is unwilling to defer the due date by agreement.

Subdivision (a)(1)(E)'s enumeration of exempt categories is exclusive. Although a case-specific order can alter or excuse initial disclosure, local rules or "standing" orders that purport to create general exemptions are invalid. See Rule 83.

The time for initial disclosure is extended to 14 days after the subdivision (f) conference unless the court orders otherwise. This change is integrated with corresponding changes requiring that the subdivision (f) conference be held 21 days before the Rule 16(b) scheduling conference or scheduling order, and that the report on the subdivision (f) conference be submitted to the court 14 days after the meeting. These changes provide a more orderly opportunity for the parties to review the disclosures, and for the court to consider the report. In many instances, the subdivision (f) conference and the effective preparation of the case would benefit from disclosure before the conference, and earlier disclosure is encouraged.

The presumptive disclosure date does not apply if a party objects to initial disclosure during the subdivision (f) conference and states its objection in the subdivision (f) discovery plan. The right to object to initial disclosure is not intended to afford parties an opportunity to "opt out" of disclosure unilaterally. It does provide an opportunity for an objecting party to present to the court its position that disclosure would be "inappropriate in the circumstances of the action." Making the objection permits the objecting party to present the question to the judge before any party is required to make disclosure. The court must then rule on the objection and determine what disclosures—if any—should be made. Ordinarily, this determination would be included in the Rule 16(b) scheduling order, but the court could handle the matter in a different fashion. Even when circumstances warrant suspending some disclosure obligations, others—such as the damages and insurance information called for by subdivisions (a)(1)(C) and (D)—may continue to be appropriate.

The presumptive disclosure date is also inapplicable to a party who is "first served or otherwise joined" after the subdivision (f) conference. This phrase refers to the date of service of a claim on a party in a defensive posture (such as a defendant or third-party defendant), and the date of joinder of a party added as a claimant or an intervenor. Absent court order or stipulation, a new party has 30 days in which to make its initial disclosures. But it is expected that later-added parties will ordinarily be treated the same as the original parties when the original parties have stipulated to forgo initial disclosure, or the court has ordered disclosure in a modified form.

Subdivision (a)(3). The amendment to Rule 5(d) forbids filing disclosures under subdivisions (a)(1) and (a)(2) until they are used in the proceeding, and this change is reflected in an amendment to subdivision (a)(4). Disclosures under subdivision (a)(3), however, may be important to the court in connection with the final pretrial conference or otherwise in preparing for trial. The requirement that objections to certain matters be filed points up the court's need to be provided with these materials. Accordingly, the requirement that subdivision (a)(3) materials be filed has been moved from subdivision (a)(4) to subdivision (a)(3), and it has also been made clear that they—and any objections—should be filed "promptly."

Subdivision (a)(4). The filing requirement has been removed from this subdivision. Rule 5(d) has been amended to provide that disclosures under subdivisions (a)(1) and (a)(2) must not be filed until used in the proceeding. Subdivision (a)(3) has been amended to require that the disclosures it directs, and objections to them, be filed promptly. Subdivision (a)(4) continues to require that all disclosures under subdivisions (a)(1), (a)(2), and (a)(3) be in writing, signed, and served.

"Shall" is replaced by "must" under the program to conform amended rules to current style conventions when there is no ambiguity.

Subdivision (b)(1). In 1978, the Committee published for comment a proposed amendment, suggested by the Section of Litigation of the American Bar Association, to refine the scope of discovery by deleting the "subject matter" language. This proposal was withdrawn, and the Committee has since then made other changes in the discovery rules to address concerns about overbroad discovery. Concerns about costs and delay of discovery have persisted nonetheless, and other bar groups have repeatedly renewed similar proposals for amendment to this subdivision to delete the "subject matter" language. Nearly one-third of the lawyers surveyed in 1997 by the Federal Judicial Center endorsed narrowing the scope of discovery as a means of reducing litigation expense without interfering with fair case resolutions. Discovery and Disclosure Practice, supra, at 44–45 (1997). The Committee has heard that in some instances, particularly cases involving large quantities of discovery, parties seek to justify discovery requests that sweep far beyond the claims and defenses of the parties on the ground that they nevertheless have a bearing on the "subject matter" involved in the action.

The amendments proposed for subdivision (b)(1) include one element of these earlier proposals but also differ from these proposals in significant ways. The similarity is that the amendments describe the scope of party-controlled discovery in terms of matter relevant to the claim or defense of any party. The court, however, retains authority to order discovery of any matter relevant to the subject matter involved in the action for good cause. The amendment is designed to involve the court more actively in regulating the breadth of sweeping or contentious discovery. The Committee has been informed repeatedly by lawyers that involvement of the court in managing discovery is an important method of controlling problems of inappropriately broad discovery. Increasing the availability of judicial officers to resolve discovery disputes and increasing court management of discovery were both strongly endorsed by the attorneys surveyed by the Federal Judicial Center. See Discovery and Disclosure Practice, supra, at 44. Under the amended provisions, if there is an objection that discovery goes beyond material relevant to the parties' claims or defenses, the court would become involved to determine whether the discovery is relevant to the claims or defenses and, if not, whether good cause exists for authorizing it so long as it is relevant to the subject matter of the action. The good-cause standard warranting broader discovery is meant to be flexible.

The Committee intends that the parties and the court focus on the actual claims and defenses involved in the action. The dividing line between information relevant to the claims and defenses and that relevant only to the subject matter of the action cannot be defined with precision. A variety of types of information not directly pertinent to the incident in suit could be relevant to the claims or defenses raised in a given action. For example, other incidents of the same type, or involving the same product, could be properly discoverable under the revised standard. Information about organizational arrangements or filing systems of a party could be discoverable if likely to yield or lead to the discovery of admissible information. Similarly, information that could be used to impeach a likely witness, although not otherwise relevant to the claims or defenses, might be properly discoverable. In each instance, the determination whether such information is discoverable because it is relevant to the claims or defenses depends on the circumstances of the pending action.

The rule change signals to the court that it has the authority to confine discovery to the claims and defenses asserted in the pleadings, and signals to the parties that they have no entitlement to discovery to develop new claims or defenses that are not already identified in the pleadings. In general, it is hoped that reasonable lawyers can cooperate to manage discovery without the need for judicial intervention. When judicial intervention is invoked, the actual scope of discovery should be determined according to the reasonable needs of the action. The court may permit broader discovery in a particular case depending on the circumstances of the case, the nature of the claims and defenses, and the scope of the discovery requested.

The amendments also modify the provision regarding discovery of information not admissible in evidence. As added in 1946, this sentence was designed to make clear that otherwise relevant material could not be withheld because it was hearsay or otherwise inadmissible. The Committee was concerned that the "reasonably calculated to lead to the discovery of admissible evidence" standard set forth in this sentence might swallow any other limitation on the scope of discovery. Accordingly, this sentence has been amended to clarify that information must be relevant to be discoverable, even though inadmissible, and that discovery of such material is permitted if reasonably calculated to lead to the discovery of admissible evidence. As used here, "relevant" means within the scope of discovery as defined in this subdivision, and it would include information relevant to the subject matter involved in the action if the court has ordered discovery to that limit based on a showing of good cause.

Finally, a sentence has been added calling attention to the limitations of subdivision (b)(2)(i), (ii), and (iii). These limitations apply to discovery that is otherwise within the scope of subdivision (b)(1). The Committee has been told repeatedly that courts have not implemented these limitations with the vigor that was contemplated. See 8 Federal Practice & Procedure §2008.1 at 121. This otherwise redundant cross-reference has been added to emphasize the need for active judicial use of subdivision (b)(2) to control excessive discovery. Cf. Crawford-El v. Britton, 118 S. Ct. 1584, 1597 (1998) (quoting Rule 26(b)(2)(iii) and stating that "Rule 26 vests the trial judge with broad discretion to tailor discovery narrowly").

Subdivision (b)(2). Rules 30, 31, and 33 establish presumptive national limits on the numbers of depositions and interrogatories. New Rule 30(d)(2) establishes a presumptive limit on the length of depositions. Subdivision (b)(2) is amended to remove the previous permission for local rules that establish different presumptive limits on these discovery activities. There is no reason to believe that unique circumstances justify varying these nationally-applicable presumptive limits in certain districts. The limits can be modified by court order or agreement in an individual action, but "standing" orders imposing different presumptive limits are not authorized. Because there is no national rule limiting the number of Rule 36 requests for admissions, the rule continues to authorize local rules that impose numerical limits on them. This change is not intended to interfere with differentiated case management in districts that use this technique by case-specific order as part of their Rule 16 process.

Subdivision (d). The amendments remove the prior authority to exempt cases by local rule from the moratorium on discovery before the subdivision (f) conference, but the categories of proceedings exempted from initial disclosure under subdivision (a)(1)(E) are excluded from subdivision (d). The parties may agree to disregard the moratorium where it applies, and the court may so order in a case, but "standing" orders altering the moratorium are not authorized.

Subdivision (f). As in subdivision (d), the amendments remove the prior authority to exempt cases by local rule from the conference requirement. The Committee has been informed that the addition of the conference was one of the most successful changes made in the 1993 amendments, and it therefore has determined to apply the conference requirement nationwide. The categories of proceedings exempted from initial disclosure under subdivision (a)(1)(E) are exempted from the conference requirement for the reasons that warrant exclusion from initial disclosure. The court may order that the conference need not occur in a case where otherwise required, or that it occur in a case otherwise exempted by subdivision (a)(1)(E). "Standing" orders altering the conference requirement for categories of cases are not authorized.

The rule is amended to require only a "conference" of the parties, rather than a "meeting." There are important benefits to face-to-face discussion of the topics to be covered in the conference, and those benefits may be lost if other means of conferring were routinely used when face-to-face meetings would not impose burdens. Nevertheless, geographic conditions in some districts may exact costs far out of proportion to these benefits. The amendment allows the court by case-specific order to require a face-to-face meeting, but "standing" orders so requiring are not authorized.

As noted concerning the amendments to subdivision (a)(1), the time for the conference has been changed to at least 21 days before the Rule 16 scheduling conference, and the time for the report is changed to no more than 14 days after the Rule 26(f) conference. This should ensure that the court will have the report well in advance of the scheduling conference or the entry of the scheduling order.

Since Rule 16 was amended in 1983 to mandate some case management activities in all courts, it has included deadlines for completing these tasks to ensure that all courts do so within a reasonable time. Rule 26(f) was fit into this scheme when it was adopted in 1993. It was never intended, however, that the national requirements that certain activities be completed by a certain time should delay case management in districts that move much faster than the national rules direct, and the rule is therefore amended to permit such a court to adopt a local rule that shortens the period specified for the completion of these tasks.

"Shall" is replaced by "must," "does," or an active verb under the program to conform amended rules to current style conventions when there is no ambiguity.

GAP Report. The Advisory Committee recommends that the amendments to Rules 26(a)(1)(A) and (B) be changed so that initial disclosure applies to information the disclosing party "may use to support" its claims or defenses. It also recommends changes in the Committee Note to explain that disclosure requirement. In addition, it recommends inclusion in the Note of further explanatory matter regarding the exclusion from initial disclosure provided in new Rule 26(a)(1)(E) for actions for review on an administrative record and the impact of these exclusions on bankruptcy proceedings. Minor wording improvements in the Note are also proposed.

The Advisory Committee recommends changing the rule to authorize the court to expand discovery to any "matter"—not "information"—relevant to the subject matter involved in the action. In addition, it recommends additional clarifying material in the Committee Note about the impact of the change on some commonly disputed discovery topics, the relationship between cost-bearing under Rule 26(b)(2) and expansion of the scope of discovery on a showing of good cause, and the meaning of "relevant" in the revision to the last sentence of current subdivision (b)(1). In addition, some minor clarifications of language changes have been proposed for the Committee Note.

The Advisory Committee recommends adding a sentence to the published amendments to Rule 26(f) authorizing local rules shortening the time between the attorney conference and the court's action under Rule 16(b), and addition to the Committee

Note of explanatory material about this change to the rule. This addition can be made without republication in response to public comments.

Committee Notes on Rules—2006 Amendment

Subdivision (a). Rule 26(a)(1)(B) is amended to parallel Rule 34(a) by recognizing that a party must disclose electronically stored information as well as documents that it may use to support its claims or defenses. The term "electronically stored information" has the same broad meaning in Rule 26(a)(1) as in Rule 34(a). This amendment is consistent with the 1993 addition of Rule 26(a)(1)(B). The term "data compilations" is deleted as unnecessary because it is a subset of both documents and electronically stored information.

Changes Made After Publication and Comment. As noted in the introduction [omitted], this provision was not included in the published rule. It is included as a conforming amendment, to make Rule 26(a)(1) consistent with the changes that were included in the published proposals.

[Subdivision (a)(1)(E).] Civil forfeiture actions are added to the list of exemptions from Rule 26(a)(1) disclosure requirements. These actions are governed by new Supplemental Rule G. Disclosure is not likely to be useful.

Subdivision (b)(2). The amendment to Rule 26(b)(2) is designed to address issues raised by difficulties in locating, retrieving, and providing discovery of some electronically stored information. Electronic storage systems often make it easier to locate and retrieve information. These advantages are properly taken into account in determining the reasonable scope of discovery in a particular case. But some sources of electronically stored information can be accessed only with substantial burden and cost. In a particular case, these burdens and costs may make the information on such sources not reasonably accessible.

It is not possible to define in a rule the different types of technological features that may affect the burdens and costs of accessing electronically stored information. Information systems are designed to provide ready access to information used in regular ongoing activities. They also may be designed so as to provide ready access to information that is not regularly used. But a system may retain information on sources that are accessible only by incurring substantial burdens or costs. Subparagraph (B) is added to regulate discovery from such sources.

Under this rule, a responding party should produce electronically stored information that is relevant, not privileged, and reasonably accessible, subject to the (b)(2)(C) limitations that apply to all discovery. The responding party must also identify, by category or type, the sources containing potentially responsive information that it is neither searching nor producing. The identification should, to the extent possible, provide enough detail to enable the requesting party to evaluate the burdens and costs of providing the discovery and the likelihood of finding responsive information on the identified sources.

A party's identification of sources of electronically stored information as not reasonably accessible does not relieve the party of its common-law or statutory duties to preserve evidence. Whether a responding party is required to preserve unsearched sources of potentially responsive information that it believes are not reasonably accessible depends on the circumstances of each case. It is often useful for the parties to discuss this issue early in discovery.

The volume of—and the ability to search—much electronically stored information means that in many cases the responding party will be able to produce information from reasonably accessible sources that will fully satisfy the parties' discovery needs. In many circumstances the requesting party should obtain and evaluate the information from such sources before insisting that the responding party search and produce information contained on sources that are not reasonably accessible. If the requesting party continues to seek discovery of information from sources identified as not reasonably accessible, the parties should discuss the burdens and costs of accessing and retrieving the information, the needs that may establish good cause for requiring all or part of the requested discovery even if the information sought is not reasonably accessible, and conditions on obtaining and producing the information that may be appropriate.

If the parties cannot agree whether, or on what terms, sources identified as not reasonably accessible should be searched and discoverable information produced, the issue may be raised either by a motion to compel discovery or by a motion for a protective order. The parties must confer before bringing either motion. If the parties do not resolve the issue and the court must decide, the responding party must show that the identified sources of information are not reasonably accessible because of undue burden or cost. The requesting party may need discovery to test this assertion. Such discovery might take the form of requiring the responding party to conduct a sampling of information contained on the sources identified as not reasonably accessible; allowing some form of inspection of such sources; or taking depositions of witnesses knowledgeable about the responding party's information systems.

Once it is shown that a source of electronically stored information is not reasonably accessible, the requesting party may still obtain discovery by showing good cause, considering the limitations of Rule 26(b)(2)(C) that balance the costs and potential benefits of discovery. The decision whether to require a responding party to search for and produce information that is not reasonably accessible depends not only on the burdens and costs of doing so, but also on whether those burdens and costs can be justified in the circumstances of the case. Appropriate considerations may include: (1) the specificity of the discovery request; (2) the quantity of information available from other and more easily accessed sources; (3) the failure to produce relevant information that seems likely to have existed but is no longer available on more easily accessed sources; (4) the likelihood of finding relevant, responsive information that cannot be obtained from other, more easily accessed sources; (5) predictions as to the importance and usefulness of the further information; (6) the importance of the issues at stake in the litigation; and (7) the parties' resources.

The responding party has the burden as to one aspect of the inquiry—whether the identified sources are not reasonably accessible in light of the burdens and costs required to search for, retrieve, and produce whatever responsive information may be found. The requesting party has the burden of showing that its need for the discovery outweighs the burdens and costs of locating, retrieving, and producing the information. In some cases, the court will be able to determine whether the identified sources are not reasonably accessible and whether the requesting party has shown good cause for some or all of the discovery, consistent with the limitations of Rule 26(b)(2)(C), through a single proceeding or presentation. The good-cause determination, however, may be complicated because the court and parties may know little about what information the sources identified as not reasonably accessible might contain, whether it is relevant, or how valuable it may be to the litigation. In such cases, the parties may need some focused discovery, which may include sampling of the sources, to learn more about what burdens and costs are involved in accessing the information, what the information consists of, and how valuable it is for the litigation in light of information that can be obtained by exhausting other opportunities for discovery.

The good-cause inquiry and consideration of the Rule 26(b)(2)(C) limitations are coupled with the authority to set conditions for discovery. The conditions may take the form of limits on the amount, type, or sources of information required to be accessed and produced. The conditions may also include payment by the requesting party of part or all of the reasonable costs of obtaining information from sources that are not reasonably accessible. A requesting party's willingness to share or bear the access costs may be weighed by the court in determining whether there is good cause. But the producing party's burdens in reviewing the information for relevance and privilege may weigh against permitting the requested discovery.

The limitations of Rule 26(b)(2)(C) continue to apply to all discovery of electronically stored information, including that stored on reasonably accessible electronic sources.

Changes Made after Publication and Comment. This recommendation modifies the version of the proposed rule amendment as published. Responding to comments that the published proposal seemed to require identification of information that cannot be identified because it is not reasonably accessible, the rule text was clarified by requiring identification of sources that are not reasonably accessible. The test of reasonable accessibility was clarified by adding "because of undue burden or cost."

The published proposal referred only to a motion by the requesting party to compel discovery. The rule text has been changed to recognize that the responding party may wish to determine its search and potential preservation obligations by moving for a protective order.

The provision that the court may for good cause order discovery from sources that are not reasonably accessible is expanded in two ways. It now states specifically that the requesting party is the one who must show good cause, and it refers to consideration of the limitations on discovery set out in present Rule 26(b)(2)(i), (ii), and (iii).

The published proposal was added at the end of present Rule 26(b)(2). It has been relocated to become a new subparagraph (B), allocating present Rule 26(b)(2) to new subparagraphs (A) and (C). The Committee Note was changed to reflect the rule text revisions. It also was shortened. The shortening was accomplished in part by deleting references to problems that are likely to become antique as technology continues to evolve, and in part by deleting passages that were at a level of detail better suited for a practice manual than a Committee Note.

The changes from the published proposed amendment to Rule 26(b)(2) are set out below. [Omitted]

Subdivision (b)(5). The Committee has repeatedly been advised that the risk of privilege waiver, and the work necessary to avoid it, add to the costs and delay of discovery. When the review is of electronically stored information, the risk of waiver, and the time and effort required to avoid it, can increase substantially because of the volume of electronically stored information and the difficulty in ensuring that all information to be produced has in fact been reviewed. Rule 26(b)(5)(A) provides a procedure for a party that has withheld information on the basis of privilege or protection as trial-preparation material to make the claim so that the requesting party can decide whether to contest the claim and the court can resolve the dispute. Rule 26(b)(5)(B) is added to provide a procedure for a party to assert a claim of privilege or trial-preparation material protection after information is produced in discovery in the action and, if the claim is contested, permit any party that received the information to present the matter to the court for resolution.

Rule 26(b)(5)(B) does not address whether the privilege or protection that is asserted after production was waived by the production. The courts have developed principles to determine whether, and under what circumstances, waiver results from inadvertent production of privileged or protected information. Rule 26(b)(5)(B) provides a procedure for presenting and addressing these issues. Rule 26(b)(5)(B) works in tandem with Rule 26(f), which is amended to direct the parties to discuss privilege issues in preparing their discovery plan, and which, with amended Rule 16(b), allows the parties to ask the court to include in an order any agreements the parties reach regarding issues of privilege or trial-preparation material protection. Agreements reached under Rule 26(f)(4) and orders including such agreements entered under Rule 16(b)(6) may be considered when a court determines whether a waiver has occurred. Such agreements and orders ordinarily control if they adopt procedures different from those in Rule 26(b)(5)(B).

A party asserting a claim of privilege or protection after production must give notice to the receiving party. That notice should be in writing unless the circumstances preclude it. Such circumstances could include the assertion of the claim during a deposition. The notice should be as specific as possible in identifying the information and stating the basis for the claim. Because the receiving party must decide whether to challenge the claim and may sequester the information and submit it to the court for a ruling on whether the claimed privilege or protection applies and whether it has been waived, the notice should be sufficiently detailed so as to enable the receiving party and the court to understand the basis for the claim and to determine whether waiver has occurred. Courts will continue to examine whether a claim of privilege or protection was made at a reasonable time when delay is part of the waiver determination under the governing law.

After receiving notice, each party that received the information must promptly return, sequester, or destroy the information and any copies it has. The option of sequestering or destroying the information is included in part because the receiving party may have incorporated the information in protected trial-preparation materials. No receiving party may use or disclose the information pending resolution of the privilege claim. The receiving party may present to the court the questions whether the information is privileged or protected as trial-preparation material, and whether the privilege or protection has been waived. If it does so, it must provide the court with the grounds for the privilege or protection specified in the producing party's notice, and serve all parties. In presenting the question, the party may use the content of the information only to the extent permitted by the applicable law of privilege, protection for trial-preparation material, and professional responsibility.

If a party disclosed the information to nonparties before receiving notice of a claim of privilege or protection as trial-preparation material, it must take reasonable steps to retrieve the information and to return it, sequester it until the claim is resolved, or destroy it.

Whether the information is returned or not, the producing party must preserve the information pending the court's ruling on whether the claim of privilege or of protection is properly asserted and whether it was waived. As with claims made under Rule 26(b)(5)(A), there may be no ruling if the other parties do not contest the claim.

Changes Made After Publication and Comment. The rule recommended for approval is modified from the published proposal. The rule is expanded to include trial-preparation protection claims in addition to privilege claims.

The published proposal referred to production "without intending to waive a claim of privilege." This reference to intent was deleted because many courts include intent in the factors that determine whether production waives privilege.

The published proposal required that the producing party give notice "within a reasonable time." The time requirement was deleted because it seemed to implicate the question whether production effected a waiver, a question not addressed by the rule, and also because a receiving party cannot practicably ignore a notice that it believes was unreasonably delayed. The notice procedure was further changed to require that the producing party state the basis for the claim.

Two statements in the published Note have been brought into the rule text. The first provides that the receiving party may not use or disclose the information until the claim is resolved. The second provides that if the receiving party disclosed the information before being notified, it must take reasonable steps to retrieve it.1

The rule text was expanded by adding a provision that the receiving party may promptly present the information to the court under seal for a determination of the claim.

The published proposal provided that the producing party must comply with Rule 26(b)(5)(A) after making the claim. This provision was deleted as unnecessary.

Changes are made in the Committee Note to reflect the changes in the rule text.

The changes from the published rule are shown below. [Omitted]

Subdivision (f). Rule 26(f) is amended to direct the parties to discuss discovery of electronically stored information during their discovery-planning conference. The rule focuses on "issues relating to disclosure or discovery of electronically stored information"; the discussion is not required in cases not involving electronic discovery, and the amendment imposes no additional requirements in those cases. When the parties do anticipate disclosure or discovery of electronically stored information, discussion at the outset may avoid later difficulties or ease their resolution.

When a case involves discovery of electronically stored information, the issues to be addressed during the Rule 26(f) conference depend on the nature and extent of the contemplated discovery and of the parties' information systems. It may be important for the parties to discuss those systems, and accordingly important for counsel to become familiar with those systems before the conference. With that information, the parties can develop a discovery plan that takes into account the capabilities of their computer systems. In appropriate cases identification of, and early discovery from, individuals with special knowledge of a party's computer systems may be helpful.

The particular issues regarding electronically stored information that deserve attention during the discovery planning stage depend on the specifics of the given case. See Manual for Complex Litigation (4th) §40.25(2) (listing topics for discussion in a proposed order regarding meet-and-confer sessions). For example, the parties may specify the topics for such discovery and the time period for which discovery will be sought. They may identify the various sources of such information within a party's control that should be searched for electronically stored information. They may discuss whether the information is reasonably accessible to the party that has it, including the burden or cost of retrieving and reviewing the information. See Rule 26(b)(2)(B). Rule 26(f)(3) explicitly directs the parties to discuss the form or forms in which electronically stored information might be produced. The parties may be able to reach agreement on the forms of production, making discovery more efficient. Rule 34(b) is amended to permit a requesting party to specify the form or forms in which it wants electronically stored information produced. If the requesting party does not specify a form, Rule 34(b) directs the responding party to state the forms it intends to use in the production. Early discussion of the forms of production may facilitate the application of Rule 34(b) by allowing the parties to determine what forms of production will meet both parties' needs. Early identification of disputes over the forms of production may help avoid the expense and delay of searches or productions using inappropriate forms.

Rule 26(f) is also amended to direct the parties to discuss any issues regarding preservation of discoverable information during their conference as they develop a discovery plan. This provision applies to all sorts of discoverable information, but can be particularly important with regard to electronically stored information. The volume and dynamic nature of electronically stored information may complicate preservation obligations. The ordinary operation of computers involves both the automatic creation and the automatic deletion or overwriting of certain information. Failure to address preservation issues early in the litigation increases uncertainty and raises a risk of disputes.

The parties' discussion should pay particular attention to the balance between the competing needs to preserve relevant evidence and to continue routine operations critical to ongoing activities. Complete or broad cessation of a party's routine computer operations could paralyze the party's activities. Cf. Manual for Complex Litigation (4th) §11.422 ("A blanket preservation order may be prohibitively expensive and unduly burdensome for parties dependent on computer systems for their day-to-day operations.") The parties should take account of these considerations in their discussions, with the goal of agreeing on reasonable preservation steps.

The requirement that the parties discuss preservation does not imply that courts should routinely enter preservation orders. A preservation order entered over objections should be narrowly tailored. Ex parte preservation orders should issue only in exceptional circumstances.

Rule 26(f) is also amended to provide that the parties should discuss any issues relating to assertions of privilege or of protection as trial-preparation materials, including whether the parties can facilitate discovery by agreeing on procedures for asserting claims of privilege or protection after production and whether to ask the court to enter an order that includes any agreement the parties reach. The Committee has repeatedly been advised about the discovery difficulties that can result from efforts to guard against waiver of privilege and work-product protection. Frequently parties find it necessary to spend large amounts of time reviewing materials requested through discovery to avoid waiving privilege. These efforts are necessary because materials subject to a claim of privilege or protection are often difficult to identify. A failure to withhold even one such item may result in an argument that there has been a waiver of privilege as to all other privileged materials on that subject matter. Efforts to avoid the risk of waiver can impose substantial costs on the party producing the material and the time required for the privilege review can substantially delay access for the party seeking discovery.

These problems often become more acute when discovery of electronically stored information is sought. The volume of such data, and the informality that attends use of e-mail and some other types of electronically stored information, may make privilege determinations more difficult, and privilege review correspondingly more expensive and time consuming. Other aspects of electronically stored information pose particular difficulties for privilege review. For example, production may be sought of information automatically included in electronic files but not apparent to the creator or to readers. Computer programs may retain draft language, editorial comments, and other deleted matter (sometimes referred to as "embedded data" or "embedded edits") in an electronic file but not make them apparent to the reader. Information describing the history, tracking, or management of an electronic file (sometimes called "metadata") is usually not apparent to the reader viewing a hard copy or a screen image. Whether this information should be produced may be among the topics discussed in the Rule 26(f) conference. If it is, it may need to be reviewed to ensure that no privileged information is included, further complicating the task of privilege review.

Parties may attempt to minimize these costs and delays by agreeing to protocols that minimize the risk of waiver. They may agree that the responding party will provide certain requested materials for initial examination without waiving any privilege or protection—sometimes known as a "quick peek." The requesting party then designates the documents it wishes to have actually produced. This designation is the Rule 34 request. The responding party then responds in the usual course, screening only those documents actually requested for formal production and asserting privilege claims as provided in Rule 26(b)(5)(A). On other occasions, parties enter agreements—sometimes called "clawback agreements"—that production without intent to waive privilege or protection should not be a waiver so long as the responding party identifies the documents mistakenly produced, and that the documents should be returned under those circumstances. Other voluntary arrangements may be appropriate depending on the circumstances of each litigation. In most circumstances, a party who receives information under such an arrangement cannot assert that production of the information waived a claim of privilege or of protection as trial-preparation material.

Although these agreements may not be appropriate for all cases, in certain cases they can facilitate prompt and economical discovery by reducing delay before the discovering party obtains access to documents, and by reducing the cost and burden of review by the producing party. A case-management or other order including such agreements may further facilitate the discovery process. Form 35 is amended to include a report to the court about any agreement regarding protections against inadvertent forfeiture or waiver of privilege or protection that the parties have reached, and Rule 16(b) is amended to recognize that the court may include such an agreement in a case-management or other order. If the parties agree to entry of such an order, their proposal should be included in the report to the court.

Rule 26(b)(5)(B) is added to establish a parallel procedure to assert privilege or protection as trial-preparation material after production, leaving the question of waiver to later determination by the court.

Changes Made After Publication and Comment. The Committee recommends a modified version of what was published. Rule 26(f)(3) was expanded to refer to the form "or forms" of production, in parallel with the like change in Rule 34. Different forms may be suitable for different sources of electronically stored information.

The published Rule 26(f)(4) proposal described the parties' views and proposals concerning whether, on their agreement, the court should enter an order protecting the right to assert privilege after production. This has been revised to refer to the parties' views and proposals concerning any issues relating to claims of privilege, including—if the parties agree on a procedure to assert such claims after production—whether to ask the court to include their agreement in an order. As with Rule 16(b)(6), this change was made to avoid any implications as to the scope of the protection that may be afforded by court adoption of the parties' agreement.

Rule 26(f)(4) also was expanded to include trial-preparation materials.

The Committee Note was revised to reflect the changes in the rule text.

The changes from the published rule are shown below. [Omitted]

Committee Notes on Rules—2007 Amendment

The language of Rule 26 has been amended as part of the general restyling of the Civil Rules to make them more easily understood and to make style and terminology consistent throughout the rules. These changes are intended to be stylistic only.

Former Rule 26(a)(5) served as an index of the discovery methods provided by later rules. It was deleted as redundant. Deletion does not affect the right to pursue discovery in addition to disclosure.

Former Rule 26(b)(1) began with a general statement of the scope of discovery that appeared to function as a preface to each of the five numbered paragraphs that followed. This preface has been shifted to the text of paragraph (1) because it does not accurately reflect the limits embodied in paragraphs (2), (3), or (4), and because paragraph (5) does not address the scope of discovery.

The reference to discovery of "books" in former Rule 26(b)(1) was deleted to achieve consistent expression throughout the discovery rules. Books remain a proper subject of discovery.

Amended Rule 26(b)(3) states that a party may obtain a copy of the party's own previous statement "on request." Former Rule 26(b)(3) expressly made the request procedure available to a nonparty witness, but did not describe the procedure to be used by a party. This apparent gap is closed by adopting the request procedure, which ensures that a party need not invoke Rule 34 to obtain a copy of the party's own statement.

Rule 26(e) stated the duty to supplement or correct a disclosure or discovery response "to include information thereafter acquired." This apparent limit is not reflected in practice; parties recognize the duty to supplement or correct by providing information that was not originally provided although it was available at the time of the initial disclosure or response. These words are deleted to reflect the actual meaning of the present rule.

Former Rule 26(e) used different phrases to describe the time to supplement or correct a disclosure or discovery response. Disclosures were to be supplemented "at appropriate intervals." A prior discovery response must be "seasonably * * * amend[ed]." The fine distinction between these phrases has not been observed in practice. Amended Rule 26(e)(1)(A) uses the same phrase for disclosures and discovery responses. The party must supplement or correct "in a timely manner."

Former Rule 26(g)(1) did not call for striking an unsigned disclosure. The omission was an obvious drafting oversight. Amended Rule 26(g)(2) includes disclosures in the list of matters that the court must strike unless a signature is provided "promptly * * * after being called to the attorney's or party's attention."

Former Rule 26(b)(2)(A) referred to a "good faith" argument to extend existing law. Amended Rule 26(b)(1)(B)(i) changes this reference to a "nonfrivolous" argument to achieve consistency with Rule 11(b)(2).

As with the Rule 11 signature on a pleading, written motion, or other paper, disclosure and discovery signatures should include not only a postal address but also a telephone number and electronic-mail address. A signer who lacks one or more of those addresses need not supply a nonexistent item.

Rule 11(b)(2) recognizes that it is legitimate to argue for establishing new law. An argument to establish new law is equally legitimate in conducting discovery.

Changes Made After Publication and Comment. See Note to Rule 1, supra.

Committee Notes on Rules—2010 Amendment

Rule 26. Rules 26(a)(2) and (b)(4) are amended to address concerns about expert discovery. The amendments to Rule 26(a)(2) require disclosure regarding expected expert testimony of those expert witnesses not required to provide expert reports and limit the expert report to facts or data (rather than "data or other information," as in the current rule) considered by the witness. Rule 26(b)(4) is amended to provide work-product protection against discovery regarding draft expert disclosures or reports and—with three specific exceptions—communications between expert witnesses and counsel.

In 1993, Rule 26(b)(4)(A) was revised to authorize expert depositions and Rule 26(a)(2) was added to provide disclosure, including—for many experts—an extensive report. Many courts read the disclosure provision to authorize discovery of all communications between counsel and expert witnesses and all draft reports. The Committee has been told repeatedly that routine discovery into attorney-expert communications and draft reports has had undesirable effects. Costs have risen. Attorneys may employ two sets of experts—one for purposes of consultation and another to testify at trial—because disclosure of their collaborative interactions with expert consultants would reveal their most sensitive and confidential case analyses. At the same time, attorneys often feel compelled to adopt a guarded attitude toward their interaction with testifying experts that impedes effective communication, and experts adopt strategies that protect against discovery but also interfere with their work.

Subdivision (a)(2)(B). Rule 26(a)(2)(B)(ii) is amended to provide that disclosure include all "facts or data considered by the witness in forming" the opinions to be offered, rather than the "data or other information" disclosure prescribed in 1993. This amendment is intended to alter the outcome in cases that have relied on the 1993 formulation in requiring disclosure of all attorney-expert communications and draft reports. The amendments to Rule 26(b)(4) make this change explicit by providing work-product protection against discovery regarding draft reports and disclosures or attorney-expert communications.

The refocus of disclosure on "facts or data" is meant to limit disclosure to material of a factual nature by excluding theories or mental impressions of counsel. At the same time, the intention is that "facts or data" be interpreted broadly to require disclosure of any material considered by the expert, from whatever source, that contains factual ingredients. The disclosure obligation extends to any facts or data "considered" by the expert in forming the opinions to be expressed, not only those relied upon by the expert.

Subdivision (a)(2)(C). Rule 26(a)(2)(C) is added to mandate summary disclosures of the opinions to be offered by expert witnesses who are not required to provide reports under Rule 26(a)(2)(B) and of the facts supporting those opinions. This disclosure is considerably less extensive than the report required by Rule 26(a)(2)(B). Courts must take care against requiring undue detail, keeping in mind that these witnesses have not been specially retained and may not be as responsive to counsel as those who have.

This amendment resolves a tension that has sometimes prompted courts to require reports under Rule 26(a)(2)(B) even from witnesses exempted from the report requirement. An (a)(2)(B) report is required only from an expert described in (a)(2)(B).

A witness who is not required to provide a report under Rule 26(a)(2)(B) may both testify as a fact witness and also provide expert testimony under Evidence Rule 702, 703, or 705. Frequent examples include physicians or other health care professionals and employees of a party who do not regularly provide expert testimony. Parties must identify such witnesses under Rule 26(a)(2)(A) and provide the disclosure required under Rule 26(a)(2)(C). The (a)(2)(C) disclosure obligation does not include facts unrelated to the expert opinions the witness will present.

Subdivision (a)(2)(D). This provision (formerly Rule 26(a)(2)(C)) is amended slightly to specify that the time limits for disclosure of contradictory or rebuttal evidence apply with regard to disclosures under new Rule 26(a)(2)(C), just as they do with regard to reports under Rule 26(a)(2)(B).

Subdivision (b)(4). Rule 26(b)(4)(B) is added to provide work-product protection under Rule 26(b)(3)(A) and (B) for drafts of expert reports or disclosures. This protection applies to all witnesses identified under Rule 26(a)(2)(A), whether they are required to provide reports under Rule 26(a)(2)(B) or are the subject of disclosure under Rule 26(a)(2)(C). It applies regardless of the form in which the draft is recorded, whether written, electronic, or otherwise. It also applies to drafts of any supplementation under Rule 26(e); see Rule 26(a)(2)(E).

Rule 26(b)(4)(C) is added to provide work-product protection for attorney-expert communications regardless of the form of the communications, whether oral, written, electronic, or otherwise. The addition of Rule 26(b)(4)(C) is designed to protect counsel's work product and ensure that lawyers may interact with retained experts without fear of exposing those communications to searching discovery. The protection is limited to communications between an expert witness required to provide a report under Rule 26(a)(2)(B) and the attorney for the party on whose behalf the witness will be testifying, including any "preliminary" expert opinions. Protected "communications" include those between the party's attorney and assistants of the expert witness. The rule does not itself protect communications between counsel and other expert witnesses, such as those for whom disclosure is required under Rule 26(a)(2)(C). The rule does not exclude protection under other doctrines, such as privilege or independent development of the work-product doctrine.

The most frequent method for discovering the work of expert witnesses is by deposition, but Rules 26(b)(4)(B) and (C) apply to all forms of discovery.

Rules 26(b)(4)(B) and (C) do not impede discovery about the opinions to be offered by the expert or the development, foundation, or basis of those opinions. For example, the expert's testing of material involved in litigation, and notes of any such testing, would not be exempted from discovery by this rule. Similarly, inquiry about communications the expert had with anyone other than the party's counsel about the opinions expressed is unaffected by the rule. Counsel are also free to question expert witnesses about alternative analyses, testing methods, or approaches to the issues on which they are testifying, whether or not the expert considered them in forming the opinions expressed. These discovery changes therefore do not affect the gatekeeping functions called for by Daubert v. Merrell Dow Pharmaceuticals, Inc., 509 U.S. 579 (1993), and related cases.

The protection for communications between the retained expert and "the party's attorney" should be applied in a realistic manner, and often would not be limited to communications with a single lawyer or a single law firm. For example, a party may be involved in a number of suits about a given product or service, and may retain a particular expert witness to testify on that party's behalf in several of the cases. In such a situation, the protection applies to communications between the expert witness and the attorneys representing the party in any of those cases. Similarly, communications with in-house counsel for the party would often be regarded as protected even if the in-house attorney is not counsel of record in the action. Other situations may also justify a pragmatic application of the "party's attorney" concept.

Although attorney-expert communications are generally protected by Rule 26(b)(4)(C), the protection does not apply to the extent the lawyer and the expert communicate about matters that fall within three exceptions. But the discovery authorized by the exceptions does not extend beyond those specific topics. Lawyer-expert communications may cover many topics and, even when the excepted topics are included among those involved in a given communication, the protection applies to all other aspects of the communication beyond the excepted topics.

First, under Rule 26(b)(4)(C)(i) attorney-expert communications regarding compensation for the expert's study or testimony may be the subject of discovery. In some cases, this discovery may go beyond the disclosure requirement in Rule 26(a)(2)(B)(vi). It is not limited to compensation for work forming the opinions to be expressed, but extends to all compensation for the study and testimony provided in relation to the action. Any communications about additional benefits to the expert, such as further work in the event of a successful result in the present case, would be included. This exception includes compensation for work done by a person or organization associated with the expert. The objective is to permit full inquiry into such potential sources of bias.

Second, under Rule 26(b)(4)(C)(ii) discovery is permitted to identify facts or data the party's attorney provided to the expert and that the expert considered in forming the opinions to be expressed. The exception applies only to communications "identifying" the facts or data provided by counsel; further communications about the potential relevance of the facts or data are protected.

Third, under Rule 26(b)(4)(C)(iii) discovery regarding attorney-expert communications is permitted to identify any assumptions that counsel provided to the expert and that the expert relied upon in forming the opinions to be expressed. For example, the party's attorney may tell the expert to assume the truth of certain testimony or evidence, or the correctness of another expert's conclusions. This exception is limited to those assumptions that the expert actually did rely on in forming the opinions to be expressed. More general attorney-expert discussions about hypotheticals, or exploring possibilities based on hypothetical facts, are outside this exception.

Under the amended rule, discovery regarding attorney-expert communications on subjects outside the three exceptions in Rule 26(b)(4)(C), or regarding draft expert reports or disclosures, is permitted only in limited circumstances and by court order. A party seeking such discovery must make the showing specified in Rule 26(b)(3)(A)(ii)—that the party has a substantial need for the discovery and cannot obtain the substantial equivalent without undue hardship. It will be rare for a party to be able to make such a showing given the broad disclosure and discovery otherwise allowed regarding the expert's testimony. A party's failure to provide required disclosure or discovery does not show the need and hardship required by Rule 26(b)(3)(A); remedies are provided by Rule 37.

In the rare case in which a party does make this showing, the court must protect against disclosure of the attorney's mental impressions, conclusions, opinions, or legal theories under Rule 26(b)(3)(B). But this protection does not extend to the expert's own development of the opinions to be presented; those are subject to probing in deposition or at trial.

Former Rules 26(b)(4)(B) and (C) have been renumbered (D) and (E), and a slight revision has been made in (E) to take account of the renumbering of former (B).

Changes Made After Publication and Comment. Small changes to rule language were made to conform to style conventions. In addition, the protection for draft expert disclosures or reports in proposed Rule 26(b)(4)(B) was changed to read "regardless of the form in which the draft is recorded." Small changes were also made to the Committee Note to recognize this change to rule language and to address specific issues raised during the public comment period.

Committee Notes on Rules—2015 Amendment

Rule 26(b)(1) is changed in several ways.

Information is discoverable under revised Rule 26(b)(1) if it is relevant to any party's claim or defense and is proportional to the needs of the case. The considerations that bear on proportionality are moved from present Rule 26(b)(2)(C)(iii), slightly rearranged and with one addition.

Most of what now appears in Rule 26(b)(2)(C)(iii) was first adopted in 1983. The 1983 provision was explicitly adopted as part of the scope of discovery defined by Rule 26(b)(1). Rule 26(b)(1) directed the court to limit the frequency or extent of use of discovery if it determined that "the discovery is unduly burdensome or expensive, taking into account the needs of the case, the amount in controversy, limitations on the parties' resources, and the importance of the issues at stake in the litigation." At the same time, Rule 26(g) was added. Rule 26(g) provided that signing a discovery request, response, or objection certified that the request, response, or objection was "not unreasonable or unduly burdensome or expensive, given the needs of the case, the discovery already had in the case, the amount in controversy, and the importance of the issues at stake in the litigation." The parties thus shared the responsibility to honor these limits on the scope of discovery.

The 1983 Committee Note stated that the new provisions were added "to deal with the problem of over-discovery. The objective is to guard against redundant or disproportionate discovery by giving the court authority to reduce the amount of discovery that may be directed to matters that are otherwise proper subjects of inquiry. The new sentence is intended to encourage judges to be more aggressive in identifying and discouraging discovery overuse. The grounds mentioned in the amended rule for limiting discovery reflect the existing practice of many courts in issuing protective orders under Rule 26(c). . . . On the whole, however, district judges have been reluctant to limit the use of the discovery devices."

The clear focus of the 1983 provisions may have been softened, although inadvertently, by the amendments made in 1993. The 1993 Committee Note explained: "[F]ormer paragraph (b)(1) [was] subdivided into two paragraphs for ease of reference and to avoid renumbering of paragraphs (3) and (4)." Subdividing the paragraphs, however, was done in a way that could be read to separate the proportionality provisions as "limitations," no longer an integral part of the (b)(1) scope provisions. That appearance was immediately offset by the next statement in the Note: "Textual changes are then made in new paragraph (2) to enable the court to keep tighter rein on the extent of discovery."

The 1993 amendments added two factors to the considerations that bear on limiting discovery: whether "the burden or expense of the proposed discovery outweighs its likely benefit," and "the importance of the proposed discovery in resolving the issues." Addressing these and other limitations added by the 1993 discovery amendments, the Committee Note stated that "[t]he revisions in Rule 26(b)(2) are intended to provide the court with broader discretion to impose additional restrictions on the scope and extent of discovery. . . ."

The relationship between Rule 26(b)(1) and (2) was further addressed by an amendment made in 2000 that added a new sentence at the end of (b)(1): "All discovery is subject to the limitations imposed by Rule 26(b)(2)(i), (ii), and (iii) [now Rule 26(b)(2)(C)]." The Committee Note recognized that "[t]hese limitations apply to discovery that is otherwise within the scope of subdivision (b)(1)." It explained that the Committee had been told repeatedly that courts were not using these limitations as originally intended. "This otherwise redundant cross-reference has been added to emphasize the need for active judicial use of subdivision (b)(2) to control excessive discovery."

The present amendment restores the proportionality factors to their original place in defining the scope of discovery. This change reinforces the Rule 26(g) obligation of the parties to consider these factors in making discovery requests, responses, or objections.

Restoring the proportionality calculation to Rule 26(b)(1) does not change the existing responsibilities of the court and the parties to consider proportionality, and the change does not place on the party seeking discovery the burden of addressing all proportionality considerations.

Nor is the change intended to permit the opposing party to refuse discovery simply by making a boilerplate objection that it is not proportional. The parties and the court have a collective responsibility to consider the proportionality of all discovery and consider it in resolving discovery disputes.

The parties may begin discovery without a full appreciation of the factors that bear on proportionality. A party requesting discovery, for example, may have little information about the burden or expense of responding. A party requested to provide discovery may have little information about the importance of the discovery in resolving the issues as understood by the requesting party. Many of these uncertainties should be addressed and reduced in the parties' Rule 26(f) conference and in scheduling and pretrial conferences with the court. But if the parties continue to disagree, the discovery dispute could be brought before the court and the parties' responsibilities would remain as they have been since 1983. A party claiming undue burden or expense ordinarily has far better information—perhaps the only information—with respect to that part of the determination. A party claiming that a request is important to resolve the issues should be able to explain the ways in which the underlying information bears on the issues as that party understands them. The court's responsibility, using all the information provided by the parties, is to consider these and all the other factors in reaching a case-specific determination of the appropriate scope of discovery.

The direction to consider the parties' relative access to relevant information adds new text to provide explicit focus on considerations already implicit in present Rule 26(b)(2)(C)(iii). Some cases involve what often is called "information asymmetry." One party—often an individual plaintiff—may have very little discoverable information. The other party may have vast amounts of information, including information that can be readily retrieved and information that is more difficult to retrieve. In practice these circumstances often mean that the burden of responding to discovery lies heavier on the party who has more information, and properly so.

Restoring proportionality as an express component of the scope of discovery warrants repetition of parts of the 1983 and 1993 Committee Notes that must not be lost from sight. The 1983 Committee Note explained that "[t]he rule contemplates greater judicial involvement in the discovery process and thus acknowledges the reality that it cannot always operate on a self-regulating basis." The 1993 Committee Note further observed that "[t]he information explosion of recent decades has greatly increased both the potential cost of wide-ranging discovery and the potential for discovery to be used as an instrument for delay or oppression." What seemed an explosion in 1993 has been exacerbated by the advent of e-discovery. The present amendment again reflects the need for continuing and close judicial involvement in the cases that do not yield readily to the ideal of effective party management. It is expected that discovery will be effectively managed by the parties in many cases. But there will be important occasions for judicial management, both when the parties are legitimately unable to resolve important differences and when the parties fall short of effective, cooperative management on their own.

It also is important to repeat the caution that the monetary stakes are only one factor, to be balanced against other factors. The 1983 Committee Note recognized "the significance of the substantive issues, as measured in philosophic, social, or institutional terms. Thus the rule recognizes that many cases in public policy spheres, such as employment practices, free speech, and other matters, may have importance far beyond the monetary amount involved." Many other substantive areas also may involve litigation that seeks relatively small amounts of money, or no money at all, but that seeks to vindicate vitally important personal or public values.

So too, consideration of the parties' resources does not foreclose discovery requests addressed to an impecunious party, nor justify unlimited discovery requests addressed to a wealthy party. The 1983 Committee Note cautioned that "[t]he court must apply the standards in an even-handed manner that will prevent use of discovery to wage a war of attrition or as a device to coerce a party, whether financially weak or affluent."

The burden or expense of proposed discovery should be determined in a realistic way. This includes the burden or expense of producing electronically stored information. Computer-based methods of searching such information continue to develop, particularly for cases involving large volumes of electronically stored information. Courts and parties should be willing to consider the opportunities for reducing the burden or expense of discovery as reliable means of searching electronically stored information become available.

A portion of present Rule 26(b)(1) is omitted from the proposed revision. After allowing discovery of any matter relevant to any party's claim or defense, the present rule adds: "including the existence, description, nature, custody, condition, and location of any documents or other tangible things and the identity and location of persons who know of any discoverable matter." Discovery of such matters is so deeply entrenched in practice that it is no longer necessary to clutter the long text of Rule 26 with these examples. The discovery identified in these examples should still be permitted under the revised rule when relevant and proportional to the needs of the case. Framing intelligent requests for electronically stored information, for example, may require detailed information about another party's information systems and other information resources.

The amendment deletes the former provision authorizing the court, for good cause, to order discovery of any matter relevant to the subject matter involved in the action. The Committee has been informed that this language is rarely invoked. Proportional discovery relevant to any party's claim or defense suffices, given a proper understanding of what is relevant to a claim or defense. The distinction between matter relevant to a claim or defense and matter relevant to the subject matter was introduced in 2000. The 2000 Note offered three examples of information that, suitably focused, would be relevant to the parties' claims or defenses. The examples were "other incidents of the same type, or involving the same product"; "information about organizational arrangements or filing systems"; and "information that could be used to impeach a likely witness." Such discovery is not foreclosed by the amendments. Discovery that is relevant to the parties' claims or defenses may also support amendment of the pleadings to add a new claim or defense that affects the scope of discovery.

The former provision for discovery of relevant but inadmissible information that appears "reasonably calculated to lead to the discovery of admissible evidence" is also deleted. The phrase has been used by some, incorrectly, to define the scope of discovery. As the Committee Note to the 2000 amendments observed, use of the "reasonably calculated" phrase to define the scope of discovery "might swallow any other limitation on the scope of discovery." The 2000 amendments sought to prevent such misuse by adding the word "Relevant" at the beginning of the sentence, making clear that " 'relevant' means within the scope of discovery as defined in this subdivision . . . ." The "reasonably calculated" phrase has continued to create problems, however, and is removed by these amendments. It is replaced by the direct statement that "Information within this scope of discovery need not be admissible in evidence to be discoverable." Discovery of nonprivileged information not admissible in evidence remains available so long as it is otherwise within the scope of discovery.

Rule 26(b)(2)(C)(iii) is amended to reflect the transfer of the considerations that bear on proportionality to Rule 26(b)(1). The court still must limit the frequency or extent of proposed discovery, on motion or on its own, if it is outside the scope permitted by Rule 26(b)(1).

Rule 26(c)(1)(B) is amended to include an express recognition of protective orders that allocate expenses for disclosure or discovery. Authority to enter such orders is included in the present rule, and courts already exercise this authority. Explicit recognition will forestall the temptation some parties may feel to contest this authority. Recognizing the authority does not imply that cost-shifting should become a common practice. Courts and parties should continue to assume that a responding party ordinarily bears the costs of responding.

Rule 26(d)(2) is added to allow a party to deliver Rule 34 requests to another party more than 21 days after that party has been served even though the parties have not yet had a required Rule 26(f) conference. Delivery may be made by any party to the party that has been served, and by that party to any plaintiff and any other party that has been served. Delivery does not count as service; the requests are considered to be served at the first Rule 26(f) conference. Under Rule 34(b)(2)(A) the time to respond runs from service. This relaxation of the discovery moratorium is designed to facilitate focused discussion during the Rule 26(f) conference. Discussion at the conference may produce changes in the requests. The opportunity for advance scrutiny of requests delivered before the Rule 26(f) conference should not affect a decision whether to allow additional time to respond.

Rule 26(d)(3) is renumbered and amended to recognize that the parties may stipulate to case-specific sequences of discovery.

Rule 26(f)(3) is amended in parallel with Rule 16(b)(3) to add two items to the discovery plan—issues about preserving electronically stored information and court orders under Evidence Rule 502.

References in Text

1 In response to concerns about the proposal raised at the June 15–16, 2005, Standing Committee meeting, the Committee Note was revised to emphasize that the courts will continue to examine whether a privilege claim was made at a reasonable time, as part of substantive law.

Rule 27. Depositions to Perpetuate Testimony

(a) Before an Action Is Filed.

(1) Petition. A person who wants to perpetuate testimony about any matter cognizable in a United States court may file a verified petition in the district court for the district where any expected adverse party resides. The petition must ask for an order authorizing the petitioner to depose the named persons in order to perpetuate their testimony. The petition must be titled in the petitioner's name and must show:

(A) that the petitioner expects to be a party to an action cognizable in a United States court but cannot presently bring it or cause it to be brought;

(B) the subject matter of the expected action and the petitioner's interest;

(C) the facts that the petitioner wants to establish by the proposed testimony and the reasons to perpetuate it;

(D) the names or a description of the persons whom the petitioner expects to be adverse parties and their addresses, so far as known; and

(E) the name, address, and expected substance of the testimony of each deponent.

(2) Notice and Service. At least 21 days before the hearing date, the petitioner must serve each expected adverse party with a copy of the petition and a notice stating the time and place of the hearing. The notice may be served either inside or outside the district or state in the manner provided in Rule 4. If that service cannot be made with reasonable diligence on an expected adverse party, the court may order service by publication or otherwise. The court must appoint an attorney to represent persons not served in the manner provided in Rule 4 and to cross-examine the deponent if an unserved person is not otherwise represented. If any expected adverse party is a minor or is incompetent, Rule 17(c) applies.

(3) Order and Examination. If satisfied that perpetuating the testimony may prevent a failure or delay of justice, the court must issue an order that designates or describes the persons whose depositions may be taken, specifies the subject matter of the examinations, and states whether the depositions will be taken orally or by written interrogatories. The depositions may then be taken under these rules, and the court may issue orders like those authorized by Rules 34 and 35. A reference in these rules to the court where an action is pending means, for purposes of this rule, the court where the petition for the deposition was filed.

(4) Using the Deposition. A deposition to perpetuate testimony may be used under Rule 32(a) in any later-filed district-court action involving the same subject matter if the deposition either was taken under these rules or, although not so taken, would be admissible in evidence in the courts of the state where it was taken.

(b) Pending Appeal.

(1) In General. The court where a judgment has been rendered may, if an appeal has been taken or may still be taken, permit a party to depose witnesses to perpetuate their testimony for use in the event of further proceedings in that court.

(2) Motion. The party who wants to perpetuate testimony may move for leave to take the depositions, on the same notice and service as if the action were pending in the district court. The motion must show:

(A) the name, address, and expected substance of the testimony of each deponent; and

(B) the reasons for perpetuating the testimony.

(3) Court Order. If the court finds that perpetuating the testimony may prevent a failure or delay of justice, the court may permit the depositions to be taken and may issue orders like those authorized by Rules 34 and 35. The depositions may be taken and used as any other deposition taken in a pending district-court action.

(c) Perpetuation by an Action. This rule does not limit a court's power to entertain an action to perpetuate testimony.

———

(As amended Dec. 27, 1946, eff. Mar. 19, 1948; Dec. 29, 1948, eff. Oct. 20, 1949; Mar. 1, 1971, eff. July 1, 1971; Mar. 2, 1987, eff. Aug. 1, 1987; Apr. 25, 2005, eff. Dec. 1, 2005; Apr. 30, 2007, eff. Dec. 1, 2007; Mar. 26, 2009, eff. Dec. 1, 2009.)

Notes of Advisory Committee on Rules—1937

Note to Subdivision (a). This rule offers a simple method of perpetuating testimony in cases where it is usually allowed under equity practice or under modern statutes. See Arizona v. California, 292 U.S. 341 (1934); Todd Engineering Dry Dock and Repair Co. v. United States, 32 F.(2d) 734 (C.C.A.5th, 1929); Hall v. Stout, 4 Del. ch. 269 (1871). For comparable state statutes see Ark.Civ.Code (Crawford, 1934) §§666–670; Calif.Code Civ.Proc. (Deering, 1937) 2083–2089; Ill.Rev.Stat. (1937) ch. 51, §§39–46; Iowa Code (1935) §§11400–11407; 2 Mass.Gen.Laws (Ter.Ed., 1932) ch. 233, §46–63; N.Y.C.P.A. (1937) §295; Ohio Gen.Code Ann. ((Throckmorton, 1936) §12216–12222; Va.Code Ann. (Michie, 1936) §6235; Wisc.Stat. (1935) §§326.27–326.29. The appointment of an attorney to represent absent parties or parties not personally notified, or a guardian ad litem to represent minors and incompetents, is provided for in several of the above statutes.

Note to Subdivision (b). This follows the practice approved in Richter v. Union Trust Co., 115 U.S. 55 (1885), by extending the right to perpetuate testimony to cases pending an appeal.

Note to Subdivision (c). This preserves the right to employ a separate action to perpetuate testimony under U.S.C., Title 28, [former] §644 (Depositions under dedimus potestatem and in perpetuam) as an alternate method.

Notes of Advisory Committee on Rules—1946 Amendment

Since the second sentence in subdivision (a)(3) refers only to depositions, it is arguable that Rules 34 and 35 are inapplicable in proceedings to perpetuate testimony. The new matter [in subdivisions (a)(3) and (b)] clarifies. A conforming change is also made in subdivision (b).

Notes of Advisory Committee on Rules—1948 Amendment

The only changes are in nomenclature to conform to the official designation of a district court in Title 28, U.S.C., §132(a).

Notes of Advisory Committee on Rules—1971 Amendment

The reference intended in this subdivision is to the rule governing the use of depositions in court proceedings. Formerly Rule 26(d), that rule is now Rule 32(a). The subdivision is amended accordingly.

Notes of Advisory Committee on Rules—1987 Amendment

The amendments are technical. No substantive change is intended.

Committee Notes on Rules—2005 Amendment

The outdated cross-reference to former Rule 4(d) is corrected to incorporate all Rule 4 methods of service. Former Rule 4(d) has been allocated to many different subdivisions of Rule 4. Former Rule 4(d) did not cover all categories of defendants or modes of service, and present Rule 4 reaches further than all of former Rule 4. But there is no reason to distinguish between the different categories of defendants and modes of service encompassed by Rule 4. Rule 4 service provides effective notice. Notice by such means should be provided to any expected adverse party that comes within Rule 4.

Other changes are made to conform Rule 27(a)(2) to current style conventions.

Changes Made After Publication and Comment. Only style changes are recommended in the published draft.

Committee Notes on Rules—2007 Amendment

The language of Rule 27 has been amended as part of the general restyling of the Civil Rules to make them more easily understood and to make style and terminology consistent throughout the rules. These changes are intended to be stylistic only.

Committee Notes on Rules—2009 Amendment

The time set in the former rule at 20 days has been revised to 21 days. See the Note to Rule 6.

Rule 28. Persons Before Whom Depositions May Be Taken

(a) Within the United States.

(1) In General. Within the United States or a territory or insular possession subject to United States jurisdiction, a deposition must be taken before:

(A) an officer authorized to administer oaths either by federal law or by the law in the place of examination; or

(B) a person appointed by the court where the action is pending to administer oaths and take testimony.

(2) Definition of "Officer." The term "officer" in Rules 30, 31, and 32 includes a person appointed by the court under this rule or designated by the parties under Rule 29(a).

(b) In a Foreign Country.

(1) In General. A deposition may be taken in a foreign country:

(A) under an applicable treaty or convention;

(B) under a letter of request, whether or not captioned a "letter rogatory";

(C) on notice, before a person authorized to administer oaths either by federal law or by the law in the place of examination; or

(D) before a person commissioned by the court to administer any necessary oath and take testimony.

(2) Issuing a Letter of Request or a Commission. A letter of request, a commission, or both may be issued:

(A) on appropriate terms after an application and notice of it; and

(B) without a showing that taking the deposition in another manner is impracticable or inconvenient.

(3) Form of a Request, Notice, or Commission. When a letter of request or any other device is used according to a treaty or convention, it must be captioned in the form prescribed by that treaty or convention. A letter of request may be addressed "To the Appropriate Authority in [name of country]." A deposition notice or a commission must designate by name or descriptive title the person before whom the deposition is to be taken.

(4) Letter of Request—Admitting Evidence. Evidence obtained in response to a letter of request need not be excluded merely because it is not a verbatim transcript, because the testimony was not taken under oath, or because of any similar departure from the requirements for depositions taken within the United States.

(c) Disqualification. A deposition must not be taken before a person who is any party's relative, employee, or attorney; who is related to or employed by any party's attorney; or who is financially interested in the action.

(As amended Dec. 27, 1946, eff. Mar. 19, 1948; Jan. 21, 1963, eff. July 1, 1963; Apr. 29, 1980, eff. Aug. 1, 1980; Mar. 2, 1987, eff. Aug. 1, 1987; Apr. 22, 1993, eff. Dec. 1, 1993; Apr. 1, 2007, eff. Dec. 1, 2007.)

Notes of Advisory Committee on Rules—1937

In effect this rule is substantially the same as U.S.C., Title 28, [former] §639 (Depositions de bene esse; when and where taken; notice). U.S.C., Title 28, [former] §642 (Depositions, acknowledgements, and affidavits taken by notaries public) does not conflict with subdivision (a).

Notes of Advisory Committee on Rules—1946 Amendment

The added language [in subdivision (a)] provides for the situation, occasionally arising, when depositions must be taken in an isolated place where there is no one readily available who has the power to administer oaths and take testimony according to the terms of the rule as originally stated. In addition, the amendment affords a more convenient method of securing depositions in the case where state lines intervene between the location of various witnesses otherwise rather closely grouped. The amendment insures that the person appointed shall have adequate power to perform his duties. It has been held that a person authorized to act in the premises, as, for example, a master, may take testimony outside the district of his appointment. Consolidated Fastener Co. v. Columbian Button & Fastener Co. (C.C.N.D.N.Y. 1898) 85 Fed. 54; Mathieson Alkali Works v. Arnold, Hoffman & Co. (C.C.A.1st, 1929) 31 F.(2d) 1.

Notes of Advisory Committee on Rules—1963 Amendment

The amendment of clause (1) is designed to facilitate depositions in foreign countries by enlarging the class of persons before whom the depositions may be taken on notice. The class is no longer confined, as at present, to a secretary of embassy or legation, consul general, consul, vice consul, or consular agent of the United States. In a country that regards the taking of testimony by a foreign official in aid of litigation pending in a court of another country as an infringement upon its sovereignty, it will be expedient to notice depositions before officers of the country in which the examination is taken. See generally Symposium, Letters Rogatory (Grossman ed. 1956); Doyle, Taking Evidence by Deposition and Letters Rogatory and Obtaining Documents in Foreign Territory, Proc. A.B.A., Sec. Int'l & Comp. L. 37 (1959); Heilpern, Procuring Evidence Abroad, 14 Tul.L.Rev. 29 (1939); Jones, International Judicial Assistance: Procedural Chaos and a Program for Reform, 62 Yale L.J. 515, 526–29 (1953); Smit, International Aspects of Federal Civil Procedure, 61 Colum.L.Rev. 1031, 1056–58 (1961).

Clause (2) of amended subdivision (b), like the corresponding provision of subdivision (a) dealing with depositions taken in the United States, makes it clear that the appointment of a person by commission in itself confers power upon him to administer any necessary oath.

It has been held that a letter rogatory will not be issued unless the use of a notice or commission is shown to be impossible or impractical. See, e.g., United States v. Matles, 154 F.Supp. 574 (E.D.N.Y. 1957); The Edmund Fanning, 89 F.Supp. 282 (E.D.N.Y. 1950); Branyan v. Koninklijke Luchtvaart Maatschappij, 13 F.R.D. 425 (S.D.N.Y. 1953). See also Ali Akber Kiachif v. Philco International Corp., 10 F.R.D. 277 (S.D.N.Y. 1950). The intent of the fourth sentence of the amended subdivision is to overcome this judicial antipathy and to permit a sound choice between depositions under a letter rogatory and on notice or by commission in the light of all the circumstances. In a case in which the foreign country will compel a witness to attend or testify in aid of a letter rogatory but not in aid of a commission, a letter rogatory may be preferred on the ground that it is less expensive to execute, even if there is plainly no need for compulsive process. A letter rogatory may also be preferred when it cannot be demonstrated that a witness will be recalcitrant or when the witness states that he is willing to testify voluntarily, but the contingency exists that he will change his mind at the last moment. In the latter case, it may be advisable to issue both a commission and a letter rogatory, the latter to be executed if the former fails. The choice between a letter rogatory and a commission may be conditioned by other factors, including the nature and extent of the assistance that the foreign country will give to the execution of either.

In executing a letter rogatory the courts of other countries may be expected to follow their customary procedure for taking testimony. See United States v. Paraffin Wax, 2255 Bags, 23 F.R.D. 289 (E.D.N.Y. 1959). In many non-common-law countries the judge questions the witness, sometimes without first administering an oath, the attorneys put any supplemental questions either to the witness or through the judge, and the judge dictates a summary of the testimony, which the witness acknowledges as correct. See Jones, supra, at 530–32; Doyle, supra, at 39–41. The last sentence of the amended subdivision provides, contrary to the implications of some authority, that evidence recorded in such a fashion need not be excluded on that account. See The Mandu, 11 F.Supp. 845 (E.D.N.Y. 1935). But cf. Nelson v. United States, 17 Fed.Cas. 1340 (No. 10,116) (C.C.D.Pa. 1816); Winthrop v. Union Ins. Co., 30 Fed.Cas. 376 (No. 17901) (C.C.D.Pa. 1807). The specific reference to the lack of an oath or a verbatim transcript is intended to be illustrative. Whether or to what degree the value or weight of the evidence may be affected by the method of taking or recording the testimony is left for determination according to the circumstances of the particular case, cf. Uebersee Finanz-Korporation, A.G. v. Brownell, 121 F.Supp. 420 (D.D.C. 1954); Danisch v. Guardian Life Ins. Co., 19 F.R.D. 235 (S.D.N.Y. 1956); the testimony may indeed be so devoid of substance or probative value as to warrant its exclusion altogether.

Some foreign countries are hostile to allowing a deposition to be taken in their country, especially by notice or commission, or to lending assistance in the taking of a deposition. Thus compliance with the terms of amended subdivision (b) may not in all cases ensure completion of a deposition abroad. Examination of the law and policy of the particular foreign country in advance of attempting a deposition is therefore advisable. See 4 Moore's Federal Practice 28.05–28.08 (2d ed. 1950).

Notes of Advisory Committee on Rules—1980 Amendment

The amendments are clarifying.

Notes of Advisory Committee on Rules—1987 Amendment

The amendments are technical. No substantive change is intended.

Notes of Advisory Committee on Rules—1993 Amendment

This revision is intended to make effective use of the Hague Convention on the Taking of Evidence Abroad in Civil or Commercial Matters, and of any similar treaties that the United States may enter into in the future which provide procedures for taking depositions abroad. The party taking the deposition is ordinarily obliged to conform to an applicable treaty or convention if an effective deposition can be taken by such internationally approved means, even though a verbatim transcript is not available or testimony cannot be taken under oath. For a discussion of the impact of such treaties upon the discovery process, and of the application of principles of comity upon discovery in countries not signatories to a convention, see Société Nationale Industrielle Aérospatiale v. United States District Court, 482 U.S. 522 (1987).

The term "letter of request" has been substituted in the rule for the term "letter rogatory" because it is the primary method provided by the Hague Convention. A letter rogatory is essentially a form of letter of request. There are several other minor changes that are designed merely to carry out the intent of the other alterations.

Committee Notes on Rules—2007 Amendment

The language of Rule 28 has been amended as part of the general restyling of the Civil Rules to make them more easily understood and to make style and terminology consistent throughout the rules. These changes are intended to be stylistic only.

Rule 29. Stipulations About Discovery Procedure

Unless the court orders otherwise, the parties may stipulate that:

(a) a deposition may be taken before any person, at any time or place, on any notice, and in the manner specified—in which event it may be used in the same way as any other deposition; and

(b) other procedures governing or limiting discovery be modified—but a stipulation extending the time for any form of discovery must have court approval if it would interfere with the time set for completing discovery, for hearing a motion, or for trial.

(As amended Mar. 30, 1970, eff. July 1, 1970; Apr. 22, 1993, eff. Dec. 1, 1993; Apr. 30, 2007, eff. Dec. 1, 2007.)

Notes of Advisory Committee on Rules—1970 Amendment

There is no provision for stipulations varying the procedures by which methods of discovery other than depositions are governed. It is common practice for parties to agree on such variations, and the amendment recognizes such agreements and provides a formal mechanism in the rules for giving them effect. Any stipulation varying the procedures may be superseded by court order, and stipulations extending the time for response to discovery under Rules 33, 34, and 36 require court approval.

Notes of Advisory Committee on Rules—1993 Amendment

This rule is revised to give greater opportunity for litigants to agree upon modifications to the procedures governing discovery or to limitations upon discovery. Counsel are encouraged to agree on less expensive and time-consuming methods to obtain information, as through voluntary exchange of documents, use of interviews in lieu of depositions, etc. Likewise, when more depositions or interrogatories are needed than allowed under these rules or when more time is needed to complete a deposition than allowed under a local rule, they can, by agreeing to the additional discovery, eliminate the need for a special motion addressed to the court.

Under the revised rule, the litigants ordinarily are not required to obtain the court's approval of these stipulations. By order or local rule, the court can, however, direct that its approval be obtained for particular types of stipulations; and, in any event, approval must be obtained if a stipulation to extend the 30-day period for responding to interrogatories, requests for production, or requests for admissions would interfere with dates set by the court for completing discovery, for hearing of a motion, or for trial.

Committee Notes on Rules—2007 Amendment

The language of Rule 29 has been amended as part of the general restyling of the Civil Rules to make them more easily understood and to make style and terminology consistent throughout the rules. These changes are intended to be stylistic only.

Rule 30. Depositions by Oral Examination

(a) When a Deposition May Be Taken.

(1) Without Leave. A party may, by oral questions, depose any person, including a party, without leave of court except as provided in Rule 30(a)(2). The deponent's attendance may be compelled by subpoena under Rule 45.

(2) With Leave. A party must obtain leave of court, and the court must grant leave to the extent consistent with Rule 26(b)(1) and (2):

(A) if the parties have not stipulated to the deposition and:

(i) the deposition would result in more than 10 depositions being taken under this rule or Rule 31 by the plaintiffs, or by the defendants, or by the third-party defendants;

(ii) the deponent has already been deposed in the case; or

(iii) the party seeks to take the deposition before the time specified in Rule 26(d), unless the party certifies in the notice, with supporting facts, that the deponent is expected to leave the United States and be unavailable for examination in this country after that time; or

(B) if the deponent is confined in prison.

(b) Notice of the Deposition; Other Formal Requirements.

(1) Notice in General. A party who wants to depose a person by oral questions must give reasonable written notice to every other party. The notice must state the time and place of the deposition and, if known, the deponent's name and address. If the name is unknown, the notice must provide a general description sufficient to identify the person or the particular class or group to which the person belongs.

(2) Producing Documents. If a subpoena duces tecum is to be served on the deponent, the materials designated for production, as set out in the subpoena, must be listed in the notice or in an attachment. The notice to a party deponent may be accompanied by a request under Rule 34 to produce documents and tangible things at the deposition.

(3) Method of Recording.

(A) Method Stated in the Notice. The party who notices the deposition must state in the notice the method for recording the testimony. Unless the court orders otherwise, testimony may be recorded by audio, audiovisual, or stenographic means. The noticing party bears the recording costs. Any party may arrange to transcribe a deposition.

(B) Additional Method. With prior notice to the deponent and other parties, any party may designate another method for recording the testimony in addition to that specified in the original notice. That party bears the expense of the additional record or transcript unless the court orders otherwise.

(4) By Remote Means. The parties may stipulate—or the court may on motion order—that a deposition be taken by telephone or other remote means. For the purpose of this rule and Rules 28(a), 37(a)(2), and 37(b)(1), the deposition takes place where the deponent answers the questions.

(5) Officer's Duties.

(A) Before the Deposition. Unless the parties stipulate otherwise, a deposition must be conducted before an officer appointed or designated under Rule 28. The officer must begin the deposition with an on-the-record statement that includes:

(i) the officer's name and business address;

(ii) the date, time, and place of the deposition;

(iii) the deponent's name;

(iv) the officer's administration of the oath or affirmation to the deponent; and

(v) the identity of all persons present.

(B) Conducting the Deposition; Avoiding Distortion. If the deposition is recorded nonstenographically, the officer must repeat the items in Rule 30(b)(5)(A)(i)–(iii) at the beginning of each unit of the recording medium. The deponent's and attorneys' appearance or demeanor must not be distorted through recording techniques.

(C) After the Deposition. At the end of a deposition, the officer must state on the record that the deposition is complete and must set out any stipulations made by the attorneys about custody of the transcript or recording and of the exhibits, or about any other pertinent matters.

(6) Notice or Subpoena Directed to an Organization. In its notice or subpoena, a party may name as the deponent a public or private corporation, a partnership, an association, a governmental agency, or other entity and must describe with reasonable particularity the matters for examination. The named organization must then designate one or more officers, directors, or managing agents, or designate other persons who consent to testify on its behalf; and it may set out the matters on which each person designated will testify. A subpoena must advise a nonparty organization of its duty to make this designation. The persons designated must testify about information known or reasonably available to the organization. This paragraph (6) does not preclude a

deposition by any other procedure allowed by these rules.

(c) Examination and Cross-Examination; Record of the Examination; Objections; Written Questions.

(1) Examination and Cross-Examination. The examination and cross-examination of a deponent proceed as they would at trial under the Federal Rules of Evidence, except Rules 103 and 615. After putting the deponent under oath or affirmation, the officer must record the testimony by the method designated under Rule 30(b)(3)(A). The testimony must be recorded by the officer personally or by a person acting in the presence and under the direction of the officer.

(2) Objections. An objection at the time of the examination—whether to evidence, to a party's conduct, to the officer's qualifications, to the manner of taking the deposition, or to any other aspect of the deposition—must be noted on the record, but the examination still proceeds; the testimony is taken subject to any objection. An objection must be stated concisely in a nonargumentative and nonsuggestive manner. A person may instruct a deponent not to answer only when necessary to preserve a privilege, to enforce a limitation ordered by the court, or to present a motion under Rule 30(d)(3).

(3) Participating Through Written Questions. Instead of participating in the oral examination, a party may serve written questions in a sealed envelope on the party noticing the deposition, who must deliver them to the officer. The officer must ask the deponent those questions and record the answers verbatim.

(d) Duration; Sanction; Motion to Terminate or Limit.

(1) Duration. Unless otherwise stipulated or ordered by the court, a deposition is limited to one day of 7 hours. The court must allow additional time consistent with Rule 26(b)(1) and (2) if needed to fairly examine the deponent or if the deponent, another person, or any other circumstance impedes or delays the examination.

(2) Sanction. The court may impose an appropriate sanction—including the reasonable expenses and attorney's fees incurred by any party—on a person who impedes, delays, or frustrates the fair examination of the deponent.

(3) Motion to Terminate or Limit.

(A) Grounds. At any time during a deposition, the deponent or a party may move to terminate or limit it on the ground that it is being conducted in bad faith or in a manner that unreasonably annoys, embarrasses, or oppresses the deponent or party. The motion may be filed in the court where the action is pending or the deposition is being taken. If the objecting deponent or party so demands, the deposition must be suspended for the time necessary to obtain an order.

(B) Order. The court may order that the deposition be terminated or may limit its scope and manner as provided in Rule 26(c). If terminated, the deposition may be resumed only by order of the court where the action is pending.

(C) Award of Expenses. Rule 37(a)(5) applies to the award of expenses.

(e) Review by the Witness; Changes.

(1) Review; Statement of Changes. On request by the deponent or a party before the deposition is completed, the deponent must be allowed 30 days after being notified by the officer that the transcript or recording is available in which:

(A) to review the transcript or recording; and

(B) if there are changes in form or substance, to sign a statement listing the changes and the reasons for making them.

(2) Changes Indicated in the Officer's Certificate. The officer must note in the certificate prescribed by Rule 30(f)(1) whether a review was requested and, if so, must attach any changes the deponent makes during the 30-day period.

(f) Certification and Delivery; Exhibits; Copies of the Transcript or Recording; Filing.

(1) Certification and Delivery. The officer must certify in writing that the witness was duly sworn and that the deposition accurately records the witness's testimony. The certificate must accompany the record of the deposition. Unless the court orders otherwise, the officer must seal the deposition in an envelope or package bearing the title of the action and marked "Deposition of [witness's name]" and must promptly send it to the attorney who arranged for the transcript or recording. The attorney must store it under conditions that will protect it against loss, destruction, tampering, or deterioration.

(2) Documents and Tangible Things.

(A) Originals and Copies. Documents and tangible things produced for inspection during a deposition must, on a party's request, be marked for identification and attached to the deposition. Any party may inspect and copy them. But if the person who produced them wants to keep the originals, the person may:

(i) offer copies to be marked, attached to the deposition, and then used as originals—after giving all parties a fair opportunity to verify the copies by comparing them with the originals; or

(ii) give all parties a fair opportunity to inspect and copy the originals after they are marked—in which event the originals may be used as if attached to the deposition.

(B) Order Regarding the Originals. Any party may move for an order that the originals be attached to the deposition pending final disposition of the case.

(3) Copies of the Transcript or Recording. Unless otherwise stipulated or ordered by the court, the officer must retain the stenographic notes of a deposition taken stenographically or a copy of the recording of a deposition taken by another method. When paid reasonable charges, the officer must furnish a copy of the transcript or recording to any party or the deponent.

(4) Notice of Filing. A party who files the deposition must promptly notify all other parties of the filing.

(g) Failure to Attend a Deposition or Serve a Subpoena; Expenses. A party who, expecting a deposition to be taken, attends in person or by an attorney may recover reasonable expenses for attending, including attorney's fees, if the noticing party failed to:

(1) attend and proceed with the deposition; or

(2) serve a subpoena on a nonparty deponent, who consequently did not attend.

(As amended Jan. 21, 1963, eff. July 1, 1963; Mar. 30, 1970, eff. July 1, 1970; Mar. 1, 1971, eff. July 1, 1971; Nov. 20, 1972, eff. July 1, 1975; Apr. 29, 1980, eff. Aug. 1, 1980; Mar. 2, 1987, eff. Aug. 1, 1987; Apr. 22, 1993, eff. Dec. 1, 1993; Apr. 17, 2000, eff. Dec. 1, 2000; Apr. 30, 2007, eff. Dec. 1, 2007; Apr. 29, 2015, eff. Dec. 1, 2015.)

Notes of Advisory Committee on Rules—1937

Note to Subdivision (a). This is in accordance with common practice. See U.S.C., Title 28, [former] §639 (Depositions de bene esse; when and where taken; notice), the relevant provisions of which are incorporated in this rule; Calif.Code Civ.Proc. (Deering, 1937) §2031; and statutes cited in respect to notice in the Note to Rule 26(a). The provision for enlarging or shortening the time of notice has been added to give flexibility to the rule.

Note to Subdivisions (b) and (d). These are introduced as a safeguard for the protection of parties and deponents on account of the unlimited right of discovery given by Rule 26.

Note to Subdivisions (c) and (e). These follow the general plan of [former] Equity Rule 51 (Evidence Taken Before Examiners, Etc.) and U. S. C., Title 28, [former] §§640 (Depositions de bene esse; mode of taking), and [former] 641 (Same; transmission to court), but are more specific. They also permit the deponent to require the officer to make changes in the deposition if the deponent is not satisfied with it. See also [former] Equity Rule 50 (Stenographer–Appointment–Fees).

Note to Subdivision (f). Compare [former] Equity Rule 55 (Depositions Deemed Published When Filed).

Note to Subdivision (g). This is similar to 2 Minn. Stat. (Mason, 1927) §9833, but is more extensive.

Notes of Advisory Committee on Rules—1963 Amendment

This amendment corresponds to the change in Rule 4(d)(4). See the Advisory Committee's Note to that amendment.

Notes of Advisory Committee on Rules—1970 Amendment

Subdivision (a). This subdivision contains the provisions of existing Rule 26(a), transferred here as part of the rearrangement relating to Rule 26. Existing Rule 30(a) is transferred to 30(b). Changes in language have been made to conform to the new arrangement.

This subdivision is further revised in regard to the requirement of leave of court for taking a deposition. The present procedure, requiring a plaintiff to obtain leave of court if he serves notice of taking a deposition within 20 days after commencement of the action, is changed in several respects. First, leave is required by reference to the time the deposition is to be taken rather than the date of serving notice of taking. Second, the 20-day period is extended to 30 days and runs from the service of summons and complaint on any defendant, rather than the commencement of the action. Cf. Ill. S.Ct.R. 19–1, S–H Ill.Ann.Stat. §101.19–1. Third, leave is not required beyond the time that defendant initiates discovery, thus showing that he has retained counsel. As under the present practice, a party not afforded a reasonable opportunity to appear at a deposition, because he has not yet been served with process, is protected against use of the deposition at trial against him. See Rule 32(a), transferred from 26(d). Moreover, he can later redepose the witness if he so desires.

The purpose of requiring the plaintiff to obtain leave of court is, as stated by the Advisory Committee that proposed the present language of Rule 26(a), to protect "a defendant who has not had an opportunity to retain counsel and inform himself as to the nature of the suit." Note to 1948 amendment of Rule 26(a), quoted in 3A Barron & Holtzoff, Federal Practice and Procedure 455–456 (Wright ed. 1958). In order to assure defendant of this opportunity, the period is lengthened to 30 days. This protection, however, is relevant to the time of taking the deposition, not to the time that notice is served. Similarly, the protective period should run from the service of process rather than the filing of the complaint with the court. As stated in the note to Rule 26(d), the courts have used the service of notice as a convenient reference point for assigning priority in taking depositions, but with the elimination of priority in new Rule 26(d) the reference point is no longer needed. The new procedure is consistent in principle with the provisions of Rules 33, 34, and 36 as revised.

Plaintiff is excused from obtaining leave even during the initial 30-day period if he gives the special notice provided in subdivision (b)(2). The required notice must state that the person to be examined is about to go out of the district where the action is pending and more than 100 miles from the place of trial, or out of the United States, or on a voyage to sea, and will be unavailable for examination unless deposed within the 30-day period. These events occur most often in maritime litigation, when seamen are transferred from one port to another or are about to go to sea. Yet, there are analogous situations in nonmaritime litigation, and although the maritime problems are more common, a rule limited to claims in the admiralty and maritime jurisdiction is not justified.

In the recent unification of the civil and admiralty rules, this problem was temporarily met through addition in Rule 26(a) of a provision that depositions de bene esse may continue to be taken as to admiralty and maritime claims within the meaning of Rule 9(h). It was recognized at the time that "a uniform rule applicable alike to what are now civil actions and suits in admiralty" was clearly preferable, but the de bene esse procedure was adopted "for the time being at least." See Advisory Committee's note in Report of the Judicial Conference: Proposed Amendments to Rules of Civil Procedure 43–44 (1966).

The changes in Rule 30(a) and the new Rule 30(b)(2) provide a formula applicable to ordinary civil as well as maritime claims. They replace the provision for depositions de bene esse. They authorize an early deposition without leave of court where the witness is about to depart and, unless his deposition is promptly taken, (1) it will be impossible or very difficult to depose him before trial or (2) his deposition can later be taken but only with substantially increased effort and expense. Cf. S.S. Hai Chang, 1966 A.M.C. 2239 (S.D.N.Y. 1966), in which the deposing party is required to prepay expenses and counsel fees of the other party's lawyer when the action is pending in New York and depositions are to be taken on the West Coast. Defendant is protected by a provision that the deposition cannot be used against him if he was unable through exercise of diligence to obtain counsel to represent him.

The distance of 100 miles from place of trial is derived from the de bene esse provision and also conforms to the reach of a subpoena of the trial court, as provided in Rule 45(e). See also S.D.N.Y. Civ.R. 5(a). Some parts of the de bene esse provision are omitted from Rule 30(b)(2). Modern deposition practice adequately covers the witness who lives more than 100 miles away from place of trial. If a witness is aged or infirm, leave of court can be obtained.

Subdivision (b). Existing Rule 30(b) on protective orders has been transferred to Rule 26(c), and existing Rule 30(a) relating to the notice of taking deposition has been transferred to this subdivision. Because new material has been added, subsection numbers have been inserted.

Subdivision (b)(1). If a subpoena duces tecum is to be served, a copy thereof or a designation of the materials to be produced must accompany the notice. Each party is thereby enabled to prepare for the deposition more effectively.

Subdivision (b)(2). This subdivision is discussed in the note to subdivision (a), to which it relates.

Subdivision (b)(3). This provision is derived from existing Rule 30(a), with a minor change of language.

Subdivision (b)(4). In order to facilitate less expensive procedures, provision is made for the recording of testimony by other than stenographic means—e.g., by mechanical, electronic, or photographic means. Because these methods give rise to problems of accuracy and trustworthiness, the party taking the deposition is required to apply for a court order. The order is to specify how the testimony is to be recorded, preserved, and filed, and it may contain whatever additional safeguards the court deems necessary.

Subdivision (b)(5). A provision is added to enable a party, through service of notice, to require another party to produce documents or things at the taking of his deposition. This may now be done as to a nonparty deponent through use of a subpoena duces tecum as authorized by Rule 45, but some courts have held that documents may be secured from a party only under Rule 34. See 2A Barron & Holtzoff, Federal Practice and Procedure §644.1 n. 83.2, §792 n. 16 (Wright ed. 1961). With the elimination of "good cause" from Rule 34, the reason for this restrictive doctrine has disappeared. Cf. N.Y.C.P.L.R. §3111.

Whether production of documents or things should be obtained directly under Rule 34 or at the deposition under this rule will depend on the nature and volume of the documents or things. Both methods are made available. When the documents are few and simple, and closely related to the oral examination, ability to proceed via this rule will facilitate discovery. If the discovering party insists on examining many and complex documents at the taking of the deposition, thereby causing undue burdens on others, the latter may, under Rules 26(c) or 30(d), apply for a court order that the examining party proceed via Rule 34 alone.

Subdivision (b)(6). A new provision is added, whereby a party may name a corporation, partnership, association, or governmental agency as the deponent and designate the matters on which he requests examination, and the organization shall then name one or more of its officers, directors, or managing agents, or other persons consenting to appear and testify on its behalf with respect to matters known or reasonably available to the organization. Cf. Alberta Sup.Ct.R. 255. The organization may designate persons other than officers, directors, and managing agents, but only with their consent. Thus, an employee or agent who has an independent or conflicting interest in the litigation—for example, in a personal injury case—can refuse to testify on behalf of the organization.

This procedure supplements the existing practice whereby the examining party designates the corporate official to be deposed. Thus, if the examining party believes that certain officials who have not testified pursuant to this subdivision have added information, he may depose them. On the other hand, a court's decision whether to issue a protective order may take account of the availability and use made of the procedures provided in this subdivision.

The new procedure should be viewed as an added facility for discovery, one which may be advantageous to both sides as well as an improvement in the deposition process. It will reduce the difficulties now encountered in determining, prior to the taking of a deposition, whether a particular employee or agent is a "managing agent." See Note, Discovery Against Corporations Under the Federal Rules, 47 Iowa L.Rev. 1006–1016 (1962). It will curb the "bandying" by which officers or managing agents of a corporation are deposed in turn but each disclaims knowledge of facts that are clearly known to persons in the organization and thereby to it. Cf. Haney v. Woodward & Lothrop, Inc., 330 F.2d 940, 944 (4th Cir. 1964). The provisions should also assist organizations which find that an unnecessarily large number of their officers and agents are being deposed by a party uncertain of who in the organization has knowledge. Some courts have held that under the existing rules a corporation should not be burdened with choosing which person is to appear for it. E.g., United States v. Gahagan Dredging Corp., 24 F.R.D. 328, 329 (S.D.N.Y. 1958). This burden is not essentially different from that of answering interrogatories under Rule 33, and is in any case lighter than that of an examining party ignorant of who in the corporation has knowledge.

Subdivision (c). A new sentence is inserted at the beginning, representing the transfer of existing Rule 26(c) to this subdivision. Another addition conforms to the new provision in subdivision (b)(4).

The present rule provides that transcription shall be carried out unless all parties waive it. In view of the many depositions taken from which nothing useful is discovered, the revised language provides that transcription is to be performed if any party requests it. The fact of the request is relevant to the exercise of the court's discretion in determining who shall pay for transcription.

Parties choosing to serve written questions rather than participate personally in an oral deposition are directed to serve their questions on the party taking the deposition, since the officer is often not identified in advance. Confidentiality is preserved, since the questions may be served in a sealed envelope.

Subdivision (d). The assessment of expenses incurred in relation to motions made under this subdivision (d) is made subject to the provisions of Rule 37(a). The standards for assessment of expenses are more fully set out in Rule 37(a), and these standards should apply to the essentially similar motions of this subdivision.

Subdivision (e). The provision relating to the refusal of a witness to sign his deposition is tightened through insertion of a 30-day time period.

Subdivision (f)(1). A provision is added which codifies in a flexible way the procedure for handling exhibits related to the deposition and at the same time assures each party that he may inspect and copy documents and things produced by a nonparty witness in response to subpoena duces tecum. As a general rule and in the absence of agreement to the contrary or order of the court, exhibits produced without objection are to be annexed to and returned with the deposition, but a witness may substitute copies for purposes of marking and he may obtain return of the exhibits. The right of the parties to inspect exhibits for identification and to make copies is assured. Cf. N.Y.C.P.L.R. §3116(c).

Notes of Advisory Committee on Rules—1971 Amendment

The subdivision permits a party to name a corporation or other form of organization as a deponent in the notice of examination and to describe in the notice the matters about which discovery is desired. The organization is then obliged to designate natural persons to testify on its behalf. The amendment clarifies the procedure to be followed if a party desires to examine a non-party organization through persons designated by the organization. Under the rules, a subpoena rather than a notice of examination is served on a non-party to compel attendance at the taking of a deposition. The amendment provides that a subpoena may name a non-party organization as the deponent and may indicate the matters about which discovery is desired. In that event, the non-party organization must respond by designating natural persons, who are then obliged to testify as to matters known or reasonably available to the organization. To insure that a non-party organization that is not represented by counsel has knowledge of its duty to designate, the amendment directs the party seeking discovery to advise of the duty in the body of the subpoena.

Notes of Advisory Committee on Rules—1972 Amendment

Subdivision (c). Existing. Rule 43(b), which is to be abrogated, deals with the use of leading questions, the calling, interrogation, impeachment, and scope of cross-examination of adverse parties, officers, etc. These topics are dealt with in many places in the Rules of Evidence. Moreover, many pertinent topics included in the Rules of Evidence are not mentioned in Rule 43(b), e.g. privilege. A reference to the Rules of Evidence generally is therefore made in subdivision (c) of Rule 30.

Notes of Advisory Committee on Rules—1980 Amendment

Subdivision (b)(4). It has been proposed that electronic recording of depositions be authorized as a matter of course, subject to the right of a party to seek an order that a deposition be recorded by stenographic means. The Committee is not satisfied that a case has been made for a reversal of present practice. The amendment is made to encourage parties to agree to the use of electronic recording of depositions so that conflicting claims with respect to the potential of electronic recording for reducing costs of depositions can be appraised in the light of greater experience. The provision that the parties may stipulate that depositions may be recorded by other than stenographic means seems implicit in Rule 29. The amendment makes it explicit. The provision that the stipulation or order shall designate the person before whom the deposition is to be taken is added to encourage the naming of the recording technician as that person, eliminating the necessity of the presence of one whose only function is to administer the oath. See Rules 28(a) and 29.

Subdivision (b)(7). Depositions by telephone are now authorized by Rule 29 upon stipulation of the parties. The amendment authorizes that method by order of the court. The final sentence is added to make it clear that when a deposition is taken by telephone it is taken in the district and at the place where the witness is to answer the questions rather than that where the questions are propounded.

Subdivision (f)(1). For the reasons set out in the Note following the amendment of Rule 5(d), the court may wish to permit the parties to retain depositions unless they are to be used in the action. The amendment of the first paragraph permits the court to so order.

The amendment of the second paragraph is clarifying. The purpose of the paragraph is to permit a person who produces materials at a deposition to offer copies for marking and annexation to the deposition. Such copies are a "substitute" for the originals, which are not to be marked and which can thereafter be used or even disposed of by the person who produces them. In the light of that purpose, the former language of the paragraph had been justly termed "opaque." Wright & Miller, Federal Practice and Procedure: Civil §2114.

Notes of Advisory Committee on Rules—1987 Amendment

The amendments are technical. No substantive change is intended.

Effective Date of Amendment Proposed November 20, 1972

Amendment of this rule embraced by the order entered by the Supreme Court of the United States on November 20, 1972, effective on the 180th day beginning after January 2, 1975, see section 3 of Pub. L. 93–595, Jan. 2, 1975, 88 Stat. 1959, set out as a note under section 2074 of this title.

Notes of Advisory Committee on Rules—1993 Amendment

Subdivision (a). Paragraph (1) retains the first and third sentences from the former subdivision (a) without significant modification. The second and fourth sentences are relocated.

Paragraph (2) collects all provisions bearing on requirements of leave of court to take a deposition.

Paragraph (2)(A) is new. It provides a limit on the number of depositions the parties may take, absent leave of court or stipulation with the other parties. One aim of this revision is to assure judicial review under the standards stated in Rule 26(b)(2) before any side will be allowed to take more than ten depositions in a case without agreement of the other parties. A second objective is to emphasize that counsel have a professional obligation to develop a mutual cost-effective plan for discovery in the case. Leave to take additional depositions should be granted when consistent with the principles of Rule 26(b)(2), and in some cases the ten-per-side limit should be reduced in accordance with those same principles. Consideration should ordinarily be given at the planning meeting of the parties under Rule 26(f) and at the time of a scheduling conference under Rule 16(b) as to enlargements or reductions in the number of depositions, eliminating the need for special motions.

A deposition under Rule 30(b)(6) should, for purposes of this limit, be treated as a single deposition even though more than one person may be designated to testify.

In multi-party cases, the parties on any side are expected to confer and agree as to which depositions are most needed, given the presumptive limit on the number of depositions they can take without leave of court. If these disputes cannot be amicably resolved, the court can be requested to resolve the dispute or permit additional depositions.

Paragraph (2)(B) is new. It requires leave of court if any witness is to be deposed in the action more than once. This requirement does not apply when a deposition is temporarily recessed for convenience of counsel or the deponent or to enable additional materials to be gathered before resuming the deposition. If significant travel costs would be incurred to resume the deposition, the parties should consider the feasibility of conducting the balance of the examination by telephonic means.

Paragraph (2)(C) revises the second sentence of the former subdivision (a) as to when depositions may be taken. Consistent with the changes made in Rule 26(d), providing that formal discovery ordinarily not commence until after the litigants have met and conferred as directed in revised Rule 26(f), the rule requires leave of court or agreement of the parties if a deposition is to be taken before that time (except when a witness is about to leave the country).

Subdivision (b). The primary change in subdivision (b) is that parties will be authorized to record deposition testimony by nonstenographic means without first having to obtain permission of the court or agreement from other counsel.

Former subdivision (b)(2) is partly relocated in subdivision (a)(2)(C) of this rule. The latter two sentences of the first paragraph are deleted, in part because they are redundant to Rule 26(g) and in part because Rule 11 no longer applies to discovery requests. The second paragraph of the former subdivision (b)(2), relating to use of depositions at trial where a party was unable to obtain counsel in time for an accelerated deposition, is relocated in Rule 32.

New paragraph (2) confers on the party taking the deposition the choice of the method of recording, without the need to obtain prior court approval for one taken other than stenographically. A party choosing to record a deposition only by videotape or audiotape should understand that a transcript will be required by Rule 26(a)(3)(B) and Rule 32(c) if the deposition is later to be offered as evidence at trial or on a dispositive motion under Rule 56. Objections to the nonstenographic recording of a deposition, when warranted by the circumstances, can be presented to the court under Rule 26(c).

Paragraph (3) provides that other parties may arrange, at their own expense, for the recording of a deposition by a means (stenographic, visual, or sound) in addition to the method designated by the person noticing the deposition. The former provisions of this paragraph, relating to the court's power to change the date of a deposition, have been eliminated as redundant in view of Rule 26(c)(2).

Revised paragraph (4) requires that all depositions be recorded by an officer designated or appointed under Rule 28 and contains special provisions designed to provide basic safeguards to assure the utility and integrity of recordings taken other than stenographically.

Paragraph (7) is revised to authorize the taking of a deposition not only by telephone but also by other remote electronic means, such as satellite television, when agreed to by the parties or authorized by the court.

Subdivision (c). Minor changes are made in this subdivision to reflect those made in subdivision (b) and to complement the new provisions of subdivision (d)(1), aimed at reducing the number of interruptions during depositions.

In addition, the revision addresses a recurring problem as to whether other potential deponents can attend a deposition. Courts have disagreed, some holding that witnesses should be excluded through invocation of Rule 615 of the evidence rules, and others holding that witnesses may attend unless excluded by an order under Rule 26(c)(5). The revision provides that other witnesses are not automatically excluded from a deposition simply by the request of a party. Exclusion, however, can be ordered under Rule 26(c)(5) when appropriate; and, if exclusion is ordered, consideration should be given as to whether the excluded witnesses likewise should be precluded from reading, or being otherwise informed about, the testimony given in the earlier depositions. The revision addresses only the matter of attendance by potential deponents, and does not attempt to resolve issues concerning attendance by others, such as members of the public or press.

Subdivision (d). The first sentence of new paragraph (1) provides that any objections during a deposition must be made concisely and in a non-argumentative and non-suggestive manner. Depositions frequently have been unduly prolonged, if not unfairly frustrated, by lengthy objections and colloquy, often suggesting how the deponent should respond. While objections may, under the revised rule, be made during a deposition, they ordinarily should be limited to those that under Rule 32(d)(3) might be waived if not made at that time, i.e., objections on grounds that might be immediately obviated, removed, or cured, such as to the form of a question or the responsiveness of an answer. Under Rule 32(b), other objections can, even without the so-called "usual stipulation" preserving objections, be raised for the first time at trial and therefore should be kept to a minimum during a deposition.

Directions to a deponent not to answer a question can be even more disruptive than objections. The second sentence of new paragraph (1) prohibits such directions except in the three circumstances indicated: to claim a privilege or protection against disclosure (e.g., as work product), to enforce a court directive limiting the scope or length of permissible discovery, or to suspend a deposition to enable presentation of a motion under paragraph (3).

Paragraph (2) is added to this subdivision to dispel any doubts regarding the power of the court by order or local rule to establish limits on the length of depositions. The rule also explicitly authorizes the court to impose the cost resulting from obstructive tactics that unreasonably prolong a deposition on the person engaged in such obstruction. This sanction may be imposed on a non-party witness as well as a party or attorney, but is otherwise congruent with Rule 26(g).

It is anticipated that limits on the length of depositions prescribed by local rules would be presumptive only, subject to modification by the court or by agreement of the parties. Such modifications typically should be discussed by the parties in their meeting under Rule 26(f) and included in the scheduling order required by Rule 16(b). Additional time, moreover, should be allowed under the revised rule when justified under the principles stated in Rule 26(b)(2). To reduce the number of special motions, local rules should ordinarily permit—and indeed encourage—the parties to agree to additional time, as when, during the taking of a deposition, it becomes clear that some additional examination is needed.

Paragraph (3) authorizes appropriate sanctions not only when a deposition is unreasonably prolonged, but also when an attorney engages in other practices that improperly frustrate the fair examination of the deponent, such as making improper objections or giving directions not to answer prohibited by paragraph (1). In general, counsel should not engage in any conduct during a deposition that would not be allowed in the presence of a judicial officer. The making of an excessive number of unnecessary objections may itself constitute sanctionable conduct, as may the refusal of an attorney to agree with other counsel on a fair apportionment of the time allowed for examination of a deponent or a refusal to agree to a reasonable request for some additional time to complete a deposition, when that is permitted by the local rule or order.

Subdivision (e). Various changes are made in this subdivision to reduce problems sometimes encountered when depositions are taken stenographically. Reporters frequently have difficulties obtaining signatures—and the return of depositions—from deponents. Under the revision pre-filing review by the deponent is required only if requested before the deposition is completed. If review is requested, the deponent will be allowed 30 days to review the transcript or recording and to indicate any changes in form or substance. Signature of the deponent will be required only if review is requested and changes are made.

Subdivision (f). Minor changes are made in this subdivision to reflect those made in subdivision (b). In courts which direct that depositions not be automatically filed, the reporter can transmit the transcript or recording to the attorney taking the deposition (or ordering the transcript or record), who then becomes custodian for the court of the original record of the deposition. Pursuant to subdivision (f)(2), as under the prior rule, any other party is entitled to secure a copy of the deposition from the officer designated to take the deposition; accordingly, unless ordered or agreed, the officer must retain a copy of the recording or the stenographic notes.

Committee Notes on Rules—2000 Amendment

Subdivision (d). Paragraph (1) has been amended to clarify the terms regarding behavior during depositions. The references to objections "to evidence" and limitations "on evidence" have been removed to avoid disputes about what is "evidence" and whether an objection is to, or a limitation is on, discovery instead. It is intended that the rule apply to any objection to a question or other issue arising during a deposition, and to any limitation imposed by the court in connection with a deposition, which might relate to duration or other matters.

The current rule places limitations on instructions that a witness not answer only when the instruction is made by a "party." Similar limitations should apply with regard to anyone who might purport to instruct a witness not to answer a question. Accordingly, the rule is amended to apply the limitation to instructions by any person. The amendment is not intended to confer new authority on nonparties to instruct witnesses to refuse to answer deposition questions. The amendment makes it clear that, whatever the legitimacy of giving such instructions, the nonparty is subject to the same limitations as parties.

Paragraph (2) imposes a presumptive durational limitation of one day of seven hours for any deposition. The Committee has been informed that overlong depositions can result in undue costs and delays in some circumstances. This limitation contemplates that there will be reasonable breaks during the day for lunch and other reasons, and that the only time to be counted is the time occupied by the actual deposition. For purposes of this durational limit, the deposition of each person designated under Rule 30(b)(6) should be considered a separate deposition. The presumptive duration may be extended, or otherwise altered, by agreement. Absent agreement, a court order is needed. The party seeking a court order to extend the examination, or otherwise alter the limitations, is expected to show good cause to justify such an order.

Parties considering extending the time for a deposition—and courts asked to order an extension—might consider a variety of factors. For example, if the witness needs an interpreter, that may prolong the examination. If the examination will cover events occurring over a long period of time, that may justify allowing additional time. In cases in which the witness will be questioned about numerous or lengthy documents, it is often desirable for the interrogating party to send copies of the documents to the witness sufficiently in advance of the deposition so that the witness can become familiar with them. Should the witness nevertheless not read the documents in advance, thereby prolonging the deposition, a court could consider that a reason for extending the time limit. If the examination reveals that documents have been requested but not produced, that may justify further examination once production has occurred. In multi-party cases, the need for each party to examine the witness may warrant additional time, although duplicative questioning should be avoided and parties with similar interests should strive to designate one lawyer to question about areas of common interest. Similarly, should the lawyer for the witness want to examine the witness, that may require additional time. Finally, with regard to expert witnesses, there may more often be a need for additional time—even after the submission of the report required by Rule 26(a)(2)—for full exploration of the theories upon which the witness relies.

It is expected that in most instances the parties and the witness will make reasonable accommodations to avoid the need for resort to the court. The limitation is phrased in terms of a single day on the assumption that ordinarily a single day would be preferable to a deposition extending over multiple days; if alternative arrangements would better suit the parties, they may agree to them. It is also assumed that there will be reasonable breaks during the day. Preoccupation with timing is to be avoided.

The rule directs the court to allow additional time where consistent with Rule 26(b)(2) if needed for a fair examination of the deponent. In addition, if the deponent or another person impedes or delays the examination, the court must authorize extra time. The amendment makes clear that additional time should also be allowed where the examination is impeded by an "other circumstance," which might include a power outage, a health emergency, or other event.

In keeping with the amendment to Rule 26(b)(2), the provision added in 1993 granting authority to adopt a local rule limiting the time permitted for depositions has been removed. The court may enter a case-specific order directing shorter depositions for all depositions in a case or with regard to a specific witness. The court may also order that a deposition be taken for limited periods on several days.

Paragraph (3) includes sanctions provisions formerly included in paragraph (2). It authorizes the court to impose an appropriate sanction on any person responsible for an impediment that frustrated the fair examination of the deponent. This could include the deponent, any party, or any other person involved in the deposition. If the impediment or delay results from an "other circumstance" under paragraph (2), ordinarily no sanction would be appropriate.

Former paragraph (3) has been renumbered (4) but is otherwise unchanged.

Subdivision (f)(1). This subdivision is amended because Rule 5(d) has been amended to direct that discovery materials, including depositions, ordinarily should not be filed. The rule already has provisions directing that the lawyer who arranged for the transcript or recording preserve the deposition. Rule 5(d) provides that, once the deposition is used in the proceeding, the attorney must file it with the court.

"Shall" is replaced by "must" or "may" under the program to conform amended rules to current style conventions when there is no ambiguity.

GAP Report. The Advisory Committee recommends deleting the requirement in the published proposed amendments that the deponent consent to extending a deposition beyond one day, and adding an amendment to Rule 30(f)(1) to conform to the published amendment to Rule 5(d) regarding filing of depositions. It also recommends conforming the Committee Note with regard to the deponent veto, and adding material to the Note to provide direction on computation of the durational limitation on depositions, to provide examples of situations in which the parties might agree—or the court order—that a deposition be extended, and to make clear that no new authority to instruct a witness is conferred by the amendment. One minor wording improvement in the Note is also suggested.

Committee Notes on Rules—2007 Amendment

The language of Rule 30 has been amended as part of the general restyling of the Civil Rules to make them more easily understood and to make style and terminology consistent throughout the rules. These changes are intended to be stylistic only.

The right to arrange a deposition transcription should be open to any party, regardless of the means of recording and regardless of who noticed the deposition.

"[O]ther entity" is added to the list of organizations that may be named as deponent. The purpose is to ensure that the deposition process can be used to reach information known or reasonably available to an organization no matter what abstract fictive concept is used to describe the organization. Nothing is gained by wrangling over the place to fit into current rule language such entities as limited liability companies, limited partnerships, business trusts, more exotic common-law creations, or forms developed in other countries.

Committee Notes on Rules—2015 Amendment

Rule 30 is amended in parallel with Rules 31 and 33 to reflect the recognition of proportionality in Rule 26(b)(1).

Rule 31. Depositions by Written Questions

(a) When a Deposition May Be Taken.

(1) Without Leave. A party may, by written questions, depose any person, including a party, without leave of court except as provided in Rule 31(a)(2). The deponent's attendance may be compelled by subpoena under Rule 45.

(2) With Leave. A party must obtain leave of court, and the court must grant leave to the extent consistent with Rule 26(b)(1) and (2):

(A) if the parties have not stipulated to the deposition and:

(i) the deposition would result in more than 10 depositions being taken under this rule or Rule 30 by the plaintiffs, or by the defendants, or by the third-party defendants;

(ii) the deponent has already been deposed in the case; or

(iii) the party seeks to take a deposition before the time specified in Rule 26(d); or

(B) if the deponent is confined in prison.

(3) Service; Required Notice. A party who wants to depose a person by written questions must serve them on every other party, with a notice stating, if known, the deponent's name and address. If the name is unknown, the notice must provide a general description sufficient to identify the person or the particular class or group to which the person belongs. The notice must also state the name or descriptive title and the address of the officer before whom the deposition will be taken.

(4) Questions Directed to an Organization. A public or private corporation, a partnership, an association, or a governmental agency may be deposed by written questions in accordance with Rule 30(b)(6).

(5) Questions from Other Parties. Any questions to the deponent from other parties must be served on all parties as follows: cross-questions, within 14 days after being served with the notice and direct questions; redirect questions, within 7 days after being served with cross-questions; and recross-questions, within 7 days after being served with redirect questions. The court may, for good cause, extend or shorten these times.

(b) Delivery to the Officer; Officer's Duties. The party who noticed the deposition must deliver to the officer a copy of all the questions served and of the notice. The officer must promptly proceed in the manner provided in Rule 30(c), (e), and (f) to:

(1) take the deponent's testimony in response to the questions;

(2) prepare and certify the deposition; and

(3) send it to the party, attaching a copy of the questions and of the notice.

(c) Notice of Completion or Filing.

(1) Completion. The party who noticed the deposition must notify all other parties when it is completed.

(2) Filing. A party who files the deposition must promptly notify all other parties of the filing.

(As amended Mar. 30, 1970, eff. July 1, 1970; Mar. 2, 1987, eff. Aug. 1, 1987; Apr. 22, 1993, eff. Dec. 1, 1993; Apr. 30, 2007, eff. Dec. 1, 2007; Apr. 29, 2015, eff. Dec. 1, 2015.)

Notes of Advisory Committee on Rules—1937

This rule is in accordance with common practice. In most of the states listed in the Note to Rule 26(a), provisions similar to this rule will be found in the statutes which in their respective statutory compilations follow those cited in the Note to Rule 26(a).

Notes of Advisory Committee on Rules—1970 Amendment

Confusion is created by the use of the same terminology to describe both the taking of a deposition upon "written interrogatories" pursuant to this rule and the serving of "written interrogatories" upon parties pursuant to Rule 33. The distinction between these two modes of discovery will be more readily and clearly grasped through substitution of the word "questions" for "interrogatories" throughout this rule.

Subdivision (a). A new paragraph is inserted at the beginning of this subdivision to conform to the rearrangement of provisions in Rules 26(a), 30(a), and 30(b).

The revised subdivision permits designation of the deponent by general description or by class or group. This conforms to the practice for depositions on oral examination.

The new procedure provided in Rule 30(b)(6) for taking the deposition of a corporation or other organization through persons designated by the organization is incorporated by reference.

The service of all questions, including cross, redirect, and recross, is to be made on all parties. This will inform the parties and enable them to participate fully in the procedure.

The time allowed for service of cross, redirect, and recross questions has been extended. Experience with the existing time limits shows them to be unrealistically short. No special restriction is placed on the time for serving the notice of taking the deposition and the first set of questions. Since no party is required to serve cross questions less than 30 days after the notice and questions are served, the defendant has sufficient time to obtain counsel. The court may for cause shown enlarge or shorten the time.

Subdivision (d). Since new Rule 26(c) provides for protective orders with respect to all discovery, and expressly provides that the court may order that one discovery device be used in place of another, subdivision (d) is eliminated as unnecessary.

Notes of Advisory Committee on Rules—1987 Amendment

The amendments are technical. No substantive change is intended.

Notes of Advisory Committee on Rules—1993 Amendment

Subdivision (a). The first paragraph of subdivision (a) is divided into two subparagraphs, with provisions comparable to those made in the revision of Rule 30. Changes are made in the former third paragraph, numbered in the revision as paragraph (4), to reduce the total time for developing cross-examination, redirect, and recross questions from 50 days to 28 days.

Committee Notes on Rules—2007 Amendment

The language of Rule 31 has been amended as part of the general restyling of the Civil Rules to make them more easily understood and to make style and terminology consistent throughout the rules. These changes are intended to be stylistic only.

The party who noticed a deposition on written questions must notify all other parties when the deposition is completed, so that they may make use of the deposition. A deposition is completed when it is recorded and the deponent has either waived or exercised the right of review under Rule 30(e)(1).

Committee Notes on Rules—2015 Amendment

Rule 31 is amended in parallel with Rules 30 and 33 to reflect the recognition of proportionality in Rule 26(b)(1).

Rule 32. Using Depositions in Court Proceedings

(a) Using Depositions.

(1) In General. At a hearing or trial, all or part of a deposition may be used against a party on these conditions:

(A) the party was present or represented at the taking of the deposition or had reasonable notice of it;

(B) it is used to the extent it would be admissible under the Federal Rules of Evidence if the deponent were present and testifying; and

(C) the use is allowed by Rule 32(a)(2) through (8).

(2) Impeachment and Other Uses. Any party may use a deposition to contradict or impeach the testimony given by the deponent as a witness, or for any other purpose allowed by the Federal Rules of Evidence.

(3) Deposition of Party, Agent, or Designee. An adverse party may use for any purpose the deposition of a party or anyone who, when deposed, was the party's officer, director, managing agent, or designee under Rule 30(b)(6) or 31(a)(4).

(4) Unavailable Witness. A party may use for any purpose the deposition of a witness, whether or not a party, if the court finds:

(A) that the witness is dead;

(B) that the witness is more than 100 miles from the place of hearing or trial or is outside the United States, unless it appears that the witness's absence was procured by the party offering the deposition;

(C) that the witness cannot attend or testify because of age, illness, infirmity, or imprisonment;

(D) that the party offering the deposition could not procure the witness's attendance by subpoena; or

(E) on motion and notice, that exceptional circumstances make it desirable—in the interest of justice and with due regard to the importance of live testimony in open court—to permit the deposition to be used.

(5) Limitations on Use.

(A) Deposition Taken on Short Notice. A deposition must not be used against a party who, having received less than 14 days' notice of the deposition, promptly moved for a protective order under Rule 26(c)(1)(B) requesting that it not be taken or be taken at a different time or place—and this motion was still pending when the deposition was taken.

(B) Unavailable Deponent; Party Could Not Obtain an Attorney. A deposition taken without leave of court under the unavailability provision of Rule 30(a)(2)(A)(iii) must not be used against a party who shows that, when served with the notice, it could not, despite diligent efforts, obtain an attorney to represent it at the deposition.

(6) Using Part of a Deposition. If a party offers in evidence only part of a deposition, an adverse party may require the offeror to introduce other parts that in fairness should be considered with the part introduced, and any party may itself introduce any other parts.

(7) Substituting a Party. Substituting a party under Rule 25 does not affect the right to use a deposition previously taken.

(8) Deposition Taken in an Earlier Action. A deposition lawfully taken and, if required, filed in any federal- or state-court action may be used in a later action involving the same subject matter between the same parties, or their representatives or successors in interest, to the same extent as if taken in the later action. A deposition previously taken may also be used as allowed by the Federal Rules of Evidence.

(b) Objections to Admissibility. Subject to Rules 28(b) and 32(d)(3), an objection may be made at a hearing or trial to the admission of any deposition testimony that would be inadmissible if the witness were present and testifying.

(c) Form of Presentation. Unless the court orders otherwise, a party must provide a transcript of any deposition testimony the party offers, but may provide the court with the testimony in nontranscript form as well. On any party's request, deposition testimony offered in a jury trial for any purpose other than impeachment must be presented in nontranscript form, if available, unless the court for good cause orders otherwise.

(d) Waiver of Objections.

(1) To the Notice. An objection to an error or irregularity in a deposition notice is waived unless promptly served in writing on the party giving the notice.

(2) To the Officer's Qualification. An objection based on disqualification of the officer before whom a deposition is to be taken is waived if not made:

(A) before the deposition begins; or

(B) promptly after the basis for disqualification becomes known or, with reasonable diligence, could have been known.

(3) To the Taking of the Deposition.

(A) Objection to Competence, Relevance, or Materiality. An objection to a deponent's competence—or to the competence, relevance, or materiality of testimony—is not waived by a failure to make the objection before or during the deposition, unless the ground for it might have been corrected at that time.

(B) Objection to an Error or Irregularity. An objection to an error or irregularity at an oral examination is waived if:

(i) it relates to the manner of taking the deposition, the form of a question or answer, the oath or affirmation, a party's conduct, or other matters that might have been corrected at that time; and

(ii) it is not timely made during the deposition.

(C) Objection to a Written Question. An objection to the form of a written question under Rule 31 is waived if not served in writing on the party submitting the question within the time for serving responsive questions or, if the question is a recross-question, within 7 days after being served with it.

(4) To Completing and Returning the Deposition. An objection to how the officer transcribed the testimony—or prepared, signed, certified, sealed, endorsed, sent, or otherwise dealt with the deposition—is waived unless a motion to suppress is made promptly after the error or irregularity becomes known or, with reasonable diligence, could have been known.

(As amended Mar. 30, 1970, eff. July 1, 1970; Nov. 20, 1972, eff. July 1, 1975; Apr. 29, 1980, eff. Aug. 1, 1980; Mar. 2, 1987, eff. Aug. 1, 1987; Apr. 22, 1993, eff. Dec. 1, 1993; Apr. 30, 2007, eff. Dec. 1, 2007; Mar. 26, 2009, eff. Dec. 1, 2009.)

Notes of Advisory Committee on Rules—1937

This rule is in accordance with common practice. In most of the states listed in the Note to Rule 26, provisions similar to this rule will be found in the statutes which in their respective statutory compilations follow those cited in the Note to Rule 26.

Notes of Advisory Committee on Rules—1970 Amendment

As part of the rearrangement of the discovery rules, existing subdivisions (d), (e), and (f) of Rule 26 are transferred to Rule 32 as new subdivisions (a), (b), and (c). The provisions of Rule 32 are retained as subdivision (d) of Rule 32 with appropriate changes in the lettering and numbering of subheadings. The new rule is given a suitable new title. A beneficial byproduct of the rearrangement is that provisions which are naturally related to one another are placed in one rule.

A change is made in new Rule 32(a), whereby it is made clear that the rules of evidence are to be applied to depositions offered at trial as though the deponent were then present and testifying at trial. This eliminates the possibility of certain technical hearsay objections which are based, not on the contents of deponent's testimony, but on his absence from court. The language of present Rule 26(d) does not appear to authorize these technical objections, but it is not entirely clear. Note present Rule 26(e), transferred to Rule 32(b); see 2A Barron & Holtzoff, Federal Practice and Procedure 164–166 (Wright ed. 1961).

An addition in Rule 32(a)(2) provides for use of a deposition of a person designated by a corporation or other organization, which is a party, to testify on its behalf. This complements the new procedure for taking the deposition of a corporation or other organization provided in Rules 30(b)(6) and 31(a). The addition is appropriate, since the deposition is in substance and effect that of the corporation or other organization which is a party.

A change is made in the standard under which a party offering part of a deposition in evidence may be required to introduce additional parts of the deposition. The new standard is contained in a proposal made by the Advisory Committee on Rules of Evidence. See Rule 1–07 and accompanying Note, Preliminary Draft of Proposed Rules of Evidence for the United States District Courts and Magistrates 21–22 (March, 1969).

References to other rules are changed to conform to the rearrangement, and minor verbal changes have been made for clarification. The time for objecting to written questions served under Rule 31 is slightly extended.

Notes of Advisory Committee on Rules—1972 Amendment

Subdivision (e). The concept of "making a person one's own witness" appears to have had significance principally in two respects: impeachment and waiver of incompetency. Neither retains any vitality under the Rules of Evidence. The old prohibition against impeaching one's own witness is eliminated by Evidence Rule 607. The lack of recognition in the Rules of Evidence of state rules of incompetency in the Dead Man's area renders it unnecessary to consider aspects of waiver arising from calling the incompetent party witness. Subdivision (c) is deleted because it appears to be no longer necessary in the light of the Rules of Evidence.

Notes of Advisory Committee on Rules—1980 Amendment

Subdivision (a)(1). Rule 801(d) of the Federal Rules of Evidence permits a prior inconsistent statement of a witness in a deposition to be used as substantive evidence. And Rule 801(d)(2) makes the statement of an agent or servant admissible against the principal under the circumstances described in the Rule. The language of the present subdivision is, therefore, too narrow.

Subdivision (a)(4). The requirement that a prior action must have been dismissed before depositions taken for use in it can be used in a subsequent action was doubtless an oversight, and the courts have ignored it. See Wright & Miller, Federal Practice and Procedure: Civil §2150. The final sentence is added to reflect the fact that the Federal Rules of Evidence permit a broader use of depositions previously taken under certain circumstances. For example, Rule 804(b)(1) of the Federal Rules of Evidence provides that if a witness is unavailable, as that term is defined by the rule, his deposition in any earlier proceeding can be used against a party to the prior proceeding who had an opportunity and similar motive to develop the testimony of the witness.

Notes of Advisory Committee on Rules—1987 Amendment

The amendment is technical. No substantive change is intended.

Notes of Advisory Committee on Rules—1993 Amendment

Subdivision (a). The last sentence of revised subdivision (a) not only includes the substance of the provisions formerly contained in the second paragraph of Rule 30(b)(2), but adds a provision to deal with the situation when a party, receiving minimal notice of a proposed deposition, is unable to obtain a court ruling on its motion for a protective order seeking to delay or change the place of the deposition. Ordinarily a party does not obtain protection merely by the filing of a motion for a protective order under Rule 26(c); any protection is dependent upon the court's ruling. Under the revision, a party receiving less than 11 days notice of a deposition can, provided its motion for a protective order is filed promptly, be spared the risks resulting from nonattendance at the deposition held before its motion is ruled upon. Although the revision of Rule 32(a) covers only the risk that the deposition could be used against the non-appearing movant, it should also follow that, when the proposed deponent is the movant, the deponent would have "just cause" for failing to appear for purposes of Rule 37(d)(1). Inclusion of this provision is not intended to signify that 11 days' notice is the minimum advance notice for all depositions or that greater than 10 days should necessarily be deemed sufficient in all situations.

Subdivision (c). This new subdivision, inserted at the location of a subdivision previously abrogated, is included in view of the increased opportunities for video-recording and audio-recording of depositions under revised Rule 30(b). Under this rule a party may offer deposition testimony in any of the forms authorized under Rule 30(b) but, if offering it in a nonstenographic form, must provide the court with a transcript of the portions so offered. On request of any party in a jury trial, deposition testimony offered other than for impeachment purposes is to be presented in a nonstenographic form if available, unless the court directs otherwise. Note that under Rule 26(a)(3)(B) a party expecting to use nonstenographic deposition testimony as substantive evidence is required to provide other parties with a transcript in advance of trial.

Committee Notes on Rules—2007 Amendment

The language of Rule 32 has been amended as part of the general restyling of the Civil Rules to make them more easily understood and to make style and terminology consistent throughout the rules. These changes are intended to be stylistic only.

Former Rule 32(a) applied "[a]t the trial or upon the hearing of a motion or an interlocutory proceeding." The amended rule describes the same events as "a hearing or trial."

The final paragraph of former Rule 32(a) allowed use in a later action of a deposition "lawfully taken and duly filed in the former action." Because of the 2000 amendment of Rule 5(d), many depositions are not filed. Amended Rule 32(a)(8) reflects this change by excluding use of an unfiled deposition only if filing was required in the former action.

Committee Notes on Rules—2009 Amendment

The times set in the former rule at less than 11 days and within 5 days have been revised to 14 days and 7 days. See the Note to Rule 6.

Effective Date of Amendment Proposed November 20, 1972

Amendment of this rule embraced by the order entered by the Supreme Court of the United States on November 20, 1972, effective on the 180th day beginning after January 2, 1975, see section 3 of Pub. L. 93–595, Jan. 2, 1975, 88 Stat. 1959, set out as a note under section 2074 of this title.

Rule 33. Interrogatories to Parties

(a) In General.

(1) Number. Unless otherwise stipulated or ordered by the court, a party may serve on any other party no more than 25 written interrogatories, including all discrete subparts. Leave to serve additional interrogatories may be granted to the extent consistent with Rule 26(b)(1) and (2).

(2) Scope. An interrogatory may relate to any matter that may be inquired into under Rule 26(b). An interrogatory is not objectionable merely because it asks for an opinion or contention that relates to fact or the application of law to fact, but the court may order that the interrogatory need not be answered until designated discovery is complete, or until a pretrial conference or some other time.

(b) Answers and Objections.

(1) Responding Party. The interrogatories must be answered:

(A) by the party to whom they are directed; or

(B) if that party is a public or private corporation, a partnership, an association, or a governmental agency, by any officer or agent, who must furnish the information available to the party.

(2) Time to Respond. The responding party must serve its answers and any objections within 30 days after being served with the interrogatories. A shorter or longer time may be stipulated to under Rule 29 or be ordered by the court.

(3) Answering Each Interrogatory. Each interrogatory must, to the extent it is not objected to, be answered separately and fully in writing under oath.

(4) Objections. The grounds for objecting to an interrogatory must be stated with specificity. Any ground not stated in a timely objection is waived unless the court, for good cause, excuses the failure.

(5) Signature. The person who makes the answers must sign them, and the attorney who objects must sign any objections.

(c) Use. An answer to an interrogatory may be used to the extent allowed by the Federal Rules of Evidence.

(d) Option to Produce Business Records. If the answer to an interrogatory may be determined by examining, auditing, compiling, abstracting, or summarizing a party's business records (including electronically stored information), and if the burden of deriving or ascertaining the answer will be substantially the same for either party, the responding party may answer by:

(1) specifying the records that must be reviewed, in sufficient detail to enable the interrogating party to locate and identify them as readily as the responding party could; and

(2) giving the interrogating party a reasonable opportunity to examine and audit the records and to make copies, compilations, abstracts, or summaries.

(As amended Dec. 27, 1946, eff. Mar. 19, 1948; Mar. 30, 1970, eff. July 1, 1970; Apr. 29, 1980, eff. Aug. 1, 1980; Apr. 22, 1993, eff. Dec. 1, 1993; Apr. 12, 2006, eff. Dec. 1, 2006; Apr. 30, 2007, eff. Dec. 1, 2007; Apr. 29, 2015, eff. Dec. 1, 2015.)

Notes of Advisory Committee on Rules—1937

This rule restates the substance of [former] Equity Rule 58 (Discovery—Interrogatories—Inspection and Production of Documents—Admission of Execution or Genuineness), with modifications to conform to these rules.

Notes of Advisory Committee on Rules—1946 Amendment

The added second sentence in the first paragraph of Rule 33 conforms with a similar change in Rule 26(a) and will avoid litigation as to when the interrogatories may be served. Original Rule 33 does not state the times at which parties may serve written interrogatories upon each other. It has been the accepted view, however, that the times were the same in Rule 33 as those stated in Rule 26(a). United States v. American Solvents & Chemical Corp. of California (D.Del. 1939) 30 F.Supp. 107; Sheldon v. Great Lakes Transit Corp. (W.D.N.Y. 1942) 5 Fed.Rules Serv. 33.11, Case 3; Musher Foundation, Inc. v. Alba Trading Co. (S.D.N.Y. 1941) 42 F.Supp. 281; 2 Moore's Federal Practice, (1938) 2621. The time within which leave of court must be secured by a plaintiff has been fixed at 10 days, in view of the fact that a defendant has 10 days within which to make objections in any case, which should give him ample time to engage counsel and prepare.

Further in the first paragraph of Rule 33, the word "service" is substituted for "delivery" in conformance with the use of the word "serve" elsewhere in the rule and generally throughout the rules. See also Note to Rule 13(a) herein. The portion of the rule dealing with practice on objections has been revised so as to afford a clearer statement of the procedure. The addition of the words "to interrogatories to which objection is made" insures that only the answers to the objectionable interrogatories may be deferred, and that the answers to interrogatories not objectionable shall be forthcoming within the time prescribed in the rule. Under the original wording, answers to all interrogatories may be withheld until objections, sometimes to but a few interrogatories, are determined. The amendment expedites the procedure of the rule and serves to eliminate the strike value of objections to minor interrogatories. The elimination of the last sentence of the original rule is in line with the policy stated subsequently in this note.

The added second paragraph in Rule 33 contributes clarity and specificity as to the use and scope of interrogatories to the parties. The field of inquiry will be as broad as the scope of examination under Rule 26(b). There is no reason why interrogatories should be more limited than depositions, particularly when the former represent an inexpensive means of securing useful information. See Hoffman v. Wilson Line, Inc. (E.D.Pa. 1946) 9 Fed.Rules Serv. 33.514, Case 2; Brewster v. Technicolor, Inc. (S.D.N.Y. 1941) 5 Fed.Rules Serv. 33.319, Case 3; Kingsway Press, Inc. v. Farrell Publishing Corp. (S.D.N.Y. 1939) 30 F.Supp. 775. Under present Rule 33 some courts have unnecessarily restricted the breadth of inquiry on various grounds. See Auer v. Hershey Creamery Co. (D.N.J. 1939) 2 Fed.Rules Serv. 33.31, Case 2, 1 F.R.D. 14; Tudor v. Leslie (D.Mass. 1940) 4 Fed.Rules Serv. 33.324, Case 1. Other courts have read into the rule the requirement that interrogation should be directed only towards "important facts", and have tended to fix a more or less arbitrary limit as to the number of interrogatories which could be asked in any case. See Knox v. Alter (W.D.Pa. 1942) 6 Fed.Rules Serv. 33.352, Case 1; Byers Theaters, Inc. v. Murphy (W.D.Va. 1940) 3 Fed.Rules Serv. 33.31, Case 3, 1 F.R.D. 286; Coca-Cola Co. v. Dixi-Cola Laboratories, Inc. (D.Md. 1939) 30 F.Supp. 275. See also comment on these restrictions in Holtzoff, Instruments of Discovery Under Federal Rules of Civil Procedure (1942) 41 Mich.L.Rev. 205, 216–217. Under amended Rule 33, the party interrogated is given the right to invoke such protective orders under Rule 30(b) as are appropriate to the situation. At the same time, it is provided that the number of or number of sets of interrogatories to be served may not be limited arbitrarily or as a general policy to any particular number, but that a limit may be fixed only as justice requires to avoid annoyance, expense, embarrassment or oppression in individual cases. The party interrogated, therefore, must show the necessity for limitation on that basis. It will be noted that in accord with this change the last sentence of the present rule, restricting the sets of interrogatories to be served, has been stricken. In J. Schoeneman, Inc. v. Brauer (W.D.Mo. 1940) 3 Fed.Rules Serv. 33.31, Case 2, the court said: "Rule 33 . . . has been interpreted . . . as being just as broad in its implications as in the case of depositions . . . It makes no difference therefore, how many interrogatories are propounded. If the inquiries are pertinent the opposing party cannot complain." To the same effect, see Canuso v. City of Niagara Falls (W.D.N.Y. 1945) 8 Fed.Rules Serv. 33.352, Case 1; Hoffman v. Wilson Line, Inc., supra.

By virtue of express language in the added second paragraph of Rule 33, as amended, any uncertainty as to the use of the answers to interrogatories is removed. The omission of a provision on this score in the original rule has caused some difficulty. See, e.g., Bailey v. New England Mutual Life Ins. Co. (S.D.Cal. 1940) 4 Fed.Rules Serv. 33.46, Case 1.

The second sentence of the second paragraph in Rule 33, as amended, concerns the situation where a party wishes to serve interrogatories on a party after having taken his deposition, or vice versa. It has been held that an oral examination of a party, after the submission to him and answer of interrogatories, would be permitted. Howard v. State Marine Corp. (S.D.N.Y. 1940) 4 Fed.Rules Serv. 33.62, Case 1, 1 F.R.D. 499; Stevens v. Minder Construction Co. (S.D.N.Y. 1943) 7 Fed.Rules Serv. 30b.31, Case 2. But objections have been sustained to interrogatories served after the oral deposition of a party had been taken. McNally v. Simons (S.D.N.Y. 1940) 3 Fed.Rules Serv. 33.61, Case 1, 1 F.R.D. 254; Currier v. Currier (S.D.N.Y. 1942) 6 Fed.Rules Serv. 33.61, Case 1. Rule 33, as amended, permits either interrogatories after a deposition or a deposition after interrogatories. It may be quite desirable or necessary to elicit additional information by the inexpensive method of interrogatories where a deposition has already been taken. The party to be interrogated, however, may seek a protective order from the court under Rule 30(b) where the additional deposition or interrogation works a hardship or injustice on the party from whom it is sought.

Notes of Advisory Committee on Rules—1970 Amendment

Subdivision (a). The mechanics of the operation of Rule 33 are substantially revised by the proposed amendment, with a view to reducing court intervention. There is general agreement that interrogatories spawn a greater percentage of objections and motions than any other discovery device. The Columbia Survey shows that, although half of the litigants resorted to depositions and about one-third used interrogatories, about 65 percent of the objections were made with respect to interrogatories and 26 percent related to depositions. See also Speck, The Use of Discovery in United States District Courts, 60 Yale L.J. 1132, 1144, 1151 (1951); Note, 36 Minn.L.Rev. 364, 379 (1952).

The procedures now provided in Rule 33 seem calculated to encourage objections and court motions. The time periods now allowed for responding to interrogatories—15 days for answers and 10 days for objections—are too short. The Columbia Survey shows that tardy response to interrogatories is common, virtually expected. The same was reported in Speck, supra, 60 Yale L.J. 1132, 1144. The time pressures tend to encourage objections as a means of gaining time to answer.

The time for objections is even shorter than for answers, and the party runs the risk that if he fails to object in time he may have waived his objections. E.g., Cleminshaw v. Beech Aircraft Corp., 21 F.R.D. 300 (D.Del. 1957); see 4 Moore's Federal Practice, 33.27 (2d ed. 1966); 2A Barron & Holtzoff, Federal Practice and Procedure 372–373 (Wright ed. 1961). It often seems easier to object than to seek an extension of time. Unlike Rules 30(d) and 37(a), Rule 33 imposes no sanction of expenses on a party whose objections are clearly unjustified.

Rule 33 assures that the objections will lead directly to court, through its requirement that they be served with a notice of hearing. Although this procedure does preclude an out-of-court resolution of the dispute, the procedure tends to discourage informal negotiations. If answers are served and they are thought inadequate, the interrogating party may move under Rule 37(a) for an order compelling adequate answers. There is no assurance that the hearing on objections and that on inadequate answers will be heard together.

The amendment improves the procedure of Rule 33 in the following respects:

(1) The time allowed for response is increased to 30 days and this time period applies to both answers and objections, but a defendant need not respond in less than 45 days after service of the summons and complaint upon him. As is true under existing law, the responding party who believes that some parts or all of the interrogatories are objectionable may choose to seek a protective order under new Rule 26(c) or may serve objections under this rule. Unless he applies for a protective order, he is required to serve answers or objections in response to the interrogatories, subject to the sanctions provided in Rule 37(d). Answers and objections are served together, so that a response to each interrogatory is encouraged, and any failure to respond is easily noted.

(2) In view of the enlarged time permitted for response, it is no longer necessary to require leave of court for service of interrogatories. The purpose of this requirement—that defendant have time to obtain counsel before a response must be made—is adequately fulfilled by the requirement that interrogatories be served upon a party with or after service of the summons and complaint upon him.

Some would urge that the plaintiff nevertheless not be permitted to serve interrogatories with the complaint. They fear that a routine practice might be invited, whereby form interrogatories would accompany most complaints. More fundamentally, they feel that, since very general complaints are permitted in present-day pleading, it is fair that the defendant have a right to take the lead in serving interrogatories. (These views apply also to Rule 36.) The amendment of Rule 33 rejects these views, in favor of allowing both parties to go forward with discovery, each free to obtain the information he needs respecting the case.

(3) If objections are made, the burden is on the interrogating party to move under Rule 37(a) for a court order compelling answers, in the course of which the court will pass on the objections. The change in the burden of going forward does not alter the existing obligation of an objecting party to justify his objections. E.g., Pressley v. Boehlke, 33 F.R.D. 316 (W.D.N.C. 1963). If the discovering party asserts than an answer is incomplete or evasive, again he may look to Rule 37(a) for relief, and he should add this assertion to his motion to overrule objections. There is no requirement that the parties consult informally concerning their differences, but the new procedure should encourage consultation, and the court may by local rule require it.

The proposed changes are similar in approach to those adopted by California in 1961. See Calif.Code Civ.Proc. §2030(a). The experience of the Los Angeles Superior Court is informally reported as showing that the California amendment resulted in a significant reduction in court motions concerning interrogatories. Rhode Island takes a similar approach. See R. 33, R.I.R.Civ.Proc. Official Draft, p. 74 (Boston Law Book Co.).

A change is made in subdivision (a) which is not related to the sequence of procedures. The restriction to "adverse" parties is eliminated. The courts have generally construed this restriction as precluding interrogatories unless an issue between the parties is disclosed by the pleadings—even though the parties may have conflicting interests. E.g., Mozeika v. Kaufman Construction Co., 25 F.R.D. 233 (E.D.Pa. 1960) (plaintiff and third-party defendant); Biddle v. Hutchinson, 24 F.R.D. 256 (M.D.Pa. 1959) (codefendants). The resulting distinctions have often been highly technical. In Schlagenhauf v. Holder, 379 U.S. 104 (1964), the Supreme Court rejected a contention that examination under Rule 35 could be had only against an "opposing" party, as not in keeping "with the aims of a liberal, nontechnical application of the Federal Rules." 379 U.S. at 116. Eliminating the requirement of "adverse" parties from Rule 33 brings it into line with all other discovery rules.

A second change in subdivision (a) is the addition of the term "governmental agency" to the listing of organizations whose answers are to be made by any officer or agent of the organization. This does not involve any change in existing law. Compare the similar listing in Rule 30(b)(6).

The duty of a party to supplement his answers to interrogatories is governed by a new provision in Rule 26(e).

Subdivision (b). There are numerous and conflicting decisions on the question whether and to what extent interrogatories are limited to matters "of fact," or may elicit opinions, contentions, and legal conclusions. Compare, e.g., Payer, Hewitt & Co. v. Bellanca Corp., 26 F.R.D. 219 (D.Del. 1960) (opinions bad); Zinsky v. New York Central R.R., 36 F.R.D. 680 (N.D.Ohio 1964) (factual opinion or contention good, but legal theory bad); United States v. Carter Products, Inc., 28 F.R.D. 373 (S.D.N.Y.1961) (factual contentions and legal theories bad) with Taylor v. Sound Steamship Lines, Inc., 100 F.Supp. 388 (D.Conn. 1951) (opinions good), Bynum v. United States, 36 F.R.D. 14 (E.D.La. 1964) (contentions as to facts constituting negligence good). For lists of the many conflicting authorities, see 4 Moore's Federal Practice 33.17 (2d ed. 1966); 2A Barron & Holtzoff, Federal Practice and Procedure §768 (Wright ed. 1961).

Rule 33 is amended to provide that an interrogatory is not objectionable merely because it calls for an opinion or contention that relates to fact or the application of law to fact. Efforts to draw sharp lines between facts and opinions have invariably been unsuccessful, and the clear trend of the cases is to permit "factual" opinions. As to requests for opinions or contentions that call for the application of law to fact, they can be most useful in narrowing and sharpening the issues, which is a major purpose of discovery. See Diversified Products Corp. v. Sports Center Co., 42 F.R.D. 3 (D.Md. 1967); Moore, supra; Field & McKusick, Maine Civil Practice §26.18 (1959). On the other hand, under the new language interrogatories may not extend to issues of "pure law," i.e., legal issues unrelated to the facts of the case. Cf. United States v. Maryland & Va. Milk Producers Assn., Inc., 22 F.R.D. 300 (D.D.C. 1958).

Since interrogatories involving mixed questions of law and fact may create disputes between the parties which are best resolved after much or all of the other discovery has been completed, the court is expressly authorized to defer an answer. Likewise, the court may delay determination until pretrial conference, if it believes that the dispute is best resolved in the presence of the judge.

The principal question raised with respect to the cases permitting such interrogatories is whether they reintroduce undesirable aspects of the prior pleading practice, whereby parties were chained to misconceived contentions or theories, and ultimate determination on the merits was frustrated. See James, The Revival of Bills of Particulars under the Federal Rules, 71 Harv.L.Rev. 1473 (1958). But there are few if any instances in the recorded cases demonstrating that such frustration has occurred. The general rule governing the use of answers to interrogatories is that under ordinary circumstances they do not limit proof. See e.g., McElroy v. United Air Lines, Inc., 21 F.R.D. 100 (W.D.Mo. 1967); Pressley v. Boehlke, 33 F.R.D. 316, 317 (W.D.N.C. 1963). Although in exceptional circumstances reliance on an answer may cause such prejudice that the court will hold the answering party bound to his answer, e.g., Zielinski v. Philadelphia Piers, Inc., 139 F.Supp. 408 (E.D.Pa. 1956), the interrogating party will ordinarily not be entitled to rely on the unchanging character of the answers he receives and cannot base prejudice on such reliance. The rule does not affect the power of a court to permit withdrawal or amendment of answers to interrogatories.

The use of answers to interrogatories at trial is made subject to the rules of evidence. The provisions governing use of depositions, to which Rule 33 presently refers, are not entirely apposite to answers to interrogatories, since deposition practice contemplates that all parties will ordinarily participate through cross-examination. See 4 Moore's Federal Practice 33.29[1] (2 ed. 1966).

Certain provisions are deleted from subdivision (b) because they are fully covered by new Rule 26(c) providing for protective orders and Rules 26(a) and 26(d). The language of the subdivision is thus simplified without any change of substance.

Subdivision (c). This is a new subdivision, adopted from Calif.Code Civ.Proc. §2030(c), relating especially to interrogatories which require a party to engage in burdensome or expensive research into his own business records in order to give an answer. The subdivision gives the party an option to make the records available and place the burden of research on the party who seeks the information. "This provision, without undermining the liberal scope of interrogatory discovery, places the burden of discovery upon its potential benefitee," Louisell, Modern California Discovery, 124–125 (1963), and alleviates a problem which in the past has troubled Federal courts. See Speck, The Use of Discovery in United States District Courts, 60 Yale L.J. 1132, 1142–1144 (1951). The interrogating party is protected against abusive use of this provision through the requirement that the burden of ascertaining the answer be substantially the same for both sides. A respondent may not impose on an interrogating party a mass of records as to which research is feasible only for one familiar with the records. At the same time, the respondent unable to invoke this subdivision does not on that account lose the protection available to him under new Rule 26(c) against oppressive or unduly burdensome or expensive interrogatories. And even when the respondent successfully invokes the subdivision, the court is not deprived of its usual power, in appropriate cases, to require that the interrogating party reimburse the respondent for the expense of assembling his records and making them intelligible.

Notes of Advisory Committee on Rules—1980 Amendment

Subdivision (c). The Committee is advised that parties upon whom interrogatories are served have occasionally responded by directing the interrogating party to a mass of business records or by offering to make all of their records available, justifying the response by the option provided by this subdivision. Such practices are an abuse of the option. A party who is permitted by the terms of this subdivision to offer records for inspection in lieu of answering an interrogatory should offer them in a manner that permits the same direct and economical access that is available to the party. If the information sought exists in the form of compilations, abstracts or summaries then available to the responding party, those should be made available to the interrogating party. The final sentence is added to make it clear that a responding party has the duty to specify, by category and location, the records from which answers to interrogatories can be derived.

Notes of Advisory Committee on Rules—1993 Amendment

Purpose of Revision. The purpose of this revision is to reduce the frequency and increase the efficiency of interrogatory practice. The revision is based on experience with local rules. For ease of reference, subdivision (a) is divided into two subdivisions and the remaining subdivisions renumbered.

Subdivision (a). Revision of this subdivision limits interrogatory practice. Because Rule 26(a)(1)–(3) requires disclosure of much of the information previously obtained by this form of discovery, there should be less occasion to use it. Experience in over half of the district courts has confirmed that limitations on the number of interrogatories are useful and manageable. Moreover, because the device can be costly and may be used as a means of harassment, it is desirable to subject its use to the control of the court consistent with the principles stated in Rule 26(b)(2), particularly in multi-party cases where it has not been unusual for the same interrogatory to be propounded to a party by more than one of its adversaries.

Each party is allowed to serve 25 interrogatories upon any other party, but must secure leave of court (or a stipulation from the opposing party) to serve a larger number. Parties cannot evade this presumptive limitation through the device of joining as "subparts" questions that seek information about discrete separate subjects. However, a question asking about communications of a particular type should be treated as a single interrogatory even though it requests that the time, place, persons present, and contents be stated separately for each such communication.

As with the number of depositions authorized by Rule 30, leave to serve additional interrogatories is to be allowed when consistent with Rule 26(b)(2). The aim is not to prevent needed discovery, but to provide judicial scrutiny before parties make potentially excessive use of this discovery device. In many cases it will be appropriate for the court to permit a larger number of interrogatories in the scheduling order entered under Rule 16(b).

Unless leave of court is obtained, interrogatories may not be served prior to the meeting of the parties under Rule 26(f).

When a case with outstanding interrogatories exceeding the number permitted by this rule is removed to federal court, the interrogating party must seek leave allowing the additional interrogatories, specify which twenty-five are to be answered, or resubmit interrogatories that comply with the rule. Moreover, under Rule 26(d), the time for response would be measured from the date of the parties' meeting under Rule 26(f). See Rule 81(c), providing that these rules govern procedures after removal.

Subdivision (b). A separate subdivision is made of the former second paragraph of subdivision (a). Language is added to paragraph (1) of this subdivision to emphasize the duty of the responding party to provide full answers to the extent not objectionable. If, for example, an interrogatory seeking information about numerous facilities or products is deemed objectionable, but an interrogatory seeking information about a lesser number of facilities or products would not have been objectionable, the interrogatory should be answered with respect to the latter even though an objection is raised as to the balance of the facilities or products. Similarly, the fact that additional time may be needed to respond to some questions (or to some aspects of questions) should not justify a delay in responding to those questions (or other aspects of questions) that can be answered within the prescribed time.

Paragraph (4) is added to make clear that objections must be specifically justified, and that unstated or untimely grounds for objection ordinarily are waived. Note also the provisions of revised Rule 26(b)(5), which require a responding party to indicate when it is withholding information under a claim of privilege or as trial preparation materials.

These provisions should be read in light of Rule 26(g), authorizing the court to impose sanctions on a party and attorney making an unfounded objection to an interrogatory.

Subdivisions (c) and (d). The provisions of former subdivisions (b) and (c) are renumbered.

Committee Notes on Rules—2006 Amendment

Rule 33(d) is amended to parallel Rule 34(a) by recognizing the importance of electronically stored information. The term "electronically stored information" has the same broad meaning in Rule 33(d) as in Rule 34(a). Much business information is stored only in electronic form; the Rule 33(d) option should be available with respect to such records as well.

Special difficulties may arise in using electronically stored information, either due to its form or because it is dependent on a particular computer system. Rule 33(d) allows a responding party to substitute access to documents or electronically stored information for an answer only if the burden of deriving the answer will be substantially the same for either party. Rule 33(d) states that a party electing to respond to an interrogatory by providing electronically stored information must ensure that the interrogating party can locate and identify it "as readily as can the party served," and that the responding party must give the interrogating party a "reasonable opportunity to examine, audit, or inspect" the information. Depending on the circumstances, satisfying these provisions with regard to electronically stored information may require the responding party to provide some combination of technical support, information on application software, or other assistance. The key question is whether such support enables the interrogating party to derive or ascertain the answer from the electronically stored information as readily as the responding party. A party that wishes to invoke Rule 33(d) by specifying electronically stored information may be required to provide direct access to its electronic information system, but only if that is necessary to afford the requesting party an adequate opportunity to derive or ascertain the answer to the interrogatory. In that situation, the responding party's need to protect sensitive interests of confidentiality or privacy may mean that it must derive or ascertain and provide the answer itself rather than invoke Rule 33(d).

Changes Made after Publication and Comment. No changes are made to the rule text. The Committee Note is changed to reflect the sensitivities that limit direct access by a requesting party to a responding party's information system. If direct access to the responding party's system is the only way to enable a requesting party to locate and identify the records from which the answer may be ascertained, the responding party may choose to derive or ascertain the answer itself.

Committee Notes on Rules—2007 Amendment

The language of Rule 33 has been amended as part of the general restyling of the Civil Rules to make them more easily understood and to make style and terminology consistent throughout the rules. These changes are intended to be stylistic only.

The final sentence of former Rule 33(a) was a redundant cross-reference to the discovery moratorium provisions of Rule 26(d). Rule 26(d) is now familiar, obviating any need to carry forward the redundant cross-reference.

Former Rule 33(b)(5) was a redundant reminder of Rule 37(a) procedure and is omitted as no longer useful.

Former Rule 33(c) stated that an interrogatory "is not necessarily objectionable merely because an answer * * * involves an opinion or contention * * *." "[I]s not necessarily" seemed to imply that the interrogatory might be objectionable merely for this reason. This implication has been ignored in practice. Opinion and contention interrogatories are used routinely. Amended Rule 33(a)(2) embodies the current meaning of Rule 33 by omitting "necessarily."

Changes Made After Publication and Comment. See Note to Rule 1, supra.

Committee Notes on Rules—2015 Amendment

Rule 33 is amended in parallel with Rules 30 and 31 to reflect the recognition of proportionality in Rule 26(b)(1).

Rule 34. Producing Documents, Electronically Stored Information, and Tangible Things, or Entering onto Land, for Inspection and Other Purposes

(a) In General. A party may serve on any other party a request within the scope of Rule 26(b):

(1) to produce and permit the requesting party or its representative to inspect, copy, test, or sample the following items in the responding party's possession, custody, or control:

(A) any designated documents or electronically stored information—including writings, drawings, graphs, charts, photographs, sound recordings, images, and other data or data compilations—stored in any medium from which information can be obtained either directly or, if necessary, after translation by the responding party into a reasonably usable form; or

(B) any designated tangible things; or

(2) to permit entry onto designated land or other property possessed or controlled by the responding party, so that the requesting party may inspect, measure, survey, photograph, test, or sample the property or any designated object or operation on it.

(b) Procedure.

(1) Contents of the Request. The request:

(A) must describe with reasonable particularity each item or category of items to be inspected;

(B) must specify a reasonable time, place, and manner for the inspection and for performing the related acts; and

(C) may specify the form or forms in which electronically stored information is to be produced.

(2) Responses and Objections.

(A) Time to Respond. The party to whom the request is directed must respond in writing within 30 days after being served or—if the request was delivered under Rule 26(d)(2)—within 30 days after the parties' first Rule 26(f) conference. A shorter or longer time may be stipulated to under Rule 29 or be ordered by the court.

(B) Responding to Each Item. For each item or category, the response must either state that inspection and related activities will be permitted as requested or state with specificity the grounds for objecting to the request, including the reasons. The responding party may state that it will produce copies of documents or of electronically stored information instead of permitting inspection. The production must then be completed no later than the time for inspection specified in the request or another reasonable time specified in the response.

(C) Objections. An objection must state whether any responsive materials are being withheld on the basis of that objection. An objection to part of a request must specify the part and permit inspection of the rest.

(D) Responding to a Request for Production of Electronically Stored Information. The response may state an objection to a requested form for producing electronically stored information. If the responding party objects to a requested form—or if no form was specified in the request—the party must state the form or forms it intends to use.

(E) Producing the Documents or Electronically Stored Information. Unless otherwise stipulated or ordered by the court, these procedures apply to producing documents or electronically stored information:

(i) A party must produce documents as they are kept in the usual course of business or must organize and label them to correspond to the categories in the request;

(ii) If a request does not specify a form for producing electronically stored information, a party must produce it in a form or forms in which it is ordinarily maintained or in a reasonably usable form or forms; and

(iii) A party need not produce the same electronically stored information in more than one form.

(c) Nonparties. As provided in Rule 45, a nonparty may be compelled to produce documents and tangible things or to permit an inspection.

———

(As amended Dec. 27, 1946, eff. Mar. 19, 1948; Mar. 30, 1970, eff. July 1, 1970; Apr. 29, 1980, eff. Aug. 1, 1980; Mar. 2, 1987, eff. Aug. 1, 1987; Apr. 30, 1991, eff. Dec. 1, 1991; Apr. 22, 1993, eff. Dec. 1, 1993; Apr. 12, 2006, eff. Dec. 1, 2006; Apr. 30, 2007, eff. Dec. 1, 2007; Apr. 29, 2015, eff. Dec. 1, 2015.)

Notes of Advisory Committee on Rules—1937

In England orders are made for the inspection of documents, English Rules Under the Judicature Act (The Annual Practice, 1937) O. 31, r.r. 14, et seq., or for the inspection of tangible property or for entry upon land, O. 50, r.3. Michigan provides for inspection of damaged property when such damage is the ground of the action. Mich.Court Rules Ann. (Searl, 1933) Rule 41, §2.

Practically all states have statutes authorizing the court to order parties in possession or control of documents to permit other parties to inspect and copy them before trial. See Ragland, Discovery Before Trial (1932), Appendix, p. 267, setting out the statutes.

Compare [former] Equity Rule 58 (Discovery—Interrogatories—Inspection and Production of Documents—Admission of Execution or Genuineness) (fifth paragraph).

Notes of Advisory Committee on Rules—1946 Amendment

The changes in clauses (1) and (2) correlate the scope of inquiry permitted under Rule 34 with that provided in Rule 26(b), and thus remove any ambiguity created by the former differences in language. As stated in Olson Transportation Co. v. Socony-Vacuum Oil Co. (E.D.Wis. 1944) 8 Fed.Rules Serv. 34.41, Case 2, ". . . Rule 34 is a direct and simple method of discovery." At the same time the addition of the words following the term "parties" makes certain that the person in whose custody, possession, or control the evidence reposes may have the benefit of the applicable protective orders stated in Rule 30(b). This change should be considered in the light of the proposed expansion of Rule 30(b).

An objection has been made that the word "designated" in Rule 34 has been construed with undue strictness in some district court cases so as to require great and impracticable specificity in the description of documents, papers, books, etc., sought to be inspected. The Committee, however, believes that no amendment is needed, and that the proper meaning of "designated" as requiring specificity has already been delineated by the Supreme Court. See Brown v. United States (1928) 276 U.S. 134, 143 ("The subpoena . . . specifies . . . with reasonable particularity the subjects to which the documents called for related."); Consolidated Rendering Co. v. Vermont (1908) 207 U.S. 541, 543–544 ("We see no reason why all such books, papers and correspondence which related to the subject of inquiry, and were described with reasonable detail, should not be called for and the company directed to produce them. Otherwise, the State would be compelled to designate each particular paper which it desired, which presupposes an accurate knowledge of such papers, which the tribunal desiring the papers would probably rarely, if ever, have.").

Notes of Advisory Committee on Rules—1970 Amendment

Rule 34 is revised to accomplish the following major changes in the existing rule: (1) to eliminate the requirement of good cause; (2) to have the rule operate extrajudicially; (3) to include testing and sampling as well as inspecting or photographing tangible things; and (4) to make clear that the rule does not preclude an independent action for analogous discovery against persons not parties.

Subdivision (a). Good cause is eliminated because it has furnished an uncertain and erratic protection to the parties from whom production is sought and is now rendered unnecessary by virtue of the more specific provisions added to Rule 26(b) relating to materials assembled in preparation for trial and to experts retained or consulted by parties.

The good cause requirement was originally inserted in Rule 34 as a general protective provision in the absence of experience with the specific problems that would arise thereunder. As the note to Rule 26(b)(3) on trial preparation materials makes clear, good cause has been applied differently to varying classes of documents, though not without confusion. It has often been said in court opinions that good cause requires a consideration of need for the materials and of alternative means of obtaining them, i.e., something more than relevance and lack of privilege. But the overwhelming proportion of the cases in which the formula of good cause has been applied to require a special showing are those involving trial preparation. In practice, the courts have not treated documents as having a special immunity to discovery simply because of their being documents. Protection may be afforded to claims of privacy or secrecy or of undue burden or expense under what is now Rule 26(c) (previously Rule 30(b)). To be sure, an appraisal of "undue" burden inevitably entails consideration of the needs of the party seeking discovery. With special provisions added to govern trial preparation materials and experts, there is no longer any occasion to retain the requirement of good cause.

The revision of Rule 34 to have it operate extrajudicially, rather than by court order, is to a large extent a reflection of existing law office practice. The Columbia Survey shows that of the litigants seeking inspection of documents or things, only about 25 percent filed motions for court orders. This minor fraction nevertheless accounted for a significant number of motions. About half of these motions were uncontested and in almost all instances the party seeking production ultimately prevailed. Although an extrajudicial procedure will not drastically alter existing practice under Rule 34—it will conform to it in most cases—it has the potential of saving court time in a substantial though proportionately small number of cases tried annually.

The inclusion of testing and sampling of tangible things and objects or operations on land reflects a need frequently encountered by parties in preparation for trial. If the operation of a particular machine is the basis of a claim for negligent injury, it will often be necessary to test its operating parts or to sample and test the products it is producing. Cf. Mich.Gen.Ct.R. 310.1(1) (1963) (testing authorized).

The inclusive description of "documents" is revised to accord with changing technology. It makes clear that Rule 34 applies to electronic data compilations from which information can be obtained only with the use of detection devices, and that when the data can as a practical matter be made usable by the discovering party only through respondent's devices, respondent may be required to use his devices to translate the data into usable form. In many instances, this means that respondent will have to supply a print-out of computer data. The burden thus placed on respondent will vary from case to case, and the courts have ample power under Rule 26(c) to protect respondent against undue burden of expense, either by restricting discovery or requiring that the discovering party pay costs. Similarly, if the discovering party needs to check the electronic source itself, the court may protect respondent with respect to preservation of his records, confidentially of nondiscoverable matters, and costs.

Subdivision (b). The procedure provided in Rule 34 is essentially the same as that in Rule 33, as amended, and the discussion in the note appended to that rule is relevant to Rule 34 as well. Problems peculiar to Rule 34 relate to the specific arrangements that must be worked out for inspection and related acts of copying, photographing, testing, or sampling. The rule provides that a request for inspection shall set forth the items to be inspected either by item or category, describing each with reasonable particularity, and shall specify a reasonable time, place, and manner of making the inspection.

Subdivision (c). Rule 34 as revised continues to apply only to parties. Comments from the bar make clear that in the preparation of cases for trial it is occasionally necessary to enter land or inspect large tangible things in the possession of a person not a party, and that some courts have dismissed independent actions in the nature of bills in equity for such discovery on the ground that Rule 34 is preemptive. While an ideal solution to this problem is to provide for discovery against persons not parties in Rule 34, both the jurisdictional and procedural problems are very complex. For the present, this subdivision makes clear that Rule 34 does not preclude independent actions for discovery against persons not parties.

Notes of Advisory Committee on Rules—1980 Amendment

Subdivision (b). The Committee is advised that, "It is apparently not rare for parties deliberately to mix critical documents with others in the hope of obscuring significance." Report of the Special Committee for the Study of Discovery Abuse, Section of Litigation of the American Bar Association (1977) 22. The sentence added by this subdivision follows the recommendation of the Report.

Notes of Advisory Committee on Rules—1987 Amendment

The amendment is technical. No substantive change is intended.

Notes of Advisory Committee on Rules—1991 Amendment

This amendment reflects the change effected by revision of Rule 45 to provide for subpoenas to compel non-parties to produce documents and things and to submit to inspections of premises. The deletion of the text of the former paragraph is not intended to preclude an independent action for production of documents or things or for permission to enter upon land, but such actions may no longer be necessary in light of this revision.

Notes of Advisory Committee on Rules—1993 Amendment

The rule is revised to reflect the change made by Rule 26(d), preventing a party from seeking formal discovery prior to the meeting of the parties required by Rule 26(f). Also, like a change made in Rule 33, the rule is modified to make clear that, if a request for production is objectionable only in part, production should be afforded with respect to the unobjectionable portions.

When a case with outstanding requests for production is removed to federal court, the time for response would be measured from the date of the parties' meeting. See Rule 81(c), providing that these rules govern procedures after removal.

Committee Notes on Rules—2006 Amendment

Subdivision (a). As originally adopted, Rule 34 focused on discovery of "documents" and "things." In 1970, Rule 34(a) was amended to include discovery of data compilations, anticipating that the use of computerized information would increase. Since then, the growth in electronically stored information and in the variety of systems for creating and storing such information has been dramatic. Lawyers and judges interpreted the term "documents" to include electronically stored information because it was obviously improper to allow a party to evade discovery obligations on the basis that the label had not kept pace with changes in information technology. But it has become increasingly difficult to say that all forms of electronically stored information, many dynamic in nature, fit within the traditional concept of a "document." Electronically stored information may exist in dynamic databases and other forms far different from fixed expression on paper. Rule 34(a) is amended to confirm that discovery of electronically stored information stands on equal footing with discovery of paper documents. The change clarifies that Rule 34 applies to information that is fixed in a tangible form and to information that is stored in a medium from which it can be retrieved and examined. At the same time, a Rule 34 request for production of "documents" should be understood to encompass, and the response should include, electronically stored information unless discovery in the action has clearly distinguished between electronically stored information and "documents."

Discoverable information often exists in both paper and electronic form, and the same or similar information might exist in both. The items listed in Rule 34(a) show different ways in which information may be recorded or stored. Images, for example, might be hard-copy documents or electronically stored information. The wide variety of computer systems currently in use, and the rapidity of technological change, counsel against a limiting or precise definition of electronically stored information. Rule 34(a)(1) is expansive and includes any type of information that is stored electronically. A common example often sought in discovery is electronic communications, such as e-mail. The rule covers—either as documents or as electronically stored information—information "stored in any medium," to encompass future developments in computer technology. Rule 34(a)(1) is intended to be broad enough to cover all current types of computer-based information, and flexible enough to encompass future changes and developments.

References elsewhere in the rules to "electronically stored information" should be understood to invoke this expansive approach. A companion change is made to Rule 33(d), making it explicit that parties choosing to respond to an interrogatory by permitting access to responsive records may do so by providing access to electronically stored information. More generally, the term used in Rule 34(a)(1) appears in a number of other amendments, such as those to Rules 26(a)(1), 26(b)(2), 26(b)(5)(B), 26(f), 34(b), 37(f), and 45. In each of these rules, electronically stored information has the same broad meaning it has under Rule 34(a)(1). References to "documents" appear in discovery rules that are not amended, including Rules 30(f), 36(a), and 37(c)(2). These references should be interpreted to include electronically stored information as circumstances warrant.

The term "electronically stored information" is broad, but whether material that falls within this term should be produced, and in what form, are separate questions that must be addressed under Rules 26(b), 26(c), and 34(b).

The Rule 34(a) requirement that, if necessary, a party producing electronically stored information translate it into reasonably usable form does not address the issue of translating from one human language to another. See In re Puerto Rico Elect. Power Auth., 687 F.2d 501, 504–510 (1st Cir. 1989).

Rule 34(a)(1) is also amended to make clear that parties may request an opportunity to test or sample materials sought under the rule in addition to inspecting and copying them. That opportunity may be important for both electronically stored information and hard-copy materials. The current rule is not clear that such testing or sampling is authorized; the amendment expressly permits it. As with any other form of discovery, issues of burden and intrusiveness raised by requests to test or sample can be addressed under Rules 26(b)(2) and 26(c). Inspection or testing of certain types of electronically stored information or of a responding party's electronic information system may raise issues of confidentiality or privacy. The addition of testing and sampling to Rule 34(a) with regard to documents and electronically stored information is not meant to create a routine right of direct access to a party's electronic information system, although such access might be justified in some circumstances. Courts should guard against undue intrusiveness resulting from inspecting or testing such systems.

Rule 34(a)(1) is further amended to make clear that tangible things must—like documents and land sought to be examined—be designated in the request.

Subdivision (b). Rule 34(b) provides that a party must produce documents as they are kept in the usual course of business or must organize and label them to correspond with the categories in the discovery request. The production of electronically stored information should be subject to comparable requirements to protect against deliberate or inadvertent production in ways that raise unnecessary obstacles for the requesting party. Rule 34(b) is amended to ensure similar protection for electronically stored information.

The amendment to Rule 34(b) permits the requesting party to designate the form or forms in which it wants electronically stored information produced. The form of production is more important to the exchange of electronically stored information than of hard-copy materials, although a party might specify hard copy as the requested form. Specification of the desired form or forms may facilitate the orderly, efficient, and cost-effective discovery of electronically stored information. The rule recognizes that different forms of production may be appropriate for different types of electronically stored information. Using current technology, for example, a party might be called upon to produce word processing documents, e-mail messages, electronic spreadsheets, different image or sound files, and material from databases. Requiring that such diverse types of electronically stored information all be produced in the same form could prove impossible, and even if possible could increase the cost and burdens of producing and using the information. The rule therefore provides that the requesting party may ask for different forms of production for different types of electronically stored information.

The rule does not require that the requesting party choose a form or forms of production. The requesting party may not have a preference. In some cases, the requesting party may not know what form the producing party uses to maintain its electronically stored information, although Rule 26(f)(3) is amended to call for discussion of the form of production in the parties' prediscovery conference.

The responding party also is involved in determining the form of production. In the written response to the production request that Rule 34 requires, the responding party must state the form it intends to use for producing electronically stored information if the requesting party does not specify a form or if the responding party objects to a form that the requesting party specifies. Stating the intended form before the production occurs may permit the parties to identify and seek to resolve disputes before the expense and work of the production occurs. A party that responds to a discovery request by simply producing electronically stored information in a form of its choice, without identifying that form in advance of the production in the response required by Rule 34(b), runs a risk that the requesting party can show that the produced form is not reasonably usable and that it is entitled to production of some or all of the information in an additional form. Additional time might be required to permit a responding party to assess the appropriate form or forms of production.

If the requesting party is not satisfied with the form stated by the responding party, or if the responding party has objected to the form specified by the requesting party, the parties must meet and confer under Rule 37(a)(2)(B) in an effort to resolve the matter before the requesting party can file a motion to compel. If they cannot agree and the court resolves the dispute, the court is not limited to the forms initially chosen by the requesting party, stated by the responding party, or specified in this rule for situations in which there is no court order or party agreement.

If the form of production is not specified by party agreement or court order, the responding party must produce electronically stored information either in a form or forms in which it is ordinarily maintained or in a form or forms that are reasonably usable. Rule 34(a) requires that, if necessary, a responding party "translate" information it produces into a "reasonably usable" form. Under some circumstances, the responding party may need to provide some reasonable amount of technical support, information on application software, or other reasonable assistance to enable the requesting party to use the information. The rule does not require a party to produce electronically stored information in the form it [sic] which it is ordinarily maintained, as long as it is produced in a reasonably usable form. But the option to produce in a reasonably usable form does not mean that a responding party is free to convert electronically stored information from the form in which it is ordinarily maintained to a different form that makes it more difficult or burdensome for the requesting party to use the information efficiently in the litigation. If the responding party ordinarily maintains the information it is producing in a way that makes it searchable by electronic means, the information should not be produced in a form that removes or significantly degrades this feature.

Some electronically stored information may be ordinarily maintained in a form that is not reasonably usable by any party. One example is "legacy" data that can be used only by superseded systems. The questions whether a producing party should be required to convert such information to a more usable form, or should be required to produce it at all, should be addressed under Rule 26(b)(2)(B).

Whether or not the requesting party specified the form of production, Rule 34(b) provides that the same electronically stored information ordinarily be produced in only one form.

Changes Made after Publication and Comment. The proposed amendment recommended for approval has been modified from the published version. The sequence of "documents or electronically stored information" is changed to emphasize that the parenthetical exemplifications apply equally to illustrate "documents" and "electronically stored information." The reference to "detection devices" is deleted as redundant with "translated" and as archaic.

The references to the form of production are changed in the rule and Committee Note to refer also to "forms." Different forms may be appropriate or necessary for different sources of information.

The published proposal allowed the requesting party to specify a form for production and recognized that the responding party could object to the requested form. This procedure is now amplified by directing that the responding party state the form or forms it intends to use for production if the request does not specify a form or if the responding party objects to the requested form.

The default forms of production to be used when the parties do not agree on a form and there is no court order are changed in part. As in the published proposal, one default form is "a form or forms in which [electronically stored information] is ordinarily maintained." The alternative default form, however, is changed from "an electronically searchable form" to "a form or forms that are reasonably usable." "[A]n electronically searchable form" proved to have several defects. Some electronically stored information cannot be searched electronically. In addition, there often are many different levels of electronic searchability—the published default would authorize production in a minimally searchable form even though more easily searched forms might be available at equal or less cost to the responding party.

The provision that absent court order a party need not produce the same electronically stored information in more than one form was moved to become a separate item for the sake of emphasis.

The Committee Note was changed to reflect these changes in rule text, and also to clarify many aspects of the published Note. In addition, the Note was expanded to add a caveat to the published amendment that establishes the rule that documents—and now electronically stored information—may be tested and sampled as well as inspected and copied. Fears were expressed that testing and sampling might imply routine direct access to a party's information system. The Note states that direct access is not a routine right, "although such access might be justified in some circumstances."

The changes in the rule text since publication are set out below. [Omitted]

Committee Notes on Rules—2007 Amendment

The language of Rule 34 has been amended as part of the general restyling of the Civil Rules to make them more easily understood and to make style and terminology consistent throughout the rules. These changes are intended to be stylistic only.

The final sentence in the first paragraph of former Rule 34(b) was a redundant cross-reference to the discovery moratorium provisions of Rule 26(d). Rule 26(d) is now familiar, obviating any need to carry forward the redundant cross-reference.

The redundant reminder of Rule 37(a) procedure in the second paragraph of former Rule 34(b) is omitted as no longer useful.

Changes Made After Publication and Comment. See Note to Rule 1, supra.

Committee Notes on Rules—2015 Amendment

Several amendments are made in Rule 34, aimed at reducing the potential to impose unreasonable burdens by objections to requests to produce.

Rule 34(b)(2)(A) is amended to fit with new Rule 26(d)(2). The time to respond to a Rule 34 request delivered before the parties' Rule 26(f) conference is 30 days after the first Rule 26(f) conference.

Rule 34(b)(2)(B) is amended to require that objections to Rule 34 requests be stated with specificity. This provision adopts the language of Rule 33(b)(4), eliminating any doubt that less specific objections might be suitable under Rule 34. The specificity of the objection ties to the new provision in Rule 34(b)(2)(C) directing that an objection must state whether any responsive materials are being withheld on the basis of that objection. An objection may state that a request is overbroad, but if the objection recognizes that some part of the request is appropriate the objection should state the scope that is not overbroad. Examples would be a statement that the responding party will limit the search to documents or electronically stored information created within a given period of time prior to the events in suit, or to specified sources. When there is such an objection, the statement of what has been withheld can properly identify as matters "withheld" anything beyond the scope of the search specified in the objection.

Rule 34(b)(2)(B) is further amended to reflect the common practice of producing copies of documents or electronically stored information rather than simply permitting inspection. The response to the request must state that copies will be produced. The production must be completed either by the time for inspection specified in the request or by another reasonable time specifically identified in the response. When it is necessary to make the production in stages the response should specify the beginning and end dates of the production.

Rule 34(b)(2)(C) is amended to provide that an objection to a Rule 34 request must state whether anything is being withheld on the basis of the objection. This amendment should end the confusion that frequently arises when a producing party states several objections and still produces information, leaving the requesting party uncertain whether any relevant and responsive information has been withheld on the basis of the objections. The producing party does not need to provide a detailed description or log of all documents withheld, but does need to alert other parties to the fact that documents have been withheld and thereby facilitate an informed discussion of the objection. An objection that states the limits that have controlled the search for responsive and relevant materials qualifies as a statement that the materials have been "withheld."

Rule 35. Physical and Mental Examinations

(a) Order for an Examination.

(1) In General. The court where the action is pending may order a party whose mental or physical condition—including blood group—is in controversy to submit to a physical or mental examination by a suitably licensed or certified examiner. The court has the same authority to order a party to produce for examination a person who is in its custody or under its legal control.

(2) Motion and Notice; Contents of the Order. The order:

(A) may be made only on motion for good cause and on notice to all parties and the person to be examined; and

(B) must specify the time, place, manner, conditions, and scope of the examination, as well as the person or persons who will perform it.

(b) Examiner's Report.

(1) Request by the Party or Person Examined. The party who moved for the examination must, on request, deliver to the requester a copy of the examiner's report, together with like reports of all earlier examinations of the same condition. The request may be made by the party against whom the examination order was issued or by the person examined.

(2) Contents. The examiner's report must be in writing and must set out in detail the examiner's findings, including diagnoses, conclusions, and the results of any tests.

(3) Request by the Moving Party. After delivering the reports, the party who moved for the examination may request—and is entitled to receive—from the party against whom the examination order was issued like reports of all earlier or later examinations of the same condition. But those reports need not be delivered by the party with custody or control of the person examined if the party shows that it could not obtain them.

(4) Waiver of Privilege. By requesting and obtaining the examiner's report, or by deposing the examiner, the party examined waives any privilege it may have—in that action or any other action involving the same controversy—concerning testimony about all examinations of the same condition.

(5) Failure to Deliver a Report. The court on motion may order—on just terms—that a party deliver the report of an examination. If the report is not provided, the court may exclude the examiner's testimony at trial.

(6) Scope. This subdivision (b) applies also to an examination made by the parties' agreement, unless the agreement states otherwise. This subdivision does not preclude obtaining an examiner's report or deposing an examiner under other rules.

(As amended Mar. 30, 1970, eff. July 1, 1970; Mar. 2, 1987, eff. Aug. 1, 1987; Pub. L. 100–690, title VII, §7047(b), Nov. 18, 1988, 102 Stat. 4401; Apr. 30, 1991, eff. Dec. 1, 1991; Apr. 30, 2007, eff. Dec. 1, 2007.)

Notes of Advisory Committee on Rules—1937

Physical examination of parties before trial is authorized by statute or rule in a number of states. See Ariz.Rev.Code Ann. (Struckmeyer, 1928) §4468; Mich.Court Rules Ann. (Searl, 1933) Rule 41, §2; 2 N.J.Comp.Stat. (1910), N.Y.C.P.A. (1937) §306; 1 S.D.Comp.Laws (1929) §2716A; 3 Wash.Rev.Stat.Ann. (Remington, 1932) §1230–1.

Mental examination of parties is authorized in Iowa. Iowa Code (1935) ch. 491–F1. See McCash, The Evolution of the Doctrine of Discovery and Its Present Status in Iowa, 20 Ia.L.Rev. 68 (1934).

The constitutionality of legislation providing for physical examination of parties was sustained in Lyon v. Manhattan Railway Co., 142 N.Y. 298, 37 N.E. 113 (1894), and McGovern v. Hope, 63 N.J.L. 76, 42 Atl. 830 (1899). In Union Pacific Ry. Co. v. Botsford, 141 U.S. 250 (1891), it was held that the court could not order the physical examination of a party in the absence of statutory authority. But in Camden and Suburban Ry. Co. v. Stetson, 177 U.S. 172 (1900) where there was statutory authority for such examination, derived from a state statute made operative by the conformity act, the practice was sustained. Such authority is now found in the present rule made operative by the Act of June 19, 1934, ch. 651, U.S.C., Title 28, §§723b [see 2072] (Rules in actions at law; Supreme Court authorized to make) and 723c [see 2072] (Union of equity and action at law rules; power of Supreme Court).

Notes of Advisory Committee on Rules—1970 Amendment

Subdivision (a). Rule 35(a) has hitherto provided only for an order requiring a party to submit to an examination. It is desirable to extend the rule to provide for an order against the party for examination of a person in his custody or under his legal control. As appears from the provisions of amended Rule 37(b)(2) and the comment under that rule, an order to "produce" the third person imposes only an obligation to use good faith efforts to produce the person.

The amendment will settle beyond doubt that a parent or guardian suing to recover for injuries to a minor may be ordered to produce the minor for examination. Further, the amendment expressly includes blood examination within the kinds of examinations that can be ordered under the rule. See Beach v. Beach, 114 F.2d 479 (D.C. Cir. 1940). Provisions similar to the amendment have been adopted in at least 10 States: Calif.Code Civ.Proc. §2032; Ida.R.Civ.P. 35; Ill.S-H Ann. c. 110A, §215; Md.R.P. 420; Mich.Gen. Ct.R. 311; Minn.R.Civ.P. 35; Mo.Vern.Ann.R.Civ.P. 60.01; N.Dak.R.Civ.P. 35; N.Y.C.P.L. §3121; Wyo.R.Civ.P. 35.

The amendment makes no change in the requirements of Rule 35 that, before a court order may issue, the relevant physical or mental condition must be shown to be "in controversy" and "good cause" must be shown for the examination. Thus, the amendment has no effect on the recent decision of the Supreme Court in Schlagenhauf v. Holder, 379 U.S. 104 (1964), stressing the importance of these requirements and applying them to the facts of the case. The amendment makes no reference to employees of a party. Provisions relating to employees in the State statutes and rules cited above appear to have been virtually unused.

Subdivision (b)(1). This subdivision is amended to correct an imbalance in Rule 35(b)(1) as heretofore written. Under that text, a party causing a Rule 35(a) examination to be made is required to furnish to the party examined, on request, a copy of the examining physician's report. If he delivers this copy, he is in turn entitled to receive from the party examined reports of all examinations of the same condition previously or later made. But the rule has not in terms entitled the examined party to receive from the party causing the Rule 35(a) examination any reports of earlier examinations of the same condition to which the latter may have access. The amendment cures this defect. See La.Stat.Ann., Civ.Proc. art. 1495 (1960); Utah R.Civ.P.35(c).

The amendment specifies that the written report of the examining physician includes results of all tests made, such as results of X-rays and cardiograms. It also embodies changes required by the broadening of Rule 35(a) to take in persons who are not parties.

Subdivision (b)(3). This new subdivision removes any possible doubt that reports of examination may be obtained although no order for examination has been made under Rule 35(a). Examinations are very frequently made by agreement, and sometimes before the party examined has an attorney. The courts have uniformly ordered that reports be supplied, see 4 Moore's Federal Practice 35.06, n.1 (2d ed. 1966); 2A Barron & Holtzoff, Federal Practice and Procedure §823, n. 22 (Wright ed. 1961), and it appears best to fill the technical gap in the present rule.

The subdivision also makes clear that reports of examining physicians are discoverable not only under Rule 35(b) but under other rules as well. To be sure, if the report is privileged, then discovery is not permissible under any rule other than Rule 35(b) and it is permissible under Rule 35(b) only if the party requests a copy of the report of examination made by the other party's doctor. Sher v. De Haven, 199 F.2d 777 (D.C. Cir. 1952), cert. denied 345 U.S. 936 (1953). But if the report is unprivileged and is subject to discovery under the provisions of rules other than Rule 35(b)—such as Rules 34 or 26(b)(3) or (4)—discovery should not depend upon whether the person examined demands a copy of the report. Although a few cases have suggested the contrary, e.g., Galloway v. National Dairy Products Corp., 24 F.R.D. 362 (E.D.Pa. 1959), the better considered district court decisions hold that Rule 35(b) is not preemptive. E.g., Leszynski v. Russ, 29 F.R.D. 10, 12 (D.Md. 1961) and cases cited. The question was recently given full consideration in Buffington v. Wood, 351 F.2d 292 (3d Cir. 1965), holding that Rule 35(b) is not preemptive.

Notes of Advisory Committee on Rules—1987 Amendment

The amendments are technical. No substantive change is intended.

Notes of Advisory Committee on Rules—1991 Amendment

The revision authorizes the court to require physical or mental examinations conducted by any person who is suitably licensed or certified.

The rule was revised in 1988 by Congressional enactment to authorize mental examinations by licensed clinical psychologists. This revision extends that amendment to include other certified or licensed professionals, such as dentists or occupational therapists, who are not physicians or clinical psychologists, but who may be well-qualified to give valuable testimony about the physical or mental condition that is the subject of dispute.

The requirement that the examiner be suitably licensed or certified is a new requirement. The court is thus expressly authorized to assess the credentials of the examiner to assure that no person is subjected to a court-ordered examination by an examiner whose testimony would be of such limited value that it would be unjust to require the person to undergo the invasion of privacy associated with the examination. This authority is not wholly new, for under the former rule, the court retained discretion to refuse to order an examination, or to restrict an examination. 8 WRIGHT & MILLER, FEDERAL PRACTICE & PROCEDURE §2234 (1986 Supp.). The revision is intended to encourage the exercise of this discretion, especially with respect to examinations by persons having narrow qualifications.

The court's responsibility to determine the suitability of the examiner's qualifications applies even to a proposed examination by a physician. If the proposed examination and testimony calls for an expertise that the proposed examiner does not have, it should not be ordered, even if the proposed examiner is a physician. The rule does not, however, require that the license or certificate be conferred by the jurisdiction in which the examination is conducted.

Committee Notes on Rules—2007 Amendment

The language of Rule 35 has been amended as part of the general restyling of the Civil Rules to make them more easily understood and to make style and terminology consistent throughout the rules. These changes are intended to be stylistic only.

Amendment by Public Law

1988—Subd. (a). Pub. L. 100–690, §7047(b)(1), substituted "physical examination by a physician, or mental examination by a physician or psychologist" for "physical or mental examination by a physician".

Subd. (b). Pub. L. 100–690, §7047(b)(2), inserted "or psychologist" in heading, in two places in par. (1), and in two places in par. (3).

Subd. (c). Pub. L. 100–690, §7047(b)(3), added subd. (c).

Rule 36. Requests for Admission

(a) Scope and Procedure.

(1) Scope. A party may serve on any other party a written request to admit, for purposes of the pending action

only, the truth of any matters within the scope of Rule 26(b)(1) relating to:

(A) facts, the application of law to fact, or opinions about either; and

(B) the genuineness of any described documents.

(2) Form; Copy of a Document. Each matter must be separately stated. A request to admit the genuineness of a document must be accompanied by a copy of the document unless it is, or has been, otherwise furnished or made available for inspection and copying.

(3) Time to Respond; Effect of Not Responding. A matter is admitted unless, within 30 days after being served, the party to whom the request is directed serves on the requesting party a written answer or objection addressed to the matter and signed by the party or its attorney. A shorter or longer time for responding may be stipulated to under Rule 29 or be ordered by the court.

(4) Answer. If a matter is not admitted, the answer must specifically deny it or state in detail why the answering party cannot truthfully admit or deny it. A denial must fairly respond to the substance of the matter; and when good faith requires that a party qualify an answer or deny only a part of a matter, the answer must specify the part admitted and qualify or deny the rest. The answering party may assert lack of knowledge or information as a reason for failing to admit or deny only if the party states that it has made reasonable inquiry and that the information it knows or can readily obtain is insufficient to enable it to admit or deny.

(5) Objections. The grounds for objecting to a request must be stated. A party must not object solely on the ground that the request presents a genuine issue for trial.

(6) Motion Regarding the Sufficiency of an Answer or Objection. The requesting party may move to determine the sufficiency of an answer or objection. Unless the court finds an objection justified, it must order that an answer be served. On finding that an answer does not comply with this rule, the court may order either that the matter is admitted or that an amended answer be served. The court may defer its final decision until a pretrial conference or a specified time before trial. Rule 37(a)(5) applies to an award of expenses.

(b) Effect of an Admission; Withdrawing or Amending It. A matter admitted under this rule is conclusively established unless the court, on motion, permits the admission to be withdrawn or amended. Subject to Rule 16(e), the court may permit withdrawal or amendment if it would promote the presentation of the merits of the action and if the court is not persuaded that it would prejudice the requesting party in maintaining or defending the action on the merits. An admission under this rule is not an admission for any other purpose and cannot be used against the party in any other proceeding.

(As amended Dec. 27, 1946, eff. Mar. 19, 1948; Mar. 30, 1970, eff. July 1, 1970; Mar. 2, 1987, eff. Aug. 1, 1987; Apr. 22, 1993, eff. Dec. 1, 1993; Apr. 30, 2007, eff. Dec. 1, 2007.)

Notes of Advisory Committee on Rules—1937

Compare similar rules: [Former] Equity Rule 58 (last paragraph, which provides for the admission of the execution and genuineness of documents); English Rules Under the Judicature Act (The Annual Practice, 1937) O. 32; Ill.Rev.Stat. (1937) ch. 110, §182 and Rule 18 (Ill.Rev.Stat. (1937) ch. 110, §259.18); 2 Mass.Gen.Laws (Ter.Ed., 1932) ch. 231, §69; Mich.Court Rules Ann. (Searl, 1933) Rule 42; N.J.Comp.Stat. (2 Cum.Supp. 1911–1924) N.Y.C.P.A. (1937) §§322, 323; Wis.Stat. (1935) §327.22.

Notes of Advisory Committee on Rules—1946 Amendment

The first change in the first sentence of Rule 36(a) and the addition of the new second sentence, specifying when requests for admissions may be served, bring Rule 36 in line with amended Rules 26(a) and 33. There is no reason why these rules should not be treated alike. Other provisions of Rule 36(a) give the party whose admissions are requested adequate protection.

The second change in the first sentence of the rule [subdivision (a)] removes any uncertainty as to whether a party can be called upon to admit matters of fact other than those set forth in relevant documents described in and exhibited with the request. In Smyth v. Kaufman (C.C.A.2d, 1940) 114 F.(2d) 40, it was held that the word "therein", now stricken from the rule [said subdivision] referred to the request and that a matter of fact not related to any document could be presented to the other party for admission or denial. The rule of this case is now clearly stated.

The substitution of the word "served" for "delivered" in the third sentence of the amended rule [said subdivision] is in conformance with the use of the word "serve" elsewhere in the rule and generally throughout the rules. See also Notes to Rules 13(a) and 33 herein. The substitution [in said subdivision] of "shorter or longer" for "further" will enable a court to designate a lesser period than 10 days for answer. This conforms with a similar provision already contained in Rule 33.

The addition of clause (2) [in said subdivision] specifies the method by which a party may challenge the propriety of a request to admit. There has been considerable difference of judicial opinion as to the correct method, if any, available to secure relief from an allegedly improper request. See Commentary, Methods of Objecting to Notice to Admit (1942) 5 Fed.Rules Serv. 835; International Carbonic Engineering Co. v. Natural Carbonic Products, Inc. (S.D.Cal. 1944) 57 F.Supp. 248. The changes in clause (1) are merely of a clarifying and conforming nature.

The first of the added last two sentences [in said subdivision] prevents an objection to a part of a request from holding up the answer, if any, to the remainder. See similar proposed change in Rule 33. The last sentence strengthens the rule by making the denial accurately reflect the party's position. It is taken, with necessary changes, from Rule 8(b).

Notes of Advisory Committee on Rules—1970 Amendment

Rule 36 serves two vital purposes, both of which are designed to reduce trial time. Admissions are sought, first to facilitate proof with respect to issues that cannot be eliminated from the case, and secondly, to narrow the issues by eliminating those that can be. The changes made in the rule are designed to serve these purposes more effectively. Certain disagreements in the courts about the proper scope of the rule are resolved. In addition, the procedural operation of the rule is brought into line with other discovery procedures, and the binding effect of an admission is clarified. See generally Finman, The Request for Admissions in Federal Civil Procedure, 71 Yale L.J. 371 (1962).

Subdivision (a). As revised, the subdivision provides that a request may be made to admit any matter within the scope of Rule 26(b) that relate to statements or opinions of fact or of the application of law to fact. It thereby eliminates the requirement that the matters be "of fact." This change resolves conflicts in the court decisions as to whether a request to admit matters of "opinion" and matters involving "mixed law and fact" is proper under the rule. As to "opinion," compare, e.g., Jackson Bluff Corp. v. Marcelle, 20 F.R.D. 139 (E.D.N.Y. 1957); California v. The S.S. Jules Fribourg, 19 F.R.D. 432 (N.D.Calif. 1955), with e.g., Photon, Inc. v. Harris Intertype, Inc., 28 F.R.D. 327 (D.Mass. 1961); Hise v. Lockwood Grader Corp., 153 F.Supp 276 (D.Nebr. 1957). As to "mixed law and fact" the majority of courts sustain objections, e.g., Minnesota Mining and Mfg. Co. v. Norton Co., 36 F.R.D. 1 (N.D.Ohio 1964), but McSparran v. Hanigan, 225 F.Supp. 628 (E.D.Pa. 1963) is to the contrary.

Not only is it difficult as a practical matter to separate "fact" from "opinion," see 4 Moore's Federal Practice 36.04 (2d ed. 1966); cf. 2A Barron & Holtzoff, Federal Practice and Procedure 317 (Wright ed. 1961), but an admission on a matter of opinion may facilitate proof or narrow the issues or both. An admission of a matter involving the application of law to fact may, in a given case, even more clearly narrow the issues. For example, an admission that an employee acted in the scope of his employment may remove a major issue from the trial. In McSparran v. Hanigan, supra, plaintiff admitted that "the premises on which said accident occurred, were occupied or under the control" of one of the defendants, 225 F.Supp. at 636. This admission, involving law as well as fact, removed one of the issues from the lawsuit and thereby reduced the proof required at trial. The amended provision does not authorize requests for admissions of law unrelated to the facts of the case.

Requests for admission involving the application of law to fact may create disputes between the parties which are best resolved in the presence of the judge after much or all of the other discovery has been completed. Power is therefore expressly conferred upon the court to defer decision until a pretrial conference is held or until a designated time prior to trial. On the other hand, the court should not automatically defer decision; in many instances, the importance of the admission lies in enabling the requesting party to avoid the burdensome accumulation of proof prior to the pretrial conference.

Courts have also divided on whether an answering party may properly object to request for admission as to matters which that party regards as "in dispute." Compare, e.g., Syracuse Broadcasting Corp. v. Newhouse, 271 F.2d 910, 917 (2d Cir. 1959); Driver v. Gindy Mfg. Corp., 24 F.R.D. 473 (E.D.Pa. 1959); with e.g., McGonigle v. Baxter, 27 F.R.D. 504 (E.D.Pa. 1961); United States v. Ehbauer, 13 F.R.D. 462 (W.D.Mo. 1952). The proper response in such cases is an answer. The very purpose of the request is to ascertain whether the answering party is prepared to admit or regards the matter as presenting a genuine issue for trial. In his answer, the party may deny, or he may give his reason for inability to admit or deny the existence of a genuine issue. The party runs no risk of sanctions if the matter is genuinely in issue, since Rule 37(c) provides a sanction of costs only when there are no good reasons for a failure to admit.

On the other hand, requests to admit may be so voluminous and so framed that the answering party finds the task of identifying what is in dispute and what is not unduly burdensome. If so, the responding party may obtain a protective order under Rule 26(c). Some of the decisions sustaining objections on "disputability" grounds could have been justified by the burdensome character of the requests. See, e.g., Syracuse Broadcasting Corp. v. Newhouse, supra.

Another sharp split of authority exists on the question whether a party may base his answer on lack of information or knowledge without seeking out additional information. One line of cases has held that a party may answer on the basis of such knowledge as he has at the time he answers. E.g., Jackson Buff Corp. v. Marcelle, 20 F.R.D. 139 (E.D.N.Y. 1957); Sladek v. General Motors Corp., 16 F.R.D. 104 (S.D.Iowa 1954). A larger group of cases, supported by commentators, has taken the view that if the responding party lacks knowledge, he must inform himself in reasonable fashion. E.g., Hise v. Lockwood Grader Corp., 153 F.Supp. 276 (D.Nebr. 1957); E. H. Tate Co. v. Jiffy Enterprises, Inc., 16 F.R.D. 571 (E.D.Pa. 1954); Finman, supra, 71 Yale L.J. 371, 404–409; 4 Moore's Federal Practice 36.04 (2d ed. 1966); 2A Barron & Holtzoff, Federal Practice and Procedure 509 (Wright ed. 1961).

The rule as revised adopts the majority view, as in keeping with a basic principle of the discovery rules that a reasonable burden may be imposed on the parties when its discharge will facilitate preparation for trial and ease the trial process. It has been argued against this view that one side should not have the burden of "proving" the other side's case. The revised rule requires only that the answering party make reasonable inquiry and secure such knowledge and information as are readily obtainable by him. In most instances, the investigation will be necessary either to his own case or to preparation for rebuttal. Even when it is not, the information may be close enough at hand to be "readily obtainable." Rule 36 requires only that the party state that he has taken these steps. The sanction for failure of a party to inform himself before he answers lies in the award of costs after trial, as provided in Rule 37(c).

The requirement that the answer to a request for admission be sworn is deleted, in favor of a provision that the answer be signed by the party or by his attorney. The provisions of Rule 36 make it clear that admissions function very much as pleadings do. Thus, when a party admits in part and denies in part, his admission is for purposes of the pending action only and may not be used against him in any other proceeding. The broadening of the rule to encompass mixed questions of law and fact reinforces this feature. Rule 36 does not lack a sanction for false answers; Rule 37(c) furnishes an appropriate deterrent.

The existing language describing the available grounds for objection to a request for admission is eliminated as neither necessary nor helpful. The statement that objection may be made to any request, which is "improper" adds nothing to the provisions that the party serve an answer or objection addressed to each matter and that he state his reasons for any objection. None of the other discovery rules set forth grounds for objection, except so far as all are subject to the general provisions of Rule 26.

Changes are made in the sequence of procedures in Rule 36 so that they conform to the new procedures in Rules 33 and 34. The major changes are as follows:

(1) The normal time for response to a request for admissions is lengthened from 10 to 30 days, conforming more closely to prevailing practice. A defendant need not respond, however, in less than 45 days after service of the summons and complaint upon him. The court may lengthen or shorten the time when special situations require it.

(2) The present requirement that the plaintiff wait 10 days to serve requests without leave of court is eliminated. The revised provision accords with those in Rules 33 and 34.

(3) The requirement that the objecting party move automatically for a hearing on his objection is eliminated, and the burden is on the requesting party to move for an order. The change in the burden of going forward does not modify present law on burden of persuasion. The award of expenses incurred in relation to the motion is made subject to the comprehensive provisions of Rule 37(a)(4).

(4) A problem peculiar to Rule 36 arises if the responding party serves answers that are not in conformity with the requirements of the rule—for example, a denial is not "specific," or the explanation of inability to admit or deny is not "in detail." Rule 36 now makes no provision for court scrutiny of such answers before trial, and it seems to contemplate that defective answers bring about admissions just as effectively as if no answer had been served. Some cases have so held. E.g., Southern Ry. Co. v. Crosby, 201 F.2d 878 (4th Cir. 1953); United States v. Laney, 96 F.Supp. 482 (E.D.S.C. 1951).

Giving a defective answer the automatic effect of an admission may cause unfair surprise. A responding party who purported to deny or to be unable to admit or deny will for the first time at trial confront the contention that he has made a binding admission. Since it is not always easy to know whether a denial is "specific" or an explanation is "in detail," neither party can know how the court will rule at trial and whether proof must be prepared. Some courts, therefore, have entertained motions to rule on defective answers. They have at times ordered that amended answers be served, when the defects were technical, and at other times have declared that the matter was admitted. E.g., Woods v. Stewart, 171 F.2d 544 (5th Cir. 1948); SEC v. Kaye, Real & Co., 122 F.Supp. 639 (S.D.N.Y. 1954); Seib's Hatcheries, Inc. v. Lindley, 13 F.R.D. 113 (W.D.Ark. 1952). The rule as revised conforms to the latter practice.

Subdivision (b). The rule does not now indicate the extent to which a party is bound by his admission. Some courts view admissions as the equivalent of sworn testimony E.g., Ark.-Tenn Distributing Corp. v. Breidt, 209 F.2d 359 (3d Cir. 1954); United States v. Lemons, 125 F.Supp. 686 (W.D.Ark. 1954); 4 Moore's Federal Practice 36.08 (2d ed. 1966 Supp.). At least in some jurisdictions a party may rebut his own testimony, e.g., Alamo v. Del Rosario, 98 F.2d 328 (D.C.Cir. 1938), and by analogy an admission made pursuant to Rule 36 may likewise be thought rebuttable. The courts in Ark-Tenn and Lemons, supra, reasoned in this way, although the results reached may be supported on different grounds. In McSparran v. Hanigan, 225 F.Supp. 628, 636–637 (E.D.Pa. 1963), the court held that an admission is conclusively binding, though noting the confusion created by prior decisions.

The new provisions give an admission a conclusively binding effect, for purposes only of the pending action, unless the admission is withdrawn or amended. In form and substance a Rule 36 admission is comparable to an admission in pleadings or a stipulation drafted by counsel for use at trial, rather than to an evidentiary admission of a party. Louisell, Modern California Discovery §8.07 (1963); 2A Barron & Holtzoff, Federal Practice and Procedure §838 (Wright ed. 1961). Unless the party securing an admission can depend on its binding effect, he cannot safely avoid the expense of preparing to prove the very matters on which he has secured the admission, and the purpose of the rule is defeated. Field & McKusick, Maine Civil Practice §36.4 (1959); Finman, supra, 71 Yale L.J. 371, 418–426; Comment, 56 Nw.U.L.Rev. 679, 682–683 (1961).

Provision is made for withdrawal or amendment of an admission. This provision emphasizes the importance of having the action resolved on the merits, while at the same time assuring each party that justified reliance on an admission in preparation for trial will not operate to his prejudice. Cf. Moosman v. Joseph P. Blitz, Inc., 358 F.2d 686 (2d Cir. 1966).

Notes of Advisory Committee on Rules—1987 Amendment

The amendments are technical. No substantive change is intended.

Notes of Advisory Committee on Rules—1993 Amendment

The rule is revised to reflect the change made by Rule 26(d), preventing a party from seeking formal discovery until after the meeting of the parties required by Rule 26(f).

Committee Notes on Rules—2007 Amendment

The language of Rule 36 has been amended as part of the general restyling of the Civil Rules to make them more easily understood and to make style and terminology consistent throughout the rules. These changes are intended to be stylistic only.

The final sentence of the first paragraph of former Rule 36(a) was a redundant cross-reference to the discovery moratorium provisions of Rule 26(d). Rule 26(d) is now familiar, obviating any need to carry forward the redundant cross-reference. The redundant reminder of Rule 37(c) in the second paragraph was likewise omitted.

Changes Made After Publication and Comment. See Note to Rule 1, supra.

Rule 37. Failure to Make Disclosures or to Cooperate in Discovery; Sanctions

(a) Motion for an Order Compelling Disclosure or Discovery.

(1) In General. On notice to other parties and all affected persons, a party may move for an order compelling disclosure or discovery. The motion must include a certification that the movant has in good faith conferred or attempted to confer with the person or party failing to make disclosure or discovery in an effort to obtain it without court action.

(2) Appropriate Court. A motion for an order to a party must be made in the court where the action is pending. A motion for an order to a nonparty must be made in the court where the discovery is or will be taken.

(3) Specific Motions.

(A) To Compel Disclosure. If a party fails to make a disclosure required by Rule 26(a), any other party may move to compel disclosure and for appropriate sanctions.

(B) To Compel a Discovery Response. A party seeking discovery may move for an order compelling an answer, designation, production, or inspection. This motion may be made if:

(i) a deponent fails to answer a question asked under Rule 30 or 31;

(ii) a corporation or other entity fails to make a designation under Rule 30(b)(6) or 31(a)(4);

(iii) a party fails to answer an interrogatory submitted under Rule 33; or

(iv) a party fails to produce documents or fails to respond that inspection will be permitted—or fails to permit inspection—as requested under Rule 34.

(C) Related to a Deposition. When taking an oral deposition, the party asking a question may complete or adjourn the examination before moving for an order.

(4) Evasive or Incomplete Disclosure, Answer, or Response. For purposes of this subdivision (a), an evasive or incomplete disclosure, answer, or response must be treated as a failure to disclose, answer, or respond.

(5) Payment of Expenses; Protective Orders.

(A) If the Motion Is Granted (or Disclosure or Discovery Is Provided After Filing). If the motion is granted—or if the disclosure or requested discovery is provided after the motion was filed—the court must, after giving an opportunity to be heard, require the party or deponent whose conduct necessitated the motion, the party or attorney advising that conduct, or both to pay the movant's reasonable expenses incurred in making the motion, including attorney's fees. But the court must not order this payment if:

(i) the movant filed the motion before attempting in good faith to obtain the disclosure or discovery without court action;

(ii) the opposing party's nondisclosure, response, or objection was substantially justified; or

(iii) other circumstances make an award of expenses unjust.

(B) If the Motion Is Denied. If the motion is denied, the court may issue any protective order authorized under Rule 26(c) and must, after giving an opportunity to be heard, require the movant, the attorney filing the motion, or both to pay the party or deponent who opposed the motion its reasonable expenses incurred in opposing the motion, including attorney's fees. But the court must not order this payment if the motion was substantially justified or other circumstances make an award of expenses unjust.

(C) If the Motion Is Granted in Part and Denied in Part. If the motion is granted in part and denied in part, the court may issue any protective order authorized under Rule 26(c) and may, after giving an opportunity to be heard, apportion the reasonable expenses for the motion.

(b) Failure to Comply with a Court Order.

(1) Sanctions Sought in the District Where the Deposition Is Taken. If the court where the discovery is taken orders a deponent to be sworn or to answer a question and the deponent fails to obey, the failure may be treated as contempt of court. If a deposition-related motion is transferred to the court where the action is pending, and that court orders a deponent to be sworn or to answer a question and the deponent fails to obey, the failure may be treated as contempt of either the court where the discovery is taken or the court where the action is pending.

(2) Sanctions Sought in the District Where the Action Is Pending.

(A) For Not Obeying a Discovery Order. If a party or a party's officer, director, or managing agent—or a witness designated under Rule 30(b)(6) or 31(a)(4)—fails to obey an order to provide or permit discovery, including an order under Rule 26(f), 35, or 37(a), the court where the action is pending may issue further just orders. They may include the following:

(i) directing that the matters embraced in the order or other designated facts be taken as established for purposes of the action, as the prevailing party claims;

(ii) prohibiting the disobedient party from supporting or opposing designated claims or defenses, or from introducing designated matters in evidence;

(iii) striking pleadings in whole or in part;

(iv) staying further proceedings until the order is obeyed;

(v) dismissing the action or proceeding in whole or in part;

(vi) rendering a default judgment against the disobedient party; or

(vii) treating as contempt of court the failure to obey any order except an order to submit to a physical or mental examination.

(B) For Not Producing a Person for Examination. If a party fails to comply with an order under Rule 35(a) requiring it to produce another person for examination, the court may issue any of the orders listed in Rule 37(b)(2)(A)(i)–(vi), unless the disobedient party shows that it cannot produce the other person.

(C) Payment of Expenses. Instead of or in addition to the orders above, the court must order the disobedient party, the attorney advising that party, or both to pay the reasonable expenses, including attorney's fees, caused by the failure, unless the failure was substantially justified or other circumstances make an award of expenses unjust.

(c) Failure to Disclose, to Supplement an Earlier Response, or to Admit.

(1) Failure to Disclose or Supplement. If a party fails to provide information or identify a witness as required by Rule 26(a) or (e), the party is not allowed to use that information or witness to supply evidence on a motion, at a hearing, or at a trial, unless the failure was substantially justified or is harmless. In addition to or instead of this sanction, the court, on motion and after giving an opportunity to be heard:

(A) may order payment of the reasonable expenses, including attorney's fees, caused by the failure;

(B) may inform the jury of the party's failure; and

(C) may impose other appropriate sanctions, including any of the orders listed in Rule 37(b)(2)(A)(i)–(vi).

(2) Failure to Admit. If a party fails to admit what is requested under Rule 36 and if the requesting party later proves a document to be genuine or the matter true, the requesting party may move that the party who failed to admit pay the reasonable expenses, including attorney's fees, incurred in making that proof. The court must so order unless:

(A) the request was held objectionable under Rule 36(a);

(B) the admission sought was of no substantial importance;

(C) the party failing to admit had a reasonable ground to believe that it might prevail on the matter; or

(D) there was other good reason for the failure to admit.

(d) Party's Failure to Attend Its Own Deposition, Serve Answers to Interrogatories, or Respond to a Request for Inspection.

(1) In General.

(A) Motion; Grounds for Sanctions. The court where the action is pending may, on motion, order sanctions if:

(i) a party or a party's officer, director, or managing agent—or a person designated under Rule 30(b)(6) or 31(a)(4)—fails, after being served with proper notice, to appear for that person's deposition; or

(ii) a party, after being properly served with interrogatories under Rule 33 or a request for inspection under Rule 34, fails to serve its answers, objections, or written response.

(B) Certification. A motion for sanctions for failing to answer or respond must include a certification that the movant has in good faith conferred or attempted to confer with the party failing to act in an effort to obtain the answer or response without court action.

(2) Unacceptable Excuse for Failing to Act. A failure described in Rule 37(d)(1)(A) is not excused on the ground that the discovery sought was objectionable, unless the party failing to act has a pending motion for a protective order under Rule 26(c).

(3) Types of Sanctions. Sanctions may include any of the orders listed in Rule 37(b)(2)(A)(i)–(vi). Instead of or in addition to these sanctions, the court must require the party failing to act, the attorney advising that party, or both to pay the reasonable expenses, including attorney's fees, caused by the failure, unless the failure was substantially justified or other circumstances make an award of expenses unjust.

(e) Failure to Preserve Electronically Stored Information. If electronically stored information that should have been preserved in the anticipation or conduct of litigation is lost because a party failed to take reasonable steps to preserve it, and it cannot be restored or replaced through additional discovery, the court:

(1) upon finding prejudice to another party from loss of the information, may order measures no greater than necessary to cure the prejudice; or

(2) only upon finding that the party acted with the intent to deprive another party of the information's use in the litigation may:

(A) presume that the lost information was unfavorable to the party;

(B) instruct the jury that it may or must presume the information was unfavorable to the party; or

(C) dismiss the action or enter a default judgment.

(f) Failure to Participate in Framing a Discovery Plan. If a party or its attorney fails to participate in good faith in developing and submitting a proposed discovery plan as required by Rule 26(f), the court may, after giving an opportunity to be heard, require that party or attorney to pay to any other party the reasonable expenses, including attorney's fees, caused by the failure.

(As amended Dec. 29, 1948, eff. Oct. 20, 1949; Mar. 30, 1970, eff. July 1, 1970; Apr. 29, 1980, eff. Aug. 1, 1980; Pub. L. 96–481, §205(a), Oct. 21, 1980, 94 Stat. 2330, eff. Oct. 1, 1981; Mar. 2, 1987, eff. Aug. 1, 1987; Apr. 22, 1993, eff. Dec. 1, 1993; Apr. 17, 2000, eff. Dec. 1, 2000; Apr. 12, 2006, eff. Dec. 1, 2006; Apr. 30, 2007, eff. Dec. 1, 2007; Apr. 16, 2013, eff. Dec. 1, 2013; Apr. 29, 2015, eff. Dec. 1, 2015.)

Notes of Advisory Committee on Rules—1937

The provisions of this rule authorizing orders establishing facts or excluding evidence or striking pleadings, or authorizing judgments of dismissal or default, for refusal to answer questions or permit inspection or otherwise make discovery, are in accord with Hammond Packing Co. v. Arkansas, 212 U.S. 322 (1909), which distinguishes between the justifiable use of such measures as a means of compelling the production of evidence, and their unjustifiable use, as in Hovey v. Elliott, 167 U.S. 409 (1897), for the mere purpose of punishing for contempt.

Notes of Advisory Committee on Rules—1948 Amendment

The amendment substitutes the present statutory reference.

Notes of Advisory Committee on Rules—1970 Amendment

Rule 37 provides generally for sanctions against parties or persons unjustifiably resisting discovery. Experience has brought to light a number of defects in the language of the rule as well as instances in which it is not serving the purposes for which it was designed. See Rosenberg, Sanctions to Effectuate Pretrial Discovery, 58 Col.L.Rev. 480 (1958). In addition, changes being made in other discovery rules requiring conforming amendments to Rule 37.

Rule 37 sometimes refers to a "failure" to afford discovery and at other times to a "refusal" to do so. Taking note of this dual terminology, courts have imported into "refusal" a requirement of "wilfullness." See Roth v. Paramount Pictures Corp., 8 F.R.D. 31 (W.D.Pa. 1948); Campbell v. Johnson, 101 F.Supp. 705, 707 (S.D.N.Y. 1951). In Societe Internationale v. Rogers, 357 U.S. 197 (1958), the Supreme Court concluded that the rather random use of these two terms in Rule 37 showed no design to use them with consistently distinctive meanings, that "refused" in Rule 37(b)(2) meant simply a failure to comply, and that wilfullness was relevant only to the selection of sanctions, if any, to be imposed. Nevertheless, after the decision in Societe, the court in Hinson v. Michigan Mutual Liability Co., 275 F.2d 537 (5th Cir. 1960) once again ruled that "refusal" required wilfullness. Substitution of "failure" for "refusal" throughout Rule 37 should eliminate this confusion and bring the rule into harmony with the Societe Internationale decision. See Rosenberg, supra, 58 Col.L.Rev. 480, 489–490 (1958).

Subdivision (a). Rule 37(a) provides relief to a party seeking discovery against one who, with or without stated objections, fails to afford the discovery sought. It has always fully served this function in relation to depositions, but the amendments being made to Rules 33 and 34 give Rule 37(a) added scope and importance. Under existing Rule 33, a party objecting to interrogatories must make a motion for court hearing on his objections. The changes now made in Rules 33 and 37(a) make it clear that the interrogating party must move to compel answers, and the motion is provided for in Rule 37(a). Existing Rule 34, since it requires a court order prior to production of documents or things or permission to enter on land, has no relation to Rule 37(a). Amendments of Rules 34 and 37(a) create a procedure similar to that provided for Rule 33.

Subdivision (a)(1). This is a new provision making clear to which court a party may apply for an order compelling discovery. Existing Rule 37(a) refers only to the court in which the deposition is being taken; nevertheless, it has been held that the court where the action is pending has "inherent power" to compel a party deponent to answer. Lincoln Laboratories, Inc. v. Savage Laboratories, Inc., 27 F.R.D. 476 (D.Del. 1961). In relation to Rule 33 interrogatories and Rule 34 requests for inspection, the court where the action is pending is the appropriate enforcing tribunal. The new provision eliminates the need to resort to inherent power by spelling out the respective roles of the court where the action is pending and the court where the deposition is taken. In some instances, two courts are available to a party seeking to compel answers from a party deponent. The party seeking discovery may choose the court to which he will apply, but the court has power to remit the party to the other court as a more appropriate forum.

Subdivision (a)(2). This subdivision contains the substance of existing provisions of Rule 37(a) authorizing motions to compel answers to questions put at depositions and to interrogatories. New provisions authorize motions for orders compelling designation under Rules 30(b)(6) and 31(a) and compelling inspection in accordance with a request made under Rule 34. If the court denies a motion, in whole or part, it may accompany the denial with issuance of a protective order. Compare the converse provision in Rule 26(c).

Subdivision (a)(3). This new provision makes clear that an evasive or incomplete answer is to be considered, for purposes of subdivision (a), a failure to answer. The courts have consistently held that they have the power to compel adequate answers. E.g., Cone Mills Corp. v. Joseph Bancroft & Sons Co., 33 F.R.D. 318 (D.Del. 1963). This power is recognized and incorporated into the rule.

Subdivision (a)(4). This subdivision amends the provisions for award of expenses, including reasonable attorney's fees, to the prevailing party or person when a motion is made for an order compelling discovery. At present, an award of expenses is made only if the losing party or person is found to have acted without substantial justification. The change requires that expenses be awarded unless the conduct of the losing party or person is found to have been substantially justified. The test of "substantial justification" remains, but the change in language is intended to encourage judges to be more alert to abuses occurring in the discovery process.

On many occasions, to be sure, the dispute over discovery between the parties is genuine, though ultimately resolved one way or the other by the court. In such cases, the losing party is substantially justified in carrying the matter to court. But the rules should deter the abuse implicit in carrying or forcing a discovery dispute to court when no genuine dispute exists. And the potential or actual imposition of expenses is virtually the sole formal sanction in the rules to deter a party from pressing to a court hearing frivolous requests for or objections to discovery.

The present provision of Rule 37(a) that the court shall require payment if it finds that the defeated party acted without "substantial justification" may appear adequate, but in fact it has been little used. Only a handful of reported cases include an award of expenses, and the Columbia Survey found that in only one instance out of about 50 motions decided under Rule 37(a) did the court award expenses. It appears that the courts do not utilize the most important available sanction to deter abusive resort to the judiciary.

The proposed change provides in effect that expenses should ordinarily be awarded unless a court finds that the losing party acted justifiably in carrying his point to court. At the same time, a necessary flexibility is maintained, since the court retains the power to find that other circumstances make an award of expenses unjust—as where the prevailing party also acted unjustifiably. The amendment does not significantly narrow the discretion of the court, but rather presses the court to address itself to abusive practices. The present provision that expenses may be imposed upon either the party or his attorney or both is unchanged. But it is not contemplated that expenses will be imposed upon the attorney merely because the party is indigent.

Subdivision (b). This subdivision deals with sanctions for failure to comply with a court order. The present captions for subsections (1) and (2) entitled, "Contempt" and "Other Consequences," respectively, are confusing. One of the consequences listed in (2) is the arrest of the party, representing the exercise of the contempt power. The contents of the subsections show that the first authorizes the sanction of contempt (and no other) by the court in which the deposition is taken, whereas the second subsection authorizes a variety of sanctions, including contempt, which may be imposed by the court in which the action is pending. The captions of the subsections are changed to deflect their contents.

The scope of Rule 37(b)(2) is broadened by extending it to include any order "to provide or permit discovery," including orders issued under Rules 37(a) and 35. Various rules authorize orders for discovery—e.g., Rule 35 (b)(1), Rule 26(c) as revised. Rule 37(d). See Rosenberg, supra, 58 Col.L.Rev. 480, 484–486. Rule 37(b)(2) should provide comprehensively for enforcement of all these orders. Cf. Societe Internationale v. Rogers, 357 U.S. 197, 207 (1958). On the other hand, the reference to Rule 34 is deleted to conform to the changed procedure in that rule.

A new subsection (E) provides that sanctions which have been available against a party for failure to comply with an order under Rule 35(a) to submit to examination will now be available against him for his failure to comply with a Rule 35(a) order to produce a third person for examination, unless he shows that he is unable to produce the person. In this context, "unable" means in effect "unable in good faith." See Societe Internationale v. Rogers, 357 U.S. 197 (1958).

Subdivision (b)(2) is amplified to provide for payment of reasonable expenses caused by the failure to obey the order. Although Rules 37(b)(2) and 37(d) have been silent as to award of expenses, courts have nevertheless ordered them on occasion. E.g., United Sheeplined Clothing Co. v. Arctic Fur Cap Corp., 165 F.Supp. 193 (S.D.N.Y.1958); Austin Theatre, Inc. v. Warner Bros. Picture, Inc., 22 F.R.D. 302 (S.D.N.Y. 1958). The provision places the burden on the disobedient party to avoid expenses by showing that his failure is justified or that special circumstances make an award of expenses unjust. Allocating the burden in this way conforms to the changed provisions as to expenses in Rule 37(a), and is particularly appropriate when a court order is disobeyed.

An added reference to directors of a party is similar to a change made in subdivision (d) and is explained in the note to that subdivision. The added reference to persons designated by a party under Rules 30(b)(6) or 31(a) to testify on behalf of the party carries out the new procedure in those rules for taking a deposition of a corporation or other organization.

Subdivision (c). Rule 37(c) provides a sanction for the enforcement of Rule 36 dealing with requests for admission. Rule 36 provides the mechanism whereby a party may obtain from another party in appropriate instances either (1) and admission, or (2) a sworn and specific denial, or (3) a sworn statement "setting forth in detail the reasons why he cannot truthfully admit or deny." If the party obtains the second or third of these responses, in proper form, Rule 36 does not provide for a pretrial hearing on whether the response is warranted by the evidence thus far accumulated. Instead, Rule 37(c) is intended to provide posttrial relief in the form of a requirement that the party improperly refusing the admission pay the expenses of the other side in making the necessary proof at trial.

Rule 37(c), as now written, addresses itself in terms only to the sworn denial and is silent with respect to the statement of reasons for an inability to admit or deny. There is no apparent basis for this distinction, since the sanction provided in Rule 37(c) should deter all unjustified failures to admit. This omission in the rule has caused confused and diverse treatment in the courts. One court has held that if a party gives inadequate reasons, he should be treated before trial as having denied the request, so that Rule 37(c) may apply. Bertha Bldg. Corp. v. National Theatres Corp., 15 F.R.D. 339 (E.D.N.Y. 1954). Another has held that the party should be treated as having admitted the request. Heng Hsin Co. v. Stern, Morgenthau & Co., 20 Fed.Rules Serv. 36a.52, Case 1 (S.D.N.Y. Dec. 10, 1954). Still another has ordered a new response, without indicating what the outcome should be if the new response were inadequate. United States Plywood Corp. v. Hudson Lumber Co., 127 F.Supp. 489, 497–498 (S.D.N.Y. 1954). See generally Finman, The Request for Admissions in Federal Civil Procedure, 71 Yale L.J. 371, 426–430 (1962). The amendment eliminates this defect in Rule 37(c) by bringing within its scope all failures to admit.

Additional provisions in Rule 37(c) protect a party from having to pay expenses if the request for admission was held objectionable under Rule 36(a) or if the party failing to admit had reasonable ground to believe that he might prevail on the matter. The latter provision emphasizes that the true test under Rule 37(c) is not whether a party prevailed at trial but whether he acted reasonably in believing that he might prevail.

Subdivision (d). The scope of subdivision (d) is broadened to include responses to requests for inspection under Rule 34, thereby conforming to the new procedures of Rule 34.

Two related changes are made in subdivision (d): the permissible sanctions are broadened to include such orders "as are just"; and the requirement that the failure to appear or respond be "wilful" is eliminated. Although Rule 37(d) in terms provides for only three sanctions, all rather severe, the courts have interpreted it as permitting softer sanctions than those which it sets forth. E.g., Gill v. Stolow, 240 F.2d 669 (2d Cir. 1957); Saltzman v. Birrell, 156 F.Supp. 538 (S.D.N.Y. 1957); 2A Barron & Holtzoff, Federal Practice and Procedure 554–557 (Wright ed. 1961). The rule is changed to provide the greater flexibility as to sanctions which the cases show is needed.

The resulting flexibility as to sanctions eliminates any need to retain the requirement that the failure to appear or respond be "wilful." The concept of "wilful failure" is at best subtle and difficult, and the cases do not supply a bright line. Many courts have imposed sanctions without referring to wilfullness. E.g., Milewski v. Schneider Transportation Co., 238 F.2d 397 (6th Cir. 1956); Dictograph Products, Inc. v. Kentworth Corp., 7 F.R.D. 543 (W.D.Ky. 1947). In addition, in view of the possibility of light sanctions, even a negligent failure should come within Rule 37(d). If default is caused by counsel's ignorance of Federal practice, cf. Dunn. v. Pa. R.R., 96 F. Supp. 597 (N.D.Ohio 1951), or by his preoccupation with another aspect of the case, cf. Maurer-Neuer, Inc. v. United Packinghouse Workers, 26 F.R.D. 139 (D.Kans. 1960), dismissal of the action and default judgment are not justified, but the imposition of expenses and fees may well be. "Wilfullness" continues to play a role, along with various other factors, in the choice of sanctions. Thus, the scheme conforms to Rule 37(b) as construed by the Supreme Court in Societe Internationale v. Rogers, 357 U.S. 197, 208 (1958).

A provision is added to make clear that a party may not properly remain completely silent even when he regards a notice to take his deposition or a set of interrogatories or requests to inspect as improper and objectionable. If he desires not to appear or not to respond, he must apply for a protective order. The cases are divided on whether a protective order must be sought. Compare Collins v. Wayland, 139 F.2d 677 (9th Cir. 1944), cert. den. 322 U.S. 744; Bourgeois v. El Paso Natural Gas Co., 20 F.R.D. 358 (S.D.N.Y. 1957); Loosley v. Stone, 15 F.R.D. 373 (S.D.Ill. 1954), with Scarlatos v. Kulukundis, 21 F.R.D. 185 (S.D.N.Y. 1957); Ross v. True Temper Corp., 11 F.R.D 307 (N.D.Ohio 1951). Compare also Rosenberg, supra, 58 Col.L.Rev. 480, 496 (1958) with 2A Barron & Holtzoff, Federal Practice and Procedure 530–531 (Wright ed. 1961). The party from whom discovery is sought is afforded, through Rule 26(c), a fair and effective procedure whereby he can challenge the request made. At the same time, the total non-compliance with which Rule 37(d) is concerned may impose severe inconvenience or hardship on the discovering party and substantially delay the discovery process. Cf. 2B Barron & Holtzoff, Federal Practice and Procedure 306–307 (Wright ed. 1961) (response to a subpoena).

The failure of an officer or managing agent of a party to make discovery as required by present Rule 37(d) is treated as the failure of the party. The rule as revised provides similar treatment for a director of a party. There is slight warrant for the present distinction between officers and managing agents on the one hand and directors on the other. Although the legal power over a director to compel his making discovery may not be as great as over officers or managing agents, Campbell v. General Motors Corp., 13 F.R.D. 331 (S.D.N.Y. 1952), the practical differences are negligible. That a director's interests are normally aligned with those of his corporation is shown by the provisions of old Rule 26(d)(2), transferred to 32(a)(2) (deposition of director of party may be used at trial by an adverse party for any purpose) and of Rule 43(b) (director of party may be treated at trial as a hostile witness on direct examination by any adverse party). Moreover, in those rare instances when a corporation is unable through good faith efforts to compel a director to make discovery, it is unlikely that the court will impose sanctions. Cf. Societe Internationale v. Rogers, 357 U.S. 197 (1958).

Subdivision (e). The change in the caption conforms to the language of 28 U.S.C. §1783, as amended in 1964.

Subdivision (f). Until recently, costs of a civil action could be awarded against the United States only when expressly provided by Act of Congress, and such provision was rarely made. See H.R.Rept.No. 1535, 89th Cong., 2d Sess., 2–3 (1966). To avoid any conflict with this doctrine, Rule 37(f) has provided that expenses and attorney's fees may not be imposed upon the United States under Rule 37. See 2A Barron & Holtzoff, Federal Practice and Procedure 857 (Wright ed. 1961).

A major change in the law was made in 1966, 80 Stat. 308, 28 U.S.C. §2412 (1966), whereby a judgment for costs may ordinarily be awarded to the prevailing party in any civil action brought by or against the United States. Costs are not to include the fees and expenses of attorneys. In light of this legislative development, Rule 37(f) is amended to permit the award of expenses and fees against the United States under Rule 37, but only to the extent permitted by statute. The amendment brings Rule 37(f) into line with present and future statutory provisions.

Notes of Advisory Committee on Rules—1980 Amendment

Subdivision (b)(2). New Rule 26(f) provides that if a discovery conference is held, at its close the court shall enter an order respecting the subsequent conduct of discovery. The amendment provides that the sanctions available for violation of other court orders respecting discovery are available for violation of the discovery conference order.

Subdivision (e). Subdivision (e) is stricken. Title 28, U.S.C. §1783 no longer refers to sanctions. The subdivision otherwise duplicates Rule 45(e)(2).

Subdivision (g). New Rule 26(f) imposes a duty on parties to participate in good faith in the framing of a discovery plan by agreement upon the request of any party. This subdivision authorizes the court to award to parties who participate in good faith in an attempt to frame a discovery plan the expenses incurred in the attempt if any party or his attorney fails to participate in good faith and thereby causes additional expense.

Failure of United States to Participate in Good Faith in Discovery. Rule 37 authorizes the court to direct that parties or attorneys who fail to participate in good faith in the discovery process pay the expenses, including attorney's fees, incurred by other parties as a result of that failure. Since attorneys' fees cannot ordinarily be awarded against the United States (28 U.S.C. §2412), there is often no practical remedy for the misconduct of its officers and attorneys. However, in the case of a government attorney who fails to participate in good faith in discovery, nothing prevents a court in an appropriate case from giving written notification of that fact to the Attorney General of the United States and other appropriate heads of offices or agencies thereof.

Notes of Advisory Committee on Rules—1987 Amendment

The amendments are technical. No substantive change is intended.

Notes of Advisory Committee on Rules—1993 Amendment

Subdivision (a). This subdivision is revised to reflect the revision of Rule 26(a), requiring disclosure of matters without a discovery request.

Pursuant to new subdivision (a)(2)(A), a party dissatisfied with the disclosure made by an opposing party may under this rule move for an order to compel disclosure. In providing for such a motion, the revised rule parallels the provisions of the former rule dealing with failures to answer particular interrogatories. Such a motion may be needed when the information to be disclosed might be helpful to the party seeking the disclosure but not to the party required to make the disclosure. If the party required to make the disclosure would need the material to support its own contentions, the more effective enforcement of the disclosure requirement will be to exclude the evidence not disclosed, as provided in subdivision (c)(1) of this revised rule.

Language is included in the new paragraph and added to the subparagraph (B) that requires litigants to seek to resolve discovery disputes by informal means before filing a motion with the court. This requirement is based on successful experience with similar local rules of court promulgated pursuant to Rule 83.

The last sentence of paragraph (2) is moved into paragraph (4).

Under revised paragraph (3), evasive or incomplete disclosures and responses to interrogatories and production requests are treated as failures to disclose or respond. Interrogatories and requests for production should not be read or interpreted in an artificially restrictive or hypertechnical manner to avoid disclosure of information fairly covered by the discovery request, and to do so is subject to appropriate sanctions under subdivision (a).

Revised paragraph (4) is divided into three subparagraphs for ease of reference, and in each the phrase "after opportunity for hearing" is changed to "after affording an opportunity to be heard" to make clear that the court can consider such questions on written submissions as well as on oral hearings.

Subparagraph (A) is revised to cover the situation where information that should have been produced without a motion to compel is produced after the motion is filed but before it is brought on for hearing. The rule also is revised to provide that a party should not be awarded its expenses for filing a motion that could have been avoided by conferring with opposing counsel.

Subparagraph (C) is revised to include the provision that formerly was contained in subdivision (a)(2) and to include the same requirement of an opportunity to be heard that is specified in subparagraphs (A) and (B).

Subdivision (c). The revision provides a self-executing sanction for failure to make a disclosure required by Rule 26(a), without need for a motion under subdivision (a)(2)(A).

Paragraph (1) prevents a party from using as evidence any witnesses or information that, without substantial justification, has not been disclosed as required by Rules 26(a) and 26(e)(1). This automatic sanction provides a strong inducement for disclosure of material that the disclosing party would expect to use as evidence, whether at a trial, at a hearing, or on a motion, such as one under Rule 56. As disclosure of evidence offered solely for impeachment purposes is not required under those rules, this preclusion sanction likewise does not apply to that evidence.

Limiting the automatic sanction to violations "without substantial justification," coupled with the exception for violations that are "harmless," is needed to avoid unduly harsh penalties in a variety of situations: e.g., the inadvertent omission from a Rule 26(a)(1)(A) disclosure of the name of a potential witness known to all parties; the failure to list as a trial witness a person so listed by another party; or the lack of knowledge of a pro se litigant of the requirement to make disclosures. In the latter situation, however, exclusion would be proper if the requirement for disclosure had been called to the litigant's attention by either the court or another party.

Preclusion of evidence is not an effective incentive to compel disclosure of information that, being supportive of the position of the opposing party, might advantageously be concealed by the disclosing party. However, the rule provides the court with a wide range of other sanctions—such as declaring specified facts to be established, preventing contradictory evidence, or, like spoliation of evidence, allowing the jury to be informed of the fact of nondisclosure—that, though not self-executing, can be imposed when found to be warranted after a hearing. The failure to identify a witness or document in a disclosure statement would be admissible under the Federal Rules of Evidence under the same principles that allow a party's interrogatory answers to be offered against it.

Subdivision (d). This subdivision is revised to require that, where a party fails to file any response to interrogatories or a Rule 34 request, the discovering party should informally seek to obtain such responses before filing a motion for sanctions.

The last sentence of this subdivision is revised to clarify that it is the pendency of a motion for protective order that may be urged as an excuse for a violation of subdivision (d). If a party's motion has been denied, the party cannot argue that its subsequent failure to comply would be justified. In this connection, it should be noted that the filing of a motion under Rule 26(c) is not self-executing—the relief authorized under that rule depends on obtaining the court's order to that effect.

Subdivision (g). This subdivision is modified to conform to the revision of Rule 26(f).

Committee Notes on Rules—2000 Amendment

Subdivision (c)(1). When this subdivision was added in 1993 to direct exclusion of materials not disclosed as required, the duty to supplement discovery responses pursuant to Rule 26(e)(2) was omitted. In the face of this omission, courts may rely on inherent power to sanction for failure to supplement as required by Rule 26(e)(2), see 8 Federal Practice & Procedure §2050 at 607–09, but that is an uncertain and unregulated ground for imposing sanctions. There is no obvious occasion for a Rule 37(a) motion in connection with failure to supplement, and ordinarily only Rule 37(c)(1) exists as rule-based authority for sanctions if this supplementation obligation is violated.

The amendment explicitly adds failure to comply with Rule 26(e)(2) as a ground for sanctions under Rule 37(c)(1), including exclusion of withheld materials. The rule provides that this sanction power only applies when the failure to supplement was "without substantial justification." Even if the failure was not substantially justified, a party should be allowed to use the material that was not disclosed if the lack of earlier notice was harmless.

"Shall" is replaced by "is" under the program to conform amended rules to current style conventions when there is no ambiguity.

GAP Report. The Advisory Committee recommends that the published amendment proposal be modified to state that the exclusion sanction can apply to failure "to amend a prior response to discovery as required by Rule 26(e)(2)." In addition, one minor phrasing change is recommended for the Committee Note.

Committee Notes on Rules—2006 Amendment

Subdivision (f). Subdivision (f) is new. It focuses on a distinctive feature of computer operations, the routine alteration and deletion of information that attends ordinary use. Many steps essential to computer operation may alter or destroy information, for reasons that have nothing to do with how that information might relate to litigation. As a result, the ordinary operation of computer systems creates a risk that a party may lose potentially discoverable information without culpable conduct on its part. Under Rule 37(f), absent exceptional circumstances, sanctions cannot be imposed for loss of electronically stored information resulting from the routine, good-faith operation of an electronic information system.

Rule 37(f) applies only to information lost due to the "routine operation of an electronic information system"—the ways in which such systems are generally designed, programmed, and implemented to meet the party's technical and business needs. The "routine operation" of computer systems includes the alteration and overwriting of information, often without the operator's specific direction or awareness, a feature with no direct counterpart in hard-copy documents. Such features are essential to the operation of electronic information systems.

Rule 37(f) applies to information lost due to the routine operation of an information system only if the operation was in good faith. Good faith in the routine operation of an information system may involve a party's intervention to modify or suspend certain features of that routine operation to prevent the loss of information, if that information is subject to a preservation obligation. A preservation obligation may arise from many sources, including common law, statutes, regulations, or a court order in the case. The good faith requirement of Rule 37(f) means that a party is not permitted to exploit the routine operation of an information system to thwart discovery obligations by allowing that operation to continue in order to destroy specific stored information that it is required to preserve. When a party is under a duty to preserve information because of pending or reasonably anticipated litigation, intervention in the routine operation of an information system is one aspect of what is often called a "litigation hold." Among the factors that bear on a party's good faith in the routine operation of an information system are the steps the party took to comply with a court order in the case or party agreement requiring preservation of specific electronically stored information.

Whether good faith would call for steps to prevent the loss of information on sources that the party believes are not reasonably accessible under Rule 26(b)(2) depends on the circumstances of each case. One factor is whether the party reasonably believes that the information on such sources is likely to be discoverable and not available from reasonably accessible sources.

The protection provided by Rule 37(f) applies only to sanctions "under these rules." It does not affect other sources of authority to impose sanctions or rules of professional responsibility.

This rule restricts the imposition of "sanctions." It does not prevent a court from making the kinds of adjustments frequently used in managing discovery if a party is unable to provide relevant responsive information. For example, a court could order the responding party to produce an additional witness for deposition, respond to additional interrogatories, or make similar attempts to provide substitutes or alternatives for some or all of the lost information.

Changes Made after Publication and Comment. The published rule barred sanctions only if the party who lost electronically stored information took reasonable steps to preserve the information after it knew or should have known the information was discoverable in the action. A footnote invited comment on an alternative standard that barred sanctions unless the party recklessly or intentionally failed to preserve the information. The present proposal establishes an intermediate standard, protecting against sanctions if the information was lost in the "good faith" operation of an electronic information system. The present proposal carries forward a related element that was a central part of the published proposal—the information must have been lost in the system's "routine operation." The change to a good-faith test made it possible to eliminate the reference to information "discoverable in the action," removing a potential source of confusion as to the duty to preserve information on sources that are identified as not reasonably accessible under Rule 26(b)(2)(B).

The change to a good-faith standard is accompanied by addition of a provision that permits sanctions for loss of information in good- faith routine operation in "exceptional circumstances." This provision recognizes that in some circumstances a court should provide remedies to protect an entirely innocent party requesting discovery against serious prejudice arising from the loss of potentially important information.

As published, the rule included an express exception that denied protection if a party "violated an order in the action requiring it to preserve electronically stored information." This exception was deleted for fear that it would invite routine applications for preservation orders, and often for overbroad orders. The revised Committee Note observes that violation of an order is an element in determining whether a party acted in good faith.

The revised proposal broadens the rule's protection by applying to operation of "an" electronic information system, rather than "the party's" system. The change protects a party who has contracted with an outside firm to provide electronic information storage, avoiding potential arguments whether the system can be characterized as "the party's." The party remains obliged to act in good faith to avoid loss of information in routine operations conducted by the outside firm.

The Committee Note is changed to reflect the changes in the rule text.

The changes from the published version of the proposed rule text are set out below. [Omitted]

Committee Notes on Rules—2007 Amendment

The language of Rule 37 has been amended as part of the general restyling of the Civil Rules to make them more easily understood and to make style and terminology consistent throughout the rules. These changes are intended to be stylistic only.

Changes Made After Publication and Comment. See Note to Rule 1, supra.

Committee Notes on Rules—2013 Amendment

Rule 37(b) is amended to conform to amendments made to Rule 45, particularly the addition of Rule 45(f) providing for transfer of a subpoena-related motion to the court where the action is pending. A second sentence is added to Rule 37(b)(1) to deal with contempt of orders entered after such a transfer. The Rule 45(f) transfer provision is explained in the Committee Note to Rule 45.

Changes Made After Publication and Comment. No changes were made after publication and comment.

Committee Notes on Rules—2015 Amendment

Subdivision (a). Rule 37(a)(3)(B)(iv) is amended to reflect the common practice of producing copies of documents or electronically stored information rather than simply permitting inspection. This change brings item (iv) into line with paragraph (B), which provides a motion for an order compelling "production, or inspection."

Subdivision (e). Present Rule 37(e), adopted in 2006, provides: "Absent exceptional circumstances, a court may not impose sanctions under these rules on a party for failing to provide electronically stored information lost as a result of the routine, good-faith operation of an electronic information system." This limited rule has not adequately addressed the serious problems resulting from the continued exponential growth in the volume of such information. Federal circuits have established significantly different standards for imposing sanctions or curative measures on parties who fail to preserve electronically stored information. These developments have caused litigants to expend excessive effort and money on preservation in order to avoid the risk of severe sanctions if a court finds they did not do enough.

New Rule 37(e) replaces the 2006 rule. It authorizes and specifies measures a court may employ if information that should have been preserved is lost, and specifies the findings necessary to justify these measures. It therefore forecloses reliance on inherent authority or state law to determine when certain measures should be used. The rule does not affect the validity of an independent tort claim for spoliation if state law applies in a case and authorizes the claim.

The new rule applies only to electronically stored information, also the focus of the 2006 rule. It applies only when such information is lost. Because electronically stored information often exists in multiple locations, loss from one source may often be harmless when substitute information can be found elsewhere.

The new rule applies only if the lost information should have been preserved in the anticipation or conduct of litigation and the party failed to take reasonable steps to preserve it. Many court decisions hold that potential litigants have a duty to preserve relevant information when litigation is reasonably foreseeable. Rule 37(e) is based on this common-law duty; it does not attempt to create a new duty to preserve. The rule does not apply when information is lost before a duty to preserve arises.

In applying the rule, a court may need to decide whether and when a duty to preserve arose. Courts should consider the extent to which a party was on notice that litigation was likely and that the information would be relevant. A variety of events may alert a party to the prospect of litigation. Often these events provide only limited information about that prospective litigation, however, so that the scope of information that should be preserved may remain uncertain. It is important not to be blinded to this reality by hindsight arising from familiarity with an action as it is actually filed.

Although the rule focuses on the common-law obligation to preserve in the anticipation or conduct of litigation, courts may sometimes consider whether there was an independent requirement that the lost information be preserved. Such requirements arise from many sources—statutes, administrative regulations, an order in another case, or a party's own information-retention protocols. The court should be sensitive, however, to the fact that such independent preservation requirements may be addressed to a wide variety of concerns unrelated to the current litigation. The fact that a party had an independent obligation to preserve information does not necessarily mean that it had such a duty with respect to the litigation, and the fact that the party failed to observe some other preservation obligation does not itself prove that its efforts to preserve were not reasonable with respect to a particular case.

The duty to preserve may in some instances be triggered or clarified by a court order in the case. Preservation orders may become more common, in part because Rules 16(b)(3)(B)(iii) and 26(f)(3)(C) are amended to encourage discovery plans and orders that address preservation. Once litigation has commenced, if the parties cannot reach agreement about preservation issues, promptly seeking judicial guidance about the extent of reasonable preservation may be important.

The rule applies only if the information was lost because the party failed to take reasonable steps to preserve the information. Due to the ever-increasing volume of electronically stored information and the multitude of devices that generate such information, perfection in preserving all relevant electronically stored information is often impossible. As under the current rule, the routine, good-faith operation of an electronic information system would be a relevant factor for the court to consider in evaluating whether a party failed to take reasonable steps to preserve lost information, although the prospect of litigation may call for reasonable steps to preserve information by intervening in that routine operation. This rule recognizes that "reasonable steps" to preserve suffice; it does not call for perfection. The court should be sensitive to the party's sophistication with regard to litigation in evaluating preservation efforts; some litigants, particularly individual litigants, may be less familiar with preservation obligations than others who have considerable experience in litigation.

Because the rule calls only for reasonable steps to preserve, it is inapplicable when the loss of information occurs despite the party's reasonable steps to preserve. For example, the information may not be in the party's control. Or information the party has preserved may be destroyed by events outside the party's control—the computer room may be flooded, a "cloud" service may fail, a malign software attack may disrupt a storage system, and so on. Courts may, however, need to assess the extent to which a party knew of and protected against such risks.

Another factor in evaluating the reasonableness of preservation efforts is proportionality. The court should be sensitive to party resources; aggressive preservation efforts can be extremely costly, and parties (including governmental parties) may have limited staff and resources to devote to those efforts. A party may act reasonably by choosing a less costly form of information preservation, if it is substantially as effective as more costly forms. It is important that counsel become familiar with their clients' information systems and digital data—including social media—to address these issues. A party urging that preservation requests are disproportionate may need to provide specifics about these matters in order to enable meaningful discussion of the appropriate preservation regime.

When a party fails to take reasonable steps to preserve electronically stored information that should have been preserved in the anticipation or conduct of litigation, and the information is lost as a result, Rule 37(e) directs that the initial focus should be on whether the lost information can be restored or replaced through additional discovery. Nothing in the rule limits the court's powers under Rules 16 and 26 to authorize additional discovery. Orders under Rule 26(b)(2)(B) regarding discovery from sources that would ordinarily be considered inaccessible or under Rule 26(c)(1)(B) on allocation of expenses may be pertinent to solving such problems. If the information is restored or replaced, no further measures should be taken. At the same time, it is important to emphasize that efforts to restore or replace lost information through discovery should be proportional to the apparent importance of the lost information to claims or defenses in the litigation. For example, substantial measures should not be employed to restore or replace information that is marginally relevant or duplicative.

Subdivision (e)(1). This subdivision applies only if information should have been preserved in the anticipation or conduct of litigation, a party failed to take reasonable steps to preserve the information, information was lost as a result, and the information could not be restored or replaced by additional discovery. In addition, a court may resort to (e)(1) measures only "upon finding prejudice to another party from loss of the information." An evaluation of prejudice from the loss of information necessarily includes an evaluation of the information's importance in the litigation.

The rule does not place a burden of proving or disproving prejudice on one party or the other. Determining the content of lost information may be a difficult task in some cases, and placing the burden of proving prejudice on the party that did not lose the information may be unfair. In other situations, however, the content of the lost information may be fairly evident, the information may appear to be unimportant, or the abundance of preserved information may appear sufficient to meet the needs of all parties. Requiring the party seeking curative measures to prove prejudice may be reasonable in such situations. The rule leaves judges with discretion to determine how best to assess prejudice in particular cases.

Once a finding of prejudice is made, the court is authorized to employ measures "no greater than necessary to cure the prejudice." The range of such measures is quite broad if they are necessary for this purpose. There is no all-purpose hierarchy of the severity of various measures; the severity of given measures must be calibrated in terms of their effect on the particular case. But authority to order measures no greater than necessary to cure prejudice does not require the court to adopt measures to cure every possible prejudicial effect. Much is entrusted to the court's discretion.

In an appropriate case, it may be that serious measures are necessary to cure prejudice found by the court, such as forbidding the party that failed to preserve information from putting on certain evidence, permitting the parties to present evidence and argument to the jury regarding the loss of information, or giving the jury instructions to assist in its evaluation of such evidence or argument, other than instructions to which subdivision (e)(2) applies. Care must be taken, however, to ensure that curative measures under subdivision (e)(1) do not have the effect of measures that are permitted under subdivision (e)(2) only on a finding of intent to deprive another party of the lost information's use in the litigation. An example of an inappropriate (e)(1) measure might be an order striking pleadings related to, or precluding a party from offering any evidence in support of, the central or only claim or defense in the case. On the other hand, it may be appropriate to exclude a specific item of evidence to offset prejudice caused by failure to preserve other evidence that might contradict the excluded item of evidence.

Subdivision (e)(2). This subdivision authorizes courts to use specified and very severe measures to address or deter failures to preserve electronically stored information, but only on finding that the party that lost the information acted with the intent to deprive another party of the information's use in the litigation. It is designed to provide a uniform standard in federal court for use of these serious measures when addressing failure to preserve electronically stored information. It rejects cases such as Residential Funding Corp. v. DeGeorge Financial Corp., 306 F.3d 99 (2d Cir. 2002), that authorize the giving of adverse-inference instructions on a finding of negligence or gross negligence.

Adverse-inference instructions were developed on the premise that a party's intentional loss or destruction of evidence to prevent its use in litigation gives rise to a reasonable inference that the evidence was unfavorable to the party responsible for loss or destruction of the evidence. Negligent or even grossly negligent behavior does not logically support that inference. Information lost through negligence may have been favorable to either party, including the party that lost it, and inferring that it was unfavorable to that party may tip the balance at trial in ways the lost information never would have. The better rule for the negligent or grossly negligent loss of electronically stored information is to preserve a broad range of measures to cure prejudice caused by its loss, but to limit the most severe measures to instances of intentional loss or destruction.

Similar reasons apply to limiting the court's authority to presume or infer that the lost information was unfavorable to the party who lost it when ruling on a pretrial motion or presiding at a bench trial. Subdivision (e)(2) limits the ability of courts to draw adverse inferences based on the loss of information in these circumstances, permitting them only when a court finds that the information was lost with the intent to prevent its use in litigation.

Subdivision (e)(2) applies to jury instructions that permit or require the jury to presume or infer that lost information was unfavorable to the party that lost it. Thus, it covers any instruction that directs or permits the jury to infer from the loss of information that it was in fact unfavorable to the party that lost it. The subdivision does not apply to jury instructions that do not involve such an inference. For example, subdivision (e)(2) would not prohibit a court from allowing the parties to present evidence to the jury concerning the loss and likely relevance of information and instructing the jury that it may consider that evidence, along with all the other evidence in the case, in making its decision. These measures, which would not involve instructing a jury it may draw an adverse inference from loss of information, would be available under subdivision (e)(1) if no greater than necessary to cure prejudice. In addition, subdivision (e)(2) does not limit the discretion of courts to give traditional missing evidence instructions based on a party's failure to present evidence it has in its possession at the time of trial.

Subdivision (e)(2) requires a finding that the party acted with the intent to deprive another party of the information's use in the litigation. This finding may be made by the court when ruling on a pretrial motion, when presiding at a bench trial, or when deciding whether to give an adverse inference instruction at trial. If a court were to conclude that the intent finding should be made by a jury, the court's instruction should make clear that the jury may infer from the loss of the information that it was unfavorable to the party that lost it only if the jury first finds that the party acted with the intent to deprive another party of the information's use in the litigation. If the jury does not make this finding, it may not infer from the loss that the information was unfavorable to the party that lost it.

Subdivision (e)(2) does not include a requirement that the court find prejudice to the party deprived of the information. This is because the finding of intent required by the subdivision can support not only an inference that the lost information was unfavorable to the party that intentionally destroyed it, but also an inference that the opposing party was prejudiced by the loss of information that would have favored its position. Subdivision (e)(2) does not require any further finding of prejudice.

Courts should exercise caution, however, in using the measures specified in (e)(2). Finding an intent to deprive another party of the lost information's use in the litigation does not require a court to adopt any of the measures listed in subdivision (e)(2). The remedy should fit the wrong, and the severe measures authorized by this subdivision should not be used when the information lost was relatively unimportant or lesser measures such as those specified in subdivision (e)(1) would be sufficient to redress the loss.

Amendment by Public Law

1980—Subd. (f). Pub. L. 96–481 repealed subd. (f) which provided that except to the extent permitted by statute, expenses and fees may not be awarded against the United States under this rule.

Effective Date of 1980 Amendment

Amendment by Pub. L. 96–481 effective Oct. 1, 1981, and applicable to adversary adjudication defined in section 504(b)(1)(C) of Title 5, and to civil actions and adversary adjudications described in section 2412 of Title 28, Judiciary and Judicial Procedure, which are pending on, or commenced on or after Oct. 1, 1981, see section 208 of Pub. L. 96–481, set out as an Effective Date note under section 504 of Title 5, Government Organization and Employees.

TITLE VI. TRIALS

Rule 38. Right to a Jury Trial; Demand

(a) Right Preserved. The right of trial by jury as declared by the Seventh Amendment to the Constitution—or as provided by a federal statute—is preserved to the parties inviolate.

(b) Demand. On any issue triable of right by a jury, a party may demand a jury trial by:

(1) serving the other parties with a written demand—which may be included in a pleading—no later than 14 days after the last pleading directed to the issue is served; and

(2) filing the demand in accordance with Rule 5(d).

(c) Specifying Issues. In its demand, a party may specify the issues that it wishes to have tried by a jury; otherwise, it is considered to have demanded a jury trial on all the issues so triable. If the party has demanded a jury trial on only some issues, any other party may—within 14 days after being served with the demand or within a shorter time ordered by the court—serve a demand for a jury trial on any other or all factual issues triable by jury.

(d) Waiver; Withdrawal. A party waives a jury trial unless its demand is properly served and filed. A proper demand may be withdrawn only if the parties consent.

(e) Admiralty and Maritime Claims. These rules do not create a right to a jury trial on issues in a claim that is an admiralty or maritime claim under Rule 9(h).

(As amended Feb. 28, 1966, eff. July 1, 1966; Mar. 2, 1987, eff. Aug. 1, 1987; Apr. 22, 1993, eff. Dec. 1, 1993; Apr. 30, 2007, eff. Dec. 1, 2007; Mar. 26, 2009, eff. Dec. 1, 2009.)

Notes of Advisory Committee on Rules—1937

This rule provides for the preservation of the constitutional right of trial by jury as directed in the enabling act (act of June 19, 1934, 48 Stat. 1064, U.S.C., Title 28, §723c [see 2072]), and it and the next rule make definite provision for claim and waiver of jury trial, following the method used in many American states and in England and the British Dominions. Thus the claim must be made at once on initial pleading or appearance under Ill.Rev.Stat. (1937) ch. 110, §188; 6 Tenn.Code Ann. (Williams, 1934) §8734; compare Wyo.Rev.Stat.Ann. (1931) §89–1320 (with answer or reply); within 10 days after the pleadings are completed or the case is at issue under 2 Conn.Gen.Stat. (1930) §5624; Hawaii Rev.Laws (1935) §4101; 2 Mass.Gen.Laws (Ter.Ed. 1932) ch. 231, §60; 3 Mich.Comp.Laws (1929) §14263; Mich.Court Rules Ann. (Searl, 1933) Rule 33 (15 days); England (until 1933) O. 36, r.r. 2 and 6; and Ontario Jud.Act (1927) §57(1) (4 days, or, where prior notice of trial, 2 days from such notice); or at a definite time varying under different codes, from 10 days before notice of trial to 10 days after notice, or, as in many, when the case is called for assignment, Ariz.Rev.Code Ann. (Struckmeyer, 1928) §3802; Calif.Code Civ.Proc. (Deering, 1937) §631, par. 4; Iowa Code (1935) §10724; 4 Nev.Comp.Laws (Hillyer, 1929) §8782; N.M.Stat.Ann. (Courtright, 1929) §105–814; N.Y.C.P.A. (1937) §426, subdivision 5 (applying to New York, Bronx, Richmond, Kings, and Queens Counties); R.I.Pub.Laws (1929), ch. 1327, amending R.I.Gen.Laws (1923) ch. 337, §6; Utah Rev.Stat.Ann.

(1933) §104–23–6; 2 Wash.Rev.Stat.Ann. (Remington, 1932) §316; England (4 days after notice of trial), Administration of Justice Act (1933) §6 and amended rule under the Judicature Act (The Annual Practice, 1937), O. 36, r. 1; Australia High Court Procedure Act (1921) §12, Rules, O. 33, r. 2; Alberta Rules of Ct. (1914) 172, 183, 184; British Columbia Sup.Ct.Rules (1925) O. 36, r.r. 2, 6, 11, and 16; New Brunswick Jud. Act (1927) O. 36, r.r. 2 and 5. See James, Trial by Jury and the New Federal Rules of Procedure (1936), 45 Yale L.J. 1022.

Rule 81(c) provides for claim for jury trial in removed actions.

The right to trial by jury as declared in U.S.C., Title 28, §770 [now 1873] (Trial of issues of fact; by jury; exceptions), and similar statutes, is unaffected by this rule. This rule modifies U.S.C., Title 28, [former] §773 (Trial of issues of fact; by court).

Notes of Advisory Committee on Rules—1966 Amendment

See Note to Rule 9(h), supra.

Notes of Advisory Committee on Rules—1987 Amendment

The amendments are technical. No substantive change is intended.

Notes of Advisory Committee on Rules—1993 Amendment

Language requiring the filing of a jury demand as provided in subdivision (d) is added to subdivision (b) to eliminate an apparent ambiguity between the two subdivisions. For proper scheduling of cases, it is important that jury demands not only be served on other parties, but also be filed with the court.

Committee Notes on Rules—2007 Amendment

The language of Rule 38 has been amended as part of the general restyling of the Civil Rules to make them more easily understood and to make style and terminology consistent throughout the rules. These changes are intended to be stylistic only.

Committee Notes on Rules—2009 Amendment

The times set in the former rule at 10 days have been revised to 14 days. See the Note to Rule 6.

Rule 39. Trial by Jury or by the Court

(a) When a Demand Is Made. When a jury trial has been demanded under Rule 38, the action must be designated on the docket as a jury action. The trial on all issues so demanded must be by jury unless:

(1) the parties or their attorneys file a stipulation to a nonjury trial or so stipulate on the record; or

(2) the court, on motion or on its own, finds that on some or all of those issues there is no federal right to a jury trial.

(b) When No Demand Is Made. Issues on which a jury trial is not properly demanded are to be tried by the court. But the court may, on motion, order a jury trial on any issue for which a jury might have been demanded.

(c) Advisory Jury; Jury Trial by Consent. In an action not triable of right by a jury, the court, on motion or on its own:

(1) may try any issue with an advisory jury; or

(2) may, with the parties' consent, try any issue by a jury whose verdict has the same effect as if a jury trial had been a matter of right, unless the action is against the United States and a federal statute provides for a nonjury trial.

(As amended Apr. 30, 2007, eff. Dec. 1, 2007.)

Notes of Advisory Committee on Rules—1937

The provisions for express waiver of jury trial found in U.S.C., Title 28, [former] §773 (Trial of issues of fact; by court) are incorporated in this rule. See rule 38, however, which extends the provisions for waiver of jury. U.S.C., Title 28, [former] §772 (Trial of issues of fact; in equity in patent causes) is unaffected by this rule. When certain of the issues are to be tried by jury and others by the court, the court may determine the sequence in which such issues shall be tried. See Liberty Oil Co. v. Condon Nat. Bank, 260 U.S. 235 (1922).

A discretionary power in the courts to send issues of fact to the jury is common in state procedure. Compare Calif.Code Civ.Proc. (Deering, 1937) §592; 1 Colo.Stat.Ann. (1935) Code Civ.Proc., ch. 12, §191; Conn.Gen.Stat. (1930) §5625; 2 Minn.Stat. (Mason, 1927) §9288; 4 Mont.Rev.Codes Ann. (1935) §9327; N.Y.C.P.A. (1937) §430; 2 Ohio Gen.Code Ann. (Page, 1926) §11380; 1 Okla.Stat.Ann. (Harlow, 1931) §351; Utah Rev.Stat.Ann. (1933) §104–23–5; 2 Wash.Rev.Stat.Ann. (Remington, 1932) §315; Wis.Stat. (1935) §270.07. See [former] Equity Rule 23 (Matters Ordinarily Determinable at Law When Arising in Suit in Equity to be Disposed of Therein) and U.S.C., Title 28, [former] §772 (Trial of issues of fact; in equity in patent causes); Colleton Merc. Mfg. Co. v. Savannah River Lumber Co., 280 Fed. 358 (C.C.A.4th, 1922); Fed. Res. Bk. of San Francisco v. Idaho Grimm Alfalfa Seed Growers' Ass'n, 8 F.(2d) 922 (C.C.A.9th, 1925), cert. den. 270 U.S. 646 (1926); Watt v. Starke, 101 U.S. 247, 25 L.Ed. 826 (1879).

Committee Notes on Rules—2007 Amendment

The language of Rule 39 has been amended as part of the general restyling of the Civil Rules to make them more easily understood and to make style and terminology consistent throughout the rules. These changes are intended to be stylistic only.

Rule 40. Scheduling Cases for Trial

Each court must provide by rule for scheduling trials. The court must give priority to actions entitled to priority by a federal statute.

(As amended Apr. 30, 2007, eff. Dec. 1, 2007.)

Notes of Advisory Committee on Rules—1937

U.S.C., Title 28, [former] §769 (Notice of case for trial) is modified. See [former] Equity Rule 56 (On Expiration of Time for Depositions, Case Goes on Trial Calendar). See also [former] Equity Rule 57 (Continuances).

For examples of statutes giving precedence, see U.S.C., Title 28, §47 [now 1253, 2101, 2325] (Injunctions as to orders of Interstate Commerce Commission); §380 [now 1253, 2101, 2284] (Injunctions alleged unconstitutionality of state statutes); §380a [now 1253, 2101, 2284] (Same; Constitutionality of federal statute); [former] §768 (Priority of cases where a state is party); Title 15, §28 (Antitrust laws; suits against monopolies expedited); Title 22, §240 (Petition for restoration of property seized as munitions of war, etc.); and Title 49, [former] §44 (Proceedings in equity under interstate commerce laws; expedition of suits).

Committee Notes on Rules—2007 Amendment

The language of Rule 40 has been amended as part of the general restyling of the Civil Rules to make them more easily understood

and to make style and terminology consistent throughout the rules. These changes are intended to be stylistic only.

The best methods for scheduling trials depend on local conditions. It is useful to ensure that each district adopts an explicit rule for scheduling trials. It is not useful to limit or dictate the provisions of local rules.

Rule 41. Dismissal of Actions

(a) Voluntary Dismissal.

(1) By the Plaintiff.

(A) Without a Court Order. Subject to Rules 23(e), 23.1(c), 23.2, and 66 and any applicable federal statute, the plaintiff may dismiss an action without a court order by filing:

(i) a notice of dismissal before the opposing party serves either an answer or a motion for summary judgment; or

(ii) a stipulation of dismissal signed by all parties who have appeared.

(B) Effect. Unless the notice or stipulation states otherwise, the dismissal is without prejudice. But if the plaintiff previously dismissed any federal- or state-court action based on or including the same claim, a notice of dismissal operates as an adjudication on the merits.

(2) By Court Order; Effect. Except as provided in Rule 41(a)(1), an action may be dismissed at the plaintiff's request only by court order, on terms that the court considers proper. If a defendant has pleaded a counterclaim before being served with the plaintiff's motion to dismiss, the action may be dismissed over the defendant's objection only if the counterclaim can remain pending for independent adjudication. Unless the order states otherwise, a dismissal under this paragraph (2) is without prejudice.

(b) Involuntary Dismissal; Effect. If the plaintiff fails to prosecute or to comply with these rules or a court order, a defendant may move to dismiss the action or any claim against it. Unless the dismissal order states otherwise, a dismissal under this subdivision (b) and any dismissal not under this rule—except one for lack of jurisdiction, improper venue, or failure to join a party under Rule 19—operates as an adjudication on the merits.

(c) Dismissing a Counterclaim, Crossclaim, or Third-Party Claim. This rule applies to a dismissal of any counterclaim, crossclaim, or third-party claim. A claimant's voluntary dismissal under Rule 41(a)(1)(A)(i) must be made:

(1) before a responsive pleading is served; or

(2) if there is no responsive pleading, before evidence is introduced at a hearing or trial.

(d) Costs of a Previously Dismissed Action. If a plaintiff who previously dismissed an action in any court files an action based on or including the same claim against the same defendant, the court:

(1) may order the plaintiff to pay all or part of the costs of that previous action; and

(2) may stay the proceedings until the plaintiff has complied.

———

(As amended Dec. 27, 1946, eff. Mar. 19, 1948; Jan. 21, 1963, eff. July 1, 1963; Feb. 28, 1966, eff. July 1, 1966; Dec. 4, 1967, eff. July 1, 1968; Mar. 2, 1987, eff. Aug. 1, 1987; Apr. 30, 1991, eff. Dec. 1, 1991; Apr. 30, 2007, eff. Dec. 1, 2007.)

Notes of Advisory Committee on Rules—1937

Note to Subdivision (a). Compare Ill.Rev.Stat. (1937) ch. 110, §176, and English Rules Under the Judicature Act (The Annual Practice, 1937) O. 26.

Provisions regarding dismissal in such statutes as U.S.C., Title 8, §164 [see 1329] (Jurisdiction of district courts in immigration cases) and U.S.C., Title 31, §232 [now 3730] (Liability of persons making false claims against United States; suits) are preserved by paragraph (1).

Note to Subdivision (b). This provides for the equivalent of a nonsuit on motion by the defendant after the completion of the presentation of evidence by the plaintiff. Also, for actions tried without a jury, it provides the equivalent of the directed verdict practice for jury actions which is regulated by Rule 50.

Notes of Advisory Committee on Rules—1946 Amendment

Subdivision (a). The insertion of the reference to Rule 66 correlates Rule 41(a)(1) with the express provisions concerning dismissal set forth in amended Rule 66 on receivers.

The change in Rule 41(a)(1)(i) gives the service of a motion for summary judgment by the adverse party the same effect in preventing unlimited dismissal as was originally given only to the service of an answer. The omission of reference to a motion for summary judgment in the original rule was subject to criticism. 3 Moore's Federal Practice (1938) 3037–3038, n. 12. A motion for summary judgment may be forthcoming prior to answer, and if well taken will eliminate the necessity for an answer. Since such a motion may require even more research and preparation than the answer itself, there is good reason why the service of the motion, like that of the answer, should prevent a voluntary dismissal by the adversary without court approval.

The word "generally" has been stricken from Rule 41(a)(1)(ii) in order to avoid confusion and to conform with the elimination of the necessity for special appearances by original Rule 12(b).

Subdivision (b). In some cases tried without a jury, where at the close of plaintiff's evidence the defendant moves for dismissal under Rule 41(b) on the ground that plaintiff's evidence is insufficient for recovery, the plaintiff's own evidence may be conflicting or present questions of credibility. In ruling on the defendant's motion, questions arise as to the function of the judge in evaluating the testimony and whether findings should be made if the motion is sustained. Three circuits hold that as the judge is the trier of the facts in such a situation his function is not the same as on a motion to direct a verdict, where the jury is the trier of the facts, and that the judge in deciding such a motion in a non-jury case may pass on conflicts of evidence and credibility, and if he performs that function of evaluating the testimony and grants the motion on the merits, findings are required. Young v. United States (C.C.A.9th, 1940) 111 F.(2d) 823; Gary Theatre Co. v. Columbia Pictures Corporation (C.C.A.7th, 1941) 120 F.(2d) 891; Bach v. Friden Calculating Machine Co., Inc. (C.C.A.6th, 1945) 148 F.(2d) 407. Cf. Mateas v. Fred Harvey, a Corporation (C.C.A.9th, 1945) 146 F.(2d) 989. The Third Circuit has held that on such a motion the function of the court is the same as on a motion to direct in a jury case, and that the court should only decide whether there is evidence which would support a judgment for the plaintiff, and, therefore, findings are not required by Rule 52. Federal Deposit Insurance Corp. v. Mason

(C.C.A.3d, 1940) 115 F.(2d) 548; Schad v. Twentieth Century-Fox Film Corp. (C.C.A.3d, 1943) 136 F.(2d) 991. The added sentence in Rule 41(b) incorporates the view of the Sixth, Seventh and Ninth Circuits. See also 3 Moore's Federal Practice (1938) Cum. Supplement §41.03, under "Page 3045"; Commentary, The Motion to Dismiss in Non-Jury Cases (1946) 9 Fed.Rules Serv., Comm.Pg. 41b.14.

Notes of Advisory Committee on Rules—1963 Amendment

Under the present text of the second sentence of this subdivision, the motion for dismissal at the close of the plaintiff's evidence may be made in a case tried to a jury as well as in a case tried without a jury. But, when made in a jury-tried case, this motion overlaps the motion for a directed verdict under Rule 50(a), which is also available in the same situation. It has been held that the standard to be applied in deciding the Rule 41(b) motion at the close of the plaintiff's evidence in a jury-tried case is the same as that used upon a motion for a directed verdict made at the same stage; and, just as the court need not make findings pursuant to Rule 52(a) when it directs a verdict, so in a jury-tried case it may omit these findings in granting the Rule 41(b) motion. See generally O'Brien v. Westinghouse Electric Corp., 293 F.2d 1, 5–10 (3d Cir. 1961).

As indicated by the discussion in the O'Brien case, the overlap has caused confusion. Accordingly, the second and third sentences of Rule 41(b) are amended to provide that the motion for dismissal at the close of the plaintiff's evidence shall apply only to nonjury cases (including cases tried with an advisory jury). Hereafter the correct motion in jury-tried cases will be the motion for a directed verdict. This involves no change of substance. It should be noted that the court upon a motion for a directed verdict may in appropriate circumstances deny that motion and grant instead a new trial, or a voluntary dismissal without prejudice under Rule 41(a)(2). See 6 Moore's Federal Practice §59.08[5] (2d ed. 1954); cf. Cone v. West Virginia Pulp & Paper Co., 330 U.S. 212, 217, 67 S.Ct. 752, 91 L.Ed. 849 (1947).

The first sentence of Rule 41(b), providing for dismissal for failure to prosecute or to comply with the Rules or any order of court, and the general provisions of the last sentence remain applicable in jury as well as nonjury cases.

The amendment of the last sentence of Rule 41(b) indicates that a dismissal for lack of an indispensable party does not operate as an adjudication on the merits. Such a dismissal does not bar a new action, for it is based merely "on a plaintiff's failure to comply with a precondition requisite to the Court's going forward to determine the merits of his substantive claim." See Costello v. United States, 365 U.S. 265, 284–288, 81 S.Ct. 534, 5 L.Ed.2d 551 & n. 5 (1961); Mallow v. Hinde, 12 Wheat. (25 U.S.) 193, 6 L.Ed. 599 (1827); Clark, Code Pleading 602 (2d ed. 1947); Restatement of Judgments §49, comm. a, b (1942). This amendment corrects an omission from the rule and is consistent with an earlier amendment, effective in 1948, adding "the defense of failure to join an indispensable party" to clause (1) of Rule 12(h).

Notes of Advisory Committee on Rules—1966 Amendment

The terminology is changed to accord with the amendment of Rule 19. See that amended rule and the Advisory Committee's Note thereto.

Notes of Advisory Committee on Rules—1968 Amendment

The amendment corrects an inadvertent error in the reference to amended Rule 23.

Notes of Advisory Committee on Rules—1987 Amendment

The amendment is technical. No substantive change is intended.

Notes of Advisory Committee on Rules—1991 Amendment

Language is deleted that authorized the use of this rule as a means of terminating a non-jury action on the merits when the plaintiff has failed to carry a burden of proof in presenting the plaintiff's case. The device is replaced by the new provisions of Rule 52(c), which authorize entry of judgment against the defendant as well as the plaintiff, and earlier than the close of the case of the party against whom judgment is rendered. A motion to dismiss under Rule 41 on the ground that a plaintiff's evidence is legally insufficient should now be treated as a motion for judgment on partial findings as provided in Rule 52(c).

Committee Notes on Rules—2007 Amendment

The language of Rule 41 has been amended as part of the general restyling of the Civil Rules to make them more easily understood and to make style and terminology consistent throughout the rules. These changes are intended to be stylistic only.

When Rule 23 was amended in 1966, Rules 23.1 and 23.2 were separated from Rule 23. Rule 41(a)(1) was not then amended to reflect the Rule 23 changes. In 1968 Rule 41(a)(1) was amended to correct the cross-reference to what had become Rule 23(e), but Rules 23.1 and 23.2 were inadvertently overlooked. Rules 23.1 and 23.2 are now added to the list of exceptions in Rule 41(a)(1)(A). This change does not affect established meaning. Rule 23.2 explicitly incorporates Rule 23(e), and thus was already absorbed directly into the exceptions in Rule 41(a)(1). Rule 23.1 requires court approval of a compromise or dismissal in language parallel to Rule 23(e) and thus supersedes the apparent right to dismiss by notice of dismissal.

Rule 42. Consolidation; Separate Trials

(a) Consolidation. If actions before the court involve a common question of law or fact, the court may:

(1) join for hearing or trial any or all matters at issue in the actions;

(2) consolidate the actions; or

(3) issue any other orders to avoid unnecessary cost or delay.

(b) Separate Trials. For convenience, to avoid prejudice, or to expedite and economize, the court may order a separate trial of one or more separate issues, claims, crossclaims, counterclaims, or third-party claims. When ordering a separate trial, the court must preserve any federal right to a jury trial.

(As amended Feb. 28, 1966, eff. July 1, 1966; Apr. 30, 2007, eff. Dec. 1, 2007.)

Notes of Advisory Committee on Rules—1937

Subdivision (a) is based upon U.S.C., Title 28, [former] §734 (Orders to save costs; consolidation of causes of like nature) but insofar as the statute differs from this rule, it is modified.

For comparable statutes dealing with consolidation see Ark.Dig.Stat. (Crawford & Moses, 1921) §1081; Calif.Code Civ.Proc. (Deering, 1937) §1048; N.M.Stat.Ann. (Courtright, 1929) §105–828; N.Y.C.P.A. (1937) §§96, 96a, and 97; American Judicature Society, Bulletin XIV (1919) Art.26.

For severance or separate trials see Calif.Code Civ.Proc. (Deering, 1937) §1048; N.Y.C.P.A. (1937) §96; American Judicature Society,

Bulletin XIV (1919) Art. 3, §2 and Art. 10, §10. See also the third sentence of Equity Rule 29 (Defenses—How Presented) providing for discretionary separate hearing and disposition before trial of pleas in bar or abatement, and see also Rule 12(d) of these rules for preliminary hearings of defenses and objections.

For the entry of separate judgments, see Rule 54(b) (Judgment at Various Stages).

Notes of Advisory Committee on Rules—1966 Amendment

In certain suits in admiralty separation for trial of the issues of liability and damages (or of the extent of liability other than damages, such as salvage and general average) has been conducive to expedition and economy, especially because of the statutory right to interlocutory appeal in admiralty cases (which is of course preserved by these Rules). While separation of issues for trial is not to be routinely ordered, it is important that it be encouraged where experience has demonstrated its worth. Cf. Weinstein, Routine Bifurcation of Negligence Trials, 14 Vand.L.Rev. 831 (1961).

In cases (including some cases within the admiralty and maritime jurisdiction) in which the parties have a constitutional or statutory right of trial by jury, separation of issues may give rise to problems. See e.g., United Air Lines, Inc. v. Wiener, 286 F.2d 302 (9th Cir. 1961). Accordingly, the proposed change in Rule 42 reiterates the mandate of Rule 38 respecting preservation of the right to jury trial.

Committee Notes on Rules—2007 Amendment

The language of Rule 42 has been amended as part of the general restyling of the Civil Rules to make them more easily understood and to make style and terminology consistent throughout the rules. These changes are intended to be stylistic only.

Rule 43. Taking Testimony

(a) In Open Court. At trial, the witnesses' testimony must be taken in open court unless a federal statute, the Federal Rules of Evidence, these rules, or other rules adopted by the Supreme Court provide otherwise. For good cause in compelling circumstances and with appropriate safeguards, the court may permit testimony in open court by contemporaneous transmission from a different location.
(b) Affirmation Instead of an Oath. When these rules require an oath, a solemn affirmation suffices.
(c) Evidence on a Motion. When a motion relies on facts outside the record, the court may hear the matter on affidavits or may hear it wholly or partly on oral testimony or on depositions.
(d) Interpreter. The court may appoint an interpreter of its choosing; fix reasonable compensation to be paid from funds provided by law or by one or more parties; and tax the compensation as costs.

———

(As amended Feb. 28, 1966, eff. July 1, 1966; Nov. 20, 1972, and Dec. 18, 1972, eff. July 1, 1975; Mar. 2, 1987, eff. Aug. 1, 1987; Apr. 23, 1996, eff. Dec. 1, 1996; Apr. 30, 2007, eff. Dec. 1, 2007.)

Notes of Advisory Committee on Rules—1937

Note to Subdivision (a). The first sentence is a restatement of the substance of U.S.C., Title 28, [former] §635 (Proof in common-law actions), §637 [see 2072, 2073] (Proof in equity and admiralty), and [former] Equity Rule 46 (Trial—Testimony Usually Taken in Open Court—Rulings on Objections to Evidence). This rule abolishes in patent and trade-mark actions, the practice under [former] Equity Rule 48 of setting forth in affidavits the testimony in chief of expert witnesses whose testimony is directed to matters of opinion. The second and third sentences on admissibility of evidence and Subdivision (b) on contradiction and cross-examination modify U.S.C., Title 28, §725 [now 1652] (Laws of states as rules of decision) insofar as that statute has been construed to prescribe conformity to state rules of evidence. Compare Callihan and Ferguson, Evidence and the New Federal Rules of Civil Procedure, 45 Yale L.J. 622 (1936), and Same: 2, 47 Yale L.J. 195 (1937). The last sentence modifies to the extent indicated U.S.C., Title 28, [former] §631 (Competency of witnesses governed by State laws).

Note to Subdivision (b). See 4 Wigmore on Evidence (2d ed., 1923) §1885 et seq.

Note to Subdivision (c). See [former] Equity Rule 46 (Trial—Testimony Usually Taken in Open Court—Rulings on Objections to Evidence). With the last sentence compare Dowagiac v. Lochren, 143 Fed. 211 (C.C.A.8th, 1906). See also Blease v. Garlington, 92 U.S. 1 (1876); Nelson v. United States, 201 U.S. 92. 114 (1906); Unkle v. Wills, 281 Fed. 29 (C.C.A.8th 1922).

See Rule 61 for harmless error in either the admission or exclusion of evidence.

Note to Subdivision (d). See [former] Equity Rule 78 (Affirmation in Lieu of Oath) and U.S.C., Title 1, §1 (Words importing singular number, masculine gender, etc.; extended application), providing for affirmation in lieu of oath.

Notes of Advisory Committee on Rules—1946 Supplementary Note Regarding Rules 43 and 44

These rules have been criticized and suggested improvements offered by commentators. 1 Wigmore on Evidence (3d ed. 1940) 200–204; Green, The Admissibility of Evidence Under the Federal Rules (1941) 55 Harv.L.Rev. 197. Cases indicate, however, that the rule is working better than these commentators had expected. Boerner v. United States (C.C.A.2d, 1941) 117 F.(2d) 387, cert. den. (1941) 313 U.S. 587; Mosson v. Liberty Fast Freight Co. (C.C.A.2d, 1942) 124 F.(2d) 448; Hartford Accident & Indemnity Co. v. Olivier (C.C.A.5th, 1941) 123 F.(2d) 709; Anzano v. Metropolitan Life Ins. Co. of New York (C.C.A.3d, 1941) 118 F.(2d) 430; Franzen v. E. I. DuPont De Nemours & Co. (C.C.A.3d, 1944) 146 F.(2d) 837; Fakouri v. Cadais (C.C.A.5th, 1945) 147 F.(2d) 667; In re C. & P. Co. (S.D.Cal. 1945) 63 F.Supp. 400, 408. But cf. United States v. Aluminum Co. of America (S.D.N.Y. 1938) 1 Fed.Rules Serv. 43a.3, Case 1; Note (1946) 46 Col.L.Rev. 267. While consideration of a comprehensive and detailed set of rules of evidence seems very desirable, it has not been feasible for the Committee so far to undertake this important task. Such consideration should include the adaptability to federal practice of all or parts of the proposed Code of Evidence of the American Law Institute. See Armstrong, Proposed Amendments to Federal Rules of Civil Procedure, 4 F.R.D. 124, 137–138.

Notes of Advisory Committee on Rules—1966 Amendment

This new subdivision authorizes the court to appoint interpreters (including interpreters for the deaf), to provide for their compensation, and to tax the compensation as costs. Compare proposed subdivision (b) of Rule 28 of the Federal Rules of Criminal Procedure.

Notes of Advisory Committee on Rules—1972 Amendment

Rule 43, entitled Evidence, has heretofore served as the basic rule of evidence for civil cases in federal courts. Its very general provisions are superseded by the detailed provisions of the new Rules of Evidence. The original title and many of the provisions of the rule are, therefore, no longer appropriate.

Subdivision (a). The provision for taking testimony in open court is not duplicated in the Rules of Evidence and is retained. Those dealing with admissibility of evidence and competency of witnesses, however, are no longer needed or appropriate since those topics are covered at large in the Rules of Evidence. They are accordingly deleted. The language is broadened, however, to take account of acts of Congress dealing with the taking of testimony, as well as of the Rules of Evidence and any other rules adopted by the Supreme Court.

Subdivision (b). The subdivision is no longer needed or appropriate since the matters with which it deals are treated in the Rules of Evidence. The use of leading questions, both generally and in the interrogation of an adverse party or witness identified with him, is the subject of Evidence Rule 611(c). Who may impeach is treated in Evidence Rule 601 and scope of cross-examination is covered in Evidence Rule 611(b). The subdivision is accordingly deleted.

Subdivision (c). Offers of proof and making a record of excluded evidence are treated in Evidence Rule 103. The subdivision is no longer needed or appropriate and is deleted.

Notes of Advisory Committee on Rules—1987 Amendment

The amendment is technical. No substantive change is intended.

Notes of Advisory Committee on Rules—1996 Amendment

Rule 43(a) is revised to conform to the style conventions adopted for simplifying the present Civil Rules. The only intended changes of meaning are described below.

The requirement that testimony be taken "orally" is deleted. The deletion makes it clear that testimony of a witness may be given in open court by other means if the witness is not able to communicate orally. Writing or sign language are common examples. The development of advanced technology may enable testimony to be given by other means. A witness unable to sign or write by hand may be able to communicate through a computer or similar device.

Contemporaneous transmission of testimony from a different location is permitted only on showing good cause in compelling circumstances. The importance of presenting live testimony in court cannot be forgotten. The very ceremony of trial and the presence of the factfinder may exert a powerful force for truthtelling. The opportunity to judge the demeanor of a witness face-to-face is accorded great value in our tradition. Transmission cannot be justified merely by showing that it is inconvenient for the witness to attend the trial.

The most persuasive showings of good cause and compelling circumstances are likely to arise when a witness is unable to attend trial for unexpected reasons, such as accident or illness, but remains able to testify from a different place. Contemporaneous transmission may be better than an attempt to reschedule the trial, particularly if there is a risk that other—and perhaps more important—witnesses might not be available at a later time.

Other possible justifications for remote transmission must be approached cautiously. Ordinarily depositions, including video depositions, provide a superior means of securing the testimony of a witness who is beyond the reach of a trial subpoena, or of resolving difficulties in scheduling a trial that can be attended by all witnesses. Deposition procedures ensure the opportunity of all parties to be represented while the witness is testifying. An unforeseen need for the testimony of a remote witness that arises during trial, however, may establish good cause and compelling circumstances. Justification is particularly likely if the need arises from the interjection of new issues during trial or from the unexpected inability to present testimony as planned from a different witness.

Good cause and compelling circumstances may be established with relative ease if all parties agree that testimony should be presented by transmission. The court is not bound by a stipulation, however, and can insist on live testimony. Rejection of the parties' agreement will be influenced, among other factors, by the apparent importance of the testimony in the full context of the trial.

A party who could reasonably foresee the circumstances offered to justify transmission of testimony will have special difficulty in showing good cause and the compelling nature of the circumstances. Notice of a desire to transmit testimony from a different location should be given as soon as the reasons are known, to enable other parties to arrange a deposition, or to secure an advance ruling on transmission so as to know whether to prepare to be present with the witness while testifying.

No attempt is made to specify the means of transmission that may be used. Audio transmission without video images may be sufficient in some circumstances, particularly as to less important testimony. Video transmission ordinarily should be preferred when the cost is reasonable in relation to the matters in dispute, the means of the parties, and the circumstances that justify transmission. Transmission that merely produces the equivalent of a written statement ordinarily should not be used.

Safeguards must be adopted that ensure accurate identification of the witness and that protect against influence by persons present with the witness. Accurate transmission likewise must be assured.

Other safeguards should be employed to ensure that advance notice is given to all parties of foreseeable circumstances that may lead the proponent to offer testimony by transmission. Advance notice is important to protect the opportunity to argue for attendance of the witness at trial. Advance notice also ensures an opportunity to depose the witness, perhaps by video record, as a means of supplementing transmitted testimony.

Committee Notes on Rules—2007 Amendment

The language of Rule 43 has been amended as part of the general restyling of the Civil Rules to make them more easily understood and to make style and terminology consistent throughout the rules. These changes are intended to be stylistic only.

References in Text

Effective Date of Amendments Proposed November 20, 1972, and December 18, 1972

Amendments of this rule embraced by orders entered by the Supreme Court of the United States on November 20, 1972, and December 18, 1972, effective on the 180th day beginning after January 2, 1975, see section 3 of Pub. L. 93–595, Jan. 2, 1975, 88 Stat. 1959, set out as a note under section 2074 of this title.

Rule 44. Proving an Official Record

(a) Means of Proving.

(1) Domestic Record. Each of the following evidences an official record—or an entry in it—that is otherwise admissible and is kept within the United States, any state, district, or commonwealth, or any territory subject to the administrative or judicial jurisdiction of the United States:

(A) an official publication of the record; or

(B) a copy attested by the officer with legal custody of the record—or by the officer's deputy—and accompanied by a certificate that the officer has custody. The certificate must be made under seal:

(i) by a judge of a court of record in the district or political subdivision where the record is kept; or

(ii) by any public officer with a seal of office and with official duties in the district or political subdivision where the record is kept.

(2) Foreign Record.

(A) In General. Each of the following evidences a foreign official record—or an entry in it—that is otherwise admissible:

(i) an official publication of the record; or

(ii) the record—or a copy—that is attested by an authorized person and is accompanied either by a final certification of genuineness or by a certification under a treaty or convention to which the United States and the country where the record is located are parties.

(B) Final Certification of Genuineness. A final certification must certify the genuineness of the signature and official position of the attester or of any foreign official whose certificate of genuineness relates to the attestation or is in a chain of certificates of genuineness relating to the attestation. A final certification may be made by a secretary of a United States embassy or legation; by a consul general, vice consul, or consular agent of the United States; or by a diplomatic or consular official of the foreign country assigned or accredited to the United States.

(C) Other Means of Proof. If all parties have had a reasonable opportunity to investigate a foreign record's authenticity and accuracy, the court may, for good cause, either:

(i) admit an attested copy without final certification; or

(ii) permit the record to be evidenced by an attested summary with or without a final certification.

(b) Lack of a Record. A written statement that a diligent search of designated records revealed no record or entry of a specified tenor is admissible as evidence that the records contain no such record or entry. For domestic records, the statement must be authenticated under Rule 44(a)(1). For foreign records, the statement must comply with (a)(2)(C)(ii).

(c) Other Proof. A party may prove an official record—or an entry or lack of an entry in it—by any other method authorized by law.

(As amended Feb. 28, 1966, eff. July 1, 1966; Mar. 2, 1987, eff. Aug. 1, 1987; Apr. 30, 1991, eff. Dec. 1, 1991; Apr. 30, 2007, eff. Dec. 1, 2007.)

Notes of Advisory Committee on Rules—1937

This rule provides a simple and uniform method of proving public records, and entry or lack of entry therein, in all cases including those specifically provided for by statutes of the United States. Such statutes are not superseded, however, and proof may also be made according to their provisions whenever they differ from this rule. Some of those statutes are:

U.S.C., Title 28:

- §661 [now 1733] (Copies of department or corporation records and papers; admissibility; seal)
- §662 [now 1733] (Same; in office of General Counsel of the Treasury)
- §663 [now 1733] (Instruments and papers of Comptroller of Currency; admissibility)
- §664 [now 1733] (Organization certificates of national banks; admissibility)
- §665 [now 1733] (Transcripts from books of Treasury in suits against delinquents; admissibility)
- §666 [now 1733] (Same; certificate by Secretary or Assistant Secretary)
- §670 [now 1743] (Admissibility of copies of statements of demands by Post Office Department)
- §671 [now 1733] (Admissibility of copies of post office records and statement of accounts)
- §672 [former] (Admissibility of copies of records in General Land Office)
- §673 [now 1744] (Admissibility of copies of records, and so forth, of Patent Office)
- §674 [now 1745] (Copies of foreign letters patent as prima facie evidence)
- §675 [former] (Copies of specifications and drawings of patents admissible)
- §676 [now 1736] (Extracts from Journals of Congress admissible when injunction of secrecy removed)
- §677 [now 1740] (Copies of records in offices of United States consuls admissible)
- §678 [former] (Books and papers in certain district courts)
- §679 [former] (Records in clerks' offices, western district of North Carolina)
- §680 [former] (Records in clerks' offices of former district of California)
- §681 [now 1734] (Original records lost or destroyed; certified copy admissible)
- §682 [now 1734] (Same; when certified copy not obtainable)
- §685 [now 1735] (Same; certified copy of official papers)
- §687 [now 1738] (Authentication of legislative acts; proof of judicial proceedings of State)
- §688 [now 1739] (Proofs of records in offices not pertaining to courts)
- §689 [now 1742] (Copies of foreign records relating to land titles)
- §695 [now 1732] (Writings and records made in regular course of business; admissibility)
- §695e [now 1741] (Foreign documents on record in public offices; certification)

U.S.C., Title 1:

- §30 [now 112] (Statutes at large; contents; admissibility in evidence)

- §30a [now 113] ("Little and Brown's" edition of laws and treaties competent evidence of Acts of Congress)
- §54 [now 204] (Codes and supplements as establishing prima facie the laws of United States and District of Columbia, etc.)
- §55 [now 208] (Copies of supplements to Code of Laws of United States and of District of Columbia Code and supplements; conclusive evidence of original)

U.S.C., Title 5:

- §490 [former] (Records of Department of Interior; authenticated copies as evidence)

U.S.C., Title 6:

- §7 [now Title 31, §9306] (Surety Companies as sureties; appointment of agents; service of process)

U.S.C., Title 8:

- §9a [see 1435(c)] (Citizenship of children of persons naturalized under certain laws; repatriation of native-born women married to aliens prior to September 22, 1922; copies of proceedings)
- §356 [see 1443] (Regulations for execution of naturalization laws; certified copies of papers as evidence)
- §399b(d) [see 1443] (Certifications of naturalization records; authorization; admissibility as evidence)

U.S.C., Title 11:

- §44(d), (e), (f), (g) [former] (Bankruptcy court proceedings and orders as evidence)
- §204 [former] (Extensions extended, etc.; evidence of confirmation)
- §207(j) [former] (Corporate reorganizations; certified copy of decree as evidence)

U.S.C., Title 15:

- §127 (Trade-mark records in Patent Office; copies as evidence)

U.S.C., Title 20:

- §52 (Smithsonian Institution; evidence of title to site and buildings)

U.S.C., Title 25:

- §6 (Bureau of Indian Affairs; seal; authenticated and certified documents; evidence)

U.S.C., Title 31:

- §46 [now 704] (Laws governing General Accounting Office; copies of books, records, etc., thereof as evidence)

U.S.C., Title 38:

- §11g [see 302] (Seal of Veterans' Administration; authentication of copies of records)

U.S.C., Title 40:

- §238 [former] (National Archives; seal; reproduction of archives; fee; admissibility in evidence of reproductions)
- §270c [now 3133(a)] (Bonds of contractors for public works; right of person furnishing labor or material to copy of bond)

U.S.C., Title 43:

- §§57–59 (Copies of land surveys, etc., in certain states and districts admissible as evidence)
- §83 (General Land Office registers and receivers; transcripts of records as evidence)

U.S.C., Title 46:

- §823 [former] (Records of Maritime Commission; copies; publication of reports; evidence)

U.S.C., Title 47:

- §154(m) (Federal Communications Commission; copies of reports and decisions as evidence)
- §412 (Documents filed with Federal Communications Commission as public records; prima facie evidence; confidential records)

U.S.C., Title 49:

- §14(3) [see 706] (Interstate Commerce Commission reports and decisions; printing and distribution of copies)
- §16(13) [former] (Copies of schedules, tariffs, etc., filed with Interstate Commerce Commission as evidence)
- §19a(i) [former] (Valuation of property of carriers by Interstate Commerce Commission; final published valuations as evidence)

Notes of Advisory Committee on Rules—1946 Supplementary Note Regarding Rules 43 and 44

For supplementary note of Advisory Committee on this rule, see note under rule 43.

Notes of Advisory Committee on Rules—1966 Amendment

Subdivision (a)(1). These provisions on proof of official records kept within the United States are similar in substance to those heretofore appearing in Rule 44. There is a more exact description of the geographical areas covered. An official record kept in one of the areas enumerated qualifies for proof under subdivision (a)(1) even though it is not a United States official record. For example, an official record kept in one of these areas by a government in exile falls within subdivision (a)(1). It also falls within subdivision (a)(2) which may be availed of alternatively. Cf. Banco de Espana v. Federal Reserve Bank, 114 F.2d 438 (2d Cir. 1940).

Subdivision (a)(2). Foreign official records may be proved, as heretofore, by means of official publications thereof. See United States v. Aluminum Co. of America, 1 F.R.D. 71 (S.D.N.Y. 1939). Under this rule, a document that, on its face, appears to be an official publication, is admissible, unless a party opposing its admission into evidence shows that it lacks that character.

The rest of subdivision (a)(2) aims to provide greater clarity, efficiency, and flexibility in the procedure for authenticating copies of foreign official records.

The reference to attestation by "the officer having the legal custody of the record," hitherto appearing in Rule 44, has been found inappropriate for official records kept in foreign countries where the assumed relation between custody and the authority to attest does not obtain. See 2B Barron & Holtzoff, Federal Practice & Procedure §992 (Wright ed. 1961). Accordingly it is provided that an attested copy may be obtained from any person authorized by the law of the foreign country to make the attestation without regard to whether he is charged with responsibility for maintaining the record or keeping it in his custody.

Under Rule 44 a United States foreign service officer has been called on to certify to the authority of the foreign official attesting the copy as well as the genuineness of his signature and his official position. See Schlesinger, Comparative Law 57 (2d ed. 1959); Smit, International Aspects of Federal Civil Procedure, 61 Colum.L.Rev. 1031, 1063 (1961); 22 C.F.R. §92.41(a), (e) (1958).

This has created practical difficulties. For example, the question of the authority of the foreign officer might raise issues of foreign law which were beyond the knowledge of the United States officer. The difficulties are met under the amended rule by eliminating the element of the authority of the attesting foreign official from the scope of the certifying process, and by specifically permitting use of the chain-certificate method. Under this method, it is sufficient if the original attestation purports to have been issued by an authorized person and is accompanied by a certificate of another foreign official whose certificate may in turn be followed by that of a foreign official of higher rank. The process continues until a foreign official is reached as to whom the United States foreign service official (or a diplomatic or consular officer of the foreign country assigned or accredited to the United States) has adequate information upon which to base a "final certification." See New York Life Ins. Co. v. Aronson, 38 F.Supp. 687 (W.D.Pa. 1941); 22 C.F.R. §92.37 (1958).

The final certification (a term used in contradistinction to the certificates prepared by the foreign officials in a chain) relates to the incumbency and genuineness of signature of the foreign official who attested the copy of the record or, where the chain-certificate method is used, of a foreign official whose certificate appears in the chain, whether that certificate is the last in the chain or not. A final certification may be prepared on the basis of material on file in the consulate or any other satisfactory information.

Although the amended rule will generally facilitate proof of foreign official records, it is recognized that in some situations it may be difficult or even impossible to satisfy the basic requirements of the rule. There may be no United States consul in a particular foreign country; the foreign officials may not cooperate, peculiarities may exist or arise hereafter in the law or practice of a foreign country. See United States v. Grabina, 119 F.2d 863 (2d Cir. 1941); and, generally, Jones, International Judicial Assistance: Procedural Chaos and a Program for Reform, 62 Yale L.J. 515, 548–49 (1953). Therefore the final sentence of subdivision (a)(2) provides the court with discretion to admit an attested copy of a record without a final certification, or an attested summary of a record with or without a final certification. See Rep. of Comm. on Comparative Civ. Proc. & Prac., Proc. A.B.A., Sec. Int'l & Comp. L. 123, 130–131 (1952); Model Code of Evidence §§517, 519 (1942). This relaxation should be permitted only when it is shown that the party has been unable to satisfy the basic requirements of the amended rule despite his reasonable efforts. Moreover, it is specially provided that the parties must be given a reasonable opportunity in these cases to examine into the authenticity and accuracy of the copy or summary.

Subdivision (b). This provision relating to proof of lack of record is accommodated to the changes made in subdivision (a).

Subdivision (c). The amendment insures that international agreements of the United States are unaffected by the rule. Several consular conventions contain provisions for reception of copies or summaries of foreign official records. See, e.g., Consular Conv. with Italy, May 8, 1878, art. X, 20 Stat. 725, T.S. No. 178 (Dept. State 1878). See also 28 U.S.C. §§1740–42, 1745; Fakouri v. Cadais, 149 F.2d 321 (5th Cir. 1945), cert. denied, 326 U.S. 742 (1945); 5 Moore's Federal Practice, par. 44.05 (2d ed. 1951).

Notes of Advisory Committee on Rules—1987 Amendment

The amendments are technical. No substantive change is intended.

Notes of Advisory Committee on Rules—1991 Amendment

The amendment to paragraph (a)(1) strikes the references to specific territories, two of which are no longer subject to the jurisdiction of the United States, and adds a generic term to describe governments having a relationship with the United States such that their official records should be treated as domestic records.

The amendment to paragraph (a)(2) adds a sentence to dispense with the final certification by diplomatic officers when the United States and the foreign country where the record is located are parties to a treaty or convention that abolishes or displaces the requirement. In that event the treaty or convention is to be followed. This changes the former procedure for authenticating foreign official records only with respect to records from countries that are parties to the Hague Convention Abolishing the Requirement of Legalization for Foreign Public Documents. Moreover, it does not affect the former practice of attesting the records, but only changes the method of certifying the attestation.

The Hague Public Documents Convention provides that the requirement of a final certification is abolished and replaced with a model apostille, which is to be issued by officials of the country where the records are located. See Hague Public Documents Convention, Arts. 2–4. The apostille certifies the signature, official position, and seal of the attesting officer. The authority who issues the apostille must maintain a register or card index showing the serial number of the apostille and other relevant information recorded on it. A foreign court can then check the serial number and information on the apostille with the issuing authority in order to guard against the use of fraudulent apostilles. This system provides a reliable method for maintaining the integrity of the authentication process, and the apostille can be accorded greater weight than the normal authentication procedure because foreign officials are more likely to know the precise capacity under their law of the attesting officer than would an American official. See generally Comment, The United States and the Hague Convention Abolishing the Requirement of Legalization for Foreign Public Documents, 11 HARV. INT'L L.J. 476, 482, 488 (1970).

Committee Notes on Rules—2007 Amendment

The language of Rule 44 has been amended as part of the general restyling of the Civil Rules to make them more easily understood and to make style and terminology consistent throughout the rules. These changes are intended to be stylistic only.

Rule 44.1. Determining Foreign Law

A party who intends to raise an issue about a foreign country's law must give notice by a pleading or other writing. In determining foreign law, the court may consider any relevant material or source, including testimony, whether or not submitted by a party or admissible under the Federal Rules of Evidence. The court's determination must be treated as a ruling on a question of law.

(As added Feb. 28, 1966, eff. July 1, 1966; amended Nov. 20, 1972, eff. July 1, 1975; Mar. 2, 1987, eff. Aug. 1, 1987; Apr. 30, 2007, eff. Dec. 1, 2007.)

Notes of Advisory Committee on Rules—1966

Rule 44.1 is added by amendment to furnish Federal courts with a uniform and effective procedure for raising and determining an issue concerning the law of a foreign country.

To avoid unfair surprise, the first sentence of the new rule requires that a party who intends to raise an issue of foreign law shall give notice thereof. The uncertainty under Rule 8(a) about whether foreign law must be pleaded—compare Siegelman v. Cunard White Star, Ltd., 221 F.2d 189 (2d Cir. 1955), and Pedersen v. United States, 191 F.Supp. 95 (D.Guam 1961), with Harrison v. United Fruit Co., 143 F.Supp. 598 (S.D.N.Y. 1956)—is eliminated by the provision that the notice shall be "written" and "reasonable." It may, but need not be, incorporated in the pleadings. In some situations the pertinence of foreign law is apparent from the outset; accordingly the necessary investigation of that law will have been accomplished by the party at the pleading stage, and the notice can be given conveniently in the pleadings. In other situations the pertinence of foreign law may remain doubtful until the case is further developed. A requirement that notice of foreign law be given only through the medium of the pleadings would tend in the latter instances to force the party to engage in a peculiarly burdensome type of investigation which might turn out to be unnecessary; and correspondingly the adversary would be forced into a possible wasteful investigation. The liberal provisions for amendment of the pleadings afford help if the pleadings are used as the medium of giving notice of the foreign law; but it seems best to permit a written notice to be given outside of and later than the pleadings, provided the notice is reasonable.

The new rule does not attempt to set any definite limit on the party's time for giving the notice of an issue of foreign law; in some cases the issue may not become apparent until the trial and notice then given may still be reasonable. The stage which the case has reached at the time of the notice, the reason proffered by the party for his failure to give earlier notice, and the importance to the case as a whole of the issue of foreign law sought to be raised, are among the factors which the court should consider in deciding a question of the reasonableness of a notice. If notice is given by one party it need not be repeated by any other and serves as a basis for presentation of material on the foreign law by all parties.

The second sentence of the new rule describes the materials to which the court may resort in determining an issue of foreign law. Heretofore the district courts, applying Rule 43(a), have looked in certain cases to State law to find the rules of evidence by which the content of foreign-country law is to be established. The State laws vary; some embody procedures which are inefficient, time consuming and expensive. See, generally, Nussbaum, Proving the Law of Foreign Countries, 3 Am.J.Comp.L. 60 (1954). In all events the ordinary rules of evidence are often inapposite to the problem of determining foreign law and have in the past prevented examination of material which could have provided a proper basis for the determination. The new rule permits consideration by the court of any relevant material, including testimony, without regard to its admissibility under Rule 43. Cf. N.Y.Civ.Prac.Law & Rules, R. 4511 (effective Sept. 1, 1963); 2 Va.Code Ann. tit. 8, §8–273; 2 W.Va.Code Ann. §5711.

In further recognition of the peculiar nature of the issue of foreign law, the new rule provides that in determining this law the court is not limited by material presented by the parties; it may engage in its own research and consider any relevant material thus found. The court may have at its disposal better foreign law materials than counsel have presented, or may wish to reexamine and amplify material that has been presented by counsel in partisan fashion or in insufficient detail. On the other hand, the court is free to insist on a complete presentation by counsel.

There is no requirement that the court give formal notice to the parties of its intention to engage in its own research on an issue of foreign law which has been raised by them, or of its intention to raise and determine independently an issue not raised by them. Ordinarily the court should inform the parties of material it has found diverging substantially from the material which they have presented; and in general the court should give the parties an opportunity to analyze and counter new points upon which it proposes to rely. See Schlesinger, Comparative Law 142 (2d ed. 1959); Wyzanski, A Trial Judge's Freedom and Responsibility, 65 Harv.L.Rev. 1281, 1296 (1952); cf. Siegelman v. Cunard White Star, Ltd., supra, 221 F.2d at 197. To require, however, that the court give formal notice from time to time as it proceeds with its study of the foreign law would add an element of undesirable rigidity to the procedure for determining issues of foreign law.

The new rule refrains from imposing an obligation on the court to take "judicial notice" of foreign law because this would put an extreme burden on the court in many cases; and it avoids use of the concept of "judicial notice" in any form because of the uncertain meaning of that concept as applied to foreign law. See, e.g., Stern, Foreign Law in the Courts: Judicial Notice and Proof, 45 Calif.L.Rev. 23, 43 (1957). Rather the rule provides flexible procedures for presenting and utilizing material on issues of foreign law by which a sound result can be achieved with fairness to the parties.

Under the third sentence, the court's determination of an issue of foreign law is to be treated as a ruling on a question of "law," not "fact," so that appellate review will not be narrowly confined by the "clearly erroneous" standard of Rule 52(a). Cf. Uniform Judicial Notice of Foreign Law Act §3; Note, 72 Harv.L.Rev. 318 (1958).

The new rule parallels Article IV of the Uniform Interstate and International Procedure Act, approved by the Commissioners on Uniform State Laws in 1962, except that section 4.03 of Article IV states that "[t]he court, not the jury" shall determine foreign law. The new rule does not address itself to this problem, since the Rules refrain from allocating functions as between the court and the jury. See Rule 38(a). It has long been thought, however, that the jury is not the appropriate body to determine issues of foreign law. See, e.g., Story, Conflict of Laws, §638 (1st ed. 1834, 8th ed. 1883); 1 Greenleaf, Evidence, §486 (1st ed. 1842, 16th ed. 1899); 4 Wigmore, Evidence §2558 (1st ed. 1905); 9 id. §2558 (3d ed. 1940). The majority of the States have committed such issues to determination by the court. See Article 5 of the Uniform Judicial Notice of Foreign Law Act, adopted by twenty-six states, 9A U.L.A. 318 (1957) (Suppl. 1961, at 134); N.Y.Civ.Prac.Law & Rules, R. 4511 (effective Sept. 1, 1963); Wigmore, loc. cit. And Federal courts that have considered the problem in recent years have reached the same conclusion without reliance on statute. See Janson v. Swedish American Line, 185 F.2d 212, 216 (1st Cir. 1950); Bank of Nova Scotia v. San Miguel, 196 F.2d 950, 957, n. 6 (1st Cir. 1952); Liechti v. Roche, 198 F.2d 174 (5th Cir. 1952); Daniel Lumber Co. v. Empresas Hondurenas, S.A., 215 F.2d 465 (5th Cir. 1954).

Notes of Advisory Committee on Rules—1972 Amendment

Since the purpose of the provision is to free the judge, in determining foreign law, from any restrictions imposed by evidence rules, a general reference to the Rules of Evidence is appropriate and is made.

Notes of Advisory Committee on Rules—1987 Amendment

The amendment is technical. No substantive change is intended.

Committee Notes on Rules—2007 Amendment

The language of Rule 44.1 has been amended as part of the general restyling of the Civil Rules to make them more easily understood and to make style and terminology consistent throughout the rules. These changes are intended to be stylistic only.

References in Text

Effective Date of Amendment Proposed November 20, 1972

Amendment of this rule embraced by the order entered by the Supreme Court of the United States on November 20, 1972, effective on the 180th day beginning after January 2, 1973, see section 3 of Pub. L. 93–595, Jan. 2, 1975, 88 Stat. 1959, set out as a note under section 2074 of this title.

Rule 45. Subpoena

(a) In General.

(1) Form and Contents.

(A) Requirements—In General. Every subpoena must:

(i) state the court from which it issued;

(ii) state the title of the action and its civil-action number;

(iii) command each person to whom it is directed to do the following at a specified time and place: attend and testify; produce designated documents, electronically stored information, or tangible things in that person's possession, custody, or control; or permit the inspection of premises; and

(iv) set out the text of Rule 45(d) and (e).

(B) Command to Attend a Deposition—Notice of the Recording Method. A subpoena commanding attendance at a deposition must state the method for recording the testimony.

(C) Combining or Separating a Command to Produce or to Permit Inspection; Specifying the Form for Electronically Stored Information. A command to produce documents, electronically stored information, or tangible things or to permit the inspection of premises may be included in a subpoena commanding attendance at a deposition, hearing, or trial, or may be set out in a separate subpoena. A subpoena may specify the form or forms in which electronically stored information is to be produced.

(D) Command to Produce; Included Obligations. A command in a subpoena to produce documents, electronically stored information, or tangible things requires the responding person to permit inspection, copying, testing, or sampling of the materials.

(2) Issuing Court. A subpoena must issue from the court where the action is pending.

(3) Issued by Whom. The clerk must issue a subpoena, signed but otherwise in blank, to a party who requests it. That party must complete it before service. An attorney also may issue and sign a subpoena if the attorney is authorized to practice in the issuing court.

(4) Notice to Other Parties Before Service. If the subpoena commands the production of documents, electronically stored information, or tangible things or the inspection of premises before trial, then before it is served on the person to whom it is directed, a notice and a copy of the subpoena must be served on each party.

(b) Service.

(1) By Whom and How; Tendering Fees. Any person who is at least 18 years old and not a party may serve a subpoena. Serving a subpoena requires delivering a copy to the named person and, if the subpoena requires that person's attendance, tendering the fees for 1 day's attendance and the mileage allowed by law. Fees and mileage need not be tendered when the subpoena issues on behalf of the United States or any of its officers or agencies.

(2) Service in the United States. A subpoena may be served at any place within the United States.

(3) Service in a Foreign Country. 28 U.S.C. §1783 governs issuing and serving a subpoena directed to a United States national or resident who is in a foreign country.

(4) Proof of Service. Proving service, when necessary, requires filing with the issuing court a statement showing the date and manner of service and the names of the persons served. The statement must be certified by the server.

(c) Place of Compliance.

(1) For a Trial, Hearing, or Deposition. A subpoena may command a person to attend a trial, hearing, or deposition only as follows:

(A) within 100 miles of where the person resides, is employed, or regularly transacts business in person; or

(B) within the state where the person resides, is employed, or regularly transacts business in person, if the person

(i) is a party or a party's officer; or

(ii) is commanded to attend a trial and would not incur substantial expense.

(2) For Other Discovery. A subpoena may command:

(A) production of documents, electronically stored information, or tangible things at a place within 100 miles of where the person resides, is employed, or regularly transacts business in person; and

(B) inspection of premises at the premises to be inspected.

(d) Protecting a Person Subject to a Subpoena; Enforcement.

(1) Avoiding Undue Burden or Expense; Sanctions. A party or attorney responsible for issuing and serving a subpoena must take reasonable steps to avoid imposing undue burden or expense on a person subject to the subpoena. The court for the district where compliance is required must enforce this duty and impose an appropriate sanction—which may include lost earnings and reasonable attorney's fees—on a party or attorney who fails to comply.

(2) Command to Produce Materials or Permit Inspection.

(A) Appearance Not Required. A person commanded to produce documents, electronically stored information, or tangible things, or to permit the inspection of premises, need not appear in person at the place of production or inspection unless also commanded to appear for a deposition, hearing, or trial.

(B) Objections. A person commanded to produce documents or tangible things or to permit inspection may serve on the party or attorney designated in the subpoena a written objection to inspecting, copying, testing, or sampling any or all of the materials or to inspecting the premises—or to producing electronically stored information in the form or forms requested. The objection must be served before the earlier of the time specified for compliance or 14 days after the subpoena is served. If an objection is made, the following rules apply:

(i) At any time, on notice to the commanded person, the serving party may move the court for the district where compliance is required for an order compelling production or inspection.

(ii) These acts may be required only as directed in the order, and the order must protect a person who is neither a party nor a party's officer from significant expense resulting from compliance.

(3) Quashing or Modifying a Subpoena.

(A) When Required. On timely motion, the court for the district where compliance is required must quash or modify a subpoena that:

(i) fails to allow a reasonable time to comply;

(ii) requires a person to comply beyond the geographical limits specified in Rule 45(c);

(iii) requires disclosure of privileged or other protected matter, if no exception or waiver applies; or

(iv) subjects a person to undue burden.

(B) When Permitted. To protect a person subject to or affected by a subpoena, the court for the district where compliance is required may, on motion, quash or modify the subpoena if it requires:

(i) disclosing a trade secret or other confidential research, development, or commercial information; or

(ii) disclosing an unretained expert's opinion or information that does not describe specific occurrences in dispute and results from the expert's study that was not requested by a party.

(C) Specifying Conditions as an Alternative. In the circumstances described in Rule 45(d)(3)(B), the court may, instead of quashing or modifying a subpoena, order appearance or production under specified conditions if the serving party:

(i) shows a substantial need for the testimony or material that cannot be otherwise met without undue hardship; and

(ii) ensures that the subpoenaed person will be reasonably compensated.

(e) Duties in Responding to a Subpoena.

(1) Producing Documents or Electronically Stored Information. These procedures apply to producing documents or electronically stored information:

(A) Documents. A person responding to a subpoena to produce documents must produce them as they are kept in the ordinary course of business or must organize and label them to correspond to the categories in the demand.

(B) Form for Producing Electronically Stored Information Not Specified. If a subpoena does not specify a form for producing electronically stored information, the person responding must produce it in a form or forms in which it is ordinarily maintained or in a reasonably usable form or forms.

(C) Electronically Stored Information Produced in Only One Form. The person responding need not produce the same electronically stored information in more than one form.

(D) Inaccessible Electronically Stored Information. The person responding need not provide discovery of electronically stored information from sources that the person identifies as not reasonably accessible because of undue burden or cost. On motion to compel discovery or for a protective order, the person responding must show that the information is not reasonably accessible because of undue burden or cost. If that showing is made, the court may nonetheless order discovery from such sources if the requesting party shows good cause, considering the limitations of Rule 26(b)(2)(C). The court may specify conditions for the discovery.

(2) Claiming Privilege or Protection.

(A) Information Withheld. A person withholding subpoenaed information under a claim that it is privileged or subject to protection as trial-preparation material must:

(i) expressly make the claim; and

(ii) describe the nature of the withheld documents, communications, or tangible things in a manner that, without revealing information itself privileged or protected, will enable the parties to assess the claim.

(B) Information Produced. If information produced in response to a subpoena is subject to a claim of privilege or of protection as trial-preparation material, the person making the claim may notify any party that received the information of the claim and the basis for it. After being notified, a party must promptly return, sequester, or destroy the specified information and any copies it has; must not use or disclose the information until the claim is resolved; must take reasonable steps to retrieve the information if the party disclosed it before being notified; and may promptly present the information under seal to the court for the district where compliance is required for a determination of the claim. The person who produced the information must preserve the information until the claim is resolved.

(f) Transferring a Subpoena-Related Motion. When the court where compliance is required did not issue the subpoena, it may transfer a motion under this rule to the issuing court if the person subject to the subpoena consents or if the court finds exceptional circumstances. Then, if the attorney for a person subject to a subpoena is authorized to practice in the court where the motion was made, the attorney may file papers and appear on the motion as an officer of the issuing court. To enforce its order, the issuing court may transfer the order to the court where the motion was made.

(g) Contempt. The court for the district where compliance is required—and also, after a motion is transferred, the issuing court—may hold in contempt a person who, having been served, fails without adequate excuse to obey the subpoena or an order related to it.

———

(As amended Dec. 27, 1946, eff. Mar. 19, 1948; Dec. 29, 1948, eff. Oct. 20, 1949; Mar. 30, 1970, eff. July 1, 1970; Apr. 29, 1980, eff. Aug. 1, 1980; Apr. 29, 1985, eff. Aug. 1, 1985; Mar. 2, 1987, eff. Aug. 1, 1987; Apr. 30, 1991, eff. Dec. 1, 1991; Apr. 25, 2005, eff. Dec. 1, 2005; Apr. 12, 2006, eff. Dec. 1, 2006; Apr. 30, 2007, eff. Dec. 1, 2007; Apr. 16, 2013, eff. Dec. 1, 2013.)

Notes of Advisory Committee on Rules—1937

This rule applies to subpoenas ad testificandum and duces tecum issued by the district courts for attendance at a hearing or a trial, or to take depositions. It does not apply to the enforcement of subpoenas issued by administrative officers and commissions pursuant to statutory authority. The enforcement of such subpoenas by the district courts is regulated by appropriate statutes. Many of these statutes do not place any territorial limits on the validity of subpoenas so issued, but provide that they may be served anywhere within the United States. Among such statutes are the following:

- U.S.C., Title 7, §§222 and 511n (Secretary of Agriculture)
- U.S.C., Title 15, §49 (Federal Trade Commission)
- U.S.C., Title 15, §§77v(b), 78u(c), 79r(d) (Securities and Exchange Commission)
- U.S.C., Title 16, §§797(g) and 825f (Federal Power Commission)
- U.S.C., Title 19, §1333(b) (Tariff Commission)
- U.S.C., Title 22, §§268, 270d and 270e (International Commissions, etc.)
- U.S.C., Title 26, §§614, 619(b) [see 7456] (Board of Tax Appeals)
- U.S.C., Title 26, §1523(a) [see 7608] (Internal Revenue Officers)
- U.S.C., Title 29, §161 (Labor Relations Board)
- U.S.C., Title 33, §506 (Secretary of Army)
- U.S.C., Title 35, §§54–56 [now 24] (Patent Office proceedings)
- U.S.C., Title 38, [former] §133 (Veterans' Administration)
- U.S.C., Title 41, §39 (Secretary of Labor)
- U.S.C., Title 45, §157 Third. (h) (Board of Arbitration under Railway Labor Act)
- U.S.C., Title 45, §222(b) (Investigation Commission under Railroad Retirement Act of 1935)
- U.S.C., Title 46 [App.], §1124(b) (Maritime Commission)
- U.S.C., Title 47, §409(c) and (d) (Federal Communications Commission)
- U.S.C., Title 49, §12(2) and (3) [see 721(c) and 13301(c)] (Interstate Commerce Commission)
- U.S.C., Title 49, §173a [see 46104] (Secretary of Commerce)

Note to Subdivisions (a) and (b). These simplify the form of subpoena as provided in U.S.C., Title 28, [former] §655 (Witnesses; subpoena; form; attendance under); and broaden U.S.C., Title 28, [former] §636 (Production of books and writings) to include all actions, and to extend to any person. With the provision for relief from an oppressive or unreasonable subpoena duces tecum, compare N.Y.C.P.A. (1937) §411.

Note to Subdivision (c). This provides for the simple and convenient method of service permitted under many state codes; e.g., N.Y.C.P.A. (1937) §§220, 404, J.Ct.Act, §191; 3 Wash.Rev.Stat.Ann. (Remington, 1932) §1218. Compare Equity Rule 15 (Process, by Whom Served).

For statutes governing fees and mileage of witnesses see:

U.S.C., Title 28:

- §600a [now 1871] (Per diem; mileage)
- §600c [now 1821, 1825] (Amount per diem and mileage for witnesses; subsistence)
- §600d [former] (Fees and mileage in certain states)
- §601 [former] (Witnesses; fees; enumeration)
- §602 [now 1824] (Fees and mileage of jurors and witnesses)
- §603 [see Title 5, §§5515, 5537] (No officer of court to have witness fees)

Note to Subdivision (d). The method provided in paragraph (1) for the authorization of the issuance of subpoenas has been employed in some districts. See Henning v. Boyle, 112 Fed. 397 (S.D.N.Y., 1901). The requirement of an order for the issuance of a subpoena duces tecum is in accordance with U.S.C., Title 28, [former] §647 (Deposition under dedimus potestatem; subpoena duces tecum). The provisions of paragraph (2) are in accordance with common practice. See U.S.C., Title 28, [former] §648 (Deposition under dedimus potestatem; witnesses, when required to attend); N.Y.C.P.A. (1937) §300; 1 N.J.Rev.Stat. (1937) 2:27–174.

Note to Subdivision (e). The first paragraph continues the substance of U.S.C., Title 28, [former] §654 (Witnesses; subpoenas; may run into another district). Compare U.S.C., Title 11, [former] §69 (Referees in bankruptcy; contempts before) (production of books and writings) which is not affected by this rule. For examples of statutes which allow the court, upon proper application and cause shown, to authorize the clerk of the court to issue a subpoena for a witness who lives in another district and at a greater distance than 100 miles from the place of the hearing or trial, see:

U.S.C., Title 15:

- §23 (Suits by United States; subpoenas for witnesses) (under antitrust laws).

U.S.C., Title 38:

- §445 [now 1984] (Actions on claims; jurisdiction; parties; procedure; limitation; witnesses; definitions) (Veterans; insurance contracts).

The second paragraph continues the present procedure applicable to certain witnesses who are in foreign countries. See U.S.C., Title 28, §§711 [now 1783] (Letters rogatory to take testimony of witness, addressed to court of foreign country; failure of witness to appear; subpoena) and 713 [now 1783] (Service of subpoena on witness in foreign country).

Note to Subdivision (f). Compare [former] Equity Rule 52 (Attendance of Witnesses Before Commissioner, Master, or Examiner).

Notes of Advisory Committee on Rules—1946 Amendment

Subdivision (b). The added words, "or tangible things" in subdivision (b) merely make the rule for the subpoena duces tecum at the trial conform to that of subdivision (d) for the subpoena at the taking of depositions.

The insertion of the words "or modify" in clause (1) affords desirable flexibility.

Subdivision (d). The added last sentence of amended subdivision (d)(1) properly gives the subpoena for documents or tangible things the same scope as provided in Rule 26(b), thus promoting uniformity. The requirement in the last sentence of original Rule 45(d)(1)—to the effect that leave of court should be obtained for the issuance of such a subpoena—has been omitted. This requirement is unnecessary and oppressive on both counsel and court, and it has been criticized by district judges. There is no satisfactory reason for a differentiation between a subpoena for the production of documentary evidence by a witness at a trial (Rule 45(a)) and for the production of the same evidence at the taking of a deposition. Under this amendment, the person subpoenaed may obtain the protection afforded by any of the orders permitted under Rule 30(b) or Rule 45(b). See Application of Zenith Radio Corp. (E.D.Pa. 1941) 4 Fed.Rules Serv. 30b.21, Case 1, 1 F.R.D. 627; Fox v. House (E.D.Okla. 1939) 29 F.Supp. 673; United States of America for the Use of Tilo Roofing Co., Inc. v. J. Slotnik Co. (D.Conn. 1944) 3 F.R.D. 408.

The changes in subdivision (d)(2) give the court the same power in the case of residents of the district as is conferred in the case of non-residents, and permit the court to fix a place for attendance which may be more convenient and accessible for the parties than that specified in the rule.

Notes of Advisory Committee on Rules—1948 Amendment

The amendment substitutes the present statutory reference.

Notes of Advisory Committee on Rules—1970 Amendment

At present, when a subpoena duces tecum is issued to a deponent, he is required to produce the listed materials at the deposition, but is under no clear compulsion to permit their inspection and copying. This results in confusion and uncertainty before the time the deposition is taken, with no mechanism provided whereby the court can resolve the matter. Rule 45(d)(1), as revised, makes clear that the subpoena authorizes inspection and copying of the materials produced. The deponent is afforded full protection since he can object, thereby forcing the party serving the subpoena to obtain a court order if he wishes to inspect and copy. The procedure is thus analogous to that provided in Rule 34.

The changed references to other rules conform to changes made in those rules. The deletion of words in the clause describing the proper scope of the subpoena conforms to a change made in the language of Rule 34. The reference to Rule 26(b) is unchanged but encompasses new matter in that subdivision. The changes make it clear that the scope of discovery through a subpoena is the same as that applicable to Rule 34 and the other discovery rules.

Notes of Advisory Committee on Rules—1980 Amendment

Subdivision (d)(1). The amendment defines the term "proof of service" as used in the first sentence of the present subdivision. For want of a definition, the district court clerks have been obliged to fashion their own, with results that vary from district to district. All that seems required is a simple certification on a copy of the notice to take a deposition that the notice has been served on every other party to the action. That is the proof of service required by Rule 25(d) of both the Federal Rules of Appellate Procedure and the Supreme Court Rules.

Subdivision (e)(1). The amendment makes the reach of a subpoena of a district court at least as extensive as that of the state courts of general jurisdiction in the state in which the district court is held. Under the present rule the reach of a district court subpoena is often greater, since it extends throughout the district. No reason appears why it should be less, as it sometimes is because of the accident of district lines. Restrictions upon the reach of subpoenas are imposed to prevent undue inconvenience to witnesses. State statutes and rules of court are quite likely to reflect the varying degrees of difficulty and expense attendant upon local travel.

Notes of Advisory Committee on Rules—1985 Amendment

Present Rule 45(d)(2) has two sentences setting forth the territorial scope of deposition subpoenas. The first sentence is directed to depositions taken in the judicial district in which the deponent resides; the second sentence addresses situations in which the deponent is not a resident of the district in which the deposition is to take place. The Rule, as currently constituted, creates anomalous situations that often cause logistical problems in conducting litigation.

The first sentence of the present Rule states that a deponent may be required to attend only in the county wherein that person resides or is employed or transacts business in person, that is, where the person lives or works. Under this provision a deponent can be compelled, without court order, to travel from one end of that person's home county to the other, no matter how far that may be. The second sentence of the Rule is somewhat more flexible, stating that someone who does not reside in the district in which the deposition is to be taken can be required to attend in the county where the person is served with the subpoena, or within 40 miles from the place of service.

Under today's conditions there is no sound reason for distinguishing between residents of the district or county in which a deposition is to be taken and nonresidents, and the Rule is amended to provide that any person may be subpoenaed to attend a deposition within a specified radius from that person's residence, place of business, or where the person was served. The 40-mile radius has been increased to 100 miles.

Notes of Advisory Committee on Rules—1987 Amendment

The amendments are technical. No substantive change is intended.

Notes of Advisory Committee on Rules—1991 Amendment

Purposes of Revision. The purposes of this revision are (1) to clarify and enlarge the protections afforded persons who are required to assist the court by giving information or evidence; (2) to facilitate access outside the deposition procedure provided by Rule 30 to documents and other information in the possession of persons who are not parties; (3) to facilitate service of subpoenas for depositions or productions of evidence at places distant from the district in which an action is proceeding; (4) to enable the court to compel a witness found within the state in which the court sits to attend trial; (5) to clarify the organization of the text of the rule.

Subdivision (a). This subdivision is amended in seven significant respects.

First, Paragraph (a)(3) modifies the requirement that a subpoena be issued by the clerk of court. Provision is made for the issuance of subpoenas by attorneys as officers of the court. This revision perhaps culminates an evolution. Subpoenas were long issued by specific order of the court. As this became a burden to the court, general orders were made authorizing clerks to issue subpoenas on request. Since 1948, they have been issued in blank by the clerk of any federal court to any lawyer, the clerk serving as stationer to the bar. In allowing counsel to issue the subpoena, the rule is merely a recognition of present reality.

Although the subpoena is in a sense the command of the attorney who completes the form, defiance of a subpoena is nevertheless an act in defiance of a court order and exposes the defiant witness to contempt sanctions. In ICC v. Brimson, 154 U.S. 447 (1894), the Court upheld a statute directing federal courts to issue subpoenas to compel testimony before the ICC. In CAB v. Hermann, 353 U.S. 322 (1957), the Court approved as established practice the issuance of administrative subpoenas as a matter of absolute agency right. And in NLRB v. Warren Co., 350 U.S. 107 (1955), the Court held that the lower court had no discretion to withhold sanctions against a contemnor who violated such subpoenas. The 1948 revision of Rule 45 put the attorney in a position similar to that of the administrative agency, as a public officer entitled to use the court's contempt power to investigate facts in dispute. Two courts of appeals have touched on the issue and have described lawyer-issued subpoenas as mandates of the court. Waste Conversion, Inc. v. Rollins Environmental Services (NJ), Inc., 893 F.2d 605 (3d cir., 1990); Fisher v. Marubent Cotton Corp., 526 F.2d 1338, 1340 (8th cir., 1975). Cf. Young v. United States ex rel Vuitton et Fils S.A., 481 U.S. 787, 821 (1987) (Scalia, J., concurring). This revision makes the rule explicit that the attorney acts as an officer of the court in issuing and signing subpoenas.

Necessarily accompanying the evolution of this power of the lawyer as officer of the court is the development of increased responsibility and liability for the misuse of this power. The latter development is reflected in the provisions of subdivision (c) of this rule, and also in the requirement imposed by paragraph (3) of this subdivision that the attorney issuing a subpoena must sign it.

Second, Paragraph (a)(3) authorizes attorneys in distant districts to serve as officers authorized to issue commands in the name of the court. Any attorney permitted to represent a client in a federal court, even one admitted pro hac vice, has the same authority as a clerk to issue a subpoena from any federal court for the district in which the subpoena is served and enforced. In authorizing attorneys to issue subpoenas from distant courts, the amended rule effectively authorizes service of a subpoena anywhere in the United States by an attorney representing any party. This change is intended to ease the administrative burdens of inter-district law practice. The former rule resulted in delay and expense caused by the need to secure forms from clerks' offices some distance from the place at which the action proceeds. This change does not enlarge the burden on the witness.

Pursuant to Paragraph (a)(2), a subpoena for a deposition must still issue from the court in which the deposition or production would be compelled. Accordingly, a motion to quash such a subpoena if it overbears the limits of the subpoena power must, as under the previous rule, be presented to the court for the district in which the deposition would occur. Likewise, the court in whose name the subpoena is issued is responsible for its enforcement.

Third, in order to relieve attorneys of the need to secure an appropriate seal to affix to a subpoena issued as an officer of a distant court, the requirement that a subpoena be under seal is abolished by the provisions of Paragraph (a)(1).

Fourth, Paragraph (a)(1) authorizes the issuance of a subpoena to compel a non-party to produce evidence independent of any deposition. This revision spares the necessity of a deposition of the custodian of evidentiary material required to be produced. A party seeking additional production from a person subject to such a subpoena may serve an additional subpoena requiring additional production at the same time and place.

Fifth, Paragraph (a)(2) makes clear that the person subject to the subpoena is required to produce materials in that person's control whether or not the materials are located within the district or within the territory within which the subpoena can be served. The non-party witness is subject to the same scope of discovery under this rule as that person would be as a party to whom a request is addressed pursuant to Rule 34.

Sixth, Paragraph (a)(1) requires that the subpoena include a statement of the rights and duties of witnesses by setting forth in full the text of the new subdivisions (c) and (d).

Seventh, the revised rule authorizes the issuance of a subpoena to compel the inspection of premises in the possession of a non-party. Rule 34 has authorized such inspections of premises in the possession of a party as discovery compelled under Rule 37, but prior practice required an independent proceeding to secure such relief ancillary to the federal proceeding when the premises were not in the possession of a party. Practice in some states has long authorized such use of a subpoena for this purpose without apparent adverse consequence.

Subdivision (b). Paragraph (b)(1) retains the text of the former subdivision (c) with minor changes.

The reference to the United States marshal and deputy marshal is deleted because of the infrequency of the use of these officers for this purpose. Inasmuch as these officers meet the age requirement, they may still be used if available.

A provision requiring service of prior notice pursuant to Rule 5 of compulsory pretrial production or inspection has been added to paragraph (b)(1). The purpose of such notice is to afford other parties an opportunity to object to the production or inspection, or to serve a demand for additional documents or things. Such additional notice is not needed with respect to a deposition because of the requirement of notice imposed by Rule 30 or 31. But when production or inspection is sought independently of a deposition, other parties may need notice in order to monitor the discovery and in order to pursue access to any information that may or should be produced.

Paragraph (b)(2) retains language formerly set forth in subdivision (e) and extends its application to subpoenas for depositions or production.

Paragraph (b)(3) retains language formerly set forth in paragraph (d)(1) and extends its applications to subpoenas for trial or hearing or production.

Subdivision (c). This provision is new and states the rights of witnesses. It is not intended to diminish rights conferred by Rules 26–37 or any other authority.

Paragraph (c)(1) gives specific application to the principle stated in Rule 26(g) and specifies liability for earnings lost by a non-party witness as a result of a misuse of the subpoena. No change in existing law is thereby effected. Abuse of a subpoena is an actionable tort, Board of Ed. v. Farmingdale Classroom Teach. Ass'n, 38 N.Y.2d 397, 380 N.Y.S.2d 635, 343 N.E.2d 278 (1975), and the duty of the attorney to the non-party is also embodied in Model Rule of Professional Conduct 4.4. The liability of the attorney is correlative to the expanded power of the attorney to issue subpoenas. The liability may include the cost of fees to collect attorneys' fees owed as a result of a breach of this duty.

Paragraph (c)(2) retains language from the former subdivision (b) and paragraph (d)(1). The 10-day period for response to a subpoena is extended to 14 days to avoid the complex calculations associated with short time periods under Rule 6 and to allow a bit more time for such objections to be made.

A non-party required to produce documents or materials is protected against significant expense resulting from involuntary assistance to the court. This provision applies, for example, to a non-party required to provide a list of class members. The court is not required to fix the costs in advance of production, although this will often be the most satisfactory accommodation to protect the party seeking discovery from excessive costs. In some instances, it may be preferable to leave uncertain costs to be determined after the materials have been produced, provided that the risk of uncertainty is fully disclosed to the discovering party. See, e.g., United States v. Columbia Broadcasting Systems, Inc., 666 F.2d 364 (9th Cir. 1982).

Paragraph (c)(3) explicitly authorizes the quashing of a subpoena as a means of protecting a witness from misuse of the subpoena power. It replaces and enlarges on the former subdivision (b) of this rule and tracks the provisions of Rule 26(c). While largely repetitious, this rule is addressed to the witness who may read it on the subpoena, where it is required to be printed by the revised paragraph (a)(1) of this rule.

Subparagraph (c)(3)(A) identifies those circumstances in which a subpoena must be quashed or modified. It restates the former provisions with respect to the limits of mandatory travel that are set forth in the former paragraphs (d)(2) and (e)(1), with one important change. Under the revised rule, a federal court can compel a witness to come from any place in the state to attend trial, whether or not the local state law so provides. This extension is subject to the qualification provided in the next paragraph, which authorizes the court to condition enforcement of a subpoena compelling a non-party witness to bear substantial expense to attend trial. The traveling non-party witness may be entitled to reasonable compensation for the time and effort entailed.

Clause (c)(3)(A)(iv) requires the court to protect all persons from undue burden imposed by the use of the subpoena power. Illustratively, it might be unduly burdensome to compel an adversary to attend trial as a witness if the adversary is known to have no personal knowledge of matters in dispute, especially so if the adversary would be required to incur substantial travel burdens.

Subparagraph (c)(3)(B) identifies circumstances in which a subpoena should be quashed unless the party serving the subpoena shows a substantial need and the court can devise an appropriate accommodation to protect the interests of the witness. An additional circumstance in which such action is required is a request for costly production of documents; that situation is expressly governed by subparagraph (b)(2)(B).

Clause (c)(3)(B)(i) authorizes the court to quash, modify, or condition a subpoena to protect the person subject to or affected by the subpoena from unnecessary or unduly harmful disclosures of confidential information. It corresponds to Rule 26(c)(7).

Clause (c)(3)(B)(ii) provides appropriate protection for the intellectual property of the non-party witness; it does not apply to the expert retained by a party, whose information is subject to the provisions of Rule 26(b)(4). A growing problem has been the use of subpoenas to compel the giving of evidence and information by unretained experts. Experts are not exempt from the duty to give evidence, even if they cannot be compelled to prepare themselves to give effective testimony, e.g., Carter-Wallace, Inc. v. Otte, 474 F.2d 529 (2d Cir. 1972), but compulsion to give evidence may threaten the intellectual property of experts denied the opportunity to bargain for the value of their services. See generally Maurer, Compelling the Expert Witness: Fairness and Utility Under the Federal Rules of Civil Procedure, 19 GA.L.REV. 71 (1984); Note, Discovery and Testimony of Unretained Experts, 1987 DUKE L.J. 140. Arguably the compulsion to testify can be regarded as a "taking" of intellectual property. The rule establishes the right of such persons to withhold their expertise, at least unless the party seeking it makes the kind of showing required for a conditional denial of a motion to quash as provided in the final sentence of subparagraph (c)(3)(B); that requirement is the same as that necessary to secure work product under Rule 26(b)(3) and gives assurance of reasonable compensation. The Rule thus approves the accommodation of competing interests exemplified in United States v. Columbia Broadcasting Systems Inc., 666 F.2d 364 (9th Cir. 1982). See also Wright v. Jeep Corporation, 547 F. Supp. 871 (E.D. Mich. 1982).

As stated in Kaufman v. Edelstein, 539 F.2d 811, 822 (2d Cir. 1976), the district court's discretion in these matters should be informed by "the degree to which the expert is being called because of his knowledge of facts relevant to the case rather than in order to give opinion testimony; the difference between testifying to a previously formed or expressed opinion and forming a new one; the possibility that, for other reasons, the witness is a unique expert; the extent to which the calling party is able to show the unlikelihood that any comparable witness will willingly testify; and the degree to which the witness is able to show that he has been oppressed by having continually to testify. . . ."

Clause (c)(3)(B)(iii) protects non-party witnesses who may be burdened to perform the duty to travel in order to provide testimony at trial. The provision requires the court to condition a subpoena requiring travel of more than 100 miles on reasonable compensation.

Subdivision (d). This provision is new. Paragraph (d)(1) extends to non-parties the duty imposed on parties by the last paragraph of Rule 34(b), which was added in 1980.

Paragraph (d)(2) is new and corresponds to the new Rule 26(b)(5). Its purpose is to provide a party whose discovery is constrained by a claim of privilege or work product protection with information sufficient to evaluate such a claim and to resist if it seems unjustified. The person claiming a privilege or protection cannot decide the limits of that party's own entitlement.

A party receiving a discovery request who asserts a privilege or protection but fails to disclose that claim is at risk of waiving the privilege or protection. A person claiming a privilege or protection who fails to provide adequate information about the privilege or protection claim to the party seeking the information is subject to an order to show cause why the person should not be held in contempt under subdivision (e). Motions for such orders and responses to motions are subject to the sanctions provisions of Rules 7 and 11.

A person served a subpoena that is too broad may be faced with a burdensome task to provide full information regarding all that person's claims to privilege or work product protection. Such a person is entitled to protection that may be secured through an objection made pursuant to paragraph (c)(2).

Subdivision (e). This provision retains most of the language of the former subdivision (f).

"Adequate cause" for a failure to obey a subpoena remains undefined. In at least some circumstances, a non-party might be guilty of contempt for refusing to obey a subpoena even though the subpoena manifestly overreaches the appropriate limits of the subpoena power. E.g., Walker v. City of Birmingham, 388 U.S. 307 (1967). But, because the command of the subpoena is not in fact one uttered by a judicial officer, contempt should be very sparingly applied when the non-party witness has been overborne by a party or attorney. The language added to subdivision (f) is intended to assure that result where a non-party has been commanded, on the signature of an attorney, to travel greater distances than can be compelled pursuant to this rule.

Committee Notes on Rules—2005 Amendment

This amendment closes a small gap in regard to notifying witnesses of the manner for recording a deposition. A deposition subpoena must state the method for recording the testimony.

Rule 30(b)(2) directs that the party noticing a deposition state in the notice the manner for recording the testimony, but the notice need not be served on the deponent. The deponent learns of the recording method only if the deponent is a party or is informed by a party. Rule 30(b)(3) permits another party to designate an additional method of recording with prior notice to the deponent and the other parties. The deponent thus has notice of the recording method when an additional method is designated. This amendment completes the notice provisions to ensure that a nonparty deponent has notice of the recording method when the recording method is described only in the deposition notice.

A subpoenaed witness does not have a right to refuse to proceed with a deposition due to objections to the manner of recording. But under rare circumstances, a nonparty witness might have a ground for seeking a protective order under Rule 26(c) with regard to the manner of recording or the use of the deposition if recorded in a certain manner. Should such a witness not learn of the manner of recording until the deposition begins, undesirable delay or complication might result. Advance notice of the recording method affords an opportunity to raise such protective issues.

Other changes are made to conform Rule 45(a)(2) to current style conventions.

Changes Made After Publication and Comment. Only a small style change has been made in the proposal as published.

Committee Notes on Rules—2006 Amendment

Rule 45 is amended to conform the provisions for subpoenas to changes in other discovery rules, largely related to discovery of electronically stored information. Rule 34 is amended to provide in greater detail for the production of electronically stored information. Rule 45(a)(1)(C) is amended to recognize that electronically stored information, as defined in Rule 34(a), can also be sought by subpoena. Like Rule 34(b), Rule 45(a)(1) is amended to provide that the subpoena can designate a form or forms for production of electronic data. Rule 45(c)(2) is amended, like Rule 34(b), to authorize the person served with a subpoena to object to the requested form or forms. In addition, as under Rule 34(b), Rule 45(d)(1)(B) is amended to provide that if the subpoena does not specify the form or forms for electronically stored information, the person served with the subpoena must produce electronically stored information in a form or forms in which it is usually maintained or in a form or forms that are reasonably usable. Rule 45(d)(1)(C) is added to provide that the person producing electronically stored information should not have to produce the same information in more than one form unless so ordered by the court for good cause.

As with discovery of electronically stored information from parties, complying with a subpoena for such information may impose burdens on the responding person. Rule 45(c) provides protection against undue impositions on nonparties. For example, Rule 45(c)(1) directs that a party serving a subpoena "shall take reasonable steps to avoid imposing undue burden or expense on a person subject to the subpoena," and Rule 45(c)(2)(B) permits the person served with the subpoena to object to it and directs that an order requiring compliance "shall protect a person who is neither a party nor a party's officer from significant expense resulting from" compliance. Rule 45(d)(1)(D) is added to provide that the responding person need not provide discovery of electronically stored information from sources the party identifies as not reasonably accessible, unless the court orders such discovery for good cause, considering the limitations of Rule 26(b)(2)(C), on terms that protect a nonparty against significant expense. A parallel provision is added to Rule 26(b)(2).

Rule 45(a)(1)(B) is also amended, as is Rule 34(a), to provide that a subpoena is available to permit testing and sampling as well as inspection and copying. As in Rule 34, this change recognizes that on occasion the opportunity to perform testing or sampling may be important, both for documents and for electronically stored information. Because testing or sampling may present particular issues of burden or intrusion for the person served with the subpoena, however, the protective provisions of Rule 45(c) should be enforced with vigilance when such demands are made. Inspection or testing of certain types of electronically stored information or of a person's electronic information system may raise issues of confidentiality or privacy. The addition of sampling and testing to Rule 45(a) with regard to documents and electronically stored information is not meant to create a routine right of direct access to a person's electronic information system, although such access might be justified in some circumstances. Courts should guard against undue intrusiveness resulting from inspecting or testing such systems.

Rule 45(d)(2) is amended, as is Rule 26(b)(5), to add a procedure for assertion of privilege or of protection as trial-preparation materials after production. The receiving party may submit the information to the court for resolution of the privilege claim, as under Rule 26(b)(5)(B).

Other minor amendments are made to conform the rule to the changes described above.

Changes Made After Publication and Comment. The Committee recommends a modified version of the proposal as published. The changes were made to maintain the parallels between Rule 45 and the other rules that address discovery of electronically stored information. These changes are fully described in the introduction to Rule 45 and in the discussions of the other rules. [Omitted]

The changes from the published proposed amendment are shown below. [Omitted]

Committee Notes on Rules—2007 Amendment

The language of Rule 45 has been amended as part of the general restyling of the Civil Rules to make them more easily understood and to make style and terminology consistent throughout the rules. These changes are intended to be stylistic only.

The reference to discovery of "books" in former Rule 45(a)(1)(C) was deleted to achieve consistent expression throughout the discovery rules. Books remain a proper subject of discovery.

Former Rule 45(b)(1) required "prior notice" to each party of any commanded production of documents and things or inspection of premises. Courts have agreed that notice must be given "prior" to the return date, and have tended to converge on an interpretation that requires notice to the parties before the subpoena is served on the person commanded to produce or permit inspection. That interpretation is adopted in amended Rule 45(b)(1) to give clear notice of general present practice.

The language of former Rule 45(d)(2) addressing the manner of asserting privilege is replaced by adopting the wording of Rule 26(b)(5). The same meaning is better expressed in the same words.

Changes Made After Publication and Comment. See Note to Rule 1, supra.

Committee Notes on Rules—2013 Amendment

Rule 45 was extensively amended in 1991. The goal of the present amendments is to clarify and simplify the rule. The amendments recognize the court where the action is pending as the issuing court, permit nationwide service of a subpoena, and collect in a new subdivision (c) the previously scattered provisions regarding place of compliance. These changes resolve a conflict that arose after the 1991 amendment about a court's authority to compel a party or party officer to travel long distances to testify at trial; such testimony may now be required only as specified in new Rule 45(c). In addition, the amendments introduce authority in new Rule 45(f) for the court where compliance is required to transfer a subpoena-related motion to the court where the action is pending on consent of the person subject to the subpoena or in exceptional circumstances.

Subdivision (a). This subdivision is amended to provide that a subpoena issues from the court where the action is pending. Subdivision (a)(3) specifies that an attorney authorized to practice in that court may issue a subpoena, which is consistent with current practice.

In Rule 45(a)(1)(D), "person" is substituted for "party" because the subpoena may be directed to a nonparty.

Rule 45(a)(4) is added to highlight and slightly modify a notice requirement first included in the rule in 1991. Under the 1991 amendments, Rule 45(b)(1) required prior notice of the service of a "documents only" subpoena to the other parties. Rule 45(b)(1) was clarified in 2007 to specify that this notice must be served before the subpoena is served on the witness.

The Committee has been informed that parties serving subpoenas frequently fail to give the required notice to the other parties. The amendment moves the notice requirement to a new provision in Rule 45(a) and requires that the notice include a copy of the subpoena. The amendments are intended to achieve the original purpose of enabling the other parties to object or to serve a subpoena for additional materials.

Parties desiring access to information produced in response to the subpoena will need to follow up with the party serving it or the person served to obtain such access. The rule does not limit the court's authority to order notice of receipt of produced materials or access to them. The party serving the subpoena should in any event make reasonable provision for prompt access.

Subdivision (b). The former notice requirement in Rule 45(b)(1) has been moved to new Rule 45(a)(4).

Rule 45(b)(2) is amended to provide that a subpoena may be served at any place within the United States, removing the complexities prescribed in prior versions.

Subdivision (c). Subdivision (c) is new. It collects the various provisions on where compliance can be required and simplifies them. Unlike the prior rule, place of service is not critical to place of compliance. Although Rule 45(a)(1)(A)(iii) permits the subpoena to direct a place of compliance, that place must be selected under Rule 45(c).

Rule 45(c)(1) addresses a subpoena to testify at a trial, hearing, or deposition. Rule 45(c)(1)(A) provides that compliance may be required within 100 miles of where the person subject to the subpoena resides, is employed, or regularly conducts business in person. For parties and party officers, Rule 45(c)(1)(B)(i) provides that compliance may be required anywhere in the state where the person resides, is employed, or regularly conducts business in person. When an order under Rule 43(a) authorizes testimony from a remote location, the witness can be commanded to testify from any place described in Rule 45(c)(1).

Under Rule 45(c)(1)(B)(ii), nonparty witnesses can be required to travel more than 100 miles within the state where they reside, are employed, or regularly transact business in person only if they would not, as a result, incur "substantial expense." When travel over 100 miles could impose substantial expense on the witness, the party that served the subpoena may pay that expense and the court can condition enforcement of the subpoena on such payment.

Because Rule 45(c) directs that compliance may be commanded only as it provides, these amendments resolve a split in interpreting Rule 45's provisions for subpoenaing parties and party officers. Compare In re Vioxx Products Liability Litigation, 438 F. Supp. 2d 664 (E.D. La. 2006) (finding authority to compel a party officer from New Jersey to testify at trial in New Orleans), with Johnson v. Big Lots Stores, Inc., 251 F.R.D. 213 (E.D. La. 2008) (holding that Rule 45 did not require attendance of plaintiffs at trial in New Orleans when they would have to travel more than 100 miles from outside the state). Rule 45(c)(1)(A) does not authorize a subpoena for trial to require a party or party officer to travel more than 100 miles unless the party or party officer resides, is employed, or regularly transacts business in person in the state.

Depositions of parties, and officers, directors, and managing agents of parties need not involve use of a subpoena. Under Rule 37(d)(1)(A)(i), failure of such a witness whose deposition was properly noticed to appear for the deposition can lead to Rule 37(b) sanctions (including dismissal or default but not contempt) without regard to service of a subpoena and without regard to the geographical limitations on compliance with a subpoena. These amendments do not change that existing law; the courts retain their authority to control the place of party depositions and impose sanctions for failure to appear under Rule 37(b).

For other discovery, Rule 45(c)(2) directs that inspection of premises occur at those premises, and that production of documents, tangible things, and electronically stored information may be commanded to occur at a place within 100 miles of where the person subject to the subpoena resides, is employed, or regularly conducts business in person. Under the current rule, parties often agree that production, particularly of electronically stored information, be transmitted by electronic means. Such arrangements facilitate discovery, and nothing in these amendments limits the ability of parties to make such arrangements.

Rule 45(d)(3)(A)(ii) directs the court to quash any subpoena that purports to compel compliance beyond the geographical limits specified in Rule 45(c).

Subdivision (d). Subdivision (d) contains the provisions formerly in subdivision (c). It is revised to recognize the court where the action is pending as the issuing court, and to take account of the addition of Rule 45(c) to specify where compliance with a subpoena is required.

Subdivision (f). Subdivision (f) is new. Under Rules 45(d)(2)(B), 45(d)(3), and 45(e)(2)(B), subpoena-related motions and applications are to be made to the court where compliance is required under Rule 45(c). Rule 45(f) provides authority for that court to transfer the motion to the court where the action is pending. It applies to all motions under this rule, including an application under Rule 45(e)(2)(B) for a privilege determination.

Subpoenas are essential to obtain discovery from nonparties. To protect local nonparties, local resolution of disputes about subpoenas is assured by the limitations of Rule 45(c) and the requirements in Rules 45(d) and (e) that motions be made in the court in which compliance is required under Rule 45(c). But transfer to the court where the action is pending is sometimes warranted. If the person subject to the subpoena consents to transfer, Rule 45(f) provides that the court where compliance is required may do so.

In the absence of consent, the court may transfer in exceptional circumstances, and the proponent of transfer bears the burden of showing that such circumstances are present. The prime concern should be avoiding burdens on local nonparties subject to subpoenas, and it should not be assumed that the issuing court is in a superior position to resolve subpoena-related motions. In some circumstances, however, transfer may be warranted in order to avoid disrupting the issuing court's management of the underlying litigation, as when that court has already ruled on issues presented by the motion or the same issues are likely to arise in discovery in many districts. Transfer is appropriate only if such interests outweigh the interests of the nonparty served with the subpoena in obtaining local resolution of the motion. Judges in compliance districts may find it helpful to consult with the judge in the issuing court presiding over the underlying case while addressing subpoena-related motions.

If the motion is transferred, judges are encouraged to permit telecommunications methods to minimize the burden a transfer imposes on nonparties, if it is necessary for attorneys admitted in the court where the motion is made to appear in the court in which the action is pending. The rule provides that if these attorneys are authorized to practice in the court where the motion is made, they may file papers and appear in the court in which the action is pending in relation to the motion as officers of that court.

After transfer, the court where the action is pending will decide the motion. If the court rules that discovery is not justified, that should end the matter. If the court orders further discovery, it is possible that retransfer may be important to enforce the order. One consequence of failure to obey such an order is contempt, addressed in Rule 45(g). Rule 45(g) and Rule 37(b)(1) are both amended to provide that disobedience of an order enforcing a subpoena after transfer is contempt of the issuing court and the court where compliance is required under Rule 45(c). In some instances, however, there may be a question about whether the issuing court can impose contempt sanctions on a distant nonparty. If such circumstances arise, or if it is better to supervise compliance in the court where compliance is required, the rule provides authority for retransfer for enforcement. Although changed circumstances may prompt a modification of such an order, it is not expected that the compliance court will reexamine the resolution of the underlying motion.

Subdivision (g). Subdivision (g) carries forward the authority of former subdivision (e) to punish disobedience of subpoenas as contempt. It is amended to make clear that, in the event of transfer of a subpoena-related motion, such disobedience constitutes contempt of both the court where compliance is required under Rule 45(c) and the court where the action is pending. If necessary for effective enforcement, Rule 45(f) authorizes the issuing court to transfer its order after the motion is resolved.

The rule is also amended to clarify that contempt sanctions may be applied to a person who disobeys a subpoena-related order, as well as one who fails entirely to obey a subpoena. In civil litigation, it would be rare for a court to use contempt sanctions without first ordering compliance with a subpoena, and the order might not require all the compliance sought by the subpoena. Often contempt proceedings will be initiated by an order to show cause, and an order to comply or be held in contempt may modify the subpoena's command. Disobedience of such an order may be treated as contempt.

The second sentence of former subdivision (e) is deleted as unnecessary.

Changes Made After Publication and Comment. As described in the Report, the published preliminary draft was modified in several ways after the public comment period. The words "before trial" were restored to the notice provision that was moved to new Rule 45(a)(4). The place of compliance in new Rule 45(c)(2)(A) was changed to a place "within 100 miles of where the person resides, is employed or regularly conducts business." In new Rule 45(f), the party consent feature was removed, meaning consent of the person subject to the subpoena is sufficient to permit transfer to the issuing court. In addition, style changes were made after consultation with the Standing Committee's Style Consultant. In the Committee Note, clarifications were made in response to points raised during the public comment period.

Rule 46. Objecting to a Ruling or Order

A formal exception to a ruling or order is unnecessary. When the ruling or order is requested or made, a party need only state the action that it wants the court to take or objects to, along with the grounds for the request or objection. Failing to object does not prejudice a party who had no opportunity to do so when the ruling or order was made.

(As amended Mar. 2, 1987, eff. Aug. 1, 1987; Apr. 30, 2007, eff. Dec. 1, 2007.)

Notes of Advisory Committee on Rules—1937

Abolition of formal exceptions is often provided by statute. See Ill.Rev.Stat. (1937), ch. 110, §204; Neb.Comp.Stat. (1929) §20–1139; N.M.Stat.Ann. (Courtright, 1929) §105–830; 2 N.D.Comp.Laws Ann. (1913) §7653; Ohio Code Ann. (Throckmorton, 1936) §11560; 1 S.D.Comp.Laws (1929) §2542; Utah Rev.Stat.Ann. (1933) §§104–39–2, 104–24–18; Va.Rules of Court, Rule 22, 163 Va. v, xii (1935); Wis.Stat. (1935) §270.39. Compare N.Y.C.P.A. (1937) §§583, 445, and 446, all as amended by L. 1936, ch. 915. Rule 51 deals with objections to the court's instructions to the jury.

U.S.C., Title 28, [former] §§776 (Bill of exceptions; authentication; signing of by judge) and [former] 875 (Review of findings in cases tried without a jury) are superseded insofar as they provide for formal exceptions, and a bill of exceptions.

Notes of Advisory Committee on Rules—1987 Amendment

The amendments are technical. No substantive change is intended.

Committee Notes on Rules—2007 Amendment

The language of Rule 46 has been amended as part of the general restyling of the Civil Rules to make them more easily understood and to make style and terminology consistent throughout the rules. These changes are intended to be stylistic only.

Rule 47. Selecting Jurors

(a) Examining Jurors. The court may permit the parties or their attorneys to examine prospective jurors or may itself do so. If the court examines the jurors, it must permit the parties or their attorneys to make any further inquiry it considers proper, or must itself ask any of their additional questions it considers proper.
(b) Peremptory Challenges. The court must allow the number of peremptory challenges provided by 28 U.S.C. §1870.
(c) Excusing a Juror. During trial or deliberation, the court may excuse a juror for good cause.

(As amended Feb. 28, 1966, eff. July 1, 1966; Apr. 30, 1991, eff. Dec. 1, 1991; Apr. 30, 2007, eff. Dec. 1, 2007.)

Notes of Advisory Committee on Rules—1937

Note to Subdivision (a). This permits a practice found very useful by Federal trial judges. For an example of a state practice in which the examination by the court is supplemented by further inquiry by counsel, see Rule 27 of the Code of Rules for the District Courts of Minnesota, 186 Minn. xxxiii (1932), 3 Minn.Stat. (Mason, supp. 1936) Appendix, 4, p. 1062.

Note to Subdivision (b). The provision for an alternate juror is one often found in modern state codes. See N.C.Code (1935) §2330(a); Ohio Gen.Code Ann. (Page, Supp. 1926–1935) §11419–47; Pa.Stat.Ann. (Purdon, Supp. 1936) Title 17, §1153; compare U.S.C., Title 28, [former] §417a (Alternate jurors in criminal trials); 1 N.J.Rev.Stat. (1937) 2:91A–1, 2:91A–2, 2:91A–3.

Provisions for qualifying, drawing, and challenging of jurors are found in U.S.C., Title 28:

- §411 [now 1861] (Qualifications and exemptions)
- §412 [now 1864] (Manner of drawing)
- §413 [now 1865] (Apportioned in district)
- §415 [see 1862] (Not disqualified because of race or color)
- §416 [now 1867] (Venire; service and return)
- §417 [now 1866] (Talesmen for petit jurors)
- §418 [now 1866] (Special juries)
- §423 [now 1869] (Jurors not to serve more than once a year)
- §424 [now 1870] (Challenges)

and D.C. Code (1930) Title 18, §§341–360 (Juries and Jury Commission) and Title 6, §366 (Peremptory challenges.

Notes of Advisory Committee on Rules—1966 Amendment

The revision of this subdivision brings it into line with the amendment of Rule 24(c) of the Federal Rules of Criminal Procedure. That rule previously allowed four alternate jurors, as contrasted with the two allowed in civil cases, and the amendments increase the number of a maximum of six in all cases. The Advisory Committee's Note to amended Criminal Rule 24(c) points to experience demonstrating that four alternates may not be enough in some lengthy criminal trials; and the same may be said of civil trials. The Note adds:

"The words 'or are found to be' are added to the second sentence to make clear that an alternate juror may be called in the situation where it is first discovered during the trial that a juror was unable or disqualified to perform his duties at the time he was sworn."

Notes of Advisory Committee on Rules—1991 Amendment

Subdivision (b). The former provision for alternate jurors is stricken and the institution of the alternate juror abolished.

The former rule reflected the long-standing assumption that a jury would consist of exactly twelve members. It provided for additional jurors to be used as substitutes for jurors who are for any reason excused or disqualified from service after the commencement of the trial. Additional jurors were traditionally designated at the outset of the trial, and excused at the close of the evidence if they had not been promoted to full service on account of the elimination of one of the original jurors.

The use of alternate jurors has been a source of dissatisfaction with the jury system because of the burden it places on alternates who are required to listen to the evidence but denied the satisfaction of participating in its evaluation.

Subdivision (c). This provision makes it clear that the court may in appropriate circumstances excuse a juror during the jury deliberations without causing a mistrial. Sickness, family emergency or juror misconduct that might occasion a mistrial are examples of appropriate grounds for excusing a juror. It is not grounds for the dismissal of a juror that the juror refuses to join with fellow jurors in reaching a unanimous verdict.

Committee Notes on Rules—2007 Amendment

The language of Rule 47 has been amended as part of the general restyling of the Civil Rules to make them more easily understood and to make style and terminology consistent throughout the rules. These changes are intended to be stylistic only.

Rule 48. Number of Jurors; Verdict; Polling

(a) Number of Jurors. A jury must begin with at least 6 and no more than 12 members, and each juror must participate in the verdict unless excused under Rule 47(c).
(b) Verdict. Unless the parties stipulate otherwise, the verdict must be unanimous and must be returned by a jury of at least 6 members.
(c) Polling. After a verdict is returned but before the jury is discharged, the court must on a party's request, or may on its own, poll the jurors individually. If the poll reveals a lack of unanimity or lack of assent by the number of jurors that the parties stipulated to, the court may direct the jury to deliberate further or may order a new trial.

(As amended Apr. 30, 1991, eff. Dec. 1, 1991; Apr. 30, 2007, eff. Dec. 1, 2007; Mar. 26, 2009, eff. Dec. 1, 2009.)

Notes of Advisory Committee on Rules—1937

For provisions in state codes, compare Utah Rev.Stat.Ann. (1933) §48–O–5 (In civil cases parties may agree in open court on lesser number of jurors); 2 Wash.Rev.Stat.Ann. (Remington, 1932) §323 (Parties may consent to any number of jurors not less than three).

Notes of Advisory Committee on Rules—1991 Amendment

The former rule was rendered obsolete by the adoption in many districts of local rules establishing six as the standard size for a civil jury.

It appears that the minimum size of a jury consistent with the Seventh Amendment is six. Cf. Ballew v. Georgia, 435 U.S. 223 (1978) (holding that a conviction based on a jury of less than six is a denial of due process of law). If the parties agree to trial before a smaller jury, a verdict can be taken, but the parties should not other than in exceptional circumstances be encouraged to waive the right to a jury of six, not only because of the constitutional stature of the right, but also because smaller juries are more erratic and less effective in serving to distribute responsibility for the exercise of judicial power.

Because the institution of the alternate juror has been abolished by the proposed revision of Rule 47, it will ordinarily be prudent and necessary, in order to provide for sickness or disability among jurors, to seat more than six jurors. The use of jurors in excess of six increases the representativeness of the jury and harms no interest of a party. Ray v. Parkside Surgery Center, 13 F.R. Serv. 585 (6th cir. 1989).

If the court takes the precaution of seating a jury larger than six, an illness occurring during the deliberation period will not result in a mistrial, as it did formerly, because all seated jurors will participate in the verdict and a sufficient number will remain to render a unanimous verdict of six or more.

In exceptional circumstances, as where a jury suffers depletions during trial and deliberation that are greater than can reasonably be expected, the parties may agree to be bound by a verdict rendered by fewer than six jurors. The court should not, however, rely upon the availability of such an agreement, for the use of juries smaller than six is problematic for reasons fully explained in Ballew v. Georgia, supra.

Committee Notes on Rules—2007 Amendment

The language of Rule 48 has been amended as part of the general restyling of the Civil Rules to make them more easily understood and to make style and terminology consistent throughout the rules. These changes are intended to be stylistic only.

Committee Notes on Rules—2009 Amendment

Jury polling is added as new subdivision (c), which is drawn from Criminal Rule 31(d) with minor revisions to reflect Civil Rules Style and the parties' opportunity to stipulate to a nonunanimous verdict.

Rule 49. Special Verdict; General Verdict and Questions

(a) Special Verdict.

(1) In General. The court may require a jury to return only a special verdict in the form of a special written finding on each issue of fact. The court may do so by:

(A) submitting written questions susceptible of a categorical or other brief answer;

(B) submitting written forms of the special findings that might properly be made under the pleadings and evidence; or

(C) using any other method that the court considers appropriate.

(2) Instructions. The court must give the instructions and explanations necessary to enable the jury to make its findings on each submitted issue.

(3) Issues Not Submitted. A party waives the right to a jury trial on any issue of fact raised by the pleadings or evidence but not submitted to the jury unless, before the jury retires, the party demands its submission to the jury. If the party does not demand submission, the court may make a finding on the issue. If the court makes no finding, it is considered to have made a finding consistent with its judgment on the special verdict.

(b) General Verdict with Answers to Written Questions.

(1) In General. The court may submit to the jury forms for a general verdict, together with written questions on one or more issues of fact that the jury must decide. The court must give the instructions and explanations necessary to enable the jury to render a general verdict and answer the questions in writing, and must direct the jury to do both.

(2) Verdict and Answers Consistent. When the general verdict and the answers are consistent, the court must approve, for entry under Rule 58, an appropriate judgment on the verdict and answers.

(3) Answers Inconsistent with the Verdict. When the answers are consistent with each other but one or more is inconsistent with the general verdict, the court may:

(A) approve, for entry under Rule 58, an appropriate judgment according to the answers, notwithstanding the general verdict;

(B) direct the jury to further consider its answers and verdict; or

(C) order a new trial.

(4) Answers Inconsistent with Each Other and the Verdict. When the answers are inconsistent with each other and one or more is also inconsistent with the general verdict, judgment must not be entered; instead, the court must direct the jury to further consider its answers and verdict, or must order a new trial.

(As amended Jan. 21, 1963, eff. July 1, 1963; Mar. 2, 1987, eff. Aug. 1, 1987; Apr. 30, 2007, eff. Dec. 1, 2007.)

Notes of Advisory Committee on Rules—1937

The Federal courts are not bound to follow state statutes authorizing or requiring the court to ask a jury to find a special verdict or to answer interrogatories. Victor American Fuel Co. v. Peccarich, 209 Fed. 568 (C.C.A.8th, 1913) cert. den. 232 U.S. 727 (1914); Spokane and I. E. R. Co. v. Campbell, 217 Fed. 518 (C.C.A.9th, 1914), affd. 241 U.S. 497 (1916); Simkins, Federal Practice (1934) §186. The power of a territory to adopt by statute the practice under Subdivision (b) has been sustained. Walker v. New Mexico and Southern Pacific R. R., 165 U.S. 593 (1897); Southwestern Brewery and Ice Co. v. Schmidt, 226 U.S. 162 (1912).

Compare Wis.Stat. (1935) §§270.27, 270.28 and 270.30 Green, A New Development in Jury Trial (1927), 13 A.B.A.J. 715; Morgan, A Brief History of Special Verdicts and Special Interrogatories (1923), 32 Yale L.J. 575.

The provisions of U.S.C., Title 28, [former] §400(3) (Declaratory judgments authorized; procedure) permitting the submission of issues of fact to a jury are covered by this rule.

Notes of Advisory Committee on Rules—1963 Amendment

This amendment conforms to the amendment of Rule 58. See the Advisory Committee's Note to Rule 58, as amended.

Notes of Advisory Committee on Rules—1987 Amendment

The amendments are technical. No substantive change is intended.

Committee Notes on Rules—2007 Amendment

The language of Rule 49 has been amended as part of the general restyling of the Civil Rules to make them more easily understood and to make style and terminology consistent throughout the rules. These changes are intended to be stylistic only.

Rule 50. Judgment as a Matter of Law in a Jury Trial; Related Motion for a New Trial; Conditional Ruling

(a) Judgment as a Matter of Law.

(1) In General. If a party has been fully heard on an issue during a jury trial and the court finds that a reasonable jury would not have a legally sufficient evidentiary basis to find for the party on that issue, the court may:

(A) resolve the issue against the party; and

(B) grant a motion for judgment as a matter of law against the party on a claim or defense that, under the controlling law, can be maintained or defeated only with a favorable finding on that issue.

(2) Motion. A motion for judgment as a matter of law may be made at any time before the case is submitted to the jury. The motion must specify the judgment sought and the law and facts that entitle the movant to the judgment.

(b) Renewing the Motion After Trial; Alternative Motion for a New Trial. If the court does not grant a motion for judgment as a matter of law made under Rule 50(a), the court is considered to have submitted the action to the jury subject to the court's later deciding the legal questions raised by the motion. No later than 28 days after the entry of judgment—or if the motion addresses a jury issue not decided by a verdict, no later than 28 days after the jury was discharged—the movant may file a renewed motion for judgment as a matter of law and may include an alternative or joint request for a new trial under Rule 59. In ruling on the renewed motion, the court may:

(1) allow judgment on the verdict, if the jury returned a verdict;

(2) order a new trial; or

(3) direct the entry of judgment as a matter of law.

(c) Granting the Renewed Motion; Conditional Ruling on a Motion for a New Trial.

(1) In General. If the court grants a renewed motion for judgment as a matter of law, it must also conditionally rule on any motion for a new trial by determining whether a new trial should be granted if the judgment is later vacated or reversed. The court must state the grounds for conditionally granting or denying the motion for a new trial.

(2) Effect of a Conditional Ruling. Conditionally granting the motion for a new trial does not affect the judgment's finality; if the judgment is reversed, the new trial must proceed unless the appellate court orders otherwise. If the motion for a new trial is conditionally denied, the appellee may assert error in that denial; if the judgment is reversed, the case must proceed as the appellate court orders.

(d) Time for a Losing Party's New-Trial Motion. Any motion for a new trial under Rule 59 by a party against whom judgment as a matter of law is rendered must be filed no later than 28 days after the entry of the judgment.

(e) Denying the Motion for Judgment as a Matter of Law; Reversal on Appeal. If the court denies the motion for judgment as a matter of law, the prevailing party may, as appellee, assert grounds entitling it to a new trial should the appellate court conclude that the trial court erred in denying the motion. If the appellate court reverses the judgment, it may order a new trial, direct the trial court to determine whether a new trial should be granted, or direct the entry of judgment.

(As amended Jan. 21, 1963, eff. July 1, 1963; Mar. 2, 1987, eff. Aug. 1, 1987; Apr. 30, 1991, eff. Dec. 1, 1991; Apr. 22, 1993, eff. Dec. 1, 1993; Apr. 27, 1995, eff. Dec. 1, 1995; Apr. 12, 2006, eff. Dec. 1, 2006; Apr. 30, 2007, eff. Dec. 1, 2007; Mar. 26, 2009, eff. Dec. 1, 2009.)

Notes of Advisory Committee on Rules—1937

Note to Subdivision (a). The present federal rule is changed to the extent that the formality of an express reservation of rights against waiver is no longer necessary. See Sampliner v. Motion Picture Patents Co., 254 U.S. 233 (1920); Union Indemnity Co. v. United States, 74 F.(2d) 645 (C.C.A.6th, 1935). The requirement that specific grounds for the motion for a directed verdict must be stated settles a conflict in the federal cases. See Simkins, Federal Practice (1934) §189.

Note to Subdivision (b). For comparable state practice upheld under the conformity act, see Baltimore and Carolina Line v. Redman, 295 U.S. 654 (1935); compare Slocum v. New York Life Ins. Co., 228 U.S. 364 (1913).

See Northern Ry. Co. v. Page, 274 U.S. 65 (1927), following the Massachusetts practice of alternative verdicts, explained in Thorndike, Trial by Jury in United States Courts, 26 Harv.L.Rev. 732 (1913). See also Thayer, Judicial Administration, 63 U. of Pa.L.Rev. 585, 600–601, and note 32 (1915); Scott, Trial by Jury and the Reform of Civil Procedure, 31 Harv.L.Rev. 669, 685 (1918); Comment, 34 Mich.L.Rev. 93, 98 (1935).

Notes of Advisory Committee on Rules—1963 Amendment

Subdivision (a). The practice, after the court has granted a motion for a directed verdict, of requiring the jury to express assent to a verdict they did not reach by their own deliberations serves no useful purpose and may give offense to the members of the jury. See 2B Barron & Holtzoff, Federal Practice and Procedure §1072, at 367 (Wright ed. 1961); Blume, Origin and Development of the Directed Verdict, 48 Mich.L.Rev. 555, 582–85, 589–90 (1950). The final sentence of the subdivision, added by amendment, provides that the court's order granting a motion for a directed verdict is effective in itself, and that no action need be taken by the foreman or other members of the jury. See Ariz.R.Civ.P. 50(c); cf. Fed.R.Crim.P. 29 (a). No change is intended in the standard to be applied in deciding the motion. To assure this interpretation, and in the interest of simplicity, the traditional term, "directed verdict," is retained.

Subdivision (b). A motion for judgment notwithstanding the verdict will not lie unless it was preceded by a motion for a directed verdict made at the close of all the evidence.

The amendment of the second sentence of this subdivision sets the time limit for making the motion for judgment n.o.v. at 10 days after the entry of judgment, rather than 10 days after the reception of the verdict. Thus the time provision is made consistent with that contained in Rule 59(b) (time for motion for new trial) and Rule 52(b) (time for motion to amend findings by the court).

Subdivision (c) deals with the situation where a party joins a motion for a new trial with his motion for judgment n.o.v. or prays for a new trial in the alternative, and the motion for judgment n.o.v. is granted. The procedure to be followed in making rulings on the motion for the new trial, and the consequences of the rulings thereon, were partly set out in Montgomery Ward & Co. v. Duncan, 311 U.S. 243, 253, 61 S.Ct. 189, 85 L.Ed. 147 (1940), and have been further elaborated in later cases. See Cone v. West Virginia Pulp & Paper Co., 330 U.S. 212, 67 S.Ct. 752, 91 L.Ed. 849 (1947); Globe Liquor Co., Inc. v. San Roman, 332 U.S. 571, 68 S.Ct. 246, 92 L.Ed. 177 (1948); Fountain v. Filson, 336 U.S. 681, 69 S.Ct. 754, 93 L.Ed. 971 (1949); Johnson v. New York, N.H. & H.R.R. Co., 344 U.S. 48, 73 S.Ct. 125, 97 L.Ed. 77 (1952). However, courts as well as counsel have often misunderstood the procedure, and it will be helpful to summarize the proper practice in the text of the rule. The amendments do not alter the effects of a jury verdict or the scope of appellate review.

In the situation mentioned, subdivision (c)(1) requires that the court make a "conditional" ruling on the new-trial motion, i.e., a ruling which goes on the assumption that the motion for judgment n.o.v. was erroneously granted and will be reversed or vacated; and the court is required to state its grounds for the conditional ruling. Subdivision (c)(1) then spells out the consequences of a reversal of the judgment in the light of the conditional ruling on the new-trial motion.

If the motion for new trial has been conditionally granted, and the judgment is reversed, "the new trial shall proceed unless the appellate court has otherwise ordered." The party against whom the judgment n.o.v. was entered below may, as appellant, besides seeking to overthrow that judgment, also attack the conditional grant of the new trial. And the appellate court, if it reverses the judgment n.o.v., may in an appropriate case also reverse the conditional grant of the new trial and direct that judgment be entered on the verdict. See Bailey v. Slentz, 189 F.2d 406 (10th Cir. 1951); Moist Cold Refrigerator Co. v. Lou Johnson Co., 249 F.2d 246 (9th Cir. 1957), cert. denied, 356 U.S. 968, 78 S.Ct. 1008, 2 L.Ed.2d 1074 (1958); Peters v. Smith, 221 F.2d 721 (3d Cir.1955); Dailey v. Timmer, 292 F.2d 824 (3d Cir. 1961), explaining Lind v. Schenley Industries, Inc., 278 F.2d 79 (3d Cir.), cert. denied, 364 U.S. 835, 81 S.Ct. 58, 5 L.Ed.2d 60 (1960); Cox v. Pennsylvania R.R., 120 A.2d 214 (D.C.Mun.Ct.App. 1956); 3 Barron & Holtzoff, Federal Practice and Procedure §1302.1 at 346–47 (Wright ed. 1958); 6 Moore's Federal Practice 59.16 at 3915 n. 8a (2d ed. 1954).

If the motion for a new trial has been conditionally denied, and the judgment is reversed, "subsequent proceedings shall be in accordance with the order of the appellate court." The party in whose favor judgment n.o.v. was entered below may, as appellee, besides seeking to uphold that judgment, also urge on the appellate court that the trial court committed error in conditionally denying the new trial. The appellee may assert this error in his brief, without taking a cross-appeal. Cf. Patterson v. Pennsylvania R.R., 238 F.2d 645, 650 (6th Cir. 1956); Hughes v. St. Louis Nat. L. Baseball Club, Inc., 359 Mo. 993, 997, 224 S.W.2d 989, 992 (1949). If the appellate court concludes that the judgment cannot stand, but accepts the appellee's contention that there was error in the conditional denial of the new trial, it may order a new trial in lieu of directing the entry of judgment upon the verdict.

Subdivision (c)(2), which also deals with the situation where the trial court has granted the motion for judgment n.o.v., states that the verdict-winner may apply to the trial court for a new trial pursuant to Rule 59 after the judgment n.o.v. has been entered against him. In arguing to the trial court in opposition to the motion for judgment n.o.v., the verdict-winner may, and often will, contend that he is entitled, at the least, to a new trial, and the court has a range of discretion to grant a new trial or (where plaintiff won the verdict) to order a dismissal of the action without prejudice instead of granting judgment n.o.v. See Cone v. West Virginia Pulp & Paper Co., supra, 330 U.S. at 217, 218 67 S.Ct. at 755, 756, 91 L.Ed. 849. Subdivision (c)(2) is a reminder that the verdict-winner is entitled, even after entry of judgment n.o.v. against him, to move for a new trial in the usual course. If in these circumstances the motion is granted, the judgment is superseded.

In some unusual circumstances, however, the grant of the new-trial motion may be only conditional, and the judgment will not be superseded. See the situation in Tribble v. Bruin, 279 F.2d 424 (4th Cir. 1960) (upon a verdict for plaintiff, defendant moves for and obtains judgment n.o.v.; plaintiff moves for a new trial on the ground of inadequate damages; trial court might properly have granted plaintiff's motion, conditional upon reversal of the judgment n.o.v.).

Even if the verdict-winner makes no motion for a new trial, he is entitled upon his appeal from the judgment n.o.v. not only to urge that that judgment should be reversed and judgment entered upon the verdict, but that errors were committed during the trial which at the least entitle him to a new trial.

Subdivision (d) deals with the situation where judgment has been entered on the jury verdict, the motion for judgment n.o.v. and any motion for a new trial having been denied by the trial court. The verdict-winner, as appellee, besides seeking to uphold the judgment, may urge upon the appellate court that in case the trial court is found to have erred in entering judgment on the verdict, there are grounds for granting him a new trial instead of directing the entry of judgment for his opponent. In appropriate cases the appellate court is not precluded from itself directing that a new trial be had. See Weade v. Dichmann, Wright & Pugh, Inc., 337 U.S. 801, 69 S.Ct. 1326, 93 L.Ed. 1704 (1949). Nor is it precluded in proper cases from remanding the case for a determination by the trial court as to whether a new trial should be granted. The latter course is advisable where the grounds urged are suitable for the exercise of trial court discretion.

Subdivision (d) does not attempt a regulation of all aspects of the procedure where the motion for judgment n.o.v. and any accompanying motion for a new trial are denied, since the problems have not been fully canvassed in the decisions and the procedure is in some respects still in a formative stage. It is, however, designed to give guidance on certain important features of the practice.

Notes of Advisory Committee on Rules—1987 Amendment

The amendments are technical. No substantive change is intended.

Notes of Advisory Committee on Rules—1991 Amendment

Subdivision (a). The revision of this subdivision aims to facilitate the exercise by the court of its responsibility to assure the fidelity of its judgment to the controlling law, a responsibility imposed by the Due Process Clause of the Fifth Amendment. Cf. Galloway v. United States, 319 U.S. 372 (1943).

The revision abandons the familiar terminology of direction of verdict for several reasons. The term is misleading as a description of the relationship between judge and jury. It is also freighted with anachronisms some of which are the subject of the text of former subdivision (a) of this rule that is deleted in this revision. Thus, it should not be necessary to state in the text of this rule that a motion made pursuant to it is not a waiver of the right to jury trial, and only the antiquities of directed verdict practice suggest that it might have been. The term "judgment as a matter of law" is an almost equally familiar term and appears in the text of Rule 56; its use in Rule 50 calls attention to the relationship between the two rules. Finally, the change enables the rule to refer to preverdict and post-verdict motions with a terminology that does not conceal the common identity of two motions made at different times in the proceeding.

If a motion is denominated a motion for directed verdict or for judgment notwithstanding the verdict, the party's error is merely formal. Such a motion should be treated as a motion for judgment as a matter of law in accordance with this rule.

Paragraph (a)(1) articulates the standard for the granting of a motion for judgment as a matter of law. It effects no change in the existing standard. That existing standard was not expressed in the former rule, but was articulated in long-standing case law. See generally Cooper, Directions for Directed Verdicts: A Compass for Federal Courts, 55 MINN. L. REV. 903 (1971). The expressed standard makes clear that action taken under the rule is a performance of the court's duty to assure enforcement of the controlling law and is not an intrusion on any responsibility for factual determinations conferred on the jury by the Seventh Amendment or any other provision of federal law. Because this standard is also used as a reference point for entry of summary judgment under 56(a), it serves to link the two related provisions.

The revision authorizes the court to perform its duty to enter judgment as a matter of law at any time during the trial, as soon as it is apparent that either party is unable to carry a burden of proof that is essential to that party's case. Thus, the second sentence of paragraph (a)(1) authorizes the court to consider a motion for judgment as a matter of law as soon as a party has completed a presentation on a fact essential to that party's case. Such early action is appropriate when economy and expedition will be served. In no event, however, should the court enter judgment against a party who has not been apprised of the materiality of the dispositive fact and been afforded an opportunity to present any available evidence bearing on that fact. In order further to facilitate the exercise of the authority provided by this rule, Rule 16 is also revised to encourage the court to schedule an order of trial that proceeds first with a presentation on an issue that is likely to be dispositive, if such an issue is identified in the course of pretrial. Such scheduling can be appropriate where the court is uncertain whether favorable action should be taken under Rule 56. Thus, the revision affords the court the alternative of denying a motion for summary judgment while scheduling a separate trial of the issue under Rule 42(b) or scheduling the trial to begin with a presentation on that essential fact which the opposing party seems unlikely to be able to maintain.

Paragraph (a)(2) retains the requirement that a motion for judgment be made prior to the close of the trial, subject to renewal after a jury verdict has been rendered. The purpose of this requirement is to assure the responding party an opportunity to cure any deficiency in that party's proof that may have been overlooked until called to the party's attention by a late motion for judgment. Cf. Farley Transp. Co. v. Santa Fe Trail Transp. Co., 786 F.2d 1342 (9th Cir. 1986) ("If the moving party is then permitted to make a later attack on the evidence through a motion for judgment notwithstanding the verdict or an appeal, the opposing party may be prejudiced by having lost the opportunity to present additional evidence before the case was submitted to the jury"); Benson v. Allphin, 786 F.2d 268 (7th Cir. 1986) ("the motion for directed verdict at the close of all the evidence provides the nonmovant an opportunity to do what he can to remedy the deficiencies in his case . . .); McLaughlin v. The Fellows Gear Shaper Co., 4 F.R.Serv. 3d 607 (3d Cir. 1986) (per Adams, J., dissenting: "This Rule serves important practical purposes in ensuring that neither party is precluded from presenting the most persuasive case possible and in preventing unfair surprise after a matter has been submitted to the jury"). At one time, this requirement was held to be of constitutional stature, being compelled by the Seventh Amendment. Cf. Slocum v. New York Insurance Co., 228 U.S. 364 (1913). But cf. Baltimore & Carolina Line v. Redman, 295 U.S. 654 (1935).

The second sentence of paragraph (a)(2) does impose a requirement that the moving party articulate the basis on which a judgment as a matter of law might be rendered. The articulation is necessary to achieve the purpose of the requirement that the motion be made before the case is submitted to the jury, so that the responding party may seek to correct any overlooked deficiencies in the proof. The revision thus alters the result in cases in which courts have used various techniques to avoid the requirement that a motion for a directed verdict be made as a predicate to a motion for judgment notwithstanding the verdict. E.g., Benson v. Allphin, 788 F.2d 268 (7th cir. 1986) ("this circuit has allowed something less than a formal motion for directed verdict to preserve a party's right to move for judgment notwithstanding the verdict"). See generally 9 WRIGHT & MILLER, FEDERAL PRACTICE AND PROCEDURE §2537 (1971 and Supp.). The information required with the motion may be supplied by explicit reference to materials and argument previously supplied to the court.

This subdivision deals only with the entry of judgment and not with the resolution of particular factual issues as a matter of law. The court may, as before, properly refuse to instruct a jury to decide an issue if a reasonable jury could on the evidence presented decide that issue in only one way.

Subdivision (b). This provision retains the concept of the former rule that the post-verdict motion is a renewal of an earlier motion made at the close of the evidence. One purpose of this concept was to avoid any question arising under the Seventh Amendment. Montgomery Ward & Co. v. Duncan, 311 U.S. 243 (1940). It remains useful as a means of defining the appropriate issue posed by the post-verdict motion. A post-trial motion for judgment can be granted only on grounds advanced in the pre-verdict motion. E.g., Kutner Buick, Inc. v. American Motors Corp., 848 F.2d 614 (3d cir. 1989).

Often it appears to the court or to the moving party that a motion for judgment as a matter of law made at the close of the evidence should be reserved for a post-verdict decision. This is so because a jury verdict for the moving party moots the issue and because a pre-verdict ruling gambles that a reversal may result in a new trial that might have been avoided. For these reasons, the court may often wisely decline to rule on a motion for judgment as a matter of law made at the close of the evidence, and it is not inappropriate for the moving party to suggest such a postponement of the ruling until after the verdict has been rendered.

In ruling on such a motion, the court should disregard any jury determination for which there is no legally sufficient evidentiary basis enabling a reasonable jury to make it. The court may then decide such issues as a matter of law and enter judgment if all other material issues have been decided by the jury on the basis of legally sufficient evidence, or by the court as a matter of law.

The revised rule is intended for use in this manner with Rule 49. Thus, the court may combine facts established as a matter of law either before trial under Rule 56 or at trial on the basis of the evidence presented with other facts determined by the jury under instructions provided under Rule 49 to support a proper judgment under this rule.

This provision also retains the former requirement that a post-trial motion under the rule must be made within 10 days after entry of a contrary judgment. The renewed motion must be served and filed as provided by Rule 5. A purpose of this requirement is to meet the requirements of F.R.App.P. 4(a)(4).

Subdivision (c). Revision of this subdivision conforms the language to the change in diction set forth in subdivision (a) of this revised rule.

Subdivision (d). Revision of this subdivision conforms the language to that of the previous subdivisions.

Notes of Advisory Committee on Rules—1993 Amendment

This technical amendment corrects an ambiguity in the text of the 1991 revision of the rule, which, as indicated in the Notes, was not intended to change the existing standards under which "directed verdicts" could be granted. This amendment makes clear that judgments as a matter of law in jury trials may be entered against both plaintiffs and defendants and with respect to issues or defenses that may not be wholly dispositive of a claim or defense.

Notes of Advisory Committee on Rules—1995 Amendment

The only change, other than stylistic, intended by this revision is to prescribe a uniform explicit time for filing of post-judgment motions under this rule—no later than 10 days after entry of the judgment. Previously, there was an inconsistency in the wording of Rules 50, 52, and 59 with respect to whether certain post-judgment motions had to be filed, or merely served, during that period. This inconsistency caused special problems when motions for a new trial were joined with other post-judgment motions. These motions affect the finality of the judgment, a matter often of importance to third persons as well as the parties and the court. The Committee believes that each of these rules should be revised to require filing before end of the 10-day period. Filing is an event that can be determined with certainty from court records. The phrase "no later than" is used—rather than "within"—to include post-judgment motions that sometimes are filed before actual entry of the judgment by the clerk. It should be noted that under Rule 6(a) Saturdays, Sundays, and legal holidays are excluded in measuring the 10-day period, and that under Rule 5 the motions when filed are to contain a certificate of service on other parties.

Committee Notes on Rules—2006 Amendment

The language of Rule 50(a) has been amended as part of the general restyling of the Civil Rules to make them more easily understood and to make style and terminology consistent throughout the rules. These changes are intended to be stylistic only.

Rule 50(b) is amended to permit renewal of any Rule 50(a) motion for judgment as a matter of law, deleting the requirement that a motion be made at the close of all the evidence. Because the Rule 50(b) motion is only a renewal of the preverdict motion, it can be granted only on grounds advanced in the preverdict motion. The earlier motion informs the opposing party of the challenge to the sufficiency of the evidence and affords a clear opportunity to provide additional evidence that may be available. The earlier motion also alerts the court to the opportunity to simplify the trial by resolving some issues, or even all issues, without submission to the jury. This fulfillment of the functional needs that underlie present Rule 50(b) also satisfies the Seventh Amendment. Automatic reservation of the legal questions raised by the motion conforms to the decision in Baltimore & Carolina Line v. Redman, 297 U.S. 654 (1935).

This change responds to many decisions that have begun to move away from requiring a motion for judgment as a matter of law at the literal close of all the evidence. Although the requirement has been clearly established for several decades, lawyers continue to overlook it. The courts are slowly working away from the formal requirement. The amendment establishes the functional approach that courts have been unable to reach under the present rule and makes practice more consistent and predictable.

Many judges expressly invite motions at the close of all the evidence. The amendment is not intended to discourage this useful practice.

Finally, an explicit time limit is added for making a posttrial motion when the trial ends without a verdict or with a verdict that does not dispose of all issues suitable for resolution by verdict. The motion must be made no later than 10 days after the jury was discharged.

Changes Made After Publication and Comment. This recommendation modifies the version of the proposal as published. The only changes made in the rule text after publication are matters of style. One sentence in the Committee Note was changed by adopting the wording of the 1991 Committee Note describing the grounds that may be used to support a renewed motion for judgment as a matter of law. A paragraph also was added to the Committee Note to explain the style revisions in subdivision (a). The changes from the published rule text are set out below. [Omitted]

Committee Notes on Rules—2007 Amendment

The language of Rule 50 has been amended as part of the general restyling of the Civil Rules to make them more easily understood and to make style and terminology consistent throughout the rules. These changes are intended to be stylistic only.

Former Rule 50(b) stated that the court reserves ruling on a motion for judgment as a matter of law made at the close of all the evidence "[i]f, for any reason, the court does not grant" the motion. The words "for any reason" reflected the proposition that the reservation is automatic and inescapable. The ruling is reserved even if the court explicitly denies the motion. The same result follows under the amended rule. If the motion is not granted, the ruling is reserved.

Amended Rule 50(e) identifies the appellate court's authority to direct the entry of judgment. This authority was not described in former Rule 50(d), but was recognized in Weisgram v. Marley Co., 528 U.S. 440 (2000), and in Neely v. Martin K. Eby Construction Company, 386 U.S. 317 (1967). When Rule 50(d) was drafted in 1963, the Committee Note stated that "[s]ubdivision (d) does not attempt a regulation of all aspects of the procedure where the motion for judgment n.o.v. and any accompanying motion for a new trial are denied * * *." Express recognition of the authority to direct entry of judgment does not otherwise supersede this caution.

Committee Notes on Rules—2009 Amendment

Former Rules 50, 52, and 59 adopted 10-day periods for their respective post-judgment motions. Rule 6(b) prohibits any expansion of those periods. Experience has proved that in many cases it is not possible to prepare a satisfactory post-judgment motion in 10 days, even under the former rule that excluded intermediate Saturdays, Sundays, and legal holidays. These time periods are particularly sensitive because Appellate Rule 4 integrates the time to appeal with a timely motion under these rules. Rather than introduce the prospect of uncertainty in appeal time by amending Rule 6(b) to permit additional time, the former 10-day periods are expanded to 28 days. Rule 6(b) continues to prohibit expansion of the 28-day period.

Changes Made after Publication and Comment. The 30-day period proposed in the August 2007 publication is shortened to 28 days.

Rule 51. Instructions to the Jury; Objections; Preserving a Claim of Error

(a) Requests.

(1) Before or at the Close of the Evidence. At the close of the evidence or at any earlier reasonable time that the court orders, a party may file and furnish to every other party written requests for the jury instructions it wants the court to give.

(2) After the Close of the Evidence. After the close of the evidence, a party may:

(A) file requests for instructions on issues that could not reasonably have been anticipated by an earlier time that the court set for requests; and

(B) with the court's permission, file untimely requests for instructions on any issue.

(b) Instructions. The court:

(1) must inform the parties of its proposed instructions and proposed action on the requests before instructing the jury and before final jury arguments;

(2) must give the parties an opportunity to object on the record and out of the jury's hearing before the instructions and arguments are delivered; and

(3) may instruct the jury at any time before the jury is discharged.

(c) Objections.

(1) How to Make. A party who objects to an instruction or the failure to give an instruction must do so on the record, stating distinctly the matter objected to and the grounds for the objection.

(2) When to Make. An objection is timely if:

(A) a party objects at the opportunity provided under Rule 51(b)(2); or

(B) a party was not informed of an instruction or action on a request before that opportunity to object, and the party objects promptly after learning that the instruction or request will be, or has been, given or refused.

(d) Assigning Error; Plain Error.

(1) Assigning Error. A party may assign as error:

(A) an error in an instruction actually given, if that party properly objected; or

(B) a failure to give an instruction, if that party properly requested it and—unless the court rejected the request in a definitive ruling on the record—also properly objected.

(2) Plain Error. A court may consider a plain error in the instructions that has not been preserved as required by Rule 51(d)(1) if the error affects substantial rights.

(As amended Mar. 2, 1987, eff. Aug. 1, 1987; Mar. 27, 2003, eff. Dec. 1, 2003; Apr. 30, 2007, eff. Dec. 1, 2007.)

Notes of Advisory Committee on Rules—1937

Supreme Court Rule 8 requires exceptions to the charge of the court to the jury which shall distinctly state the several matters of law in the charge to which exception is taken. Similar provisions appear in the rules of the various Circuit Courts of Appeals.

Notes of Advisory Committee on Rules—1987 Amendment

Although Rule 51 in its present form specifies that the court shall instruct the jury only after the arguments of the parties are completed, in some districts (typically those in states where the practice is otherwise) it is common for the parties to stipulate to instruction before the arguments. The purpose of the amendment is to give the court discretion to instruct the jury either before or after argument. Thus, the rule as revised will permit resort to the long-standing federal practice or to an alternative procedure, which has been praised because it gives counsel the opportunity to explain the instructions, argue their application to the facts and thereby give the jury the maximum assistance in determining the issues and arriving at a good verdict on the law and the evidence. As an ancillary benefit, this approach aids counsel by supplying a natural outline so that arguments may be directed to the essential fact issues which the jury must decide. See generally Raymond, Merits and Demerits of the Missouri System of Instructing Juries, 5 St. Louis U.L.J. 317 (1959). Moreover, if the court instructs before an argument, counsel then know the precise words the court has chosen and need not speculate as to the words the court will later use in its instructions. Finally, by instructing ahead of argument the court has the attention of the jurors when they are fresh and can given their full attention to the court's instructions. It is more difficult to hold the attention of jurors after lengthy arguments.

Committee Notes on Rules—2003 Amendment

Rule 51 is revised to capture many of the interpretations that have emerged in practice. The revisions in text will make uniform the conclusions reached by a majority of decisions on each point. Additions also are made to cover some practices that cannot now be anchored in the text of Rule 51.

Scope. Rule 51 governs instructions to the trial jury on the law that governs the verdict. A variety of other instructions cannot practicably be brought within Rule 51. Among these instructions are preliminary instructions to a venire, and cautionary or limiting instructions delivered in immediate response to events at trial.

Requests. Subdivision (a) governs requests. Apart from the plain error doctrine recognized in subdivision (d)(2), a court is not obliged to instruct the jury on issues raised by the evidence unless a party requests an instruction. The revised rule recognizes the court's authority to direct that requests be submitted before trial.

The close-of-the-evidence deadline may come before trial is completed on all potential issues. Trial may be formally bifurcated or may be sequenced in some less formal manner. The close of the evidence is measured by the occurrence of two events: completion of all intended evidence on an identified phase of the trial and impending submission to the jury with instructions.

The risk in directing a pretrial request deadline is that trial evidence may raise new issues or reshape issues the parties thought they had understood. Courts need not insist on pretrial requests in all cases. Even if the request time is set before trial or early in the trial, subdivision (a)(2)(A) permits requests after the close of the evidence to address issues that could not reasonably have been anticipated at the earlier time for requests set by the court.

Subdivision (a)(2)(B) expressly recognizes the court's discretion to act on an untimely request. The most important consideration in exercising the discretion confirmed by subdivision (a)(2)(B) is the importance of the issue to the case—the closer the issue lies to the "plain error" that would be recognized under subdivision (d)(2), the better the reason to give an instruction. The cogency of the reason for failing to make a timely request also should be considered. To be considered under subdivision (a)(2)(B) a request should be made before final instructions and before final jury arguments. What is a "final" instruction and argument depends on the sequence of submitting the case to the jury. If separate portions of the case are submitted to the jury in sequence, the final arguments and final instructions are those made on submitting to the jury the portion of the case addressed by the arguments and instructions.

Instructions. Subdivision (b)(1) requires the court to inform the parties, before instructing the jury and before final jury arguments related to the instruction, of the proposed instructions as well as the proposed action on instruction requests. The time limit is addressed to final jury arguments to reflect the practice that allows interim arguments during trial in complex cases; it may not be feasible to develop final instructions before such interim arguments. It is enough that counsel know of the intended instructions before making final arguments addressed to the issue. If the trial is sequenced or bifurcated, the final arguments addressed to an issue may occur before the close of the entire trial.

Subdivision (b)(2) complements subdivision (b)(1) by carrying forward the opportunity to object established by present Rule 51. It makes explicit the opportunity to object on the record, ensuring a clear memorial of the objection.

Subdivision (b)(3) reflects common practice by authorizing instructions at any time after trial begins and before the jury is discharged.

Objections. Subdivision (c) states the right to object to an instruction or the failure to give an instruction. It carries forward the formula of present Rule 51 requiring that the objection state distinctly the matter objected to and the grounds of the objection, and makes explicit the requirement that the objection be made on the record. The provisions on the time to object make clear that it is timely to object promptly after learning of an instruction or action on a request when the court has not provided advance information as required by subdivision (b)(1). The need to repeat a request by way of objection is continued by new subdivision (d)(1)(B) except where the court made a definitive ruling on the record.

Preserving a claim of error and plain error. Many cases hold that a proper request for a jury instruction is not alone enough to preserve the right to appeal failure to give the instruction. The request must be renewed by objection. This doctrine is appropriate when the court may not have sufficiently focused on the request, or may believe that the request has been granted in substance although in different words. But this doctrine may also prove a trap for the unwary who fail to add an objection after the court has made it clear that the request has been considered and rejected on the merits. Subdivision (d)(1)(B) establishes authority to review the failure to grant a timely request, despite a failure to add an objection, when the court has made a definitive ruling on the record rejecting the request.

Many circuits have recognized that an error not preserved under Rule 51 may be reviewed in exceptional circumstances. The language adopted to capture these decisions in subdivision (d)(2) is borrowed from Criminal Rule 52. Although the language is the same, the context of civil litigation often differs from the context of criminal prosecution; actual application of the plain-error standard takes account of the differences. The Supreme Court has summarized application of Criminal Rule 52 as involving four elements: (1) there must be an error; (2) the error must be plain; (3) the error must affect substantial rights; and (4) the error must seriously affect the fairness, integrity, or public reputation of judicial proceedings. Johnson v. U.S., 520 U.S. 461, 466–467, 469–470 (1997). (The Johnson case quoted the fourth element from its decision in a civil action, U.S. v. Atkinson, 297 U.S. 157, 160 (1936): "In exceptional circumstances, especially in criminal cases, appellate courts, in the public interest, may, of their own motion, notice errors to which no exception has been taken, if the errors are obvious, or if they otherwise substantially affect the fairness, integrity, or public reputation of judicial proceedings.")

The court's duty to give correct jury instructions in a civil action is shaped by at least four factors.

The factor most directly implied by a "plain" error rule is the obviousness of the mistake. The importance of the error is a second major factor. The costs of correcting an error reflect a third factor that is affected by a variety of circumstances. In a case that seems close to the fundamental error line, account also may be taken of the impact a verdict may have on nonparties.

Changes Made After Publication and Comment. The changes made after publication and comment are indicated by double-underlining and overstriking on the texts that were published in August 2001.

Rule 51(d) was revised to conform the plain-error provision to the approach taken in Criminal Rule 52(b). The Note was revised as described in the Recommendation.

Committee Notes on Rules—2007 Amendment

The language of Rule 51 has been amended as part of the general restyling of the Civil Rules to make them more easily understood and to make style and terminology consistent throughout the rules. These changes are intended to be stylistic only.

Rule 52. Findings and Conclusions by the Court; Judgment on Partial Findings

(a) Findings and Conclusions.

(1) In General. In an action tried on the facts without a jury or with an advisory jury, the court must find the facts specially and state its conclusions of law separately. The findings and conclusions may be stated on the record after the close of the evidence or may appear in an opinion or a memorandum of decision filed by the court. Judgment must be entered under Rule 58.

(2) For an Interlocutory Injunction. In granting or refusing an interlocutory injunction, the court must similarly state the findings and conclusions that support its action.

(3) For a Motion. The court is not required to state findings or conclusions when ruling on a motion under Rule 12 or 56 or, unless these rules provide otherwise, on any other motion.

(4) Effect of a Master's Findings. A master's findings, to the extent adopted by the court, must be considered the court's findings.

(5) Questioning the Evidentiary Support. A party may later question the sufficiency of the evidence supporting the findings, whether or not the party requested findings, objected to them, moved to amend them, or moved for partial findings.

(6) Setting Aside the Findings. Findings of fact, whether based on oral or other evidence, must not be set aside unless clearly erroneous, and the reviewing court must give due regard to the trial court's opportunity to judge the witnesses' credibility.

(b) Amended or Additional Findings. On a party's motion filed no later than 28 days after the entry of judgment, the court may amend its findings—or make additional findings—and may amend the judgment accordingly. The motion may accompany a motion for a new trial under Rule 59.

(c) Judgment on Partial Findings. If a party has been fully heard on an issue during a nonjury trial and the court finds against the party on that issue, the court may enter judgment against the party on a claim or defense that, under the controlling law, can be maintained or defeated only with a favorable finding on that issue. The court may, however, decline to render any judgment until the close of the evidence. A judgment on partial findings must be supported by findings of fact and conclusions of law as required by Rule 52(a).

(As amended Dec. 27, 1946, eff. Mar. 19, 1948; Jan. 21, 1963, eff. July 1, 1963; Apr. 28, 1983, eff. Aug. 1, 1983; Apr. 29, 1985, eff. Aug. 1, 1985; Apr. 30, 1991, eff. Dec. 1, 1991; Apr. 22, 1993, eff. Dec. 1, 1993; Apr. 27, 1995, eff. Dec. 1, 1995; Apr. 30, 2007, eff. Dec. 1, 2007; Mar. 26, 2009, eff. Dec. 1, 2009.)

Notes of Advisory Committee on Rules—1937

See [former] Equity Rule 70½, as amended Nov. 25, 1935 (Findings of Fact and Conclusions of Law), and U.S.C., Title 28, [former] §764 (Opinion, findings, and conclusions in action against United States) which are substantially continued in this rule. The provisions of U.S.C., Title 28, [former] §§773 (Trial of issues of fact; by court) and [former] 875 (Review in cases tried without a jury) are superseded insofar as they provide a different method of finding facts and a different method of appellate review. The rule stated in the third sentence of Subdivision (a) accords with the decisions on the scope of the review in modern federal equity practice. It is applicable to all classes of findings in cases tried without a jury whether the finding is of a fact concerning which there was conflict of testimony, or of a fact deduced or inferred from uncontradicted testimony. See Silver King Coalition Mines, Co. v. Silver King Consolidated Mining Co., 204 Fed. 166 (C.C.A.8th, 1913), cert. den. 229 U.S. 624 (1913); Warren v. Keep, 155 U.S. 265 (1894); Furrer v. Ferris, 145 U.S. 132 (1892); Tilghman v. Proctor, 125 U.S. 136, 149 (1888); Kimberly v. Arms, 129 U.S. 512, 524 (1889). Compare Kaeser & Blair, Inc., v. Merchants' Ass'n, 64 F.(2d) 575, 576 (C.C.A.6th, 1933); Dunn v. Trefry, 260 Fed. 147, 148 (C.C.A.1st, 1919).

In the following states findings of fact are required in all cases tried without a jury (waiver by the parties being permitted as indicated at the end of the listing): Arkansas, Civ.Code (Crawford, 1934) §364; California, Code Civ.Proc. (Deering, 1937) §§632, 634; Colorado, 1 Stat.Ann. (1935) Code Civ.Proc. §§232, 291 (in actions before referees or for possession of and damages to land); Connecticut, Gen.Stats. §§5660, 5664; Idaho, 1 Code Ann. (1932) §§7–302 through 7–305; Massachusetts (equity cases), 2 Gen.Laws (Ter.Ed., 1932) ch. 214, §23; Minnesota, 2 Stat. (Mason, 1927) §9311; Nevada, 4 Comp.Laws (Hillyer, 1929) §8783–8784; New Jersey, Sup.Ct. Rule 113, 2 N.J.Misc. 1197, 1239 (1924); New Mexico, Stat.Ann. (Courtright, 1929) §105–813; North Carolina, Code (1935) §569; North Dakota, 2 Comp.Laws Ann. (1913) §7641; Oregon, 2 Code Ann. (1930) §2–502; South Carolina, Code (Michie, 1932) §649; South Dakota, 1 Comp.Laws (1929) §§2525–2526; Utah, Rev.Stat.Ann. (1933) §104–26–2, 104–26–3; Vermont (where jury trial waived), Pub. Laws (1933) §2069; Washington, 2 Rev.Stat.Ann. (Remington, 1932) §367; Wisconsin, Stat. (1935) §270.33. The parties may waive this requirement for findings in California, Idaho, North Dakota, Nevada, New Mexico, Utah, and South Dakota.

In the following states the review of findings of fact in all non-jury cases, including jury waived cases, is assimilated to the equity review: Alabama, Code Ann. (Michie, 1928) §§9498, 8599; California, Code Civ.Proc. (Deering, 1937) §956a; but see 20 Calif.Law Rev. 171 (1932); Colorado, Johnson v. Kountze, 21 Colo. 486, 43 Pac. 445 (1895), semble; Illinois, Baker v. Hinricks, 359 Ill. 138, 194 N.E. 284 (1934), Weininger v. Metropolitan Fire Ins. Co., 359 Ill. 584, 195 N.E. 420, 98 A.L.R. 169 (1935); Minnesota, State Bank of Gibbon v. Walter, 167 Minn. 37, 38, 208 N.W. 423 (1926), Waldron v. Page, 191 Minn. 302, 253 N.W. 894 (1934); New Jersey, N.J.Comp.Stat. (2 Cum.Supp. 1911–1924) Title 163, §303, as interpreted in Bussy v. Hatch, 95 N.J.L. 56, 111 A. 546 (1920); New York, York Mortgage Corporation v. Clotar Const. Corp., 254 N.Y. 128, 133, 172 N.E. 265 (1930); North Dakota, Comp.Laws Ann. (1913) §7846, as amended by N.D.Laws 1933, ch. 208, Milnor Holding Co. v. Holt, 63 N.D. 362, 370, 248 N.W. 315 (1933); Oklahoma, Wichita Mining and Improvement Co. v. Hale, 20 Okla. 159, 167, 94 Pac. 530 (1908); South Dakota, Randall v. Burk Township, 4 S.D. 337, 57 N.W. 4 (1893); Texas, Custard v. Flowers, 14 S.W.2d 109 (1929); Utah, Rev.Stat.Ann. (1933) §104–41–5; Vermont, Roberge v. Troy, 105 Vt. 134, 163 Atl. 770 (1933); Washington, 2 Rev.Stat.Ann. (Remington, 1932) §§309–316; McCullough v. Puget Sound Realty Associates, 76 Wash. 700, 136 Pac. 1146 (1913), but see Cornwall v. Anderson, 85 Wash. 369, 148 Pac. 1 (1915); West Virginia, Kinsey v. Carr, 60 W.Va. 449, 55 S.E. 1004 (1906), semble; Wisconsin, Stat. (1935) §251.09; Campbell v. Sutliff, 193 Wis. 370, 214 N.W. 374 (1927), Gessler v. Erwin Co., 182 Wis. 315, 193 N.W. 363 (1924).

For examples of an assimilation of the review of findings of fact in cases tried without a jury to the review at law as made in several states, see Clark and Stone, Review of Findings of Fact, 4 U. of Chi.L.Rev. 190, 215 (1937).

Notes of Advisory Committee on Rules—1946 Amendment

Subdivision (a). The amended rule makes clear that the requirement for findings of fact and conclusions of law thereon applies in a case with an advisory jury. This removes an ambiguity in the rule as originally stated, but carries into effect what has been considered its intent. 3 Moore's Federal Practice (1938) 3119; Hurwitz v. Hurwitz (App.D.C. 1943) 136 F.(2d) 796.

The two sentences added at the end of Rule 52(a) eliminate certain difficulties which have arisen concerning findings and conclusions. The first of the two sentences permits findings of fact and conclusions of law to appear in an opinion or memorandum of decision. See, e.g., United States v. One 1941 Ford Sedan (S.D.Tex. 1946) 65 F.Supp. 84. Under original Rule 52(a) some courts have expressed the view that findings and conclusions could not be incorporated in an opinion. Detective

Comics, Inc. v. Bruns Publications (S.D.N.Y. 1939) 28 F.Supp. 399; Pennsylvania Co. for Insurance on Lives & Granting Annuities v. Cincinnati & L. E. R. Co. (S.D.Ohio 1941) 43 F.Supp. 5; United States v. Aluminum Co. of America (S.D.N.Y. 1941) 5 Fed.Rules Serv. 52a.11, Case 3; see also s.c., 44 F.Supp. 97. But, to the contrary, see Wellman v. United States (D.Mass. 1938) 25 F.Supp. 868; Cook v. United States (D.Mass. 1939) 26 F.Supp. 253; Proctor v. White (D.Mass. 1939) 28 F.Supp. 161; Green Valley Creamery, Inc. v. United States (C.C.A.1st, 1939) 108 F.(2d) 342. See also Matton Oil Transfer Corp. v. The Dynamic (C.C.A.2d, 1941) 123 F.(2d) 999; Carter Coal Co. v. Litz (C.C.A.4th, 1944) 140 F.(2d) 934; Woodruff v. Heiser (C.C.A.10th, 1945) 150 F.(2d) 869; Coca-Cola Co. v. Busch (E.D.Pa. 1943) 7 Fed.Rules Serv. 59b.2, Case 4; Oglebay, Some Developments in Bankruptcy Law (1944) 18 J. of Nat'l Ass'n of Ref. 68, 69. Findings of fact aid in the process of judgment and in defining for future cases the precise limitations of the issues and the determination thereon. Thus they not only aid the appellate court on review (Hurwitz v. Hurwitz (App.D.C. 1943) 136 F.(2d) 796) but they are an important factor in the proper application of the doctrines of res judicata and estoppel by judgment. Nordbye, Improvements in Statement of Findings of Fact and Conclusions of Law, 1 F.R.D. 25, 26–27; United States v. Forness (C.C.A.2d, 1942) 125 F.(2d) 928, cert. den. (1942) 316 U.S. 694. These findings should represent the judge's own determination and not the long, often argumentative statements of successful counsel. United States v. Forness, supra; United States v. Crescent Amusement Co. (1944) 323 U.S. 173. Consequently, they should be a part of the judge's opinion and decision, either stated therein or stated separately. Matton Oil Transfer Corp. v. The Dynamic, supra. But the judge need only make brief, definite, pertinent findings and conclusions upon the contested matters; there is no necessity for over-elaboration of detail or particularization of facts. United States v. Forness, supra; United States v. Crescent Amusement Co., supra. See also Petterson Lighterage & Towing Corp. v. New York Central R. Co. (C.C.A.2d, 1942) 126 F.(2d) 992; Brown Paper Mill Co., Inc. v. Irwin (C.C.A.8th, 1943) 134 F.(2d) 337; Allen Bradley Co. v. Local Union No. 3, I.B.E.W. (C.C.A.2d, 1944) 145 F.(2d) 215, rev'd on other grounds (1945) 325 U.S. 797; Young v. Murphy (N.D.Ohio 1946) 9 Fed.Rules Serv. 52a.11, Case 2.

The last sentence of Rule 52(a) as amended will remove any doubt that findings and conclusions are unnecessary upon decision of a motion, particularly one under Rule 12 or Rule 56, except as provided in amended Rule 41(b). As so holding, see Thomas v. Peyser (App.D.C. 1941) 118 F.(2d) 369; Schad v. Twentieth Century-Fox Corp. (C.C.A.3d, 1943) 136 F.(2d) 991; Prudential Ins. Co. of America v. Goldstein (E.D.N.Y. 1942) 43 F.Supp. 767; Somers Coal Co. v. United States (N.D.Ohio 1942) 6 Fed.Rules Serv. 52a.1, Case 1; Pen-Ken Oil & Gas Corp. v. Warfield Natural Gas Co. (E.D.Ky. 1942) 5 Fed.Rules Serv. 52a.1, Case 3; also Commentary, Necessity of Findings of Fact (1941) 4 Fed.Rules Serv. 936.

Notes of Advisory Committee on Rules—1963 Amendment

This amendment conforms to the amendment of Rule 58. See the Advisory Committee's Note to Rule 58, as amended.

Notes of Advisory Committee on Rules—1983 Amendment

Rule 52(a) has been amended to revise its penultimate sentence to provide explicitly that the district judge may make the findings of fact and conclusions of law required in nonjury cases orally. Nothing in the prior text of the rule forbids this practice, which is widely utilized by district judges. See Christensen, A Modest Proposal for Immeasurable Improvement, 64 A.B.A.J. 693 (1978). The objective is to lighten the burden on the trial court in preparing findings in nonjury cases. In addition, the amendment should reduce the number of published district court opinions that embrace written findings.

Notes of Advisory Committee on Rules—1985 Amendment

Rule 52(a) has been amended (1) to avoid continued confusion and conflicts among the circuits as to the standard of appellate review of findings of fact by the court, (2) to eliminate the disparity between the standard of review as literally stated in Rule 52(a) and the practice of some courts of appeals, and (3) to promote nationwide uniformity. See Note, Rule 52(a): Appellate Review of Findings of Fact Based on Documentary or Undisputed Evidence, 49 Va. L. Rev. 506, 536 (1963).

Some courts of appeal have stated that when a trial court's findings do not rest on demeanor evidence and evaluation of a witness' credibility, there is no reason to defer to the trial court's findings and the appellate court more readily can find them to be clearly erroneous. See, e.g., Marcum v. United States, 621 F.2d 142, 144–45 (5th Cir. 1980). Others go further, holding that appellate review may be had without application of the "clearly erroneous" test since the appellate court is in as good a position as the trial court to review a purely documentary record. See, e.g., Atari, Inc. v. North American Philips Consumer Electronics Corp., 672 F.2d 607, 614 (7th Cir.), cert. denied, 459 U.S. 880 (1982); Lydle v. United States, 635 F.2d 763, 765 n. 1 (6th Cir. 1981); Swanson v. Baker Indus., Inc., 615 F.2d 479, 483 (8th Cir. 1980); Taylor v. Lombard, 606 F.2d 371, 372 (2d Cir. 1979), cert. denied, 445 U.S. 946 (1980); Jack Kahn Music Co. v. Baldwin Piano & Organ Co., 604 F.2d 755, 758 (2d Cir. 1979); John R. Thompson Co. v. United States, 477 F.2d 164, 167 (7th Cir. 1973).

A third group has adopted the view that the "clearly erroneous" rule applies in all nonjury cases even when findings are based solely on documentary evidence or on inferences from undisputed facts. See, e.g., Maxwell v. Sumner, 673 F.2d 1031, 1036 (9th Cir.), cert. denied, 459 U.S. 976 (1982); United States v. Texas Education Agency, 647 F.2d 504, 506–07 (5th Cir. 1981), cert. denied, 454 U.S. 1143 (1982); Constructora Maza, Inc. v. Banco de Ponce, 616 F.2d 573, 576 (1st Cir. 1980); In re Sierra Trading Corp., 482 F.2d 333, 337 (10th Cir. 1973); Case v. Morrisette, 475 F.2d 1300, 1306–07 (D.C. Cir. 1973).

The commentators also disagree as to the proper interpretation of the Rule. Compare Wright, The Doubtful Omniscience of Appellate Courts, 41 Minn. L. Rev. 751, 769–70 (1957) (language and intent of Rule support view that "clearly erroneous" test should apply to all forms of evidence), and 9 C. Wright & A. Miller, Federal Practice and Procedure: Civil §2587, at 740 (1971) (language of the Rule is clear), with 5A J. Moore, Federal Practice 52.04, 2687–88 (2d ed. 1982) (Rule as written supports broader review of findings based on non-demeanor testimony).

The Supreme Court has not clearly resolved the issue. See, Bose Corp. v. Consumers Union of United States, Inc., 466 U.S. 485, 104 S. Ct. 1949, 1958 (1984); Pullman Standard v. Swint, 456 U.S. 273, 293 (1982); United States v. General Motors Corp., 384 U.S. 127, 141 n. 16 (1966); United States v. United States Gypsum Co., 333 U.S. 364, 394–96 (1948).

The principal argument advanced in favor of a more searching appellate review of findings by the district court based solely on documentary evidence is that the rationale of Rule 52(a) does not apply when the findings do not rest on the trial court's assessment of credibility of the witnesses but on an evaluation of documentary proof and the drawing of inferences from it, thus eliminating the need for any special deference to the trial court's findings. These considerations are outweighed by the public interest in the stability and judicial economy that would be promoted by recognizing that the trial court, not the appellate tribunal, should be the finder of the facts. To permit courts of appeals to share more actively in the fact-finding function would tend to undermine the legitimacy of the district courts in the eyes of litigants, multiply appeals by encouraging appellate retrial of some factual issues, and needlessly reallocate judicial authority.

Notes of Advisory Committee on Rules—1991 Amendment

Subdivision (c) is added. It parallels the revised Rule 50(a), but is applicable to non-jury trials. It authorizes the court to enter judgment at any time that it can appropriately make a dispositive finding of fact on the evidence.

The new subdivision replaces part of Rule 41(b), which formerly authorized a dismissal at the close of the plaintiff's case if the plaintiff had failed to carry an essential burden of proof. Accordingly, the reference to Rule 41 formerly made in subdivision (a) of this rule is deleted.

As under the former Rule 41(b), the court retains discretion to enter no judgment prior to the close of the evidence.

Judgment entered under this rule differs from a summary judgment under Rule 56 in the nature of the evaluation made by the court. A judgment on partial findings is made after the court has heard all the evidence bearing on the crucial issue of fact, and the finding is reversible only if the appellate court finds it to be "clearly erroneous." A summary judgment, in contrast, is made on the basis of facts established on account of the absence of contrary evidence or presumptions; such establishments of fact are rulings on questions of law as provided in Rule 56(a) and are not shielded by the "clear error" standard of review.

Notes of Advisory Committee on Rules—1993 Amendment

This technical amendment corrects an ambiguity in the text of the 1991 revision of the rule, similar to the revision being made to Rule 50. This amendment makes clear that judgments as a matter of law in nonjury trials may be entered against both plaintiffs and defendants and with respect to issues or defenses that may not be wholly dispositive of a claim or defense.

Notes of Advisory Committee on Rules—1995 Amendment

The only change, other than stylistic, intended by this revision is to require that any motion to amend or add findings after a nonjury trial must be filed no later than 10 days after entry of the judgment. Previously, there was an inconsistency in the wording of Rules 50, 52, and 59 with respect to whether certain post-judgment motions had to be filed, or merely served, during that period. This inconsistency caused special problems when motions for a new trial were joined with other post-judgment motions. These motions affect the finality of the judgment, a matter often of importance to third persons as well as the parties and the court. The Committee believes that each of these rules should be revised to require filing before end of the 10-day period. Filing is an event that can be determined with certainty from court records. The phrase "no later than" is used—rather than "within"—to include post-judgment motions that sometimes are filed before actual entry of the judgment by the clerk. It should be noted that under Rule 6(a) Saturdays, Sundays, and legal holidays are excluded in measuring the 10-day period, and that under Rule 5 the motions when filed are to contain a certificate of service on other parties.

Committee Notes on Rules—2007 Amendment

The language of Rule 52 has been amended as part of the general restyling of the Civil Rules to make them more easily understood and to make style and terminology consistent throughout the rules. These changes are intended to be stylistic only.

Former Rule 52(a) said that findings are unnecessary on decisions of motions "except as provided in subdivision (c) of this rule." Amended Rule 52(a)(3) says that findings are unnecessary "unless these rules provide otherwise." This change reflects provisions in other rules that require Rule 52 findings on deciding motions. Rules 23(e), 23(h), and 54(d)(2)(C) are examples.

Amended Rule 52(a)(5) includes provisions that appeared in former Rule 52(a) and 52(b). Rule 52(a) provided that requests for findings are not necessary for purposes of review. It applied both in an action tried on the facts without a jury and also in granting or refusing an interlocutory injunction. Rule 52(b), applicable to findings "made in actions tried without a jury," provided that the sufficiency of the evidence might be "later questioned whether or not in the district court the party raising the question objected to the findings, moved to amend them, or moved for partial findings." Former Rule 52(b) did not explicitly apply to decisions granting or refusing an interlocutory injunction. Amended Rule 52(a)(5) makes explicit the application of this part of former Rule 52(b) to interlocutory injunction decisions.

Former Rule 52(c) provided for judgment on partial findings, and referred to it as "judgment as a matter of law." Amended Rule 52(c) refers only to "judgment," to avoid any confusion with a Rule 50 judgment as a matter of law in a jury case. The standards that govern judgment as a matter of law in a jury case have no bearing on a decision under Rule 52(c).

Committee Notes on Rules—2009 Amendment

Former Rules 50, 52, and 59 adopted 10-day periods for their respective post-judgment motions. Rule 6(b) prohibits any expansion of those periods. Experience has proved that in many cases it is not possible to prepare a satisfactory post-judgment motion in 10 days, even under the former rule that excluded intermediate Saturdays, Sundays, and legal holidays. These time periods are particularly sensitive because Appellate Rule 4 integrates the time to appeal with a timely motion under these rules. Rather than introduce the prospect of uncertainty in appeal time by amending Rule 6(b) to permit additional time, the former 10-day periods are expanded to 28 days. Rule 6(b) continues to prohibit expansion of the 28-day period.

Changes Made after Publication and Comment. The 30-day period proposed in the August 2007 publication is shortened to 28 days.

Rule 53. Masters

(a) Appointment.

(1) Scope. Unless a statute provides otherwise, a court may appoint a master only to:

(A) perform duties consented to by the parties;

(B) hold trial proceedings and make or recommend findings of fact on issues to be decided without a jury if appointment is warranted by:

(i) some exceptional condition; or

(ii) the need to perform an accounting or resolve a difficult computation of damages; or

(C) address pretrial and posttrial matters that cannot be effectively and timely addressed by an available district judge or magistrate judge of the district.

(2) Disqualification. A master must not have a relationship to the parties, attorneys, action, or court that would require disqualification of a judge under 28 U.S.C. §455, unless the parties, with the court's approval,

consent to the appointment after the master discloses any potential grounds for disqualification.

(3) Possible Expense or Delay. In appointing a master, the court must consider the fairness of imposing the likely expenses on the parties and must protect against unreasonable expense or delay.

(b) Order Appointing a Master.

(1) Notice. Before appointing a master, the court must give the parties notice and an opportunity to be heard. Any party may suggest candidates for appointment.

(2) Contents. The appointing order must direct the master to proceed with all reasonable diligence and must state:

(A) the master's duties, including any investigation or enforcement duties, and any limits on the master's authority under Rule 53(c);

(B) the circumstances, if any, in which the master may communicate ex parte with the court or a party;

(C) the nature of the materials to be preserved and filed as the record of the master's activities;

(D) the time limits, method of filing the record, other procedures, and standards for reviewing the master's orders, findings, and recommendations; and

(E) the basis, terms, and procedure for fixing the master's compensation under Rule 53(g).

(3) Issuing. The court may issue the order only after:

(A) the master files an affidavit disclosing whether there is any ground for disqualification under 28 U.S.C. §455; and

(B) if a ground is disclosed, the parties, with the court's approval, waive the disqualification.

(4) Amending. The order may be amended at any time after notice to the parties and an opportunity to be heard.

(c) Master's Authority.

(1) In General. Unless the appointing order directs otherwise, a master may:

(A) regulate all proceedings;

(B) take all appropriate measures to perform the assigned duties fairly and efficiently; and

(C) if conducting an evidentiary hearing, exercise the appointing court's power to compel, take, and record evidence.

(2) Sanctions. The master may by order impose on a party any noncontempt sanction provided by Rule 37 or 45, and may recommend a contempt sanction against a party and sanctions against a nonparty.

(d) Master's Orders. A master who issues an order must file it and promptly serve a copy on each party. The clerk must enter the order on the docket.

(e) Master's Reports. A master must report to the court as required by the appointing order. The master must file the report and promptly serve a copy on each party, unless the court orders otherwise.

(f) Action on the Master's Order, Report, or Recommendations.

(1) Opportunity for a Hearing; Action in General. In acting on a master's order, report, or recommendations, the court must give the parties notice and an opportunity to be heard; may receive evidence; and may adopt or affirm, modify, wholly or partly reject or reverse, or resubmit to the master with instructions.

(2) Time to Object or Move to Adopt or Modify. A party may file objections to—or a motion to adopt or modify—the master's order, report, or recommendations no later than 21 days after a copy is served, unless the court sets a different time.

(3) Reviewing Factual Findings. The court must decide de novo all objections to findings of fact made or recommended by a master, unless the parties, with the court's approval, stipulate that:

(A) the findings will be reviewed for clear error; or

(B) the findings of a master appointed under Rule 53(a)(1)(A) or (C) will be final.

(4) Reviewing Legal Conclusions. The court must decide de novo all objections to conclusions of law made or recommended by a master.

(5) Reviewing Procedural Matters. Unless the appointing order establishes a different standard of review, the court may set aside a master's ruling on a procedural matter only for an abuse of discretion.

(g) Compensation.

(1) Fixing Compensation. Before or after judgment, the court must fix the master's compensation on the basis and terms stated in the appointing order, but the court may set a new basis and terms after giving notice and an opportunity to be heard.

(2) Payment. The compensation must be paid either:

(A) by a party or parties; or

(B) from a fund or subject matter of the action within the court's control.

(3) Allocating Payment. The court must allocate payment among the parties after considering the nature and amount of the controversy, the parties' means, and the extent to which any party is more responsible than other parties for the reference to a master. An interim allocation may be amended to reflect a decision on the merits.

(h) Appointing a Magistrate Judge. A magistrate judge is subject to this rule only when the order referring a matter to the magistrate judge states that the reference is made under this rule.

(As amended Feb. 28, 1966, eff. July 1, 1966; Apr. 28, 1983, eff. Aug. 1, 1983; Mar. 2, 1987, eff. Aug. 1, 1987; Apr. 30, 1991, eff. Dec. 1, 1991; Apr. 22, 1993, eff. Dec. 1, 1993; Mar. 27, 2003, eff. Dec. 1, 2003; Apr. 30, 2007, eff. Dec. 1, 2007; Mar. 26, 2009, eff. Dec. 1, 2009.)

Notes of Advisory Committee on Rules—1937

Note to Subdivision (a). This is a modification of [former] Equity Rule 68 (Appointment and Compensation of Masters).

Note to Subdivision (b). This is substantially the first sentence of [former] Equity Rule 59 (Reference to Master—Exceptional, Not Usual) extended to actions formerly legal. See Ex parte Peterson 253 U.S. 300, 40 S.Ct. 543, 64 L.Ed. 919 (1920).

Note to Subdivision (c). This is [former] Equity Rules 62 (Powers of Master) and 65 (Claimants Before Master Examinable by Him) with slight modifications. Compare [former] Equity Rules 49

(Evidence Taken Before Examiners, Etc.) and 51 (Evidence Taken Before Examiners, Etc.).

Note to Subdivision (d). (1) This is substantially a combination of the second sentence of [former] Equity Rule 59 (Reference to Master—Exceptional, Not Usual) and [former] Equity Rule 60 (Proceedings Before Master). Compare [former] Equity Rule 53 (Notice of Taking Testimony Before Examiner, Etc.).

(2) This is substantially [former] Equity Rule 52 (Attendance of Witnesses Before Commissioner, Master, or Examiner).

(3) This is substantially [former] Equity Rule 63 (Form of Accounts Before Master).

Note to Subdivision (e). This contains the substance of [former] Equity Rules 61 (Master's Report—Documents Identified but not Set Forth), 61½ (Master's Report—Presumption as to Correctness—Review), and 66 (Return of Master's Report—Exceptions—Hearing), with modifications as to the form and effect of the report and for inclusion of reports by auditors, referees, and examiners, and references in actions formerly legal. Compare [former] Equity Rules 49 (Evidence Taken Before Examiners, Etc.) and 67 (Costs on Exceptions to Master's Report). See Camden v. Stuart, 144 U.S. 104, 12 S.Ct. 585, 36 L.Ed. 363 (1892); Ex parte Peterson, 253 U.S. 300, 40 S.Ct. 543, 64 L.Ed. 919 (1920).

Notes of Advisory Committee on Rules—1966 Amendment

These changes are designed to preserve the admiralty practice whereby difficult computations are referred to a commissioner or assessor, especially after an interlocutory judgment determining liability. As to separation of issues for trial see Rule 42(b).

Notes of Advisory Committee on Rules—1983 Amendment

Subdivision (a). The creation of full-time magistrates, who serve at government expense and have no nonjudicial duties competing for their time, eliminates the need to appoint standing masters. Thus the prior provision in Rule 53(a) authorizing the appointment of standing masters is deleted. Additionally, the definition of "master" in subdivision (a) now eliminates the superseded office of commissioner.

The term "special master" is retained in Rule 53 in order to maintain conformity with 28 U.S.C. §636(b)(2), authorizing a judge to designate a magistrate "to serve as a special master pursuant to the applicable provisions of this title and the Federal Rules of Civil Procedure for the United States District Courts." Obviously, when a magistrate serves as a special master, the provisions for compensation of masters are inapplicable, and the amendment to subdivision (a) so provides.

Although the existence of magistrates may make the appointment of outside masters unnecessary in many instances, see, e.g., Gautreaux v. Chicago Housing Authority, 384 F.Supp. 37 (N.D.Ill. 1974), mandamus denied sub nom., Chicago Housing Authority v. Austin, 511 F.2d 82 (7th Cir. 1975); Avco Corp. v. American Tel. & Tel. Co., 68 F.R.D. 532 (S.D. Ohio 1975), such masters may prove useful when some special expertise is desired or when a magistrate is unavailable for lengthy and detailed supervision of a case.

Subdivision (b). The provisions of 28 U.S.C. §636(b)(2) not only permit magistrates to serve as masters under Rule 53(b) but also eliminate the exceptional condition requirement of Rule 53(b) when the reference is made with the consent of the parties. The amendment to subdivision (b) brings Rule 53 into harmony with the statute by exempting magistrates, appointed with the consent of the parties, from the general requirement that some exceptional condition requires the reference. It should be noted that subdivision (b) does not address the question, raised in recent decisional law and commentary, as to whether the exceptional condition requirement is applicable when private masters who are not magistrates are appointed with the consent of the parties. See Silberman, Masters and Magistrates Part II: The American Analogue, 50 N.Y.U. L.Rev. 1297, 1354 (1975).

Subdivision (c). The amendment recognizes the abrogation of Federal Rule 43(c) by the Federal Rules of Evidence.

Subdivision (f). The new subdivision responds to confusion flowing from the dual authority for references of pretrial matters to magistrates. Such references can be made, with or without the consent of the parties, pursuant to Rule 53 or under 28 U.S.C. §636(b)(1)(A) and (b)(1)(B). There are a number of distinctions between references made under the statute and under the rule. For example, under the statute nondispositive pretrial matters may be referred to a magistrate, without consent, for final determination with reconsideration by the district judge if the magistrate's order is clearly erroneous or contrary to law. Under the rule, however, the appointment of a master, without consent of the parties, to supervise discovery would require some exceptional condition (Rule 53(b)) and would subject the proceedings to the report procedures of Rule 53(e). If an order of reference does not clearly articulate the source of the court's authority the resulting proceedings could be subject to attack on grounds of the magistrate's noncompliance with the provisions of Rule 53. This subdivision therefore establishes a presumption that the limitations of Rule 53 are not applicable unless the reference is specifically made subject to Rule 53.

A magistrate serving as a special master under 28 U.S.C. §636(b)(2) is governed by the provisions of Rule 53, with the exceptional condition requirement lifted in the case of a consensual reference.

Notes of Advisory Committee on Rules—1987 Amendment

The amendments are technical. No substantive change is intended.

Notes of Advisory Committee on Rules—1991 Amendment

The purpose of the revision is to expedite proceedings before a master. The former rule required only a filing of the master's report, with the clerk then notifying the parties of the filing. To receive a copy, a party would then be required to secure it from the clerk. By transmitting directly to the parties, the master can save some efforts of counsel. Some local rules have previously required such action by the master.

Notes of Advisory Committee on Rules—1993 Amendment

This revision is made to conform the rule to changes made by the Judicial Improvements Act of 1990.

Committee Notes on Rules—2003 Amendment

Rule 53 is revised extensively to reflect changing practices in using masters. From the beginning in 1938, Rule 53 focused primarily on special masters who perform trial functions. Since then, however, courts have gained experience with masters appointed to perform a variety of pretrial and post-trial functions. See Willging, Hooper, Leary, Miletich, Reagan, & Shapard, Special Masters' Incidence and Activity (Federal Judicial Center 2000). This revised Rule 53 recognizes that in appropriate circumstances masters may properly be appointed to perform these functions and regulates such appointments. Rule 53 continues to address trial masters as well, but permits appointment of a trial master in an action to be tried to a jury only if the parties consent. The new rule clarifies the provisions that govern the appointment and function of masters for all purposes. Rule 53(g) also changes the standard of review for findings of fact made or recommended by a master. The core of the original Rule 53 remains, including its prescription that appointment of a master must be the exception and not the rule.

Special masters are appointed in many circumstances outside the Civil Rules. Rule 53 applies only to proceedings that Rule 1 brings within its reach.

Subdivision (a)(1). District judges bear primary responsibility for the work of their courts. A master should be appointed only in limited circumstances. Subdivision (a)(1) describes three different standards, relating to appointments by consent of the parties, appointments for trial duties, and appointments for pretrial or post-trial duties.

Consent Masters. Subparagraph (a)(1)(A) authorizes appointment of a master with the parties' consent. Party consent does not require that the court make the appointment; the court retains unfettered discretion to refuse appointment.

Trial Masters. Use of masters for the core functions of trial has been progressively limited. These limits are reflected in the provisions of subparagraph (a)(1)(B) that restrict appointments to exercise trial functions. The Supreme Court gave clear direction to this trend in La Buy v. Howes Leather Co., 352 U.S. 249 (1957); earlier roots are sketched in Los Angeles Brush Mfg. Corp. v. James, 272 U.S. 701 (1927). As to nonjury trials, this trend has developed through elaboration of the "exceptional condition" requirement in present Rule 53(b). This phrase is retained, and will continue to have the same force as it has developed. Although the provision that a reference "shall be the exception and not the rule" is deleted, its meaning is embraced for this setting by the exceptional condition requirement.

Subparagraph (a)(1)(B)(ii) carries forward the approach of present Rule 53(b), which exempts from the "exceptional condition" requirement "matters of account and of difficult computation of damages." This approach is justified only as to essentially ministerial determinations that require mastery of much detailed information but that do not require extensive determinations of credibility. Evaluations of witness credibility should only be assigned to a trial master when justified by an exceptional condition.

The use of a trial master without party consent is abolished as to matters to be decided by a jury unless a statute provides for this practice.

Abolition of the direct power to appoint a trial master as to issues to be decided by a jury leaves the way free to appoint a trial master with the consent of all parties. A trial master should be appointed in a jury case, with consent of the parties and concurrence of the court, only if the parties waive jury trial with respect to the issues submitted to the master or if the master's findings are to be submitted to the jury as evidence in the manner provided by former Rule 53(e)(3). In no circumstance may a master be appointed to preside at a jury trial.

The central function of a trial master is to preside over an evidentiary hearing on the merits of the claims or defenses in the action. This function distinguishes the trial master from most functions of pretrial and post-trial masters. If any master is to be used for such matters as a preliminary injunction hearing or a determination of complex damages issues, for example, the master should be a trial master. The line, however, is not distinct. A pretrial master might well conduct an evidentiary hearing on a discovery dispute, and a post-trial master might conduct evidentiary hearings on questions of compliance.

Rule 53 has long provided authority to report the evidence without recommendations in nonjury trials. This authority is omitted from Rule 53(a)(1)(B). In some circumstances a master may be appointed under Rule 53(a)(1)(A) or (C) to take evidence and report without recommendations.

For nonjury cases, a master also may be appointed to assist the court in discharging trial duties other than conducting an evidentiary hearing.

Pretrial and Post-Trial Masters. Subparagraph (a)(1)(C) authorizes appointment of a master to address pretrial or post-trial matters. Appointment is limited to matters that cannot be addressed effectively and in a timely fashion by an available district judge or magistrate judge of the district. A master's pretrial or post-trial duties may include matters that could be addressed by a judge, such as reviewing discovery documents for privilege, or duties that might not be suitable for a judge. Some forms of settlement negotiations, investigations, or administration of an organization are familiar examples of duties that a judge might not feel free to undertake.

Magistrate Judges. Particular attention should be paid to the prospect that a magistrate judge may be available for special assignments. United States magistrate judges are authorized by statute to perform many pretrial functions in civil actions. 28 U.S.C. §636(b)(1). Ordinarily a district judge who delegates these functions should refer them to a magistrate judge acting as magistrate judge.

There is statutory authority to appoint a magistrate judge as special master. 28 U.S.C. §636(b)(2). In special circumstances, or when expressly authorized by a statute other than §636(b)(2), it may be appropriate to appoint a magistrate judge as a master when needed to perform functions outside those listed in §636(b)(1). There is no apparent reason to appoint a magistrate judge to perform as master duties that could be performed in the role of magistrate judge. Party consent is required for trial before a magistrate judge, moreover, and this requirement should not be undercut by resort to Rule 53 unless specifically authorized by statute; see 42 U.S.C. §2000e–5(f)(5).

Pretrial Masters. The appointment of masters to participate in pretrial proceedings has developed extensively over the last two decades as some district courts have felt the need for additional help in managing complex litigation. This practice is not well regulated by present Rule 53, which focuses on masters as trial participants. Rule 53 is amended to confirm the authority to appoint—and to regulate the use of—pretrial masters.

A pretrial master should be appointed only when the need is clear. Direct judicial performance of judicial functions may be particularly important in cases that involve important public issues or many parties. At the extreme, a broad delegation of pretrial responsibility as well as a delegation of trial responsibilities can run afoul of Article III.

A master also may be appointed to address matters that blur the divide between pretrial and trial functions. The court's responsibility to interpret patent claims as a matter of law, for example, may be greatly assisted by appointing a master who has expert knowledge of the field in which the patent operates. Review of the master's findings will be de novo under Rule 53(g)(4), but the advantages of initial determination by a master may make the process more effective and timely than disposition by the judge acting alone. Determination of foreign law may present comparable difficulties. The decision whether to appoint a master to address such matters is governed by subdivision (a)(1)(C), not the trial-master provisions of subdivision (a)(1)(B).

Post-Trial Masters. Courts have come to rely on masters to assist in framing and enforcing complex decrees. Present Rule 53 does not directly address this practice. Amended Rule 53 authorizes appointment of post-trial masters for these and similar purposes. The constraint of subdivision (a)(1)(C) limits this practice to cases in which the master's duties cannot be performed effectively and in a timely fashion by an available district judge or magistrate judge of the district.

Reliance on a master is appropriate when a complex decree requires complex policing, particularly when a party has proved resistant or intransigent. This practice has been recognized by the Supreme Court, see Local 28, Sheet Metal Workers' Internat. Assn. v. EEOC, 478 U.S. 421, 481–482 (1986). The master's role in enforcement may extend to investigation in ways that are quite unlike the traditional role of judicial officers in an adversary system.

Expert Witness Overlap. This rule does not address the difficulties that arise when a single person is appointed to perform overlapping roles as master and as court-appointed expert witness under Evidence Rule 706. Whatever combination of functions is involved, the Rule 53(a)(1)(B) limit that confines trial masters to issues to be decided by the court does not apply to a person who also is appointed as an expert witness under Evidence Rule 706.

Subdivision (a)(2) and (3). Masters are subject to the Code of Conduct for United States Judges, with exceptions spelled out in the Code. Special care must be taken to ensure that there is no actual or apparent conflict of interest involving a master. The standard of disqualification is established by 28 U.S.C. §455. The affidavit required by Rule 53(b)(3) provides an important source of information about possible grounds for disqualification, but careful inquiry should be made at the time of making the initial appointment. The disqualification standards established by §455 are strict. Because a master is not a public judicial officer, it may be appropriate to permit the parties to consent to appointment of a particular person as master in circumstances that would require disqualification of a judge. The judge must be careful to ensure that no party feels any pressure to consent, but with such assurances—and with the judge's own determination that there is no troubling conflict of interests or disquieting appearance of impropriety—consent may justify an otherwise barred appointment.

One potential disqualification issue is peculiar to the master's role. It may happen that a master who is an attorney represents a client whose litigation is assigned to the judge who appointed the attorney as master. Other parties to the litigation may fear that the attorney-master will gain special respect from the judge. A flat prohibition on appearance before the appointing judge during the time of service as master, however, might in some circumstances unduly limit the opportunity to make a desirable appointment. These matters may be regulated to some extent by state rules of professional responsibility. The question of present conflicts, and the possibility of future conflicts, can be considered at the time of appointment. Depending on the circumstances, the judge may consider it appropriate to impose a non-appearance condition on the lawyer-master, and perhaps on the master's firm as well.

Subdivision (b). The order appointing a pretrial master is vitally important in informing the master and the parties about the nature and extent of the master's duties and authority. Care must be taken to make the order as precise as possible. The parties must be given notice and opportunity to be heard on the question whether a master should be appointed and on the terms of the appointment. To the extent possible, the notice should describe the master's proposed duties, time to complete the duties, standards of review, and compensation. Often it will be useful to engage the parties in the process of identifying the master, inviting nominations, and reviewing potential candidates. Party involvement may be particularly useful if a pretrial master is expected to promote settlement.

The hearing requirement of Rule 53(b)(1) can be satisfied by an opportunity to make written submissions unless the circumstances require live testimony.

Rule 53(b)(2) requires precise designation of the master's duties and authority. Clear identification of any investigating or enforcement duties is particularly important. Clear delineation of topics for any reports or recommendations is also an important part of this process. And it is important to protect against delay by establishing a time schedule for performing the assigned duties. Early designation of the procedure for fixing the master's compensation also may provide useful guidance to the parties.

Ex parte communications between a master and the court present troubling questions. Ordinarily the order should prohibit such communications, assuring that the parties know where authority is lodged at each step of the proceedings. Prohibiting ex parte communications between master and court also can enhance the role of a settlement master by assuring the parties that settlement can be fostered by confidential revelations that will not be shared with the court. Yet there may be circumstances in which the master's role is enhanced by the opportunity for ex parte communications with the court. A master assigned to help coordinate multiple proceedings, for example, may benefit from off-the-record exchanges with the court about logistical matters. The rule does not directly regulate these matters. It requires only that the court exercise its discretion and address the topic in the order of appointment.

Similarly difficult questions surround ex parte communications between a master and the parties. Ex parte communications may be essential in seeking to advance settlement. Ex parte communications also may prove useful in other settings, as with in camera review of documents to resolve privilege questions. In most settings, however, ex parte communications with the parties should be discouraged or prohibited. The rule requires that the court address the topic in the order of appointment.

Subdivision (b)(2)(C) provides that the appointment order must state the nature of the materials to be preserved and filed as the record of the master's activities, and (b)(2)(D) requires that the order state the method of filing the record. It is not feasible to prescribe the nature of the record without regard to the nature of the master's duties. The records appropriate to discovery duties may be different from those appropriate to encouraging settlement, investigating possible violations of a complex decree, or making recommendations for trial findings. A basic requirement, however, is that the master must make and file a complete record of the evidence considered in making or recommending findings of fact on the basis of evidence. The order of appointment should routinely include this requirement unless the nature of the appointment precludes any prospect that the master will make or recommend evidence-based findings of fact. In some circumstances it may be appropriate for a party to file materials directly with the court as provided by Rule 5(e), but in many circumstances filing with the court may be inappropriate. Confidentiality is important with respect to many materials that may properly be considered by a master. Materials in the record can be transmitted to the court, and filed, in connection with review of a master's order, report, or recommendations under subdivisions (f) and (g). Independently of review proceedings, the court may direct filing of any materials that it wishes to make part of the public record.

The provision in subdivision (b)(2)(D) that the order must state the standards for reviewing the master's orders, findings, or recommendations is a reminder of the provisions of subdivision (g)(3) that recognize stipulations for review less searching than the presumptive requirement of de novo decision by the court. Subdivision (b)(2)(D) does not authorize the court to supersede the limits of subdivision (g)(3).

In setting the procedure for fixing the master's compensation, it is useful at the outset to establish specific guidelines to control total expense. The court has power under subdivision (h) to change the basis and terms for determining compensation after notice to the parties.

Subdivision (b)(3) permits entry of the order appointing a master only after the master has filed an affidavit disclosing whether there is any ground for disqualification under 28 U.S.C. §455. If the affidavit discloses a possible ground for disqualification, the order can enter only if the court determines that there is no ground for disqualification or if the parties, knowing of the ground for disqualification, consent with the court's approval to waive the disqualification.

The provision in Rule 53(b)(4) for amending the order of appointment is as important as the provisions for the initial order. Anything that could be done in the initial order can be done by amendment. The hearing requirement can be satisfied by an opportunity to make written submissions unless the circumstances require live testimony.

Subdivision (c). Subdivision (c) is a simplification of the provisions scattered throughout present Rule 53. It is intended to provide the broad and flexible authority necessary to discharge the master's responsibilities. The most important delineation of a master's authority and duties is provided by the Rule 53(b) appointing order.

Subdivision (d). The subdivision (d) provisions for evidentiary hearings are reduced from the extensive provisions in current Rule 53. This simplification of the rule is not intended to diminish the authority that may be delegated to a master. Reliance is placed on the broad and general terms of subdivision (c).

Subdivision (e). Subdivision (e) provides that a master's order must be filed and entered on the docket. It must be promptly served on the parties, a task ordinarily accomplished by mailing or other means as permitted by Rule 5(b). In some circumstances it may be appropriate to have the clerk's office assist the master in mailing the order to the parties.

Subdivision (f). Subdivision (f) restates some of the provisions of present Rule 53(e)(1). The report is the master's primary means of communication with the court. The materials to be provided to support review of the report will depend on the nature of the report. The master should provide all portions of the record preserved under Rule 53(b)(2)(C) that the master deems relevant to the report. The parties may designate additional materials from the record, and may seek permission to supplement the record with evidence. The court may direct that additional materials from the record be provided and filed. Given the wide array of tasks that may be assigned to a pretrial master, there may be circumstances that justify sealing a report or review record against public access—a report on continuing or failed settlement efforts is the most likely example. A post-trial master may be assigned duties in formulating a decree that deserve similar protection. Such circumstances may even justify denying access to the report or review materials by the parties, although this step should be taken only for the most compelling reasons. Sealing is much less likely to be appropriate with respect to a trial master's report.

Before formally making an order, report, or recommendations, a master may find it helpful to circulate a draft to the parties for review and comment. The usefulness of this practice depends on the nature of the master's proposed action.

Subdivision (g). The provisions of subdivision (g)(1), describing the court's powers to afford a hearing, take evidence, and act on a master's order, report, or recommendations are drawn from present Rule 53(e)(2), but are not limited, as present Rule 53(e)(2) is limited, to the report of a trial master in a nonjury action. The requirement that the court must afford an opportunity to be heard can be satisfied by taking written submissions when the court acts on the report without taking live testimony.

The subdivision (g)(2) time limits for objecting to—or seeking adoption or modification of—a master's order, report, or recommendations, are important. They are not jurisdictional. Although a court may properly refuse to entertain untimely review proceedings, the court may excuse the failure to seek timely review. The basic time period is lengthened to 20 days because the present 10-day period may be too short to permit thorough study and response to a complex report dealing with complex litigation. If no party asks the court to act on a master's report, the court is free to adopt the master's action or to disregard it at any relevant point in the proceedings.

Subdivision (g)(3) establishes the standards of review for a master's findings of fact or recommended findings of fact. The court must decide de novo all objections to findings of fact made or recommended by the master unless the parties stipulate, with the court's consent, that the findings will be reviewed for clear error or—with respect to a master appointed on the parties' consent or appointed to address pretrial or post-trial matters—that the findings will be final. Clear-error review is more likely to be appropriate with respect to findings that do not go to the merits of the underlying claims or defenses, such as findings of fact bearing on a privilege objection to a discovery request. Even if no objection is made, the court is free to decide the facts de novo; to review for clear error if an earlier approved stipulation provided clear-error review; or to withdraw its consent to a stipulation for clear-error review or finality, and then to decide de novo. If the court withdraws its consent to a stipulation for finality or clear-error review, it may reopen the opportunity to object.

Under Rule 53(g)(4), the court must decide de novo all objections to conclusions of law made or recommended by a master. As with findings of fact, the court also may decide conclusions of law de novo when no objection is made.

Apart from factual and legal questions, masters often make determinations that, when made by a trial court, would be treated as matters of procedural discretion. The court may set a standard for review of such matters in the order of appointment, and may amend the order to establish the standard. If no standard is set by the original or amended order appointing the master, review of procedural matters is for abuse of discretion. The subordinate role of the master means that the trial court's review for abuse of discretion may be more searching than the review that an appellate court makes of a trial court.

If a master makes a recommendation on any matter that does not fall within Rule 53(g)(3), (4), or (5), the court may act on the recommendation under Rule 53(g)(1).

Subdivision (h). The need to pay compensation is a substantial reason for care in appointing private persons as masters.

Payment of the master's fees must be allocated among the parties and any property or subject-matter within the court's control. The amount in controversy and the means of the parties may provide some guidance in making the allocation. The nature of the dispute also may be important—parties pursuing matters of public interest, for example, may deserve special protection. A party whose unreasonable behavior has occasioned the need to appoint a master, on the other hand, may properly be charged all or a major portion of the master's fees. It may be proper to revise an interim allocation after decision on the merits. The revision need not await a decision that is final for purposes of appeal, but may be made to reflect disposition of a substantial portion of the case.

The basis and terms for fixing compensation should be stated in the order of appointment. The court retains power to alter the initial basis and terms, after notice and an opportunity to be heard, but should protect the parties against unfair surprise.

The provision of former Rule 53(a) that the "provision for compensation shall not apply when a United States Magistrate Judge is designated to serve as a master" is deleted as unnecessary. Other provisions of law preclude compensation.

Subdivision (i). Rule 53(i) carries forward unchanged former Rule 53(f).

Changes Made After Publication and Comment. Subdivision (a)(3), barring appearance by a master as attorney before the appointing judge during the period of the appointment, is deleted. Subdivision (a)(4) is renumbered as (a)(3).

Subdivision (b)(2) is amended by adding new material to the subparagraph (A), (B,) (C), and (D) specifications of issues that must be addressed in the order appointing a master. (A) now requires a statement of any investigation or enforcement duties. (B) now establishes a presumption that ex parte communications between master and court are limited to administrative matters; the court may, in its discretion, permit ex parte communications on other matters. (C) directs that the order address not only preservation but also filing of the record. (D) requires that the order state the method of filing the record.

Subdivision (b)(3) is changed by requiring an opportunity to be heard on an order amending an appointment order. It also is renumbered as (b)(4).

Subdivision (b)(4), renumbered as (b)(3), is redrafted to express the original meaning more clearly.

Subdivision (c) has a minor style change.

Subdivision (g)(1) is amended to state that in acting on a master's recommendations the court "must" afford an opportunity to be heard.

Subdivision (g)(3) is changed to narrow still further the opportunities to depart from de novo determination of objections to a master's findings or recommendations for findings of fact.

Subdivision (g)(4) is changed by deleting the opportunity of the parties to stipulate that a master's conclusions of law will be final.

Committee Notes on Rules—2007 Amendment

The language of Rule 53 has been amended as part of the general restyling of the Civil Rules to make them more easily understood and to make style and terminology consistent throughout the rules. These changes are intended to be stylistic only.

Committee Notes on Rules—2009 Amendment

The time set in the former rule at 20 days has been revised to 21 days. See the Note to Rule 6.

TITLE VII. JUDGMENT

Rule 54. Judgment; Costs

(a) Definition; Form. "Judgment" as used in these rules includes a decree and any order from which an appeal lies. A judgment should not include recitals of pleadings, a master's report, or a record of prior proceedings.

(b) Judgment on Multiple Claims or Involving Multiple Parties. When an action presents more than one claim for relief—whether as a claim, counterclaim, crossclaim, or third-party claim—or when multiple parties are involved, the court may direct entry of a final judgment as to one or more, but fewer than all, claims or parties only if the court expressly determines that there is no just reason for delay. Otherwise, any order or other decision, however designated, that adjudicates fewer than all the claims or the rights and liabilities of fewer than all the parties does not end the action as to any of the claims or parties and may be revised at any time before the entry of a judgment adjudicating all the claims and all the parties' rights and liabilities.

(c) Demand for Judgment; Relief to Be Granted. A default judgment must not differ in kind from, or exceed in amount, what is demanded in the pleadings. Every other final judgment should grant the relief to which each party is entitled, even if the party has not demanded that relief in its pleadings.

(d) Costs; Attorney's Fees.

(1) Costs Other Than Attorney's Fees. Unless a federal statute, these rules, or a court order provides otherwise, costs—other than attorney's fees—should be allowed to the prevailing party. But costs against the United States, its officers, and its agencies may be imposed only to the extent allowed by law. The clerk may tax costs on 14 days' notice. On motion served within the next 7 days, the court may review the clerk's action.

(2) Attorney's Fees.

(A) Claim to Be by Motion. A claim for attorney's fees and related nontaxable expenses must be made by motion unless the substantive law requires those fees to be proved at trial as an element of damages.

(B) Timing and Contents of the Motion. Unless a statute or a court order provides otherwise, the motion must:

(i) be filed no later than 14 days after the entry of judgment;

(ii) specify the judgment and the statute, rule, or other grounds entitling the movant to the award;

(iii) state the amount sought or provide a fair estimate of it; and

(iv) disclose, if the court so orders, the terms of any agreement about fees for the services for which the claim is made.

(C) Proceedings. Subject to Rule 23(h), the court must, on a party's request, give an opportunity for adversary submissions on the motion in accordance with Rule 43(c) or 78. The court may decide issues of liability for fees before receiving submissions on the value of services. The court must find the facts and state its conclusions of law as provided in Rule 52(a).

(D) Special Procedures by Local Rule; Reference to a Master or a Magistrate Judge. By local rule, the court may establish special procedures to resolve fee-related issues without extensive evidentiary hearings. Also, the court may refer issues concerning the value of services to a special master under Rule 53 without regard to the limitations of Rule 53(a)(1), and may refer a motion for attorney's fees to a magistrate judge under Rule 72(b) as if it were a dispositive pretrial matter.

(E) Exceptions. Subparagraphs (A)–(D) do not apply to claims for fees and expenses as sanctions for violating these rules or as sanctions under 28 U.S.C. §1927.

(As amended Dec. 27, 1946, eff. Mar. 19, 1948; Apr. 17, 1961, eff. July 19, 1961; Mar. 2, 1987, eff. Aug. 1, 1987; Apr. 22, 1993, eff. Dec. 1, 1993; Apr. 29, 2002, eff. Dec. 1, 2002; Mar. 27, 2003, eff. Dec. 1, 2003; Apr. 30, 2007, eff. Dec. 1, 2007; Mar. 26, 2009, eff. Dec. 1, 2009.)

Notes of Advisory Committee on Rules—1937

Note to Subdivision (a). The second sentence is derived substantially from [former] Equity Rule 71 (Form of Decree).

Note to Subdivision (b). This provides for the separate judgment of equity and code practice. See Wis.Stat. (1935) §270.54; Compare N.Y.C.P.A. (1937) §476.

Note to Subdivision (c). For the limitation on default contained in the first sentence, see 2 N.D.Comp.Laws Ann. (1913) §7680; N.Y.C.P.A. (1937) §479. Compare English Rules Under the Judicature Act (The Annual Practice, 1937) O. 13, r.r. 3–12. The remainder is a usual code provision. It makes clear that a judgment should give the relief to which a party is entitled, regardless of whether it is legal or equitable or both. This necessarily includes the deficiency judgment in foreclosure cases formerly provided for by Equity Rule 10 (Decree for Deficiency in Foreclosures, Etc.).

Note to Subdivision (d). For the present rule in common law actions, see Ex parte Peterson, 253 U.S. 300, 40 S.Ct. 543, 64 L.Ed. 919 (1920); Payne, Costs in Common Law Actions in the Federal Courts (1935), 21 Va.L.Rev. 397.

The provisions as to costs in actions in forma pauperis contained in U.S.C., Title 28, §§832–836 [now 1915] are unaffected by this rule. Other sections of U.S.C., Title 28, which are unaffected by this rule are: §§815 [former] (Costs; plaintiff not entitled to, when), 821 [now 1928] (Costs; infringement of patent; disclaimer), 825 (Costs; several actions), 829 [now 1927] (Costs; attorney liable for, when), and 830 [now 1920] (Costs; bill of; taxation).

The provisions of the following and similar statutes as to costs against the United States and its officers and agencies are specifically continued:

- U.S.C., Title 15, §§77v(a), 78aa, 79y (Securities and Exchange Commission)
- U.S.C., Title 16, §825p (Federal Power Commission)
- U.S.C., Title 26, [former] §§1569(d) and 1645(d) (Internal revenue actions)
- U.S.C., Title 26, [former] §1670(b)(2) (Reimbursement of costs of recovery against revenue officers)
- U.S.C., Title 28, [former] §817 (Internal revenue actions)
- U.S.C., Title 28, §836 [now 1915] (United States—actions in forma pauperis)
- U.S.C., Title 28, §842 [now 2006] (Actions against revenue officers)
- U.S.C., Title 28, §870 [now 2408] (United States—in certain cases)
- U.S.C., Title 28, [former] §906 (United States—foreclosure actions)
- U.S.C., Title 47, §401 (Communications Commission)
- The provisions of the following and similar statutes as to costs are unaffected:
- U.S.C., Title 7, §210(f) (Actions for damages based on an order of the Secretary of Agriculture under Stockyards Act)
- U.S.C., Title 7, §499g(c) (Appeals from reparations orders of Secretary of Agriculture under Perishable Commodities Act)
- U.S.C., Title 8, [former] §45 (Action against district attorneys in certain cases)
- U.S.C., Title 15, §15 (Actions for injuries due to violation of antitrust laws)
- U.S.C., Title 15, §72 (Actions for violation of law forbidding importation or sale of articles at less than market value or wholesale prices)
- U.S.C., Title 15, §77k (Actions by persons acquiring securities registered with untrue statements under Securities Act of 1933)
- U.S.C., Title 15, §78i(e) (Certain actions under the Securities Exchange Act of 1934)
- U.S.C., Title 15, §78r (Similar to 78i(e))
- U.S.C., Title 15, §96 (Infringement of trade-mark—damages)
- U.S.C., Title 15, §99 (Infringement of trade-mark—injunctions)
- U.S.C., Title 15, §124 (Infringement of trade-mark—damages)
- U.S.C., Title 19, §274 (Certain actions under customs law)
- U.S.C., Title 30, §32 (Action to determine right to possession of mineral lands in certain cases)
- U.S.C., Title 31, §§232 [now 3730] and [former] 234 (Action for making false claims upon United States)
- U.S.C., Title 33, §926 (Actions under Harbor Workers' Compensation Act)
- U.S.C., Title 35, §67 [now 281, 284] (Infringement of patent—damages)
- U.S.C., Title 35, §69 [now 282] (Infringement of patent—pleading and proof)
- U.S.C., Title 35, §71 [now 288] (Infringement of patent—when specification too broad)
- U.S.C., Title 45, §153p (Actions for non-compliance with an order of National R. R. Adjustment Board for payment of money)
- U.S.C., Title 46, [former] §38 (Action for penalty for failure to register vessel)
- U.S.C., Title 46, [former] §829 (Action based on non-compliance with an order of Maritime Commission for payment of money)
- U.S.C., Title 46, §941 [now 31304] (Certain actions under Ship Mortgage Act)
- U.S.C., Title 46 [App.], §1227 (Actions for damages for violation of certain provisions of the Merchant Marine Act, 1936)
- U.S.C., Title 47, §206 (Actions for certain violations of Communications Act of 1934)

- U.S.C., Title 49, §16(2) [see 11704, 15904] (Action based on non-compliance with an order of I. C. C. for payment of money)

Notes of Advisory Committee on Rules—1946 Amendment

The historic rule in the federal courts has always prohibited piecemeal disposal of litigation and permitted appeals only from final judgments except in those special instances covered by statute. Hohorst v. Hamburg-American Packet Co. (1893) 148 U.S. 262; Rexford v. Brunswick-Balke-Collender Co. (1913) 228 U.S. 339; Collins v. Miller (1920) 252 U.S. 364. Rule 54(b) was originally adopted in view of the wide scope and possible content of the newly created "civil action" in order to avoid the possible injustice of a delay in judgment of a distinctly separate claim to await adjudication of the entire case. It was not designed to overturn the settled federal rule stated above, which, indeed, has more recently been reiterated in Catlin v. United States (1945) 324 U.S. 229. See also United States v. Florian (1941) 312 U.S. 656, rev'g (and restoring the first opinion in) Florian v. United States (C.C.A.7th, 1940) 114 F.(2d) 990; Reeves v. Beardall (1942) 316 U.S. 283.

Unfortunately, this was not always understood, and some confusion ensued. Hence situations arose where district courts made a piecemeal disposition of an action and entered what the parties thought amounted to a judgment, although a trial remained to be had on other claims similar or identical with those disposed of. In the interim the parties did not know their ultimate rights, and accordingly took an appeal, thus putting the finality of the partial judgment in question. While most appellate courts have reached a result generally in accord with the intent of the rule, yet there have been divergent precedents and division of views which have served to render the issues more clouded to the parties appellant. It hardly seems a case where multiplicity of precedents will tend to remove the problem from debate. The problem is presented and discussed in the following cases: Atwater v. North American Coal Corp. (C.C.A.2d, 1940) 111 F.(2d) 125; Rosenblum v. Dingfelder (C.C.A.2d, 1940) 111 F.(2d) 406; Audi-Vision, Inc. v. RCA Mfg. Co., Inc. (C.C.A.2d, 1943) 136 F.(2d) 621; Zalkind v. Scheinman (C.C.A.2d, 1943) 139 F.(2d) 895; Oppenheimer v. F. J. Young & Co., Inc. (C.C.A.2d, 1944) 144 F.(2d) 387; Libbey-Owens-Ford Glass Co. v. Sylvania Industrial Corp. (C.C.A.2d, 1946) 154 F.(2d) 814, cert. den. (1946) 66 S.Ct. 1353; Zarati Steamship Co. v. Park Bridge Corp. (C.C.A.2d, 1946) 154 F.(2d) 377; Baltimore and Ohio R. Co. v. United Fuel Gas Co. (C.C.A.4th, 1946) 154 F.(2d) 545; Jefferson Electric Co. v. Sola Electric Co. (C.C.A.7th, 1941) 122 F.(2d) 124; Leonard v. Socony-Vacuum Oil Co. (C.C.A.7th, 1942) 130 F.(2d) 535; Markham v. Kasper (C.C.A.7th, 1945) 152 F.(2d) 270; Hanney v. Franklin Fire Ins. Co. of Philadelphia (C.C.A.9th, 1944) 142 F.(2d) 864; Toomey v. Toomey (App.D.C. 1945) 149 F.(2d) 19.

In view of the difficulty thus disclosed, the Advisory Committee in its two preliminary drafts of proposed amendments attempted to redefine the original rule with particular stress upon the interlocutory nature of partial judgments which did not adjudicate all claims arising out of a single transaction or occurrence. This attempt appeared to meet with almost universal approval from those of the profession commenting upon it, although there were, of course, helpful suggestions for additional changes in language or clarification of detail. But cf. Circuit Judge Frank's dissenting opinion in Libbey-Owens-Ford Glass Co. v. Sylvania Industrial Corp., supra, n. 21 of the dissenting opinion. The Committee, however, became convinced on careful study of its own proposals that the seeds of ambiguity still remained, and that it had not completely solved the problem of piecemeal appeals. After extended consideration, it concluded that a retention of the older federal rule was desirable, and that this rule needed only the exercise of a discretionary power to afford a remedy in the infrequent harsh case to provide a simple, definite, workable rule. This is afforded by amended Rule 54(b). It re-establishes an ancient policy with clarity and precision. For the possibility of staying execution where not all claims are disposed of under Rule 54(b), see amended Rule 62(h).

Notes of Advisory Committee on Rules—1961 Amendment

This rule permitting appeal, upon the trial court's determination of "no just reason for delay," from a judgment upon one or more but fewer than all the claims in an action, has generally been given a sympathetic construction by the courts and its validity is settled. Reeves v. Beardall, 316 U.S. 283 (1942); Sears, Roebuck & Co. v. Mackey, 351 U.S. 427 (1956); Cold Metal Process Co. v. United Engineering & Foundry Co., 351 U.S. 445 (1956).

A serious difficulty has, however, arisen because the rule speaks of claims but nowhere mentions parties. A line of cases has developed in the circuits consistently holding the rule to be inapplicable to the dismissal, even with the requisite trial court determination, of one or more but fewer than all defendants jointly charged in an action, i.e. charged with various forms of concerted or related wrongdoing or related liability. See Mull v. Ackerman, 279 F.2d 25 (2d Cir. 1960); Richards v. Smith, 276 F.2d 652 (5th Cir. 1960); Hardy v. Bankers Life & Cas. Co., 222 F.2d 827 (7th Cir. 1955); Steiner v. 20th Century-Fox Film Corp., 220 F.2d 105 (9th Cir. 1955). For purposes of Rule 54(b) it was arguable that there were as many "claims" as there were parties defendant and that the rule in its present text applied where less than all of the parties were dismissed, cf. United Artists Corp. v. Masterpiece Productions, Inc., 221 F.2d 213, 215 (2d Cir. 1955); Bowling Machines, Inc. v. First Nat. Bank, 283 F.2d 39 (1st Cir. 1960); but the Courts of Appeals are now committed to an opposite view.

The danger of hardship through delay of appeal until the whole action is concluded may be at least as serious in the multiple-parties situations as in multiple-claims cases, see Pabellon v. Grace Line, Inc., 191 F.2d 169, 179 (2d Cir. 1951), cert. denied, 342 U.S. 893 (1951), and courts and commentators have urged that Rule 54(b) be changed to take in the former. See Reagan v. Traders & General Ins. Co., 255 F.2d 845 (5th Cir. 1958); Meadows v. Greyhound Corp., 235 F.2d 233 (5th Cir. 1956); Steiner v. 20th Century-Fox Film Corp., supra; 6 Moore's Federal Practice 54.34[2] (2d ed. 1953); 3 Barron & Holtzoff, Federal Practice & Procedure §1193.2 (Wright ed. 1958); Developments in the Law—Multiparty Litigation, 71 Harv.L.Rev. 874, 981 (1958); Note, 62 Yale L.J. 263, 271 (1953); Ill.Ann.Stat. ch. 110, §50(2) (Smith-Hurd 1956). The amendment accomplishes this purpose by referring explicitly to parties.

There has been some recent indication that interlocutory appeal under the provisions of 28 U.S.C. §1292(b), added in 1958, may now be available for the multiple-parties cases here considered. See Jaftex Corp. v. Randolph Mills, Inc., 282 F.2d 508 (2d Cir. 1960). The Rule 54(b) procedure seems preferable for those cases, and §1292(b) should be held inapplicable to them when the rule is enlarged as here proposed. See Luckenbach Steamship Co., Inc., v. H. Muehlstein & Co., Inc., 280 F.2d 755, 757 (2d Cir. 1960); 1 Barron & Holtzoff, supra, §58.1, p. 321 (Wright ed. 1960).

Notes of Advisory Committee on Rules—1987 Amendment

The amendment is technical. No substantive change is intended.

Notes of Advisory Committee on Rules—1993 Amendment

Subdivision (d). This revision adds paragraph (2) to this subdivision to provide for a frequently recurring form of litigation not initially contemplated by the rules—disputes over the amount of attorneys' fees to be awarded in the large number of actions in which prevailing parties may be entitled to such awards or in which the court must determine the fees to be paid from a common fund. This revision seeks to harmonize and clarify procedures that have been developed through case law and local rules.

Paragraph (1). Former subdivision (d), providing for taxation of costs by the clerk, is renumbered as paragraph (1) and revised to exclude applications for attorneys' fees.

Paragraph (2). This new paragraph establishes a procedure for presenting claims for attorneys' fees, whether or not denominated as "costs." It applies also to requests for reimbursement of expenses, not taxable as costs, when recoverable under governing law incident to the award of fees. Cf. West Virginia Univ. Hosp. v. Casey, ____ U.S. ____ (1991), holding, prior to the Civil Rights Act of 1991, that expert witness fees were not recoverable under 42 U.S.C. §1988. As noted in subparagraph (A), it does not, however, apply to fees recoverable as an element of damages, as when sought under the terms of a contract; such damages typically are to be claimed in a pleading and may involve issues to be resolved by a jury. Nor, as provided in subparagraph (E), does it apply to awards of fees as sanctions authorized or mandated under these rules or under 28 U.S.C. §1927.

Subparagraph (B) provides a deadline for motions for attorneys' fees—14 days after final judgment unless the court or a statute specifies some other time. One purpose of this provision is to assure that the opposing party is informed of the claim before the time for appeal has elapsed. Prior law did not prescribe any specific time limit on claims for attorneys' fees. White v. New Hampshire Dep't of Employment Sec., 455 U.S. 445 (1982). In many nonjury cases the court will want to consider attorneys' fee issues immediately after rendering its judgment on the merits of the case. Note that the time for making claims is specifically stated in some legislation, such as the Equal Access to Justice Act, 28 U.S.C. §2412(d)(1)(B) (30-day filing period).

Prompt filing affords an opportunity for the court to resolve fee disputes shortly after trial, while the services performed are freshly in mind. It also enables the court in appropriate circumstances to make its ruling on a fee request in time for any appellate review of a dispute over fees to proceed at the same time as review on the merits of the case.

Filing a motion for fees under this subdivision does not affect the finality or the appealability of a judgment, though revised Rule 58 provides a mechanism by which prior to appeal the court can suspend the finality to resolve a motion for fees. If an appeal on the merits of the case is taken, the court may rule on the claim for fees, may defer its ruling on the motion, or may deny the motion without prejudice, directing under subdivision (d)(2)(B) a new period for filing after the appeal has been resolved. A notice of appeal does not extend the time for filing a fee claim based on the initial judgment, but the court under subdivision (d)(2)(B) may effectively extend the period by permitting claims to be filed after resolution of the appeal. A new period for filing will automatically begin if a new judgment is entered following a reversal or remand by the appellate court or the granting of a motion under Rule 59.

The rule does not require that the motion be supported at the time of filing with the evidentiary material bearing on the fees. This material must of course be submitted in due course, according to such schedule as the court may direct in light of the circumstances of the case. What is required is the filing of a motion sufficient to alert the adversary and the court that there is a claim for fees and the amount of such fees (or a fair estimate).

If directed by the court, the moving party is also required to disclose any fee agreement, including those between attorney and client, between attorneys sharing a fee to be awarded, and between adversaries made in partial settlement of a dispute where the settlement must be implemented by court action as may be required by Rules 23(e) and 23.1 or other like provisions. With respect to the fee arrangements requiring court approval, the court may also by local rule require disclosure immediately after such arrangements are agreed to. E.g., Rule 5 of United States District Court for the Eastern District of New York; cf. In re "Agent Orange" Product Liability Litigation (MDL 381), 611 F. Supp. 1452, 1464 (E.D.N.Y. 1985).

In the settlement of class actions resulting in a common fund from which fees will be sought, courts frequently have required that claims for fees be presented in advance of hearings to consider approval of the proposed settlement. The rule does not affect this practice, as it permits the court to require submissions of fee claims in advance of entry of judgment.

Subparagraph (C) assures the parties of an opportunity to make an appropriate presentation with respect to issues involving the evaluation of legal services. In some cases, an evidentiary hearing may be needed, but this is not required in every case. The amount of time to be allowed for the preparation of submissions both in support of and in opposition to awards should be tailored to the particular case.

The court is explicitly authorized to make a determination of the liability for fees before receiving submissions by the parties bearing on the amount of an award. This option may be appropriate in actions in which the liability issue is doubtful and the evaluation issues are numerous and complex.

The court may order disclosure of additional information, such as that bearing on prevailing local rates or on the appropriateness of particular services for which compensation is sought.

On rare occasion, the court may determine that discovery under Rules 26–37 would be useful to the parties. Compare Rules Governing Section 2254 Cases in the U.S. District Courts, Rule 6. See Note, Determining the Reasonableness of Attorneys' Fees—the Discoverability of Billing Records, 64 B.U.L. Rev. 241 (1984). In complex fee disputes, the court may use case management techniques to limit the scope of the dispute or to facilitate the settlement of fee award disputes.

Fee awards should be made in the form of a separate judgment under Rule 58 since such awards are subject to review in the court of appeals. To facilitate review, the paragraph provides that the court set forth its findings and conclusions as under Rule 52(a), though in most cases this explanation could be quite brief.

Subparagraph (D) explicitly authorizes the court to establish procedures facilitating the efficient and fair resolution of fee claims. A local rule, for example, might call for matters to be presented through affidavits, or might provide for issuance of proposed findings by the court, which would be treated as accepted by the parties unless objected to within a specified time. A court might also consider establishing a schedule reflecting customary fees or factors affecting fees within the community, as implicitly suggested by Justice O'Connor in Pennsylvania v. Delaware Valley Citizens' Council, 483 U.S. 711, 733 (1987) (O'Connor, J., concurring) (how particular markets compensate for contingency). Cf. Thompson v. Kennickell, 710 F. Supp. 1 (D.D.C. 1989) (use of findings in other cases to promote consistency). The parties, of course, should be permitted to show that in the circumstances of the case such a schedule should not be applied or that different hourly rates would be appropriate.

The rule also explicitly permits, without need for a local rule, the court to refer issues regarding the amount of a fee award in a particular case to a master under Rule 53. The district judge may designate a magistrate judge to act as a master for this purpose or may refer a motion for attorneys' fees to a magistrate judge for proposed findings and recommendations under Rule 72(b). This authorization eliminates any controversy as to whether such references are permitted under Rule 53(b) as "matters of account and of difficult computation of damages" and whether motions for attorneys' fees can be treated as the equivalent of a dispositive pretrial matter that can be referred to a magistrate judge. For consistency and efficiency, all such matters might be referred to the same magistrate judge.

Subparagraph (E) excludes from this rule the award of fees as sanctions under these rules or under 28 U.S.C. §1927.

Committee Notes on Rules—2002 Amendment

Subdivision (d)(2)(C) is amended to delete the requirement that judgment on a motion for attorney fees be set forth in a separate document. This change complements the amendment of Rule 58(a)(1), which deletes the separate document requirement for an order disposing of a motion for attorney fees under Rule 54. These changes are made to support amendment of Rule 4 of the Federal Rules of Appellate Procedure. It continues to be important that a district court make clear its meaning when it intends an order to be the final disposition of a motion for attorney fees.

The requirement in subdivision (d)(2)(B) that a motion for attorney fees be not only filed but also served no later than 14 days after entry of judgment is changed to require filing only, to establish a parallel with Rules 50, 52, and 59. Service continues to be required under Rule 5(a).

Committee Notes on Rules—2003 Amendment

Rule 54(d)(2)(D) is revised to reflect amendments to Rule 53.

Committee Notes on Rules—2007 Amendment

The language of Rule 54 has been amended as part of the general restyling of the Civil Rules to make them more easily understood and to make style and terminology consistent throughout the rules. These changes are intended to be stylistic only.

The words "or class member" have been removed from Rule 54(d)(2)(C) because Rule 23(h)(2) now addresses objections by class members to attorney-fee motions. Rule 54(d)(2)(C) is amended to recognize that Rule 23(h) now controls those aspects of attorney-fee motions in class actions to which it is addressed.

Committee Notes on Rules—2009 Amendment

Former Rule 54(d)(1) provided that the clerk may tax costs on 1 day's notice. That period was unrealistically short. The new 14-day period provides a better opportunity to prepare and present a response. The former 5-day period to serve a motion to review the clerk's action is extended to 7 days to reflect the change in the Rule 6(a) method for computing periods of less than 11 days.

Rule 55. Default; Default Judgment

(a) Entering a Default. When a party against whom a judgment for affirmative relief is sought has failed to plead or otherwise defend, and that failure is shown by affidavit or otherwise, the clerk must enter the party's default.

(b) Entering a Default Judgment.

(1) By the Clerk. If the plaintiff's claim is for a sum certain or a sum that can be made certain by computation, the clerk—on the plaintiff's request, with an affidavit showing the amount due—must enter judgment for that amount and costs against a defendant who has been defaulted for not appearing and who is neither a minor nor an incompetent person.

(2) By the Court. In all other cases, the party must apply to the court for a default judgment. A default judgment may be entered against a minor or incompetent person only if represented by a general guardian, conservator, or other like fiduciary who has appeared. If the party against whom a default judgment is sought has appeared personally or by a representative, that party or its representative must be served with written notice of the application at least 7 days before the hearing. The court may conduct hearings or make referrals—preserving any federal statutory right to a jury trial—when, to enter or effectuate judgment, it needs to:

(A) conduct an accounting;
(B) determine the amount of damages;
(C) establish the truth of any allegation by evidence; or
(D) investigate any other matter.

(c) Setting Aside a Default or a Default Judgment. The court may set aside an entry of default for good cause, and it may set aside a final default judgment under Rule 60(b).

(d) Judgment Against the United States. A default judgment may be entered against the United States, its officers, or its agencies only if the claimant establishes a claim or right to relief by evidence that satisfies the court.

(As amended Mar. 2, 1987, eff. Aug. 1, 1987; Apr. 30, 2007, eff. Dec. 1, 2007; Mar. 26, 2009, eff. Dec. 1, 2009; Apr. 29, 2015, eff. Dec. 1, 2015.)

Notes of Advisory Committee on Rules—1937

This represents the joining of the equity decree pro confesso ([former] Equity Rules 12 (Issue of Subpoena—Time for Answer), 16 (Defendant to Answer—Default—Decree Pro Confesso), 17 (Decree Pro Confesso to be Followed by Final Decree—Setting Aside Default), 29 (Defenses—How Presented), 31 (Reply—When Required—When Cause at Issue)) and the judgment by default now governed by U.S.C., Title 28, [former] §724 (Conformity act). For dismissal of an action for failure to comply with these rules or any order of the court, see rule 41(b).

Note to Subdivision (a). The provision for the entry of default comes from the Massachusetts practice, 2 Mass.Gen.Laws (Ter.Ed., 1932) ch. 231, §57. For affidavit of default, see 2 Minn.Stat. (Mason, 1927) §9256.

Note to Subdivision (b). The provision in paragraph (1) for the entry of judgment by the clerk when plaintiff claims a sum certain is found in the N.Y.C.P.A. (1937) §485, in Calif.Code Civ.Proc. (Deering, 1937) §585(1), and in Conn.Practice Book (1934) §47. For provisions similar to paragraph (2), compare Calif.Code, supra, §585(2); N.Y.C.P.A. (1937) §490; 2 Minn.Stat. (Mason, 1927) §9256(3); 2 Wash.Rev.Stat.Ann. (Remington, 1932) §411(2). U.S.C., Title 28, §785 (Action to recover forfeiture in bond) and similar statutes are preserved by the last clause of paragraph (2).

Note to Subdivision (e). This restates substantially the last clause of U.S.C., Title 28, [former] §763 (Action against the United States under the Tucker Act). As this rule governs in all actions against the United States, U.S.C., Title 28, [former] §45 (Practice and procedure in certain cases under the interstate commerce laws) and similar statutes are modified insofar as they contain anything inconsistent therewith.

Notes of Advisory Committee on Rules—1946 Supplementary Note

Note. The operation of Rule 55(b) (Judgment) is directly affected by the Soldiers' and Sailors' Civil Relief Act of 1940 ([former] 50 U.S.C. [App.] §501 et seq.) [now 50 U.S.C. 3901 et seq.]. Section 200 of the Act [former 50 U.S.C. Appendix, §520] imposes specific requirements which must be fulfilled before a default judgment can be entered (e.g., Ledwith v. Storkan (D.Neb. 1942) 6 Fed.Rules Serv. 60b.24, Case 2, 2 F.R.D. 539, and also provides for the vacation of a judgment in certain circumstances. See discussion in Commentary, Effect of Conscription Legislation on the Federal Rules (1940) 3 Fed.Rules Serv. 725; 3 Moore's Federal Practice (1938) Cum.Supplement §55.02.

Notes of Advisory Committee on Rules—1987 Amendment

The amendments are technical. No substantive change is intended.

Committee Notes on Rules—2007 Amendment

The language of Rule 55 has been amended as part of the general restyling of the Civil Rules to make them more easily understood and to make style and terminology consistent throughout the rules. These changes are intended to be stylistic only.

Former Rule 55(a) directed the clerk to enter a default when a party failed to plead or otherwise defend "as provided by these rules." The implication from the reference to defending "as provided by these rules" seemed to be that the clerk should enter a default even if a party did something showing an intent to defend, but that act was not specifically described by the rules. Courts in fact have rejected that implication. Acts that show an intent to defend have frequently prevented a default even though not connected to any particular rule. "[A]s provided by these rules" is deleted to reflect Rule 55(a)'s actual meaning.

Amended Rule 55 omits former Rule 55(d), which included two provisions. The first recognized that Rule 55 applies to described claimants. The list was incomplete and unnecessary. Rule 55(a) applies Rule 55 to any party against whom a judgment for affirmative relief is requested. The second provision was a redundant reminder that Rule 54(c) limits the relief available by default judgment.

Committee Notes on Rules—2009 Amendment

The time set in the former rule at 3 days has been revised to 7 days. See the Note to Rule 6.

Committee Notes on Rules—2015 Amendment

Rule 55(c) is amended to make plain the interplay between Rules 54(b), 55(c), and 60(b). A default judgment that does not dispose of all of the claims among all parties is not a final judgment unless the court directs entry of final judgment under Rule 54(b). Until final judgment is entered, Rule 54(b) allows revision of the default judgment at any time. The demanding standards set by Rule 60(b) apply only in seeking relief from a final judgment.

Rule 56. Summary Judgment

(a) Motion for Summary Judgment or Partial Summary Judgment. A party may move for summary judgment, identifying each claim or defense—or the part of each claim or defense—on which summary judgment is sought. The court shall grant summary judgment if the movant shows that there is no genuine dispute as to any material fact and the movant is entitled to judgment as a matter of law. The court should state on the record the reasons for granting or denying the motion.

(b) Time to File a Motion. Unless a different time is set by local rule or the court orders otherwise, a party may file a motion for summary judgment at any time until 30 days after the close of all discovery.

(c) Procedures.

(1) Supporting Factual Positions. A party asserting that a fact cannot be or is genuinely disputed must support the assertion by:

(A) citing to particular parts of materials in the record, including depositions, documents, electronically stored information, affidavits or declarations, stipulations (including those made for purposes of the motion only), admissions, interrogatory answers, or other materials; or

(B) showing that the materials cited do not establish the absence or presence of a genuine dispute, or that an adverse party cannot produce admissible evidence to support the fact.

(2) Objection That a Fact Is Not Supported by Admissible Evidence. A party may object that the material cited to support or dispute a fact cannot be presented in a form that would be admissible in evidence.

(3) Materials Not Cited. The court need consider only the cited materials, but it may consider other materials in the record.

(4) Affidavits or Declarations. An affidavit or declaration used to support or oppose a motion must be made on personal knowledge, set out facts that would be admissible in evidence, and show that the affiant or declarant is competent to testify on the matters stated.

(d) When Facts Are Unavailable to the Nonmovant. If a nonmovant shows by affidavit or declaration that, for specified reasons, it cannot present facts essential to justify its opposition, the court may:

(1) defer considering the motion or deny it;

(2) allow time to obtain affidavits or declarations or to take discovery; or

(3) issue any other appropriate order.

(e) Failing to Properly Support or Address a Fact. If a party fails to properly support an assertion of fact or fails to properly address another party's assertion of fact as required by Rule 56(c), the court may:

(1) give an opportunity to properly support or address the fact;

(2) consider the fact undisputed for purposes of the motion;

(3) grant summary judgment if the motion and supporting materials—including the facts considered undisputed—show that the movant is entitled to it; or

(4) issue any other appropriate order.

(f) Judgment Independent of the Motion. After giving notice and a reasonable time to respond, the court may:

(1) grant summary judgment for a nonmovant;

(2) grant the motion on grounds not raised by a party; or

(3) consider summary judgment on its own after identifying for the parties material facts that may not be genuinely in dispute.

(g) Failing to Grant All the Requested Relief. If the court does not grant all the relief requested by the motion, it may enter an order stating any material fact—including an item of damages or other relief—that is not genuinely in dispute and treating the fact as established in the case.

(h) Affidavit or Declaration Submitted in Bad Faith. If satisfied that an affidavit or declaration under this rule is submitted in bad faith or solely for delay, the court—after notice and a reasonable time to respond—may order the submitting party to pay the other party the reasonable expenses, including attorney's fees, it incurred as a result. An offending party or attorney may also be held in contempt or subjected to other appropriate sanctions.

(As amended Dec. 27, 1946, eff. Mar. 19, 1948; Jan. 21, 1963, eff. July 1, 1963; Mar. 2, 1987, eff. Aug. 1, 1987; Apr. 30, 2007, eff. Dec. 1, 2007; Mar. 26, 2009, eff. Dec. 1, 2009; Apr. 28, 2010, eff. Dec. 1, 2010.)

Notes of Advisory Committee on Rules—1937

This rule is applicable to all actions, including those against the United States or an officer or agency thereof.

Summary judgment procedure is a method for promptly disposing of actions in which there is no genuine issue as to any material fact. It has been extensively used in England for more than 50 years and has been adopted in a number of American states. New York, for example, has made great use of it. During the first nine years after its adoption there, the records of New York county alone show 5,600 applications for summary judgments. Report of the Commission on the Administration of Justice in New York State (1934), p. 383. See also Third Annual Report of the Judicial Council of the State of New York (1937), p. 30.

In England it was first employed only in cases of liquidated claims, but there has been a steady enlargement of the scope of the remedy until it is now used in actions to recover land or chattels and in all other actions at law, for liquidated or unliquidated claims, except for a few designated torts and breach of promise of marriage. English Rules Under the Judicature Act (The Annual Practice, 1937) O. 3, r. 6; Orders 14, 14A, and 15; see also O. 32, r. 6, authorizing an application for judgment at any time upon admissions. In Michigan (3 Comp.Laws (1929) §14260) and Illinois (Ill.Rev.Stat. (1937) ch. 110, §§181, 259.15, 259.16), it is not limited to liquidated demands. New York (N.Y.R.C.P. (1937) Rule 113; see also Rule 107) has brought so many classes of actions under the operation of the rule that the Commission on Administration of Justice in New York State (1934) recommend that all restrictions be removed and that the remedy be available "in any action" (p. 287). For the history and nature of the summary judgment procedure and citations of state statutes, see Clark and Samenow, The Summary Judgment (1929), 38 Yale L.J. 423.

Note to Subdivision (d). See Rule 16 (Pre-Trial Procedure; Formulating Issues) and the Note thereto.

Note to Subdivisions (e) and (f). These are similar to rules in Michigan. Mich.Court Rules Ann. (Searl, 1933) Rule 30.

Notes of Advisory Committee on Rules—1946 Amendment

Subdivision (a). The amendment allows a claimant to move for a summary judgment at any time after the expiration of 20 days from the commencement of the action or after service of a motion for summary judgment by the adverse party. This will normally operate to permit an earlier motion by the claimant than under the original rule, where the phrase "at any time after the pleading in answer thereto has been served" operates to prevent a claimant from moving for summary judgment, even in a case clearly proper for its exercise, until a formal answer has been filed. Thus in Peoples Bank v. Federal Reserve Bank of San Francisco (N.D.Cal. 1944) 58 F.Supp. 25, the plaintiff's counter-motion for a summary judgment was stricken as premature, because the defendant had not filed an answer. Since Rule 12(a) allows at least 20 days for an answer, that time plus the 10 days required in Rule 56(c) means that under original Rule 56(a) a minimum period of 30 days necessarily has to elapse in every case before the claimant can be heard on his right to a summary judgment. An extension of time by the court or the service of preliminary motions of any kind will prolong that period even further. In many cases this merely represents unnecessary delay. See United States v. Adler's Creamery, Inc. (C.C.A.2d, 1939) 107 F.(2d) 987. The changes are in the interest of more expeditious litigation. The 20-day period, as provided, gives the defendant an opportunity to secure counsel and determine a course of action. But in a case where the defendant himself serves a motion for summary judgment within that time, there is no reason to restrict the plaintiff and the amended rule so provides.

Subdivision (c). The amendment of Rule 56(c), by the addition of the final sentence, resolves a doubt expressed in Sartor v. Arkansas Natural Gas Corp. (1944) 321 U.S. 620. See also Commentary, Summary Judgment as to Damages (1944) 7 Fed.Rules Serv. 974; Madeirense Do Brasil S/A v. Stulman-Emrick Lumber Co. (C.C.A.2d, 1945) 147 F.(2d) 399, cert. den. (1945) 325 U.S. 861. It makes clear that although the question of recovery depends on the amount of damages, the summary judgment rule is applicable and summary judgment may be granted in a proper case. If the case is not fully adjudicated it may be dealt with as provided in subdivision (d) of Rule 56, and the right to summary recovery determined by a preliminary order, interlocutory in character, and the precise amount of recovery left for trial.

Subdivision (d). Rule 54(a) defines "judgment" as including a decree and "any order from which an appeal lies." Subdivision (d) of Rule 56 indicates clearly, however, that a partial summary "judgment" is not a final judgment, and, therefore, that it is not appealable, unless in the particular case some statute allows an appeal from the interlocutory order involved. The partial summary judgment is merely a pretrial adjudication that certain issues shall be deemed established for the trial of the case. This adjudication is more nearly akin to the preliminary order under Rule 16, and likewise serves the purpose of speeding up litigation by eliminating before trial matters wherein there is no genuine issue of fact. See Leonard v. Socony-Vacuum Oil Co. (C.C.A.7th, 1942) 130 F.(2d) 535; Biggins v. Oltmer Iron Works (C.C.A.7th, 1946) 154 F.(2d) 214; 3 Moore's Federal Practice (1938). 3190–3192. Since interlocutory appeals are not allowed, except where specifically provided by statute (see 3 Moore, op. cit. supra, 3155–3156) this interpretation is in line with that policy, Leonard v. Socony-Vacuum Oil Co., supra. See also Audi Vision Inc., v. RCA Mfg. Co. (C.C.A.2d, 1943) 136 F.(2d) 621; Toomey v. Toomey

(App.D.C. 1945) 149 F.(2d) 19; Biggins v. Oltmer Iron Works, supra; Catlin v. United States (1945) 324 U.S. 229.

Notes of Advisory Committee on Rules—1963 Amendment

Subdivision (c). By the amendment "answers to interrogatories" are included among the materials which may be considered on motion for summary judgment. The phrase was inadvertently omitted from the rule, see 3 Barron & Holtzoff, Federal Practice and Procedure 159–60 (Wright ed. 1958), and the courts have generally reached by interpretation the result which will hereafter be required by the text of the amended rule. See Annot., 74 A.L.R.2d 984 (1960).

Subdivision (e). The words "answers to interrogatories" are added in the third sentence of this subdivision to conform to the amendment of subdivision (c).

The last two sentences are added to overcome a line of cases, chiefly in the Third Circuit, which has impaired the utility of the summary judgment device. A typical case is as follows: A party supports his motion for summary judgment by affidavits or other evidentiary matters sufficient to show that there is no genuine issue as to a material fact. The adverse party, in opposing the motion, does not produce any evidentiary matter, or produces some but not enough to establish that there is a genuine issue for trial. Instead, the adverse party rests on averments of his pleadings which on their face present an issue. In this situation Third Circuit cases have taken the view that summary judgment must be denied, at least if the averments are "well-pleaded," and not suppositious, conclusory, or ultimate. See Frederick Hart & Co., Inc. v. Recordgraph Corp., 169 F.2d 580 (3d Cir. 1948); United States ex rel. Kolton v. Halpern, 260 F.2d 590 (3d Cir. 1958); United States ex rel. Nobles v. Ivey Bros. Constr. Co., Inc., 191 F.Supp. 383 (D.Del. 1961); Jamison v. Pennsylvania Salt Mfg. Co., 22 F.R.D. 238 (W.D.Pa. 1958); Bunny Bear, Inc. v. Dennis Mitchell Industries, 139 F.Supp. 542 (E.D.Pa. 1956); Levy v. Equitable Life Assur. Society, 18 F.R.D. 164 (E.D.Pa. 1955).

The very mission of the summary judgment procedure is to pierce the pleadings and to assess the proof in order to see whether there is a genuine need for trial. The Third Circuit doctrine, which permits the pleadings themselves to stand in the way of granting an otherwise justified summary judgment, is incompatible with the basic purpose of the rule. See 6 Moore's Federal Practice 2069 (2d ed. 1953); 3 Barron & Holtzoff, supra, §1235.1.

It is hoped that the amendment will contribute to the more effective utilization of the salutary device of summary judgment.

The amendment is not intended to derogate from the solemnity of the pleadings. Rather it recognizes that, despite the best efforts of counsel to make his pleadings accurate, they may be overwhelmingly contradicted by the proof available to his adversary.

Nor is the amendment designed to affect the ordinary standards applicable to the summary judgment motion. So, for example: Where an issue as to a material fact cannot be resolved without observation of the demeanor of witnesses in order to evaluate their credibility, summary judgment is not appropriate. Where the evidentiary matter in support of the motion does not establish the absence of a genuine issue, summary judgment must be denied even if no opposing evidentiary matter is presented. And summary judgment may be inappropriate where the party opposing it shows under subdivision (f) that he cannot at the time present facts essential to justify his opposition.

Notes of Advisory Committee on Rules—1987 Amendment

The amendments are technical. No substantive change is intended.

Committee Notes on Rules—2007 Amendment

The language of Rule 56 has been amended as part of the general restyling of the Civil Rules to make them more easily understood and to make style and terminology consistent throughout the rules. These changes are intended to be stylistic only.

Former Rule 56(a) and (b) referred to summary-judgment motions on or against a claim, counterclaim, or crossclaim, or to obtain a declaratory judgment. The list was incomplete. Rule 56 applies to third-party claimants, intervenors, claimants in interpleader, and others. Amended Rule 56(a) and (b) carry forward the present meaning by referring to a party claiming relief and a party against whom relief is sought.

Former Rule 56(c), (d), and (e) stated circumstances in which summary judgment "shall be rendered," the court "shall if practicable" ascertain facts existing without substantial controversy, and "if appropriate, shall" enter summary judgment. In each place "shall" is changed to "should." It is established that although there is no discretion to enter summary judgment when there is a genuine issue as to any material fact, there is discretion to deny summary judgment when it appears that there is no genuine issue as to any material fact. Kennedy v. Silas Mason Co., 334 U.S. 249, 256–257 (1948). Many lower court decisions are gathered in 10A Wright, Miller & Kane, Federal Practice & Procedure: Civil 3d, §2728. "Should" in amended Rule 56(c) recognizes that courts will seldom exercise the discretion to deny summary judgment when there is no genuine issue as to any material fact. Similarly sparing exercise of this discretion is appropriate under Rule 56(e)(2). Rule 56(d)(1), on the other hand, reflects the more open-ended discretion to decide whether it is practicable to determine what material facts are not genuinely at issue.

Former Rule 56(d) used a variety of different phrases to express the Rule 56(c) standard for summary judgment—that there is no genuine issue as to any material fact. Amended Rule 56(d) adopts terms directly parallel to Rule 56(c).

Committee Notes on Rules—2009 Amendment

The timing provisions for summary judgment are outmoded. They are consolidated and substantially revised in new subdivision (c)(1). The new rule allows a party to move for summary judgment at any time, even as early as the commencement of the action. If the motion seems premature both subdivision (c)(1) and Rule 6(b) allow the court to extend the time to respond. The rule does set a presumptive deadline at 30 days after the close of all discovery.

The presumptive timing rules are default provisions that may be altered by an order in the case or by local rule. Scheduling orders are likely to supersede the rule provisions in most cases, deferring summary-judgment motions until a stated time or establishing different deadlines. Scheduling orders tailored to the needs of the specific case, perhaps adjusted as it progresses, are likely to work better than default rules. A scheduling order may be adjusted to adopt the parties' agreement on timing, or may require that discovery and motions occur in stages—including separation of expert-witness discovery from other discovery.

Local rules may prove useful when local docket conditions or practices are incompatible with the general Rule 56 timing provisions.

If a motion for summary judgment is filed before a responsive pleading is due from a party affected by the motion, the time for responding to the motion is 21 days after the responsive pleading is due.

Committee Notes on Rules—2010 Amendment

Rule 56 is revised to improve the procedures for presenting and deciding summary-judgment motions and to make the procedures more consistent with those already used in many courts. The standard for granting summary judgment remains unchanged. The language of subdivision (a) continues to require that there be no genuine dispute as to any material fact and that the movant be entitled to judgment as a matter of law. The amendments will not affect continuing development of the decisional law construing and applying these phrases.

Subdivision (a). Subdivision (a) carries forward the summary-judgment standard expressed in former subdivision (c), changing only one word—genuine "issue" becomes genuine "dispute." "Dispute" better reflects the focus of a summary-judgment determination. As explained below, "shall" also is restored to the place it held from 1938 to 2007.

The first sentence is added to make clear at the beginning that summary judgment may be requested not only as to an entire case but also as to a claim, defense, or part of a claim or defense. The subdivision caption adopts the common phrase "partial summary judgment" to describe disposition of less than the whole action, whether or not the order grants all the relief requested by the motion.

"Shall" is restored to express the direction to grant summary judgment. The word "shall" in Rule 56 acquired significance over many decades of use. Rule 56 was amended in 2007 to replace "shall" with "should" as part of the Style Project, acting under a convention that prohibited any use of "shall." Comments on proposals to amend Rule 56, as published in 2008, have shown that neither of the choices available under the Style Project conventions—"must" or "should"—is suitable in light of the case law on whether a district court has discretion to deny summary judgment when there appears to be no genuine dispute as to any material fact. Compare Anderson v. Liberty Lobby, Inc., 477 U.S. 242, 255 (1986) ("Neither do we suggest that the trial courts should act other than with caution in granting summary judgment or that the trial court may not deny summary judgment in a case in which there is reason to believe that the better course would be to proceed to a full trial. Kennedy v. Silas Mason Co., 334 U.S. 249 * * * (1948))," with Celotex Corp. v. Catrett, 477 U.S. 317, 322 (1986) ("In our view, the plain language of Rule 56(c) mandates the entry of summary judgment, after adequate time for discovery and upon motion, against a party who fails to make a showing sufficient to establish the existence of an element essential to that party's case, and on which that party will bear the burden of proof at trial."). Eliminating "shall" created an unacceptable risk of changing the summary-judgment standard. Restoring "shall" avoids the unintended consequences of any other word.

Subdivision (a) also adds a new direction that the court should state on the record the reasons for granting or denying the motion. Most courts recognize this practice. Among other advantages, a statement of reasons can facilitate an appeal or subsequent trial-court proceedings. It is particularly important to state the reasons for granting summary judgment. The form and detail of the statement of reasons are left to the court's discretion.

The statement on denying summary judgment need not address every available reason. But identification of central issues may help the parties to focus further proceedings.

Subdivision (b). The timing provisions in former subdivisions (a) and (c) are superseded. Although the rule allows a motion for summary judgment to be filed at the commencement of an action, in many cases the motion will be premature until the nonmovant has had time to file a responsive pleading or other pretrial proceedings have been had. Scheduling orders or other pretrial orders can regulate timing to fit the needs of the case.

Subdivision (c). Subdivision (c) is new. It establishes a common procedure for several aspects of summary-judgment motions synthesized from similar elements developed in the cases or found in many local rules.

Subdivision (c)(1) addresses the ways to support an assertion that a fact can or cannot be genuinely disputed. It does not address the form for providing the required support. Different courts and judges have adopted different forms including, for example, directions that the support be included in the motion, made part of a separate statement of facts, interpolated in the body of a brief or memorandum, or provided in a separate statement of facts included in a brief or memorandum.

Subdivision (c)(1)(A) describes the familiar record materials commonly relied upon and requires that the movant cite the particular parts of the materials that support its fact positions. Materials that are not yet in the record—including materials referred to in an affidavit or declaration—must be placed in the record. Once materials are in the record, the court may, by order in the case, direct that the materials be gathered in an appendix, a party may voluntarily submit an appendix, or the parties may submit a joint appendix. The appendix procedure also may be established by local rule. Pointing to a specific location in an appendix satisfies the citation requirement. So too it may be convenient to direct that a party assist the court in locating materials buried in a voluminous record.

Subdivision (c)(1)(B) recognizes that a party need not always point to specific record materials. One party, without citing any other materials, may respond or reply that materials cited to dispute or support a fact do not establish the absence or presence of a genuine dispute. And a party who does not have the trial burden of production may rely on a showing that a party who does have the trial burden cannot produce admissible evidence to carry its burden as to the fact.

Subdivision (c)(2) provides that a party may object that material cited to support or dispute a fact cannot be presented in a form that would be admissible in evidence. The objection functions much as an objection at trial, adjusted for the pretrial setting. The burden is on the proponent to show that the material is admissible as presented or to explain the admissible form that is anticipated. There is no need to make a separate motion to strike. If the case goes to trial, failure to challenge admissibility at the summary-judgment stage does not forfeit the right to challenge admissibility at trial.

Subdivision (c)(3) reflects judicial opinions and local rules provisions stating that the court may decide a motion for summary judgment without undertaking an independent search of the record. Nonetheless, the rule also recognizes that a court may consider record materials not called to its attention by the parties.

Subdivision (c)(4) carries forward some of the provisions of former subdivision (e)(1). Other provisions are relocated or omitted. The requirement that a sworn or certified copy of a paper referred to in an affidavit or declaration be attached to the affidavit or declaration is omitted as unnecessary given the requirement in subdivision (c)(1)(A) that a statement or dispute of fact be supported by materials in the record.

A formal affidavit is no longer required. 28 U.S.C. §1746 allows a written unsworn declaration, certificate, verification, or statement subscribed in proper form as true under penalty of perjury to substitute for an affidavit.

Subdivision (d). Subdivision (d) carries forward without substantial change the provisions of former subdivision (f).

A party who seeks relief under subdivision (d) may seek an order deferring the time to respond to the summary-judgment motion.

Subdivision (e). Subdivision (e) addresses questions that arise when a party fails to support an assertion of fact or fails to properly address another party's assertion of fact as required by Rule 56(c). As explained below, summary judgment cannot be granted by default even if there is a complete failure to respond to the motion, much less when an attempted response fails to comply with Rule 56(c) requirements. Nor should it be denied by default even if the movant completely fails to reply to a nonmovant's response. Before deciding on other possible action, subdivision (e)(1) recognizes that the court may afford an opportunity to properly support or address the fact. In many circumstances this opportunity will be the court's preferred first step.

Subdivision (e)(2) authorizes the court to consider a fact as undisputed for purposes of the motion when response or reply requirements are not satisfied. This approach reflects the "deemed admitted" provisions in many local rules. The fact is considered undisputed only for purposes of the motion; if summary judgment is denied, a party who failed to make a proper Rule 56 response or reply remains free to contest the fact in further proceedings. And the court may choose not to consider the fact as undisputed, particularly if the court knows of record materials that show grounds for genuine dispute.

Subdivision (e)(3) recognizes that the court may grant summary judgment only if the motion and supporting materials—including the facts considered undisputed under subdivision (e)(2)—show that the movant is entitled to it. Considering some facts undisputed does not of itself allow summary judgment. If there is a proper response or reply as to some facts, the court cannot grant summary judgment without determining whether those facts can be genuinely disputed. Once the court has determined the set of facts—both those it has chosen to consider undisputed for want of a proper response or reply and any that cannot be genuinely disputed despite a procedurally proper response or reply—it must determine the legal consequences of these facts and permissible inferences from them.

Subdivision (e)(4) recognizes that still other orders may be appropriate. The choice among possible orders should be designed to encourage proper presentation of the record. Many courts take extra care with pro se litigants, advising them of the need to respond and the risk of losing by summary judgment if an adequate response is not filed. And the court may seek to reassure itself by some examination of the record before granting summary judgment against a pro se litigant.

Subdivision (f). Subdivision (f) brings into Rule 56 text a number of related procedures that have grown up in practice. After giving notice and a reasonable time to respond the court may grant summary judgment for the nonmoving party; grant a motion on legal or factual grounds not raised by the parties; or consider summary judgment on its own. In many cases it may prove useful first to invite a motion; the invited motion will automatically trigger the regular procedure of subdivision (c).

Subdivision (g). Subdivision (g) applies when the court does not grant all the relief requested by a motion for summary judgment. It becomes relevant only after the court has applied the summary-judgment standard carried forward in subdivision (a) to each claim, defense, or part of a claim or defense, identified by the motion. Once that duty is discharged, the court may decide whether to apply the summary-judgment standard to dispose of a material fact that is not genuinely in dispute. The court must take care that this determination does not interfere with a party's ability to accept a fact for purposes of the motion only. A nonmovant, for example, may feel confident that a genuine dispute as to one or a few facts will defeat the motion, and prefer to avoid the cost of detailed response to all facts stated by the movant. This position should be available without running the risk that the fact will be taken as established under subdivision (g) or otherwise found to have been accepted for other purposes.

If it is readily apparent that the court cannot grant all the relief requested by the motion, it may properly decide that the cost of determining whether some potential fact disputes may be eliminated by summary disposition is greater than the cost of resolving those disputes by other means, including trial. Even if the court believes that a fact is not genuinely in dispute it may refrain from ordering that the fact be treated as established. The court may conclude that it is better to leave open for trial facts and issues that may be better illuminated by the trial of related facts that must be tried in any event.

Subdivision (h). Subdivision (h) carries forward former subdivision (g) with three changes. Sanctions are made discretionary, not mandatory, reflecting the experience that courts seldom invoke the independent Rule 56 authority to impose sanctions. See Cecil & Cort, Federal Judicial Center Memorandum on Federal Rule of Civil Procedure 56(g) Motions for Sanctions (April 2, 2007). In addition, the rule text is expanded to recognize the need to provide notice and a reasonable time to respond. Finally, authority to impose other appropriate sanctions also is recognized.

Changes Made After Publication and Comment.

Subdivision (a). "[S]hould grant" was changed to "shall grant."

"[T]he movant shows that" was added.

Language about identifying the claim or defense was moved up from subdivision (c)(1) as published.

Subdivision (b). The specifications of times to respond and to reply were deleted.

Words referring to an order "in the case" were deleted.

Subdivision (c). The detailed "point-counterpoint" provisions published as subdivision (c)(1) and (2) were deleted.

The requirement that the court give notice before granting summary judgment on the basis of record materials not cited by the parties was deleted.

The provision that a party may accept or dispute a fact for purposes of the motion only was deleted.

Subdivision (e). The language was revised to reflect elimination of the point-counterpoint procedure from subdivision (c). The new language reaches failure to properly support an assertion of fact in a motion.

Subdivision (f). The provision requiring notice before denying summary judgment on grounds not raised by a party was deleted.

Subdivision (h). Recognition of the authority to impose other appropriate sanctions was added.

Other changes. Many style changes were made to express more clearly the intended meaning of the published proposal.

Rule 57. Declaratory Judgment

These rules govern the procedure for obtaining a declaratory judgment under 28 U.S.C. §2201. Rules 38 and 39 govern a demand for a jury trial. The existence of another adequate remedy does not preclude a declaratory judgment that is otherwise appropriate. The court may order a speedy hearing of a declaratory-judgment action.

———

(As amended Dec. 29, 1948, eff. Oct. 20, 1949; Apr. 30, 2007, eff. Dec. 1, 2007.)

Notes of Advisory Committee on Rules—1937

The fact that a declaratory judgment may be granted "whether or not further relief is or could be prayed" indicates that declaratory relief is alternative or cumulative and not exclusive or extraordinary. A declaratory judgment is appropriate when it will "terminate the controversy" giving rise to the proceeding. Inasmuch as it often involves only an issue of law on undisputed or relatively undisputed facts, it operates frequently as a summary proceeding, justifying docketing the case for early hearing as on a motion, as provided for in California (Code Civ.Proc. (Deering, 1937) §1062a), Michigan (3 Comp.Laws (1929) §13904), and Kentucky (Codes (Carroll, 1932) Civ.Pract. §639a–3).

The "controversy" must necessarily be "of a justiciable nature, thus excluding an advisory decree upon a hypothetical state of facts." Ashwander v. Tennessee Valley Authority, 297 U.S. 288, 325, 56 S.Ct. 466, 473, 80 L.Ed. 688, 699 (1936). The existence or nonexistence of any right, duty, power, liability, privilege, disability, or immunity or of any fact upon which such legal relations depend, or of a status, may be declared. The petitioner must have a practical interest in the declaration sought and all parties having an interest therein or adversely affected must be made parties or be cited. A declaration may not be rendered if a special statutory proceeding has been provided for the adjudication of some special type of case, but general ordinary or extraordinary legal remedies, whether regulated by statute or not, are not deemed special statutory proceedings.

When declaratory relief will not be effective in settling the controversy, the court may decline to grant it. But the fact that another remedy would be equally effective affords no ground for declining declaratory relief. The demand for relief shall state with precision the declaratory judgment desired, to which may be joined a demand for coercive relief, cumulatively or in the alternative; but when coercive relief only is sought but is deemed ungrantable or inappropriate, the court may sua sponte, if it serves a useful purpose, grant instead a declaration of rights. Hasselbring v. Koepke, 263 Mich. 466, 248 N.W. 869, 93 A.L.R. 1170 (1933). Written instruments, including ordinances and statutes, may be construed before or after breach at the petition of a properly interested party, process being served on the private parties or public officials interested. In other respects the Uniform Declaratory Judgment Act affords a guide to the scope and function of the Federal act. Compare Aetna Life Insurance Co. v. Haworth, 300 U.S. 227, 57 S.Ct. 461 (1937); Nashville, Chattanooga & St. Louis Ry. v. Wallace, 288 U.S. 249 (1933); Gully, Tax Collector v. Interstate Natural Gas Co., 82 F.(2d) 145 (C.C.A.5th, 1936); Ohio Casualty Ins. Co. v. Plummer, 13 F.Supp. 169 (S.D.Tex., 1935); Borchard, Declaratory Judgments (1934), passim.

Notes of Advisory Committee on Rules—1948 Amendment

The amendment substitutes the present statutory reference.

Committee Notes on Rules—2007 Amendment

The language of Rule 57 has been amended as part of the general restyling of the Civil Rules to make them more easily understood and to make style and terminology consistent throughout the rules. These changes are intended to be stylistic only.

Rule 58. Entering Judgment

(a) Separate Document. Every judgment and amended judgment must be set out in a separate document, but a separate document is not required for an order disposing of a motion:

(1) for judgment under Rule 50(b);

(2) to amend or make additional findings under Rule 52(b);

(3) for attorney's fees under Rule 54;

(4) for a new trial, or to alter or amend the judgment, under Rule 59; or

(5) for relief under Rule 60.

(b) Entering Judgment.

(1) Without the Court's Direction. Subject to Rule 54(b) and unless the court orders otherwise, the clerk must, without awaiting the court's direction, promptly prepare, sign, and enter the judgment when:

(A) the jury returns a general verdict;

(B) the court awards only costs or a sum certain; or

(C) the court denies all relief.

(2) Court's Approval Required. Subject to Rule 54(b), the court must promptly approve the form of the judgment, which the clerk must promptly enter, when:

(A) the jury returns a special verdict or a general verdict with answers to written questions; or

(B) the court grants other relief not described in this subdivision (b).

(c) Time of Entry. For purposes of these rules, judgment is entered at the following times:

(1) if a separate document is not required, when the judgment is entered in the civil docket under Rule 79(a); or

(2) if a separate document is required, when the judgment is entered in the civil docket under Rule 79(a) and the earlier of these events occurs:

(A) it is set out in a separate document; or

(B) 150 days have run from the entry in the civil docket.

(d) Request for Entry. A party may request that judgment be set out in a separate document as required by Rule 58(a).

(e) Cost or Fee Awards. Ordinarily, the entry of judgment may not be delayed, nor the time for appeal extended, in order to tax costs or award fees. But if a timely motion for attorney's fees is made under Rule 54(d)(2), the court may act before a notice of appeal has been filed and become effective to order that the motion have the same effect under Federal Rule of Appellate Procedure 4(a)(4) as a timely motion under Rule 59.

(As amended Dec. 27, 1946, eff. Mar. 19, 1948; Jan. 21, 1963, eff. July 1, 1963; Apr. 22, 1993, eff. Dec. 1, 1993; Apr. 29, 2002, eff. Dec. 1, 2002; Apr. 30, 2007, eff. Dec. 1, 2007.)

Notes of Advisory Committee on Rules—1937

See Wis.Stat. (1935) §270.31 (judgment entered forthwith on verdict of jury unless otherwise ordered), §270.65 (where trial is by the court, entered by direction of the court), §270.63 (entered by clerk on judgment on admitted claim for money). Compare 1 Idaho Code Ann. (1932) §7–1101, and 4 Mont.Rev.Codes Ann. (1935) §9403, which provides that judgment in jury cases be entered by clerk within 24 hours after verdict unless court otherwise directs. Conn. Practice Book (1934) §200, provides that all judgments shall be entered within one week after rendition. In some States such as Washington, 2 Rev.Stat.Ann. (Remington, 1932) §431, in jury cases the judgment is entered two days after the return of verdict to give time for making motion for new trial; §435 (ibid.), provides that all judgments shall be entered by the clerk, subject to the court's direction.

Notes of Advisory Committee on Rules—1946 Amendment

The reference to Rule 54(b) is made necessary by the amendment of that rule.

Two changes have been made in Rule 58 in order to clarify the practice. The substitution of the more inclusive phrase "all relief be denied" for the words "there be no recovery", makes it clear that the clerk shall enter the judgment forthwith in the situations specified without awaiting the filing of a formal judgment approved by the court. The phrase "all relief be denied" covers cases such as the denial of a bankrupt's discharge and similar situations where the relief sought is refused but there is literally no denial of a "recovery".

The addition of the last sentence in the rule emphasizes that judgments are to be entered promptly by the clerk without waiting for the taxing of costs. Certain district court rules, for example, Civil Rule 22 of the Southern District of New York—until its annulment Oct. 1, 1945, for conflict with this rule—and the like rule of the Eastern District of New York, are expressly in conflict with this provision, although the federal law is of long standing and well settled. Fowler v. Hamill (1891) 139 U.S. 549; Craig v. The Hartford (C.C.Cal. 1856) Fed.Case No. 3,333; Tuttle v. Claflin (C.C.A.2d, 1895) 60 Fed. 7, cert. den. (1897) 166 U.S. 721; Prescott & A. C. Ry. Co. v. Atchison, T. & S. F. R. Co. (C.C.A.2d, 1897) 84 Fed. 213; Stallo v. Wagner (C.C.A.2d, 1917) 245 Fed. 636, 639–40; Brown v. Parker (C.C.A.8th, 1899) 97 Fed. 446; Allis-Chalmers v. United States (C.C.A.7th, 1908) 162 Fed. 679. And this applies even though state law is to the contrary. United States v. Nordbye (C.C.A.8th, 1935) 75 F.(2d) 744, 746, cert. den. (1935) 296 U.S. 572. Inasmuch as it has been held that failure of the clerk thus enter judgment is a "misprision" "not to be excused" (The Washington (C.C.A.2d, 1926) 16 F.(2d) 206), such a district court rule may have serious consequences for a district court clerk. Rules of this sort also provide for delay in entry of the judgment contrary to Rule 58. See Commissioner of Internal Revenue v. Bedford's Estate (1945) 325 U.S. 283.

Notes of Advisory Committee on Rules—1963 Amendment

Under the present rule a distinction has sometimes been made between judgments on general jury verdicts, on the one hand, and, on the other, judgments upon decisions of the court that a party shall recover only money or costs or that all relief shall be denied. In the first situation, it is clear that the clerk should enter the judgment without awaiting a direction by the court unless the court otherwise orders. In the second situation it was intended that the clerk should similarly enter the judgment forthwith upon the court's decision; but because of the separate listing in the rule, and the use of the phrase "upon receipt . . . of the direction," the rule has sometimes been interpreted as requiring the clerk to await a separate direction of the court. All these judgments are usually uncomplicated, and should be handled in the same way. The amended rule accordingly deals with them as a single group in clause (1) (substituting the expression "only a sum certain" for the present expression "only money"), and requires the clerk to prepare, sign, and enter them forthwith, without awaiting court direction, unless the court makes a contrary order. (The clerk's duty is ministerial and may be performed by a deputy clerk in the name of the clerk. See 28 U.S.C. §956; cf. Gilbertson v. United States, 168 Fed. 672 (7th Cir. 1909).) The more complicated judgments described in clause (2) must be approved by the court before they are entered.

Rule 58 is designed to encourage all reasonable speed in formulating and entering the judgment when the case has been decided. Participation by the attorneys through the submission of forms of judgment involves needless expenditure of time and effort and promotes delay, except in special cases where counsel's assistance can be of real value. See Matteson v. United States, 240 F.2d 517, 518–19 (2d Cir. 1956). Accordingly, the amended rule provides that attorneys shall not submit forms of judgment unless directed to do so by the court. This applies to the judgments mentioned in clause (2) as well as clause (1).

Hitherto some difficulty has arisen, chiefly where the court has written an opinion or memorandum containing some apparently directive or dispositive words, e.g., "the plaintiff's motion [for summary judgment] is granted," see United States v. F. & M. Schaefer Brewing Co., 356 U.S. 227, 229, 78 S.Ct. 674, 2 L.Ed.2d 721 (1958). Clerks on occasion have viewed these opinions or memoranda as being in themselves a sufficient basis for entering judgment in the civil docket as provided by Rule 79(a). However, where the opinion or memorandum has not contained all the elements of a judgment, or where the judge has later signed a formal judgment, it has become a matter of doubt whether the purported entry of judgment was effective, starting the time running for postverdict motions and for the purpose of appeal. See id.; and compare Blanchard v. Commonwealth Oil Co., 294 F.2d 834 (5th Cir. 1961); United States v. Higginson, 238 F.2d 439 (1st Cir. 1956); Danzig v. Virgin Isle Hotel, Inc., 278 F.2d 580 (3d Cir. 1960); Sears v. Austin, 282 F.2d 340 (9th Cir. 1960), with Matteson v. United States, supra; Erstling v. Southern Bell Tel. & Tel. Co., 255 F.2d 93 (5th Cir. 1958); Barta v. Oglala Sioux Tribe, 259 F.2d 553 (8th Cir. 1958), cert. denied, 358 U.S. 932, 79 S.Ct. 320, 3 L.Ed.2d 304 (1959); Beacon Fed. S. & L. Assn. v. Federal Home L. Bank Bd., 266 F.2d 246 (7th Cir.), cert. denied, 361 U.S. 823, 80 S.Ct. 70, 4 L.Ed.2d 67 (1959); Ram v. Paramount Film D. Corp., 278 F.2d 191 (4th Cir. 1960).

The amended rule eliminates these uncertainties by requiring that there be a judgment set out on a separate document—distinct from any opinion or memorandum—which provides the basis for the entry of judgment. That judgments shall be on separate documents is also indicated in Rule 79(b); and see General Rule 10 of the U.S. District Courts for the Eastern and Southern Districts of New York; Ram v. Paramount Film D. Corp., supra, at 194.

See the amendment of Rule 79(a) and the new specimen forms of judgment, Forms 31 and 32.

See also Rule 55(b)(1) and (2) covering the subject of judgments by default.

Notes of Advisory Committee on Rules—1993 Amendment

Ordinarily the pendency or post-judgment filing of a claim for attorney's fees will not affect the time for appeal from the underlying judgment. See Budinich v. Becton Dickinson & Co., 486 U.S. 196 (1988). Particularly if the claim for fees involves substantial issues or is likely to be affected by the appellate decision, the district court may prefer to defer consideration of the claim for fees until after the appeal is resolved. However, in many cases it may be more efficient to decide fee questions before an appeal is taken so that appeals relating to the fee award can be heard at the same time as appeals relating to the merits of the case. This revision permits, but does not require, the court to delay the finality of the judgment for appellate purposes under revised Fed. R. App. P. 4(a) until the fee dispute is decided. To accomplish this result requires entry of an order by the district court before the time a notice of appeal becomes effective for appellate purposes. If the order is entered, the motion for attorney's fees is treated in the same manner as a timely motion under Rule 59.

Committee Notes on Rules—2002 Amendment

Rule 58 has provided that a judgment is effective only when set forth on a separate document and entered as provided in Rule 79(a). This simple separate document requirement has been ignored in many cases. The result of failure to enter judgment on a separate document is that the time for making motions under Rules 50, 52, 54(d)(2)(B), 59, and some motions under Rule 60, never begins to run. The time to appeal under Appellate Rule 4(a) also does not begin to run. There have been few visible problems with respect to Rule 50, 52, 54(d)(2)(B), 59, or 60 motions, but there have been many and horridly confused problems under Appellate Rule 4(a). These amendments are designed to work in conjunction with Appellate Rule 4(a) to ensure that appeal time does not linger on indefinitely, and to maintain the integration of the time periods set for Rules 50, 52, 54(d)(2)(B), 59, and 60 with Appellate Rule 4(a).

Rule 58(a) preserves the core of the present separate document requirement, both for the initial judgment and for any amended judgment. No attempt is made to sort through the confusion that some courts have found in addressing the elements of a separate document. It is easy to prepare a separate document that recites the terms of the judgment without offering additional explanation or citation of authority. Forms 31 and 32 provide examples.

Rule 58 is amended, however, to address a problem that arises under Appellate Rule 4(a). Some courts treat such orders as those that deny a motion for new trial as a "judgment," so that appeal time does not start to run until the order is entered on a separate document. Without attempting to address the question whether such orders are appealable, and thus judgments as defined by Rule 54(a), the amendment provides that entry on a separate document is not required for an order disposing of the motions listed in Appellate Rule 4(a). The enumeration of motions drawn from the Appellate Rule 4(a) list is generalized by omitting details that are important for appeal time purposes but that would unnecessarily complicate the separate document requirement. As one example, it is not required that any of the enumerated motions be timely. Many of the enumerated motions are frequently made before judgment is entered. The exemption of the order disposing of the motion does not excuse the obligation to set forth the judgment itself on a separate document. And if disposition of the motion results in an amended judgment, the amended judgment must be set forth on a separate document.

Rule 58(b) discards the attempt to define the time when a judgment becomes "effective." Taken in conjunction with the Rule 54(a) definition of a judgment to include "any order from which an appeal lies," the former Rule 58 definition of effectiveness could cause strange difficulties in implementing pretrial orders that are appealable under interlocutory appeal provisions or under expansive theories of finality. Rule 58(b) replaces the definition of effectiveness with a new provision that defines the time when judgment is entered. If judgment is promptly set forth on a separate document, as should be done when required by Rule 58(a)(1), the new provision will not change the effect of Rule 58. But in the cases in which court and clerk fail to comply with this simple requirement, the motion time periods set by Rules 50, 52, 54, 59, and 60 begin to run after expiration of 150 days from entry of the judgment in the civil docket as required by Rule 79(a).

A companion amendment of Appellate Rule 4(a)(7) integrates these changes with the time to appeal.

The new all-purpose definition of the entry of judgment must be applied with common sense to other questions that may turn on the time when judgment is entered. If the 150-day provision in Rule 58(b)(2)(B)—designed to integrate the time for post-judgment motions with appeal time—serves no purpose, or would defeat the purpose of another rule, it should be disregarded. In theory, for example, the separate document requirement continues to apply to an interlocutory order that is appealable as a final decision under collateral-order doctrine. Appealability under collateral-order doctrine should not be complicated by failure to enter the order as a judgment on a separate document—there is little reason to force trial judges to speculate about the potential appealability of every order, and there is no means to ensure that the trial judge will always reach the same conclusion as the court of appeals. Appeal time should start to run when the collateral order is entered without regard to creation of a separate document and without awaiting expiration of the 150 days provided by Rule 58(b)(2). Drastic surgery on Rules 54(a) and 58 would be required to address this and related issues, however, and it is better to leave this conundrum to the pragmatic disregard that seems its present fate. The present amendments do not seem to make matters worse, apart from one false appearance. If a pretrial order is set forth on a separate document that meets the requirements of Rule 58(b), the time to move for reconsideration seems to begin to run, perhaps years before final judgment. And even if there is no separate document, the time to move for reconsideration seems to begin 150 days after entry in the civil docket. This apparent problem is resolved by Rule 54(b), which expressly permits revision of all orders not made final under Rule 54(b) "at any time before the entry of judgment adjudicating all the claims and the rights and liabilities of all the parties."

New Rule 58(d) replaces the provision that attorneys shall not submit forms of judgment except on direction of the court. This provision was added to Rule 58 to avoid the delays that were frequently encountered by the former practice of directing the attorneys for the prevailing party to prepare a form of judgment, and also to avoid the occasionally inept drafting that resulted from attorney-prepared judgments. See 11 Wright, Miller & Kane, Federal Practice & Procedure: Civil 2d, §2786. The express direction in Rule 58(a)(2) for prompt action by the clerk, and by the court if court action is required, addresses this concern. The new provision allowing any party to move for entry of judgment on a separate document will protect all needs for prompt commencement of the periods for motions, appeals, and execution or other enforcement.

Changes Made After Publication and Comments. Minor style changes were made. The definition of the time of entering judgment in Rule 58(b) was extended to reach all Civil Rules, not only the Rules described in the published version—Rules 50, 52, 54(d)(2)(B), 59, 60, and 62. And the time of entry was extended from 60 days to 150 days after entry in the civil docket without a required separate document.

Committee Notes on Rules—2007 Amendment

The language of Rule 58 has been amended as part of the general restyling of the Civil Rules to make them more easily understood and to make style and terminology consistent throughout the rules. These changes are intended to be stylistic only.

Rule 59. New Trial; Altering or Amending a Judgment

(a) In General.

(1) Grounds for New Trial. The court may, on motion, grant a new trial on all or some of the issues—and to any party—as follows:

(A) after a jury trial, for any reason for which a new trial has heretofore been granted in an action at law in federal court; or

(B) after a nonjury trial, for any reason for which a rehearing has heretofore been granted in a suit in equity in federal court.

(2) Further Action After a Nonjury Trial. After a nonjury trial, the court may, on motion for a new trial, open the judgment if one has been entered, take additional testimony, amend findings of fact and conclusions of law or make new ones, and direct the entry of a new judgment.

(b) Time to File a Motion for a New Trial. A motion for a new trial must be filed no later than 28 days after the entry of judgment.

(c) Time to Serve Affidavits. When a motion for a new trial is based on affidavits, they must be filed with the motion. The opposing party has 14 days after being served to file opposing affidavits. The court may permit reply affidavits.

(d) New Trial on the Court's Initiative or for Reasons Not in the Motion. No later than 28 days after the entry of judgment, the court, on its own, may order a new trial for any reason that would justify granting one on a party's motion. After giving the parties notice and an opportunity to be heard, the court may grant a timely motion for a new trial for a reason not stated in the motion. In either event, the court must specify the reasons in its order.

(e) Motion to Alter or Amend a Judgment. A motion to alter or amend a judgment must be filed no later than 28 days after the entry of the judgment.

(As amended Dec. 27, 1946, eff. Mar. 19, 1948; Feb. 28, 1966, eff. July 1, 1966; Apr. 27, 1995, eff. Dec. 1, 1995; Apr. 30, 2007, eff. Dec. 1, 2007; Mar. 26, 2009, eff. Dec. 1, 2009.)

Notes of Advisory Committee on Rules—1937

This rule represents an amalgamation of the petition for rehearing of [former] Equity Rule 69 (Petition for Rehearing) and the motion for new trial of U.S.C., Title 28, §391 [see 2111] (New trials; harmless error), made in the light of the experience and provision of the code States. Compare Calif.Code Civ.Proc. (Deering, 1937) §§656–663a, U.S.C., Title 28, §391 [see 2111] (New trials; harmless error) is thus substantially continued in this rule. U.S.C., Title 28, [former] §840 (Executions; stay on conditions) is modified insofar as it contains time provisions inconsistent with Subdivision (b). For the effect of the motion for new trial upon the time for taking an appeal see Morse v. United States, 270 U.S. 151 (1926); Aspen Mining and Smelting Co. v. Billings, 150 U.S. 31 (1893).

For partial new trials which are permissible under Subdivision (a), see Gasoline Products Co., Inc., v. Champlin Refining Co., 283 U.S. 494 (1931); Schuerholz v. Roach, 58 F.(2d) 32 (C.C.A.4th, 1932); Simmons v. Fish, 210 Mass. 563, 97 N.E. 102, Ann.Cas.1912D, 588 (1912) (sustaining and recommending the practice and citing Federal cases and cases in accord from about sixteen States and contra from three States). The procedure in several States provides specifically for partial new trials. Ariz.Rev.Code Ann. (Struckmeyer, 1928) §3852; Calif.Code Civ.Proc. (Deering, 1937) §§657, 662; Ill.Rev.Stat. (1937) ch. 110, §216 (par. (f)); Md.Ann.Code (Bagby, 1924) Art. 5, §§25, 26; Mich.Court Rules Ann. (Searl, 1933) Rule 47, §2; Miss.Sup.Ct. Rule 12, 161 Miss. 903, 905 (1931); N.J.Sup.Ct. Rules 131, 132, 147, 2 N.J.Misc. 1197, 1246–1251, 1255 (1924); 2 N.D.Comp.Laws Ann. (1913), §7844, as amended by N.D.Laws 1927, ch. 214.

Notes of Advisory Committee on Rules—1946 Amendment

Subdivision (b). With the time for appeal to a circuit court of appeals reduced in general to 30 days by the proposed amendment of Rule 73(a), the utility of the original "except" clause, which permits a motion for a new trial on the ground of newly discovered evidence to be made before the expiration of the time for appeal, would have been seriously restricted. It was thought advisable, therefore, to take care of this matter in another way. By amendment of Rule 60(b), newly discovered evidence is made the basis for relief from a judgment, and the maximum time limit has been extended to one year. Accordingly the amendment of Rule 59(b) eliminates the "except" clause and its specific treatment of newly discovered evidence as a ground for a motion for new trial. This ground remains, however, as a basis for a motion for new trial served not later than 10 days after the entry of judgment. See also Rule 60(b).

As to the effect of a motion under subdivision (b) upon the running of appeal time, see amended Rule 73(a) and Note.

Subdivision (e). This subdivision has been added to care for a situation such as that arising in Boaz v. Mutual Life Ins. Co. of New York (C.C.A.8th, 1944) 146 F.(2d) 321, and makes clear that the district court possesses the power asserted in that case to alter or amend a judgment after its entry. The subdivision deals only with alteration or amendment of the original judgment in a case and does not relate to a judgment upon motion as provided in Rule 50(b). As to the effect of a motion under subdivision (e) upon the running of appeal time, see amended Rule 73(a) and Note.

The title of Rule 59 has been expanded to indicate the inclusion of this subdivision.

Notes of Advisory Committee on Rules—1966 Amendment

By narrow interpretation of Rule 59(b) and (d), it has been held that the trial court is without power to grant a motion for a new trial, timely served, by an order made more than 10 days after the entry of judgment, based upon a ground not stated in the motion but perceived and relied on by the trial court sua sponte.

Freid v. McGrath, 133 F.2d 350 (D.C.Cir. 1942); National Farmers Union Auto. & Cas. Co. v. Wood, 207 F.2d 659 (10th Cir. 1953); Bailey v. Slentz, 189 F.2d 406 (10th Cir. 1951); Marshall's U.S. Auto Supply, Inc. v. Cashman, 111 F.2d 140 (10th Cir. 1940), cert. denied, 311 U.S. 667 (1940); but see Steinberg v. Indemnity Ins. Co., 36 F.R.D. 253 (E.D.La. 1964).

The result is undesirable. Just as the court has power under Rule 59(d) to grant a new trial of its own initiative within the 10 days, so it should have power, when an effective new trial motion has been made and is pending, to decide it on grounds thought meritorious by the court although not advanced in the motion. The second sentence added by amendment to Rule 59(d) confirms the court's power in the latter situation, with provision that the parties be afforded a hearing before the power is exercised. See 6 Moore's Federal Practice, par. 59.09[2] (2d ed. 1953).

In considering whether a given ground has or has not been advanced in the motion made by the party, it should be borne in mind that the particularity called for in stating the grounds for a new trial motion is the same as that required for all motions by Rule 7(b)(1). The latter rule does not require ritualistic detail but rather a fair indication to court and counsel of the substance of the grounds relied on. See Lebeck v. William A. Jarvis Co., 250 F.2d 285 (3d Cir. 1957); Tsai v. Rosenthal, 297 F.2d 614 (8th Cir. 1961); General Motors Corp. v. Perry, 303 F.2d 544 (7th Cir. 1962); cf. Grimm v. California Spray-Chemical Corp., 264 F.2d 145 (9th Cir. 1959); Cooper v. Midwest Feed Products Co., 271 F.2d 177 (8th Cir. 1959).

Notes of Advisory Committee on Rules—1995 Amendment

The only change, other than stylistic, intended by this revision is to add explicit time limits for filing motions for a new trial, motions to alter or amend a judgment, and affidavits opposing a new trial motion. Previously, there was an inconsistency in the wording of Rules 50, 52, and 59 with respect to whether certain post-judgment motions had to be filed, or merely served, during the prescribed period. This inconsistency caused special problems when motions for a new trial were joined with other post-judgment motions. These motions affect the finality of the judgment, a matter often of importance to third persons as well as the parties and the court. The Committee believes that each of these rules should be revised to require filing before end of the 10-day period. Filing is an event that can be determined with certainty from court records. The phrase "no later than" is used—rather than "within"—to include post-judgment motions that sometimes are filed before actual entry of the judgment by the clerk. It should be noted that under Rule 5 the motions when filed are to contain a certificate of service on other parties. It also should be noted that under Rule 6(a) Saturdays, Sundays, and legal holidays are excluded in measuring the 10-day period, but that Bankruptcy Rule 9006(a) excludes intermediate Saturdays, Sundays, and legal holidays only in computing periods less than 8 days.

Committee Notes on Rules—2007 Amendment

The language of Rule 59 has been amended as part of the general restyling of the Civil Rules to make them more easily understood and to make style and terminology consistent throughout the rules. These changes are intended to be stylistic only.

Committee Notes on Rules—2009 Amendment

Former Rules 50, 52, and 59 adopted 10-day periods for their respective post-judgment motions. Rule 6(b) prohibits any expansion of those periods. Experience has proved that in many cases it is not possible to prepare a satisfactory post-judgment motion in 10 days, even under the former rule that excluded intermediate Saturdays, Sundays, and legal holidays. These time periods are particularly sensitive because Appellate Rule 4 integrates the time to appeal with a timely motion under these rules. Rather than introduce the prospect of uncertainty in appeal time by amending Rule 6(b) to permit additional time, the former 10-day periods are expanded to 28 days. Rule 6(b) continues to prohibit expansion of the 28-day period.

Former Rule 59(c) set a 10-day period after being served with a motion for new trial to file opposing affidavits. It also provided that the period could be extended for up to 20 days for good cause or by stipulation. The apparent 20-day limit on extending the time to file opposing affidavits seemed to conflict with the Rule 6(b) authority to extend time without any specific limit. This tension between the two rules may have been inadvertent. It is resolved by deleting the former Rule 59(c) limit. Rule 6(b) governs. The underlying 10-day period was extended to 14 days to reflect the change in the Rule 6(a) method for computing periods of less than 11 days.

Changes Made after Publication and Comment. The 30-day period proposed in the August 2007 publication is shortened to 28 days.

Rule 60. Relief from a Judgment or Order

(a) Corrections Based on Clerical Mistakes; Oversights and Omissions. The court may correct a clerical mistake or a mistake arising from oversight or omission whenever one is found in a judgment, order, or other part of the record. The court may do so on motion or on its own, with or without notice. But after an appeal has been docketed in the appellate court and while it is pending, such a mistake may be corrected only with the appellate court's leave.

(b) Grounds for Relief from a Final Judgment, Order, or Proceeding. On motion and just terms, the court may relieve a party or its legal representative from a final judgment, order, or proceeding for the following reasons:

(1) mistake, inadvertence, surprise, or excusable neglect;

(2) newly discovered evidence that, with reasonable diligence, could not have been discovered in time to move for a new trial under Rule 59(b);

(3) fraud (whether previously called intrinsic or extrinsic), misrepresentation, or misconduct by an opposing party;

(4) the judgment is void;

(5) the judgment has been satisfied, released, or discharged; it is based on an earlier judgment that has been reversed or vacated; or applying it prospectively is no longer equitable; or

(6) any other reason that justifies relief.

(c) Timing and Effect of the Motion.

(1) Timing. A motion under Rule 60(b) must be made within a reasonable time—and for reasons (1), (2), and (3) no more than a year after the entry of the judgment or order or the date of the proceeding.

(2) Effect on Finality. The motion does not affect the judgment's finality or suspend its operation.

(d) Other Powers to Grant Relief. This rule does not limit a court's power to:

(1) entertain an independent action to relieve a party from a judgment, order, or proceeding;

(2) grant relief under 28 U.S.C. §1655 to a defendant who was not personally notified of the action; or

(3) set aside a judgment for fraud on the court.

(e) Bills and Writs Abolished. The following are abolished: bills of review, bills in the nature of bills of review, and writs of coram nobis, coram vobis, and audita querela.

(As amended Dec. 27, 1946, eff. Mar. 19, 1948; Dec. 29, 1948, eff. Oct. 20, 1949; Mar. 2, 1987, eff. Aug. 1, 1987; Apr. 30, 2007, eff. Dec. 1, 2007.)

Notes of Advisory Committee on Rules—1937

Note to Subdivision (a). See [former] Equity Rule 72 (Correction of Clerical Mistakes in Orders and Decrees); Mich.Court Rules Ann. (Searl, 1933) Rule 48, §3; 2 Wash.Rev.Stat.Ann. (Remington, 1932) §464(3); Wyo.Rev.Stat.Ann. (Courtright, 1931) §89–2301(3). For an example of a very liberal provision for the correction of clerical errors and for amendment after judgment, see Va.Code Ann. (Michie, 1936) §§6329, 6333.

Note to Subdivision (b). Application to the court under this subdivision does not extend the time for taking an appeal, as distinguished from the motion for new trial. This section is based upon Calif.Code Civ.Proc. (Deering, 1937) §473. See also N.Y.C.P.A. (1937) §108; 2 Minn.Stat. (Mason, 1927) §9283.

For the independent action to relieve against mistake, etc., see Dobie, Federal Procedure, pages 760–765, compare 639; and Simkins, Federal Practice, ch. CXXI (pp. 820–830) and ch. CXXII (pp. 831–834), compare §214.

Notes of Advisory Committee on Rules—1946 Amendment

Subdivision (a). The amendment incorporates the view expressed in Perlman v. 322 West Seventy-Second Street Co., Inc. (C.C.A.2d, 1942) 127 F.(2d) 716; 3 Moore's Federal Practice (1938) 3276, and further permits correction after docketing, with leave of the appellate court. Some courts have thought that upon the taking of an appeal the district court lost its power to act. See Schram v. Safety Investment Co. (E.D.Mich. 1942) 45 F.Supp. 636; also Miller v. United States (C.C.A.7th, 1940) 114 F.(2d) 267.

Subdivision (b). When promulgated, the rules contained a number of provisions, including those found in Rule 60(b), describing the practice by a motion to obtain relief from judgments, and these rules, coupled with the reservation in Rule 60(b) of the right to entertain a new action to relieve a party from a judgment, were generally supposed to cover the field. Since the rules have been in force, decisions have been rendered that the use of bills of review, coram nobis, or audita querela, to obtain relief from final judgments is still proper, and that various remedies of this kind still exist although they are not mentioned in the rules and the practice is not prescribed in the rules. It is obvious that the rules should be complete in this respect and define the practice with respect to any existing rights or remedies to obtain relief from final judgments. For extended discussion of the old common law writs and equitable remedies, the interpretation of Rule 60, and proposals for change, see Moore and Rogers, Federal Relief from Civil Judgments (1946) 55 Yale L.J. 623. See also 3 Moore's Federal Practice (1938) 3254 et seq.; Commentary, Effect of Rule 60b on Other Methods of Relief From Judgment (1941) 4 Fed.Rules Serv. 942, 945; Wallace v. United States (C.C.A.2d, 1944) 142 F.(2d) 240, cert. den. (1944) 323 U.S. 712.

The reconstruction of Rule 60(b) has for one of its purposes a clarification of this situation. Two types of procedure to obtain relief from judgments are specified in the rules as it is proposed to amend them. One procedure is by motion in the court and in the action in which the judgment was rendered. The other procedure is by a new or independent action to obtain relief from a judgment, which action may or may not be begun in the court which rendered the judgment. Various rules, such as the one dealing with a motion for new trial and for amendment of judgments, Rule 59, one for amended findings, Rule 52, and one for judgment notwithstanding the verdict, Rule 50(b), and including the provisions of Rule 60(b) as amended, prescribe the various types of cases in which the practice by motion is permitted. In each case there is a limit upon the time within which resort to a motion is permitted, and this time limit may not be enlarged under Rule 6(b). If the right to make a motion is lost by the expiration of the time limits fixed in these rules, the only other procedural remedy is by a new or independent action to set aside a judgment upon those principles which have heretofore been applied in such an action. Where the independent action is resorted to, the limitations of time are those of laches or statutes of limitations. The Committee has endeavored to ascertain all the remedies and types of relief heretofore available by coram nobis, coram vobis, audita querela, bill of review, or bill in the nature of a bill of review. See Moore and Rogers, Federal Relief from Civil Judgments (1946) 55 Yale L.J. 623, 659–682. It endeavored then to amend the rules to permit, either by motion or by independent action, the granting of various kinds of relief from judgments which were permitted in the federal courts prior to the adoption of these rules, and the amendment concludes with a provision abolishing the use of bills of review and the other common law writs referred to, and requiring the practice to be by motion or by independent action.

To illustrate the operation of the amendment, it will be noted that under Rule 59(b) as it now stands, without amendment, a motion for new trial on the ground of newly discovered evidence is permitted within ten days after the entry of the judgment, or after that time upon leave of the court. It is proposed to amend Rule 59(b) by providing that under that rule a motion for new trial shall be served not later than ten days after the entry of the judgment, whatever the ground be for the motion, whether error by the court or newly discovered evidence. On the other hand, one of the purposes of the bill of review in equity was to afford relief on the ground of newly discovered evidence long after the entry of the judgment. Therefore, to permit relief by a motion similar to that heretofore obtained on bill of review, Rule 60(b) as amended permits an application for relief to be made by motion, on the ground of newly discovered evidence, within one year after judgment. Such a motion under Rule 60(b) does not affect the finality of the judgment, but a motion under Rule 59, made within 10 days, does affect finality and the running of the time for appeal.

If these various amendments, including principally those to Rule 60(b), accomplish the purpose for which they are intended, the federal rules will deal with the practice in every sort of case in which relief from final judgments is asked, and prescribe the practice. With reference to the question whether, as the rules now exist, relief by coram nobis, bills of review, and so forth, is permissible, the generally accepted view is that the remedies are still available, although the precise relief obtained in a particular case by use of these ancillary remedies is shrouded in ancient lore and mystery. See Wallace v. United States (C.C.A.2d, 1944) 142 F.(2d) 240, cert. den. (1944) 323 U.S. 712; Fraser v. Doing (App.D.C. 1942) 130 F.(2d) 617; Jones v. Watts (C.C.A.5th, 1944) 142 F.(2d) 575; Preveden v. Hahn (S.D.N.Y. 1941) 36 F.Supp. 952; Cavallo v. Agwilines, Inc. (S.D.N.Y. 1942) 6 Fed.Rules Serv. 60b.31, Case 2, 2 F.R.D. 526; McGinn v. United States (D.Mass. 1942) 6 Fed.Rules Serv. 60b.51, Case 3, 2 F.R.D. 562; City of Shattuck, Oklahoma ex rel. Versluis v. Oliver (W.D.Okla. 1945) 8 Fed.Rules Serv. 60b.31, Case 3; Moore and Rogers, Federal Relief from Civil

Judgments (1946) 55 Yale L.J. 623, 631–653; 3 Moore's Federal Practice (1938) 3254 et seq.; Commentary, Effect of Rule 60b on Other Methods of Relief From Judgment, op. cit. supra. Cf. Norris v. Camp (C.C.A.10th, 1944) 144 F.(2d) 1; Reed v. South Atlantic Steamship Co. of Delaware (D.Del. 1942) 6 Fed.Rules Serv. 60b.31, Case 1; Laughlin v. Berens (D.D.C. 1945) 8 Fed.Rules Serv. 60b.51, Case 1, 73 W.L.R. 209.

The transposition of the words "the court" and the addition of the word "and" at the beginning of the first sentence are merely verbal changes. The addition of the qualifying word "final" emphasizes the character of the judgments, orders or proceedings from which Rule 60(b) affords relief; and hence interlocutory judgments are not brought within the restrictions of the rule, but rather they are left subject to the complete power of the court rendering them to afford such relief from them as justice requires.

The qualifying pronoun "his" has been eliminated on the basis that it is too restrictive, and that the subdivision should include the mistake or neglect of others which may be just as material and call just as much for supervisory jurisdiction as where the judgment is taken against the party through his mistake, inadvertence, etc.

Fraud, whether intrinsic or extrinsic, misrepresentation, or other misconduct of an adverse party are express grounds for relief by motion under amended subdivision (b). There is no sound reason for their exclusion. The incorporation of fraud and the like within the scope of the rule also removes confusion as to the proper procedure. It has been held that relief from a judgment obtained by extrinsic fraud could be secured by motion within a "reasonable time," which might be after the time stated in the rule had run. Fiske v. Buder (C.C.A.8th, 1942) 125 F.(2d) 841; see also inferentially Bucy v. Nevada Construction Co. (C.C.A.9th, 1942) 125 F.(2d) 213. On the other hand, it has been suggested that in view of the fact that fraud was omitted from original Rule 60(b) as a ground for relief, an independent action was the only proper remedy. Commentary, Effect of Rule 60b on Other Methods of Relief From Judgment (1941) 4 Fed.Rules Serv. 942, 945. The amendment settles this problem by making fraud an express ground for relief by motion; and under the saving clause, fraud may be urged as a basis for relief by independent action insofar as established doctrine permits. See Moore and Rogers, Federal Relief from Civil Judgments (1946) 55 Yale L.J. 623, 653–659; 3 Moore's Federal Practice (1938) 3267 et seq. And the rule expressly does not limit the power of the court, when fraud has been perpetrated upon it, to give relief under the saving clause. As an illustration of this situation, see Hazel-Atlas Glass Co. v. Hartford Empire Co. (1944) 322 U.S. 238.

The time limit for relief by motion in the court and in the action in which the judgment was rendered has been enlarged from six months to one year.

It should be noted that Rule 60(b) does not assume to define the substantive law as to the grounds for vacating judgments, but merely prescribes the practice in proceedings to obtain relief.

It should also be noted that under §200(4) of the Soldiers' and Sailors' Civil Relief Act of 1940 ([former] 50 U.S.C. [App.] §501 et seq. [§520(4)]), a judgment rendered in any action or proceeding governed by the section may be vacated under certain specified circumstances upon proper application to the court.

Notes of Advisory Committee on Rules—1948 Amendment

The amendment substitutes the present statutory reference.

Notes of Advisory Committee on Rules—1987 Amendment

The amendment is technical. No substantive change is intended.

Committee Notes on Rules—2007 Amendment

The language of Rule 60 has been amended as part of the general restyling of the Civil Rules to make them more easily understood and to make style and terminology consistent throughout the rules. These changes are intended to be stylistic only.

The final sentence of former Rule 60(b) said that the procedure for obtaining any relief from a judgment was by motion as prescribed in the Civil Rules or by an independent action. That provision is deleted as unnecessary. Relief continues to be available only as provided in the Civil Rules or by independent action.

Rule 61. Harmless Error

Unless justice requires otherwise, no error in admitting or excluding evidence—or any other error by the court or a party—is ground for granting a new trial, for setting aside a verdict, or for vacating, modifying, or otherwise disturbing a judgment or order. At every stage of the proceeding, the court must disregard all errors and defects that do not affect any party's substantial rights.

(As amended Apr. 30, 2007, eff. Dec. 1, 2007.)

Notes of Advisory Committee on Rules—1937

A combination of U.S.C., Title 28, §§391 [see 2111] (New trials; harmless error) and [former] 777 (Defects of form; amendments) with modifications. See McCandless v. United States, 298 U.S. 342 (1936). Compare [former] Equity Rule 72 (Correction of Clerical Mistakes in Orders and Decrees); and last sentence of [former] Equity Rule 46 (Trial—Testimony Usually Taken in Open Court—Rulings on Objections to Evidence). For the last sentence see the last sentence of [former] Equity Rule 19 (Amendments Generally).

Committee Notes on Rules—2007 Amendment

The language of Rule 61 has been amended as part of the general restyling of the Civil Rules to make them more easily understood and to make style and terminology consistent throughout the rules. These changes are intended to be stylistic only.

Rule 62. Stay of Proceedings to Enforce a Judgment

(a) Automatic Stay; Exceptions for Injunctions, Receiverships, and Patent Accountings. Except as stated in this rule, no execution may issue on a judgment, nor may proceedings be taken to enforce it, until 14 days have passed after its entry. But unless the court orders otherwise, the following are not stayed after being entered, even if an appeal is taken:

(1) an interlocutory or final judgment in an action for an injunction or a receivership; or

(2) a judgment or order that directs an accounting in an action for patent infringement.

(b) Stay Pending the Disposition of a Motion. On appropriate terms for the opposing party's security, the court may stay the execution of a judgment—or any proceedings to enforce it—pending disposition of any of the following motions:

(1) under Rule 50, for judgment as a matter of law;
(2) under Rule 52(b), to amend the findings or for additional findings;
(3) under Rule 59, for a new trial or to alter or amend a judgment; or
(4) under Rule 60, for relief from a judgment or order.

(c) Injunction Pending an Appeal. While an appeal is pending from an interlocutory order or final judgment that grants, dissolves, or denies an injunction, the court may suspend, modify, restore, or grant an injunction on terms for bond or other terms that secure the opposing party's rights. If the judgment appealed from is rendered by a statutory three-judge district court, the order must be made either:
(1) by that court sitting in open session; or
(2) by the assent of all its judges, as evidenced by their signatures.

(d) Stay with Bond on Appeal. If an appeal is taken, the appellant may obtain a stay by supersedeas bond, except in an action described in Rule 62(a)(1) or (2). The bond may be given upon or after filing the notice of appeal or after obtaining the order allowing the appeal. The stay takes effect when the court approves the bond.

(e) Stay Without Bond on an Appeal by the United States, Its Officers, or Its Agencies. The court must not require a bond, obligation, or other security from the appellant when granting a stay on an appeal by the United States, its officers, or its agencies or on an appeal directed by a department of the federal government.

(f) Stay in Favor of a Judgment Debtor Under State Law. If a judgment is a lien on the judgment debtor's property under the law of the state where the court is located, the judgment debtor is entitled to the same stay of execution the state court would give.

(g) Appellate Court's Power Not Limited. This rule does not limit the power of the appellate court or one of its judges or justices:
(1) to stay proceedings—or suspend, modify, restore, or grant an injunction—while an appeal is pending; or
(2) to issue an order to preserve the status quo or the effectiveness of the judgment to be entered.

(h) Stay with Multiple Claims or Parties. A court may stay the enforcement of a final judgment entered under Rule 54(b) until it enters a later judgment or judgments, and may prescribe terms necessary to secure the benefit of the stayed judgment for the party in whose favor it was entered.

(As amended Dec. 27, 1946, eff. Mar. 19, 1948; Dec. 29, 1948, eff. Oct. 20, 1949; Apr. 17, 1961, eff. July 19, 1961; Mar. 2, 1987, eff. Aug. 1, 1987; Apr. 30, 2007, eff. Dec. 1, 2007; Mar. 26, 2009, eff. Dec. 1, 2009.)

Notes of Advisory Committee on Rules—1937

Note to Subdivision (a). The first sentence states the substance of the last sentence of U.S.C., Title 28, [former] §874 (Supersedeas). The remainder of the subdivision states the substance of the last clause of U.S.C., Title 28, [former] §227 (Appeals in proceedings for injunctions; receivers; and admiralty), and of [former] §227a (Appeals in suits in equity for infringement of letters patent for inventions; stay of proceedings for accounting), but extended to include final as well as interlocutory judgments.

Note to Subdivision (b). This modifies U.S.C., Title 28, [former] §840 (Executions; stay on conditions).

Note to Subdivision (c). Compare [former] Equity Rule 74 (Injunction Pending Appeal); and Cumberland Telephone and Telegraph Co. v. Louisiana Public Service Commission, 260 U.S. 212 (1922). See Simkins, Federal Practice (1934) §916 in regard to the effect of appeal on injunctions and the giving of bonds. See U.S.C., [former] Title 6 (Official and Penal Bonds) for bonds by surety companies. For statutes providing for a specially constituted district court of three judges, see:

U.S.C., Title 7:

- §217 (Proceedings for suspension of orders of Secretary of Agriculture under Stockyards Act)—by reference.
- §499k (Injunctions; application of injunction laws governing orders of Interstate Commerce Commission to orders of Secretary of Agriculture under Perishable Commodities Act)—by reference.

U.S.C., Title 15:

- §28 (Antitrust laws; suits against monopolies expedited)

U.S.C., Title 28:

- §47 [now 2325] (Injunctions as to orders of Interstate Commerce Commission, etc.)
- §380 [now 2284] (Injunctions; alleged unconstitutionality of State statutes.)
- §380a [now 2284] (Same; constitutionality of federal statute)

U.S.C., Title 49:

- §44 [former] (Suits in equity under interstate commerce laws; expedition of suits)

Note to Subdivision (d). This modifies U.S.C., Title 28, [former] §874 (Supersedeas). See Rule 36(2), Rules of the Supreme Court of the United States, which governs supersedeas bonds on direct appeals to the Supreme Court, and Rule 73(d), of these rules, which governs supersedeas bonds on appeals to a circuit court of appeals. The provisions governing supersedeas bonds in both kinds of appeals are substantially the same.

Note to Subdivision (e). This states the substance of U.S.C., Title 28, §870 [now 2408] (Bond; not required of the United States).

Note to Subdivision (f). This states the substance of U.S.C., Title 28, [former] §841 (Executions; stay of one term) with appropriate modification to conform to the provisions of Rule 6(c) as to terms of court.

Notes of Advisory Committee on Rules—1946 Amendment

Subdivision (a). [This subdivision not amended]. Sections 203 and 204 of the Soldiers' and Sailors' Civil Relief Act of 1940 ([former] 50 U.S.C. [App.] §501 et seq. [§§523, 524] [now 50 U.S.C. §§3933, 3934]) provide under certain circumstances for the issuance and continuance of a stay of execution of any judgment or order entered against a person in military service. See Bowsman v. Peterson (D.Neb. 1942) 45 F.Supp. 741. Section 201 of the Act [50 U.S.C. §3931] permits under certain circumstances the issuance of a stay of any action or proceeding at any stage thereof, where either the plaintiff or defendant is a person in military service. See also Note to Rule 64 herein.

Subdivision (b). This change was necessary because of the proposed addition to Rule 59 of subdivision (e).

Subdivision (h). In proposing to revise Rule 54(b), the Committee thought it advisable to include a separate provision in Rule 62 for stay of enforcement of a final judgment in cases involving multiple claims.

Notes of Advisory Committee on Rules—1948 Amendment

Section 210 of the Judicial Code, as amended, U.S.C., Title 28, §47a, is repealed by revised Title 28 and its provisions that stays pending appeals to the Supreme Court in Interstate Commerce Commission cases may be granted only by that court or a justice thereof are not included in revised Title 28. Prior to this repeal the additional general reference in subdivision (g) to "other statutes of the United States", was needed as a safety residual provision due to the specific reference to Section 210 of the Judicial Code. With the repeal of this latter section there is no need for the residual provision, which has no present applicability; and to the extent that any statute is enacted providing "that stays pending appeals to the Supreme Court may be granted only by that court or a justice thereof" it will govern and will not be inconsistent or repugnant to subdivision (g) as amended.

Notes of Advisory Committee on Rules—1961 Amendment

These changes conform to the amendment of Rule 54(b).

Notes of Advisory Committee on Rules—1987 Amendment

The amendment is technical. No substantive change is intended.

Committee Notes on Rules—2007 Amendment

The language of Rule 62 has been amended as part of the general restyling of the Civil Rules to make them more easily understood and to make style and terminology consistent throughout the rules. These changes are intended to be stylistic only.

The final sentence of former Rule 62(a) referred to Rule 62(c). It is deleted as an unnecessary [sic]. Rule 62(c) governs of its own force.

Committee Notes on Rules—2009 Amendment

The time set in the former rule at 10 days has been revised to 14 days. See the Note to Rule 6.

Rule 62.1. Indicative Ruling on a Motion for Relief That is Barred by a Pending Appeal

(a) Relief Pending Appeal. If a timely motion is made for relief that the court lacks authority to grant because of an appeal that has been docketed and is pending, the court may:

(1) defer considering the motion;

(2) deny the motion; or

(3) state either that it would grant the motion if the court of appeals remands for that purpose or that the motion raises a substantial issue.

(b) Notice to the Court of Appeals. The movant must promptly notify the circuit clerk under Federal Rule of Appellate Procedure 12.1 if the district court states that it would grant the motion or that the motion raises a substantial issue.

(c) Remand. The district court may decide the motion if the court of appeals remands for that purpose.

———

(As added Mar. 26, 2009, eff. Dec. 1, 2009.)

Committee Notes on Rules—2009

This new rule adopts for any motion that the district court cannot grant because of a pending appeal the practice that most courts follow when a party makes a Rule 60(b) motion to vacate a judgment that is pending on appeal. After an appeal has been docketed and while it remains pending, the district court cannot grant a Rule 60(b) motion without a remand. But it can entertain the motion and deny it, defer consideration, or state that it would grant the motion if the the [sic] court of appeals remands for that purpose or state that the motion raises a substantial issue. Experienced lawyers often refer to the suggestion for remand as an "indicative ruling." (Appellate Rule 4(a)(4) lists six motions that, if filed within the relevant time limit, suspend the effect of a notice of appeal filed before or after the motion is filed until the last such motion is disposed of. The district court has authority to grant the motion without resorting to the indicative ruling procedure.)

This clear procedure is helpful whenever relief is sought from an order that the court cannot reconsider because the order is the subject of a pending appeal. Rule 62.1 does not attempt to define the circumstances in which an appeal limits or defeats the district court's authority to act in the face of a pending appeal. The rules that govern the relationship between trial courts and appellate courts may be complex, depending in part on the nature of the order and the source of appeal jurisdiction. Rule 62.1 applies only when those rules deprive the district court of authority to grant relief without appellate permission. If the district court concludes that it has authority to grant relief without appellate permission, it can act without falling back on the indicative ruling procedure.

To ensure proper coordination of proceedings in the district court and in the appellate court, the movant must notify the circuit clerk under Federal Rule of Appellate Procedure 12.1 if the district court states that it would grant the motion or that the motion raises a substantial issue. Remand is in the court of appeals' discretion under Appellate Rule 12.1.

Often it will be wise for the district court to determine whether it in fact would grant the motion if the court of appeals remands for that purpose. But a motion may present complex issues that require extensive litigation and that may either be mooted or be presented in a different context by decision of the issues raised on appeal. In such circumstances the district court may prefer to state that the motion raises a substantial issue, and to state the reasons why it prefers to decide only if the court of appeals agrees that it would be useful to decide the motion before decision of the pending appeal. The district court is not bound to grant the motion after stating that the motion raises a substantial issue; further proceedings on remand may show that the motion ought not be granted.

Changes Made After Publication and Comment. The rule text is changed by substituting "for that purpose" for "further proceedings"; the reason is discussed above.

Minor changes are made in the Committee Note to make it conform to the Committee Note for proposed Appellate Rule 12.1.

Rule 63. Judge's Inability to Proceed

If a judge conducting a hearing or trial is unable to proceed, any other judge may proceed upon certifying familiarity with the record and determining that the case may be completed without prejudice to the parties. In a hearing or a nonjury trial, the successor judge must, at a party's request, recall any witness whose testimony is material and disputed and who is available to testify again without undue burden. The successor judge may also recall any other witness.

(As amended Mar. 2, 1987, eff. Aug. 1, 1987; Apr. 30, 1991, eff. Dec. 1, 1991; Apr. 30, 2007, eff. Dec. 1, 2007.)

Notes of Advisory Committee on Rules—1937

This rule adapts and extends the provisions of U.S.C., Title 28, [former] §776 (Bill of exceptions; authentication; signing of by judge) to include all duties to be performed by the judge after verdict or judgment. The statute is therefore superseded.

Notes of Advisory Committee on Rules—1987 Amendment

The amendments are technical. No substantive change is intended.

Notes of Advisory Committee on Rules—1991 Amendment

The revision substantially displaces the former rule. The former rule was limited to the disability of the judge, and made no provision for disqualification or possible other reasons for the withdrawal of the judge during proceedings. In making provision for other circumstances, the revision is not intended to encourage judges to discontinue participation in a trial for any but compelling reasons. Cf. United States v. Lane, 708 F.2d 1394, 1395–1397 (9th cir. 1983). Manifestly, a substitution should not be made for the personal convenience of the court, and the reasons for a substitution should be stated on the record.

The former rule made no provision for the withdrawal of the judge during the trial, but was limited to disqualification after trial. Several courts concluded that the text of the former rule prohibited substitution of a new judge prior to the points described in the rule, thus requiring a new trial, whether or not a fair disposition was within reach of a substitute judge. E.g., Whalen v. Ford Motor Credit Co., 684 F.2d 272 (4th Cir. 1982, en banc) cert. denied, 459 U.S. 910 (1982) (jury trial); Arrow-Hart, Inc. v. Philip Carey Co., 552 F.2d 711 (6th Cir. 1977) (non-jury trial). See generally Comment, The Case of the Dead Judge: Fed.R.Civ.P. 63: Whalen v. Ford Motor Credit Co., 67 MINN. L. REV. 827 (1983).

The increasing length of federal trials has made it likely that the number of trials interrupted by the disability of the judge will increase. An efficient mechanism for completing these cases without unfairness is needed to prevent unnecessary expense and delay. To avoid the injustice that may result if the substitute judge proceeds despite unfamiliarity with the action, the new Rule provides, in language similar to Federal Rule of Criminal Procedure 25(a), that the successor judge must certify familiarity with the record and determine that the case may be completed before that judge without prejudice to the parties. This will necessarily require that there be available a transcript or a videotape of the proceedings prior to substitution. If there has been a long but incomplete jury trial, the prompt availability of the transcript or videotape is crucial to the effective use of this rule, for the jury cannot long be held while an extensive transcript is prepared without prejudice to one or all parties.

The revised text authorizes the substitute judge to make a finding of fact at a bench trial based on evidence heard by a different judge. This may be appropriate in limited circumstances. First, if a witness has become unavailable, the testimony recorded at trial can be considered by the successor judge pursuant to F.R.Ev. 804, being equivalent to a recorded deposition available for use at trial pursuant to Rule 32. For this purpose, a witness who is no longer subject to a subpoena to compel testimony at trial is unavailable. Secondly, the successor judge may determine that particular testimony is not material or is not disputed, and so need not be reheard. The propriety of proceeding in this manner may be marginally affected by the availability of a videotape record; a judge who has reviewed a trial on videotape may be entitled to greater confidence in his or her ability to proceed.

The court would, however, risk error to determine the credibility of a witness not seen or heard who is available to be recalled. Cf. Anderson v. City of Bessemer City NC, 470 U.S. 564, 575 (1985); Marshall v. Jerrico Inc, 446 U.S. 238, 242 (1980). See also United States v. Radatz, 447 U.S. 667 (1980).

Committee Notes on Rules—2007 Amendment

The language of Rule 63 has been amended as part of the general restyling of the Civil Rules to make them more easily understood and to make style and terminology consistent throughout the rules. These changes are intended to be stylistic only.

TITLE VIII. PROVISIONAL AND FINAL REMEDIES

Rule 64. Seizing a Person or Property

(a) Remedies Under State Law—In General. At the commencement of and throughout an action, every remedy is available that, under the law of the state where the court is located, provides for seizing a person or property to secure satisfaction of the potential judgment. But a federal statute governs to the extent it applies.
(b) Specific Kinds of Remedies. The remedies available under this rule include the following—however designated and regardless of whether state procedure requires an independent action:

- arrest;
- attachment;
- garnishment;
- replevin;
- sequestration; and
- other corresponding or equivalent remedies.

(As amended Apr. 30, 2007, eff. Dec. 1, 2007.)

Notes of Advisory Committee on Rules—1937

This rule adopts the existing Federal law, except that it specifies the applicable State law to be that of the time when the remedy is sought. Under U.S.C., Title 28, [former] §726 (Attachments as provided by State laws) the plaintiff was entitled to remedies by attachment or other process which were on June 1, 1872, provided by the applicable State law, and the district courts might, from time to time, by general rules, adopt such State laws as might be in force. This statute is superseded as are district court rules which are rendered unnecessary by the rule.

Lis pendens. No rule concerning lis pendens is stated, for this would appear to be a matter of substantive law affecting State laws of property. It has been held that in the absence of a State statute expressly providing for the recordation of notice of the pendency of Federal actions, the commencement of a Federal action is notice to all persons affected. King v. Davis, 137 Fed. 198 (W.D.Va., 1903). It has been held, however, that when a State statute does so provide expressly, its provisions are binding. United States v. Calcasieu Timber Co., 236 Fed. 196 (C.C.A.5th, 1916).

For statutes of the United States on attachment, see e.g.:

U.S.C., Title 28:

- §737 [now 2710] (Attachment in postal suits)
- §738 [now 2711] (Attachment; application for warrant)
- §739 [now 2712] (Attachment; issue of warrant)
- §740 [now 2713] (Attachment; trial of ownership of property)
- §741 [now 2714] (Attachment; investment of proceeds of attached property)
- §742 [now 2715] (Attachment; publication of attachment)
- §743 [now 2716] (Attachment; personal notice of attachment)
- §744 [now 2717] (Attachment; discharge; bond)
- §745 [former] (Attachment; accrued rights not affected)
- §746 (Attachments dissolved in conformity with State laws)

For statutes of the United States on garnishment, see e.g.:

U.S.C., Title 28:

- §748 [now 2405] (Garnishees in suits by United States against a corporation)
- §749 [now 2405] (Same; issue tendered on denial of indebtedness)
- §750 [now 2405] (Same; garnishee failing to appear)

For statutes of the United States on arrest, see e.g.:

U.S.C., Title 28:

- §376 [now 1651] (Writs of ne exeat)
- §755 [former] (Special bail in suits for duties and penalties)
- §756 [former] (Defendant giving bail in one district and committed in another)
- §757 [former] (Defendant giving bail in one district and committed in another; defendant held until judgment in first suit)
- §758 [former] (Bail and affidavits; taking by commissioners)
- §759 [former] (Calling of bail in Kentucky)
- §760 [former] (Clerks may take bail de bene esse)
- §843 [now 2007] (Imprisonment for debt)
- §844 [now 2007] (Imprisonment for debt; discharge according to State laws)
- §845 [now 2007] (Imprisonment for debt; jail limits)

For statutes of the United States on replevin, see, e.g.:

U.S.C., Title 28:

- §747 [now 2463] (Replevy of property taken under revenue laws)

Notes of Advisory Committee on Rules—1946 Supplementary Note

Sections 203 and 204 of the Soldiers' and Sailors' Civil Relief Act of 1940 ([former] 50 U.S.C. [App.] §501 et seq. [§§523, 524] [now 50 U.S.C. §§3933, 3934]) provide under certain circumstances for the issuance and continuance of a stay of the execution of any judgment entered against a person in military service, or the vacation or stay of any attachment or garnishment directed against such person's property, money, or debts in the hands of another. See also Note to Rule 62 herein.

Committee Notes on Rules—2007 Amendment

The language of Rule 64 has been amended as part of the general restyling of the Civil Rules to make them more easily understood and to make style and terminology consistent throughout the rules. These changes are intended to be stylistic only.

Former Rule 64 stated that the Civil Rules govern an action in which any remedy available under Rule 64(a) is used. The Rules were said to govern from the time the action is commenced if filed in federal court, and from the time of removal if removed from state court. These provisions are deleted as redundant. Rule 1 establishes that the Civil Rules apply to all actions in a district court, and Rule 81(c)(1) adds reassurance that the Civil Rules apply to a removed action "after it is removed."

Rule 65. Injunctions and Restraining Orders

(a) Preliminary Injunction.

(1) Notice. The court may issue a preliminary injunction only on notice to the adverse party.

(2) Consolidating the Hearing with the Trial on the Merits. Before or after beginning the hearing on a motion for a preliminary injunction, the court may advance the trial on the merits and consolidate it with the hearing. Even when consolidation is not ordered, evidence that is received on the motion and that would be admissible at trial becomes part of the trial record and need not be repeated at trial. But the court must preserve any party's right to a jury trial.

(b) Temporary Restraining Order.

(1) Issuing Without Notice. The court may issue a temporary restraining order without written or oral notice to the adverse party or its attorney only if:

(A) specific facts in an affidavit or a verified complaint clearly show that immediate and irreparable injury, loss, or damage will result to the movant before the adverse party can be heard in opposition; and

(B) the movant's attorney certifies in writing any efforts made to give notice and the reasons why it should not be required.

(2) Contents; Expiration. Every temporary restraining order issued without notice must state the date and hour it was issued; describe the injury and state why it is irreparable; state why the order was issued without notice; and be promptly filed in the clerk's office and entered in the record. The order expires at the time after entry—not to exceed 14 days—that the court sets, unless before that time the court, for good cause, extends it for a like period or the adverse party consents to a longer extension. The reasons for an extension must be entered in the record.

(3) Expediting the Preliminary-Injunction Hearing. If the order is issued without notice, the motion for a preliminary injunction must be set for hearing at the earliest possible time, taking precedence over all other matters except hearings on older matters of the same character. At the hearing, the party who obtained the order must proceed with the motion; if the party does not, the court must dissolve the order.

(4) Motion to Dissolve. On 2 days' notice to the party who obtained the order without notice—or on shorter notice set by the court—the adverse party may appear and move to dissolve or modify the order. The court must then hear and decide the motion as promptly as justice requires.

(c) Security. The court may issue a preliminary injunction or a temporary restraining order only if the movant gives security in an amount that the court considers proper to pay the costs and damages sustained by any party found to have been wrongfully enjoined or restrained. The United States, its officers, and its agencies are not required to give security.

(d) Contents and Scope of Every Injunction and Restraining Order.

(1) Contents. Every order granting an injunction and every restraining order must:

(A) state the reasons why it issued;

(B) state its terms specifically; and

(C) describe in reasonable detail—and not by referring to the complaint or other document—the act or acts restrained or required.

(2) Persons Bound. The order binds only the following who receive actual notice of it by personal service or otherwise:

(A) the parties;

(B) the parties' officers, agents, servants, employees, and attorneys; and

(C) other persons who are in active concert or participation with anyone described in Rule 65(d)(2)(A) or (B).

(e) Other Laws Not Modified. These rules do not modify the following:

(1) any federal statute relating to temporary restraining orders or preliminary injunctions in actions affecting employer and employee;

(2) 28 U.S.C. §2361, which relates to preliminary injunctions in actions of interpleader or in the nature of interpleader; or

(3) 28 U.S.C. §2284, which relates to actions that must be heard and decided by a three-judge district court.

(f) Copyright Impoundment. This rule applies to copyright-impoundment proceedings.

(As amended Dec. 27, 1946, eff. Mar. 19, 1948; Dec. 29, 1948, eff. Oct. 20, 1949; Feb. 28, 1966, eff. July 1, 1966; Mar. 2, 1987, eff. Aug. 1, 1987; Apr. 23, 2001, eff. Dec. 1, 2001; Apr. 30, 2007, eff. Dec. 1, 2007; Mar. 26, 2009, eff. Dec. 1, 2009.)

Notes of Advisory Committee on Rules—1937

Note to Subdivisions (a) and (b). These are taken from U.S.C., Title 28, [former] §381 (Injunctions; preliminary injunctions and temporary restraining orders).

Note to Subdivision (c). Except for the last sentence, this is substantially U.S.C., Title 28, [former] §382 (Injunctions; security on issuance of). The last sentence continues the following and similar statutes which expressly except the United States or an officer or agency thereof from such security requirements: U.S.C., Title 15, §§77t(b), 78u(e), and 79r(f) (Securities and Exchange Commission).

It also excepts the United States or an officer or agency thereof from such security requirements in any action in which a restraining order or interlocutory judgment of injunction issues in its favor whether there is an express statutory exception from such security requirements or not.

See U.S.C., [former] Title 6 (Official and Penal Bonds) for bonds by surety companies.

Note to Subdivision (d). This is substantially U.S.C., Title 28, [former] §383 (Injunctions; requisites of order; binding effect).

Note to Subdivision (e). The words "relating to temporary restraining orders and preliminary injunctions in actions affecting employer and employee" are words of description and not of limitation.

Compare [former] Equity Rule 73 (Preliminary Injunctions and Temporary Restraining Orders) which is substantially equivalent to the statutes.

For other statutes dealing with injunctions which are continued, see e.g.:

U.S.C., Title 28:

- §46 [now 2324] (Suits to enjoin orders of Interstate Commerce Commission to be against United States)
- §47 [now 2325] (Injunctions as to orders of Interstate Commerce Commission; appeal to Supreme Court; time for taking)
- §378 [former] (Injunctions; when granted)
- §379 [now 2283] (Injunctions; stay in State courts)
- §380 [now 1253, 2101, 2281, 2284] (Injunctions; alleged unconstitutionality of State statutes; appeal to Supreme Court)
- §380a [now 1253, 2101, 2281, 2284] (Injunctions; constitutionality of Federal statute; application for hearing; appeal to Supreme Court)

U.S.C., Title 7:

- §216 (Court proceedings to enforce orders; injunction)
- §217 (Proceedings for suspension of orders)

U.S.C., Title 15:

- §4 (Jurisdiction of courts; duty of district attorney; procedure)
- §25 (Restraining violations; procedure)
- §26 (Injunctive relief for private parties; exceptions)
- §77t(b) (Injunctions and prosecution of offenses)

Notes of Advisory Committee on Rules—1946 Amendment

It has been held that in actions on preliminary injunction bonds the district court has discretion to grant relief in the same proceeding or to require the institution of a new action on the bond. Russell v. Farley (1881) 105 U.S. 433, 466. It is believed, however, that in all cases the litigant should have a right to proceed on the bond in the same proceeding, in the manner provided in Rule 73(f) for a similar situation. The paragraph added to Rule 65(c) insures this result and is in the interest of efficiency. There is no reason why Rules 65(c) and 73(f) should operate differently. Compare §50(n) of the Bankruptcy Act, 11 U.S.C. §78(n), under which actions on all bonds furnished pursuant to the Act may be proceeded upon summarily in the bankruptcy court. See 2 Collier on Bankruptcy (14th ed. by Moore and Oglebay) 1853–1854.

Notes of Advisory Committee on Rules—1948 Amendment

Specific enumeration of statutes dealing with labor injunctions is undesirable due to the enactment of amendatory or new legislation from time to time. The more general and inclusive reference, "any statute of the United States", does not change the intent of subdivision (e) of Rule 65, and the subdivision will have continuing applicability without the need of subsequent readjustment to labor legislation.

The amendment relative to actions of interpleader or in the nature of interpleader substitutes the present statutory reference and will embrace any future amendment to statutory interpleader provided for in Title 28, U.S.C., §2361.

The Act of August 24, 1937, provided for a district court of three judges to hear and determine an action to enjoin the enforcement of any Act of Congress for repugnance to the Constitution of the United States. The provisions of that Act dealing with the procedure for the issuance of temporary restraining orders and interlocutory and final injunctions have been included in revised Title 28, U.S.C., §2284, which, however, has been broadened to apply to all actions required to be heard and determined by a district court of three judges. The amendatory saving clause of subdivision (e) of Rule 65 has been broadened accordingly.

Notes of Advisory Committee on Rules—1966 Amendment

Subdivision (a)(2). This new subdivision provides express authority for consolidating the hearing of an application for a preliminary injunction with the trial on the merits. The authority can be exercised with particular profit when it appears that a substantial part of evidence offered on the application will be relevant to the merits and will be presented in such form as to qualify for admission on the trial proper. Repetition of evidence is thereby avoided. The fact that the proceedings have been consolidated should cause no delay in the disposition of the application for the preliminary injunction, for the evidence will be directed in the first instance to that relief, and the preliminary injunction, if justified by the proof, may be issued in the course of the consolidated proceedings. Furthermore, to consolidate the proceedings will tend to expedite the final disposition of the action. It is believed that consolidation can be usefully availed of in many cases.

The subdivision further provides that even when consolidation is not ordered, evidence received in connection with an application for a preliminary injunction for a preliminary injunction which would be admissible on the trial on the merits forms part of the trial record. This evidence need not be repeated on the trial. On the the other hand, repetition is not altogether prohibited. That would be impractical and unwise. For example, a witness testifying comprehensively on the trial who has previously testified upon the application for a preliminary injunction might sometimes be hamstrung in telling his story if he could not go over some part of his prior testimony to connect it with his present testimony. So also, some repetition of testimony may be called for where the trial is conducted by a judge who did not hear the application for the preliminary injunction. In general, however, repetition can be avoided with an increase of efficiency in the conduct of the case and without any distortion of the presentation of evidence by the parties.

Since an application for a preliminary injunction may be made in an action in which, with respect to all or part of the merits, there is a right to trial by jury, it is appropriate to add the caution appearing in the last sentence of the subdivision. In such a case the jury will have to hear all the evidence bearing on its verdict, even if some part of the evidence has already been heard by the judge alone on the application for the preliminary injunction.

The subdivision is believed to reflect the substance of the best current practice and introduces no novel conception.

Subdivision (b). In view of the possibly drastic consequence of a temporary restraining order, the opposition should be heard, if feasible, before the order is granted. Many judges have properly insisted that, when time does not permit of formal notice of the application to the adverse party, some expedient, such as telephonic notice to the attorney for the adverse party, be resorted to if this can reasonably be done. On occasion, however, temporary restraining orders have been issued without any notice when it was feasible for some fair, although informal, notice to be given. See the emphatic criticisms in Pennsylvania Rd. Co. v. Transport Workers Union, 278 F.2d 693, 694 (3d Cir. 1960); Arvida Corp. v. Sugarman, 259 F.2d 428, 429 (2d Cir. 1958); Lummus Co. v. Commonwealth Oil Ref. Co., Inc., 297 F.2d 80, 83 (2d Cir. 1961), cert. denied, 368 U.S. 986 (1962).

Heretofore the first sentence of subdivision (b), in referring to a notice "served" on the "adverse party" on which a "hearing" could be held, perhaps invited the interpretation that the order might be granted without notice if the circumstances did not permit of a formal hearing on the basis of a formal notice. The subdivision is amended to make it plain that informal notice, which may be communicated to the attorney rather than the adverse party, is to be preferred to no notice at all.

Before notice can be dispensed with, the applicant's counsel must give his certificate as to any efforts made to give notice and the reasons why notice should not be required. This certificate is in addition to the requirement of an affidavit or verified complaint setting forth the facts as to the irreparable injury which would result before the opposition could be heard.

The amended subdivision continues to recognize that a temporary restraining order may be issued without any notice when the circumstances warrant.

Subdivision (c). Original Rules 65 and 73 contained substantially identical provisions for summary proceedings against sureties on bonds required or permitted by the rules. There was fragmentary coverage of the same subject in the Admiralty Rules. Clearly, a single comprehensive rule is required, and is incorporated as Rule 65.1.

Notes of Advisory Committee on Rules—1987 Amendment

The amendments are technical. No substantive change is intended.

Committee Notes on Rules—2001 Amendment

New subdivision (f) is added in conjunction with abrogation of the antiquated Copyright Rules of Practice adopted for proceedings under the 1909 Copyright Act. Courts have naturally turned to Rule 65 in response to the apparent inconsistency of the former Copyright Rules with the discretionary impoundment procedure adopted in 1976, 17 U.S.C. §503(a). Rule 65 procedures also have assuaged well-founded doubts whether the Copyright Rules satisfy more contemporary requirements of due process. See, e.g., Religious Technology Center v. Netcom On-Line Communications Servs., Inc., 923 F.Supp. 1231, 1260–1265 (N.D.Cal.1995); Paramount Pictures Corp. v. Doe, 821 F.Supp. 82 (E.D.N.Y.1993); WPOW, Inc. v. MRLJ Enterprises, 584 F.Supp. 132 (D.D.C.1984).

A common question has arisen from the experience that notice of a proposed impoundment may enable an infringer to defeat the court's capacity to grant effective relief. Impoundment may be ordered on an ex parte basis under subdivision (b) if the applicant makes a strong showing of the reasons why notice is likely to defeat effective relief. Such no-notice procedures are authorized in trademark infringement proceedings, see 15 U.S.C. §1116(d), and courts have provided clear illustrations of the kinds of showings that support ex parte relief. See Matter of Vuitton et Fils S.A., 606 F.2d 1 (2d Cir.1979); Vuitton v. White, 945 F.2d 569 (3d Cir.1991). In applying the tests for no-notice relief, the court should ask whether impoundment is necessary, or whether adequate protection can be had by a less intrusive form of no-notice relief shaped as a temporary restraining order.

This new subdivision (f) does not limit use of trademark procedures in cases that combine trademark and copyright claims. Some observers believe that trademark procedures should be adopted for all copyright cases, a proposal better considered by Congressional processes than by rulemaking processes.

Changes Made After Publication and Comments No change has been made.

Committee Notes on Rules—2007 Amendment

The language of Rule 65 has been amended as part of the general restyling of the Civil Rules to make them more easily understood and to make style and terminology consistent throughout the rules. These changes are intended to be stylistic only.

The final sentence of former Rule 65(c) referred to Rule 65.1. It is deleted as unnecessary. Rule 65.1 governs of its own force.

Rule 65(d)(2) clarifies two ambiguities in former Rule 65(d). The former rule was adapted from former 28 U.S.C. §363, but omitted a comma that made clear the common doctrine that a party must have actual notice of an injunction in order to be bound by it.Amended Rule 65(d) restores the meaning of the earlier statute, and also makes clear the proposition that an injunction can be enforced against a person who acts in concert with a party's officer, agent, servant, employee, or attorney.

Changes Made After Publication and Comment. See Note to Rule 1, supra.

Committee Notes on Rules—2009 Amendment

The time set in the former rule at 10 days has been revised to 14 days. See the Note to Rule 6.

Rule 65.1. Proceedings Against a Surety

Whenever these rules (including the Supplemental Rules for Admiralty or Maritime Claims and Asset Forfeiture Actions) require or allow a party to give security, and security is given through a bond or other undertaking with one or more sureties, each surety submits to the court's jurisdiction and irrevocably appoints the court clerk as its agent for receiving service of any papers that affect its liability on the bond or undertaking. The surety's liability may be enforced on motion without an independent action. The motion and any notice that the court orders may be served on the court clerk, who must promptly mail a copy of each to every surety whose address is known.

———

(As added Feb. 28, 1966, eff. July 1, 1966; amended Mar. 2, 1987, eff. Aug. 1, 1987; Apr. 12, 2006, eff. Dec. 1, 2006; Apr. 30, 2007, eff. Dec. 1, 2007.)

Notes of Advisory Committee on Rules—1966

See Note to Rule 65.

Notes of Advisory Committee on Rules—1987 Amendment

The amendments are technical. No substantive change is intended.

Committee Notes on Rules—2006 Amendment

Rule 65.1 is amended to conform to the changed title of the Supplemental Rules.

Committee Notes on Rules—2007 Amendment

The language of Rule 65.1 has been amended as part of the general restyling of the Civil Rules to make them more easily understood and to make style and terminology consistent throughout the rules. These changes are intended to be stylistic only.

Rule 66. Receivers

These rules govern an action in which the appointment of a receiver is sought or a receiver sues or is sued. But the practice in administering an estate by a receiver or a similar court-appointed officer must accord with the historical practice in federal courts or with a local rule. An action in which a receiver has been appointed may be dismissed only by court order.

———

(As amended Dec. 27, 1946, eff. Mar. 19, 1948; Dec. 29, 1948, eff. Oct. 20, 1949; Apr. 30, 2007, eff. Dec. 1, 2007.)

Notes of Advisory Committee on Rules—1946 Amendment

The title of Rule 66 has been expanded to make clear the subject of the rule, i.e., federal equity receivers.

The first sentence added to Rule 66 prevents a dismissal by any party, after a federal equity receiver has been appointed, except upon leave of court. A party should not be permitted to oust the court and its officer without the consent of that court. See Civil Rule 31(e), Eastern District of Washington.

The second sentence added at the beginning of the rule deals with suits by or against a federal equity receiver. The first clause thereof eliminates the formal ceremony of an ancillary appointment before suit can be brought by a receiver, and is in accord with the more modern state practice, and with more expeditious and less expensive judicial administration. 2 Moore's Federal Practice (1938) 2088–2091. For the rule necessitating ancillary appointment, see Sterrett v. Second Nat. Bank (1918) 248 U.S. 73; Kelley v. Queeney (W.D.N.Y. 1941) 41 F.Supp. 1015; see also McCandless v. Furlaud (1934) 293 U.S. 67. This rule has been extensively criticized. First, Extraterritorial Powers of Receivers (1932) 27 Ill.L.Rev. 271; Rose, Extraterritorial Actions by Receivers (1933) 17 Minn.L.Rev. 704; Laughlin, The Extraterritorial Powers of Receivers (1932) 45 Harv.L.Rev. 429; Clark and Moore, A New Federal Civil Procedure—II, Pleadings and Parties (1935) 44 Yale L.J. 1291, 1312–1315; Note (1932) 30 Mich.L.Rev. 1322. See also comment in Bicknell v. Lloyd-Smith (C.C.A.2d, 1940) 109 F.(2d) 527, cert. den. (1940) 311 U.S. 650. The second clause of the sentence merely incorporates the well-known and general rule that, absent statutory authorization, a federal receiver cannot be sued without leave of the court which appointed him, applied in the federal courts since Barton v. Barbour (1881) 104 U.S. 126. See also 1 Clark on Receivers (2d ed.) §549. Under 28 U.S.C. §125, leave of court is unnecessary when a receiver is sued "in respect of any act or transaction of his in carrying on the business" connected with the receivership property, but such suit is subject to the general equity jurisdiction of the court in which the receiver was appointed, so far as justice necessitates.

Capacity of a state court receiver to sue or be sued in federal court is governed by Rule 17(b).

The last sentence added to Rule 66 assures the application of the rules in all matters except actual administration of the receivership estate itself. Since this implicitly carries with it the applicability of those rules relating to appellate procedure, the express reference thereto contained in Rule 66 has been stricken as superfluous. Under Rule 81(a)(1) the rules do not apply to bankruptcy proceedings except as they may be made applicable by order of the Supreme Court. Rule 66 is applicable to what is commonly known as a federal "chancery" or "equity" receiver, or similar type of court officer. It is not designed to regulate or affect receivers in bankruptcy, which are governed by the Bankruptcy Act and the General Orders. Since the Federal Rules are applicable in bankruptcy by virtue of General Orders in Bankruptcy 36 and 37 [following section 53 of Title 11, U.S.C.] only to the extent that they are not inconsistent with the Bankruptcy Act or the General Orders, Rule 66 is not applicable to bankruptcy receivers. See 1 Collier on Bankruptcy (14th ed. by Moore and Oglebay) 2.23–2.36.

Notes of Advisory Committee on Rules—1948 Amendment

Title 28, U.S.C., §§754 and 959(a), state the capacity of a federal receiver to sue or be sued in a federal court, and a repetitive statement of the statute in Rule 66 is confusing and undesirable. See also Note to Rule 17(b), supra.

Committee Notes on Rules—2007 Amendment

The language of Rule 66 has been amended as part of the general restyling of the Civil Rules to make them more easily understood and to make style and terminology consistent throughout the rules. These changes are intended to be stylistic only.

Rule 67. Deposit into Court

(a) Depositing Property. If any part of the relief sought is a money judgment or the disposition of a sum of money or some other deliverable thing, a party—on notice to every other party and by leave of court—may deposit with the court all or part of the money or thing, whether or not that party claims any of it. The depositing party must deliver to the clerk a copy of the order permitting deposit.

(b) Investing and Withdrawing Funds. Money paid into court under this rule must be deposited and withdrawn in accordance with 28 U.S.C. §§2041 and 2042 and any like statute. The money must be deposited in an interest-bearing account or invested in a court-approved, interest-bearing instrument.

(As amended Dec. 29, 1948, eff. Oct. 20, 1949; Apr. 28, 1983, eff. Aug. 1, 1983; Apr. 30, 2007, eff. Dec. 1, 2007.)

Notes of Advisory Committee on Rules—1937

This rule provides for deposit in court generally, continuing similar special provisions contained in such statutes as U.S.C., Title 28, §41(26) [now 1335, 1397, 2361] (Original jurisdiction of bills of interpleader, and of bills in the nature of interpleader). See generally Howard v. United States, 184 U.S. 676 (1902); United States Supreme Court Admiralty Rules (1920), Rules 37 (Bringing Funds into Court), 41 (Funds in Court Registry), and 42 (Claims Against Proceeds in Registry). With the first sentence, compare English Rules Under the Judicature Act (The Annual Practice, 1937) O. 22, r. 1(1).

Notes of Advisory Committee on Rules—1948 Amendment

The first amendment substitutes the present statutory reference.

Since the Act of June 26, 1934, was amended by Act of December 21, 1944, 58 Stat. 845, correcting references are made.

Notes of Advisory Committee on Rules—1983 Amendment

Rule 67 has been amended in three ways. The first change is the addition of the clause in the first sentence. Some courts have construed the present rule to permit deposit only when the party making it claims no interest in the fund or thing deposited. E.g., Blasin-Stern v. Beech-Nut Life Savers Corp., 429 F.Supp. 533 (D. Puerto Rico 1975); Dinkins v. General Aniline & Film Corp., 214 F.Supp. 281 (S.D.N.Y. 1963). However, there are situations in which a litigant may wish to be relieved of responsibility for a sum or thing, but continue to claim an interest in all or part of it. In these cases the deposit-in-court procedure should be available; in addition to the advantages to the party making the deposit, the procedure gives other litigants assurance that any judgment will be collectable. The amendment is intended to accomplish that.

The second change is the addition of a requirement that the order of deposit be served on the clerk of the court in which the sum or thing is to be deposited. This is simply to assure that the clerk knows what is being deposited and what his responsibilities are with respect to the deposit. The latter point is particularly important since the rule as amended contemplates that deposits will be placed in interest-bearing accounts; the clerk must know what treatment has been ordered for the particular deposit.

The third change is to require that any money be deposited in an interest-bearing account or instrument approved by the court.

Committee Notes on Rules—2007 Amendment

The language of Rule 67 has been amended as part of the general restyling of the Civil Rules to make them more easily understood and to make style and terminology consistent throughout the rules. These changes are intended to be stylistic only.

Rule 68. Offer of Judgment

(a) Making an Offer; Judgment on an Accepted Offer. At least 14 days before the date set for trial, a party defending against a claim may serve on an opposing party an offer to allow judgment on specified terms, with the costs then accrued. If, within 14 days after being served, the opposing party serves written notice accepting the offer, either party may then file the offer and notice of acceptance, plus proof of service. The clerk must then enter judgment.

(b) Unaccepted Offer. An unaccepted offer is considered withdrawn, but it does not preclude a later offer. Evidence of an unaccepted offer is not admissible except in a proceeding to determine costs.

(c) Offer After Liability is Determined. When one party's liability to another has been determined but the extent of liability remains to be determined by further proceedings, the party held liable may make an offer of judgment. It must be served within a reasonable time—but at least 14 days—before the date set for a hearing to determine the extent of liability.

(d) Paying Costs After an Unaccepted Offer. If the judgment that the offeree finally obtains is not more favorable than the unaccepted offer, the offeree must pay the costs incurred after the offer was made.

(As amended Dec. 27, 1946, eff. Mar. 19, 1948; Feb. 28, 1966, eff. July 1, 1966; Mar. 2, 1987, eff. Aug. 1, 1987; Apr. 30, 2007, eff. Dec. 1, 2007; Mar. 26, 2009, eff. Dec. 1, 2009.)

Notes of Advisory Committee on Rules—1937

See 2 Minn. Stat. (Mason, 1927) §9323; 4 Mont. Rev. Codes Ann. (1935) §9770; N.Y.C.P.A. (1937) §177.

For the recovery of costs against the United States, see Rule 54(d).

Notes of Advisory Committee on Rules—1946 Amendment

The third sentence of Rule 68 has been altered to make clear that evidence of an unaccepted offer is admissible in a proceeding to determine the costs of the action but is not otherwise admissible.

The two sentences substituted for the deleted last sentence of the rule assure a party the right to make a second offer where the situation permits—as, for example, where a prior offer was not accepted but the plaintiff's judgment is nullified and a new trial ordered, whereupon the defendant desires to make a second offer. It is implicit, however, that as long as the case continues—whether there be a first, second or third trial—and the defendant makes no further offer, his first and only offer will operate to save him the costs from the time of that offer if the plaintiff ultimately obtains a judgment less than the sum offered. In the case of successive offers not accepted, the offeror is saved the costs incurred after the making of the offer which was equal to or greater than the judgment ultimately obtained. These provisions should serve to encourage settlements and avoid protracted litigation.

The phrase "before the trial begins", in the first sentence of the rule, has been construed in Cover v. Chicago Eye Shield Co. (C.C.A.7th, 1943) 136 F.(2d) 374, cert. den. (1943) 320 U.S. 749.

Notes of Advisory Committee on Rules—1966 Amendment

This logical extension of the concept of offer of judgment is suggested by the common admiralty practice of determining liability before the amount of liability is determined.

Notes of Advisory Committee on Rules—1987 Amendment

The amendments are technical. No substantive change is intended.

Committee Notes on Rules—2007 Amendment

The language of Rule 68 has been amended as part of the general restyling of the Civil Rules to make them more easily understood and to make style and terminology consistent throughout the rules. These changes are intended to be stylistic only.

Committee Notes on Rules—2009 Amendment

Former Rule 68 allowed service of an offer of judgment more than 10 days before the trial begins, or—if liability has been determined—at least 10 days before a hearing to determine the extent of liability. It may be difficult to know in advance when trial will begin or when a hearing will be held. The time is now measured from the date set for trial or hearing; resetting the date establishes a new time for serving the offer.

The former 10-day periods are extended to 14 days to reflect the change in the Rule 6(a) method for computing periods less than 11 days.

Rule 69. Execution

(a) In General.

(1) Money Judgment; Applicable Procedure. A money judgment is enforced by a writ of execution, unless the court directs otherwise. The procedure on execution—and in proceedings supplementary to and in aid of judgment or execution—must accord with the procedure of the state where the court is located, but a federal statute governs to the extent it applies.

(2) Obtaining Discovery. In aid of the judgment or execution, the judgment creditor or a successor in interest whose interest appears of record may obtain discovery from any person—including the judgment debtor—as provided in these rules or by the procedure of the state where the court is located.

(b) Against Certain Public Officers. When a judgment has been entered against a revenue officer in the circumstances stated in 28 U.S.C. §2006, or against an officer of Congress in the circumstances stated in 2 U.S.C. §118 1, the judgment must be satisfied as those statutes provide.

(As amended Dec. 29, 1948, eff. Oct. 20, 1949; Mar. 30, 1970, eff. July 1, 1970; Mar. 2, 1987, eff. Aug. 1, 1987; Apr. 30, 2007, eff. Dec. 1, 2007.)

Notes of Advisory Committee on Rules—1937

Note to Subdivision (a). This follows in substance U.S.C., Title 28, [former] §§727 (Executions as provided by State laws) and 729 [now Title 42, §1988] (Proceedings in vindication of civil rights), except that, as in the similar case of attachments (see note to Rule 64), the rule specifies the applicable State law to be that of the time when the remedy is sought, and thus renders unnecessary, as well as supersedeas, local district court rules.

Statutes of the United States on execution, when applicable, govern under this rule. Among these are:

U.S.C., Title 12:

- §91 (Transfers by bank and other acts in contemplation of insolvency)
- §632 (Jurisdiction of United States district courts in cases arising out of foreign banking jurisdiction where Federal reserve bank a party)

U.S.C., Title 19:

- §199 (Judgments for customs duties, how payable)

U.S.C., Title 26:

- §1610(a) [former] (Surrender of property subject to distraint)

U.S.C., Title 28:

- §122 [now 1656] (Creation of new district or transfer of territory; lien)
- §350 [now 2101] (Time for making application for appeal or certiorari; stay pending application for certiorari)
- §489 [now 547] (District Attorneys; reports to Department of Justice)
- §574 [now 1921] (Marshals, fees enumerated)
- §786 [former] (Judgments for duties; collected in coin)
- §811 [now 1961] (Interest on judgments)
- §838 [former] (Executions; run in all districts of State)
- §839 [now 2413] (Executions; run in every State and Territory)
- §840 [former] (Executions; stay on conditions), as modified by Rule 62(b).
- §841 [former] (Executions; stay of one term), as modified by Rule 62(f)

- §842 [now 2006] (Executions; against officers of revenue in cases of probable cause), as incorporated in Subdivision (b) of this rule
- §843 [now 2007] (Imprisonment for debt)
- §844 [now 2007] (Imprisonment for debt; discharge according to State laws)
- §845 [now 2007] (Imprisonment for debt; jail limits)
- §846 [now 2005] (Fieri Facias; appraisal of goods; appraisers)
- §847 [now 2001] (Sales; real property under order or decree)
- §848 [now 2004] (Sales; personal property under order or decree)
- §849 [now 2002] (Sales; necessity of notice)
- §850 [now 2003] (Sales; death of marshal after levy or after sale)
- §869 [former] (Bond in former error and on appeal) as incorporated in Rule 73(c)
- §874 [former] (Supersedeas), as modified by Rules 62(d) and 73(d)

U.S.C., Title 31:

- §195 [now 3715] (Purchase on execution)

U.S.C., Title 33:

- §918 (Collection of defaulted payments)

U.S.C., Title 49:

- §74(g) [former] (Causes of action arising out of Federal control of railroads; execution and other process)

Special statutes of the United States on exemption from execution are also continued. Among these are:

U.S.C., Title 2:

- §118 (Actions against officers of Congress for official acts)

U.S.C., Title 5:

- §729 [see 8346, 8470] (Federal employees retirement annuities not subject to assignment, execution, levy, or other legal process)

U.S.C., Title 10:

- §610 [now 3690, 8690] (Exemption of enlisted men from arrest on civil process)

U.S.C., Title 22:

- §21(h) [see 4060] (Foreign service retirement and disability system; establishment; rules and regulations; annuities; nonassignable; exemption from legal process)

U.S.C., Title 33:

- §916 (Assignment and exemption from claims of creditors) Longshoremen's and Harborworkers' Compensation Act)

U.S.C., Title 38:

- §54 [see 5301] (Attachment, levy or seizure of moneys due pensioners prohibited)
- §393 [former] (Army and Navy Medal of Honor Roll; pensions additional to other pensions; liability to attachment, etc.) Compare Title 34, §365(c) (Medal of Honor Roll; special pension to persons enrolled)
- §618 [see 5301] (Benefits exempt from seizure under process and taxation; no deductions for indebtedness to United States)

U.S.C., Title 43:

- §175 (Exemption from execution of homestead land)

U.S.C., Title 48:

- §1371o (Panama Canal and railroad retirement annuities, exemption from execution and so forth)

Notes of Advisory Committee on Rules—1946 Supplementary Note

With respect to the provisions of the Soldiers' and Sailors' Civil Relief Act of 1940 ([former] 50 U.S.C. [App.] §501 et seq. [now 50 U.S.C. §3901 et seq.]) see Notes to Rules 62 and 64 herein.

Notes of Advisory Committee on Rules—1948 Amendment

The amendment substitutes the present statutory reference.

Notes of Advisory Committee on Rules—1970 Amendment

The amendment assures that, in aid of execution on a judgment, all discovery procedures provided in the rules are available and not just discovery via the taking of a deposition. Under the present language, one court has held that Rule 34 discovery is unavailable to the judgment creditor. M. Lowenstein & Sons, Inc. v. American Underwear Mfg. Co., 11 F.R.D. 172 (E.D.Pa. 1951). Notwithstanding the language, and relying heavily on legislative history referring to Rule 33, the Fifth Circuit has held that a judgment creditor may invoke Rule 33 interrogatories. United States v. McWhirter, 376 F.2d 102 (5th Cir. 1967). But the court's reasoning does not extend to discovery except as provided in Rules 26–33. One commentator suggests that the existing language might properly be stretched to all discovery, 7 Moore's Federal Practice 69.05[1] (2d ed. 1966), but another believes that a rules amendment is needed. 3 Barron & Holtzoff, Federal Practice and Procedure 1484 (Wright ed. 1958). Both commentators and the court in McWhirter are clear that, as a matter of policy, Rule 69 should authorize the use of all discovery devices provided in the rules.

Notes of Advisory Committee on Rules—1987 Amendment

The amendments are technical. No substantive change is intended.

Committee Notes on Rules—2007 Amendment

The language of Rule 69 has been amended as part of the general restyling of the Civil Rules to make them more easily understood and to make style and terminology consistent throughout the rules. These changes are intended to be stylistic only.

Amended Rule 69(b) incorporates directly the provisions of 2 U.S.C. §118 and 28 U.S.C. §2006, deleting the incomplete statement in former Rule 69(b) of the circumstances in which execution does not issue against an officer.

References in Text

2 U.S.C. §118, referred to in subd. (b), was editorially reclassified as 2 U.S.C. 5503.

1 See References in Text note below.

Rule 70. Enforcing a Judgment for a Specific Act

(a) Party's Failure to Act; Ordering Another to Act. If a judgment requires a party to convey land, to deliver a deed or other document, or to perform any other specific act and the party fails to comply within the time specified, the court may order the act to be done—at the disobedient party's expense—by another person appointed by the

court. When done, the act has the same effect as if done by the party.
(b) Vesting Title. If the real or personal property is within the district, the court—instead of ordering a conveyance—may enter a judgment divesting any party's title and vesting it in others. That judgment has the effect of a legally executed conveyance.
(c) Obtaining a Writ of Attachment or Sequestration. On application by a party entitled to performance of an act, the clerk must issue a writ of attachment or sequestration against the disobedient party's property to compel obedience.
(d) Obtaining a Writ of Execution or Assistance. On application by a party who obtains a judgment or order for possession, the clerk must issue a writ of execution or assistance.
(e) Holding in Contempt. The court may also hold the disobedient party in contempt.

(As amended Apr. 30, 2007, eff. Dec. 1, 2007.)

Notes of Advisory Committee on Rules—1937

Compare [former] Equity Rules 7 (Process, Mesne and Final), 8 (Enforcement of Final Decrees), and 9 (Writ of Assistance). To avoid possible confusion, both old and new denominations for attachment (sequestration) and execution (assistance) are used in this rule. Compare with the provision in this rule that the judgment may itself vest title, 6 Tenn.Ann.Code (Williams, 1934), §10594; 2 Conn.Gen.Stat. (1930), §5455; N.M.Stat.Ann. (Courtright, 1929), §117–117; 2 Ohio Gen.Code Ann. (Page, 1926), §11590; and England, Supreme Court of Judicature Act (1925), §47.

Committee Notes on Rules—2007 Amendment

The language of Rule 70 has been amended as part of the general restyling of the Civil Rules to make them more easily understood and to make style and terminology consistent throughout the rules. These changes are intended to be stylistic only.

Rule 71. Enforcing Relief For or Against a Nonparty

When an order grants relief for a nonparty or may be enforced against a nonparty, the procedure for enforcing the order is the same as for a party.

(As amended Mar. 2, 1987, eff. Aug. 1, 1987; Apr. 30, 2007, eff. Dec. 1, 2007.)

Notes of Advisory Committee on Rules—1937

Compare [former] Equity Rule 11 (Process in Behalf of and Against Persons Not Parties). Compare also Terrell v. Allison, 21 Wall. 289, 22 L.Ed. 634 (U.C., 1875); Farmers' Loan and Trust Co. v. Chicago and A. Ry. Co., 44 Fed. 653 (C.C.Ind., 1890); Robert Findlay Mfg. Co. v. Hygrade Lighting Fixture Corp., 288 Fed. 80 (E.D.N.Y., 1923); Thompson v. Smith, Fed.Cas.No. 13,977 (C.C.Minn., 1870).

Notes of Advisory Committee on Rules—1987 Amendment

The amendments are technical. No substantive change is intended.

Committee Notes on Rules—2007 Amendment

The language of Rule 71 has been amended as part of the general restyling of the Civil Rules to make them more easily understood and to make style and terminology consistent throughout the rules. These changes are intended to be stylistic only.

TITLE IX. SPECIAL PROCEEDINGS

Rule 71.1. Condemning Real or Personal Property

(a) Applicability of Other Rules. These rules govern proceedings to condemn real and personal property by eminent domain, except as this rule provides otherwise.
(b) Joinder of Properties. The plaintiff may join separate pieces of property in a single action, no matter whether they are owned by the same persons or sought for the same use.
(c) Complaint.
(1) Caption. The complaint must contain a caption as provided in Rule 10(a). The plaintiff must, however, name as defendants both the property—designated generally by kind, quantity, and location—and at least one owner of some part of or interest in the property.
(2) Contents. The complaint must contain a short and plain statement of the following:
(A) the authority for the taking;
(B) the uses for which the property is to be taken;
(C) a description sufficient to identify the property;
(D) the interests to be acquired; and
(E) for each piece of property, a designation of each defendant who has been joined as an owner or owner of an interest in it.
(3) Parties. When the action commences, the plaintiff need join as defendants only those persons who have or claim an interest in the property and whose names are then known. But before any hearing on compensation, the plaintiff must add as defendants all those persons who have or claim an interest and whose names have become known or can be found by a reasonably diligent search of the records, considering both the property's character and value and the interests to be acquired. All others may be made defendants under the designation "Unknown Owners."
(4) Procedure. Notice must be served on all defendants as provided in Rule 71.1(d), whether they were named as defendants when the action commenced or were added later. A defendant may answer as provided in Rule 71.1(e). The court, meanwhile, may order any distribution of a deposit that the facts warrant.
(5) Filing; Additional Copies. In addition to filing the complaint, the plaintiff must give the clerk at least one copy for the defendants' use and additional copies at the request of the clerk or a defendant.
(d) Process.
(1) Delivering Notice to the Clerk. On filing a complaint, the plaintiff must promptly deliver to the clerk joint or several notices directed to the named defendants. When adding defendants, the plaintiff must deliver to the clerk additional notices directed to the new defendants.
(2) Contents of the Notice.

(A) Main Contents. Each notice must name the court, the title of the action, and the defendant to whom it is directed. It must describe the property sufficiently to identify it, but need not describe any property other than that to be taken from the named defendant. The notice must also state:

(i) that the action is to condemn property;
(ii) the interest to be taken;
(iii) the authority for the taking;
(iv) the uses for which the property is to be taken;
(v) that the defendant may serve an answer on the plaintiff's attorney within 21 days after being served with the notice;
(vi) that the failure to so serve an answer constitutes consent to the taking and to the court's authority to proceed with the action and fix the compensation; and
(vii) that a defendant who does not serve an answer may file a notice of appearance.

(B) Conclusion. The notice must conclude with the name, telephone number, and e-mail address of the plaintiff's attorney and an address within the district in which the action is brought where the attorney may be served.

(3) Serving the Notice.

(A) Personal Service. When a defendant whose address is known resides within the United States or a territory subject to the administrative or judicial jurisdiction of the United States, personal service of the notice (without a copy of the complaint) must be made in accordance with Rule 4.

(B) Service by Publication.

(i) A defendant may be served by publication only when the plaintiff's attorney files a certificate stating that the attorney believes the defendant cannot be personally served, because after diligent inquiry within the state where the complaint is filed, the defendant's place of residence is still unknown or, if known, that it is beyond the territorial limits of personal service. Service is then made by publishing the notice—once a week for at least 3 successive weeks—in a newspaper published in the county where the property is located or, if there is no such newspaper, in a newspaper with general circulation where the property is located. Before the last publication, a copy of the notice must also be mailed to every defendant who cannot be personally served but whose place of residence is then known. Unknown owners may be served by publication in the same manner by a notice addressed to "Unknown Owners."

(ii) Service by publication is complete on the date of the last publication. The plaintiff's attorney must prove publication and mailing by a certificate, attach a printed copy of the published notice, and mark on the copy the newspaper's name and the dates of publication.

(4) Effect of Delivery and Service. Delivering the notice to the clerk and serving it have the same effect as serving a summons under Rule 4.

(5) Amending the Notice; Proof of Service and Amending the Proof. Rule 4(a)(2) governs amending the notice. Rule 4(l) governs proof of service and amending it.

(e) Appearance or Answer.

(1) Notice of Appearance. A defendant that has no objection or defense to the taking of its property may serve a notice of appearance designating the property in which it claims an interest. The defendant must then be given notice of all later proceedings affecting the defendant.

(2) Answer. A defendant that has an objection or defense to the taking must serve an answer within 21 days after being served with the notice. The answer must:

(A) identify the property in which the defendant claims an interest;
(B) state the nature and extent of the interest; and
(C) state all the defendant's objections and defenses to the taking.

(3) Waiver of Other Objections and Defenses; Evidence on Compensation. A defendant waives all objections and defenses not stated in its answer. No other pleading or motion asserting an additional objection or defense is allowed. But at the trial on compensation, a defendant—whether or not it has previously appeared or answered—may present evidence on the amount of compensation to be paid and may share in the award.

(f) Amending Pleadings. Without leave of court, the plaintiff may—as often as it wants—amend the complaint at any time before the trial on compensation. But no amendment may be made if it would result in a dismissal inconsistent with Rule 71.1(i)(1) or (2). The plaintiff need not serve a copy of an amendment, but must serve notice of the filing, as provided in Rule 5(b), on every affected party who has appeared and, as provided in Rule 71.1(d), on every affected party who has not appeared. In addition, the plaintiff must give the clerk at least one copy of each amendment for the defendants' use, and additional copies at the request of the clerk or a defendant. A defendant may appear or answer in the time and manner and with the same effect as provided in Rule 71.1(e).

(g) Substituting Parties. If a defendant dies, becomes incompetent, or transfers an interest after being joined, the court may, on motion and notice of hearing, order that the proper party be substituted. Service of the motion and notice on a nonparty must be made as provided in Rule 71.1(d)(3).

(h) Trial of the Issues.

(1) Issues Other Than Compensation; Compensation. In an action involving eminent domain under federal law, the court tries all issues, including compensation, except when compensation must be determined:

(A) by any tribunal specially constituted by a federal statute to determine compensation; or
(B) if there is no such tribunal, by a jury when a party demands one within the time to answer or within any additional time the court sets, unless the court appoints a commission.

(2) Appointing a Commission; Commission's Powers and Report.

(A) Reasons for Appointing. If a party has demanded a jury, the court may instead appoint a three-person commission to determine compensation because of the character, location, or quantity of the property to be condemned or for other just reasons.

(B) Alternate Commissioners. The court may appoint up to two additional persons to serve as alternate commissioners to hear the case and replace commissioners who, before a decision is filed, the court finds unable or disqualified to perform their duties. Once the commission renders its final decision, the court must discharge any alternate who has not replaced a commissioner.

(C) Examining the Prospective Commissioners. Before making its appointments, the court must advise the parties of the identity and qualifications of each prospective commissioner and alternate, and may permit the parties to examine them. The parties may not suggest appointees, but for good cause may object to a prospective commissioner or alternate.

(D) Commission's Powers and Report. A commission has the powers of a master under Rule 53(c). Its action and report are determined by a majority. Rule 53(d), (e), and (f) apply to its action and report.

(i) Dismissal of the Action or a Defendant.

(1) Dismissing the Action.

(A) By the Plaintiff. If no compensation hearing on a piece of property has begun, and if the plaintiff has not acquired title or a lesser interest or taken possession, the plaintiff may, without a court order, dismiss the action as to that property by filing a notice of dismissal briefly describing the property.

(B) By Stipulation. Before a judgment is entered vesting the plaintiff with title or a lesser interest in or possession of property, the plaintiff and affected defendants may, without a court order, dismiss the action in whole or in part by filing a stipulation of dismissal. And if the parties so stipulate, the court may vacate a judgment already entered.

(C) By Court Order. At any time before compensation has been determined and paid, the court may, after a motion and hearing, dismiss the action as to a piece of property. But if the plaintiff has already taken title, a lesser interest, or possession as to any part of it, the court must award compensation for the title, lesser interest, or possession taken.

(2) Dismissing a Defendant. The court may at any time dismiss a defendant who was unnecessarily or improperly joined.

(3) Effect. A dismissal is without prejudice unless otherwise stated in the notice, stipulation, or court order.

(j) Deposit and Its Distribution.

(1) Deposit. The plaintiff must deposit with the court any money required by law as a condition to the exercise of eminent domain and may make a deposit when allowed by statute.

(2) Distribution; Adjusting Distribution. After a deposit, the court and attorneys must expedite the proceedings so as to distribute the deposit and to determine and pay compensation. If the compensation finally awarded to a defendant exceeds the amount distributed to that defendant, the court must enter judgment against the plaintiff for the deficiency. If the compensation awarded to a defendant is less than the amount distributed to that defendant, the court must enter judgment against that defendant for the overpayment.

(k) Condemnation Under a State's Power of Eminent Domain. This rule governs an action involving eminent domain under state law. But if state law provides for trying an issue by jury—or for trying the issue of compensation by jury or commission or both—that law governs.

(l) Costs. Costs are not subject to Rule 54(d).

(As added Apr. 30, 1951, eff. Aug. 1, 1951; amended Jan. 21, 1963, eff. July 1, 1963; Apr. 29, 1985, eff. Aug. 1, 1985; Mar. 2, 1987, eff. Aug. 1, 1987; Apr. 25, 1988, eff. Aug. 1, 1988; Pub. L. 100–690, title VII, §7050, Nov. 18, 1988, 102 Stat. 4401; Apr. 22, 1993, eff. Dec. 1, 1993; Mar. 27, 2003, eff. Dec. 1, 2003; Apr. 30, 2007, eff. Dec. 1, 2007; Mar. 26, 2009, eff. Dec. 1, 2009.)

Notes of Advisory Committee on Rules—1951

Supplementary report

The Court will remember that at its conference on December 2, 1948, the discussion was confined to subdivision (h) of the rule (* * *), the particular question being whether the tribunal to award compensation should be a commission or a jury in cases where the Congress has not made specific provision on the subject. The Advisory Committee was agreed from the outset that a rule should not be promulgated which would overturn the decision of the Congress as to the kind of tribunal to fix compensation, provided that the system established by Congress was found to be working well. We found two instances where the Congress had specified the kind of tribunal to fix compensation. One case was the District of Columbia (U.S.C., [former] Title 40, §§361–386) where a rather unique system exists under which the court is required in all cases to order the selection of a "jury" of five from among not less than twenty names drawn from "the special box provided by law." They must have the usual qualifications of jurors and in addition must be freeholders of the District and not in the service of the United States or the District. That system has been in effect for many years, and our inquiry revealed that it works well under the conditions prevailing in the District, and is satisfactory to the courts of the District, the legal profession and to property owners.

The other instance is that of the Tennessee Valley Authority, where the act of Congress (U.S.C., Title 16, §831x) provides that compensation is fixed by three disinterested commissioners appointed by the court, whose award goes before the District Court for confirmation or modification. The Advisory Committee made a thorough inquiry into the practical operation of the TVA commission system. We obtained from counsel for the TVA the results of their experience, which afforded convincing proof that the commission system is preferable under the conditions affecting TVA and that the jury system would not work satisfactorily. We then, under date of February 6, 1947, wrote every Federal judge who had ever sat in a TVA condemnation case, asking his views as to whether the commission system is satisfactory and whether a jury system should be preferred. Of 21 responses from the judges 17 approved the commission system and opposed the substitution of a jury system for the TVA. Many of the judges went further and opposed the use of juries in any condemnation cases. Three of the judges preferred the jury system, and one dealt only with the TVA provision for a three judge district court. The Advisory Committee has not considered abolition of the three judge requirement of the TVA Act, because it seemed to raise a question of jurisdiction, which cannot be altered by rule. Nevertheless the Department of Justice continued its advocacy of the jury system for its asserted expedition and economy; and others favored a uniform procedure. In consequence of these divided counsels the Advisory Committee was itself divided, but in its May 1948 Report to the Court recommended the following rule as approved by a majority (* * *):

(h) Trial. If the action involves the exercise of the power of eminent domain under the law of the United States, any tribunal specially constituted by an Act of Congress governing the case for the trial of the issue of just compensation shall be the tribunal for the determination of that issue; but if there is no such specially constituted tribunal any party may have a trial by jury of the issue of just compensation by filing a demand therefor within the time allowed for answer or within such further time as the court may fix. Trial of all issues shall otherwise be by the court.

The effect of this was to preserve the existing systems in the District of Columbia and in TVA cases, but to provide for a jury to fix compensation in all other cases.

Before the Court's conference of December 2, 1948, the Chief Justice informed the Committee that the Court was particularly interested in the views expressed by Judge John Paul, judge of the United States District Court for the Western District of Virginia, in a letter from him to the chairman of the Advisory Committee, dated February 13, 1947. Copies of all the letters from judges who had sat in TVA cases had been made available to the Court, and this letter from Judge Paul is one of them. Judge Paul strongly opposed jury trials and recommended the commission system in large projects like the TVA, and his views seemed to have impressed the Court and to have been the occasion for the conference.

The reasons which convinced the Advisory Committee that the use of commissioners instead of juries is desirable in TVA cases were these:

1. The TVA condemns large areas of land of similar kind, involving many owners. Uniformity in awards is essential. The commission system tends to prevent discrimination and provide for uniformity in compensation. The jury system tends to lack of uniformity. Once a reasonable and uniform standard of values for the area has been settled by a commission, litigation ends and settlements result.

2. Where large areas are involved many small landowners reside at great distances from the place where a court sits. It is a great hardship on humble people to have to travel long distances to attend a jury trial. A commission may travel around and receive the evidence of the owner near his home.

3. It is impracticable to take juries long distances to view the premises.

4. If the cases are tried by juries the burden on the time of the courts is excessive.

These considerations are the very ones Judge Paul stressed in his letter. He pointed out that they applied not only to the TVA but to other large governmental projects, such as flood control, hydroelectric power, reclamation, national forests, and others. So when the representatives of the Advisory Committee appeared at the Court's conference December 2, 1948, they found it difficult to justify the proposed provision in subdivision (h) of the rule that a jury should be used to fix compensation in all cases where Congress had not specified the tribunal. If our reasons for preserving the TVA system were sound, provision for a jury in similar projects of like magnitude seemed unsound.

Aware of the apparent inconsistency between the acceptance of the TVA system and the provision for a jury in all other cases, the members of the Committee attending the conference of December 2, 1948, then suggested that in the other cases the choice of jury or commission be left to the discretion of the District Court, going back to a suggestion previously made by Committee members and reported at page 15 of the Preliminary Draft of June 1947. They called the attention of the Court to the fact that the entire Advisory Committee had not been consulted about this suggestion and proposed that the draft be returned to the Committee for further consideration, and that was done.

The proposal we now make for subdivision (h) is as follows:

(h) Trial. If the action involves the exercise of the power of eminent domain under the law of the United States, any tribunal specially constituted by an Act of Congress governing the case for the trial of the issue of just compensation shall be the tribunal for the determination of that issue; but if there is no such specially constituted tribunal any party may have a trial by jury of the issue of just compensation by filing a demand therefor within the time allowed for answer or within such further time as the court may fix, unless the court in its discretion orders that, because of the character, location, or quantity of the property to be condemned, or for other reasons in the interest of justice, the issue of compensation shall be determined by a commission of three persons appointed by it. If a commission is appointed it shall have the powers of a master provided in subdivision (c) of Rule 53 proceedings before it shall be governed by the provisions of paragraphs (1) and (2) of subdivision (d) of Rule 53. Its action and report shall be determined by a majority and its findings and report shall have the effect, and be dealt with by the court in accordance with the practice, prescribed in paragraph (2) of subdivision (e) of Rule 53. Trial of all issues shall otherwise be by the court.

In the 1948 draft the Committee had been almost evenly divided as between jury or commission and that made it easy for us to agree on the present draft. It would be difficult to state in a rule the various conditions to control the District Court in its choice and we have merely stated generally the matters which should be considered by the District Court.

The rule as now drafted seems to meet Judge Paul's objection. In large projects like the TVA the court may decide to use a commission. In a great number of cases involving only sites for buildings or other small areas, where use of a jury is appropriate, a jury may be chosen. The District Court's discretion may also be influenced by local preference or habit, and the preference of the Department of Justice and the reasons for its preference will doubtless be given weight. The Committee is convinced that there are some types of cases in which use of a commission is preferable and others in which a jury may be appropriately used, and that it would be a mistake to provide that the same kind of tribunal should be used in all cases. We think the available evidence clearly leads to that conclusion.

When this suggestion was made at the conference of December 2, 1948, representatives of the Department of Justice opposed it, expressing opposition to the use of a commission in any case. Their principal ground for opposition to commissions was then based on the assertion that the commission system is too expensive because courts allow commissioners too large compensation. The obvious answer to that is that the compensation of commissioners ought to be fixed or limited by law, as was done in the TVA Act, and the agency dealing with appropriations—either the Administrative Office or some other interested department of the government—should correct that evil, if evil there be, by obtaining such legislation. Authority to promulgate rules of procedure does not include power to fix compensation of government employees. The Advisory Committee is not convinced that even without such legislation the commission system is more expensive than the jury system. The expense of jury trials includes not only the per diem and mileage of the jurors impaneled for a case but like items for the entire venire. In computing cost of jury trials, the salaries of court officials, judges, clerks, marshals and deputies must be considered. No figures have been given to the Committee to establish that the cost of the commission system is the greater.

We earnestly recommend the rule as now drafted for promulgation by the Court, in the public interest.

The Advisory Committee have given more time to this rule, including time required for conferences with the Department of Justice to hear statements of its representatives, than has been required by any other rule. The rule may not be perfect but if faults develop in practice they may be promptly cured. Certainly the present conformity system is atrocious.

Under state practices, just compensation is normally determined by one of three methods: by commissioners; by commissioners with a right of appeal to and trial de novo before a jury; and by a jury, without a commission. A trial to the court or to the court including a master are, however, other methods that are occasionally used. Approximately 5 states use only commissioners; 23 states use commissioners with a trial de novo before a jury; and 18 states use only the jury. This classification is advisedly stated in approximate terms, since the same state may utilize diverse methods, depending upon different types of condemnations or upon the locality of the property, and since the methods used in a few states do not permit of a categorical classification. To reject the proposed rule and leave the situation as it is would not satisfy the views of the Department of Justice. The Department and the Advisory Committee agree that the use of a commission, with appeal to a jury, is a wasteful system.

The Department of Justice has a voluminous "Manual on Federal Eminent Domain," the 1940 edition of which has 948 pages with an appendix of 73 more pages. The title page informs us the preparation of the manual was begun during the incumbency of Attorney General Cummings, was continued under Attorney General Murphy, and completed during the incumbency of Attorney General Jackson. The preface contains the following statement:

It should also be mentioned that the research incorporated in the manual would be of invaluable assistance in the drafting of a new uniform code, or rules of court, for federal condemnation proceedings, which are now greatly confused, not only by the existence of over seventy federal statutes governing condemnations for different purposes—statutes which sometimes conflict with one another—but also by the countless problems occasioned by the requirements of conformity to state law. Progress of the work has already demonstrated that the need for such reform exists.

It is not surprising that more than once Attorneys General have asked the Advisory Committee to prepare a federal rule and rescue the government from this morass.

The Department of Justice has twice tried and failed to persuade the Congress to provide that juries shall be used in all condemnation cases. The debates in Congress show that part of the opposition to the Department of Justice's bills came from representatives opposed to jury trials in all cases, and in part from a preference for the conformity system. Our present proposal opens the door for district judges to yield to local preferences on the subject. It does much for the Department's points of view. It is a great improvement over the present so-called conformity system. It does away with the wasteful "double" system prevailing in 23 states where awards by commissions are followed by jury trials.

Aside from the question as to the choice of a tribunal to award compensation, the proposed rule would afford a simple and improved procedure.

We turn now to an itemized explanation of the other changes we have made in the 1948 draft. Some of these result from recent amendments to the Judicial Code. Others result from a reconsideration by the Advisory Committee of provisions which we thought could be improved.

1. In the amended Judicial Code, the district courts are designated as "United States District Courts" instead of "District Courts of the United States," and a corresponding change has been made in the rule.

2. After the 1948 draft was referred back to the committee, the provision in subdivision (c)(2), relating to naming defendants, * * * which provided that the plaintiff shall add as defendants all persons having or claiming an interest in that property whose names can be ascertained by a search of the records to the extent commonly made by competent searchers of title in the vicinity "in light of the type and value of the property involved," the phrase in quotation marks was changed to read "in the light of the character and value of the property involved and the interests to be acquired."

The Department of Justice made a counter proposal * * * that there be substituted the words "reasonably diligent search of the records, considering the type." When the American Bar Association thereafter considered the draft, it approved the Advisory Committee's draft of this subdivision, but said that it had no objection to the Department's suggestion. Thereafter, in an effort to eliminate controversy, the Advisory Committee accepted the Department's suggestion as to (c)(2), using the word "character" instead of the word "type."

The Department of Justice also suggested that in subdivision (d)(3)(2) relating to service by publication, the search for a defendant's residence as a preliminary to publication be limited to the state in which the complaint is filed. Here again the American Bar Association's report expressed the view that the Department's suggestion was unobjectionable and the Advisory Committee thereupon adopted it.

3. Subdivision (k) of the 1948 draft is as follows:

(k) Condemnation Under a State's Power of Eminent Domain. If the action involves the exercise of the power of eminent domain under the law of a state, the practice herein prescribed may be altered to the extent necessary to observe and enforce any condition affecting the substantial rights of a litigant attached by the state law to the exercise of the state's power of eminent domain.

Occasionally condemnation cases under a state's power of eminent domain reach a United States District Court because of diversity of citizenship. Such cases are rare, but provision should be made for them.

The 1948 draft of (k) required a district court to decide whether a provision of state law specifying the tribunal to award compensation is or is not a "condition" attached to the exercise of the state's power. On reconsideration we concluded that it would be wise to redraft (k) so as to avoid that troublesome question. As to conditions in state laws which affect the substantial rights of a litigant, the district courts would be bound to give them effect without any rule on the subject. Accordingly we present two alternative revisions. One suggestion supported by a majority of the Advisory Committee is as follows:

(k) Condemnation Under a State's Power of Eminent Domain. The practice herein prescribed governs in actions involving the exercise of the power of eminent domain under the law of a state, provided that if the state law makes provision for trial of any issue by jury, or for trial of the issue of compensation by jury or commission or both, that provision shall be followed.

The other is as follows:

(k) Condemnation Under a State's Power of Eminent Domain. The practice herein prescribed governs in actions involving the exercise of the power of eminent domain under the law of a state, provided that if the state law gives a right to a trial by jury such a trial shall in any case be allowed to the party demanding it within the time permitted by these rules, and in that event no hearing before a commission shall be had.

The first proposal accepts the state law as to the tribunals to fix compensation, and in that respect leaves the parties in precisely the same situation as if the case were pending in a state court, including the use of a commission with appeal to a jury, if the state law so provides. It has the effect of avoiding any question as to whether the decisions in Erie R. Co. v. Tompkins and later cases have application to a situation of this kind.

The second proposal gives the parties a right to a jury trial if that is provided for by state law, but prevents the use of both commission and jury. Those members of the Committee who favor the second proposal do so because of the obvious objections to the double trial, with a commission and appeal to a jury. As the decisions in Erie R. Co. v. Tompkins and later cases may have a bearing on this point, and the Committee is divided, we think both proposals should be placed before the Court.

4. The provision * * * of the 1948 draft * * * prescribing the effective date of the rule was drafted before the recent amendment of the Judicial Code on that subject. On May 10, 1950, the President approved an act which amended section 2072 of Title 28, United States Code, to read as follows:

Such rules shall not take effect until they have been reported to Congress by the Chief Justice at or after the beginning of a regular session thereof but not later than the first day of May, and until the expiration of 90 days after they have been thus reported.

To conform to the statute now in force, we suggest a provision as follows:

Effective Date. This Rule 71A and the amendment to Rule 81(a) will take effect on August 1, 1951. Rule 71A governs all proceedings in actions brought after it takes effect and also all further proceedings in actions then pending, except to the extent that in the opinion of the court its application in a particular action pending when the rule takes effect would not be feasible or would work injustice, in which event the former procedure applies.

If the rule is not reported to Congress by May 1, 1951, this provision must be altered.

5. We call attention to the fact that the proposed rule does not contain a provision for the procedure to be followed in order to exercise the right of the United States to take immediate possession or title, when the condemnation proceeding is begun. There are several statutes conferring such a right which are cited in the original notes to the May 1948 draft * * *. The existence of this right is taken into account in the rule. In paragraph (c)(2), * * * it is stated: "Upon the commencement of the action, the plaintiff need join as defendants only the persons having or claiming an interest in the property whose names are then known." That is to enable the United States to exercise the right to immediate title or possession without the delay involved in ascertaining the names of all interested parties. The right is also taken into account in the provision relating to dismissal (paragraph (i) subdivisions (1), (2), and (3), * * *); also in paragraph (j) relating to deposits and their distribution.

The Advisory Committee considered whether the procedure for exercising the right should be specified in the rule and decided against it, as the procedure now being followed seems to be giving no trouble, and to draft a rule to fit all the statutes on the subject might create confusion.

The American Bar Association has taken an active interest in a rule for condemnation cases. In 1944 its House of Delegates adopted a resolution which among other things resolved:

That before adoption by the Supreme Court of the United States of any redraft of the proposed rule, time and opportunity should be afforded to the bar to consider and make recommendations concerning any such redraft.

Accordingly, in 1950 the revised draft was submitted to the American Bar Association and its section of real property, probate and trust law appointed a committee to consider it. That committee was supplied with copies of the written statement from the Department of Justice giving the reasons relied on by the Department for preferring a rule to use juries in all cases. The Advisory Committee's report was approved at a meeting of the section of real property law, and by the House of Delegates at the annual meeting of September 1950. The American Bar Association report gave particular attention to the question whether juries or commissions should be used to fix compensation, approved the Advisory Committee's solution appearing in their latest draft designed to allow use of commissions in projects comparable to the TVA, and rejected the proposal for use of juries in all cases.

In November 1950 a committee of the Federal Bar Association, the chairman of which was a Special Assistant to the Attorney General, made a report which reflected the attitude of the Department of Justice on the condemnation rule.

Aside from subdivision (h) about the tribunal to award compensation the final draft of the condemnation rule here presented has the approval of the American Bar Association and, we understand, the Department of Justice, and we do not know of any opposition to it. Subdivision (h) has the unanimous approval of the Advisory Committee and has been approved by the American Bar Association. The use of commissions in TVA cases, and, by fair inference, in cases comparable to the TVA, is supported by 17 out of 20 judges who up to 1947 had sat in TVA cases. The legal staff of the TVA has vigorously objected to the substitution of juries for commissions in TVA cases. We regret to report that the Department of Justice still asks that subdivision (h) be altered to provide for jury trials in all cases where Congress has not specified the tribunal. We understand that the Department approves the proposal that the system prevailing in 23 states for the "double" trial, by commission with appeal to and trial de novo before a jury, should be abolished, and also asks that on demand a jury should be substituted for a commission, in those states where use of a commission alone is now required. The Advisory Committee has no evidence that commissions do not operate satisfactorily in the case of projects comparable to the TVA.

Original report

General Statement. 1. Background. When the Advisory Committee was formulating its recommendations to the Court concerning rules of procedure, which subsequently became the Federal Rules of 1938, the Committee concluded at an early stage not to fix the procedure in condemnation cases. This is a matter principally involving the exercise of the federal power of eminent domain, as very few condemnation cases involving the state's power reach the United States District Courts. The Committee's reasons at that time were that inasmuch as condemnation proceedings by the United States are governed by statutes of the United States, prescribing different procedure for various agencies and departments of the government, or, in the absence of such statutes, by local state practice under the Conformity Act ([former] 40 U.S.C. sec. 258), it would be extremely difficult to draft a uniform rule satisfactory to the various agencies and departments of the government and to private parties; and that there was no general demand for a uniform rule. The Committee continued in that belief until shortly before the preparation of the April 1937 Draft of the Rules, when the officials of the Department of Justice having to do with condemnation cases urgently requested the Committee to propose rules on this subject. The Committee undertook the task and drafted a Condemnation Rule which appeared for the first time as Rule 74 of the April 1937 Draft. After the publication and distribution of this initial draft many objections were urged against it by counsel for various governmental agencies, whose procedure in condemnation cases was prescribed by federal statutes. Some of these agencies wanted to be excepted in whole or in part from the operation of the uniform rule proposed in April 1937. And the Department of Justice changed its position and stated that it preferred to have government condemnations conducted by local attorneys familiar with the state practice, which was applied under the Conformity Act where the Acts of Congress do not prescribe the practice; that it preferred to work under the Conformity Act without a uniform rule of procedure. The profession generally showed little interest in the proposed uniform rule. For these reasons the Advisory Committee in its Final Report to the Court in November 1937 proposed that all of Rule 74 be stricken and that the Federal Rules be made applicable only to appeals in condemnation cases. See note to Rule 74 of the Final Report.

Some six or seven years later when the Advisory Committee was considering the subject of amendments to the Federal Rules both government officials and the profession generally urged the adoption of some uniform procedure. This demand grew out of the volume of condemnation proceedings instituted during the war, and the general feeling of dissatisfaction with the diverse condemnation procedures that were applicable in the federal courts. A strongly held belief was that both the sovereign's power to condemn and the property owner's right to compensation could be promoted by a simplified rule. As a consequence the Committee proposed a Rule 71A on the subject of condemnation in its Preliminary Draft of May 1944. In the Second Preliminary Draft of May 1945 this earlier proposed Rule 71A was, however, omitted. The Committee did not then feel that it had sufficient time to prepare a revised draft satisfactorily to it which would meet legitimate objections made to the draft of May 1944. To avoid unduly delaying the proposed amendments to existing rules the Committee concluded to proceed in the regular way with the preparation of the amendments to these rules and deal with the question of a condemnation rule as an independent matter. As a consequence it made no recommendations to the Court on condemnation in its Final Report of Proposed Amendments of June 1946; and the amendments which the Court adopted in December 1946 did not deal with condemnation. After concluding its task relative to amendments, the Committee returned to a consideration of eminent domain, its proposed Rule 71A of May 1944, the suggestions and criticisms that had been presented in the interim, and in June 1947 prepared and distributed to the profession another draft of a proposed condemnation rule. This draft contained several alternative provisions, specifically called attention to and asked for opinion relative to these matters, and in particular as to the constitution of the tribunal to award compensation. The present draft was based on the June 1947 formulation, in light of the advice of the profession on both matters of substance and form.

2. Statutory Provisions. The need for a uniform condemnation rule in the federal courts arises from the fact that by various statutes Congress has prescribed diverse procedures for certain condemnation proceedings, and, in the absence of such statutes, has prescribed conformity to local state practice under [former] 40 U.S.C. §258. This general conformity adds to the diversity of procedure since in the United States there are multifarious methods of procedure in existence. Thus in 1931 it was said that there were 269 different methods of judicial procedure in different classes of condemnation cases and 56 methods of nonjudicial or administrative procedure. First Report of Judicial Council of Michigan, 1931, §46, pp. 55–56. These numbers have not decreased. Consequently, the general requirement of conformity to state practice and procedure, particularly where the condemnor is the United States, leads to expense, delay and uncertainty. In advocacy of a uniform federal rule, see Armstrong, Proposed Amendments to Federal Rules for Civil Procedure 1944, 4 F.R.D. 124, 134; id., Report of the Advisory Committee on Federal Rules of Civil Procedure Recommending Amendments, 1946, 5 F.R.D. 339, 357.

There are a great variety of Acts of Congress authorizing the exercise of the power of eminent domain by the United States and its officers and agencies. These statutes for the most part do not specify the exact procedure to be followed, but where procedure is prescribed, it is by no means uniform.

The following are instances of Acts which merely authorize the exercise of the power without specific declaration as to the procedure:

U.S.C., Title 16:

- §404c–11 (Mammoth Cave National Park; acquisition of lands, interests in lands or other property for park by the Secretary of the Interior).
- §426d (Stones River National Park; acquisition of land for parks by the Secretary of the Army).
- §450aa (George Washington Carver National Monument; acquisition of land by the Secretary of the Interior).
- §517 (National forest reservation; title to lands to be acquired by the Secretary of Agriculture).

U.S.C., Title 42:

- §§1805(b)(5), 1813(b) (Atomic Energy Act).

The following are instances of Acts which authorized condemnation and declare that the procedure is to conform with that of similar actions in state courts:

U.S.C., Title 16:

- §423k (Richmond National Battlefield Park; acquisition of lands by the Secretary of the Interior).
- §714 (Exercise by water power licensee of power of eminent domain).

U.S.C., Title 24:

- §78 (Condemnation of land for the former National Home for Disabled Volunteer Soldiers).

U.S.C., Title 33:

- §591 (Condemnation of lands and materials for river and harbor improvement by the Secretary of the Army).

U.S.C., Title 40:

- §257 [now 3113] (Condemnation of realty for sites for public building and for other public uses by the Secretary of the Treasury authorized).
- §258 [former] (Same procedure).

U.S.C., Title 50:

- §171 (Acquisition of land by the Secretary of the Army for national defense).
- §172 (Acquisition of property by the Secretary of the Army, etc., for production of lumber).
- §632 App. (Second War Powers Act, 1942; acquisition of real property for war purposes by the Secretary of the Army, the Secretary of the Navy and others).

The following are Acts in which a more or less complete code of procedure is set forth in connection with the taking:

U.S.C., Title 16:

- §831x (Condemnation by Tennessee Valley Authority).

U.S.C., Title 40:

- §§361–386 [former] (Acquisition of lands in District of Columbia for use of United States; condemnation).

3. Adjustment of Rule to Statutory Provisions. While it was apparent that the principle of uniformity should be the basis for a rule to replace the multiple diverse procedures set out above, there remained a serious question as to whether an exception could properly be made relative to the method of determining compensation. Where Congress had provided for conformity to state law the following were the general methods in use: an initial determination by commissioners, with appeal to a judge; an initial award, likewise made by commissioners, but with the appeal to a jury; and determination by a jury without a previous award by commissioners. In two situations Congress had specified the tribunal to determine the issue of compensation: condemnation by the Tennessee Valley Authority; and condemnation in the District of Columbia. Under the TVA procedure the initial determination of value is by three disinterested commissioners, appointed by the court, from a locality other than the one in which the land lies. Either party may except to the award of the commission; in that case the exceptions are to be heard by three district judges (unless the parties stipulate for a lesser number), with a right of appeal to the circuit court of appeals. The TVA is a regional agency. It is faced with the necessity of acquiring a very substantial acreage within a relatively small area, and charged with the task of carrying on within the Tennessee Valley and in cooperation with the local people a permanent program involving navigation and flood control, electric power, soil conservation, and general regional development. The success of this program is partially dependent upon the good will and cooperation of the people of the Tennessee Valley, and this in turn partially depends upon the land acquisition program. Disproportionate awards among landowners would create dissatisfaction and ill will. To secure uniformity in treatment Congress provided the rather unique procedure of the three-judge court to review de novo the initial award of the commissioners. This procedure has worked to the satisfaction of the property owners and the TVA. A full statement of the TVA position and experience is set forth in Preliminary Draft of Proposed Rule to Govern Condemnation Cases (June, 1947) 15–19. A large majority of the district judges with experience under this procedure approve it, subject to some objection to the requirement for a three-judge district court to review commissioners' awards. A statutory three-judge requirement is, however, jurisdictional and must be strictly followed. Stratton v. St. Louis, Southwestern Ry. Co., 1930, 51 S.Ct. 8, 282 U.S. 10, 75 L.Ed. 135; Ayrshire Collieries Corp. v. United States, 1947, 67 S.Ct. 1168, 331 U.S. 132, 91 L.Ed. 1391. Hence except insofar as the TVA statute itself authorizes the parties to stipulate for a court of less than three judges, the requirement must be followed, and would seem to be beyond alteration by court rule even if change were thought desirable. Accordingly the TVA procedure is retained for the determination of compensation in TVA condemnation cases. It was also thought desirable to retain the specific method Congress had prescribed for the District of Columbia, which is a so-called jury of five appointed by the court. This is a local matter and the specific treatment accorded by Congress has given local satisfaction.

Aside from the foregoing limited exceptions dealing with the TVA and the District of Columbia, the question was whether a uniform method for determining compensation should be a commission with appeal to a district judge, or a commission with appeal to a jury, or a jury without a commission. Experience with the commission on a nationwide basis, and in particular with the utilization of a commission followed by an appeal to a jury, has been that the commission is time consuming and expensive. Furthermore, it is largely a futile procedure where it is preparatory to jury trial. Since in the bulk of states a land owner is entitled eventually to a jury trial, since the jury is a traditional tribunal for the determination of questions of value, and since experience with juries has proved satisfactory to both government and land owner, the right to jury trial is adopted as the general rule. Condemnation involving the TVA and the District of Columbia are the two exceptions. See Note to Subdivision (h), infra.

Note to Subdivision (a). As originally promulgated the Federal Rules governed appeals in condemnation proceedings but were not otherwise applicable. Rule 81(a)(7). Pre-appeal procedure, in the main, conformed to state procedure. See statutes and discussion, supra. The purpose of Rule 71A is to provide a uniform procedure for condemnation in the federal district courts, including the District of Columbia. To achieve this purpose Rule 71A prescribes such specialized procedure as is required by condemnation proceedings, otherwise it utilizes the general framework of the Federal Rules where specific detail is unnecessary. The adoption of Rule 71A, of course, renders paragraph (7) of Rule 81(a) unnecessary.

The promulgation of a rule for condemnation procedure is within the rule-making power. The Enabling Act [Act of June 19, 1934, c. 651, §§1, 2 (48 Stat. 1064), 28 U.S.C. §§723b, 723c [see 2072]] gives the Supreme Court "the power to prescribe, by general rules * * * the forms of process, writs, pleadings, and motions, and the practice and procedure in civil actions at law." Such rules, however, must not abridge, enlarge, or modify substantive rights. In Kohl v. United States, 1875, 91 U.S. 367, 23 L.Ed. 449, a proceeding instituted by the United States to appropriate land for a post-office site under a statute enacted for such purpose, the Supreme Court held that "a proceeding to take land in virtue of the government's eminent domain, and determining the compensation to be made for it, is * * * a suit at common law, when initiated in a court." See also Madisonville Traction Co. v. Saint Bernard Mining Co., 1905, 25 S.Ct. 251, 196 U.S. 239, 23 L.Ed. 449, infra, under subdivision (k). And the Conformity Act, [former] 40 U.S.C. §258, which is superseded by Rule 71A, deals only with "practice, pleadings, forms and proceedings and not with matters of substantive laws." United States v. 243.22 Acres of Land in Village of Farmingdale, Town of Babylon, Suffolk County, N.Y., D.C.N.Y. 1942, 43 F.Supp. 561, affirmed 129 F.2d 678, certiorari denied, 63 S.Ct. 441, 317 U.S. 698, 87 L.Ed. 558.

Rule 71A affords a uniform procedure for all cases of condemnation invoking the national power of eminent domain, and, to the extent stated in subdivision (k), for cases invoking a state's power of eminent domain; and supplants all statutes prescribing a different procedure. While the almost exclusive utility of the rule is for the condemnation of real property, it also applies to the condemnation of personal property, either as an incident to real property or as the sole object of the proceeding, when permitted or required by statute. See 38 U.S.C. [former] §438j (World War Veterans' Relief Act); 42 U.S.C. §§1805, 1811, 1813 (Atomic Energy Act); 50 U.S.C. §79 (Nitrates Act); 50 U.S.C. §§161–166 (Helium Gas Act). Requisitioning of personal property with the right in the owner to sue the United States, where the compensation cannot be agreed upon (see 42 U.S.C. §1813, supra, for example) will continue to be the normal method of acquiring personal property and Rule 71A in no way interferes with or restricts any such right. Only where the law requires or permits the formal procedure of condemnation to be utilized will the rule have any applicability to the acquisition of personal property.

Rule 71A is not intended to and does not supersede the Act of February 26, 1931, ch. 307, §§1–5 (46 Stat. 1421), 40 U.S.C. §§258a–258e [now 40 U.S.C. 3114, 3115, 3118], which is a supplementary condemnation statute, permissive in its nature and designed to permit the prompt acquisition of title by the United States, pending the condemnation proceeding, upon a deposit in court. See United States v. 76,800 Acres, More or Less, of Land, in Bryan and Liberty Counties, Ga., D.C.Ga. 1942, 44 F.Supp. 653; United States v. 17,280 Acres of Land, More or Less, Situated in Saunders County, Nebr., D.C.Neb. 1942, 47 F.Supp. 267. The same is true insofar as the following or any other statutes authorize the acquisition of title or the taking of immediate possession:

U.S.C., Title 33:

- §594 (When immediate possession of land may be taken; for a work of river and harbor improvements).

U.S.C., Title 42:

- §1813(b) (When immediate possession may be taken under Atomic Energy Act).

U.S.C., Title 50:

- §171 (Acquisition of land by the Secretary of the Army for national defense).
- §632 App. (Second War Powers Act, 1942; acquisition of real property for war purposes by the Secretary of the Army, the Secretary of the Navy, and others).

Note to Subdivision (b). This subdivision provides for broad joinder in accordance with the tenor of other rules such as Rule 18. To require separate condemnation proceedings for each piece of property separately owned would be unduly burdensome and would serve no useful purpose. And a restriction that only properties may be joined which are to be acquired for the same public use would also cause difficulty. For example, a unified project to widen a street, construct a bridge across a navigable river, and for the construction of approaches to the level of the bridge on both sides of the river might involve acquiring property for different public uses. Yet it is eminently desirable that the plaintiff may in one proceeding condemn all the property interests and rights necessary to carry out this project. Rule 21 which allows the court to sever and proceed separately with any claim against a party, and Rule 42(b) giving the court broad discretion to order separate trials give adequate protection to all defendants in condemnation proceedings.

Note to Subdivision (c). Since a condemnation proceeding is in rem and since a great many property owners are often involved, paragraph (1) requires the property to be named and only one of the owners. In other respects the caption will contain the name of the court, the title of the action, file number, and a designation of the pleading as a complaint in accordance with Rule 10(a).

Since the general standards of pleading are stated in other rules, paragraph (2) prescribes only the necessary detail for condemnation proceedings. Certain statutes allow the United States to acquire title or possession immediately upon commencement of an action. See the Act of February 26, 1931, ch. 307 §§1–5 (46 Stat. 1421), 40 U.S.C. §§258a–258e [now 40 U.S.C. 3114, 3115, 3118], supra; and 33 U.S.C. §594, 42 U.S.C. §1813(b), 50 U.S.C. §§171, 632, supra. To carry out the purpose of such statutes and to aid the condemnor in instituting the action even where title is not acquired at the outset, the plaintiff is initially required to join as defendants only the persons having or claiming an interest in the property whose names are then known. This in no way prejudices the property owner, who must eventually be joined as a defendant, served with process, and allowed to answer before there can be any hearing involving the compensation to be paid for his piece of property. The rule requires the plaintiff to name all persons having or claiming an interest in the property of whom the plaintiff has learned and, more importantly, those appearing of record. By charging the plaintiff with the necessity to make "a search of the records of the extent commonly made by competent searchers of title in the vicinity in light of the type and value of the property involved" both the plaintiff and property owner are protected. Where a short term interest in property of little value is involved, as a two or three year easement over a vacant land for purposes of ingress and egress to other property, a search of the records covering a long period of time is not required. Where on the other hand fee simple title in valuable property is being condemned the search must necessarily cover a much longer period of time and be commensurate with the interests involved. But even here the search is related to the type made by competent title searchers in the vicinity. A search that extends back to the original patent may be feasible in some midwestern and western states and be proper under certain circumstances. In the Atlantic seaboard states such a search is normally not feasible nor desirable. There is a common sense business accommodation of what title searchers can and should do. For state statutes requiring persons appearing as owners or otherwise interested in the property to be named as defendants, see 3 Colo. Stat. Ann., 1935, c. 61, §2; Ill. Ann. Stat. (Smith-Hurd) c. 47, §2; 1 Iowa Code, 1946, §472.3; Kans. Stat. Ann., 1935, §26–101; 2 Mass. Laws Ann., 1932, ch. 80A, §4; 7 Mich. Stat. Ann., 1936, §8.2; 2 Minn. Stat., Mason, 1927, §6541; 20 N.J. Stat. Ann., 1939, §1–2; 3 Wash. Revised Stat., Remington, 1932, Title 6, §891. For state provisions allowing persons whose names are not known to be designated under the descriptive term of "unknown owner", see Hawaii

Revised Laws, 1945, c. 8, §310 ("such [unknown] defendant may be joined in the petition under a fictitious name."; Ill. Ann. Stat., Smith-Hurd), c. 47, §2 ("Persons interested, whose names are unknown, may be made parties defendant by the description of the unknown owners; . . ."); Maryland Code Ann., 1939, Ar. 33A, §1 ("In case any owner or owners is or are not known, he or they may be described in such petition as the unknown owner or owners, or the unknown heir or heirs of a deceased owner."); 2 Mass. Laws Ann., 1932, c. 80A, §4 ("Persons not in being, unascertained or unknown who may have an interest in any of such land shall be made parties respondent by such description as seems appropriate, * * *"); New Mex. Stat. Ann., 1941, §25–901 ("the owners * * * shall be parties defendant, by name, if the names are known, and by description of the unknown owners of the land therein described, if their names are unknown."); Utah Code Ann., 1943, §104–61–7 ("The names of all owners and claimants of the property, if known, or a statement that they are unknown, who must be styled defendants").

The last sentence of paragraph (2) enables the court to expedite the distribution of a deposit, in whole or in part, as soon as pertinent facts of ownership, value and the like are established. See also subdivision (j).

The signing of the complaint is governed by Rule 11.

Note to Subdivision (d). In lieu of a summons, which is the initial process in other civil actions under Rule 4 (a), subdivision (d) provides for a notice which is to contain sufficient information so that the defendant in effect obtains the plaintiff's statement of his claim against the defendant to whom the notice is directed. Since the plaintiff's attorney is an officer of the court and to prevent unduly burdening the clerk of the court, paragraph (1) of subdivision (d) provides that plaintiff's attorney shall prepare and deliver a notice or notices to the clerk. Flexibility is provided by the provision for joint or several notices, and for additional notices. Where there are only a few defendants it may be convenient to prepare but one notice directed to all the defendants. In other cases where there are many defendants it will be more convenient to prepare two or more notices; but in any event a notice must be directed to each named defendant. Paragraph (2) provides that the notice is to be signed by the plaintiff's attorney. Since the notice is to be delivered to the clerk, the issuance of the notice will appear of record in the court. The clerk should forthwith deliver the notice or notices for service to the marshal or to a person specially appointed to serve the notice. Rule 4 (a). The form of the notice is such that, in addition to informing the defendant of the plaintiff's statement of claim, it tells the defendant precisely what his rights are. Failure on the part of the defendant to serve an answer constitutes a consent to the taking and to the authority of the court to proceed to fix compensation therefor, but it does not preclude the defendant from presenting evidence as to the amount of compensation due him or in sharing the award of distribution. See subdivision (e); Form 28.

While under Rule 4(f) the territorial limits of a summons are normally the territorial limits of the state in which the district court is held, the territorial limits for personal service of a notice under Rule 71A (d)(3) are those of the nation. This extension of process is here proper since the aim of the condemnation proceeding is not to enforce any personal liability and the property owner is helped, not imposed upon, by the best type of service possible. If personal service cannot be made either because the defendant's whereabouts cannot be ascertained, or, if ascertained, the defendant cannot be personally served, as where he resides in a foreign country such as Canada or Mexico, then service by publication is proper. The provisions for this type of service are set forth in the rule and are in no way governed by 28 U.S.C. §118.

Note to Subdivision (e). Departing from the scheme of Rule 12, subdivision (e) requires all defenses and objections to be presented in an answer and does not authorize a preliminary motion. There is little need for the latter in condemnation proceedings. The general standard of pleading is governed by other rules, particularly Rule 8, and this subdivision (e) merely prescribes what matters the answer should set forth. Merely by appearing in the action a defendant can receive notice of all proceedings affecting him. And without the necessity of answering a defendant may present evidence as to the amount of compensation due him, and he may share in the distribution of the award. See also subdivision (d)(2); Form 28.

Note to Subdivision (f). Due to the number of persons who may be interested in the property to be condemned, there is a likelihood that the plaintiff will need to amend his complaint, perhaps many times, to add new parties or state new issues. This subdivision recognizes that fact and does not burden the court with applications by the plaintiff for leave to amend. At the same time all defendants are adequately protected; and their need to amend the answer is adequately protected by Rule 15, which is applicable by virtue of subdivision (a) of this Rule 71A.

Note to Subdivision (g). A condemnation action is a proceeding in rem. Commencement of the action as against a defendant by virtue of his joinder pursuant to subdivision (c)(2) is the point of cut-off and there is no mandatory requirement for substitution because of a subsequent change of interest, although the court is given ample power to require substitution. Rule 25 is inconsistent with subdivision (g) and hence inapplicable. Accordingly, the time periods of Rule 25 do not govern to require dismissal nor to prevent substitution.

Note to Subdivision (h). This subdivision prescribes the method for determining the issue of just compensation in cases involving the federal power of eminent domain. The method of jury trial provided by subdivision (h) will normally apply in cases involving the state power by virtue of subdivision (k).

Congress has specially constituted a tribunal for the trial of the issue of just compensation in two instances: condemnation under the Tennessee Valley Authority Act; and condemnation in the District of Columbia. These tribunals are retained for reasons set forth in the General Statement: 3. Adjustment of Rule to Statutory Provisions, supra. Subdivision (h) also has prospective application so that if Congress should create another special tribunal, that tribunal will determine the issue of just compensation. Subject to these exceptions the general method of trial of that issue is to be by jury if any party demands it, otherwise that issue, as well as all other issues, are to be tried by the court.

As to the TVA procedure that is continued, U.S.C., Title 16, §831x requires that three commissioners be appointed to fix the compensation; that exceptions to their award are to be heard by three district judges (unless the parties stipulate for a lesser number) and that the district judges try the question de novo; that an appeal to the circuit court of appeals may be taken within 30 days from the filing of the decision of the district judges; and that the circuit court of appeals shall on the record fix compensation "without regard to the awards of findings theretofore made by the commissioners or the district judges." The mode of fixing compensation in the District of Columbia, which is also continued, is prescribed in U.S.C., [former] Title 40, §§361–386. Under §371 the court is required in all cases to order the selection of a jury of five from among not less than 20 names, drawn "from the special box provided by law." They must have the usual qualifications of jurors and in addition must be freeholders of the District, and not in the service of the United States or the District. A special oath is administered to the chosen jurors. The trial proceeds in the ordinary way, except that the jury is allowed to separate after they have begun to consider their verdict.

There is no constitutional right to jury trial in a condemnation proceeding. Bauman v. Ross, 1897, 17 S.Ct. 966, 167 U.S. 548, 42 L.Ed. 270. See, also, Hines, Does the Seventh Amendment to the Constitution of the United States Require Jury Trials in all Condemnation Proceedings? 1925, 11 Va.L.Rev. 505; Blair, Federal Condemnation Proceedings and the Seventh Amendment 1927, 41 Harv.L.Rev. 29; 3 Moore's Federal Practice 1938, 3007. Prior to Rule 71A, jury trial in federal condemnation proceedings was, however, enjoyed under the general conformity statute, [former] 40 U.S.C. §258, in states which provided for jury trial. See generally, 2 Lewis, Eminent Domain 3d ed. 1909, §§509, 510; 3 Moore, op. cit. supra. Since the general conformity statute is superseded by Rule 71A, see supra under subdivision (a), and since it was believed that the rule to be substituted should likewise give a right to jury trial, subdivision (h) establishes that method as the general one for determining the issue of just compensation.

Note to Subdivision (i). Both the right of the plaintiff to dismiss by filing a notice of dismissal and the right of the court to permit a dismissal are circumscribed to the extent that where the plaintiff has acquired the title or a lesser interest or possession, viz, any property interest for which just compensation should be paid, the action may not be dismissed, without the defendant's consent, and the property owner remitted to another court, such as the Court of Claims, to recover just compensation for the property right taken. Circuity of action is thus prevented without increasing the liability of the plaintiff to pay just compensation for any interest that is taken. Freedom of dismissal is accorded, where both the condemnor and condemnee agree, up to the time of the entry of judgment vesting plaintiff with title. And power is given to the court, where the parties agree, to vacate the judgment and thus revest title in the property owner. In line with Rule 21, the court may at any time drop a defendant who has been unnecessarily or improperly joined as where it develops that he has no interest.

Note to Subdivision (j). Whatever the substantive law is concerning the necessity of making a deposit will continue to govern. For statutory provisions concerning deposit in court in condemnation proceedings by the United States, see U.S.C., Title 40, §258a [now 40 U.S.C. 3114(a)–(d)]; U.S.C., Title 33, §594—acquisition of title and possession statutes referred to in note to subdivision (a), supra. If the plaintiff is invoking the state's power of eminent domain the necessity of deposit will be governed by the state law. For discussion of such law, see 1 Nichols, Eminent Domain, 2d ed. 1917, §§209–216. For discussion of the function of deposit and the power of the court to enter judgment in cases both of deficiency and overpayment, see United States v. Miller, 1943, 63 S.Ct. 276, 317 U.S. 369, 87 L.Ed. 336, 147 A.L.R. 55, rehearing denied, 63 S.Ct. 557, 318 U.S. 798, 87 L.Ed. 1162 (judgment in favor of plaintiff for overpayment ordered).

The court is to make distribution of the deposit as promptly as the facts of the case warrant. See also subdivision (c)(2).

Note to Subdivision (k). While the overwhelming number of cases that will be brought in the federal courts under this rule will be actions involving the federal power of eminent domain, a small percentage of cases may be instituted in the federal court or removed thereto on the basis of diversity or alienage which will involve the power of eminent domain under the law of a state. See Boom Co. v. Patterson, 1878, 98 U.S. 403, 25 L.Ed. 206; Searl v. School District No. 2, 1888, 8 S.Ct. 460, 124 U.S. 197, 31 L.Ed. 415; Madisonville Traction Co. v. Saint Bernard Mining Co., 1905, 25 S.Ct. 251, 196 U.S. 239, 49 L.Ed. 462. In the Madisonville case, and in cases cited therein, it has been held that condemnation actions brought by state corporations in the exercise of a power delegated by the state might be governed by procedure prescribed by the laws of the United States, whether the cases were begun in or removed to the federal court. See also Franzen v. Chicago, M. & St. P. Ry. Co., C.C.A.7th, 1921, 278 F. 370, 372.

Any condition affecting the substantial right of a litigant attached by state law is to be observed and enforced, such as making a deposit in court where the power of eminent domain is conditioned upon so doing. (See also subdivision (j)). Subject to this qualification, subdivision (k) provides that in cases involving the state power of eminent domain, the practice prescribed by other subdivisions of Rule 71A shall govern.

Note to Subdivision (l). Since the condemnor will normally be the prevailing party and since he should not recover his costs against the property owner, Rule 54(d), which provides generally that costs shall go to the prevailing party, is made inapplicable. Without attempting to state what the rule on costs is, the effect of subdivision (1) is that costs shall be awarded in accordance with the law that has developed in condemnation cases. This has been summarized as follows: "Costs of condemnation proceedings are not assessable against the condemnee, unless by stipulation he agrees to assume some or all of them. Such normal expenses of the proceeding as bills for publication of notice, commissioners' fees, the cost of transporting commissioners and jurors to take a view, fees for attorneys to represent defendants who have failed to answer, and witness' fees, are properly charged to the government, though not taxed as costs. Similarly, if it is necessary that a conveyance be executed by a commissioner, the United States pay his fees and those for recording the deed. However, the distribution of the award is a matter in which the United States has no legal interest. Expenses incurred in ascertaining the identity of distributees and deciding between conflicting claimants are properly chargeable against the award, not against the United States, although United States attorneys are expected to aid the court in such matters as amici curiae." Lands Division Manual 861. For other discussion and citation, see Grand River Dam Authority v. Jarvis, C.C.A.10th, 1942, 124 F.2d 914. Costs may not be taxed against the United States except to the extent permitted by law. United States v. 125.71 Acres of Land in Loyalhanna Tp., Westmoreland County, Pa., D.C.Pa. 1944, 54 F.Supp. 193; Lands Division Manual 859. Even if it were thought desirable to allow the property owner's costs to be taxed against the United States, this is a matter for legislation and not court rule.

Notes of Advisory Committee on Rules—1963 Amendment

This amendment conforms to the amendment of Rule 4(f).

Notes of Advisory Committee on Rules—1985 Amendment

Rule 71A(h) provides that except when Congress has provided otherwise, the issue of just compensation in a condemnation case may be tried by a jury if one of the parties so demands, unless the court in its discretion orders the issue determined by a commission of three persons. In 1980, the Comptroller General of the United States in a Report to Congress recommended that use of the commission procedure should be encouraged in order to improve and expedite the trial of condemnation cases. The Report noted that long delays were being caused in many districts by such factors as crowded dockets, the precedence given criminal cases, the low priority accorded condemnation matters, and the high turnover of Assistant United States Attorneys. The Report concluded that revising Rule 71A to make the use of the commission procedure more attractive might alleviate the situation.

Accordingly, Rule 71A(h) is being amended in a number of respects designed to assure the quality and utility of a Rule 71A commission. First, the amended Rule will give the court discretion to appoint, in addition to the three members of a commission, up to two additional persons as alternate commissioners who would hear the case and be available, at any time up to the filing of the decision by the three-member commission, to replace any commissioner who becomes unable or disqualified to continue. The discretion to appoint alternate commissioners can be particularly useful in protracted cases, avoiding expensive retrials that have been required in some cases because of the death or disability of a commissioner. Prior to replacing a commissioner an alternate would not be present at, or participate in, the commission's deliberations.

Second, the amended Rule requires the court, before appointment, to advise the parties of the identity and qualifications of each prospective commissioner and alternate. The court then may authorize the examination of prospective appointees by the parties and each party has the right to challenge for cause. The objective is to insure that unbiased and competent commissioners are appointed.

The amended Rule does not prescribe a qualification standard for appointment to a commission, although it is understood that only persons possessing background and ability to appraise real estate valuation testimony and to award fair and just compensation on the basis thereof would be appointed. In most situations the chairperson should be a lawyer and all members should have some background qualifying them to weigh proof of value in the real estate field and, when possible, in the particular real estate market embracing the land in question.

The amended Rule should give litigants greater confidence in the commission procedure by affording them certain rights to participate in the appointment of commission members that are roughly comparable to the practice with regard to jury selection. This is accomplished by giving the court permission to allow the parties to examine prospective commissioners and by recognizing the right of each party to object to the appointment of any person for cause.

Notes of Advisory Committee on Rules—1987 Amendment

The amendments are technical. No substantive change is intended.

Notes of Advisory Committee on Rules—1988 Amendment

The amendment is technical. No substantive change is intended.

Notes of Advisory Committee on Rules—1993 Amendment

The references to the subdivisions of Rule 4 are deleted in light of the revision of that rule.

Committee Notes on Rules—2003 Amendment

The references to specific subdivisions of Rule 53 are deleted or revised to reflect amendments of Rule 53.

Committee Notes on Rules—2007 Amendment

The language of Rule 71A has been amended as part of the general restyling of the Civil Rules to make them more easily understood and to make style and terminology consistent throughout the rules. These changes are intended to be stylistic only.

Former Rule 71A has been redesignated as Rule 71.1 to conform to the designations used for all other rules added within the original numbering system.

Rule 71.1(e) allows a defendant to appear without answering. Former form 28 (now form 60) includes information about this right in the Rule 71.1(d)(2) notice. It is useful to confirm this practice in the rule.

The information that identifies the attorney is changed to include telephone number and electronic-mail address, in line with similar amendments to Rules 11(a) and 26(g)(1).

Committee Notes on Rules—2009 Amendment

The times set in the former rule at 20 days have been revised to 21 days. See the Note to Rule 6.

Amendment by Public Law

1988—Subd. (e). Pub. L. 100–690, which directed amendment of subd. (e) by striking "taking of the defendants property" and inserting "taking of the defendant's property", could not be executed because of the intervening amendment by the Court by order dated Apr. 25, 1988, eff. Aug. 1, 1988.

Rule 72. Magistrate Judges: Pretrial Order

(a) Nondispositive Matters. When a pretrial matter not dispositive of a party's claim or defense is referred to a magistrate judge to hear and decide, the magistrate judge must promptly conduct the required proceedings and, when appropriate, issue a written order stating the decision. A party may serve and file objections to the order within 14 days after being served with a copy. A party may not assign as error a defect in the order not timely objected to. The district judge in the case must consider timely objections and modify or set aside any part of the order that is clearly erroneous or is contrary to law.

(b) Dispositive Motions and Prisoner Petitions.

(1) Findings and Recommendations. A magistrate judge must promptly conduct the required proceedings when assigned, without the parties' consent, to hear a pretrial matter dispositive of a claim or defense or a prisoner petition challenging the conditions of confinement. A record must be made of all evidentiary proceedings and may, at the magistrate judge's discretion, be made of any other proceedings. The magistrate judge must enter a recommended disposition, including, if appropriate, proposed findings of fact. The clerk must promptly mail a copy to each party.

(2) Objections. Within 14 days after being served with a copy of the recommended disposition, a party may serve and file specific written objections to the proposed findings and recommendations. A party may respond to another party's objections within 14 days after being served with a copy. Unless the district judge orders otherwise, the objecting party must promptly arrange for transcribing the record, or whatever portions of it the parties agree to or the magistrate judge considers sufficient.

(3) Resolving Objections. The district judge must determine de novo any part of the magistrate judge's

disposition that has been properly objected to. The district judge may accept, reject, or modify the recommended disposition; receive further evidence; or return the matter to the magistrate judge with instructions.

(As added Apr. 28, 1983, eff. Aug. 1, 1983; amended Apr. 30, 1991, eff. Dec. 1, 1991; Apr. 22, 1993, eff. Dec. 1, 1993; Apr. 30, 2007, eff. Dec. 1, 2007; Mar. 26, 2009, eff. Dec. 1, 2009.)

Notes of Advisory Committee on Rules—1983

Subdivision (a). This subdivision addresses court-ordered referrals of nondispositive matters under 28 U.S.C. §636(b)(1)(A). The rule calls for a written order of the magistrate's disposition to preserve the record and facilitate review. An oral order read into the record by the magistrate will satisfy this requirement.

No specific procedures or timetables for raising objections to the magistrate's rulings on nondispositive matters are set forth in the Magistrates Act. The rule fixes a 10-day period in order to avoid uncertainty and provide uniformity that will eliminate the confusion that might arise if different periods were prescribed by local rule in different districts. It also is contemplated that a party who is successful before the magistrate will be afforded an opportunity to respond to objections raised to the magistrate's ruling.

The last sentence of subdivision (a) specifies that reconsideration of a magistrate's order, as provided for in the Magistrates Act, shall be by the district judge to whom the case is assigned. This rule does not restrict experimentation by the district courts under 28 U.S.C. §636(b)(3) involving references of matters other than pretrial matters, such as appointment of counsel, taking of default judgments, and acceptance of jury verdicts when the judge is unavailable.

Subdivision (b). This subdivision governs court-ordered referrals of dispositive pretrial matters and prisoner petitions challenging conditions of confinement, pursuant to statutory authorization in 28 U.S.C. §636(b)(1)(B). This rule does not extend to habeas corpus petitions, which are covered by the specific rules relating to proceedings under Sections 2254 and 2255 of Title 28.

This rule implements the statutory procedures for making objections to the magistrate's proposed findings and recommendations. The 10-day period, as specified in the statute, is subject to Rule 6(e) which provides for an additional 3-day period when service is made by mail. Although no specific provision appears in the Magistrates Act, the rule specifies a 10-day period for a party to respond to objections to the magistrate's recommendation.

Implementing the statutory requirements, the rule requires the district judge to whom the case is assigned to make a de novo determination of those portions of the report, findings, or recommendations to which timely objection is made. The term "de novo" signifies that the magistrate's findings are not protected by the clearly erroneous doctrine, but does not indicate that a second evidentiary hearing is required. See United States v. Raddatz, 417 U.S. 667 (1980). See also Silberman, Masters and Magistrates Part II: The American Analogue, 50 N.Y.U. L.Rev. 1297, 1367 (1975). When no timely objection is filed, the court need only satisfy itself that there is no clear error on the face of the record in order to accept the recommendation. See Campbell v. United States Dist. Court, 501 F.2d 196, 206 (9th Cir. 1974), cert. denied, 419 U.S. 879, quoted in House Report No. 94–1609, 94th Cong. 2d Sess. (1976) at 3. Compare Park Motor Mart, Inc. v. Ford Motor Co., 616 F.2d 603 (1st Cir. 1980). Failure to make timely objection to the magistrate's report prior to its adoption by the district judge may constitute a waiver of appellate review of the district judge's order. See United States v. Walters, 638 F.2d 947 (6th Cir. 1981).

Notes of Advisory Committee on Rules—1991 Amendment

This amendment is intended to eliminate a discrepancy in measuring the 10 days for serving and filing objections to a magistrate's action under subdivisions (a) and (b) of this Rule. The rule as promulgated in 1983 required objections to the magistrate's handling of nondispositive matters to be served and filed within 10 days of entry of the order, but required objections to dispositive motions to be made within 10 days of being served with a copy of the recommended disposition. Subdivision (a) is here amended to conform to subdivision (b) to avoid any confusion or technical defaults, particularly in connection with magistrate orders that rule on both dispositive and nondispositive matters.

The amendment is also intended to assure that objections to magistrate's orders that are not timely made shall not be considered. Compare Rule 51.

Notes of Advisory Committee on Rules—1993 Amendment

This revision is made to conform the rule to changes made by the Judicial Improvements Act of 1990.

Committee Notes on Rules—2007 Amendment

The language of Rule 72 has been amended as part of the general restyling of the Civil Rules to make them more easily understood and to make style and terminology consistent throughout the rules. These changes are intended to be stylistic only.

Committee Notes on Rules—2009 Amendment

The times set in the former rule at 10 days have been revised to 14 days. See the Note to Rule 6.

Rule 73. Magistrate Judges: Trial by Consent; Appeal

(a) Trial by Consent. When authorized under 28 U.S.C. §636(c), a magistrate judge may, if all parties consent, conduct a civil action or proceeding, including a jury or nonjury trial. A record must be made in accordance with 28 U.S.C. §636(c)(5).

(b) Consent Procedure.

(1) In General. When a magistrate judge has been designated to conduct civil actions or proceedings, the clerk must give the parties written notice of their opportunity to consent under 28 U.S.C. §636(c). To signify their consent, the parties must jointly or separately file a statement consenting to the referral. A district judge or magistrate judge may be informed of a party's response to the clerk's notice only if all parties have consented to the referral.

(2) Reminding the Parties About Consenting. A district judge, magistrate judge, or other court official may remind the parties of the magistrate judge's availability, but must also advise them that they are free to withhold consent without adverse substantive consequences.

(3) Vacating a Referral. On its own for good cause—or when a party shows extraordinary circumstances—the

district judge may vacate a referral to a magistrate judge under this rule.

(c) Appealing a Judgment. In accordance with 28 U.S.C. §636(c)(3), an appeal from a judgment entered at a magistrate judge's direction may be taken to the court of appeals as would any other appeal from a district-court judgment.

(As added Apr. 28, 1983, eff. Aug. 1, 1983; amended Mar. 2, 1987, eff. Aug. 1, 1987; Apr. 22, 1993, eff. Dec. 1, 1993; Apr. 11, 1997, eff. Dec. 1, 1997; Apr. 30, 2007, eff. Dec. 1, 2007.)

Notes of Advisory Committee on Rules—1983

Subdivision (a). This subdivision implements the broad authority of the 1979 amendments to the Magistrates Act, 28 U.S.C. §636(c), which permit a magistrate to sit in lieu of a district judge and exercise civil jurisdiction over a case, when the parties consent. See McCabe, The Federal Magistrate Act of 1979, 16 Harv. J. Legis. 343, 364–79 (1979). In order to exercise this jurisdiction, a magistrate must be specially designated under 28 U.S.C. §636(c)(1) by the district court or courts he serves. The only exception to a magistrate's exercise of civil jurisdiction, which includes the power to conduct jury and nonjury trials and decide dispositive motions, is the contempt power. A hearing on contempt is to be conducted by the district judge upon certification of the facts and an order to show cause by the magistrate. See 28 U.S.C. §639(e). In view of 28 U.S.C. §636(c)(1) and this rule, it is unnecessary to amend Rule 58 to provide that the decision of a magistrate is a "decision by the court" for the purposes of that rule and a "final decision of the district court" for purposes of 28 U.S.C. §1291 governing appeals.

Subdivision (b). This subdivision implements the blind consent provision of 28 U.S.C. §636(c)(2) and is designed to ensure that neither the judge nor the magistrate attempts to induce a party to consent to reference of a civil matter under this rule to a magistrate. See House Rep. No. 96–444, 96th Cong. 1st Sess. 8 (1979).

The rule opts for a uniform approach in implementing the consent provision by directing the clerk to notify the parties of their opportunity to elect to proceed before a magistrate and by requiring the execution and filing of a consent form or forms setting forth the election. However, flexibility at the local level is preserved in that local rules will determine how notice shall be communicated to the parties, and local rules will specify the time period within which an election must be made.

The last paragraph of subdivision (b) reiterates the provision in 28 U.S.C. §636(c)(6) for vacating a reference to the magistrate.

Subdivision (c). Under 28 U.S.C. §636(c)(3), the normal route of appeal from the judgment of a magistrate—the only route that will be available unless the parties otherwise agree in advance—is an appeal by the aggrieved party "directly to the appropriate United States court of appeals from the judgment of the magistrate in the same manner as an appeal from any other judgment of a district court." The quoted statutory language indicates Congress' intent that the same procedures and standards of appealability that govern appeals from district court judgments govern appeals from magistrates' judgments.

Subdivision (d). 28 U.S.C. §636(c)(4) offers parties who consent to the exercise of civil jurisdiction by a magistrate an alternative appeal route to that provided in subdivision (c) of this rule. This optional appellate route was provided by Congress in recognition of the fact that not all civil cases warrant the same appellate treatment. In cases where the amount in controversy is not great and there are no difficult questions of law to be resolved, the parties may desire to avoid the expense and delay of appeal to the court of appeals by electing an appeal to the district judge. See McCabe, The Federal Magistrate Act of 1979, 16 Harv. J. Legis. 343, 388 (1979). This subdivision provides that the parties may elect the optional appeal route at the time of reference to a magistrate. To this end, the notice by the clerk under subdivision (b) of this rule shall explain the appeal option and the corollary restriction on review by the court of appeals. This approach will avoid later claims of lack of consent to the avenue of appeal. The choice of the alternative appeal route to the judge of the district court should be made by the parties in their forms of consent. Special appellate rules to govern appeals from a magistrate to a district judge appear in new Rules 74 through 76.

Notes of Advisory Committee on Rules—1987 Amendment

The amendment is technical. No substantive change is intended.

Notes of Advisory Committee on Rules—1993 Amendment

This revision is made to conform the rule to changes made by the Judicial Improvements Act of 1990. The Act requires that, when being reminded of the availability of a magistrate judge, the parties be advised that withholding of consent will have no "adverse substantive consequences." They may, however, be advised if the withholding of consent will have the adverse procedural consequence of a potential delay in trial.

Notes of Advisory Committee on Rules—1997 Amendment

The Federal Courts Improvement Act of 1996 repealed the former provisions of 28 U.S.C. §636(c)(4) and (5) that enabled parties that had agreed to trial before a magistrate judge to agree also that appeal should be taken to the district court. Rule 73 is amended to conform to this change. Rules 74, 75, and 76 are abrogated for the same reason. The portions of Form 33 and Form 34 that referred to appeals to the district court also are deleted.

Committee Notes on Rules—2007 Amendment

The language of Rule 73 has been amended as part of the general restyling of the Civil Rules to make them more easily understood and to make style and terminology consistent throughout the rules. These changes are intended to be stylistic only.

Rule 74. [Abrogated (Apr. 11, 1997, eff. Dec. 1, 1997).]

Notes of Advisory Committee on Rules—1997 Amendment

Rule 74 is abrogated for the reasons described in the Note to Rule 73.

Committee Notes on Rules—2007

Rule 74 was abrogated in 1997 to reflect repeal of the statute providing for appeal from a magistrate judge's judgment to the district court. The rule number is reserved for possible future use.

Rule 75. [Abrogated (Apr. 11, 1997, eff. Dec. 1, 1997).]

Notes of Advisory Committee on Rules—1997 Amendment

Rule 75 is abrogated for the reasons described in the Note to Rule 73.

Committee Notes on Rules—2007

Rule 75 was abrogated in 1997 to reflect repeal of the statute providing for appeal from a magistrate judge's judgment to the district court. The rule number is reserved for possible future use.

Rule 76. [Abrogated (Apr. 11, 1997, eff. Dec. 1, 1997).]

Notes of Advisory Committee on Rules—1997 Amendment

Rule 76 is abrogated for the reasons described in the Note to Rule 73.

Committee Notes on Rules—2007

Rule 76 was abrogated in 1997 to reflect repeal of the statute providing for appeal from a magistrate judge's judgment to the district court. The rule number is reserved for possible future use.

TITLE X. DISTRICT COURTS AND CLERKS: CONDUCTING BUSINESS; ISSUING ORDERS

Rule 77. Conducting Business; Clerk's Authority; Notice of an Order or Judgment

(a) When Court Is Open. Every district court is considered always open for filing any paper, issuing and returning process, making a motion, or entering an order.

(b) Place for Trial and Other Proceedings. Every trial on the merits must be conducted in open court and, so far as convenient, in a regular courtroom. Any other act or proceeding may be done or conducted by a judge in chambers, without the attendance of the clerk or other court official, and anywhere inside or outside the district. But no hearing—other than one ex parte—may be conducted outside the district unless all the affected parties consent.

(c) Clerk's Office Hours; Clerk's Orders.

(1) Hours. The clerk's office—with a clerk or deputy on duty—must be open during business hours every day except Saturdays, Sundays, and legal holidays. But a court may, by local rule or order, require that the office be open for specified hours on Saturday or a particular legal holiday other than one listed in Rule 6(a)(6)(A).

(2) Orders. Subject to the court's power to suspend, alter, or rescind the clerk's action for good cause, the clerk may:

(A) issue process;

(B) enter a default;

(C) enter a default judgment under Rule 55(b)(1); and

(D) act on any other matter that does not require the court's action.

(d) Serving Notice of an Order or Judgment.

(1) Service. Immediately after entering an order or judgment, the clerk must serve notice of the entry, as provided in Rule 5(b), on each party who is not in default for failing to appear. The clerk must record the service on the docket. A party also may serve notice of the entry as provided in Rule 5(b).

(2) Time to Appeal Not Affected by Lack of Notice. Lack of notice of the entry does not affect the time for appeal or relieve—or authorize the court to relieve—a party for failing to appeal within the time allowed, except as allowed by Federal Rule of Appellate Procedure (4)(a).

(As amended Dec. 27, 1946, eff. Mar. 19, 1948; Jan. 21, 1963, eff. July 1, 1963; Dec. 4, 1967, eff. July 1, 1968; Mar. 1, 1971, eff. July 1, 1971; Mar. 2, 1987, eff. Aug. 1, 1987; Apr. 30, 1991, eff. Dec. 1, 1991; Apr. 23, 2001, eff. Dec. 1, 2001; Apr. 30, 2007, eff. Dec. 1, 2007; Apr. 25, 2014, eff. Dec. 1, 2014.)

Notes of Advisory Committee on Rules—1937

This rule states the substance of U.S.C., Title 28, §13 [now 452] (Courts open as courts of admiralty and equity). Compare [former] Equity Rules 1 (District Court Always Open For Certain Purposes—Orders at Chambers), 2 (Clerk's Office Always Open, Except, Etc.), 4 (Notice of Orders), and 5 (Motions Grantable of Course by Clerk).

Notes of Advisory Committee on Rules—1946 Amendment

Rule 77(d) has been amended to avoid such situations as the one arising in Hill v. Hawes (1944) 320 U.S. 520. In that case, an action instituted in the District Court for the District of Columbia, the clerk failed to give notice of the entry of a judgment for defendant as required by Rule 77(d). The time for taking an appeal then was 20 days under Rule 10 of the Court of Appeals (later enlarged by amendment to thirty days), and due to lack of notice of the entry of judgment the plaintiff failed to file his notice of appeal within the prescribed time. On this basis the trial court vacated the original judgment and then reentered it, whereupon notice of appeal was filed. The Court of Appeals dismissed the appeal as taken too late. The Supreme Court, however, held that although Rule 77(d) did not purport to attach any consequence to the clerk's failure to give notice as specified, the terms of the rule were such that the appellant was entitled to rely on it, and the trial court in such a case, in the exercise of a sound discretion, could vacate the former judgment and enter a new one, so that the appeal would be within the allowed time.

Because of Rule 6(c), which abolished the old rule that the expiration of the term ends a court's power over its judgment, the effect of the decision in Hill v. Hawes is to give the district court power, in its discretion and without time limit, and long after the term may have expired, to vacate a judgment and reenter it for the purpose of reviving the right of appeal. This seriously affects the finality of judgments. See also proposed Rule 6(c) and Note; proposed Rule 60(b) and Note; and proposed Rule 73(a) and Note.

Rule 77(d) as amended makes it clear that notification by the clerk of the entry of a judgment has nothing to do with the starting of the time for appeal; that time starts to run from the date of entry of judgment and not from the date of notice of the entry. Notification by the clerk is merely for the convenience of litigants. And lack of such notification in itself has no effect upon the time for appeal; but in considering an application for extension of time for appeal as provided in Rule 73(a), the court may take into account, as one of the factors affecting its decision, whether the clerk failed to give notice as provided in Rule 77(d) or the party failed to receive the clerk's notice. It need not, however, extend the time for appeal merely because the clerk's notice was not sent or received. It would, therefore, be entirely unsafe for a party to rely on absence of notice from the clerk of the entry of a judgment, or to rely on the adverse party's failure to serve notice of the entry of a judgment. Any party may, of course, serve timely notice of the entry of a judgment upon the adverse party and thus preclude a successful application, under Rule 73(a), for the extension of the time for appeal.

Notes of Advisory Committee on Rules—1963 Amendment

Subdivision (c). The amendment authorizes closing of the clerk's office on Saturday as far as civil business is concerned. However, a district court may require its clerk's office to remain open for specified hours on Saturdays or "legal holidays" other than those enumerated. ("Legal holiday" is defined in Rule 6(a), as amended.) The clerk's offices of many district courts have customarily remained open on some of the days appointed as holidays by State law. This practice could be continued by local rule or order.

Subdivision (d). This amendment conforms to the amendment of Rule 5(a). See the Advisory Committee's Note to that amendment.

Notes of Advisory Committee on Rules—1968 Amendment

The provisions of Rule 73(a) are incorporated in Rule 4(a) of the Federal Rules of Appellate Procedure.

Notes of Advisory Committee on Rules—1971 Amendment

The amendment adds Columbus Day to the list of legal holidays. See the Note accompanying the amendment of Rule 6(a).

Notes of Advisory Committee on Rules—1987 Amendment

The amendments are technical. No substantive change is intended. The Birthday of Martin Luther King, Jr. is added to the list of national holidays in Rule 77.

Notes of Advisory Committee on Rules—1991 Amendment

This revision is a companion to the concurrent amendment to Rule 4 of the Federal Rules of Appellate Procedure. The purpose of the revisions is to permit district courts to ease strict sanctions now imposed on appellants whose notices of appeal are filed late because of their failure to receive notice of entry of a judgment. See, e.g. Tucker v. Commonwealth Land Title Ins. Co., 800 F.2d 1054 (11th Cir. 1986); Ashby Enterprises, Ltd. v. Weitzman, Dym & Associates, 780 F.2d 1043 (D.C. Cir. 1986); In re OPM Leasing Services, Inc., 769 F.2d 911 (2d Cir. 1985); Spika v. Village of Lombard, Ill., 763 F.2d 282 (7th Cir. 1985); Hall v. Community Mental Health Center of Beaver County, 772 F.2d 42 (3d Cir. 1985); Wilson v. Atwood v. Stark, 725 F.2d 255 (5th Cir. en banc), cert dismissed, 105 S.Ct. 17 (1984); Case v. BASF Wyandotte, 727 F.2d 1034 (Fed. Cir. 1984), cert. denied, 105 S.Ct. 386 (1984); Hensley v. Chesapeake & Ohio R.R.Co., 651 F.2d 226 (4th Cir. 1981); Buckeye Cellulose Corp. v. Electric Construction Co., 569 F.2d 1036 (8th Cir. 1978).

Failure to receive notice may have increased in frequency with the growth in the caseload in the clerks' offices. The present strict rule imposes a duty on counsel to maintain contact with the court while a case is under submission. Such contact is more difficult to maintain if counsel is outside the district, as is increasingly common, and can be a burden to the court as well as counsel.

The effect of the revisions is to place a burden on prevailing parties who desire certainty that the time for appeal is running. Such parties can take the initiative to assure that their adversaries receive effective notice. An appropriate procedure for such notice is provided in Rule 5.

The revised rule lightens the responsibility but not the workload of the clerks' offices, for the duty of that office to give notice of entry of judgment must be maintained.

Committee Notes on Rules—2001 Amendment

Rule 77(d) is amended to reflect changes in Rule 5(b). A few courts have experimented with serving Rule 77(d) notices by electronic means on parties who consent to this procedure. The success of these experiments warrants express authorization. Because service is made in the manner provided in Rule 5(b), party consent is required for service by electronic or other means described in Rule 5(b)(2)(D). The same provision is made for a party who wishes to ensure actual communication of the Rule 77(d) notice by also serving notice.

Changes Made After Publication and Comments Rule 77(d) was amended to correct an oversight in the published version. The clerk is to note "service," not "mailing," on the docket.

Committee Notes on Rules—2007 Amendment

The language of Rule 77 has been amended as part of the general restyling of the Civil Rules to make them more easily understood and to make style and terminology consistent throughout the rules. These changes are intended to be stylistic only.

Committee Notes on Rules—2014 Amendment

The amendment corrects an inadvertent failure to revise the cross-reference to Rule 6(a) when what was Rule 6(a)(4)(A) became Rule 6(a)(6)(A).

Rule 78. Hearing Motions; Submission on Briefs

(a) Providing a Regular Schedule for Oral Hearings. A court may establish regular times and places for oral hearings on motions.
(b) Providing for Submission on Briefs. By rule or order, the court may provide for submitting and determining motions on briefs, without oral hearings.

(As amended Mar. 2, 1987, eff. Aug. 1, 1987; Apr. 30, 2007, eff. Dec. 1, 2007.)

Notes of Advisory Committee on Rules—1937

Compare [former] Equity Rule 6 (Motion Day) with the first paragraph of this rule. The second paragraph authorizes a procedure found helpful for the expedition of business in some of the Federal and State courts. See Rule 43(e) of these rules dealing with evidence on motions. Compare Civil Practice Rules of the Municipal Court of Chicago (1935), Rules 269, 270, 271.

Notes of Advisory Committee on Rules—1987 Amendment

The amendment is technical. No substantive change is intended.

Committee Notes on Rules—2007 Amendment

The language of Rule 78 has been amended as part of the general restyling of the Civil Rules to make them more easily understood and to make style and terminology consistent throughout the rules. These changes are intended to be stylistic only.

Rule 16 has superseded any need for the provision in former Rule 78 for orders for the advancement, conduct, and hearing of actions.

Rule 79. Records Kept by the Clerk

(a) Civil Docket.

(1) In General. The clerk must keep a record known as the "civil docket" in the form and manner prescribed by the Director of the Administrative Office of the United States Courts with the approval of the Judicial Conference of the United States. The clerk must enter each civil action in the docket. Actions must be assigned consecutive file numbers, which must be noted in the docket where the first entry of the action is made.

(2) Items to be Entered. The following items must be marked with the file number and entered chronologically in the docket:

(A) papers filed with the clerk;

(B) process issued, and proofs of service or other returns showing execution; and

(C) appearances, orders, verdicts, and judgments.

(3) Contents of Entries; Jury Trial Demanded. Each entry must briefly show the nature of the paper filed or writ issued, the substance of each proof of service or other return, and the substance and date of entry of each order and judgment. When a jury trial has been properly demanded or ordered, the clerk must enter the word "jury" in the docket.

(b) Civil Judgments and Orders. The clerk must keep a copy of every final judgment and appealable order; of every order affecting title to or a lien on real or personal property; and of any other order that the court directs to be kept. The clerk must keep these in the form and manner prescribed by the Director of the Administrative Office of the United States Courts with the approval of the Judicial Conference of the United States.

(c) Indexes; Calendars. Under the court's direction, the clerk must:

(1) keep indexes of the docket and of the judgments and orders described in Rule 79(b); and

(2) prepare calendars of all actions ready for trial, distinguishing jury trials from nonjury trials.

(d) Other Records. The clerk must keep any other records required by the Director of the Administrative Office of the United States Courts with the approval of the Judicial Conference of the United States.

(As amended Dec. 27, 1946, eff. Mar. 19, 1948; Dec. 29, 1948, eff. Oct. 20, 1949; Jan. 21, 1963, eff. July 1, 1963; Apr. 30, 2007, eff. Dec. 1, 2007.)

Notes of Advisory Committee on Rules—1937

Compare [former] Equity Rule 3 (Books Kept by Clerk and Entries Therein). In connection with this rule, see also the following statutes of the United States:

U.S.C., Title 5:

- §301 [see Title 28, §526] (Officials for investigation of official acts, records and accounts of marshals, attorneys, clerks of courts, United States commissioners, referees and trustees)
- §318 [former] (Accounts of district attorneys)

U.S.C., Title 28:

- §556 [former] (Clerks of district courts; books open to inspection)
- §567 [now 751] (Same; accounts)
- §568 [now 751] (Same; reports and accounts of moneys received; dockets)
- §813 [former] (Indices of judgment debtors to be kept by clerks)

And see "Instructions to United States Attorneys, Marshals, Clerks and Commissioners" issued by the Attorney General of the United States.

Notes of Advisory Committee on Rules—1946 Amendment

Subdivision (a). The amendment substitutes the Director of the Administrative Office of the United States Courts, acting subject to the approval of the Judicial Conference of Senior Circuit Judges, in the place of the Attorney General as a consequence of and in accordance with the provisions of the act establishing the Administrative Office and transferring functions thereto. Act of August 7, 1939, c. 501, §§1–7, 53 Stat. 1223, 28 U.S.C. §§444–450 [now 601–610].

Subdivision (b). The change in this subdivision does not alter the nature of the judgments and orders to be recorded in permanent form but it does away with the express requirement that they be recorded in a book. This merely gives latitude for the preservation of court records in other than book form, if that shall seem advisable, and permits with the approval of the Judicial Conference the adoption of such modern, space-saving methods as microphotography. See Proposed Improvements in the Administration of the Offices of Clerks of United States District Courts, prepared by the Bureau of the Budget (1941) 38–42. See also Rule 55, Federal Rules of Criminal Procedure [following section 687 of Title 18 U.S.C.].

Subdivision (c). The words "Separate and" have been deleted as unduly rigid. There is no sufficient reason for requiring that the indices in all cases be separate; on the contrary, the requirement frequently increases the labor of persons searching the records as well as the labor of the clerk's force preparing them. The matter should be left to administrative discretion.

The other changes in the subdivision merely conform with those made in subdivision (b) of the rule.

Subdivision (d). Subdivision (d) is a new provision enabling the Administrative Office, with the approval of the Judicial Conference, to carry out any improvements in clerical procedure with respect to books and records which may be deemed advisable. See report cited in Note to subdivision (b), supra.

Notes of Advisory Committee on Rules—1948 Amendment

The change in nomenclature conforms to the official designation in Title 28, U.S.C., §231.

Notes of Advisory Committee on Rules—1963 Amendment

The terminology is clarified without any change of the prescribed practice. See amended Rule 58, and the Advisory Committee's Note thereto.

Committee Notes on Rules—2007 Amendment

The language of Rule 79 has been amended as part of the general restyling of the Civil Rules to make them more easily understood and to make style and terminology consistent throughout the rules. These changes are intended to be stylistic only.

Rule 80. Stenographic Transcript as Evidence

If stenographically reported testimony at a hearing or trial is admissible in evidence at a later trial, the testimony may be proved by a transcript certified by the person who reported it.

(As amended Dec. 27, 1946, eff. Mar. 19, 1948; Apr. 30, 2007, eff. Dec. 1, 2007.)

Notes of Advisory Committee on Rules—1937

Note to Subdivision (a). This follows substantially [former] Equity Rule 50 (Stenographer—Appointment—Fees). [This subdivision was abrogated. See amendment note of Advisory Committee below.]

Note to Subdivision (b). See Reports of Conferences of Senior Circuit Judges with the Chief Justice of the United States (1936), 22 A.B.A.J. 818, 819; (1937), 24 A.B.A.J. 75, 77. [This subdivision was abrogated. See amendment note of Advisory Committee below.]

Note to Subdivision (c). Compare Iowa Code (1935) §11353.

Notes of Advisory Committee on Rules—1946 Amendment

Subdivisions (a) and (b) of Rule 80 have been abrogated because of Public Law 222, 78th Cong., c. 3, 2d Sess., approved Jan. 20, 1944, 28 U.S.C. §9a [now 550, 604, 753, 1915, 1920], providing for the appointment of official stenographers for each district court, prescribing their duties, providing for the furnishing of transcripts, the taxation of the fees therefor as costs, and other related matters. This statute has now been implemented by Congressional appropriation available for the fiscal year beginning July 1, 1945.

Subdivision (c) of Rule 80 (Stenographic Report or Transcript as Evidence) has been retained unchanged.

Committee Notes on Rules—2007 Amendment

The language of Rule 80 has been amended as part of the general restyling of the Civil Rules to make them more easily understood and to make style and terminology consistent throughout the rules. These changes are intended to be stylistic only.

TITLE XI. GENERAL PROVISIONS

Rule 81. Applicability of the Rules in General; Removed Actions

(a) Applicability to Particular Proceedings.

(1) Prize Proceedings. These rules do not apply to prize proceedings in admiralty governed by 10 U.S.C. §§7651–7681.

(2) Bankruptcy. These rules apply to bankruptcy proceedings to the extent provided by the Federal Rules of Bankruptcy Procedure.

(3) Citizenship. These rules apply to proceedings for admission to citizenship to the extent that the practice in those proceedings is not specified in federal statutes and has previously conformed to the practice in civil actions. The provisions of 8 U.S.C. §1451 for service by publication and for answer apply in proceedings to cancel citizenship certificates.

(4) Special Writs. These rules apply to proceedings for habeas corpus and for quo warranto to the extent that the practice in those proceedings:

(A) is not specified in a federal statute, the Rules Governing Section 2254 Cases, or the Rules Governing Section 2255 Cases; and

(B) has previously conformed to the practice in civil actions.

(5) Proceedings Involving a Subpoena. These rules apply to proceedings to compel testimony or the production of documents through a subpoena issued by a United States officer or agency under a federal statute, except as otherwise provided by statute, by local rule, or by court order in the proceedings.

(6) Other Proceedings. These rules, to the extent applicable, govern proceedings under the following laws, except as these laws provide other procedures:

(A) 7 U.S.C. §§292, 499g(c), for reviewing an order of the Secretary of Agriculture;

(B) 9 U.S.C., relating to arbitration;

(C) 15 U.S.C. §522, for reviewing an order of the Secretary of the Interior;

(D) 15 U.S.C. §715d(c), for reviewing an order denying a certificate of clearance;

(E) 29 U.S.C. §§159, 160, for enforcing an order of the National Labor Relations Board;

(F) 33 U.S.C. §§918, 921, for enforcing or reviewing a compensation order under the Longshore and Harbor Workers' Compensation Act; and

(G) 45 U.S.C. §159, for reviewing an arbitration award in a railway-labor dispute.

(b) Scire Facias and Mandamus. The writs of scire facias and mandamus are abolished. Relief previously available through them may be obtained by appropriate action or motion under these rules.

(c) Removed Actions.

(1) Applicability. These rules apply to a civil action after it is removed from a state court.

(2) Further Pleading. After removal, repleading is unnecessary unless the court orders it. A defendant who did not answer before removal must answer or present other defenses or objections under these rules within the longest of these periods:

(A) 21 days after receiving—through service or otherwise—a copy of the initial pleading stating the claim for relief;

(B) 21 days after being served with the summons for an initial pleading on file at the time of service; or

(C) 7 days after the notice of removal is filed.

(3) Demand for a Jury Trial.

(A) As Affected by State Law. A party who, before removal, expressly demanded a jury trial in accordance with state law need not renew the demand after removal. If the state law did not require an express demand for a jury trial, a party need not make one after removal unless the court orders the parties to do so within a specified time. The court must so order at a party's request and may so order on its own. A party who fails to make a demand when so ordered waives a jury trial.

(B) Under Rule 38. If all necessary pleadings have been served at the time of removal, a party entitled to a jury trial under Rule 38 must be given one if the party serves a demand within 14 days after:

(i) it files a notice of removal; or

(ii) it is served with a notice of removal filed by another party.

(d) Law Applicable.

(1) "State Law" Defined. When these rules refer to state law, the term "law" includes the state's statutes and the state's judicial decisions.

(2) "State" Defined. The term "state" includes, where appropriate, the District of Columbia and any United States commonwealth or territory.
(3) "Federal Statute" Defined in the District of Columbia. In the United States District Court for the District of Columbia, the term "federal statute" includes any Act of Congress that applies locally to the District.

———

(As amended Dec. 28, 1939, eff. Apr. 3, 1941; Dec. 27, 1946, eff. Mar. 19, 1948; Dec. 29, 1948, eff. Oct. 20, 1949; Apr. 30, 1951, eff. Aug. 1, 1951; Jan. 21, 1963, eff. July 1, 1963; Feb. 28, 1966, eff. July 1, 1966; Dec. 4, 1967, eff. July 1, 1968; Mar. 1, 1971, eff. July 1, 1971; Mar. 2, 1987, eff. Aug. 1, 1987; Apr. 23, 2001, eff. Dec. 1, 2001; Apr. 29, 2002, eff. Dec. 1, 2002; Apr. 30, 2007, eff. Dec. 1, 2007; Mar. 26, 2009, eff. Dec. 1, 2009.)

Notes of Advisory Committee on Rules—1937

Note to Subdivision (a). Paragraph (1): Compare the enabling act, act of June 19, 1934, U.S.C., Title 28, §§723b [see 2072] (Rules in actions at law; Supreme Court authorized to make) and 723c [see 2072] (Union of equity and action at law rules; power of Supreme Court). For the application of these rules in bankruptcy and copyright proceedings, see Orders xxxvi and xxxvii in Bankruptcy and Rule 1 of Rules of Practice and Procedure under §25 of the copyright act, act of March 4, 1909, U.S.C., Title 17, §25 [see 412, 501 to 504] (Infringement and rules of procedure).

For examples of statutes which are preserved by paragraph (2) see: U.S.C., Title 8, ch. 9 [former] (Naturalization); Title 28, ch. 14 [now 153] (Habeas corpus); Title 28, §§377a–377c (Quo warranto); and such forfeiture statutes as U.S.C., Title 7, §116 (Misbranded seeds, confiscation), and Title 21, §14 [see 334(b)] (Pure Food and Drug Act—condemnation of adulterated or misbranded food; procedure). See also 443 Cans of Frozen Eggs Product v. U.S., 226 U.S. 172, 33 S.Ct. 50 (1912).

For examples of statutes which under paragraph (7) will continue to govern procedure in condemnation cases, see U.S.C., [former] Title 40, §258 (Condemnation of realty for sites for public building, etc., procedure); U.S.C., Title 16, §831x (Condemnation by Tennessee Valley Authority); U.S.C., [former] Title 40, §120 (Acquisition of lands for public use in District of Columbia); [former] Title 40, ch. 7 (Acquisition of lands in District of Columbia for use of United States; condemnation).

Note to Subdivision (b). Some statutes which will be affected by this subdivision are:

U.S.C., Title 7:

- §222 (Federal Trade Commission powers adopted for enforcement of Stockyards Act) (By reference to Title 15, §49)

U.S.C., Title 15:

- §49 (Enforcement of Federal Trade Commission orders and antitrust laws)
- §77t(c) (Enforcement of Securities and Exchange Commission orders and Securities Act of 1933)
- §78u(f) (Same; Securities Exchange Act of 1934)
- §79r(g) (Same; Public Utility Holding Company Act of 1935)

U.S.C., Title 16:

- §820 (Proceedings in equity for revocation or to prevent violations of license of Federal Power Commission licensee)
- §825m(b) (Mandamus to compel compliance with Federal Water Power Act, etc.)

U.S.C., Title 19:

- §1333(c) (Mandamus to compel compliance with orders of Tariff Commission, etc.)

U.S.C., Title 28:

- §377 [now 1651] (Power to issue writs)
- §572 [now 1923] (Fees, attorneys, solicitors and proctors)
- §778 [former] (Death of parties; substitution of executor or administrator). Compare Rule 25(a) (Substitution of parties; death), and the note thereto.

U.S.C., Title 33:

- §495 (Removal of bridges over navigable waters)

U.S.C., Title 45:

- §88 (Mandamus against Union Pacific Railroad Company)
- §153(p) (Mandamus to enforce orders of Adjustment Board under Railway Labor Act)
- §185 (Same; National Air Transport Adjustment Board) (By reference to §153)

U.S.C., Title 47:

- §11 (Powers of Federal Communications Commission)
- §401(a) (Enforcement of Federal Communications Act and orders of Commission)
- §406 (Same; compelling furnishing of facilities; mandamus)

U.S.C., Title 49:

- §19a(l) [see 11703(a), 14703, 15903(a)] (Mandamus to compel compliance with Interstate Commerce Act)
- §20(9) [see 11703(a), 14703, 15903(a)] (Jurisdiction to compel compliance with interstate commerce laws by mandamus)

For comparable provisions in state practice see Ill. Rev. Stat. (1937), ch. 110, §179; Calif. Code Civ. Proc. (Deering, 1937) §802.

Note to Subdivision (c). Such statutes as the following dealing with the removal of actions are substantially continued and made subject to these rules:

U.S.C., Title 28:

- §71 [now 1441, 1445, 1447] (Removal of suits from state courts)
- §72 [now 1446, 1447] (Same; procedure)
- §73 [former] (Same; suits under grants of land from different states)
- §74 [now 1443, 1446, 1447] (Same; causes against persons denied civil rights)
- §75 [now 1446] (Same; petitioner in actual custody of state court)
- §76 [now 1442, 1446, 1447] (Same; suits and prosecutions against revenue officers)
- §77 [now 1442] (Same; suits by aliens)
- §78 [now 1449] (Same; copies of records refused by clerk of state court)
- §79 [now 1450] (Same; previous attachment bonds or orders)
- §80 [now 1359, 1447, 1919] (Same; dismissal or remand)
- §81 [now 1447] (Same; proceedings in suits removed)
- §82 [former] (Same; record; filing and return)
- §83 [now 1447, 1448] (Service of process after removal)

U.S.C., Title 28, §72 [now 1446, 1447], supra, however, is modified by shortening the time for pleading in removed actions.

Note to Subdivision (e). The last sentence of this subdivision modifies U.S.C., Title 28, §725 [now 1652] (Laws of States as rules of decision) in so far as that statute has been construed to govern matters of procedure and to exclude state judicial decisions relative thereto.

Notes of Advisory Committee on Rules—1946 Amendment

Subdivision (a). Despite certain dicta to the contrary [Lynn v. United States (C.C.A.5th, 1940) 110 F.(2d) 586; Mount Tivy Winery, Inc. v. Lewis (N.D.Cal. 1942) 42 F.Supp. 636], it is manifest that the rules apply to actions against the United States under the Tucker Act [28 U.S.C., §§41(20), 250, 251, 254, 257, 258, 287, 289, 292, 761–765 [now 791, 1346, 1401, 1402, 1491, 1493, 1496, 1501, 1503, 2071, 2072, 2411, 2412, 2501, 2506, 2509, 2510]]. See United States to use of Foster Wheeler Corp. v. American Surety Co. of New York (E.D.N.Y. 1939) 25 F.Supp. 700; Boerner v. United States (E.D.N.Y. 1939) 26 F.Supp. 769; United States v. Gallagher (C.C.A.9th, 1945) 151 F.(2d) 556. Rules 1 and 81 provide that the rules shall apply to all suits of a civil nature, whether cognizable as cases at law or in equity, except those specifically excepted; and the character of the various proceedings excepted by express statement in Rule 81, as well as the language of the rules generally, shows that the term "civil action" [Rule 2] includes actions against the United States. Moreover, the rules in many places expressly make provision for the situation wherein the United States is a party as either plaintiff or defendant. See Rules 4(d)(4), 12(a), 13(d), 25(d), 37(f), 39(c), 45(c), 54(d), 55(e), 62(e), and 65(c). In United States v. Sherwood (1941) 312 U.S. 584, the Solicitor General expressly conceded in his brief for the United States that the rules apply to Tucker Act cases. The Solicitor General stated: "The Government, of course, recognizes that the Federal Rules of Civil Procedure apply to cases brought under the Tucker Act." (Brief for the United States, p. 31). Regarding Lynn v. United States, supra, the Solicitor General said: "In Lynn v. United States . . . the Circuit Court of Appeals for the Fifth Circuit went beyond the Government's contention there, and held that an action under the Tucker Act is neither an action at law nor a suit in equity and, seemingly, that the Federal Rules of Civil Procedure are, therefore, inapplicable. We think the suggestion is erroneous. Rules 4(d), 12(a), 39(c), and 55(e) expressly contemplate suits against the United States, and nothing in the enabling Act (48 Stat. 1064) [see 28 U.S.C. 2072] suggests that the Rules are inapplicable to Tucker Act proceedings, which in terms are to accord with court rules and their subsequent modifications (Sec. 4, Act of March 3, 1887, 24 Stat. 505) [see 28 U.S.C. 2071, 2072]." (Brief for the United States, p. 31, n. 17.)

United States v. Sherwood, supra, emphasizes, however, that the application of the rules in Tucker Act cases affects only matters of procedure and does not operate to extend jurisdiction. See also Rule 82. In the Sherwood case, the New York Supreme Court, acting under §795 of the New York Civil Practice Act, made an order authorizing Sherwood, as a judgment creditor, to maintain a suit under the Tucker Act to recover damages from the United States for breach of its contract with the judgment debtor, Kaiser, for construction of a post office building. Sherwood brought suit against the United States and Kaiser in the District Court for the Eastern District of New York. The question before the United States Supreme Court was whether a United States District Court had jurisdiction to entertain a suit against the United States wherein private parties were joined as parties defendant. It was contended that either the Federal Rules of Civil Procedure or the Tucker Act, or both, embodied the consent of the United States to be sued in litigations in which issues between the plaintiff and third persons were to be adjudicated. Regarding the effect of the Federal Rules, the Court declared that nothing in the rules, so far as they may be applicable in Tucker Act cases, authorized the maintenance of any suit against the United States to which it had not otherwise consented. The matter involved was not one of procedure but of jurisdiction, the limits of which were marked by the consent of the United States to be sued. The jurisdiction thus limited is unaffected by the Federal Rules of Civil Procedure.

Subdivision (a)(2). The added sentence makes it clear that the rules have not superseded the requirements of U.S.C., Title 28, §466 [now 2253]. Schenk v. Plummer (C.C.A. 9th, 1940) 113 F.(2d) 726.

For correct application of the rules in proceedings for forfeiture of property for violation of a statute of the United States, such as under U.S.C., Title 22, §405 (seizure of war materials intended for unlawful export) or U.S.C., Title 21, §334(b) (Federal Food, Drug, and Cosmetic Act; formerly Title 21, §14, Pure Food and Drug Act), see Reynal v. United States (C.C.A. 5th, 1945) 153 F.(2d) 929; United States v. 108 Boxes of Cheddar Cheese (S.D.Iowa 1943) 3 F.R.D. 40.

Subdivision (a)(3). The added sentence makes it clear that the rules apply to appeals from proceedings to enforce administrative subpoenas. See Perkins v. Endicott Johnson Corp. (C.C.A. 2d 1942) 128 F.(2d) 208, aff'd on other grounds (1943) 317 U.S. 501; Walling v. News Printing, Inc. (C.C.A. 3d, 1945) 148 F.(2d) 57; McCrone v. United States (1939) 307 U.S. 61. And, although the provision allows full recognition of the fact that the rigid application of the rules in the proceedings themselves may conflict with the summary determination desired [Goodyear Tire & Rubber Co. v. National Labor Relations Board (C.C.A. 6th, 1941) 122 F.(2d) 450; Cudahy Packing Co. v. National Labor Relations Board (C.C.A. 10th, 1941) 117 F.(2d) 692], it is drawn so as to permit application of any of the rules in the proceedings whenever the district court deems them helpful. See, e.g., Peoples Natural Gas Co. v. Federal Power Commission (App. D.C. 1942) 127 F.(2d) 153, cert. den. (1942) 316 U.S. 700; Martin v. Chandis Securities Co. (C.C.A. 9th, 1942) 128 F.(2d) 731. Compare the application of the rules in summary proceedings in bankruptcy under General Order 37. See 1 Collier on Bankruptcy (14th ed. by Moore and Oglebay) 326–327; 2 Collier, op. cit. supra, 1401–1402; 3 Collier, op. cit. supra, 228–231; 4 Collier, op. cit. supra, 1199–1202.

Subdivision (a)(6). Section 405 of U.S.C., Title 8 originally referred to in the last sentence of paragraph (6), has been repealed and §738 [see 1451], U.S.C., Title 8, has been enacted in its stead. The last sentence of paragraph (6) has, therefore, been amended in accordance with this change. The sentence has also been amended so as to refer directly to the statute regarding the provision of time for answer, thus avoiding any confusion attendant upon a change in the statute.

That portion of subdivision (a)(6) making the rules applicable to proceedings for enforcement or review of compensation orders under the Longshoremen's and Harbor Workers' Compensation Act [33 U.S.C. §901 et seq.] was added by an amendment made pursuant to order of the Court, December 28, 1939, effective three months subsequent to the adjournment of the 76th Congress, January 3, 1941.

Subdivision (c). The change in subdivision (c) effects more speedy trials in removed actions. In some states many of the courts have only two terms a year. A case, if filed 20 days before a term, is returnable to that term, but if filed less than 20 days before a term, is returnable to the following term, which convenes six months later. Hence, under the original wording of Rule 81(c), where a case is filed less than 20 days before the term and is removed within a few days but before answer, it is possible for the defendant to delay interposing his answer or presenting his defenses by motion for six months or more. The rule as amended prevents this result.

Subdivision (f). The use of the phrase "the United States or an officer or agency thereof" in the rules (as e.g., in Rule 12(a) and amended Rule 73(a)) could raise the question of whether "officer" includes a collector of internal revenue, a former collector, or the personal representative of a deceased collector, against whom suits for tax refunds are frequently instituted. Difficulty might ensue for the reason that a suit against a collector or his representative has been held to be a personal action. Sage v. United States (1919) 250 U.S. 33; Smietanka v. Indiana Steel Co. (1921) 257 U.S. 1; United States v. Nunnally Investment Co. (1942) 316 U.S. 258. The addition of subdivision (f) to Rule 81 dispels any doubts on the matter and avoids further litigation.

Notes of Advisory Committee on Rules—1948 Amendment

Subdivision (a)—Paragraph (1).—The Copyright Act of March 4, 1909, as amended, was repealed and Title 17, U.S.C., enacted into positive law by the Act of July 30, 1947, c. 391, §§1, 2, 61 Stat. 652. The first amendment, therefore, reflects this change. The second amendment involves a matter of nomenclature and reflects the official designation of the United States District Court for the District of Columbia in Title 28, U.S.C. §§88, 132.

Paragraph (2).—The amendment substitutes the present statutory reference.

Paragraph (3).—The Arbitration Act of February 12, 1925, was repealed and Title 9, U.S.C., enacted into positive law by the Act of July 30, 1947, c. 392, §§1, 2, 61 Stat. 669, and the amendment reflects this change. The Act of May 20, 1926, c. 347, §9 (44 Stat. 585), U.S.C., Title 45, §159, deals with the review by the district court of an award of a board of arbitration under the Railway Labor Act, and provides, inter alia, for an appeal within 10 days from a final judgment of the district court to the court of appeals. It is not clear whether Title 28, U.S.C., repealed this time period and substituted the time periods provided for in Title 28, U.S.C., §2107, normally a minimum of 30 days. If there has been no repeal, then the 10-day time period of 45 U.S.C., §159, applies by virtue of the "unless" clause in Rule 73(a); if there has been a repeal, then the other time periods stated in Rule 73(a), normally a minimum of 30 days, apply. For discussion, see Note to Rule 73 (§), supra.

Paragraph (4).—The nomenclature of the district courts is changed to conform to the official designation in Title 28, U.S.C., §132(a).

Paragraph (5).—The nomenclature of the district courts is changed to conform to the official designation in Title 28, U.S.C., §132(a). The Act of July 5, 1935, c. 372, §§9 and 10, was amended by Act of June 23, 1947, c. 120, 61 Stat. 143, 146, and will probably be amended from time to time. Insertion in Rule 81(a)(5) of the words "as amended", and deletion of the subsection reference "(e), (g), and (i)" of U.S.C., Title 29, §160, make correcting references and are sufficiently general to include future statutory amendment.

Paragraph (6).—The Chinese Exclusion Acts were repealed by the Act of December 17, 1943, c. 344, §1, 57 Stat. 600, and hence the reference to the Act of September 13, 1888, as amended, is deleted. The Longshoremen's and Harbor Workers' Compensation Act of March 4, 1927, was amended by Act of June 25, 1936, c. 804, 49 Stat. 1921, and hence the words "as amended" have been added to reflect this change and, as they are sufficiently general, to include future statutory amendment. The Nationality Act of October 14, 1940, c. 876, 54 Stat. 1137, 1172, repealed and replaced the Act of June 29, 1906, as amended, and correcting statutory references are, therefore, made.

Subdivision (c).—In the first sentence the change in nomenclature conforms to the official designation of district courts in Title 28, U.S.C., §132(a); and the word "all" is deleted as superfluous. The need for revision of the third sentence is occasioned by the procedure for removal set forth in revised Title 28, U.S.C., §1446. Under the prior removal procedure governing civil actions, 28 U.S.C., §72 (1946), the petition for removal had to be first presented to and filed with the state court, except in the case of removal on the basis of prejudice or local influence, within the time allowed "to answer or plead to the declaration or complaint of the plaintiff"; and the defendant had to file a transcript of the record in the federal court within thirty days from the date of filing his removal petition. Under §1446(a) removal is effected by a defendant filing with the proper United States district court "a verified petition containing a short and plain statement of the facts which entitled him or them to removal together with a copy of all process, pleadings, and orders served upon him or them in such action." And §1446(b) provides: "The petition for removal of a civil action or proceeding may be filed within twenty days after commencement of the action or service of process, whichever is later." This subsection (b) gives trouble in states where an action may be both commenced and service of process made without serving or otherwise giving the defendant a copy of the complaint or other initial pleading. To cure this statutory defect, the Judge's Committee appointed pursuant to action of the Judicial Conference and headed by Judge Albert B. Maris is proposing an amendment to §1446(b) to read substantially as follows: "The petition for removal of a civil action or proceedings shall be filed within 20 days after the receipt through service or otherwise by the defendant of a copy of the initial pleading setting forth the claim for relief upon which the action or proceeding is based." The revised third sentence of Rule 81(c) is geared to this proposed statutory amendment; and it gives the defendant at least 5 days after removal within which to present his defenses.*

The change in the last sentence of subdivision (c) reflects the fact that a transcript of the record is no longer required under §1446, and safeguards the right to demand a jury trial, where the right has not already been waived and where the parties are at issue—"all necessary pleadings have been served." Only, rarely will the last sentence of Rule 81(c) have any applicability, since removal will normally occur before the pleadings are closed, and in this usual situation Rule 38(b) applies and safeguards the right to jury trial. See Moore's Federal practice (1st ed.) 3020.

Subdivision (d).—This subdivision is abrogated because it is obsolete and unnecessary under Title 28, U.S.C. Sections 88, 132, and 133 provide that the District of Columbia constitutes a judicial district, the district court of that district is the United States District Court for the District of Columbia, and the personnel of that court are district judges. Sections 41, 43, and 44 provide that the District of Columbia is a judicial circuit, the court of appeals of that circuit is the United States Court of Appeals for the District of Columbia, and the personnel of that court are circuit judges.

Subdivision (e).—The change in nomenclature conforms to the official designation of the United States District Court for the District of Columbia in Title 28, U.S.C., §§132(a), 88.

Notes of Advisory Committee on Rules—1963 Amendment

Subdivision (a)(4). This change reflects the transfer of functions from the Secretary of Commerce to the Secretary of the Interior made by 1939 Reorganization Plan No. II, §4(e), 53 Stat. 1433.

Subdivision (a)(6). The proper current reference is to the 1952 statute superseding the 1940 statute.

Subdivision (c). Most of the cases have held that a party who has made a proper express demand for jury trial in the State court is not required to renew the demand after removal of the action. Zakoscielny v. Waterman Steamship Corp., 16 F.R.D. 314 (D.Md. 1954); Talley v. American Bakeries Co., 15 F.R.D. 391 (E.D.Tenn. 1954); Rehrer v. Service Trucking Co., 15 F.R.D. 113 (D.Del. 1953); 5 Moore's Federal Practice 38.39[3] (2d ed. 1951); 1 Barron & Holtzoff, Federal Practice and Procedure §132 (Wright ed. 1960). But there is some authority to the contrary. Petsel v. Chicago, B. & Q.R. Co., 101 F.Supp. 1006 (S.D.Iowa 1951) Nelson v. American Nat. Bank & Trust Co., 9 F.R.D. 680 (E.D.Tenn. 1950). The amendment adopts the preponderant view.

In order still further to avoid unintended waivers of jury trial, the amendment provides that where by State law applicable in the court from which the case is removed a party is entitled to jury trial without making an express demand, he need not make a demand after removal. However, the district court for calendar or other purposes may on its own motion direct the parties to state whether they demand a jury, and the court must make such a direction upon the request of any party. Under the amendment a district court may find it convenient to establish a routine practice of giving these directions to the parties in appropriate cases.

Subdivision (f). The amendment recognizes the change of nomenclature made by Treasury Dept. Order 150–26(2), 18 Fed. Reg. 3499 (1953).

As to a special problem arising under Rule 25 (Substitution of parties) in actions for refund of taxes, see the Advisory Committee's Note to the amendment of Rule 25(d), effective July 19, 1961; and 4 Moore's Federal Practice §25.09 at 531 (2d ed. 1950).

Notes of Advisory Committee on Rules—1966 Amendment

See Note to Rule 1, supra.

Statutory proceedings to forfeit property for violation of the laws of the United States, formerly governed by the admiralty rules, will be governed by the unified and supplemental rules. See Supplemental Rule A.

Upon the recommendation of the judges of the United States District Court for the District of Columbia, the Federal Rules of Civil Procedure are made applicable to probate proceedings in that court. The exception with regard to adoption proceedings is removed because the court no longer has jurisdiction of those matters; and the words "mental health" are substituted for "lunacy" to conform to the current characterization in the District.

The purpose of the amendment to paragraph (3) is to permit the deletion from Rule 73(a) of the clause "unless a shorter time is provided by law." The 10 day period fixed for an appeal under 45 U.S.C. §159 is the only instance of a shorter time provided for appeals in civil cases. Apart from the unsettling effect of the clause, it is eliminated because its retention would preserve the 15 day period heretofore allowed by 28 U.S.C. §2107 for appeals from interlocutory decrees in admiralty, it being one of the purposes of the amendment to make the time for appeals in civil and admiralty cases uniform under the unified rules. See Advisory Committee's Note to subdivision (a) of Rule 73.

Notes of Advisory Committee on Rules—1968 Amendment

The amendments eliminate inappropriate references to appellate procedure.

Notes of Advisory Committee on Rules—1971 Amendment

Title 28, U.S.C., §2243 now requires that the custodian of a person detained must respond to an application for a writ of habeas corpus "within three days unless for good cause additional time, not exceeding twenty days, is allowed." The amendment increases to forty days the additional time that the district court may allow in habeas corpus proceedings involving persons in custody pursuant to a judgment of a state court. The substantial increase in the number of such proceedings in recent years has placed a considerable burden on state authorities. Twenty days has proved in practice too short a time in which to prepare and file the return in many such cases. Allowance of additional time should, of course, be granted only for good cause.

While the time allowed in such a case for the return of the writ may not exceed forty days, this does not mean that the state must necessarily be limited to that period of time to provide for the federal court the transcript of the proceedings of a state trial or plenary hearing if the transcript must be prepared after the habeas corpus proceeding has begun in the federal court.

Notes of Advisory Committee on Rules—1987 Amendment

The amendments are technical. No substantive change is intended.

Committee Notes on Rules—2001 Amendment

Former Copyright Rule 1 made the Civil Rules applicable to copyright proceedings except to the extent the Civil Rules were inconsistent with Copyright Rules. Abrogation of the Copyright Rules leaves the Civil Rules fully applicable to copyright proceedings. Rule 81(a)(1) is amended to reflect this change.

The District of Columbia Court Reform and Criminal Procedure Act of 1970, Pub.L. 91–358, 84 Stat. 473, transferred mental health proceedings formerly held in the United States District Court for the District of Columbia to local District of Columbia courts. The provision that the Civil Rules do not apply to these proceedings is deleted as superfluous.

The reference to incorporation of the Civil Rules in the Federal Rules of Bankruptcy Procedure has been restyled.

Changes Made After Publication and Comments The Committee Note was amended to correct the inadvertent omission of a negative. As revised, it correctly reflects the language that is stricken from the rule.

Committee Notes on Rules—2002 Amendment

This amendment brings Rule 81(a)(2) into accord with the Rules Governing §2254 and §2255 proceedings. In its present form, Rule 81(a)(2) includes return-time provisions that are inconsistent with the provisions in the Rules Governing §§2254 and 2255. The inconsistency should be eliminated, and it is better that the time provisions continue to be set out in the other rules without duplication in Rule 81. Rule 81 also directs that the writ be directed to the person having custody of the person detained. Similar directions exist in the §2254 and §2255 rules, providing additional detail for applicants subject to future custody. There is no need for partial duplication in Rule 81.

The provision that the civil rules apply to the extent that practice is not set forth in the §2254 and §2255 rules dovetails with the provisions in Rule 11 of the §2254 rules and Rule 12 of the §2255 rules.

Changes Made After Publication and Comment. The only change since publication is deletion of an inadvertent reference to §2241 proceedings.

Committee Notes on Rules—2007 Amendment

The language of Rule 81 has been amended as part of the general restyling of the Civil Rules to make them more easily understood and to make style and terminology consistent throughout the rules. These changes are intended to be stylistic only.

Rule 81(c) has been revised to reflect the amendment of 28 U.S.C. §1446(a) that changed the procedure for removal from a petition for removal to a notice of removal.

Former Rule 81(e), drafted before the decision in Erie R.R. v. Tompkins, 304 U.S. 64 (1938), defined state law to include "the statutes of that state and the state judicial decisions construing them." The Erie decision reinterpreted the Rules of Decision Act, now 28 U.S.C. §1652, recognizing that the "laws" of the states include the common law established by judicial decisions. Long-established practice reflects this understanding, looking to state common law as well as statutes and court rules when a Civil Rule directs use of state law. Amended Rule 81(d)(1) adheres to this practice, including all state judicial decisions, not only those that construe state statutes.

Former Rule 81(f) is deleted. The office of district director of internal revenue was abolished by restructuring under the Internal Revenue Service Restructuring and Reform Act of 1998, Pub. L. 105–206, July 22, 1998, 26 U.S.C. §1 Note.

Committee Notes on Rules—2009 Amendment

The times set in the former rule at 5, 10, and 20 days have been revised to 7, 14, and 21 days, respectively. See the Note to Rule 6.

Several Rules incorporate local state practice. Rule 81(d) now provides that "the term 'state' includes, where appropriate, the District of Columbia." The definition is expanded to include any commonwealth or territory of the United States. As before, these entities are included only "where appropriate." They are included for the reasons that counsel incorporation of state practice. For example, state holidays are recognized in computing time under Rule 6(a). Other, quite different, examples are Rules 64(a), invoking state law for prejudgment remedies, and 69(a)(1), relying on state law for the procedure on execution. Including commonwealths and territories in these and other rules avoids the gaps that otherwise would result when the federal rule relies on local practice rather than provide a uniform federal approach. Including them also establishes uniformity between federal courts and local courts in areas that may involve strong local interests, little need for uniformity among federal courts, or difficulty in defining a uniform federal practice that integrates effectively with local practice.

Adherence to a local practice may be refused as not "appropriate" when the local practice would impair a significant federal interest.

Changes Made after Publication and Comment. The reference to a "possession" was deleted in deference to the concerns expressed by the Department of Justice.

The Rules Governing Section 2254 Cases and the Rules Governing Section 2255 Cases, referred to in subd. (a)(4)(A), are set out in notes under the respective sections in Title 28, Judiciary and Judicial Procedure.

The Longshore and Harbor Workers' Compensation Act, referred to in subd. (a)(6)(F), is act Mar. 4, 1927, ch. 509, 44 Stat. 1424, which is classified generally to chapter 18 (§901 et seq.) of Title 33, Navigation and Navigable Waters. For complete classification of this Act to the Code, see section 901 of Title 33 and Tables.

Effective Date of Abrogation

Abrogation of par. (7) of subdivision (a) of this rule as effective August 1, 1951, see Effective Date note under Rule 71A.

* Note.—The Supreme Court made these changes in the committee's proposed amendment to Rule 81(c): The phrase, "or within 20 days after the service of summons upon such initial pleading, then filed," was inserted following the phrase, "within 20 days after the receipt through service or otherwise of a copy of the initial pleading setting forth the claim for relief upon which the action or proceeding is based", because in several states suit is commenced by service of summons upon the defendant, notifying him that the plaintiff's pleading has been filed with the clerk of court. Thus, he may never receive a copy of the initial pleading. The added phrase is intended to give the defendant 20 days after the service of such summons in which to answer in a removed action, or 5 days after the filing of the petition for removal, whichever is longer. In these states, the 20-day period does not begin to run until such pleading is actually filed. The last word of the third sentence was changed from "longer" to "longest" because of the added phrase.

The phrase, "and who has not already waived his right to such trial," which previously appeared in the fourth sentence of subsection (c) of Rule 81, was deleted in order to afford a party who has waived his right to trial by jury in a state court an opportunity to assert that right upon removal to a federal court.

Rule 82. Jurisdiction and Venue Unaffected

These rules do not extend or limit the jurisdiction of the district courts or the venue of actions in those courts. An admiralty or maritime claim under Rule 9(h) is governed by 28 U.S.C. §1390.

(As amended Dec. 29, 1948, eff. Oct. 20, 1949; Feb. 28, 1966, eff. July 1, 1966; Apr. 23, 2001, eff. Dec. 1, 2001; Apr. 30, 2007, eff. Dec. 1, 2007; Apr. 28, 2016, eff. Dec. 1, 2016.)

Notes of Advisory Committee on Rules—1937

These rules grant extensive power of joining claims and counterclaims in one action, but, as this rule states, such grant does not extend federal jurisdiction. The rule is declaratory of existing practice under the [former] Federal Equity Rules with regard to such provisions as [former] Equity Rule 26 on Joinder of Causes of Action and [former] Equity Rule 30 on Counterclaims. Compare Shulman and Jaegerman, Some Jurisdictional Limitations on Federal Procedure, 45 Yale L.J. 393 (1936).

Notes of Advisory Committee on Rules—1948 Amendment

The change in nomenclature conforms to the official designation of district courts in Title 28, U.S.C., §132(a).

Notes of Advisory Committee on Rules—1966 Amendment

Title 28, U.S.C. §1391(b) provides: "A civil action wherein jurisdiction is not founded solely on diversity of citizenship may be brought only in the judicial district where all defendants reside, except as otherwise provided by law." This provision cannot appropriately be applied to what were formerly suits in admiralty. The rationale of decisions holding it inapplicable rests largely on the use of the term "civil action"; i.e., a suit in admiralty is not a "civil action" within the statute. By virtue of the amendment to Rule 1, the provisions of Rule 2 convert suits in admiralty into civil actions. The added sentence is necessary to avoid an undesirable change in existing law with respect to venue.

Committee Notes on Rules—2001 Amendment

The final sentence of Rule 82 is amended to delete the reference to 28 U.S.C. §1393, which has been repealed.

Style Comment

The recommendation that the change be made without publication carries with it a recommendation that style changes not be made. Styling would carry considerable risks. The first sentence of Rule 82, for example, states that the Civil Rules do not "extend or limit the jurisdiction of the United States district courts." That sentence is a flat lie if "jurisdiction" includes personal or quasi-in rem jurisdiction. The styling project on this rule requires publication and comment.

Committee Notes on Rules—2007 Amendment

The language of Rule 82 has been amended as part of the general restyling of the Civil Rules to make them more easily understood and to make style and terminology consistent throughout the rules. These changes are intended to be stylistic only.

Committee Notes on Rules—2016 Amendment

Rule 82 is amended to reflect the enactment of 28 U.S.C. §1390 and the repeal of §1392.

Rule 83. Rules by District Courts; Judge's Directives

(a) Local Rules.

(1) In General. After giving public notice and an opportunity for comment, a district court, acting by a majority of its district judges, may adopt and amend rules governing its practice. A local rule must be consistent with—but not duplicate—federal statutes and rules adopted under 28 U.S.C. §§2072 and 2075, and must conform to any uniform numbering system prescribed by the Judicial Conference of the United States. A local rule takes effect on the date specified by the district court and remains in effect unless amended by the court or abrogated by the judicial council of the circuit. Copies of rules and amendments must, on their adoption, be furnished to the judicial council and the Administrative Office of the United States Courts and be made available to the public.

(2) Requirement of Form. A local rule imposing a requirement of form must not be enforced in a way that causes a party to lose any right because of a nonwillful failure to comply.

(b) Procedure When There Is No Controlling Law. A judge may regulate practice in any manner consistent with federal law, rules adopted under 28 U.S.C. §§2072 and 2075, and the district's local rules. No sanction or other disadvantage may be imposed for noncompliance with any requirement not in federal law, federal rules, or the local rules unless the alleged violator has been furnished in the particular case with actual notice of the requirement.

(As amended Apr. 29, 1985, eff. Aug. 1, 1985; Apr. 27, 1995, eff. Dec. 1, 1995; Apr. 30, 2007, eff. Dec. 1, 2007.)

Notes of Advisory Committee on Rules—1937

This rule substantially continues U.S.C., Title 28, §731 [now 2071] (Rules of practice in district courts) with the additional requirement that copies of such rules and amendments be furnished to the Supreme Court of the United States. See [former] Equity Rule 79 (Additional Rules by District Court). With the last sentence compare United States Supreme Court Admiralty Rules (1920), Rule 44 (Right of Trial Courts To Make Rules of Practice) (originally promulgated in 1842).

Notes of Advisory Committee on Rules—1985 Amendment

Rule 83, which has not been amended since the Federal Rules were promulgated in 1938, permits each district to adopt local rules not inconsistent with the Federal Rules by a majority of the judges. The only other requirement is that copies be furnished to the Supreme Court.

The widespread adoption of local rules and the modest procedural prerequisites for their promulgation have led many commentators to question the soundness of the process as well as the validity of some rules, See 12 C. Wright & A. Miller, Federal Practice and Procedure: Civil §3152, at 217 (1973); Caballero, Is There an Over-Exercise of Local Rule-Making Powers by the United States District Courts?, 24 Fed. Bar News 325 (1977). Although the desirability of local rules for promoting uniform practice within a district is widely accepted, several commentators also have suggested reforms to increase the quality, simplicity, and uniformity of the local rules. See Note, Rule 83 and the Local Federal Rules, 67 Colum.L.Rev. 1251 (1967), and Comment, The Local Rules of Civil Procedure in the Federal District Courts—A Survey, 1966 Duke L.J. 1011.

The amended Rule attempts, without impairing the procedural validity of existing local rules, to enhance the local rulemaking process by requiring appropriate public notice of proposed rules and an opportunity to comment on them. Although some district courts apparently consult the local bar before promulgating rules, many do not, which has led to criticism of a process that has district judges consulting only with each other. See 12 C. Wright & A. Miller, supra, §3152, at 217; Blair, The New Local Rules for Federal Practice In Iowa, 23 Drake L.Rev. 517 (1974). The new language subjects local rulemaking to scrutiny similar to that accompanying the Federal Rules, administrative rulemaking, and legislation. It attempts to assure that the expert advice of practitioners and scholars is made available to the district court before local rules are promulgated. See Weinstein, Reform of Court Rule-Making Procedures 84–87, 127–37, 151 (1977).

The amended Rule does not detail the procedure for giving notice and an opportunity to be heard since conditions vary from district to district. Thus, there is no explicit requirement for a public hearing, although a district may consider that procedure appropriate in all or some rulemaking situations. See generally, Weinstein, supra, at 117–37, 151. The new Rule does not foreclose any other form of consultation. For example, it can be accomplished through the mechanism of an "Advisory Committee" similar to that employed by the Supreme Court in connection with the Federal Rules themselves.

The amended Rule provides that a local rule will take effect upon the date specified by the district court and will remain in effect unless amended by the district court or abrogated by the judicial council. The effectiveness of a local rule should not be deferred until approved by the judicial council because that might unduly delay promulgation of a local rule that should become effective immediately, especially since some councils do not meet frequently. Similarly, it was thought that to delay a local rule's effectiveness for a fixed period of time would be arbitrary and that to require the judicial council to abrogate a local rule within a specified time would be inconsistent with its power under 28 U.S.C. §332 (1976) to nullify a local rule at any time. The expectation is that the judicial council will examine all local rules, including those currently in effect, with an eye toward determining whether they are valid and consistent with the Federal Rules, promote inter-district uniformity and efficiency, and do not undermine the basic objectives of the Federal Rules.

The amended Rule requires copies of local rules to be sent upon their promulgation to the judicial council and the Administrative Office of the United States Courts rather than to the Supreme Court. The Supreme Court was the appropriate filing place in 1938, when Rule 83 originally was promulgated, but the establishment of the Administrative Office makes it a more logical place to develop a centralized file of local rules. This procedure is consistent with both the Criminal and the Appellate Rules. See Fed.R.Crim.P. 57(a); Fed.R.App.P. 47. The Administrative Office also will be able to provide improved utilization of the file because of its recent development of a Local Rules Index.

The practice pursued by some judges of issuing standing orders has been controversial, particularly among members of the practicing bar. The last sentence in Rule 83 has been amended to make certain that standing orders are not inconsistent with the Federal Rules or any local district court rules. Beyond that, it is hoped that each district will adopt procedures, perhaps by local rule, for promulgating and reviewing single-judge standing orders.

Notes of Advisory Committee on Rules—1995 Amendment

Subdivison (a). This rule is amended to reflect the requirement that local rules be consistent not only with the national rules but also with Acts of Congress. The amendment also states that local rules should not repeat Acts of Congress or national rules.

The amendment also requires that the numbering of local rules conform with any uniform numbering system that may be prescribed by the Judicial Conference. Lack of uniform numbering might create unnecessary traps for counsel and litigants. A uniform numbering system would make it easier for an increasingly national bar and for litigants to locate a local rule that applies to a particular procedural issue.

Paragraph (2) is new. Its aim is to protect against loss of rights in the enforcement of local rules relating to matters of form. For example, a party should not be deprived of a right to a jury trial because its attorney, unaware of—or forgetting—a local rule directing that jury demands be noted in the caption of the case, includes a jury demand only in the body of the pleading. The proscription of paragraph (2) is narrowly drawn—covering only violations attributable to nonwillful failure to comply and only those involving local rules directed to matters of form. It does not limit the court's power to impose substantive penalties upon a party if it or its attorney contumaciously or willfully violates a local rule, even one involving merely a matter of form. Nor does it affect the court's power to enforce local rules that involve more than mere matters of form—for example, a local rule requiring parties to identify evidentiary matters relied upon to support or oppose motions for summary judgment.

Subdivision (b). This rule provides flexibility to the court in regulating practice when there is no controlling law. Specifically, it permits the court to regulate practice in any manner consistent with Acts of Congress, with rules adopted under 28 U.S.C. §§2072 and 2075, and with the district local rules.

This rule recognizes that courts rely on multiple directives to control practice. Some courts regulate practice through the published Federal Rules and the local rules of the court. Some courts also have used internal operating procedures, standing orders, and other internal directives. Although such directives continue to be authorized, they can lead to problems. Counsel or litigants may be unaware of various directives. In addition, the sheer volume of directives may impose an unreasonable barrier. For example, it may be difficult to obtain copies of the directives. Finally, counsel or litigants may be unfairly sanctioned for failing to comply with a directive. For these reasons, the amendment to this rule disapproves imposing any sanction or other disadvantage on a person for noncompliance with such an internal directive, unless the alleged violator has been furnished actual notice of the requirement in a particular case.

There should be no adverse consequence to a party or attorney for violating special requirements relating to practice before a particular court unless the party or attorney has actual notice of those requirements. Furnishing litigants with a copy outlining the judge's practices—or attaching instructions to a notice setting a case for conference or trial—would suffice to give actual notice, as would an order in a case specifically adopting by reference a judge's standing order and indicating how copies can be obtained.

Committee Notes on Rules—2007 Amendment

The language of Rule 83 has been amended as part of the general restyling of the Civil Rules to make them more easily understood and to make style and terminology consistent throughout the rules. These changes are intended to be stylistic only.

Rule 84. [Abrogated (Apr. 29, 2015, eff. Dec. 1, 2015).]

Committee Notes on Rules—2015 Amendment

Rule 84 was adopted when the Civil Rules were established in 1938 "to indicate, subject to the provisions of these rules, the simplicity and brevity of statement which the rules contemplate." The purpose of providing illustrations for the rules, although useful when the rules were adopted, has been fulfilled. Accordingly, recognizing that there are many alternative sources for forms, including the website of the Administrative Office of the United States Courts, the websites of many district courts, and local law libraries that contain many commercially published forms, Rule 84 and the Appendix of Forms are no longer necessary and have been abrogated. The abrogation of Rule 84 does not alter existing pleading standards or otherwise change the requirements of Civil Rule 8.

Rule 85. Title

These rules may be cited as the Federal Rules of Civil Procedure.

(As amended Apr. 30, 2007, eff. Dec. 1, 2007.)

Committee Notes on Rules—2007 Amendment

The language of Rule 85 has been amended as part of the general restyling of the Civil Rules to make them more easily understood

and to make style and terminology consistent throughout the rules. These changes are intended to be stylistic only.

Rule 86. Effective Dates

(a) In General. These rules and any amendments take effect at the time specified by the Supreme Court, subject to 28 U.S.C. §2074. They govern:

(1) proceedings in an action commenced after their effective date; and

(2) proceedings after that date in an action then pending unless:

(A) the Supreme Court specifies otherwise; or

(B) the court determines that applying them in a particular action would be infeasible or work an injustice.

(b) December 1, 2007 Amendments. If any provision in Rules 1–5.1, 6–73, or 77–86 conflicts with another law, priority in time for the purpose of 28 U.S.C. §2072(b) is not affected by the amendments taking effect on December 1, 2007.

(As amended Dec. 27, 1946, eff. Mar. 19, 1948; Dec. 29, 1948, eff. Oct. 20, 1949; Apr. 17, 1961, eff. July 19, 1961; Jan. 21 and Mar. 18, 1963, eff. July 1, 1963; Apr. 30, 2007, eff. Dec. 1, 2007.)

Notes of Advisory Committee on Rules—1937

See [former] Equity Rule 81 (These Rules Effective February 1, 1913—Old Rules Abrogated).

Notes of Advisory Committee on Rules—1948 Amendment

By making the general amendments effective on the day following the adjournment of the first regular session of Congress to which they are transmitted, subdivision (c), supra, departs slightly from the prior practice of making amendments effective on the day which is three months subsequent to the adjournment of Congress or on September 1 of that year, whichever day is later. The reason for this departure is that no added period of time is needed for the Bench and Bar to acquaint themselves with the general amendments, which effect a change in nomenclature to conform to revised Title 28, substitute present statutory references to this Title and cure the omission or defect occasioned by the statutory revision in relation to the substitution of public officers, to a cost bond on appeal, and to procedure after removal (see Rules 25(d), 73(c), 81(c)).

Committee Notes on Rules—2007 Amendment

The language of Rule 86 has been amended as part of the general restyling of the Civil Rules to make them more easily understood and to make style and terminology consistent throughout the rules. These changes are intended to be stylistic only.

The subdivisions that provided a list of the effective dates of the original Civil Rules and amendments made up to 1963 are deleted as no longer useful.

Rule 86(b) is added to clarify the relationship of amendments taking effect on December 1, 2007, to other laws for the purpose of applying the "supersession" clause in 28 U.S.C. §2072(b). Section 2072(b) provides that a law in conflict with an Enabling Act Rule "shall be of no further force or effect after such rule[] ha[s] taken effect." The amendments that take effect on December 1, 2007, result from the general restyling of the Civil Rules and from a small number of technical revisions adopted on a parallel track. None of these amendments is intended to affect resolution of any conflict that might arise between a rule and another law. Rule 86(b) makes this intent explicit. Any conflict that arises should be resolved by looking to the date the specific conflicting rule provision first became effective.

Effective Date of 1966 Amendment; Transmission to Congress; Rescission

Sections 2–4 of the Order of the Supreme Court, dated Feb. 28, 1966, 383 U.S. 1031, provided:

"2. That the foregoing amendments and additions to the Rules of Civil Procedure shall take effect on July 1, 1966, and shall govern all proceedings in actions brought thereafter and also in all further proceedings in actions then pending, except to the extent that in the opinion of the court their application in a particular action then pending would not be feasible or would work injustice, in which event the former procedure applies.

"3. That the Chief Justice be, and he hereby is, authorized to transmit to the Congress the foregoing amendments and additions to the Rules of Civil Procedure in accordance with the provisions of Title 28, U.S.C., §§2072 and 2073.

"4. That: (a) subdivision (c) of Rule 6 of the Rules of Civil Procedure for the United States District Courts promulgated by this court on December 20, 1937, effective September 16, 1938; (b) Rule 2 of the Rules for Practice and Procedure under section 25 of An Act To amend and consolidate the Acts respecting copyright, approved March 4, 1909, promulgated by this court on June 1, 1909, effective July 1, 1909; and (c) the Rules of Practice in Admiralty and Maritime Cases, promulgated by this court on December 6, 1920, effective March 7, 1921, as revised, amended and supplemented be, and they hereby are, rescinded, effective July 1, 1966."

APPENDIX OF FORMS

[Abrogated (Apr. 29, 2015, eff. Dec. 1, 2015).]

SUPPLEMENTAL RULES FOR ADMIRALTY OR MARITIME CLAIMS AND ASSET FORFEITURE ACTIONS

Notes of Advisory Committee on Rules

The amendments to the Federal Rules of Civil Procedure to unify the civil and admiralty procedure, together with the Supplemental Rules for Certain Admiralty and Maritime Claims, completely superseded the Admiralty Rules, effective July 1, 1966. Accordingly, the latter were rescinded.

Notes of Advisory Committee on Rules—1985 Amendment

Since their promulgation in 1966, the Supplemental Rules for Certain Admiralty and Maritime Claims have preserved the special procedures of arrest and attachment unique to admiralty law. In recent years, however, these Rules have been challenged as violating the principles of procedural due process enunciated in the United States Supreme Court's decision in Sniadach v. Family Finance Corp., 395 U.S. 337 (1969), and later developed in Fuentes v. Shevin, 407 U.S. 67 (1972); Mitchell v. W. T. Grant Co., 416 U.S. 600 (1974); and North Georgia Finishing, Inc. v. Di-Chem, Inc., 419 U.S. 601 (1975). These Supreme Court decisions provide five basic criteria for a constitutional seizure of property: (1) effective notice to persons having interests in the property seized, (2) judicial review prior to attachment, (3) avoidance of conclusory allegations in the complaint, (4) security posted by the plaintiff to protect the owner of the property under attachment, and (5) a meaningful and timely hearing after attachment.

Several commentators have found the Supplemental Rules lacking on some or all five grounds. E.g., Batiza & Partridge, The Constitutional Challenge to Maritime Seizures, 26 Loy. L. Rev. 203 (1980); Morse, The Conflict Between the Supreme Court Admiralty Rules and Sniadach-Fuentes: A Collision Course?, 3 Fla. St. U.L. Rev. 1 (1975). The federal courts have varied in their disposition of challenges to the Supplemental Rules. The Fourth and Fifth Circuits have affirmed the constitutionality of Rule C. Amstar Corp. v. S/S Alexandros T., 664 F.2d 904 (4th Cir. 1981); Merchants National Bank of Mobile v. The Dredge General G. L. Gillespie, 663 F.2d 1338 (5th Cir. 1981), cert. dismissed, 456 U.S. 966 (1982). However, a district court in the Ninth Circuit found Rule C unconstitutional. Alyeska Pipeline Service Co. v. The Vessel Bay Ridge, 509 F. Supp. 1115 (D. Alaska 1981), appeal dismissed, 703 F.2d 381 (9th Cir. 1983). Rule B(1) has received similar inconsistent treatment. The Ninth and Eleventh Circuits have upheld its constitutionality. Polar Shipping, Ltd. v. Oriental Shipping Corp., 680 F.2d 627 (9th Cir. 1982); Schiffahartsgesellschaft Leonhardt & Co. v. A. Bottacchi S. A. de Navegacion, 732 F.2d 1543 (11th Cir. 1984). On the other hand, a Washington district court has found it to be constitutionally deficient. Grand Bahama Petroleum Co. v. Canadian Transportation Agencies, Ltd., 450 F. Supp. 447 (W.D. Wash. 1978). The constitutionality of both rules was questioned in Techem Chem Co. v. M/T Choyo Maru, 416 F. Supp. 960 (D. Md. 1976). Thus, there is uncertainty as to whether the current rules prescribe constitutionally sound procedures for guidance of courts and counsel. See generally Note, Due Process in Admiralty Arrest and Attachment, 56 Tex. L. Rev. 1091 (1978).

Due to the controversy and uncertainty that have surrounded the Supplemental Rules, local admiralty bars and the Maritime Law Association of the United States have sought to strengthen the constitutionality of maritime arrest and attachment by encouraging promulgation of local admiralty rules providing for prompt post-seizure hearings. Some districts also adopted rules calling for judicial scrutiny of applications for arrest or attachment. Nonetheless, the result has been a lack of uniformity and continued concern over the constitutionality of the existing practice. The amendments that follow are intended to provide rules that meet the requirements prescribed by the Supreme Court and to develop uniformity in the admiralty practice.

Rule A. Scope of Rules

(1) These Supplemental Rules apply to:
- (A) the procedure in admiralty and maritime claims within the meaning of Rule 9(h) with respect to the following remedies:
  - (i) maritime attachment and garnishment,
  - (ii) actions in rem,
  - (iii) possessory, petitory, and partition actions, and
  - (iv) actions for exoneration from or limitation of liability;
- (B) forfeiture actions in rem arising from a federal statute; and
- (C) the procedure in statutory condemnation proceedings analogous to maritime actions in rem, whether within the admiralty and maritime jurisdiction or not. Except as otherwise provided, references in these Supplemental Rules to actions in rem include such analogous statutory condemnation proceedings.

(2) The Federal Rules of Civil Procedure also apply to the foregoing proceedings except to the extent that they are inconsistent with these Supplemental Rules.

(As added Feb. 28, 1966, eff. July 1, 1966; amended Apr. 12, 2006, eff. Dec. 1, 2006.)

Notes of Advisory Committee on Rules

Certain distinctively maritime remedies must be preserved in unified rules. The commencement of an action by attachment or garnishment has heretofore been practically unknown in federal jurisprudence except in admiralty, although the amendment of Rule 4(e) effective July 1, 1963, makes available that procedure in accordance with state law. The maritime proceeding in rem is unique, except as it has been emulated by statute, and is closely related to the substantive maritime law relating to liens. Arrest of the vessel or other maritime property is an historic remedy in controversies over title or right to possession, and in disputes among co-owners over the vessel's employment. The statutory right to limit liability is limited to owners of vessels, and has its own complexities. While the unified federal rules are generally applicable to these distinctive proceedings, certain special rules dealing with them are needed.

Arrest of the person and imprisonment for debt are not included because these remedies are not peculiarly maritime. The practice is not uniform but conforms to state law. See 2 Benedict §286; 28 U.S.C., §2007; FRCP 64, 69. The relevant provisions of Admiralty Rules 2, 3, and 4 are unnecessary or obsolete.

No attempt is here made to compile a complete and self-contained code governing these distinctively maritime remedies. The more limited objective is to carry forward the relevant provisions of the former Rules of Practice for Admiralty and Maritime Cases, modernized and revised to some extent but still in the context of history and precedent. Accordingly, these Rules are not to be construed as limiting or impairing the traditional power of a district court, exercising the admiralty and maritime jurisdiction, to adapt its procedures and its remedies in the individual case, consistently with these rules, to secure the just, speedy, and inexpensive determination of every action. (See Swift & Co., Packers v. Compania Columbiana Del Caribe, S/A, 339 U.S. 684, (1950); Rule 1). In addition, of course, the district courts retain the power to make local rules not inconsistent with these rules. See Rule 83; cf. Admiralty Rule 44.

Committee Notes on Rules—2006 Amendment

Rule A is amended to reflect the adoption of Rule G to govern procedure in civil forfeiture actions. Rule G(1) contemplates application of other Supplemental Rules to the extent that Rule G does not address an issue. One example is the Rule E(4)(c) provision for arresting intangible property.

Rule B. In Personam Actions: Attachment and Garnishment

(1) When Available; Complaint, Affidavit, Judicial Authorization, and Process. In an in personam action:
- (a) If a defendant is not found within the district when a verified complaint praying for attachment and the affidavit required by Rule B(1)(b) are filed, a verified complaint may contain a prayer for process to attach the defendant's tangible or intangible personal property—up to the amount sued for—in the hands of garnishees named in the process.
- (b) The plaintiff or the plaintiff's attorney must sign and file with the complaint an affidavit stating that, to the affiant's knowledge, or on information and belief, the

defendant cannot be found within the district. The court must review the complaint and affidavit and, if the conditions of this Rule B appear to exist, enter an order so stating and authorizing process of attachment and garnishment. The clerk may issue supplemental process enforcing the court's order upon application without further court order.

(c) If the plaintiff or the plaintiff's attorney certifies that exigent circumstances make court review impracticable, the clerk must issue the summons and process of attachment and garnishment. The plaintiff has the burden in any post-attachment hearing under Rule E(4)(f) to show that exigent circumstances existed.

(d)

(i) If the property is a vessel or tangible property on board a vessel, the summons, process, and any supplemental process must be delivered to the marshal for service.

(ii) If the property is other tangible or intangible property, the summons, process, and any supplemental process must be delivered to a person or organization authorized to serve it, who may be (A) a marshal; (B) someone under contract with the United States; (C) someone specially appointed by the court for that purpose; or, (D) in an action brought by the United States, any officer or employee of the United States.

(e) The plaintiff may invoke state-law remedies under Rule 64 for seizure of person or property for the purpose of securing satisfaction of the judgment.

(2) Notice to Defendant. No default judgment may be entered except upon proof—which may be by affidavit—that:

(a) the complaint, summons, and process of attachment or garnishment have been served on the defendant in a manner authorized by Rule 4;

(b) the plaintiff or the garnishee has mailed to the defendant the complaint, summons, and process of attachment or garnishment, using any form of mail requiring a return receipt; or

(c) the plaintiff or the garnishee has tried diligently to give notice of the action to the defendant but could not do so.

(3) Answer.

(a) By Garnishee. The garnishee shall serve an answer, together with answers to any interrogatories served with the complaint, within 21 days after service of process upon the garnishee. Interrogatories to the garnishee may be served with the complaint without leave of court. If the garnishee refuses or neglects to answer on oath as to the debts, credits, or effects of the defendant in the garnishee's hands, or any interrogatories concerning such debts, credits, and effects that may be propounded by the plaintiff, the court may award compulsory process against the garnishee. If the garnishee admits any debts, credits, or effects, they shall be held in the garnishee's hands or paid into the registry of the court, and shall be held in either case subject to the further order of the court.

(b) By Defendant. The defendant shall serve an answer within 30 days after process has been executed, whether by attachment of property or service on the garnishee.

(As added Feb. 28, 1966, eff. July 1, 1966; amended Apr. 29, 1985, eff. Aug. 1, 1985; Mar. 2, 1987, eff. Aug. 1, 1987; Apr. 17, 2000, eff. Dec. 1, 2000; Apr. 25, 2005, eff. Dec. 1, 2005; Mar. 26, 2009, eff. Dec. 1, 2009.)

Notes of Advisory Committee on Rules

Subdivision (1)

This preserves the traditional maritime remedy of attachment and garnishment, and carries forward the relevant substance of Admiralty Rule 2. In addition, or in the alternative, provision is made for the use of similar state remedies made available by the amendment of Rule 4(e) effective July 1, 1963. On the effect of appearance to defend against attachment see Rule E(8).

The rule follows closely the language of Admiralty Rule 2. No change is made with respect to the property subject to attachment. No change is made in the condition that makes the remedy available. The rules have never defined the clause, "if the defendant shall not be found within the district," and no definition is attempted here. The subject seems one best left for the time being to development on a case-by-case basis. The proposal does shift from the marshal (on whom it now rests in theory) to the plaintiff the burden of establishing that the defendant cannot be found in the district.

A change in the context of the practice is brought about by Rule 4(f), which will enable summons to be served throughout the state instead of, as heretofore, only within the district. The Advisory Committee considered whether the rule on attachment and garnishment should be correspondingly changed to permit those remedies only when the defendant cannot be found within the state and concluded that the remedy should not be so limited.

The effect is to enlarge the class of cases in which the plaintiff may proceed by attachment or garnishment although jurisdiction of the person of the defendant may be independently obtained. This is possible at the present time where, for example, a corporate defendant has appointed an agent within the district to accept service of process but is not carrying on activities there sufficient to subject it to jurisdiction. (Seawind Compania, S.A. v. Crescent Line, Inc., 320 F.2d 580 (2d Cir. 1963)), or where, though the foreign corporation's activities in the district are sufficient to subject it personally to the jurisdiction, there is in the district no officer on whom process can be served (United States v. Cia. Naviera Continental, S.A., 178 F.Supp. 561, (S.D.N.Y. 1959)).

Process of attachment or garnishment will be limited to the district. See Rule E(3)(a).

Subdivision (2)

The former Admiralty Rules did not provide for notice to the defendant in attachment and garnishment proceedings. None is required by the principles of due process, since it is assumed that the garnishee or custodian of the property attached will either notify the defendant or be deprived of the right to plead the judgment as a defense in an action against him by the defendant. Harris v. Balk, 198 U.S. 215 (1905); Pennoyer v. Neff, 95 U.S. 714 (1878). Modern conceptions of fairness, however, dictate that actual notice be given to persons known to claim an interest in the property that is the subject of the action where that is reasonably practicable. In attachment and garnishment proceedings the persons whose interests will be affected by the judgment are identified by the complaint. No substantial burden is imposed on the plaintiff by a simple requirement that he notify the defendant of the action by mail.

In the usual case the defendant is notified of the pendency of the proceedings by the garnishee or otherwise, and appears to claim the property and to make his answer. Hence notice by mail is not routinely required in all cases, but only in those in which the defendant has not appeared prior to the time when a default judgment is demanded. The rule therefore provides only that no default judgment shall be entered except upon proof of notice, or of inability to give notice despite diligent efforts to do so. Thus the burden of giving notice is further minimized.

In some cases the plaintiff may prefer to give notice by serving process in the usual way instead of simply by mail. (Rule 4(d).) In particular, if the defendant is in a foreign country the plaintiff may wish to utilize the modes of notice recently provided to facilitate compliance with foreign laws and procedures (Rule 4(i)). The rule provides for these alternatives.

The rule does not provide for notice by publication because there is no problem concerning unknown claimants, and publication has little utility in proportion to its expense where the identity of the defendant is known.

Subdivision (3)

Subdivision (a) incorporates the substance of Admiralty Rule 36.

The Admiralty Rules were silent as to when the garnishee and the defendant were to answer. See also 2 Benedict ch. XXIV.

The rule proceeds on the assumption that uniform and definite periods of time for responsive pleadings should be substituted for return days (see the discussion under Rule C(6), below). Twenty days seems sufficient time for the garnishee to answer (cf. FRCP 12(a)), and an additional 10 days should suffice for the defendant. When allowance is made for the time required for notice to reach the defendant this gives the defendant in attachment and garnishment approximately the same time that defendants have to answer when personally served.

Notes of Advisory Committee on Rules—1985 Amendment

Rule B(1) has been amended to provide for judicial scrutiny before the issuance of any attachment or garnishment process. Its purpose is to eliminate doubts as to whether the Rule is consistent with the principles of procedural due process enunciated by the Supreme Court in Sniadach v. Family Finance Corp., 395 U.S. 337 (1969); and later developed in Fuentes v. Shevin, 407 U.S. 67 (1972); Mitchell v. W. T. Grant Co., 416 U.S. 600 (1974); and North Georgia Finishing, Inc. v. Di-Chem, Inc., 419 U.S. 601 (1975). Such doubts were raised in Grand Bahama Petroleum Co. v. Canadian Transportation Agencies, Ltd., 450 F. Supp. 447 (W.D. Wash. 1978); and Schiffahartsgesellschaft Leonhardt & Co. v. A. Bottacchi S.A. de Navegacion, 552 F. Supp. 771 (S.D. Ga. 1982), which was reversed, 732 F.2d 1543 (11th Cir. 1984). But compare Polar Shipping Ltd. v. Oriental Shipping Corp., 680 F.2d 627 (9th Cir. 1982), in which a majority of the panel upheld the constitutionality of Rule B because of the unique commercial context in which it is invoked. The practice described in Rule B(1) has been adopted in some districts by local rule. E.g., N.D. Calif. Local Rule 603.3; W.D. Wash. Local Admiralty Rule 15(d).

The rule envisions that the order will issue when the plaintiff makes a prima facie showing that he has a maritime claim against the defendant in the amount sued for and the defendant is not present in the district. A simple order with conclusory findings is contemplated. The reference to review by the "court" is broad enough to embrace review by a magistrate as well as by a district judge.

The new provision recognizes that in some situations, such as when the judge is unavailable and the ship is about to depart from the jurisdiction, it will be impracticable, if not impossible, to secure the judicial review contemplated by Rule B(1). When "exigent circumstances" exist, the rule enables the plaintiff to secure the issuance of the summons and process of attachment and garnishment, subject to a later showing that the necessary circumstances actually existed. This provision is intended to provide a safety valve without undermining the requirement of preattachment scrutiny. Thus, every effort to secure judicial review, including conducting a hearing by telephone, should be pursued before resorting to the exigent-circumstances procedure.

Rule B(1) also has been amended so that the garnishee shall be named in the "process" rather than in the "complaint." This should solve the problem presented in Filia Compania Naviera, S.A. v. Petroship, S.A., 1983 A.M.C. 1 (S.D.N.Y. 1982), and eliminate any need for an additional judicial review of the complaint and affidavit when a garnishee is added.

Notes of Advisory Committee on Rules—1987 Amendment

The amendments are technical. No substantive change is intended.

Committee Notes on Rules—2000 Amendment

Rule B(1) is amended in two ways, and style changes have been made.

The service provisions of Rule C(3) are adopted in paragraph (d), providing alternatives to service by a marshal if the property to be seized is not a vessel or tangible property on board a vessel.

The provision that allows the plaintiff to invoke state attachment and garnishment remedies is amended to reflect the 1993 amendments of Civil Rule 4. Former Civil Rule 4(e), incorporated in Rule B(1), allowed general use of state quasi-in-rem jurisdiction if the defendant was not an inhabitant of, or found within, the state. Rule 4(e) was replaced in 1993 by Rule 4(n)(2), which permits use of state law to seize a defendant's assets only if personal jurisdiction over the defendant cannot be obtained in the district where the action is brought. Little purpose would be served by incorporating Rule 4(n)(2) in Rule B, since maritime attachment and garnishment are available whenever the defendant is not found within the district, a concept that allows attachment or garnishment even in some circumstances in which personal jurisdiction also can be asserted. In order to protect against any possibility that elimination of the reference to state quasi-in-rem jurisdiction remedies might seem to defeat continued use of state security devices, paragraph (e) expressly incorporates Civil Rule 64. Because Rule 64 looks only to security, not jurisdiction, the former reference to Rule E(8) is deleted as no longer relevant.

Rule B(2)(a) is amended to reflect the 1993 redistribution of the service provisions once found in Civil Rule 4(d) and (i). These provisions are now found in many different subdivisions of Rule 4. The new reference simply incorporates Rule 4, without designating the new subdivisions, because the function of Rule B(2) is simply to describe the methods of notice that suffice to support a default judgment. Style changes also have been made.

Committee Notes on Rules—2005 Amendment

Rule B(1) is amended to incorporate the decisions in Heidmar, Inc. v. Anomina Ravennate Di Armamento Sp.A. of Ravenna, 132 F.3d 264, 267–268 (5th Cir. 1998), and Navieros InterAmericanos, S.A. v. M/V Vasilia Express, 120 F.3d 304, 314–315 (1st Cir. 1997). The time for determining whether a defendant is "found" in the district is set at the time of filing the verified complaint that prays for attachment and the affidavit required by Rule B(1)(b). As provided by Rule B(1)(b), the affidavit must be filed with the complaint. A defendant cannot defeat the security purpose of attachment by appointing an agent for service of process after the complaint and affidavit are filed. The complaint praying for attachment need not be the initial complaint. So long as the defendant is not found in the district, the prayer for attachment may be made in an amended complaint; the affidavit that the defendant cannot be found must be filed with the amended complaint.

Changes Made After Publication and Comment. No changes have been made since publication.

Committee Notes on Rules—2009 Amendment

The time set in the former rule at 20 days has been revised to 21 days. See the Note to Rule 6.

Rule C. In Rem Actions: Special Provisions

(1) When Available. An action in rem may be brought:

(a) To enforce any maritime lien;

(b) Whenever a statute of the United States provides for a maritime action in rem or a proceeding analogous thereto.

Except as otherwise provided by law a party who may proceed in rem may also, or in the alternative, proceed in personam against any person who may be liable.

Statutory provisions exempting vessels or other property owned or possessed by or operated by or for the United States from arrest or seizure are not affected by this rule. When a statute so provides, an action against the United States or an instrumentality thereof may proceed on in rem principles.

(2) Complaint. In an action in rem the complaint must:

(a) be verified;

(b) describe with reasonable particularity the property that is the subject of the action; and

(c) state that the property is within the district or will be within the district while the action is pending.

(3) Judicial Authorization and Process.

(a) Arrest Warrant.

(i) The court must review the complaint and any supporting papers. If the conditions for an in rem action appear to exist, the court must issue an order directing the clerk to issue a warrant for the arrest of the vessel or other property that is the subject of the action.

(ii) If the plaintiff or the plaintiff's attorney certifies that exigent circumstances make court review impracticable, the clerk must promptly issue a summons and a warrant for the arrest of the vessel or other property that is the subject of the action. The plaintiff has the burden in any post-arrest hearing under Rule E(4)(f) to show that exigent circumstances existed.

(b) Service.

(i) If the property that is the subject of the action is a vessel or tangible property on board a vessel, the warrant and any supplemental process must be delivered to the marshal for service.

(ii) If the property that is the subject of the action is other property, tangible or intangible, the warrant and any supplemental process must be delivered to a person or organization authorized to enforce it, who may be: (A) a marshal; (B) someone under contract with the United States; (C) someone specially appointed by the court for that purpose; or, (D) in an action brought by the United States, any officer or employee of the United States.

(c) Deposit in Court. If the property that is the subject of the action consists in whole or in part of freight, the proceeds of property sold, or other intangible property, the clerk must issue—in addition to the warrant—a summons directing any person controlling the property to show cause why it should not be deposited in court to abide the judgment.

(d) Supplemental Process. The clerk may upon application issue supplemental process to enforce the court's order without further court order.

(4) Notice. No notice other than execution of process is required when the property that is the subject of the action has been released under Rule E(5). If the property is not released within 14 days after execution, the plaintiff must promptly—or within the time that the court allows—give public notice of the action and arrest in a newspaper designated by court order and having general circulation in the district, but publication may be terminated if the property is released before publication is completed. The notice must specify the time under Rule C(6) to file a statement of interest in or right against the seized property and to answer. This rule does not affect the notice requirements in an action to foreclose a preferred ship mortgage under 46 U.S.C. §§31301 et seq., as amended.

(5) Ancillary Process. In any action in rem in which process has been served as provided by this rule, if any part of the property that is the subject of the action has not been brought within the control of the court because it has been removed or sold, or because it is intangible property in the hands of a person who has not been served with process, the court may, on motion, order any person having possession or control of such property or its proceeds to show cause why it should not be delivered into the custody of the marshal or other person or organization having a warrant for the arrest of the property, or paid into court to abide the judgment; and, after hearing, the court may enter such judgment as law and justice may require.

(6) Responsive Pleading; Interrogatories.

(a) Statement of Interest; Answer. In an action in rem:

(i) a person who asserts a right of possession or any ownership interest in the property that is the subject of the action must file a verified statement of right or interest:

(A) within 14 days after the execution of process, or

(B) within the time that the court allows;

(ii) the statement of right or interest must describe the interest in the property that supports the person's demand for its restitution or right to defend the action;
(iii) an agent, bailee, or attorney must state the authority to file a statement of right or interest on behalf of another; and
(iv) a person who asserts a right of possession or any ownership interest must serve an answer within 21 days after filing the statement of interest or right.

(b) *Interrogatories*. Interrogatories may be served with the complaint in an in rem action without leave of court. Answers to the interrogatories must be served with the answer to the complaint.

(As added Feb. 28, 1966, eff. July 1, 1966; amended Apr. 29, 1985, eff. Aug. 1, 1985; Mar. 2, 1987, eff. Aug. 1, 1987; Apr. 30, 1991, eff. Dec. 1, 1991; Apr. 17, 2000, eff. Dec. 1, 2000; Apr. 29, 2002, eff. Dec. 1, 2002; Apr. 25, 2005, eff. Dec. 1, 2005; Apr. 12, 2006, eff. Dec. 1, 2006; Apr. 23, 2008, eff. Dec. 1, 2008; Mar. 26, 2009, eff. Dec. 1, 2009.)

Notes of Advisory Committee on Rules

Subdivision (1).

This rule is designed not only to preserve the proceeding in rem as it now exists in admiralty cases, but to preserve the substance of Admiralty Rules 13–18. The general reference to enforcement of any maritime lien is believed to state the existing law, and is an improvement over the enumeration in the former Admiralty Rules, which is repetitious and incomplete (e.g., there was no reference to general average). The reference to any maritime lien is intended to include liens created by state law which are enforceable in admiralty.

The main concern of Admiralty Rules 13–18 was with the question whether certain actions might be brought in rem or also, or in the alternative, in personam. Essentially, therefore, these rules deal with questions of substantive law, for in general an action in rem may be brought to enforce any maritime lien, and no action in personam may be brought when the substantive law imposes no personal liability.

These rules may be summarized as follows:

1. Cases in which the plaintiff may proceed in rem and/or in personam:

a. Suits for seamen's wages;

b. Suits by materialmen for supplies, repairs, etc.;

c. Suits for pilotage;

d. Suits for collision damages;

e. Suits founded on mere maritime hypothecation;

f. Suits for salvage.

2. Cases in which the plaintiff may proceed only in personam:

a. Suits for assault and beating.

3. Cases in which the plaintiff may proceed only in rem:

a. Suits on bottomry bonds.

The coverage is complete, since the rules omit mention of many cases in which the plaintiff may proceed in rem or in personam. This revision proceeds on the principle that it is preferable to make a general statement as to the availability of the remedies, leaving out conclusions on matters of substantive law. Clearly it is not necessary to enumerate the cases listed under Item 1, above, nor to try to complete the list.

The rule eliminates the provision of Admiralty Rule 15 that actions for assault and beating may be brought only in personam. A preliminary study fails to disclose any reason for the rule. It is subject to so many exceptions that it is calculated to receive rather than to inform. A seaman may sue in rem when he has been beaten by a fellow member of the crew so vicious as to render the vessel unseaworthy. The Rolph, 293 Fed. 269, aff'd 299 Fed. 52 (9th Cir. 1923), or where the theory of the action is that a beating by the master is a breach of the obligation under the shipping articles to treat the seaman with proper kindness. The David Evans, 187 Fed. 775 (D. Hawaii 1911); and a passenger may sue in rem on the theory that the assault is a breach of the contract of passage, The Western States, 159 Fed. 354 (2d Cir. 1908). To say that an action for money damages may be brought only in personam seems equivalent to saying that a maritime lien shall not exist; and that, in turn, seems equivalent to announcing a rule of substantive law rather than a rule of procedure. Dropping the rule will leave it to the courts to determine whether a lien exists as a matter of substantive law.

The specific reference to bottomry bonds is omitted because, as a matter of hornbook substantive law, there is no personal liability on such bonds.

Subdivision (2).

This incorporates the substance of Admiralty Rules 21 and 22.

Subdivision (3).

Derived from Admiralty Rules 10 and 37. The provision that the warrant is to be issued by the clerk is new, but is assumed to state existing law.

There is remarkably little authority bearing on Rule 37, although the subject would seem to be an important one. The rule appears on its face to have provided for a sort of ancillary process, and this may well be the case when tangible property, such as a vessel, is arrested, and intangible property such as freight is incidentally involved. It can easily happen, however, that the only property against which the action may be brought is intangible, as where the owner of a vessel under charter has a lien on subfreights. See 2 Benedict §299 and cases cited. In such cases it would seem that the order to the person holding the fund is equivalent to original process, taking the place of the warrant for arrest. That being so, it would also seem that (1) there should be some provision for notice, comparable to that given when tangible property is arrested, and (2) it should not be necessary, as Rule 37 provided, to petition the court for issuance of the process, but that it should issue as of course. Accordingly the substance of Rule 37 is included in the rule covering ordinary process, and notice will be required by Rule C(4). Presumably the rules omit any requirement of notice in these cases because the holder of the funds (e.g., the cargo owner) would be required on general principles (cf. Harris v. Balk, 198 U.S. 215 (1905) to notify his obligee (e.g., the charterer); but in actions in rem such notice seems plainly inadequate because there may be adverse claims to the fund (e.g., there may be liens against the subfreights for seamen's wages, etc.). Compare Admiralty Rule 9.

Subdivision (4).

This carries forward the notice provision of Admiralty Rule 10, with one modification. Notice by publication is too expensive and ineffective a formality to be routinely required. When, as usually happens, the vessel or other property is released on bond or otherwise there is no point in publishing notice; the vessel is freed from the claim of the plaintiff and no other interest in the vessel can be affected by the proceedings. If however, the vessel is not released, general notice is required in order that all persons, including unknown claimants, may appear and be heard, and in order that the judgment in rem shall be binding on all the world.

Subdivision (5).

This incorporates the substance of Admiralty Rule 9.

There are remarkably few cases dealing directly with the rule. In The George Prescott, 10 Fed. Cas. 222 (No. 5,339) (E.D.N.Y. 1865), the master and crew of a vessel libeled her for wages, and other lienors also filed libels. One of the lienors suggested to the court that prior to the arrest of the vessel the master had removed the sails, and asked that he be ordered to produce them. He admitted removing the sails and selling them, justifying on the ground that he held a mortgage on the vessel. He was ordered to pay the proceeds into court. Cf. United States v. The Zarko, 187 F.Supp. 371 (S.D.Cal. 1960), where an armature belonging to a vessel subject to a preferred ship mortgages was in possession of a repairman claiming a lien.

It is evident that, though the rule has had a limited career in the reported cases, it is a potentially important one. It is also evident that the rule is framed in terms narrower than the principle that supports it. There is no apparent reason for limiting it to ships and their appurtenances (2 Benedict §299). Also, the reference to "third parties" in the existing rule seems unfortunate. In The George Prescott, the person who removed and sold the sails was a plaintiff in the action, and relief against him was just as necessary as if he had been a stranger.

Another situation in which process of this kind would seem to be useful is that in which the principal property that is the subject of the action is a vessel, but her pending freight is incidentally involved. The warrant of arrest, and notice of its service, should be all that is required by way of original process and notice; ancillary process without notice should suffice as to the incidental intangibles.

The distinction between Admiralty Rules 9 and 37 is not at once apparent, but seems to be this: Where the action was against property that could not be seized by the marshal because it is intangible, the original process was required to be similar to that issued against a garnishee, and general notice was required (though not provided for by the present rule; cf. Advisory Committee's Note to Rule C(3)). Under Admiralty Rule 9 property had been arrested and general notice had been given, but some of the property had been removed or for some other reason could not be arrested. Here no further notice was necessary.

The rule also makes provision for this kind of situation: The proceeding is against a vessel's pending freight only; summons has been served on the person supposedly holding the funds, and general notice has been given; it develops that another person holds all or part of the funds. Ancillary process should be available here without further notice.

Subdivision (6).

Adherence to the practice of return days seems unsatisfactory. The practice varies significantly from district to district. A uniform rule should be provided so that any claimant or defendant can readily determine when he is required to file or serve a claim or answer.

A virtue of the return-day practice is that it requires claimants to come forward and identify themselves at an early stage of the proceedings—before they could fairly be required to answer. The draft is designed to preserve this feature of the present practice by requiring early filing of the claim. The time schedule contemplated in the draft is closely comparable to the present practice in the Southern District of New York, where the claimant has a minimum of 8 days to claim and three weeks thereafter to answer.

This rule also incorporates the substance of Admiralty Rule 25. The present rule's emphasis on "the true and bona fide owner" is omitted, since anyone having the right to possession can claim (2 Benedict §324).

Notes of Advisory Committee on Rules—1985 Amendment

Rule C(3) has been amended to provide for judicial scrutiny before the issuance of any warrant of arrest. Its purpose is to eliminate any doubt as to the rule's constitutionality under the Sniadach line of cases. Sniadach v. Family Finance Corp., 395 U.S. 337 (1969); Fuentes v. Shevin, 407 U.S. 67 (1972); Mitchell v. W. T. Grant Co., 416 U.S. 600 (1974); and North Georgia Finishing, Inc. v. Di-Chem, Inc., 419 U.S. 601 (1975). This was thought desirable even though both the Fourth and the Fifth Circuits have upheld the existing rule. Amstar Corp. v. S/S Alexandros T., 664 F.2d 904 (4th Cir. 1981); Merchants National Bank of Mobile v. The Dredge General G. L. Gillespie, 663 F.2d 1338 (5th Cir. 1981), cert. dismissed, 456 U.S. 966 (1982). A contrary view was taken by Judge Tate in the Merchants National Bank case and by the district court in Alyeska Pipeline Service Co. v. The Vessel Bay Ridge, 509 F. Supp. 1115 (D. Alaska 1981), appeal dismissed, 703 F.2d 381 (9th Cir. 1983).

The rule envisions that the order will issue upon a prima facie showing that the plaintiff has an action in rem against the defendant in the amount sued for and that the property is within the district. A simple order with conclusory findings is contemplated. The reference to review by the "court" is broad enough to embrace a magistrate as well as a district judge.

The new provision recognizes that in some situations, such as when a judge is unavailable and the vessel is about to depart from the jurisdiction, it will be impracticable, if not impossible, to secure the judicial review contemplated by Rule C(3). When "exigent circumstances" exist, the rule enables the plaintiff to secure the issuance of the summons and warrant of arrest, subject to a later showing that the necessary circumstances actually existed. This provision is intended to provide a safety valve without undermining the requirement of pre-arrest scrutiny. Thus, every effort to secure judicial review, including conducting a hearing by telephone, should be pursued before invoking the exigent-circumstances procedure.

The foregoing requirements for prior court review or proof of exigent circumstances do not apply to actions by the United States for forfeitures for federal statutory violations. In such actions a prompt hearing is not constitutionally required, United States v. Eight Thousand Eight Hundred and Fifty Dollars, 103 S.Ct. 2005 (1983); Calero-Toledo v. Pearson Yacht Leasing Co., 416 U.S. 663 (1974), and could prejudice the government in its prosecution of the claimants as defendants in parallel criminal proceedings since the forfeiture hearing could be misused by the defendants to obtain by way of civil discovery information to which they would not otherwise be entitled and subject the government and the courts to the unnecessary burden and expense of two hearings rather than one.

Notes of Advisory Committee on Rules—1987 Amendment

The amendments are technical. No substantive change is intended.

Notes of Advisory Committee on Rules—1991 Amendment

These amendments are designed to conform the rule to Fed.R.Civ.P. 4, as amended. As with recent amendments to Rule 4, it is intended to relieve the Marshals Service of the burden of using its limited personnel and facilities for execution of process in routine circumstances. Doing so may involve a contractual arrangement with a person or organization retained by the government to perform these services, or the use of other government officers and employees, or the special appointment by the court of persons available to perform suitably.

The seizure of a vessel, with or without cargo, remains a task assigned to the Marshal. Successful arrest of a vessel frequently requires the enforcement presence of an armed government official and the cooperation of the United States Coast Guard and other governmental authorities. If the marshal is called upon to seize the vessel, it is expected that the same officer will also be responsible for the seizure of any property on board the vessel at the time of seizure that is to be the object of arrest or attachment.

Committee Notes on Rules—2000 Amendment

Style changes have been made throughout the revised portions of Rule C. Several changes of meaning have been made as well.

Subdivision 2. In rem jurisdiction originally extended only to property within the judicial district. Since 1986, Congress has enacted a number of jurisdictional and venue statutes for forfeiture and criminal matters that in some circumstances permit a court to exercise authority over property outside the district. 28 U.S.C. §1355(b)(1) allows a forfeiture action in the district where an act or omission giving rise to forfeiture occurred, or in any other district where venue is established by §1395 or by any other statute. Section 1355(b)(2) allows an action to be brought as provided in (b)(1) or in the United States District Court for the District of Columbia when the forfeiture property is located in a foreign country or has been seized by authority of a foreign government. Section 1355(d) allows a court with jurisdiction under §1355(b) to cause service in any other district of process required to bring the forfeiture property before the court. Section 1395 establishes venue of a civil proceeding for forfeiture in the district where the forfeiture accrues or the defendant is found; in any district where the property is found; in any district into which the property is brought, if the property initially is outside any judicial district; or in any district where the vessel is arrested if the proceeding is an admiralty proceeding to forfeit a vessel. Section 1395(e) deals with a vessel or cargo entering a port of entry closed by the President, and transportation to or from a state or section declared to be in insurrection. 18 U.S.C. §981(h) creates expanded jurisdiction and venue over property located elsewhere that is related to a criminal prosecution pending in the district. These amendments, and related amendments of Rule E(3), bring these Rules into step with the new statutes. No change is made as to admiralty and maritime proceedings that do not involve a forfeiture governed by one of the new statutes.

Subdivision (2) has been separated into lettered paragraphs to facilitate understanding.

Subdivision (3). Subdivision (3) has been rearranged and divided into lettered paragraphs to facilitate understanding.

Paragraph (b)(i) is amended to make it clear that any supplemental process addressed to a vessel or tangible property on board a vessel, as well as the original warrant, is to be served by the marshal.

Subdivision (4). Subdivision (4) has required that public notice state the time for filing an answer, but has not required that the notice set out the earlier time for filing a statement of interest or claim. The amendment requires that both times be stated.

A new provision is added, allowing termination of publication if the property is released more than 10 days after execution but before publication is completed. Termination will save money, and also will reduce the risk of confusion as to the status of the property.

Subdivision (6). Subdivision (6) has applied a single set of undifferentiated provisions to civil forfeiture proceedings and to in rem admiralty proceedings. Because some differences in procedure are desirable, these proceedings are separated by adopting a new paragraph (a) for civil forfeiture proceedings and recasting the present rule as paragraph (b) for in rem admiralty proceedings. The provision for interrogatories and answers is carried forward as paragraph (c). Although this established procedure for serving interrogatories with the complaint departs from the general provisions of Civil Rule 26(d), the special needs of expedition that often arise in admiralty justify continuing the practice.

Both paragraphs (a) and (b) require a statement of interest or right rather than the "claim" formerly required. The new wording permits parallel drafting, and facilitates cross-references in other rules. The substantive nature of the statement remains the same as the former claim. The requirements of (a) and (b) are, however, different in some respects.

In a forfeiture proceeding governed by paragraph (a), a statement must be filed by a person who asserts an interest in or a right against the property involved. This category includes every right against the property, such as a lien, whether or not it establishes ownership or a right to possession. In determining who has an interest in or a right against property, courts may continue to rely on precedents that have developed the meaning of "claims" or "claimants" for the purpose of civil forfeiture proceedings.

In an admiralty and maritime proceeding governed by paragraph (b), a statement is filed only by a person claiming a right of possession or ownership. Other claims against the property are advanced by intervention under Civil Rule 24, as it may be supplemented by local admiralty rules. The reference to ownership includes every interest that qualifies as ownership under domestic or foreign law. If an ownership interest is asserted, it makes no difference whether its character is legal, equitable, or something else.

Paragraph (a) provides more time than paragraph (b) for filing a statement. Admiralty and maritime in rem proceedings often present special needs for prompt action that do not commonly arise in forfeiture proceedings.

Paragraphs (a) and (b) do not limit the right to make a restricted appearance under Rule E(8).

Committee Notes on Rules—2002 Amendment

Rule C(3) is amended to reflect the provisions of 18 U.S.C. §985, enacted by the Civil Asset Forfeiture Reform Act of 2000, 114 Stat. 202, 214–215. Section 985 provides, subject to enumerated exceptions, that real property that is the subject of a civil forfeiture action is not to be seized until an order of forfeiture is entered. A civil forfeiture action is initiated by filing a complaint, posting notice, and serving notice on the property owner. The summons and arrest procedure is no longer appropriate.

Rule C(6)(a)(i)(A) is amended to adopt the provision enacted by 18 U.S.C. §983(a)(4)(A), shortly before Rule C(6)(a)(i)(A) took effect, that sets the time for filing a verified statement as 30 days rather than 20 days, and that sets the first alternative event for measuring the 30 days as the date of service of the Government's complaint.

Rule C(6)(a)(iii) is amended to give notice of the provision enacted by 18 U.S.C. §983(a)(4)(B) that requires that the answer in a forfeiture proceeding be filed within 20 days. Without this notice, unwary litigants might rely on the provision of Rule 5(d) that allows a reasonable time for filing after service.

Rule C(6)(b)(iv) is amended to change the requirement that an answer be filed within 20 days to a requirement that it be served within 20 days. Service is the ordinary requirement, as in Rule 12(a). Rule 5(d) requires filing within a reasonable time after service.

Changes Made After Publication and Comments. No changes have been made since publication.

Committee Notes on Rules—2005 Amendment

Rule C(6)(b)(i)(A) is amended to delete the reference to a time 10 days after completed publication under Rule C(4). This change corrects an oversight in the amendments made in 2000. Rule C(4) requires publication of notice only if the property that is the subject of the action is not released within 10 days after execution of process. Execution of process will always be earlier than publication.

Changes Made After Publication and Comment. No changes have been made since publication.

Committee Notes on Rules—2006 Amendment

Rule C is amended to reflect the adoption of Rule G to govern procedure in civil forfeiture actions.

Committee Notes on Rules—2008 Amendment

Supplemental Rule C(6)(a)(i) is amended to correct an inadvertent omission in the 2006 amendment to Rule C. The amendment is technical and stylistic in nature. No substantive change is intended.

Committee Notes on Rules—2009 Amendment

The times set in the former rule at 10 or 20 days have been revised to 14 or 21 days. See the Note to Rule 6.

Rule D. Possessory, Petitory, and Partition Actions

In all actions for possession, partition, and to try title maintainable according to the course of the admiralty practice with respect to a vessel, in all actions so maintainable with respect to the possession of cargo or other maritime property, and in all actions by one or more part owners against the others to obtain security for the return of the vessel from any voyage undertaken without their consent, or by one or more part owners against the others to obtain possession of the vessel for any voyage on giving security for its safe return, the process shall be by a warrant of arrest of the vessel, cargo, or other property, and by notice in the manner provided by Rule B(2) to the adverse party or parties.

(As added Feb. 28, 1966, eff. July 1, 1966.)

Notes of Advisory Committee on Rules

This carries forward the substance of Admiralty Rule 19.

Rule 19 provided the remedy of arrest in controversies involving title and possession in general. See The Tilton, 23 Fed. Cas. 1277 (No. 14, 054) (C.C.D. Mass. 1830). In addition it provided that remedy in controversies between co-owners respecting the employment of a vessel. It did not deal comprehensively with controversies between co-owners, omitting the remedy of partition. Presumably the omission is traceable to the fact that, when the rules were originally promulgated, concepts of substantive law (sometimes stated as concepts of jurisdiction) denied the remedy of partition except where the parties in disagreement were the owners of equal shares. See The Steamboat Orleans, 36 U.S. (11 Pet.) 175 (1837). The Supreme Court has now removed any doubt as to the jurisdiction of the district courts to partition a vessel, and has held in addition that no fixed principle of federal admiralty law limits the remedy to the case of equal shares. Madruga v. Superior Court, 346 U.S. 556 (1954). It is therefore appropriate to include a reference to partition in the rule.

Rule E. Actions in Rem and Quasi in Rem: General Provisions

(1) Applicability. Except as otherwise provided, this rule applies to actions in personam with process of maritime attachment and garnishment, actions in rem, and petitory, possessory, and partition actions, supplementing Rules B, C, and D.

(2) Complaint; Security.

(a) Complaint. In actions to which this rule is applicable the complaint shall state the circumstances from which the claim arises with such particularity that the defendant or claimant will be able, without moving for a more definite statement, to commence an investigation of the facts and to frame a responsive pleading.

(b) Security for Costs. Subject to the provisions of Rule 54(d) and of relevant statutes, the court may, on the filing of the complaint or on the appearance of any defendant, claimant, or any other party, or at any later time, require the plaintiff, defendant, claimant, or other party to give security, or additional security, in such sum as the court shall direct to pay all costs and expenses that shall be awarded against the party by any interlocutory order or by the final judgment, or on appeal by any appellate court.

(3) Process.

(a) In admiralty and maritime proceedings process in rem or of maritime attachment and garnishment may be served only within the district.

(b) Issuance and Delivery. Issuance and delivery of process in rem, or of maritime attachment and garnishment, shall be held in abeyance if the plaintiff so requests.

(4) Execution of Process; Marshal's Return; Custody of Property; Procedures for Release.

(a) In General. Upon issuance and delivery of the process, or, in the case of summons with process of attachment and garnishment, when it appears that the defendant

cannot be found within the district, the marshal or other person or organization having a warrant shall forthwith execute the process in accordance with this subdivision (4), making due and prompt return.

(b) Tangible Property. If tangible property is to be attached or arrested, the marshal or other person or organization having the warrant shall take it into the marshal's possession for safe custody. If the character or situation of the property is such that the taking of actual possession is impracticable, the marshal or other person executing the process shall affix a copy thereof to the property in a conspicuous place and leave a copy of the complaint and process with the person having possession or the person's agent. In furtherance of the marshal's custody of any vessel the marshal is authorized to make a written request to the collector of customs not to grant clearance to such vessel until notified by the marshal or deputy marshal or by the clerk that the vessel has been released in accordance with these rules.

(c) Intangible Property. If intangible property is to be attached or arrested the marshal or other person or organization having the warrant shall execute the process by leaving with the garnishee or other obligor a copy of the complaint and process requiring the garnishee or other obligor to answer as provided in Rules B(3)(a) and C(6); or the marshal may accept for payment into the registry of the court the amount owed to the extent of the amount claimed by the plaintiff with interest and costs, in which event the garnishee or other obligor shall not be required to answer unless alias process shall be served.

(d) Directions With Respect to Property in Custody. The marshal or other person or organization having the warrant may at any time apply to the court for directions with respect to property that has been attached or arrested, and shall give notice of such application to any or all of the parties as the court may direct.

(e) Expenses of Seizing and Keeping Property; Deposit. These rules do not alter the provisions of Title 28, U.S.C., §1921, as amended, relative to the expenses of seizing and keeping property attached or arrested and to the requirement of deposits to cover such expenses.

(f) Procedure for Release From Arrest or Attachment. Whenever property is arrested or attached, any person claiming an interest in it shall be entitled to a prompt hearing at which the plaintiff shall be required to show why the arrest or attachment should not be vacated or other relief granted consistent with these rules. This subdivision shall have no application to suits for seamen's wages when process is issued upon a certification of sufficient cause filed pursuant to Title 46, U.S.C. §§603 and 604 1 or to actions by the United States for forfeitures for violation of any statute of the United States.

(5) Release of Property.

(a) Special Bond. Whenever process of maritime attachment and garnishment or process in rem is issued the execution of such process shall be stayed, or the property released, on the giving of security, to be approved by the court or clerk, or by stipulation of the parties, conditioned to answer the judgment of the court or of any appellate court. The parties may stipulate the amount and nature of such security. In the event of the inability or refusal of the parties so to stipulate the court shall fix the principal sum of the bond or stipulation at an amount sufficient to cover the amount of the plaintiff's claim fairly stated with accrued interest and costs; but the principal sum shall in no event exceed (i) twice the amount of the plaintiff's claim or (ii) the value of the property on due appraisement, whichever is smaller. The bond or stipulation shall be conditioned for the payment of the principal sum and interest thereon at 6 per cent per annum.

(b) General Bond. The owner of any vessel may file a general bond or stipulation, with sufficient surety, to be approved by the court, conditioned to answer the judgment of such court in all or any actions that may be brought thereafter in such court in which the vessel is attached or arrested. Thereupon the execution of all such process against such vessel shall be stayed so long as the amount secured by such bond or stipulation is at least double the aggregate amount claimed by plaintiffs in all actions begun and pending in which such vessel has been attached or arrested. Judgments and remedies may be had on such bond or stipulation as if a special bond or stipulation had been filed in each of such actions. The district court may make necessary orders to carry this rule into effect, particularly as to the giving of proper notice of any action against or attachment of a vessel for which a general bond has been filed. Such bond or stipulation shall be indorsed by the clerk with a minute of the actions wherein process is so stayed. Further security may be required by the court at any time.

If a special bond or stipulation is given in a particular case, the liability on the general bond or stipulation shall cease as to that case.

(c) Release by Consent or Stipulation; Order of Court or Clerk; Costs. Any vessel, cargo, or other property in the custody of the marshal or other person or organization having the warrant may be released forthwith upon the marshal's acceptance and approval of a stipulation, bond, or other security, signed by the party on whose behalf the property is detained or the party's attorney and expressly authorizing such release, if all costs and charges of the court and its officers shall have first been paid. Otherwise no property in the custody of the marshal, other person or organization having the warrant, or other officer of the court shall be released without an order of the court; but such order may be entered as of course by the clerk, upon the giving of approved security as provided by law and these rules, or upon the dismissal or discontinuance of the action; but the marshal or other person or organization having the warrant shall not deliver any property so released until the costs and charges of the officers of the court shall first have been paid.

(d) Possessory, Petitory, and Partition Actions. The foregoing provisions of this subdivision (5) do not apply to petitory, possessory, and partition actions. In such cases the property arrested shall be released only by

order of the court, on such terms and conditions and on the giving of such security as the court may require.

(6) Reduction or Impairment of Security. Whenever security is taken the court may, on motion and hearing, for good cause shown, reduce the amount of security given; and if the surety shall be or become insufficient, new or additional sureties may be required on motion and hearing.

(7) Security on Counterclaim.

(a) When a person who has given security for damages in the original action asserts a counterclaim that arises from the transaction or occurrence that is the subject of the original action, a plaintiff for whose benefit the security has been given must give security for damages demanded in the counterclaim unless the court, for cause shown, directs otherwise. Proceedings on the original claim must be stayed until this security is given, unless the court directs otherwise.

(b) The plaintiff is required to give security under Rule E(7)(a) when the United States or its corporate instrumentality counterclaims and would have been required to give security to respond in damages if a private party but is relieved by law from giving security.

(8) Restricted Appearance. An appearance to defend against an admiralty and maritime claim with respect to which there has issued process in rem, or process of attachment and garnishment, may be expressly restricted to the defense of such claim, and in that event is not an appearance for the purposes of any other claim with respect to which such process is not available or has not been served.

(9) Disposition of Property; Sales.

(a) Interlocutory Sales; Delivery.

(i) On application of a party, the marshal, or other person having custody of the property, the court may order all or part of the property sold—with the sales proceeds, or as much of them as will satisfy the judgment, paid into court to await further orders of the court—if:

(A) the attached or arrested property is perishable, or liable to deterioration, decay, or injury by being detained in custody pending the action;

(B) the expense of keeping the property is excessive or disproportionate; or

(C) there is an unreasonable delay in securing release of the property.

(ii) In the circumstances described in Rule E(9)(a)(i), the court, on motion by a defendant or a person filing a statement of interest or right under Rule C(6), may order that the property, rather than being sold, be delivered to the movant upon giving security under these rules.

(b) Sales, Proceeds. All sales of property shall be made by the marshal or a deputy marshal, or by other person or organization having the warrant, or by any other person assigned by the court where the marshal or other person or organization having the warrant is a party in interest; and the proceeds of sale shall be forthwith paid into the registry of the court to be disposed of according to law.

(10) Preservation of Property. When the owner or another person remains in possession of property attached or arrested under the provisions of Rule E(4)(b) that permit execution of process without taking actual possession, the court, on a party's motion or on its own, may enter any order necessary to preserve the property and to prevent its removal.

(As added Feb. 28, 1966, eff. July 1, 1966; amended Apr. 29, 1985, eff. Aug. 1, 1985; Mar. 2, 1987, eff. Aug. 1, 1987; Apr. 30, 1991, eff. Dec. 1, 1991; Apr. 17, 2000, eff. Dec. 1, 2000; Apr. 12, 2006, eff. Dec. 1, 2006.)

Notes of Advisory Committee on Rules

Subdivisions (1), (2).

Adapted from Admiralty Rule 24. The rule is based on the assumption that there is no more need for security for costs in maritime personal actions than in civil cases generally, but that there is reason to retain the requirement for actions in which property is seized. As to proceedings for limitation of liability see Rule F(1).

Subdivision (3).

The Advisory Committee has concluded for practical reasons that process requiring seizure of property should continue to be served only within the geographical limits of the district. Compare Rule B(1), continuing the condition that process of attachment and garnishment may be served only if the defendant is not found within the district.

The provisions of Admiralty Rule 1 concerning the persons by whom process is to be served will be superseded by FRCP 4(c).

Subdivision (4).

This rule is intended to preserve the provisions of Admiralty Rules 10 and 36 relating to execution of process, custody of property, seized by the marshal, and the marshal's return. It is also designed to make express provision for matters not heretofore covered.

The provision relating to clearance in subdivision (b) is suggested by Admiralty Rule 44 of the District of Maryland.

Subdivision (d) is suggested by English Rule 12, Order 75.

28 U.S.C. §1921 as amended in 1962 contains detailed provisions relating to the expenses of seizing and preserving property attached or arrested.

Subdivision (5).

In addition to Admiralty Rule 11 (see Rule E(9)), the release of property seized on process of attachment or in rem was dealt with by Admiralty Rules 5, 6, 12, and 57, and 28 U.S.C., §2464 (formerly Rev. Stat. §941). The rule consolidates these provisions and makes them uniformly applicable to attachment and garnishment and actions in rem.

The rule restates the substance of Admiralty Rule 5. Admiralty Rule 12 dealt only with ships arrested on in rem process. Since the same ground appears to be covered more generally by 28 U.S.C., §2464, the subject matter of Rule 12 is omitted. The substance of Admiralty Rule 57 is retained. 28 U.S.C., §2464 is incorporated with changes of terminology, and with a substantial change as to the amount of the bond. See 2 Benedict 395 n. 1a; The Lotosland, 2 F. Supp. 42 (S.D.N.Y. 1933). The provision for general bond is enlarged to include the contingency of attachment as well as arrest of the vessel.

Subdivision (6).

Adapted from Admiralty Rule 8.

Subdivision (7).

Derived from Admiralty Rule 50.

Title 46, U.S.C., §783 extends the principle of Rule 50 to the Government when sued under the Public Vessels Act, presumably on the theory that the credit of the Government is the equivalent of the best security. The rule adopts this principle and extends it to all cases in which the Government is defendant although the Suits in Admiralty Act contains no parallel provisions.

Subdivision (8).

Under the liberal joinder provisions of unified rules the plaintiff will be enabled to join with maritime actions in rem, or maritime actions in personam with process of attachment and garnishment, claims with respect to which such process is not available, including nonmaritime claims. Unification should not, however, have the result that, in order to defend against an admiralty and maritime claim with respect to which process in rem or quasi in rem has been served, the claimant or defendant must subject himself personally to the jurisdiction of the court with reference to other claims with respect to which such process is not available or has not been served, especially when such other claims are nonmaritime. So far as attachment and garnishment are concerned this principle holds true whether process is issued according to admiralty tradition and the Supplemental Rules or according to Rule 4(e) as incorporated by Rule B(1).

A similar problem may arise with respect to civil actions other than admiralty and maritime claims within the meaning of Rule 9(h). That is to say, in an ordinary civil action, whether maritime or not, there may be joined in one action claims with respect to which process of attachment and garnishment is available under state law and Rule 4(e) and claims with respect to which such process is not available or has not been served. The general Rules of Civil Procedure do not specify whether an appearance in such cases to defend the claim with respect to which process of attachment and garnishment has issued is an appearance for the purposes of the other claims. In that context the question has been considered best left to case-by-case development. Where admiralty and maritime claims within the meaning of Rule 9(h) are concerned, however, it seems important to include a specific provision to avoid an unfortunate and unintended effect of unification. No inferences whatever as to the effect of such an appearance in an ordinary civil action should be drawn from the specific provision here and the absence of such a provision in the general Rules.

Subdivision (9).

Adapted from Admiralty Rules 11, 12, and 40. Subdivision (a) is necessary because of various provisions as to disposition of property in forfeiture proceedings. In addition to particular statutes, note the provisions of 28 U.S.C., §§2461–65.

The provision of Admiralty Rule 12 relating to unreasonable delay was limited to ships but should have broader application. See 2 Benedict 404. Similarly, both Rules 11 and 12 were limited to actions in rem, but should equally apply to attached property.

Notes of Advisory Committee on Rules—1985 Amendment

Rule E(4)(f) makes available the type of prompt post-seizure hearing in proceedings under Supplemental Rules B and C that the Supreme Court has called for in a number of cases arising in other contexts. See North Georgia Finishing, Inc. v. Di-Chem, Inc., 419 U.S. 601 (1975); Mitchell v. W. T. Grant Co., 416 U.S. 600 (1974). Although post-attachment and post-arrest hearings always have been available on motion, an explicit statement emphasizing promptness and elaborating the procedure has been lacking in the Supplemental Rules. Rule E(4)(f) is designed to satisfy the constitutional requirement of due process by guaranteeing to the shipowner [sic] a prompt post-seizure hearing at which he can attack the complaint, the arrest, the security demanded, or any other alleged deficiency in the proceedings. The amendment also is intended to eliminate the previously disparate treatment under local rules of defendants whose property has been seized pursuant to Supplemental Rules B and C.

The new Rule E(4)(f) is based on a proposal by the Maritime Law Association of the United States and on local admiralty rules in the Eastern, Northern, and Southern Districts of New York. E.D.N.Y. Local Rule 13; N.D.N.Y. Local Rule 13; S.D.N.Y. Local Rule 12. Similar provisions have been adopted by other maritime districts. E.g., N.D. Calif. Local Rule 603.4; W.D. La. Local Admiralty Rule 21. Rule E(4)(f) will provide uniformity in practice and reduce constitutional uncertainties.

Rule E(4)(f) is triggered by the defendant or any other person with an interest in the property seized. Upon an oral or written application similar to that used in seeking a temporary restraining order, see Rule 65(b), the court is required to hold a hearing as promptly as possible to determine whether to allow the arrest or attachment to stand. The plaintiff has the burden of showing why the seizure should not be vacated. The hearing also may determine the amount of security to be granted or the propriety of imposing counter-security to protect the defendant from an improper seizure.

The foregoing requirements for prior court review or proof of exigent circumstances do not apply to actions by the United States for forfeitures for federal statutory violations. In such actions a prompt hearing is not constitutionally required, United States v. Eight Thousand Eight Hundred and Fifty Dollars, 103 S.Ct. 2005 (1983); Calero-Toledo v. Pearson Yacht Leasing Co., 416 U.S. 663 (1974), and could prejudice the government in its prosecution of the claimants as defendants in parallel criminal proceedings since the forfeiture hearing could be misused by the defendants to obtain by way of civil discovery information to which they would not otherwise be entitled and subject the government and the courts to the unnecessary burden and expense of two hearings rather than one.

Notes of Advisory Committee on Rules—1987 Amendment

The amendments are technical. No substantive change is intended.

Notes of Advisory Committee on Rules—1991 Amendment

These amendments are designed to conform this rule to Fed.R.Civ.P. 4, as amended. They are intended to relieve the Marshals Service of the burden of using its limited personnel and facilities for execution of process in routine circumstances. Doing so may involve a contractual arrangement with a person or organization retained by the government to perform these services, or the use of other government officers and employees, or the special appointment by the court of persons available to perform suitably.

Committee Notes on Rules—2000 Amendment

Style changes have been made throughout the revised portions of Rule E. Several changes of meaning have been made as well.

Subdivision (3). Subdivision (3) is amended to reflect the distinction drawn in Rule C(2)(c) and (d). Service in an admiralty or maritime proceeding still must be made within the district, as reflected in Rule C(2)(c), while service in forfeiture proceedings may be made outside the district when authorized by statute, as reflected in Rule C(2)(d).

Subdivision (7). Subdivision (7)(a) is amended to make it clear that a plaintiff need give security to meet a counterclaim only when the counterclaim is asserted by a person who has given security to respond in damages in the original action.

Subdivision (8). Subdivision (8) is amended to reflect the change in Rule B(1)(e) that deletes the former provision incorporating state quasi-in-rem jurisdiction. A restricted appearance is not appropriate when state law is invoked only for security under Civil Rule 64, not as a basis of quasi-in-rem jurisdiction. But if state law allows a special, limited, or restricted appearance as an incident of the remedy adopted from state law, the state practice applies through Rule 64 "in the manner provided by" state law.

Subdivision (9). Subdivision 9(b)(ii) is amended to reflect the change in Rule C(6) that substitutes a statement of interest or right for a claim.

Subdivision (10). Subdivision 10 is new. It makes clear the authority of the court to preserve and to prevent removal of attached or arrested property that remains in the possession of the owner or other person under Rule E(4)(b).

Committee Notes on Rules—2006 Amendment

Rule E is amended to reflect the adoption of Rule G to govern procedure in civil forfeiture actions.

References in Text

Sections 603 and 604 of Title 46, referred to in subd. (4)(f), were repealed by Pub. L. 98–89, §4(b), Aug. 26, 1983, 97 Stat. 600, section 1 of which enacted Title 46, Shipping.

1 See References in Text note below.

Rule F. Limitation of Liability

(1) Time for Filing Complaint; Security. Not later than six months after receipt of a claim in writing, any vessel owner may file a complaint in the appropriate district court, as provided in subdivision (9) of this rule, for limitation of liability pursuant to statute. The owner (a) shall deposit with the court, for the benefit of claimants, a sum equal to the amount or value of the owner's interest in the vessel and pending freight, or approved security therefor, and in addition such sums, or approved security therefor, as the court may from time to time fix as necessary to carry out the provisions of the statutes as amended; or (b) at the owner's option shall transfer to a trustee to be appointed by the court, for the benefit of claimants, the owner's interest in the vessel and pending freight, together with such sums, or approved security therefor, as the court may from time to time fix as necessary to carry out the provisions of the statutes as amended. The plaintiff shall also give security for costs and, if the plaintiff elects to give security, for interest at the rate of 6 percent per annum from the date of the security.

(2) Complaint. The complaint shall set forth the facts on the basis of which the right to limit liability is asserted and all facts necessary to enable the court to determine the amount to which the owner's liability shall be limited. The complaint may demand exoneration from as well as limitation of liability. It shall state the voyage if any, on which the demands sought to be limited arose, with the date and place of its termination; the amount of all demands including all unsatisfied liens or claims of lien, in contract or in tort or otherwise, arising on that voyage, so far as known to the plaintiff, and what actions and proceedings, if any, are pending thereon; whether the vessel was damaged, lost, or abandoned, and, if so, when and where; the value of the vessel at the close of the voyage or, in case of wreck, the value of her wreckage, strippings, or proceeds, if any, and where and in whose possession they are; and the amount of any pending freight recovered or recoverable. If the plaintiff elects to transfer the plaintiff's interest in the vessel to a trustee, the complaint must further show any prior paramount liens thereon, and what voyages or trips, if any, she has made since the voyage or trip on which the claims sought to be limited arose, and any existing liens arising upon any such subsequent voyage or trip, with the amounts and causes thereof, and the names and addresses of the lienors, so far as known; and whether the vessel sustained any injury upon or by reason of such subsequent voyage or trip.

(3) Claims Against Owner; Injunction. Upon compliance by the owner with the requirements of subdivision (1) of this rule all claims and proceedings against the owner or the owner's property with respect to the matter in question shall cease. On application of the plaintiff the court shall enjoin the further prosecution of any action or proceeding against the plaintiff or the plaintiff's property with respect to any claim subject to limitation in the action.

(4) Notice to Claimants. Upon the owner's compliance with subdivision (1) of this rule the court shall issue a notice to all persons asserting claims with respect to which the complaint seeks limitation, admonishing them to file their respective claims with the clerk of the court and to serve on the attorneys for the plaintiff a copy thereof on or before a date to be named in the notice. The date so fixed shall not be less than 30 days after issuance of the notice. For cause shown, the court may enlarge the time within which claims may be filed. The notice shall be published in such newspaper or newspapers as the court may direct once a week for four successive weeks prior to the date fixed for the filing of claims. The plaintiff not later than the day of second publication shall also mail a copy of the notice to every person known to have made any claim against the vessel or the plaintiff arising out of the voyage or trip on which the claims sought to be limited arose. In cases involving death a copy of such notice shall be mailed to the decedent at the decedent's last known address, and also to any person who shall be known to have made any claim on account of such death.

(5) Claims and Answer. Claims shall be filed and served on or before the date specified in the notice provided for in subdivision (4) of this rule. Each claim shall specify the facts upon which the claimant relies in support of the claim, the items thereof, and the dates on which the same accrued. If a claimant desires to contest either the right to exoneration from or the right to limitation of liability the claimant shall file and serve an answer to the complaint unless the claim has included an answer.

(6) Information To Be Given Claimants. Within 30 days after the date specified in the notice for filing claims, or within such time as the court thereafter may allow, the plaintiff shall mail to the attorney for each claimant (or if the claimant has no attorney to the claimant) a list setting forth (a) the name of each claimant, (b) the name and address of the claimant's attorney (if the claimant is known to have one), (c) the nature of the claim, i.e., whether property loss, property damage, death, personal injury etc., and (d) the amount thereof.

(7) Insufficiency of Fund or Security. Any claimant may by motion demand that the funds deposited in court or the security given by the plaintiff be increased on the ground that they are less than the value of the plaintiff's interest in the vessel and pending freight. Thereupon the court shall cause due appraisement to be made of the value of the plaintiff's interest in the vessel and pending freight; and if the court finds that the deposit or security is either insufficient or excessive it shall order its increase or reduction. In like manner any claimant may demand that the deposit or security be increased on the ground that it is insufficient to carry out the provisions of the statutes relating to claims in respect of loss of life or bodily injury; and, after notice and hearing, the court may similarly order that the deposit or security be increased or reduced.

(8) Objections to Claims: Distribution of Fund. Any interested party may question or controvert any claim without filing an objection thereto. Upon determination of liability the fund deposited or secured, or the proceeds of the vessel and pending freight, shall be divided pro rata, subject to all relevant provisions of law, among the several claimants in proportion to the amounts of their respective claims, duly proved, saving, however, to all parties any priority to which they may be legally entitled.

(9) Venue; Transfer. The complaint shall be filed in any district in which the vessel has been attached or arrested to answer for any claim with respect to which the plaintiff seeks to limit liability; or, if the vessel has not been attached or arrested, then in any district in which the owner has been sued with respect to any such claim. When the vessel has not been attached or arrested to answer the matters aforesaid, and suit has not been commenced against the owner, the proceedings may be had in the district in which the vessel may be, but if the vessel is not within any district and no suit has been commenced in any district, then the complaint may be filed in any district. For the convenience of parties and witnesses, in the interest of justice, the court may transfer the action to any district; if venue is wrongly laid the court shall dismiss or, if it be in the interest of justice, transfer the action to any district in which it could have been brought. If the vessel shall have been sold, the proceeds shall represent the vessel for the purposes of these rules.

(As added Feb. 28, 1966, eff. July 1, 1966; amended Mar. 2, 1987, eff. Aug. 1, 1987.)

Notes of Advisory Committee on Rules

Subdivision (1).

The amendments of 1936 to the Limitation Act superseded to some extent the provisions of Admiralty Rule 51, especially with respect to the time of filing the complaint and with respect to security. The rule here incorporates in substance the 1936 amendment of the Act (46 U.S.C., §185) with a slight modification to make it clear that the complaint may be filed at any time not later than six months after a claim has been lodged with the owner.

Subdivision (2).

Derived from Admiralty Rules 51 and 53.

Subdivision (3).

This is derived from the last sentence of 36 [46] U.S.C. §185 and the last paragraph of Admiralty Rule 51.

Subdivision (4).

Derived from Admiralty Rule 51.

Subdivision (5).

Derived from Admiralty Rules 52 and 53.

Subdivision (6).

Derived from Admiralty Rule 52.

Subdivision (7).

Derived from Admiralty Rules 52 and 36 [46] U.S.C., §185.

Subdivision (8).

Derived from Admiralty Rule 52.

Subdivision (9).

Derived from Admiralty Rule 54. The provision for transfer is revised to conform closely to the language of 28 U.S.C. §§1404(a) and 1406(a), though it retains the existing rule's provision for transfer to any district for convenience. The revision also makes clear what has been doubted: that the court may transfer if venue is wrongly laid.

Notes of Advisory Committee on Rules—1987 Amendment

The amendments are technical. No substantive change is intended.

Rule G. Forfeiture Actions in Rem

(1) Scope. This rule governs a forfeiture action in rem arising from a federal statute. To the extent that this rule does not address an issue, Supplemental Rules C and E and the Federal Rules of Civil Procedure also apply.

(2) Complaint. The complaint must:

(a) be verified;

(b) state the grounds for subject-matter jurisdiction, in rem jurisdiction over the defendant property, and venue;

(c) describe the property with reasonable particularity;

(d) if the property is tangible, state its location when any seizure occurred and—if different—its location when the action is filed;
(e) identify the statute under which the forfeiture action is brought; and
(f) state sufficiently detailed facts to support a reasonable belief that the government will be able to meet its burden of proof at trial.

(3) Judicial Authorization and Process.

(a) Real Property. If the defendant is real property, the government must proceed under 18 U.S.C. §985.

(b) Other Property; Arrest Warrant. If the defendant is not real property:

(i) the clerk must issue a warrant to arrest the property if it is in the government's possession, custody, or control;
(ii) the court—on finding probable cause—must issue a warrant to arrest the property if it is not in the government's possession, custody, or control and is not subject to a judicial restraining order; and
(iii) a warrant is not necessary if the property is subject to a judicial restraining order.

(c) Execution of Process.

(i) The warrant and any supplemental process must be delivered to a person or organization authorized to execute it, who may be: (A) a marshal or any other United States officer or employee; (B) someone under contract with the United States; or (C) someone specially appointed by the court for that purpose.
(ii) The authorized person or organization must execute the warrant and any supplemental process on property in the United States as soon as practicable unless:

(A) the property is in the government's possession, custody, or control; or
(B) the court orders a different time when the complaint is under seal, the action is stayed before the warrant and supplemental process are executed, or the court finds other good cause.

(iii) The warrant and any supplemental process may be executed within the district or, when authorized by statute, outside the district.
(iv) If executing a warrant on property outside the United States is required, the warrant may be transmitted to an appropriate authority for serving process where the property is located.

(4) Notice.

(a) Notice by Publication.

(i) When Publication Is Required. A judgment of forfeiture may be entered only if the government has published notice of the action within a reasonable time after filing the complaint or at a time the court orders. But notice need not be published if:

(A) the defendant property is worth less than $1,000 and direct notice is sent under Rule G(4)(b) to every person the government can reasonably identify as a potential claimant; or
(B) the court finds that the cost of publication exceeds the property's value and that other means of notice would satisfy due process.

(ii) Content of the Notice. Unless the court orders otherwise, the notice must:

(A) describe the property with reasonable particularity;
(B) state the times under Rule G(5) to file a claim and to answer; and
(C) name the government attorney to be served with the claim and answer.

(iii) Frequency of Publication. Published notice must appear:

(A) once a week for three consecutive weeks; or
(B) only once if, before the action was filed, notice of nonjudicial forfeiture of the same property was published on an official internet government forfeiture site for at least 30 consecutive days, or in a newspaper of general circulation for three consecutive weeks in a district where publication is authorized under Rule G(4)(a)(iv).

(iv) Means of Publication. The government should select from the following options a means of publication reasonably calculated to notify potential claimants of the action:

(A) if the property is in the United States, publication in a newspaper generally circulated in the district where the action is filed, where the property was seized, or where property that was not seized is located;
(B) if the property is outside the United States, publication in a newspaper generally circulated in a district where the action is filed, in a newspaper generally circulated in the country where the property is located, or in legal notices published and generally circulated in the country where the property is located; or
(C) instead of (A) or (B), posting a notice on an official internet government forfeiture site for at least 30 consecutive days.

(b) Notice to Known Potential Claimants.

(i) Direct Notice Required. The government must send notice of the action and a copy of the complaint to any person who reasonably appears to be a potential claimant on the facts known to the government before the end of the time for filing a claim under Rule G(5)(a)(ii)(B).
(ii) Content of the Notice. The notice must state:

(A) the date when the notice is sent;
(B) a deadline for filing a claim, at least 35 days after the notice is sent;
(C) that an answer or a motion under Rule 12 must be filed no later than 21 days after filing the claim; and
(D) the name of the government attorney to be served with the claim and answer.

(iii) Sending Notice.

(A) The notice must be sent by means reasonably calculated to reach the potential claimant.
(B) Notice may be sent to the potential claimant or to the attorney representing the potential claimant with respect to the seizure of the property or in a

related investigation, administrative forfeiture proceeding, or criminal case.

(C) Notice sent to a potential claimant who is incarcerated must be sent to the place of incarceration.

(D) Notice to a person arrested in connection with an offense giving rise to the forfeiture who is not incarcerated when notice is sent may be sent to the address that person last gave to the agency that arrested or released the person.

(E) Notice to a person from whom the property was seized who is not incarcerated when notice is sent may be sent to the last address that person gave to the agency that seized the property.

(iv) When Notice Is Sent. Notice by the following means is sent on the date when it is placed in the mail, delivered to a commercial carrier, or sent by electronic mail.

(v) Actual Notice. A potential claimant who had actual notice of a forfeiture action may not oppose or seek relief from forfeiture because of the government's failure to send the required notice.

(5) Responsive Pleadings.

(a) Filing a Claim.

(i) A person who asserts an interest in the defendant property may contest the forfeiture by filing a claim in the court where the action is pending. The claim must:

(A) identify the specific property claimed;

(B) identify the claimant and state the claimant's interest in the property;

(C) be signed by the claimant under penalty of perjury; and

(D) be served on the government attorney designated under Rule G(4)(a)(ii)(C) or (b)(ii)(D).

(ii) Unless the court for good cause sets a different time, the claim must be filed:

(A) by the time stated in a direct notice sent under Rule G(4)(b);

(B) if notice was published but direct notice was not sent to the claimant or the claimant's attorney, no later than 30 days after final publication of newspaper notice or legal notice under Rule G(4)(a) or no later than 60 days after the first day of publication on an official internet government forfeiture site; or

(C) if notice was not published and direct notice was not sent to the claimant or the claimant's attorney:

(1) if the property was in the government's possession, custody, or control when the complaint was filed, no later than 60 days after the filing, not counting any time when the complaint was under seal or when the action was stayed before execution of a warrant issued under Rule G(3)(b); or

(2) if the property was not in the government's possession, custody, or control when the complaint was filed, no later than 60 days after the government complied with 18 U.S.C. §985(c) as to real property, or 60 days after process was executed on the property under Rule G(3).

(iii) A claim filed by a person asserting an interest as a bailee must identify the bailor, and if filed on the bailor's behalf must state the authority to do so.

(b) Answer. A claimant must serve and file an answer to the complaint or a motion under Rule 12 within 21 days after filing the claim. A claimant waives an objection to in rem jurisdiction or to venue if the objection is not made by motion or stated in the answer.

(6) Special Interrogatories.

(a) Time and Scope. The government may serve special interrogatories limited to the claimant's identity and relationship to the defendant property without the court's leave at any time after the claim is filed and before discovery is closed. But if the claimant serves a motion to dismiss the action, the government must serve the interrogatories within 21 days after the motion is served.

(b) Answers or Objections. Answers or objections to these interrogatories must be served within 21 days after the interrogatories are served.

(c) Government's Response Deferred. The government need not respond to a claimant's motion to dismiss the action under Rule G(8)(b) until 21 days after the claimant has answered these interrogatories.

(7) Preserving, Preventing Criminal Use, and Disposing of Property; Sales.

(a) Preserving and Preventing Criminal Use of Property. When the government does not have actual possession of the defendant property the court, on motion or on its own, may enter any order necessary to preserve the property, to prevent its removal or encumbrance, or to prevent its use in a criminal offense.

(b) Interlocutory Sale or Delivery.

(i) Order to Sell. On motion by a party or a person having custody of the property, the court may order all or part of the property sold if:

(A) the property is perishable or at risk of deterioration, decay, or injury by being detained in custody pending the action;

(B) the expense of keeping the property is excessive or is disproportionate to its fair market value;

(C) the property is subject to a mortgage or to taxes on which the owner is in default; or

(D) the court finds other good cause.

(ii) Who Makes the Sale. A sale must be made by a United States agency that has authority to sell the property, by the agency's contractor, or by any person the court designates.

(iii) Sale Procedures. The sale is governed by 28 U.S.C. §§2001, 2002, and 2004, unless all parties, with the court's approval, agree to the sale, aspects of the sale, or different procedures.

(iv) Sale Proceeds. Sale proceeds are a substitute res subject to forfeiture in place of the property that was sold. The proceeds must be held in an interest-bearing account maintained by the United States pending the conclusion of the forfeiture action.

(v) Delivery on a Claimant's Motion. The court may order that the property be delivered to the claimant pending the conclusion of the action if the claimant shows circumstances that would permit sale under Rule G(7)(b)(i) and gives security under these rules.

(c) Disposing of Forfeited Property. Upon entry of a forfeiture judgment, the property or proceeds from selling the property must be disposed of as provided by law.

(8) Motions.

(a) Motion To Suppress Use of the Property as Evidence. If the defendant property was seized, a party with standing to contest the lawfulness of the seizure may move to suppress use of the property as evidence. Suppression does not affect forfeiture of the property based on independently derived evidence.

(b) Motion To Dismiss the Action.

(i) A claimant who establishes standing to contest forfeiture may move to dismiss the action under Rule 12(b).

(ii) In an action governed by 18 U.S.C. §983(a)(3)(D) the complaint may not be dismissed on the ground that the government did not have adequate evidence at the time the complaint was filed to establish the forfeitability of the property. The sufficiency of the complaint is governed by Rule G(2).

(c) Motion To Strike a Claim or Answer.

(i) At any time before trial, the government may move to strike a claim or answer:

(A) for failing to comply with Rule G(5) or (6), or

(B) because the claimant lacks standing.

(ii) The motion:

(A) must be decided before any motion by the claimant to dismiss the action; and

(B) may be presented as a motion for judgment on the pleadings or as a motion to determine after a hearing or by summary judgment whether the claimant can carry the burden of establishing standing by a preponderance of the evidence.

(d) Petition To Release Property.

(i) If a United States agency or an agency's contractor holds property for judicial or nonjudicial forfeiture under a statute governed by 18 U.S.C. §983(f), a person who has filed a claim to the property may petition for its release under §983(f).

(ii) If a petition for release is filed before a judicial forfeiture action is filed against the property, the petition may be filed either in the district where the property was seized or in the district where a warrant to seize the property issued. If a judicial forfeiture action against the property is later filed in another district—or if the government shows that the action will be filed in another district—the petition may be transferred to that district under 28 U.S.C. §1404.

(e) Excessive Fines. A claimant may seek to mitigate a forfeiture under the Excessive Fines Clause of the Eighth Amendment by motion for summary judgment or by motion made after entry of a forfeiture judgment if:

(i) the claimant has pleaded the defense under Rule 8; and

(ii) the parties have had the opportunity to conduct civil discovery on the defense.

(9) Trial. Trial is to the court unless any party demands trial by jury under Rule 38.

(As added Apr. 12, 2006, eff. Dec. 1, 2006; amended Mar. 26, 2009, eff. Dec. 1, 2009.)

Committee Notes on Rules—2006

Rule G is added to bring together the central procedures that govern civil forfeiture actions. Civil forfeiture actions are in rem proceedings, as are many admiralty proceedings. As the number of civil forfeiture actions has increased, however, reasons have appeared to create sharper distinctions within the framework of the Supplemental Rules. Civil forfeiture practice will benefit from distinctive provisions that express and focus developments in statutory, constitutional, and decisional law. Admiralty practice will be freed from the pressures that arise when the needs of civil forfeiture proceedings counsel interpretations of common rules that may not be suitable for admiralty proceedings.

Rule G generally applies to actions governed by the Civil Asset Forfeiture Reform Act of 2000 (CAFRA) and also to actions excluded from it. The rule refers to some specific CAFRA provisions; if these statutes are amended, the rule should be adapted to the new provisions during the period required to amend the rule.

Rule G is not completely self-contained. Subdivision (1) recognizes the need to rely at times on other Supplemental Rules and the place of the Supplemental Rules within the basic framework of the Civil Rules.

Supplemental Rules A, C, and E are amended to reflect the adoption of Rule G.

Subdivision (1)

Rule G is designed to include the distinctive procedures that govern a civil forfeiture action. Some details, however, are better supplied by relying on Rules C and E. Subdivision (1) incorporates those rules for issues not addressed by Rule G. This general incorporation is at times made explicit—subdivision (7)(b)(v), for example, invokes the security provisions of Rule E. But Rules C and E are not to be invoked to create conflicts with Rule G. They are to be used only when Rule G, fairly construed, does not address the issue.

The Civil Rules continue to provide the procedural framework within which Rule G and the other Supplemental Rules operate. Both Rule G(1) and Rule A state this basic proposition. Rule G, for example, does not address pleadings amendments. Civil Rule 15 applies, in light of the circumstances of a forfeiture action.

Subdivision (2)

Rule E(2)(a) requires that the complaint in an admiralty action "state the circumstances from which the claim arises with such particularity that the defendant or claimant will be able, without moving for a more definite statement, to commence an investigation of the facts and to frame a responsive pleading." Application of this standard to civil forfeiture actions has evolved to the standard stated in subdivision (2)(f). The complaint must state sufficiently detailed facts to support a reasonable belief that the government will be able to meet its burden of proof at trial. See U.S. v. Mondragon, 313 F.3d 862 (4th Cir. 2002). Subdivision (2)(f) carries this forfeiture case law forward without change.

Subdivision (3)

Subdivision (3) governs in rem process in a civil forfeiture action.

Paragraph (a). Paragraph (a) reflects the provisions of 18 U.S.C. §985.

Paragraph (b). Paragraph (b) addresses arrest warrants when the defendant is not real property. Subparagraph (i) directs the clerk to issue a warrant if the property is in the government's possession, custody, or control. If the property is not in the government's possession, custody, or control and is not subject to a restraining order, subparagraph (ii) provides that a warrant issues only if the court finds probable cause to arrest the property. This provision departs from former Rule C(3)(a)(i), which authorized issuance of summons and warrant by the clerk without a probable-cause finding. The probable-cause finding better protects the interests of persons interested in the property. Subparagraph (iii) recognizes that a warrant is not necessary if the property is subject to a judicial restraining order. The government remains free, however, to seek a warrant if it anticipates that the restraining order may be modified or vacated.

Paragraph (c). Subparagraph (ii) requires that the warrant and any supplemental process be served as soon as practicable unless the property is already in the government's possession, custody, or control. But it authorizes the court to order a different time. The authority to order a different time recognizes that the government may have secured orders sealing the complaint in a civil forfeiture action or have won a stay after filing. The seal or stay may be ordered for reasons, such as protection of an ongoing criminal investigation, that would be defeated by prompt service of the warrant. Subparagraph (ii) does not reflect any independent ground for ordering a seal or stay, but merely reflects the consequences for execution when sealing or a stay is ordered. A court also may order a different time for service if good cause is shown for reasons unrelated to a seal or stay. Subparagraph (iv) reflects the uncertainty surrounding service of an arrest warrant on property not in the United States. It is not possible to identify in the rule the appropriate authority for serving process in all other countries. Transmission of the warrant to an appropriate authority, moreover, does not ensure that the warrant will be executed. The rule requires only that the warrant be transmitted to an appropriate authority.

Subdivision (4)

Paragraph (a). Paragraph (a) reflects the traditional practice of publishing notice of an in rem action.

Subparagraph (i) recognizes two exceptions to the general publication requirement. Publication is not required if the defendant property is worth less than $1,000 and direct notice is sent to all reasonably identifiable potential claimants as required by subdivision (4)(b). Publication also is not required if the cost would exceed the property's value and the court finds that other means of notice would satisfy due process. Publication on a government-established internet forfeiture site, as contemplated by subparagraph (iv), would be at a low marginal publication cost, which would likely be the cost to compare to the property value.

Subparagraph (iv) states the basic criterion for selecting the means and method of publication. The purpose is to adopt a means reasonably calculated to reach potential claimants. The government should choose from among these means a method that is reasonably likely to reach potential claimants at a cost reasonable in the circumstances.

If the property is in the United States and newspaper notice is chosen, publication may be where the action is filed, where the property was seized, or—if the property was not seized—where the property is located. Choice among these places is influenced by the probable location of potential claimants.

If the property is not in the United States, account must be taken of the sensitivities that surround publication of legal notices in other countries. A foreign country may forbid local publication. If potential claimants are likely to be in the United States, publication in the district where the action is filed may be the best choice. If potential claimants are likely to be located abroad, the better choice may be publication by means generally circulated in the country where the property is located.

Newspaper publication is not a particularly effective means of notice for most potential claimants. Its traditional use is best defended by want of affordable alternatives. Paragraph (iv)(C) contemplates a government-created internet forfeiture site that would provide a single easily identified means of notice. Such a site could allow much more direct access to notice as to any specific property than publication provides.

Paragraph (b). Paragraph (b) is entirely new. For the first time, Rule G expressly recognizes the due process obligation to send notice to any person who reasonably appears to be a potential claimant.

Subparagraph (i) states the obligation to send notice. Many potential claimants will be known to the government because they have filed claims during the administrative forfeiture stage. Notice must be sent, however, no matter what source of information makes it reasonably appear that a person is a potential claimant. The duty to send notice terminates when the time for filing a claim expires.

Notice of the action does not require formal service of summons in the manner required by Rule 4 to initiate a personal action. The process that begins an in rem forfeiture action is addressed by subdivision (3). This process commonly gives notice to potential claimants. Publication of notice is required in addition to this process. Due process requirements have moved beyond these traditional means of notice, but are satisfied by practical means that are reasonably calculated to accomplish actual notice.

Subparagraph (ii)(B) directs that the notice state a deadline for filing a claim that is at least 35 days after the notice is sent. This provision applies both in actions that fall within 18 U.S.C. §983(a)(4)(A) and in other actions. Section 983(a)(4)(A) states that a claim should be filed no later than 30 days after service of the complaint. The variation introduced by subparagraph (ii)(B) reflects the procedure of §983(a)(2)(B) for nonjudicial forfeiture proceedings. The nonjudicial procedure requires that a claim be filed "not later than the deadline set forth in a personal notice letter (which may be not earlier than 35 days after the date the letter is sent) * * *." This procedure is as suitable in a civil forfeiture action as in a nonjudicial forfeiture proceeding. Thirty-five days after notice is sent ordinarily will extend the claim time by no more than a brief period; a claimant anxious to expedite proceedings can file the claim before the deadline; and the government has flexibility to set a still longer period when circumstances make that desirable.

Subparagraph (iii) begins by stating the basic requirement that notice must be sent by means reasonably calculated to reach the potential claimant. No attempt is made to list the various means that may be reasonable in different circumstances. It may be reasonable, for example, to rely on means that have already been established for communication with a particular potential claimant. The government's interest in choosing a means likely to accomplish actual notice is bolstered by its desire to avoid post-forfeiture challenges based on arguments that a different method would have been more likely to accomplish actual notice. Flexible rule language accommodates the rapid evolution of communications technology.

Notice may be directed to a potential claimant through counsel, but only to counsel already representing the claimant with respect to the seizure of the property, or in a related investigation, administrative forfeiture proceeding, or criminal case.

Subparagraph (iii)(C) reflects the basic proposition that notice to a potential claimant who is incarcerated must be sent to the place of incarceration. Notice directed to some other place, such as a pre-incarceration residence, is less likely to reach the potential claimant. This provision does not address due process questions that may arise if a particular prison has deficient procedures for delivering notice to prisoners. See Dusenbery v. U.S., 534 U.S. 161 (2002).

Items (D) and (E) of subparagraph (iii) authorize the government to rely on an address given by a person who is not incarcerated. The address may have been given to the agency that arrested or released the person, or to the agency that seized the property. The government is not obliged to undertake an independent investigation to verify the address.

Subparagraph (iv) identifies the date on which notice is considered to be sent for some common means, without addressing the circumstances for choosing among the identified means or other means. The date of sending should be determined by analogy for means not listed. Facsimile transmission, for example, is sent upon transmission. Notice by personal delivery is sent on delivery.

Subparagraph (v), finally, reflects the purpose to effect actual notice by providing that a potential claimant who had actual notice of a forfeiture proceeding cannot oppose or seek relief from forfeiture because the government failed to comply with subdivision (4)(b).

Subdivision (5)

Paragraph (a). Paragraph (a) establishes that the first step of contesting a civil forfeiture action is to file a claim. A claim is required by 18 U.S.C. §983(a)(4)(A) for actions covered by §983. Paragraph (a) applies this procedure as well to actions not covered by §983. "Claim" is used to describe this first pleading because of the statutory references to claim and claimant. It functions in the same way as the statement of interest prescribed for an admiralty proceeding by Rule C(6), and is not related to the distinctive meaning of "claim" in admiralty practice.

If the claimant states its interest in the property to be as bailee, the bailor must be identified. A bailee who files a claim on behalf of a bailor must state the bailee's authority to do so.

The claim must be signed under penalty of perjury by the person making it. An artificial body that can act only through an agent may authorize an agent to sign for it. Excusable inability of counsel to obtain an appropriate signature may be grounds for an extension of time to file the claim.

Paragraph (a)(ii) sets the time for filing a claim. Item (C) applies in the relatively rare circumstance in which notice is not published and the government did not send direct notice to the claimant because it did not know of the claimant or did not have an address for the claimant.

Paragraph (b). Under 18 U.S.C. §983(a)(4)(B), which governs many forfeiture proceedings, a person who asserts an interest by filing a claim "shall file an answer to the Government's complaint for forfeiture not later than 20 days after the date of the filing of the claim." Paragraph (b) recognizes that this statute works within the general procedures established by Civil Rule 12. Rule 12(a)(4) suspends the time to answer when a Rule 12 motion is served within the time allowed to answer. Continued application of this rule to proceedings governed by §983(a)(4)(B) serves all of the purposes advanced by Rule 12(a)(4), see U.S. v. $8,221,877.16, 330 F.3d 141 (3d Cir. 2003); permits a uniform procedure for all civil forfeiture actions; and recognizes that a motion under Rule 12 can be made only after a claim is filed that provides background for the motion.

Failure to present an objection to in rem jurisdiction or to venue by timely motion or answer waives the objection. Waiver of such objections is familiar. An answer may be amended to assert an objection initially omitted. But Civil Rule 15 should be applied to an amendment that for the first time raises an objection to in rem jurisdiction by analogy to the personal jurisdiction objection provision in Civil Rule 12(h)(1)(B). The amendment should be permitted only if it is permitted as a matter of course under Rule 15(a).

A claimant's motion to dismiss the action is further governed by subdivisions (6)(c), (8)(b), and (8)(c).

Subdivision (6)

Subdivision (6) illustrates the adaptation of an admiralty procedure to the different needs of civil forfeiture. Rule C(6) permits interrogatories to be served with the complaint in an in rem action without limiting the subjects of inquiry. Civil forfeiture practice does not require such an extensive departure from ordinary civil practice. It remains useful, however, to permit the government to file limited interrogatories at any time after a claim is filed to gather information that bears on the claimant's standing. Subdivisions (8)(b) and (c) allow a claimant to move to dismiss only if the claimant has standing, and recognize the government's right to move to dismiss a claim for lack of standing. Subdivision (6) interrogatories are integrated with these provisions in that the interrogatories are limited to the claimant's identity and relationship to the defendant property. If the claimant asserts a relationship to the property as bailee, the interrogatories can inquire into the bailor's interest in the property and the bailee's relationship to the bailor. The claimant can accelerate the time to serve subdivision (6) interrogatories by serving a motion to dismiss—the interrogatories must be served within 20 days after the motion is served. Integration is further accomplished by deferring the government's obligation to respond to a motion to dismiss until 20 days after the claimant moving to dismiss has answered the interrogatories.

Special interrogatories served under Rule G(6) do not count against the presumptive 25-interrogatory limit established by Rule 33(a). Rule 33 procedure otherwise applies to these interrogatories.

Subdivision (6) supersedes the discovery "moratorium" of Rule 26(d) and the broader interrogatories permitted for admiralty proceedings by Rule C(6).

Subdivision (7)

Paragraph (a). Paragraph (a) is adapted from Rule E(9)(b). It provides for preservation orders when the government does not have actual possession of the defendant property. It also goes beyond Rule E(9) by recognizing the need to prevent use of the defendant property in ongoing criminal offenses.

Paragraph (b). Paragraph (b)(i)(C) recognizes the authority, already exercised in some cases, to order sale of property subject to a defaulted mortgage or to defaulted taxes. The authority is narrowly confined to mortgages and tax liens; other lien interests may be addressed, if at all, only through the general good-cause provision. The court must carefully weigh the competing interests in each case.

Paragraph (b)(i)(D) establishes authority to order sale for good cause. Good cause may be shown when the property is subject to diminution in value. Care should be taken before ordering sale to avoid diminished value.

Paragraph (b)(iii) recognizes that if the court approves, the interests of all parties may be served by their agreement to sale, aspects of the sale, or sale procedures that depart from governing statutory procedures.

Paragraph (c) draws from Rule E(9)(a), (b), and (c). Disposition of the proceeds as provided by law may require resolution of disputed issues. A mortgagee's claim to the property or sale proceeds, for example, may be disputed on the ground that the mortgage is not genuine. An undisputed lien claim, on the other hand, may be recognized by payment after an interlocutory sale.

Subdivision (8)

Subdivision (8) addresses a number of issues that are unique to civil forfeiture actions.

Paragraph (a). Standing to suppress use of seized property as evidence is governed by principles distinct from the principles that govern claim standing. A claimant with standing to contest forfeiture may not have standing to seek suppression. Rule G does not of itself create a basis of suppression standing that does not otherwise exist.

Paragraph (b). Paragraph (b)(i) is one element of the system that integrates the procedures for determining a claimant's standing to claim and for deciding a claimant's motion to dismiss the action. Under paragraph (c)(ii), a motion to dismiss the action cannot be addressed until the court has decided any government motion to strike the claim or answer. This procedure is reflected in the (b)(i) reminder that a motion to dismiss the forfeiture action may be made only by a claimant who establishes claim standing. The government, moreover, need not respond to a claimant's motion to dismiss until 20 days after the claimant has answered any subdivision (6) interrogatories.

Paragraph (b)(ii) mirrors 18 U.S.C. §983(a)(3)(D). It applies only to an action independently governed by §983(a)(3)(D), implying nothing as to actions outside §983(a)(3)(D). The adequacy of the complaint is measured against the pleading requirements of subdivision (2), not against the quality of the evidence available to the government when the complaint was filed.

Paragraph (c). As noted with paragraph (b), paragraph (c) governs the procedure for determining whether a claimant has standing. It does not address the principles that govern claim standing.

Paragraph (c)(i)(A) provides that the government may move to strike a claim or answer for failure to comply with the pleading requirements of subdivision (5) or to answer subdivision (6) interrogatories. As with other pleadings, the court should strike a claim or answer only if satisfied that an opportunity should not be afforded to cure the defects under Rule 15. Not every failure to respond to subdivision (6) interrogatories warrants an order striking the claim. But the special role that subdivision (6) plays in the scheme for determining claim standing may justify a somewhat more demanding approach than the general approach to discovery sanctions under Rule 37.

Paragraph (c)(ii) directs that a motion to strike a claim or answer be decided before any motion by the claimant to dismiss the action. A claimant who lacks standing is not entitled to challenge the forfeiture on the merits.

Paragraph (c)(ii) further identifies three procedures for addressing claim standing. If a claim fails on its face to show facts that support claim standing, the claim can be dismissed by judgment on the pleadings. If the claim shows facts that would support claim standing, those facts can be tested by a motion for summary judgment. If material facts are disputed, precluding a grant of summary judgment, the court may hold an evidentiary hearing. The evidentiary hearing is held by the court without a jury. The claimant has the burden to establish claim standing at a hearing; procedure on a government summary judgment motion reflects this allocation of the burden.

Paragraph (d). The hardship release provisions of 18 U.S.C. §983(f) do not apply to a civil forfeiture action exempted from §983 by §983(i).

Paragraph (d)(ii) reflects the venue provisions of 18 U.S.C. §983(f)(3)(A) as a guide to practitioners. In addition, it makes clear the status of a civil forfeiture action as a "civil action" eligible for transfer under 28 U.S.C. §1404. A transfer decision must be made on the circumstances of the particular proceeding. The district where the forfeiture action is filed has the advantage of bringing all related proceedings together, avoiding the waste that flows from consideration of different parts of the same forfeiture proceeding in the court where the warrant issued or the court where the property was seized. Transfer to that court would serve consolidation, the purpose that underlies nationwide enforcement of a seizure warrant. But there may be offsetting advantages in retaining the petition where it was filed. The claimant may not be able to litigate, effectively or at all, in a distant court. Issues relevant to the petition may be better litigated where the property was seized or where the warrant issued. One element, for example, is whether the claimant has sufficient ties to the community to provide assurance that the property will be available at the time of trial. Another is whether continued government possession would prevent the claimant from working. Determining whether seizure of the claimant's automobile prevents work may turn on assessing the realities of local public transit facilities.

Paragraph (e). The Excessive Fines Clause of the Eighth Amendment forbids an excessive forfeiture. U.S. v. Bajakajian, 524 U.S. 321 (1998). 18 U.S.C. §983(g) provides a "petition" "to determine whether the forfeiture was constitutionally excessive" based on finding "that the forfeiture is grossly disproportional to the offense." Paragraph (e) describes the procedure for §983(g) mitigation petitions and adopts the same procedure for forfeiture actions that fall outside §983(g). The procedure is by motion, either for summary judgment or for mitigation after a forfeiture judgment is entered. The claimant must give notice of this defense by pleading, but failure to raise the defense in the initial answer may be cured by amendment under Rule 15. The issues that bear on mitigation often are separate from the issues that determine forfeiture. For that reason it may be convenient to resolve the issue by summary judgment before trial on the forfeiture issues. Often, however, it will be more convenient to determine first whether the property is to be forfeited. Whichever time is chosen to address mitigation, the parties must have had the opportunity to conduct civil discovery on the defense. The extent and timing of discovery are governed by the ordinary rules.

Subdivision (9)

Subdivision (9) serves as a reminder of the need to demand jury trial under Rule 38. It does not expand the right to jury trial. See U.S. v. One Parcel of Property Located at 32 Medley Lane, 2005 WL 465241 (D.Conn. 2005), ruling that the court, not the jury, determines whether a forfeiture is constitutionally excessive.

Changes Made After Publication and Comment. Rule G(6)(a) was amended to delete the provision that special interrogatories addressed to a claimant's standing are "under Rule 33." The government was concerned that some forfeitures raise factually complex standing issues that require many interrogatories, severely depleting the presumptive 25-interrogatory limit in Rule 33. The Committee Note is amended to state that the interrogatories do not count against the limit, but that Rule 33 governs the procedure.

Rule G(7)(a) was amended to recognize the court's authority to enter an order necessary to prevent use of the defendant property in a criminal offense.

Rule G(8)(c) was revised to clarify the use of three procedures to challenge a claimant's standing—judgment on the pleadings, summary judgment, or an evidentiary hearing.

Several other rule text changes were made to add clarity on small points or to conform to Style conventions.

Changes were made in the Committee Note to explain some of the rule text revisions, to add clarity on a few points, and to delete statements about complex matters that seemed better left to case-law development.

Committee Notes on Rules—2009 Amendment

The times set in the former rule at 20 days have been revised to 21 days. See the Note to Rule 6.

28 USC Chapter 85
District Courts; Jurisdiction

§1330. Actions against foreign states

(a) The district courts shall have original jurisdiction without regard to amount in controversy of any nonjury civil action against a foreign state as defined in section 1603(a) of this title as to any claim for relief in personam with respect to which the foreign state is not entitled to immunity either under sections 1605–1607 of this title or under any applicable international agreement.

(b) Personal jurisdiction over a foreign state shall exist as to every claim for relief over which the district courts have jurisdiction under subsection (a) where service has been made under section 1608 of this title.

(c) For purposes of subsection (b), an appearance by a foreign state does not confer personal jurisdiction with respect to any claim for relief not arising out of any transaction or occurrence enumerated in sections 1605–1607 of this title.

§1331. Federal question

The district courts shall have original jurisdiction of all civil actions arising under the Constitution, laws, or treaties of the United States.

§1332. Diversity of citizenship; amount in controversy; costs

(a) The district courts shall have original jurisdiction of all civil actions where the matter in controversy exceeds the sum or value of $75,000, exclusive of interest and costs, and is between—
  (1) citizens of different States;
  (2) citizens of a State and citizens or subjects of a foreign state, except that the district courts shall not have original jurisdiction under this subsection of an action between citizens of a State and citizens or subjects of a foreign state who are lawfully admitted for permanent residence in the United States and are domiciled in the same State;
  (3) citizens of different States and in which citizens or subjects of a foreign state are additional parties; and
  (4) a foreign state, defined in section 1603(a) of this title, as plaintiff and citizens of a State or of different States.

(b) Except when express provision therefor is otherwise made in a statute of the United States, where the plaintiff who files the case originally in the Federal courts is finally adjudged to be entitled to recover less than the sum or value of $75,000, computed without regard to any setoff or counterclaim to which the defendant may be adjudged to be entitled, and exclusive of interest and costs, the district court may deny costs to the plaintiff and, in addition, may impose costs on the plaintiff.

(c) For the purposes of this section and section 1441 of this title—
  (1) a corporation shall be deemed to be a citizen of every State and foreign state by which it has been incorporated and of the State or foreign state where it has its principal place of business, except that in any direct action against the insurer of a policy or contract of liability insurance, whether incorporated or unincorporated, to which action the insured is not joined as a party-defendant, such insurer shall be deemed a citizen of—
    (A) every State and foreign state of which the insured is a citizen;
    (B) every State and foreign state by which the insurer has been incorporated; and
    (C) the State or foreign state where the insurer has its principal place of business; and
  (2) the legal representative of the estate of a decedent shall be deemed to be a citizen only of the same State as the decedent, and the legal representative of an infant or incompetent shall be deemed to be a citizen only of the same State as the infant or incompetent.

(d)
  (1) In this subsection—
    (A) the term "class" means all of the class members in a class action;
    (B) the term "class action" means any civil action filed under rule 23 of the Federal Rules of Civil Procedure or similar State statute or rule of judicial procedure authorizing an action to be brought by 1 or more representative persons as a class action;
    (C) the term "class certification order" means an order issued by a court approving the treatment of some or all aspects of a civil action as a class action; and
    (D) the term "class members" means the persons (named or unnamed) who fall within the definition of the proposed or certified class in a class action.
  (2) The district courts shall have original jurisdiction of any civil action in which the matter in controversy exceeds the sum or value of $5,000,000, exclusive of interest and costs, and is a class action in which—
    (A) any member of a class of plaintiffs is a citizen of a State different from any defendant;
    (B) any member of a class of plaintiffs is a foreign state or a citizen or subject of a foreign state and any defendant is a citizen of a State; or
    (C) any member of a class of plaintiffs is a citizen of a State and any defendant is a foreign state or a citizen or subject of a foreign state.
  (3) A district court may, in the interests of justice and looking at the totality of the circumstances, decline to exercise jurisdiction under paragraph (2) over a class action in which greater than one-third but less than two-thirds of the members of all proposed plaintiff classes in the aggregate and the primary defendants are citizens of the State in which the action was originally filed based on consideration of—

(A) whether the claims asserted involve matters of national or interstate interest;
(B) whether the claims asserted will be governed by laws of the State in which the action was originally filed or by the laws of other States;
(C) whether the class action has been pleaded in a manner that seeks to avoid Federal jurisdiction;
(D) whether the action was brought in a forum with a distinct nexus with the class members, the alleged harm, or the defendants;
(E) whether the number of citizens of the State in which the action was originally filed in all proposed plaintiff classes in the aggregate is substantially larger than the number of citizens from any other State, and the citizenship of the other members of the proposed class is dispersed among a substantial number of States; and
(F) whether, during the 3-year period preceding the filing of that class action, 1 or more other class actions asserting the same or similar claims on behalf of the same or other persons have been filed.

(4) A district court shall decline to exercise jurisdiction under paragraph (2)—
(A)
(i) over a class action in which—
(I) greater than two-thirds of the members of all proposed plaintiff classes in the aggregate are citizens of the State in which the action was originally filed;
(II) at least 1 defendant is a defendant—
(aa) from whom significant relief is sought by members of the plaintiff class;
(bb) whose alleged conduct forms a significant basis for the claims asserted by the proposed plaintiff class; and
(cc) who is a citizen of the State in which the action was originally filed; and
(III) principal injuries resulting from the alleged conduct or any related conduct of each defendant were incurred in the State in which the action was originally filed; and
(ii) during the 3-year period preceding the filing of that class action, no other class action has been filed asserting the same or similar factual allegations against any of the defendants on behalf of the same or other persons; or
(B) two-thirds or more of the members of all proposed plaintiff classes in the aggregate, and the primary defendants, are citizens of the State in which the action was originally filed.

(5) Paragraphs (2) through (4) shall not apply to any class action in which—
(A) the primary defendants are States, State officials, or other governmental entities against whom the district court may be foreclosed from ordering relief; or
(B) the number of members of all proposed plaintiff classes in the aggregate is less than 100.

(6) In any class action, the claims of the individual class members shall be aggregated to determine whether the matter in controversy exceeds the sum or value of $5,000,000, exclusive of interest and costs.

(7) Citizenship of the members of the proposed plaintiff classes shall be determined for purposes of paragraphs (2) through (6) as of the date of filing of the complaint or amended complaint, or, if the case stated by the initial pleading is not subject to Federal jurisdiction, as of the date of service by plaintiffs of an amended pleading, motion, or other paper, indicating the existence of Federal jurisdiction.

(8) This subsection shall apply to any class action before or after the entry of a class certification order by the court with respect to that action.

(9) Paragraph (2) shall not apply to any class action that solely involves a claim—
(A) concerning a covered security as defined under 16(f)(3) [1] of the Securities Act of 1933 (15 U.S.C. 78p(f)(3) [2]) and section 28(f)(5)(E) of the Securities Exchange Act of 1934 (15 U.S.C. 78bb(f)(5)(E));
(B) that relates to the internal affairs or governance of a corporation or other form of business enterprise and that arises under or by virtue of the laws of the State in which such corporation or business enterprise is incorporated or organized; or
(C) that relates to the rights, duties (including fiduciary duties), and obligations relating to or created by or pursuant to any security (as defined under section 2(a)(1) of the Securities Act of 1933 (15 U.S.C. 77b(a)(1)) and the regulations issued thereunder).

(10) For purposes of this subsection and section 1453, an unincorporated association shall be deemed to be a citizen of the State where it has its principal place of business and the State under whose laws it is organized.

(11)
(A) For purposes of this subsection and section 1453, a mass action shall be deemed to be a class action removable under paragraphs (2) through (10) if it otherwise meets the provisions of those paragraphs.
(B)
(i) As used in subparagraph (A), the term "mass action" means any civil action (except a civil action within the scope of

section 1711(2)) in which monetary relief claims of 100 or more persons are proposed to be tried jointly on the ground that the plaintiffs' claims involve common questions of law or fact, except that jurisdiction shall exist only over those plaintiffs whose claims in a mass action satisfy the jurisdictional amount requirements under subsection (a).

(ii) As used in subparagraph (A), the term "mass action" shall not include any civil action in which—

(I) all of the claims in the action arise from an event or occurrence in the State in which the action was filed, and that allegedly resulted in injuries in that State or in States contiguous to that State;

(II) the claims are joined upon motion of a defendant;

(III) all of the claims in the action are asserted on behalf of the general public (and not on behalf of individual claimants or members of a purported class) pursuant to a State statute specifically authorizing such action; or

(IV) the claims have been consolidated or coordinated solely for pretrial proceedings.

(C)

(i) Any action(s) removed to Federal court pursuant to this subsection shall not thereafter be transferred to any other court pursuant to section 1407, or the rules promulgated thereunder, unless a majority of the plaintiffs in the action request transfer pursuant to section 1407.

(ii) This subparagraph will not apply—

(I) to cases certified pursuant to rule 23 of the Federal Rules of Civil Procedure; or

(II) if plaintiffs propose that the action proceed as a class action pursuant to rule 23 of the Federal Rules of Civil Procedure.

(D) The limitations periods on any claims asserted in a mass action that is removed to Federal court pursuant to this subsection shall be deemed tolled during the period that the action is pending in Federal court.

(e) The word "States", as used in this section, includes the Territories, the District of Columbia, and the Commonwealth of Puerto Rico.

§1333. Admiralty, maritime and prize cases

The district courts shall have original jurisdiction, exclusive of the courts of the States, of:

(1) Any civil case of admiralty or maritime jurisdiction, saving to suitors in all cases all other remedies to which they are otherwise entitled.

(2) Any prize brought into the United States and all proceedings for the condemnation of property taken as prize.

§1334. Bankruptcy cases and proceedings

(a) Except as provided in subsection (b) of this section, the district courts shall have original and exclusive jurisdiction of all cases under title 11.

(b) Except as provided in subsection (e)(2), and notwithstanding any Act of Congress that confers exclusive jurisdiction on a court or courts other than the district courts, the district courts shall have original but not exclusive jurisdiction of all civil proceedings arising under title 11, or arising in or related to cases under title 11.

(c)

(1) Except with respect to a case under chapter 15 of title 11, nothing in this section prevents a district court in the interest of justice, or in the interest of comity with State courts or respect for State law, from abstaining from hearing a particular proceeding arising under title 11 or arising in or related to a case under title 11.

(2) Upon timely motion of a party in a proceeding based upon a State law claim or State law cause of action, related to a case under title 11 but not arising under title 11 or arising in a case under title 11, with respect to which an action could not have been commenced in a court of the United States absent jurisdiction under this section, the district court shall abstain from hearing such proceeding if an action is commenced, and can be timely adjudicated, in a State forum of appropriate jurisdiction.

(d) Any decision to abstain or not to abstain made under subsection (c) (other than a decision not to abstain in a proceeding described in subsection (c)(2)) is not reviewable by appeal or otherwise by the court of appeals under section 158(d), 1291, or 1292 of this title or by the Supreme Court of the United States under section 1254 of this title. Subsection (c) and this subsection shall not be construed to limit the applicability of the stay provided for by section 362 of title 11, United States Code, as such section applies to an action affecting the property of the estate in bankruptcy.

(e) The district court in which a case under title 11 is commenced or is pending shall have exclusive jurisdiction—

(1) of all the property, wherever located, of the debtor as of the commencement of such case, and of property of the estate; and

(2) over all claims or causes of action that involve construction of section 327 of title 11, United States

Code, or rules relating to disclosure requirements under section 327.

§1335. Interpleader

(a) The district courts shall have original jurisdiction of any civil action of interpleader or in the nature of interpleader filed by any person, firm, or corporation, association, or society having in his or its custody or possession money or property of the value of $500 or more, or having issued a note, bond, certificate, policy of insurance, or other instrument of value or amount of $500 or more, or providing for the delivery or payment or the loan of money or property of such amount or value, or being under any obligation written or unwritten to the amount of $500 or more, if
 (1) Two or more adverse claimants, of diverse citizenship as defined in subsection (a) or (d) of section 1332 of this title, are claiming or may claim to be entitled to such money or property, or to any one or more of the benefits arising by virtue of any note, bond, certificate, policy or other instrument, or arising by virtue of any such obligation; and if
 (2) the plaintiff has deposited such money or property or has paid the amount of or the loan or other value of such instrument or the amount due under such obligation into the registry of the court, there to abide the judgment of the court, or has given bond payable to the clerk of the court in such amount and with such surety as the court or judge may deem proper, conditioned upon the compliance by the plaintiff with the future order or judgment of the court with respect to the subject matter of the controversy.

(b) Such an action may be entertained although the titles or claims of the conflicting claimants do not have a common origin, or are not identical, but are adverse to and independent of one another.

§1336. Surface Transportation Board's orders

(a) Except as otherwise provided by Act of Congress, the district courts shall have jurisdiction of any civil action to enforce, in whole or in part, any order of the Surface Transportation Board, and to enjoin or suspend, in whole or in part, any order of the Surface Transportation Board for the payment of money or the collection of fines, penalties, and forfeitures.

(b) When a district court or the United States Court of Federal Claims refers a question or issue to the Surface Transportation Board for determination, the court which referred the question or issue shall have exclusive jurisdiction of a civil action to enforce, enjoin, set aside, annul, or suspend, in whole or in part, any order of the Surface Transportation Board arising out of such referral.

(c) Any action brought under subsection (b) of this section shall be filed within 90 days from the date that the order of the Surface Transportation Board becomes final.

§1337. Commerce and antitrust regulations; amount in controversy, costs

(a) The district courts shall have original jurisdiction of any civil action or proceeding arising under any Act of Congress regulating commerce or protecting trade and commerce against restraints and monopolies: *Provided, however*, That the district courts shall have original jurisdiction of an action brought under section 11706 or 14706 of title 49, only if the matter in controversy for each receipt or bill of lading exceeds $10,000, exclusive of interest and costs.

(b) Except when express provision therefor is otherwise made in a statute of the United States, where a plaintiff who files the case under section 11706 or 14706 of title 49, originally in the Federal courts is finally adjudged to be entitled to recover less than the sum or value of $10,000, computed without regard to any setoff or counterclaim to which the defendant may be adjudged to be entitled, and exclusive of any interest and costs, the district court may deny costs to the plaintiff and, in addition, may impose costs on the plaintiff.

(c) The district courts shall not have jurisdiction under this section of any matter within the exclusive jurisdiction of the Court of International Trade under chapter 95 of this title.

§1338. Patents, plant variety protection, copyrights, mask works, designs, trademarks, and unfair competition

(a) The district courts shall have original jurisdiction of any civil action arising under any Act of Congress relating to patents, plant variety protection, copyrights and trademarks. No State court shall have jurisdiction over any claim for relief arising under any Act of Congress relating to patents, plant variety protection, or copyrights. For purposes of this subsection, the term "State" includes any State of the United States, the District of Columbia, the Commonwealth of Puerto Rico, the United States Virgin Islands, American Samoa, Guam, and the Northern Mariana Islands.

(b) The district courts shall have original jurisdiction of any civil action asserting a claim of unfair competition when joined with a substantial and related claim under the copyright, patent, plant variety protection or trademark laws.

(c) Subsections (a) and (b) apply to exclusive rights in mask works under chapter 9 of title 17, and to exclusive rights in designs under chapter 13 of title 17, to the same extent as such subsections apply to copyrights.

§1339. Postal matters

The district courts shall have original jurisdiction of any civil action arising under any Act of Congress relating to the postal service.

§1340. Internal revenue; customs duties

The district courts shall have original jurisdiction of any civil action arising under any Act of Congress providing for internal revenue, or revenue from imports or tonnage except matters within the jurisdiction of the Court of International Trade.

§1341. Taxes by States

The district courts shall not enjoin, suspend or restrain the assessment, levy or collection of any tax under State law where a plain, speedy and efficient remedy may be had in the courts of such State.

§1342. Rate orders of State agencies

The district courts shall not enjoin, suspend or restrain the operation of, or compliance with, any order affecting rates chargeable by a public utility and made by a State administrative agency or a rate-making body of a State political subdivision, where:

(1) Jurisdiction is based solely on diversity of citizenship or repugnance of the order to the Federal Constitution; and,
(2) The order does not interfere with interstate commerce; and,
(3) The order has been made after reasonable notice and hearing; and,
(4) A plain, speedy and efficient remedy may be had in the courts of such State.

§1343. Civil rights and elective franchise

(a) The district courts shall have original jurisdiction of any civil action authorized by law to be commenced by any person:
   (1) To recover damages for injury to his person or property, or because of the deprivation of any right or privilege of a citizen of the United States, by any act done in furtherance of any conspiracy mentioned in section 1985 of Title 42;
   (2) To recover damages from any person who fails to prevent or to aid in preventing any wrongs mentioned in section 1985 of Title 42 which he had knowledge were about to occur and power to prevent;
   (3) To redress the deprivation, under color of any State law, statute, ordinance, regulation, custom or usage, of any right, privilege or immunity secured by the Constitution of the United States or by any Act of Congress providing for equal rights of citizens or of all persons within the jurisdiction of the United States;
   (4) To recover damages or to secure equitable or other relief under any Act of Congress providing for the protection of civil rights, including the right to vote.
(b) For purposes of this section—
   (1) the District of Columbia shall be considered to be a State; and
   (2) any Act of Congress applicable exclusively to the District of Columbia shall be considered to be a statute of the District of Columbia.

§1344. Election disputes

The district courts shall have original jurisdiction of any civil action to recover possession of any office, except that of elector of President or Vice President, United States Senator, Representative in or delegate to Congress, or member of a state legislature, authorized by law to be commenced, where in it appears that the sole question touching the title to office arises out of denial of the right to vote, to any citizen offering to vote, on account of race, color or previous condition of servitude.

The jurisdiction under this section shall extend only so far as to determine the rights of the parties to office by reason of the denial of the right, guaranteed by the Constitution of the United States and secured by any law, to enforce the right of citizens of the United States to vote in all the States.

§1345. United States as plaintiff

Except as otherwise provided by Act of Congress, the district courts shall have original jurisdiction of all civil actions, suits or proceedings commenced by the United States, or by any agency or officer thereof expressly authorized to sue by Act of Congress.

§1346. United States as defendant

(a) The district courts shall have original jurisdiction, concurrent with the United States Court of Federal Claims, of:
   (1) Any civil action against the United States for the recovery of any internal-revenue tax alleged to have been erroneously or illegally assessed or collected, or any penalty claimed to have been collected without authority or any sum alleged to have been excessive or in any manner wrongfully collected under the internal-revenue laws;
   (2) Any other civil action or claim against the United States, not exceeding $10,000 in amount, founded either upon the Constitution, or any Act of Congress, or any regulation of an executive department, or upon any express or implied contract with the United States, or for liquidated or unliquidated damages in cases not sounding in tort, except that the district courts shall not have jurisdiction of any civil action or claim against the United States founded upon any express or implied contract with the United States or for liquidated or unliquidated damages in cases not sounding in tort which are subject to sections 7104(b)(1) and 7107(a)(1) of title 41. For the purpose of this paragraph, an express or implied contract with the Army and Air Force Exchange Service, Navy Exchanges, Marine Corps Exchanges, Coast Guard Exchanges, or Exchange Councils of the National

Aeronautics and Space Administration shall be considered an express or implied contract with the United States.

(b)

(1) Subject to the provisions of chapter 171 of this title, the district courts, together with the United States District Court for the District of the Canal Zone and the District Court of the Virgin Islands, shall have exclusive jurisdiction of civil actions on claims against the United States, for money damages, accruing on and after January 1, 1945, for injury or loss of property, or personal injury or death caused by the negligent or wrongful act or omission of any employee of the Government while acting within the scope of his office or employment, under circumstances where the United States, if a private person, would be liable to the claimant in accordance with the law of the place where the act or omission occurred.

(2) No person convicted of a felony who is incarcerated while awaiting sentencing or while serving a sentence may bring a civil action against the United States or an agency, officer, or employee of the Government, for mental or emotional injury suffered while in custody without a prior showing of physical injury.

(c) The jurisdiction conferred by this section includes jurisdiction of any set-off, counterclaim, or other claim or demand whatever on the part of the United States against any plaintiff commencing an action under this section.

(d) The district courts shall not have jurisdiction under this section of any civil action or claim for a pension.

(e) The district courts shall have original jurisdiction of any civil action against the United States provided in section 6226, 6228(a), 7426, or 7428 (in the case of the United States district court for the District of Columbia) or section 7429 of the Internal Revenue Code of 1986.

(f) The district courts shall have exclusive original jurisdiction of civil actions under section 2409a to quiet title to an estate or interest in real property in which an interest is claimed by the United States.

(g) Subject to the provisions of chapter 179, the district courts of the United States shall have exclusive jurisdiction over any civil action commenced under section 453(2) of title 3, by a covered employee under chapter 5 of such title.

§1347. Partition action where United States is joint tenant

The district courts shall have original jurisdiction of any civil action commenced by any tenant in common or joint tenant for the partition of lands where the United States is one of the tenants in common or joint tenants.

§1348. Banking association as party

The district courts shall have original jurisdiction of any civil action commenced by the United States, or by direction of any officer thereof, against any national banking association, any civil action to wind up the affairs of any such association, and any action by a banking association established in the district for which the court is held, under chapter 2 of Title 12, to enjoin the Comptroller of the Currency, or any receiver acting under his direction, as provided by such chapter.

All national banking associations shall, for the purposes of all other actions by or against them, be deemed citizens of the States in which they are respectively located.

§1349. Corporation organized under federal law as party

The district courts shall not have jurisdiction of any civil action by or against any corporation upon the ground that it was incorporated by or under an Act of Congress, unless the United States is the owner of more than one-half of its capital stock.

§1350. Alien's action for tort

The district courts shall have original jurisdiction of any civil action by an alien for a tort only, committed in violation of the law of nations or a treaty of the United States.

§1351. Consuls, vice consuls, and members of a diplomatic mission as defendant

The district courts shall have original jurisdiction, exclusive of the courts of the States, of all civil actions and proceedings against—

(1) consuls or vice consuls of foreign states; or

(2) members of a mission or members of their families (as such terms are defined in section 2 of the Diplomatic Relations Act).

§1352. Bonds executed under federal law

The district courts shall have original jurisdiction, concurrent with State courts, of any action on a bond executed under any law of the United States, except matters within the jurisdiction of the Court of International Trade under section 1582 of this title.

§1353. Indian allotments

The district courts shall have original jurisdiction of any civil action involving the right of any person, in whole or in part of Indian blood or descent, to any allotment of land under any Act of Congress or treaty.

The judgment in favor of any claimant to an allotment of land shall have the same effect, when properly certified to the Secretary of the Interior, as if such allotment had been allowed and approved by him; but this provision shall not apply to any lands held on or before December 21, 1911, by either of the Five Civilized Tribes, the Osage Nation of Indians, nor to any of the lands within the Quapaw Indian Agency.

§1354. Land grants from different states

The district courts shall have original jurisdiction of actions between citizens of the same state claiming lands under grants from different states.

§1355. Fine, penalty or forfeiture

(a) The district courts shall have original jurisdiction, exclusive of the courts of the States, of any action or proceeding for the recovery or enforcement of any fine, penalty, or forfeiture, pecuniary or otherwise, incurred under any Act of Congress, except matters within the jurisdiction of the Court of International Trade under section 1582 of this title.

(b)
- (1) A forfeiture action or proceeding may be brought in—
  - (A) the district court for the district in which any of the acts or omissions giving rise to the forfeiture occurred, or
  - (B) any other district where venue for the forfeiture action or proceeding is specifically provided for in section 1395 of this title or any other statute.
- (2) Whenever property subject to forfeiture under the laws of the United States is located in a foreign country, or has been detained or seized pursuant to legal process or competent authority of a foreign government, an action or proceeding for forfeiture may be brought as provided in paragraph (1), or in the United States District court [1] for the District of Columbia.

(c) In any case in which a final order disposing of property in a civil forfeiture action or proceeding is appealed, removal of the property by the prevailing party shall not deprive the court of jurisdiction. Upon motion of the appealing party, the district court or the court of appeals shall issue any order necessary to preserve the right of the appealing party to the full value of the property at issue, including a stay of the judgment of the district court pending appeal or requiring the prevailing party to post an appeal bond.

(d) Any court with jurisdiction over a forfeiture action pursuant to subsection (b) may issue and cause to be served in any other district such process as may be required to bring before the court the property that is the subject of the forfeiture action.

§1356. Seizures not within admiralty and maritime jurisdiction

The district courts shall have original jurisdiction, exclusive of the courts of the States, of any seizure under any law of the United States on land or upon waters not within admiralty and maritime jurisdiction, except matters within the jurisdiction of the Court of International Trade under section 1582 of this title.

§1357. Injuries under Federal laws

The district courts shall have original jurisdiction of any civil action commenced by any person to recover damages for any injury to his person or property on account of any act done by him, under any Act of Congress, for the protection or collection of any of the revenues, or to enforce the right of citizens of the United States to vote in any State.

§1358. Eminent domain

The district courts shall have original jurisdiction of all proceedings to condemn real estate for the use of the United States or its departments or agencies.

§1359. Parties collusively joined or made

A district court shall not have jurisdiction of a civil action in which any party, by assignment or otherwise, has been improperly or collusively made or joined to invoke the jurisdiction of such court.

§1360. State civil jurisdiction in actions to which Indians are parties

(a) Each of the States listed in the following table shall have jurisdiction over civil causes of action between Indians or to which Indians are parties which arise in the areas of Indian country listed opposite the name of the State to the same extent that such State has jurisdiction over other civil causes of action, and those civil laws of such State that are of general application to private persons or private property shall have the same force and effect within such Indian country as they have elsewhere within the State:

State of	Indian country affected
Alaska	All Indian country within the State.
California	All Indian country within the State.
Minnesota	All Indian country within the State, except the Red Lake Reservation.
Nebraska	All Indian country within the State.
Oregon	All Indian country within the State, except the Warm Springs Reservation.
Wisconsin	All Indian country within the State.

(b) Nothing in this section shall authorize the alienation, encumbrance, or taxation of any real or personal property, including water rights, belonging to any Indian or any Indian tribe, band, or community that is held in trust by the United States or is subject to a restriction against alienation imposed by the United States; or shall authorize regulation of the use of such property in a manner inconsistent with any Federal treaty, agreement, or statute or with any regulation made pursuant thereto; or shall confer jurisdiction upon the State to adjudicate, in probate proceedings or otherwise, the ownership or right to possession of such property or any interest therein.

(c) Any tribal ordinance or custom heretofore or hereafter adopted by an Indian tribe, band, or community in the exercise of any authority which it may possess shall, if not inconsistent with any applicable civil law of the State, be given full force and effect in the determination of civil causes of action pursuant to this section.

§1361. Action to compel an officer of the United States to perform his duty

The district courts shall have original jurisdiction of any action in the nature of mandamus to compel an officer or employee of the United States or any agency thereof to perform a duty owed to the plaintiff.

§1362. Indian tribes

The district courts shall have original jurisdiction of all civil actions, brought by any Indian tribe or band with a governing body duly recognized by the Secretary of the Interior, wherein the matter in controversy arises under the Constitution, laws, or treaties of the United States.

§1363. Jurors' employment rights

The district courts shall have original jurisdiction of any civil action brought for the protection of jurors' employment under section 1875 of this title.

§1364. Direct actions against insurers of members of diplomatic missions and their families

(a) The district courts shall have original and exclusive jurisdiction, without regard to the amount in controversy, of any civil action commenced by any person against an insurer who by contract has insured an individual, who is, or was at the time of the tortious act or omission, a member of a mission (within the meaning of section 2(3) of the Diplomatic Relations Act (22 U.S.C. 254a(3))) or a member of the family of such a member of a mission, or an individual described in section 19 of the Convention on Privileges and Immunities of the United Nations of February 13, 1946, against liability for personal injury, death, or damage to property.

(b) Any direct action brought against an insurer under subsection (a) shall be tried without a jury, but shall not be subject to the defense that the insured is immune from suit, that the insured is an indispensable party, or in the absence of fraud or collusion, that the insured has violated a term of the contract, unless the contract was cancelled before the claim arose.

§1365. Senate actions

(a) The United States District Court for the District of Columbia shall have original jurisdiction, without regard to the amount in controversy, over any civil action brought by the Senate or any authorized committee or subcommittee of the Senate to enforce, to secure a declaratory judgment concerning the validity of, or to prevent a threatened refusal or failure to comply with, any subpena or order issued by the Senate or committee or subcommittee of the Senate to any entity acting or purporting to act under color or authority of State law or to any natural person to secure the production of documents or other materials of any kind or the answering of any deposition or interrogatory or to secure testimony or any combination thereof. This section shall not apply to an action to enforce, to secure a declaratory judgment concerning the validity of, or to prevent a threatened refusal to comply with, any subpena or order issued to an officer or employee of the executive branch of the Federal Government acting within his or her official capacity, except that this section shall apply if the refusal to comply is based on the assertion of a personal privilege or objection and is not based on a governmental privilege or objection the assertion of which has been authorized by the executive branch of the Federal Government.

(b) Upon application by the Senate or any authorized committee or subcommittee of the Senate, the district court shall issue an order to an entity or person refusing, or failing to comply with, or threatening to refuse or not to comply with, a subpena or order of the Senate or committee or subcommittee of the Senate requiring such entity or person to comply forthwith. Any refusal or failure to obey a lawful order of the district court issued pursuant to this section may be held by such court to be a contempt thereof. A contempt proceeding shall be commenced by an order to show cause before the court why the entity or person refusing or failing to obey the court order should not be held in contempt of court. Such contempt proceeding shall be tried by the court and shall be summary in manner. The purpose of sanctions imposed as a result of such contempt proceeding shall be to compel obedience to the order of the court. Process in any such action or contempt proceeding may be served in any judicial district wherein the entity or party refusing, or failing to comply, or threatening to refuse or not to comply, resides, transacts business, or may be found, and subpenas for witnesses who are required to attend such proceeding may run into any other district. Nothing in this section shall confer upon such court jurisdiction to affect by injunction or otherwise the issuance or effect of any subpena or order of the Senate or any committee or subcommittee of the Senate or to review, modify, suspend, terminate, or set aside any such subpena or order. An action, contempt proceeding, or sanction brought or imposed pursuant to this section shall not abate upon adjournment sine die by the Senate at the end of a Congress if the Senate or the committee or subcommittee of the Senate which issued the subpena or order certifies to the court that it maintains its interest in securing the documents, answers, or testimony during such adjournment.

(c) [(c) Repealed. Pub. L. 98–620, title IV, §402(29)(D), Nov. 8, 1984, 98 Stat. 3359.]

(d) The Senate or any committee or subcommittee of the Senate commencing and prosecuting a civil action or contempt proceeding under this section may be represented in such action by such attorneys as the Senate may designate.

(e) A civil action commenced or prosecuted under this section, may not be authorized pursuant to the Standing Order of the Senate "authorizing suits by Senate Committees" (S. Jour. 572, May 28, 1928).

(f) For the purposes of this section the term "committee" includes standing, select, or special committees of the Senate established by law or resolution.

§1366. Construction of references to laws of the United States or Acts of Congress

For the purposes of this chapter, references to laws of the United States or Acts of Congress do not include laws applicable exclusively to the District of Columbia.

§1367. Supplemental jurisdiction

(a) Except as provided in subsections (b) and (c) or as expressly provided otherwise by Federal statute, in any civil action of which the district courts have original jurisdiction, the district courts shall have supplemental jurisdiction over all other claims that are so related to claims in the action within such original jurisdiction that they form part of the same case or controversy under Article III of the United States Constitution. Such supplemental jurisdiction shall include claims that involve the joinder or intervention of additional parties.

(b) In any civil action of which the district courts have original jurisdiction founded solely on section 1332 of this title, the district courts shall not have supplemental jurisdiction under subsection (a) over claims by plaintiffs against persons made parties under Rule 14, 19, 20, or 24 of the Federal Rules of Civil Procedure, or over claims by persons proposed to be joined as plaintiffs under Rule 19 of such rules, or seeking to intervene as plaintiffs under Rule 24 of such rules, when exercising supplemental jurisdiction over such claims would be inconsistent with the jurisdictional requirements of section 1332.

(c) The district courts may decline to exercise supplemental jurisdiction over a claim under subsection (a) if—

(1) the claim raises a novel or complex issue of State law,

(2) the claim substantially predominates over the claim or claims over which the district court has original jurisdiction,

(3) the district court has dismissed all claims over which it has original jurisdiction, or

(4) in exceptional circumstances, there are other compelling reasons for declining jurisdiction.

(d) The period of limitations for any claim asserted under subsection (a), and for any other claim in the same action that is voluntarily dismissed at the same time as or after the dismissal of the claim under subsection (a), shall be tolled while the claim is pending and for a period of 30 days after it is dismissed unless State law provides for a longer tolling period.

(e) As used in this section, the term "State" includes the District of Columbia, the Commonwealth of Puerto Rico, and any territory or possession of the United States.

§1368. Counterclaims in unfair practices in international trade.

The district courts shall have original jurisdiction of any civil action based on a counterclaim raised pursuant to section 337(c) of the Tariff Act of 1930, to the extent that it arises out of the transaction or occurrence that is the subject matter of the opposing party's claim in the proceeding under section 337(a) of that Act.

§1369. Multiparty, multiforum jurisdiction

(a) In General.—The district courts shall have original jurisdiction of any civil action involving minimal diversity between adverse parties that arises from a single accident, where at least 75 natural persons have died in the accident at a discrete location, if—

(1) a defendant resides in a State and a substantial part of the accident took place in another State or other location, regardless of whether that defendant is also a resident of the State where a substantial part of the accident took place;

(2) any two defendants reside in different States, regardless of whether such defendants are also residents of the same State or States; or

(3) substantial parts of the accident took place in different States.

(b) Limitation of Jurisdiction of District Courts.—The district court shall abstain from hearing any civil action described in subsection (a) in which—

(1) the substantial majority of all plaintiffs are citizens of a single State of which the primary defendants are also citizens; and

(2) the claims asserted will be governed primarily by the laws of that State.

(c) Special Rules and Definitions.—For purposes of this section—

(1) minimal diversity exists between adverse parties if any party is a citizen of a State and any adverse party is a citizen of another State, a citizen or subject of a foreign state, or a foreign state as defined in section 1603(a) of this title;

(2) a corporation is deemed to be a citizen of any State, and a citizen or subject of any foreign state, in which it is incorporated or has its principal place of business, and is deemed to be a resident of any

State in which it is incorporated or licensed to do business or is doing business;

(3) the term "injury" means—

(A) physical harm to a natural person; and

(B) physical damage to or destruction of tangible property, but only if physical harm described in subparagraph (A) exists;

(4) the term "accident" means a sudden accident, or a natural event culminating in an accident, that results in death incurred at a discrete location by at least 75 natural persons; and

(5) the term "State" includes the District of Columbia, the Commonwealth of Puerto Rico, and any territory or possession of the United States.

(d) Intervening Parties.—In any action in a district court which is or could have been brought, in whole or in part, under this section, any person with a claim arising from the accident described in subsection (a) shall be permitted to intervene as a party plaintiff in the action, even if that person could not have brought an action in a district court as an original matter.

(e) Notification of Judicial Panel on Multidistrict Litigation.—A district court in which an action under this section is pending shall promptly notify the judicial panel on multidistrict litigation of the pendency of the action.

28 USC Chapter 87
District Courts; Venue

§1390. Scope

(a) Venue Defined.—As used in this chapter, the term "venue" refers to the geographic specification of the proper court or courts for the litigation of a civil action that is within the subject-matter jurisdiction of the district courts in general, and does not refer to any grant or restriction of subject-matter jurisdiction providing for a civil action to be adjudicated only by the district court for a particular district or districts.
(b) Exclusion of Certain Cases.—Except as otherwise provided by law, this chapter shall not govern the venue of a civil action in which the district court exercises the jurisdiction conferred by section 1333, except that such civil actions may be transferred between district courts as provided in this chapter.
(c) Clarification Regarding Cases Removed From State Courts.—This chapter shall not determine the district court to which a civil action pending in a State court may be removed, but shall govern the transfer of an action so removed as between districts and divisions of the United States district courts.

§1391. Venue generally

(a) Applicability of Section.—Except as otherwise provided by law—
  (1) this section shall govern the venue of all civil actions brought in district courts of the United States; and
  (2) the proper venue for a civil action shall be determined without regard to whether the action is local or transitory in nature.
(b) Venue in General.—A civil action may be brought in—
  (1) a judicial district in which any defendant resides, if all defendants are residents of the State in which the district is located;
  (2) a judicial district in which a substantial part of the events or omissions giving rise to the claim occurred, or a substantial part of property that is the subject of the action is situated; or
  (3) if there is no district in which an action may otherwise be brought as provided in this section, any judicial district in which any defendant is subject to the court's personal jurisdiction with respect to such action.
(c) Residency.—For all venue purposes—
  (1) a natural person, including an alien lawfully admitted for permanent residence in the United States, shall be deemed to reside in the judicial district in which that person is domiciled;
  (2) an entity with the capacity to sue and be sued in its common name under applicable law, whether or not incorporated, shall be deemed to reside, if a defendant, in any judicial district in which such defendant is subject to the court's personal jurisdiction with respect to the civil action in question and, if a plaintiff, only in the judicial district in which it maintains its principal place of business; and
  (3) a defendant not resident in the United States may be sued in any judicial district, and the joinder of such a defendant shall be disregarded in determining where the action may be brought with respect to other defendants.
(d) Residency of Corporations in States With Multiple Districts.—For purposes of venue under this chapter, in a State which has more than one judicial district and in which a defendant that is a corporation is subject to personal jurisdiction at the time an action is commenced, such corporation shall be deemed to reside in any district in that State within which its contacts would be sufficient to subject it to personal jurisdiction if that district were a separate State, and, if there is no such district, the corporation shall be deemed to reside in the district within which it has the most significant contacts.
(e) Actions Where Defendant Is Officer or Employee of the United States.—
  (1) In general.—A civil action in which a defendant is an officer or employee of the United States or any agency thereof acting in his official capacity or under color of legal authority, or an agency of the United States, or the United States, may, except as otherwise provided by law, be brought in any judicial district in which (A) a defendant in the action resides, (B) a substantial part of the events or omissions giving rise to the claim occurred, or a substantial part of property that is the subject of the action is situated, or (C) the plaintiff resides if no real property is involved in the action. Additional persons may be joined as parties to any such action in accordance with the Federal Rules of Civil Procedure and with such other venue requirements as would be applicable if the United States or one of its officers, employees, or agencies were not a party.
  (2) Service.—The summons and complaint in such an action shall be served as provided by the Federal Rules of Civil Procedure except that the delivery of the summons and complaint to the officer or agency as required by the rules may be made by certified mail beyond the territorial limits of the district in which the action is brought.
(f) Civil Actions Against a Foreign State.—A civil action against a foreign state as defined in section 1603(a) of this title may be brought—
  (1) in any judicial district in which a substantial part of the events or omissions giving rise to the claim occurred, or a substantial part of property that is the subject of the action is situated;
  (2) in any judicial district in which the vessel or cargo of a foreign state is situated, if the claim is asserted under section 1605(b) of this title;
  (3) in any judicial district in which the agency or instrumentality is licensed to do business or is doing business, if the action is brought against an agency or instrumentality of a foreign state as defined in section 1603(b) of this title; or

(4) in the United States District Court for the District of Columbia if the action is brought against a foreign state or political subdivision thereof.

(g) Multiparty, Multiforum Litigation.—A civil action in which jurisdiction of the district court is based upon section 1369 of this title may be brought in any district in which any defendant resides or in which a substantial part of the accident giving rise to the action took place.

§1394. Banking association's action against Comptroller of Currency

Any civil action by a national banking association to enjoin the Comptroller of the Currency, under the provisions of any Act of Congress relating to such associations, may be prosecuted in the judicial district where such association is located.

§1395. Fine, penalty or forfeiture

(a) A civil proceeding for the recovery of a pecuniary fine, penalty or forfeiture may be prosecuted in the district where it accrues or the defendant is found.

(b) A civil proceeding for the forfeiture of property may be prosecuted in any district where such property is found.

(c) A civil proceeding for the forfeiture of property seized outside any judicial district may be prosecuted in any district into which the property is brought.

(d) A proceeding in admiralty for the enforcement of fines, penalties and forfeitures against a vessel may be brought in any district in which the vessel is arrested.

(e) Any proceeding for the forfeiture of a vessel or cargo entering a port of entry closed by the President in pursuance of law, or of goods and chattels coming from a State or section declared by proclamation of the President to be in insurrection, or of any vessel or vehicle conveying persons or property to or from such State or section or belonging in whole or in part to a resident thereof, may be prosecuted in any district into which the property is taken and in which the proceeding is instituted.

§1396. Internal revenue taxes

Any civil action for the collection of internal revenue taxes may be brought in the district where the liability for such tax accrues, in the district of the taxpayer's residence, or in the district where the return was filed.

§1397. Interpleader

Any civil action of interpleader or in the nature of interpleader under section 1335 of this title may be brought in the judicial district in which one or more of the claimants reside.

§1398. Interstate Commerce Commission's orders

(a) Except as otherwise provided by law, a civil action brought under section 1336(a) of this title shall be brought only in a judicial district in which any of the parties bringing the action resides or has its principal office.

(b) A civil action to enforce, enjoin, set aside, annul, or suspend, in whole or in part, an order of the Interstate Commerce Commission made pursuant to the referral of a question or issue by a district court or by the United States Court of Federal Claims, shall be brought only in the court which referred the question or issue.

§1399. Partition action involving United States

Any civil action by any tenant in common or joint tenant for the partition of lands, where the United States is one of the tenants in common or joint tenants, may be brought only in the judicial district where such lands are located or, if located in different districts in the same State, in any of such districts.

§1400. Patents and copyrights, mask works, and designs

(a) Civil actions, suits, or proceedings arising under any Act of Congress relating to copyrights or exclusive rights in mask works or designs may be instituted in the district in which the defendant or his agent resides or may be found.

(b) Any civil action for patent infringement may be brought in the judicial district where the defendant resides, or where the defendant has committed acts of infringement and has a regular and established place of business.

§1401. Stockholder's derivative action

Any civil action by a stockholder on behalf of his corporation may be prosecuted in any judicial district where the corporation might have sued the same defendants.

§1402. United States as defendant

(a) Any civil action in a district court against the United States under subsection (a) of section 1346 of this title may be prosecuted only:

   (1) Except as provided in paragraph (2), in the judicial district where the plaintiff resides;

   (2) In the case of a civil action by a corporation under paragraph (1) of subsection (a) of section 1346, in the judicial district in which is located the principal place of business or principal office or agency of the corporation; or if it has no principal place of business or principal office or agency in any judicial district (A) in the judicial district in which is located the office to which was made the return of the tax in respect of which the claim is made, or (B) if no return was made, in the judicial district in which lies the District of Columbia. Notwithstanding the foregoing provisions of this paragraph a district court, for the convenience of the parties and witnesses, in the interest of justice, may transfer any such action to any other district or division.

(b) Any civil action on a tort claim against the United States under subsection (b) of section 1346 of this title may be prosecuted only in the judicial district where the plaintiff resides or wherein the act or omission complained of occurred.

(c) Any civil action against the United States under subsection (e) of section 1346 of this title may be prosecuted only in the judicial district where the property is situated at the time of levy, or if no levy is made, in the judicial district in which the event occurred which gave rise to the cause of action.

(d) Any civil action under section 2409a to quiet title to an estate or interest in real property in which an interest is claimed by the United States shall be brought in the district court of the district where the property is located or, if located in different districts, in any of such districts.

§1403. Eminent domain

Proceedings to condemn real estate for the use of the United States or its departments or agencies shall be brought in the district court of the district where the land is located or, if located in different districts in the same State, in any of such districts.

§1404. Change of venue

(a) For the convenience of parties and witnesses, in the interest of justice, a district court may transfer any civil action to any other district or division where it might have been brought or to any district or division to which all parties have consented.

(b) Upon motion, consent or stipulation of all parties, any action, suit or proceeding of a civil nature or any motion or hearing thereof, may be transferred, in the discretion of the court, from the division in which pending to any other division in the same district. Transfer of proceedings in rem brought by or on behalf of the United States may be transferred under this section without the consent of the United States where all other parties request transfer.

(c) A district court may order any civil action to be tried at any place within the division in which it is pending.

(d) Transfers from a district court of the United States to the District Court of Guam, the District Court for the Northern Mariana Islands, or the District Court of the Virgin Islands shall not be permitted under this section. As otherwise used in this section, the term "district court" includes the District Court of Guam, the District Court for the Northern Mariana Islands, and the District Court of the Virgin Islands, and the term "district" includes the territorial jurisdiction of each such court.

§1405. Creation or alteration of district or division

Actions or proceedings pending at the time of the creation of a new district or division or transfer of a county or territory from one division or district to another may be tried in the district or division as it existed at the institution of the action or proceeding, or in the district or division so created or to which the county or territory is so transferred as the parties shall agree or the court direct.

§1406. Cure or waiver of defects

(a) The district court of a district in which is filed a case laying venue in the wrong division or district shall dismiss, or if it be in the interest of justice, transfer such case to any district or division in which it could have been brought.

(b) Nothing in this chapter shall impair the jurisdiction of a district court of any matter involving a party who does not interpose timely and sufficient objection to the venue.

(c) As used in this section, the term "district court" includes the District Court of Guam, the District Court for the Northern Mariana Islands, and the District Court of the Virgin Islands, and the term "district" includes the territorial jurisdiction of each such court.

§1407. Multidistrict litigation

(a) When civil actions involving one or more common questions of fact are pending in different districts, such actions may be transferred to any district for coordinated or consolidated pretrial proceedings. Such transfers shall be made by the judicial panel on multidistrict litigation authorized by this section upon its determination that transfers for such proceedings will be for the convenience of parties and witnesses and will promote the just and efficient conduct of such actions. Each action so transferred shall be remanded by the panel at or before the conclusion of such pretrial proceedings to the district from which it was transferred unless it shall have been previously terminated: *Provided, however*, That the panel may separate any claim, cross-claim, counter-claim, or third-party claim and remand any of such claims before the remainder of the action is remanded.

(b) Such coordinated or consolidated pretrial proceedings shall be conducted by a judge or judges to whom such actions are assigned by the judicial panel on multidistrict litigation. For this purpose, upon request of the panel, a circuit judge or a district judge may be designated and assigned temporarily for service in the transferee district by the Chief Justice of the United States or the chief judge of the circuit, as may be required, in accordance with the provisions of chapter 13 of this title. With the consent of the transferee district court, such actions may be assigned by the panel to a judge or judges of such district. The judge or judges to whom such actions are assigned, the members of the judicial panel on multidistrict litigation, and other circuit and district judges designated when needed by the panel may exercise the powers of a district judge in any district for the purpose of conducting pretrial depositions in such coordinated or consolidated pretrial proceedings.

(c) Proceedings for the transfer of an action under this section may be initiated by—

(i) the judicial panel on multidistrict litigation upon its own initiative, or

(ii) motion filed with the panel by a party in any action in which transfer for coordinated or consolidated pretrial proceedings under this section may be appropriate. A copy of such motion shall be filed in the district court in which the moving party's action is pending.

The panel shall give notice to the parties in all actions in which transfers for coordinated or consolidated pretrial proceedings are contemplated, and such notice shall specify the time and place of any hearing to determine whether such transfer shall be made. Orders of the panel to set a hearing and other orders of the panel issued prior to the order either directing or denying transfer shall be filed in the office of the clerk of the district court in which a transfer hearing is to be or has been held. The panel's order of transfer shall be based upon a record of such hearing at which material evidence may be offered by any party to an action pending in any district that would be affected by the proceedings under this section, and shall be supported by findings of fact and conclusions of law based upon such record. Orders of transfer and such other orders as the panel may make thereafter shall be filed in the office of the clerk of the district court of the transferee district and shall be effective when thus filed. The clerk of the transferee district court shall forthwith transmit a certified copy of the panel's order to transfer to the clerk of the district court from which the action is being transferred. An order denying transfer shall be filed in each district wherein there is a case pending in which the motion for transfer has been made.

(d) The judicial panel on multidistrict litigation shall consist of seven circuit and district judges designated from time to time by the Chief Justice of the United States, no two of whom shall be from the same circuit. The concurrence of four members shall be necessary to any action by the panel.

(e) No proceedings for review of any order of the panel may be permitted except by extraordinary writ pursuant to the provisions of title 28, section 1651, United States Code. Petitions for an extraordinary writ to review an order of the panel to set a transfer hearing and other orders of the panel issued prior to the order either directing or denying transfer shall be filed only in the court of appeals having jurisdiction over the district in which a hearing is to be or has been held. Petitions for an extraordinary writ to review an order to transfer or orders subsequent to transfer shall be filed only in the court of appeals having jurisdiction over the transferee district. There shall be no appeal or review of an order of the panel denying a motion to transfer for consolidated or coordinated proceedings.

(f) The panel may prescribe rules for the conduct of its business not inconsistent with Acts of Congress and the Federal Rules of Civil Procedure.

(g) Nothing in this section shall apply to any action in which the United States is a complainant arising under the antitrust laws. "Antitrust laws" as used herein include those acts referred to in the Act of October 15, 1914, as amended (38 Stat. 730; 15 U.S.C. 12), and also include the Act of June 19, 1936 (49 Stat. 1526; 15 U.S.C. 13, 13a, and 13b) and the Act of September 26, 1914, as added March 21, 1938 (52 Stat. 116, 117; 15 U.S.C. 56); but shall not include section 4A of the Act of October 15, 1914, as added July 7, 1955 (69 Stat. 282; 15 U.S.C. 15a).

(h) Notwithstanding the provisions of section 1404 or subsection (f) of this section, the judicial panel on multidistrict litigation may consolidate and transfer with or without the consent of the parties, for both pretrial purposes and for trial, any action brought under section 4C of the Clayton Act.

§1408. Venue of cases under title 11

Except as provided in section 1410 of this title, a case under title 11 may be commenced in the district court for the district—

(1) in which the domicile, residence, principal place of business in the United States, or principal assets in the United States, of the person or entity that is the subject of such case have been located for the one hundred and eighty days immediately preceding such commencement, or for a longer portion of such one-hundred-and-eighty-day period than the domicile, residence, or principal place of business, in the United States, or principal assets in the United States, of such person were located in any other district; or

(2) in which there is pending a case under title 11 concerning such person's affiliate, general partner, or partnership.

§1409. Venue of proceedings arising under title 11 or arising in or related to cases under title 11

(a) Except as otherwise provided in subsections (b) and (d), a proceeding arising under title 11 or arising in or related to a case under title 11 may be commenced in the district court in which such case is pending.

(b) Except as provided in subsection (d) of this section, a trustee in a case under title 11 may commence a proceeding arising in or related to such case to recover a money judgment of or property worth less than $1,000 or a consumer debt of less than $15,000, or a debt (excluding a consumer debt) against a noninsider of less than $10,000, only in the district court for the district in which the defendant resides.

(c) Except as provided in subsection (b) of this section, a trustee in a case under title 11 may commence a proceeding arising in or related to such case as statutory successor to the debtor or creditors under section 541 or 544(b) of title 11 in the district court for the district where the State or Federal court sits in which, under applicable nonbankruptcy venue provisions, the debtor or creditors, as the case may be, may have commenced an action on which such proceeding is based if the case under title 11 had not been commenced.

(d) A trustee may commence a proceeding arising under title 11 or arising in or related to a case under title 11 based on a claim arising after the commencement of such case from the operation of the business of the debtor only in the district court for the district where a

State or Federal court sits in which, under applicable nonbankruptcy venue provisions, an action on such claim may have been brought.

(e) A proceeding arising under title 11 or arising in or related to a case under title 11, based on a claim arising after the commencement of such case from the operation of the business of the debtor, may be commenced against the representative of the estate in such case in the district court for the district where the State or Federal court sits in which the party commencing such proceeding may, under applicable nonbankruptcy venue provisions, have brought an action on such claim, or in the district court in which such case is pending.

§1410. Venue of cases ancillary to foreign proceedings

A case under chapter 15 of title 11 may be commenced in the district court of the United States for the district—

(1) in which the debtor has its principal place of business or principal assets in the United States;

(2) if the debtor does not have a place of business or assets in the United States, in which there is pending against the debtor an action or proceeding in a Federal or State court; or

(3) in a case other than those specified in paragraph (1) or (2), in which venue will be consistent with the interests of justice and the convenience of the parties, having regard to the relief sought by the foreign representative.

§1411. Jury trials

(a) Except as provided in subsection (b) of this section, this chapter and title 11 do not affect any right to trial by jury that an individual has under applicable nonbankruptcy law with regard to a personal injury or wrongful death tort claim.

(b) The district court may order the issues arising under section 303 of title 11 to be tried without a jury.

§1412. Change of venue

A district court may transfer a case or proceeding under title 11 to a district court for another district, in the interest of justice or for the convenience of the parties.

§1413. Venue of cases under chapter 5 of title 3

Notwithstanding the preceding provisions of this chapter, a civil action under section 1346(g) may be brought in the United States district court for the district in which the employee is employed or in the United States District Court for the District of Columbia.

28 USC Chapter 91
District Courts; Removal of Cases from State Courts

§1441. Removal of civil actions

(a) Generally.— Except as otherwise expressly provided by Act of Congress, any civil action brought in a State court of which the district courts of the United States have original jurisdiction, may be removed by the defendant or the defendants, to the district court of the United States for the district and division embracing the place where such action is pending.

(b) Removal Based on Diversity of Citizenship.—

(1) In determining whether a civil action is removable on the basis of the jurisdiction under section 1332 (a) of this title, the citizenship of defendants sued under fictitious names shall be disregarded.

(2) A civil action otherwise removable solely on the basis of the jurisdiction under section 1332 (a) of this title may not be removed if any of the parties in interest properly joined and served as defendants is a citizen of the State in which such action is brought.

(c) Joinder of Federal Law Claims and State Law Claims.—

(1) If a civil action includes—

(A) a claim arising under the Constitution, laws, or treaties of the United States (within the meaning of section 1331 of this title), and

(B) a claim not within the original or supplemental jurisdiction of the district court or a claim that has been made nonremovable by statute,

the entire action may be removed if the action would be removable without the inclusion of the claim described in subparagraph (B).

(2) Upon removal of an action described in paragraph (1), the district court shall sever from the action all claims described in paragraph (1)(B) and shall remand the severed claims to the State court from which the action was removed. Only defendants against whom a claim described in paragraph (1)(A) has been asserted are required to join in or consent to the removal under paragraph (1).

(d) Actions Against Foreign States.— Any civil action brought in a State court against a foreign state as defined in section 1603 (a) of this title may be removed by the foreign state to the district court of the United States for the district and division embracing the place where such action is pending. Upon removal the action shall be tried by the court without jury. Where removal is based upon this subsection, the time limitations of section 1446 (b) of this chapter may be enlarged at any time for cause shown.

(e) Multiparty, Multiforum Jurisdiction.—

(1) Notwithstanding the provisions of subsection (b) of this section, a defendant in a civil action in a State court may remove the action to the district court of the United States for the district and division embracing the place where the action is pending if—

(A) the action could have been brought in a United States district court under section 1369 of this title; or

(B) the defendant is a party to an action which is or could have been brought, in whole or in part, under section 1369 in a United States district court and arises from the same accident as the action in State court, even if the action to be removed could not have been brought in a district court as an original matter.

The removal of an action under this subsection shall be made in accordance with section 1446 of this title, except that a notice of removal may also be filed before trial of the action in State court within 30 days after the date on which the defendant first becomes a party to an action under section 1369 in a United States district court that arises from the same accident as the action in State court, or at a later time with leave of the district court.

(2) Whenever an action is removed under this subsection and the district court to which it is removed or transferred under section 1407 (j) [1] has made a liability determination requiring further proceedings as to damages, the district court shall remand the action to the State court from which it had been removed for the determination of damages, unless the court finds that, for the convenience of parties and witnesses and in the interest of justice, the action should be retained for the determination of damages.

(3) Any remand under paragraph (2) shall not be effective until 60 days after the district court has issued an order determining liability and has certified its intention to remand the removed action for the determination of damages. An appeal with respect to the liability determination of the district court may be taken during that 60-day period to the court of appeals with appellate jurisdiction over the district court. In the event a party files such an appeal, the remand shall not be effective until the appeal has been finally disposed of. Once the remand has become effective, the liability determination shall not be subject to further review by appeal or otherwise.

(4) Any decision under this subsection concerning remand for the determination of damages shall not be reviewable by appeal or otherwise.

(5) An action removed under this subsection shall be deemed to be an action under section 1369 and an action in which jurisdiction is based on section 1369 of this title for purposes of this section and sections 1407, 1697, and 1785 of this title.

(6) Nothing in this subsection shall restrict the authority of the district court to transfer or dismiss an action on the ground of inconvenient forum.

(f) Derivative Removal Jurisdiction.— The court to which a civil action is removed under this section is not precluded from hearing and determining any claim in such civil action because the State court from which such civil action is removed did not have jurisdiction over that claim.

§1442. Federal officers or agencies sued or prosecuted

(a) A civil action or criminal prosecution that is commenced in a State court and that is against or directed to any of the following may be removed by them to the district court of the United States for the district and division embracing the place wherein it is pending:
  (1) The United States or any agency thereof or any officer (or any person acting under that officer) of the United States or of any agency thereof, in an official or individual capacity, for or relating to any act under color of such office or on account of any right, title or authority claimed under any Act of Congress for the apprehension or punishment of criminals or the collection of the revenue.
  (2) A property holder whose title is derived from any such officer, where such action or prosecution affects the validity of any law of the United States.
  (3) Any officer of the courts of the United States, for or relating to any act under color of office or in the performance of his duties;
  (4) Any officer of either House of Congress, for or relating to any act in the discharge of his official duty under an order of such House.

(b) A personal action commenced in any State court by an alien against any citizen of a State who is, or at the time the alleged action accrued was, a civil officer of the United States and is a nonresident of such State, wherein jurisdiction is obtained by the State court by personal service of process, may be removed by the defendant to the district court of the United States for the district and division in which the defendant was served with process.

(c) Solely for purposes of determining the propriety of removal under subsection (a), a law enforcement officer, who is the defendant in a criminal prosecution, shall be deemed to have been acting under the color of his office if the officer—
  (1) protected an individual in the presence of the officer from a crime of violence;
  (2) provided immediate assistance to an individual who suffered, or who was threatened with, bodily harm; or
  (3) prevented the escape of any individual who the officer reasonably believed to have committed, or was about to commit, in the presence of the officer, a crime of violence that resulted in, or was likely to result in, death or serious bodily injury.

(d) In this section, the following definitions apply:
  (1) The terms "civil action" and "criminal prosecution" include any proceeding (whether or not ancillary to another proceeding) to the extent that in such proceeding a judicial order, including a subpoena for testimony or documents, is sought or issued. If removal is sought for a proceeding described in the previous sentence, and there is no other basis for removal, only that proceeding may be removed to the district court.
  (2) The term "crime of violence" has the meaning given that term in section 16 of title 18.
  (3) The term "law enforcement officer" means any employee described in subparagraph (A), (B), or (C) of section 8401(17) of title 5 and any special agent in the Diplomatic Security Service of the Department of State.
  (4) The term "serious bodily injury" has the meaning given that term in section 1365 of title 18.
  (5) The term "State" includes the District of Columbia, United States territories and insular possessions, and Indian country (as defined in section 1151 of title 18).
  (6) The term "State court" includes the Superior Court of the District of Columbia, a court of a United States territory or insular possession, and a tribal court.

§1442a. Members of armed forces sued or prosecuted

A civil or criminal prosecution in a court of a State of the United States against a member of the armed forces of the United States on account of an act done under color of his office or status, or in respect to which he claims any right, title, or authority under a law of the United States respecting the armed forces thereof, or under the law of war, may at any time before the trial or final hearing thereof be removed for trial into the district court of the United States for the district where it is pending in the manner prescribed by law, and it shall thereupon be entered on the docket of the district court, which shall proceed as if the cause had been originally commenced therein and shall have full power to hear and determine the cause.

§1443. Civil rights cases

Any of the following civil actions or criminal prosecutions, commenced in a State court may be removed by the defendant to the district court of the United States for the district and division embracing the place wherein it is pending:
  (1) Against any person who is denied or cannot enforce in the courts of such State a right under any law providing for the equal civil rights of citizens of the United States, or of all persons within the jurisdiction thereof;
  (2) For any act under color of authority derived from any law providing for equal rights, or for refusing to do any act on the ground that it would be inconsistent with such law.

§1444. Foreclosure action against United States

Any action brought under section 2410 of this title against the United States in any State court may be removed by the United States to the district court of the United States for the district and division in which the action is pending.

§1445. Nonremovable actions

(a) A civil action in any State court against a railroad or its receivers or trustees, arising under sections 1–4 and 5–

10 of the Act of April 22, 1908 (45 U.S.C. 51–54, 55–60), may not be removed to any district court of the United States.

(b) A civil action in any State court against a carrier or its receivers or trustees to recover damages for delay, loss, or injury of shipments, arising under section 11706 or 14706 of title 49, may not be removed to any district court of the United States unless the matter in controversy exceeds $10,000, exclusive of interest and costs.

(c) A civil action in any State court arising under the workmen's compensation laws of such State may not be removed to any district court of the United States.

(d) A civil action in any State court arising under section 40302 of the Violence Against Women Act of 1994 may not be removed to any district court of the United States.

§1446. Procedure for removal of civil actions

(a) Generally.—A defendant or defendants desiring to remove any civil action from a State court shall file in the district court of the United States for the district and division within which such action is pending a notice of removal signed pursuant to Rule 11 of the Federal Rules of Civil Procedure and containing a short and plain statement of the grounds for removal, together with a copy of all process, pleadings, and orders served upon such defendant or defendants in such action.

(b) Requirements; Generally.—

(1) The notice of removal of a civil action or proceeding shall be filed within 30 days after the receipt by the defendant, through service or otherwise, of a copy of the initial pleading setting forth the claim for relief upon which such action or proceeding is based, or within 30 days after the service of summons upon the defendant if such initial pleading has then been filed in court and is not required to be served on the defendant, whichever period is shorter.

(2)

(A) When a civil action is removed solely under section 1441(a), all defendants who have been properly joined and served must join in or consent to the removal of the action.

(B) Each defendant shall have 30 days after receipt by or service on that defendant of the initial pleading or summons described in paragraph (1) to file the notice of removal.

(C) If defendants are served at different times, and a later-served defendant files a notice of removal, any earlier-served defendant may consent to the removal even though that earlier-served defendant did not previously initiate or consent to removal.

(3) Except as provided in subsection (c), if the case stated by the initial pleading is not removable, a notice of removal may be filed within thirty days after receipt by the defendant, through service or otherwise, of a copy of an amended pleading, motion, order or other paper from which it may first be ascertained that the case is one which is or has become removable.

(c) Requirements; Removal Based on Diversity of Citizenship.—

(1) A case may not be removed under subsection (b)(3) on the basis of jurisdiction conferred by section 1332 more than 1 year after commencement of the action, unless the district court finds that the plaintiff has acted in bad faith in order to prevent a defendant from removing the action.

(2) If removal of a civil action is sought on the basis of the jurisdiction conferred by section 1332(a), the sum demanded in good faith in the initial pleading shall be deemed to be the amount in controversy, except that—

(A) the notice of removal may assert the amount in controversy if the initial pleading seeks—

(i) nonmonetary relief; or

(ii) a money judgment, but the State practice either does not permit demand for a specific sum or permits recovery of damages in excess of the amount demanded; and

(B) removal of the action is proper on the basis of an amount in controversy asserted under subparagraph (A) if the district court finds, by the preponderance of the evidence, that the amount in controversy exceeds the amount specified in section 1332(a).

(3)

(A) If the case stated by the initial pleading is not removable solely because the amount in controversy does not exceed the amount specified in section 1332(a), information relating to the amount in controversy in the record of the State proceeding, or in responses to discovery, shall be treated as an "other paper" under subsection (b)(3).

(B) If the notice of removal is filed more than 1 year after commencement of the action and the district court finds that the plaintiff deliberately failed to disclose the actual amount in controversy to prevent removal, that finding shall be deemed bad faith under paragraph (1).

(d) Notice to Adverse Parties and State Court.—Promptly after the filing of such notice of removal of a civil action the defendant or defendants shall give written notice thereof to all adverse parties and shall file a copy of the notice with the clerk of such State court, which shall effect the removal and the State court shall proceed no further unless and until the case is remanded.

(e) Counterclaim in 337 Proceeding.—With respect to any counterclaim removed to a district court pursuant to section 337(c) of the Tariff Act of 1930, the district court shall resolve such counterclaim in the same manner as an original complaint under the Federal Rules of Civil

Procedure, except that the payment of a filing fee shall not be required in such cases and the counterclaim shall relate back to the date of the original complaint in the proceeding before the International Trade Commission under section 337 of that Act.

(g) Where the civil action or criminal prosecution that is removable under section 1442(a) is a proceeding in which a judicial order for testimony or documents is sought or issued or sought to be enforced, the 30-day requirement of subsection (b) of this section and paragraph (1) of section 1455(b) is satisfied if the person or entity desiring to remove the proceeding files the notice of removal not later than 30 days after receiving, through service, notice of any such proceeding.

§1447. Procedure after removal generally

(a) In any case removed from a State court, the district court may issue all necessary orders and process to bring before it all proper parties whether served by process issued by the State court or otherwise.

(b) It may require the removing party to file with its clerk copies of all records and proceedings in such State court or may cause the same to be brought before it by writ of certiorari issued to such State court.

(c) A motion to remand the case on the basis of any defect other than lack of subject matter jurisdiction must be made within 30 days after the filing of the notice of removal under section 1446(a). If at any time before final judgment it appears that the district court lacks subject matter jurisdiction, the case shall be remanded. An order remanding the case may require payment of just costs and any actual expenses, including attorney fees, incurred as a result of the removal. A certified copy of the order of remand shall be mailed by the clerk to the clerk of the State court. The State court may thereupon proceed with such case.

(d) An order remanding a case to the State court from which it was removed is not reviewable on appeal or otherwise, except that an order remanding a case to the State court from which it was removed pursuant to section 1442 or 1443 of this title shall be reviewable by appeal or otherwise.

(e) If after removal the plaintiff seeks to join additional defendants whose joinder would destroy subject matter jurisdiction, the court may deny joinder, or permit joinder and remand the action to the State court.

§1448. Process after removal

In all cases removed from any State court to any district court of the United States in which any one or more of the defendants has not been served with process or in which the service has not been perfected prior to removal, or in which process served proves to be defective, such process or service may be completed or new process issued in the same manner as in cases originally filed in such district court.
This section shall not deprive any defendant upon whom process is served after removal of his right to move to remand the case.

§1449. State court record supplied

Where a party is entitled to copies of the records and proceedings in any suit or prosecution in a State court, to be used in any district court of the United States, and the clerk of such State court, upon demand, and the payment or tender of the legal fees, fails to deliver certified copies, the district court may, on affidavit reciting such facts, direct such record to be supplied by affidavit or otherwise. Thereupon such proceedings, trial, and judgment may be had in such district court, and all such process awarded, as if certified copies had been filed in the district court.

§1450. Attachment or sequestration; securities

Whenever any action is removed from a State court to a district court of the United States, any attachment or sequestration of the goods or estate of the defendant in such action in the State court shall hold the goods or estate to answer the final judgment or decree in the same manner as they would have been held to answer final judgment or decree had it been rendered by the State court.
All bonds, undertakings, or security given by either party in such action prior to its removal shall remain valid and effectual notwithstanding such removal.
All injunctions, orders, and other proceedings had in such action prior to its removal shall remain in full force and effect until dissolved or modified by the district court.

§1451. Definitions

For purposes of this chapter—

(1) The term "State court" includes the Superior Court of the District of Columbia.

(2) The term "State" includes the District of Columbia.

§1452. Removal of claims related to bankruptcy cases

(a) A party may remove any claim or cause of action in a civil action other than a proceeding before the United States Tax Court or a civil action by a governmental unit to enforce such governmental unit's police or regulatory power, to the district court for the district where such civil action is pending, if such district court has jurisdiction of such claim or cause of action under section 1334 of this title.

(b) The court to which such claim or cause of action is removed may remand such claim or cause of action on any equitable ground. An order entered under this subsection remanding a claim or cause of action, or a decision to not remand, is not reviewable by appeal or otherwise by the court of appeals under section 158(d), 1291, or 1292 of this title or by the Supreme Court of the United States under section 1254 of this title.

§1453. Removal of class actions

(a) Definitions.—In this section, the terms "class", "class action", "class certification order", and "class member" shall have the meanings given such terms under section 1332(d)(1).

(b) In General.—A class action may be removed to a district court of the United States in accordance with section 1446 (except that the 1-year limitation under section 1446(c)(1) shall not apply), without regard to whether any defendant is a citizen of the State in which the action is brought, except that such action may be removed by any defendant without the consent of all defendants.

(c) Review of Remand Orders.—
  (1) In general.—Section 1447 shall apply to any removal of a case under this section, except that notwithstanding section 1447(d), a court of appeals may accept an appeal from an order of a district court granting or denying a motion to remand a class action to the State court from which it was removed if application is made to the court of appeals not more than 10 days after entry of the order.
  (2) Time period for judgment.—If the court of appeals accepts an appeal under paragraph (1), the court shall complete all action on such appeal, including rendering judgment, not later than 60 days after the date on which such appeal was filed, unless an extension is granted under paragraph (3).
  (3) Extension of time period.—The court of appeals may grant an extension of the 60-day period described in paragraph (2) if—
    (A) all parties to the proceeding agree to such extension, for any period of time; or
    (B) such extension is for good cause shown and in the interests of justice, for a period not to exceed 10 days.
  (4) Denial of appeal.—If a final judgment on the appeal under paragraph (1) is not issued before the end of the period described in paragraph (2), including any extension under paragraph (3), the appeal shall be denied.

(d) Exception.—This section shall not apply to any class action that solely involves—
  (1) a claim concerning a covered security as defined under section 16(f)(3) of the Securities Act of 1933 (15 U.S.C. 78p(f)(3) 1) and section 28(f)(5)(E) of the Securities Exchange Act of 1934 (15 U.S.C. 78bb(f)(5)(E));
  (2) a claim that relates to the internal affairs or governance of a corporation or other form of business enterprise and arises under or by virtue of the laws of the State in which such corporation or business enterprise is incorporated or organized; or
  (3) a claim that relates to the rights, duties (including fiduciary duties), and obligations relating to or created by or pursuant to any security (as defined under section 2(a)(1) of the Securities Act of 1933 (15 U.S.C. 77b(a)(1)) and the regulations issued thereunder).

§1454. Patent, plant variety protection, and copyright cases

(a) In General.—A civil action in which any party asserts a claim for relief arising under any Act of Congress relating to patents, plant variety protection, or copyrights may be removed to the district court of the United States for the district and division embracing the place where the action is pending.

(b) Special Rules.—The removal of an action under this section shall be made in accordance with section 1446, except that if the removal is based solely on this section—
  (1) the action may be removed by any party; and
  (2) the time limitations contained in section 1446(b) may be extended at any time for cause shown.

(c) Clarification of Jurisdiction in Certain Cases.—The court to which a civil action is removed under this section is not precluded from hearing and determining any claim in the civil action because the State court from which the civil action is removed did not have jurisdiction over that claim.

(d) Remand.—If a civil action is removed solely under this section, the district court—
  (1) shall remand all claims that are neither a basis for removal under subsection (a) nor within the original or supplemental jurisdiction of the district court under any Act of Congress; and
  (2) may, under the circumstances specified in section 1367(c), remand any claims within the supplemental jurisdiction of the district court under section 1367.

§1455. Procedure for removal of criminal prosecutions

(a) Notice of Removal.—A defendant or defendants desiring to remove any criminal prosecution from a State court shall file in the district court of the United States for the district and division within which such prosecution is pending a notice of removal signed pursuant to Rule 11 of the Federal Rules of Civil Procedure and containing a short and plain statement of the grounds for removal, together with a copy of all process, pleadings, and orders served upon such defendant or defendants in such action.

(b) Requirements.—(1) A notice of removal of a criminal prosecution shall be filed not later than 30 days after the arraignment in the State court, or at any time before trial, whichever is earlier, except that for good cause shown the United States district court may enter an order granting the defendant or defendants leave to file the notice at a later time.
  (1) A notice of removal of a criminal prosecution shall include all grounds for such removal. A failure to state grounds that exist at the time of the filing of the notice shall constitute a waiver of such grounds, and a second notice may be filed only on grounds not existing at the time of the original notice. For good cause shown, the United States district court may grant relief from the limitations of this paragraph.

(2) The filing of a notice of removal of a criminal prosecution shall not prevent the State court in which such prosecution is pending from proceeding further, except that a judgment of conviction shall not be entered unless the prosecution is first remanded.

(3) The United States district court in which such notice is filed shall examine the notice promptly. If it clearly appears on the face of the notice and any exhibits annexed thereto that removal should not be permitted, the court shall make an order for summary remand.

(4) If the United States district court does not order the summary remand of such prosecution, it shall order an evidentiary hearing to be held promptly and, after such hearing, shall make such disposition of the prosecution as justice shall require. If the United States district court determines that removal shall be permitted, it shall so notify the State court in which prosecution is pending, which shall proceed no further.

(c) Writ of Habeas Corpus.—If the defendant or defendants are in actual custody on process issued by the State court, the district court shall issue its writ of habeas corpus, and the marshal shall thereupon take such defendant or defendants into the marshal's custody and deliver a copy of the writ to the clerk of such State court.

Appendix A
Official Forms

Form Number	Form Name
AO 85	Notice, Consent, and Reference of a Civil Action to a Magistrate Judge
AO 85A	Notice, Consent, and Reference of a Dispositive Motion to a Magistrate Judge
AO 88	Subpoena to Appear and Testify at a Hearing or Trial in a Civil Action
AO 88A	Subpoena to Testify at a Deposition in a Civil Action
AO 88B	Subpoena to Produce Documents, Information, or Objects or to Perm t Inspection of Premises in a Civil Action
AO 239	Application to Proceed in District Court Without Prepaying Fees or Costs (Long Form)
AO 240	Application to Proceed in District Court Without Prepaying Fees or Costs (Short Form)
AO 240A	Order to Proceed Without Prepaying Fees or Costs
AO 398	Notice of a Lawsuit and Request to Waive Service of a Summons
AO 399	Waiver of the Service of Summons
AO 440	Summons in a Civil Action
AO 441	Summons on Third-Party Complaint
AO 445	Warrant for the Arrest of a Witness in a Civil Case
AO 450	Judgment in a Civil Case
AO 451	Clerk's Certification of a Judgment to be Registered in Another District
JS 44	Civil Cover Sheet
Pro Se 1	Complaint for a Civil Case
Pro Se 2	Complaint and Request for Injunction
Pro Se 3	Defendant's Answer to the Complaint
Pro Se 4	Complaint for a Civil Case Alleging Breach of Contract
Pro Se 5	Complaint for a Civil Case Alleging Negligence
Pro Se 6	Complaint for a Civil Case Alleging that the Defendant Owes the Plaintiff a Sum of Money
Pro Se 7	Complaint for Employment Discrimination
Pro Se 8	Complaint for Violations of Fair Labor Standards
Pro Se 9	Complaint for Specific Performance or Damages Based on a Contract to Convey Real Property
Pro Se 10	Complaint for the Conversion of Property
Pro Se 11	Third Party Complaint
Pro Se 12	Complaint for Interpleader and Declaratory Relief
Pro Se 13	Complaint for Review of Social Security Decision
Pro Se 14	Complaint for Violation of Civil Rights (Prisoner)
Pro Se 15	Complaint for Violation of Civil Rights (Non-Prisoner)

UNITED STATES DISTRICT COURT

for the

______________________ *Plaintiff*	)	
v.	)	Civil Action No.
______________________ *Defendant*	)	

NOTICE, CONSENT, AND REFERENCE OF A CIVIL ACTION TO A MAGISTRATE JUDGE

Notice of a magistrate judge's availability. A United States magistrate judge of this court is available to conduct all proceedings in this civil action (including a jury or nonjury trial) and to order the entry of a final judgment. The judgment may then be appealed directly to the United States court of appeals like any other judgment of this court. A magistrate judge may exercise this authority only if all parties voluntarily consent.

You may consent to have your case referred to a magistrate judge, or you may withhold your consent without adverse substantive consequences. The name of any party withholding consent will not be revealed to any judge who may otherwise be involved with your case.

Consent to a magistrate judge's authority. The following parties consent to have a United States magistrate judge conduct all proceedings in this case including trial, the entry of final judgment, and all post-trial proceedings.

Printed names of parties and attorneys	*Signatures of parties or attorneys*	*Dates*

Reference Order

IT IS ORDERED: This case is referred to a United States magistrate judge to conduct all proceedings and order the entry of a final judgment in accordance with 28 U.S.C. § 636(c) and Fed. R. Civ. P. 73.

Date: ______________

____
District Judge's signature

____
Printed name and title

Note: Return this form to the clerk of court only if you are consenting to the exercise of jurisdiction by a United States magistrate judge. Do not return this form to a judge.

UNITED STATES DISTRICT COURT

for the

______________________________)
Plaintiff)
v.) Civil Action No.
______________________________)
Defendant)

NOTICE, CONSENT, AND REFERENCE OF A DISPOSITIVE MOTION TO A MAGISTRATE JUDGE

Notice of a magistrate judge's availability. A United States magistrate judge of this court is available to conduct all proceedings and enter a final order dispositive of each motion. A magistrate judge may exercise this authority only if all parties voluntarily consent.

You may consent to have motions referred to a magistrate judge, or you may withhold your consent without adverse substantive consequences. The name of any party withholding consent will not be revealed to any judge who may otherwise be involved with your case.

Consent to a magistrate judge's consideration of a dispositive motion. The following parties consent to have a United States magistrate judge conduct any and all proceedings and enter a final order as to each motion identified below *(identify each motion by document number and title).*

Motions: ______________________________

____

____

Printed names of parties and attorneys	*Signatures of parties or attorneys*	*Dates*

Reference Order

IT IS ORDERED: The motions are referred to a United States magistrate judge to conduct all proceedings and enter a final order on the motions identified above in accordance with 28 U.S.C. § 636(c).

Date: ______________

____
District Judge's signature

____
Printed name and title

Note: Return this form to the clerk of court only if you are consenting to the exercise of jurisdiction by a United States magistrate judge. Do not return this form to a judge.

UNITED STATES DISTRICT COURT
for the

______________________ *Plaintiff*	))	
v.	)	Civil Action No.
______________________ *Defendant*	))	

SUBPOENA TO APPEAR AND TESTIFY AT A HEARING OR TRIAL IN A CIVIL ACTION

To:

____
(Name of person to whom this subpoena is directed)

YOU ARE COMMANDED to appear in the United States district court at the time, date, and place set forth below to testify at a hearing or trial in this civil action. When you arrive, you must remain at the court until the judge or a court officer allows you to leave.

Place:	Courtroom No.:
	Date and Time:

You must also bring with you the following documents, electronically stored information, or objects *(leave blank if not applicable)*:

The following provisions of Fed. R. Civ. P. 45 are attached – Rule 45(c), relating to the place of compliance; Rule 45(d), relating to your protection as a person subject to a subpoena; and Rule 45(e) and (g), relating to your duty to respond to this subpoena and the potential consequences of not doing so.

Date: ______________

CLERK OF COURT

OR

______________________ *Signature of Clerk or Deputy Clerk*

______________________ *Attorney's signature*

The name, address, e-mail address, and telephone number of the attorney representing *(name of party)* ______________ ______________________, who issues or requests this subpoena, are:

Notice to the person who issues or requests this subpoena

If this subpoena commands the production of documents, electronically stored information, or tangible things before trial, a notice and a copy of the subpoena must be served on each party in this case before it is served on the person to whom it is directed. Fed. R. Civ. P. 45(a)(4).

Civil Action No.

PROOF OF SERVICE

(This section should not be filed with the court unless required by Fed. R. Civ. P. 45.)

I received this subpoena for *(name of individual and title, if any)* ____________________
on *(date)* __________ .

❒ I served the subpoena by delivering a copy to the named person as follows: ____________________

____________________ on *(date)* __________ ; or

❒ I returned the subpoena unexecuted because: ____________________
____________________ .

Unless the subpoena was issued on behalf of the United States, or one of its officers or agents, I have also tendered to the witness the fees for one day's attendance, and the mileage allowed by law, in the amount of $ __________ .

My fees are $ __________ for travel and $ __________ for services, for a total of $ 0.00 .

I declare under penalty of perjury that this information is true.

Date: __________

____
Server's signature

____
Printed name and title

____
Server's address

Additional information regarding attempted service, etc.:

Federal Rule of Civil Procedure 45 (c), (d), (e), and (g) (Effective 12/1/13)

(c) Place of Compliance.

(1) ***For a Trial, Hearing, or Deposition.*** A subpoena may command a person to attend a trial, hearing, or deposition only as follows:

(A) within 100 miles of where the person resides, is employed, or regularly transacts business in person; or

(B) within the state where the person resides, is employed, or regularly transacts business in person, if the person

(i) is a party or a party's officer; or

(ii) is commanded to attend a trial and would not incur substantial expense.

(2) ***For Other Discovery.*** A subpoena may command:

(A) production of documents, electronically stored information, or tangible things at a place within 100 miles of where the person resides, is employed, or regularly transacts business in person; and

(B) inspection of premises at the premises to be inspected.

(d) Protecting a Person Subject to a Subpoena; Enforcement.

(1) ***Avoiding Undue Burden or Expense; Sanctions.*** A party or attorney responsible for issuing and serving a subpoena must take reasonable steps to avoid imposing undue burden or expense on a person subject to the subpoena. The court for the district where compliance is required must enforce this duty and impose an appropriate sanction—which may include lost earnings and reasonable attorney's fees—on a party or attorney who fails to comply.

(2) ***Command to Produce Materials or Permit Inspection.***

(A) *Appearance Not Required.* A person commanded to produce documents, electronically stored information, or tangible things, or to permit the inspection of premises, need not appear in person at the place of production or inspection unless also commanded to appear for a deposition, hearing, or trial.

(B) *Objections.* A person commanded to produce documents or tangible things or to permit inspection may serve on the party or attorney designated in the subpoena a written objection to inspecting, copying, testing, or sampling any or all of the materials or to inspecting the premises—or to producing electronically stored information in the form or forms requested. The objection must be served before the earlier of the time specified for compliance or 14 days after the subpoena is served. If an objection is made, the following rules apply:

(i) At any time, on notice to the commanded person, the serving party may move the court for the district where compliance is required for an order compelling production or inspection.

(ii) These acts may be required only as directed in the order, and the order must protect a person who is neither a party nor a party's officer from significant expense resulting from compliance.

(3) ***Quashing or Modifying a Subpoena.***

(A) *When Required.* On timely motion, the court for the district where compliance is required must quash or modify a subpoena that:

(i) fails to allow a reasonable time to comply;

(ii) requires a person to comply beyond the geographical limits specified in Rule 45(c);

(iii) requires disclosure of privileged or other protected matter, if no exception or waiver applies; or

(iv) subjects a person to undue burden.

(B) *When Permitted.* To protect a person subject to or affected by a subpoena, the court for the district where compliance is required may, on motion, quash or modify the subpoena if it requires:

(i) disclosing a trade secret or other confidential research, development, or commercial information; or

(ii) disclosing an unretained expert's opinion or information that does not describe specific occurrences in dispute and results from the expert's study that was not requested by a party.

(C) *Specifying Conditions as an Alternative.* In the circumstances described in Rule 45(d)(3)(B), the court may, instead of quashing or modifying a subpoena, order appearance or production under specified conditions if the serving party:

(i) shows a substantial need for the testimony or material that cannot be otherwise met without undue hardship; and

(ii) ensures that the subpoenaed person will be reasonably compensated.

(e) Duties in Responding to a Subpoena.

(1) ***Producing Documents or Electronically Stored Information.*** These procedures apply to producing documents or electronically stored information:

(A) *Documents.* A person responding to a subpoena to produce documents must produce them as they are kept in the ordinary course of business or must organize and label them to correspond to the categories in the demand.

(B) *Form for Producing Electronically Stored Information Not Specified.* If a subpoena does not specify a form for producing electronically stored information, the person responding must produce it in a form or forms in which it is ordinarily maintained or in a reasonably usable form or forms.

(C) *Electronically Stored Information Produced in Only One Form.* The person responding need not produce the same electronically stored information in more than one form.

(D) *Inaccessible Electronically Stored Information.* The person responding need not provide discovery of electronically stored information from sources that the person identifies as not reasonably accessible because of undue burden or cost. On motion to compel discovery or for a protective order, the person responding must show that the information is not reasonably accessible because of undue burden or cost. If that showing is made, the court may nonetheless order discovery from such sources if the requesting party shows good cause, considering the limitations of Rule 26(b)(2)(C). The court may specify conditions for the discovery.

(2) ***Claiming Privilege or Protection.***

(A) *Information Withheld.* A person withholding subpoenaed information under a claim that it is privileged or subject to protection as trial-preparation material must:

(i) expressly make the claim; and

(ii) describe the nature of the withheld documents, communications, or tangible things in a manner that, without revealing information itself privileged or protected, will enable the parties to assess the claim.

(B) *Information Produced.* If information produced in response to a subpoena is subject to a claim of privilege or of protection as trial-preparation material, the person making the claim may notify any party that received the information of the claim and the basis for it. After being notified, a party must promptly return, sequester, or destroy the specified information and any copies it has; must not use or disclose the information until the claim is resolved; must take reasonable steps to retrieve the information if the party disclosed it before being notified; and may promptly present the information under seal to the court for the district where compliance is required for a determination of the claim. The person who produced the information must preserve the information until the claim is resolved.

(g) Contempt.

The court for the district where compliance is required—and also, after a motion is transferred, the issuing court—may hold in contempt a person who, having been served, fails without adequate excuse to obey the subpoena or an order related to it.

For access to subpoena materials, see Fed. R. Civ. P. 45(a) Committee Note (2013).

UNITED STATES DISTRICT COURT

for the

____________________ *Plaintiff*	)	
v.	)	Civil Action No.
____________________ *Defendant*	)	

SUBPOENA TO TESTIFY AT A DEPOSITION IN A CIVIL ACTION

To:

____

(Name of person to whom this subpoena is directed)

❒ *Testimony:* **YOU ARE COMMANDED** to appear at the time, date, and place set forth below to testify at a deposition to be taken in this civil action. If you are an organization, you must designate one or more officers, directors, or managing agents, or designate other persons who consent to testify on your behalf about the following matters, or those set forth in an attachment:

Place:	Date and Time:

The deposition will be recorded by this method: ____________________

❒ *Production:* You, or your representatives, must also bring with you to the deposition the following documents, electronically stored information, or objects, and must permit inspection, copying, testing, or sampling of the material:

The following provisions of Fed. R. Civ. P. 45 are attached – Rule 45(c), relating to the place of compliance; Rule 45(d), relating to your protection as a person subject to a subpoena; and Rule 45(e) and (g), relating to your duty to respond to this subpoena and the potential consequences of not doing so.

Date: __________

CLERK OF COURT

OR

____________________ *Signature of Clerk or Deputy Clerk*

____________________ *Attorney's signature*

The name, address, e-mail address, and telephone number of the attorney representing *(name of party)* ____________________, who issues or requests this subpoena, are:

Notice to the person who issues or requests this subpoena

If this subpoena commands the production of documents, electronically stored information, or tangible things before trial, a notice and a copy of the subpoena must be served on each party in this case before it is served on the person to whom it is directed. Fed. R. Civ. P. 45(a)(4).

Civil Action No.

PROOF OF SERVICE

(This section should not be filed with the court unless required by Fed. R. Civ. P. 45.)

I received this subpoena for *(name of individual and title, if any)* ______________________
on *(date)* ____________ .

❒ I served the subpoena by delivering a copy to the named individual as follows: ____________

____ on *(date)* ____________ ; or

❒ I returned the subpoena unexecuted because: ______________________________

____ .

Unless the subpoena was issued on behalf of the United States, or one of its officers or agents, I have also tendered to the witness the fees for one day's attendance, and the mileage allowed by law, in the amount of

$ ______________ .

My fees are $ ____________ for travel and $ ____________ for services, for a total of $ 0.00 .

I declare under penalty of perjury that this information is true.

Date: ____________

____
Server's signature

____
Printed name and title

____
Server's address

Additional information regarding attempted service, etc.:

Federal Rule of Civil Procedure 45 (c), (d), (e), and (g) (Effective 12/1/13)

(c) Place of Compliance.

(1) ***For a Trial, Hearing, or Deposition.*** A subpoena may command a person to attend a trial, hearing, or deposition only as follows:

(A) within 100 miles of where the person resides, is employed, or regularly transacts business in person; or

(B) within the state where the person resides, is employed, or regularly transacts business in person, if the person

(i) is a party or a party's officer; or

(ii) is commanded to attend a trial and would not incur substantial expense.

(2) ***For Other Discovery.*** A subpoena may command:

(A) production of documents, electronically stored information, or tangible things at a place within 100 miles of where the person resides, is employed, or regularly transacts business in person; and

(B) inspection of premises at the premises to be inspected.

(d) Protecting a Person Subject to a Subpoena; Enforcement.

(1) ***Avoiding Undue Burden or Expense; Sanctions.*** A party or attorney responsible for issuing and serving a subpoena must take reasonable steps to avoid imposing undue burden or expense on a person subject to the subpoena. The court for the district where compliance is required must enforce this duty and impose an appropriate sanction—which may include lost earnings and reasonable attorney's fees—on a party or attorney who fails to comply.

(2) ***Command to Produce Materials or Permit Inspection.***

(A) *Appearance Not Required.* A person commanded to produce documents, electronically stored information, or tangible things, or to permit the inspection of premises, need not appear in person at the place of production or inspection unless also commanded to appear for a deposition, hearing, or trial.

(B) *Objections.* A person commanded to produce documents or tangible things or to permit inspection may serve on the party or attorney designated in the subpoena a written objection to inspecting, copying, testing, or sampling any or all of the materials or to inspecting the premises—or to producing electronically stored information in the form or forms requested. The objection must be served before the earlier of the time specified for compliance or 14 days after the subpoena is served. If an objection is made, the following rules apply:

(i) At any time, on notice to the commanded person, the serving party may move the court for the district where compliance is required for an order compelling production or inspection.

(ii) These acts may be required only as directed in the order, and the order must protect a person who is neither a party nor a party's officer from significant expense resulting from compliance.

(3) ***Quashing or Modifying a Subpoena.***

(A) *When Required.* On timely motion, the court for the district where compliance is required must quash or modify a subpoena that:

(i) fails to allow a reasonable time to comply;

(ii) requires a person to comply beyond the geographical limits specified in Rule 45(c);

(iii) requires disclosure of privileged or other protected matter, if no exception or waiver applies; or

(iv) subjects a person to undue burden.

(B) *When Permitted.* To protect a person subject to or affected by a subpoena, the court for the district where compliance is required may, on motion, quash or modify the subpoena if it requires:

(i) disclosing a trade secret or other confidential research, development, or commercial information; or

(ii) disclosing an unretained expert's opinion or information that does not describe specific occurrences in dispute and results from the expert's study that was not requested by a party.

(C) *Specifying Conditions as an Alternative.* In the circumstances described in Rule 45(d)(3)(B), the court may, instead of quashing or modifying a subpoena, order appearance or production under specified conditions if the serving party:

(i) shows a substantial need for the testimony or material that cannot be otherwise met without undue hardship; and

(ii) ensures that the subpoenaed person will be reasonably compensated.

(e) Duties in Responding to a Subpoena.

(1) ***Producing Documents or Electronically Stored Information.*** These procedures apply to producing documents or electronically stored information:

(A) *Documents.* A person responding to a subpoena to produce documents must produce them as they are kept in the ordinary course of business or must organize and label them to correspond to the categories in the demand.

(B) *Form for Producing Electronically Stored Information Not Specified.* If a subpoena does not specify a form for producing electronically stored information, the person responding must produce it in a form or forms in which it is ordinarily maintained or in a reasonably usable form or forms.

(C) *Electronically Stored Information Produced in Only One Form.* The person responding need not produce the same electronically stored information in more than one form.

(D) *Inaccessible Electronically Stored Information.* The person responding need not provide discovery of electronically stored information from sources that the person identifies as not reasonably accessible because of undue burden or cost. On motion to compel discovery or for a protective order, the person responding must show that the information is not reasonably accessible because of undue burden or cost. If that showing is made, the court may nonetheless order discovery from such sources if the requesting party shows good cause, considering the limitations of Rule 26(b)(2)(C). The court may specify conditions for the discovery.

(2) ***Claiming Privilege or Protection.***

(A) *Information Withheld.* A person withholding subpoenaed information under a claim that it is privileged or subject to protection as trial-preparation material must:

(i) expressly make the claim; and

(ii) describe the nature of the withheld documents, communications, or tangible things in a manner that, without revealing information itself privileged or protected, will enable the parties to assess the claim.

(B) *Information Produced.* If information produced in response to a subpoena is subject to a claim of privilege or of protection as trial-preparation material, the person making the claim may notify any party that received the information of the claim and the basis for it. After being notified, a party must promptly return, sequester, or destroy the specified information and any copies it has; must not use or disclose the information until the claim is resolved; must take reasonable steps to retrieve the information if the party disclosed it before being notified; and may promptly present the information under seal to the court for the district where compliance is required for a determination of the claim. The person who produced the information must preserve the information until the claim is resolved.

(g) Contempt.

The court for the district where compliance is required—and also, after a motion is transferred, the issuing court—may hold in contempt a person who, having been served, fails without adequate excuse to obey the subpoena or an order related to it.

For access to subpoena materials, see Fed. R. Civ. P. 45(a) Committee Note (2013).

UNITED STATES DISTRICT COURT

for the

______________________________ *Plaintiff* v. ______________________________ *Defendant*	))))))	Civil Action No.

SUBPOENA TO PRODUCE DOCUMENTS, INFORMATION, OR OBJECTS OR TO PERMIT INSPECTION OF PREMISES IN A CIVIL ACTION

To:

____

(Name of person to whom this subpoena is directed)

❒ *Production:* **YOU ARE COMMANDED** to produce at the time, date, and place set forth below the following documents, electronically stored information, or objects, and to permit inspection, copying, testing, or sampling of the material:

Place:	Date and Time:

❒ *Inspection of Premises:* **YOU ARE COMMANDED** to permit entry onto the designated premises, land, or other property possessed or controlled by you at the time, date, and location set forth below, so that the requesting party may inspect, measure, survey, photograph, test, or sample the property or any designated object or operation on it.

Place:	Date and Time:

The following provisions of Fed. R. Civ. P. 45 are attached – Rule 45(c), relating to the place of compliance; Rule 45(d), relating to your protection as a person subject to a subpoena; and Rule 45(e) and (g), relating to your duty to respond to this subpoena and the potential consequences of not doing so.

Date: ______________

CLERK OF COURT

OR

______________________________ *Signature of Clerk or Deputy Clerk*

______________________________ *Attorney's signature*

The name, address, e-mail address, and telephone number of the attorney representing *(name of party)* ______________ ______________________________ , who issues or requests this subpoena, are:

Notice to the person who issues or requests this subpoena

If this subpoena commands the production of documents, electronically stored information, or tangible things or the inspection of premises before trial, a notice and a copy of the subpoena must be served on each party in this case before it is served on the person to whom it is directed. Fed. R. Civ. P. 45(a)(4).

Civil Action No.

PROOF OF SERVICE

(This section should not be filed with the court unless required by Fed. R. Civ. P. 45.)

I received this subpoena for *(name of individual and title, if any)* ____________________

on *(date)* ____________ .

❐ I served the subpoena by delivering a copy to the named person as follows: ____________

____

____________________________ on *(date)* ____________ ; or

❐ I returned the subpoena unexecuted because: ____________________

____ .

Unless the subpoena was issued on behalf of the United States, or one of its officers or agents, I have also tendered to the witness the fees for one day's attendance, and the mileage allowed by law, in the amount of

$ ____________ .

My fees are $ ____________ for travel and $ ____________ for services, for a total of $ 0.00 .

I declare under penalty of perjury that this information is true.

Date: ____________

____
Server's signature

____
Printed name and title

____
Server's address

Additional information regarding attempted service, etc.:

Federal Rule of Civil Procedure 45 (c), (d), (e), and (g) (Effective 12/1/13)

(c) Place of Compliance.

(1) ***For a Trial, Hearing, or Deposition.*** A subpoena may command a person to attend a trial, hearing, or deposition only as follows:

(A) within 100 miles of where the person resides, is employed, or regularly transacts business in person; or

(B) within the state where the person resides, is employed, or regularly transacts business in person, if the person

(i) is a party or a party's officer; or

(ii) is commanded to attend a trial and would not incur substantial expense.

(2) ***For Other Discovery.*** A subpoena may command:

(A) production of documents, electronically stored information, or tangible things at a place within 100 miles of where the person resides, is employed, or regularly transacts business in person; and

(B) inspection of premises at the premises to be inspected.

(d) Protecting a Person Subject to a Subpoena; Enforcement.

(1) ***Avoiding Undue Burden or Expense; Sanctions.*** A party or attorney responsible for issuing and serving a subpoena must take reasonable steps to avoid imposing undue burden or expense on a person subject to the subpoena. The court for the district where compliance is required must enforce this duty and impose an appropriate sanction—which may include lost earnings and reasonable attorney's fees—on a party or attorney who fails to comply.

(2) ***Command to Produce Materials or Permit Inspection.***

(A) *Appearance Not Required.* A person commanded to produce documents, electronically stored information, or tangible things, or to permit the inspection of premises, need not appear in person at the place of production or inspection unless also commanded to appear for a deposition, hearing, or trial.

(B) *Objections.* A person commanded to produce documents or tangible things or to permit inspection may serve on the party or attorney designated in the subpoena a written objection to inspecting, copying, testing, or sampling any or all of the materials or to inspecting the premises—or to producing electronically stored information in the form or forms requested. The objection must be served before the earlier of the time specified for compliance or 14 days after the subpoena is served. If an objection is made, the following rules apply:

(i) At any time, on notice to the commanded person, the serving party may move the court for the district where compliance is required for an order compelling production or inspection.

(ii) These acts may be required only as directed in the order, and the order must protect a person who is neither a party nor a party's officer from significant expense resulting from compliance.

(3) ***Quashing or Modifying a Subpoena.***

(A) *When Required.* On timely motion, the court for the district where compliance is required must quash or modify a subpoena that:

(i) fails to allow a reasonable time to comply;

(ii) requires a person to comply beyond the geographical limits specified in Rule 45(c);

(iii) requires disclosure of privileged or other protected matter, if no exception or waiver applies; or

(iv) subjects a person to undue burden.

(B) *When Permitted.* To protect a person subject to or affected by a subpoena, the court for the district where compliance is required may, on motion, quash or modify the subpoena if it requires:

(i) disclosing a trade secret or other confidential research, development, or commercial information; or

(ii) disclosing an unretained expert's opinion or information that does not describe specific occurrences in dispute and results from the expert's study that was not requested by a party.

(C) *Specifying Conditions as an Alternative.* In the circumstances described in Rule 45(d)(3)(B), the court may, instead of quashing or modifying a subpoena, order appearance or production under specified conditions if the serving party:

(i) shows a substantial need for the testimony or material that cannot be otherwise met without undue hardship; and

(ii) ensures that the subpoenaed person will be reasonably compensated.

(e) Duties in Responding to a Subpoena.

(1) ***Producing Documents or Electronically Stored Information.*** These procedures apply to producing documents or electronically stored information:

(A) *Documents.* A person responding to a subpoena to produce documents must produce them as they are kept in the ordinary course of business or must organize and label them to correspond to the categories in the demand.

(B) *Form for Producing Electronically Stored Information Not Specified.* If a subpoena does not specify a form for producing electronically stored information, the person responding must produce it in a form or forms in which it is ordinarily maintained or in a reasonably usable form or forms.

(C) *Electronically Stored Information Produced in Only One Form.* The person responding need not produce the same electronically stored information in more than one form.

(D) *Inaccessible Electronically Stored Information.* The person responding need not provide discovery of electronically stored information from sources that the person identifies as not reasonably accessible because of undue burden or cost. On motion to compel discovery or for a protective order, the person responding must show that the information is not reasonably accessible because of undue burden or cost. If that showing is made, the court may nonetheless order discovery from such sources if the requesting party shows good cause, considering the limitations of Rule 26(b)(2)(C). The court may specify conditions for the discovery.

(2) ***Claiming Privilege or Protection.***

(A) *Information Withheld.* A person withholding subpoenaed information under a claim that it is privileged or subject to protection as trial-preparation material must:

(i) expressly make the claim; and

(ii) describe the nature of the withheld documents, communications, or tangible things in a manner that, without revealing information itself privileged or protected, will enable the parties to assess the claim.

(B) *Information Produced.* If information produced in response to a subpoena is subject to a claim of privilege or of protection as trial-preparation material, the person making the claim may notify any party that received the information of the claim and the basis for it. After being notified, a party must promptly return, sequester, or destroy the specified information and any copies it has; must not use or disclose the information until the claim is resolved; must take reasonable steps to retrieve the information if the party disclosed it before being notified; and may promptly present the information under seal to the court for the district where compliance is required for a determination of the claim. The person who produced the information must preserve the information until the claim is resolved.

(g) Contempt.

The court for the district where compliance is required—and also, after a motion is transferred, the issuing court—may hold in contempt a person who, having been served, fails without adequate excuse to obey the subpoena or an order related to it.

For access to subpoena materials, see Fed. R. Civ. P. 45(a) Committee Note (2013).

UNITED STATES DISTRICT COURT

for the

_______________ Plaintiff/Petitioner	))	
v.	)	Civil Action No.
_______________ Defendant/Respondent	))	

APPLICATION TO PROCEED IN DISTRICT COURT WITHOUT PREPAYING FEES OR COSTS (Long Form)

Affidavit in Support of the Application

I am a plaintiff or petitioner in this case and declare that I am unable to pay the costs of these proceedings and that I am entitled to the relief requested. I declare under penalty of perjury that the information below is true and understand that a false statement may result in a dismissal of my claims.

Signed: _______________

Instructions

Complete all questions in this application and then sign it. Do not leave any blanks: if the answer to a question is "0," "none," or "not applicable (N/A)," write that response. If you need more space to answer a question or to explain your answer, attach a separate sheet of paper identified with your name, your case's docket number, and the question number.

Date: _______________

1. For both you and your spouse estimate the average amount of money received from each of the following sources during the past 12 months. Adjust any amount that was received weekly, biweekly, quarterly, semiannually, or annually to show the monthly rate. Use gross amounts, that is, amounts before any deductions for taxes or otherwise.

Income source	Average monthly income amount during the past 12 months		Income amount expected next month	
	You	Spouse	You	Spouse
Employment	$	$	$	$
Self-employment	$	$	$	$
Income from real property *(such as rental income)*	$	$	$	$
Interest and dividends	$	$	$	$
Gifts	$	$	$	$
Alimony	$	$	$	$
Child support	$	$	$	$

Retirement *(such as social security, pensions, annuities, insurance)*	$	$	$	$
Disability *(such as social security, insurance payments)*	$	$	$	$
Unemployment payments	$	$	$	$
Public-assistance *(such as welfare)*	$	$	$	$
Other *(specify)*:	$	$	$	$
Total monthly income:	$ 0.00	$ 0.00	$ 0.00	$ 0.00

2. List your employment history for the past two years, most recent employer first. *(Gross monthly pay is before taxes or other deductions.)*

Employer	**Address**	**Dates of employment**	**Gross monthly pay**
			$
			$

3. List your spouse's employment history for the past two years, most recent employer first. *(Gross monthly pay is before taxes or other deductions.)*

Employer	**Address**	**Dates of employment**	**Gross monthly pay**
			$
			$
			$

4. How much cash do you and your spouse have? $ ____________

Below, state any money you or your spouse have in bank accounts or in any other financial institution.

Financial institution	**Type of account**	**Amount you have**	**Amount your spouse has**
		$	$
		$	$
		$	$

If you are a prisoner, you must attach a statement certified by the appropriate institutional officer showing all receipts, expenditures, and balances during the last six months in your institutional accounts. If you have multiple accounts, perhaps because you have been in multiple institutions, attach one certified statement of each account.

5. List the assets, and their values, which you own or your spouse owns. Do not list clothing and ordinary household furnishings.

Assets owned by you or your spouse	
Home *(Value)*	$
Other real estate *(Value)*	$
Motor vehicle #*1* *(Value)*	$
Make and year:	
Model:	
Registration #:	
Motor vehicle #*2* *(Value)*	$
Make and year:	
Model:	
Registration #:	
Other assets *(Value)*	$
Other assets *(Value)*	$

6. State every person, business, or organization owing you or your spouse money, and the amount owed.

Person owing you or your spouse money	**Amount owed to you**	**Amount owed to your spouse**
	$	**$**
	$	**$**
	$	**$**

7. State the persons who rely on you or your spouse for support.

Name (or, if under 18, initials only)	**Relationship**	**Age**

8. Estimate the average monthly expenses of you and your family. Show separately the amounts paid by your spouse. Adjust any payments that are made weekly, biweekly, quarterly, semiannually, or annually to show the monthly rate.

	You	**Your spouse**
Rent or home-mortgage payment *(including lot rented for mobile home)* Are real estate taxes included? ❒ Yes ❒ No Is property insurance included? ❒ Yes ❒ No	$	$
Utilities *(electricity, heating fuel, water, sewer, and telephone)*	$	$
Home maintenance *(repairs and upkeep)*	$	$
Food	$	$
Clothing	$	$
Laundry and dry-cleaning	$	$
Medical and dental expenses	$	$
Transportation *(not including motor vehicle payments)*	$	$
Recreation, entertainment, newspapers, magazines, etc.	$	$
Insurance *(not deducted from wages or included in mortgage payments)*		
Homeowner's or renter's:	$	$
Life:	$	$
Health:	$	$
Motor vehicle:	$	$
Other:	$	$
Taxes *(not deducted from wages or included in mortgage payments) (specify):*	$	$
Installment payments		
Motor vehicle:	$	$
Credit card *(name)*:	$	$
Department store *(name)*:	$	$
Other:	$	$
Alimony, maintenance, and support paid to others	$	$

Regular expenses for operation of business, profession, or farm *(attach detailed statement)*	$	$
Other *(specify)*:	$	$
Total monthly expenses:	$ 0.00	$ 0.00

9. Do you expect any major changes to your monthly income or expenses or in your assets or liabilities during the next 12 months?

   ❐ Yes ❐ No If yes, describe on an attached sheet.

10. Have you spent — or will you be spending — any money for expenses or attorney fees in conjunction with this lawsuit? ❐ Yes ❐ No

    If yes, how much? $ ____________________

11. Provide any other information that will help explain why you cannot pay the costs of these proceedings.

12. Identify the city and state of your legal residence.

    Your daytime phone number: ____________________

    Your age: ________ Your years of schooling: __________

UNITED STATES DISTRICT COURT

for the

_______________________ *Plaintiff/Petitioner*	)	
v.	)	Civil Action No.
_______________________ *Defendant/Respondent*	)	

APPLICATION TO PROCEED IN DISTRICT COURT WITHOUT PREPAYING FEES OR COSTS (Short Form)

I am a plaintiff or petitioner in this case and declare that I am unable to pay the costs of these proceedings and that I am entitled to the relief requested.

In support of this application, I answer the following questions under penalty of perjury:

1. *If incarcerated.* I am being held at: ____________________________________ . If employed there, or have an account in the institution, I have attached to this document a statement certified by the appropriate institutional officer showing all receipts, expenditures, and balances during the last six months for any institutional account in my name. I am also submitting a similar statement from any other institution where I was incarcerated during the last six months.

2. *If not incarcerated.* If I am employed, my employer's name and address are:

My gross pay or wages are: $ ______________, and my take-home pay or wages are: $ ______________ per *(specify pay period)* ____________________ .

3. *Other Income.* In the past 12 months, I have received income from the following sources *(check all that apply)*:

(a) Business, profession, or other self-employment	❒ Yes	❒ No
(b) Rent payments, interest, or dividends	❒ Yes	❒ No
(c) Pension, annuity, or life insurance payments	❒ Yes	❒ No
(d) Disability, or worker's compensation payments	❒ Yes	❒ No
(e) Gifts, or inheritances	❒ Yes	❒ No
(f) Any other sources	❒ Yes	❒ No

If you answered "Yes" to any question above, describe below or on separate pages each source of money and state the amount that you received and what you expect to receive in the future.

4. Amount of money that I have in cash or in a checking or savings account: $ ____________________ .

5. Any automobile, real estate, stock, bond, security, trust, jewelry, art work, or other financial instrument or thing of value that I own, including any item of value held in someone else's name *(describe the property and its approximate value)*:

6. Any housing, transportation, utilities, or loan payments, or other regular monthly expenses *(describe and provide the amount of the monthly expense)*:

7. Names (or, if under 18, initials only) of all persons who are dependent on me for support, my relationship with each person, and how much I contribute to their support:

8. Any debts or financial obligations *(describe the amounts owed and to whom they are payable)*:

Declaration: I declare under penalty of perjury that the above information is true and understand that a false statement may result in a dismissal of my claims.

Date: ____________________

____
Applicant's signature

____
Printed name

UNITED STATES DISTRICT COURT

for the

______________________ Plaintiff	)	
v.	)	Civil Action No.
______________________ Defendant	)	

ORDER TO PROCEED WITHOUT PREPAYING FEES OR COSTS

IT IS ORDERED: The plaintiff's application under 28 U.S.C. § 1915 to proceed without prepaying fees or costs is:

❒ Granted:

The clerk is ordered to file the complaint and issue a summons. The United States marshal is ordered to serve the summons with a copy of the complaint and this order on the defendant(s). The United States will advance the costs of service. Prisoner plaintiffs are responsible for full payment of the filing fee.

❒ Granted Conditionally:

The clerk is ordered to file the complaint. Upon receipt of the completed summons and USM-285 form for each defendant, the clerk will issue a summons. If the completed summons and USM-285 forms are not submitted as directed, the complaint may be dismissed. The United States marshal is ordered to serve the completed summons with a copy of the complaint and this order on the defendant(s). The United States will advance the costs of service. Prisoner plaintiffs are responsible for full payment of the filing fee.

❒ Denied:

This application is denied for these reasons:

Date: ______________

____
Judge's signature

____
Printed name and title

UNITED STATES DISTRICT COURT

for the

_______________________________)
Plaintiff)
v.) Civil Action No.
_______________________________)
Defendant)

NOTICE OF A LAWSUIT AND REQUEST TO WAIVE SERVICE OF A SUMMONS

To: ____
(Name of the defendant or - if the defendant is a corporation, partnership, or association - an officer or agent authorized to receive service)

Why are you getting this?

A lawsuit has been filed against you, or the entity you represent, in this court under the number shown above. A copy of the complaint is attached.

This is not a summons, or an official notice from the court. It is a request that, to avoid expenses, you waive formal service of a summons by signing and returning the enclosed waiver. To avoid these expenses, you must return the signed waiver within _____ days *(give at least 30 days, or at least 60 days if the defendant is outside any judicial district of the United States)* from the date shown below, which is the date this notice was sent. Two copies of the waiver form are enclosed, along with a stamped, self-addressed envelope or other prepaid means for returning one copy. You may keep the other copy.

What happens next?

If you return the signed waiver, I will file it with the court. The action will then proceed as if you had been served on the date the waiver is filed, but no summons will be served on you and you will have 60 days from the date this notice is sent (see the date below) to answer the complaint (or 90 days if this notice is sent to you outside any judicial district of the United States).

If you do not return the signed waiver within the time indicated, I will arrange to have the summons and complaint served on you. And I will ask the court to require you, or the entity you represent, to pay the expenses of making service.

Please read the enclosed statement about the duty to avoid unnecessary expenses.

I certify that this request is being sent to you on the date below.

Date: _______________

____
Signature of the attorney or unrepresented party

____
Printed name

____
Address

____
E-mail address

____
Telephone number

UNITED STATES DISTRICT COURT
for the

______________________________)
Plaintiff)
v.) Civil Action No.
______________________________)
Defendant)

WAIVER OF THE SERVICE OF SUMMONS

To: ______________________________
(Name of the plaintiff's attorney or unrepresented plaintiff)

I have received your request to waive service of a summons in this action along with a copy of the complaint, two copies of this waiver form, and a prepaid means of returning one signed copy of the form to you.

I, or the entity I represent, agree to save the expense of serving a summons and complaint in this case.

I understand that I, or the entity I represent, will keep all defenses or objections to the lawsuit, the court's jurisdiction, and the venue of the action, but that I waive any objections to the absence of a summons or of service.

I also understand that I, or the entity I represent, must file and serve an answer or a motion under Rule 12 within 60 days from ______________, the date when this request was sent (or 90 days if it was sent outside the United States). If I fail to do so, a default judgment will be entered against me or the entity I represent.

Date: ____________

____
Signature of the attorney or unrepresented party

____
Printed name of party waiving service of summons

____
Printed name

____
Address

____
E-mail address

____
Telephone number

Duty to Avoid Unnecessary Expenses of Serving a Summons

Rule 4 of the Federal Rules of Civil Procedure requires certain defendants to cooperate in saving unnecessary expenses of serving a summons and complaint. A defendant who is located in the United States and who fails to return a signed waiver of service requested by a plaintiff located in the United States will be required to pay the expenses of service, unless the defendant shows good cause for the failure.

"Good cause" does *not* include a belief that the lawsuit is groundless, or that it has been brought in an improper venue, or that the court has no jurisdiction over this matter or over the defendant or the defendant's property.

If the waiver is signed and returned, you can still make these and all other defenses and objections, but you cannot object to the absence of a summons or of service.

If you waive service, then you must, within the time specified on the waiver form, serve an answer or a motion under Rule 12 on the plaintiff and file a copy with the court. By signing and returning the waiver form, you are allowed more time to respond than if a summons had been served.

UNITED STATES DISTRICT COURT

for the

______________________________ *Plaintiff(s)*	)	
v.	)	Civil Action No.
______________________________ *Defendant(s)*	)	

SUMMONS IN A CIVIL ACTION

To: *(Defendant's name and address)*

A lawsuit has been filed against you.

Within 21 days after service of this summons on you (not counting the day you received it) — or 60 days if you are the United States or a United States agency, or an officer or employee of the United States described in Fed. R. Civ. P. 12 (a)(2) or (3) — you must serve on the plaintiff an answer to the attached complaint or a motion under Rule 12 of the Federal Rules of Civil Procedure. The answer or motion must be served on the plaintiff or plaintiff's attorney, whose name and address are:

If you fail to respond, judgment by default will be entered against you for the relief demanded in the complaint. You also must file your answer or motion with the court.

CLERK OF COURT

Date: ______________________

____
Signature of Clerk or Deputy Clerk

Civil Action No.

PROOF OF SERVICE

(This section should not be filed with the court unless required by Fed. R. Civ. P. 4 (l))

This summons for *(name of individual and title, if any)* ______________________
was received by me on *(date)* ______________ .

❒ I personally served the summons on the individual at *(place)* ______________________
______________________ on *(date)* ______________ ; or

❒ I left the summons at the individual's residence or usual place of abode with *(name)* ______________
______________________ , a person of suitable age and discretion who resides there,
on *(date)* ______________ , and mailed a copy to the individual's last known address; or

❒ I served the summons on *(name of individual)* ______________________ , who is
designated by law to accept service of process on behalf of *(name of organization)* ______________
______________________ on *(date)* ______________ ; or

❒ I returned the summons unexecuted because ______________________ ; or

❒ Other *(specify)*:

My fees are $ __________ for travel and $ __________ for services, for a total of $ 0.00 .

I declare under penalty of perjury that this information is true.

Date: ______________

____
Server's signature

____
Printed name and title

____
Server's address

Additional information regarding attempted service, etc:

UNITED STATES DISTRICT COURT

for the

_______________ *Plaintiff*	)	
v.	)	Civil Action No.
_______________ *Defendant, Third-party plaintiff*	)	
v.	)	
_______________ *Third-party defendant*	)	

SUMMONS ON A THIRD-PARTY COMPLAINT

To: *(Third-party defendant's name and address)*

A lawsuit has been filed against defendant ____________________, who as third-party plaintiff is making this claim against you to pay part or all of what the defendant may owe to the plaintiff ________________________.

Within 21 days after service of this summons on you (not counting the day you received it) — or 60 days if you are the United States or a United States agency, or an officer or employee of the United States described in Fed. R. Civ. P. 12 (a)(2) or (3) — you must serve on the plaintiff and on the defendant an answer to the attached complaint or a motion under Rule 12 of the Federal Rules of Civil Procedure. The answer or motion must be served on the defendant or defendant's attorney, whose name and address are:

It must also be served on the plaintiff or plaintiff's attorney, whose name and address are:

If you fail to respond, judgment by default will be entered against you for the relief demanded in the third-party complaint. You also must file the answer or motion with the court and serve it on any other parties.

A copy of the plaintiff's complaint is also attached. You may – but are not required to – respond to it.

Date: ______________

CLERK OF COURT

____
Signature of Clerk or Deputy Clerk

Civil Action No.

PROOF OF SERVICE

(This section should not be filed with the court unless required by Fed. R. Civ. P. 4 (l))

This summons for *(name of individual and title, if any)* ______________________________
was received by me on *(date)* ______________ .

❒ I personally served the summons on the individual at *(place)* ______________________________
______________________________ on *(date)* ______________ ; or

❒ I left the summons at the individual's residence or usual place of abode with *(name)* ______________
______________________________ , a person of suitable age and discretion who resides there,
on *(date)* ______________ , and mailed a copy to the individual's last known address; or

❒ I served the summons on *(name of individual)* ______________________________ , who is
designated by law to accept service of process on behalf of *(name of organization)* ______________
______________________________ on *(date)* ______________ ; or

❒ I returned the summons unexecuted because ______________________________ ; or

❒ Other *(specify)*: ______________________________
______________________________ .

My fees are $ ________ for travel and $ ________ for services, for a total of $ 0.00 .

I declare under penalty of perjury that this information is true.

Date: ______________

____
Server's signature

____
Printed name and title

____
Server's address

Additional information regarding attempted service, etc:

UNITED STATES DISTRICT COURT
for the

______________________________ *Plaintiff* v.	)))))	Civil Action No.
______________________________ *Defendant*		

WARRANT FOR THE ARREST OF A WITNESS IN A CIVIL ACTION

To: Any authorized law enforcement officer

YOU ARE COMMANDED to arrest and bring before this court *(name of person to be arrested)* ______________ ______________________________ , a witness who has been served with a subpoena to appear in this case and has failed to do so.

YOU ARE FURTHER COMMANDED to detain this witness until this court orders discharge from custody.

Date: ______________

CLERK OF COURT

City and state: ______________________

____
Signature of Clerk or Deputy Clerk

Return

This warrant was received on *(date)* ____________ and the person was arrested on *(date)* ____________ at *(city and state)* ______________________ .

Date: ______________

____
Arresting officer's signature

____
Printed name and title

This second page contains personal identifiers provided for law-enforcement use only and therefore should not be filed in court with the executed warrant unless under seal.

(Not for Public Disclosure)

Name of witness: ______________________

Known aliases: ______________________

Last known residence: ______________________

Prior addresses to which witness may still have ties: ______________________

____

Last known employment: ______________________

Last known telephone numbers: ______________________

Place of birth: ______________________

Date of birth: ______________________

Social Security number: ______________________

Height: ______________ Weight: ______________

Sex: ______________ Race: ______________

Hair: ______________ Eyes: ______________

Scars, tattoos, other distinguishing marks: ______________________

____

____

History of violence, weapons, drug use: ______________________

____

Known family, friends, and other associates *(name, relation, address, phone number)*:

____

FBI number: ______________________

Complete description of auto: ______________________

____

Investigative agency and address: ______________________

____

UNITED STATES DISTRICT COURT

for the

______________________________)
Plaintiff)
v.) Civil Action No.
______________________________)
Defendant)

JUDGMENT IN A CIVIL ACTION

The court has ordered that *(check one)*:

❒ the plaintiff *(name)* ____________________ recover from the defendant *(name)* ____________________ the amount of ____________________ dollars ($ ________), which includes prejudgment interest at the rate of ______ %, plus post judgment interest at the rate of ______ % per annum, along with costs.

❒ the plaintiff recover nothing, the action be dismissed on the merits, and the defendant *(name)* ____________________ recover costs from the plaintiff *(name)* ____________________ .

❒ other: .

This action was *(check one)*:

❒ tried by a jury with Judge ____________________ presiding, and the jury has rendered a verdict.

❒ tried by Judge ____________________ without a jury and the above decision was reached.

❒ decided by Judge ____________________ on a motion for .

Date: ________________ *CLERK OF COURT*

____
Signature of Clerk or Deputy Clerk

UNITED STATES DISTRICT COURT

for the

_______________ *Plaintiff*	)	
v.	)	Civil Action No.
_______________ *Defendant*	)	

CLERK'S CERTIFICATION OF A JUDGMENT TO BE REGISTERED IN ANOTHER DISTRICT

I certify that the attached judgment is a copy of a judgment entered by this court on *(date)* _______________ .

I also certify that, as appears from this court's records, no motion listed in Fed. R. App. P. 4(a)(4)(A) is pending before this court, the time for appeal has expired, and no appeal has been filed or, if one was filed, it is no longer pending.

Date: _______________

CLERK OF COURT

____

Signature of Clerk or Deputy Clerk

JS 44 (Rev. 06/17)

CIVIL COVER SHEET

The JS 44 civil cover sheet and the information contained herein neither replace nor supplement the filing and service of pleadings or other papers as required by law, except as provided by local rules of court. This form, approved by the Judicial Conference of the United States in September 1974, is required for the use of the Clerk of Court for the purpose of initiating the civil docket sheet. *(SEE INSTRUCTIONS ON NEXT PAGE OF THIS FORM.)*

I. (a) PLAINTIFFS

(b) County of Residence of First Listed Plaintiff ______________
(EXCEPT IN U.S. PLAINTIFF CASES)

(c) Attorneys *(Firm Name, Address, and Telephone Number)*

DEFENDANTS

County of Residence of First Listed Defendant ______________
(IN U.S. PLAINTIFF CASES ONLY)

NOTE: IN LAND CONDEMNATION CASES, USE THE LOCATION OF THE TRACT OF LAND INVOLVED.

Attorneys *(If Known)*

II. BASIS OF JURISDICTION *(Place an "X" in One Box Only)*

- ❒ 1 U.S. Government Plaintiff
- ❒ 3 Federal Question *(U.S. Government Not a Party)*
- ❒ 2 U.S. Government Defendant
- ❒ 4 Diversity *(Indicate Citizenship of Parties in Item III)*

III. CITIZENSHIP OF PRINCIPAL PARTIES *(Place an "X" in One Box for Plaintiff and One Box for Defendant)*

(For Diversity Cases Only)

	PTF	DEF		PTF	DEF
Citizen of This State	❒ 1	❒ 1	Incorporated *or* Principal Place of Business In This State	❒ 4	❒ 4
Citizen of Another State	❒ 2	❒ 2	Incorporated *and* Principal Place of Business In Another State	❒ 5	❒ 5
Citizen or Subject of a Foreign Country	❒ 3	❒ 3	Foreign Nation	❒ 6	❒ 6

IV. NATURE OF SUIT *(Place an "X" in One Box Only)*

Click here for: Nature of Suit Code Descriptions.

CONTRACT

- ❒ 110 Insurance
- ❒ 120 Marine
- ❒ 130 Miller Act
- ❒ 140 Negotiable Instrument
- ❒ 150 Recovery of Overpayment & Enforcement of Judgment
- ❒ 151 Medicare Act
- ❒ 152 Recovery of Defaulted Student Loans (Excludes Veterans)
- ❒ 153 Recovery of Overpayment of Veteran's Benefits
- ❒ 160 Stockholders' Suits
- ❒ 190 Other Contract
- ❒ 195 Contract Product Liability
- ❒ 196 Franchise

REAL PROPERTY

- ❒ 210 Land Condemnation
- ❒ 220 Foreclosure
- ❒ 230 Rent Lease & Ejectment
- ❒ 240 Torts to Land
- ❒ 245 Tort Product Liability
- ❒ 290 All Other Real Property

TORTS

PERSONAL INJURY

- ❒ 310 Airplane
- ❒ 315 Airplane Product Liability
- ❒ 320 Assault, Libel & Slander
- ❒ 330 Federal Employers' Liability
- ❒ 340 Marine
- ❒ 345 Marine Product Liability
- ❒ 350 Motor Vehicle
- ❒ 355 Motor Vehicle Product Liability
- ❒ 360 Other Personal Injury
- ❒ 362 Personal Injury - Medical Malpractice

PERSONAL INJURY

- ❒ 365 Personal Injury - Product Liability
- ❒ 367 Health Care/ Pharmaceutical Personal Injury Product Liability
- ❒ 368 Asbestos Personal Injury Product Liability

PERSONAL PROPERTY

- ❒ 370 Other Fraud
- ❒ 371 Truth in Lending
- ❒ 380 Other Personal Property Damage
- ❒ 385 Property Damage Product Liability

CIVIL RIGHTS

- ❒ 440 Other Civil Rights
- ❒ 441 Voting
- ❒ 442 Employment
- ❒ 443 Housing/ Accommodations
- ❒ 445 Amer. w/Disabilities - Employment
- ❒ 446 Amer. w/Disabilities - Other
- ❒ 448 Education

PRISONER PETITIONS

Habeas Corpus:

- ❒ 463 Alien Detainee
- ❒ 510 Motions to Vacate Sentence
- ❒ 530 General
- ❒ 535 Death Penalty

Other:

- ❒ 540 Mandamus & Other
- ❒ 550 Civil Rights
- ❒ 555 Prison Condition
- ❒ 560 Civil Detainee - Conditions of Confinement

FORFEITURE/PENALTY

- ❒ 625 Drug Related Seizure of Property 21 USC 881
- ❒ 690 Other

LABOR

- ❒ 710 Fair Labor Standards Act
- ❒ 720 Labor/Management Relations
- ❒ 740 Railway Labor Act
- ❒ 751 Family and Medical Leave Act
- ❒ 790 Other Labor Litigation
- ❒ 791 Employee Retirement Income Security Act

IMMIGRATION

- ❒ 462 Naturalization Application
- ❒ 465 Other Immigration Actions

BANKRUPTCY

- ❒ 422 Appeal 28 USC 158
- ❒ 423 Withdrawal 28 USC 157

PROPERTY RIGHTS

- ❒ 820 Copyrights
- ❒ 830 Patent
- ❒ 835 Patent - Abbreviated New Drug Application
- ❒ 840 Trademark

SOCIAL SECURITY

- ❒ 861 HIA (1395ff)
- ❒ 862 Black Lung (923)
- ❒ 863 DIWC/DIWW (405(g))
- ❒ 864 SSID Title XVI
- ❒ 865 RSI (405(g))

FEDERAL TAX SUITS

- ❒ 870 Taxes (U.S. Plaintiff or Defendant)
- ❒ 871 IRS—Third Party 26 USC 7609

OTHER STATUTES

- ❒ 375 False Claims Act
- ❒ 376 Qui Tam (31 USC 3729(a))
- ❒ 400 State Reapportionment
- ❒ 410 Antitrust
- ❒ 430 Banks and Banking
- ❒ 450 Commerce
- ❒ 460 Deportation
- ❒ 470 Racketeer Influenced and Corrupt Organizations
- ❒ 480 Consumer Credit
- ❒ 490 Cable/Sat TV
- ❒ 850 Securities/Commodities/ Exchange
- ❒ 890 Other Statutory Actions
- ❒ 891 Agricultural Acts
- ❒ 893 Environmental Matters
- ❒ 895 Freedom of Information Act
- ❒ 896 Arbitration
- ❒ 899 Administrative Procedure Act/Review or Appeal of Agency Decision
- ❒ 950 Constitutionality of State Statutes

V. ORIGIN *(Place an "X" in One Box Only)*

- ❒ 1 Original Proceeding
- ❒ 2 Removed from State Court
- ❒ 3 Remanded from Appellate Court
- ❒ 4 Reinstated or Reopened
- ❒ 5 Transferred from Another District *(specify)*
- ❒ 6 Multidistrict Litigation - Transfer
- ❒ 8 Multidistrict Litigation - Direct File

VI. CAUSE OF ACTION

Cite the U.S. Civil Statute under which you are filing ***(Do not cite jurisdictional statutes unless diversity)***:

Brief description of cause:

VII. REQUESTED IN COMPLAINT:

❒ CHECK IF THIS IS A **CLASS ACTION** UNDER RULE 23, F.R.Cv.P.

DEMAND $

CHECK YES only if demanded in complaint:
JURY DEMAND: ❒ Yes ❒ No

VIII. RELATED CASE(S) IF ANY

(See instructions): JUDGE ______________ DOCKET NUMBER ______________

DATE SIGNATURE OF ATTORNEY OF RECORD

FOR OFFICE USE ONLY

RECEIPT # AMOUNT APPLYING IFP JUDGE MAG. JUDGE

INSTRUCTIONS FOR ATTORNEYS COMPLETING CIVIL COVER SHEET FORM JS 44

Authority For Civil Cover Sheet

The JS 44 civil cover sheet and the information contained herein neither replaces nor supplements the filings and service of pleading or other papers as required by law, except as provided by local rules of court. This form, approved by the Judicial Conference of the United States in September 1974, is required for the use of the Clerk of Court for the purpose of initiating the civil docket sheet. Consequently, a civil cover sheet is submitted to the Clerk of Court for each civil complaint filed. The attorney filing a case should complete the form as follows:

I.(a) Plaintiffs-Defendants. Enter names (last, first, middle initial) of plaintiff and defendant. If the plaintiff or defendant is a government agency, use only the full name or standard abbreviations. If the plaintiff or defendant is an official within a government agency, identify first the agency and then the official, giving both name and title.

(b) County of Residence. For each civil case filed, except U.S. plaintiff cases, enter the name of the county where the first listed plaintiff resides at the time of filing. In U.S. plaintiff cases, enter the name of the county in which the first listed defendant resides at the time of filing. (NOTE: In land condemnation cases, the county of residence of the "defendant" is the location of the tract of land involved.)

(c) Attorneys. Enter the firm name, address, telephone number, and attorney of record. If there are several attorneys, list them on an attachment, noting in this section "(see attachment)".

II. Jurisdiction. The basis of jurisdiction is set forth under Rule 8(a), F.R.Cv.P., which requires that jurisdictions be shown in pleadings. Place an "X" in one of the boxes. If there is more than one basis of jurisdiction, precedence is given in the order shown below.
United States plaintiff. (1) Jurisdiction based on 28 U.S.C. 1345 and 1348. Suits by agencies and officers of the United States are included here.
United States defendant. (2) When the plaintiff is suing the United States, its officers or agencies, place an "X" in this box.
Federal question. (3) This refers to suits under 28 U.S.C. 1331, where jurisdiction arises under the Constitution of the United States, an amendment to the Constitution, an act of Congress or a treaty of the United States. In cases where the U.S. is a party, the U.S. plaintiff or defendant code takes precedence, and box 1 or 2 should be marked.
Diversity of citizenship. (4) This refers to suits under 28 U.S.C. 1332, where parties are citizens of different states. When Box 4 is checked, the citizenship of the different parties must be checked. (See Section III below; **NOTE: federal question actions take precedence over diversity cases.**)

III. Residence (citizenship) of Principal Parties. This section of the JS 44 is to be completed if diversity of citizenship was indicated above. Mark this section for each principal party.

IV. Nature of Suit. Place an "X" in the appropriate box. If there are multiple nature of suit codes associated with the case, pick the nature of suit code that is most applicable. Click here for: Nature of Suit Code Descriptions.

V. Origin. Place an "X" in one of the seven boxes.
Original Proceedings. (1) Cases which originate in the United States district courts.
Removed from State Court. (2) Proceedings initiated in state courts may be removed to the district courts under Title 28 U.S.C., Section 1441. When the petition for removal is granted, check this box.
Remanded from Appellate Court. (3) Check this box for cases remanded to the district court for further action. Use the date of remand as the filing date.
Reinstated or Reopened. (4) Check this box for cases reinstated or reopened in the district court. Use the reopening date as the filing date.
Transferred from Another District. (5) For cases transferred under Title 28 U.S.C. Section 1404(a). Do not use this for within district transfers or multidistrict litigation transfers.
Multidistrict Litigation – Transfer. (6) Check this box when a multidistrict case is transferred into the district under authority of Title 28 U.S.C. Section 1407.
Multidistrict Litigation – Direct File. (8) Check this box when a multidistrict case is filed in the same district as the Master MDL docket.
PLEASE NOTE THAT THERE IS NOT AN ORIGIN CODE 7. Origin Code 7 was used for historical records and is no longer relevant due to changes in statue.

VI. Cause of Action. Report the civil statute directly related to the cause of action and give a brief description of the cause. **Do not cite jurisdictional statutes unless diversity.** Example: U.S. Civil Statute: 47 USC 553 Brief Description: Unauthorized reception of cable service

VII. Requested in Complaint. Class Action. Place an "X" in this box if you are filing a class action under Rule 23, F.R.Cv.P.
Demand. In this space enter the actual dollar amount being demanded or indicate other demand, such as a preliminary injunction.
Jury Demand. Check the appropriate box to indicate whether or not a jury is being demanded.

VIII. Related Cases. This section of the JS 44 is used to reference related pending cases, if any. If there are related pending cases, insert the docket numbers and the corresponding judge names for such cases.

Date and Attorney Signature. Date and sign the civil cover sheet.

UNITED STATES DISTRICT COURT

for the

__________ District of __________

__________ Division

____________________ *Plaintiff(s)* *(Write the full name of each plaintiff who is filing this complaint. If the names of all the plaintiffs cannot fit in the space above, please write "see attached" in the space and attach an additional page with the full list of names.)* **-v-** ____________________ *Defendant(s)* *(Write the full name of each defendant who is being sued. If the names of all the defendants cannot fit in the space above, please write "see attached" in the space and attach an additional page with the full list of names.)*	)	Case No. ____________________ *(to be filled in by the Clerk's Office)* Jury Trial: *(check one)* ☐ Yes ☐ No

COMPLAINT FOR A CIVIL CASE

I. The Parties to This Complaint

A. The Plaintiff(s)

Provide the information below for each plaintiff named in the complaint. Attach additional pages if needed.

Name ____________________

Street Address ____________________

City and County ____________________

State and Zip Code ____________________

Telephone Number ____________________

E-mail Address ____________________

B. The Defendant(s)

Provide the information below for each defendant named in the complaint, whether the defendant is an individual, a government agency, an organization, or a corporation. For an individual defendant, include the person's job or title *(if known)*. Attach additional pages if needed.

Defendant No. 1

Name ______

Job or Title *(if known)* ______

Street Address ______

City and County ______

State and Zip Code ______

Telephone Number ______

E-mail Address *(if known)* ______

Defendant No. 2

Name ______

Job or Title *(if known)* ______

Street Address ______

City and County ______

State and Zip Code ______

Telephone Number ______

E-mail Address *(if known)* ______

Defendant No. 3

Name ______

Job or Title *(if known)* ______

Street Address ______

City and County ______

State and Zip Code ______

Telephone Number ______

E-mail Address *(if known)* ______

Defendant No. 4

Name ______

Job or Title *(if known)* ______

Street Address ______

City and County ______

State and Zip Code ______

Telephone Number ______

E-mail Address *(if known)* ______

II. Basis for Jurisdiction

Federal courts are courts of limited jurisdiction (limited power). Generally, only two types of cases can be heard in federal court: cases involving a federal question and cases involving diversity of citizenship of the parties. Under 28 U.S.C. § 1331, a case arising under the United States Constitution or federal laws or treaties is a federal question case. Under 28 U.S.C. § 1332, a case in which a citizen of one State sues a citizen of another State or nation and the amount at stake is more than $75,000 is a diversity of citizenship case. In a diversity of citizenship case, no defendant may be a citizen of the same State as any plaintiff.

What is the basis for federal court jurisdiction? *(check all that apply)*

☐ Federal question ☐ Diversity of citizenship

Fill out the paragraphs in this section that apply to this case.

A. If the Basis for Jurisdiction Is a Federal Question

List the specific federal statutes, federal treaties, and/or provisions of the United States Constitution that are at issue in this case.

B. If the Basis for Jurisdiction Is Diversity of Citizenship

1. The Plaintiff(s)

a. If the plaintiff is an individual

The plaintiff, *(name)* ____________________, is a citizen of the State of *(name)* ____________________.

b. If the plaintiff is a corporation

The plaintiff, *(name)* ____________________, is incorporated under the laws of the State of *(name)* ____________________, and has its principal place of business in the State of *(name)* ____________________.

(If more than one plaintiff is named in the complaint, attach an additional page providing the same information for each additional plaintiff.)

2. The Defendant(s)

a. If the defendant is an individual

The defendant, *(name)* ____________________, is a citizen of the State of *(name)* ____________________. Or is a citizen of *(foreign nation)* ____________________.

b. If the defendant is a corporation

The defendant, *(name)* ____________________, is incorporated under the laws of the State of *(name)* ____________________, and has its principal place of business in the State of *(name)* ____________________.
Or is incorporated under the laws of *(foreign nation)* ____________________,
and has its principal place of business in *(name)* ____________________.

(If more than one defendant is named in the complaint, attach an additional page providing the same information for each additional defendant.)

3. The Amount in Controversy

The amount in controversy–the amount the plaintiff claims the defendant owes or the amount at stake–is more than $75,000, not counting interest and costs of court, because *(explain)*:

III. Statement of Claim

Write a short and plain statement of the claim. Do not make legal arguments. State as briefly as possible the facts showing that each plaintiff is entitled to the damages or other relief sought. State how each defendant was involved and what each defendant did that caused the plaintiff harm or violated the plaintiff's rights, including the dates and places of that involvement or conduct. If more than one claim is asserted, number each claim and write a short and plain statement of each claim in a separate paragraph. Attach additional pages if needed.

IV. Relief

State briefly and precisely what damages or other relief the plaintiff asks the court to order. Do not make legal arguments. Include any basis for claiming that the wrongs alleged are continuing at the present time. Include the amounts of any actual damages claimed for the acts alleged and the basis for these amounts. Include any punitive or exemplary damages claimed, the amounts, and the reasons you claim you are entitled to actual or punitive money damages.

V. Certification and Closing

Under Federal Rule of Civil Procedure 11, by signing below, I certify to the best of my knowledge, information, and belief that this complaint: (1) is not being presented for an improper purpose, such as to harass, cause unnecessary delay, or needlessly increase the cost of litigation; (2) is supported by existing law or by a nonfrivolous argument for extending, modifying, or reversing existing law; (3) the factual contentions have evidentiary support or, if specifically so identified, will likely have evidentiary support after a reasonable opportunity for further investigation or discovery; and (4) the complaint otherwise complies with the requirements of Rule 11.

A. For Parties Without an Attorney

I agree to provide the Clerk's Office with any changes to my address where case–related papers may be served. I understand that my failure to keep a current address on file with the Clerk's Office may result in the dismissal of my case.

Date of signing: ____________________

Signature of Plaintiff ____________________

Printed Name of Plaintiff ____________________

B. For Attorneys

Date of signing: ____________________

Signature of Attorney ____________________

Printed Name of Attorney ____________________

Bar Number ____________________

Name of Law Firm ____________________

Street Address ____________________

State and Zip Code ____________________

Telephone Number ____________________

E-mail Address ____________________

UNITED STATES DISTRICT COURT

for the

_________ District of _________

_________ Division

________________________ *Plaintiff(s)* *(Write the full name of each plaintiff who is filing this complaint. If the names of all the plaintiffs cannot fit in the space above, please write "see attached" in the space and attach an additional page with the full list of names.)* **-v-** ________________________ *Defendant(s)* *(Write the full name of each defendant who is being sued. If the names of all the defendants cannot fit in the space above, please write "see attached" in the space and attach an additional page with the full list of names.)*	)	Case No. ________________ *(to be filled in by the Clerk's Office)*

COMPLAINT AND REQUEST FOR INJUNCTION

I. The Parties to This Complaint

A. The Plaintiff(s)

Provide the information below for each plaintiff named in the complaint. Attach additional pages if needed.

Name	________________
Street Address	________________
City and County	________________
State and Zip Code	________________
Telephone Number	________________
E-mail Address	________________

B. The Defendant(s)

Provide the information below for each defendant named in the complaint, whether the defendant is an individual, a government agency, an organization, or a corporation. For an individual defendant, include the person's job or title *(if known)*. Attach additional pages if needed.

Defendant No. 1

Name ________________

Job or Title *(if known)* ________________

Street Address ________________

City and County ________________

State and Zip Code ________________

Telephone Number ________________

E-mail Address *(if known)* ________________

Defendant No. 2

Name ________________

Job or Title *(if known)* ________________

Street Address ________________

City and County ________________

State and Zip Code ________________

Telephone Number ________________

E-mail Address *(if known)* ________________

Defendant No. 3

Name ________________

Job or Title *(if known)* ________________

Street Address ________________

City and County ________________

State and Zip Code ________________

Telephone Number ________________

E-mail Address *(if known)* ________________

Defendant No. 4

Name ________________

Job or Title *(if known)* ________________

Street Address ________________

City and County ________________

State and Zip Code ________________

Telephone Number ________________

E-mail Address *(if known)* ________________

II. Basis for Jurisdiction

Federal courts are courts of limited jurisdiction (limited power). Generally, only two types of cases can be heard in federal court: cases involving a federal question and cases involving diversity of citizenship of the parties. Under 28 U.S.C. § 1331, a case arising under the United States Constitution or federal laws or treaties is a federal question case. Under 28 U.S.C. § 1332, a case in which a citizen of one State sues a citizen of another State or nation and the amount at stake is more than $75,000 is a diversity of citizenship case. In a diversity of citizenship case, no defendant may be a citizen of the same State as any plaintiff.

What is the basis for federal court jurisdiction? *(check all that apply)*

☐ Federal question ☐ Diversity of citizenship

Fill out the paragraphs in this section that apply to this case.

A. If the Basis for Jurisdiction Is a Federal Question

List the specific federal statutes, federal treaties, and/or provisions of the United States Constitution that are at issue in this case.

B. If the Basis for Jurisdiction Is Diversity of Citizenship

1. The Plaintiff(s)

a. If the plaintiff is an individual

The plaintiff, *(name)* ________________, is a citizen of the State of *(name)* ________________.

b. If the plaintiff is a corporation

The plaintiff, *(name)* ________________, is incorporated under the laws of the State of *(name)* ________________, and has its principal place of business in the State of *(name)* ________________.

(If more than one plaintiff is named in the complaint, attach an additional page providing the same information for each additional plaintiff.)

2. The Defendant(s)

a. If the defendant is an individual

The defendant, *(name)* ________________, is a citizen of the State of *(name)* ________________. Or is a citizen of *(foreign nation)* ________________.

b. If the defendant is a corporation

The defendant, *(name)* ____________________, is incorporated under the laws of the State of *(name)* ____________________, and has its principal place of business in the State of *(name)* ____________________.
Or is incorporated under the laws of *(foreign nation)* ____________________,
and has its principal place of business in *(name)* ____________________.

(If more than one defendant is named in the complaint, attach an additional page providing the same information for each additional defendant.)

3. The Amount in Controversy

The amount in controversy–the amount the plaintiff claims the defendant owes or the amount at stake–is more than $75,000, not counting interest and costs of court, because *(explain)*:

III. Statement of Claim

Write a short and plain statement of the claim. Do not make legal arguments. State as briefly as possible the facts showing that each plaintiff is entitled to the injunction or other relief sought. State how each defendant was involved and what each defendant did that caused the plaintiff harm or violated the plaintiff's rights, including the dates and places of that involvement or conduct. If more than one claim is asserted, number each claim and write a short and plain statement of each claim in a separate paragraph. Attach additional pages if needed.

A. Where did the events giving rise to your claim(s) occur?

B. What date and approximate time did the events giving rise to your claim(s) occur?

C. What are the facts underlying your claim(s)? *(For example: What happened to you? Who did what? Was anyone else involved? Who else saw what happened?)*

IV. Irreparable Injury

Explain why monetary damages at a later time would not adequately compensate you for the injuries you sustained, are sustaining, or will sustain as a result of the events described above, or why such compensation could not be measured.

V. Relief

State briefly and precisely what damages or other relief the plaintiff asks the court to order. Do not make legal arguments. Include any basis for claiming that the wrongs alleged are continuing at the present time. Include the amounts of any actual damages claimed for the acts alleged and the basis for these amounts. Include any punitive or exemplary damages claimed, the amounts, and the reasons you claim you are entitled to actual or punitive money damages.

VI. Certification and Closing

Under Federal Rule of Civil Procedure 11, by signing below, I certify to the best of my knowledge, information, and belief that this complaint: (1) is not being presented for an improper purpose, such as to harass, cause unnecessary delay, or needlessly increase the cost of litigation; (2) is supported by existing law or by a nonfrivolous argument for extending, modifying, or reversing existing law; (3) the factual contentions have evidentiary support or, if specifically so identified, will likely have evidentiary support after a reasonable opportunity for further investigation or discovery; and (4) the complaint otherwise complies with the requirements of Rule 11.

A. For Parties Without an Attorney

I agree to provide the Clerk's Office with any changes to my address where case–related papers may be served. I understand that my failure to keep a current address on file with the Clerk's Office may result in the dismissal of my case.

Date of signing: ____________________

Signature of Plaintiff ____________________

Printed Name of Plaintiff ____________________

B. For Attorneys

Date of signing: ____________________

Signature of Attorney ____________________

Printed Name of Attorney ____________________

Bar Number ____________________

Name of Law Firm ____________________

Street Address ____________________

State and Zip Code ____________________

Telephone Number ____________________

E-mail Address ____________________

UNITED STATES DISTRICT COURT

for the

_________ District of _________

_________ Division

______________________________ Plaintiff(s) *(Write the full name of each plaintiff who is filing this complaint. If the names of all the plaintiffs cannot fit in the space above, please write "see attached" in the space and attach an additional page with the full list of names.)*	)	Case No. ______________ *(to be filled in by the Clerk's Office)*
-v-	)	Jury Trial: *(check one)* ☐ Yes ☐ No
______________________________ Defendant(s) *(Write the full name of each defendant who is being sued. If the names of all the defendants cannot fit in the space above, please write "see attached" in the space and attach an additional page with the full list of names.)*	)	

THE DEFENDANT'S ANSWER TO THE COMPLAINT

I. The Parties Filing This Answer to the Complaint

Provide the information below for each defendant filing this answer or other response to the allegations in the plaintiff's complaint. Attach additional pages if needed.

Name	______________
Street Address	______________
City and County	______________
State and Zip Code	______________
Telephone Number	______________
E-mail Address	______________

II. The Answer and Defenses to the Complaint

A. Answering the Claims for Relief

On a separate page or pages, write a short and plain statement of the answer to the allegations in the complaint. Number the paragraphs. The answer should correspond to each paragraph in the complaint, with paragraph 1 of the answer corresponding to paragraph 1 of the complaint, etc. For each paragraph in the complaint, state whether: the defendant admits the allegations in that paragraph; denies the allegations; lacks sufficient knowledge to admit or deny the allegations; or admits certain allegations but denies, or lacks sufficient knowledge to admit or deny, the rest.

B. Presenting Defenses to the Claims for Relief

Write a short and plain statement identifying the defenses to the claims, using one or more of the following alternatives that apply.

1. The court does not have subject–matter jurisdiction over the claims because *(briefly explain why there is no federal–question jurisdiction or diversity–of–citizenship jurisdiction; see the complaint form for more information)*

2. The court does not have personal jurisdiction over the defendant because *(briefly explain)*

3. The venue where the court is located is improper for this case because *(briefly explain)*

4. The defendant was served but the process–the form of the summons–was insufficient because *(briefly explain)*

5. The manner of serving the defendant with the summons and complaint was insufficient because *(briefly explain)*

6. The complaint fails to state a claim upon which relief can be granted because *(briefly explain why the facts alleged, even if true, are not enough to show the plaintiff's right to recover)*

7. Another party *(name)* ________________ needs to be joined (added) in the case. The reason is *(briefly explain why joining another party is required)*

a. If the basis for subject–matter jurisdiction is diversity of citizenship, state the effect of adding the other party:

The other party is a citizen of the State of *(name)* ____________________.

Or is a citizen of *(foreign nation)* ____________________. The amount of damages sought from this other party is *(specify the amount)* ____________________.

b. If the claim by this other party is based on an alleged violation of a federal constitutional or statutory right, state the basis:

C. Asserting Affirmative Defenses to the Claims for Relief

Identify an affirmative defense or avoidance that provides a basis for the defendant to avoid liability for one or more of the plaintiff's claims even if the basis for the claim is met. Any affirmative defense or avoidance must be identified in the answer. Include any of the following that apply, as well as any others that may apply.

The plaintiff's claim for *(specify the claim)*

is barred by *(identify one or more of the following that apply)*:

1. Accord and satisfaction *(briefly explain)*

2. Arbitration and award *(briefly explain)*

3. Assumption of risk *(briefly explain)*

4. Contributory or comparative negligence of the plaintiff *(briefly explain)*

5. Duress *(briefly explain)*

6. Estoppel *(briefly explain)*

7. Failure of consideration *(briefly explain)*

8. Fraud *(briefly explain)*

9. Illegality *(briefly explain)*

10. Injury by fellow employee *(briefly explain)*

11. Laches (Delay) *(briefly explain)*

12. License *(briefly explain)*

13. Payment *(briefly explain)*

14. Release *(briefly explain)*

15. Res judicata *(briefly explain)*

16. Statute of frauds *(briefly explain)*

17. Statute of limitations *(briefly explain)*

18. Waiver *(briefly explain)*

19. Other *(briefly explain)*

D. Asserting Claims Against the Plaintiff (Counterclaim) or Against Another Defendant (Cross–Claim)

For either a counterclaim against the plaintiff or a cross–claim against another defendant, state briefly the facts showing why the defendant asserting the counterclaim or cross–claim is entitled to the damages or other relief sought. Do not make legal arguments. State how each opposing party was involved and what each did that caused the defendant harm or violated the defendant's rights, including the dates and places of that involvement or conduct. If more than one counterclaim or cross–claim is asserted, number each claim and write a short and plain statement of each claim in a separate paragraph. Attach additional pages if needed.

1. The defendant has the following claim against the plaintiff *(specify the claim and explain it; include a further statement of jurisdiction, if needed)*:

2. The defendant has the following claim against one or more of the other defendants *(specify the claim and explain it; include a further statement of jurisdiction, if needed)*:

3. State briefly and precisely what damages or other relief the party asserting a counterclaim or cross–claim asks the court to order. Do not make legal arguments. Include any basis for claiming that the wrongs alleged are continuing at the present time. Include the amounts of any actual damages claimed for the acts alleged and the basis for these amounts. Include any punitive or exemplary damages claimed, the amounts, and the reasons that are alleged to entitle the party to actual or punitive money damages.

a. The defendant asserting the counterclaim or cross–claim against *(specify who the claim is against)* ____________________ alleges that the following injury or damages resulted *(specify)*:

b. The defendant seeks the following damages or other relief *(specify)*:

III. Certification and Closing

Under Federal Rule of Civil Procedure 11, by signing below, I certify to the best of my knowledge, information, and belief that this answer: (1) is not being presented for an improper purpose, such as to harass, cause unnecessary delay, or needlessly increase the cost of litigation; (2) is supported by existing law or by a nonfrivolous argument for extending, modifying, or reversing existing law; (3) the factual contentions have evidentiary support or, if specifically so identified, will likely have evidentiary support after a reasonable opportunity for further investigation or discovery; and (4) the answer otherwise complies with the requirements of Rule 11.

A. For Parties Without an Attorney

I agree to provide the Clerk's Office with any changes to my address where case–related papers may be served. I understand that my failure to keep a current address on file with the Clerk's Office may result in the dismissal of my case.

Date of signing: ________________

Signature of Defendant ________________

Printed Name of Defendant ________________

B. For Attorneys

Date of signing: ________________

Signature of Attorney ________________

Printed Name of Attorney ________________

Bar Number ________________

Name of Law Firm ________________

Street Address ________________

State and Zip Code ________________

Telephone Number ______________________

E-mail Address ______________________

UNITED STATES DISTRICT COURT

for the

__________ District of __________

__________ Division

______________________________ *Plaintiff(s)* *(Write the full name of each plaintiff who is filing this complaint. If the names of all the plaintiffs cannot fit in the space above, please write "see attached" in the space and attach an additional page with the full list of names.)* **-v-** ______________________________ *Defendant(s)* *(Write the full name of each defendant who is being sued. If the names of all the defendants cannot fit in the space above, please write "see attached" in the space and attach an additional page with the full list of names.)*	)))))))))))))))	Case No. ______________________ *(to be filled in by the Clerk's Office)* Jury Trial: *(check one)* ☐ Yes ☐ No

COMPLAINT FOR A CIVIL CASE ALLEGING BREACH OF CONTRACT
(28 U.S.C. § 1332; Diversity of Citizenship)

I. The Parties to This Complaint

A. The Plaintiff(s)

Provide the information below for each plaintiff named in the complaint. Attach additional pages if needed.

Name	______________________
Street Address	______________________
City and County	______________________
State and Zip Code	______________________
Telephone Number	______________________
E-mail Address	______________________

B. The Defendant(s)

Provide the information below for each defendant named in the complaint, whether the defendant is an individual, a government agency, an organization, or a corporation. For an individual defendant, include the person's job or title *(if known)*. Attach additional pages if needed.

Defendant No. 1

Name __________
Job or Title *(if known)* __________
Street Address __________
City and County __________
State and Zip Code __________
Telephone Number __________
E-mail Address *(if known)* __________

Defendant No. 2

Name __________
Job or Title *(if known)* __________
Street Address __________
City and County __________
State and Zip Code __________
Telephone Number __________
E-mail Address *(if known)* __________

Defendant No. 3

Name __________
Job or Title *(if known)* __________
Street Address __________
City and County __________
State and Zip Code __________
Telephone Number __________
E-mail Address *(if known)* __________

Defendant No. 4

Name __________
Job or Title *(if known)* __________
Street Address __________
City and County __________
State and Zip Code __________
Telephone Number __________
E-mail Address *(if known)* __________

II. Basis for Jurisdiction

Federal courts are courts of limited jurisdiction (limited power). Under 28 U.S.C. § 1332, federal courts may hear cases in which a citizen of one State sues a citizen of another State or nation and the amount at stake is more than $75,000. In that kind of case, called a diversity of citizenship case, no defendant may be a citizen of the same State as any plaintiff. Explain how these jurisdictional requirements have been met.

A. The Plaintiff(s)

1. If the plaintiff is an individual

   The plaintiff, *(name)* ______________________________, is a citizen of the State of *(name)* ____________________________.

2. If the plaintiff is a corporation

   The plaintiff, *(name)* ______________________________, is incorporated under the laws of the State of *(name)* ______________________________, and has its principal place of business in the State of *(name)* ____________________________.

(If more than one plaintiff is named in the complaint, attach an additional page providing the same information for each additional plaintiff.)

B. The Defendant(s)

1. If the defendant is an individual

   The defendant, *(name)* ______________________________, is a citizen of the State of *(name)* ______________________________. Or is a citizen of *(foreign nation)* ____________________________.

2. If the defendant is a corporation

   The defendant, *(name)* ______________________________, is incorporated under the laws of the State of *(name)* ______________________________, and has its principal place of business in the State of *(name)* ____________________________. Or is incorporated under the laws of *(foreign nation)* ____________________________, and has its principal place of business in *(name)* ____________________________.

(If more than one defendant is named in the complaint, attach an additional page providing the same information for each additional defendant.)

C. The Amount in Controversy

The amount in controversy–the amount the plaintiff claims the defendant owes or the amount at stake–is more than $75,000, not counting interest and costs of court, because *(explain)*:

III. Statement of Claim

Write a short and plain statement of the claim. Do not make legal arguments. State as briefly as possible the facts showing that each plaintiff is entitled to the damages or other relief sought. State how each defendant was involved and what each defendant did that caused the plaintiff harm or violated the plaintiff's rights, including the dates and places of that involvement or conduct. If more than one claim is asserted, number each claim and write a short and plain statement of each claim in a separate paragraph. Attach additional pages if needed.

The plaintiff, *(name)* ____________________, and the defendant, *(name)* ____________________, made an agreement or contract on *(date)* __________. The agreement or contract was *(oral or written)* __________. Under that agreement or contract, the parties were required to *(specify what the agreement or contract required each party to do)*

The defendant failed to comply because *(specify what the defendant did or failed to do that failed to comply with what the agreement or contract required)*

The plaintiff has complied with the plaintiff's obligations under the contract.

IV. Relief

State briefly and precisely what damages or other relief the plaintiff asks the court to order. Do not make legal arguments. Include any basis for claiming that the wrongs alleged are continuing at the present time. Include the amounts of any actual damages claimed for the acts alleged and the basis for these amounts. Include any punitive or exemplary damages claimed, the amounts, and the reasons you claim you are entitled to actual or punitive money damages.

V. Certification and Closing

Under Federal Rule of Civil Procedure 11, by signing below, I certify to the best of my knowledge, information, and belief that this complaint: (1) is not being presented for an improper purpose, such as to harass, cause unnecessary delay, or needlessly increase the cost of litigation; (2) is supported by existing law or by a nonfrivolous argument for extending, modifying, or reversing existing law; (3) the factual contentions have evidentiary support or, if specifically so identified, will likely have evidentiary support after a reasonable opportunity for further investigation or discovery; and (4) the complaint otherwise complies with the requirements of Rule 11.

A. For Parties Without an Attorney

I agree to provide the Clerk's Office with any changes to my address where case–related papers may be served. I understand that my failure to keep a current address on file with the Clerk's Office may result in the dismissal of my case.

Date of signing: ______________

Signature of Plaintiff ______________

Printed Name of Plaintiff ______________

B. For Attorneys

Date of signing: ______________

Signature of Attorney ______________

Printed Name of Attorney ______________

Bar Number ______________

Name of Law Firm ______________

Street Address ______________

State and Zip Code ______________

Telephone Number ______________

E-mail Address ______________

UNITED STATES DISTRICT COURT

for the

_________ District of _________

_________ Division

_______________ *Plaintiff(s)* *(Write the full name of each plaintiff who is filing this complaint. If the names of all the plaintiffs cannot fit in the space above, please write "see attached" in the space and attach an additional page with the full list of names.)* **-v-** _______________ *Defendant(s)* *(Write the full name of each defendant who is being sued. If the names of all the defendants cannot fit in the space above, please write "see attached" in the space and attach an additional page with the full list of names.)*	)	Case No. _______________ *(to be filled in by the Clerk's Office)* Jury Trial: *(check one)* ☐ Yes ☐ No

COMPLAINT FOR A CIVIL CASE ALLEGING NEGLIGENCE
(28 U.S.C. § 1332; Diversity of Citizenship)

I. The Parties to This Complaint

A. The Plaintiff(s)

Provide the information below for each plaintiff named in the complaint. Attach additional pages if needed.

Name _______________
Street Address _______________
City and County _______________
State and Zip Code _______________
Telephone Number _______________
E-mail Address _______________

B. The Defendant(s)

Provide the information below for each defendant named in the complaint, whether the defendant is an individual, a government agency, an organization, or a corporation. For an individual defendant, include the person's job or title *(if known)*. Attach additional pages if needed.

Defendant No. 1

Name ______________________________

Job or Title *(if known)* ______________________________

Street Address ______________________________

City and County ______________________________

State and Zip Code ______________________________

Telephone Number ______________________________

E-mail Address *(if known)* ______________________________

Defendant No. 2

Name ______________________________

Job or Title *(if known)* ______________________________

Street Address ______________________________

City and County ______________________________

State and Zip Code ______________________________

Telephone Number ______________________________

E-mail Address *(if known)* ______________________________

Defendant No. 3

Name ______________________________

Job or Title *(if known)* ______________________________

Street Address ______________________________

City and County ______________________________

State and Zip Code ______________________________

Telephone Number ______________________________

E-mail Address *(if known)* ______________________________

Defendant No. 4

Name ______________________________

Job or Title *(if known)* ______________________________

Street Address ______________________________

City and County ______________________________

State and Zip Code ______________________________

Telephone Number ______________________________

E-mail Address *(if known)* ______________________________

II. Basis for Jurisdiction

Federal courts are courts of limited jurisdiction (limited power). Under 28 U.S.C. § 1332, federal courts may hear cases in which a citizen of one State sues a citizen of another State or nation and the amount at stake is more than $75,000. In that kind of case, called a diversity of citizenship case, no defendant may be a citizen of the same State as any plaintiff. Explain how these jurisdictional requirements have been met.

A. The Plaintiff(s)

1. If the plaintiff is an individual

   The plaintiff, *(name)* ____________________, is a citizen of the State of *(name)* ____________________.

2. If the plaintiff is a corporation

   The plaintiff, *(name)* ____________________, is incorporated under the laws of the State of *(name)* ____________________, and has its principal place of business in the State of *(name)* ____________________.

(If more than one plaintiff is named in the complaint, attach an additional page providing the same information for each additional plaintiff.)

B. The Defendant(s)

1. If the defendant is an individual

   The defendant, *(name)* ____________________, is a citizen of the State of *(name)* ____________________. Or is a citizen of *(foreign nation)* ____________________.

2. If the defendant is a corporation

   The defendant, *(name)* ____________________, is incorporated under the laws of the State of *(name)* ____________________, and has its principal place of business in the State of *(name)* ____________________. Or is incorporated under the laws of *(foreign nation)* ____________________, and has its principal place of business in *(name)* ____________________.

(If more than one defendant is named in the complaint, attach an additional page providing the same information for each additional defendant.)

C. The Amount in Controversy

The amount in controversy–the amount the plaintiff claims the defendant owes or the amount at stake–is more than $75,000, not counting interest and costs of court, because *(explain)*:

III. Statement of Claim

Write a short and plain statement of the claim. Do not make legal arguments. State as briefly as possible the facts showing that each plaintiff is entitled to the damages or other relief sought. State how each defendant was involved and what each defendant did that caused the plaintiff harm or violated the plaintiff's rights, including the dates and places of that involvement or conduct. If more than one claim is asserted, number each claim and write a short and plain statement of each claim in a separate paragraph. Attach additional pages if needed.

On *(date)* ____________, at *(place)* ______________________________,
the defendant(s): (1) performed acts that a person of ordinary prudence in the same or similar circumstances would not have done; or (2) failed to perform acts that a person of ordinary prudence would have done under the same or similar circumstances because *(describe the acts or failures to act and why they were negligent)*

The acts or omissions caused or contributed to the cause of the plaintiff's injuries by *(explain)*

IV. Relief

State briefly and precisely what damages or other relief the plaintiff asks the court to order. Do not make legal arguments. Include any basis for claiming that the wrongs alleged are continuing at the present time. Include the amounts of any actual damages claimed for the acts alleged and the basis for these amounts. Include any punitive or exemplary damages claimed, the amounts, and the reasons you claim you are entitled to actual or punitive money damages.

V. Certification and Closing

Under Federal Rule of Civil Procedure 11, by signing below, I certify to the best of my knowledge, information, and belief that this complaint: (1) is not being presented for an improper purpose, such as to harass, cause unnecessary delay, or needlessly increase the cost of litigation; (2) is supported by existing law or by a nonfrivolous argument for extending, modifying, or reversing existing law; (3) the factual contentions have evidentiary support or, if specifically so identified, will likely have evidentiary support after a reasonable opportunity for further investigation or discovery; and (4) the complaint otherwise complies with the requirements of Rule 11.

A. For Parties Without an Attorney

I agree to provide the Clerk's Office with any changes to my address where case–related papers may be served. I understand that my failure to keep a current address on file with the Clerk's Office may result in the dismissal of my case.

Date of signing: ________________

Signature of Plaintiff ________________

Printed Name of Plaintiff ________________

B. For Attorneys

Date of signing: ________________

Signature of Attorney ________________

Printed Name of Attorney ________________

Bar Number ________________

Name of Law Firm ________________

Street Address ________________

State and Zip Code ________________

Telephone Number ________________

E-mail Address ________________

UNITED STATES DISTRICT COURT

for the

__________ District of __________

__________ Division

Case No. ____________________

(to be filled in by the Clerk's Office)

Jury Trial: *(check one)* ☐ Yes ☐ No

____

Plaintiff(s)

(Write the full name of each plaintiff who is filing this complaint. If the names of all the plaintiffs cannot fit in the space above, please write "see attached" in the space and attach an additional page with the full list of names.)

-v-

____

Defendant(s)

(Write the full name of each defendant who is being sued. If the names of all the defendants cannot fit in the space above, please write "see attached" in the space and attach an additional page with the full list of names.)

COMPLAINT FOR A CIVIL CASE ALLEGING THAT THE DEFENDANT OWES PLAINTIFF A SUM OF MONEY

(28 U.S.C. § 1332; Diversity of Citizenship)

I. The Parties to This Complaint

A. The Plaintiff(s)

Provide the information below for each plaintiff named in the complaint. Attach additional pages if needed.

Name ____________________

Street Address ____________________

City and County ____________________

State and Zip Code ____________________

Telephone Number ____________________

E-mail Address ____________________

B. The Defendant(s)

Provide the information below for each defendant named in the complaint, whether the defendant is an individual, a government agency, an organization, or a corporation. For an individual defendant, include the person's job or title *(if known)*. Attach additional pages if needed.

Defendant No. 1

Name ______________________________

Job or Title *(if known)* ______________________________

Street Address ______________________________

City and County ______________________________

State and Zip Code ______________________________

Telephone Number ______________________________

E-mail Address *(if known)* ______________________________

Defendant No. 2

Name ______________________________

Job or Title *(if known)* ______________________________

Street Address ______________________________

City and County ______________________________

State and Zip Code ______________________________

Telephone Number ______________________________

E-mail Address *(if known)* ______________________________

Defendant No. 3

Name ______________________________

Job or Title *(if known)* ______________________________

Street Address ______________________________

City and County ______________________________

State and Zip Code ______________________________

Telephone Number ______________________________

E-mail Address *(if known)* ______________________________

Defendant No. 4

Name ______________________________

Job or Title *(if known)* ______________________________

Street Address ______________________________

City and County ______________________________

State and Zip Code ______________________________

Telephone Number ______________________________

E-mail Address *(if known)* ______________________________

II. Basis for Jurisdiction

Federal courts are courts of limited jurisdiction (limited power). Under 28 U.S.C. § 1332, federal courts may hear cases in which a citizen of one State sues a citizen of another State or nation and the amount at stake is more than $75,000. In that kind of case, called a diversity of citizenship case, no defendant may be a citizen of the same State as any plaintiff. Explain how these jurisdictional requirements have been met.

A. The Plaintiff(s)

1. If the plaintiff is an individual

   The plaintiff, *(name)* ____________________, is a citizen of the State of *(name)* ____________________.

2. If the plaintiff is a corporation

   The plaintiff, *(name)* ____________________, is incorporated under the laws of the State of *(name)* ____________________, and has its principal place of business in the State of *(name)* ____________________.

(If more than one plaintiff is named in the complaint, attach an additional page providing the same information for each additional plaintiff.)

B. The Defendant(s)

1. If the defendant is an individual

   The defendant, *(name)* ____________________, is a citizen of the State of *(name)* ____________________. Or is a citizen of *(foreign nation)* ____________________.

2. If the defendant is a corporation

   The defendant, *(name)* ____________________, is incorporated under the laws of the State of *(name)* ____________________, and has its principal place of business in the State of *(name)* ____________________.
   Or is incorporated under the laws of *(foreign nation)* ____________________, and has its principal place of business in *(name)* ____________________.

(If more than one defendant is named in the complaint, attach an additional page providing the same information for each additional defendant.)

C. The Amount in Controversy

The amount in controversy–the amount the plaintiff claims the defendant owes or the amount at stake–is more than $75,000, not counting interest and costs of court, because *(explain)*:

III. Statement of Claim

Write a short and plain statement of the claim. Do not make legal arguments. State as briefly as possible the facts showing that each plaintiff is entitled to the damages or other relief sought. State how each defendant was involved and what each defendant did that caused the plaintiff harm or violated the plaintiff's rights, including the dates and places of that involvement or conduct. If more than one claim is asserted, number each claim and write a short and plain statement of each claim in a separate paragraph. Attach additional pages if needed.

The defendant, *(name)* ____________________, owes the plaintiff *(specify the amount)* $ ________, because *(use one or more of the following, as appropriate)*:

A. On a Promissory Note

On *(date)* ________, the defendant signed and delivered a note promising to pay the plaintiff on *(date)* ________ the sum of *(specify the amount)* $ ________ with interest at the rate of *(specify the amount)* ________ percent. The defendant has not paid the amount due and owes *(state the amount of unpaid principal and interest)* $ ________. A copy of the note is attached as an exhibit or is summarized below. *(Attach the note or summarize what the document says.)*

B. On an Account Between the Parties

The defendant owes the plaintiff *(specify the amount)* $ ________. This debt arises from an account between the parties, based on *(state the basis, such as an agreement between a credit–card company and a credit–card holder)*

The plaintiff sent the defendant a statement of the account listing the transactions over a certain period and showing the bills sent, the payments received or credits approved, and the balance due. The defendant owes *(specify the amount)* $ ________. Copies of the bills or account statements are attached as exhibits or summarized below. *(Attach the statements or summarize what they say.)*

C. **For Goods Sold and Delivered**

The defendant owes the plaintiff *(specify the amount)* $ ____________, for goods sold and delivered by the plaintiff to the defendant from *(date)* __________ to *(date)* ____________.

D. **For Money Loaned**

The defendant owes the plaintiff *(specify the amount)* $ ____________, for money the plaintiff loaned the defendant on *(date)* ____________.

E. **For Money Paid by Mistake**

The defendant owes the plaintiff *(specify the amount)* $ ____________ for money paid by mistake to the defendant on *(date)* ____________, when the defendant received the payment from *(specify who paid and describe the circumstances of the payment)*

____

F. **For Money Had and Received**

The defendant was paid money *(specify the amount)* $ ____________ on *(date)* ____________ by *(identify who paid and describe the circumstances of the payment)*

____

It is unjust for the defendant not to pay the plaintiff the money received because *(explain the reason, such as that the money was intended to be paid to the plaintiff, or was paid by coercion, duress, or fraud, or was an overpayment or a deposit to be returned)*

____

IV. Relief

State briefly and precisely what damages or other relief the plaintiff asks the court to order. Do not make legal arguments. Include any basis for claiming that the wrongs alleged are continuing at the present time. Include the amounts of any actual damages claimed for the acts alleged and the basis for these amounts. Include any punitive or exemplary damages claimed, the amounts, and the reasons you claim you are entitled to actual or punitive money damages.

V. Certification and Closing

Under Federal Rule of Civil Procedure 11, by signing below, I certify to the best of my knowledge, information, and belief that this complaint: (1) is not being presented for an improper purpose, such as to harass, cause unnecessary delay, or needlessly increase the cost of litigation; (2) is supported by existing law or by a nonfrivolous argument for extending, modifying, or reversing existing law; (3) the factual contentions have evidentiary support or, if specifically so identified, will likely have evidentiary support after a reasonable opportunity for further investigation or discovery; and (4) the complaint otherwise complies with the requirements of Rule 11.

A. For Parties Without an Attorney

I agree to provide the Clerk's Office with any changes to my address where case–related papers may be served. I understand that my failure to keep a current address on file with the Clerk's Office may result in the dismissal of my case.

Date of signing: ____________________

Signature of Plaintiff ____________________

Printed Name of Plaintiff ____________________

B. For Attorneys

Date of signing: ____________________

Signature of Attorney ____________________

Printed Name of Attorney ____________________

Bar Number ____________________

Name of Law Firm ____________________

Street Address ____________________

State and Zip Code ____________________

Telephone Number ____________________

E-mail Address ____________________

UNITED STATES DISTRICT COURT

for the

__________ District of __________

__________ Division

____________________ *Plaintiff(s)* *(Write the full name of each plaintiff who is filing this complaint. If the names of all the plaintiffs cannot fit in the space above, please write "see attached" in the space and attach an additional page with the full list of names.)* **-v-** ____________________ *Defendant(s)* *(Write the full name of each defendant who is being sued. If the names of all the defendants cannot fit in the space above, please write "see attached" in the space and attach an additional page with the full list of names.)*	)	Case No. ____________________ *(to be filled in by the Clerk's Office)* Jury Trial: *(check one)* ☐ Yes ☐ No

COMPLAINT FOR EMPLOYMENT DISCRIMINATION

I. The Parties to This Complaint

A. The Plaintiff(s)

Provide the information below for each plaintiff named in the complaint. Attach additional pages if needed.

Name ____________________

Street Address ____________________

City and County ____________________

State and Zip Code ____________________

Telephone Number ____________________

E-mail Address ____________________

B. The Defendant(s)

Provide the information below for each defendant named in the complaint, whether the defendant is an individual, a government agency, an organization, or a corporation. For an individual defendant, include the person's job or title *(if known)*. Attach additional pages if needed.

Defendant No. 1

Name __________

Job or Title *(if known)* __________

Street Address __________

City and County __________

State and Zip Code __________

Telephone Number __________

E-mail Address *(if known)* __________

Defendant No. 2

Name __________

Job or Title *(if known)* __________

Street Address __________

City and County __________

State and Zip Code __________

Telephone Number __________

E-mail Address *(if known)* __________

Defendant No. 3

Name __________

Job or Title *(if known)* __________

Street Address __________

City and County __________

State and Zip Code __________

Telephone Number __________

E-mail Address *(if known)* __________

Defendant No. 4

Name __________

Job or Title *(if known)* __________

Street Address __________

City and County __________

State and Zip Code __________

Telephone Number __________

E-mail Address *(if known)* __________

C. Place of Employment

The address at which I sought employment or was employed by the defendant(s) is

Name	
Street Address	
City and County	
State and Zip Code	
Telephone Number	

II. Basis for Jurisdiction

This action is brought for discrimination in employment pursuant to *(check all that apply)*:

- ☐ Title VII of the Civil Rights Act of 1964, as codified, 42 U.S.C. §§ 2000e to 2000e-17 (race, color, gender, religion, national origin).

  (Note: In order to bring suit in federal district court under Title VII, you must first obtain a Notice of Right to Sue letter from the Equal Employment Opportunity Commission.)

- ☐ Age Discrimination in Employment Act of 1967, as codified, 29 U.S.C. §§ 621 to 634.

  (Note: In order to bring suit in federal district court under the Age Discrimination in Employment Act, you must first file a charge with the Equal Employment Opportunity Commission.)

- ☐ Americans with Disabilities Act of 1990, as codified, 42 U.S.C. §§ 12112 to 12117.

  (Note: In order to bring suit in federal district court under the Americans with Disabilities Act, you must first obtain a Notice of Right to Sue letter from the Equal Employment Opportunity Commission.)

- ☐ Other federal law *(specify the federal law)*:

- ☐ Relevant state law *(specify, if known)*:

- ☐ Relevant city or county law *(specify, if known)*:

III. Statement of Claim

Write a short and plain statement of the claim. Do not make legal arguments. State as briefly as possible the facts showing that each plaintiff is entitled to the damages or other relief sought. State how each defendant was involved and what each defendant did that caused the plaintiff harm or violated the plaintiff's rights, including the dates and places of that involvement or conduct. If more than one claim is asserted, number each claim and write a short and plain statement of each claim in a separate paragraph. Attach additional pages if needed.

A. The discriminatory conduct of which I complain in this action includes *(check all that apply)*:

- ☐ Failure to hire me.
- ☐ Termination of my employment.
- ☐ Failure to promote me.
- ☐ Failure to accommodate my disability.
- ☐ Unequal terms and conditions of my employment.
- ☐ Retaliation.
- ☐ Other acts *(specify)*: ______________________

(Note: Only those grounds raised in the charge filed with the Equal Employment Opportunity Commission can be considered by the federal district court under the federal employment discrimination statutes.)

B. It is my best recollection that the alleged discriminatory acts occurred on date(s)

____

C. I believe that defendant(s) *(check one)*:

- ☐ is/are still committing these acts against me.
- ☐ is/are not still committing these acts against me.

D. Defendant(s) discriminated against me based on my *(check all that apply and explain)*:

- ☐ race ______________________
- ☐ color ______________________
- ☐ gender/sex ______________________
- ☐ religion ______________________
- ☐ national origin ______________________
- ☐ age *(year of birth)* __________ *(only when asserting a claim of age discrimination.)*
- ☐ disability or perceived disability *(specify disability)*

____

E. The facts of my case are as follows. Attach additional pages if needed.

(Note: As additional support for the facts of your claim, you may attach to this complaint a copy of your charge filed with the Equal Employment Opportunity Commission, or the charge filed with the relevant state or city human rights division.)

IV. Exhaustion of Federal Administrative Remedies

A. It is my best recollection that I filed a charge with the Equal Employment Opportunity Commission or my Equal Employment Opportunity counselor regarding the defendant's alleged discriminatory conduct on *(date)*

B. The Equal Employment Opportunity Commission *(check one)*:

- ☐ has not issued a Notice of Right to Sue letter.
- ☐ issued a Notice of Right to Sue letter, which I received on *(date)* __________.

(Note: Attach a copy of the Notice of Right to Sue letter from the Equal Employment Opportunity Commission to this complaint.)

C. Only litigants alleging age discrimination must answer this question.

Since filing my charge of age discrimination with the Equal Employment Opportunity Commission regarding the defendant's alleged discriminatory conduct *(check one)*:

- ☐ 60 days or more have elapsed.
- ☐ less than 60 days have elapsed.

V. Relief

State briefly and precisely what damages or other relief the plaintiff asks the court to order. Do not make legal arguments. Include any basis for claiming that the wrongs alleged are continuing at the present time. Include the amounts of any actual damages claimed for the acts alleged and the basis for these amounts. Include any punitive or exemplary damages claimed, the amounts, and the reasons you claim you are entitled to actual or punitive money damages.

VI. Certification and Closing

Under Federal Rule of Civil Procedure 11, by signing below, I certify to the best of my knowledge, information, and belief that this complaint: (1) is not being presented for an improper purpose, such as to harass, cause unnecessary delay, or needlessly increase the cost of litigation; (2) is supported by existing law or by a nonfrivolous argument for extending, modifying, or reversing existing law; (3) the factual contentions have evidentiary support or, if specifically so identified, will likely have evidentiary support after a reasonable opportunity for further investigation or discovery; and (4) the complaint otherwise complies with the requirements of Rule 11.

A. For Parties Without an Attorney

I agree to provide the Clerk's Office with any changes to my address where case–related papers may be served. I understand that my failure to keep a current address on file with the Clerk's Office may result in the dismissal of my case.

Date of signing: ____________

Signature of Plaintiff ______________________________

Printed Name of Plaintiff ______________________________

B. For Attorneys

Date of signing: ____________

Signature of Attorney ______________________________

Printed Name of Attorney ______________________________

Bar Number ______________________________

Name of Law Firm ______________________________

Street Address ______________________________

State and Zip Code ______________________________

Telephone Number ______________________________

E-mail Address ______________________________

UNITED STATES DISTRICT COURT

for the

_________ District of _________

_________ Division

_______________ *Plaintiff(s)* *(Write the full name of each plaintiff who is filing this complaint. If the names of all the plaintiffs cannot fit in the space above, please write "see attached" in the space and attach an additional page with the full list of names.)* **-v-** _______________ *Defendant(s)* *(Write the full name of each defendant who is being sued. If the names of all the defendants cannot fit in the space above, please write "see attached" in the space and attach an additional page with the full list of names.)*	))))))))))))))))	Case No. _______________ *(to be filled in by the Clerk's Office)* Jury Trial: *(check one)* ☐ Yes ☐ No

COMPLAINT FOR VIOLATION OF FAIR LABOR STANDARDS

I. The Parties to This Complaint

A. The Plaintiff(s)

Provide the information below for each plaintiff named in the complaint. Attach additional pages if needed.

Name	_______________
Street Address	_______________
City and County	_______________
State and Zip Code	_______________
Telephone Number	_______________
E-mail Address	_______________

B. The Defendant(s)

Provide the information below for each defendant named in the complaint, whether the defendant is an individual, a government agency, an organization, or a corporation. For an individual defendant, include the person's job or title *(if known)*. Attach additional pages if needed.

Defendant No. 1

Name

Job or Title *(if known)*

Street Address

City and County

State and Zip Code

Telephone Number

E-mail Address *(if known)*

Defendant No. 2

Name

Job or Title *(if known)*

Street Address

City and County

State and Zip Code

Telephone Number

E-mail Address *(if known)*

Defendant No. 3

Name

Job or Title *(if known)*

Street Address

City and County

State and Zip Code

Telephone Number

E-mail Address *(if known)*

Defendant No. 4

Name

Job or Title *(if known)*

Street Address

City and County

State and Zip Code

Telephone Number

E-mail Address *(if known)*

C. Place of Employment

The address at which I am employed or was employed by the defendant(s) is

Name	
Street Address	
City and County	
State and Zip Code	
Telephone Number	

II. Basis for Jurisdiction

This action is brought pursuant to *(check all that apply)*:

- ☐ Fair Labor Standards Act, as codified, 29 U.S.C. §§ 201 to 209.
- ☐ Relevant state law
- ☐ Relevant city or county law

III. Statement of Claim

State as briefly as possible the facts of your case. You may wish to include further details such as the names of other persons involved in the events giving rise to your claims. Do not cite any cases. If more than one claim is asserted, number each claim and write a short and plain statement of each claim in a separate paragraph. Attach additional pages if needed.

A. Nature of employer's business:

B. Dates of employment:

C. Employee's job title and a description of the kind of work done:

D. Rate, method, and frequency of wage payment:

E. Number of hours actually worked each week in which a violation is claimed:

F. Description of the alleged violation(s) *(check all that apply)*:

☐ Failure to pay the minimum wage *(explain)*

☐ Failure to pay required overtime *(explain)*

☐ Other violation(s) *(explain)*

G. Date(s) of the alleged violation(s):

H. Additional facts:

IV. Relief

State briefly and precisely what damages or other relief the plaintiff asks the court to order. Do not make legal arguments. Include any basis for claiming that the wrongs alleged are continuing at the present time. Include the amounts of any actual damages claimed for the acts alleged and the basis for these amounts. Include any punitive or exemplary damages claimed, the amounts, and the reasons you claim you are entitled to actual or punitive money damages.

V. Certification and Closing

Under Federal Rule of Civil Procedure 11, by signing below, I certify to the best of my knowledge, information, and belief that this complaint: (1) is not being presented for an improper purpose, such as to harass, cause unnecessary delay, or needlessly increase the cost of litigation; (2) is supported by existing law or by a nonfrivolous argument for extending, modifying, or reversing existing law; (3) the factual contentions have evidentiary support or, if specifically so identified, will likely have evidentiary support after a reasonable opportunity for further investigation or discovery; and (4) the complaint otherwise complies with the requirements of Rule 11.

A. For Parties Without an Attorney

I agree to provide the Clerk's Office with any changes to my address where case–related papers may be served. I understand that my failure to keep a current address on file with the Clerk's Office may result in the dismissal of my case.

Date of signing: ________________

Signature of Plaintiff ________________________________

Printed Name of Plaintiff ________________________________

B. For Attorneys

Date of signing: ________________

Signature of Attorney ________________________________

Printed Name of Attorney ________________________________

Bar Number ________________________________

Name of Law Firm ____________________

Street Address ____________________

State and Zip Code ____________________

Telephone Number ____________________

E-mail Address ____________________

UNITED STATES DISTRICT COURT

for the

__________ District of __________

__________ Division

Case No. ____________________

(to be filled in by the Clerk's Office)

____

Plaintiff(s)

(Write the full name of each plaintiff who is filing this complaint. If the names of all the plaintiffs cannot fit in the space above, please write "see attached" in the space and attach an additional page with the full list of names.)

-v-

____

Defendant(s)

(Write the full name of each defendant who is being sued. If the names of all the defendants cannot fit in the space above, please write "see attached" in the space and attach an additional page with the full list of names.)

COMPLAINT TO REQUIRE PERFORMANCE OF A CONTRACT TO CONVEY REAL PROPERTY

(28 U.S.C. § 1332; Diversity of Citizenship)

I. The Parties to This Complaint

A. The Plaintiff(s)

Provide the information below for each plaintiff named in the complaint. Attach additional pages if needed.

Name ____________________

Street Address ____________________

City and County ____________________

State and Zip Code ____________________

Telephone Number ____________________

E-mail Address ____________________

B. The Defendant(s)

Provide the information below for each defendant named in the complaint, whether the defendant is an individual, a government agency, an organization, or a corporation. For an individual defendant, include the person's job or title *(if known)*. Attach additional pages if needed.

Defendant No. 1

Name __________

Job or Title *(if known)* __________

Street Address __________

City and County __________

State and Zip Code __________

Telephone Number __________

E-mail Address *(if known)* __________

Defendant No. 2

Name __________

Job or Title *(if known)* __________

Street Address __________

City and County __________

State and Zip Code __________

Telephone Number __________

E-mail Address *(if known)* __________

Defendant No. 3

Name __________

Job or Title *(if known)* __________

Street Address __________

City and County __________

State and Zip Code __________

Telephone Number __________

E-mail Address *(if known)* __________

Defendant No. 4

Name __________

Job or Title *(if known)* __________

Street Address __________

City and County __________

State and Zip Code __________

Telephone Number __________

E-mail Address *(if known)* __________

II. Basis for Jurisdiction

Federal courts are courts of limited jurisdiction (limited power). Under 28 U.S.C. § 1332, federal courts may hear cases in which a citizen of one State sues a citizen of another State or nation and the amount at stake is more than $75,000. In that kind of case, called a diversity of citizenship case, no defendant may be a citizen of the same State as any plaintiff. Explain how these jurisdictional requirements have been met.

A. The Plaintiff(s)

1. If the plaintiff is an individual

The plaintiff, *(name)* ____________________, is a citizen of the State of *(name)* ____________________.

2. If the plaintiff is a corporation

The plaintiff, *(name)* ____________________, is incorporated under the laws of the State of *(name)* ____________________, and has its principal place of business in the State of *(name)* ____________________.

(If more than one plaintiff is named in the complaint, attach an additional page providing the same information for each additional plaintiff.)

B. The Defendant(s)

1. If the defendant is an individual

The defendant, *(name)* ____________________, is a citizen of the State of *(name)* ____________________. Or is a citizen of *(foreign nation)* ____________________.

2 If the defendant is a corporation

The defendant, *(name)* ____________________, is incorporated under the laws of the State of *(name)* ____________________, and has its principal place of business in the State of *(name)* ____________________. Or is incorporated under the laws of *(foreign nation)* ____________________, and has its principal place of business in *(name)* ____________________.

(If more than one defendant is named in the complaint, attach an additional page providing the same information for each additional defendant.)

C. **The Amount in Controversy**

The amount in controversy–the amount the plaintiff claims the defendant owes or the amount at stake–is more than $75,000, not counting interest and costs of court, because *(explain)*:

III. Statement of Claim

A. Describe the real property owned by the defendant(s) that is the subject of this complaint. Include the address or location of the property.

B. Describe the terms of the contract you entered into with the defendant(s) to purchase the real property at issue. Attach the contract as an exhibit.

1. When did you enter into the contract with the defendant(s)?

2. What is the purchase price you agreed to pay?

3. Describe your obligations under the contract. Include any terms regarding required deposits.

4. Describe the defendant(s)' obligations under the contract, including the obligation to convey the real property at issue.

C. Describe when and how you complied with, or attempted to comply with, all of your obligations under the contract, including payment of the purchase price. If you have not complied with all of your obligations under the contract, explain how you are ready and able to comply with those obligations.

D. Describe when and how you requested that the defendant(s) convey the real property at issue and when and how the defendant(s) refused to do so. Attach copies of any correspondence with the defendant(s).

IV. Relief

What is your requested form of relief? *(check all that apply)*

☐ Specific performance of the contract. *(Explain why specific performance is the only adequate remedy and why damages would not suffice.)*

☐ Damages sustained as a result of the defendant(s)' refusal to comply with the contract. *(Describe the damages you are requesting.)*

☐ If specific performance cannot be granted, damages in the amount of $ ______________ .

(Describe the damages you are requesting.)

☐ Other relief.

V. Certification and Closing

Under Federal Rule of Civil Procedure 11, by signing below, I certify to the best of my knowledge, information, and belief that this complaint: (1) is not being presented for an improper purpose, such as to harass, cause unnecessary delay, or needlessly increase the cost of litigation; (2) is supported by existing law or by a nonfrivolous argument for extending, modifying, or reversing existing law; (3) the factual contentions have evidentiary support or, if specifically so identified, will likely have evidentiary support after a reasonable opportunity for further investigation or discovery; and (4) the complaint otherwise complies with the requirements of Rule 11.

A. For Parties Without an Attorney

I agree to provide the Clerk's Office with any changes to my address where case–related papers may be served. I understand that my failure to keep a current address on file with the Clerk's Office may result in the dismissal of my case.

Date of signing: ______________

Signature of Plaintiff ______________

Printed Name of Plaintiff ______________

B. For Attorneys

Date of signing: ______________

Signature of Attorney ______________________________

Printed Name of Attorney ______________________________

Bar Number ______________________________

Name of Law Firm ______________________________

Street Address ______________________________

State and Zip Code ______________________________

Telephone Number ______________________________

E-mail Address ______________________________

UNITED STATES DISTRICT COURT

for the

__________ District of __________

__________ Division

____________________ *Plaintiff(s)* *(Write the full name of each plaintiff who is filing this complaint. If the names of all the plaintiffs cannot fit in the space above, please write "see attached" in the space and attach an additional page with the full list of names.)* -v- ____________________ *Defendant(s)* *(Write the full name of each defendant who is being sued. If the names of all the defendants cannot fit in the space above, please write "see attached" in the space and attach an additional page with the full list of names.)*	)	Case No. ____________________ *(to be filled in by the Clerk's Office)* Jury Trial: *(check one)* ☐ Yes ☐ No

COMPLAINT FOR THE CONVERSION OF PROPERTY

(28 U.S.C. § 1332; Diversity of Citizenship)

I. The Parties to This Complaint

A. The Plaintiff(s)

Provide the information below for each plaintiff named in the complaint. Attach additional pages if needed.

Name ____________________

Street Address ____________________

City and County ____________________

State and Zip Code ____________________

Telephone Number ____________________

E-mail Address ____________________

B. The Defendant(s)

Provide the information below for each defendant named in the complaint, whether the defendant is an individual, a government agency, an organization, or a corporation. For an individual defendant, include the person's job or title *(if known)*. Attach additional pages if needed.

Defendant No. 1

Name ______________________________

Job or Title *(if known)* ______________________________

Street Address ______________________________

City and County ______________________________

State and Zip Code ______________________________

Telephone Number ______________________________

E-mail Address *(if known)* ______________________________

Defendant No. 2

Name ______________________________

Job or Title *(if known)* ______________________________

Street Address ______________________________

City and County ______________________________

State and Zip Code ______________________________

Telephone Number ______________________________

E-mail Address *(if known)* ______________________________

Defendant No. 3

Name ______________________________

Job or Title *(if known)* ______________________________

Street Address ______________________________

City and County ______________________________

State and Zip Code ______________________________

Telephone Number ______________________________

E-mail Address *(if known)* ______________________________

Defendant No. 4

Name ______________________________

Job or Title *(if known)* ______________________________

Street Address ______________________________

City and County ______________________________

State and Zip Code ______________________________

Telephone Number ______________________________

E-mail Address *(if known)* ______________________________

II. Basis for Jurisdiction

Federal courts are courts of limited jurisdiction (limited power). Under 28 U.S.C. § 1332, federal courts may hear cases in which a citizen of one State sues a citizen of another State or nation and the amount at stake is more than $75,000. In that kind of case, called a diversity of citizenship case, no defendant may be a citizen of the same State as any plaintiff. Explain how these jurisdictional requirements have been met.

A. The Plaintiff(s)

1. If the plaintiff is an individual

The plaintiff, *(name)* ______________________, is a citizen of the State of *(name)* ______________________.

2. If the plaintiff is a corporation

The plaintiff, *(name)* ______________________, is incorporated under the laws of the State of *(name)* ______________________, and has its principal place of business in the State of *(name)* ______________________.

(If more than one plaintiff is named in the complaint, attach an additional page providing the same information for each additional plaintiff.)

B. The Defendant(s)

1. If the defendant is an individual

The defendant, *(name)* ______________________, is a citizen of the State of *(name)* ______________________. Or is a citizen of *(foreign nation)* ______________________.

2 If the defendant is a corporation

The defendant, *(name)* ______________________, is incorporated under the laws of the State of *(name)* ______________________, and has its principal place of business in the State of *(name)* ______________________. Or is incorporated under the laws of *(foreign nation)* ______________________, and has its principal place of business in *(name)* ______________________.

(If more than one defendant is named in the complaint, attach an additional page providing the same information for each additional defendant.)

C. The Amount in Controversy

The amount in controversy–the amount the plaintiff claims the defendant owes or the amount at stake–is more than $75,000, not counting interest and costs of court, because *(explain)*:

III. Statement of Claim

A. Describe the property that you own that is the subject of this complaint, including its value.

B. How and when did you come to own the property?

C. How and when did the defendant(s) obtain possession of the property? Describe with particularity, the actions the defendant(s) took to convert the property.

D. *(If the defendant(s) rightfully came into possession of the property):* Describe how and when you notified the defendant(s) that the property belonged to you. Describe how and when you demanded that the defendant(s) deliver or return the property, and what response you received from the defendant(s). Attach a copy of any written correspondence with the defendant(s), if such copies exist.

IV. Relief

State briefly and precisely what damages or other relief the plaintiff asks the court to order. Do not make legal arguments. Include any basis for claiming that the wrongs alleged are continuing at the present time. Include the amounts of any actual damages claimed for the acts alleged and the basis for these amounts. Include any punitive or exemplary damages claimed, the amounts, and the reasons you claim you are entitled to actual or punitive money damages.

V. Certification and Closing

Under Federal Rule of Civil Procedure 11, by signing below, I certify to the best of my knowledge, information, and belief that this complaint: (1) is not being presented for an improper purpose, such as to harass, cause unnecessary delay, or needlessly increase the cost of litigation; (2) is supported by existing law or by a nonfrivolous argument for extending, modifying, or reversing existing law; (3) the factual contentions have evidentiary support or, if specifically so identified, will likely have evidentiary support after a reasonable opportunity for further investigation or discovery; and (4) the complaint otherwise complies with the requirements of Rule 11.

A. For Parties Without an Attorney

I agree to provide the Clerk's Office with any changes to my address where case–related papers may be served. I understand that my failure to keep a current address on file with the Clerk's Office may result in the dismissal of my case.

Date of signing: ________________

Signature of Plaintiff ________________

Printed Name of Plaintiff ________________

B. For Attorneys

Date of signing: ________________

Signature of Attorney ________________

Printed Name of Attorney ________________

Bar Number ________________

Name of Law Firm ________________

Street Address ________________

State and Zip Code ________________

Telephone Number ________________

E-mail Address ________________

UNITED STATES DISTRICT COURT

for the

_________ District of _________

_________ Division

______________________________ *Plaintiff(s)* *(Write the full name of each plaintiff who is filing this complaint. If the names of all the plaintiffs cannot fit in the space above, please write "see attached" in the space and attach an additional page with the full list of names.)* **-v-** ______________________________ *Defendant, Third–party plaintiff(s)* *(Write the full name of each defendant/third–party plaintiff. If the names of all the defendants/third–party plaintiffs cannot fit in the space above, please write "see attached" in the space and attach an additional page with the full list of names.)* **-v-** ______________________________ *Third–party defendant(s)* *(Write the full name of each third–party defendant. If the names of all the third–party defendants cannot fit in the space above, please write "see attached" in the space and attach an additional page with the full list of names.)*	)	Case No. ______________________ *(to be filled in by the Clerk's Office)* Jury Trial: *(check one)* ☐ Yes ☐ No

THIRD – PARTY COMPLAINT

I. The Parties to This Complaint

A. The Plaintiff(s)

Provide the information below for each plaintiff named in the complaint. Attach additional pages if needed.

Name	______________________
Street Address	______________________
City and County	______________________
State and Zip Code	______________________
Telephone Number	______________________
E-mail Address *(if known)*	______________________

B. The Defendant(s)/Third–Party Plaintiff(s)

Provide the information below for each defendant/third–party plaintiff named in the complaint. Attach additional pages if needed.

Name _______________
Street Address _______________
City and County _______________
State and Zip Code _______________
Telephone Number _______________
E-mail Address _______________

C. The Third–Party Defendant(s)

Provide the information below for each third–party defendant named in the complaint, whether the third–party defendant is an individual, a government agency, an organization, or a corporation. For an individual third–party defendant, include the person's job or title *(if known)*. Attach additional pages if needed.

Third–Party Defendant No. 1

Name _______________
Job or Title *(if known)* _______________
Street Address _______________
City and County _______________
State and Zip Code _______________
Telephone Number _______________
E-mail Address *(if known)* _______________

Third–Party Defendant No. 2

Name _______________
Job or Title *(if known)* _______________
Street Address _______________
City and County _______________
State and Zip Code _______________
Telephone Number _______________
E-mail Address *(if known)* _______________

Third–Party Defendant No. 3

Name	
Job or Title *(if known)*	
Street Address	
City and County	
State and Zip Code	
Telephone Number	
E-mail Address *(if known)*	

Third–Party Defendant No. 4

Name	
Job or Title *(if known)*	
Street Address	
City and County	
State and Zip Code	
Telephone Number	
E-mail Address *(if known)*	

II. Initial Complaint

A. Identify the initial complaint filed against you and the date it was filed. Describe the events that gave rise to the plaintiff's complaint, the nature of the claims asserted, and the relief sought. Attach the complaint as an exhibit.

B. State whether you have filed an answer to the complaint and, if so, briefly summarize what admissions or denials that answer asserted. Attach the answer as an exhibit.

III. Third–Party Complaint

A. Describe the nature of the relationship between you and the third–party defendant. Attach any contracts or documents showing the nature of the relationship.

B. Explain why, if the plaintiff received any judgment against you, you will be entitled to judgment against the third–party defendant for contribution to or indemnification for the amount of damages and costs awarded to the plaintiff. Include the percentage of the plaintiff's recovery that the third–party defendant will be required to contribute. Describe the facts, or relevant provisions of state law, that demonstrate you are entitled to collect from the third–party defendant.

IV. Certification and Closing

Under Federal Rule of Civil Procedure 11, by signing below, I certify to the best of my knowledge, information, and belief that this complaint: (1) is not being presented for an improper purpose, such as to harass, cause unnecessary delay, or needlessly increase the cost of litigation; (2) is supported by existing law or by a nonfrivolous argument for extending, modifying, or reversing existing law; (3) the factual contentions have evidentiary support or, if specifically so identified, will likely have evidentiary support after a reasonable opportunity for further investigation or discovery; and (4) the complaint otherwise complies with the requirements of Rule 11.

A. For Parties Without an Attorney

I agree to provide the Clerk's Office with any changes to my address where case–related papers may be served. I understand that my failure to keep a current address on file with the Clerk's Office may result in the dismissal of my case.

Date of signing: ______________

Signature of Defendant/Third–Party Plaintiff ______________

Printed Name of Defendant/Third–Party Plaintiff ______________

B. For Attorneys

Date of signing: ______________

Signature of Attorney ______________

Printed Name of Attorney ______________

Bar Number ______________

Name of Law Firm ______________________

Street Address ______________________

State and Zip Code ______________________

Telephone Number ______________________

E-mail Address ______________________

UNITED STATES DISTRICT COURT

for the

__________ District of __________

__________ Division

______________________________ *Plaintiff(s)* *(Write the full name of each plaintiff who is filing this complaint. If the names of all the plaintiffs cannot fit in the space above, please write "see attached" in the space and attach an additional page with the full list of names.)* **-v-** ______________________________ *Defendant(s)* *(Write the full name of each defendant who is being sued. If the names of all the defendants cannot fit in the space above, please write "see attached" in the space and attach an additional page with the full list of names.)*	)))))))))))))))	Case No. ______________________ *(to be filled in by the Clerk's Office)*

COMPLAINT FOR INTERPLEADER AND DECLARATORY RELIEF

I. The Parties to This Complaint

A. The Plaintiff(s) in Interpleader

Provide the information below for each plaintiff named in the complaint. Attach additional pages if needed.

Name	______________________
Street Address	______________________
City and County	______________________
State and Zip Code	______________________
Telephone Number	______________________
E-mail Address	______________________

B. The Defendant(s) in Interpleader

Provide the information below for each defendant named in the complaint, whether the defendant is an individual, a government agency, an organization, or a corporation. For an individual defendant, include the person's job or title *(if known)*. Attach additional pages if needed.

Defendant No. 1

Name ______________________

Job or Title *(if known)* ______________________

Street Address ______________________

City and County ______________________

State and Zip Code ______________________

Telephone Number ______________________

E-mail Address *(if known)* ______________________

Defendant No. 2

Name ______________________

Job or Title *(if known)* ______________________

Street Address ______________________

City and County ______________________

State and Zip Code ______________________

Telephone Number ______________________

E-mail Address *(if known)* ______________________

Defendant No. 3

Name ______________________

Job or Title *(if known)* ______________________

Street Address ______________________

City and County ______________________

State and Zip Code ______________________

Telephone Number ______________________

E-mail Address *(if known)* ______________________

Defendant No. 4

Name ______________________

Job or Title *(if known)* ______________________

Street Address ______________________

City and County ______________________

State and Zip Code ______________________

Telephone Number ______________________

E-mail Address *(if known)* ______________________

II. Basis for Jurisdiction and Venue

There are two types of interpleader actions, each brought under a different provision. Which type of interpleader action are you bringing? *(check one)*

- ☐ I am bringing this interpleader action under Federal Rule of Civil Procedure 22. *(Fill out Section A below.)*
- ☐ I am bringing this interpleader action under 28 U.S.C. § 1335. *(Fill out Section B below.)*

A. Interpleader Action Under Rule 22

1. Jurisdiction is proper because the action *(check all that apply)*:

   ☐ arises under a federal statute, a federal treaty, and/or a provision of the United States Constitution *(specify the relevant statutory, treaty, and/or constitutional provisions)*:

   ____

   ☐ meets the jurisdictional requirements of 28 U.S.C. § 1332, under which no plaintiff may be a citizen of the same State as any defendant, and the amount at stake must exceed the sum or value of $75,000:

   a. The Plaintiff(s)

      i. If the plaintiff is an individual

      The plaintiff, *(name)* ______________________________, is a citizen of the State of *(name)* ______________________________.

      ii. If the plaintiff is a corporation

      The plaintiff, *(name)* ______________________________, is incorporated under the laws of the State of *(name)* ______________________________, and has its principal place of business in the State of *(name)* ______________________________.

      (If more than one plaintiff is named in the complaint, attach an additional page providing the same information for each additional plaintiff.)

b. The Defendant(s)

i. If the defendant is an individual

The defendant, *(name)* ____________________, is a citizen of the State of *(name)* ____________________.
Or is a citizen of *(foreign nation)* ____________________.

ii. If the defendant is a corporation

The defendant, *(name)* ____________________, is incorporated under the laws of the State of *(name)* ____________________, and has its principal place of business in the State of *(name)* ____________________. Or is incorporated under the laws of *(foreign nation)* ____________________, and has its principal place of business in *(name)* ____________________.

(If more than one defendant is named in the complaint, attach an additional page providing the same information for each additional defendant.)

c. The Amount in Controversy

The amount in controversy–the amount the plaintiff claims the defendant owes or the amount at stake–is more than $75,000, not counting interest and costs of court, because *(explain)*:

____

2. Venue is proper under 28 U.S.C. § 1391 because *(check one)*:

☐ all of the defendants live in ____________________ *(a common State)* and at least one defendant lives ____________________ *(county, State)*, which is located in this court's judicial district.

☐ a substantial part of the property that is the subject of this complaint for interpleader is situated in ____________________ *(county, State)*, which is located in this court's judicial district.

☐ there is no district in which this action may otherwise be brought. The court has personal jurisdiction over the defendants for the following reasons *(identify the connections the defendants have with the judicial district)*:

B. **Interpleader Action Under 28 U.S.C. § 1335**

1. In order for this court to have jurisdiction over this action, at least two defendants must be citizens of different States as defined in 28 U.S.C. § 1332(a) or (c), and the value of the property in controversy must be at least $500.

a. Interpleader Defendant No. 1

i. If the defendant is an individual

The defendant, *(name)* ____________________, is a citizen of the State of *(name)* ____________________. Or is a citizen of *(foreign nation)* ____________________.

ii. If the defendant is a corporation

The defendant, *(name)* ____________________, is incorporated under the laws of the State of *(name)* ____________________, and has its principal place of business in the State of *(name)* ____________________. Or is incorporated under the laws of *(foreign nation)* ____________________, and has its principal place of business in *(name)* ____________________.

b. Interpleader Defendant No. 2

i. If the defendant is an individual

The defendant, *(name)* ____________________, is a citizen of the State of *(name)* ____________________. Or is a citizen of *(foreign nation)* ____________________.

ii. If the defendant is a corporation

The defendant, *(name)* ____________________, is incorporated under the laws of the State of *(name)* ____________________, and has its principal place of business in the State of *(name)* ____________________. Or is incorporated under the laws of *(foreign nation)* ____________________, and has its principal place of business in *(name)* ____________________.

c. The Property in Controversy

The property in controversy is worth $ ____________________.

2. Venue is proper under 28 U.S.C. § 1397 because at least one defendant, *(name)* ____________________, resides in ____________________ *(county, State)*, which is located in this court's judicial district.

III. Statement of Interpleader Action

A. Describe the property that is the subject of this interpleader action, and explain why you are in possession of the property. Explain why each of the defendants claims an entitlement to the property.

B. Plaintiff has *(check one)*:

- ☐ deposited *(the property at issue)* ____________________ into the registry of the court
- ☐ given a bond payable to the clerk of court in the amount of $ ____________, which the court has deemed proper and which is conditioned upon compliance by the plaintiff with the future order or judgment of the court with respect to the subject matter of the controversy.

C. Explain why you are in great doubt as to which defendant(s) is/are entitled to the property subject to the interpleader action. Explain why you cannot determine which claim(s) is/are valid without exposing yourself to potential double litigation.

IV. Relief

The plaintiff requests that *(check all that apply)*:

- ☐ Each defendant be restrained from instituting any action against the plaintiff for recovery of the property or any part of it.
- ☐ The defendants be required to interplead and settle among themselves their rights to the property and that the plaintiff be discharged from all liability.

- [ ] The plaintiff recover costs and reasonable attorney's fees.
- [ ] The court grant any further relief as may be just and proper under the circumstances of this case.

V. Certification and Closing

Under Federal Rule of Civil Procedure 11, by signing below, I certify to the best of my knowledge, information, and belief that this complaint: (1) is not being presented for an improper purpose, such as to harass, cause unnecessary delay, or needlessly increase the cost of litigation; (2) is supported by existing law or by a nonfrivolous argument for extending, modifying, or reversing existing law; (3) the factual contentions have evidentiary support or, if specifically so identified, will likely have evidentiary support after a reasonable opportunity for further investigation or discovery; and (4) the complaint otherwise complies with the requirements of Rule 11.

A. For Parties Without an Attorney

I agree to provide the Clerk's Office with any changes to my address where case–related papers may be served. I understand that my failure to keep a current address on file with the Clerk's Office may result in the dismissal of my case.

Date of signing: ______________________

Signature of Plaintiff ______________________

Printed Name of Plaintiff ______________________

B. For Attorneys

Date of signing: ______________________

Signature of Attorney ______________________

Printed Name of Attorney ______________________

Bar Number ______________________

Name of Law Firm ______________________

Street Address ______________________

State and Zip Code ______________________

Telephone Number ______________________

E-mail Address ______________________

UNITED STATES DISTRICT COURT

for the

__________ District of __________

__________ Division

______________________________	)	Case No. ____________________
Plaintiff(s)	)	*(to be filled in by the Clerk's Office)*
(Write the full name of each plaintiff who is filing this complaint. If the names of all the plaintiffs cannot fit in the space above, please write "see attached" in the space and attach an additional page with the full list of names.)	)	
-v-	)	
______________________________	)	
Defendant	)	
(Write the full name of the current Commissioner of the Social Security Administration. Do not include address here.)	)	

COMPLAINT FOR REVIEW OF A SOCIAL SECURITY DISABILITY OR SUPPLEMENTAL SECURITY INCOME DECISION

NOTICE

Federal Rules of Civil Procedure 5.2 addresses the privacy and security concerns resulting from public access to electronic court files. Under this rule, papers filed with the court should *not* contain: an individual's full social security number or full birth date; the full name of a person known to be a minor; or a complete financial account number. A filing may include *only*: the last four digits of a social security number; the year of an individual's birth; a minor's initials; and the last four digits of a financial account number.

Except as noted in this form, plaintiff need not send exhibits, affidavits, grievance or witness statements, or any other materials to the Clerk's Office with this complaint.

In order for your complaint to be filed, it must be accompanied by the filing fee or an application to proceed in forma pauperis.

I. The Parties to This Complaint

A. The Plaintiff(s)

Provide the information below for each plaintiff named in the complaint. Attach additional pages if needed.

Name __________

Street Address __________

City and County __________

State and Zip Code __________

Telephone Number __________

E-mail Address __________

Last Four Digits of Your Social Security Number *(Do not include full number)* __________

B. The Defendant

Provide the information below for the defendant named in the complaint. Attach additional pages if needed.

Defendant *(The current Commissioner of the Social Security Administration)*

Name __________

Street Address __________

City and County __________

State and Zip Code __________

(Regional Office of the Social Security Administration General Counsel.)

Telephone Number __________

E-mail Address *(if known)* __________

II. Basis for Jurisdiction

This is an action seeking court review of a decision of the Commissioner of the Social Security Administration. Jurisdiction for such proceedings can be based on two statutes. If this complaint seeks review of a decision regarding Disability Insurance Benefits under Title II of the Social Security Act, jurisdiction is proper under 42 U.S.C. § 405(g). If this complaint seeks review of a decision regarding Supplemental Security Income under Title XVI of the Social Security Act, jurisdiction is proper under 42 U.S.C. § 1383(c)(3). Please check the type of claim you are filing.

Claim Type	For Clerk's Office Use Only
☐ Disability Insurance Benefits Claim (Title II)	COA: 42:0405id NOS: 864
☐ Supplemental Security Income Claim (Title XVI)	COA: 42:1383 NOS: 863/864
☐ Child Disability Claim	COA: 42:0405wc NOS: 863
☐ Widow or Widower Claim	COA: 42:0405ww NOS: 863

An appeal from a decision of the Commissioner must be filed within 60 days of the date on which you received notice that the Commissioner's decision became final. When did you receive notice that the Commissioner's decision was final? *(This is likely the date on which you received notice from the Social Security Appeals Council that your appeal was denied.)*

Please attach a copy of the Commissioner's final decision, and a copy of the notice you received that your appeal was denied from the Social Security Appeals Council.

III. Statement of Claim

Federal courts may overturn decisions by the Commissioner of Social Security only if the decision was not supported by substantial evidence in the record or was based on legal error. Why should this court overturn the Commissioner's decision? *(Check all that apply)*

☐ The Commissioner found the following facts to be true, but these facts are not supported by substantial evidence in the record. *(Explain why the Commissioner's factual findings are not supported by substantial evidence in the record.)*

☐ The Commissioner's decision was based on legal error. *(Identify all legal errors.)*

IV. Relief

State what you want the court to do *(check all that apply)*:

☐ Issue a summons directing the defendant to appear before the court.

☐ Order the defendant to submit a certified copy of the transcript and record, including evidence upon which the findings and decision are based.

☐ Modify the defendant's decision and grant monthly maximum insurance benefits to the plaintiff, retroactive to the date of initial disability.

☐ In the alternative, remand to the defendant for reconsideration of the evidence.

☐ Grant any further relief as may be just and proper under the circumstances of this case.

V. Certification and Closing

Under Federal Rule of Civil Procedure 11, by signing below, I certify to the best of my knowledge, information, and belief that this complaint: (1) is not being presented for an improper purpose, such as to harass, cause unnecessary delay, or needlessly increase the cost of litigation; (2) is supported by existing law or by a nonfrivolous argument for extending, modifying, or reversing existing law; (3) the factual contentions have evidentiary support or, if specifically so identified, will likely have evidentiary support after a reasonable opportunity for further investigation or discovery; and (4) the complaint otherwise complies with the requirements of Rule 11.

A. For Parties Without an Attorney

I agree to provide the Clerk's Office with any changes to my address where case–related papers may be served. I understand that my failure to keep a current address on file with the Clerk's Office may result in the dismissal of my case.

Date of signing: ______________________

Signature of Plaintiff ______________________

Printed Name of Plaintiff ______________________

B. For Attorneys

Date of signing: ______________________

Signature of Attorney ______________________

Printed Name of Attorney ______________________

Bar Number ______________________

Name of Law Firm ______________________

Street Address ______________________

State and Zip Code ______________________

Telephone Number ______________________

E-mail Address ______________________

UNITED STATES DISTRICT COURT

for the

__________ District of __________

__________ Division

______________________________ *Plaintiff(s)* *(Write the full name of each plaintiff who is filing this complaint. If the names of all the plaintiffs cannot fit in the space above, please write "see attached" in the space and attach an additional page with the full list of names.)* **-v-** ______________________________ *Defendant(s)* *(Write the full name of each defendant who is being sued. If the names of all the defendants cannot fit in the space above, please write "see attached" in the space and attach an additional page with the full list of names. Do not include addresses here.)*	)))))))))))))))	Case No. ____________________ *(to be filled in by the Clerk's Office)*

COMPLAINT FOR VIOLATION OF CIVIL RIGHTS

(Prisoner Complaint)

NOTICE

Federal Rules of Civil Procedure 5.2 addresses the privacy and security concerns resulting from public access to electronic court files. Under this rule, papers filed with the court should *not* contain: an individual's full social security number or full birth date; the full name of a person known to be a minor; or a complete financial account number. A filing may include *only*: the last four digits of a social security number; the year of an individual's birth; a minor's initials; and the last four digits of a financial account number.

Except as noted in this form, plaintiff need not send exhibits, affidavits, grievance or witness statements, or any other materials to the Clerk's Office with this complaint.

In order for your complaint to be filed, it must be accompanied by the filing fee or an application to proceed in forma pauperis.

I. The Parties to This Complaint

A. The Plaintiff(s)

Provide the information below for each plaintiff named in the complaint. Attach additional pages if needed.

Name ____________________

All other names by which you have been known: ____________________

ID Number ____________________

Current Institution ____________________

Address ____________________

____________________ City ____________________ State ____________________ Zip Code

B. The Defendant(s)

Provide the information below for each defendant named in the complaint, whether the defendant is an individual, a government agency, an organization, or a corporation. Make sure that the defendant(s) listed below are identical to those contained in the above caption. For an individual defendant, include the person's job or title *(if known)* and check whether you are bringing this complaint against them in their individual capacity or official capacity, or both. Attach additional pages if needed.

Defendant No. 1

Name ____________________

Job or Title *(if known)* ____________________

Shield Number ____________________

Employer ____________________

Address ____________________

____________________ City ____________________ State ____________________ Zip Code

☐ Individual capacity ☐ Official capacity

Defendant No. 2

Name ____________________

Job or Title *(if known)* ____________________

Shield Number ____________________

Employer ____________________

Address ____________________

____________________ City ____________________ State ____________________ Zip Code

☐ Individual capacity ☐ Official capacity

Defendant No. 3

Name __________

Job or Title *(if known)* __________

Shield Number __________

Employer __________

Address __________

City *State* *Zip Code*

☐ Individual capacity ☐ Official capacity

Defendant No. 4

Name __________

Job or Title *(if known)* __________

Shield Number __________

Employer __________

Address __________

City *State* *Zip Code*

☐ Individual capacity ☐ Official capacity

II. Basis for Jurisdiction

Under 42 U.S.C. § 1983, you may sue state or local officials for the "deprivation of any rights, privileges, or immunities secured by the Constitution and [federal laws]." Under *Bivens v. Six Unknown Named Agents of Federal Bureau of Narcotics, 403 U.S. 388 (1971)*, you may sue federal officials for the violation of certain constitutional rights.

A. Are you bringing suit against *(check all that apply)*:

☐ Federal officials (a *Bivens* claim)

☐ State or local officials (a § 1983 claim)

B. Section 1983 allows claims alleging the "deprivation of any rights, privileges, or immunities secured by the Constitution and [federal laws]." 42 U.S.C. § 1983. If you are suing under section 1983, what federal constitutional or statutory right(s) do you claim is/are being violated by state or local officials?

C. Plaintiffs suing under *Bivens* may only recover for the violation of certain constitutional rights. If you are suing under *Bivens*, what constitutional right(s) do you claim is/are being violated by federal officials?

D. Section 1983 allows defendants to be found liable only when they have acted "under color of any statute, ordinance, regulation, custom, or usage, of any State or Territory or the District of Columbia." 42 U.S.C. § 1983. If you are suing under section 1983, explain how each defendant acted under color of state or local law. If you are suing under *Bivens*, explain how each defendant acted under color of federal law. Attach additional pages if needed.

III. Prisoner Status

Indicate whether you are a prisoner or other confined person as follows *(check all that apply)*:

- ☐ Pretrial detainee
- ☐ Civilly committed detainee
- ☐ Immigration detainee
- ☐ Convicted and sentenced state prisoner
- ☐ Convicted and sentenced federal prisoner
- ☐ Other *(explain)* ______

IV. Statement of Claim

State as briefly as possible the facts of your case. Describe how each defendant was personally involved in the alleged wrongful action, along with the dates and locations of all relevant events. You may wish to include further details such as the names of other persons involved in the events giving rise to your claims. Do not cite any cases or statutes. If more than one claim is asserted, number each claim and write a short and plain statement of each claim in a separate paragraph. Attach additional pages if needed.

A. If the events giving rise to your claim arose outside an institution, describe where and when they arose.

B. If the events giving rise to your claim arose in an institution, describe where and when they arose.

C. What date and approximate time did the events giving rise to your claim(s) occur?

D. What are the facts underlying your claim(s)? *(For example: What happened to you? Who did what? Was anyone else involved? Who else saw what happened?)*

V. Injuries

If you sustained injuries related to the events alleged above, describe your injuries and state what medical treatment, if any, you required and did or did not receive.

VI. Relief

State briefly what you want the court to do for you. Make no legal arguments. Do not cite any cases or statutes. If requesting money damages, include the amounts of any actual damages and/or punitive damages claimed for the acts alleged. Explain the basis for these claims.

VII. Exhaustion of Administrative Remedies Administrative Procedures

The Prison Litigation Reform Act ("PLRA"), 42 U.S.C. § 1997e(a), requires that "[n]o action shall be brought with respect to prison conditions under section 1983 of this title, or any other Federal law, by a prisoner confined in any jail, prison, or other correctional facility until such administrative remedies as are available are exhausted."

Administrative remedies are also known as grievance procedures. Your case may be dismissed if you have not exhausted your administrative remedies.

A. Did your claim(s) arise while you were confined in a jail, prison, or other correctional facility?

☐ Yes

☐ No

If yes, name the jail, prison, or other correctional facility where you were confined at the time of the events giving rise to your claim(s).

____

B. Does the jail, prison, or other correctional facility where your claim(s) arose have a grievance procedure?

☐ Yes

☐ No

☐ Do not know

C. Does the grievance procedure at the jail, prison, or other correctional facility where your claim(s) arose cover some or all of your claims?

☐ Yes

☐ No

☐ Do not know

If yes, which claim(s)?

____

D. Did you file a grievance in the jail, prison, or other correctional facility where your claim(s) arose concerning the facts relating to this complaint?

☐ Yes

☐ No

If no, did you file a grievance about the events described in this complaint at any other jail, prison, or other correctional facility?

☐ Yes

☐ No

E. If you did file a grievance:

1. Where did you file the grievance?

2. What did you claim in your grievance?

3. What was the result, if any?

4. What steps, if any, did you take to appeal that decision? Is the grievance process completed? If not, explain why not. *(Describe all efforts to appeal to the highest level of the grievance process.)*

F. If you did not file a grievance:

1. If there are any reasons why you did not file a grievance, state them here:

2. If you did not file a grievance but you did inform officials of your claim, state who you informed, when and how, and their response, if any:

G. Please set forth any additional information that is relevant to the exhaustion of your administrative remedies.

(Note: You may attach as exhibits to this complaint any documents related to the exhaustion of your administrative remedies.)

VIII. Previous Lawsuits

The "three strikes rule" bars a prisoner from bringing a civil action or an appeal in federal court without paying the filing fee if that prisoner has "on three or more prior occasions, while incarcerated or detained in any facility, brought an action or appeal in a court of the United States that was dismissed on the grounds that it is frivolous, malicious, or fails to state a claim upon which relief may be granted, unless the prisoner is under imminent danger of serious physical injury." 28 U.S.C. § 1915(g).

To the best of your knowledge, have you had a case dismissed based on this "three strikes rule"?

☐ Yes

☐ No

If yes, state which court dismissed your case, when this occurred, and attach a copy of the order if possible.

A. Have you filed other lawsuits in state or federal court dealing with the same facts involved in this action?

☐ Yes

☐ No

B. If your answer to A is yes, describe each lawsuit by answering questions 1 through 7 below. *(If there is more than one lawsuit, describe the additional lawsuits on another page, using the same format.)*

1. Parties to the previous lawsuit

   Plaintiff(s) ________________

   Defendant(s) ________________

2. Court *(if federal court, name the district; if state court, name the county and State)*

   ____

3. Docket or index number

   ____

4. Name of Judge assigned to your case

   ____

5. Approximate date of filing lawsuit

   ____

6. Is the case still pending?

   ☐ Yes

   ☐ No

   If no, give the approximate date of disposition. ________________

7. What was the result of the case? *(For example: Was the case dismissed? Was judgment entered in your favor? Was the case appealed?)*

   ____

C. Have you filed other lawsuits in state or federal court otherwise relating to the conditions of your imprisonment?

☐ Yes

☐ No

D. If your answer to C is yes, describe each lawsuit by answering questions 1 through 7 below. *(If there is more than one lawsuit, describe the additional lawsuits on another page, using the same format.)*

1. Parties to the previous lawsuit

   Plaintiff(s) __________

   Defendant(s) __________

2. Court *(if federal court, name the district; if state court, name the county and State)*

   ____

3. Docket or index number

   ____

4. Name of Judge assigned to your case

   ____

5. Approximate date of filing lawsuit

   ____

6. Is the case still pending?

   ☐ Yes

   ☐ No

   If no, give the approximate date of disposition __________

7. What was the result of the case? *(For example: Was the case dismissed? Was judgment entered in your favor? Was the case appealed?)*

   ____

IX. Certification and Closing

Under Federal Rule of Civil Procedure 11, by signing below, I certify to the best of my knowledge, information, and belief that this complaint: (1) is not being presented for an improper purpose, such as to harass, cause unnecessary delay, or needlessly increase the cost of litigation; (2) is supported by existing law or by a nonfrivolous argument for extending, modifying, or reversing existing law; (3) the factual contentions have evidentiary support or, if specifically so identified, will likely have evidentiary support after a reasonable opportunity for further investigation or discovery; and (4) the complaint otherwise complies with the requirements of Rule 11.

A. For Parties Without an Attorney

I agree to provide the Clerk's Office with any changes to my address where case–related papers may be served. I understand that my failure to keep a current address on file with the Clerk's Office may result in the dismissal of my case.

Date of signing: ________________

Signature of Plaintiff ________________

Printed Name of Plaintiff ________________

Prison Identification # ________________

Prison Address ________________

City *State* *Zip Code*

B. For Attorneys

Date of signing: ________________

Signature of Attorney ________________

Printed Name of Attorney ________________

Bar Number ________________

Name of Law Firm ________________

Address ________________

City *State* *Zip Code*

Telephone Number ________________

E-mail Address ________________

UNITED STATES DISTRICT COURT

for the

__________ District of __________

__________ Division

____ *Plaintiff(s)* *(Write the full name of each plaintiff who is filing this complaint. If the names of all the plaintiffs cannot fit in the space above, please write "see attached" in the space and attach an additional page with the full list of names.)* **-v-** ____ *Defendant(s)* *(Write the full name of each defendant who is being sued. If the names of all the defendants cannot fit in the space above, please write "see attached" in the space and attach an additional page with the full list of names. Do not include addresses here.)*	)))))))))))))))	Case No. ____________________ *(to be filled in by the Clerk's Office)* Jury Trial: *(check one)* ☐ Yes ☐ No

COMPLAINT FOR VIOLATION OF CIVIL RIGHTS

(Non-Prisoner Complaint)

NOTICE

Federal Rules of Civil Procedure 5.2 addresses the privacy and security concerns resulting from public access to electronic court files. Under this rule, papers filed with the court should *not* contain: an individual's full social security number or full birth date; the full name of a person known to be a minor; or a complete financial account number. A filing may include *only*: the last four digits of a social security number; the year of an individual's birth; a minor's initials; and the last four digits of a financial account number.

Except as noted in this form, plaintiff need not send exhibits, affidavits, grievance or witness statements, or any other materials to the Clerk's Office with this complaint.

In order for your complaint to be filed, it must be accompanied by the filing fee or an application to proceed in forma pauperis.

I. The Parties to This Complaint

A. The Plaintiff(s)

Provide the information below for each plaintiff named in the complaint. Attach additional pages if needed.

Name ______________________

Address ______________________

______________ ______ ______________
City *State* *Zip Code*

County ______________________

Telephone Number ______________________

E-Mail Address ______________________

B. The Defendant(s)

Provide the information below for each defendant named in the complaint, whether the defendant is an individual, a government agency, an organization, or a corporation. For an individual defendant, include the person's job or title (if known) and check whether you are bringing this complaint against them in their individual capacity or official capacity, or both. Attach additional pages if needed.

Defendant No. 1

Name ______________________

Job or Title *(if known)* ______________________

Address ______________________

______________ ______ ______________
City *State* *Zip Code*

County ______________________

Telephone Number ______________________

E-Mail Address *(if known)* ______________________

☐ Individual capacity ☐ Official capacity

Defendant No. 2

Name ______________________

Job or Title *(if known)* ______________________

Address ______________________

______________ ______ ______________
City *State* *Zip Code*

County ______________________

Telephone Number ______________________

E-Mail Address *(if known)* ______________________

☐ Individual capacity ☐ Official capacity

Defendant No. 3

Name ______

Job or Title *(if known)* ______

Address ______

______ ______ ______
City *State* *Zip Code*

County ______

Telephone Number ______

E-Mail Address *(if known)* ______

☐ Individual capacity ☐ Official capacity

Defendant No. 4

Name ______

Job or Title *(if known)* ______

Address ______

______ ______ ______
City *State* *Zip Code*

County ______

Telephone Number ______

E-Mail Address *(if known)* ______

☐ Individual capacity ☐ Official capacity

II. Basis for Jurisdiction

Under 42 U.S.C. § 1983, you may sue state or local officials for the "deprivation of any rights, privileges, or immunities secured by the Constitution and [federal laws]." Under *Bivens v. Six Unknown Named Agents of Federal Bureau of Narcotics, 403 U.S. 388 (1971)*, you may sue federal officials for the violation of certain constitutional rights.

A. Are you bringing suit against *(check all that apply)*:

☐ Federal officials (a *Bivens* claim)

☐ State or local officials (a § 1983 claim)

B. Section 1983 allows claims alleging the "deprivation of any rights, privileges, or immunities secured by the Constitution and [federal laws]." 42 U.S.C. § 1983. If you are suing under section 1983, what federal constitutional or statutory right(s) do you claim is/are being violated by state or local officials?

______

C. Plaintiffs suing under *Bivens* may only recover for the violation of certain constitutional rights. If you are suing under *Bivens*, what constitutional right(s) do you claim is/are being violated by federal officials?

D. Section 1983 allows defendants to be found liable only when they have acted "under color of any statute, ordinance, regulation, custom, or usage, of any State or Territory or the District of Columbia." 42 U.S.C. § 1983. If you are suing under section 1983, explain how each defendant acted under color of state or local law. If you are suing under *Bivens*, explain how each defendant acted under color of federal law. Attach additional pages if needed.

III. Statement of Claim

State as briefly as possible the facts of your case. Describe how each defendant was personally involved in the alleged wrongful action, along with the dates and locations of all relevant events. You may wish to include further details such as the names of other persons involved in the events giving rise to your claims. Do not cite any cases or statutes. If more than one claim is asserted, number each claim and write a short and plain statement of each claim in a separate paragraph. Attach additional pages if needed.

A. Where did the events giving rise to your claim(s) occur?

B. What date and approximate time did the events giving rise to your claim(s) occur?

C. What are the facts underlying your claim(s)? *(For example: What happened to you? Who did what? Was anyone else involved? Who else saw what happened?)*

IV. Injuries

If you sustained injuries related to the events alleged above, describe your injuries and state what medical treatment, if any, you required and did or did not receive.

V. Relief

State briefly what you want the court to do for you. Make no legal arguments. Do not cite any cases or statutes. If requesting money damages, include the amounts of any actual damages and/or punitive damages claimed for the acts alleged. Explain the basis for these claims.

VI. Certification and Closing

Under Federal Rule of Civil Procedure 11, by signing below, I certify to the best of my knowledge, information, and belief that this complaint: (1) is not being presented for an improper purpose, such as to harass, cause unnecessary delay, or needlessly increase the cost of litigation; (2) is supported by existing law or by a nonfrivolous argument for extending, modifying, or reversing existing law; (3) the factual contentions have evidentiary support or, if specifically so identified, will likely have evidentiary support after a reasonable opportunity for further investigation or discovery; and (4) the complaint otherwise complies with the requirements of Rule 11.

A. For Parties Without an Attorney

I agree to provide the Clerk's Office with any changes to my address where case–related papers may be served. I understand that my failure to keep a current address on file with the Clerk's Office may result in the dismissal of my case.

Date of signing: ____________________

Signature of Plaintiff ________________________________

Printed Name of Plaintiff ________________________________

B. For Attorneys

Date of signing: ____________________

Signature of Attorney ________________________________

Printed Name of Attorney ________________________________

Bar Number ________________________________

Name of Law Firm ________________________________

Address ________________________________

________________ ________ ____________
City *State* *Zip Code*

Telephone Number ________________________________

E-mail Address ________________________________

www.ingramcontent.com/pod-product-compliance
Lightning Source LLC
Chambersburg PA
CBHW080648220326
41598CB00033B/5136

* 9 7 8 1 6 4 0 0 2 0 2 0 7 *